Manual of Curatorship

A Guide to Museum Practice

Second edition

Editorial Board

John M. A. Thompson, BA, MA, FMA, Chairman
Douglas A. Bassett, BSC, PhD, FGS, FMA
Antony J. Duggan, MD, BS, FRCP, FIBIOL, DTM, FMA
Geoffrey D. Lewis, MA, FSA, HonFMA
Alexander Fenton, CBE, MA, BA, DLitt, HonDLitt, FSA, FRSE, FRSGS

Manual of Curatorship

A Guide to Museum Practice

Butterworth-Heinemann Ltd
Linacre House, Jordan Hill, Oxford OX2 8DP

 PART OF REED INTERNATIONAL BOOKS

OXFORD   LONDON   BOSTON
MUNICH   NEW DELHI   SINGAPORE   SYDNEY
TOKYO   TORONTO   WELLINGTON

First published 1984
Reprinted (with revisions) 1986
Second edition 1992

© Museums Association 1984, 1992

British Library Cataloguing in Publication Data
Thompson, John M. A.
   Manual of curatorship: a guide to museum practice.
   I. Title
   069.5

   ISBN 0 7506 0351 8

Library of Congress Cataloguing in Publication Data
Manual of curatorship: a guide to museum practice/[edited by] John
   M. A. Thompson.
   p.   cm.
   Originally published: London; Boston: Butterworths, 1984.
   Includes bibliographical references and index.
   ISBN 0 7506 0351 8
   1. Museum techniques – Handbooks, manuals, etc.   2. Museums –
   Administration – Handbooks, manuals, etc. I. Thompson, John M. A.
   AM151.M32   1992
   069'.5–dc20   91–43671
                                                             CIP

Composition by Genesis Typesetting, Laser Quay, Rochester, Kent
Printed and bound in Great Britain

Contents

Section Two: Management and Administration
Section Editor
John Thompson

Section Three: Conservation
Section Editor
Peter N. Lowell

Section Four: Collections Research
Section Editor
Alexander Fenton

Section Five: User Services
Section Editor
Douglas A. Bassett

Foreword

The museums and galleries of the United Kingdom hold a substantial part of our common heritage in the form of collections of great aesthetic interest and inestimable scientific value. Museums are now enjoyed by millions of people each year, providing services which know no boundaries in appealing to young and old alike and to people from all walks of life.

It is vital that those working in museums, and those responsible for directing and funding them, can work to develop museums and improve their services at a time of increasing leisure and when they can contribute so much to education and tourism.

I welcome the new edition of this Manual as an invaluable work of reference for all those involved in museums in the widest sense, and I congratulate the Museums Association on this initiative.

David Mellor
Secretary of State
for National Heritage

Preface

The second edition of *The Manual of Curatorship; a Guide to Museum Practice*, is for the practical use of all concerned with the management and administration of museums. It is a comprehensive reference work for museum professionals involved in the diversity of activities which characterize museums in the 1990s. Although its value lies primarily in its usefulness for the museum professional, it will also be of relevance to governing bodies responsible for museums whether local authority, independent, national trustee, university or company. The work of the many supporting organizations, such as Friends and associated bodies, volunteer groups, training and technical organizations, and others who make regular use of the services that museums provide, should benefit from the information it contains.

The second edition has followed the successful method adopted for the first edition, that is an edited work based on original contributions from museum professionals arising from their own experience. For the second edition, a number of contributions have also been commissioned from professionals providing services to museums in areas such as security, architectural services and the law, and several contributions from museum professionals have also benefited from the advice of other specialists.

The overall aim has been to present the current practices and issues involved in curatorship and, where appropriate, to indicate future trends and directions. As a standard work of reference, it consists of practical material based on a firm, theoretical foundation. The arrangement has continued to reflect the multi-disciplinary nature of curatorship and therefore it has not been considered practical to incorporate detailed material of a specialist nature if it could be found in other existing published sources available to the museum professional. The requirement for specialist information has been met by the references being as extensive and up to date as possible, with annotations where necessary, thus serving as a primary, bibliographical source. Although the work has its main foundation on museum practice specific to the United Kingdom, the Editorial Board is confident that the experience of the contributors, drawn from a wide range of museums and related organizations and institutions, will again give the work universal relevance in the way it addresses the fundamental requirements of curatorship as practiced in museums and galleries in the 1990s.

Several changes have been introduced in the form and organization of the volume for ease of reference and to reflect the views of the Board over the content of the sections in the first edition. The first is the sub-division of the collections management section into the separate sections of collections conservation and collections research, each with its own editor. This has resulted in a substantial review of these areas which represent a major part of the volume and reflect the changes in practice and techniques that have taken place during the 1980s. Secondly, the visitor services section has been re-named user services to reflect the wider range of service provided by museums than simply for those who come through the doors and the more purposeful and structured use of museums by the community. Thirdly, the management and administration section now follows the history, survey and typological description of museums in Section One. Finally in response to the late 20th century appetite of museum practitioners to form sub-groups, alliances and new institutions to serve the needs of an increasingly complex operational environment, a glossary of acronyms as well as an expanded index has been included.

The contents of the Manual have been substantially reviewed in the light of the changes that have occurred in museums practice during the intervening years. In many cases, authors have revised and updated those contributions which have remained relevant, and the opportunity has been taken to commission a large proportion of new contributions. Some of the areas covered include marketing, volunteers, legislation, security, information technology and the role of the Director. The Board remains conscious that there are areas of activity in museums which, although not addressed fully in the second edition, will be the subject of further attention in subsequent revisions and editions. In addition, the rapidly expanding areas of training and information technology in particular, cannot be adequately addressed in a work such as the Manual and users of the Manual should consult specialist publications produced by the main practising bodies in the United Kingdom such MDA (Museums Documentation Association) and the MTI (Museum Training Institute).

Due to the widespread differences between countries and as a matter of editorial policy, the legislative implications of curatorship have been confined to United Kingdom practice and to the general international codes which apply. An innovation in the second edition is to include an extended contribution on an interpretation of the law affecting museums by Patrick Sudbury and C. K. Wilson.

With the application of scientific and technological advances to the key functions of museums and as they continue to evolve in response to changing social and economic factors, there are new and exciting opportunities both now and in the future for meeting the needs of the museum user. In turn, the role of the museum professional is changing as new and improved skills are required in the face of these changes and developments. At the same time, expanding areas of activity are changing the face of museums with increasing rapidity. It is therefore inevitable that parts of the Manual will age within a relatively brief period as the difference between the first and second editions already illustrates. In order that the Manual should continue to reflect the current state of museum practice, the Board will plan for further revisions at regular intervals by commissioning new material and for this to be included in future editions.

The Editorial Board wishes to make it clear that each contribution reflects the opinion of the author, not Board members, and to the best of our knowledge all sources have been quoted or referred to as far as known.

John Thompson

Acknowledgements

On behalf of the Editorial Board, I would like to thank the many contributors who have spent much time between the first and second editions of the Manual revising and updating previous material and to those who have contributed new articles. The Board has once again been overwhelmed by the support for the Manual from members of the profession and those sympathetic towards its aims.

During the later stages of this project, the Board has received considerable assistance from the publications staff of the Museums Association, notably Michael Wright and Maurice Davies in liaising with the publishers on technical matters and in assisting me in maintaining the continuity of the project.

Ann Berne, Senior Commissioning Editor of Butterworths Scientific (now Butterworth–Heinemann) who was responsible for the technical aspects of the production, worked tirelessly to maintain progress with the publication arrangements, assisting the Board in focusing on the areas requiring further revision and alteration. Latterly Neil Warnock-Smith, Division Publisher and Angela Leopard, Desk Editor have taken on this responsibility. Thanks are also due to Blaise Vyner, formerly Director, Cleveland County Museums, and a regional Councillor of the Museums Association, for reading the manuscript and making valuable suggestions, some of which have been included and others which will assist in planning the contents of the next edition.

Finally, I would like to extend my thanks to the members of the Editorial Board, three of whom have continued from the first edition, namely Geoffrey Lewis, Anthony Duggan and Douglas Bassett. David Prince, Researcher for the first edition and a Board member, resigned during this period for business reasons. Dr Alexander Fenton, Director of Research, Royal Museum of Scotland, joined the Board to take responsibility for the research section, and we are grateful to him for undertaking a major revision of this section within a tight time scale. Anthony Duggan resigned following the completion of the first draft of the collections management section after a long association with the project which extended back into the early 1970s. Work on the conservation section continued under the guidance of Dr Peter Lowell, Head of Conservation for Tyne and Wear Museums.

Herbert Coutts, Curator of the City of Edinburgh Museums, has once again provided valuable advice to the Board over specific legislative arrangements for Scottish museums which has been incorporated into the extended section on legislation prepared by Patrick Sudbury and C. K. Wilson. The Museums Training Institute have helped in updating the bibliography in specific areas.

In addition to editing sections, several Board members have again taken on responsibility for the preparation of articles, and for preparing indices and glossaries. In particular, I am grateful to Geoffrey Lewis and Douglas Bassett for the immense amount of time they have devoted to the additional tasks.

John Thompson

Contributors

Frank Atkinson, OBE, MA, BSC, FSA, FMA, Museum Consultant; formerly Director, Beamish, The North of England Open Air Museum

Donald M. Bailey, FSA, Curator, Department of Greek and Roman Antiquities, British Museum, London

Douglas A. Bassett, BSC, PhD, FGS, FMA, Formerly Director, National Museum of Wales, Cardiff

Michael Belcher, NDD, MPhil, FMA, FCSD, FBIM, FRSA, Vice Principal, Berkshire College of Art & Design

David Bomford, MSC, Senior Restorer of Paintings, National Gallery, London

Michael Bottomley, BA, DAA, Principal Archivist, West Yorkshire Archive Service

Susan M. Bradley, BSC, CChem, MRSC, Head of Conservation Research, British Museum, London

Peter Brears, DipAD, FMA, FSA, Director, Leeds City Museums

Roy Brigden, BA, FMA, Keeper, Museum of English Rural Life, Reading

John Burnett, MA, MSC, FSA (SCOT), Head of Documentation, National Museums of Scotland, Edinburgh

Sue Cackett, MSC, BA, Curator (Materials Science), Science Museum, London

Peter Cannon-Brookes, MA, PhD, FRSA, FMA, FIIC, International Museum Consultant

John Cherry, MA, FSA, FRHistS, Acting Keeper, Department of Medieval and Later Antiquities, British Museum, London

David T-D Clarke, MA, FSA, FMA, FRNS, Formerly Curator, Colchester & Essex Museum

Michael Compton, CBE, Formerly Keeper, Museum Services, Tate Gallery, London

Michael Corfield, DipCons, FSA, FIIC, Head of Artefact Conservation, Ancient Monuments Laboratory, London

Neil Cossons, OBE, DSOCSC, DLitt, MA, FSA, FMA, Director, Science Museum, London

Christine Daintith, DipCons, National Trust, London

Richard Dennis, BSC, Technical Information Officer, Rentokil Research & Development Division, East Grinstead

Michael Diamond, MA, FMA, FRSA, Director, City Museum & Art Gallery, Birmingham

James Dimond, BA, DipCon, Assistant Conservation Officer, Area Museum Service for South East England, London

Jennifer K. Dinsmore, MSC Senior Conservator, Stone, Wall Paintings and Mosaics, Conservation section, British Museum, London

Philip S. Doughty, MSC, FMA, FGS, Geology Department, Ulster Museum, Belfast

Bryan Dovey, QPM, FBIM, Museums Security Adviser, Museums & Galleries Commission, London

Antony J. Duggan, MD, FRCP, FIBiol, FMA, Formerly Director, Wellcome Museum of Medical Science, London

Dennis Farr, CBE, MA, DLitt, FRSA, FMA, Director, Courtauld Institute Galleries, London

Alexander Fenton, CBE, MA, BA DLitt, Hon DLitt, FRSE, FSA, FSA (SCOT), FRSGS, Director, European Ethnological Research Centre, National Museums of Scotland, Edinburgh and Director, School of Scottish Studies

Anne Fleming, Deputy Curator, National Film Archive, British Film Institute, London

Jean M. Glover, MBE certEd, FMA, FIIC, conscert, Senior Textile Conservation Officer, North West Museums Service, Blackburn

Patrick Greene, OBE, BSC, PhD, FSA, FMA, Director, Museum of Science & Industry, Manchester

John C. Hallam, FMA, Industrial Museum Consultant, Formerly Principal Keeper of Science and Engineering, Tyne & Wear Museums

Max Hebditch, MA, FSA, FMA, Director, Museum of London

Eilean Hooper-Greenhill, BA, ATC, DipEd, MA, PhD, FMA, Lecturer, Department of Museum Studies, University of Leicester

C. V. Horie, BSC, FIIC, FMA, Keeper of Conservation, Manchester Museum

M. V. Hounsome, BSC, PhD, CBiol, MIBiol, MBOU, Keeper of Zoology, Manchester Museum

Francis M. P. Howie, BSC, Museum Safety and Conservation Advisor, National History Museum, London

William D. Jones, BA, PhD, Assistant Keeper, National Museum of Wales (Welsh Industrial & Maritime Museum), Cardiff

John Kent, BA, PhD, FBA, FSA, FMA, Formerly Keeper, Deptartment of Coins & Medals, British Museum, London

John R. Kenyon, BA, ALA, FSA, FRHists, Librarian, National Museum of Wales, Cardiff

John Kitchin, Head of the Furniture Conservation Section of the Victoria & the Albert Museum, London

Geoffrey Lewis, MA, FSA, FMA, HONFMA, Formerly Director of Museum Studies, University of Leicester

Peter Lewis, BA, MLitt, Director, Beamish, North of England Open Air Museum

Peter Longman, Director, Museums & Galleries Commission, London

Ian H. Longworth, MA, PhD, FSA, FSA (scot), Keeper, Department of Prehistoric & Romano-British Antiquities, British Museum, London

Brian Loughbrough, MA, FMA, Arts Director, Nottingham City Council

Peter N. Lowell, BSC, DPhil, Tyne and Wear Museums Service, Newcastle upon Tyne

Richard Marks, MA, PhD, FSA, Director, Royal Pavilion, Art Gallery & Museums, Brighton

Elizabeth Martin, DipAD, ATD, CertEd, Senior Conservator (Photographs), Victoria & Albert Museum, London

Jane McAusland, FIIC, Freelance conservator of art on paper

Hazel Newey, BSC, AMA, FIIC, Head of Metals Conservation, British Museum, London

Gwyn Miles, BSC, Surveyor of Collections, Victoria & Albert Museum, London

Andrew Oddy, MA, BSC, FSA, Keeper of Conservation, British Museum, London

Roy Perry, MSC, Head of Cryptogams, National Museum of Wales, Cardiff

Tim H. Pettigrew, MSC, Registrar, Tyne & Wear Museums, Newcastle upon Tyne

David R. Prince, BEd, PhD, FRGS, Prince Research Consultants, London

Elizabeth Pye, MA, FIIC, Senior Lecturer, Head of Conservation & Museum Studies, UCL Institute of Archaeology, London

Trevor Skempton, DiplArch, RIBA, City Architect, Newcastle upon Tyne

Theo Skinner, BSC, DipAarchcons, Royal Museum of Scotland, Edinburgh

Sarah Staniforth, BA, DipCons, Adviser for Paintings, Conservation and Environmental Control, National Trust

Geoff Stansfield, BSC, FMA, Department of Museum Studies, Leicester

Sheila M. Stone, MA, FMA, Curator, Northampton Museums & Art Gallery

Patrick Sudbury, MSC, PhD, FMA, Assistant Director, National Museums and Galleries on Merseyside, Liverpool

James Tate, BSC, PhD, CPhys, MInstP, FSA(scot), National Museums of Scotland, Edinburgh

Barry A. Thomas, BSC, PhD, Keeper of Botany, National Museum of Wales, Cardiff, formerly Head of Life Sciences Department & Dean of Science & Mathematics, University of London Goldsmiths' College

John Thompson, BA, MA, FMA, Museums Professional and Consultant, formerly Director of Tyne & Wear Museums, Newcastle upon Tyne

Mel Twelves, DipInstM, Principal Marketing & Commercial Officer, Tyne & Wear Museums, Newcastle-upon-Tyne

Giles Velarde, FCSD, FMA, Museum Design Consultant, London

Alan Warhurst, CBE, MA, FSA, FMA, Director, Manchester Museum

C. K. Wilson, LLB, Formerly County Solicitor & Secretary, Merseyside County Council

Sir David M. Wilson, FBA, Formerly Director, British Museum, London

SECTION ONE

THE MUSEUM CONTEXT

Section Editor

Geoffrey Lewis

1

Introduction

Geoffrey Lewis

The emergence, development and organization of museums makes interesting reading. It is largely a story of continuous development to meet changing social needs without overall strategic planning. The result is a fascinatingly variegated, some would say idiosyncratic, museum scene. This section, then, attempts to put the museums of the UK into context, both nationally and internationally.

The first characteristic of the country's museums is their diversity, which would be difficult to parallel elsewhere in the world. They vary from the British Museum, maintaining its universal and encyclopaedic stance – albeit now only within the humanities – to the smallest museum catering for the interests of its community. Closer examination soon reveals that the early global, encyclopaedic concept is also present in some of the larger museums of provincial Britain – Birmingham, Glasgow and Liverpool, for example – and the university museums of, say, Cambridge, Manchester and Oxford. These are on a scale and with a quality to their collections which stand the closest comparison with the principal museums of many nations.

The UK's museums are a product of the country's history. The influence of a colonial power with wide trade connections not only carried the museum idea out of Europe but had its impact on collecting at home and, indeed, on the concept of the nation's heritage. It is no accident that England contains no national museum of antiquities, history or natural history in the continental European style; rather, attention was paid to an Empire and further afield. The result is a lack of nationalistic expression in the national museums. It is this, however, that provides such strength to the predominantly regional museums centred on such major centres as Bristol, Leicester and Sheffield. Much of the country's national heritage is in the provinces and this accounts for the richness of many of the provincial collections.

This richness is not peculiar to large museums. The large conurbations do not necessarily coincide with rich heritage areas. And so it is that the museums of Chester, Devizes, Lincoln, St Albans, Truro or York, for example, all reflect an archaeological and historic heritage that is national rather than parochial; the same could be said for some of the smallest museums in the country.

Although the record reveals that the UK was in the vanguard of public museum provision, it is also clear that the art of collecting, conserving, inventorying, exhibiting and interpreting cultural property is of far greater antiquity and by no means peculiarly British. Indeed, British writers on the theory and practice of museum work have been few, although the formation of the premier museums' association in Britain over a century ago, gave some impetus to this. But there is still a reluctance to write on museological subjects. Curators have tended to gain more satisfaction from technical accomplishment and contributions to one of the disciplines reflected in museum collections, than to rigorous study of curatorial work in all its manifestations.

There is, however, some movement here. Massive social change, the impact of mass travel, greater leisure, better education, increased environmental awareness and more conscious economic goals have all contributed to this. Museums, as with any other public service, must be accountable. This has resulted in an increasing curatorial awareness and vastly improved technical competence in conserving collections, in display and exhibition, educational work and other visitor facilities. It has brought into the museum a number of new skills and, with such increasing specialization, the curator's work has itself become more specialized and managerial. The training of museum staff – in which the UK has also been at the forefront – has done much to facilitate such massive change, but it continues to be a vital

3

factor in this. The development and definition of professional standards is another significant issue. Initially this took the form of codes of ethics, but more recently work has been directed, where possible, to measurable standards, both to facilitate the setting of realistic objectives and to demonstrate value for money in professional terms.

Despite such massive change, the legal and organizational structures within which museums conduct their business have changed little in their basic form and have increased greatly in complexity; from 1992 there will be an added, European, dimension. This is despite recommendations in the past, by Government and profession alike, to achieve some semblance of structure, order and co-ordination to museums in the UK. Nor is there yet a mandatory requirement to preserve the nation's cultural heritage in museums. The Museums & Galleries Commission was given new terms of reference 10 years ago and, although its powers as a co-ordinating body and a forum for developing a national strategy are ill-defined, it has made some progress in this direction. The need for major reform, however, is urgent.

Bibliography

AUDIT COMMISSION (1991), *The Road to Wigan Pier? Managing Local Authority Museums and Art Galleries*, HMSO, London

CA'ZORZI, A. (1989), *The Public Administration and Funding of Culture in the European Community*, Office for Official Publications of the European Communities, Luxembourg

HUDSON, K. (1990), *1992:Prayer or Promise?*, HMSO, London

LORD, B., LORD, G. D. and NICKS, J. (1989), *The Cost of Collecting: Collection Management in UK Museums*, Office of Arts and Libraries, HMSO, London

MIDDLETON, V. (1990), *New Visions for Independent Museums in the UK*, Association of Independent Museums, Singleton

MUSEUMS & GALLERIES COMMISSION (1983), *Review of Museums in Northern Ireland*, HMSO, London

MUSEUMS & GALLERIES COMMISSION (1984), *Review of Area Museum Councils and Services*, HMSO, London

MUSEUMS & GALLERIES COMMISSION (1986), *Museums in Scotland*, HMSO, London

MUSEUMS & GALLERIES COMMISSION (1987), *Museum Professional Training and Career Structure*, HMSO, London

MUSEUMS & GALLERIES COMMISSION (1988), *The National Museums*, HMSO, London

MUSEUMS & GALLERIES COMMISSION (1990), *The Museums of the Armed Forces*, HMSO, London

MUSEUMS & GALLERIES COMMISSION (1991), *Local Authorities and Museums*, HMSO, London

MUSEUMS ASSOCIATION (1987), *Museums UK: The Findings of the Museums Data-Base Project*, Museums Association, London

NATIONAL AUDIT OFFICE (1988), *Management of the Collections of the English National Museums and Galleries. Report by the Comptroller and Auditor General*, HMSO, London

POLICY STUDIES INSTITUTE (1988), *The Economic Importance of the Arts in Britain*, Policy Studies Institute, London

STANDING COMMISSION ON MUSEUMS AND GALLERIES (1979), *Framework for System for Museums*, HMSO, London

STANDING COMMISSION ON MUSEUMS AND GALLERIES (1981), *Report on Museums in Wales*, HMSO, London

WOODHEAD, P. and STANSFIELD, G. (1989), *Keyguide to Information Sources in Museum Studies*, Mansell Publishing, London

2

Museums and their precursors: a brief world survey

Geoffrey Lewis

The term museum,[1] like most words, has changed in meaning with time. Today it conveys concepts not only of preserving the material evidence of the human and natural world but also of a major force in interpreting these things. The idea is perceived positively and the availability of museums as a public facility is considered desirable in developed and developing countries alike. For countries with a significant past, museums may be seen to have a vital cultural and even economic role to play. Museums today are, to quote part of the International Council of Museums (1990) definition of a museum, 'in the service of society and of its development'.

The derivation of the word 'museum' is of far greater antiquity. In classical Greece a *mouseion* was a place of contemplation, a philosophical institution or a temple of the Muses. For the Romans the word 'museum' related to places for philosophical discussion. It was not until the fifteenth century that the term was used to describe a collection in Renaissance Florence and then it carried with it connotations of comprehensiveness and encyclopaedic knowledge.[2] However, since the eighteenth century a museum has been, by popular usage, a building used for the storage and exhibition of historic and natural objects.

The classical associations of the term with the Muses and contemplation, together with a strong tendency for museums to collect, preserve and exhibit only 'high' art, the exotic and the unusual have had a marked influence on public perception in the past and these traits are very visible in many museums today. This is not a slavish maintenance of a latter-day classical tradition. Museums are a preservation agency and interpretive medium, fostered by an inherent human propensity towards inquisitiveness and acquisitiveness which is combined with a desire to communicate with others.

The motivation for acquisition may vary[3] but is to be found from earliest times in the grave-goods accompanying Palaeolithic burials, a characteristic by no means peculiar to prehistoric societies. The earliest evidence of communication through another medium is also of Palaeolithic origin, occurring in the cave and mobiliary art of the latter part of this period. In due course came the development of writing, probably independently in both China and Sumerian Mesopotamia. By the third millennium BC such remarkable State archives as that at Ebla were being formed. But, while these are manifestations of the wish to record, to communicate and of an inquisitiveness about the past, the museum idea goes further. This requires the *original* material and not some secondary source to communicate. It is therefore to this also that we look in tracing the history of the museum idea. The story is far from complete and cannot be considered to become an evolving continuum until the European middle ages.

The earliest recorded instance of the use of historical material to communicate information dates from the beginning of the second millennium BC when earlier inscriptions, albeit copies, were being used in a school at Larsa, Mesopotamia (Woolley and Mallowan, 1962). Personal collections, however, would have been fairly common, certainly among the aristocracy. Examples of these may be quoted from eighteenth-dynasty Egypt: Tuthmosis III (1504–1450 BC) formed a fine collection of Asian flora and fauna, brought back from his campaigns; Amenophis III (1417–1379 BC) was a collector, especially of blue enamel.

A clearer spirit of historical enquiry appears during the time of the Babylonian empire. The Kings Nebuchadrezzar (605–562 BC)[4] and Nabonidus (c. 555–539 BC) certainly collected antiquities and even excavated and restored parts of their city, Ur 'of the Chaldees'. But it is to Nabonidus' daughter, En-nigaldi-Nanna, that credit must be given for creating what the archaeological evidence suggests was a school museum. During Woolley's excavation of the temple at Ur, a number of antiquities pre-dating it by up to 1600 years were found in two rooms connecting with the boys' school there. What appears to have been a 'museum label' was also found on which were included copies of brick inscriptions of Amar-Suena (nineteenth century BC) which had been discovered close to the temple 100 years previously. The scribe wrote out the inscriptions for 'the marvel of the beholders' (Woolley and Moorey, 1982).

Classical collecting

To this strong evidence of the educational use of historical material for teaching must be added the reasonable assumption that Aristotle (384–322 BC) used his natural history collection similarly at the Lyceum in Athens. That most celebrated museum, founded by Ptolemy Sotor in Alexandria, Egypt, in about 290 BC, is attributed to Aristotlian influence and it is likely that one of Aristotle's followers, Demetrius of Phaleron, advised on its creation. There is little doubt that this Alexandrian museum contained some objects and that it was associated with a botanical and zoological park. But the emphasis on collecting specimens and objects was not here. It was a philosophical institution, a college of scholars, a prototype university with a large library and facilities for the state-supported philosophers to engage in their studies. Such scholars as Euclid and Archimedes worked here. It was not a museum in the sense that the word is used today.

In classical Greece many collections of works of art were formed in temples from votive offerings to the deity concerned and housed in treasuries where they could be viewed by visitors on payment of a small charge. This was not just for the devout but for the tourist as well. The administration of these treasuries included many features familiar to the curator: the offerings were inventoried in some detail and active conservation measures taken to preserve them; many of the objects were on open display but others were shown in cases. Such a treasury, dedicated by the Athenians to commemorate their victory at Marathon in 490 BC and now restored, exists at Delphi. The fifth century BC also saw the display of paintings by different artists in one wing of the Propylaea on the Acropolis at Athens. Paintings were sometimes provided with shutters to protect them. The extensive collection of works of art by the Greek aristocracy does not seem to have been in vogue before Hellenistic times.

The fall of the Greek empire in the second century BC saw the conquering Romans removing many of these works of art as spoils of war; these reappeared in their own temples and also formed the basis of many private collections. Indeed the Romans became avid collectors which in turn gave rise to an antique trade and also the copying of many of the Greek masterpieces. The Emperor Hadrian, at his villa near Tivoli, erected copies of some of the structures he had visited during his tours of the empire to form a facility not so far removed from the idea of an open-air museum. For paintings, special galleries were sometimes built, with due attention being paid, for protection, to orienting the building to receive a north light (Bazin, 1967).

The Roman temples contained more than works of art among their exhibits. They were also places where the unusual and the curious were displayed, often brought back by travellers or soldiers from the far-flung provinces. Thus at Hierapolis, Indian jewels, the jaw of a snake and elephant tusks were among the items shown in the temple of the Syrian goddess; the temple of Hercules at Rome contained a number of animal hides, while rare plants, foreign weapons and an obsolete flute were amongst the collections at Carthage.

Ignoring the etymological difficulties that arise, it is necessary to ask whether this great awareness of art in classical Rome led to the formation of museums as we know them today. Certainly there was considerable public exhibition of art and curios. On a number of occasions public opinion took issue with the aristocracy for keeping works of art for their own enjoyment: Julius Caesar actually dedicated his own collection to temples while Agrippa, who avowed that the best art should belong to the people, opened his collections to the public. But no organized structure existed for the administration and upkeep of these collections, the initiative being left to the owners and few followed his example. As Bazin (1967) states: 'Rome had no museum *per se* but all Rome was a museum'.

Early Islamic collecting

With the rise of Islam in the sixth century AD and the spread of its culture and learning during the succeeding centuries across the southern Mediterranean lands and as far east as Indonesia, there is abundant evidence of art, expressed mainly in three-dimensional objects. There is considerable evidence of collecting at this time but not in furtherance of the museum idea. Rather it arises mainly from religious motives and takes the form of treasuries associated with the tombs of Muslim martyrs. The best known of these is the shrine of the Imam Aliar-Rida (*c.* AD 765–818) at Meshed in north-east Iran. The subject of pilgrimage to this day, many fine gifts have been made to the shrine and these are now housed in an adjacent museum. An important factor which has contributed to the preservation of cultural property was the idea of *al-waqf.*[6] This involved giving property, in perpetuity, for the public good and religious benefit and was formalized as a concept by Mohammad himself. In this way collections were formed, many of which have now been passed to museums.

Collections were also formed from the spoils of war. After the defeat of the Umayyads in the middle of the eighth century AD, the Abbasid caliphs and princes are recorded as having amassed works of art such as textiles, weapons and glass as trophies of their victory. The Fatimids (AD 909–1160), who reigned in Egypt and founded an academy at Cairo in the eleventh century also collected, housing their *Khanzaneh* in certain of their palaces for the pleasure of their caliphs and princes. This material was, however, destroyed at the end of the dynasty.

Early oriental collecting

It has been a characteristic of the Chinese peoples from antiquity to look to the past for guidance and this has expressed itself in collecting from very early times. Hoards of fine gold and bronze artefacts dating from the Shang dynasty (c. 1600–1025 BC) have been found during excavations in the Honan Province[7] and the remarkable collection of Qin dynasty (221–207 BC) terracotta warriors and horses in the Shanxi Province near Xi'an is an example of this. Collecting was almost certainly the prerogative of the rich and, by the time of the Empire, an activity of the emperors who acted as patrons to calligraphers and painters. Wu Ti (190–220 BC) amassed paintings and calligraphs in an imperial academy and this tradition seems to have continued in China over a very long period. Hsien Ti (AD 190–220) established a room devoted to portraits of his ministers. By the time of the Tang dynasty (AD 618–907), the collecting of treasures and books was popular and by no means restricted to the Emperor.

In Japan, the past and its personalities were also venerated and collections gathered by the aristocracy often found their way to the temples. One such offering was made by the widow of Emperor Shomu (AD 724–756) to the Buddha Vairochana and a special building, the Shoso-in, was constructed and its fine contents still exist today. Another early collection is that of the Buddhist Shingon sect, specializing in works of art from the Heian period (AD 794–1185). Since 1985 this has been available to the public in the Toji treasure house at Kyoto.

Medieval Europe

The destruction of Roman civilization in Western Europe in the fifth and sixth centuries AD brought to an end many of its customs and institutions, not least the mass appreciation and display of art. The main preoccupation now was economic and social self-sufficiency. Communities concerned with a primitive economy were more likely to find satisfaction from the talisman and their ruling families from easily realizable precious metal and stones. But a further factor was the re-introduction and spread of Christianity. For those under the influence of Augustinian teaching, the collection of things relating to the pagan classical world would have been unacceptable. However, with the rise of Christianity and of princely families it became commonplace for church and state to have treasuries and these became the main source of collections throughout medieval Europe.

As the church assumed greater power, so its holdings increased, sometimes in close collaboration with the ruling families of the time. But on a number of occasions sovereigns made demands on ecclesiastical treasuries to assist in financing wars and other state expenses, a fate which periodically affected French collections as late as the eighteenth century. Thus, while the motivation for establishing both ecclesiastical and secular treasuries at this time served cultural purposes, there can be little doubt of their economic significance as well.

For the church some of the collections were of a purely religious nature, embracing much sought-after relics of Christendom. Many of these allegedly unique items were duplicated in different churches in Europe. The catacombs of the Pechersky Monastery at Kiev are reputed to have been the source of a substantial trade in saints' bones in medieval times.[8] Because of their reputed therapeutic qualities they were the subject of pilgrimage and, therefore, of gifts.

The Renaissance

By the twelfth century new social, political and intellectual forces were being felt in Europe which would eventually lead to the Renaissance. These included an awakening of interest in classical learning and values. Private collecting and evidence of pilgrims visiting the ancient monuments of Rome can be found. Indeed, in 1162, Trajan's Column was effectively the subject of a preservation order as a monument in honour of the Roman people. The evidence for collecting is not peculiar to Italy. If the outstanding collection administered by Abbot Bernard Suger (c. AD 1081–1151) at the Royal Abbey of St Denis in France comprised mainly ecclesiastical objects, that of his contemporary Henry of Blois, Bishop of Winchester and Abbot of Glastonbury (c. AD 1099–1171), included classical statues which he brought back from Rome in 1151. Henry, Duke of Saxony and Bavaria (AD 1129–1195) also had a collection including an alleged 'griffin's claw', which originated in Palestine. The following century, Henry III, King of England (AD 1207–1272) had a collection which included pictures, jewels, relics and plate.

However, nowhere was the new prosperity more apparent than in Venice, which maintained maritime supremacy in the Mediterranean at this time. Although normally neutral in their dealings, the Venetians did join the Fourth Crusade at the beginning of the fourteenth century and captured Constantinople. Among the spoils brought back to Venice were the Greek bronze horses from Nero's hippodrome which now grace the portico of the Cathedral of St Mark. The latin occupation of Constantinople saw the beginning in the decline of Byzantine art which had flourished for over half a millennium.

By the following century a number of fine collections had been established, particularly by the great bourgeois families of Florence. Outstanding among these was that assembled by Cosimo (the Elder) de'Medici (1389–1464) and developed by members of the family. By the time of his grandson, Lorenzo the Magnificent (1449–1492), the collection included books, intaglios, precious stones, medals, tapestries, Byzantine icons, Flemish and other contemporary paintings and sculpture, a number of which had been specially commissioned. The fact that Jan van Eyck's *St Jerome* was purchased for 30 florins and 'the horn of a unicorn' for 6000 florins gives an insight into the relative value of the pieces in the Medici collection. The vicissitudes that affected the Medici after Lorenzo's death led to the pillaging of the collections on at least three occasions until Cosimo I (1519–1574) began to reassemble it; he also added to it, including artefacts from Etruscan sites and a fine collection of natural history specimens. To house the collections, additions to palaces as well as new ones were constructed by the Medicis. Francesco I (1541–1587), however, was responsible for converting the upper floor of the Uffizi into a picture gallery which was completed in 1582. The Medici collection continued to flourish until it was bequeathed by the last member of the Medici family, Anna Maria, in 1743 on the following terms:

> That these things being for the ornament of the State, for the benefit of the people and for an inducement to the curiosity of foreigners, nothing shall be alienated or taken away from the capital or from the territories of the Grand Duchy (translation Hale, 1977).

Many other collections formed by the ruling houses and the rich existed in fifteenth-century Italy. Furthermore, many of the collections were available to visitors, often on payment of a small fee, and they were popular enough to be listed in tourist guides of the period. Amongst them was the now increasing Vatican collection, towards which considerable resources were being devoted. The forming of collections was not restricted to Italy from whence there was an active trade in antiquities and art; indeed, in 1534, the Pope attempted to ban this export trade but without much effect. One of the principal recipient countries was France. There the royal collections were much enlarged by the king, Francis I, many of which were kept at Fontainebleau and to which were added curiosities brought to France by merchants and explorers.

The first recorded instance of the use of the word *museum* to describe a collection related to the de'Medici material at the time of Lorenzo the Magnificent. Other terms used more frequently were, from the sixteenth century, *gallery* to denote a place where paintings and sculpture were exhibited while, later, the word *cabinet* was used to describe either a collection of curiosities or the place where decorative art material was housed. Both terms were used in English and French. In German, *Kabinett* or *Kammer* were used, normally prefixed to give it greater precision, for example *Naturalienkabinett*, *Wunderkammer* (normally natural science collections) and *Rüstkammer* (arms and armour).

In Central Europe, the Dukes of Bavaria, Wilhelm IV and Albrecht V, both established collections in Munich, the latter erecting a gallery to hold the paintings between 1563 and 1567. This building, now the Mint, is probably the oldest surviving purpose-built 'museum'. Albrecht also built a long-vaulted Antiquarium at the Munich Residenz for his collection of antiquities between 1569 and 1571. Vespasiano Ganzaga, Duke of Sabbioneta, similarly built an Antiquarium for his Roman collection in 1580–1584 as an annexe to the Casino del Giardino near Mantua, Italy. At Ambras Castle, near Innsbruck, Ferdinand of Tyrol established a number of different types of collection: a Kunstkammer, an Antiquarium and a Rustkammer, all of which are open to the public today.

The spirit of the Renaissance, with its emphasis on experiment and observation, led to the formation of scientific collections. Collections of natural history material were particularly common in sixteenth-century Italy, over 250 such collections being recorded there alone. Perhaps the first herbarium collected for scientific purposes was that of Luca Ghini (1490–1556) at Padua. Konrad von Gesner (1516–1565),[9] whose *Historiae animalium* was an outstanding contribution to the natural history of his time, also gathered an important collection. This was acquired by Felix Potter (1536–1614), another notable naturalist, part of whose collection is held in the Natural History Museum at Basle. Ulisse Aldrovandi (1522–1605), whose large collection of plant, animal and mineral illustrations, prepared for his encyclopaedic work on natural history, found its way into the University of Bologna's museum in

1743. Another important Italian collection was that of Ferrante Imperato at Naples. Of particular interest during the sixteenth century was the exotic natural history introduced to Europe as a result of exploration and trading, but the indigenous fauna and flora were not ignored.

The sixteenth century saw many changes in Europe, not least the changing balance of sea power. Throughout medieval times the principal route from Africa and the Orient to central and northern Europe had been through the ports of Venice and Genoa. Thus the influence of the Italian Renaissance had spread through Europe and there the trade in antiquities, classical and exotic, had centred. This now changed as Spain and Portugal, France, the Netherlands and also Britain commenced trans-ocean exploration, trade and, eventually, colonization.

Among the well-known private collections in Northern Europe were those of Olaf Worm (1588–1654) in Copenhagen and Bernard Paludanius (1550–1633). Both of these followed the cabinet of curiosities pattern and visitors were admitted to them. In due course they became part of public museum collections.[10] Taylor (1948) notes that only one painting was to be found in the palace of Gustavus Adolphus in Stockholm, although it should be recorded that this King was responsible for the appointment of a *Riksantikvarie* in 1630 to look after Sweden's national antiquities. His daughter Christina, however, set out to improve the country's holdings of foreign culture and, when her troops occupied Prague, much of the fine collection of Rudolph II was transferred to Stockholm. When she abdicated and left the country in 1654 many of the works of art went with her, but she left behind a number of Dutch and German paintings which contributed to the formation of the National Museum in Stockholm.

The Enlightenment

By this time the age of applying system and scientific method to an understanding of humankind and nature was already underway. A century earlier Nicolas Copernicus had led the way for a revolution in astronomy; Francis Bacon had propounded the need to establish an inductive empiricism and expressed the need for useful knowledge to be catalogued, while René Descartes, who ended his days at Christina of Sweden's court, was seeking mathematical solutions to rationalize religion and science. Moreover, many of the collections were already more than just an assemblage of curiosities; they were well ordered. As early as 1565, Samuel van Quiccheberg, a Flemish doctor, had written that collections should ideally represent a systematic classification of all materials in the universe and this

work undoubtedly influenced the Tradescents of England in ordering their collection. Indeed, such general guidance was readily available in published form by 1727 for the amateur collector; it dealt with the problems of classification, collection care and sources to supplement collections and was to be found in Casper F. Neickel's *Museographia*, published in Leipzig. But the naturalists and antiquarians had still to await Linnaeus and Thomsen, both Scandinavians who, in 1735 and 1836, respectively, provided the beginning of modern classification for their material. These frameworks, necessary to bring better order and understanding to the natural and prehistoric worlds, were constructed and developed from collections. An important part of Linneaus's collection is now housed at the Linnaean Society in London, while that used by Thomsen is at the Danish National Museum of Antiquities, of which he was the first curator.

This was the age of the development of learned societies of which many also formed collections. In Florence the *Accademia del Cimento* was founded by the Medici in 1650, by no means the first such society in Italy; another, the Etruscan Academy founded in 1726, arranged excavations and in due course opened its *Galleria del publico* to show archaeology and art objects in its collection. At Haarlem the natural history cabinet of the *Hollandsche Maatschappij der Wetenschappen* was opened in 1778 as a result of Pieter Teyler van der Hulst's benefaction. The development of the collection thereafter changed direction towards natural philosophy and, as a result, Teyler's Museum today holds an important collection of eighteenth century scientific instruments (Turner, 1973). There is no doubt that this society and the *Accademia* in Florence became centres for scientific experimentation for their members (Bedini, 1965). Many other countries in Europe had similar societies, their collections being formed primarily for the benefit of their own members but often, in later years, contributing to the foundation of public museums.

The first public museums

The point in time when corporate bodies began to acquire or form collections with the clear intention of making them available for the public benefit must be regarded as a watershed in the history of museums and an important step nearer the idea of a museum as it is known today. However, the development of public collections and their ready availability was gradual and much influenced by prevailing social and philosophical considerations.

The Venetian Republic appears to have been one of the earliest public bodies to receive collections, bequeathed by the Grimani family in 1523 and 1583; these collections went to form the basis for the present archaeological museum in Venice. Sixteenth-century Switzerland saw many paintings, antiquities and manuscripts taken over by a number of the municipalities as a result of the Reformation and these were in due course to contribute to some of its leading museums, for example, the National Swiss Museum, Zurich, and the Historical Museum, Berne. Another Swiss city, Basel, purchased the important Amerbach collection in 1661 to prevent it leaving the country and this was installed in a house within the university library to which there was public access (Ackermann, 1985). In France, Abbot Boisot bequeathed his collection to the Abbey of St Vincent at Besançon in 1694. This bequest, which included his collection of books, paintings and medallions, was subject to them being available to the public to read and study on two occasions each week (Poulot, 1983).

In England, John Tradescant and his son formed a fine biological and artefact collection which was available for public visiting at Lambeth from 1625. Later in the century this became the founding collection for the Ashmolean Museum, when it was given to the University of Oxford by Elias Ashmole and opened to the public in purpose-built premises in 1683 (MacGregor, 1983). This can be regarded as the first public museum in England. The British Museum, established by Act of Parliament from collections acquired for the nation, opened in 1759.

The French capital had to wait rather longer for its first truly public museum, the Louvre, to which visitors were admitted in 1793. It was based on the magnificent royal collections, the inaccessibility of which had been the subject of public disquiet for at least 50 years. Louis XV had already tried to appease this by exhibiting about 100 of the paintings in the Palais Luxembourg in 1750, but this was closed to the public in 1779. However, the campaign had continued. When Diderot published the ninth volume of his *Encyclopédie* in 1765 he included a detailed scheme for a national museum in the Louvre, which would also accommodate the Academies; in this the proposals suggested a latter-day Alexandrian *mouseion*.

In fact proposals were already afoot to use the *Grand Gallerie* of the Louvre as a museum, and in 1784 a Conservateur was appointed to prepare it. But in the event it was not to be a museum of the royal collection but of the nationalized collections following the creation of the French Republic in 1792 and, therefore, a public museum in the true sense of the phrase. The Muséum Central des Arts, as the Louvre was first known, was created by decree the following year and opened to the public in August. However, because of the condition of the gallery it was open only for a short time, not fully re-opening until 1801. The museum collection, however, grew rapidly. The *Convention Nationale* instructed Napoleon to

appropriate works of art during his European campaigns and, as a result, many looted collections found their way to the Louvre. It was no accident that for about a decade from 1803 the institution was known as the Musée Napoléon and during this period undoubtedly contained the finest collection in Europe. Following the Congress of Vienna in 1815, much of the material was returned to its owners, this constituting the first major example of the restitution of cultural property.[11]

The latter years of the eighteenth century and the beginning of the nineteenth century saw the opening of a number of collections to the public in different parts of Europe. Many of these resulted from royal favour rather than public benefaction. Thus the opening of the Schloss Belvedere in Vienna as an art gallery around 1784 was the direct result of Joseph II's wish for some of the royal paintings to be displayed for the public benefit. Chretian de Mechel, who was responsible for the collection, arranged the collection by schools because, a great public collection of this type, he said, should be 'more for one's instruction than delight'. This approach was controversial if not novel, but it marked an important move in the ordered presentation of paintings for the public benefit (Bazin, 1967). Admission to the Schloss was possible on three days a week. Also in Austria, but representing the founding of a truly public museum at the outset, was the Archduke Johann's gift of his natural science and historical collections to the Styrian people in 1811. Today, the Joanneum continues to follow its donor's stipulation that it should be 'for the welfare of the community . . . to cultivate the minds of Styrian youth, to serve the advancement of knowledge and to stimulate the diligence and industry of the Styrian people' (Waidacher, 1986).

In Spain, the royal collections at the Escorial Palace were certainly available to visitors on request from the seventeenth century, but it was not until the reign of Charles III that this was taken a stage further. In 1774 he brought together in the reconstructed Goyeneche Palace some of his works of art and natural history collections with the idea that the St Ferdinand Royal Academy of Fine Art should be based there and that an Academy of Science should also be created. In 1785, however, the King directed that a new building should be erected to serve as a Museum of Natural Science. The premises were completed about 20 years later and if it had not been for the Spanish War of Independence the original intention might have been realized in 1808. The usurper, Joseph Bonaparte, proposed the establishment of a public museum of paintings and also the transfer of 50 pictures to the Musée Napoléon in Paris; only the latter was effected. The new museum building, however, was requisitioned and damaged during these troubles and it was not until 1818 that the re-instated Ferdinand VII ordered its repair anad preparation to display some of the royal pictures. And so the Prado Museum eventually opened its doors to the public of Madrid on 19 November 1819. Today one of the world's great art galleries, there is some evidence (Sanchez Canton, 1973, pp. 68–70) that it also displayed natural specimens in its early days. The collections were nationalized after the revolution of 1868 and, since 1870, have been administered by the State.

In Portugal the earliest public museum seems to have been the Museum of Natural History, opened in 1772 by the University in Coimbra in specially designed accommodation (Braz Teixeira, 1985). The national museum of Belgium came into being following the recognition of Brussels as the capital of the new State in 1830. It was based on the Royal Arsenal with collections dating from the sixteenth century. A Royal Decree of 1835 establishing the museum indicates that it was created in the interest of historical and artistic study. In 1847 it was renamed the Musée Royal d'Armures, d'Antiquités et d'Ethnologie, thus recognizing its important ethnology department and collection (Schotsmans, 1985).

Another country occupied by Napoleon was The Netherlands. Here the collecting tradition did not rest with royal families but with official bodies, particularly the municipalities. Notwithstanding this, some of the art treasures were seized and dispatched to Paris as war trophies. Perhaps as an indirect result of this, the idea of a national art gallery was mooted for some of the remaining paintings in Haarlem and these were transferred to the Huis den Bosch which opened in 1800; for a small fee the public could visit the museum for a guided tour. This museum, however, was short-lived, being transferred to Amsterdam in 1808 by Louis Bonaparte to become the Koninklijk Museum to which several paintings were loaned by the city of Amsterdam. In 1815 it was renamed the Rijksmuseum. This museum suffered severe accommodation problems and the modern paintings were transferred to Haarlem. It was not until 1885 that the present purpose-built Rijksmuseum was opened in Amsterdam by which time the collections had expanded considerably, drawing on the many private art collections that had been built up in this international trading nation.

It was the return of the looted royal works of art from France to Berlin and their public exhibition in the Unter den Linden Academy that gave the impetus to the erection of the Altes Museum by Frederick William III and the acquisition of a large number of paintings by the State to supplement the royal collection. It was not opened to the public, however, until 1830. The Altes Museum was the first building in what was to become a major planned museum development over the next century on the peninsula formed by the rivers Spree and Kupfergraben, later known as the Museum-insel; first the Neues Museum (1855), linked by bridge with the earlier museum, followed by the National Gallery (1875), the Kaiser Friedrich Museum (1904) and, finally, as one complex in the Renaissance tradition, the Deutsches Museum, the Pergamon Museum and the Vorderasiastische Museum, completed in 1930.

Thus, while most of the early museums of Europe came into existence by the accident of circumstances with collections available at the time and often housed in a building redundant from some other purpose, the Berlin development was from the outset based on a clear plan. The Altes Museum was in fact conceived by art historians and directed by one, unlike its counterparts in Britain and France where artists seem to have been preferred to head the art museums. As Wilhelm von Humboldt, Chairman of the Commission for the establishment of the Altes Museum reported to the king in 1830: 'the Royal gallery here is different in that it covers systematically all periods of painting and provides a visual history of art from its beginnings' (quoted in Klessmann, 1971); other galleries at Dusseldorf and Vienna had, in fact, followed this approach in 1756 and 1784, respectively. The subsequent development of the site extends this philosophy of the scientific approach to collections with their division into different subjects.

The collections of the Alte Pinakothek, opened in Munich in 1836, were also displayed chronologically by schools; as Leo von Klenze, the architect, explained: the gallery 'was intended for the whole nation, not just to artists who will be favourably disposed to their nature' (quoted in Dube, 1970). The architect required the building to be situated in an open space, protected from fire, dust and vibration and that internally the rooms should be separately accessible, lit by skylights or north-facing windows and moderately heated both for the conservation of the pictures and the comfort of the visitors. Thus were displayed the finest pictures of the Dukes of Wittelsbach.

The last of the important major royal collections to be displayed to the public was that of the Russian Tsars. Remarkable for the fact that it was built up over the relatively short period of about 150 years and that the fine-art collection was entirely of non-Russian work – a feature which it still retains – it also included the fine picture collection of Sir Robert Walpole whose heirs sold it to Catherine the Great in 1778 for £30,000. The Tsars' collection was the subject of a Napoleonic request in 1812 and certain of the works were dispatched to Paris from what is now St Petersburg but were returned the following year. As the collection continued to grow it spread from the Winter Palace into the adjacent Hermitage. Following a severe fire in the Winter Palace, Leo van

Klenze, who designed the Alte Pinakothek in Munich, was commissioned to plan new adjacent premises to house the collection, known as the New Hermitage. The building and collection were opened by Nicholas I in 1852 and the public allowed to enter on presentation of an admission ticket and provided they wore full regimental uniform or tail coats (Piotrovsky, 1978). These regulations were rescinded in the following decade and the Hermitage took on the role of a public museum, although it remained nominally under royal administration until the revolution of 1917.

It was at the beginning of the nineteenth century that the first realization of the role of the museum in contributing to national consciousness arose in Europe. With it came the recognition that the museum was the appropriate institution for the preservation of a nation's historic heritage. In Budapest the national museum, which originated in 1802, was built from money raised from voluntary taxes and was to figure prominently later in the fight for Hungarian independence. In Prague a revival in nationalism led to the founding of a museum in 1818 specifically to foster cultural identity and the study of the Czech and Slovak peoples. Although a national museum for Poland was considered as early as 1775, it was not established until 1862; there were, however, at least two early nineteenth-century museums: the museum of the Princess Czartoryski in the park at Pulawy and the palace museum at Wilanów, both near Warsaw (Fijalkowski, 1986). The Danish government, responding to a suggestion that it should collect and preserve the nation's early archaeological heritage, established the National Museum of Antiquities in Copenhagen in 1819. The Swedish State, which had been collecting national antiquities since the seventeenth century did not make them available to the public until the Statens Historiska Museum was opened in Stockholm in 1847. In a sense the Musée des Monuments Français, created in Paris in 1795, served a similar purpose until its dissolution in 1816 to be followed by the Musée de Cluny and, eventually, the Musée des Antiquités Nationales in the Château de Saint-Germain-en-Laye in 1862.

Museum development outside Europe

The concept of the public museum as defined here is essentially European in origin and the idea seems to have been transmitted to other parts of the world through trading and colonialism. As far as Britain is concerned there is no evidence of Government policy to establish museums in the colonies; rather it was left to the British colonies to take the initiative. In consequence, museum development, as in the UK itself, was haphazard.

The American continent

The earliest recorded museum in North America was in the English colonies. In 1773 the Charleston Library Society of South Carolina announced its intention of forming a collection of the 'natural productions, either animal vegetable or mineral' with a view to displaying the practical and commercial aspects of agriculture and medicine in the province. The resulting museum, although its activities were interrupted by the War of Independence and not revived until 1785, reflected two features which were to characterize museum development in the USA: an overtly educational role and an origin resulting from the initiative of a local society.

There were, however, a number of private collectors in the USA, some operating early in the eighteenth century. Among these were John Winthrop (1681–1747) who collected shells, particularly in New England, and John Bartram (1699–1777) who collected widely in Pennsylvania, Georgia, Carolina and Florida. Other collectors included Thomas Say (1787–1834) and Prince Alexander Maximilian Neuwied (1782–1867), whose large zoological collection is in the American Museum of Natural History, New York. However, perhaps the best known of these early collectors was Charles Wilson Peale (1741–1827).

Mr Peale opened his museum in his home at Philadelphia in 1785. This was European in concept but, in advance of its time, with the clear intention of the instruction and entertainment of all classes. It soon outgrew its accommodation and moved a number of times to larger premises. As a private museum it went through a number of economic vicissitudes and, after being declined both by the city and the nation, finally became incorporated in 1821 as the Philadelphia Museum Company. This enterprise continued after Peale's death and was known on both sides of the Atlantic. In 1840 James Silk Buckingham, a protagonist for municipal museums in Britain, visited it and he described the collection in his book *The Eastern and Western States of America*; he arranged for an exhibition of the Museum's fine Chinese collection in London. However, the Museum waned and the dispersal of its collections commenced in 1845, to be completed nine years later (Sellars, 1980; Miller and Ward, 1991).

The national museum for the USA cannot really be considered as being established until 1858, and then after a long gestation period (Oehser, 1970). Collections had been forming, however, for some time and there had been a keeper of the Cabinet since 1850. The origins of the national museum lie in the remarkable bequest of James Macie Smithson (1765–1829), a son of Hugh Smithson, first Duke of Northumberland and Elizabeth Macie. The first beneficiaries under James Smithson's Will having died, the alternative provisions became operative:

> to the United States of America, to be founded at Washington, under the name Smithsonian Institution, an Establishment for the increase and diffusion of knowledge among men.

And so in 1838 just over £100,000 (about $500,000) was shipped across the Atlantic. It was not until 1846, however, that the US Senate approved an Act establishing the Smithsonian Institution which *inter alia* provided for the creation of a building to house 'all objects of art and curious research, and all objects of natural history, plants and geological and mineralogical specimens' belonging to the USA, together with the Smithson material. The objects were to 'be arranged in such order . . . as best facilitate the examination and study of them'; additions to the collection were authorized which 'may be obtained . . . by exchanges of duplicate specimens . . . by donation . . . or otherwise'.

The first Secretary of the Smithsonian Institution, Joseph Henry, laid the foundations on which the Institution, including its museums, would develop. In his view 'Smithson was well aware that knowledge should not be viewed as existing in isolated parts'; and this approach was an important factor in the development of the museum. In one respect Henry's view was not accepted in that he would have preferred the museum to be separate from the main Institution. When Spencer Baird was appointed Keeper of the Cabinet in 1850, however, the museum side of the enterprise developed, eventually to dominate it, even though in the late 1930s there was still an official view that the Smithsonian was not a museum.

The US National Museum, as it was then known, opened in 1858 under Baird who eventually succeeded Henry. Another Assistant Secretary, George Browne Goode, joined the staff in 1877 having already been an honorary curator of the Museum, and continued the work, becoming one of the leading curators of his time. Today the Smithsonian complex, once described as 'the octopus on the Mall' includes the National Museum of Natural History, the Museum of American History, the National Air and Space Museum, the National Gallery of Art, the Freer Gallery, the National Portrait Gallery, the Museum of African Art and the Hirshhorn Museum and Sculpture Garden. A zoo and the Anacostia Neighbourhood Museum also form part of the Institution.

The first art museum of any standing in the USA was the Wadsworth Atheneum, founded at Hartford in 1842. It was not until 1870 that the Metropolitan Museum of Art was established in New York; the Museum of Fine Arts in Boston was founded in the same year. Another of the well-known institutions, the American Museum of Natural History, was

founded in 1869. Both of these New York institutions established an important precedent, to be followed subsequently by a number of other museums in the USA, whereby the city authorities agreed to provide and maintain the buildings while the trustees accepted responsibility for the collections and professional staff.

The predominance of history museums, particularly historic-house museums, in the USA is due largely to the work of the historical societies, of which the earliest was The Massachusetts Historical Society, founded in Boston in 1791. The first historic house to be preserved as a museum was Hasbronck House, Newburgh – George Washington's headquarters – but this was purchased by the state of New York in 1850. The second, purchased through private initiative 3 years later, was Mount Vernon, Virginia, also with Washington connections. Both were established at a period of civil unrest and can be regarded as patriotic gestures.

The earliest museum collection in Canada seems to have been in the eastern Maritime Provinces. Key (1973) records that the Picton Academy of Nova Scotia had a museum, probably by 1822; certainly it was described some seven years later as having 'the most extensive collection of zoology in the country'. He also attributes the development of many of the community museums there to the Mechanics' Institute movement, the earliest of which appears to be that founded at Halifax, Nova Scotia in 1831. The natural history collections of this Museum, by now defunct, were transferred to the new Provincial Museum in Halifax about 35 years later.

Montreal also had some early collections. *Le Musée del Vecchio* was operated for a short time from 1824 by an Italian entrepreneur. The Natural History Society of Montreal certainly had a fine collection by 1826 (Murray, 1904, Vol. 3), part of which was transferred to the Redpath Museum at McGill University, as also had that of the Literary and Historical Society of Quebec. In Quebec City a museum was opened by a sculptor and gilder, Pierre Chasseur, in the same year and this collection was purchased by the Government of Quebec in 1836 to become the first public museum in Canada; it was destroyed by fire in 1854.

The National Museum commenced as an adjunct of the Geological Survey of Canada in 1843 at Montreal and, although it was transferred to Ottawa in 1880, it remained part of the Survey until a separate Director of the Museum was appointed in 1920 and later separated administratively. In this it was unlike the National Gallery of Canada which had a common founding with the Royal Canadian Academy of Arts in 1880 and operated under an Advisory Council until this was replaced with a Board of Trustees in 1951. Under the *National Museums Act 1967* the Canadian National Museums operated as a unit but this has now been reversed and the four museums (the National Gallery, the Canadian Museum of Civilization and the National Museums of Natural History and of Technology) have a degree of autonomy. The 1967 statute did much to encourage museum development at a national, provincial and local level in the run up to Canada's centennial year and for nearly 20 years thereafter.

The origins of Ontario's provincial museum are to be found in the *Public School Act 1853* which provided for the purchase of books, publications and objects suitable for a Canadian Library and Museum. The resulting collection, mainly copies of paintings and statues, and intended primarily for trainee teachers, was exhibited to the public at the Toronto Normal School. This collection soon developed; in 1896 the Canada Institute's fine archaeological collection was moved to the same premises and the combined collection became known as the Ontario Provincial Museum. The colleges of the University of Toronto also developed a number of teaching collections, although one of these was destroyed by fire in 1890. Eventually, these and other collections were brought together to form the Royal Ontario Museum, established by a special statute in 1912 in purpose-built premises and opened to the public two years later (Dickson, 1986). The Art Gallery of Ontario was opened in 1913. A feature of the Canadian museum scene is the number of historical society museums that exist, particularly in Ontario. These appear to have commenced in the last decade of the nineteenth century and have continued to increase ever since (Miers and Markham, 1932). The appearance of museums in British Columbia and the Prairie Provinces also dates to the end of that century.

The earliest museums in South America were also the result of colonial influence. The first recorded example was at Rio de Janeiro and was formed from a collection of paintings given by the King of Portugal. It opened to the public in 1815 and is now the national museum (Coleman, 1939). Another early museum was the Museo del Pais, Buenos Aires, resulting from an initiative by Bernardino Rivadavia in 1812 and opened in 1823, shortly after independence. Now known as the Argentine Museum of Natural History it has occupied its present purpose-built premises since 1937 adjacent to the University of Buenos Aires with which it is closely associated (Lascano Gonzalez, 1980). Other museums developed in Latin America as part of wider cultural provision by governments, for example in Costa Rica, where the decade 1880–1890 saw the establishment of the National Archives, National Library, National Theatre as well at the National Museum in 1887 (San Romàn Johanning, 1987).

Africa

Early museum development in Africa commenced in the south of the continent. The first, the South African Museum in Cape Town, was founded by 'the father of South African zoology', Dr Andrew Smith, in 1825 (Barry, 1975). As might be expected, the earliest of the North African museums was in Egypt, established in 1863 and which formed the basis for three well-known present-day museums in Cairo (the Egyptian Museum, the Coptic Museum and the Museum of Islamic Art), all of which opened in the first decade of the twentieth century. Much of the remainder of North Africa was under Ottoman rule at this time and there is some evidence that antiquities were sent from these countries to the museum at Constantinople (Istanbul). A museum was, however, created in Algeria in 1884 by a geographical and archaeological society in Oran and four years later the Musée Alaoui (now the national museum) was inaugurated in Tunis. Other earlier museums in Africa were founded in Tananarive, Madagascar (1897); Bulawayo (1901) and Harare, Zimbabwe (1902); Kampala, Uganda and Cherchell, Algeria (1908); and Nairobi, Kenya (1909).

Asia

Perhaps the earliest museum on the Asian continent was that of the Asiatic Society of Bengal which, although conceived 18 years previously, eventually opened in 1814. This society maintained the museum in Calcutta for a number of years, considerably adding to its predominantly geological and natural history collections. In 1875 the Indian Museum collection was vested in trustees in a new building provided by the government. A number of other government museums were founded in India during the second half of the nineteenth century: Madras (1851), Lucknow (1863), Bangalore (1865), Mathura (1874), Jaipur (1886), and Baroda (1894). Pakistan's Lahore Museum is the oldest and largest in the country, dating to 1864. The National Museum in Colombo, Sri Lanka, was opened in 1877.

Another early Asian museum which owes its foundation to a learned society is the National Museum of Indonesia at Jakarta. The Batavia Society of Arts and Sciences, established in 1778, began a collection of books and artefacts which formed the nucleus of the present museum which was inaugurated in 1868. The Singapore National Museum also had early origins in that it is based on collections from the Raffles Museum and Library which was established in 1823. In the Philippines, even earlier origins are claimed for the University of Santo Tomas Museum of Arts and Sciences, Manila. Although only established in 1927, the founding collection included the *Gabineta di Fisica* dating to 1682. Other South-East Asian museums with nineteenth-century origins include the national Museum of Thailand in Bangkok originally opened in 1874, the Perak and Sarawak museums in Malaysia dating from 1886 and 1891 respectively.

Despite the long-established tradition of collecting in China, the emergence of public museums was not early. Shanghai witnessed the establishment of the Sikowei Museum in 1868 and a further museum four years later under the aegis of the Royal Asiatic Society[7]: both museums appear to have been intended for a restricted, overseas audience. The Museums Department of the State Administrative Bureau of Museums and Archaeological Data (1980) records the first museum of modern type as being the Nantung Centre of Natural History, founded in 1905.

In Japan, a government order protecting old wares and objects was made in 1871 and the following year a museum to encourage industry and the development of natural resources was opened. These collections formed the basis of the museums known as the Tokyo National Museum and the National Science Museum (Tsurita, 1960). The latter museum had a strong educational bias when it opened to the public in 1877 and included aids for scientific teaching, school equipment as well as a natural science collection (Greenwood, 1888).

Australasia

The collection of specimens of Australia's remarkable natural history and the shipment of material to England was commonplace at the beginning of the nineteenth century. The Governor of New South Wales was a member of the Newcastle upon Tyne Literary and Philosophical Society and sent material to them, as did Sir Joseph Banks. There were also close links with John Hunter's museum in London (Strahan *et al*, 1979). The first recorded collection in Australia dates to 1821 and was established in Sydney by the Philosophical Society of Australasia. This Society appears to have continued only for one year after which time the collections were probably stored in the Colonial Secretary's office. However, when a new incumbent, Alexander Macleay, arrived in 1826, he brought with him a deep interest in natural history. He was a Fellow and past Honorary Secretary of the Linnaean Society in London.

It is thought likely that Alexander Macleay was responsible for establishing what was to become the Australian Museum in Sydney. Certainly representations were made to the Colonial Office in 1827, but the appointment of a zoologist to run the Museum did not occur until 1829. The following year, the local newspaper refers to 'a beautiful collection of Australian curiosities, the property of the Government' which Mr Holmes (the zoologist) 'between the hours of ten and three politely shows . . . to any

respectable individuals who may think fit to call'. The Museum remained in temporary quarters for over 25 years but received corporate status under the administration of trustees through the *Australian Museum Trust Act 1853*. The Museum moved into its present, purpose-built premises in 1857. Alexander Macleay's own fine collection of European insects, however, formed the basis for the University of Sydney's Macleay Museum, opened in 1874 through a legacy from a descendant of the family. The National Art Gallery of New South Wales in Sydney was much later and a permanent gallery was not opened until 1897 (Markham and Richards, 1933).

In Melbourne the National Gallery of Victoria commenced as the Museum of Art in part of the Public Library in 1861 but did not have its own trustees until after World War II, or a separate building until the present fine gallery was opened in 1968 (Cox, 1970). The National Museum of Victoria commenced as an independent institution in 1854 (Prescott, 1954) to be followed in 1870 by what was to become known as the Science Museum of Victoria (Perry, 1972). By this time the library, museums and art gallery had been incorporated under one body of trustees. These were national institutions in the sense that they were financed by the Government of a Crown State Colony.

The Ancanthe Museum to the north of Hobart, Tasmania, was probably the earliest purpose-built museum in Australia, having been erected in 1842. Although a private museum, it was subsequently merged with the collections of the Royal Society of Tasmania. Other museums founded during the mid-nineteenth century were the Queensland Museum, Brisbane (1855), the Museum of the Swan River Mechanics' Institute in Perth (1860) and the Adelaide Museum (1861). Most of the major art galleries in Australia opened later in the same century.

In New Zealand the initiative of the Mechanics' Institute at Taranaki led to the formation of a collection of ethnographic material and curiosities in the late 1840s which survived for about half a century. The earliest museum, however, is the Nelson Provincial Museum at Stoke, dating to about 1841, to be followed by the Dominion Museum at Auckland (now the Auckland Institute and Museum) 11 years later. The Christchurch Museum which opened in 1861 was supported financially by the Provincial Government until it was abolished in 1875 (Markham and Oliver, 1933). The National Museum in Wellington did not open until 1865 and was the result of a jointly sponsored venture by the Government and the New Zealand Geological Society (Thompson, 1981). The present building, opened in 1936, also resulted from joint collaboration in which the Government provided a matching contribution to funds raised in Wellington, and brought together the National Museum and the National Art Gallery in one building which was first opened as the Wellington Public Gallery in 1906.

The twentieth century

By the beginning of the twentieth century the world museum scene had changed significantly. With the increasing population movement to urban centres in the industrialized nations, many of these communities developed their own museums. In Europe, this tended to be through local government while in the USA the initiative was by individual patronage or local groups of citizens. In certain countries a more centralized State museum system developed, for example in France and in the USSR, the latter much encouraged by Leninist philosophy to protect the cultural heritage and make it available to the people; elsewhere museum development was less controlled.

While many of the earliest museums were encyclopaedic in character, reflecting the spirit of their age, in the twentieth century more specialized museums began to emerge. One such important development was the proliferation of 'folk museums'. The idea originated in Sweden where Artur Hazelius opened his museum of Scandinavian folklore (now the *Nordiska Museet*) at Stockholm in 1873. Before long, however, his work had extended beyond easily transportable artefacts to buildings and, in 1891, the first open-air museum was opened at Skansen.

Such a conscious attempt to preserve and display a nation's more recent past, or aspects of it, was increasingly to characterize much museum activity as the century progressed. In certain cases such museums were exploited for propaganda purposes. This was a feature of post-World War I Germany when over 2000 *Heimatmuseen* were created (Bazin, 1967; Cruz-Ramirez, 1985) and of communist Russia where, for example, the opening of the new Central Lenin Museum, Moscow, in 1936 prompted the newspaper *Pravda* to report that it was 'a new powerful propaganda weapon for Leninism'. The use of museums to promote cultural identity occurs in many parts of the world. The Council of Europe, for example, has encouraged its member states to develop 'European Rooms' in museums to present a public view of the European heritage.[12] An example of this can be found at the Norwich Castle Museum (Cheetham, 1981).

Science museums were much earlier in origin. Private cabinets of scientific instruments such as that of Bonnier de la Mosson, could be found before the mid-eighteenth century (Hill, 1986). The museum of Pieter Teyler in Haarlem (Turner, 1973) and the *Conservatoire National des Arts et Métiers* in Paris, however, did not open to the public until towards the end of that century (Danilov, 1982). The application of science to industry was reflected during the following century at the *Conservatoire* and in London's embryonic Science Museum at South Kensington, both institutions benefiting considerably from the international exhibitions in their respective countries. But the Deutsches Museum in Munich, when it finally transferred from its temporary home in 1925, set the pace in interpreting science and technology for a lay audience.

Following World War II rapid technological change brought a concern not only to preserve and interpret industrial artefacts but also to recreate industrial environments, their impact on communities and the rapidly disappearing processes involved. Important catalysts to these developments were an increasing public interest in the past and developing tourism. In the UK, the North of England Open Air Museum at Beamish and the Ironbridge Gorge Museum, which commenced with corporate identity in 1970, typify this movement (Cossons, 1980). Related to these developments but involving a mainly simulated location and re-sited buildings is the Sovereign Hill Goldmining Township and Historical Park at Ballarat, Victoria, Australia, which also opened in 1970. A similar project was developed in France in 1972 at the Museum of Man and Industry at Le Creusot-Montceau-les-Mines to the south-west of Dijon (de Varine-Bohan, 1973; Evrard, 1980); here the day-to-day participation of the local community in the Museum is a key element of its operation and it can be regarded as one of the earliest of the so-called ecomuseums (UNESCO, 1985b).

On-site preservation of historic environments for museum purposes has also become an increasing trend. One of the better known is Colonial Williamsburg, the restored capital of eighteenth-century Virginia in the USA. This project was founded in 1926 (Kocher *et al.*, 1961). More recent examples include the restoration of the walled medieval cities of Suzdal and Vladimir in the USSR (Aksenova, 1978) and the rehabilitation of the total environment of the small island of Goreé, off the west coast of Senegal, Africa, with its slave-trade associations (UNESCO, 1985a) and the development of the Museum of Qin Shi Huang which preserves the remarkable terracotta warriors and horses associated with this mausoleum at Xi'an in China (Wu, 1985).

The changing philosophy towards museums in the second half of the twentieth century, however, has by no means been exclusively among the industrialized nations. In Latin America, Asia and Africa there have been strong moves to integrate the museum more fully with the community it serves. At a meeting of curators from Latin American countries held in Santiago in 1972, the museum was recognized as a medium of long-life education through which an awareness of the social, economic and political aspects of scientific, technological and environmental development could be created (UNESCO, 1973).

Nations newly gaining independence also closely examined the role of museums and their contribution in a developing State. This has been particularly marked in Africa and, according to Diop (1973), where a country has inherited a colonial museum this is 'like most European museums . . . 'a sort of warehouse in which exhibits were deprived of their true essence in a totally inanimate setting'. In Nigeria a network of national museums has been created because they were seen both as an important means of preserving the heritage and as a medium through which national cultural unity could be fostered (Afigbo and Okita, 1985). At Jos, a representative series of traditional buildings was created to form a Museum of Traditional Nigerian Architecture – it is impractical to re-site traditional buildings – while other museums developed workshops where traditional crafts could be demonstrated and the products sold. In the National Museum in Niamey, Niger, there are two craft workshops, one worked by professional craft-workers and the other specially provided to train the blind and physically handicapped in craft-work in order that they can take their place in the community. The products are sold in the museum shop and exported to Europe and North America (Saley, 1976).

This re-appraisal of the role of the museum has led curators and governing bodies far more into the realm of operations research. In Canada a survey of a population sample was used to provide evidence of the public perception of the museums' role (Dixon, 1974). In the UK similar work has been undertaken, although based on smaller samples, and considerable attention has also been paid to the numbers and types of visitor using museum services. The results have shown that few museums attract a true cross-section of the public and this has led to an examination of the issues. In Toronto, the Art Gallery of Ontario organized a seminar on the topic 'Are art galleries obsolete?'. As a keynote speaker at that seminar said:

> To some, the art gallery has become a sanctuary of scholarship with aesthetic selectivity. To others it is a club and fashionable warehouse for the wealthy. In such instituations, art, at best, is seen as a cultural artifact and rarely as an instrument of illuminating the human perception and visual awareness of the public (Cameron, 1969).

Concern about the elitist position of many museums generally led to an active 'democratization' process in Canada and other countries to involve a far greater cross-section of the public. Such policies are also found among the international and supranational governmental organizations.[13]

In the USA action to relate more closely to social issues in the community was also taken by a number of museums. For example, the Anacostia Neighbourhood Museum, Washington, DC (Kinard, 1985), and the New York City Museum organized temporary exhibitions on such issues as rat infestation and drugs, respectively. An increased awareness of the part that museums can play in multi-cultural communities at both national and local levels as well as with the mentally and physically disabled is also apparent in a number of countries.

Concern about the effectiveness of museum communication through display has led to a number of studies. Both the British Museum (Natural History) and the Royal Ontario Museum in Toronto have been in the vanguard of this work, examining exhibit evaluation techniques as part of long-established research programmes into the effectiveness of museum exhibits. Considerable experimentation with art museums has also taken place. One aspect of this has been in the closer association of such museums with other forms of art provision. In Australia, the Art Gallery of Victoria at Melbourne, although in a separate building, forms part of an arts-centre complex; the same is true of the Tel Aviv Museum of Art in Israel. The Georges Pompidou National Centre for Art and Culture in Paris combines a gallery of modern art and special exhibition galleries with other cultural activities (Fradier, 1978). The idea of associating or combining the museum function with other cultural or educational institutions has also developed at a local level, particularly as part of a cultural-centre concept. Such institutions tend to accentuate their special exhibition programmes.

The temporary-exhibition programme and in the largest museums the 'block-buster', almost became the measure of success in the search for wider audiences during the 1970s. The considerable outlay involved and the occasional unsuccessful show – in financial terms – has led to a more cautious approach to this type of exhibition. In addition, the needs of other sections of the public were not being met; as Bazin (1967) wryly notes 'of all the visitors, the connoisseur is the one who is short-changed'.

That museum visiting has much increased is amply borne out by the national attendance statistics that are available. In the UK the information available suggests that the number of visits is of the order of 75 million per year. In the USSR an annual attendance was recorded of 140 million to State museums alone (USSR Ministry of Culture, 1980); another USSR group, the community museums, reported 27 million visits a year with 80 per cent of these being young people under the age of 27 (Khokhlov, 1985). In the USA more than 300 million museum visits are recorded every year (AAM, 1984).

Such statistics reflect an increasing public demand on museums; however, they also reflect that a large number of new museums have been opened during the last 20 years. Some of these result from national programmes such as, for example, the Australian bicentenary celebrations in 1988 (as was the case with Canada in 1967). Most of the new museums, however, have been created through local initiative to preserve an aspect of the local natural or human environment. Thus they have resulted from local archaeological discoveries, the availability of a local collection, the closing-down of a local industry or a threat to some aspect of the human or natural history of a specific locality. This phenomenon is widespread and can be found, for example, amongst groups of history enthusiasts in New Zealand or the UK, in small communities in the USSR or on the kibbutzim of Israel.

New, larger, museums are rare and in the main have been based on collections already held in museums. Examples include: the Musée d'Orsay in Paris (Almeida, 1987); the national galleries of Australia and Canada in Canberra and Ottawa, respectively; the Museon in The Hague (van den Bossche, 1987); the Ethnographical Museum, Antwerp; the Canadian Museum of Civilization, also in Ottawa (MacDonald and Cardinal, 1986); and the Power House project in Sydney, Australia. Of a different character are the Cité des Sciences et de l'Industrie at La Villette in Paris, which reflects the participative approach to museum display (Natali and Landry, 1986; Decrosse *et al*, 1987), or the exciting network of regional and district science centres now being developed in India, based on four national science museums in Bangalore, Bombay, Calcutta and Delhi (Ghose, 1986). In addition, a number of major museums have undergone extensive reorganization and display: the British Museum (Natural History); the Louvre with its 'pyramid' development; the Royal Ontario Museum, Toronto; the Armoury of the Kremlin in Moscow (Tsoukanov, 1987), and many others.

Much of this development has taken place in the economic recession of the 1980s with its consequent restraints on government expenditure and, for a number of countries, a fundamental change in the structure of public-sector funding. The change towards plural funding was anticipated in an International Council of Museums (ICOM) report on the financing of museums (de la Torre and Monreal, 1982). The study pointed out that there was a need to search for new and innovative solutions to the finance of museums in both developing and industrialized countries. It also suggested that potential funding agencies should take into account not only the ratio of museums to population, but also other factors such as population distribution, the extent of the country's heritage and the adult literacy rate. The report also showed, on the figures then available to the investigators, that two-thirds of the world's museums are in the industrialized countries. Thus, while there is one museum to every 43,000 inhabitants in Europe, in Africa the ratio is one museum to every 1.3 million inhabitants. As the twentieth century draws to a close, this gap appears to be widening with the major growth in museums occurring in the industrialized countries.

Notes

1   This term is used to mean a museum or art gallery or both unless the context indicates otherwise.
2   In this sense the term has been used to describe compilations, not necessarily of objects. For example, see Caw, G. *The Poetical Museum* (1784) or Farmer, J. S. *Museum Dramatists* (1906), both books claiming to cover their subject comprehensively.
3   Wittlin (1970, pp. 4–60) discusses the motivation for forming collections.
4   von Holst (1967, p. 21) suggests that Nebuchadrezzar's collecting had religious and political motives.
5   Kenyon (1927, p. 7) questioned the interpretation of the evidence, but no alternative hypothesis has since been offered.
6   I am grateful to Hadyieh Akerba-Abaza for this information and generally for her work in 'Legislation relating to the protection of cultural property with particular reference to the Arab States', M.A. dissertation, University of Leicester, 1981.
7   Information in C.-H. Ho, 'The growth and use of collections before the advent of modern museums in the 20th century', M.A. dissertation, University of Leicester, 1978.
8   I am grateful to Raymond Singleton for this information.
9   Gesner published a catalogue of Johann Kentmann's collection at Dresden in 1565; other early catalogues of collections include those of Olaf Worm in Copenhagen (1655), John Tradescant in London (1656), the Gottorffische Kunstkammer (1666), Ferdinando Cospi in Bologna (1677), the Royal Society of London (1681) and King Christian V of Denmark at Copenhagen (1696). (See Newton, 1891).
10 For discussion on a number of European cabinets, see Impey and MacGregor (1985).
11 For a detailed study see Quynn (1945); an excellent summary is given by Taylor (1948, Chap. 5).
12 For fuller discussions on the European Communities and the art market, see Pescatore (1988); also *International Journal of Museum Management and Curatorship* **1** (4), 303–338 (1982) and **2** (1), 11–26 (1983).
13 On cultural democracy see, for example, Key (1973, pp. 234–235) concerning Canadian national museum policy; also Simpson (1976) and UNESCO (1982, pp. 25–27, 43).
14 According to this study the ratio of museums to inhabitants in the following selected countries was: Australia 1 : 14,000; Canada 1 : 23,000; France 1 : 43,000; India 1 : 1,831,000; Japan 1 : 77,000; New Zealand 1 : 27,000; Nigeria 1 : 3,177,000; USSR 1 : 189,000; UK 1 : 55,000; USA 1 : 41,000.

References

ACKERMANN, H. C. (1985), 'The Basle Cabinets of Art and Curiosities in the Sixteenth and Seventeenth Centuries', in Impey, O. and MacGregor, A., *The Origins of Museums: the Cabinet of Curiosities in Sixteenth- and Seventeenth-Century Europe*, Clarendon Press, Oxford

AFIGBO, A. E. AND OKITA, S. I. O. (1985), *The Museum and Nation Building*, New Africa Publishing Co., Owerri, Imo State

AKSENOVA, A. I. (1978), 'Vladimir and Suzdal, museum cities', *Museum*, 30 (2), 116–121

ALMEIDA, M. T. (1987), 'The display of the permanent collections at the Musée d'Orsay, Paris', *Museum*, 39 (2), 113–119

AMERICAN ASSOCIATION OF MUSEUMS (AAM) (1984), *Museums for a New Century: A Report of the Commission on Museums for a New Century*, AAM, Washington, DC

BARRY, T. H. (1975), '150 years – an assessment', *South African Museums Association Bulletin*, 11 (7), 249–260

BAZIN, G. (1967), *The Museum Age*, Desoer, Brussels

BEDINI, S. A. (1965). 'The evolution of science museums', *Technology and Culture*, 6, 1–29

BRAZ TEIXEIRA, M. (1985), 'Os Primeiros Museus Criados em Portugal', *Bibliotecas, Arquivos e Museus Lisboa*, 1 (1), 185–239

CAMERON, D. R. (1969), *Are Art Galleries Obsolete?*, Peter Martin Associates, Toronto

CAW, G. (1784), *The Poetical Museum. Containing songs and poems on almost every subject. Mostly from periodical publications*, G. Caw, Hawick

CHEETHAM, F. (1981), 'Norfolk in Europe', *Museums Journal*, 80 (4), 183–185

COLEMAN, L. V. (1939), *The Museum in America*, Vols 1–3, American Association of Museums, Washington, DC

COSSONS, N. (1980), 'The museum in the valley, Ironbridge Gorge', *Museum*, 32 (3), 138–153

CRUZ-RAMIREZ, A. (1985), 'The Heimatmuseum: a perverted forerunner', *Museum*, 37 (4), 242–244

COX, L. B. (1970), *The National Gallery of Victoria 1861–1968: A Search for a Collection*, National Gallery of Victoria, Melbourne

DANILOV, V. J. (1982), *Science and Technology Centers*, MIT Press, Cambridge, MA

DECROSSE, A., LANDRY, J. AND NATALI, J.-P. (1987), 'Explora: the permanent exhibition of the Centre for Science and Industry at La Villette, Paris', *Museum*, 39 (3), 176–191

DE LA TORRE, M. AND MONREAL, L. (1982), *Museums: An Investment for Development*, ICOM, Paris

DE VARINE-BOHAN, H. (1973), 'A fragmented museum: the Museum of Man and Industry, Le Creusot-Montceau-les-Mines', *Museum*, 25 (4), 242–249

DICKSON, L. (1986), *The Museum Makers: the Story of the Royal Ontario Museum*, Royal Ontario Museum, Toronto

DIOP, A. S. G. (1973), 'Museological activity in African countries: its role and purpose', *Museum*, 25 (4), 250–256

DIXON, B., COURTNEY, A. E. and BAILEY, R. H. (1974), *The Museum and the Canadian Public*, Arts and Culture Branch, Department of the Secretary of State, Toronto

DUBE, W. (1970), *The Munich Gallery: Alte Pinakothek*, Thames and Hudson, London

EVRARD, M. (1980), 'Le Creusot-Montceau-les-Mines: the life of an ecomuseum; assessment of ten years', *Museum*, 32 (4), 226–234

FARMER, J. S. (Ed) (1906), *The Museum Dramatists*, Gibbings & Co. for the Early English Drama Society, London

FIJALKOWSKI, W. (1986), 'The residence-museum at Wilanów', *The International Journal of Museum Management and Curatorship*, 5 (2), 109–126

FRADIER, G. (1978), 'The Georges Pompidou National Centre for Art and Culture, Paris', *Museum*, 30 (2), 77–87

GHOSE, S. (1986), 'Science Museums beyond their four walls', *Museum*, 38 (2), 100–106

GREENWOOD, T. (1888), *Museums and Galleries*, Simpkin Marshall, London

HALE, J. R. (1977), *Florence and the Medici: The Pattern of Control*, Thames and Hudson, London

HILL, C. R. (1986), 'The cabinet of Bonnier de la Mosson (1702–1744)', *Annals of Science*, 43, 147–174

IMPEY, O. AND MACGREGOR, A. (Eds) (1985), *The Origins of Museums*, Oxford University Press, Oxford

INTERNATIONAL COUNCIL OF MUSEUMS (1990), *ICOM Statutes; Code of Professional Ethics*, ICOM, Paris

KENYON, F. G. (1927), *Museums and National Life*, Clarendon Press, Oxford

KEY, A. F. (1973), *Beyond Four Walls: the Origins and Development of Canadian Museums*, McClelland and Stewart, Toronto

KHOKHLOV, V. V. (1985), 'Community museums in the USSR', *Museum*, 37 (1), 46–49

KINARD, J. R. (1985), 'The neighbourhood museum as a catalyst for social change', *Museum*, 37 (4), 217–221

KLESSMAN, R. (1971), *The Berlin Gallery*, Thames and Hudson, London

KOCHER, A. et al. (1961), *Colonial Williamsburg: its Buildings and Gardens*, Holt, Rinehart and Winston, New York

LASCANO GONZALEZ, A. (1980), *El Museo de Ciencias Naturales de Buenos Aires: su Historia*, Ediciones Culturales Argentinas, Buenos Aires

MACDONALD, G. AND CARDINAL, D. J. (1986), 'Building Canada's National Museum of Man: an interprofessional dialogue', *Museum*, 38 (1), 9–15

MACGREGOR, A. (1983), *Tradescant's Rarities: Essays on the Foundation of the Ashmolean Museum*, Clarendon Press, Oxford

MARKHAM, S. F. AND OLIVER, W. R. B. (1933), *A Report on the Museums and Art Galleries of New Zealand*, Museums Association, London

MARKHAM, S. F. AND RICHARDS, H. C. (1933), *A Report on the Museums and Art Galleries of Australia*, Museums Association, London

MIERS, H. A. AND MARKHAM, S. F. (1932), *The Museums of Canada*, Museums Association, London

MILLER, L. B. and WARD, D. C. (Eds) (1991), *New Perspectives on Charles Willson Peale: a 250th Anniversary Celebration*, Smithsonian Institution, Washington, DC and University of Pittsburg Press

MURRAY, D. (1904), *Museums: Their History and their Use*, Vols 1–3, James MacLehose and Sons, Glasgow

MUSEUMS DEPARTMENT, ADMINISTRATIVE BUREAU OF MUSEUMS AND ARCHAEOLOGICAL DATA (1980), 'Museums in China today', *Museum*, 34 (4), 170–182

NATALI, J.-P. AND LANDRY, J. (1986), 'The Cité des Sciences et de l'Industrie, La Villette (Paris)', *Museum*, 38 (2), 124–136

NEICKEL, F. (1727), *Museographia*, Michael Hubert, Leipzig

NEWTON, A. (1891), 'Notes on some old museums', *Report of proceedings . . . at the Annual General Meeting held at Cambridge . . . 1891*, 28–48, Museums Association, London

OEHSER, P. H. (1970), *The Smithsonian Institution*, Praeger, New York

PERRY, W. (1972), *The Science Museum of Victoria: A History of its First Hundred Years*, Science Museum of Victoria, Melbourne

PESCATORE, P. (1988), 'Le commerce d l'art et le Marché Commun', in *La Vente Internationale d'Oeuvres d'Art*, Lalive, P. (Ed.), Faculté de Droit de Geneva

PIOTROVSKY, B. B. (1978), 'Introduction', in *Western European Painting in The Hermitage*, Aurora, St Petersburg

POULOT, D. (1983), 'Les finalités des musées du XVIIᵉ siecle au XIXᵉ siecle', in *Quels Musées, pour quelles Fins, Aujourd'hui?*, 13–29, La Documentation Française, Paris

PRESCOTT, R. I. M. (1954), *Collections of a Century: The History of the First Hundred Years of the National Museum of Victoria*, National Museum of Victoria, Melbourne

QUYNN, D. M. (1945), 'The art confiscations of the Napoleonic Wars', *American History Review*, **1** (3)

SALEY, M. (1976), 'Action to help the blind and physically handicapped, Niger National Museum, Niamey', *Museum*, **28** (4), 210–211

SANCHEZ CANTON, F. J. (1973), *The Prado*, Thames and Hudson, London

SAN ROMAN JOHANNING, L. (1987), *National Museum of Costa Rica: over One Hundred Years of History*, Ministry of Culture, Youth and Sports, San José

SCHOTSMANS, J. (1985), 'Historique des musées/Geschiedenis van de musea 1835–1885', in *Liber Memorialis 1835–1985*, 11–29, Koninklijke Musea voor Kunst en Geschiedenis/Musées Royaux d'Art et d'Histore, Brussels

SELLARS, C. C. (1980), *Mr Peale's Museum*, Norton, New York

SIMPSON, J. A. (1976), *Towards Cultural Democracy*, Council of Europe, Strasbourg

STRAHAN, R. *et al.* (1979), *Rare and Curious Specimens – An Illustrated History of the Australian Museum*, The Australian Museum, Sydney

TAYLOR, F. H. (1948), *The Taste of Angels*, Little, Brown and Co., Boston, MA

THOMPSON, K. W. (1981), *Art Galleries and Museums in New Zealand*, A. H. and A. W. Reed, Wellington

TSOUKANOV, M. P. (1987), 'The new exhibition in the Armoury of the Kremlin in Moscow', *Museum*, **39** (2), 96–101

TSURUTA, S. (1960), 'Museum administration in Japan', in *Museums in Japan*, 1–34, Japanese National Commission for Unesco, Kasal, Tokyo

TURNER, G. L. E. (1973), 'A very scientific century', in Lefebvre, E. and de Bruijn, J. G. (Eds), *Martinus van Marum: Life and Work*, Vol. IV, Noordhoff, Leyden

UNESCO (1973), 'The role of museums in today's Latin America', *Museum*, **25** (3), 128–202

UNESCO (1982), *World Conference on Cultural Policies, Final Report*, UNESCO, Paris

UNESCO (1985a), *Goreé: Island of Memories*, UNESCO, Paris

UNESCO (1985b), 'Images of the ecomuseum', *Museum*, **37** (4), 182–244

USSR MINISTRY OF CULTURE (1980), *Museums in the USSR*, USSR Central Museum of the Revolution, Moscow

VAN DEN BOSSCHE, J. O. J. (1987), 'The Museon in a new perspective', *Museum*, **39** (3), 157–161

VON HOLST, N. (1967), *Creators, Collectors and Connoisseurs*, Thames and Hudson, London

WAIDACHER, F. (1986), '175 years of service to the community: the Joanneum, Styria's provincial museum', *Museum*, **38** (3), 158–164

WITTLIN, A. (1970), *Museums: In Search of a Usable Future*, MIT Press, Cambridge, MA

WOOLLEY, L. AND MALLOWAN, M. E. L. (1962), *Ur Excavations IX, The Neo-Babylonian and Persian Periods*, British Museum, London and Philadelphia

WOOLLEY, L. AND MOOREY, P. R. (1982), *Ur 'of the Chaldees'*, Herbert Press, London

WU, ZILIN (1985), 'The Museum of Qin Shi Huang Terracotta Warriors and Horses', *Museum*, **37** (3), 140–147

Bibliography

AMERICAN ASSOCIATION OF MUSEUMS (AAM) (1969), *America's Museums: The Belmont Report*, AAM, Washington, DC

BAZIN, G. (1979), *The Louvre*, Thames and Hudson, London

EUROPEAN COMMUNITIES (1978), *Community Action in the Cultural Sector* (Bulletin of the European Communities, 6/77), Commission of the European Communities, Brussels

GILMAN, B. (1977), *Le Musée: Agent d'Innovation Culturelle*, Council of Europe, Strasbourg

GOVERNMENT OF CANADA (1986), *Report and Recommendations of the Task Force charged with examining Federal Policy concerning Museums*, Department of Communications, Ottawa

LEWIS, G. D. (1987), 'Museums', in *Encyclopaedia Britannica*, **24**, 478–490

MCINTYRE, D. (1987), 'Developments in Australian museums since the 1970s: an overview', *Museum*, **39** (3), 169–175

PIOTROVSKY, B. B. (1985), 'The destruction and restoration of Leningrad's palace museums', *Museum*, **37** (3), 169–173

ROYAL ONTARIO MUSEUM (1976), *Communicating with the Museum Visitor – Guidelines for Planning*, Royal Ontario Museum, Toronto, Canada

SCHEICHER, E. *et al.* (1977), *Die Kunstkammer*, Kunsthistorishces Museum, Sammlungen Schloss Ambras, Innsbruck

SHEETS-PYENSON, S. (1988), *Cathedrals of Science*, McGill-Queen's University Press, Montreal

SHERMAN, D. J. (1989), *Worthy Monuments: Art Museums and the Politics of Culture in Nineteenth-Century France*, Harvard University Press, Cambridge, MA

TREVOR-ROPER, H. (1976), *Princes and Artists: Patronage and Ideology at Four Hapsburg Courts 1517–1633*, Thames and Hudson, London

UNESCO–ICOM DOCUMENTATION CENTRE (1981), *Directory of African Museums 1981*, ICOM, Paris

UNESCO–ICOM DOCUMENTATION CENTRE (1985), *Directory of Asian Museums 1985*, ICOM, Paris

3

Museums in Britain: a historical survey

Geoffrey Lewis

Unlike some of their continental counterparts, there is no evidence to suggest that the monarchy in Britain were great art collectors, at least until the seventeenth century. Certainly, Henry II (1207–1272) had a collection of pictures, plate and relics. Equally the Renaissance and its aftermath influenced the royal households of Britain. Poetry and music flourished under the patronage of Henry VIII (1491–1547), who also appointed the country's only King's Antiquary, John Leyland, to describe and list material of antiquarian interest in England and Wales. But it was not until the reign of Charles I (1600–1649) that the first royal collection of significance was established in England.

Charles I inherited a small collection of paintings and other *objets d'art* at the palaces of Whitehall, Windsor and Hampton. To these he added with discernment and taste. Among his major purchases were the entire Gonzaga collection from Mantua in 1627 and Raphael's original cartoons used for the Papal tapestries, 'The Acts of the Apostles', now in the Victoria and Albert Museum. About 1400 paintings and 400 sculptures were listed in the catalogue of Charles' collection. Following his execution, the majority were sold and dispersed to many private collections in Europe (MacGregor, 1989). Some, however, remained and others were returned or otherwise acquired following the Restoration. These were supplemented with taste by both Charles II as well as William and Mary – during whose reign much was lost in a disastrous fire at the Whitehall Palace in 1697. It was not until later in the eighteenth century, during the reign of George III, that royal patronage of art re-emerges strongly in Britain and by the middle of the following century the outstanding royal collection of today had been well established.

Thus the development of the British royal collection occurred in parallel with the emergence of the public museum in Europe. No royal art collection, on a scale to be found in other European countries, was available which might be opened to the public to serve this purpose. On the other hand, the Royal Menageria had been exhibited at the Tower of London from the thirteenth century and certainly the Crown Jewels and other objects, including the horn of a 'unicorn', were being visited by the public at the time of Charles II. The Royal Armoury was also established and from the sixteenth century parts of it were displayed in the White Tower. Although a number of pieces had been sold on the death of Charles I the armour made at Greenwich for Charles and his son was purchased by the Keeper of the Stores at the Tower and thus, fortunately, was saved. The Armoury was certainly open to the public regularly towards the end of the century and there is a record of a visit to it by Tsar Peter I in 1698.

But it is necessary to look elsewhere at private collecting for the founding collections that made possible the establishment of museums in Britain. In so doing, other factors must also be considered. One of these is that the sixteenth century saw the dissolution of the monasteries and the dispersal of their considerable collections. Another consideration, increasingly to have a profound effect on the nature of the country's major cultural collections, was the access to material available because of trans-ocean exploration, trade and, eventually, colonization by Britain resulting from the shift in the balance of maritime power to Northern Europe.

Private collections

There has been a long tradition of private collecting in Britain, although in medieval times this appears to have been restricted to the nobility and those associated with the church. As early as 1151 Henry of

Blois (?1101–1171), Bishop of Winchester, had sent some antiquities back from Rome to Winchester which included classical statues and a seal. Humphrey, Duke of Gloucester (1391–1447), who was influenced by the new Renaissance learning, amassed a library which was to become a major benefaction for the Bodleian Library of the University of Oxford in the fifteenth century. The outstanding collection of the following century appears to have been that of Cardinal Wolsey (1471–1530). Another one was made by Andrew Perne (?1517–1591), Master of Peterhouse, who gave his cabinet of coins and other antiquities to the University of Cambridge in 1589. Five cabinets of coins were presented to the Bodleian Library by Archbishop William Laud (1573–1645) about 1630. Of a far more eclectic nature was the collection of Sir Walter Cope (d. 1614) which included strong natural history and ethnographical sections as well as fine- and decorative-art material.

The strong interest in British antiquities is also reflected at this time. In 1586 William Camden's guide to British antiquities, *Britannia*, was published. It is likely that the original impetus for the collection of Sir Robert Cotton (1571–1631) came while he was at Westminster School where William Camden was Second Master. Certainly, they were collecting antiquities together in Northern England in 1599. Sir Robert's collection, which had a particularly strong representation of manuscripts, many concerned with the suppressed monasteries, was given to the nation by his grandson to form one of the founding collections of the British Museum.

Sir Dudley Carleton, later Viscount Dorchester (1573–1632), formed a collection for both pleasure and profit. As a British ambassador his duties enabled him to create a network of agents in different parts of the world and to acquire antiquities and paintings. Many of these he sent to England and elsewhere where there was a ready market. Rubens was among his customers and exchanged some of his paintings for antiquities to improve his cabinet at Antwerp.

An outstanding private collection of its time was that formed by Thomas Howard, twenty-first Earl of Arundel (1586–1646). He was one of the first to appreciate the importance of Asia Minor and Greece as a source of antiquities. For over 30 years he travelled to bring together a superb collection of classical marble statues and inscriptions, pottery, gems, pictures and manuscripts. He exhibited them at Arundel House in London's Strand in a gallery modelled on the Uffizi Gallery in Florence and made them available to the scholars of the time. Among them was Francis Bacon who, in 1594, suggested to Elizabeth I that a cabinet of man-made products, a library, botanical and zoological garden should be provided to further scientific work.

John Tradescant (?1577–1638) came from a much humbler background. Probably of yeoman farming stock, he spent his working life as a skilful gardener on four country estates. That the last two were owned by George Villiers, first Duke of Buckingham and Charles I, both avid collectors, may be significant but he was certainly collecting exotic plants and other material before these appointments. He visited many places in Europe as well as North Africa and also enjoyed a number of contacts elsewhere overseas. In 1625 he leased a house in Lambeth where he assembled his collections and created a garden for his foreign plants. The house was opened to the public and became a well-known London attraction, being called Tradescant's Ark. From contemporary descriptions, it contained stuffed birds and animals and a wide variety of artefacts from different parts of the world. There was certainly a printed guide to the garden and its plants, but a catalogue of the whole collection was published after Tradescant's death under the title *Museum Tradescantianum* in 1656; this is the first recorded use of the term 'museum' in England in its currently accepted form. His son, also John Tradescant (1608–1662) continued to maintain and supplement the collection which eventually became the major founding collection for the Ashmolean Museum at Oxford (MacGregor, 1983; 1985).

Another of the founding collections of the British Museum originated through Robert Harley, first Earl of Oxford (1661–1724), who formed an outstanding library of books and manuscripts. The latter comprised more than 6000 volumes of manuscripts as well as some 14,500 charters and rolls (Miller, 1973). The collection was supplemented by his son Edward, the second Earl, but after his death in 1741 much of the original collection was sold. However, the manuscripts remained and, following the recommendation of a government committee that they should be purchased for the nation for £10,000 as a further founding collection for the British Museum, Lady Oxford and her daughter Margaret, Duchess of Portland, made them available for this sum on the understanding that they should be known as the 'Harleian Collection of Manuscripts'.

Sir Hans Sloane (1660–1753), whose natural history collection originated during his stay in Jamaica as personal physician to the Governor, was to become the other founding collector of the British Museum. To this he added further specimens, classical antiquities, ethnographical material and paintings which were supplemented considerably in 1702 by William Couten's fine personal collection. Contemporary accounts of the collection[1] give some idea of its size and splendour. In his Will he directed his trustees to offer the collection to the nation in return for £20,000 and this was accepted by the Government.

Particularly well known amongst the aristocratic collections of the second half of the eighteenth century were those of Charles Lennox, Duke of Richmond (1735–1806) and the second Duchess of Portland (1715–1785). After Lennox's visit to Italy in 1758 where he had observed that art students were given access to collections, he adopted a similar practice with his paintings, classical sculpture and casts. Indeed, both collections could be viewed by friends and scholars. The Duchess of Portland's fine collection, which included the 'Berberini' or 'Portland' vase, eventually found its way into the British Museum in 1810.

Collections of a specialist nature appear in seventeenth-century Britain, reflecting the developing spirit of scientific enquiry. The collection of John Ray (1628–1705) was a fine example of this. A naturalist who travelled widely, he systematized and classified the natural world from his own observation in the field and the study of his collection. The collection passed to Samuel Dale, a physician, then to the Society of Apothecaries and finally to the British Museum in 1862. Later scientific collections include the systematically arranged physiological specimens of John Hunter (1728–1793) housed in Leicester Square, London, which eventually became the Museum of the Royal College of Surgeons in Lincoln's Inn Fields. The collection of his older brother, William Hunter (1718–1783) formed the Hunterian Museum at the University of Glasgow. Another was the more eclectic collection at Soho of Sir Joseph Banks (1743–1820) who was with James Cook on his first voyage to the Pacific and who employed Daniel Solander (of Solander box fame) as an assistant; his collection, part of which is now in the British Museum, was freely available to scholars at the time. Scientific collections were also to be found in provincial England as was the case with William Borlase (1696–1772) who undertook pioneering work on the antiquities and natural history of Cornwall (Borlase, 1754; Pool, 1986).

Of a rather different character were the privately owned museums of, for example, Richard Greene (1716–1793), Sir Ashton Lever (1729–1788) and William Bullock (flourishing 1795–1830). They had an entrepreneurial character not seen earlier (for these and others see Altick, 1978) and were intended to be visited by a curious public. Each of these had its origins in the north midlands of England. Greene's museum was at Lichfield and open to the public free of charge. The collection was very diverse but included South Sea material originating from James Cook's expeditions, firearms and fossils.

Lever's collection of natural history specimens (particularly birds) and ethnographic material was first opened to the public at Alkrington Hall to the north of Manchester. Judging from a press advertisement issued in 1773 he became 'tired out of the insolence of the common people' who visited his museum and resolved that he would refuse admittance 'to the lower class except that they come provided with a ticket from some Gentleman or Lady of my acquaintance'. Eventually the size of his collection forced him to find other accommodation and about 1774 it was transferred to London where it was exhibited for some years in Leicester Square (Mullens, 1915; 1917).

William Bullock first exhibited his collection about 1795 in Sheffield. He moved it to Liverpool in 1801 and then, eight years later, to London where it was shown in Piccadilly. A charge was made for entry. One of the major attractions was the dramatic habitat groups of many of the quadrupeds. The natural history collection was arranged in Linnaean order; other material included natural freaks, arms and armour and other historical and ethnographical material. This collection was acquired by Edinburgh University. Another of the private collections was that of James Bisset (c. 1762–1832), a miniaturist who was born in Perth but who opened a Museum and Picture Gallery in New Street, Birmingham in 1808. His collection was also primarily of natural history specimens with some ethnographic material. He moved his museum to Leamington Spa in 1812.

Society collections

From the mid-seventeenth century a new scientific movement can be discerned clearly in England. This led in 1660 to the establishment of the oldest extant learned society in the country, the Royal Society (Hunter, 1985). In 1662, when it received its royal charter, it was organizing dsicussions on the preservative qualities of spirits of wine in keeping animal material. Strong antiquarian interests in England had led to the formation of a society for the preservation of national antiquities in the sixteenth century but this does not appear to have survived long. However, a club with similar aims was formed in 1707 and the members met regularly at two London taverns; in 1718 this became the Society of Antiquaries of London which received its Royal Charter in 1751. For those interested in the classical world who had undertaken the 'Grand Tour' there was the Society of Dilettanti, formed in 1732 to encourage 'a taste for those objects which had contributed so much to their entertainment abroad'. All of these societies maintained collections for the interest of their members. It is at this time that we find galleries being established at the great English country houses to display classical sculpture and other works of art.[2]

Coffee houses were also places of popular resort for scientific and antiquarian discussion. One of these, run by 'Don Saltero' in Chelsea, fulfilled a 'museum' role throughout the eighteenth century; its collections boasted such things as 'Pontius Pilate's wife's chambermaid's sister's hat' and other equally improbable curiosities. Another coffee house, Rawthmell's, was the venue for the inaugural meeting in 1754 of a society for the encouragement of arts, manufactures and commerce, now better known as the Royal Society of Arts. The Linnaean Society was established in London in 1788.

London was not, however, the only centre where learned societies were formed. The Spalding Gentlemen's Society, founded in 1710 by Maurice Johnson, one of the leading members of the embryonic Society of Antiquaries of London, was seen as 'a cell' to that society in its earlier days. The Society maintained a library and museum for its members in Spalding and it remains the oldest society museum in Britain. Other later eighteenth-century societies, which included the formation of a museum collection among their aims were the Newcastle upon Tyne Literary and Philosophical Society (1770), the Society of Antiquaries of Scotland (1781), the Manchester Literary and Philosophical Society (1781) and the Perth Literary and Antiquarian Society (1784). Most of these provided collections for future public museums.

The first public museums

A private collection formed the basis of the first public museum in England, the Ashmolean at Oxford. Opened by James, Duke of York, in May 1683, it was based on the Tradescants' collection which had been acquired and then given to the University by Elias Ashmole. This benefaction was subject to a room being built to house it. The University of Oxford seems readily to have accepted the gift and accordingly built a new School of Natural Philosophy in Broad Street comprising a chemistry laboratory, a lecture theatre and the upper room designed to house the collection. Sometimes known as Ashmole's Repository, it was properly known as the Ashmolean Museum from the outset, the name still borne by the successor institution in Beaumont Street. The original building now houses the university's Museum of the History of Science. The museum was open to anyone on payment of a small fee for a guided tour, and in the first year the income received in the Museum amounted to nearly £92. Rules for the Museum reveal that the admission charge was on a sliding scale, calculated according to the number of visitors in the group and the period of time that the Keeper attended them in the Museum. This income was significant as it was the only source of payment for the Keeper and his assistants, Ashmole having failed to endow a chair of chemistry which would have been held by the Keeper of the Museum.

The first Keeper of the Ashmolean Museum was Dr Robert Plot, author of the natural history of two counties (Oxfordshire and Staffordshire), who gave lectures on chemistry in the Museum three times a week. The stimulus that the collection gave to the study of natural history in Oxford seems to have been limited. Plot resigned in 1691 and in a letter to his successor deplored the lack of interest taken by both the Royal Society in London and the local Philosophical Society. Nevertheless, the Ashmolean remained the centre of scientific work in Oxford for over 150 years. With the subsequent development of specialist museums in Oxford, different parts of the founding collection were passed to them (MacGregor, 1983; Ovenell, 1986).

The British Museum opened to the public in January 1759. Its collection also originated from a private collector, Sir Hans Sloane, who bequeathed it on condition that £20,000 was paid to his daughters. An Act of Parliament passed within five months of his death in 1753 provided the basis for establishing the museum from this collection, making the required payment to his daughters, purchasing the Harley collection of manuscripts for £10,000 and providing a permanent home for these collections and the Cotton Library. The latter had already been accepted by the government through earlier legislation in 1700 and 1707. The money was to be raised by lottery. Admission to the museum was to be free.

The interpretation of free public access considerably exercised the minds of the Trustees (Miller, 1973) and, as a result, strict rules governing admissions to the Museum were drawn up. With the exception of holy days it opened from Monday to Friday each week during the winter from 9 a.m. to 3 p.m.; the daytime opening was restricted to three days during the summer but on the other two days it opened from 4 p.m. to 8 p.m. for the benefit of those unable to come at the normal times. To gain admission it was necessary to apply for a ticket, return to collect it and then come again to visit the collection on the day and time authorized. Only 10 tickets were issued for each hour and visitors were conducted round the Museum in parties of five. Despite this, François de la Rochefoucauld noted with approval in 1784 that the Museum was expressly 'for the instruction and gratification of the public', no doubt reflecting the prevailing conditions in France and also the different approaches of the two countries, perhaps expressed best in Bazin's (1967) words: 'The institution's approach to art is from the standpoint of archaeology'. In its early years the British Museum attracted about 10,000 visitors annually.

The early nineteenth century

In 1799 a new Principal Librarian was appointed to the British Museum. There were already considerable problems for him to face, not least a building too small to hold its collections and in a very poor state of repair for lack of funds. The Egyptian material, including the Rosetta Stone, had to be stored in wooden sheds in the garden when it arrived early in 1802. The poor state of repair of the Museum was alleviated when, in 1815, building maintenance became the responsibility of a government department rather than the Trustees. The congestion was relieved when the Townley Gallery was opened in 1808 to house the Museum's rapidly expanding antiquities collection. The library also increased considerably in size and when the King's Library was also offered to the Museum in 1823 a master plan was drawn up to rebuild the British Museum completely. Designed by Sir Robert Smirke this took place in stages over a period of nearly half a century to form the building that we know today. The King's Library came first with a picture gallery to house the national collection above it. In the event the gallery was not needed for this purpose.

Compared with many other European countries, the creation of a national public art gallery in Britain came late. An important opportunity was lost in 1778 when the British Government declined to build an art gallery to house the Walpole collection and it was sold to Catherine the Great for the Hermitage in present-day St Petersburg. The Royal Academy of Arts, established in 1768, partially fulfilled the role of a national gallery but the lobby for a separate institution continued. One of the lobbyists was Noel Desenfans who published a plan for a national gallery in 1799. This came to nothing. When Sir Francis Bourgeois inherited Desenfans collection and came to find a permanent institution to preserve and exhibit it, as required in the Will, he chose to leave them to Dulwich College which had had a small picture gallery since the early seventeenth century. This collection now forms the Dulwich Picture Gallery and is housed in its purpose-built premises, opened in 1813.

The idea of establishing a national gallery of art had its critics. One of these was John Constable who feared that its influence would bring 'an end of the art in poor old England'. But the prospect that the fine collection of paintings belonging to the late John Julius Angerstein (1735–1823) might be dispersed abroad again precipitated the issue of a national public art collection. It was at about this time that Sir George Beaumont (1753–1827) and the Rev. William Holwell Carr (1758–1830) promised to give their important collections of paintings to the nation, subject to suitable premises being available to house them. The British Government agreed to buy 38 of Angerstein's paintings for £57,000 to form a National Gallery and this collection was opened to the public in Angerstein's town house at 100 Pall Mall in May 1824 (Potterton, 1977). Other collec-

tions followed by gift and purchase, including the bequests of Carr and Beaumont, in 1831 and 1836, respectively, and the gallery moved into its purpose-built premises in Trafalgar Square in 1838.

The Ashmolean Museum at Oxford had seen little change during the eighteenth century but, shortly after 1823, displays were rearranged systematically and much of the founding collection relegated to stores (MacGregor, 1983). However, the practice of using collections for teaching purposes in universities becomes more apparent. The Woodward geological collection had been acquired by the University of Cambridge in 1727 but, when Sedgwick was appointed to the Chair of Geology in 1818, this was considerably expanded to form the basis of the Museum now named after him. Similarly, the bequest of Viscount Fitzwilliam (1745–1816) founded the well-known museum of that name at Cambridge, although it did not move into the present purpose-built premises until 1848; it is worthy of note that Lord Fitzwilliam had been deterred from giving his collection to the British Museum because of the Trustees' powers and willingness to dispose of duplicate specimens at that time. Glasgow University's museum was opened in 1804 following the bequest, some 20 years previously, of Dr William Hunter. Other educational institutions were also forming collections at this time. Stonyhurst College, near Blackburn, certainly had one in 1794 while Ampleforth College, is reputed to have established a collection in 1802.

Trading companies also formed collections. In the case of the East India Company there is a reference as early as 1669 to a collection of rarities held 'to gratify the curiosity of the public' (Hunter, 1985). However, for its museum, founded in 1801, the Company's employees were encouraged specifically to contribute specimens. This museum was established with the declared intention of promoting Asian studies and was open to the public who gained admission by ticket. It was no doubt seen more as a cabinet of curiosities but was an acknowledged public attraction in London. Its collections played an important role in furnishing the Indian pavilion of the Great Exhibition of 1851. When the collections were transferred to the Government in 1857 they became known as the India Museum. After a separate existence for 77 years these collections were dispersed, many of them going to the South Kensington Museum (Desmond, 1982).

The number of learned societies increased greatly in the nineteenth century. At Liverpool, the Royal Institution, founded in 1814, housed a natural history museum as well as a picture gallery and continued to fulfill this function long after the town council had established their museum. The Royal Institution of Cornwall started its museum at Truro in 1818 where it remains the county's principal museum. The

Yorkshire Philosophical Society was responsible for establishing the Yorkshire Museum at York in 1823 (Pyrah, 1988), while the Scarborough Philosophical Society built its museum in 1829 in the form of a rotunda at the suggestion of William Smith so that the geological collections could be displayed in stratigraphic sequence (Brears and Davies, 1989).

The strong antiquarian movement in Britain during the eighteenth and nineteenth centuries led to the digging of many sites, particularly burial mounds. Both private collectors, especially the landed gentry and the clergy, and the learned societies were involved and this resulted in the accumulation of many discoveries (Pearce, 1990). By the mid-1840s the British Archaeological Association and the Royal Archaeological Institute of Great Britain and Ireland, two recently formed rival societies, became concerned that, unlike many other European countries, there was no national museum of antiquities in England. In answer to this criticism the British Museum opened two small rooms for British antiquities by 1850, but another 16 years elapsed before a Department of British and Medieval Antiquities was formed (Kendrick, 1951). In the absence of a national lead, however, many of the important discoveries remained outside of London, eventually to find their way into provincial museums, either society or local authority run.

For the operatives of the new industrial society of the time, experimental classes were organized in Glasgow, Edinburgh and London which led to the formation of Mechanics' Institutes; the one in London was commenced in 1824. The idea spread rapidly in Britain and by 1860 there were 610 institutes with over 100,000 members (Woodward, 1979); as seen in Chapter 2, this influence also spread to the colonies. Although primarily intended to provide formal educational opportunities, the institutes soon found themselves organizing excursions to places of interest, including country houses, and arranging exhibitions, the latter often to raise funds.

The London Mechanics' Institute was responsible for the development of the 'National Repository' of new inventions and improved productions acquired to be shown at the annual exhibition of the Institution; by 1835 this collection was open daily to the public as the Museum of National Manufactures and of the Mechanical Arts in Leicester Square. Other institutes also formed museums, amongst them Keighley and Bradford; Keighley specialized in fossils and minerals but also had a technical section; Bradford attempted to develop on local lines but was less successful (Tylecote, 1957). Manchester started a natural history class in 1836 and acquired an extensive herbarium and a collection of British insects which formed the basis of a museum, for which there was a salaried curator for a time.

The municipal museum movement in Britain

The origins of municipal museums in mid-nineteenth century Britain stem from the social and political influences of the previous 40 years. This was an age of reform with the Government attempting to respond to the effects of the industrial revolution which, over a relatively short period, had created major population centres outside the metropolis, bringing with it the need for massive social reform. There was a concern that those in manufacturing industry, including the working classes, should have opportunities to extend their knowledge, particularly in the arts and principles of design (e.g. see House of Commons, 1834, 1836). The Society for the Encouragement of Arts, Manufactures and Commerce had also been prominent in promoting this since its foundation (Hudson and Luckhurst, 1954). The great success of the Mechanics' Institute exhibitions was also an important contribution in developing public opinion towards the idea of local public museums. Indeed, letters to the *Manchester Guardian* in January 1838 expressed the hope that the success of the Manchester Institute's recent exhibition would add support to the idea of opening museums and galleries to the general public. In 1844 a public meeting in Manchester suggested that local authorities should be empowered to establish and run museums from the rates.

In the following year, 1845, the necessary legislation for municipal authorities to provide museums reached the statute book. Museums were to be provided 'for the instruction and amusement' of the public. However, only six towns opened museums under the Act in the next five years: Sunderland (1846); Canterbury (1847); Warrington (1848); Dover, Leicester and Salford (1849). With the exception of Salford, these local authorities took over the collections of the local Literary and Philosophical Society or other cognate societies to provide their museums. At Canterbury, Salford and Warrington a library was also provided, probably illegally. In justification of this, the Town Clerk of Warrington explained (House of Commons, 1849) that they employed 'a skilled naturalist who is competent to stuff and prepare specimens and he and his family act also as librarians'.

Despite further legislation, empowering certain local authorities to provide libraries as well as museums, the number of municipalities that responded was small. Winchester opened a library and museum in 1851 but, as at Canterbury and Warrington and, later, Ipswich (1853) and Maidstone (1855), the library formed a small adjunct to the museum. In these early days of joint libraries and museums only Salford seems to have given its library priority in space, the museum being housed in one small room, perhaps for lack of specimens. At

Lichfield (1859) and Stockport (1860) the museum development came some years before the provision of a municipal library.

Not all of the mid-century municipal museums, however, were provided under the general enabling legislation for museums. In 1850 there was a move to establish a library, museum and art gallery in the Royal Institution at Liverpool,[3] based on its collections; an Association of Citizens was formed to promote the idea, solicit subscriptions, specimens, etc. The negotiations with the Royal Institution, however, failed. About the same time the thirteenth Earl of Derby[4] died, expressing the wish that his collection of stuffed birds and animals should be made available in Liverpool or its environs, preferably in a building administered by the public authorities. He asked that the museum be administered by trustees. Because his requirement could not be met under the existing law, the Liverpool Town Council obtained special local legislation.

The museum and reference library were opened in Liverpool late in 1852 and it was reported that the museum attracted an average attendance of over 500 people a day for some years. However, conditions were very cramped and eventually a new building was opened in 1860. This was in present-day William Brown Street, named after the member of parliament whose benefaction made the new premises possible. The event occasioned a general holiday in Liverpool. At that time the annual revenue expenditure was of the order of £3300. Some 350,000 visits to the new building and collections were recorded annually which included a number of 'excursionists' who travelled by railway to see it. The Museum continued to develop and in 1868 received a major gift of the antiquities collection of Joseph Mayer (1803–1886) (Gibson and Wright, 1988). Amongst this was the fine Anglo-Saxon collection of the Rev. Bryan Faussett (1720–1776) and the Fejérváry collection of ivories, metalwork and manuscripts both of which were purchased by Joseph Mayer, the Trustees of the British Museum pleading lack of funds to acquire the material themselves.

Other agencies were also establishing museums in provincial Britain. A new breed of local and county archaeological society was being formed, often with the purpose of forming a museum. The St Albans society (1845) appears to have been the earliest of these. The following year, two of the earliest of the county societies, Sussex and Essex, commenced museums at Lewes and Colchester, respectively. In Wiltshire the society included natural history as well as archaeological interests and founded its museum at Devizes (1854) where the Wessex archaeological collections of Sir Richard Colt Hoare (1758–1838) and William Cunnington (1754–1810) came to form an important part of the Museum. The Mechanics' Institute was responsible for the Curtis Museum at Alton in Hampshire (1855). The Gloucester Museum (1859) comprised the collection of the local historical and scientific association, while the museums at Berwick-on-Tweed (1857) and Salisbury (1860) were private collections.

In Scotland some of the larger municipal authorities began to consider museum provision. The first of these, Glasgow, received a fine collection of paintings and a building to house them on the death of Archibald McLellan (1796–1854) and these were exhibited in the McLellan Galleries until the Art Gallery and Museum at Kelvingrove was opened in 1902. In the meantime, however, a museum of historical and scientific material had been provided in other premises in Glasgow from 1870 to which a wing was added six years later to house a technological collection (Auld *et al*, 1987). Other local authorities in Scotland which provided museums were Paisley (1870) and Dundee (1873), the latter based on the collections of the Watt Institution (Blair, 1973).

Some of the larger towns in England took longer to adopt the museum powers. Birmingham did not do so until 1860 and then had to wait 25 years before the present building was opened. In the meantime a small collection of pictures and a large copper Buddha from India had been offered and these together with other works were initially exhibited in 1865, and two years later were housed on a more permanent basis in the 'Corporation Art Gallery', a small room in the Central Library. The donors of one painting expressed the wish that it 'may be the means of educating the tastes of those upon whom the reputation of Birmingham manufacturers chiefly depends'. A loan collection of applied art material from the South Kensington Museum was also exhibited here for a time and his led to a demand for a Museum of Industrial and Decorative Arts in Birmingham. Some acquisitions from the International Exhibition of 1871 were intended for this. Space soon became a problem and, until proper premises could be provided in 1885, the collections were transferred to Aston Hall, now a branch museum (Davies, 1985).

Nottingham opened its museum in 1872, based on the local Natural History Society's collection. Sheffield followed three years later, to benefit from the collections of the Literary and Philosophical Society and, in 1893, from the purchase of another collection which had been made by William Bateman (1787–1835) and his son Thomas (1821–1861), mainly from the excavation of burial mounds in the area. It had been housed at Lomberdale House, Derbyshire, for many years and was the subject of a published catalogue (Bateman, 1855). The first curator of the Sheffield Museum, Elijah Howarth, came from the Liverpool Museum where he started work as office boy in 1868; he played an important role in provincial museum development for over 50 years.

New national museums

Unlike many museums in Britain, which were precipitated into existence by the sudden availability of major collections, the South Kensington Museum was planned. Initially opened in Marlborough House as the Museum of Manufactures in 1852, it comprised a collection of plaster casts and ornamental art from the School of Design and a selection of material from the Great Exhibition of the Works of Industry of all Nations, held in Hyde Park the previous year. The latter objects were chosen 'for the excellence of their art or workmanship' and purchased with £5000 made available by the Treasury for this purpose. The Museum, which was also known as the Art Museum and the Museum of Ornamental Art during its five-year sojourn on this site, provided a popular and innovative facility which included evening opening and the provision of museum lectures. Much of its success was due to the energy and enthusiasm of Henry Cole (1808–1882), a joint secretary in the Government's Department of Science and Art of which the Museum was a part. His association continued for over 20 years, latterly as Director of the Museum.

Following the Great Exhibition, the 1851 Commissioners purchased a site at South Kensington out of profits from the Exhibition and a temporary iron-framed building was erected to house the collections from Marlborough House. This building, which became known as the 'Brompton Boilers' during its construction, was opened in 1857. It contained ornamental art; British painting; a sculpture gallery; architectural casts; an educational museum of books, maps, diagrams and models; a museum of animal products; and a collection of models and inventions under patent. It is perhaps understandable that Bazin (1967) argues that there was a certain confusion about the role of the museum, instancing also the changes in name in the first few years and, from 1857, the title South Kensington Museum which avoided precision as to its aims. There was, however, nothing imprecise about Henry Cole's oversight of this pioneering operation. He saw it as 'a national centre for consulting the best works of science and art and as a storehouse for circulating objects of science and art throughout the Kingdom' (Cole, 1884). It was an integral part of a much larger scheme to improve taste and knowledge among those concerned with the manufactures of Britain.

Closely associated with the South Kensington Museum, and connected to it, was the School of Design. Another innovatory feature of the Museum was the inclusion of a refreshment room, where wine, beer and spirits were sold. The Museum's loan scheme was inaugurated to promote good taste and design in recognized schools of art. The scheme was extended to municipal museums in 1886, although it is clear that the Birmingham Museum, for example, benefited from loans much earlier than this; the loans scheme continued until 1977. Despite Cole's clear vision, however, the scientific aspects of the collection were not developed in the same way as the decorative arts.

A decade later the opportunity arose to provide museum facilities in another, less central, part of London. With sections of the 'Brompton boiler' structure, now surplus to requirements, a museum was built at Bethnal Green as a branch to the South Kensington institution and opened in 1866. It was here that that doyen of nineteenth century private collectors in his field, Lieut-General A. H. Lane-Fox Pitt-Rivers (1827–1900), first exhibited publicly his world-wide collection of ethnographic and prehistoric material and British firearms. Pitt-Rivers was of the view that artefacts generally should be arranged typologically rather than geographically to demonstrate their development and this was followed in their display at the Bethnal Green Museum. They were shown there from 1874 to 1878 and then for five years at the South Kensington Museum. In 1883 the collection was given to the University of Oxford where it is now housed in the Pitt-Rivers Museum. He also founded a museum at Farnham in Dorset to display the finds from his excavations, particularly on Cranborne Chase. His archaeological collection is now in the Salisbury and South Wiltshire Museum.

The encouragement of an interest in industry and industrial design was also one of the main motivating forces in the establishment of the Industrial Museum of Scotland in 1854. The intention was to promote an understanding of world industry in relation to Scotland, rather than Scottish industry alone. The necessary finance was voted to the Government's Science and Art Department to purchase a site, acquire specimens and appoint staff. In 1855 a Director was appointed and in the same year the Natural History Museum of the University of Edinburgh was transferred to the Department; this collection, which commenced in 1812 and included ethnological material, remained at the University, open to the public, until it was merged in a new building. By this time the Museum had been renamed the Edinburgh Museum of Science and Art, a move away from its original aim, to take account of the nature of the two collections; it became the Royal Scottish Museum in 1904 and the Royal Museum of Scotland in 1985. For a period it organized lecture courses for artisans and in 1875 a refreshment room was opened, but this lost its licence to sell alcoholic drinks through the temperance movement in 1891. It also had a loan collection, provided guidance to several local authorities on setting up their own museums and, certainly in the later 1870s, staged loan exhibitions (Allan, 1954).

Two other significant developments in public museum provision took place in Scotland in the mid-nineteenth century. In 1851 the Museum of the Society of Antiquaries of Scotland, which commenced in 1781, was given to the Board of Trustees for Manufactures in Scotland for the benefit of the nation on the understanding that a public building would be provided to house it. This was done in 1859, although the custody of the Museum remained with the Society (Bell, 1981). The other development was the establishment of the National Gallery of Scotland in 1858 at The Mound where it is still housed. The Scottish National Portrait Gallery was opened in 1889 in a building shared with the Antiquities Museum.

Professional awakening

A national climate of increasing professionalism – for example the Civil Service had introduced promotion examinations in 1855 – combined with the increasing number of museums and with this an increasing number of issues of mutual concern among curators, eventually led to the suggestion that there should be a professional body for museums. The initial initiative came from Elijah Howarth at Sheffield who in 1877 called attention to the need for such a body in the periodical *Nature*. Occasional correspondence appeared in the same journal over the next three years from James Paton of Glasgow and J. Romilly Allen supporting the idea. However, because of 'the absence of any co-operation whatever among museums', the matter went into abeyance (Museums Association, 1890). Howarth did pursue the matter further a few years later and approached the Library Association in 1884 to see whether they would be willing to include museums within their remit. This may be regarded as surprising for, as the British Association (1887) reported three years later 'the two offices of librarian and curator are frequently combined . . . but it is rarely satisfactory for the museum'. The Library Association decided that they did not wish to increase their area of influence and the proposal was dropped.

It fell to the Yorkshire Philosophical Society to test reaction and call a meeting on the matter; 11 provincial museum curators met in 1888 at York and agreed that a Museums Association should be formed. The Association was inaugurated on 20 June 1889 at York (Lewis, 1989). From the outset, membership specifically included curators and 'representatives of the committees and councils of management' of their museums.

In the first 10 years the membership increased from 27 institutions to 45, plus associates which included five overseas members. When the British Association for the Advancement of Science reported on the provincial museums of Britain in 1887 it recorded the existence of some 217 museums; this excluded the national institutions and provincial galleries. Of the provincial museums listed, however, only 47 were rate supported, three being in Scotland and three in Wales; another nine were being assisted from municipal funds. This gives some indication of the extent of the Association's membership, although it included most of the larger provincial museums. A number of issues of mutual concern were exercising the minds of curators at this time.

One of these was the circulation of material between museums. The Royal Society of Arts had been particularly active in promoting this and, when some of the South Kensington Museum's collections were transferred to the new branch museum at Bethnal Green in 1866, the Society made a considerable grant towards this Museum; its intentions, however, were far wider, although unsuccessful: to lobby government to develop museums as a matter of policy. Proposals subsequently made by the Society to parliament included a national scheme of museums under a Minister of State and giving increased museum powers to local authorities (Hudson and Luckhurst, 1954). In this they relate closely to recommendations to be made again a century later.

Proposals were also being made by the Committee on Provincial Museums set up by the British Association (1887; 1888). One of these related to the role of the rate-supported provincial museum and the unsystematic collecting undertaken by many of them. As the report stated:

> To represent the history of the entire inorganic world and of the development and present condition of its vegetable and animal life, as far as these things are known to science, is an object worthy of a great State department but impracticable in any ordinary provincial town.

The larger provincial museums, however, actively collected on a global scale, like their national counterparts, and occasionally organized collecting expeditions abroad. The first Keeper of the Birmingham Museum did so to supplement the industrial and decorative art collections, while the Liverpool Museum's expedition to Sokotra in 1899 was for natural history and ethnographic material.

The educational potential of provincial museums for child and adult alike received particular attention in the Committee's report as well as the special assistance that museums could give to local students and science teachers. The practice of lending specimens to educational institutions for teaching purposes was introduced in the provinces by Liverpool Museum in the early 1880s. Certainly the new University College in Liverpool benefited from this, as did certain local societies who borrowed material for their soirées. In 1884 the same museum introduced its 'circulating school museum' which can be regarded as the first school loans service in Britain. The object of this innovation was 'not so much teaching as training; not so much the inculcation of facts as the illustration of the happiness that is to be obtained through habits of observation' (quoted in Chard, 1890).

Although school groups were visiting museums there is little evidence of organized class work. An exception to this was the Ancoats Hall Museum (Horsfall Museum), Manchester. This art museum was established withh a strong educational bias in 1877, and certainly 10 years later school parties were being taught by a museum teacher (Horsfall, 1892; Hindshaw, 1941). This museum also operated a loans service to schools. The first real impetus for school visits came in 1894 when the Day School Code was revised to allow instruction in a museum to be reckoned as school attendance.

The question of labelling and interpretation generally was also under debate at the time. Models were certainly used as an aid to display at Leicester and habitat groups at Liverpool. As the Chairman of the latter museum stated in 1884 'a public museum should as far as possible be self-explanatory without the aid of a guidebook'. The British Association Committee (1887) offered clear advice on museum labelling:

> Effective labelling is an art to be studied; it is like style in literature. A good writer conveys his meaning clearly, tersely, artistically. The reader grasps the thought with the least possible effort and with a pleasing sense of elegance and harmony. A good labeller produces the same effect.

But as Flower (1898) pointed out a few years later 'the majority of museums – especially of natural history – . . . confound together the two distinct objects . . . research and instruction'.

The public accessibility of museums was also a matter of debate at this time. Most museums opened on three or four weekdays with at least one other day being reserved for student access. The most common opening hours were from 10 a.m. until dusk, but with the increased availability of gas for lighting demand arose for year-long evening opening. The British Museum Trustees had already reviewed the question with expert advice on the fire hazards involved and were unanimous that the dangers were sufficient not to open at any hour that would require gaslight (House of Commons, 1861). The Trustees of the National Gallery, however, received a report from a committee of scientists (which included Michael Faraday) and agreed to introduce it. As a consequence, the Vernon and Turner galleries at South Kensington were opened three evenings a week. The South Kensington Museum had been lit by gas since it was opened in 1857. When gas lighting was introduced to Liverpool Museum in 1888 it was reported that evening openings had attracted 'all ages and classes, operatives largely predominating'. The museum at Canterbury probably had the longest opening hours, from 9 a.m. to 10 p.m. (British Association, 1887).

There were demands for more weekday opening, where this was restricted and also for Sunday opening. In 1878, the Maidstone Museum was opened on Sundays, the first municipal museum to do so. This was used by the National Sunday League to promote Sunday opening in the national museums. However, the Maidstone Town Council rescinded their decision three years later. By the time Greenwood (1888) was writing on the subject, the Natural History Museum and some of the other London museums were opening on Sundays as well as a number of museums in provincial cities. It was not until 1896, however, that the House of Commons approved a motion for all national museums and galleries to open on Sunday afternoons.

Charging for admission also had its protagonists. Admission to the British Museum had been free since it was opened in 1759, although there had been at least one attempt to introduce a charge since then. The municipal museums, however, were originally permitted to make a charge, but most of them were free, often being associated with free public libraries with which they were seen as part of the free-education movement. The private museums normally charged admission, a sum varying from one penny to one shilling, although there were normally reductions for parties and children. The Yorkshire Philosophical Society, which charged a shilling for admission to its museum and gardens, probably raised over £500 each year in this way.

Museum growth and public benefaction

The period 1870–1910 saw a considerable growth in the number of museums, particularly by the municipal authorities, some being founded to mark Queen Victoria's jubilees. Most of them were started as the result of a gift of collections. But it was also a time of considerable benevolence as far as museum buildings were concerned. Unlike libraries, there was no Andrew Carnegie to provide museum buildings, although sometimes his initiative acted as a catalyst in bringing forward a benefactor to build a museum as an addition to a Carnegie library. John Passmore Edwards, the Cornishman who built 24 libraries in London and the West Country, did not contribute significantly to museum provision either, although his libraries at Whitechapel (1892), Bodmin (1897) and Camberwell (1898) included museums or galleries, while the museum at New Ham (1898) occupied a Passmore Edwards building and now bears his name.

Of the less well-known benefactors, only a few can be mentioned. To Liverpool, already given a museum building, came the gift of its art gallery by Sir Andrew Barclay Walker in 1877 which was extended at his expense seven years later. Sheffield's first art gallery resulted from the bequest of John Newton Mappin. At Preston the museum and art gallery was erected in 1895 as part of the bequest of Edmond Robert Harris to the town. In Bradford, Lord Masham, wishing to create a memorial to Dr Edmond Cartwright – the inventor of the power-loom and woolcombing machine – offered a sum of money in 1898 for the erection of the Cartwright Hall Museum. The site for St Alban's City Museum, opened in 1899, was given by Earl Spencer. Both a new building and a founding collection were given to the London County Council by F. J. Horniman.

Local authorities were not the only recipients of private benefaction for museum purposes. The cost of the new building for the National Portrait Gallery in London, founded in 1856, was borne almost entirely by William Henry Alexander in 1896. The following year saw the opening of the National Gallery of British Art, built by Sir Henry Tate who also gave his collection of contemporary art for the gallery. Another bequest to the nation was that of Lady Wallace in 1897. This comprised both the house and art collection of the Hertford family which was opened as the Wallace Collection in 1900.

Sir Henry Tate's offer to build a national art gallery led to a stormy debate among the scientific community because a site long regarded as ear-marked for the National Science Museum was considered for this new gallery. Indeed the story of the Science Museum is one of the anachronisms of the period. Henry Cole's wish to create a national centre for the best works of science clearly took second place to the decorative arts at South Kensington. In the mid-1860s the science collection was moved to temporary quarters in Exhibition Road. Acquisitions were being made but it was not until 1874 that the first recommendation was made for a permanent building and then the Government failed to act. Further committees considered the matter, each strongly supporting the development of the museum, but by 1888 some of the collections were being dispersed because of increasing conges-tion.

One of the reasons for the long delay in providing a Science Museum was the pressing space needs of its partner in the South Kensington Museum. Its collections had vastly increased, not least from international exhibitions, and eventually a new

building was provided, the foundation stone of which was laid by Queen Victoria in 1898 who renamed it the Victoria and Albert Museum in memory of her consort. The building was opened to the public in 1909. At this time a separate administration was created for the Science Museum, although it had been under separate direction since 1893. Work commenced on the Science Museum building in 1913, but with the intervention of World War I the move into it only commenced in 1919 and it was not officially opened until 1928 (Follett, 1978). Like the British Museum before it, the old South Kensington Museum divided, amoeba like, to produce two more institutions of world renown in London.

The National Museum of Wales had a long gestation period. The earliest suggestion seems to have been made at the National Eisteddfod in 1858, but detailed discussions did not take place until about the turn of the century. The Charter of Incorporation was granted in 1907, a Director appointed in 1909 and national museum facilities opened in Cardiff in 1912; these were based on the municipal museum collection – which was founded in 1868 – together with a temporary exhibition gallery. The foundation stone for the new building was laid in the same year but completion was severely delayed by World War I and, although the Museum partially opened in 1922, the official opening did not take place until 1927 (Bassett, 1982).

New museums, mainly in the public sector, continued to be opened at a rate of about six a year until World War I reduced the flow. Despite such development, public concern was beginning to be expressed that museums were not fulfilling their full role in society. This related to both national and provincial museums. One powerful group, led by Lord Sudeley (1840–1922), lobbied considerably on the public utility of museums and was largely responsible for the introduction of guide lecturers at the British Museum in 1913. On the death of Lord Sudeley, a Sudeley Committee was formed to continue his work for a time. The British Associa-tion for the Advancement of Science began a further investigation in 1913 by setting up a committee on museums in relation to education. While this committee was deliberating, the Ministry of Recon-struction had created its Committee on Adult Education which issued a series of reports in 1918 and 1919, including recommendations on museums.

Because of the War, the British Association did not complete its report for seven years. It contained useful data about museums during this decade from which it developed a number of recommendations. These included strong proposals for the development of schools work both in the museum and through special loan collections to schools; in this the Committee had been influenced considerably by work in the USA and the scheme at Manchester Museum which commenced in 1915 for teachers seconded from the local education committee to provide classes for elementary schools in the Museum. The development of museums as research centres, the provision of temporary exhibitions, better labelling, conducted tours, public lectures and published guides were among the proposals. The Committee also reported adversely on the resources available to provincial museums, the lack of general principles and, therefore, standards both for the government and the administration of museums as well as on the salaries and training of curators (British Association, 1920).

The Ministry of Reconstruction's Committee on Adult Edcuation proposed that municipal museums and galleries should be transferred to the local education authorities. This view, which has been the subject of periodic debate in the profession over the ensuing years, was contested by the Museums Association at the time on the grounds that the Board of Education already had the means of assisting local museums. However, new legislation in 1919 which allowed the voluntary delegation of a library authority's powers to the education authority, and with it responsibility for any museums, was welcomed by Lowe (1919) considering that 'museums and art galleries had received their charter'.

A period of reassessment

The period between the two World Wars may be regarded as a time of reassessment and consolidation, but also a time when the foundations were laid which made possible some of the museum developments of the second half of the twentieth century. Further major reports on museums were issued; the Museums Association was substantially strengthened and commenced its training work; the Standing Commission on Museums and Galleries was formed; experimental work, particularly in the field of museum education, was being undertaken with the assistance of the Carnegie United Kingdom Trust (CUKT). Outside of this activity, however, many museums appear largely dormant and, in many cases, unresponsive to the profound social consequences of World War I and the severe economic depression of the 1930s.

One of the features of inter-war museum development is the appearance of museums connected with the armed forces at both a national and provincial level. The establishment of the Imperial War Museum resulted from a decision of the War Cabinet towards the end of World War I. It was first opened in 1920 at the Crystal Palace, but transferred to the Imperial Institute at South Kensington where it remained for 11 years before being housed in its present building at Lambeth in 1935. The museum was intended as a memorial for the war and only housed material relating to it (Royal Commission on National Museums and Galleries, 1929c). This was extended later to include material from World War II. Another new national museum during this period was the National Maritime Museum, formed to illustrate the maritime history of Britain. Based on the collections of the Royal Naval Museum and Sir James Caird, it opened to the public in 1935 in the Queen's House and Royal Hospital School at Greenwich.

Although the Royal Artillery Institution's museum at the Rotunda, Woolwich, had existed as a collection since 1778 and the Royal Engineer's Museum was formed in 1875, the idea of a museum associated with regimental headquarters and their recruiting areas only began to appear in the 1920s. The earliest of these seems to have been at the School of Infantry at Hythe (1920) followed by the Royal Armoured Corps Museum at Wareham (1923) together with the Royal Corps of Signals and Blackwatch museums (1924) at Catterick and Perth, respectively. By the end of the decade there were 14 such museums and their number had increased to 40 by 1939. A factor encouraging the formation of this type of museum was the creation of a Committee on Military Museums by the War Office in 1913. Initially this committee was concerned with rationalizing the collections in the Tower of London and, as a result, the Greek and Oriental armour were passed to the British Museum. It was also responsible for recommending that a representative selection of the fine arms collection at Woolwich be exhibited at the Tower of London which was realized in 1927.

Two further major reports on museums were published by the end of the 1920s. The first of these, commissioned by the CUKT following consultation with the Museums Association, surveyed the public museums in the provinces with special reference to their services and potential in education, culture and learning. At least partly concurrent with this study, a rigorous examination of the national museums with particular reference to their financial and space problems was being undertaken by a Royal Commission on National Museums and Galleries, appointed in 1927; in fact the Commissioners took evidence from many overseas museums as well as enquiring into the British provincial museum scene. Common to both enquiries, and indeed to the earlier studies by the Ministry of Reconstruction and the British Association was one person, Sir Henry Miers. He had served for eight years as an assistant in the British Museum (Natural History) before taking a university appointment which eventually led to the vice-chancellorship of the University of Manchester. He was a Trustee of the British Museum and later became President of the Museums Association.

In his report for the CUKT, Miers (1928) stated that the time was ripe for a movement that would sweep away the conventional attitude towards museums and arouse widespread enthusiasm for them. He went on to say:

> most peoples in this country do not really care for museums or believe in them; they have not hitherto played a sufficiently important part in the life of the community to make ordinary folk realize what they can do. . . . how dull many of them have become and how low the worst of them have sunk.

Miers' main conclusions were that museums should be formed in every town with sufficient population, that there should be clearly defined collecting policies with one museum in each county being reorganized to arrange exchanges, loans, circulating exhibitions for educational purposes and travelling exhibitions for rural areas. He saw the need for the national museums to institute an advisory board to promote relations with local museums, assist in establishing travelling educational museums as well as new types of museum to cover such fields as agriculture, the applied arts, folk-life and nautical history. On staffing, he stressed the need for museums to be under a full-time qualified curator rather than a librarian as was often the case – a point echoed by librarians some 20 years later (McColvin, 1942) – and that their status and salaries be improved. He saw the Museums Association as the vehicle to assist in the implementation of the proposals and, in particular, a scheme of museum education. The research and educational roles of museums were also stressed in his report.

The recommendations of the Royal Commission on National Museums and Galleries (1929a, b) in many ways endorse those of Miers for the CUKT. Common to both was the need for far closer collaboration between national and provincial museums and for an advisory body to achieve this as well as consider issues concerned with the development of the national institutions and stimulate benefaction to museums. Details of the work of the resulting Standing Commission on Museums and Galleries, its development and current activity form Chapter 5. Other conclusions from the Royal Commission study included the need for the national museums to show far greater awareness of their visitors, to differentiate between the requirements of the general public and students, to improve their displays and extend their contact with schools. They also recommended that the Circulation Department of the Victoria and Albert Museum be enlarged, that other national institutions come within the scheme as well and that a national folk and open-air museum should be created. An indirect outcome of the report was the formation of the Conference of Directors of National Institutions to assist co-ordination at that level.

Major reports recommending the development of museums in Britain have a propensity to appear just before a major downturn in the national economy or other national emergency. The Royal Commission and Carnegie reports were no exception and many of their recommendations, although still valid, remain unimplemented. If anything, the CUKT report was to have the greatest impact on the museums of Britain, particularly in the provinces. From the report, the Carnegie Trustees developed a policy of aiding museums which was to last for half a century. Its first act enabled the Museums Association to set up a permanent office and appoint its first paid Secretary in 1929. Indeed with Sir Henry Miers as its President and Frank Markham, MP as its Secretary, the Association moved forward. The following year it became incorporated under the Companies Act, ran its first training course for curators at the Science Museum and increased its membership to 500 (Lewis, 1989).

The desirability of curatorial training had been under discussion for some time. As early as 1894 a paper had been read at the annual meeting of the Museums Association (Paton, 1895) and the issue recurred on a number of occasions. Miers (1928) underlined the problem in his report and the Royal Commission on National Museums and Galleries (1929b), like others, saw an important role for national museum staff in providing initial training, anticipating that curatorial training would lead to a Diploma from the Museums Association in due course and, ultimately, perhaps a university diploma. Indeed, the National Museum of Wales, which commenced an affiliation scheme with other museums in the principality in 1922, introduced a training summer school in 1925 (Lee, 1928). Like this the teaching on the Museums Association's first course was undertaken mainly by national museum staff. By 1932, however, the Museums Association had published regulations governing the award of its in-service Diploma, and courses followed on museum administration, methods and techniques. Candidates were required to have worked in a recognized museum or art gallery and assessment was based on a thesis on museum work and an example of their curatorial skill.[5] The Diploma Scheme received financial assistance from the CUKT.

As part of their five year experimental funding for museums the CUKT made grants for development in small town museums, subject to stringent conditions relating to finance and the employment of professional staff. A system for assisting museum services in rural areas was also introduced. In 1936 grant-aid for museum reorganization was introduced by the Trustees of the CUKT and for many years a number of small museums received an expert report and subsequent financial assistance to improve their displays under this scheme. At the same time they announced that they wished to establish experimental circulating exhibit schemes to rural and other county areas; as a result two schemes were started in Leicester and Derbyshire. The Derbyshire School Museum Service was based on a local education authority. This service was stocked with material 'based on the requirements of the school curriculum' (Winstanley, 1967) rather than such specimens as might be made available in an existing museum. The Trustees also offered travel grants to enable museum staff to visit other museums at home and abroad.

Another innovation of this period was the founding of the regional federations. The first of these was the Lancashire and Cheshire Federation of Museums in 1927,[6] created to promote closer co-operation between museums in the area, particularly in encouraging the exchange of surplus specimens and sharing professional advice and facilities. This seems to have been a spontaneous development rather than promoted by the Museums Association for the Editor of the *Museums Journal* commented with apparent chagrin:[7] 'This is just the kind of co-operation for which the Museums Association was founded'. Other areas of the country soon followed the example and so, eventually, provided a country-wide network of regional organizations which, at minimum, provided a forum for the members in a region to discuss common problems. Markham (1938) usefully devotes a chapter to the progress of these organizations by the mid-1930s and they continue to operate, although now partially eclipsed by the Area Museum Services.

Although the depression of the early 1930s had a major impact on many museum revenue budgets, it does not seem materially to have affected the growth of a number of new museums. No less than 63 museums were established in the period 1931–1935, excluding regimental museums.[8] The national museums continued to make purchases. For example, the British Museum found £100,000 to buy one of its most valuable manuscripts in 1933, the *Codex Sinaiticus* and the following year, jointly with the Victoria and Albert Museum, a further £100,000 for the Eumorfopoulos collection of oriental antiquities. These purchases were achieved through remarkably successful fund-raising and short-term borrowing (Miller, 1973). Markham (1938) records that, while national museum budgets had increased by about 20 per cent over the previous 10 years, provincial museum budgets had shown little change and many salaries had been severely cut. At Liverpool Museum increases in attendance figures were attributed to the extent of unemployment in that city in 1931–1932, but a decrease the following year, particularly during the Easter and Summer holidays, was considered to result from the reduction in day trips now available on the railway. This museum's committee proposed that special tours of the Museum be arranged for the unemployed, but the evidence is sparse for any major response from museums to the social conditions of the time.

The report by Markham (1938) was undertaken on behalf of the CUKT to review progress since Miers' study published 10 years previously and to assist the Trustees in continuing to grant-aid museum development. Major museum defects listed in the report include inadequate finance, lack of space, untrained part-time and ill-paid curators and the absence of any national subject index of collections. He concludes the list of problems with:

> Much of the slowness of development is due to the fact that the very qualities that go to make up a good curator are often opposed to those that make good reformers. Many curators are so close to their problems that they tend to lose sight of the fact that they are part of a national service that needs adequate publicity.

But, at the root of the matter, Markham saw the lack of any authoritative central body with the oversight of all public museums. There was only one body in the country capable of doing this, the Government. He recommended the establishment of a Commission to consider the whole question of the provincial museums because he felt that without authoritative oversight his other recommendations would not bring museums to the standard of the best overseas examples. These recommendations went far beyond the purview of the Carnegie Trustees and were under consideration by the Board of Education when World War II broke out in 1939 and the issues were subordinated to more pressing matters.

In preparation for the War, many museums packed and transported their major holdings to safer locations, a precaution fully justified in the light of events published in wartime issues of the *Museums Journal*; even so, some valuable collections were lost. Other museum buildings were requisitioned for war purposes. Museum staff, too, were depleted as they left for war service or were dismissed for economic reasons. An indication of the impact of the War on the museum service can be seen from Markham's (1948) survey. Although he records that 160 museums had closed since 1938, nevertheless there appears to have been a greater effort than in the 1914–1918 War to maintain a museum service. Indeed, museums played a more active role in the community and involved themselves in the war effort. This included providing special classes for children evacuated to their area (e.g. Stevens, 1940), arranging lunch-time concerts and holding Ministry of Information exhibitions such as 'Dig for Victory', 'Anti-gossip' and 'Buy a Spitfire'. The journal

Nature[9] particularly acknowledged the role and achievements of the larger museums and galleries during the war and expressed the hope that smaller institutions would now emulate them. Although the Standing Commission on Museums and Galleries (1963) records the foundation of about 10 museums during the War, it is unlikely that many of them were opened to the public on a regular basis. An exception to this was Leicester's Newark Houses Museum which, although taken into trusteeship by the Corporation in 1936, was first opened to the public in July 1940.

The post-war years

During the lean war years, the Museums Association (1942) published a memorandum on the reinstatement and development of museums in the period when hostilities had ceased as a basis for discussion with the Ministry of Reconstruction; this took place in 1943. An extended version appeared at the close of the War (Museums Association, 1945) to act as a blueprint for the years ahead. Finance figured high in the list of priorities as well as Markham's suggestion for a national body which was now proposed to be concerned with all museums and to take the form of an 'arms-length' Grants Board. This, it was recommended, would assess new schemes, allocate grants, define standards and ensure that they were maintained through a system of inspection. The report envisaged finance being available for capital schemes involving new buildings and the reconstruction of old ones; providing sufficient trained and adequately paid staff to maintain the museum service, increase circulating exhibitions, provide for certain museums to act as centres in a region to advise and assist smaller museums and develop educational services, purchase and hire exhibits and generally improve museum amenities.

The proposed Grants Board was seen to have two complementary sections, one concerned with museums and the other with art galleries. The latter would also be concerned with developing a loan pool of works of art, taking over responsibilities of the Council for the Encouragement of Music and the Arts (CEMA), initiating art-appreciation education based on galleries and arts centres, acting as a central publications agency for reproductions and catalogues and advising galleries on disposal policies. The influence of a discussion document issued in 1944 by the Art Enquiry and published two years later under the title *The Visual Arts* can be seen in this. In the event, the Arts Council of Great Britain was established in 1946, taking responsibility for a number of these art functions. However, no similar body was created to help co-ordinate, finance and assist museums and galleries in their established role.

By 1946 most of the damaged national museums had been re-opened, partly or fully, the British Museum being among the last, although not all of the important items that had been removed from their premises were yet reinstated. The Museums Association held its first conference outside of London since the war commenced and amongst the items reported was the resumption of training courses for the Diploma and special refresher provisions for those involved in war service. Its continuing concern for training was also refllected in the publication of a series of notes for students in its journal from 1948 to 1950 which were also reprinted as separate booklets. With a medium-term aim of achieving chartered status for its diploma holders, the Association changed its Articles of Association in 1951. The new Articles provided for certain professional members to qualify for election to Associateship and Fellowship of the Museums Association; currently Associateship is restricted to holders of the Association's Diploma.

The Festival of Britain in 1951, held to commemorate the centenary of the Great Exhibition, involved many museums and galleries both in the preparation of the main exhibition and in special events in the institutions themselves. Some of them benefited from new galleries to commemorate the occasion, as with the Cotman collection at the Norwich Castle Museum, or as recipients in due course of displays from the main London exhibition: for example, the museums at Jewry Wall, Leicester and Worthing received archaeological models for their displays. The Festival may have been responsible, indirectly, for fostering better display design in museums; in 1951, Leicester Museum became the first provincial institution to employ a qualified designer for its exhibition work.

Indeed, the 1950s saw the beginning of a greater awareness of the need for many specialized non-curatorial skills, in the manifold functions of museums and the Museums Association introduced its Technical Certificate in 1953. This awareness was also reflected in the formation of the first specialist groups, separate from the Museums Association, such as the International Institute of Conservation (IIC) in 1950 and the reconstituted Childrens' Activities Group in 1951, now the Group for Education in Museums (GEM). In 1955 the Military Museums Federation was formed, to be followed the next year by the Ogilby Trust which has contributed much to advising and making grants available to the regimental museums. There had, however, already been in existence for some years another organization for curatorial and technical staff other than those in charge of a museum. Formed from members of a diploma course held in December 1938, the Junior Officials Group of the Museums Association was revived after World War II to become the Museum Assistants Group, now known as the Museum Professionals Group (MPG).

But, if the Festival of Britain had given an impression of prosperity in the early 1950s, the reality was a period of severe financial restraint. In 1952 economies had to be made by the national museums and, in annual conference at Oxford, the Museums Association condemned the Government's action. On the same occasion a further resolution sought the rehabilitation of those provincial museums still incapacitated by war damage. But, despite this, public interest in museums was increasing, fostered without doubt by television. For six years during the 1950s the BBC screened its highly successful quiz programme 'Animal, Vegetable or Mineral?' in which different museums challenged a panel of experts to identify objects from their collections. The entertainment value of the programme was high and resulted in increased visitors to museums generally; museum objects took on a new interest and museum people were perceived in a new light. Indeed, the chief panellist was a past president of the Museums Association, the distinguished archaeologist Sir Mortimer Wheeler.

This was clearly the time for the Association to renew its attempts to gain State aid for provincial museums. By 1949 discussions had reached the stage to provide a central fund of £250,000. An election, a static economy and dissention by a minority of local authorities conspired to prevent further progress. In 1955 a memorandum on the subject was prepared by a joint committee involving the Carnegie United Kingdom Trust, the Arts Council and the Museums Association and presented to the Chancellor of the Exchequer. By 1958 a new factor had entered the arena, regionalization, and an experimental scheme of mutual co-operation between museums had been established in south-west England. In the belief that Government might be more willing to finance regional museum organizations rather than individual museums, the Association proposed a scheme based on Regional Museums Services. A weakness in the Association's case was a lack of detailed information about provincial museum services and it sought to rectify this. Lord Bridges, who had called for an 'arms-length' body to fund the arts in his 1958 Romaines lecture, came to a similar conclusion in his report following an enquiry into the arts for the Gulbenkian Foundation and called for a general survey of material in museum collections to be made. Neither of these surveys took place. In 1960 the Standing Commission on Museums and Art Galleries was asked to undertake a review of the provincial museums and galleries with the following terms of reference:

> To ascertain the scope, nature and significance of the local collections, the manner in which they are organized, the resources available to them and the possibilities of their further development on a basis of regional co-operation.

The Commission's report *Survey of Provisional Museums and Galleries* was published in 1963 under the chairmanship of the Earl of Rosse, and marks the beginning of its close relationship with the non-national museums which has been supported by many of its reports.[10] The 1963 survey listed some 876 provincial museums and galleries with a permanent collection and open to the public. A number of its recommendations echo those of earlier reports: that there should be an increase in the Victoria and Albert Museum grant to aid purchases in provincial museums and in its travelling exhibitions, and that these should be extended to involve material from the British Museum, the Science Museum and other national institutions; that curators should be paid an acceptable salary, have adequate qualifications and not generally be subordinated to a librarian; that school museum services should be established throughout the country and, particularly, loan services for rural areas. In addition, the continuing financial condition of the Museums Association received attention with particular recommendations for Government grant to enable it to set up a training institute to develop its work and appoint an education officer of senior status.

The requirement that the report should cover problems relating to the provincial collections led to a number of topical recommendations as they related to different types of collection. The need for one museum to provide the facilities necessary to deal with the increasing archaeological discoveries in each area is reminiscent of the more general recommendations of earlier reports, as was the idea for central stores of ethnographic material in the provinces. Despite its provincial terms of reference, however, the report also recommended that a National Museum of Ethnography should be built as soon as possible, drawing attention to the earlier aborted attempt at this in 1938, that the National Army Museum should be established in central London and that type specimens should normally be housed at the British Museum (Natural History). The suggestion that museum buildings should be adapted to further their use for social purposes and staff provided for this was a clear acknowledgement of the now widely recognized role of the museum in its own community. Impetus for this had commenced as a result of the extended use of museums during the war, as well as a recognition of the success of such work in the USA.

The Commission had been asked particularly to look at regional co-operation. By the time its report was published in 1963 the south-west of England and the Midlands had Area Museum Services for their regions and north-west England was actively considering one; each of these was governed by an Area Council. The report recommended that all local authorities should prepare a co-ordinated scheme for museum improvement and development in their areas; further, that the Government should help financially in setting up the schemes, and in the costs of providing services, including capital schemes, to museums on the basis of the amount subscribed locally. The Government responded with a revenue grant of £10,000 to assist local museums. The inadequacy of such a sum produced an immediate reaction and agreement was reached that grant should in future be calculated on the basis of one-half of the net expenditure of the Area Councils; this basis was changed to half of the gross expenditure in 1966. The services provided by the Area Councils concentrated mainly in the areas of conservation and exhibition and were intended primarily for the smaller, poorer museums (Harrison, 1971). Many of these services were provided by agencies based on existing museums, but certain of the Area Services established their own facilities in a headquarters building. The development of these services can be traced in the periodic reports of the Standing Commission on Museums and Galleries and the now annual reports of its successor, the Museums & Galleries Commission.

The 1960s also saw legislative change for the British Museum, the local authority museums of England and Wales and for the transfer of the old Belfast Museum and Art Gallery to become the national museum for Northern Ireland (Nesbitt, 1979). For the former, the original statute of 1753 was replaced. All previous general legislation for local authority museums in England and Wales was also repealed. The next decade was to see the development of plans which would eventually move two important collections at the British Museum to other locations. The recommendations of the Royal Commission on National Museums and Galleries (1929b), reiterated by the Standing Commission on Museums and Galleries (1963), to set-up a national museum of ethnography came to fruition, albeit in temporary quarters, when the Museum of Mankind was opened in Burlington Gardens in 1970 (Fagg, 1972). The other move involved the British Museum Library. After considerable controversy, particularly concerning the library's location, it was eventually determined that this should be amalgamated with other national libraries, including the Science Museum Library, to form the British Library under an Act of that name in 1972. Although not on the same scale, the severance of a museum from its library had its precedents in the provinces: many of the Liverpool Museum's book holdings were transferred to the Central Library in the 1930s, while at Bristol the Museum Library was taken over to form the substantial part of the Reference Library for that city in 1892.

A matter of recurring debate in the post-World War II years has been the responsibility of museum governing bodies to their collections. In 1954 the Trustees of the National Gallery sought and obtained revised legislation which prevented them from disposing of the collections in their care. The decision of the Royal Academy to sell its Leonardo cartoon in the early 1960s, therefore, gave rise to particular public concern and a Committee of Enquiry appointed to examine the issue drew attention to the special position of property given for the public benefit (Cottesloe, 1964). The debate continued within the Museums Association (Jacob, 1971); at Government level, the Minister called for a report on the sale and gift of surplus objects in the national collections and the possibility of circulating and loaning such objects to the regions. The report, by the Standing Commission on Museums and Galleries (1973), usefully lists the legal position and the views of trustees of the national institutions on the matter. For local authority museums considerable variations in their powers of disposal remain in the current legislation.[11]

Expansion and diversification

The 10 years to 1975 were important in the development of museums in Britain. Not only did the number of new museums increase rapidly but new types of museum appeared and the response to changing social and cultural conditions among existing museums gathered pace. This expressed itself in a number of ways: an increase in the number of museum appointments to public service posts, particularly educationists and designers; a wish to know more about museum visitors and their attitude through visitor surveys of which that at Ulster (Doughty, 1968) was the first of a number to be published at this time; an increasing involvement with the natural and human heritage outside the museum; greater activity at a community level, particularly under the Government's urban-aid programme for the declining industrial cities (Thompson, 1980) and with minority groups (Thompson, 1972) which was to become more prominent in the following decade. Some of this work had an art bias, at least partly attributable to the formation during this period of a country-wide network of Regional Arts Associations established on a basis similar to the Area Museum Councils with government funding through the Arts Council.

Awareness of the archaeological heritage had been forced on museums as a result of post-war building and road development by the mid-1950s. Faced with increasing numbers of discoveries, archaeological staff in the provincial museums mounted rescue operations, often in collaboration with local societies, to salvage what they could. The incidence of archaeological sites not necessarily coinciding with major museum provision meant that many small museums, for example those at Chester, Winchester and Worthing, found themselves pre-occupied with these problems with minimal staff resources. With one or two notable exceptions, a decade passed before museums were able to recruit additional archaeological staff, particularly at county level, to cope with the work (Barton, 1974). Government grants became available for a time to assist excavation work and major rescue operations took place in many parts of the country. Government aid did not, however, extend to the long-term storage requirements of the finds until 1981 in England and three years later in Scotland.

In the wake of this intense activity came a growing interest in industrial archaeology in which museums were also involved. Perhaps the earliest excavation of an industrial site was that of an Abraham Darby furnace at Ironbridge in 1959; another, involving Sheffield City Museums, was at the Catcliffe glassworks in 1961. The same museum was also associated with the excavation of a sixteenth-century ironworks, to be destroyed by motorway construction near Barnsley. It also opened the Abbeydale Industrial Hamlet, an eighteenth-century steel and scythe works as a site museum in 1970 (Greenaway, 1970). But the major industrial-site development of this period was at Ironbridge. Here a registered charity and limited liability company was established to restore, preserve and develop an area of industrial landscape as a museum in what is regarded by many as the cradle of the industrial revolution (Cossons, 1973).

Another example of the concern to preserve and interpret the social and industrial history of a region was the development of the North of England Open Air Museum at Beamish, administered by a consortium of local authorities (Atkinson, 1985). More normally, however, this type of activity was funded through the creation of a charitable trust for the purpose, administratively independent of the public sector. At Pontypool the local authority transferred the Torfaen Museum to a charitable trust in 1974, but this was an exception rather than the rule. This increasingly numerous group of museums gave rise to the formation of the Association of Independent Museums (AIM) in 1977.

Museums also became far more involved with the interpretation of the countryside, a response to an increasing public awareness of the need to use the natural heritage wisely. This movement, which received some impetus in the early 1960s, resulted in museums providing nature trails and interpretive centres and, for example, creating field-study units such as that funded by the CUKT at Leicester Museum (see Stansfield, 1967, 1969). Conservation awareness has influenced natural history displays considerably since that time.

Expansion and diversification brought with it the need for new skills and the development of old ones, for improved standards among museum staff and for a better understanding of the purpose of museums in society. As the result of a three-year grant from the Calouste Gulbenkian Foundation, the University of Leicester established a full department of museum studies (Singleton, 1966). This development took place in close collaboration with the Museums Association and is concerned with training graduates for the museum profession and providing opportunities for research into the museum operation. A similar course, with specialization in the fine and decorative arts, commenced in the Department of the History of Art at the University of Manchester in 1971 (Smith, 1971) and a third one of the same type commenced at the Institute of Archaeology in the University of London in 1986. For over a decade from 1980, the Department of Museum Studies at Leicester also provided the compulsory course requirements for the in-service Museums Association Diploma.[5]

The 1970s saw the completion of a number of capital works involving museums. Two new purpose-built armed-services' museums were opened in London: the National Army Museum at Chelsea (Reid, 1971, 1973), thus realizing the recommendation of the Standing Commission on Museums and Galleries (1963) that the collection should be moved from Sandhurst to London; the other museum was at Hendon to form the Royal Air Force Museum in 1972, thus making available an important collection that had been amassed by the Ministry of Defence (Tanner, 1973). In the same year a much enlarged Ulster Museum was opened to the public (Warhurst, 1973). As part of its regional policy, the Science Museum opened a further branch museum, the National Railway Museum at York in 1975 incorporating collections originally held by British Rail at York and Clapham; its National Museum of Photography, Film and Television opened in 1983 at Bradford. In 1976 another purpose-built museum opened in London. Conceived as the amalgamation of the London Museum and the Guildhall Museum in the late 1950s, the Museum of London was established by the Government, the City of London and the Greater London Council[12] to preserve and interpret the history of the capital from earliest times to the present day (Simmons, 1977).

There had been unprecedented growth in Britain's educational provision in the 1960s, and this gave rise to a debate by no means new to the museums movement. This was the role of museums in education. Among the issues were the establishment of school resource centres and their impact on schools loan services and the creation of community schools with the opportunities these presented for extending museum services to a wider audience. The educationists in museums sought a far more overtly educational role for museums. A number of reports ensued;[13] one prepared by the Museums Association's Working Party on Museums in Education was accepted at the 1970 annual conference and published the following year (Museums Association, 1971a).

But the Museums Association was mainly preoccupied with attempting to achieve some semblance of structural and strategic sense to the museum service nationally. Its latest proposals saw the designation of certain museums with collections of international importance as 'national museums in the provinces' and a larger group with specialized collections of national or considerable regional importance as 'regional museums', both aided by central-government funds. The supporting paper (Museums Association, 1971b) claimed that, in their primary concern for small museums, the Area Councils were not contributing to the major problems confronting many of the larger museums. However, by the time the Association had agreed in principle to the proposals in conference, two new factors had emerged: the government was to reorganize local government and it had also appointed a committee to review the provincial museums and galleries.

This committee was formed to examine particularly the conservation and display needs of the principal local museums and galleries in England and to improve relationships between them and the national institutions. It reported two years later (Department of Education and Science, 1973). Many of its conclusions made familiar reading. On the organization of museums, the need for a new central body reappears. This would advise central and local government on provincial museums and galleries, channel funds to them according to a considered plan and be supported by both professional and administrative staff. To co-ordinate this at a regional level, provincial museum councils were proposed to continue and expand the existing work of the area museum councils. The Committee also proposed that a limited number of museums, or groups of museums, should become 'provincial centres of excellence', to foster high standards by their own performance. Like many other reports most of its recommendations remain unimplemented.

By the time this report had appeared, planning for the reorganization of local government was already well advanced. This was to take place in England (except London), Wales and Northern Ireland in 1974 and in Scotland in 1975. Based broadly on a two-tier system of government, it amalgamated many of the old local authority administrative units. While it was not the unanimous view of its members, the Museums Association lobbied strongly that museums should be a mandatory first-tier function and this was debated during the passage of

the legislation through parliament; in the event museums became a concurrent function which could be exercised by both tiers of local government.

Local government reorganization had a profound effect administratively on local services, not least museums. The joining of old authorities often brought together a number of museums under one administration for the first time. Certain of the old County Borough museums were transferred to the new County Councils, notably Liverpool to Merseyside and Leicester and Norwich to their respective counties. While the former only involved Liverpool's museums and galleries but included all assets, in Norfolk buildings and collections remained with the successor district authorities while the museum service was provided by a Joint Committee of the County Council which included district representation in its membership. In Tyne and Wear a County Museum Service was created to administer 10 museums in four of its constituent districts.

Elsewhere, some county councils commenced new museum services even where, for example in the case of South Yorkshire and Humberside, existing district museums were already providing a regional service. As museums are small units in comparison with other local authority departments, many of them found themselves amalgamated with other functions – education, recreation and leisure particularly – while, ironically, the two metropolitan county ervices each became one of the larger departments of their authority. Hopes for greater structural cohesion, so long sought, faded and as Cheetham (1974) stated 'the "unique opportunity" has largely been allowed . . . to slip away' (see also Loughbrough, 1978). Despite this it was a period of expansion for museums. New posts were created to meet the needs of new services and lacunae were filled in existing establishments, particularly in providing staff to improve public services. There was also some improvement in the level of museum-staff remuneration, either because of increased responsibilities or in providing parity with other similar staff in larger composite departments.

Change and challenge

From the later 1970s and through the following decade, museum development continued, despite the hard economic times, and the number of museums in Britain increased greatly to well over 2000.[14] But, behind this apparent well-being was a deteriorating and then changing economy; the concept of plural funding became a British as well as a world issue (see Chapter 2) and by the 1980s very different philosophies towards public-sector funding prevailed. Unlike the trustees of the national museums, which had received greater autonomy as a result of devolution two years previously, the Victoria and

Albert Museum continued as part of a government department. In order to meet government staffing reductions in 1977, a whole department of the Museum was closed with the result that the museum's circulating exhibition programme ceased after 113 years of operation, a blow from which many provincial museums have not yet recovered.

Another indicator of the financial difficulties occurred in 1980 when government directives to local authorities led to the freezing of a number of posts as they became vacant. Museums generally chose not to fill the most junior posts and for a time recruitment into the profession was much reduced. As the changed policies continued, government introduced cash limits to public-sector expenditure with rate-capping as a very real sanction on local authorities. The university museums were also in considerable difficulties resulting from government fiscal policies operated through the UGC (Warhurst, 1986; Willett, 1986; see also Chapter 9). It soon became clear that, in a labour-intensive operation such as museums and with staff costs increasing faster than the additional grant for inflation, in some museums employee expenditure would soon exceed the total revenue budget available. As a result, voluntary and sometimes forced redundancies occurred, a fate that befell some senior staff in the Victoria and Albert Museum and the Natural History Museum.

The financial restraints and government directives brought major changes in management style, particularly in larger institutions. This had already taken place in a few of the large provincial museums as a result of local government reorganization in 1974 with the introduction of more overt programme planning and the creation of a divisional structure within the museums, normally headed by an assistant director. By the mid-1980s the national museums were preparing five-year corporate plans with a number modifying their staff structures to meet the new requirements. A major issue with all the older established museums was their heavy emphasis on subject-specialist curatorial staff in relation to those directly involved with the public services. The Natural History Museum in London responded early to this in creating a Public Services Department through which a 30-year display renewal programme was developed (Miles and Alt, 1979). The initial experimental exhibitions were controversial with their incorporation of new educational technology, communication and evaluation techniques, but few specimens. The 'blockbuster' exhibition was another example of public service, the first of which, 'Treasures of Tutankhamun' shown at the British Museum in 1972, attracted almost 1,700,000 visitors.

Inevitably in a period of economic difficulty the issue of free admission to museums arose again. The Government had imposed charges on the national

museums in 1974, but this lasted only three months, a period which saw a dramatic fall in attendances. Ten years later the Trustees of several of the national museums were considering the matter again (Museum Professionals Group, 1985). The British Museum (Natural History), faced with a £1.5 million budget shortfall, introduced an admission charge; the National Maritime Museum and, later, the Science Museum also did so. The Victoria and Albert Museum decided from 1985 to give visitors the opportunity of making a £2 voluntary contribution on entrance. In all cases attendance figures initially were reported to have dropped significantly, sometimes by as much as 40 per cent. Throughout this the British Museum remained open free of charge (Wilson, 1989). Towards the end of the 1970s some local authorities had introduced entrance fees to their museums but, in terms of a revenue source, they were rarely a success; at least one local authority soon discontinued the practice (Besterman and Bott, 1982). The position of the independent museums, however, appeared to be different with a public willing to pay, particularly for an open-air experience.

The economic importance of the arts in Britain was studied in depth for the first time as a result of a government-commissioned survey which included museums and galleries (Myerscough, 1988). It revealed that, in terms of turnover, museums in Britain were worth £230 million in 1984–1985. As far as the source of museum funding was concerned, over 90 per cent of national and local authority museum income came from the public sector; independent museums relied on grants of public money totalling just over half of their income. In the context of the arts generally, the importance of museums in attracting tourism was demonstrated as was the significant economic benefit that can arise from this. The arts were shown to act as a catalyst in encouraging urban renewal, contributing significantly to the image of the locality. Arts activity also created a significant number of jobs to sustain its work; in Glasgow and Merseyside this was reported to be as high as 2.8 jobs for every arts post.

However, the government's interest did not focus only on the direct public face of museums. In 1988 the House of Commons Committee of Public Accounts took evidence and issued a report on the management of the collections of the English national museums and galleries (House of Commons, 1988). This followed a report by the Comptroller and Auditor General on the subject from the National Audit Office (1988). The committee recognized that the major difficulties faced in the custody, care and maintenance of the collections have built up over many years and will take time and substantial resources to resolve. The physical state of the nation's collections has been the subject of a number of reports over the last 20 years: the UK Group of the International Institute for Conservation (1974) drew particular attention to the paucity of conservators and conservation facilities; the Geological Curators' Group painted a particularly alarming picture on the lack of curatorial and conservation facilities in geology (Doughty, n.d.); the Scottish Museums Council (1989) survey reviews the position for each subject area underlining the poor storage conditions and general lack of environmental monitoring and control. The Standing Commission on Museums and Galleries (1980) also reported on the state of conservation needs and in 1984 received a new government grant to assist English non-national museums with their conservation and related problems. A small central conservation advisory unit was created by the Museums & Galleries Commission in 1987.

Another aspect of collection management – documentation – receives funding from the Museums & Galleries Commission through the Museum Documentation Association. Created in 1977 from the work of the Information Retrieval Group of the Museums Association (IRGMA) (Roberts *et al*, 1980) the Association services museums with advice on documentation procedures and seeks to establish standards in the field. This development coincided with the establishment of government-financed job-creation schemes and a number of museums took advantage of these. Atkinson (1978) records that a quarter of the 400 temporary posts created in the first two years of the scheme were concerned with cataloguing and related work. A number of museums were by now also maintaining environmental records of their area (Stewart, 1980). The recording of natural science material at collection level also gained momentum and in 1981 a co-ordinating body, the Federation for Natural Sciences Collection Research (FENS-CORE), was formed.

A matter of considerable concern during the 1970s and 1980s had been the definition and maintenance of professional standards. The first major statement was contained in documents approved at the Museums Association conference in 1977 relating to both museum authorities and curators (Boylan, 1977). These have led to a series of rules and guidelines for professional staff and governing bodies (Museums Association, 1991b). The recognition of museums which meet certain minimum standards commenced with the introduction of the Museums Association's accreditation scheme in 1974 (Cubbon, 1973, 1975). The scheme had limited success (Thompson, 1982). Certain museums adopted the 1977 statements and at least one Area Museum Council required this as a prerequisite to giving grant aid. This encouraged the idea of a register of museums, discussed originally in the 1960s (Clarke, 1969), which conform to minimum standards for the purpose of graint aid. The Museums & Galleries Commission undertook a pilot registration scheme with this in mind in northern England and, following its success, introduced it for the whole country in 1988. This has had a major impact on museums, many of which have improved standards to meet registration requirements.

The concern with standards and the changing work environment led to two further developments. One of these was a review of museum professional training which included an extensive study and report by the Museums & Galleries Commission (1987) followed by further studies through the Office of Arts and Libraries. As a result, an independent Museum Training Institute (MTI) was established in 1989 with its own Director to set and monitor standards and provide training materials. In the same year the Audit Commission for local authorities in England and Wales, which had already undertaken a number of studies of local government services, turned its attention to museums and art galleries with a view to developing performance indicators for museum operations. The resulting report (Audit Commission, 1991) has been welcomed generally in the profession. Similar work has also been undertaken for the national museums (Office of Arts and Libraries, 1991).

Of the museum developments in the provinces, particular mention should be made of the Burrell collection at Glasgow (Wells, 1972) which eventually opened to the public in 1983. Following the gift of the Sainsbury art collection to the University of East Anglia together with monies for the construction of an art gallery in 1973, the Sainsbury Centre for the Visual Arts was opened at Norwich four years later (Borg, 1979). The opening of the Stoke-on-Trent City Museum and Art Gallery in new purpose-built premises in 1981 was also a major event (Mountford, 1982). Although both the Glasgow and Stoke projects received grants from the government towards their realization, these were one-off awards. The long-sought-after allocation of government money for capital development only commenced in 1981, albeit on a very small scale. Another major enterprise was the raising of the Tudor ship *Mary Rose* from The Solent and its subsequent exhibition at Portsmouth. Of the recent national museum developments, the opening of the Sainsbury wing of the National Gallery is particularly significant.

The Standing Commission on Museums and Galleries was reconstituted in 1981 with new terms of reference and a new name, the Museums & Galleries Commission (MGC); in due course it was granted a Royal Charter (see Chapter 5). With new executive powers, this went some way towards the idea of a central co-ordinating body for museums, a recurring recommendation which had last featured in the report from the Department of Education and Science (1973) and been endorsed by the Standing Commission on Museums and Galleries (1979). These reports also supported the idea of designating certain of the provincial museums to receive direct government funding which was endorsed by an all-party committee of the House of Commons (1982). They did not, however, receive government support, although an interesting precedent arose with the abolition of the Greater London Council and the metropolitan counties in 1985. Certain of the museums previously administered by those authorities now receive direct government funding. In the case of the museums and art galleries administered by the old County of Merseyside, most of these have national status under a board of trustees and are funded directly by government as the National Museums and Galleries on Merseyside. With the abolition of the Inner London Education Authority in 1990, the Geffrye and Horniman museums also became trustee museums, receiving direct grant aid from the government.

Currently the museums of Britain are in a paradoxical situation: a period of increasing financial restriction during which a plethora of government reports have appeared emphasizing their social role and recommending additional development requiring further resources and better organization and management. The Museums Association (1991a) has published a national strategy for museums in response to this situation to emphasize to Government the need for planning and to provide an appropriate statutory, financial and administrative infrastructure in which progress can be made. There can be no doubt that museums are today much more closely integrated with the communities they serve and reveal a consciousness and responsibility to the public not witnessed to the same extent at any other time this century. This has led to national recognition of the important role played by museums not only in preserving key aspects of the nation's heritage but as a public service, in contributing to the quality of life, as an educational force and a significant factor in the economy of the country. Such recognition augurs well for the future of museums.

Notes

[1] See, for example, *Gentleman's Magazine*, 18 July 1748, reproduced in Wittlin (1970, p. 249).
[2] Galleries were built at Chatsworth (1696), Chiswick House (1725), Castle Howard (1759), Holkham Hall (1759), Townley's Villa, Park Street (1772), Somerset House (1780) and Petworth (1780).
[3] Unless otherwise stated references to Liverpool have been obtained from the minute books at the Liverpool Museum.

[4] The thirteenth Earl of Derby (1775–1851) spent much of his life collecting and had been President of both the Linnaean and Zoological Societies of London.
[5] For a fuller statement on the history and development of museum professional training see Lewis (1983, 1987).
[6] Now the North-Western Federation of Museums and Art Galleries.
[7] *Museums Journal, 28* (1), 1–5.
[8] Of the regimental museums listed by Cowper (1935), at least 22 were formed during the period 1931–1935, although not all of them opened to the public.
[9] *Nature*, 7 July 1945.
[10] For example, Standing Commission on Museums and Galleries (1967; 1968; 1971; 1973; 1977; 1979; 1980; 1981) and Museums and Galleries Commission (1982; 1983a, b; 1984; 1986; 1987; 1988; 1990a, b; 1991). See also Chapter 5.
[11] See *Public Libraries and Museums Act 1964; Public Libraries (Scotland) Act 1887; Education (Scotland) Act 1980; Museums (Northern Ireland) Order 1981.* See Chapter 6.
[12] When the Greater London Council was abolished in 1985, the Government and the City of London became equal partners in the funding of the Museum of London.
[13] See: Council for Museums and Galleries in Scotland (1970); Department of Education and Science (1971.; Museums Association (1971a); and Schools Council (1972).
[14] 2131 institutions were regarded as museums for the purpose of the Museums Association's Data-Base Project (Museums Association, 1987a, p. 12; 1987b).

References

ALLAN, D. A. (1954), 'The Royal Scottish Museum: general survey', in *The Royal Scottish Museum 1854–1954*, Oliver and Boyd, Edinburgh

ALTICK, R. D. (1978), *The Shows of London*, Harvard University Press, Cambridge, MA

ATKINSON, F. (1978), 'A report on job creation in museums 1976–8', *Museums Journal, 77* (4), 158–160

ATKINSON, F. (1985), 'The unselective collector', *Museums Journal, 85* (1), 9–11

AUDIT COMMISSION (1991), *The Road to Wigan Pier? Managing Local Authority Museums and Art Galleries*, HMSO, London

AULD, A. A. (Ed.) (1987), *Glasgow Art Gallery and Museum: the Building and the Collections*, Collins and Glasgow Art Gallery

BARTON, K. (1974), 'Rescuing museums', in Rahtz, P. A. (Ed.), *Rescue Archaeology*, Penguin Books, Harmondsworth

BASSETT, D. A. (1982), 'The making of a national museum', in *Transactions of the Honourable Society of Cymmrodorion*, 1982–1984, London

BATEMAN, T. (1855), *A Descriptive Catalogue of the Antiquities and Miscellaneous Objects Preserved in the Museum of Thomas Bateman at Lomberdale House, Derbyshire*, Gratton, Bakewell

BAZIN, G. (1967), *The Museum Age*, Desoer, Brussels

BELL, A. S. (1981), *The Scottish Antiquarian Tradition*, J. Donald, Edinburgh

BESTERMAN, T. and BOTT, V. (1982), 'To pay or not to pay', *Museums Journal, 82* (2), 118–119

BLAIR, J. A. (Ed.), (1973), *100 Years of Dundee Museums and Art Galleries, 1873–1973*, Dundee Museums and Art Galleries, Dundee

BORG, A. (1979), 'The Sainsbury Centre for Visual Arts', *Museums Journal, 78* (4), 167–169

BORLASE, W. (1754), *Antiquities of Cornwall*, Clarendon Press, Oxford

BOYLAN, P. J. (1977), 'Museum ethics: Museums Association policies', *Museums Journal, 77* (3), 106–111

BREARS, P. and DAVIES, S. (1989), *Treasures for the People*, Yorkshire and Humberside Museums Council, Leeds

BRITISH ASSOCIATION (1887), 'Report of the Committee on the Provincial Museums of the United Kingdom', in *Report of the British Association for the Advancement of Science 1887*, 97–130, British Association, London

BRITISH ASSOCIATION (1888), 'A further report of the Committee on the Provincial Museums of the United Kingdom', in *Report of the British Association for the Advancement of Science 1888*, 124–132, London

BRITISH ASSOCIATION (1920), 'Final report of the Committee on Museums in Relation to Education', in *Report of the British Association for the Advancement of Science 1920*, 267–280, British Association, London

CHARD, J. (1890), 'On circulating museum cabinets for schools and other educational purposes', *Report of Proceedings . . . at the First General Meeting held at Liverpool*, 54–68, Museums Association, London

CHEETHAM, F. W. (1974), 'Local government reorganization and the Norfolk Museums Service', *Museums Journal, 74* (1), 27–28

CLARKE, D. T.-D. (1969), 'Register of museums', *Museums Journal, 69* (3), 141

COLE, H. (1884), *Fifty Years of Public Work*, Bell, London

COSSONS, N. (1973), 'The Ironbridge project', *Museums Journal, 72* (4), 135–139

COTTESLOE, LORD (1964), *Report of the Committee of Enquiry into the Sale of Works of Art by Public Bodies*, HMSO, London

COUNCIL FOR MUSEUMS AND GALLERIES IN SCOTLAND (CMGS) (1970), *Report on Museums and Education*, CMGS, Edinburgh

COWPER, L. I. (1935), 'British military museums', *Museums Journal, 35* (2), 40–49

CUBBON, A. M. (1973), 'Accreditation', *Museums Journal, 73* (3), 97–98

CUBBON, A. M. (1975), 'Accreditation: the position to date', *Museums Journal, 75* (3) (Suppl.), xx–xxi

DAVIES, S. (1985), *By the Gains of Industry: Birmingham Museums and Art Gallery 1885–1895*, Birmingham Museum and Art Gallery, Birmingham

DEPARTMENT OF EDUCATION AND SCIENCE (1971), *Museums in Education*, DES, Education Survey 12, HMSO, London

DEPARTMENT OF EDUCATION AND SCIENCE (1973), *Provincial Museums and Galleries: a report of a Committee appointed by the Paymaster General*, HMSO, London

DESMOND, R. (1982), *The India Museum 1801–1879*, HMSO, London

DOUGHTY, P. S. (n.d.), *The State and Status of Geology in UK Museums*, Geological Society, London

DOUGHTY, P. S. (1968), 'The public of the Ulster Museum: a statistical survey', *Museums Journal, 68* (1/2), 19–25, 47–53

FAGG, W. (1972), 'The Museum of Mankind: ethnography in Burlington Gardens', *Museums Journal, 71* (4), 149–152

FLOWER, W. H. (1898), *Essays on Museums and Other Subjects*, MacMillan, London

FOLLETT, D. (1978), *The Rise of the Science Museum under Henry Lyons*, Science Museum, London

GREENAWAY, F. (1970), 'Abbeydale Industrial Hamlet', *Museums Journal, 70* (2), 78

GREENWOOD, T. (1888), *Museums and Art Galleries*, Simpkin Marshall, London

HARRISON, R. (1971), 'The first seven years 1963–70: reflections on the work of the Area Councils', *Museums Journal, 71* (1), 20–24

HINDSHAW, B. (1941), 'The museums and the child: pioneer work at the Horsfall Museum, Manchester', *Museums Journal, 40* (12), 325

HORSFALL, T. C. (1892), 'The Manchester Art Museum', *Report of Proceedings . . . at the Third Annual General Meeting held at Manchester*, 51–65, Museums Association, London

HOUSE OF COMMONS (1834), *Select Committee on Inquiry into Drunkenness; Report*, viii

HOUSE OF COMMONS (1836), *Select Committee on Arts and Manufacturers' Report*, v

HOUSE OF COMMONS (1849), *Select Committee on Public Libraries; Report*, 107–111

HOUSE OF COMMONS (1861), 'British Museum: lighting by gas', *Parliamentary Papers, 34*, 225

HOUSE OF COMMONS (1982), *Public and Private Funding of the Arts*, Eighth report from the Education, Science and Arts Committee, Session 1981–82, Vols 1–3, HMSO, London

HOUSE OF COMMONS (1988), *Management of the Collections of the English National Museums and Galleries*, Committee of Public Acounts, First Report, HMSO, London

HUDSON, D. and LUCKHURST, K. W. (1954), *The Royal Society of Arts, 1754–1954*, Murray, London

HUNTER, M. (1985), 'The Cabinet institutionalized: the Royal Society's "Repository" and its background', in Impey, O. and MacGregor, A. (Eds.), *The Origin of Museums: the Cabinet of Curiosities in Sixteenth- and Seventeenth-Century Europe*, Clarendon Press, Oxford

INTERNATIONAL INSTITUTE FOR CONSERVATION (1974), *Conservation in Museums and Galleries: a Survey of Facilities in the United Kingdom*, IIC UK Group, London

JACOB, J. (1971), 'The sale and disposal of museum objects: the principles involved and an account of some cases in point', *Museums Journal, 71* (3), 112–115

KENDRICK, T. D. (1951), 'The British Museum and British Antiquities', *Museums Journal, 51* (6), 139–149

LEE, A. H. (1928), 'A museum summer school', *Museums Journal, 28* (2), 50–52

LEWIS, G. (1983), 'The training of museum personnel in the United Kingdom', *Museums Journal, 83* (1), 65–71

LEWIS, G. (1987), 'Museum, profession and university: museum studies at Leicester' and 'New museum training proposals for the United Kingdom', *Museum, 39* (4), 255–260

LEWIS, G. (1989), *For Instruction and Recreation: a Centenary History of the Museums Association*, Quiller Press, London

LOUGHBROUGH, B. (1978), 'The effects of local government reorganization', *Museums Journal, 77* (4), 165–166

LOWE, E. (1919), 'The question of transferring the control of museums to the Education Authority', *Museums Journal, 19* (3), 36–37

MCCOLVIN, L. R. (1942), *The Public Library System of Great*

Britain, Library Association, London

MACGREGOR, A. (Ed.) (1983), *Tradescant's Rarities*, Oxford University Press, Oxford

MACGREGOR, A. (1985), 'The Cabinet of Curiosities in seventeenth century Britain', in Impey, O. and MacGregor, A., *The Origins of Museums*, Clarendon Press, Oxford

MACGREGOR, A. (Ed.), (1989), *The Late King's Goods: Collections, Possessions and Patronage of Charles I in the Light of the Commonwealth Sale Inventories*, Oxford University Press, Oxford

MARKHAM, S. F. (1938), *The Museums and Art Galleries of the British Isles*, CUKT, Edinburgh

MARKHAM, S. F. (1948), *Directory of Museum and Art Galleries in the British Isles*, Museums Association, London

MIDDLETON, V. T. C. (1990), *New Visions for Independent Museums in the UK*, Association of Independent Museums, Chichester

MIERS, H. A. (1928), *A Report on the Public Museums of the British Isles (other than the National Museums)*, CUKT, Edinburgh

MILES, R. S. and ALT, M. B. (1979), 'British Museum (Natural History): a new approach to the visiting public', *Museums Journal*, **78** (4), 158–162

MILLER, E. (1973), *That Noble Cabinet: a History of the British Museum*, Andre Deutsch, London

MOUNTFORD, A. (1982), 'The City Museum and Art Gallery, Stoke-on-Trent', *Museums Journal*, **81** (4), 210–220

MULLENS, W. H. (1915), 'Some museums of old London – I. The leverian Museum', *Museums Journal*, **15** (4), 123–129; **15** (5), 162–173

MULLENS, W. H. (1917), 'Some museums of old London – II. William Bullock's London Museum', *Museums Journal*, **17** (4), 51–56' **17** (9), 132–137; **17** (12), 180–187

MUSEUMS & GALLERIES COMMISSION (1982), *Countywide Consultative Committees for Museums*, HMSO, London

MUSEUMS & GALLERIES COMMISSION (1983a), *Museum Travelling Exhibitions*, HMSO, London

MUSEUMS & GALLERIES COMMISSION (1983b), *Review of Museums in Northern Ireland*, HMSO, London

MUSEUMS & GALLERIES COMMISSION (1984), *Review of the Area Museum Councils and Services*, HMSO, London

MUSEUMS & GALLERIES COMMISSION (1986), *Museums in Scotland*, HMSO, London

MUSEUMS & GALLERIES COMMISSION (1987), *Museum Professional Training and Career Structure*, HMSO, London

MUSEUMS & GALLERIES COMMISSION (1988), *The National Museums: the National Museums and Galleries of the United Kingdom*, HMSO, London

MUSEUMS & GALLERIES COMMISSION (1990a), *The Museums of the Armed Forces*, HMSO, London

MUSEUMS & GALLERIES COMMISSION (1990b), *1992: Prayer or Promise* (by Hudson, K.), HMSO, London

MUSEUMS & GALLERIES COMMISSION (1991), *Local Authorities and Museums*, HMSO, London

MUSEUMS ASSOCIATION (1890), *Report of the Proceedings . . . at the First Annual General Meeting held at Liverpool*, Museums Association, London

MUSEUMS ASSOCIATION (1942), 'Memorandum on museums and reconstruction', *Museums Journal*, **42** (4), 78–80

MUSEUMS ASSOCIATION (1945), 'Museums and art galleries – a national service', *Museums Journal*, **45** (3), 33–450

MUSEUMS ASSOCIATION (1971a), *Museums in Education*, report of a working party, Museums Association, London

MUSEUMS ASSOCIATION (1971b), *A Museum Service for the Nation*, proposals submitted to the 1970 Conference by the Council of the Museums Association, London

MUSEUMS ASSOCIATION (1987a), *Museums UK: the Findings of the Museums Data-Base Project*, Museums Association, London

MUSEUMS ASSOCIATION (1987b), *Museums UK: the Findings of the Museums Data-Base Project, Update 1*, Museums Association, London

MUSEUMS ASSOCIATION (1991a), *A National Strategy for Museums*, Museums Association, London

MUSEUMS ASSOCIATION (1991b), 'Code of Conduct for Museum Curators' and 'Code of Practice for Museum Authorities' in *Museums Yearbook 1991–1992*, Museums Association, London

MUSEUM PROFESSIONALS GROUP (1985), 'Admission charges at national museums', *Museum Professionals Group Transactions*, **21**

MYERSCOUGH, J. (1988), *The Economic Importance of the Arts in Britain*, Policy Studies Institute, London

NATIONAL AUDIT OFFICE (1988), *Management of the Collections of the English National Museums and Galleries*, Report by the Comptroller and Auditor General, HMSO, London

NESBITT, N. (1979), *The Museum in Belfast*, Ulster Museum, Belfast

OFFICE OF ARTS AND LIBRARIES (1991), *Report on the Development of Performance Indicators for the National Museums and Galleries*, OAL, London

OVENELL, R. F. (1986), *The Ashmolean Museum 1683–1894*, Clarendon Press, Oxford

PATON, J. (1895), 'The education of the museum curator', *Proceedings of the Museums Association 1894*, 95–105

PEARCE, S. (1990), *Archaeological Curatorship*, Leicester University Press, Leicester

POOL, P. A. S. (1986), *William Borlase*, Royal Institution of Cornwall, Truro

POTTERTON, H. (1977), *The National Gallery, London*, Thames and Hudson, London

PYRAH, B. J. (1988), *The History of the Yorkshire Museum and its Geological Collections*, North Yorkshire County Council, York

REID, W. (1971), 'The new National Army Museum', *Museums Journal*, **71** (2), 63–66

REID, W. (1973), 'The National Army Museum', *Museums Journal*, **73** (3), 114–116

ROBERTS, D. A., LIGHT, R. B. and STEWART, J. D. (1980), 'The Museum Documentation Association', *Museums Journal*, **80** (2), 81–85

ROYAL COMMISSION ON NATIONAL MUSEUMS AND GALLERIES (1929a), *Final Report, Part 1*, HMSO, London

ROYAL COMMISION ON NATIONAL MUSEUMS AND GALLERIES (1929b), *Final Report, Part 2*, HMSO, London

ROYAL COMMISSION ON NATIONAL MUSEUMS AND GALLERIES (1929c), *Oral Evidence, Memorandum and Appendices to the Final Report*, HMSO, London

SCHOOLS COUNCIL (1972), *Pterodactyls and Old Lace*, Evans and Methuen Educational, London

SCOTTISH MUSEUMS COUNCIL (1989), *A Conservation Survey of Museum Collections in Scotland*, Scottish Museums Council, Edinburgh

SIMMONS, J. (1977), 'The Museum of London', *Museums Journal*, **77** (1), 15–18

SINGLETON, H. R. (1966), 'The Leicester course', *Museums Journal*, **66** (3), 135–138

SMITH, A. (1971), 'The Postgraduate Course in Gallery and Museum Studies, Department of Art History, University of Manchester', *Museums Journal*, **71** (3), 100–101

STANDING COMMISSION ON MUSEUMS AND GALLERIES (1963), *Survey of Provincial Museums and Galleries* (The Rosse Report), HMSO, London

STANDING COMMISSION ON MUSEUMS AND GALLERIES (1967), *Area Museum Services, 1963–1966*, HMSO, London

STANDING COMMISSION ON MUSEUMS AND GALLERIES (1968), *Universities and Museums*, HMSO, London

STANDING COMMISSION ON MUSEUMS AND GALLERIES (1971), *Report and Recommendations on the Preservation of Technological material*, HMSO, London

STANDING COMMISSION ON MUSEUMS AND GALLERIES (1973), 'Loans from national institutions to provincial museums', in *Ninth Report 1960–1973*, HMSO, London

STANDING COMMISSION ON MUSEUMS AND GALLERIES (1977), *Report on University Museums*, HMSO, London

STANDING COMMISSION ON MUSEUMS AND GALLERIES (1979), *Framework for a System of Museums* (The Drew Report), HMSO, London

STANDING COMMISSION ON MUSEUMS AND GALLERIES (1980), *Conservation*, HMSO, London

STANDING COMMISSION ON MUSEUMS AND GALLERIES (1981), *Report on Museums in Wales*, HMSO, London

STANSFIELD, G. (1967), 'Museums in the countryside', *Museums Journal*, **67** (3), 212–218

STANSFIELD, G. (Ed.), (1969), 'Conference on countryside centres', *Museums Journal*, **69** (2), 63–73

STEVENS, F. (1940), 'Salisbury and South Wilts Museum: special war-time classes for evacuees and Salisbury children', *Museums Journal*, **40** (1), 9–10

STEWART, J. D. (1980), 'A summary of local environmental record centres in Britain', *Museums Journal*, **80** (3), 161–164

TANNER, J. (1973), 'The Royal Air Force Museum', *Museums Journal*, **73** (3), 116–118

THOMPSON, J. (1972), 'A Bradford project in community involvement', *Museums Journal*, **71** (4), 161–163

THOMPSON, J. (1980), 'Cities in decline: museums and the urban programmes 1969–79', *Museums Journal*, **79** (4), 188–190

THOMPSON, J. (1982), 'The accreditation scheme of the Museums Association 1974–82: a review', *Museums Journal*, **71** (4), 161–163

TYLECOTE, M. (1957), *The Mechanics Institutes' of Lancashire and Yorkshire before 1851*, Manchester University Press, Manchester

WARHURST, A. (1973), 'The new Ulster Museum', *Museums Journal*, **73** (1), 3–6

WARHURST, A. (1986), 'Triple crisis in university museums', *Museums Journal*, **86** (3), 137–140

WELLS, W., HOWELL, W. G. and GASSON, B. (1972), 'The Burrell collection – five years on', *Museums Journal*, **72** (3), 101–106

WILLETT, F. (1986), 'The crisis in university museums in Scotland', *Museums Journal*, **86** (3), 141–144

WILSON, D. M. (1989), *The British Museum: Purpose and Politics*, British Museum Publications, London

WINSTANLEY, B. (1967), *Children and Museums*, Blackwell, London

WITTLIN, A. (1970), *Museums: In Search of a Usable Future*, MIT Press, Cambridge, MA

WOODWARD, L. (1979), *The Age of Reform, 1815–1870*, Oxford University Press, Oxford

Bibliography

ALLWOOD, J. (1977), *The Great Exhibitions*, Studio Vista, London

GIBSON, M. and WRIGHT, S. M. (Eds.), (1988), *Joseph Mayer of Liverpool 1803–1886*, Society of Antiquaries of London and National Museums and Galleries on Merseyside, Liverpool

HOWARTH, E. and PLATNAUER, H. H. (1911), *Directory of Museums in Great Britain and Ireland . . . with a Section on Indian and Colonial Museums*, Museums Association, London

HUDSON, K. (1987), *Museums of Influence*, Cambridge University Press, Cambridge

IMPEY, O. and MACGREGOR, A. (1985), *The Origin of Museums: the Cabinet of Curiosities in Sixteenth- and Seventeenth-Century Europe*, Clarendon Press, Oxford

KELLY, T. (1977), *A History of Public Libraries in Great Britain 1845–1975*, Library Association, London

ROYAL COMMISSION ON NATIONAL MUSEUMS AND GALLERIES (1928a), *Interim Report*, HMSO, London

ROYAL COMMISSION ON NATIONAL MUSEUMS AND GALLERIES (1928b), *Oral Evidence, Memorandum and Appendices to the Interim Report*, HMSO, London

SCHADLA-HALL, T. (1989), *Tom Sheppard: Hull's Great Collector*, Highgate Publications, Beverley, East Yorkshire

TAYLOR, F. H. (1948), *The Taste of Angels*, Little, Brown & Co., Boston, MA

WILLIAMS, A. (1981), *A Heritage for Scotland: Scotland's National Museums and Galleries: the Next 25 Years*, Report of a Committee appointed by the Secretary of State for Scotland, HMSO, Glasgow

4

The organization of museums

Geoffrey Lewis

The organization of museums in the UK is among the most complex of any nation of the world. In certain countries, for example some of the African nations, cultural property is state owned and museums have a clear mandate as a preservation and interpretation agency. Other countries may not control all cultural property but they operate more centralized national museum systems – as for example in France and Italy – which give more opportunity to plan, control and foster museum provision and generally exercise uniform policies towards the protection and use of a nation's cultural materials.

In the UK, however, there are many providers and a variety of different funding sources which mitigate against a strong cohesive structure within which museum policy and development can be furthered. This is largely the result of historical accident in a country which pioneered the concept of the governmental museum nearly a quarter of a millennium ago and of the public museum before that. For convenience, this chapter also incorporates the international context in which the museums of the UK operate (see *Figure 4.1*).

Governmental organizations

This section is concerned with governmental organizations and their agencies which impinge in one way or another on museums. These organizations, and sometimes their agencies, normally have legislative powers and an executive to implement their policies. However, it should be noted that the effectiveness of all international legislation is dependent upon ratification by individual states. The principle of the sovereignty of the State is paramount in this matter.

The international scene

The *United Nations* (UN) was established by Charter in 1945 and may be regarded as the successor to the *League of Nations* which served a similar purpose during the period 1920–1946. The UN exists to promote world peace, security, justice, welfare and human rights and has its headquarters in New York. Much of its work is delegated to its four councils of which the *Economic and Social Council* is concerned with economic, social, cultural, educational and health matters; accordingly, issues relating to cultural property and museums are normally discussed here. It was here, for example, and in the UN General Assembly in 1973 that the question of the restitution of 'works of art, monuments, museum pieces . . .' to their country of origin was first discussed. The UN Economic and Social Council also oversees the work of a number of the specialized international agencies of the UN.

One of these, known popularly as the *World Bank* but including both the *International Bank for Reconstruction and Development* (IBRD) and the *International Development Association* (IDA), is concerned with financial provision through loans and credits to help raise standards of living in developing countries. Its programme has included low-interest loans to facilitate the renewal and development of national museums, seen as an important contribution to the development of tourism and, therefore, to the economy of the country concerned. There are many organs of the UN but one is active in the museum field in Latin America and Africa. This is the *United Nations Development Programme* (UNDP) which is funded from voluntary contributions from governments and other bodies.

The agency more directly involved in international museum affairs, however, is the *United Nations*

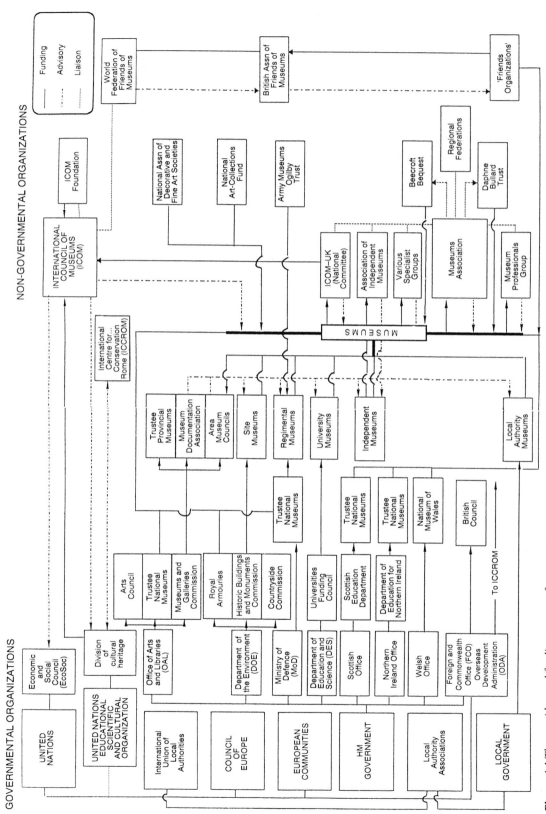

Figure 4.1 The providers and funding sources of museums

Educational, Scientific and Cultural Organization (UN-ESCO), formed in 1946 and based in Paris. Some 158 states are members of the Organization, together with three Associate Members. The UK, USA and Singapore withdrew their membership in 1985; the UK currently holds only observer status. Member States normally have a permanent delegation at the headquarters in Paris and a National Commission for UNESCO in their own country which will often assist in implementing UNESCO's programme. In Britain, the Overseas Development Administration (see below) is responsible for matters relating to UNESCO.

The General Assembly of UNESCO has approved a number of Conventions, Recommendations and Declarations relating to museums and cultural property. An early example of this was the 'Recommendation concerning the most effective means of rendering museums accessible to everyone' in 1960. Another important piece of legislation was the 'Convention on the means of prohibiting and preventing the illicit import, export and transfer of ownership of cultural property', approved in 1970; over 60 nations, including the USA and Canada, have ratified this but the UK has yet to do so.

Within the Secretariat of UNESCO, responsibility for cultural affairs rests with the Sector for Culture and Communication, a constituent part of which is the Division of Physical Heritage. This division administers matters relating to museums and monuments, including the World Heritage List, and issues a number of publications, among which is the periodical *Museum*. It works closely with the non-governmental organizations ICOM and ICO-MOS (see below) which provide professional advice and also operate joint information centres with UNESCO. In 1959 five Member States of UN-ESCO – including the UK – were responsible for the creation of an intergovernmental agency known as the *International Centre for the Study of the Preservation and Restoration of Cultural Property, Rome* (ICCROM). This agency now has over 70 members and provides a conservation advisory service, organizes training courses, undertakes research and issues publications.

At a supra-national level (or regional level in international parlance) the UK is an active member of the two major European governmental organizations. The first of these, founded in 1949, is the *Council of Europe* which is based in Strasbourg, France, and has a membership of 23 Western European States; it is likely that some Central and Eastern European States will take up membership shortly. The Council of Europe is concerned with promoting European unity, facilitating progress, safeguarding the European heritage, and furthering human rights. To this end its Committee of Ministers have drawn up a number of Conventions,

among them the 'European Convention on the Protection of the Archaeological Heritage', which was ratified by the UK in 1973, and more recently the 'European Convention on Offences Relating to Cultural Property'. The council has also worked in the fields of underwater heritage, the conservation of wildlife and habitats and sponsors the Council of Europe Prize as part of the European Museum of the Year Award. There have also been studies on museums (e.g. Rebetez, 1970; Gilman, 1977). Within the organization there is a Council for Cultural Co-operation with an advisory role and a Committee on Culture and Education with executive functions.

Of the three European Communities – coal and steel (ECSC), atomic energy (Euratom) and economic (EEC) – it is the latter that is of concern here. Although a common market is the major concern of this *European Community* it is not its sole function. In 1987 new legislation gave wider powers to the Community and, if it should be the wish of its parliament, it could become a major force in social, cultural and political affairs in Europe. In fact the Community has, since 1974, had some involvement in cultural affairs and set out a number of proposals (European Communities, 1978) which particularly encouraged exchanges between museums. One of the suggestions included the idea of European rooms in the museums of Member States, an example of which exists at the Norwich Castle Museum (Cheetham, 1981). The Community has also introduced regulations to ease customs procedures and grant relief from duty on goods in transit for exhibition purposes. As part of its policy to provide balanced development within the Community, grants have been made by the *European Investment Bank* to local authorities and other bodies in 'assisted areas' to improve the quality of life and provide environmental protection. The new Merseyside Maritime Museum has benefited considerably from such a grant.

There are four parts to the operational structure of the European Community. The *Commission of the European Communities* is responsible for day-to-day operation. However, it also initiates policy and legislation and can take action against its Member States. It comprises 17 commissioners, appointed by Member States, each of whom has specific responsibilities for an aspect of the work of the Communities. Cultural affairs is combined with audio-visual, information and communication policy for this purpose. The main decision-making body is the *Council of the European Communities* which consists of the ministers of each of the Member States, the minister concerned with the subject under discussion attending as appropriate. The Commission services the Council which in turn is required to consult the *European Parliament* on many matters and seek its opinion before making major decisions. The Parliament's secretariat is based in Luxembourg; its meetings, however, are held in Strasbourg but its committees meet in Brussels. The *European Court of Justice* completes the structure and is responsible for overseeing the Communities' treaties and determining the legality of decisions made by the Commission and the Council. Its ruling is directly binding on Member States.

A five-year plan for cultural action was drawn up by the European Commission in 1987 under the title *A Fresh Boost for Culture in the European Community* (Hebditch, 1990; Hudson, 1990). This was considered by various of its organs[1] and *inter alia* advocates a broader, more committed and more effective policy for Europe's architectural and archaeological heritage and calls for support of local and regional projects to protect and restore Europe's heritage. It also notes that the Commission is currently establishing criteria to identify 'national treasures' as defined in the Treaty of Rome[2] and indicates its wish to guarantee protection of each country's heritage with effective provisions against the theft of works of art. The reports also indicate a wish to boost training, including that for cultural administration and restoration specialists.

In examining the protection of 'national treasures', the primary aim of the Commission has been to provide for the mutual recognition of Member States' laws to prevent the unlawful dispatch of such material out of the Community area and also to look at the issues involved in returning unlawfully dispatched material.[3] In this the Commission has expressed the view that the ratification of the 1970 UNESCO Convention by all Member States would assist this problem.[4] The Commission has also issued a report on the administraton and funding of culture in the European Community (Ca'Zorzi, 1989). This reveals a diversity of approach in the public sector and suggests that Britain – after the Republic of Ireland – spends less proportionately of its national budget on culture than do its partners in Europe.[5] Other matters of interest to museums and galleries also occur in other sections of the Commission. For example, the Museum Network programme run in association with ICOM involves an experimental imaged database which may be developed as a public facility for museums.

The national scene

Legislation may come from two sources in the UK. The first of these, the *Privy Council*, advises the Crown on the issue of Royal Proclamations and on the approval of Orders in Council which may involve the granting of a Royal Charter or result from powers delegated under a Statute. Thus, the National Museum of Wales or the National Army Museum exist by virtue of Royal Charters conferred

upon them. The Ulster Museum or the National Museums and Galleries on Merseyside, however, are examples of institutions established by Orders in Council through powers given to the Privy Council under statutes, neither of which was concerned directly with museums.

The majority of the enabling legislation for museums (see Chapter 6) is through statute, passed by *Parliament*, the supreme law-making authority for the UK. The drafting of all Government Bills is undertaken by the *Parliamentary Counsel Office* unless the proposed law relates exclusively to Scotland in which case this is undertaken by the *Lord Advocate's Department*. The main responsibility for the implementation and oversight of legislation, whether by Act or Order, rests with *Government Departments*; to achieve this they may work with local authorities, Boards of Trustees for individual museums or Government agencies like the Museums & Galleries Commission (see Chapter 5). Inevitably, the *Treasury*, with its responsibility for implementing the Government's fiscal policies, has a considerable influence on all Departments and its *Public Services Sector* controls aggregate public expenditure. A number of government departments operate museums, either directly or indirectly.

In Scotland, responsibility for heritage and museum matters rests with the Secretary of State for Scotland and such matters are administered through the *Scottish Office*. Historic buildings and monuments come within the remit of the *Scottish Development Department* (SDD). Grant-aid for the national museums is channeled through the *Scottish Education Department* (SED) which also overseas the legislation relating to local museums. In Wales the funding department for the National Museum of Wales and its branches is the *Welsh Office*. The *Northern Ireland Office* operates a *Department of Education in Northern Ireland* (DENI) through which the two Ulster museums are funded and general policy matters relating to the district council museums in the Province are considered.

For England and Wales there are separate specialist ministries with supporting departments. The department responsible to the Minister for the Arts for policy formulation and financial support for the arts, libraries and museums is the *Office of Arts and Libraries* (OAL). Through its vote from Parliament it provides grant-in-aid to 11 of the national museums and their branches in England, to the Museums & Galleries Commission, the Arts Council of Great Britain, the British Library as well as for other purposes. The Government Art Collection, maintained for important Government buildings also comes within its purview. It is the Department responsible for the oversight of the legislation governing local authority museums in England and, therefore, for general policy in this area.

However, some national museums are funded through other departments. Thus the *Department of the Environment* grant aids the Royal Armouries. It also funds, through the Historic Buildings and Monuments Commission (see below), a number of site museums and interpretation centres. The *Ministry of Defence* is responsible for funding the National Army Museum and the Royal Air Force Museum. The *Lord Chancellor's Department* funds the Public Record Office Museum by virtue of his responsibilities for public records. The *Department of Education and Science*, which until 1983 was responsible for museum affairs, is indirectly responsible through the *Universities Funding Council* for the support of a number of university museums (see Chapter 9). The link in the UK to international affairs with the UN, UNESCO and generally is through the *Foreign and Commonwealth Office* (FCO) and its *Overseas Development Administration* (ODA); the British Council, which organizes a number of exhibitions overseas, is funded from this source.

There are a number of governmental advisory and executive agencies which collect information, undertake research and advise government departments or undertake specific functions on behalf of government. Two bodies of a general nature are those concerned with the auditing of public funds. Although created by Acts of Parliament in 1983, both are necessarily independent of government. The *National Audit Office* exists to provide advice and assurance to Parliament and the public about the government's financial operations. It sets auditing standards on which national museum and other governmental bodies' accounts are based; it has published a critical review on aspects of collection management in the English national museums (National Audit Office, 1988). The *Audit Commission for Local Authorities in England and Wales* performs a similar function for local government, appointing external auditors and trying to ensure that the local authorities give value for money by undertaking special studies of their services. A study on museums has been undertaken (Audit Commission, 1991). The *Commission for Local Authority Accounts in Scotland* has similar responsibilities. The *Charity Commission* operates in England and Wales to provide advice and information, to maintain a register of charities and to check and investigate any abuses of charity law. The registration of independent museums as charities gives considerable benefits. In Scotland tax relief for charities requires registration with the Inland Revenue (see Chapter 6).

The *Museums & Galleries Commission* (MGC) was established as the Standing Commission on Museums and Galleries in 1931 as an advisory body to Government on the national museums. Since 1960 it has included the provincial museums within its purview. It was renamed in 1981 and given revised terms of reference. Since then it has developed its executive functions. These include the funding of the seven English Area Museum Councils (see below), the Museum Documentation Association (see below) and, at least initially, certain museums displaced as a result of local government reorganization. It is responsible for the Local Museum Purchase Grant Fund schemes, administered on its behalf by the Victoria and Albert Museum and the Science Museum. Capital grants are also made to non-national museums for construction work to help improve the environmental conditions in which collections are housed. It has made grants to assist research, publication, training courses and marketing. The Commission, which was incorporated under Royal Charter in 1987, also provides a number of services to museums throughout the UK. These include negotiations and advice regarding the tax benefits available on heritage material, the administration of the Government Indemnity Scheme to provide cover for loans to non-national museums, advice on security in museums as well as a series of reports on professional issues. It also has a Conservation Unit, a small co-ordinating Travelling Exhibition Unit and an advisor on disability in museums. The national registration scheme for museums is also administered by the Commission. Full details about its work are given in Chapter 5.

Another government agency is the *Arts Council of Great Britain* which was created by Royal Charter in 1946 to develop understanding and practice in the arts, increase their public accessibility and generally to provide advice to government. It grant aids the arts from government funds provided through the Office of Arts and Libraries (see above), mainly through *Regional Arts Associations*. It administers the 'Glory of the Garden' scheme from which a number of museums have benefited and also arranges exhibitions, some of which are available for tour in Britain.

In 1980 the *National Heritage Memorial Fund* was established to supersede the National Land Fund as a memorial to those who have died for the UK. The enabling legislation, the *National Heritage Act 1980*, empowers the Trustees to make grants or loans to help recipients secure for the public benefit outstanding aspects of Britain's heritage, which may be land, buildings, collections of objects or individual objects. The Fund receives its monies jointly through the Department of the Environment and the Office of Arts and Libraries. It has assisted a number of museums with important purchases.

The *Historic Buildings and Monuments Commission for England* (English Heritage) was established by the *National Heritage Act 1983* and took over responsibilities from the Department of the Environment for the preservation of ancient monuments and historic buildings, their promotion – together with conservation areas – for public enjoyment and the advancement of knowledge about them. It administers a number of site museums. Part of its work involves rescue excavation and it administers grant-in-aid for this purpose and for the storage of the finds by museums. There is also a support organization known as *English Heritage*, membership of which is open to the general public. The conservation and enhancement of the countryside in England and Wales is the responsibility of the *Countryside Commission* which also, with its parallel organization the *Countryside Commission for Scotland*, has important interpretative functions. Both operate a number of visitor centres in the national parks, sometimes in association with local museums.

Advice and services in museum documentation are available through the *Museum Documentation Association* (MDA). Established from the *Information Retrieval Group of the Museums Association* (IRGMA), it commenced operations in 1977, the financial base being provided by subscriptions from national museums and a grant from the Office of Arts and Libraries through the Museums & Galleries Commission in respect of all members of the Area Museum Councils (see below). Much of the work done by the MDA is concerned with setting and promoting good standards of museum documentation through the development of manual and computerized systems, the provision of training and an advisory service.

Another specialized organization is the *Museum Training Institute* with a mandate to approve, promote and provide museum education and training in the UK. Established by the Museums Association in 1989 as a charitable company funded by the Office of Arts and Libraries and the Training Agency, and in due course from its own income, this follows a proposal in a report by the Museums & Galleries Commission (1987) on museum professional training. The Institute is establishing occupational standards in the different museum functions, which, following approval by the National Council for Vocational Qualifications (NCVQ), will form the basis of a certificate of competence from the MTI. This qualification will become the nationally recognized standard for museum work.

Although part of a network throughout Britain, the *Area Museum Councils* and their services have considerable autonomy in the region they serve. Of the nine councils,[6] seven relate to England; Northern Ireland is currently operating a pilot scheme (see Museums & Galleries Commission, 1984, 1989). The English area councils receive funding from the Office of Arts and Libraries through the Museums & Galleries Commission and those in Scotland and Wales from the Scottish Education Department and the Welsh Office, respectively. The funding base is a 50 per cent grant on gross expenditure, the difference being made up from income from services and members subscriptions. As a result, members services are provided at approximately half cost, normally with a small percentage charge for the administrative costs of the service. These services are mainly in the fields of conservation and exhibition and may be provided by Area Service sttaff and facilities or on an agency basis through a client museum. The Area Museum Councils have a co-ordinating role for their region which has become more formalized as the Museums & Galleries Commission museum registration scheme is established. Certain areas operate with Countywide Consultative Committees (see Standing Commission on Museums and Galleries, 1979; Museums & Galleries Commission, 1982).

Museum providers are treated elsewhere in this book but it should be noted that there is an international, European and national co-ordinating structure to the local authorities of the UK. At a world and regional level there are the *International Union of Local Authorities* (IULA) the *Council of European Municipalities* and, as part of the framework of the Council of Europe, the *Standing Conference of Local and Regional Authorities of Europe*. Nationally, there are a series of local authority associations representing different types of local government. These advise Government and formulate general policy relating to local authority functions, although their decisions are not binding on individual member authorities. For England, there are five associations: the *Association of London Authorities* (ALA) representing the London boroughs; the *Association of Metropolitan Authorities* (AMA) which is concerned with the functions of the 36 Metropolitan Districts in the industrial midlands and north; the *Association of County Councils* (ACC), made up of the 39 non-metropolitan or 'shire' counties; the *Association of District Councils* (ADC) which represents the interests of some 296 constituent districts of the 'shire' counties. The *National Association of Local Councils* is concerned with the 10,000 Parish, Town and Community Councils in England and Wales. Other Welsh authorities are represented by the *Welsh Counties Committee* and the *Council for the Principality*, concerned with the district councils. In Scotland the principal local authority association is the *Convention of Scottish Local Authorities* (COSLA) which represents the regions, islands and districts of Scotland.

Non-governmental organizations

Public service is a partnership between policy-maker and professional. In many cases there is an equivalent, parallel organization to such governmental bodies as those listed above, to provide professional expertise and generally represent professional interests. These non-governmental organizations have a particular role in policy formulation and implementation and, as such, will normally adopt an apolitical stance in their dealings, particularly at a national and international level. Such independence is important if a truly professional view is to be readily acceptable by all. In addition to professional bodies there is also a group of organizations, normally run by volunteers, which exist to support the work of museums; these are treated at the end of this chapter.

The international museum scene

The *International Council of Museums* (ICOM) was founded in 1946 and today has some 8000 members in 120 different countries; about 80 of these countries have a fully constituted national committee (see ICOM-UK below). ICOM may be regarded as the successor to the *International Museums Office* which operated within the League of Nations from 1922 to 1946. As the international, professional organization for museums, it is recognized – with category 'A' status – as an advisory body on museum matters to the UN Economic and Social Council and to UNESCO, where it has its headquarters in Paris. There is also an *ICOM Regional Agency for Asia and the Pacific*, an *ICOM Permanent Secretariat for Latin America and the Caribbean* and discussions are current to establish an African Agency also. ICOM holds a triennial conference and General Assembly at which general policy is determined and the officers and Executive Council elected, with the responsibility for implementing that policy. In addition to the national committees there are also some 25 specialized international committees covering many aspects of the museum operation. The chairpersons of these two groups of committees together form an advisory committee which assists in formulating policy and advising the executive council. ICOM issues occasional publications, including its *Code of Professional Ethics* and a quarterly magazine *ICOM News*.

A parallel organization concerned with the built environment was founded in 1965. This is the *International Council on Monuments and Sites* (ICOMOS) which has similar advisory status with the UN organizations and currently has a membership of about 2500 representing 72 countries. It holds occasional symposia on such topics as industrial archaeology, the conservation of urban sites, the impact of tourism on heritage preservation and other related matters. It issues a periodical *Monumentum*.

The *International Institute for the Conservation of Historic and Artistic Works* (IIC) was founded in 1950 and has a membership based on institutions and individuals (who may be Fellows or Associates). Based in London, it provides an international forum for practising conservators, publishing occasional papers, conference proceedings as well as the periodicals *Studies in Conservation* and *Art and Archaeology Technical Abstracts*. The organization maintains close links with certain national associations, for example the *United Kingdom Institute of Conservation* (UKIC).

There are a number of organizations covering other groupings of which the *Commonwealth Museums Association* (CAM) should be mentioned. Concerned with the promotion and development of museums in Commonwealth countries, membership is open to all involved in such work, whether institution or individual. It publishes *CAM Newsletter*. ICOM (see above) seeks to provide a framework for co-operation in different regions of the world. There is, however, at the time of writing, no formal professional, regional organization for Europe, although the chairpersons of ICOM's national committees in Europe occasionally hold meetings on an informal basis.

The national museum scene

At a national level, the *Museums Association* (MA) serves as the professional organization for the UK. Founded at York in 1889 and incorporated as a company limited by guarantee in 1930 (Lewis, 1989), the Association aims to unite those engaged or interested in museum work through conferences and meetings, promote legislation for the benefit of museums, disseminate information and further the position and qualifications of museum staff. To this end the Association holds an annual conference, publishes the *Museums Journal*, the *Museums Yearbook*, as well as occasional publications such as *Museums UK* and maintains close contact with government and governmental bodies. It has provided training for all levels of museum staff – at a curatorial level for some 60 years – but has now passed this responsibility to the Museums Training Institute (see above).

Although the MA has a trading company, *Museum Enterprises Ltd*, whose profits are applied for the benefit of the Association, its principal funding source is membership subscriptions. These come from institutions owning museums or providing services to the profession and individuals working in museums or related institutions who may be ordinary members, associates or fellows: associateship is awarded to holders of the Diploma of the Museums Association; fellowship is granted on the basis of the individual's contribution to museums. All such members have voting rights and, because this benefit is accorded to governing bodies, the MA is not strictly a non-governmental organization. There are also supporting members. The Association is governed by an elected council representative of the membership with a number of supporting committees.

The national branch of the International Council of Museums, *ICOM-UK*, comprises all members of the organization in that country. It has, however, separate legal identity as a limited liability company. It holds two meetings a year and arranges occasional study visits in Britain and abroad. It provides an important link with museums and colleagues in other countries. It publishes a newsletter and awards occasional bursaries to assist museum profesionals in visiting overseas museums and conferences. Another group with international links is the *United Kingdom Institute for Conservation of Historic and Artistic Works* (UKIC) which has a membership based on institutions and individuals, although only the latter have voting rights. Its aims are the education and development of conservators, improving standards of conservation and knowledge of them and disseminating such information through its publications *The Conservator* and *Conservation News*. The *Museum Professionals Group* (MPG) owes its origin to a group of Museums Association Diploma students who created it in 1939. It has subsequently been reconstituted under different names but exists to provide a forum for museum staff other than heads of museums and holds study conferences on contemporary issues as well as publishing its *Transactions* and a bulletin *News*.

There are a number of other organizations operating at a national level. One group reflects the different types of museum. Of these there is the *Conference of the Directors of the National Institutions* which was created in 1931 following a recommendation of the Royal Commission on the National Museums and Galleries to co-ordinate their work and discuss matters of mutual concern. The Directors' Conference includes all national museums in London and those in Edinburgh, Cardiff, Belfast and Liverpool. The *Group of Directors of Museums and Art Galleries in the British Isles* (GODS) comprises museum directors from all types of museum and provides a lobby for museum affairs directed at both the Museums Association and the Government. There is also a *Society of County Museum Directors* which was formed in 1974 to provide a forum for officers in charge of county museum services and provide a mechanism for co-ordinating advice given to the Association of County Councils (see above). The *Association of Independent Museums* was founded in 1977 to represent the interests of the rapidly increasing number of museums outside the local authority and national structures. It arranges a regular programme of meetings and seminars for its members, and publishes the quarterly *AIM Bulletin* as well as the *AIM Guidelines* series of handbooks. Of a slightly different character is the *University Museums Group* which comprises institutional members who represent the interests of the university museums and seek to improve their status and effectiveness as well as encouraging communication between the staff of these museums.

Other organizations operating at a national level form the *Specialist Groups* whose activities centre on an aspect of the museum function or the particular problems associated with one of the subjects reflected in museums collections. The earliest of these started when a small group interested in children in museums commenced meeting informally in 1948, but after reconstitution four years later became what is now known as the *Group for Education in Museums*. Also in 1952 a *Federation of Military Museums* was formed, some 70 institutions being involved. The real growth of these groups, however, came in the 1970s and today there are some 17 of them.[7] All arrange meetings on a regular basis and some issue their own journals and newsletters. They have consultative status with the MA.

There is also a regional structure of professional groups within the country. The first of these, known as the Federation of Lancashire and Cheshire Museums, was established in 1927. Today there is a country-wide network of federations,[8] each of which elects a representative to the Museums Association's Council. They provide a forum for the discussion of regional as well as national matters and for collaboration within and between themselves. Some have a purely professional membership while others include governing bodies as well. The federations played an important role in the establishment of the Area Museum Councils and their services (see above), although this meant a dilution of the role that they previously played.

Non-governmental support organizations

There are a wide variety of different types of support organization which assist museums and related organizations either with funding or through the promotion of good-will and as a lay voice lobbying on their behalf. Many of them are voluntary bodies with few or no support staff, although the beneficiary sometimes provides assistance.

The *ICOM Foundation* was created in 1965 as a fund-raising body to support the work of the International Council of Museums (see above). It is registered in Switzerland but administered from Paris. There is a branch organization in the USA known as *The American Friends of ICOM*. Most of the funds are raised through corporate and individual contributions together with personal subscriptions and are used to support specific aspects of ICOM's work. The Foundation normally sponsors a number of museum staff from developing countries in order that they can attend international meetings, particularly the triennial ICOM General Conference.

Friends of museums organizations have an international as well as a national co-ordinating body. The *World Federation of Friends of Museums* (WFFM) was founded in 1972 at Barcelona. Its aim is to promote the role of museums and strengthen the work of national and individual Friend's organizations. For this purpose it organizes a triennial conference and issues a Bulletin to its members. it also promotes, with ICOM, a series of multilingual guidebooks to museums known as *Museums 2000*. The membership is made up of associations and groups devoted to the support of museums throughout the world. At a national level there is the *British Association of Friends of Museums (BAFM)*. Founded in 1971, it provides a forum for Friends organizations concerned with museums, galleries, churches, gardens and areas of outstanding interest. It also provides advice and support to such organizations seeking it, holds a conference every two years and issues a newsletter and a yearbook.

The *European Museum of the Year Award Committee* has a Secretariat based in Bath. This small Committee seeks sponsors to make annual awards and also provides the judges to assess the entrants for the main award, the European Museum of the Year, which is based on national award winners of the previous year. Of the other awards administered there is one by the Council of Europe (see above) who are anxious to see applicants from Eastern as well as Western Europe. The scheme has been in operation since 1977. The Committee issues occasional publications and the *EMYA News*; it also organizes seminars, often associated with the presentation ceremony for these awards.

The idea of the European Museum of the Year award originated from a similar scheme for the museums in England and Wales introduced by an organization known as *National Heritage* or the 'Museum Action Movement'. This movement was founded in 1971 to support and encourage museums in Britain and provide an active lobby of museum supporters to promote the interests of museums. Its membership includes individuals, affiliated museums and Friends of Museums organizations. In addition to its Museum of the Year Awards – there is one for England and Wales and another for Scotland – it makes grants to small museums, organizes occasional seminars and publishes a quarterly newsletter known as *Museum News*.

Friends organizations, museum societies and similar bodies to assist and support a museum are common and their members will often act as volunteers to assist museum staff in their work. There is, however, a more specialized body known as the *National Association of Decorative and Fine Art Societies* (NADFAS) whose members assist in art

museums and galleries with routine work. This organization was formed in 1968 to co-ordinate a number of societies that had developed locally to stimulate interest in the national heritage and assist in its care.

Another group of support bodies comprises those formed specifically to provide grants for museum purchases or other museum activities. Of these, the *National Art-Collections Fund* was founded in 1903 to try to reduce the number of works of art being exported; it is supported by subscriptions, donations and bequests and assists museums and galleries with purchases who are expected to obtain funding from their own and other sources as well. The *Army Museums Ogilby Trust* was founded in 1954 and has a wider brief in that it fosters the maintenance and development of military museums as well as contributing grants to assist with purchases; its work has recently been discussed by the Museums & Galleries Commission (1990). Another specialized fund is the *Beecroft Bequest*, administered by the Museums Association, which has been available since 1961 to assist museums and galleries to purchase pictures and works of art (excluding furniture and fittings) dating not later than the eighteenth century. The *Daphne Bullard Trust*, founded in 1973 and also administered by the Museums Association, has funds to promote the work of textile and costume conservation, display and publication.

It should be noted that three foundations with wider briefs have been particularly generous to museum development in the past. These are the *Carnegie United Kingdom Trust* (CUKT), which funded museum work and the Museums Association for over 50 years and which now includes environmental conservation and interpretation projects in its present programme; the *Calouste Gulbenkian Foundation*, which actively supports the arts in Britain and has assisted a number of non-London museums with the purchase of contemporary sculpture and generally fostered contemporary art work; and the *Pilgrim Trust*, which has contributed to the preservation of the countryside and historic buildings, the acquisition of works of art and their preservation as well as archaeological excavation.

Notes

1 See the European Communities reports on 'A fresh boost for culture in the European Communities' by the Commission (COM (87) 603), Economic and Social Committee (CES (88) 460) and the European Parliament (PE DOC A 2-287/88).

2 Article 36 of the European Economic Community Treaty, 1957 reads 'restrictions or prohibitions on the importation, exporting or transfer of art objects may be maintained by member countries with a view towards the protection of national treasures having an artistic, historic or archaeological value'.

[3] See the report drawn up for the European Parliament 'Return of objects of cultural interest to their country of origin' (PE DOC A 2-104/89).

[4] Discussed in 'The protection of National Treasures possessing artistic, historic or archaeological value: needs arising from the abolition of frontiers in 1992' (Communication from the Commission of the European Communities to the Council, Brussels, 22 November 1989. Doc. COM (89) 594 final).

[5] These are the first figures gathered on public cultural spending in Europe by the Commission of the European Communities. The basis on which they have been gathered may be questioned and any comparative studies must, therefore, be treated with caution. The figures suggest that for the year 1984–1985, the UK government spent 0.221 per cent of its total budget on cultural affairs. Figures for other countries include: France 0.986 per cent; Denmark 0.788 per cent; Netherlands 0.728 per cent; Federal Republic of Germany 0.671 per cent; Republic of Ireland 0.182 per cent. The figures may also be used to suggest that the proportion of the cultural budget spent on museums is highest in the UK.

[6] The Area Museum Councils comprise: Area Museum Council for the South West (AMCSW), Area Museums Service for South Eastern England (AMSSEE), Council of Museums in Wales (CMW), East Midlands Area Museum Service (EMAMS), North of England Museums Service Ltd (NEMS), North West Museum and Art Gallery Service (NWMAGS), Scottish Museums Council (SMC), West Midlands Area Museum Service (WMAMS), and Yorkshire and Humberside Museums Council (YHMC).

[7] The specialist groups include: Association of British Transport Museums (ABTM), Biology Curators Group (BCG), Geological Curators' Group (GCG), Group for Costume and Textile Staff in Museums, Group for Education in Museums (GEM), Group for Museum Publishing and Shop Management, Group of Designers/ Interpreters in Museums, Guild of Taxidermists, Museum Ethnographers Group (MEG), Museums and Galleries Administrators Group, Museums and Galleries Disability Association (MAGDA), Science and Industry Curators Group, Social History Curators Group (SHCG), Society of Decorative Arts Curators, Society of Museum Archaeologists (SMA), Touring Exhibitions Group, Visual and Art Galleries Association, Women, Heritage and Museums (WHAM).

[8] The regional federations comprise: London Federation of Museums and Art Galleries, Midland Federation of Museums and Art Galleries, Museums North, North Western Federation of Museums and Art Galleries, Scottish Museums Federation, South Eastern Federation of Museums and Art Galleries, South Midlands Museums Federation, South Western Federation of Museums and Art Galleries, Welsh Federation of Museums and Art Galleries, and Yorkshire and Humberside Federation of Museums and Art Galleries.

References

AUDIT COMMISSION (1991), *The Road to Wigan Pier? Managing Local Authority Museums and Galleries*, HMSO, London

CA'ZORZI, A. (1989), *The Public Administration and Funding of Culture in the European Community*, Office for Official Publications of the European Communities, Luxembourg

CHEETHAM, F. (1981), 'Norfolk in Europe', *Museums Journal*, **80** (4), 183–185

EUROPEAN COMMUNITIES (1978), 'Community action in the cultural sector', *Bulletin of the European Communities*, (Suppl. 6/77), Commission of the European Communities, Brussels

GILMAN, B. (1977), *Le Musée: Agent d'Innovation Culturelle*, Council of Europe, Strasbourg

HEBDITCH, M. (1990), 'Community concerns', *Museums Journal*, **90** (5), 35–37

HUDSON, K. (1990), *1992 Prayer or Promise?*, Museums and Galleries Commission, London

LEWIS, G. (1989), *For Instruction and Recreation*, Quiller Press, London

MUSEUMS & GALLERIES COMMISSION (1982), *Countywide Consultative Committees for Museums*, HMSO, London

MUSEUMS & GALLERIES COMMISSION (1984), *Review of Area Museum Councils and Services*, HMSO, London

MUSEUMS & GALLERIES COMMISSION (1987), *Museum Professional Training and Career Structure*, HMSO, London

MUSEUMS & GALLERIES COMMISSION (1989), 'The Area Museum Councils', in *Museums and Galleries Commission Report 1988–89*, HMSO, London

MUSEUMS & GALLERIES COMMISSION (1990), *The Museums of the Armed Forces*, HMSO, London

NATIONAL AUDIT OFFICE (1988), *Management of the Collections of the English National Museums and Galleries. Report by the Comptroller and Auditor General*, HMSO, London

REBETEZ, P. (1970), *How to Visit a Museum*, Council for Cultural Co-operation, Council of Europe, Strasbourg

STANDING COMMISSION ON MUSEUMS AND GALLERIES (1979), *Framework for System for Museums*, HMSO, London

Bibliography

CLEERE, H. (1990), 'Heritage protection', *Museums Journal*, **90** (5), 37–38

COUNCIL OF EUROPE (1988), *The Art Trade: Report of the Committee on Culture and Education and Related Documents*, Council of Europe, Strasbourg

DEPARTMENT OF EDUCATION AND SCIENCE (1973), *Provincial Museums and Galleries*, HMSO, London

DEPARTMENT OF EDUCATION FOR NORTHERN IRELAND (1978), *Regional Museums in Northern Ireland*, HMSO, Belfast

LEWIS, G. (1991), 'International issues concerning museum collections', in Briat, M. and Freedberg, J. A. (Eds.) International Art Trade and Law, Volume 3, 73–94, International Chamber of Commerce Publishing, Paris and Kluwer Publishers, Deventer

MIDDLETON, V. T. C. (1990), *New Visions for Independent Museums in the U.K.*, Association of Independent Museums, Chichester

MUSEUMS & GALLERIES COMMISSION (1983), *Review of Museums in Northern Ireland*, HMSO, London

MUSEUMS & GALLERIES COMMISSION (1986), *Museums in Scotland*, HMSO, London

MUSEUMS & GALLERIES COMMISSION (1987), 'University collections', in *Museums and Galleries Commission Report 1986–87*, HMSO, London

MUSEUMS & GALLERIES COMMISSION (1988a), *The National Museums*, HMSO, London

MUSEUMS & GALLERIES COMMISSION (1988b), 'Independent museums: best philosophers', in *Museums and Galleries Commission Report 1987–88*, HMSO, London

MUSEUMS & GALLERIES COMMISSION (1991a), *Local Authorities and Museums*, HMSO, London

MUSEUM & GALLERIES COMMISSION (1991b), 'National Museums' in *Museums and Galleries Commission Report 1990–91*, HMSO, London

STANDING COMMISSION ON MUSEUMS AND GALLERIES (1981), *Report on Museums in Wales*, HMSO, London

WAKEFIELD, P. (1990), 'Export control', *Museums Journal*, **90** (5), 38

WILLIAMS, A. (1981), *A Heritage for Scotland: Scotland's National Museums and Galleries: the next 25 years*, HMSO, Glasgow

5

The Museums & Galleries Commission

Peter Longman

Introduction

In July 1927 a Royal Commission on National Museums and Galleries was set up by Royal Warrant to 'enquire into and report on the legal position, organisation, accommodation, the structural condition of building, and general cost of the institutions containing the national collections situate in London and in Edinburgh'. The Royal Commission was chaired by Viscount D'Abernon. The other 10 members included Sir Henry Miers, who later became President of the Museums Association, and was working at that time on what became known as the Miers Report on non-national museums, published in 1928. The Commissioners were faced with a formidable task, with some 20 institutions to investigate and with terms of reference which covered every aspect of museums. In September 1928 they published an *Interim Report* (Miers, 1928) drawing attention to the urgent accommodation defects in some of the national museum buildings. The recommendations made were endorsed in their entirety by the Government.

The *Final Report* was published in two parts in September 1929 and January 1930, and contained many recommendations in respect of specific institutions. The principal findings in the general context were the inadequacy of State support and lack of growth, the lack of co-operation between kindred institutions, the absence of united connection between the national and non-national institutions, and the lack of any single body which had a care for the well-being of museums and galleries as a whole. The Royal Commission saw the remedy for these defects in co-operation in the development of some form of central co-ordination. It therefore recommended that a Standing Commission be created in respect of all the national institutions which it had visited, and for others that might be added later.

The report did not envisage that the proposed body would have executive power; its influence would be derived from its central position and its prestige. It would not therefore override the existing Trustee and Government Departmental authorities. But it was considered essential that the Chairman should have ready access to the Prime Minister and to the Chancellor of the Exchequer.

The Government accepted the major part of this recommendation, and on 28 November 1930 a Treasury Minute was issued proposing that a Standing Commission should be appointed. Viscount D'Abernon (who had chaired the Royal Commission) became Chairman, and the Secretary to the Royal Commission, Mr John Beresford, continued as Secretary to the Standing Commission. Its first meeting was held on 20 March 1931.

The Standing Commission on Museums and Galleries 1931–1960

The terms of reference were based on, but not identical to, those recommended. The Standing Commission was required:

(1) to advise generally on questions relevant to the most effective development of the National Institutions as a whole, and on any specific questions which may be referred to them from time to time;
(2) to promote co-operation between the national institutions themselves and between the national and provincial institutions; and
(3) to stimulate the generosity and direct the efforts of those who aspire to become public benefactors.

Initially, all Commission members, other than the Chairman, were nominated by the various national institutions. In 1958 significant changes were made when, in addition to the nominated members

58

(reduced in number to six), six other 'independent' members were appointed directly by the Prime Minister. This had the effect of bringing the constitution closer to that originally recommended by the Royal Commission.

At first sight the names of the Commissioners appointed in these early years would appear simply to represent some well known and distinguished families, and other people prominent in various areas of public life. But from the very start the range and depth of expertise in 'museum and gallery subjects' was remarkable. They included distinguished scholars and art historians, owners of important private collections, scientists, and, more recently, eminent former museum staff. The Commission's membership has continued to maintain this balance.

For its first 30 years the Commission's Secretary was appointed on a part-time basis with clerical and administrative support from various government departments, depending on where it was housed. Meetings of the Commission were infrequent and averaged about two a year – in some years there were none – but special subcommittees did meet to consider and give advice on various specific subjects, usually on an *ad hoc* basis. Between 1933 and 1961 the Commission also published six periodic reports. These reports were chiefly concerned with the national museums and galleries, and following up the various recommendations of the Royal Commission. The Commission had some notable successes. It was instrumental in persuading the Government to take on additional staff at the British Museum and the British Museum (Natural History), to agree higher salary awards for staff in the national institutions generally, to provide a grant to support the Sir John Soane's Museum, and to increase purchase grants.

Although the Commission's terms of reference precluded it from the fourth task originally recommended by the Royal Commission – reviewing the draft estimates of national institutions – it carried out surveys and visits to advise the Treasury on the building programmes and priorities. It was also consulted generally on staffing levels, and from 1958 to 1978 it advised first the Treasury and then the Department of Education and Science on purchase grants, both on the amount required by individual institutions, and on the allocations of the total sum allotted. Since 1956 it has advised on the destination of works of art accepted in satisfaction of estate duty.

In these early years the Commission's involvement with non-national museums and galleries was limited. Commission papers show that it corresponded with the Museums Association on a proposed affiliation scheme, but its concern with non-nationals was generally restricted to ways in which the nationals could help them, either through making loans or through extending the Circulation

Department at the Victoria and Albert Museum. The Commission was not seen as a body set up to encourage government support for non-nationals, or to improve their condition. The report prepared for the Carnegie United Kingdom Trust by Markham (1938) called for an authoritative central body with oversight of all public museums. After the war the idea was developed further (Museums Association, 1945) with the proposal for a Museum and Art Gallery Grants Board, modelled on the University Grants Committee. The Commission appears not to have been involved in this proposal, although it was represented on the Joint Committee of the Carnegie United Kingdom Trust, the Arts Council and the Museums Association, which presented a memorandum to the Chancellor of the Exchequer in 1955 in an attempt to win State aid for non-national museums and a Royal Commission to consider their needs. But, although it kept in touch with the Museums Association, the Standing Commission's own efforts in this direction had been restricted to an (unsuccessful) attempt to product a list of non-national museums and galleries considered suitable to receive items accepted in lieu of tax under the 1956 Finance Act. The affairs of the non-nationals were seen to be of more direct concern to the Museums Association.

The Survey of Provincial Museums and Galleries 1960–1963

The Government's eventual response to the demand that it do something for the non-nationals came in March 1960 when it invited the Commission to undertake a survey. For the Commission this was a major undertaking, but it readily agreed to help. The post of Secretary had been put on to a full-time basis that year, so that there were now two full-time staff; additional help was brought in and a subcommittee of Commissioners set up to oversee the survey.

The terms of reference were 'to ascertain the scope, nature and significance of the local collections, the manner in which they are organised, the resources available to them, and the possibilities of their further development on a basis of regional co-operation'. At the same time the Government stressed that it did not intend to depart from its long-held principle that local museums and galleries were essentially a local responsibility, but it did admit to having been encouraged by what it referred to as the 'experiment' recently launched in the south-west of England for the regional grouping of local museums on a basis of mutual help and support. That 'experiment' later developed into the first of the Area Museum Councils which, in 1963, proved the key to unlocking central government aid for non-national museums and galleries. The Government's policy towards museums from 1960 to

1986 is the subject of a recent study by Bowers (1987).

The Commission's *Survey of Provincial Museums and Galleries* (Standing Commission on Museums and Galleries, 1963), published in 1963, is still of interest today for the mass of detailed information it contains on individual museums and galleries, their collections, and their finances. It echoed many of the earlier recommendations on the role of the national institutions, and encouraged greater co-operation between Local Authorities, as well as making recommendations on a wide range of specific subjects. But above all it was the report's encouragement (along with that of other bodies) that did much to speed the creation of a network of Area Museum Councils. The successful outcome of its recommendation that Government should provide financial support on a matching grant basis for Area Council schemes of mutual co-operation marked a breakthrough in the Government's attitude to non-national museums and galleries. It also influenced greatly the role of the Commission over the next 20 years.

Changing priorities 1964–1981

For the next few years the Commission was much concerned with the development of the Area Museum Councils (AMCs). It took the leading role in the 'Advisory Committee on the Allocation of Exchequer Grants to Area Councils' (set up by the Treasury in 1964), persuaded the Government to simplify the basis on which it contributed towards AMC expenditure in 1966, and, in 1967, produced a progress report on their development (Standing Commission on Museums and Galleries, 1967). The Commission's membership was increased in 1967 to allow for an additional 'independent' member and an additional member nominated jointly by the Area Museum Councils and the Museums Association, and it began to meeet regularly with the new Committee of Area Council Chairmen.

The Commission also attempted to follow up other recommendations of its 1963 survey. It argued successfully for increases in the Local Museum Purchase Grant Fund (LMPF), with the result that this was doubled in 1964–1965 and again in the following year; and it pressed for special Treasury grants for major purchases, and for more favourable consideration of claims by non-nationals for items accepted in lieu of tax. It was consulted by the government on the contents of what became the *Public Libraries and Museums Act 1964*, which gave local authorities the power to contribute to broad-based museum services and to accumulate funds specifically for the purchase of works of art.

The appointment in 1965 of the first Government Minister with speical responsibility for the arts promised much, but proved a disappointment as far as museums were concerned. The White Paper, *A Policy for the Arts, the First Steps* (Her Majesty's Government, 1965) resulted in additional money for the Arts Council, including a new fund for Housing the Arts. But this excluded museums, except for temporary exhibition spaces where the works of living artists could be shown. More significant for the Commission and its relation to the nationals was the decision that Government responsibility for the arts was to be transferred from the Treasury to the Department of Education and Science (DES) and the Scottish and Welsh Offices, as appropriate. As an indirect consequence of this the Commission was no longer officially invited to advise Government on the building priorities of the national institutions. The Commission did not conceal its disappointment at these developments.

The change of government in 1970 produced a change of policy and a committee to report on provincial museums and galleries was set up. But this initiative, and the welcome increase of 50% on the previously planned building programme for national museums and galleries, were overshadowed by the decision that they should levy admission charges. The Commission, along with others, expressed concern at this, and annoyance that it had not been consulted in advance.

The so-called Wright Report, published for the Minister by the Department of Education and Science (1973), called for the establishment of a Housing the Museums Fund and increased money for the AMCs and LMPF. It echoed the Commission's recommendation (1971) that a separate purchase fund be established for technological material. More significantly, it argued for the development of a structured museum service: strategic Central Government funding would be channelled through a central body, supported by provincial museum councils and a limited number of provincial 'centres of excellence', which would be charged with pastoral duties in relation to their neighbours.

The Government's response met both recommendations on the Local Museum Purchase Grant Funds and confirmed that the grants to the AMCs would be increased from £132,000 to £500,000 over the 'next few years'. (In fact they rose to £640,000 by 1975–1976 and £1.7 million by 1980–1981, far outstripping the rapid inflation rate.) Although there was not to be a Housing the Museums Fund, the Government was prepared to consider special grants towards building schemes of more than local significance. The Commission and the Museums Association promptly set about preparing a list of such schemes, but the Government declined to help any of them, suggesting instead to the Arts Council that it might help the leading contender (the new museum at Stoke-on-Trent) from its Housing the

Arts Fund! Ministerial support for the general idea of Provincial Councils and designated museums was announced, but there was no action from the Government. Attention turned instead to the 1974 reorganization of local government in England and Wales and the opportunities that it presented for improved organization at a local level.

However, the pressure for proper government funding and a new support framework did not abate, and in May 1975 the Commission began work on what was to become known as the Drew Report – *Framework for a System for Museums*, published in 1979. It developed further the strategic concepts outlined in the Wright Report, which had themselves been adumbrated in an earlier paper, *A Museum Service for the Nation* (Museums Association, 1971). The Drew Report made many other recommendations, and is probably still the best known of all reports produced by the Standing Commission. The Commission was now producing reports on topics related to non-national museums fairly regularly. These also included reports on the special needs of university museums in 1968 and 1977, on conservation in 1980, and on Countywide Consultative Committees in 1982. A full list of publications is obtainable from the Commission.

The Commission was also taking an increased interest in taxation and heritage matters. It had argued consistently since its fifth report in 1959 for tax concessions relating to bequests to museums, and for improvements to the system whereby heritage items could be accepted in lieu of tax. In the early 1970s it met with some success, but its other main recommendation, that individual one-off donations of objects to certain charitable institutions should be able to be offset against income tax, has still to be met.

But at the same time as its field of interest increased, the Commission's links with some other parts of the UK were weakening. The establishment of direct rule had brought Northern Ireland into the Commission's remit in 1974; a brief report on museums there had been published in 1965, although contacts between the Commission and Ulster remained tenuous until the 1980s. The prospect of devolution later in the 1970s made the Commission cautious about considering the particular needs of Scotland and Wales in the Drew Report, and the Williams Report (Williams, 1981) went so far as to recommend that a separate Commission be established in Scotland.

Nor did the national museums hold quite the same priority in the centre of the Commission's activity after the publication of the Drew Report. It visited them less frequently; from 1979 it travelled to a centre outside London annually for one of its regular meetings and visited local museums. From 1978 it was no longer called on to advise on the allocation of purchase grants between the nationals. The development of the Office of Arts and Libraries (then still within the DES) as the decision-making link in the chain between most of the major London nationals and the Treasury, whilst the Commission was purely advisory, with no 'teeth', reduced still further the Commission's relevance in the eyes of some of the national institutions. In truth the Commission was woefully understaffed for the tasks it had assumed. Its basic staff level was strictly controlled by the Government, and had only increased from two in 1960 to four by 1979.

Nevertheless, the Commission's periodic reports published in 1973 and 1977 still contained copious factual information on the national institutions. In the general absence of published annual reports by individual museums, much of this information was not readily available elsewhere. The texts of these two reports and their recommendations covered the whole range of national and non-national museum and gallery affairs, export control, and heritage and taxation matters. Nor did Commissioners shrink from making specific, as well as general, recommendations on the national institutions and their affairs.

In 1973 the specific recommendations included requests for financial resources for completing the new National Army and Royal Air Force Museums; and that priority should be given to completing the air conditioning at the national Gallery and the Wallace Collection, to a new building for the National Portrait Gallery, and to creating on the Chambers Street site in Edinburgh an extension for the Royal Scottish Museum and the National Museum of Antiquities of Scotland. Five years later in 1978, the National Gallery and the Wallace Collection air conditioning having been started, the Commission repeated its earlier recommendations, but added the need to rehouse the India Collection of the Victoria and Albert Museum.

In 1978 the general recommendations included the statement that national museums and galleries should generally be separated from their parent departments and placed under independent Boards of Trustees, that existing Trustee legislation should be brought into line with that of the major museums in London, and that arrangements for use of the Property Services Agency should be reviewed and made more responsive to the needs of museums so that Trustees could be given greater freedom to deal with building matters. The Report also argued that proper provision should be made in museums for shops and restaurants, and that profits from such activities should be retained by the museums as an addition to their normal maintenance grants.

Whatever the reputation of the Commission then, these recommendations now have a prophetic ring. But the most prophetic and the most surprising recommendation made by this rather self-effacing body was that its own terms of reference and future should be reviewed as soon as possible.

The new Commission 1981–1986

The general election in 1979 meant that a new government had to deal with the Commission's recommendation and with the demands for a co-ordinated national structure, which had culminated with the Drew Report. This time there was a willingness to make structural changes and to consider sympathetically the demand for additional funding for non-nationals. The Office of Arts and Libraries (OAL) was transferred out of the DES and given autonomous status. The Government was to embark on a process of devolving a wide range of its responsibilities – this included giving more national museums and galleries Trustee status and increased financial flexibility. It was also committed to reducing overall the number of civil servants.

The announcement by the Minister for the Arts on 9 September 1981 succeeded simultaneously in meeting the Government's objectives, placating (for the time being at least) the demands of the museum world, and giving the Commission a more substantial role. The Standing Commission was to be renamed the Museums & Galleries Commission (MGC), and its terms of reference changed to emphasize its concern with non-national as well as national institutions. For the first time, it was empowered to take action as appropriate, as well as to give advice and promote co-operation. From 1 April 1982 the MGC was to take on various executive functions, including allocation of the OAL grant of £1.73 million to the seven English AMCs and co-ordination of the grant to the Museum Documentation Association. It was also to be given discretion to allocate up to 10 per cent of its budget as capital grants to non-national museums, and the National Museums Security Advisor was to be transferred to the Commission from the OAL. The Minister's statement added that other changes were also in mind.

The Commission welcomed the provision for capital funding, which was the culmination of a 20-year campaign. Nevertheless, it was apprehensive about the proposed assumption of executive functions, which it feared might jeopardize its ability to provide independent advice to Government. In fact it had already acquired one executive function; earlier in the year it had agreed to assume responsibility for the National Art Slide Library, which the Victoria and Albert Museum had decided to close as an economy measure. The OAL continued to make additional money available to the MGC for this until April 1984, when the Museum again assumed responsibility for it.

Whatever its initial reservations, the Commission

and embarked, falteringly at first, but then with increasing momentum, on what turned out to be a five-year period of transformation. Its staff increased from five to 22, and its budget from £70,000 to nearly £6 million, as a succession of additional functions were rapidly assumed. In 1984 it agreed at very short notice to allocate an additional £0.5 million earmarked for conservation, whilst in the following year it took over responsibility for the Local Museum Purchase Grant Funds (£1.282 million), although these continued to be administered on its behalf by the Victoria and Albert and Science Museums. Also in 1985 it took over most of the administrative duties previously carried out by the OAL and other departments in running the Government Indemnity Scheme and the Acceptance in Lieu procedures. In 1986 the MGC became the government's channel for £1.25 million to be distributed to certain museums and galleries affected by the abolition of the GLC and Metropolitan Counties, and assumed another unexpected responsibility when it accepted the invitation to take over the conservation function previously administered by the Crafts Council.

The transformation culminated on 31 December 1986 when the MGC became legally incorporated under Royal Charter with charitable status, and on 1 April 1987, when finally it acquired its own bank account and responsibility for making its own financial arrangements. Prior to that all payments had, technically, been made on its behalf by the government. Now at last the Commission had the same legal and financial status as the Arts Council and similar bodies.

Having seen the MGC's status enhanced, Commission members were not content simply to take on new functions at the behest of government; they wished to determine their own policy and priorities for the years ahead, and they had other existing commitments. They had just completed a report on the Area Museum Councils and, at the behest of the Scottish Office, were about to undertake a review of non-national museums there, to complement similar reports published in 1981 and 1983 on Wales and Northern Ireland, which likewise had not explicitly been included in the Drew Report.

Under the Chairmanship of Lord Howard of Henderskelfe, who briefly succeeded Sir Arthur Drew in September 1984, the Commission agreed a further programme of work for the next two years. This included completing a series of visits to the national museums and galleries, with a view to producing a special report on them – a conscious attempt to make up some of the ground gradually lost during the years since 1963. In the meantime it agreed to develop further and test on a pilot basis the proposals by the Museums Association and the AMCs for a museum registration scheme, and it set up a Working Party to report on Museum Professional Training and Career Structure. Finally, it managed to persuade the Government to allow it to devote funds to implement from 1988 some of the main recommendations of its 1983 report on travelling exhibitions.

Underlying the new initiatives was a realization that the MGC also needed to professionalize its staff and modernize its image. Hitherto its staff had generally been recruited or seconded from the civil service. The new vacancies were now filled with experts from relevant specialist backgrounds. Instead of period reports, it started to publish illustrated annual reports, and in an attempt to break away from the traditional working party reports (which were gradually becoming thicker and were very time-consuming) each annual report from 1985–1986 now features a particular type of museum or problem area. The announcement of government funding levels for the following three years at the end of 1987 meant that the Commission was finally able to reassess its priorities in a more considered manner, reasonably certain that its period of rapid expansion was over.

The Commission today

The MGC's Royal Charter abolished the old nomination system of membership. The Chairman and 14 Commissioners are now appointed by the Prime Minister on an independent basis, although two of them are appointed after consultation with the Secretary of State for Scotland and one each by the Secretary of State for Wales and Northern Ireland respectively. Other than the Chairman, they are appointed for terms of up to five years, and may be re-appointed. They are all unpaid.

The Commission's small permanent staff of about 35, augmented by consultants and temporary appointments for specific assignments, is headed by the Director and it is funded by the Office of Arts and Libraries. Nearly 90% of its annual budget of some £11.4 million is distributed in grant form.

The Commission's terms of reference are now very broad, and its powers extensive. In effect, the MGC exists to help create conditions in which museums and galleries in the UK can best develop and flourish, and it can do anything it considers necessary to achieve this objective. But the money it receives from Parliament has conditions attached, and the Commission must submit annual audited accounts and a corporate plan and publish periodic reports on its activities. The Minister for the Arts has to approve the Commission's appointment of its Director, who is responsible to Parliament for its financial affairs. The pay and conditions of its staff are generally in accordance with civil service practice.

Commissioners meet monthly for a normal business meeting, but on most of these occasions they also meet less formally with representatives of other organizations such as the AMCs, or the Museums Association, or with invited groups of museum directors. Twice a year the MGC meets outside London, and combines this with a couple of days visiting museums in the area concerned. In addition, most Commissioners become members of a working party or committee, or attend other meetings and visits on an *ad hoc* basis. Other individuals, including serving museum professionals, may also be co-opted to serve on working parties or committees. The Commission values greatly its links with members of the museums profession at all levels in different types of museum throughout the UK, and relies upon them for advice (formal and informal) when considering its own advice to Government and when undertaking consultation exercises. It also works very closely with the Museums Association, the Association of Independent Museums, and the specialist groups and regional Museum Federations, as well as with the AMCs.

Much of the Commission's time is spent dealing with officials in the various Government Departments involved directly or indirectly with museums, and their Ministers. (The 19 major national museums and galleries are currently divided between six different Government Departments – and there are relatively few departments which do not have some connection with museums.) The MGC's work also brings it into regular contact with outside organizations, including the Arts Councils, English Heritage and the National Trust, Tourist Boards, major charities and grant-giving bodies, business and industry and private individuals, including politicians and journalists. But, unlike some comparable bodies, the Commission has never had any responsibility to educate the general public in the knowledge and understanding of museums, or to increase the availability of museums to the public. Whilst its Royal Charter no longer precludes such a role, the Commission has as yet no plans (or resources) to develop in this way.

The MGC's five Section Heads and a consultant report to the Director and meet weekly as a management team. The Deputy Director is head of the largest section, with overall responsibility for the Commission's grant-aiding activities and liaison with museums and galleries on professional matters, including the registration scheme and the Travelling Exhibitions Unit. The Capital Taxes Officer deals with Acceptance in Lieu, the Government Indemnity Scheme, and advises on taxation and heritage matters. The Assistant Secretary is head of Finance and Administration (which includes responsibility for publications and information) and is also available to provide advice on financial and administrative matters generally. Although the Director is the main link with national museums and galleries, he is assisted in this by other staff. The National Museums Security Advisor and the Head of the Conservation Unit complete the management team. The Commission decided in 1984 that it would avoid taking on additional executive functions if there was an alternative, and that it would make as much use as possible of fee-paid temporary consultants, rather than adding to its permanent staff complement. Posts recently created on this basis include advisers on disability and on environmental standards.

Further information on the Commission's functions and publications is provided in a series of leaflets available from its Information Officer. An Annual Report and Accounts, listing all grants offered, is published each summer. Working Party and other special reports are still published on an *ad hoc* basis.

Grants given by the MGC

During 1987 the Commission reviewed its grant schemes and the conditions under which it provided financial assistance to the AMCs. It does not generally support financially the work of national museums and galleries. Most of its grant schemes, and those of the AMCs, require applicants to raise at least half the total cost from other sources. With the exception of the English Area Museum Councils, the Museum Documentation Association, and (under special arrangements) the Tyne and Wear Museums Service the Commission does not provide revenue finding. In this it differs markedly from the Arts Council.

The Commission monitors the work of all the *Area Museum Councils* and provides advice on their activities. It receives papers for their formal meetings, and is often represented by an assessor. However, much of the assessment process is done less formally through visits and discussions. The AMCs in Scotland and Wales are funded by the Scottish Office and the Welsh Office. There is at present no AMC in Northern Ireland, although the MGC and the Northern Ireland Department of Education are jointly funding a pilot project. The grants to the English ones are subdivided into a fixed allowance towards basic administrative costs, and specified amounts towards subsidized services and grant-giving activities, but the AMC are free to determine how this money is allocated between these headings. In addition to the basic grants, contributions are available for special factors, and for one-off projects, such as capital expenditure. The three main areas for which AMCs are not permitted to aid museums are revenue costs, acquisitions, and building work.

The Commission monitors the work of the *Museum Documentation Association* (MDA) in a similar manner, and liaises with those government departments which also provide funding. Two (unpublished) reports by the MGC in October 1986 and January 1989 resulted in a restructuring of the MDA's Board, the establishment of a new corporate plan and the creation of a new managing director post.

The two *Local Museum Purchase Grant Funds* are administered on the MGC's behalf by the Victoria and Albert Museum and the Science Museum, respectively. Between them they award something like 600 grants each year but, with the level of funding separately earmarked by the government and frozen in cash terms from 1983–1984 until 1990–1991, it has been necessary in recent years to find ways of rationing the money. The Victoria and Albert fund, which helps in the field of the fine and decorative arts, is limited to a maximum of £60,000 for any one grant and for any one institution in the course of a year and, whereas grants were otherwise previously awarded automatically at a 50 per cent level, lower percentage figures are now common and applications may be deferred or turned down altogether if they are not considered to be of sufficiently high priority. The Science Museum fund can also contribute to the restoration or conservation of acquired material. These schemes cover England and Wales only; a separate fund is run by the Royal Museum of Scotland.

The *Capital Grants* scheme has always been administered on a competitive basis. Applications are sought annually and considered first by the AMCs, before being forwarded to the Commission. It is not uncommon for these funds to be over-subscribed 20-fold, even though in practice individual grants are unlikely to exceed £30,000. Priority is given to extensions and conversions which will improve the conservation, storage and security of collections, rather than new buildings and display facilities. Since 1990 the MGC and AMCs have advised on applications to the new joint OAL/Wolfson Museum Improvement Fund.

From 1984 until 1987 the MGC also administered *conservation grants*, but this overlapped with other grant schemes and the money has now been reallocated between the new Conservation Unit, the AMCs, and the Capital Grants scheme. Between 1986 and 1989 the MGC also administered *transitional grants* on a reducing basis to certain museums affected by the abolition of the GLC and Metropolitan County Councils. When this money was no longer required for that purpose it too was reallocated elsewhere to increase the budgets for research and publications and the Conservation and Travelling Exhibitions Units. The only remaining commitment is for a substantial contribution

(£945,000 in 1991–1992) towards the cost of the former *Tyne and Wear County Museums Service*, which is now run by a Joint Committee of the districts. Whilst some other museum services previously run by Metropolitan Counties or the GLC were taken over in their entirety by the government, or by other agencies, this was not considered appropriate for the Tyne and Wear Service. Whilst it is tempting to regard this as a partial implementation of the recommendations in the Wright and Drew Reports for major designated museums in the provinces to receive a measure of direct central government funding, the comparison is superficial; the Commission's grant amounts to about one-third of the basic cost of running the service and is not intended to help it provide regional or other pastoral facilities. The later decision that the MGC should take over sole funding for the *Horniman and Geffrye Museums* on the abolition of the Inner London Education Authority from 1990 to 1992 also stemmed from expediency rather than any change in government policy. Together they received over £3 million each year, but are now funded by the OAL direct.

The *Travelling Exhibitions Unit* was established during 1988; it concentrates primarily on promoting and co-ordinating information on travelling exhibitions, thus helping museums outside the capital cities to benefit more from material in the national collections and other sources. Some pump-priming financial assistance is also made available to enable exhibitions that would not otherwise be able to tour to do so. In 1991 the MGC launched a consultation exercise aimed at creating a national plan for touring.

The Commission has also run *other grant schemes*, sometimes for a limited period, to deal with particular areas of concern. These have included management and marketing, research and publications, and special aid for natural science collections and industrial material.

The museum registration scheme

The suggestion that there should be a national register of museums as a means of setting standards originated from the Museums Association (Clarke, 1969). In the early 1980s two sets of proposals – from the Association and from the Committee of Area Museum Councils – were referred to the Commission on the grounds that it alone had the authority to implement such a scheme and the financial resources to provide the necessary incentive for museums to subject themselves to the application process. In March 1987 the MGC circulated a report on the pilot scheme it had run in the area of the North of England Museums Service during the previous year, together with a consultation document which set out revised guidelines. Further revisions were made as a result of

this exercise and in March 1988 the scheme was launched on a national basis (Newbery, 1988). Implementation will take four years, and is being phased in on a regional basis.

The main advantages of registration are that it confers eligibility for grant-aid and subsidized services from the Commission and AMCs, and that many other grant-giving bodies, both independent and statutory, as well as local authorities, have stated their intention to look to the Register for assurance that the museum concerned is, in principle, worthy of support. Registration is also intended to foster confidence among potential providers of material for a museum's collection, and among the public that the museum concerned provides a basic range of services for the benefit of visitors and other users. Provisional registration may be offered to museums which are striving to reach the required standard, and grant-in-aid and subsidized services may be available to these in order to help them reach it.

The key requirements of registration are as follows.

(1) Accordance with the Museums Association's definition of a museum or, if appropriate, the MGC definition of a national museum. This implies a formal governing instrument and a long-term purpose. Privately owned museums and collections are not eligible.
(2) An acceptable constitution and a sound financial basis, and compliance with statutory and planning requirements.
(3) Publication of an acceptable statement of collection management policy. This should include details of: the acquisition and disposal policy (which should be broadly in line with the Museums Association's code of practice); the nature of the existing collection; and the source of conservation advice. There should be a basic documentation system.
(4) Provision of a range of public services/facilities appropriate to the nature, scale and location of the museum.
(5) Access to professional curatorial advice, normally through a full-time curator with an efficient line of communication to the appropriate committee of the museum's governing body; alternatively, in the case of smaller museums, the appointment of a professionally trained and experienced person, either as a member of the governing body or as a designated curatorial advisor to it.

Special arrangements are being made for the initial registration process, but subsequently museums and galleries will be able to apply at any time and will be expected to make an annual statistical return to their AMC and to renew their application every 5 years. Bodies such as AMCs and reputable training and conservation services, although outside the scope of registration, will remain eligible for financial assistance. Some other facilities sometimes run by museums, such as science centres and planetaria, or venues for temporary exhibitions, which would not necessarily qualify as museums within the Museums Association definition, will be eligible for registration and support as part of a broadly based museum service, the other components of which are registered. Special arrangements are being made for English Heritage and the National Trust, whose properties are centrally managed, and only some of which could individually be classified as museums.

Applications for registration are submitted through the appropriate AMC but considered by a special Registration Committee of the MGC. Museums failing to qualify may appeal to a separate appeals committee, comprising two members of the MGC and a senior museum professional nominated for the occasion by the Museums Association. It should be stressed that the registration of a museum does not commit the MGC or any AMC to provide funding or to accept any responsibility for the management of the museum concerned. The standards required for registration are fairly basic, but in the longer term the Commission may consider introducing a more selective system for those museums which wish to be seen to adhere to higher standards. Alternatively, the Museums Association might consider this in the context of its accreditation system.

Security in museums

The post of National Museums Security Advisor was created in 1961, and transferred to the Commission in 1981. Traditionally it has been held by a former senior police officer. The main (and original) concern was to advise on an ongoing basis on security standards in the national museums and galleries throughout the UK, and in particular to consider plans for new buildings or extensions, and changes in policy which affect security. But over the years this remit has been extended to cover non-nationals, particularly those which seek government indemnity cover for material on loan. The Security Advisor and his assistant now make hundreds of visits each year to inspect local museums and advise on improvements, and by, arrangement with the British Council, they inspect and advise on security systems in museums throughout the world where material from British collections is to be lent. Currently, the Commission is planning to extend this service to include advice on environmental conditions.

The Government Indemnity Scheme

The cost of commercial insurance for loans is now beyond the reach of many museums. Under the provisions of the Government Indemnity Scheme,

the government undertakes to meet agreed losses on items on loan valued in excess of £100, and the liability of a non-national museum or gallery borrowing them is limited to approximately one per cent of any loss. (It is usually possible to insure commercially against this one per cent). The items covered by the scheme can come from national or non-national museums or from private owners, and indemnity cover may either be granted for a temporary exhibition or, on an annual basis, for long-term loans of individual items. The legislative basis for the scheme is the *National Heritage Act 1980*, which lays down that a loan must materially increase public access to the item, or public understanding of it. The MGC administers the scheme, processing applications, checking on valuations, security and public benefit arrangements before recommending the issue of an indemnity by Ministers. National museums and the Arts Council issue their own indemnities when borrowing items.

Acceptance in Lieu and tax incentives for the heritage

The Commission's involvement with Acceptance in Lieu (AIL) has gradually increased since 1956 when the scheme was first introduced. This is a complex subject, best dealt with in simple terms by Wilson (1987), and on which further general guidance is available in leaflet form from the MGC; MGC staff will also discuss specific instances with owners, their agents, or with museums.

There are three key provisions, which are often confused. *Conditional exemption* is the means whereby an object is exempted from tax liability as long as certain conditions are fulfilled – in other words the value of the object is not taken into account when calculating death duties. The liabilities are most likely to be Capital Transfer Tax or Inheritance Tax, and the owner has to agree to keep the object (which must be of museum quality) in the UK and to make it available to public access and to look after it properly. The MGC is not directly involved with this provision. The most likely benefit to museums is that the owner may decide to lend the object in question in order to meet the public access requirement.

A *private treaty sale* (PTS) is a private sale to a museum, for which a special low price is agreed between both parties, because the tax that would otherwise have been payable has been avoided. A 'public' sale (e.g. at an auction) will render the vendor liable to pay Capital Gains Tax on any increase in value and, particularly if the item has been conditionally exempted, Capital Transfer Tax or Inheritance Tax will be due as well. Under the private treaty sale arrangement the benefit of the tax that has been thus avoided is divided between the museum and the vendor to arrive at the so-called 'special price'. If the total tax bill on a 'public' sale would have been (say) £50,000, it would be normal for the vendor to receive a quarter of that amount (i.e. £12,500) more than he or she would have done had they sold the item publicly and paid the tax due. The museum, which would otherwise have had to pay at least £37,500 more, does even better out of the PTS arrangement, although the exact division of the tax benefit (also known as the 'douceur') is negotiable between the parties.

The Commission's main involvement is in *Acceptance in Lieu* (AIL). This is what happens when the State accepts an important object in settlement of a tax debt and the object is then transferred to the ownership of a museum. To be acceptable an item has to be pre-eminent in quality, a rather higher standard than that applied for conditional exemption or a private treaty sale. There has to be an existing tax debt, either of Estate Duty, Capital Transfer Tax or Inheritance Tax. Income Tax cannot be settled in this way, nor can Companies offset Corporation Tax through the AIL mechanism.

Once an offer has been made the Commission considers whether the item is pre-eminent and its valuation reasonable. An offer may be made conditional on the item being allocated to a particular museum or gallery, or even on the item remaining *in situ* if it is historically associated with a particular house or building. Alternatively, a wish may be made as to allocation; it is unusual for a reasonable wish to be overruled. The MGC considers and advises on the appropriateness of any such conditions.

Once an offer that is not conditional as to allocation has been accepted, the Commission advertises the item's availability in the *Museums Journal* and considers the bids received from museums before making a recommendation to the Minister concerned. Ownership of the item is then transferred to the recipient institution. Land and buildings can also be accepted in lieu; the arrangements for this are dealt with by the Department of the Environment. When dealing with manuscripts and archives, the Royal Commission on Historic Manuscripts gives expert advice to the Minister. The amount of tax settled by an AIL transaction is calculated in the same way as the 'special price' in a private treaty sale. The only difference is that with AIL the 'douceur' is fixed as 25%. For many years the Commission has argued that this division of the tax benefit should be such that both parties derive an equal benefit.

The Conservation Unit

The Conservation Unit was set up in April 1987, and continues work previously done by the Crafts Council. It is intended to foster conservation generally, with a particular concern to ensure that the needs and views of private conservators receive proper attention. Unlike other parts of the MGC, the Unit also has a responsibility to the public, in particular to the owners of historic objects, buildings and works of art, to persuade them of the importance of conservation and the needs for proper standards in conservation work if the country's heritage is to be properly preserved. The Unit also provides a forum for information, advice, planning and support for the conservation profession, both in private practice and in museums and galleries, and it runs a public information service. It also awards small grants, mainly related to training and raising standards. A register of reputable conservators in the private sector has been compiled, and a series of publications and information leaflets on training and other subjects are being developed.

The way ahead

The Commission now reviews its progress and priorities annually in a corporate plan, which covers a rolling three-year period. Much of its day-to-day work is devoted to its various executive tasks and following up published reports. These include recent reports on training (which led to the creation of the Museums Training Institute), the national institutions, armed-service museums, and, in 1991, Local Authorities and museums. The Commission also co-operated with the Association of Independent Museums in the publication of a survey of that sector and the future prospects for AIM members.

The AMCs remain the Commission's top priority for additional grant aid, although it sees them increasingly involved in an advisory and co-ordinating role, working not only with museums but with other funding agencies and those responsible for regional planning. AMC grant aid and that of the Commission will continue to be concentrated on the less glamorous sides of museum activity, such as documentation, storage and conservation – the areas of museum work that other funding sources do not reach. The Commission is now working with other interested parties to develop agreed standards for collection care across the whole field of museum activity; progress is being made in the natural sciences, archaeology, and industrial material. Codes and guidelines on disability and on environmental standards are to be issued during 1992. But there are three other key areas where investment is urgently needed, where museums generally lag behind the performing arts and have missed out from not having had an effective 'arts council' of their own over the last 45 years. Each of these is essential if museums are to become better able to help themselves. The first is training, particularly management training, and on which the Commission's views were set out in its 1987 report. It now works closely with the Museum Training Institute to follow this up. The second backlog area is buildings and improvements to buildings. The Arts Council's Housing the Arts Fund managed over some 15 years to solve many of the major accommodation problems in the performing-arts field, but if museums are likewise to maximize their potential, they do need to be properly housed; the situation here has been exacerbated by the closure of the English Tourist Board's grant scheme. The third key area where investment is needed is in the establishment and maintenance of reliable basic information and trend data on museums. Pioneering work has been done by the Museums Association in its Database Project, and the introduction of registration now provides a mechanism for annual updates through the Area Museum Councils. The MGC plans to implement a scheme based on information from registration returns and involving AMCs from early in 1992.

The Commission's other major area of concern is partly a consequence of the plural funding now available to museums. Indeed, far more money is put into museums from other Government Departments and agencies then through the MGC and the AMCs. The growth in the number of museums from 700 to up to 2500 in 25 years is in part the result of this. Undoubtedly there will be casualties in the years ahead, especially as none of the other agencies has any money to pay the running costs of the new museums they help to set up. The Commission's registration scheme is part of its answer to this and will help it to strengthen its influence with the other agencies involved.

The recent growth in the Commission's activities and influence has raised expectations outside, and its staff are finding increasingly that there is a tremendous backlog of work, advice and other things that people want to see done. Rightly, Commissioners are determined that the organization cannot attempt to do everything. Today the MGC may be seen as having developed towards three different roles. In keeping with their terms of reference, Commissioners still regard themselves as the Government's advisory body on museums. Whether framed in working party reports or *ad hoc* advice to government or help to individual museums, the MGC's advisory functions still occupy a major proportion of its time. The MGC's remit spans all Government Departments. It covers the whole of the UK, and deals with all types of museum. The Commission is objective, and it has an overview. No other body possesses all these characteristics.

However, in recent years the Government has sometimes tended to see the Commission more as an executive arm, particularly to implement its policy towards the non-national museums, including administering grant aid, and as a body to deal with various other jobs which it has shed. These include doing security checks, and administering the schemes for Indemnities and AIL (on both of which the Government still takes the final decisions). The development of the Office of Arts and Libraries and other 'arts' departments in recent years has led Government to prefer to decide things itself, and made it appear less likely to seek the views of an impartial outside body, even though only one of the departments concerned employs any specialist staff.

As the Commission's publications have increased and its executive role has developed, it has also increasingly been seen by non-national museums, and by some nationals, as a pressure group – as a campaigning body for museums. The role of pressure group is not compatible with that of being the Government's official advisory body, or indeed with acting as the Government's executive arm. The Commission's credibility with Government, and the willingness of Government to confide in it and to consult it, would not be enhanced if the Commission were seen to adopt the role of pressure group or actively to play along with those who would cast it in such a role. The pressure group job, which surely needs doing, probably rests better with the Museums Association and other support bodies.

There is also a parallel danger that the MGC's ability to be objective may be called into question if it ends up having to implement as additional executive functions the results of its advice. Suggestions that it should assume the training function were turned down for this reason. Already, some would argue, its involvement with grant schemes and with the work of AMCs restricts its ability to be objective about these activities. The general view of leading figures in the museum world is that the Commission should concentrate on its advisory role, even at the expense of its executive functions, and that it should certainly not risk devaluing its advice by acting also as a campaigning body. But as the Commission's history (Museums & Galleries Commission, 1988) has demonstrated, it has always been prepared to adapt to changing demands, and to do whatever seemed best to help it in its fundamental task of helping to create conditions under which museums and galleries can best flourish.

Acknowledgements

I am grateful to two colleagues who allowed me to draw on work then unpublished but now listed in the references below. Esmé, Lady Carlisle's history of the Commission provided much of the early material for the first part of this chapter. Sue Bowers' M.A. Thesis for the City University is the only substantial

References

BOWERS, S. (1987), 'Central government policy towards museums 1960–86', M.A. Thesis, City University (Department of Arts Policy and Management), London

CLARKE, D. T.-D. (1969), 'Register of museums', *Museums Journal*, **69** (3), 141

DEPARTMENT OF EDUCATION AND SCIENCE (1973), *Provincial Museums and Galleries*, a report of a committee appointed by the Paymaster General, HMSO, London

HER MAJESTY'S GOVERNMENT (1965), *Policy for the Arts; the First Steps*, Cmnd 2601, HMSO, London

MARKHAM, S. F. (1938), *The Museums and Art Galleries of the British Isles*, CUKT, Edinburgh

MIERS, H. A. (1928), *A Report on the Public Museums and Art Galleries of the British Isles (other than the National Museums)*, Carnegie United Kingdom Trust, Edinburgh

MUSEUMS ASSOCIATION (1945), 'Museums and art galleries – a national service', *Museums Journal*, **45** (3), 33–45

MUSEUMS ASSOCIATION (1971), *A Museum Service for the nation*, proposals submitted to the 1971 Conference by the Council of the Museums Association, London

MUSEUMS & GALLERIES COMMISSION (1988), *A History of the Commission by Esme, Countess of Carlisle*, Museums & Galleries Commission, London

NEWBERY, C. (1988), 'MGC Museum Registration Scheme', *Museums Bulletin* (Apr. 1988), 277–278

ROYAL COMMISSION ON NATIONAL MUSEUMS AND GALLERIES (1928), *Interim Report*, HMSO, London

ROYAL COMMISSION ON NATIONAL MUSEUMS AND GALLERIES (1929), *Final Report, Part 1*, HMSO, London

ROYAL COMMISSION ON NATIONAL MUSEUMS AND GALLERIES (1930), *Final Report, Part 2*, HMSO, London

STANDING COMMISSION ON MUSEUMS AND GALLERIES (1963), *Survey of Provincial Museums and Galleries* (The Rosse Report), HMSO, London

STANDING COMMISSION ON MUSEUMS AND GALLERIES (1967), *Area Museum Services 1963–66*, HMSO, London

STANDING COMMISSION ON MUSEUMS AND GALLERIES (1971), *The Preservation of Technological Material*, HMSO, London

STANDING COMMISSION ON MUSEUMS AND GALLERIES (1973), *Ninth Report, 1969–1973*, HMSO, London

STANDING COMMISSION ON MUSEUMS AND GALLERIES (1978), *Tenth Report, 1973–1977*, HMSO, London

STANDING COMMISSION ON MUSEUMS AND GALLERIES (1979), *Framework for a System for Museums*, HMSO, London

WILLIAMS, A. (1981), *A Heritage for Scotland, Scotland's National Museums and Galleries: the Next 25 Years*, report by a committee appointed by the Secretary of State for Scotland, HMSO, Glasgow

WILSON, H. (1987), 'Acceptance in Lieu – barter for bargains', *NACF Magazine*, **34** (Autumn 1987), 17–20

6

Enabling legislation for museums

Geoffrey Lewis

The first legislation enabling the establishment of a public museum in Britain dates from the middle of the eighteenth century and concerns the purchase, housing and use of the founding collections for the British Museum. Although the Ashmolean Museum had opened some 70 years earlier, this had resulted from a gift to further the work of an already long-established institution, the University of Oxford, and parliamentary legislation was not sought to give the Museum a separate corporate existence. Similarly, other collections and museums held by private persons and societies to which the public had access during the seventeenth and eighteenth centuries, do not figure in British law. Indeed there is a sparsity of relevant museum legislation of substance for much of the period during which museums have existed. It is therefore of some interest to examine the parallel developments of the notion of cultural property and its public access in considering the historical context of museum legislation.

Historical background

The idea of preserving the nation's patrimony for the public benefit also first appears in British law in connection with the establishment of the British Museum. In 1700 a statute was passed to vest Sir Robert Cotton's house and library in Trustees on the death of his grandson. The collection comprised manuscripts, books, papers, parchments, records, coins, medals and other rarities and curiosities. It 'was to be kept and preserved by the name of *The Cottonian Library*, for public use and advantage'; the deterioration of the property and the collection resulted in a further Act in 1707, although the material remained in the house until 1722. Consciousness of the past at this time was not peculiar to Britain. Sweden already had royal proclamations protecting ancient monuments and 'movable' anti-

quities (Daniel, 1981), while protective legislation is reported to date from the seventeenth century in Prussia also (O'Keefe and Prott, 1984). Certainly by 1718, Peter the Great, who had an outstanding personal collection, had issued a decree requiring the reporting of discoveries involving unusual or ancient objects in Russia.

The *British Museum Act 1753* was not only the first museum enabling legislation in Britain; it appears also to have pioneered this type of legislation in the world. As such it presented a number of novel conceptions to those drafting the legislation. The first of these was the word 'museum'. The Act states that this new institution is to be administered by 'The trustees of the British Museum', from which it can be assumed that the word 'museum' was by now well established. It had certainly been used elsewhere in Europe to describe a comprehensive collection since the fifteenth century and with the Enlightenment took on an encyclopaedic connotation. In Britain the catalogue of the Tradescant collection, published in 1656, had borne the term in its title, *Musæum Tradescantianum*, and the Ashmolean Museum at Oxford had been so called since its opening. That its use related to the collection rather than the building is clear from the references to the founding collection of Sir Hans Sloane: the word 'museum' was always qualified with 'or collection'. The building to house the collections was referred to as a 'general Repository' in the legislation.

Another concept defined is the purpose of the museum with some indication of the philosophy behind such collections:

That the said Museum or collection may be preserved and maintained, not only for the inspection and entertainment of the learned and the curious, but for the general use and benefit of the public

Whereas all arts and sciences have a connexion with each

other, and discoveries in natural philosophy and other branches of speculative knowledge, for the advancement and improvement whereof the said museum or collection was intended, do and may, in many instances give help and success to the most useful experiments and inventions

It is also clear that 'free access to the said general repository, and to the collections contained therein' was intended for 'all studious and curious persons, at such times and in such manner, and under such regulations for inspection and consulting the said collections' as the Trustees might determine. The Trustees were appointed mainly to represent the families involved in the benefaction and on an *ex officio* basis including the Archbishop of Canterbury, the Speaker of the House of Commons and the Lord Chancellor as principal Trustees. This, together with the other provisions in the 1753 Act, remained the basis for governing the British Museum for over 200 years. As far as staff were concerned, the Act provided for the position of Principal Librarian, appointed by the Sovereign on the recommendation of the principal Trustees; the name 'Director' was added to the title in 1898. There were also to be sub-librarians. In this the precedent of the Ashmolean Museum in appointing a Keeper (*Custos*) was not followed.

During the 200 years that the 1753 Act remained on the statute book as the governing instrument of the British Museum, a number of supplementary Acts were passed to further its work. These included such diverse legislation as the *Act to vest the Elgin Collection of ancient Marbles and Sculpture in the Trustees of the British Museum for the Use of the Public*, in 1816, the Act of 1894 which provided for the purchase of the land and property at Bloomsbury which has assured a full island site for the Museum's development, and the *British Museum Act 1924* which gave powers to lend certain types of material to provincial museums. Two other issues, both highly relevant today, also arise during this period.

The first move to introduce entrance charges at the British Museum occurred in 1784. At the time a House of Commons Committee saw an admission charge as a means of reducing crowding at the Museum and restricting an undesirable element. The Principal Librarian had reported to them that it was unpleasant for his staff to have to take round the Museum 'the lower kind of people who in many instances . . . behaved improperly to them' (quoted in Miller, 1973). However, the bill was defeated in the House of Commons. The issue has recurred from time to time, for example in 1922 during the severe economic difficulties following the Great War, but again the measure failed. Legislation imposing charges to enter the national museums eventually reached the statute book with the *Museums and Galleries Admission Charges Act 1972*. The Government introduced admission charges in 1974 but this lasted only for three months. The legislation remains in force, however, and is the legal basis for charging to those national museums which have introduced admission fees.

The *British Museum Act 1753* required that the Sloane collection be kept entire 'without the least diminution or separation . . . for the use and benefit for the public'; all the founding collections were vested in the Trustees for ever. It was not long, however, before *An Act to enable the Trustees of the British Museum to exchange, sell or dispose of any Duplicates, etc.* was passed by Parliament and until 1832 sales of such material were made; as noted elsewhere (Chapter 3), Viscount Fitzwilliam was deterred from bequeathing his collection to the British Museum because of the Trustees' powers under this Act. The Trustees of the National Gallery obtained even wider powers. The *National Gallery Act 1856*, an Act '. . . to authorize the sale of works of art belonging to the public' gave powers of disposal to its Trustees for any material judged to be unfit or not required for a national collection. This part of the Act was repealed by the *National Gallery and Tate Gallery Act 1954* at the Trustees' request.

Most of the national museums established during the nineteenth century were formed as part of an existing Government Department rather than as a result of independent legislation. Thus the South Kensington Museum, opened in 1857 and eventually to become the Science Museum and the Victoria and Albert Museum, was part of the Government's Department of Science and Art; so was the Museum of Science and Art in Edinburgh in 1854 and now the Royal Museum of Scotland. None of these museums received separate corporate status with its own Board of Trustees until the 1980s. In Ireland a different situation prevailed and the *Dublin Science and Art Museum Act 1878* was passed to establish a national museum based on the collections of two learned societies.

By the end of the nineteenth century there was a gradual awakening to the significance of cultural material and the need to enact legislation for its protection. One example was the *Ancient Monuments Protection Act 1882*, weak though it was and late compared with many other European countries. Another is the recognition in the *Finance Act 1894* that national heritage property warranted special tax treatment when given or bequeathed to a public body (Lewis, 1990). This recognition slowly permeated into the museum legislation of the twentieth century but, as much of it is still in force, this is treated later in this chapter.

The origins of the Local Authority museums in Britain lie in the social reforms consequent upon industrialization which led to the establishment of a more appropriate local government in the population centres, reflected in the *Municipal Corporations Act 1835*. A number of parliamentary committees examining the acute social issues of the day, recommended *inter alia* the provision of educational and recreational facilities in the towns. One such committee examining the 'vices of intoxication amongst the labouring classes' recommended a partnership between central and local government and local residents to provide facilities such as open spaces, libraries, museums and reading rooms (House of Commons, 1834). As a result, a Bill to effect this was presented to Parliament in 1835 and again in the two following years. The idea developed on the basis that Local Authorities would provide the necessary capital expenditure to establish museums, with running costs being met from low charges and local benevolence. These attempts to introduce legislation were, however, unsuccessful. Another committee recommended that museums and galleries should be formed to extend knowledge of the arts and the principles of design among the people (House of Commons, 1836).

It was to take another decade before the necessary legislation was enacted, and then only for England and Wales. The *Museums Act 1845* provided for towns with a population of more than 10,000 to spend up to a one-halfpenny rate in providing museums. Known popularly as 'The Beetle Act', it was intended to facilitate 'the instruction and amusement' of the public, not least in promoting industrial design. This statute permitted the charging of an admission fee of not more than one penny and also vested all specimens acquired to be held in trust for ever by the Local Authority concerned. One of the arguments that had been used against the introduction of public museums had been the fear of damage to exhibits. Because of this the *Protection of Works of Art and Scientific and Literary Collections Act 1845* was introduced at the same time, introducing penalties for malicious damage to such material.

By 1850 much of the opposition to public libraries had been overcome. Previously there had been a concern that they might become the cause of civil agitation and that they would not be in the best interests of public morals. Even so, it was a substantially modified Bill that received the Royal Assent as the *Public Libraries and Museums Act 1850*. Local Authority museum provision in England and Wales was now subject to this legislation and it was necessary to obtain a two-thirds majority of voting ratepayers in favour of the Act before it could be adopted. In many ways this enabling legislation was a retrograde step for museums. The maximum authorized expenditure – which now included libraries as well as museums – remained at a one-halfpenny rate and the power to purchase specimens was removed. However, in common with

the free library service now being provided under this Act, museums were to be free of an admission charge. The next 20 years were to see no less than nine statutes relating to public libraries, although not all of them had museum provisions.

The provisions of the 1850 legislation were extended to the rest of Britain through the *Public Libraries (Ireland and Scotland) Act 1853*, but its severe restrictions led to further legislation, the *Public Libraries (Scotland) Act 1854*, which raised the expenditure level to a one-penny rate and allowed the purchase of specimens from public funds. These provisions were extended to England and Wales in the *Public Libraries and Museums Act 1855* and to Ireland in a separate Act. Apart from the majority necessary to adopt the statute being reduced to one-half instead of two-thirds and the population limit of 10,000 being removed for England and Wales in 1866, with consequential amendments for other parts of Britain, no further major alteration was made until 1892. In certain cases a municipality would promote its own legislation, Liverpool being a case in point. Here the *Liverpool Public Library, Museum and Gallery of Art Act 1852* provided the mechanism whereby the wishes of a major benefactor could be honoured, namely that the collections should be administered by Trustees. It also allowed the Town Council to levy a one-penny rate at a time when the general legislation restricted this to one halfpenny for these functions.

Major local government reform came to England and Wales through the *Local Government Act 1888* which brought into being County Councils, County Boroughs and Boroughs, with further legislation in 1894 introducing Urban and Rural District councils. Similar provisions were contained in Scottish legislation in 1889. There followed the revision of the enabling legislation for many of the Local Authority functions and museums were no exception. The *Museums and Gymnasiums Act 1891* enabled urban authorities to provide and maintain museums in England, Wales and Ireland but excluded London until 1901. The *Public Libraries Act 1892* repealed all previous Libraries Acts and transferred museums which had been provided under that legislation to the new library authorities in England and Wales which were permitted to provide and maintain museums. The new administrative counties were not given museum powers.

Comparison of these two Acts is interesting and underlines the inconsistency of policy that has pervaded museum provision in Britain for more than a century. The 1891 Act required museums to be opened to the public free of charge on not less than three days a week, permitting admission fees on other days; charges for the use of a museum's facilities were also authorized. The 1892 Act required that no charge be made for admission to museums established under its provisions. Nor did it make provision for the disposal of the museum by sale, a feature permissible under the 1891 Act provided the museum had been established for not less than seven years and was either too expensive to run or was considered unnecessary; the proceeds from such a sale were to be treated as capital money, the disposal of which was subject to ministerial approval. The *Museums and Gymnasiums Act 1891* permitted the levying of a separate one-halfpenny rate for museum purposes. While this was less in real terms than that authorized by the 1845 Act, it was perhaps more desirable than that available under the Libraries Act of 1892: here libraries and museums had to be funded from a charge of no more than one penny, little enough for a library to operate on but if a museum was to be provided as well this was most likely to suffer as an unequal partner. This was perhaps accentuated by the lack of definition of the role of the museum in this legislation. The 1891 statute attempted this: 'for the reception of local antiquities or other objects of interest'.

The *Museums and Gymnasiums Act 1891* was effectively repealed by the *Public Libraries Act 1919* by which time most museums were being provided by library authorities; it remained in force in Northern Ireland, however, until 1981. This new library legislation also amended the *Public Libraries Act 1892*, removing the rate limit of one penny in the pound, permitting the exercise of the library and museum function by a County Council and also allowing the delegation of a library authority's powers to the education authority. In Scotland, previous library legislation, which also enabled the provision of museums, was repealed by the *Public Libraries Consolidation (Scotland) Act 1887* which remains in force today. This permits the sale or exchange of duplicate works of art and other property provided the monies or objects received are applied for the purposes of the Act – which, of course, includes the provision and maintenance of libraries as well as museums. It is a requirement of this Scottish legislation that entry to museums is free. Current museum enabling legislation is treated below.

Current museum enabling legislation

Although recent enabling legislation has been more explicit in defining the purpose and function of museums, none carries a concise definition. The definition used originally in the *Finance Act 1975*[1] has, however, been used for other legal purposes[2] and is quoted here on the basis of this precedent:

> Any . . . institution which exists wholly or mainly for the purpose of preserving for the public benefit a collection of scientific, historic or artistic interest.

It is convenient to arrange museums into three general types, based on their administrative structure, and examine the enabling legislation of each, where necessary, under the constituent countries of the UK as different legal systems apply in them. Not all of the enabling legislation is covered here. Attention is drawn to the full list of statutes given at the end of this paper.[3]

National museums

A national museum, as defined here, is a non-departmental public body with specific legislation to give it separate legal identity. This is normally achieved through an Act of Parliament but may depend on an Order in Council, the Grant of a Royal Charter or a Deed of Trust. With the exception of the National Portrait Gallery and the Wallace Collection, which exist on the basis of Treasury minutes, all of the major Government funded museums are of this type. They operate on the devolved, 'arms-length' principle whereby the Trustees of the museum are free from direct Government control except for their accountability for the public money voted to them through the Sponsoring Department. Although mainly dependent on Government grant, the university museums are excluded here as none has a separate legal identity. Similarly the site museums administered by English Heritage together with the regimental museums in the care of one of the armed services depend on Government Department funding for their existence and are not included.

England and Wales

The *British Museum Act 1963* provides the governing instrument for both the British Museum, the Natural History Museum and their branches. There are separate Boards of Trustees for each institution. One of the British Museum's Trustees is appointed by the Sovereign but otherwise the majority of members on both Boards are appointees of the Prime Minister; of the remainder about one-quarter are appointed by the Trustees themselves and the rest are appointed by the Secretary of State on the nomination of certain learned societies.

In common with all national museums, the collections are vested in the Trustees who are responsible for their care and for ensuring appropriate public access. On the latter point a marked change of emphasis is apparent in the more recent legislation. The British Museum legislation of 1963, for example, states that the collections should be available when required by members of the public; the *National Heritage Act 1983*, however, requires the Trustees of the Victoria and Albert Museum, the Science Museum, and the Royal Armouries to secure that the objects are exhibited to the public as well as promoting the public's enjoyment and understanding through the collections and ensuring that objects are available for study and research. There is a similar requirement in the *Merseyside Museums and Galleries Order 1986* and the *Museum of London Act 1986*.

As far as the acquisition of collections is concerned, the statutes of the English national museums imply that the Trustees have a duty to add to their collections and in all enabling Acts from 1983 this duty is explicit. In no case, however, is the responsibility defined in subject, geographical or chronological terms and the decision of what to acquire is a matter for the Trustees of each museum. On the disposal of collections, the legislation is fairly consistent except in the case of the National Gallery, the Trustees of which have no powers of disposal. Otherwise this is authorized in the case of duplicates, where an item is considered unsuitable for the collections or has become so damaged as to be useless. There is, though, a greater emphasis against disposal in the phrasing of the more recent statutes which also restrict the use of any resulting money to the acquisition of further items for the collection. Items may be transferred between any of the national museums listed in Schedule 1 to the *National Gallery and Tate Gallery Act 1954*, as extended in subsequent legislation.

The question of disposal from museum collections has been a matter of discussion since the early days of the British Museum (see above). The issue was debated extensively in 1954 when the Trustees of the National Gallery successfully sought to remove their powers to sell, contained in the *National Gallery Act 1856*.

It has been the subject of study by the Standing Commission on Museums and Galleries (1973) with some further work in relation to the national museums (Museums and Galleries Commission, 1988); a consultation paper has been issued by the Office of Arts and Libraries (1988). The issue, however, extends to the non-national museums and the Audit Commission (1991) and the Museums and Galleries Commission (1991) have both called for the position to be clarified for provincial museums.

The generally held professional view of the special nature of museum collections and the need to protect them can be paralleled strongly in international legislation and the law of some European countries (Lewis, 1990). The removal of Registered status by the Museums and Galleries Commission and from membership of the Museums Association of a museum which sold items from its collection reiterates that view. But the crux of the matter is that the question of disposal is ill-defined legally, particularly with regard to the non-national museums, and there is no case law. The debate continues (see e.g., Besterman (1991); Borg (1991);

Babbidge (1991a and b); Fleming (1991a and b); Clark (1991)).

Another area of substantial change in recent legislation for national museums relates to finance. One aspect of this is the recognition of the role of commercial activities which generally promote the purpose of the museum concerned. Powers to form companies to this end are given in the relevant enabling legislation to the Victoria and Albert Museum, the Science Museum, the Royal Armouries and the National Museums and Galleries on Merseyside. Variations on funding exist, however. The *National Heritage Act 1983* provides that any expenditure incurred by the Boards of Trustees of the Victoria and Albert Museum and the Science Museum, and not funded from other sources, shall be defrayed by Parliament. The same Act does not extend this to the Royal Armouries: it only provides that Parliament may provide such sums towards expenditure as the Treasury may approve and that such payments may be subject to conditions. The latter position also applies in the *Merseyside Museums and Galleries Order 1986*.

The National Army Museum and the Royal Air Force Museum do not operate under their own Acts of Parliament. The former exists by Royal Charter which is administered by a council appointed by the Army Board. The latter originated through a Deed of Trust, there being a Board of Trustees appointed by the Secretary of State for Defence. Both museums receive their funding from the Ministry of Defence. With one exception all other English national museums are funded through the Office of Arts and Libraries; this is the Royal Armouries which receives its grant-in-aid from the Department of the Environment.

The National Museum of Wales was established on the authority of a Royal Charter, granted in 1907. The administrative structure is different: there is a Court of Governors constituted to be representative of all parts of the Principality and all appropriate interests. This has a membership of 188 and comprises appointees of the Secretary of State for Wales together with a number of *ex officio* members. A separate council acts as the executive body.

Scotland

The major enabling legislation for the national museums in Scotland is the *National Heritage (Scotland) Act 1985*. This brought together, under one Board of Trustees, the Royal Scottish Museum, previously administered as part of the Scottish Education Department, and the National Museum of Antiquities of Scotland, repealing the 1954 Act of that name. It also amended certain parts of the *National Galleries of Scotland Act 1906*.

The national galleries comprise the National Gallery of Scotland, the Scottish National Portrait Gallery and the Scottish National Gallery of Modern

Art, which are administered by a Board of Trustees appointed by the Secretary of State for Scotland. Unlike its counterpart in London, the Trustees of these galleries have powers to dispose of duplicates, unsuitable or damaged material; in this the legislation closely follows the *National Heritage Act 1983* relating to English museums. However, it goes further by permitting a disposal to any institution, if this has the approval of the Secretary of State; this applies also to the National Museums of Scotland.

In appointing the Trustees for the Royal Museum of Scotland, the Secretary of State is required to include at least one Fellow of the Society of Antiquaries of Scotland in recognition of the benefaction of the Society to the nation; similarly provision is made elsewhere in the *National Heritage (Scotland) Act 1985* for free access to the library for Fellows of the Society. On funding, the Secretary of State may pay the institutions governed by the 1985 Act such sums towards their expenditure as the Treasury may approve, subject to any conditions that may be imposed. As a result of this, the provision in the *National Galleries of Scotland Act 1906* that expenditure incurred shall be paid out of moneys provided by Parliament has been amended. The 1985 Act also authorizes the making of grants to bodies promoting the development or understanding of culture or scientific matters. Both the Galleries and the Museums may set up companies to further their work.

Northern Ireland

All previous enabling legislation for the Ulster Museum and the Ulster Folk and Transport Museum was repealed by the *Museums (Northern Ireland) Order 1981*, made under the powers conferred by the *Northern Ireland Act 1974*. The Order establishes separate Trustees for the two national museums, both Boards being made up of appointments by the Department of Education of Northern Ireland which should include representatives of the District Councils, the City of Belfast, Queen's University, the New University and the Ulster Polytechnic.

The powers of the Trustees are much wider than those elsewhere in the national museums. For example, they are empowered to exchange, sell or otherwise dispose of any movable property no longer required for the purposes of the museums or to destroy material which is useless or of no value to the museums. The Trustees may make by-laws, subject to the approval of the Department of Education of Northern Ireland; fines for offences against these are stated in the Order. The financing of the museums is through the Department which may pay the Trustees such sums as they think proper towards the expenses concerned. The Trustees are permitted to give financial assistance to bodies having similar objects to their own.

Local Government museums

So far in this review the museums concerned have had their own legal identity which has been established by legislation of one form or another specific to the business of providing museums. Indeed the existence of the legislation makes it a legal necessity to provide and maintain the museum in question. In the local government sector a different situation prevails. General legislation provides for the existence of the different types of local authority. Such legislation is mandatory and provides all necessary powers to exercise government in the area concerned: the appointment of staff; the purchase of land; providing for the financial administration of the authority, its efficient operation, etc. It also provides for the establishment and determines the composition of committees of elected representatives generally to exercise the functions of local government, certain committees being required by law, e.g. a planning committee. It is not mandatory on Local Authorities in the UK to provide a museum service and they must adopt specific legislation to do so.

England and Wales

In England and Wales, including the London Boroughs, the relevant adoptive legislation for museums is the *Libraries and Museums Act 1964*. This came into force on 1 April 1965 and was the result of a series of reports on public library provision. It repealed all previous library and museum legislation in England and Wales. Under this Act it became a duty of every library authority to provide a comprehensive and efficient library service; there is no such duty in the Act for Local Authorities to provide museums. As amended by subsequent Local Government Acts, museums may be provided by the London Boroughs, the City of London, the Council of the Isles of Scilly as well as the district and county councils of England and Wales. As a concurrent function, both a county and its constituent districts may provide a museum service. The museum may be in the Local Authority's own administrative area or elsewhere. Furthermore, under this statute, a Local Authority can contribute towards the provision and maintenance of a museum or the provision of advice, services or financial assistance to a museum anywhere in England and Wales. Parish or Town Councils are not authorized to provide museums, although it might be argued that they may do so as an amenity to the area concerned under the *Local Government Act 1972*.[4]

The 1964 Act does not define the term 'museum'; nor does it provide any statement of aims which might guide Local Authorities operating a museums service. It does, however, permit the making of an admission charge but requires any Local Authority wishing to do so to take into account the need for the museum to play its full part in the promotion of education in the area and have particular regard to the interests of children and students. The use of museum premises for meetings, exhibitions and other events of an educational and cultural nature by the Local Authority or others is authorized, it being left to the discretion of the Local Authority as to whether a rent is charged or an admission fee is made. The Act permits the use of by-laws to regulate the use of the museum facilities, which must have the approval of the Secretary of State. The maximum fine permitted for breach of such by-laws is £100. A set of model by-laws, provided by the Office of Arts and Libraries, is given in the Appendix to this chapter.

A Local Authority with a museum, or planning one under the 1964 Act, may establish a cumulative fund for the purchase of objects for exhibition. Sometimes known as the 'art fund', this means that rate-derived money can be accumulated over a number of years in order to make major purchases; otherwise all unspent money is required to be returned to the rate fund at the close of each financial year. There has been no limit on the size of this purchase fund or the annual contribution made to it since 1974. Schedule 2 of the 1964 Act provides details of how such a fund should be administered. It should be noted that, although the Act makes no provision for the disposal of collections, this schedule does provide that the proceeds of any sale of items from the collection may be paid into the art fund. The question of disposal has already been discussed above.

Certain Local Authorities have Local Acts which supplement the law[5]. For example, the *Greater Manchester Act 1981* provides for the representation of the University on the committee governing the Manchester City Art Gallery. It also authorizes the sale or exchange of art objects, subject to certain conditions, but stipulates that all money arising from a sale must be applied for the purchase of other works and art objects. In the case of a gift to the collection to which the donor attached conditions, a period of 21 years must elapse following the Act before such conditions can be revoked. The Manchester City Art Gallery has benefited from a cumulative purchase fund through a Local Act since 1882 and this statute preserves the additional advantages of this facility.

The *County of Lancashire Act 1984* also provides for the disposal of unsuitable specimens and works of art for museums in that county and the constituent districts, permitting the transfer of collections between museums – whether or not in the public sector – but requiring a delay of 35 years before this can be enforced in the case of material to which conditions are attached. Other issues are covered in the *Bournemouth Borough Council Act 1985* in respect

of the Russell-Cotes Museum. This Act removes restrictions on opening hours, names the representative of the original benefactor on the Management Committee and requires that a curator be appointed, giving details of the duties of the post.

The Museum of London is funded and managed jointly by the Government and the City of London. Special legislation makes this possible. The founding statute was the *Museum of London Act 1965* to which was added further legislation of the same name in 1986 following the abolition of the Greater London Council, originally a partner in the Museum. Together the legislation provides for the constitution of the Board of Governors and sets out its duties. London is defined in the Act as 'all Greater London and the surrounding region'; such a definition clearly gives some latitude for interpretation. The Board may dispose of items in its collection subject to certain conditions, one of which requires not less than a two-thirds majority to do so.

The *Local Government Act 1985* which abolished the Greater London Council and the Metropolitan County Councils in the following year affected the management arrangements of a number of Local Authority museums. As already noted above, the Merseyside service became the responsibility of Central Government as a national museum; three historic house museums in London, Kenwood House, Marble Hill House and Ranger's House were transferred to the Historic Buildings and Monuments Commission for England (English Heritage); the Tyne and Wear Museum Service now operates with a substantial Government grant through the Museums & Galleries Commission. The Office of Arts and Libraries provides revenue grant to the Horniman Museum and Geffrye Museum which operate under their own Trustee Boards following the abolition of the Inner London Education Authority in 1990.

Scotland
Discretionary legislation also applies to the provision of Local Authority museums in Scotland. This may be either the *Public Libraries Consolidation (Scotland) Act 1887* or the *Education (Scotland) Act 1980*. In practice most operate under the 1887 Act and, at the reorganization of local government in 1975, powers were given to the Regional, Island and District Councils to provide museums. This, however, was restricted to Islands and Districts by the *Local Government and Planning (Scotland) Act 1982*, although Section 17(1) of the Act permits the Regional Councils to make grants and loans towards expenses by museums whether provided by a District or an independent organization. Although museum provision by the Islands and Districts remains discretionary, the 1982 Act did impose a duty on these authorities to 'ensure that there is

adequate provision for the inhabitants of their area for recreational, sporting, cultural and social activities'. On the other hand, the Regions and Islands are the education authorities in Scotland and under the 1980 Education Act may provide and maintain museums in their area.

The 1887 Act, as amended by the Local Government legislation of 1973 and 1982, permits a Library Authority, or a Museum Authority, under this Act to establish a museum. For museum purposes, powers are given 'to purchase . . . statuary, pictures, engravings, maps, specimens of art and science . . . and such other articles as may be necessary for the establishment, increase and use of the . . . museums and art galleries'. Authority is also given to sell or exchange works of art or other property of which there may be duplicates, provided that any money or property received from such a transaction is applied for the purposes of the Act. The proceeds from the sale of catalogues must be treated in the same way. The legislation requires that museums established under this Act must be open to the public free of charge. By-laws may be issued, subject to the approval and confirmation of the Sheriff of the area concerned.

The *Education (Scotland) Act 1980* permits Education Authorities to acquire objects for a museum maintained by them, lend them to any person for any purpose and transfer them to the governing body of a museum not run by an Education Authority for use in that museum. Objects not required for retention in the collection may be sold, exchanged, donated or otherwise disposed of, subject to any trust or condition to the contrary. Unlike the 1887 legislation, a charge for admission may be made but, like the requirements for English and Welsh Local Authority museums, the Education Authorities must 'take into account the need to secure that the museum plays its full part in the promotion of education in their area, and shall have particular regard to the interests of children and students'.

Northern Ireland

The *Museums (Northern Ireland) Order 1981* was issued under powers given in the *Northern Ireland Act 1974* and covers both national and Local Authority museums. As far as the latter is concerned, they may be provided and maintained by District Councils either alone or with another District Council or person. A District Council can contribute towards the cost of a museum provided and maintained by another District Council or make grants to other museums, subject to any conditions set by the Department of Education for Northern Ireland. This Department, which has the oversight of museums in the province, can also make grants to a District Council to facilitate the maintenance and provision of museums. This legislation permits a District Council to make by-laws regulating admission – including making a charge – and the conduct of persons in the museum. Such by-laws can also relate to the efficient management of the museum and the preservation of property vested in, or in the custody of the District Council.

Independent museums

Nothing in British law prevents a person or group of persons from creating and operating a museum and the lack of such legislation allows for considerable flexibility of operation. However, the liability of those concerned can be considerable, the safety of the collection can be jeopardized and the financial development of the enterprise limited unless some form of legal identity is adopted.

In considering the independent sector, attention must first be given to the National Trust. This organization was founded in 1895 to preserve as much as possible of the history and beauty of the country for its people. The National Trust for Scotland was founded with similar objectives in 1931. Both organizations are incorporated by an Act of Parliament but otherwise are independent of the State. The *National Trust Acts 1907 to 1971* provide the legal basis for the organization's work in England, Wales and Northern Ireland which includes the preservation of buildings, furniture, pictures and chattels of any description having national, historic or artistic interest. Under the 1907 Act the National Trust is empowered to declare part or all of a property inalienable where its Council deems that it is being held for the benefit of the nation. A charge may be levied for admission to its properties. The National Trust legislation permits the leasing of its properties and acting in concert with and making any arrangements and agreements with a Local Authority to further its objects. Some of the Trust's properties are administered by Local Authorities on this basis.

Many of Britain's independent museums are registered as companies limited by guarantee and not having a share capital under the *Companies Act 1985*. In Northern Ireland the same principles apply but they are governed by different legislation, the *Companies Act (Northern Ireland) 1986*. Incorporation under the Companies Acts in this way gives a museum legal identity with the power to hold property and enter into contracts, at the same time limiting the liability of the members of the company in the event of it being wound up. It would be normal in such a case to have a clause in the Memorandum of Association safeguarding the collection, should the company be wound up. A few museums operate as commercial companies. Others are provided under the same legislation as a promotional or public-relations facility for an industrial company. Such museums do not normally have a legal identity of their own, having been formed as part of the commercial company concerned and, as such, have no separate accounts, with the collections considered as part of the assets of the company. Where a Declaration of Trust forms the basis for the governance of a museum without corporate status the full responsibility and liability for the Trust's affairs rests with the Trustees. In the case of an unincorporated society museum without a Trust Deed, the responsibility is with the membership.

As a public amenity with educational benefits, museums are considered eligible for charitable status, although each case is considered on its merits. Charitable status brings considerable fiscal benefits, particularly in taxation relief and also provides certain safeguards for the collection (Association of Independent Museums, 1981a and b). In England and Wales this is achieved by registration with the Charity Commission under the terms of the *Charities Act 1960*. In Northern Ireland the *Charities Act (Northern Ireland) 1964* applies and the Department of Finance for Northern Ireland has general responsibilities in the matter. In Scotland a museum seeking charitable status for tax purposes is required to apply first to HM Inspector of Taxes and, if granted, to the Capital Taxes Office if deemed necessary. A similar procedure exists in the Channel Islands and the Isle of man where application is made to the appropriate Assessor of Income Tax.

Notes

[1] *Finance Act 1975*, Schedule 6, paragraph 12; now replaced by the *Inheritance Tax Act 1984*, Schedule 3 (previously known as the Capital Transfer Tax Act 1984).
[2] For example, see the parliamentary debate on Clause 1 of the *Indecent Displays (Control) Bill*, 25 February 1981.
[3] The following is a list of the main statutes enabling the establishment and maintenance of museums:

National museums
England:
British Museum Act 1963,
Imperial War Museum Acts 1920 and 1955,
Merseyside Museums and Galleries Order 1986,
National Gallery Act 1856,
National Gallery and Tate Gallery Act 1954,
National Heritage Act 1983,
National Maritime Museum Act 1934 and 1989, and
Wellington Museum Act 1947.

Scotland:
National Galleries of Scotland Acts 1906, and
National Heritage (Scotland) Act 1985.

Northern Ireland:
Northern Ireland Act 1974, and
Museums (Northern Ireland) Order 1981.

Local Authority museums
London:
Museum of London Acts 1965 and 1986,
London Government Act 1963,
Local Government Act 1985, and
Public Libraries and Museums Act 1964.

England and Wales:
Local Government Act 1972,
Local Government Act 1985, and
Public Libraries and Museums Act 1964.

Scotland:
Local Government (Scotland) Act 1973,
Local Government and Planning (Scotland) Act 1982,
Public Libraries Consolidation (Scotland) Act 1887, and
Education (Scotland) Act 1980.

Northern Ireland:
Local Government (Northern Ireland) Act 1972,
Northern Ireland Act 1974, and
Museums (Northern Ireland) Order 1981.

Independent museums
National Trust Acts 1907 to 1971,
National Trust of Scotland Act 1931,
Charities Act 1960,
Charities Act (Northern Ireland) 1964,
Companies Act 1985, and
Companies Act (Northern Ireland) 1986.

[4] Under the *Local Government Act 1972* a Parish or Town Council can acquire a building for the benefit of its area (Section 124 (1) (b)), accept gifts (Section 139 (1)), incur expenditure if considered of benefit to the area (Section 137 (1)) and appoint staff necessary to discharge such responsibilities (Section 112). However, Parish or Town Councils are not designated as museum authorities in Section 206 of the Act and such a course would therefore be against the spirit of the legislation.
[5] Local Acts known to embody museum provisions include:
Greater London Council (General Powers) Act 1978
City of London (Various Powers) Act 1979
West Yorkshire Act 1980
Greater Manchester Act 1981
County of Lancashire Act 1984
Bournemouth Borough Council Act 1985
Clifton Suspension Bridge Act 1986
Essex Act 1987
Plymouth City Council Act 1987
West Glamorgan Act 1987

References

ASSOCIATION OF INDEPENDENT MUSEUMS (1981a), *Charitable Status for Museums*, Association of Independent Museums, Beaulieu
ASSOCIATION OF INDEPENDENT MUSEUMS (1981b), *Charitable Status for Museums – Scotland*, Association of Independent Museums, Beaulieu and Council for Museums and Galleries in Scotland, Edinburgh
AUDIT COMMISSION (1991), *The road to Wigan Pier? Managing Local Authority Museums and Galleries*, HMSO, London
BABBIDGE, A. (1991a), 'Legal, decent and honest?', *Museums Journal* 91(9), 32–34

BABBIDGE, A. (1991b), 'Disposals from museums collections', *Museum Management and Curatorship* 10(3), 255–261

BESTERMAN, T. (1991), 'The ethics of emasculation', *Museum Journal* 91(9), 25–28

BORG, A. (1991), 'Confronting disposal', *Museums Journal* 91(9), 29–31

CLARK, R. (1991), 'Scottish sense', *Museums Journal* 91(9), 34–35

DANIEL, G. (1981) *A Short History of Archaeology*, Thames and Hudson, London

FLEMING, D. (1991a), 'Changing the disposals culture', *Museums Journal* 91(9), 36–37

FLEMING, D. (1991b), 'Immaculate collections, speculative conceptions', *Museums Management and Curatorship* 10(3), 263–272

HOUSE OF COMMONS (1834), *Report of the Select Committee on the Inquiry into Drunkenness*, London

HOUSE OF COMMONS (1836), *Report of the Select Committee on Arts and Manufactures*, London

LEWIS, G. (1990), 'Heritage giving through taxation in the United Kingdom', in Lalive, P. (Ed.), *International Sales of Works of Art*, Vol. 2, International Chamber of Commerce, Paris

LEWIS, G. (1991), 'International issues concerning museum collections', in Briat, M. and Freedberg, J. A. (Eds), *International Art Trade and Law, Volume 3*, 73–94, International Chamber of Commerce Publishing, Paris and Kluwer Publishers, Deventer

MILLER, E. (1973), *That Noble Cabinet: A History of the British Museum*, Andre Deutsch, London

MUSEUMS & GALLERIES COMMISSION (1988), *The National Museums*, HMSO, London

O'KEEFE, P. J. AND PROTT, L. V. (1984), *Law and the Cultural Heritage*, Vol. 1: *Discovery and Excavation*, Professional Books Ltd/Butterworths, London

OFFICE OF ARTS AND LIBRARIES (1988), 'Powers of Disposal from Museum and Gallery Collections: a consultative paper', OAL, August 1988

STANDING COMMISSION ON MUSEUMS AND GALLERIES (1973), 'Loans from national institutions to provincial museums', in *Standing Commission on Museums and Galleries, Ninth Report 1969–1973*, HMSO, London

Appendix: Model by-laws for Local Authority museums in England and Wales, prepared by the Office of Arts and Libraries

All communications concerning these model by-laws should be addressed to: Office of Arts and Libraries, Horseguards Road, London SW1P 3AL, UK.

MUSEUMS AND ART GALLERIES
4.5

BY-LAWS
made under Section 19 of the Public Libraries and Museums Act 1964 by the

[Name of Council]

(1) In these by-laws, unless the context otherwise requires:
(a) 'The Act' means the Public Libraries and Museums Act 1964;
(b) 'The Museum Authority' means the [name of local authority];
(c) 'museum' ['art gallery'] means any museum [art gallery] [period house] maintained under the Act [and includes a vehicle [or boat] when being used for purposes connected therewith];
(d) 'the Curator' means the person appointed by the Museum Authority to be the curator, director of keeper of the museum or any other person authorized by the Museum Authority to act on his behalf;
(e) 'museum officer' means the curator or any other person employed by the Museum Authority for the purposes of its functions under the Act;
(f) 'exhibit' means any object [picture] forming part of the collection kept at the museum for purposes of exhibition to the public and includes any object [picture] for the time being shown or exhibited thereat.

(2) An act necessary for the proper execution of his duty by a museum officer shall not be deemed to be a contravention of these by-laws.

(3) No person shall give a false name or address for the purpose of entering any part of the museum or for the purpose of using any facilities provided in connection therewith.

(4) No person who is offensively unclean in person or in dress, or who is suffering from an offensive disease, shall enter or use the museum.

(5) Except with the consent of a museum officer, no person shall:
(a) cause or allow any dog (other than a guide-dog accompanying a blind person) or other animal belonging to him or under his control to enter or remain in the museum, or
(b) bring into any part of the museum a wheeled vehicle or conveyance (other than a [hand-propelled] invalid chair).

(6) No person shall, after a warning by a museum officer, remain in the museum after the time fixed for its closing.

(7) No person shall, unless duly authorized, take from the museum either
(a) any exhibit, or
(b) any catalogue or other publication or any tape player or other equipment the use of which has been allowed to him by the Museum Authority.

(8) No person shall handle or touch any exhibit unless authorized so to do by a museum officer or by the Museum Authority by notice in writing.

(9) No person shall carelessly or negligently soil, tear, cut, deface, damage, injure, or destroy any exhibit or the furniture, fittings or other contents of the museum.

(10) (a) A person having charge or possession of any exhibit which the Museum Authority is entitled to have returned to it shall deliver it up to [that Authority] [the Curator] within 14 days of the service upon him by that Authority of a notice requiring him so to do.

(b) For the purposes of this by-law, a notice may be served upon any person by delivering it to him, or by leaving it at his usual or last known place of residence, or by sending it by registered post or recorded delivery service addressed to him at that place.

(11) No person shall behave in a disorderly manner in the museum or use violent, abusive or obscene language therein.

(12) No person shall spit in the museum.

(13) No person shall, after a warning by a museum officer, persist in sleeping in the museum.

(14) No person shall wilfully obstruct any museum officer in the execution of his duty or wilfully disturb, obstruct, interrupt or annoy any other person in the proper use of the museum.

(15) Except with the consent of a museum officer, no person shall display, distribute, affix or post any bill, placard or notice in, to or upon any part of the museum.

(16) No person shall, without the consent of a museum officer, offer anything for sale in the museum.

(17) No person shall lie on the furniture or fittings of the museum or on the floor thereof [except with the consent of a museum officer, on the floor of any part of the museum for the time being set apart for the use of children].

(18) No person shall smoke or strike a light in any part of the museum set apart for the use of the public, except in any part therefore in which the Museum Authority [Curator] for the time being allows smoking. [Modifications may be required to meet particular circumstances, e.g. an open-air museum].

(19) No person shall partake of refreshments in any part of the museum set apart for the use of the public except in any part thereof in which the Museum Authority [Curator] for the time being allows for the partaking of refreshments.

(20) Except with the consent of a museum officer, no person shall allow any apparatus for the reception of sound or television broadcasting or for the repro-duction of sound to be operated in any part of the museum set apart for the use of the public.

(21) Any person who shall offend against any of the foregoing by-laws shall be liable to a fine not exceeding the sum of [here specify such reasonable fine, not exceeding 100 pounds, as the Museum Authority think fit to impose].

(22) Any person who, within the view of a museum officer, contravenes any of the foregoing by-laws may be excluded or removed from the museum by such officer if:

(a) his name and address are unknown to and cannot be ascertained by the officer; or

(b) from the nature of the contravention or from any other fact of which the officer may have knowledge or be credibly informed there is reasonable ground for belief that his continuance in the museum may result in another contravention of the by-laws or that his exclusion or removal from the museum is otherwise necessary for the proper use and regulation thereof.

(23) [If there are no by-laws in force, this by-law should be omitted:] On the coming into operation of these by-laws, the by-laws relating to the museum which were made by the [..........] on the [......] day of [..........] and were confirmed by the Secretary of State for Education and Science on the [......] day of [..........] shall be revoked.

Bibliography

CHAMBERS, G. F. AND FOBARGUE, H. W. (1899), *The Law Relating to Public Libraries and Museums and Literary and Scientific Institutions*, 4th edition, Knight and Co., London

HEWITT, A. R. (1975), *Public Library Law and the Law as to Museums and Art Galleries in England and Wales, Scotland and Northern Ireland*, 5th edition, Association of Assistant Librarians, London

KELLY, T. (1977), *A History of Public Libraries in Great Britain, 1845–1975*, The Library Association, London

MORRIS, R. J. M. (1977), *Parliament and the Public Libraries*, Mansell, London

O'KEEFE, P. J. and PROTT, L. V. (1989), *Law and the Cultural Heritage*, Vol. 3: *Movement*, Butterworths, London

PALMER, N. (1989), 'Museums and cultural property', in Virgo, P. (Ed.), *The New Museology*, Reaktion Books, London

SCOTT, M. (1985), *The Law of Public Leisure Services*, Sweet and Maxwell, London

7

National museums

Sir David M. Wilson

To compare the form, function, philosophy and policies of institutions as vital and as different as the Smithsonian Institution, the National Museum of Bulgaria, the Louvre, the Imperial War Museum and the National Anthropological Museum of Mexico is as useless as to generalize about museums in any fashion. Each museum fulfils its own function, ill or well. Each museum exists for conservation, collection and display as primary objectives, but to compare the grand panorama of the Victoria and Albert Museum with the intimacy of the Kunstindustri Museum in Copenhagen is as useless as comparing a Jaguar car with an Austin 7. In what follows I attempt to discuss national museums under three headings: (1) monolithic institutions,[1] (2) state museums of national culture, and (3) specialist national institutions. Less attention is given to the third of these categories as their functions and philosophies are often clearly perceived in their title. It is obvious, for example, that the National Portrait Gallery in London is just that; similarly, the Greek National Archaeological Museum in Athens or the Historical Folk Museum of the Land of Israel in Tel Aviv are also clearly described by their titles.

Monolithic museums

The great public collections which were created as national museums (like the British Museum) or became national museums (like the State Hermitage Museum in St Petersburg) comprise the elite of the world's museums, not merely because their collections are so rich and varied but also because they represent a vast reservoir of scholarship and expertise. The philosophies which lie behind the great monolithic museums vary, but all work towards a universal view of man's achievement or knowledge. The first major, truly universal museum was the British Museum, which split into its component parts with the departure of the natural history collections in the 1880s and of the library departments in 1973. It was founded in 1753 on the principles of the French encyclopaedists as a kind of collegiate expression of universal knowledge and curiosity: in a period when the universities were at their nadir in England, the collections of books and manuscripts formed by Sloane, Cotton, Harley and others,[2] together with antiquities and natural history specimens, provided hope for the young scholars of the day. Scholars like the poet Thomas Gray who wrote in 1759 (Toynbee and Whibley, 1971):

> The museum is my favourite Domain, where I often pass four hours in the day in the stillness & solitude of the reading room.

Here also studied Blackstone, Hume and Stukeley, the latter at least interested in objects. The Museum also provided, for the respectably dressed, stimulus to their natural curiosity.

The public function of the Museum was still secondary to the learned, collecting aspects of the Museum's services. But the most extraordinary fact is that the Museum was founded at all. In a period not renowned for public support for learning, the British Government was able to move expeditiously not only to buying annuities for Sir Hans Sloane's heirs, but was also able to provide a building to house the collections and open it to the public within six years.

The Museum prospered and collected widely, although often in the face of considerable financial opposition. The result is seen today – a collection of millions of items from all over the world illustrating the history of the world as expressed in artefacts.

The National Gallery in London, however, has an entirely different *raison d'être*. It is a national collection of great works of art – unlike practically every European gallery it was not founded from a royal or princely nucleus. In the words of Sir Michael Levey (in Ragghianti, 1973):

> It has operated on the principle that it is a gallery of art – not a mere collection of historical objects. One masterpiece is worth more in aesthetic significance than twenty minor pictures, all with some historical interest.

These two examples illustrate the difficulty of classifying great national collections and, if we were to look at the stated philosophy and aims of, say, the Victoria and Albert Museum, the Natural History Museum and the Science Museum, many more different judgements could be made.

Among the great monolithic museums of the world the State Hermitage Museum in St Petersburg is one of the most remarkable and yet in some ways typical. Its history is different from that of the British Museum in that until the Revolution it was hardly a public museum (rather it was a private palace museum of the Tsars), although from 1852 when the 'New Hermitage' was inaugurated it fulfilled many of the functions of a national museum (ethnography, ethnology, and much of the archaeological material was, located elsewhere) (Persianova, 1975). Strangely enough, Russian painting went to the Russian Museum which was not opened until 1898 in the Mikhailovsky Palace (in its first year 100,000 people visited it) (Novouspensky, 1979).

In many ways the Louvre (Ragghianti, 1968) is a similar institution to the Hermitage. Like the Hermitage it emerged after a revolution as a purely public institution. Like the Hermitage it hived off part of its collection, the ethnographic and oriental collections, for example. But housing as it does the offices of the Director General of the French museums, it has a more central role than practically any national museum in the world. Only the massive Smithsonian Institution with its semi-autonomous sections (National Gallery of Art, National Air and Space Museum, National Museum of Natural History and so on) and the *Staatliche Museen Preussischer Kulturbesitz* (with its collections of paintings, antiquities, oriental art and so on) supported federally and locally, come anywhere near the centralized control of the French collections.

To most of the general public, however, it is the great picture galleries which are the national museums of the world, the *Prado* in Madrid, the *Kunsthistorisches Museum* in Vienna or the *Rijksmuseum* in Amsterdam. The reason for this is probably that these are the museums which, above everything else, show the highest visible form of human endeavour in the arts, painting. But perhaps a contributory factor is that these museums are international. They demonstrate the breadth of man's interest more completely than do state museums of national culture. Is it not perhaps significant that the *Nasjonalgalleriet* in Oslo is described as 'national', whereas the great museums of national culture: *Universitetets Oldsaksamling* and *Norsk Folkemuseum* are not distinguished in this manner? Is it possible that universality is an element of importance of museums, or is it simply an index of size?

One great museum of monolithic structure must at least be mentioned here – the Metropolitan Museum of Art in New York (Tomkins, 1970). In many ways the variety of its collections and its very size have given it, to many people, a position equivalent to the Louvre or the Hermitage. Few non-national museums have this stature (perhaps the Uffizi is another example, but that is a state-funded museum), the Metropolitan is a private foundation, aided by city and federal money, but largely financed from outside sources. Its collections are also universal and, indeed, unlike many of the great monolithic museums it has even an interest in ethnography (although largely of 'artistic' quality) Here surely is a museum which has achieved a national character.

State museums of national culture

The existence of national museums of avowedly chauvinistic purpose throughout the world has considerable impact and influence. One of the most remarkable examples of these which illustrates many of the reasons for the existence of such institutions is the Hungarian National Museum. 'It was founded', as Fülep (1978) tells us, 'in the first half of the nineteenth century as part of a movement to preserve Hungarian historic traditions and to instill greater appreciation of the Hungarian language and culture. The movement was influenced by the ideals of the Enlightenment and the National Museum was one of its first fruits'. Its symbolic place in the history of Hungary is illustrated by the part the Museum's new building played in the Revolution of 1848 (Fülep, 1978):

> It was on the steps of the museum that Sándor Petöfi's *National Song* was first recited; the Upper House of the National Assembly met in the museum's state apartment; exhibitions on industrial and agricultural production, designed to rouse the whole country were held in its galleries. The most important of the gatherings of the unions and associations, formed for the promotion of public education, were also held within its walls.

Later, in 1956, it was a rallying point for Hungarian nationalism during the Russian invasion, an incident also reflected in Prague in 1968 when the front of the Bohemian National Museum was damaged by Russian gunfire.

The propaganda and political value of a museum in such circumstances should not be underestimated. Exhibitions like *Das politische Deutschland* in 1936 and *Nürnberg, die deutsche Stadt* in 1937 or, perhaps even more poignantly, *700 Jahre im Weichselbogen* in 1939 (Deneke and Kahsnitz, 1978), which were held in the *Germanisches Nationalmuseum* in Nuremberg, show that propaganda and political pressure can rally a country in difficult times, in a fashion rather different from the wartime concerts in the National Gallery, London.

Patriotism, chauvinism and struggling nationalism all blend imperceptibly together to produce the national museum a country needs. In the period of the Russian control of Finland, the National Museum in Helsinki was built in the national architectural style of the beginning of the century by one of Finland's greatest architects, perhaps to emphasize the autonomy of a country under foreign domination. In other cases, as with the Indian National Museum in Calcutta, enlightened colonialists emphasized the culture of the land they controlled. Founded by the Asiatic Society of Bengal in 1814 and encouraged by disinterested benefaction, this museum has grown into one of the finest national and scientific collections in the world. Interestingly enough this museum is not located in the capital city, although it is not strictly speaking nowadays the National Museum (Markham and Hargreaves, 1936).

The function of such museums is clear; they express the history and aspirations of the country in which they are placed. They are sometimes, but rarely, used for jingoistic purposes and often (as with the National Museum of Ireland) enshrine an exhibition (sometimes rather badly displayed) of the struggle to freedom with the display of personal effects of heroes of revolutions, risings or rebellions.

Such museums are largely, if not completely, run on scholarly lines for a curious public and only occasionally do circumstances push them over into excess with overweighted displays. The best such museums have produced some of the most original scholarships: the National Museum of Denmark, for example, was the source of the archaeological division of prehistory into the three Ages (Stone, Bronze and Iron). Others have set new standards in architecture and display, e.g. the National Museum of Anthropology, Mexico City, the masterpiece of Pedro Ramirez Vazquez, which is one of the wonders of the modern world (Ragghianti, 1970). Others have influenced the economic development of a country, e.g. the Geological Museum and Survey in London – while some have concentrated on small, specialized facets of history or culture – e.g. the National Portrait Gallery in London. The latter comes into my third class of national museums.

Specialist national institutions

The specialist national institutions speak for themselves. The *Musée de l'Horologie* in Geneva needs no explanation, nor does the *Mineralogisches Museum* in Berlin. The *Musée de l'Homme* in Paris – ancient and out-moded in its displays although only built in the 1930s – is another type of specialist museum; dealing universally with human anthropology it is a major force in French academic life. Museums like this, the Imperial War Museum in England (or indeed any national army museum in any country in the world), the great museum of modern art in Mexico City (or the Tate Gallery in London), the Ethnographical Museum in Belgrade, or the National Archaeological Museum in Athens have a function which is probably more important than their displays in that they provide high level academic and technical support for a superstructure of scholarship which serves both the national and international academic community. This is the main function of such specialist museums, national or private, although a nation which celebrates its naval achievements or its great generals, its main industry or its great painters through a specialist museum is putting a lot of scholarly eggs into one academic basket.

The danger with such museums is that they can fossilize through lack of sensitive national support. Sometimes it is simply their display which suffers. The recent extended refurbishing of that great scholarly institution the Wallace Collection in London, will be a salutary reminder to an English audience that neglect (although curable) can happen under the most enlightened government. As Director of a monolithic museum, I feel that the German or American experience shows that such institutions are often better served under a large umbrella. At the same time the idea of the *Direction des Musées de France*, although helpful in some cases, does not serve the nation well: the small museums suffer.

The collections

Basic to all museums are the collections, and it is here that the policy of a national museum is supremely important. A national museum's relationship to the provincial museums is often fraught with jealousies on both sides. In some cases, Sweden or Denmark for example, the disposal of all archaeological material lies in the hands of the central archaeological service which works cheek by jowl with the national museum (*Statens Historiska Museum* or *Nationalmuseet*). Only now, and reluctantly, are the national museums yielding finds to the provincial museums as these become more expert in their curatorial abilities. In England there is no such central system; in fact in England it is often difficult for the relevant part of the British Museum, which embodies a national function, to acquire objects to bring its British collections up to date, although the power of the purse sometimes helps. In France the excavator has the right to say where finds go, with the result that the *Musée des Antiquités Nationales* at St-Germain-en-Laye has made hardly any acquisitions in the last 50 years. These statements are to a lesser degree true of the fine and decorative arts, but here it is usually the financial capabilities of the museum which secure an object.

Only an ostrich would deny national/provincial competitiveness. In England the system seems to work reasonably well, in some other countries it does not and bad will is easily engendered. It is, however, one of the most difficult areas of museum relations, and can give rise to much strain and bad feeling. Only constant attention and contact can heal such breaches.

The collecting problems of monolithic museums of universal content are full of pitfalls. In such a museum 'bigger is generally better'. There is, however, a very good case for the purely aesthetic museum (the picture galleries) to collect only the highest quality (as anyone would agree who has looked at the secondary collections in the National Gallery in London). But more general museums covering the decorative arts, science, history and natural history are clearly at their best when they collect over a wide area. Few museums start with a *tabula rasa*, so the first imperative is to build on strengths. Thus a print room with a good collection of French Impressionist prints will attempt to purchase individual items so that unrepresented periods, schools or artists may be represented in the collections. On the other hand, poorly represented schools must also be acquired if possible. Thus, for example, the British Museum recently started an aggressive policy of acquiring modern prints, the first fruits of which was the highly successful American exhibition in 1980 (Carey and Griffiths, 1980).

It is now legally impossible to import major pieces of art from certain countries. The campaign for the return of cultural objects, fuelled by Third World members of UNESCO, rightly makes most curators realize that they cannot buy smuggled objects or objects without a proper pedigree. But much can be done to bring international collections up to date. Many countries allow *partage* after excavation, some will donate type series. The international art market flourishes and it is still possible, and always should be possible, to buy a Poussin from an English collection and export it (Reviewing Committee on the Export of Works of Art, 1981). Further collections of ethnographic material can, and should, continue to be made to supplement old, tired and ill-documented collections. A fresh collection was recently made *de novo* by the British Museum in India and formed the basis of the Vasna exhibition (Durrans and Knox, 1982); this is but one of many such collections brought together in the last few years without offending the laws or the susceptibilities of the countries from which objects have been brought.

A museum which does not collect is a dead museum. This is particularly true of all national museums. When one source dries up another must be found – some of the greatest collections have been built up by acquiring the unfashionable. This is still the best way to increase a museum's stock.

National museums and their public

The role of national museums in education, publicity, exhibition and information services varies widely, and should do so. The monolithic museum, possibly with a tendency towards a very high foreign tourist input, has, and must have, a different approach to a state museum of national culture. Large museums can often more easily afford large exhibitions: on the other hand they cannot afford to give much individual attention to children.

To a certain extent it is the duty of the large museum to make its own and other museums' collections available to a wide public through special exhibitions. Such exhibitions need not be blockbusters, like the Tutankhamun Exhibition in London, which beat every record everywhere in terms of attendance and profit. But special exhibitions can initiate, explain, educate and entertain in a fashion, and with a frequency, often difficult for smaller museums – no matter how prestigious – to emulate. In recent years the British Museum, for example, has staged major exhibitions in large provincial centres (e.g. Norwich, Manchester, Glasgow, Cambridge and Leeds).

The educational role of the great national museum is difficult to evaluate. For the monolithic museum it almost certainly lies in educating the teacher, providing teaching notes and facilities for school classes. Only rarely can direct contact with children be catered for (the American volunteer docent system is rarely used outside the USA for a number of reasons among them union objections). But tertiary education must be provided for, partly by educational specialists and partly by the curatorial staff. Post-graduate and specialist seminars are also a *sine qua non* in such institutions. National museums in my other two classes will find it easier to provide such services, although the problems of an institution such as the Science Museum in London with its vast number of visitors[3] will surely be similar to those of the monolithic institution.

It must be emphasized that the primary duty of museums is not didactic. This is even more true of national museums. The public must have an aesthetic, cultural, emotional experience or one of half a hundred exclamatory sensations, ranging from the spiritual to the curious when they visit the museum. The visitor must not be pandered to by labels in 'Noddy' language, by coloured flashing lights, blonde information officers or any of those caricatures and gimmicks beloved of the educational administrator venturing into the museum field. The museum's client is generally intelligent and able to read and even use libraries to look up background information. The visitor must be led to this process. Unless using his museum for political purposes, the national museum Director is usually catering for the intelligent child or adult. Imagination must be stirred, but tiresome rhetoric, fussy comparisons and gimmicky flourishes are to be avoided at all costs. Good taste and restraint are vital. It is the objects which are important: they must speak for themselves.

Notes

[1] A term borrowed from Finlay (1977).
[2] For the history of the British Museum see Caygill (1992) and the sources cited there.
[3] Such figures are difficult to determine but see Alt (1980).

References

ALT, M. B. (1980), 'Four years of visitor surveys at the British Museum (Natural History), 1976–79', *Museums Journal*, **80** (1), 10–25

CAREY, F. and GRIFFITHS, A. (1980), *American Prints 1879–1979*, British Museum Publications, London

CAYGILL, M. L. (1992), *The Story of the British Museum*, (new section) British Museum Publications, London

DENEKE, B. and KAHSNITZ, R. (1978), *Das Germanische Nationalmuseum, Nürnberg 1852–1977*, Deutscher Kunstverlag, Berlin

DURRANS, B. and KNOX, R. (1982), *India: Past into Present*, British Museum Publications, London

FINLAY, I. (1977), *Priceless Heritage, the Future of Museums*, Faber and Faber, London

FÜLEP, F. (Ed.) (1978), *The Hungarian National Museum*, Corvina Press, Budapest

MARKHAM, S. F. and HARGREAVES, H. (1936), *The Museums of India*, Museums Association, London

NOVOUSPENSKY, N. (1979), *The Russian Museum, Leningrad*, Aurora Art Publishers, St Petersburg

PERSIANOVA, O. (1975), *L'Érmitage: Guide*, Editions d'art Aurore, St Petersburg

RAGGHIANTI, C. L. (Ed.) (1968), *Great Museums of the World: Louvre, Paris*, Newsweek and Mondadori, New York

RAGGHIANTI, C. L. (Ed.) (1970), *Great Museums of the World: National Museum of Anthropology, Mexico City*, Newsweek and Mondadori, New York

RAGGHIANTI, C. L. (Ed.) (1973), *Great Museums of the World: National Gallery, London*, Newsweek and Mondadori, New York

REVIEWING COMMITTEE ON THE EXPORT OF WORKS OF ART (1981), *Twenty-seventh Report*, HMSO, London

TOMKINS, C. (1970), *Merchants and Masterpieces: the Story of the Metropolitan Museum of Art*, Longmans, London

TOYNBEE, P. and WHIBLEY, L. (Eds) (1971), *Correspondence of Thomas Gray . . .*, Vol. II, 632, Clarendon Press, Oxford

8

The national galleries

Michael Compton

The idea of a national gallery of paintings depends on the view that there is something distinctive about paintings which separates them from other man-made objects, however fine. It is a view that is implicit in writings on art from early times, although not always by any means absolute. At any rate such a view existed well before the foundation of the National Gallery in London in 1824. It was embodied in the Louvre, part of which was opened to the public as a national gallery following the Revolution in 1793, as well as in the proposals for a national gallery in London made by the dealer, Noel Desenfans in 1799. The German Romantic poet Wackenroder had written in 1797:

> Picture halls . . . ought to be temples where in subdued and silent humility we may admire the great artists. Works of art, in their essence, fit as little into the common flow of life as the thoughts of God.

The National Gallery in London represents almost the extreme position in respect of the distinctiveness of the medium of painting. Not only is painting set apart from other visual arts as a category, but it is housed a mile or more from the closely related arts of sculpture, drawing and print making in the British Museum and the Victoria and Albert Museum. It is even set apart from modern painting, but more of this distinction later on. The present function of the National Gallery, defined in the Act of 1954, is to collect works of art of acknowledged excellence, just as it was at the start. The Gallery exhibits virtually all its possessions continuously, making the minimum distinction between the great and not so great. Its layout has recently been revised. The collections are divided into five large chronological blocks, beginning with the 13th–15th centuries in the new Sainsbury wing and continuing with the 16th, the 17th, the 18th and the 19th centuries in the older

parts of the building, terminating to the right of the original entrance. Within each block there is a division into national or regional schools, although occasional juxtapositions of works of different schools are provided. The plan of the whole building, which is the aggregate of many extensions, does not permit the visitor to tour the collections without constantly backtracking. The original, and still main, entrance does not give direct access to what most would consider the natural starting point of a visit, nor to the principal public services: shop, restaurant, and temporary exhibition gallery, which are close to the second, Sainsbury entrance. The character of the main entrance to the building is that of a temple, as recommended by Wackenroder and Tieck (1797), up to which you have to climb, both approaching the door itself, and again inside, to reach the pictures. The galleries are literally elevated. The competition for the Sainsbury wing confirmed the quasi-religious concept in asking for a gallery resembling a Basilica.

The present arrangement of the pictures on the walls is more aesthetic than historical. You will often see a large vertical picture in the middle of a wall flanked by two smaller paintings and then two more on either side rather larger. The symmetry may be emphasized by the relative placement of dominant colours or other internal characteristics of the pictures. This sort of arrangement is not altogether innocent of historical association, however, since it can be related to the way an altar-piece may be featured in a church or any great painting in the grand rooms of a palace or country house. It is not surprising that studies have shown that most public attention is drawn to the picture in the centre of a wall, especially if it is large, so that the display is, to this extent, hierarchical, emphasizing certain works at the expense of others.

The attempt to place paintings in any other

context than their century and school is limited (apart from special exhibitions) to the choice of room size and shape, the choice of wall-covering, occasional pieces of furniture and statuary, an exceptional placement on the wall and, above all, the actual frame of the painting. The scholarly catalogues of the collection, certainly among the very best in the world, are primarily concerned with the identity, authorship and provenance of the work itself. Apart from identifying the iconography or subject matter, there is almost no attempt to elucidate the picture, least of all by placing it in a wide cultural ambience. This is evidently a policy, in my opinion a good one, and one that is consistent with the display policy – that is with the view that paintings are essentially apodictic. As Michael Wilson (1977) writes:

Some people criticize the clinical aspect of the modern gallery . . . But such criticism seems sometimes to betray a lack of feeling for the pictures themselves. In the attempt to recreate the period setting of a particular picture, there is a danger of giving too great an importance to historical authenticity. A painting can thus be reduced to the status of an archaeological specimen. The process becomes self-defeating . . . Originally designed to fulfill a very limited function . . . a painting may offer very much more for the imagination, and this quality places it apart from the vast majority of works of its kind. It has meaning outside its original circumstances and for people living perhaps centuries later. It is this factor which distinguishes an art gallery from an historical museum. The exhibits are there for people to find present pleasure in them. [However] Paintings are not always self-explanatory, and for the visitor confronted with examples of Western art from the 13th century to the 19th, some guidance is desirable. The gallery provides 'bats' with printed information that the visitor can carry around with him.

In any case, the Gallery rejects the theory of Alfred Dorner, which would have placed every picture in a period setting approaching those displays in the period rooms of the Victoria and Albert Museum. In this, the National Gallery resembles all of its near equivalents. The specialized art museum follows quite closely the doctrine affirmed by Sir John Fosdyke, Director of the British Museum (Royal Society of Arts, 1949):

The essential element is the material document, and I mean this in the physical sense of the actual object, not pictorial reproductions of it, still less artistic or literary illustration. The photographs, lantern slides, film strips, microfilms, cinematograph films, dioramas and diagrams which are so largely used in what is called 'visual instruction' are books adapted for community reading . . . I can imagine an extremely useful institution containing nothing but this apparatus of visual instruction but I would not call it a museum.

Certainly the architecture of the National Gallery, both internal and external, by poor as well as by distinguished architects, expresses the same understanding. It would be impossible to create within it the period rooms that Dorner called for since it is an excellent example of what he was against (Cauman, 1958):

The pared down nineteenth century version of the palace – a conventional building on the outside, on the inside a succession of bare rooms serving as a 'neutral' background for a variety of equally varied styles.

This formula also describes the Sainsbury wing extension by Robert Venturi.

The function of the present Gallery building is to protect and make visible the pictures. This accounts for the blind windows on the facade that are impregnable and do not admit side-light to dazzle the eye, reflect on surfaces or irradiate the pictures too strongly. The light is, according to the still unsurpassed nineteenth-century formulation, top-light, but in many rooms it is controlled by louvres which can reduce the amount of light on the walls and paintings to determined maxima and annual totals. The Gallery's scientists have been among the leaders of those who have studied the effects of light on the substances that paintings comprise, including pigments, media and even supports (such as paper, canvas and so on) and who have shown that light is damaging in proportion to time, intensity, and the vulnerability of materials. Light levels are, therefore, kept to a minimum compatible with the adequate perception of the works of art. At any such level the pictures themselves will appear more brightly lit if the ambience is at a lower luminosity. This is not possible, for example, in galleries where a diffusing ceiling is certain to be brighter than anything on the walls. Elsewhere the darkened and low-hung ceilings of the 1975 extension rooms make them appear oppressive. The Venturi extension also combines a degree of natural top-lighting with artificial light, but it is designed to avoid confronting the visitor with obtrusive structures of control. In general it is very difficult to reconcile the demands of conservation and perception with the powerful feeling that the gallery should be a 'real' space, not too distinct from that of other type of building. The National Gallery has made a variety of attempts to do this.

Consciousness of the need to preserve works of art and the development of appropriate technology have led to the progressive, but still incomplete, programme of installing air-conditioning. There is almost no incompatibility of the demands of pictures and viewers in respect of the most important factors – especially overall levels and rapid changes of relative humidity. The massive architecture of the older parts of the building, the linings of the walls, timber floors and the large volumes, all help to stabilize the atmosphere. However, there is a conflict in the matter of glazing pictures. Air-conditioning may permit the removal of glass, but glazing may still be necessary for vulnerable works and to prevent possible accidents or vandalism. At the same time, even the most carefully adjusted lighting cannot altogether eliminate the barrier between painting and person that glass represents. The decision to glaze or not to glaze, remains an awkward one for conservators and curators when full air-conditioning is not installed. Where there is no air-conditioning, glass, frame and backboard will limit and slow down changes of humidity and ward off pollution.

The high value given to conservation by the National Gallery is reflected in the establishment of scientists of high rank as well as conservators (restorers). Two handbooks to the Gallery published recently, as well as exhibitions, have drawn attention to the physical make-up of pictures as well as to the rewards and problems of dealing with them. Cleaning, however, has almost always been controversial. No matter how conclusive the evidence supplied by the gallery that pictures have not been flayed, doubts have been entertained quite often by the well informed, while the wide public has been more frequently outraged. As more and more of the paintings have been cleaned and restored to reveal what has survived – never identical to what was painted – and as people have become used to the bright colours that artists often used rather than to yellowing varnish, complaints have begun to die down. Certainly the policy maintained by the Gallery of revealing the pictures as they are and not attempting either to accommodate them to what people may expect, or to restore them to what they might have been, is one which is consistent both with the general attitude of the Gallery, described above, and with the archaeological truth of the object as a document comprising its own history. The requirements of conservation and delectation also determine to some extent what is collected. The Gallery would not acquire what it could not keep and what no one could enjoy. But these factors are by no means sufficient to explain either the original or the accumulated purchasing policy of the Gallery.

In its early days the Gallery 'built on strength'. That is, having acquired works by the most highly estimated artists of the day, they looked for more, instead of filling the gaps. Lord Farnborough said that the main objectives should be limited 'to the works of Raphael, Correggio and Titian . . . which . . . must be obtained whenever the opportunity presents itself'. The Gallery did for a time continue this policy which included also the works of Rubens and Rembrandt and other seventeenth-century painters. However, following an Inquiry by a Select Committee in the 1850s and the appointment of a Director with power to purchase (1855), the policy switched to one of collecting all major schools. The

primitives (roughly thirteenth to fifteenth century) were strongly favoured. The shape of the National Gallery's collection, corresponds remarkably closely to the generally estimated 'map' of painterly creativity. The biggest weaknesses are in Central and Eastern European painting and the first half of the nineteenth century. Sir Michael Levey, however, was as keen as any more historically minded Director to remedy this imbalance. Of course, such a policy may result simply from the ambition to satisfy all educated tastes, but its effect is to make possible the understanding of any painting by showing characteristic, and good examples of what went before. Nevertheless, the hang does not make the most of this potential. For example, the close connections between Italy and Flanders in the mid-fifteenth century are not highlighted by placing works in reasonable propinquity.

The National Gallery of Scotland, founded in 1858, follows the London model closely. With its shorter history and relative lack of purchase funds (which are, however, slightly weighted in its favour as a ratio of population), it can never equal the strength of the prototype. Its 'balance' is, nevertheless, fairly impartial betwen the 'schools'. However, it differs from the London Gallery in one major respect, for not far away in the same country there is another very fine collection – the municipal collection of Glasgow, including the Burrell Bequest. Glasgow is richer in its collections than any other British municipality. But the London National Gallery is far, far richer and more complete than any city art gallery. Only the old universities and the Royal collections compare with the 'provincial' collections of, say, Switzerland, Germany and USA. Yet the national collections are perhaps worth 10 to 100 of these and are proportionately more copiously endowed with purchase funds. Without trying to make the complex and academic calculations necessary, one may assert that very few of the 'developed countries' have a similar proportion of wealth at the centre.

The only remaining point to make about the National Gallery is that it gives little or no favour to the national School. It has almost no British art of the sixteenth, seventeenth or late-nineteenth centuries. It is not the kind of national museum, described in UNESCO documents, in which the inhabitants of a country can find their own cultural identity celebrated. Or, rather, it is as if the cultural identity of Britain is sought mainly in the works of art created in other countries but admired and collected here. The 'national heritage' is, in other words, not essentially what we have made, but what we have loved and learned from. Sir Charles Eastlake, the first director (1855–1865), was a strong importer of works and one who, in this sense, added greatly to our heritage.

The history and disposition of the Tate Gallery

have been, from the start, very different. First, it began in 1893 precisely as a shrine of contemporary national talent, a collection of British art for the British. It was in fact a patchwork of three relatively large gifts, or bequests from Tate, Vernon and Chantrey. Historically, this was at the time of the country's period of greatest relative national, political and economic power. Why should our art not be equally great? It was also a period when certain painters achieved a peak of social status (from which they have declined perceptibly since) and one in which exhibitions and galleries attracted very large crowds. They were a public entertainment of the type, more or less, of the medium of the film which supplanted them. This, however, did not prevent the National Gallery using the Tate, which was its satellite, as a depot, not only for lesser British works, but also for those later foreign works which it did not wish to hang.

In due course (1916) when the Lane bequest, mainly of the then relatively unappreciated Impressionist paintings, came to the nation, these were also sent to the Tate. Galleries for modern foreign art were eventually added and paid for by Sir Joseph Duveen. In the same period most of the paintings of the Turner Bequest (too large to be housed at the National, and out of balance) passed to the Tate, and galleries for it were likewise provided by Duveen. The Tate's role was extended backwards in time to include British art from the sixteenth century and modern, British and foreign sculpture (galleries again by gift of Lord Duveen).

The Tate became, then, a national gallery of the sort which does offer precisely the public an image of their identity. Of course the British collections serve other purposes: to show-off that national identity to tourists, to act as a promotional show-case for national talent, and to be a resource of reference for British artists where one may expect to find typical works of all those above a certain level of quality. It serves as an institution which preserves and exhibits the representation that it has collected, which continues to collect, which studies British art and publishes the results. It is, moreover, a visible sign of the State's respect for art, as its architecture, just as temple-like as that of the National Gallery, declares.

British art includes truly contemporary art and the Tate may buy work by quite young artists, sometimes in their twenties. Generally it does not acquire works by foreign artists when they are so young, both out of policy, and because staff and Trustees cannot be so instantly and comprehensively well-informed about foreign artists. It does buy British paintings or sculpture at a time when the reputation of artists may be changing quite rapidly, both because their own performance may be variable, and because the activities of galleries, museums and critics, not to mention the flow of word-of-mouth appreciation, have their effect. The reputation of artists and the respect given to varieties of artistic practice may spread slowly and irregularly to a wider public and even more slowly to the public at large. There exist, moreover, many kinds and qualities of imagery which may be collected and appreciated by distinct or dispersed sections of this wider public, which are not recognized or are rejected by those who advise on or decide what is collected by the Tate.

The contentiousness of contemporary art remains a constant in the judgement of a large proportion of the public. Nobody concerned is surprised that contemporary art should be shocking and yet, looked at in one way, it is indeed surprising. For, since the art is produced by people who inhabit the same culture as ourselves, and who have had broadly the same experiences, one might think that we should be able readily to perceive and respond to it. That is, the modern collection should be a shrine of 'our century' just as the British is of 'our country'. If anything, it should seem so natural to us – as our clothes and hairstyles do – that it would appear rather banal. Of course, it is true that certain contemporary clothes and hairstyles do seem shocking. These are often worn precisely in order to shock others, while at the same time acting as a sign of membership of an in-group. There is a sense in which contemporary art functions in the same way, but it is not the whole story.

Modern art was first distinguished from other art by Sir Joshua Reynolds (Wark, 1975). His fear, however, was that contemporary art was too popular:

> The works of those that have stood the test of ages, have a claim to that respect and veneration to which no modern can pretend. The duration and stability of their fame is sufficient to evince that it has not been suspended upon the slender thread of fashion and caprice, but bound to the human heart by every tie of sympathetic approbation.

Of course many people think the same – that is, that contemporary art, if it is not a conspiracy, 'is suspended on a slender thread of caprice'. Meanwhile, those within the art world are convinced that what they admire will eventually be admired by a very much larger audience. The Impressionists have often been cited as the example. There is point to this for it is enshrined in the history of the great French collections.

Just as the Louvre, created after the French Revolution, was the first 'national gallery of art', so the Luxembourg in Paris was the first 'museum of modern art'. This time it was the restored monarchy that brought it into being. The idea was that contemporary French art should be exhibited there until five (at other times 10) years after the death of the artist, when it could be dispassionately decided whether it reached the high standard that would allow it to be transferred to the Louvre. The official *Moniteur Universelle* of 1818 said, at its foundation, that it was 'to form an intermediary between the salon, where the pupil is placed next to the master, and the Royal Museum (the Louvre) where France gathers together the masterpieces of the whole world when, after their death, universal opinion has established their glory'.

In practice, pressure of public or critical opinion canonized certain artists in their life-time and the 'after death plus five or plus ten years' rule was never strictly applied. Jacques Louis David, the regicide, was admitted (since art was already to a great extent kept insulated from politics), but it was precisely the purely aesthetic problem of the Impressionists that broke the system. Very few of their works even entered the Luxembourg. Such had been the scorn with which they had been received that the Louvre could not bring itself to admit even Manet until long after his death. In due course a special museum had to be set up for the Impressionists between the Louvre and the Museum of Modern Art (which succeeded the Luxembourg in 1947) when public detestation of Impressionism *en bloc* turned to adulation. Only now is it becoming possible to put the Impressionists and Post-Impressionists in the same buildings and galleries as other forms of painting nearly contemporary with them. So it was precisely the existence of museums of art that forced the necessity for the judgements of contemporary art and brought about the separation which was in turn institutionalized by the creation of museums, or at least departments of modern art.

However, most of the phases of modern art, subsequent to Impressionism, have not found a ready and ever-growing public acceptance. The taste for Cubism and De Stijl, for example, is still a very rare one. It is as if the eventual acceptance of Impressionism has led to a third phase, what may be a virtually perpetual contemporary (that is, not yet understood) art, to be for ever contested between the friends and enemies of modernism.

Contemporary art is actually understood by very many people, but the meanings and values they see in it are simply rejected as alien. Their demand to be told what works of contemporary art mean is merely the traditional expression of hostility, so an explanation of the meaning, to the limited degree to which this is possible for any work of art, does not usually satisfy them. Accordingly, the role of the very active education department of the Tate is not so much to explain contemporary art as to introduce and to confront people with it, so that they are induced to see it as it is and to experience an understanding of it. In short, it is no more than an intensification of the role of the collection of modern art as a whole which is primarily to manifest modern art to the public. Just as the building expresses the State's commitment to art, lecturers must, first of all, express intense interest, enthusiasm and respect.

The function of exhibitions is very similar. The catalogue, which may contain both information and interpretation, is read by a relatively small proportion of the visitors (five to ten per cent) and, of course, quite rightly, few of these read much while going round. They look at the works of art using the catalogue and labels mainly to identify what they are seeing. The Tate has a considerable programme of loan exhibitions. One of the reasons for this difference is that the problems and expense of gathering works comparable to its own are simply too onerous for the intensely select National Gallery. For the Tate, they are less severe, since British and modern art do not yet command the very high prices and the very highest degree of conservationist concern that Old Masters do.

Moreover, both in relation to British and to modern art, there is proselytization. The gathering together of a large proportion of the work of a modern master can do much more to promote understanding, through the perception and development of the range and variety possible for that artist, than any verbal account alone. That is, by considering the transformations available to him or her, one may learn in effect the 'language' of the artist. Of course it is helpful to have in mind both the historical context and the art practice or culture from which the work came. The former must be brought in the heads of the visitors, it cannot really be exhibited, and this may be why the visitors to museums of modern art tend to be highly educated. The 'art' context is manifested by the surrounding permanent collections. Accordingly, they need to be fairly complete or well-balanced. As a matter of policy, the Tate's exhibitions are almost always a presentation in depth, whether of an artist, or of a type of art, that is represented necessarily more sketchily in the permanent collections.

The mutual support of collections and exhibitions is not, of course, the essential reason for the former to be balanced and, within reason, comprehensive. This derives directly from the concept of the museum of modern art itself. Insofar as it is a museum, and not an arbitrary assembly of objects for delectation and excitement – a museum collection is one whose elements are themselves mutually supporting. That is, you may discern the distinctive character of an artist's work or even of an individual painting, sculpture and so on, by comparison with others contemporary with, earlier than, or indeed later than, it. New art derives its power to express partly from the way it varies and transforms the tradition it inherits. Conversely, it gives new meanings to the manifestations of that older tradition.

The practical problem that arises is that the attempt to collect fairly rapidly the range of objects that can make really contemporary art 'meaningful' by such a means, results in the gallery collecting a larger number of works that it can easily conserve and display later on. The ever-increasing diversity of twentieth century art, the rising numbers of artists, and the spread of the practice of making art in the western European tradition, have made it necessary, on this assumption, to collect faster and faster. The Tate's British (sixteenth to nineteenth century) and its modern (twentieth century) collections (excluding prints and drawings) are each of about the same number as that of the National Gallery, covering, as it does, Europe for seven centuries. The Tate's twentieth-century foreign collection alone is already half that of the National Gallery.

In spite of the argument above, it has become increasingly clear that galleries like the Tate should not all try to collect something of everything (down to a given level) but that, like the National Gallery in its early days, each should build on strength. The Tate has in Turner an exceptional strength that cannot possibly be copied elsewhere. It has in the British collections other strengths: for example, Constable (shared anomalously with the Victoria and Albert Museum) and William Blake. In the twentieth century there are groups by some of the great British artists, such as Henry Moore and Stanley Spencer, and even some quite young artists, like Richard Long. You may find unique groups of work too, e.g. those by Giacometti, Gabo and Rothko. Nevertheless, the Tate bears a distinct responsibility because it is the only substantial museum of modern international art in England. It is the nation's unique collection of such art and has a duty to represent a balanced range so that domestic visitors can see what is being created.

In 1980 the Tate opened a small museum in St Ives, Cornwall, based on the house and works of Dame Barbara Hepworth.

In 1988 the Tate opened a branch museum in the Albert Dock buildings in Liverpool. The policy of this in relation to the mother gallery on Millbank has not yet been fully determined, partly because of limitation of funds. Its primary function is to enlarge the space available so that more of the Tate's collections can be shown. It aims at the same time to bring to a new and distant public a display of works of the same standard as those shown in London. A serious problem is that in the field of foreign art, which is so poorly represented in museums outside London, the Tate collection is not rich enough to divide between two buildings in such a way as to show in each an adequate range of artists and styles. At present the solution is to take whole groups and transfer them to Liverpool for substantial periods. Loan exhibitions form a large part of the programme in Liverpool and educational work will be relatively more intensive.

With their Trustees, the last two Directors of the Tate proposed or made major changes in its policy and structure. Sir Norman Reid (1964–79) formally divided the British and Modern collections, he created the exhibition department, education department, archive, the north-east extension and the Hepworth Museum. He initiated the Clore Gallery for the Turner collection. Sir Alan Bowness (1980–88) conceived the division of the Tate into separate museums for the historic British collection, international Modern Art and New Art, and a public Study Centre. He opened the Tate Gallery Liverpool and increased the activity of the Friends (see below). Nicholas Serota, the present Director, has rearranged the collections in a more nearly chronological order (beginning at the end furthest from the entrance), removing screens, thinning out the display and setting aside rooms for changing selections of the collection. He is considering further dispersal of the collections to new or existing regional museums. He has rearranged the responsibilities of staff and created departments for the building and for fund-raising (development).

The Tate has formed, within the association of the Friends of the Tate, who support the whole range of the Tate's functions, a special group of Patrons of New Art. They will support the art by their subscriptions and interest and will act as a pressure group to encourage the Tate itself and the higher authority – the State (which supplies overwhelmingly the great part of the funds both for activities and for purchases of the Tate Gallery and National Gallery) – to remain always aware of the need to examine constantly the newest creations of art and to represent them in the Gallery. The group also aims to foster the spirit of collecting New Art. The paucity of private collections in this country compared with many European and North American countries, is probably both a cause and the effect of the loneliness of the Tate as a public institution collecting contemporary international art. A Patrons of British Art has followed with parallel aims.

The fundamental status of the national galleries, as of other national museums, has been subtly altered by Government. The changes in the system of indemnity (Government self-insurance) and of funding – from direct parliamentary vote to 'grant-in-aid' together with the transfer of responsibility for the building to the Trustees – have implied that Government now tends to see the Trustees not simply as the custodians of the nation's collections but as the owners of the museums supported by Government. This is directly related to the view that the museums and art galleries should seek support elsewhere and even charge for entrance. Nevertheless, it should be acknowledged here that governments of both political parties have since the 1960s voted the National Gallery and the Tate considerable sums for purchase – more than £3 million and £2 million pounds a year, respectively. However, while the price of great paintings of, say, the sixteenth century, may be as high as £5 million pounds or more, many British and twentieth-century works are also priced above the level of the whole annual grant. In the case of the Tate this is spent in practice on one or two first-class and expensive works and quite a large number of lesser or cheaper ones. The annual growth rate of the collections of the Tate is perhaps 20 or more times that of the National Gallery so it cannot hope to show all that it owns. Every new work acquired must displace another to the depot.

It becomes ever more necessary, therefore, that the Tate should achieve the building programme or dispersal outlined above which will not only allow visitors to see a just proportion of the national heritage in the fields where the Tate is the national gallery, but will also allow ready and convenient access to nearly all those works which cannot at present be shown.

References

CAUMAN, S. (1958), *The Living Museum: Experiences of an Art Historian and Museum Director, Alexander Dorner*, New York University Press, New York

ROYAL SOCIETY OF ARTS (1949), *Museums in Modern Life*, Royal Society of Arts, London

WACKENRODER, W. H. and TIECK, L. (1797), *Herzensergiessungen eines Kunstliebenden Klosterbruders*, 61–62, Gillies, A. (Ed.), 1948, Basil Blackwell, Oxford, pp 61–62

WARK, R. R. (Ed.) (1975), *Discourses on Art*, Chap. 6, Yale University Press, New Haven

WILSON, M. (1977), *The National Gallery, London*, Orbis Publishing, London

Bibliography

LYNES, R. (1973), *Good Old Modern: an Intimate Portrait of the Museum of Modern Art*, Athenaeum, New York

POTTERTON, H. (1977), *The National Gallery, London*, Thames and Hudson, London

ROTHENSTEIN, J. (1962), *The Tate Gallery*, Thames and Hudson, London

ROYAL COMMISSION ON NATIONAL MUSEUMS AND GALLERIES (1928), *Interim Report*, HMSO, London

9

University museums

Alan Warhurst

University museums include a variety of institutions whose origins, collections and purposes vary greatly. The only common factors are: that their administration and finance are provided, although not always exclusively, by a parent university; that their collections and buildings are generally owned by a university; that their staff are employed by a university; and that, in one way or another, they make a contribution to the purpose of that university.

At one end of the scale, many of the museums attached to British universities are little more than aggregations of specimens which are, or have been useful to the research and teaching functions of a university department. Some of these, particularly those which are currently used for teaching, are orderly collections. At the other end of the scale are several institutions containing collections which in quantity and quality far exceed what is needed for the university's teaching and research purposes and of these the Ashmolean Museum at Oxford and the Fitzwilliam Museum at Cambridge are the best known. As well as these types of university museums there are several museum collections, some of considerable antiquity, which for different reasons have been adopted or fostered by universities. Altogether, the collections of university museums are a significant part of the nation's cultural, artistic, historical and scientific heritage.

History

If the functions of a university are considered to be teaching and research, along with a wish to stimulate and fulfil the intellectual, cultural, artistic and scientific aspirations of its students, staff and non-university public in the neighbourhood, then it need occasion no surprise that universities have long been regarded as suitable locations for museums.

The earliest public museum in Britain is generally accepted to be the Ashmolean Museum (see Chapter 3), which was opened in 1683 after Elias Ashmole donated his inherited Tradescant Collection to the University of Oxford in 1677. Although at its inception the museum was primarily for scholars of the university, the public was admitted, albeit after payment. The Sedgwick Museum owes its origin to the bequest of Dr John Woodward of his collection of fossils to Cambridge University in 1727. Dr William Hunter bequeathed his private collection to the University of Glasgow in 1783 and the Hunterian Museum was opened in 1804. The Fitzwilliam Museum was established at Cambridge in 1816 following a bequest to the university. In 1868 the collections of the Manchester Society of Natural History were accepted by Owen's College (later the Victoria University of Manchester) after having been rejected by the City of Manchester, and the Manchester Museum was opened to the public free of charge in 1888. Oxford, Cambridge, Glasgow and Manchester Universities all provided splendid new buildings by distinguished architects for their collections, an indication of their enthusiasm for their museums.

These museums were undoubtedly practical manifestations of the spirit of scientific curiosity and academic inquiry which was a feature of eighteenth and nineteenth century intellectual life. Their collections, particularly those of the natural sciences, formed an important university teaching resource by the end of the nineteenth century and by this time archaeological and ethnological collections had become important in the same way. University museums at Cambridge, Oxford, Glasgow, London and Manchester came to hold some of the most significant collections of botany, entomology, zoology and geology in the country, together with important collections of fine and applied art, British, classical and Egyptian antiqutiies, ethnology and numismatics. Their collections were important to the pursuit of research both internally within the university and to international scholarship. Elsewhere, university departments concerned with taxonomic studies or with teaching from artefacts and original or reproduced works of art, accumulated collections of appropriate material. Teaching by handling specimens or observing them at close quarters was considered more beneficial than looking at encased objects during a visit to a national or local municipal museum. Some of these collections, like their more illustrious predecessors, became of national importance, in addition to providing an essential resource for teaching and research purposes.[1]

At the same time it came to be recognized that possession of a valuable art or museum collection endowed a university with a prestigious asset: useful for teaching and research purposes, but also giving the university a sense of patronage of the arts and sciences for the intellectual benefit of its students and staff as well as the general public. When university finance was readily available in the 1960s it seemed natural that universities should take over responsibility for some private society museums which were falling on hard times, in the same way that local authorities had rescued such museums during the nineteenth century. Examples were at Bath, Manchester, Newcastle and Swansea, where potentially impoverished museums[2] with significant collections were given, as it was then thought, secure financial footing backed by Government funds channelled through the university system. Other universities acquired or formed collections by negotiations with discerning patrons as at London, Birmingham, Sussex and East Anglia,[3] or formed useful art collections such as those at Nottingham, Hull and Liverpool.[4]

During the 1980s, British universities have been subject to severe financial constraints and the ability of the university system to support museums on the same scale as hitherto must be in question.

Buildings

Universities in the nineteenth century valued their museums greatly and made generous provision for their museum buildings. Oxford and Cambridge Universities in the 1840s both employed C. R. Cockerell for the Ashmolean and Fitzwilliam Museums (although the design of the latter was actually by G. Basevi). These buildings are of high architectural quality in the classical style of the early nineteenth century. Equally interesting are the University Museum of Natural Science (1855–1860) at Oxford by Benjamin Woodward and the Manchester Museum (1888) by Alfred J. Waterhouse,

which together with the Hunterian Museum (1870) by Giles Gilbert Scott are distinguished and highly individual essays in the Gothic style of the late-nineteenth century.

The latest example of this tradition of employing eminent architects for university museum buildings is at the University of East Anglia at Norwich where the firm of Norman Foster Associates was commissioned to produce a gallery to house the Sainsbury Collection. The Sainsbury Centre for Visual Arts is a building of distinctive design and has received many accolades including a Royal Institute of British Architects (RIBA) award in 1978. More recently, the new Hunterian Art Gallery by William Whitfield set a high standard of art gallery design in 1981.

Although there are some architecturally interesting university museum buildings, the majority are now generally inadequate for their purpose. The fundamental problem is financial, for the system of university funding through the former University Grants Committee made it extremely unlikely, even in good times, that funds could be provided from that source for new museum buildings or even the rehabilitation of old ones (Standing Commission on Museums and Galleries, 1977). Consequently, new buildings have been extremely rare, and where they have arisen finance came substantially from sources other than the University Grants Committee. At Manchester, for example, a new extension opened in 1977 at a cost of £250,000 was financed by equal grants from the University's private funds and the Greater Manchester Council, which were supplemented by only a small grant from the University Grants Committee for furniture and fittings.

As far as the provision of new buildings is concerned, the funding of university museums in the past through the University Grants Committee has been unsatisfactory, despite the heroic and expensive efforts of universities to maintain buildings of great historical and architectural merit. The Standing Commission report of 1977 lists a catalogue of inadequacies in both the quantity and quality of university museum buildings. Collections both in store and on display are over-crowded and environmental control in any sophisticated form is rare outside a handful of the larger art galleries.

Administration

The administration of university museums varies greatly. Those which are primarily study collections for the teaching and research needs of a university department are usually administered as an element of that department, which will be part of a faculty of the university. In such a case the administration will probably be under the control of the head of the department, perhaps with the aid of a small committee of his staff. One or more members of the staff, probably with teaching or research interests in taxonomy or artefacts, will curate the collections. In the majority of such cases the museum will not report to the governing body of the university and the financial and other needs of the museum will not be identified outside the department concerned.

Most of the larger university museums have boards or committees which report directly or indirectly to the governing body of the university. This is a procedure favoured by the Standing Commission on Museums and Galleries (1977) in its Report on University Museums. A more flexible approach was recommended by the Commission in 1987 where such a committee is seen as having responsibility for all collections on a university campus and having a liaison role with local authorities, particularly concerning the newly introduced General Certificate of Secondary Education (Museums and Galleries Commission, 1987).

A survey by the author has shown that nearly all the university museums which the Standing Commission Report (1977) identified as having public responsibilities, have boards or committees to manage their affairs. The construction varies greatly. Frequently, there is a substantial lay element in the committee, derived either from the lay members of the governing body of the university, or from local authorities, learned societies or other museum bodies. The latter is particularly the case, where the university has taken over the responsibilities for running the museum from a private society or as part of a trust to administer the affairs of a benefaction which forms the basis of the museum.

In the majority of university museums, administrative, financial and building maintenance services are provided centrally. On any university campus there is much extremely helpful academic and technical advice which a university museum can draw on. This, together with the excellent library facilities available, can be of the greatest assistance in the running of the museum and in the pursuit of research and interpretative projects.

A survey undertaken recently shows that 20 university museums are members of the Museums Association; 22 are members of area museum councils, whereas only 10 are members of regional federations; seven are members of the International Council of Museums (ICOM). The relatively high membership of area museum councils, as opposed to regional federations, probably reflects the very reasonable membership terms and an appreciation of the usefulness of area museum council services, particularly in respect of conservation and agency grants.

Finance

Generally speaking, a university museum's finance will come from the university, which receives a block grant from the Government-funded Universities Funding Council. A university may make a bid in its grant application for the costs of running its museum or art gallery to be treated as a special factor in the calculation of its block grant. For the period 1986–1989, 16 institutions in 11 universities[5] were recognized financially in the block grants made by the University Grants Committee and its successor to those universities. The Council will not, however, oblige a university to support its museum but does now indicate the extent of the financial recognition made in the calculation of the block grant. This arrangement may to some extent underpin the finances of designated university museums, but it cannot safeguard these museums from the financial constraints which the university is obliged to implement. All other university museums and collections are funded, if they are funded at all, from monies derived from the university's block grant and departmental allocations, together with any trust funds which may have been provided for that purpose. The amount of money to be spent on a university museum will only be identified within the university where the museum has a board or committee responsible to the governing body for estimates and accounts. Even then, some or all of the staff costs may be concealed within the university budget, as may also the cost of the administrative, financial and maintenance services provided by the university generally. Some university museums have access to trust funds which may have been provided by benefactors of the university for the benefit of the museum. Commercial and industrial support for both equipment and staff in universities has long been a perfectly acceptable practice. University museums also have access to the kind of funds available to other museums, such as agency granting through the Museums & Galleries Commission, area museum councils, Victoria and Albert Museum and Science Museum grant-in-aid for specimen purchase and the National Arts Collections Fund. Few university museums charge for admission, notable exceptions being at Bath and Newcastle where former private society museums have been taken over by the Universities and a tradition for charging already existed. The university financial year runs from August to July inclusive.

No university museum can be regarded as adequately financed. The Museums & Galleries Commission does not regard the present funding arrangements for university museums as satisfactory. In 1977 the Commission favoured the indication of grants for university museums by the University Grants Committee. More recently, the Commission (1987) was inclined to accept the existing arrangements for special factor funding outlined above, but to press for firmer recognition of the needs of departmental collections which are not included in these arrangements. It recommended that more notice be taken of scientific collections and the establishment of closer and regular dialogue between the Commission and the University Grants Committee.

The Committee (1987) also recommends that those museums with collections and responsibilities of a public nature beyond the immediate needs of the universities who own them should strive for plural funding from educational, tourism and Local Authority sources. The only instance of the latter kind of support on a really substantial scale was at Manchester where there was a very significant contribution by the Metropolitan Council to the running of the Manchester Museum and the Whitworth Art Gallery. This ended with the abolition of the Greater Manchester Council in 1986. Following some interim financial support from the Office of Arts and Libraries, these institutions have been funded totally by the University of Manchester since 1989.

Staff

Few university museums have a structured staff system such as might be found in a national or Local Authority museum. More frequently, curation is the responsibility of one of the academic teaching staff of the department to which the museum is attached. Only the larger institutions have posts dignified with the titles of Director, Keeper, Assistant Keeper and so on. Whichever is the case, curatorial staff are most likely to be employed on university grades and conditions of service. Where these posts are regarded as truly academic, staff will be graded in the non-clinical academic teaching grades of Professor, Senior Lecturer or Lecturer (the term Reader implies an academic status between the first two of these and carries no financial implications). Other university categories for research and analogous staff, administrative or other related staff may also be used; the various grades within these are related to the academic teaching grades and carry the same conditions of service. University museum technicians will probably be employed on one of the technical grades, although one would expect most of the technical work being done in museums to be remunerated in the higher of these grades. There are also university grades for secretarial and clerical staff and a structure for porter (attendant) and cleaning staff on the campus.

In general, university museum curatorial staff are highly qualified academically and in some instances the Director holds a professional chair. Consequently, academic research occupies a high proportion of the time of staff. Only rarely are display and educational work for schools given the prominence they would receive in other museums. Qualified exhibition officers or design and education staff are rare.

As one would expect from the underfunding of university museums, staffing at every level is inadequate to fulfil the museums' functions properly. The Standing Commission (1977) Report reveals a catalogue of staffing inadequacies. One can only fear that continuing university cuts will have the effect of reducing staff still further (Warhurst, 1986; Willett, 1986).

Function

If the functions of a museum are to collect and care for collections, to research, interpret and educate, then university museums do not differ from other museums. They may, however, be expected to place different emphases on these functions; even amongst university museums themselves these emphases vary greatly.

University collections form an important part of the nation's museum resources. A brief summary of the more important of these is contained in the Standing Commission (1977) Report. Most of the great university natural science collections at Oxford, Cambridge, Manchester and Glasgow were formed during the nineteenth century at the height of the period of taxonomic and systematic collecting. At this time the basis for teaching the subject was also taxonomic and systematic and these large collections were directly useful within the university for undergraduate teaching and post-graduate research. In the latter half of the twentieth century, teaching in the biological sciences is dominated more by chemistry, biochemistry, behavioural science, mathematics and statistics. Huge collections of skeletal material, bird skins, insects and herbarium sheets are no longer regarded as absolutely essential to undergraduate teaching, although they are useful in certain aspects of that teaching and in giving students the feel of real things. This does not mean that university museum collections have become redundant any more than have similar collections in national and Local Authority museums. Large collections of this kind contain substantial numbers of type specimens and these, together with the sheer volume of other specimens, make the collections important for research by museum staff and visiting scholars. The large natural science collections in university museums do pose huge curatorial problems because of severe understaffing. Some of these museums, notably at Glasgow, Cambridge and Manchester have embraced computerized cataloguing in an attempt to cope with the logistics of information handling arising from the large number of specimens in their collections.

Some university art collections, particularly those of long-standing at Oxford and Cambridge, are important national resources, comparing in quality with the collections in the national institutions, in addition to their use for undergraduate teaching. Art collections such as those at Liverpool, Nottingham and Hull may be used for teaching purposes, but principally supply a cultural and aesthetic quality to university life. Collections of oriental art at Durham and London are an integral part of specific teaching and research schools, as is the case with the Petrie Collection of Egyptology at University College, London. The Courtauld and Barber Institutes at London and Birmingham, respectively, have collections of the highest quality which make a significant contribution to the study of fine art and art history in the universities.

Rich archaeological and numismatic collections are contained in the museums at Oxford, Cambridge, Manchester, Glasgow, Newcastle and Bangor. In all these places the collections form an important part of the national resource. In some universities small, but choice, collections of classical archaeology perform the same teaching and research functions as the art collections mentioned above. There are highly specialized museum collections in science and technology at Oxford and Cambridge, in agriculture at Reading and in musical instruments at Edinburgh.

One of the major problems of university collections is our scant knowledge of their extent (Warhurst, 1986; Museums and Galleries Commission, 1987). Useful surveys of collections have been carried out for the Area Museum Service for South-East England (AMSSEE) for London (AMSSEE, 1984a) and the South-East generally (AMSSEE, 1984b) and in the East Midlands. These have shown that collections of museum material are more widespread and extensive than was previously realized. The Museums and Galleries Commission has indicated that it is prepared to allocate finance towards such surveys. That for Scotland has now been published and a survey of university collections in Northern England has begun.

The problems caused by lack of knowledge of university collections and by change in the perceived usefulness of university collections are illustrated by the sale of the George Brown collection of Pacific ethographical material by the University of Newcastle to the National Museum of Osaka in 1985. Most persons who knew of this collection assumed that its custody was in safe hands, even though it may have no longer been fulfilling the function it once had in the work of the university (Benthall, 1986).

In many cases university museums will have access to laboratory and workshop facilities in the university to assist in the conservation of their collections and such laboratories are likely to be as good as, if not better than, any museum conservation laboratories and workshops. At Oxford, Cambridge, London, Cardiff, Durham and Bradford the universities support conservation laboratories in art and archaeology for research and teaching purposes. Otherwise only a small number of university museums have specialized conservation facilities and staff, and appreciable use is made of area museum services for this purpose.

Purchase funds for the acquisition of new exhibits may be found at 13 University museums, although all are of extremely modest amounts in relation to the quality of the collections. All these museums take advantage of grant-aid for specimen purchase, administered through the Victoria and Albert Museum, the Science Museum and the National Museum of Scotland. An equal number undertake field-work, excavation or natural science collecting for the purpose of adding to the collections. Museums at Oxford, Cambridge, Glasgow, London and Manchester make contributions to such field-work by other bodies both at home and abroad. These contributions, in addition to supporting the project, also help to assure a controlled influx of documented specimens to the museums.

The quality and quantity of research undertaken in university museums is high. Academic staff in a university have a responsibility to undertake research and this would apply just as much to full-time curatorial staff in a university museum as to those whose museum duties are more incidental. One example of this is the Egyptian mummy research programme at the Manchester Museum where the mummified remains of humans and animals in the museum collection have been subjected to exhaustive examination by a team of scientists on the university campus led by the Keeper of Egyptology. Specimens have been studied using up-to-date medical, chemical and physical techniques and the results have been published (David, 1979). Such a research project could probably only have been carried out on a university campus, utilizing the combined knowledge and expertise of a number of university and hospital staff.

Although most university museums assist undergraduates or post-graduate research workers in their tasks, only the Hunterian Museum, the Percival David Foundation of Chinese Art and the Sainsbury Centre for Visual Arts have postgraduate research studentships attached to the museum. It is disappointing to find that more such posts are not attached to university museums. Curators in the larger university museum collections play a full part in the wider field of academic research. Highly specialized collections such as those in Chinese ceramics at Brighton or London, or in entomology at Oxford or Manchester, are more likely to be used for research by the international scholar than by their local communities.

Some difficulty exists in deciding how far university museums should be the natural resting places for specimens and information gathered by students and staff in the course of the pursuit of higher degrees. There can be little doubt that this ought to be the case, particularly with type or figured specimens, but a lot of material is involved and it is often very difficult to recover it once the thesis has been presented. Many museum workers feel that the accession of such specimens and information to a museum collection should be an integral part of thesis requirements (Strachan, 1979).

One of the original functions of a university museum was to assist in the teaching of undergraduates. Despite the change of emphasis in university teaching, particularly in the biological sciences, most university museums feel that there is still an important role for them to play in this field. Although the large systematic collections which the older university museums have amassed no longer contribute so significantly to this particular purpose, sections of the collections are still used heavily for teaching purposes. Where a museum collection is attached to a teaching department the connection with teaching and research in that department will be strong. At Manchester University the Whitworth Art Gallery is used annually for students of the post-graduate Art Gallery and Museum Studies diploma course for learning the process of mounting a major art exhibition in co-operation with the staff of the gallery and a professional designer. There are many instances where university museum staff who are fully engaged in a curatorial role lecture to students as part of the curriculum of academic courses.

Few university museums provide an educational service for schoolchildren. The Manchester Museum is exceptional in providing such services which are staffed by qualified teachers but they are paid for by the City of Manchester Education Committee. The Hunterian Museum has used a team of three teachers funded by the Manpower Services Commission, and the Ashmolean Museum has established a voluntary guide scheme which provides teaching for children of all ages in the galleries and occasionally undertakes some visits to schools.

All museums need to identify the audience with which they are communicating. University museums face the same problem, but will have different approaches. Those which are departmental teaching museums will aim their arrangements at the undergraduate student in the department. University museums with a wider brief may not be able to do this. Even where a museum is primarily for the benefit of a campus population, probably running into several thousands of staff and students, the great majority of its visitors will inevitably be non-specialists in any particular part of the museum collection. Where a museum has to fulfil a public role as well, the relative number of non-specialist visitors will be greater still. In these cases it would not be justifiable for, say, undergraduate-level zoology

displays to be provided for the benefit of a small number of zoology students, when these could not be comprehended by undergraduates in other subjects, let alone the general public. Galleries of fine art may not feel the dilemma to the same extent.

Nonetheless, university museums have a duty to provide for the teaching of students. One solution proposed for doing this in their displays involves two levels of presentation, one for the general public and one for the undergraduate (Seyd, 1970). This has merit, particularly if the physical arrangements are designed to keep the displays separate but capable of easy cross-reference within the same gallery or even within the same case. It is a solution, however, which demands fairly expensive and resourceful design if it is to be done well. Otherwise an essentially public display might be preferred leaving any undergraduate teaching arrangements to be negotiated between the curator, the lecturer and the students to take place in study rooms or parts of stores made over for this purpose.

Whatever may be the preferred solution, university museum displays are more likely to contain larger numbers of objects and larger amounts of information than those of most other types of museum and this is probably useful in counteracting different trends in other kinds of museum. Only the Manchester Museum and the Hunterian Museum have design officers. The Whitworth Art Gallery and the Sainsbury Centre for Visual Arts have exhibition officers. Displays at the Hunterian and Manchester Museums and at Aberdeen University Anthropological Museum have won wide acclaim, including awards in Museum of the Year competitions.

A surprisingly high number of university museums have temporary exhibition programmes, most of which are achieved on very small budgets. A small number of university museums provide material for other bodies such as the Arts Council or the area museum councils to circulate. Most university museums which welcome public visits provide a point of sale for museum publications and at the Fitzwilliam Museum this is done by an independent company. Many universities have a University Press and the expertise and facilities, particularly in dealing with printers and marketing, may be helpful to university museums in their more scholarly publications. About 20 university museums organize lectures, thus fulfilling an important role for campus staff and students as well as for the general public. Eight university museums, mostly art galleries, have Friends' organizations and that of the Fitzwilliam Museum is the oldest in the country.

In 1987 a University Museums Group was formed. Membership is by institution and it has over 50 members, ranging from the large public museums to small departmental collections. Its aims are to:

represent and speak for the interests of university museums; to improve their status and effectiveness; to assist in the identification and listing of university collections: and to improve communication between staff working with university museum collections. The Group is carrying out a vigorous campaign of lobbying Government Ministers, the Universities Funding Council and any other bodies capable of having a helpful influence upon university museum collections. The Museums Association at its Conference in 1987 adopted a Policy Statement on University Museums. This identified the problems facing university museum collections and advocated a comprehensive listing of collections, a higher public profile and a more reliable method of funding through the university system.

Conclusion

This brief survey of university museums presents both a heartening and disturbing picture. We may marvel that a small number of Britain's universities has successfully nurtured some of the country's most significant collections and enabled them to survive intact into the last quarter of the twentieth century. This is an act of dedicated responsibility to academic scholarship and to the public of this country. Around the 1960s universities came to the rescue of several museums which were in straitened circumstances. Some distinguished collections might well have suffered seriously at this time but for the responsibility shown by the British university system. Many universities have recognized that an art gallery or museum can be a civilizing influence on the university campus and have formed discreet collections for the benefit of the cultural life of the considerable campus population of staff and students. And all the time universities have provided, where appropriate, collections to be used for undergraduate teaching and post-graduate research. All this has been done from the money allocated to the universities' main functions of teaching and research.

The Museums & Galleries Commission has repeatedly warned that all is not well with the financial provision for this particular part of the national heritage. While universities were expanding and financial problems seemed hardly to exist, university museums did not fare too badly. Now that the financial screw has been vigorously tightened, university museums find themselves competing for funds in a contracting financial situation. No university administration can protect its museum from the same sort of financial cuts which the teaching and research departments of that university are currently bearing. As a result, university museum provision is now being cut back at a harsher rate than any other form of museum service.

The money for national museums and university museums is provided directly or indirectly by Government. There would seem, therefore, to be a strong case for making arrangements that at least the larger university museums with wide public obligations should in some way be protected to the same extent as the national collections. Possibly the Universities Funding Council, which has now replaced the University Grants Committee, will focus its attention on this point.

Notes

[1] Other university museums founded in the nineteenth or early-twentieth centuries include: the Pitt Rivers Museum (1883), and the University Museum (1853) at Oxford; the Museum of Archaeology and Ethnology (1883) and the Museum of Classical Archaeology (1884) at Cambridge; the Anthropological Museum, Marischal College, Aberdeen (1907); the Department of Geological Sciences Museum, Birmingham (1906); the Cockburn Museum, Department of Geology, Edinburgh, (1908, with earlier ancestors); King's College Geology Department Museum (1830); University College Museum of Egyptology (the Petrie Collection), London (1913); University College of Wales, Museum and Art Collections, Aberystwyth (1872); and the School of Animal Biology, University College of North Wales, Bangor (1900).

[2] The Holbourne of Menstrie Museum, Bath University (1973); the Whitworth Art Gallery, Manchester University (1958); the Hancock Museum and the Museum of the Society of Antiquaries of Newcastle upon Tyne, Newcastle University (1958 and 1960, respectively); and the Royal Institution of South Wales Museum, University College of Swansea (1973). The future of the latter museum now lies outside the university system.

[3] The Courtauld Institute of Art (1931) and the Percival David Foundation of Chinese Art, Londonn University (1951); the Barber Institute of Fine Arts, Birmingham University (1939); the Barlow Collection of Chinese Ceramics, Bronzes and Jades, Sussex University (1974); and the Sainsbury Centre for Visual Arts, University of East Anglia (1978).

[4] University Art Gallery, Nottingham University (1936); Hull University Art Collection, Hull University (1963); and University Art Gallery, Liverpool University (1977).

[5] University museums and collections accepted by the UGC as non-departmental special factors 1986–1989: Bath, Holbourne of Menstrie Museum; Birmingham, Barber Institute of Fine Arts; Cambridge, Fitzwilliam Museum, and Museum of Archaeology and Anthropology; Durham, Oriental Museum; East Anglia, Sainsbury Centre for Visual Arts; London, Courtauld Institute Galleries, Percival David Foundation, and Petrie Museum of Egyptian Archaeology; Manchester, Manchester Museum, and Whitworth Art Gallery; Oxford, Ashmolean Museum, and Pitt Rivers Museum; Reading, Museum of English Rural Life; Aberdeen, Anthropolo-

gical Museum; and Glasgow, Hunterian Art Gallery and Museum.

Six recent additions have been made to this list. They are: Hull, Hull University Art Collection; Kent, Centre for the Study of Cartoons and Caricature; Newcastle, Greek Collection; Oxford, Bate Collection of Instruments; Reading, Ure Museum of Greek Archaeology; Edinburgh, Russell Collection of early Keyboard Instruments.

References

AREA MUSEUMS SERVICE FOR SOUTH-EAST ENGLAND (1984a), *A Survey of Museums and Collections Administered by the University of London*, AMSSEE, London

AREA MUSEUMS SERVICE FOR SOUTH-EAST ENGLAND (1984b), *Survey of University Museums in South Eastern England*, AMSSEE, London

BENTHALL, J. (1986), 'The Goerge Brown Collection', *Anthropology Today*, **2**(4), 1–3

DAVID, A. R. (Ed.) (1979), *The Manchester Museum Mummy Research Project*, Manchester Museum, Manchester

DRYSDALE, L. (1990), *A World of Learning, University Collections in Scotland*, HMSO, Edinburgh

MUSEUMS AND GALLERIES COMMISSION (1987) *Report, 1986–87*, London

SEYD, E. L. (1970), 'A university museum and the general public', *Museums Journal*, **70**(4), 180–182

STANDING COMMISSION ON MUSEUMS AND GALLERIES (1977), *Report on University Museums*, HMSO, London

STRACHAN, I. (1979), 'Palaeontological collections and the role of university museums', in Bassett, M. G. (Ed.), 'Curation of Palaeontological collections', *Special papers in Palaeontology*, **22**, 70, 73–74, The Palaeontological Association, London

WARHURST, A. (1986), 'Triple crisis in university museums', *Museums Journal*, **86**(3), 137–140

WILLETT, F. (1986), 'The crisis in university museums in Scotland', *Museums Journal*, **86**(3), 141–144

10

Local Authority museums and galleries

Brian Loughbrough

Introduction

The legacy, the pressures and some challenges

Whatever category of museum, be it national, local, private, military or university, Local Authorities are involved. Some hold collections of national or international importance, some have recently become national. Others reflect purely local community interest, while varying forms of partnership and financial support in connection with private, military and university museums are all to be found. The keyword is 'variety'. That variety stems from a long, and from a national viewpoint, largely unplanned history of development, characterized by permissive rather than mandatory legislation.

The five counties of the East Midlands Area Museum Council region illustrate the situation. Leicestershire has a large and wholly county provided service, Lincolnshire has a mainly county service, Derbyshire has a county and larger ·and smaller district services, Nottinghamshire has no county service as such, but that authority undertakes important site interpretation functions; six of the eight districts provide services. Finally, Northamptonshire has a major district service in Northampton itself and, with Area Museum Council aid, is developing a country curatorial service in partnership with certain districts such as Daventry. Even this brief description is an over-simplification since it does not take into account complications arising from the actual ownership of collections!

No Local Authority is required to provide a museum, but by the exercise of various powers most may do so (see Chapter 6). There is, however, an *expectation* that they should insofar as the expenditure is recognized in the annual Government Revenue Support Grant and various forms of additional grant aid. At the core of any review of Local Authority museums lies this key issue of finance. Competition for scarce Local Authority resources from within and without has always been intense and, in the absence of any widely *adopted* guidelines, insufficient cash has been available given the size of the task. Essential national criteria should be recognized which could be cited to promote public confidence and bolster the case for improved resources. This is likely to be the best short-term position achievable short of mandatory provision.

A word of caution is due at this point. If 'variety' is one keyword in terms of Local Authority museums, then 'independence' is another. For various reasons Local Authorities do not always readily wish to accept the opportunity or agree to the requirement laid upon them to provide services. When they choose to do so, they try to reserve the right to act in their own way. Insisting on their independence, local councils maintain that they are elected locally and are best able to determine the kind and level of service that their areas need, given the cash available and the strengths of other pressures.

The different categories of Local Authority have their own associations (see Chapter 4). They come together to make joint representation to various bodies including Central Government on the make up of the Rate Support Grant. Joint discussions also take place with the Museums Association, the Museums and Galleries Commission and the Arts Council.

Legacy and historical responsibility

For a century and more Local Authority museums have cared for collections, often in elegant, but otherwise unsuitable, buildings. They have responded to change with remarkable resilience and have initiated changes themselves showing a high degree of 'flexibility'. They have the ability to capitalize on developments in the Local Authority sector. The realization of the opportunities arising from a whole range of recent initiatives will be profoundly affected by the Local Authority sector response. Improved professional training will produce better qualified staff. More clearly defined collecting policies, collections management methods and improved conservation techniques coupled with imaginative display and interpretation skills all point to a potential new threshold. Whether that response appears under the guise of tourism infrastructure support or education or some other as yet unforeseen development, museum professional staff must be ready to apply themselves to ideas which can be achieved within the system.

In times of change and financial hardship, Local Authority museums also provide a source of both professional and financial support to others. In extreme circumstances they have become partners or adoptive parents with the private, university or military sector. In either case, the extra pressure on limited resources is considerable. Nevertheless, they have managed to respond in numerous instances, even if the level of that support is not all that those most closely concerned would wish.

Since the first edition of this Manual was published in 1984 whole categories of Local Government have changed or disappeared. There is no Greater London Council (GLC) and Metropolitan Counties have been abolished. Often the reason for the change lies far outside the museum sphere and little or no regard may be taken of their needs, yet the consequences may be profound and certainly not all detrimental (Cheetham, 1984).

What lies in the future is even more difficult to predict. The introduction of the Community Charge, the so-called 'Poll Tax', and the national non-domestic rate appear likely to put constraints on funding authorities and increase direct charges on museums themselves if full discretionary rate relief is not applied to those with charitable status. 'Privatization' is a real issue in kindred Local Authority departments. Provision of catering services in museums is already subject to competitive tendering where private concessions or franchises do not already apply. The new emphasis may provide opportunities to improve visitor services, always accepting the caveat that the core of museum provision must be maintained and developed within any new initiatives.

Visitors to Britain and generally from within Britain come for the character, quality and history that the country has to offer. Much of that product lies within the museum's care. Apart from the concern that Local Authorities have for their own residents, many have a regard to the value of tourism as a contributor to the local economy. Tourism represents four per cent of all spending on goods and services in the UK. Involvement with an industry having a total turnover in excess of £14 billion and employment for 1.4 million people (1988 figures) means that museums, and especially Local Authority museums, are indeed part of a very big business. Towns like Bradford have embarked on enterprising tourism promotions and several have entered partnerships to promote joint marketing of 'mini-breaks'.

Tourism promotion is heightening the importance of museums thanks to the work of colleagues in planning and public-relations departments. New national tourism signs which feature guide symbols already direct visitors to quite small as well as big city museums. Of course there are pressures to provide associated promotional events and it is necessary to guard against over-commitment of resources and too close an involvement with the occasional unsuitable event.

From the private and voluntary sector come other challenges, opportunities and ultimately demands on the resources of Local Authorities. Often starting in modest circumstances, voluntary groups may, through dedicated effort, secure the provision of, for example, an industrial site, a framework knitter's shop or a water pumping station. In the end the public purse is sought for publicity, occasional capital grants or even supplementary running costs. As a result, the distinctions between museum sectors becomes ever more blurred.

The financial context

The Local Authority sector accounts for somewhat less than half the public museums' spending in the country and a similar figure applies with regard to attendances. The Local Authority net spending on the arts in the year 1988–1989 was approximately £230 millions (see *Table 10.1*).

The Government's own Expenditure Plans 1987–1988 to 1989–1990 allowed for about 60 per cent of total provision for the arts and libraries programme to be met through expenditure by local authorities. Of this programme, about 85 per cent is attributable to the public library service with about 4000 public libraries and about 15 per cent to some 1000 museums supported by Local Authorities. Paragraph 13 of the Government statement in the section on Local Government expenditure is worth quoting in full.

Value for money in the arts is not measured in quantitative terms alone. Quality and *variety* are also important. Nor can existing performance indicators adequately reflect the full impact of programme expenditure. The prestige attached to the country's arts activities at home and abroad is evidence of the high regard in which they are held.

Table 10.1 Net revenue expenditure (£ million) 1988–1989

	Museums/galleries	*Arts premises/promotions*	*Grants, etc.*	*Total*	*%*
London Boroughs	5.83	42.09	14.93	62.85	27.5
Metropolitan Districts	20.83	10.96	9.91	41.70	18.3
Shire Districts	32.01	46.52	21.52	100.05	43.8
Counties	13.28	2.81	7.62	23.71	10.4
All	71.95	102.38	53.98	228.31	
%	31.5	44.8	23.6	100.0	100.0

This topic is the subject of the recently published and important current Audit Commission study, 'The Road to Wigan Pier? Managing Local Authority Museums and Art Galleries'.

When referring to the 1000 Local Authority museums it is important to remember that about half the buildings housing them were built before 1850 and a quarter before 1750. As might be expected, approximately 70 per cent are listed buildings. The consequence is that high maintenance and running costs are normal. Even the buildings themselves can be a hazard to the collections that they house, ultimately representing an extra cost factor. More-over, Local Authorities in their planning role have a part to play in the operation of listed-building legislation; they must be seen to set standards. Many new museum projects are introduced in historic buildings or sites with consequent extra costs. Relatively few entirely new buildings have been completed in recent years; one may cite splendid exceptions such as the City Museum and Art Gallery at Stoke-on-Trent and the Burrell Collection build-ing at Glasgow, but only 13 per cent of museum buildings, whether Local Authority or otherwise, are post-1960 in date (Prince and Higgins-McLoughlin, 1987).

Capital expenditure

The Local Government and Housing Act 1989 provides a new framework for the control of Local Authority capital expenditure. Each year, an Annual Capital Guideline will be issued to each Local Authority expressing the Government's view of the level of capital expenditure for particular services such as housing, transport, the urban programme and the 'other services' block. The amount of capital expenditure which may be financed from borrowing is restricted by Basic Credit Approvals issued by the Government; these may in some cases be enhanced by Supplementary Credit Approvals. Capital Re-ceipts, which are generated from the sale of assets, are available to finance new expenditure after allowing for certain specified proportions which must be set aside to meet credit liabilities. Other sources available to finance capital expenditure include various capital grants and revenue. It should be noted that there is no statutory limit on the amount of capital expenditure that may be financed from revenue, although in practice other constraints will serve to limit the availability of this method of financing.

Local Authorities formulate annual capital prog-rammes and may also produce rolling programmes covering periods of up to five years. Invariably bids for the new programme exceed available resources and need to be pruned to match. Even with rolling programmes extending over five years or more, it is difficult to secure a place for a particular museum project and retain it in face of numerous other pressures. The availability of grant aid from outside sources, such as the Historic Buildings and Monu-ments Commission and the Museums & Galleries Commission (see Chapter 5) can, however, provide a key to unlock funds.

Revenue expenditure

Nearly all capital schemes have continuing revenue consequences. A few, such as improved storage, may actually *save* money, some such as new shop/catering/visitor facilities may even *earn* money, but in the nature of this type of labour-intensive service the likelihood is that increased annual revenue expenditure will follow. Debt charges must be met, staff appointed and running costs covered. Such expenditure must be seen against the inherited responsibilities of the service and its long-term commitments which ought to be protected. Some-times an opportunity arises to carry out a capital scheme because a particular building or collection becomes available. If the curator has a choice it can be a matter of nice judgement as to the degree of 'flexibility' that the individual service ought to show in its ability to absorb a new scheme. Unfortunately, such opportunities rarely occur twice and reluctance in one instance may have unfortunate later con-sequences.

Revenue expenditure is supported by the Standard Spending Grant from Government, from local taxation in the form of the Community Charge and the national non-domestic rate and from other grants, fees and charges. The precise levels of expenditure by individual Local Authorities are carefully monitored by Government through the Department of the Environment. Government indicates what is considered to be an appropriate spending level for each authority. The formula for this calculation has varied in recent years. Those Authorities that exceed the prescribed Standard Spending Assessment level may be subject to various penalties and loss of grant. The ultimate sanction is 'capping' where Government lays down what may be spent and what Community Charge levied. In times when tight control is maintained over public expenditure, Local Authority museums face particular problems. The Standard Spending Grant is not a sufficiently precise tool to take account of an Authority having a major historical house or collections in its care and which may be enjoyed by residents from adjacent areas. Except in the case of a joint project like the North of England Open Air Museum at Beamish there are too few shared funding arrangements.

Where revenue funding is cash limited or tied to a formula such as the Retail Price Index, museums can be at a disadvantage in that inflation in their specialist field may be, and often is, much higher than elsewhere in the field of Local Authority spending. The purchase of material for collections illustrates the difficulty. Spectacular increases in prices at auction, often fuelled by foreign collectors or museums, coupled with the sheer increase in the amount of material available present a serious budget problem. In the case of a deferred export licence approval, a museum may only have a short time to raise a substantial sum. Should the Purchase Grant Scheme operated through the Museums & Galleries Commission have insufficient funds available and local fund-raising has been only of limited success, the Local Authority would be faced with the prospect of finding most of the money from its own resources. While major institutions may be able to attract grants and sponsorship towards outstanding purchases, it is much more difficult for the small Local Authority museum to obtain assistance towards an item of perhaps minor national but real local importance.

Even grant aid has its drawbacks and potential problems. Various Government and private organizations offer support on the basis of 'challenge funding'. Although it only affects a number of larger museums, the Arts Council's 'Glory of the Garden' strategy operates on a matching grant basis. The idea behind such schemes is admirable in that it seeks to 'unlock' more local funding, but where that funding can only come from the Local Authority, then the danger of incurring penalties can make the offer self-defeating. Indeed, after an extended period of financial restraint, the opportunities for making economies elsewhere in museum budgets in order to match such challenges are very limited.

Help in kind can be valuable and perhaps the most significant example in recent years has been through the attachment of Manpower Services Commission personnel. Much valuable work was undertaken, but with the more specific direction of the Employment Training scheme far fewer people are now employed. There are obvious dangers in becoming too dependent on such projects where the benefit of the museum can only be a secondary consideration to the providers.

As in the case of capital, so also are there revenue schemes with a 'challenge' element seeking to direct resources to the special problems and opportunities of inner-city areas. Through the operation of Section 11 of the *Local Government Act 1966* offers of up to 75 per cent of the cost of salaries of workers are available for those whose duties, after full consultation with the local community, can be seen to assist ethnic minority groups. The provisions take special note of those situations where English is not the first language.

This still relatively unexploited area of funding may enable Local Authority museums to respond to a sector of the public whose current interests are insufficiently represented in modern galleries. It also has financial consequences in that 25 per cent of employee costs and 100 per cent of running costs must be found by the host Authority. Similarly, the government's Urban Programme may offer help with revenue costs for a specified period in respect of approved schemes.

The structural context

Museums and different types of authorities

The earlier history of museums and attempts to enhance their work is recounted elsewhere in this book (see Chapter 3) and reference has already been made to the legacy of buildings. It is nevertheless worth emphasizing the historical continuity represented in the collections and buildings maintained by Local Authorities. The zeal of learned societies and local literary and philosophical societies, of mechanics institutes, frequently of generous private collectors and travellers has left a superb, often daunting and sometimes only partially realized, resource at the curator's disposal. That many of these collections have survived is due to the Local Authority assuming the role of Patron and disinterested, but by no means uninterested, Trustee. Preservation and survival has, therefore, been a worthwhile achievement in itself.

As more and better trained and informed staff have been able to turn their attentions to these collections, so the academic and display potential of the material has increased.

It has to be acknowledged that some of these collections have deteriorated in Local Authority care and there are sad sagas of boilers and burst pipes to be told around the country. Attempts are being made to improve the position by the direct employment of conservators or by the use of area museum facilities and agency services. In addition, attention is being given to the upgrading of security, and the introduction of improved lighting, handling techniques and environmental controls. Local Authority museums are often approached by museums in the private sector for advice in this field and are thus able to make a contribution to the general improvement in standards. The appointment of 'curatorial advisers' to meet the requirements of the Museums and Galleries Commission's registration scheme is a particular case in point.

So, who were the inheritors of this legacy in 1974 when the provisions of the *Local Government Act 1972* came into effect? The Act allowed museum powers to be exercised by all but the smallest Local Authorities (Parish and Town Councils). Moreover, these powers could be concurrent, that is to say they could be provided in the same area by two different tiers of local government. Thus museum services were inherited and developed or newly provided by some, but not all Metropolitan Counties, Metropolitan Districts, Non-metropolitan or Shire Counties and Shire Districts, a very confusing situation even though the total number of Local Authorities was much reduced. More recent changes have taken place in Scotland where the *Local Government and Planning (Scotland) Act 1982*, museum powers have been put in the hands of districts who are encouraged to work together, sharing resources. This last proviso is very important, particularly in those areas where the distances are considerable, but the population small and local taxable income modest.

Finally, and most recently, the abolition of the Greater London Council, the Metropolitan Counties and the Inner London Education Authority has had further effects leading most notably to the transfer of some provision to English Heritage, the establishment of a mechanism whereby the Museums & Galleries Commission has grant aid and Trustee oversight of the Geffrye and Horniman Museums, the creation of the National Museums on Merseyside covering those museums and galleries previously administered by the Merseyside Metropolitan County Council (Foster, 1984) and special local arrangements such as the creation of the trust supporting the North Western Museum of Science and Industry.

Whether any further changes will take place remains to be seen. In England and Wales there is a lobby which urges the creation of 'most purpose' authorities based on existing districts or amalgamations of District Councils. The Metropolitan Districts are very similar to this form already. It is suggested that authorities might come together to provide joint services where the scale of the operation justifies such an arrangement, for example, to tackle the demands of education. Others advocate 'unitary' authorities based on existing city or county councils or major parts of their present areas.

Such discussions have significance too when the post-1974 arrangements are examined in more detail. Although County Councils had taken a relatively modest role in museum provision between 1919 (when they first obtained powers) and 1974, some significant developments had taken place, for example in Derbyshire, County Durham, Oxfordshire and Lincolnshire. After 1974, however, the work of the new style County Councils became very important indeed and by 1982 represented some 40 per cent of local government museum expenditure. Since 1974 new County Councils have been the legal recipients of many museum donations and have developed extensive sophisticated services on an integrated basis. Any further restructuring of local government would have to take this valuable and significant period of service development into account.

So concerned at the fragmentation and potential overlap of services was the Standing Commission on Museums and Galleries (1979) that in the Drew Report and the subsequent *Report on Countywide Consultative Committees* (Museums & Galleries Commission, 1982), authorities were exhorted to enter into collaborative and consultative arrangements, even if they had no desire to surrender their autonomy. It has to be said that, although Area Museum Councils have fostered consultation and the Museums Association's Committee on Museum Ethics have promoted consultation and collaboration at a professional level with regard to possible conflicts in collecting policies for example, there is still a bewildering array of provision which is confusing to curators and elected members alike. Random examples quoted here and in the Introduction illustrate the position. In Hampshire, services are provided by both County and District Councils, in Leicestershire the service (including archives) is provided entirely by the County Council and the seven District Councils providing 15 museums and an archaeological unit (Cheetham, 1984). In such varied circumstances, the professional curator has a special duty to ensure that care of the collections and the maintenance of public services remain paramount while adhering to the warmest professional association with colleagues in overlapping or neighbouring authorities. The advent of registration with its requirement for defined collection policies can only be helpful in this regard. These issues are considered in more detail in *Local Authorities and Museums, Report by a Working Party*, 1991 (Museums & Galleries Commission, 1991).

Professional relationships – inter-departmental structures

The fortunes of individual museums after local government reorganization in England and Wales in 1974 were very mixed. In some districts and newly formed County services, museums achieved a new profile within the portfolios of programme area committees devoted to 'leisure', 'recreation and amenities', 'arts and cultural facilities' and similar titles. In some Authorities which did not exercise education and social services powers these new committees attracted senior and influential elected members and the voice of museums became more significant.

Others became modest appendages of what were seen as insensitive omnibus departments headed by chief officers experienced in quite unrelated disciplines, reporting to committees whose priorities lay elsewhere. The deep disquiet arising from this latter experience is still apparent. Moreover, the salary of the most senior museum person may be depressed by the hierarchical relationship to the chief officer's salary which is subject to national guidelines and based on population levels in the area served (Boylan, 1987).

A key element in the Museums Association's Code of Practice for Museum Authorities is that the senior museum professional should be heard at committees when museum matters are being discussed and most certainly when the key policy implementation document, the budget, is being considered. Similarly, the Museums & Galleries Commission rubric covering essential elements for registration draws attention to the need for adequate arrangements. Because the subject is so often hotly debated it is worth pausing for a moment to consider how the need for these requirements to be inserted came about. The problem is partially one of scale. Even before reorganization, museums often represented only a small portion of a Local Authority's services and, for administrative and financial convenience, were grouped with other functions such as libraries. Parallel to the provisions of the 1972 Act, a study on *The New Local Authorities – Management and Structure*, known as the Bains Report (The Study Group on Local Authority Management Structures, 1972), looked at how the new Local Authorities might be managed. The report argued that the cause of efficient management would be better served by creating departments that were responsible for a relatively small number of broad programme areas rather than by having up to 20 or more specialized

professional departments, each pursuing what were seen as its own narrow interests. By relating these new super-departments to similar service committees a superficially neat system emerged. Chief executive and chief officers met in management teams of varying but always small size depending on the nature of the Authority and its responsibilities. Elected members had less difficulty in identifying who was reponsible for what. In the variously titled recreation, leisure or amenities departments the chief officers were served by colleagues at second- and third-tier levels who might include specialists in baths, parks, entertainments, museums, libraries, theatres, tourism and so on. The chief officer might be drawn from one of these disciplines or none of them. There were, and still are, also examples of museums in smaller Authorities being part of the Chief Executive's office, the Secretary's/Legal Department or the Technical Services Department. Bains was anxious that the operation of the new structures should not be marked by a new 'narrow departmentalism', but that rather they should foster a coming together of the numerous professional skills that Local Authorities have to offer. Groups would be formed to tackle specific tasks drawing in the specialisms within and beyond individual service departments in order to give members the best advice. There is much to be said for this approach and, provided that the span of departmental control is not too wide, it can, and did, work well. Central to its success, however, is an appreciation at all levels of the professional concerns of the officers involved.

Where the museum is only a very small or embryonic part of the provision its needs may be served by a subcommittee or working party where a relatively junior member of the council's staff may gain experience and yet still have influence on the decision-making process. Discussions with colleagues in allied professional associations indicate a growing awareness of the concerns of museum staff and a desire to take their views into account, as well as a better appreciation of what they have to contribute. Improved communication and closer consultation on training with, among others, the Institute of Leisure and Amenity Management (ILAM), the Local Government Training Board and the establishment of the Museums Training Institute, offer the prospect of further progress.

Professional relationships – council and committee structures

Each Authority has a prescribed complement of councillors elected to represent a ward or group of wards. Their first task is to look to the needs of all and not just those who voted for them. Second, they must attend to the needs of the Authority as a whole.

They may have special knowledge and experience in certain fields, but they cannot be expected to have expertise in every issue brought before them. The normal practice, therefore, is to delegate responsibility to service committees whose members may gain a good working knowledge of the relevant programme area. Members may serve on more than one and there is often competition for places on popular committees. Senior members, usually including Service Committee Chairs, then join on some form of central policy, finance or general purposes committee.

The diagrams in *Figures 10.1* to *10.3* are for illustrative purposes. There are many local variations in committee structures and titles. Many museums fall within the ambit of the 'leisure services' group of committees, but they are also found with education and even central policy committees. With the coming of compulsory competitive tendering many authorities have set up a Direct Service Department to handle the Council's own unit and workforce and there may be a parallel committee to oversee such activity.

In former times, many Local Councillors were independent individuals claiming no political party allegiance, but their numbers have declined and recently candidates increasingly have stood as members of political parties, subscribing to a particular published manifesto and, if elected, working as one of a political 'group' within the council.

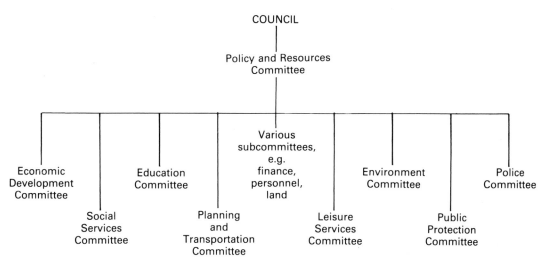

Figure 10.1 An example of a committee structure of a County Council

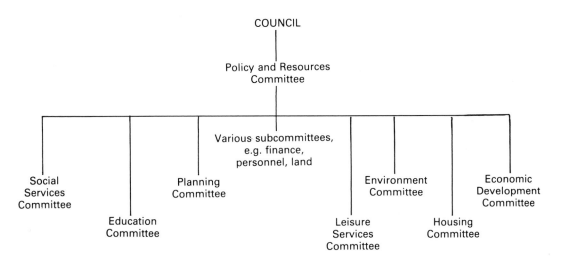

Figure 10.2 An example of a committee structure of a Metropolitan District

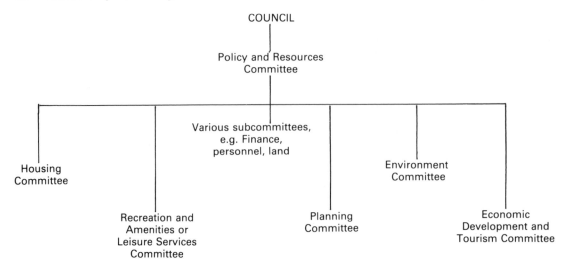

Figure 10.3 An example of a committee structure of a larger non-Metropolitan District

For all major matters or where they do not operate under delegated powers, departmental officers prepare reports for committees in accordance with standing orders and financial regulations having regard for the needs and drawing as required on the expertise of other departments. The majority of reports today are in written form because of the need for such consultations. They are the subject of scrutiny by members at preliminary meetings and indeed at political-group meetings where policy issues are involved. Technically, the only responsibility and power of a Committee Chairman is to preside over meetings, but in practice that person will often act as contact point and guide between the relevant chief officer and council members. Members may take part in regional and national meetings where they can get to know fellow members and officers. The efficient, courteous and professional conduct of such gatherings can assume an importance beyond the immediate subject matter when delegates return to their own authorities.

Members are also often very well informed about their local areas and can be useful contacts in developing outreach work. The role that museums may have in developing a sense of pride in the local community can be aided by member involvement which, in turn, helps to improve the committee climate. Museum premises are often attractive venues for promotional events involving members. Recent examples include presentations of 'best-kept-village competition' awards, a natural history book launch and the Annual General Meeting of a building preservation trust. Provided such events are well managed, do not compromise collections care or inhibit other aspects of the service, the associated spin off of publicity and information is worthwhile.

Local Government and current challenges

Internal developments

Local Authorities are big business in their own right, spending many tens, even hundreds of million pounds annually. Having labour-intensive functions they are also among the largest employers within their areas. Museums are fortunate to be part of that community of public services. There are planners and architects to help on long-term schemes, engineers, property managers, clerks of works and building surveyors, lawyers, insurance specialists, printers and many more, each with their own range of skills, contacts and specialist suppliers. By establishing good working arrangements with such fellow employees and using their advice and expertise much can be accomplished 'in house'. It is worth remembering that museums can offer a *variety* of challenging and interesting unique projects that represent a change from the more routine jobs that these colleagues encounter. Moreover, a workforce representing hundreds of local families with a museum connection is a good base from which to start.

These relationships are not all one way however. The growing emphasis on 'heritage' projects and tourism promotions means that senior officers are spending increasing amounts of time on joint projects and there are posts occupied by museum professionals which cover both fields. Biological records schemes, urban wildlife projects, industrial heritage areas and oral history recording programmes cut across traditional departmental and Local Authority boundaries bringing new friends and, it has to be said, time-consuming liaison tasks.

The older, longer established historical collections of fine and applied art, archaeology, and natural history present one kind of challenge to be met by improved documentation, conservation, reappraisal and display. The 'new' areas of activity present another where sheer scale can be a major factor. Museums of popular or folk culture, social history, agriculture, industry, technology and transport sometimes with floating or flying exhibits proliferate. Site interpretation museums and associated interactive displays are becoming more numerous. Following the rejuvenation of inner city areas, the departure of smoke stack industry and agricultural improvement, many old premises, churches, barns, tram sheds, pumping works, railway stations, mills and warehouses, all exhibits in their own right, have been dedicated to museum purposes. Technology barely a century old, like film and computing, is all part of the growing field of Local Authority responsibility. There has also been a growth in the application of the presentation skills required to meet the rising expectations of a more sophisticated audience that has become used to the adept communication of complex material.

Another aspect of change has been the transfer of responsibilities from national to local government. Three examples illustrate the situation. Following the decline in the size of the armed forces with the associated amalgamation of units there has been a gradual reduction in the number of retired soldiers who can take an interest in regimental history. This fact, together with a gradual withdrawal on the part of the Ministry of Defence, has meant numerous regimental collections have passed into Local Authority care, some with, but others without any, substantial support from military sources. A more detailed discussion may be found in *The Museums of the Armed Services, Report of a Working Party, 1990* (Museums & Galleries Commission, 1990).

Archaeological excavation units have also seen a similar transfer following the shift by the Historic Buildings and Monuments Commission to project funding. The outcome is that the balance of responsibility for rescue and research archaeology is passing to Local Authority hands, welcome though special funding such as storage grants may be.

The needs of university museums (Warhurst, 1984, 1986; and Chapter 9), subject as they are to the pressures on the University Funding Council are also a matter of concern in certain Local Authority areas. Major university museums offer public services beyond the research and teaching needs of the universities themselves. As financial priorities point towards reductions in services, it seems inevitable that universities must look to Local Authorities for help in the form of direct grants, staff secondment or even joint trusts, in order to maintain service.

The case of the special provision for the Geffrye and Horniman museums has already been mentioned. A glimpse of the challenge faced by these museums and their London Borough colleagues is afforded by the recently published information that 172 languages are represented in the London student population and that within Inner London 25 per cent of pupils speak a language other than English at home.

A feature of recent years has been the growth of the major national blockbuster exhibition, perhaps the most spectacular and certainly the captor of public imagination being the Tutankhamun show at the British Museum. Few Local Authorities can match such presentations, yet they have recognized the importance of a changing exhibition programme, maybe picking up themes from major national events. There are also opportunities in celebrations of museum centenaries themselves and other anniversaries. Local Authority records may be put to good effect in such shows like the marvellous blitz exhibition at Birmingham in 1985 which drew on photographs, incident reports and the recollections of the individuals involved. A really good temporary show can stimulate local debate and understanding such as the memorable Indian village reconstruction in Leicester in 1984. Temporary exhibitions are an important method of promoting and explaining the task and contemporary relevance of the local museum. Opportunities for a new area of temporary exhibitions have been presented by the growth of twinning arrangements with other cities abroad. Local museums can play an important part in such links and stake a claim to useful resources.

Research and fieldwork have, unhappily, been casualties of financial pressures in recent years. Few opportunities exist for Local Authority officers to undertaken projects and the normal career route has taken senior staff into management or administration rather than research. Museum organization is tackled elsewhere in this book, but it is relevant to comment here that local government structures, posts and remuneration are hierarchical. They begin with chief officers and work through a series of grades with provisions for principal officers, senior officers and six numbered scales. Management services officers do not always find it easy to cope with grading questions in this field. Responsibility for supervision of staff tends to score more highly than work complexity or care of immensely valuable assets. The Museums Association's own statement says, 'It is the policy of the Museums Association that holders of the Association's Diploma should be paid, at the minimum, on the English Government Scale 5 or its equivalent'. At November 1991 prices, that four-point incremental scale is £11,961 to £13.134. Fitting a post in with more emphasis on research is, therefore, not easy, although the system is not completely inflexible. A recent example has been the creation of a post of documentary historian to work with archaeology and social-history sections.

More attention is being paid to the subject of training, both general and specific. Local Authorities, in common with other employers, have a duty to consider the requirements of health and safety legislation. Some aspects are common to all departments, whereas others are peculiar to museums, taxidermy for example having its own code. There is a general trend to promote both initial and post-qualification training for all types of staff; much of that training is provided and funded by Local Authority museums. Museum staff themselves are often good communicators, trainers and teachers. Following 50 years of largely unpaid and freely offered contributions to the training of professional colleagues, staff have welcomed new courses in universities, colleges and institutes covering curatorial and technical skills. The work of the newly established Museums Training Institute following the recommendations of the 'Hale Report', *Museum Professional Training and Career Structure, Report by a Working Party, 1987* (Museums & Galleries Commission 1987) has concentrated on setting agreed standards and looks to further improvements in whole career development training.

A growing feature is the training of others to use museums by museum education staff. The introduction of project-based GCSE courses and the establishment of the new National Curriculum offer more new areas of work, especially for Local Authority museums.

Relations with outside bodies

The Local Authority sector has always played an important role in the affairs of the Museums Association. A major element in this relationship has been the professional training offered by the Museums Association. Its Diploma has been the most widely accepted qualification by Local Authorities and has formed the basis for appointment, salary grading and career grade enhancement. Both professional and institutional membership, recruitment through Museums Association announcements, attendance at conferences and meetings and representation on the Council have been features of the connection over many years. Indeed, Local Authority support has been vital to the successful operation of the Association. Perhaps paradoxically, it would be advantageous to Local Authority museums if the Museums Association membership could be yet wider. Apart from spreading the financial commitment it is desirable for elected members to see their local service as part of the broader national and international scene.

Building on local loyalties and pride, Friends' organizations provide welcome support and a useful alternative means of communication with decision-makers. Through their national organization, the British Association of Friends of Museums (BAFM), they can also act as a significant museum lobby, but only if those museums with proper staff resources support and inform them properly. Other more specific local societies such as restoration groups can be equally supportive, but they need input and a commitment of staff time.

At a regional level, Local Authorities have played a leading role in the expansion and growing impact of the Area Museum Councils since the 1960s, providing secretarial and financial backing as well as the core of professional advice and support for the councils' own staff. Relatively little of this work is charged except in the case of formal agencies, yet it represents a major commitment by Local Authorities to the work of all museums within the areas served.

Parallel to the Area Museum Councils are Regional Arts Associations. They too were established in the 1960s, existing to promote all current art forms and give support to practising artists and performers. Unfortunately, at first their activities tended to be separate from those of established museums and galleries. More recently, and specifically with the implementation of the Arts Council's *Glory of the Garden* strategy in which they have been closely involved, collaborative schemes have been developed. Joint exhibition working parties, the promotion of travelling shows and the presentation of art and performance in public places have all featured in a growing partnership. Museums and other Local Authority officers assist on advisory panels and so contribute to the community of arts provisions. Following considerable discussion and modification the structures and governance of the new Regional Arts Boards are being implemented with rather less local government involvement on the management bodies, as discussed in the *Wilding Review*.

Naturally, contact with national organizations is concentrated on those with a special remit to assist museums with advice and help in cash and kind, such as the Museums & Galleries Commission (Chapter 5), English Heritage, the Historic Buildings and Monuments Commission, the National Heritage Memorial Fund and the National Art-Collections Fund. The Arts Council's touring exhibitions have been very welcome visitors to Local Authority galleries and it is hoped that they can be maintained. Sadly, for many smaller museums and other non-gallery venues, there has been no replacement for the former Victoria and Albert Museum touring exhibition service since its disappearance in 1977. On the other hand, developing relationships with National Museums have resulted in loans of individual exhibits. When indemnity provisions or extra security needs have to be met on the recommendation of the national Security Adviser, however, additional Local Authority expenditure may be required. Gift horses rarely turn up without the need for some form of stabling! Other national organizations act as direct or indirect lobbies for the general museum, environment, heritage and arts cause.

Conclusion: more pressures and new initiatives

The handling of controversial collection and exhibition material is a growing local as well as national topic. Local museums have been involved in such issues as the improper use of toxic chemicals, damage to bat roosts, threats to listed buildings or sites of ecological significance. On occasion these matters can arise within an Authority when a mixture of forthright comment and tactful negotiation may be required.

When galleries show the work of contemporary artists the subject matter may well be politically or socially challenging. It is perfectly easy to demonstrate nineteenth-century social conditions separated and sanitized by time, but more awkward to hang material featuring, for example, the miners' strike without attracting accusations of bias. If museums are to present a microcosm of the changing world, then they must consider the view that it is insufficient to stick to uncontroversial subjects. In the Local Authority context, contemporary collecting and the presentation of recent historical material requires special attention to balance.

On the other hand, one should not assume the need for an intellectual hairshirt and forget that other side of recent successful promotion and communication, namely that museums are fun. Superbly demonstrated in the 1986 Manchester City Art Galleries seaside show, the various images were complemented with sandpit, deckchairs and cheerful rudery and generated lively visitor responses. The public are entitled to expect unstuffy presentation, good information and, according to the size of the museum, a whole range of other customer-care services, beginning with welcoming staff and extending to seating, refreshments, sales and conveniences. Local Authorities often take a lead and set a local example in providing improved access for people with disabilities. It used to be the case that the word 'municipal' preceding a service title implied something dull and utilitarian. Stimulated by some splendid Local Authority examples and the promotional skills of colleagues in the national and private sectors there has been a marked improvement in museum displays and visitor services. Changing economic and social circumstances offer the prospect of more users. There is more family leisure time, a growing number of active retired people representing considerable financial 'grey power', as well as many not in work for various reasons. The challenge is to generate the resources to respond to their needs.

References

AUDIT COMMISSION (1991), The Road to Wigan Pier? Managing Local Authority Museums and Art Galleries, London: HMSO

BOYLAN, P. J. (1987), 'Salaries and status', Museums Bulletin (Dec. 1989), 168

CHEETHAM, F. (1984), 'Relations between museums and employing authorities and governing bodies: local authority museums with special reference to county museums', in Thompson, J. M. A. (Ed.), Manual of Curatorship: A Guide to Museum Practice, Chap. 61, Butterworths and the Museums Association, London

FOSTER, R. A. (1984), 'The large provincial museums and galleries', in Thompson, J. M. A. (Ed.), Manual of Curatorship: A Guide to Museum Practice, Chap. 7, Butterworths and the Museums Association, London

MUSEUMS & GALLERIES COMMISSION (1982), Countywide Consultative Committees for Museums, HMSO, London

MUSEUMS & GALLERIES COMMISSION (1987), Museum Professional Training and Career Structure, Report by a Working Party, HMSO, London

MUSEUMS & GALLERIES COMMISSION (1990), The Museums of the Armed Services, Report by a Working Party, HMSO, London

MUSEUMS & GALLERIES COMMISSION (1991), Local Authorities and Museums, Report by a Working Party, HMSO, London

POLICY STUDIES INSTITUTE, Cultural Trends. Issue 8: 1990

PRINCE, D. R. and HIGGINS-MCLOUGHLIN, B. (1987), Museums U.K.: The Findings of the Museums Data-Base Project (and update), Museums Association, London

STANDING COMMISSION ON MUSEUMS AND GALLERIES (1979), Framework for a System of Museums (Drew Report), HMSO, London

THE STUDY GROUP ON LOCAL AUTHORITY MANAGEMENT STRUCTURES (1972), The New Local Authorities: Management and Structure, HMSO, London

WARHURST, A. (1984), 'University museums', in Manual of Curatorship: A Guide to Museum Practice, Chap. 8, Butterworths and the Museums Association, London

WARHURST, A. (1986), 'Triple crisis in university museums', Museums Journal, 86(3), 137–140

Bibliography

ARTS COUNCIL OF GREAT BRITAIN (1984), The Glory of the Garden: The Development of the Arts in England, London

ASSOCIATION OF DISTRICT COUNCILS (1989), Arts and the Districts, Report of the A.D.C. Working Party on the Arts, London

HM GOVERNMENT (1986), The Government's Expenditure Plans 1987–88 to 1989–90, Office of Arts and Libraries text, HMSO, London

POLICY STUDIES INSTITUTE (1989), Cultural Trends No. 1, 1989, based on data in Chartered Institute for Public Finance & Accounting, Leisure and Recreation Estimates 1988–89

THOMPSON, J. M. A. (1984), 'Accreditation', in Manual of Curatorship; A Guide to Museum Practice, Butterworths and the Museums Asssociation, London

WILDING, R. (1989), Supporting the Arts: A Review of the Structure of Arts Funding (the Wilding Review), HMSO, London

11

Independent museums

Neil Cossons

There are and always have been a substantial number of museums in Britain that are outside the established pattern of funding and management. This museum establishment has for many years consisted of two main groups, both financed almost entirely from public funds. The national museums derive their income in the main from Central Government, although it reaches them through a variety of channels. Local Authority museums are run and funded by Local Government, usually through committees of District or County Councils. Outside these two major groups are, for example, university museums, most regimental museums, and what in recent years have come to be called independent museums. It is this latter group that is considered in this chapter. There are thought to be about 1500 independent museums in Britain.

A crude definition might be that independent museums are those which are not administered directly by any Central or Local Government agency or authority. Within this group there is wide variety in the nature of constitutional framework ranging from unincorporated societies or associations to charitable companies and from those which have significant public authority financial support to others which receive little or none.

Although since the mid-1960s there has been a rapid growth in the number of independent museums the concept of a museum run by a society, club or other group of interested people dates back many years. Indeed many of the great collections now held by public authorities, and some of the buildings that house them, have their origins in the activities of literary and philosophical societies, scientific, archaeological or natural history societies, and gentlemen's clubs which, if they were still being run in this way today, would certainly place them in the category of independent museums. Similarly, the basic curatorial divisions which characterize so many

multi-disciplinary museums, derive from the nature of the collections formed by these socieities and the interests of the gifted amateurs who so frequently made up their membership. In short, the familiar pattern of public authority museums in Britain owes much to the way in which this first generation of 'independent' museums grew up reflecting as they did the needs of contemporary society for popular learning and for a point of contact with the new discoveries of science and exploration. The history of many of these societies is well documented (Lowe, 1923; Walden, 1960; Boylan, 1982). A few still exist in more or less their original form – for example, the Museum of Sussex Archaeology at Lewes set up in the 1840s by Sussex Archaeological Society – although more frequently their collections and buildings have become wholly integrated into Local Authority museum services. A few still retain an independent identity with a governing body consisting of representatives of the society and elected member nominees of the Local Authority. In many cases a large part of the funding comes from the Local Authority. For example, Torquay Natural History Society's Museum was established in 1844 and is still run by the Society in the museum which it built in 1874. Torbay Borough Council is represented on the Executive Committee and makes a substantial contribution towards operating costs. Similarly, the Devizes Museum run by Wiltshire Archaeological & Natural History Society and Salisbury & South Wiltshire Museum run by its own independent Council of Management (set up with charitable status in 1969 to replace the original governing body of 1860), both receive grants from Wiltshire County Council that are related in general terms to their curatorial and administrative salary costs. In the case of Salisbury, the District Council also makes an *ad hoc* contribution, whilst the Kennet District Council supports Devizes. The Dorset

County Museum, run by Dorset Natural History & Archaeological Society is still almost wholly independent although it enjoys a grant from the County Council more or less equivalent to salary costs. The Yorkshire Museum, on the other hand, set up by the Yorkshire Philosophical Society in 1825, passed to the Local Authority in 1960 and is now wholly run by the North Yorkshire County Council, although the Society still has three members on the museum committee and makes a nominal contribution towards costs.

The reasons for the demise of these society museums in their original form are not hard to see. Dedicated, sometimes as a matter of principle, to the concept of free admission, they were largely dependent on the subscriptions of their membership, sometimes supported by endowments. Neither source of income proved sufficient to sustain them for long after the first generation of members and, with increasing costs of maintaining collections and, more particularly, their museum buildings, the only solution was for them to be taken over by the Local Authority or to form a partnership with it. It is not insignificant that all the examples cited above charge admission to their visitors.

In the early 1960s it would have been reasonable to assume that these early society museums formed part of the transitional, formative phase of museum development in this country, a phase that had been superseded by a more formalized Local Authority based structure of museums providing a service to the population of their respective localities. In the long term this assumption may still prove to be correct. But the last 20 years have seen sharp changes in attitude on the part of the public towards the sort of material for which museums have traditionally cared. Rapid changes in the landscape as the result of urban and industrial renewal and new farming technology, increased wealth, leisure and mobility, the impact of good quality documentary television with good coverage of archaeology and natural history, are just some of the factors that have combined to create an attitude of awareness and a sensitivity towards environment and place which had not previously existed at a popular level. Many of the new museums of the last 20 years are part of the response to this awareness but, whilst some have grown out of existing Local Authority museum organizations, others are completely new, founded in the main by groups of people whose interest and enthusiasm has led them to form new independent bodies specifically to create and run museums. In this respect they differ from most of their nineteenth-century predecessors, for in these earlier examples the museum often represented only one of a number of activities which they had been set up to pursue and, today, free of their museum responsibilities, many of these soecieties successfully continue their

programme of lectures and visits and the publication of their transactions.

It is also important to appreciate that this new museum movement is only one facet of the broader-based environmental conservation interests that have developed so actively in the same period. A strong desire to participate by active engagement in the processes of environmental conservation or more passively by joining a conservation organization has led to a rapid expansion in many membership-based conservation bodies at both national and regional level. The National Trust, with 2 million members, is now one of the largest conservation bodies in the world, whilst on a smaller scale innumerable voluntary preservation groups, civic societies, nature conservation trusts and museums have sprung up anxious to protect historic town centres or endangered species, excavate archaeological sites in advance of motorway construction, revive derelict canals or save steam pumping stations from destruction.

The larger new independent museums that have grown out of this broader environmental conservation movement have a number of characteristics in common:

(1) They frequently reflect new popular interests of people in subject areas that have not, generally speaking, been covered by traditional museums or for which no existing museum could or would assume responsibility. Industrial archaeology, transport history, vernacular architecture and building preservation – often *in situ* – are some of the themes they embrace. Most of them are in fact thematic rather than multi-disciplinary museums.

(2) These people have the motivation and enthusiasm to set up and in many cases run a museum themselves, although almost invariably there is a nucleus of paid professional staff.

(3) Most of these museums are charitable trusts and many are non-profit-making companies, that is companies limited by guarantee and not having a share capital.

(4) They raise their capital by fund-raising aimed at both public- and private-sector sources.

(5) They are substantially or in some cases completely self-supporting on their revenue accounts. This is achieved in the main by charging the visitor for admission.

(6) They tend, of necessity, to be strongly market oriented.

(7) They are often outside large urban areas with existing museums services.

Many of these new museums have developed what might be called their product around a readily identifiable market of relatively affluent and mobile people. Significant reductions in the real cost of petrol have contributed towards this (Shell UK, 1981). Numbers of visitors to all types of attractions, and museums represent about one-third of the visitor market in Britain, rose spectacularly during this period too, to reach a peak in 1978. Since then there has been something of a reduction to both free and charge-admission museums.[1] Over the same quarter century or so the number of cars on the roads grew from three million to 20 million. In other words a new type of museum has become possible which could not have readily existed before. Independent museums are in part a product of this new museum-going public – there are some 70 million visits to museums in Britain each year. Their influence, however, particularly on the public conception of what a museum is or can be, has been out of all proportion to their size, their numbers and their budgets. This has been in part because of the nature of their product and in part because they have needed to market themselves energetically and sometimes quite competitively in order to develop.

It would be wrong, however, to regard these new market-oriented charge-admission museums as setting the universal pattern for museums in the future. On the contrary, whilst one set of social and economic circumstances has created conditions for the growth and development of the independent museums movement, long-established public authority museums, often based in urban areas, have responded to different pressures. Whilst clearly public authority and independent sectors have much to learn from each other it is reasonable to assume that they can fulfil a fruitful and complementary relationship in the future.

But one gap has not been filled adequately by the large independent museums any more than it has by traditional public authority museums. The need of local communities, often of very small size, to see evidence of their own history collected and preserved in their own local museum has become a strong one. Thus of the 1495 independent museums surveyed by the Association of Independent Museums, the largest single group (215 museums) consists of local history museums, most of which are very small, of relatively recent origin, and set up by local history societies or groups of enthusiasts. This desire by local communities to have their own museum which they are prepared to run themselves at little or no cost and usually on an entirely voluntary basis is clearly a strong one and the 'official' museum world has not and perhaps cannot satisfy demand in this area. The people who set up these museums are collecting primarily for themselves material which reflects their own need to identify with the place in which they live and the evidence of its history. They are not necessarily interested in visitors as such and have little interest in the tourist market which sustains larger independent museums. But they must not be dismissed out of hand as they are reflecting in their own way the same basic motives which for more than 200 years have led to the establishment of collections out of which have grown many of the great museums with which we are familiar today. What makes them distinctive, however, is the fact that they have this extremely local value and meaning, that they involve the participation of a group within the community in the curatorship of its own past, and that they are entirely voluntary in nature. A clear distinction needs to be made between these *voluntary* museums and the bigger independent museums and public authority museums in which *volunteers* often work.

A further and important new strain of museums is a direct product of the rapid changes which are taking place in the industrial landscape. 'Industrial archaeology' as a term was coined in Britain in the mid-1950s (Rix, 1955) when a few people began to recognize that the replacement of old technologies with new and the desire to sweep away the unattractive remains of past industrial activity was at the same time eliminating the evidence of an important cultural phenomenon of world significance. In the eighteenth century Britain had become the world's first industrial nation, and in the nineteenth century it was the 'workshop of the world'. Some 70 per cent of the built environment of Britain dates from the period of the Industrial Revolution and in the 1950s it was still possible to identify within that environment many of the key monuments of that period. In more recent years the decline throughout Europe of many of the traditional coal-, steam- and iron-based industries has had its most dramatic impact in the old industrial heartlands of Britain presenting a wholly new set of economic circumstances and a rate of social change unknown for nearly 200 years. An environment within which people can begin to contemplate a 'post-industrial society' has important and fascinating implications for museums and, perhaps more importantly, for the processes of curatorship. Many of the new independent museums are museums of industrial archaeology concerned with the preservation *in situ* of industrial sites and monuments, and machinery which they contain, or the preservation of industrial buildings which are being used for more traditional museum purposes. The new farm and rural museum movement which has emerged still more recently is again a reflection of the changes which have taken place in the agricultural landscape, not only as the result of new technologies, but also in response to a large-scale interest in the countryside and country pursuits on the part of increasingly urban dwellers.

The scale of this problem of de-industrialization in curatorial terms is enormous but, although industrial archaeology is still in its infancy, there is ample evidence to indicate that new and often ingenious solutions are being found to cope with sites and artefacts of great scale and complexity. Some museums, such as Ironbridge, have set out to preserve whole areas of past industrial activity, others have developed along the lines of more traditional open-air museums in which industrial buildings and artefacts have been reconstructed in special sites laid aside for them. The Black Country Museum in the West Midlands is an example. More frequently, however, industrial archaeological conservation has centred around the preservation *in situ* of specific industrial sites, on many of which working activity and, in some cases, manufacturing is an important part of the conservation, interpretation and marketing formula. Working wind and watermills abound, beam pumping engines have been preserved at, for example, Crofton in Wiltshire, Kew Bridge in London and Ryhope, Sunderland, a water-powered scythe works is regularly demonstrated at Sticklepath in Devon, Styal Mill in Cheshire is being developed as a textile museum, whilst at Chatterley Whitfield near Stoke-on-Trent the first mine in Britain to produce a million tons of coal a year and which closed in 1976 has been opened to the public who can descend below ground in the cage and walk through reconstructed workings. It would be wrong to assume that these new industrial archaeological museums have been confined to the independent sector, more that an independent body, purpose built for the project and adapted specifically to its funding and management requirements, has in many cases been the best means of achieving the objective.

The constitutional framework within which any museum operates must ensure that its collections are as far as possible safeguarded. In this respect many small independent museums have unsatisfactory constitutions as they are unincorporated societies which do not have charitable status. Thus the fate of the collections is entirely in the hands of those individuals who form the membership or governing body. The best form of protection that an independent museum can afford its collections is through the medium of charitable status. A charity for the purposes of the *Charities Act 1960*, means any institution which is established for charitable purposes and these must satisfy the essential tests of altruism and public benefit required of all charities. There is no statutory definition or test by which it can be decided if any particular purpose is charitable in law but the provision of a museum has been held to be a charitable purpose, constituting a public amenity with an associated educational advantage to the public to be derived from it. Each museum must satisfy the Charity Commission[3] that its particular purpose is charitable and details of each scheme are considered in detail by the Charity Commissioners and a decision is made on the merits of each case. The Commissioners liaise with the Inland Revenue in considering an application for charitable status. In Scotland, where there are no Charity Commissioners, a test of charitable status must satisfy the Inland Revenue.

A museum may make an application for charitable status whether it is a trust or any other undertaking and whether it is corporate or not. If a corporate structure is used the company will usually be one limited by guarantee not having a share capital rather than a company limited by shares. Alternatively, the institution in question may be a trust formed by a Declaration of Trust or it may be an unincorporated association. Often it is useful for an unincorporated association to provide in its constitution for a trust to hold its property and equally it may be useful to graft a set of rules or constitution for the running of the trust on to the basic Declaration of Trust. There is great flexibility available in the variety of structures which can be developed and it is advisable, therefore, to obtain professional advice in order to achieve the most advantageous form. The Association of Independent Museums have published a guideline on *Charitable Status for Museums*,[4] which outlines the advantages and disadvantages of various types of structure and provides a model Declaration of Trust for a charity and model Memorandum and Articles of Association for a company limited by guarantee and not having a share capital. These models have been approved as drafts by the Charity Commission.

The essential prerequisite of a museum which has any serious intent is that it should have charitable status in order to protect as far as possible the inalienability of its collections. Typically, a Declaration of Trust ensures that the collections can only be disposed of under such terms as the Trustees may think fit provided that any such disposal shall be made only for the purposes of improving, enhancing or extending the quality of the collection and in furtherance of the objects of the charity, and providing that any such item is offered first to another charitable institution, museum, school, college or university or other appropriate body by gift, exchange or private sale before it is offered to the public at large. This gives some flexibility to the Trustees in order to enable them to dispose of items in appropriate circumstances, although strictly speaking it runs contrary to the object of preserving the collection. However, by defining the Trust Fund – that is the collections and all other assets held by the trustees – as a variable fund, some discretion can be afforded to the Trustees. Without this the specific authority of the Charity Commission would be required for any disposal.

Even this may have its weaknesses, however, in the event of the museum, whether an unincorporated charity or a charitable company, being wound up through insolvency, as one of the duties of the liquidator would be to meet the debts of the institution and the collections, unless specifically protected, may be liable to be disposed of in the same way as any other assets. This can be avoided by ensuring that the collections are held under a separate Declaration of Trust from the other assets of the institution and that the trustees have the power to loan the collections to the 'parent' institution. The loan arrangements must be set out in an agreement between the two bodies in order to regulate responsibilities for maintenance, conservation, insurance and inspection and to specify the events giving rise to termination of the loan through receivership or liquidation. Thus the parent institution can hold land, property and other assets and, provided that these are not held in pursuance of any charitable objectives, they are available for securing mortgages, debentures and other charges. In the case of, for example, a site museum or open-air museum where the land and buildings on it may form a part of the collections then these too would need to be held under the separate Declaration of Trust outlined above.

Charitable status, although without the necessity for a separate Declaration of Trust, is a prerequisite for independent museum membership of the area museums councils and for receipt of grant-in-aid funds from the Science Museum or Victoria and Albert Museum[5]. In the case of the Association of Independent Museums, the main category of membership is for museums which are controlled by or registered as charitable trusts or satisfy other acceptable tests of charitable status. Although the Association accepts non-charitable independent museums as category B members, it offers strong encouragement to them to gain charitable status.

In all but the smallest museums it is usually advantageous to be incorporated as a limited company, although whether or not the body is incorporated, the persons responsible for the administration and management of the charity will have the duties and liabilities of charity trustees. The main advantages of incorporation are that the company will have a legal entity separate from its members, may hold assets in its corporate name and enter into contracts in its own name. Liability of members is limited in the event of winding up to their guarantee sum which is usually £1. The overall structure of a company limited by guarantee is the same as that of a company limited by shares and it is a generally convenient way of allowing members to participate in a venture with ultimate responsibility whilst leaving day-to-day management in the hands of a board of directors. The disadvantages of incorporation are that registration and annual running costs are involved and that the terms of the *Companies Act 1985* must be complied with in respect, for example, of keeping annual returns and accounts.

The format of a company limited by guarantee not having a share capital and registered as a charitable trust has thus become the most popular for all but the smallest independent museums. In fact many of these companies have opted for charitable status for reasons other than the degree of protection that may be afforded to their collections. Charities have a number of fiscal privileges one of the most important being the almost complete exemption from income and corporation tax, provided the funds are applied for charitable purposes only and, usually more importantly, they may in appropriate circumstances reclaim tax against gifts from individuals and companies providing a binding agreement (a covenant) has been attached to that gift. There are important advantages too in relation to Capital Gains Tax and Capital Transfer Tax; charities are statutorily eligible for 50 per cent rate relief (the other 50 per cent is at the discretion of the Local Authority) and there are numerous other minor benefits. Where a charity's trading activities, as is often the case with a museum shop for example, cannot be classed as 'occasional fund-raising through trading' and would, therefore, be free of tax on the profits, the tax may be reduced by forming a special trading company, usually as a wholly owned share-capital subsidiary which covenants its profits back to the parent charity.

Most of the new independent museums find charitable company status an admirable framework for their management, fund-raising and trading activities. An independent museum constituted in this manner lies within the public domain to the extent that it must control its affairs in a responsible manner and that its activities are for the public good. The term 'private museum' is thus an inappropriate one. At the same time its independent status can prove attractive to a potential donor, trustee, or other participant in its affairs who can readily identify with its objectives and perhaps have some active involvement in its work. Indeed, a number of charitable company museums have set up parallel 'development trusts' not only as a convenient management framework within which to raise capital or other funds for the museum but as a mechanism for providing involvement in and identity with the affairs of the institution as a whole. Therefore the first process of a development trust is the enlistment of support which in due course may be translated into a continuing flow of donations usually and preferably in the form of covenanted gifts. One of the claimed responsibilities of development trusts is that they protect the interests of the donors by ensuring that their gifts are spent on the projects for which they were intended. It must be pointed out, however, that the development trust formula, which may or may not have advantages, represents only one point of view in the complex world of fund raising and any museum contemplating a major capital-raising programme is well advised to examine as many techniques as possible, and consult several professional fund-raising organizations and other museums before embarking on a particular course of action.

The charitable company museum structure can have a number of attractions to public bodies and what might be called a second generation of new independent museums have been set up by Local Authorities. The Black Country Museum, for example, has been detached from the departmental responsibilities of the Metropolitan District Council of Dudley and set up as a charitable company. Similarly, in 1978 Torfaen Borough Council in Gwent transferred its museum and heritage functions to the then newly incorporated Torfaen Museum Trust Limited,[6] including the existing Pontypool Museum Project. Again, the benefits to a public authority of quasi-independent status require careful analysis but they may be summarized as follows:

(1) The active participation and commitment of a broad spectrum of the local community in the running of the museum can be generated through the membership of the governing body. For example, whereas elected councillors normally form the sole membership of a Local Authority committee, in a charitable company museum Trustees can be drawn from academic, industrial, business or trade union circles.

(2) Fund raising in the private sector may be easier when the museum is seen not to be a department of a Local Authority.

(3) Where a partnership of several disparate authorities – for example, a District and County Council, university or learned society – needs some formal organization in order to participate together in the running of a museum, then the charitable company may be a convenient format for funding, management and employment of staff. (The trust formed in 1982 to administer the Manchester Museum of Science and Industry is an example of this.)

Whether or not there are operational advantages in a public authority placing its museum responsibilities in the hands of a 'quango' (Cossons, 1976) is, of course, open to debate and it may be many decades before a clear picture emerges. Whilst some would argue that the structure of Government or Local Government is inappropriate to run museums (the same argument applies to the performing arts) and that museums need their own governing bodies of highly committed people drawn from all walks of life, others would say that to separate museums from the seat of political power and source of funding will in the long term be disadvantageous. What is undoubtedly true, however, is that independent museums have blossomed in the last 20 years as a reflection of a wide variety of needs within society. They have emerged spontaneously, without prompting by any of the governmental or other agencies who would seek to regulate museums on a national

or regional basis, and they have by virtue of the nature of their product and market awareness had a significant impact on the public's interpretation of the word 'museum'. There is little doubt that the best can and indeed do achieve standards of scholarship and curatorship at least as good as those of more conventional museums; by the same token the not-so-good, as in the public sector, can fall far short of the desirable standard but in so doing are much more vulnerable to closure as a result of losing their markets. Trends for the future are difficult to detect, but radical rethinking of capital funding of independent museums will undoubtedly take place, with new relationships between trusts and their trading companies being devised so that loan capital can be more effectively injected. Similarly, the strong market orientation of independent museums will push them further in the direction of providing facilities for the family unit – as opposed to the individual member of a family – with increased opportunity for participation in the work of the museum. Membership may become the most important growth point for some of them, and it is by no means far-fetched to envisage a museum in which the largest single element of revenue income is made up from the annual subscriptions of its members with visitor admission charges forming a secondary source. Although those members may not be motivated by the same enthusiasms as their predecessors of two centuries ago, their will and ability to participate will be equally important. Above all, museums will stand or fall not only by their competence to care for collections but also by their ability to care for people.

Notes

[1] The best statistical survey for England is the *English Heritage Monitor*, published annually by the English Tourist Board, Thames Tower, Black's Road, London W6 9EL, UK.

[2] The Association of Independent Museums (AIM) was established in 1978 to represent the interests of independent museums in the United Kingdom and the Republic of Ireland. It publishes a quarterly bulletin and a series of Guidelines on topics particularly relevant to independent museums and holds seminars on aspects of museum management.

[3] The address of the Charity Commission is St Alban's House, 57–60 Haymarket, London SW1Y 4QX, UK.

[4] The Association of Independent Museums' Guideline No. 3, *Charitable Status for Museums* is available for England and Wales (with comments relating to the Isle of Man, the Channel Islands and Northern Ireland) and as a separate publication for Scotland. Advice on the Scottish position is also available from the Scottish Museums Council, County House, 20–22 Torphicen Street, Edinburgh EH3 8JB, UK.

[5] The inclusion of a museum on the Museums and Galleries Commission register is likely to be the future basis of eligibility for government grant aid. The address of the Museums & Galleries Commission is 16 Queen Anne's Gate, London SW1H 9AA.

[6] For those finding use of the term 'limited' distasteful in relation to a charitable company, there is provision, under the *Companies Act 1985,* for it to be omitted. It is necessary for a statutory declaration to be filed with the Registrar of Companies stating that the company is one operating in conformity with the provision of the Act.

References

ASSOCIATION OF INDEPENDENT MUSEUMS (1981), *Charitable Status for Museums*, Guideline No. 3, AIM, Edinburgh

ASSOCIATION OF INDEPENDENT MUSEUMS (1981), *Charitable Status for Museums in Scotland*, Guideline No. 3, AIM, Edinburgh

BOYLAN, P. J. (1982), 'Why museums?', *Transactions of the Leicester Literary & Philosophical Society,* **76**, 1–24

COSSONS, N. (1976), 'The case for the cultural quango', *Museums Association Conference Proceedings, 1976,* 26–27, Museums Association, London

LOWE, E. E. (1923), 'The society and the museum', *Transactions of the Leicester Literary & Philosophical Society,* **24**, 5–20

SHELL UK (1981), *Report on Shell Shareholders' Meeting,* 4–6, Shell UK, London

RIX, M. M. (1955), 'Industrial archaeology', *Amateur Historian,* **2**, 225–229

WALDEN, T. A. (1960), 'Address by the President', *Transactions of the Leicester Literary & Philosophical Society,* **54**, 5–13

12

Ethics of curatorship in the UK

Antony J. Duggan

The background

Certain aspects of economic and academic philosophy which prevailed in Europe, and particularly in England, during the nineteenth century seriously retarded the emergence of curatorship as an honourable profession. Only in comparatively recent times has a coherent view of acceptable standards of curatorial practice become discernible. Only lately have curators admitted to each other that they have a common, if not yet characteristic, approach to their public commitments. There are curators living today who can remember when the word 'museum' was in everyday use in the vocabulary of derogation and when the word 'curator' was avoided because it conjured up the image of a recluse whose work had little or no relevance to the daily lives of others in society.

There may seem to be some paradox in this because the nineteenth century saw the establishment of some of the greatest museums in the UK. Many of today's museums owe much to philanthropy for their foundations and they were often established to fulfil the need for education and cultural enlightenment. But greater forces were at work. The thrust of the industrial revolution made cost-effectiveness a moral obligation and the amassing of profit was seen as an indicator of lofty and upright principles. At the same time fundamental advances in the knowledge of nature sustained the view that science could provide an answer to almost every question, and that the questions which it could not answer were not worth asking.

Some of the consequences are reflected in the evolution of the Museums Association. The first President of the Association was a cleric, perhaps thereby bestowing some spiritual sanction on its establishment as befitted the exquisite contradictions of the Victorian age. But of the next 19 Presidents,

12 were Fellows of the Royal Society (one of Edinburgh), one was an Earl, four were knights and another was a Member of Parliament. No doubt they were all great men who did much for museums in such of their time as they could afford. But, with the exception of Sir Jonathan Hutchinson (1908), few, if any, would be classed as curators by the standards of today. Among their many titles they would have considered that of 'curator' to have been the least; they could not have foreseen that the day would come when the practice of curatorship would require a special set of rules and guidelines. The Museums Association existed for 84 years before the curators who belonged to it adopted a Code of Conduct for themselves. Even when this chapter was written for the previous edition of this book, no code of ethics had been adopted by the membership.

The wind of change outside the museum doors has blown hard since the foundation of the Museums Association. The economic philosophy of the last 100 years has been seen to generate avarice, and the absence of ethical constraint has threatened the integrity of great houses whose very names once made the world tremble. Scientists are now generally agreed that their disciplines solve only 'convergent' problems which exist in the abstract, and that there exist 'divergent' problems in the real world of human relationships which are not susceptible to scientific analysis. Down among those 'divergent' problems lie matters of professional ethics. The hitherto covert processes of high finance and frontier scientific research are firmly in the public gaze, and their long-established domination of affairs is open to challenge.

While much of this was taking place, curators, whose responsibilities to the public only they themselves were aware of, toiled unseen and unsung to preserve much of the nation's historic and cultural heritage. Their labours commanded little in the way of remuneration and social recognition. Curatorship was (and still is) labour intensive and not income generating *per se*, although it contributes indirectly to the production of wealth in other areas such as tourism and consultancy. Science, for all its pretensions, largely bypassed the problems of conservation which daily confronted them. It is a tribute to them that so much of what was in their charge has survived into the latter part of the twentieth century. At last a new age of universal communication has dawned and aroused public inquisitiveness as to what curators actually do.

Other chapters in this book describe the responses that curators are making to the challenges which these developments have evoked. At last, curators are seen to furnish a public service which is unique, and that to be able to provide that service they must undergo a rigorous post-graduate apprenticeship. They have won the title to a minimum reward from the public purse and, gradually, the title 'curator' is acquiring an enhanced image in society. Soon, if not now, a curator is to be seen as a person prepared in every sense to respond to public demand. And it is natural for the public to insist that the curatorial house itself be kept in order. If curators claim to be professionals they must not only be well organized, have a specialized training and a canon of required knowledge, but must also demonstrate their submission to a code of ethical conduct.

The breakthrough

In the UK the need for a code of curatorial conduct began to be discussed earnestly in the early 1970s. The impetus came from the Museum Professionals Group (MPG), an affiliated body of young curators which, unlike the parent Association, is wholly professional in its membership. The Group set up a Working Party whose report, 'Towards a Code of Conduct for the Museum Profession', was published in January 1974. The developments which then ensued have been described by Boylan (1977). By that time those parts of the paper concerned with the actions and responsibilities of governing bodies had been identified and were made the basis of the Association's *Code of Practice for Museum Authorities* which was adopted at the Association's conference in Bradford in July 1977.

It proved less easy to construct a curatorial code. Although by then the need for one was generally agreed, it was a different matter when it came to agreement on what it should contain. However, a committee chaired by Kenneth Barton succeeded in framing a set of ethical guidelines which was also adopted at the Bradford conference. This modest advance paved the way ahead.

Although the guidelines contained much that is derived from sound ethical principles, there remained a conviction that they needed to be stated with greater firmness and clarity in the form of rules to which guidelines should be appended. The MPG held a symposium in London in April 1981, the proceedings of which were later published as *MPG Transactions No. 16*, under the title 'Towards a Code of Ethics in Museums' (Museum Professionals Group, 1981). In response to this fresh stimulus the Council of the Museums Association set up a Working Party to devise a *Code of Conduct for Museum Curators* containing both rules and guidelines, as proposed by Graeme Cruickshank at the London symposium.

The Working Party took two years to produce a final draft of the Code which was adopted at the Association's Annual General Meeting at Swansea in 1983 under the presidency of Lord Montagu of Beaulieu. In April 1985, the Council of the Association set up a permanent Ethics Panel to supervise matters pertaining to the Code, with specific terms of reference. There was now not only a Code, but the machinery with which to put it into motion. After 95 years the Association had succeeded in laying a professional cornerstone for curators.

Later developments and problems

Museum organizations in many countries other than the UK have recognized the need to establish codes which regulate the professional behaviour of museum staff, including curators. Some of them are referred to in the valuable document prepared by Boylan (1985) for the International Council of Museums (ICOM), in which he collated material from the codes of the USA, Brazil, Australia, Canada, Israel, New Zealand and Southern Africa. Partly on the basis of his work, ICOM itself produced its own Code of Professional Ethics in 1987, which draws extensively from the codes of many countries including that of the Museums Association in the UK.

The ICOM Code has far-reaching terms of reference. It begins with a very broad definition of a museum, even embracing zoological gardens and planetaria. If that were not enough, its code is targeted at the whole class of 'museum professionals' who are defined as all the personnel of museums with special training or experience who respect a fundamental code of professional ethics. The Code also contains a section on institutional ethics which provides 'Basic Principles for Museum Governance'.

The ICOM Code, which was requested by its members and approved by its General Assembly, is museological and implies that a 'museum worker' who does not respect its code is not a professional. The more restricted Museums Association Code applies only to those whom it deems to be curators.

It was not designed to cover a variety of other museum personnel with special training or experience who have had no part to play in framing the rules and guidelines which comprise the code. The Association's Code is applied on the assumption that a museum is managed by a professional curator (not a zoologist or an astronomer), and that the curator's role in ethical matters is an exemplary one. The staff are simply expected to conduct themselves according to the standards which they observe in their curator.

The difficulty which arises in the UK is that not all museums are managed by curators who hold the Diploma of the Museums Association, so that its ethical jurisdiction is far from countrywide. Thus an expansion of its professional membership is a prerequisite for the wider adoption of the Code. A further complication is that not all curators who belong to the Association practice in museums; some work in other cultural institutions, some teach, and others take up independent consultantships. The fact that they are not employed in museums does not release them from their ethical obligations. As with other professions, once a curator, always a curator. After all these years, the Museums Association has conceded that curators do not necessarily have to be employed in certain types of architectural construction; they are free to practice wherever they wish.

After a Code of Ethics has been adopted, it is essential for a profession to provide the means whereby the Code can be constantly maintained and implemented. As described, the Council of the Museums Association, being aware of this, set up its Ethics Panel in 1985. The Panel consists entirely of curators. It is allowed more freedom of action than is given to ordinary committees of the Association, being able to report to the president at any time. Subject to Council's approval, the Panel chooses its own members. These arrangements ensure that members can act speedily and in complete confidence.

The Panel has a duty to see that the Code is kept up to date and capable of application to new ethical problems which were not hitherto defined. In 1987, after two years work, several amendments were introduced, including a new rule to take account of ethical conduct during industrial disputes. (The Panel, of course, simply proposes new matter; it has no power to alter the code. The proposals must be ratified by the council, discussed at the professionals' meeting during conference and, hopefully, but not automatically, adopted at the Association's annual general meeting.)

The provision of advice and guidance to curators on request is the main part of the Panel's work. But its role is by no means exclusively paternalistic. The rules embodied in the code are not negotiable. Cases which are reported to the president are those in which disciplinary action is contemplated.

At this point the problem of enforcement is encountered. Since the Code was constructed and adopted through a sequence of unanimous or consensus opinions taken by the Association's professional curators over a period of 15 years, it is to be expected that they understand the need for disciplinary powers to be granted to their council in cases of serious and persistent transgression of ethical rules. However, the council recognizes (and regrets) that many professional curators in the UK do not belong to the Association and proclaim their own singular virtues which may well exclude the interests of everyone but themselves.

So what is to be done? The answer lies in the outcome of a situation in which some curators have the advantage of being professionals in the full sense of the word while others do not. Voluntary submission to a self-imposed code of ethics is the mark of a true professional, and those who make it will win, because it will be seen to benefit not only themselves, but also the public.

In the shorter term, the Museums Association has another string to its bow. Its constitution is such that a significant degree of control is exercised over it by institutional councillors who are elected by their peers among museum-owning authorities. As already described, those authorities have their own Code of Practice within the Association. The curator who has no allegiance either to the Association or its code of ethics can find little comfort in knowing that all errant curatorial behaviour can be discussed in a council which includes elected representatives of employing authorities. Those authorities have always welcomed the principle of self-restraint by the curators whom they employ, and have given their full support along the stony road which has led to the Code of Conduct.

In 1987 it was proposed that the Code should be made applicable to all professionals who work in museums, including conservators, educationalists, archivists, designers and others, some of whom already have their own Codes of Practice. A preliminary survey showed that those groups, in their majorities, welcomed the proposal without constraint. It will be a matter of negotiating the wordings of rules, modifications to the Code and possibly appendices before a comprehensive Code can be submitted for general acceptance. When this comes about it will achieve through consultation much of the sweeping embrace embodied in the present ICOM code.

Events have shown that the claim of the now defunct working party has been vindicted '. . . a code of ethics was necessary, primarily in the interests of the society which they serve, and secondly to establish themselves as a specialised and reputable group of practitioners whose standards of work were open to judgement'.

Museum collections

Ethics of collecting

It is clearly understood by curators that the exercise of their service to their governing bodies and their public depends upon the acquisition, study and preservation of artefacts in an orderly and retrievable form. The first of these activities must be regulated by ethical principles, if the other two are to be carried out satisfactorily. The consequences of indiscriminate collecting are described elsewhere in this book (Chapter 14), and are wholly undesirable; it follows that curators must submit to the necessary restrictions by adhering to a scheme known as an acquisition policy which is devised by the governing body of their museum, not only with the curators' agreement, but often at their instigation. The policy is central to practical considerations such as finance, accommodation, equipment and the available expertise (*Figure 12.1*). As these resources inevitably change with time, the policy has to be up-dated, but never in such a way as to jeopardize the items already acquired. This matter is seen as so important that both the Museums Association and the ICOM Codes treat it as a dual responsibility to be shared by the curator and the employing authority. Indeed, the Museums Association's Code of Practice recommends that the policy 'should be reviewed . . . at least once every four years'.

The curator's ethical problems begin with the act of acquiring material for his museum or gallery. It hardly needs to be said that items should never be obtained from illegal sources, and the Guidelines include the consideration of items whose owners contravene the 1970 UNESCO Convention. This point is elaborated in the Association's Code of Conduct; ICOM, however, relates it to the employing authority, even with the exhortation to

return items to their country of origin if the authority is legally free to do so. The Convention has not been officially ratified in the UK, and from time to time debates arise in cases such as that of the Elgin Marbles which were brought into the country many years before UNESCO existed. The acquisition of objects from countries under past or present military occupation serves to complicate the issue further; ICOM recommends abstinence from any such involvement. Curators may be well advised to seek expert guidance when in doubt about such matters. They must retain a clear head and a clean conscience. Basically, any curator would merit reprimand for obtaining items from a source which later turned out to be unidentifiable, particularly if they were discovered to be spurious or came on the market by means of force or deception.

At no time in the history of curatorship has provenance been of more importance than it is today. A valuable set of guidelines prepared by the Geological Curators' Group (Brunton *et al.*, 1983) gives an 'acquisition flow chart' in algorithmic form which can be usefully applied, not only to geological collecting, but to that of other natural sciences. The authors state: 'It is vital that documentation relating to the transfer of title is clear-cut and unambiguous'. That is good advice and a sound ethical principle.

No items should be acquired by taking advantage of others, and this caveat applies to many kinds of circumstances, including the out-bidding of more deserving institutions at auctions and using persuasion to obtain material from members of the public who have no special knowledge of the worth or cultural value of what they offer. The acquisition of objects from minors would be seen as unethical unless the matter is negotiated with the concurrence of the donor's parent or legal guardian.

The curator must not acquire material at the cost

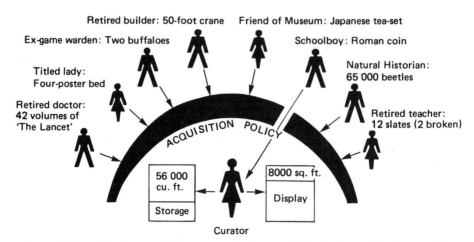

Figure 12.1 An acquisition policy is an essential instrument for the control of collections and the best use of resources

of depriving the locality of part of its heritage. This can come about in subtle ways such as the spoiling of an ecological niche by the removal of a critical plant or animal, or by the purchase of a single item from a collection, thus separating the item from its historic or scientific context.

The acquisition of objects by collecting in the field may lead to ethical problems. Questions of access to natural collecting areas in the ambience of other curators working in different disciplines under other governing bodies must be negotiated with professional diplomacy. The case illustrated in *Figure 12.2* illustrates an ethical problem in conservation rights. Fortunately, in this case a written understanding on the collecting procedure already existed between the parties concerned, permitting a straightforward solution to be found. Otherwise, a protracted investigation would have been unavoidable.

The Museums Association's Code of Conduct defines the obligations of a curator in respect of objects acquired, not only by him, but by his predecessors. Nowadays there is little excuse for allowing the forces of attrition to work unchecked on museum material. Neglect of such material and failure to grasp the opportunities that are available for its preservation must be regarded as unethical conduct by default. Losses have been incurred through the alternation of specialists from one generation of curators to another in museums whose collections are multidisciplinary. The resolution, for example, of archaeologists to put aside the natural history material accumulated by their predecessors must not prevail in such a way that previously acquired objects deteriorate or lose their value.

Difficult ethical matters arise in connection with the disposal of museum collections. There should always be a strong presumption against such disposal. In most cases the ultimate decision lies with the employing authority, and for that reason the Association's Code of Practice devotes a whole section to the subject. Nevertheless, curators are ethically bound to make their views known to the authority before a final decision is taken.

Since the first edition of this Manual appeared, the sale of items from museum collections has become a matter of widespread debate. In some quarters museums are expected to be self-financing, or at least partially so. Some of the arguments in favour of disposal appear to be logically irresistible. For example, if a painting in the basement store is threatened by flooding, the painting should be sold and the money thus raised should be used to repair the drainage system. Curators must consider this kind of logic with great care. It may be the case that when the painting was acquired by one of their percipient predecessors its value was less than that of the drains. Today's market forces have upset that equation. Should that upset demand a reappraisal of the painting's worth in terms only of the nation's heritage? To what end does such logic lead – a museum of structural integrity which has surrendered the most important items in its collections?

It would be fair to say that the state of museums in the future depends on finding the right answers to these theoretical questions. I believe that a museum which is dedicated to the raising of money takes flight from its origins and rejects its fundamental purpose. This may be an impossible precept for practising curators to follow in all respects, but they should remember that, apart from the ethical principles involved, they might eventually need guidance from those whose expertise lies in the creation of wealth. Such guidance may easily develop into domination.

Ethics of research

One reason for collecting like material is to enable curators or their staff or qualified members of the public to use it for research purposes. This apparently simple objective is heavily overlaid by problems of space, conservation and management. In large museums the situation is clear because staff of high academic standing undertake research into the collections as their chief professional task, and are expected to contribute publications of a high order to

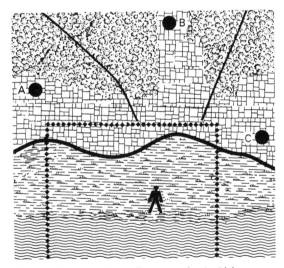

Figure 12.2 An amateur collector searches in tidal mud-flats between an embankment (thick line) and a river. He is licensed by an authority (within broken line) which controls the waterfront, but does not possess a museum. Curators of museums at A, B and C are involved with the acquisition and conservation of the finds. An agreement with all the parties concerned is essential to avoid the creation of ethical problems.

the artistic, historical or scientific literature. In such cases few ethical problems arise, but in many museums the time spent on research has to be balanced against the demands of other spheres of curatorial activity. It is unethical to pursue research at the cost of the deterioration of collections in which the researcher has no interest.

One of the most difficult aspects of this problem is to define at what point a research project ceases to be relevant to the museum's cultural and educational objectives. Serious questions are sometimes posed as to whether museum-based research is worthwhile at all, being as it is, mostly of a demonstrative rather than an experimental nature. As to whether the research is relevant or worthwhile depends, as for most research, on the motivation and ability of the research worker himself. Curatorial managers of museums sometimes find it difficult to control a research project after it has been authorized, because the nature of the programme is often open-ended, and the most important results may be derived from the most unexpected and apparently irrelevant departures. Thus the ethical problem is real, although not easy to define. A sound guideline is to examine carefully the effects of continuous research preoccupation on the museum's aims and other activities, and to decide accordingly.

Another ethical problem arises when curatorial staff withdraw material from circulation during the course of a research programme. The question may have to be answered of whether that material should be made available on request to research workers outside the museum. It is clearly unethical for a curators to impede the legitimate research of others during the course of their own investigations. Such conduct is particularly invidious when 'type' specimens are involved. It is a privilege in itself to hold the custody of such items which are deposited in museums for the purposes of verification by scholars for the rest of foreseeable time. In the natural sciences the curator is subject to rules which apply to 'type' collections of different kinds. Although such rules have not been formulated in the sphere of the arts, the ethical constraint on the curator to make original work available for study applies with the same force.

The Code of Conduct recommends that a curator whose research interests conflict with those of others (and this is likely to happen because research topics are apt to follow the caprice of fashion) should seek to join forces with them in the course of the research and its eventual publication. The sharing of space and equipment would follow as a corollary of such an arrangement, to everyone's advantage.

Ethics of publication

Difficulties may arise when curators advance on the matter of private publication. It can be argued that much of the scholarship put into works on which royalties are collected is derived from the experience gained in the service of an employer. Hence curators owe reimbursement to their employers for the professional opportunities which made their publication possible. However, the nub of the problem depends on the time and place in which the work of private publication occurs. Although the physical fact of their employment is regulated by their terms of service, their literary activities are at their disposal outside working hours. Hence authors take the view that curators may, without ethical offence, publish privately work that they undertake in their own time.

However, paragraph 71 of the National Joint Council for Local Authorities' Purple Book makes it clear that above the service grade of AP5 the curator of a Local Authority museum is the servant of that authority for 24 hours each day. When that undertaking applies it is urged that curators will obtain the consent of their employers before proceeding with private publication on the basis of their professional experience. Indeed, it would be a wise precaution for members of a museum's staff who are considering private publication of their work to inquire, first of all, into the Authority's policy regarding such matters.

Similar considerations apply to curators whose conditions are regulated by the conditions of service in national museums.

Ethics of private collecting and dealing

One of the most difficult and contentious ethical issues hinges on the right of curators to collect museum objects for themselves. The views of curators of great experience are polarized on ttheir issue. Some maintain that personal collecting is to be commended because it demonstrates curators' dedication to their discipline and their readiness to further their learning outside working hours. Others see great temptation in private collecting, particularly when curators' collections are of the same nature as that which they curate for the museum authority which employs them. By way of compromise, the Code of Conduct of the Museums Association insists that, when curators collect for themselves, they must agree with their governing body the terms under which they may do so, and the governing body must be kept informed of any changes which might alter that understanding.

In some countries private collecting by curators is proscribed. The Regulations of Israel, for example, simply state, 'A museum employee shall not collect objects in the field of interest of the department in which he is employed, except for their department'. It is doubtful whether such a prohibitive rule would find acceptance in the UK at the time of writing. At the same time, the author believes that the matter is of such importance that the personal judgements of individual curators must not be allowed to go uncontradicted. In cases where the reputation of the profession is at stake, a remedy must be available to it.

The Museums Association's Code of Conduct makes it clear that dealing by curators is an unacceptable practice. The ICOM statute declares 'In no circumstance shall . . . membership be accorded to anyone who, for reasons of commercial profit, buys or sells cultural property'. I believe that such a statement is more authoritarian than practical. Ostracism, although helpful in maintaining ICOM's unimpeachable image, is hardly likely to prevent such a widespread practice, and the very curators who are culpable are probably not members of ICOM anyway.

To define a 'collection' which is in private hands is no easy matter. It is hardly surprising to find that the homes of curators, and particularly of art curators, are furnished with items that are in good aesthetic taste and reflect the owner's knowledge and discernment. Moreover, when one item is replaced by another the prevailing market forces are likely to operate in the curator's interests, particularly if the

item is antique. Since the objective is merely to maintain a comfortable and appropriate home, such could hardly be called 'dealing' in the ethical sense. One set of Queen Anne furniture in a house shows excellent discrimination. Four sets would justify an inquiry by the Ethics Panel because the curator's motivation would be open to question.

Instances are known of the sale of cultural and scientific museum material by curators to the governing bodies of museums outside their own. Such sales demand full exposure and investigation from the ethical standpoint. The Museums Association, with its two Codes, is well placed for such work. The ethical problems which stem from artistic freedom are multiple and complex. Curators may also be artists. May they hold an exhibition of their work in the gallery of which they are in charge? May they use that gallery as a means of selling their creations? A museum is neither a platform for self-advertisement nor a market. Even if the curator were selling for charity, a collision with ethical principles could hardly be avoided.

Private collecting by curators is at best an equivocal activity; at worst it leads to dealing and a conflict of interests between curator, museum authority and the public. It is best renounced.

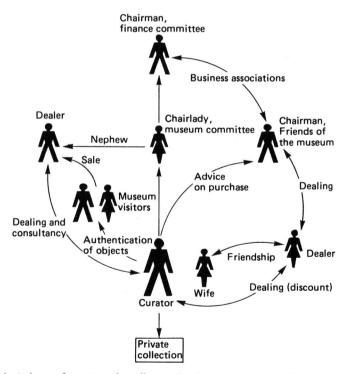

Figure 12.3 Hypothetical case of a curator who collects and authenticates privately. Such practices are 'vulnerable to abuse'. (*Code of Practice*, Part 4, Guideline 4.4)

Ethics of expertise

It is to be expected that after a time curators will become known for their understanding of the identity of objects which come into the orbit of their museum practice. Matters pertaining to identification, authentication and valuation in respect of the public at large are dealt with later. When these activities are pursued privately for personal gain, however, they bring the curator from the safety of the temple to the hazards of the marketplace. The type of situation which may arise is shown in Figure 12.3 in which curators are seen to be a link in a chain which involves profit-making at the expense of their own museum. The fact that they do not directly participate in the making of those profits does little to modify the ambiguity of their position.

When curators are asked to act as outside consultants, the terms proposed are often attractive, and their services may reflect well on the museums in which they work. Yet it cannot be denied that a consultancies may involve curators in lawsuits, the outcome of which may not turn out to be a source of congratulation, either to them or their institution. When consultancies are accepted, curators must inform their employing authority. Not to do so would be ethically unsound; the consequences of their valuation, for example, might at a later date compromise the purchasing power of their governing body, to whom they owe their first allegiance.

Scrupulous care must be taken, particularly in the sphere of art, to see that consultancy fees are on no account confused with commission on the sales which result from the consultants' advice, and if the consultants' appraisal of the matter is related to their museum it is strongly advisable for them to reject the consultancy. Figure 12.4 shows an example which, after Court action, was to the detriment of the curator's career.

Museum services

Ethics and the public

Curators must conduct their professional business with the public in a spirit of courtesy and fairness. They should regard the information which the public impart to them as confidential. Disclosure could set at risk valuable objects in private possession or material of importance to the national heritage located in the countryside. Sensitive information held on files or in computer systems is to some extent protected by law, but the harmful diffusion of information about people and their possessions can be stopped just as effectively by strictly observing the ethical principle of confidentiality. Curators

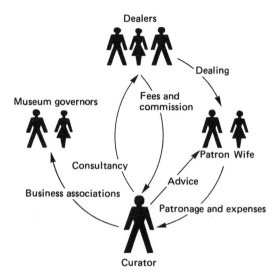

Figure 12.4 A difficult ethical position arising from the practice of consultantship by a curator (based on a published case)

should regard a leak of information, either from their files or their computer, as seriously as they would the theft of a specimen in their custody.

Curators are often asked by the public to identify objects which are brought to their museum. Providing that their knowledge is adequate for the task, there is no reason why they should not do so. Authentication should be avoided and valuations should never be made; untold trouble may otherwise lie in store. If the enquirer asks for the name of an expert who would supply the information requested, the curator should give not one but several names.

Curators have an ethical responsibility to the public in presenting displays which should be balanced and never deliberately mislead. Every care must be taken to avoid giving offence, particularly in regard to objects associated with religious beliefs and ceremonies, and human remains. The latter should always be depicted in a thematic context and never in isolation. Otherwise the display may be seen as an attempt to excite morbid curiosity. Rule 6.7 of the ICOM code deals admirably with ttheir matter.

The public reaction to art forms varies from one community to another and from one period of time to another. Even the most impeccable academic and cultural reasons for their exhibition may be insufficient justification for the expenditure of money on items which the public neither understand nor appreciate. It is true that pictures and sculptures in museums and galleries influence public taste and help it to develop in a wholesome direction. But curators should not allow their personal artistic satisfaction to be the only consideration which determines that direction.

The management of museum shops involves ethical considerations. The articles on sale and the nature of their promotion should always be in good taste and consistent with the museum's academic standpoint. Rare objects and limited editions should not be offered for sale, and the merchandise should never be of a kind which could be interpreted as the wherewithal of a genuine antique dealer. The periodical sales which are held by charitable organizations in support of a museum's funds should not be held on the museum's premises, and neither should the curatorial staff be involved in the process of trading. There is no ethical objection to such sales, some of which may be essential to the museum's economy. But the public must never be misled into the belief, no matter how erroneous, that the museum is selling off part of its collections.

Ethics and commerce

Curators must continuously conduct negotiations with suppliers of goods, auctioneers, dealers and others in the world of financial transaction. All such negotiations must be carried out with complete integrity. Curators must not accept inducements to trade or place themselves in a position of obligation to one party rather than another. All codes insist that they should not accept gifts from those with whom they do business. But ttheir is a matter of degree and intention; there is a difference between a pint of beer on signing an agreement and a crate of champagne

delivered to the curator's house the next morning. It is not asked that one should be churlish in obeying a code of ethics. There is always room for common sense. However, I believe that as in other spheres of human relationships, there is no such thing as a free lunch, and that the price tag is not necessarily of a monetary kind.

The sponsorship of museum activities by commercial institutions can create problems. Curators may find themselves under subtle pressure to orientate an exhibition with partiality to the interests of the sponsoring company. Although full acknowledgment of assistance from commercial sources must always be made, ttheir should never be done in such a way as to suggest that the museum is being used as a vehicle of promotion. In the kind of situation illustrated in Figure 12.5, the curator must ensure that the information displayed is impartial and factually correct. The illustration indicates that the media may also be involved. In my view, generally speaking the accuracy of their theirtorical perspective lasts for little more than a fortnight. The curator might be regarded, rightly or wrongly, as accountable for a subsequent distortion of the facts.

The ethical aspects of sponsorship are complex, and sometimes it is far from clear as to which party is sponsoring the other. To provide a gallery in a museum in which an auctioneer can display antiques which will come under the hammer in another place, simply to invite an increase in the museum's attendances (and, hopefully, its revenue as well) is a practice which cannot be ethically justified. Among other reasons, it will raise the bidding price of the artefacts and possibly put them beyond the purchasing powers of other museums.

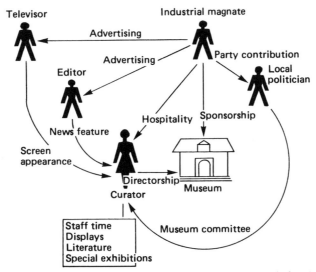

Figure 12.5 Sponsorship may give rise to ethical problems of publicity and advertising

The concern of many professional curators who find themselves involved with sponsors and their so-called 'surgeries' indicates that a Rule and Guideline for the Code is needed specifically to cover the problems that are being encountered.

Ethics and relationships with colleagues

Until a generation or so ago, curatorship was a lonely way of life, and there was little opportunity for curators to discuss professional matters with colleagues outside their own museum. Indeed, curators were given little encouragement to do otherwise. The expense of travel was beyond the means of all but those of senior rank and, in other ways too, communication was far from easy. Matters have changed completely in the last 20 years and it is now unusual for a week to pass without conducting professional affairs with a colleague beyond the museum doors. Such contacts are taken for granted by young curators of today and are eased by the modern informal mode of address. (However, the old-fashioned 'sir' and 'madam' still have their uses.)

It goes without saying that curators must treat their colleagues with deference and courtesy, but experience makes it necessary to emphasize that ttheir is of particular importance in the case of senior curators giving instructions to their staff.

When a dispute arises, care should be taken to avoid bringing it to public notice in such a way as to discredit either of the persons concerned. In particular, the matter should not be conducted so as to place a third party, such as a benefactor, in an invidious position.

Curators should be careful not to use their museum for self-advertisement, and ttheir is of special importance when dealing with newspaper reporters and television interviewers. Although it is impossible to divorce their office and their personality from their institution, they should never allow the media to provide them with an advantage over their colleagues.

Non-professionals, including volunteers, play indispensable roles in many museums, large and small, and their contributions should never go unacknowledged. However, curators should satisfy themselves of the integrity of part-time workers and ensure that they are not permitted to undertake tasks which would normally require the skills of a trained curator on the permanent staff. Similar considerations apply to curatorial trainees.

A curator must ensure that all activities are consistent with the Museums Association's *Code of Practice for Museum Authorities*. They must familiarize themselves with the procedures that operate within their governing body and clearly understand the powers and responsibilities which are delegated to them.

Practical problems

The Museums Association has nearly a decade of experience of ethical problems, and ttheir has enabled me to describe some difficulties encountered when putting the Code into use. Few problems are as clear-cut as theory would have us believe; many are overlaid by matters which must be set aside before the ethical content is revealed. Even then, some decisions have to be made by choosing 'the lesser of two evils'.

The Code emphasizes maintaining professional harmony between curators. In the event of curators finding that a colleague is in breach of the Code, what should they do? If they report the matter, do they break their own commitment to professional confidentiality and lay themselves open to a charge of rancour? Curators may agonize over such a dilemma, and before the Association set up its procedures there was no certain path for them to follow. There is now little reason why tteir ethical paradox should deter them from seeking advice from the Ethics Panel and coming to a decision.

Even mundane questions pose contradictions. A unique and fully documented collection of birds' eggs dating from the nineteenth century is put on the market and the curator is given first refusal. The money is available, but should the purchase be made for the museum? Should that once-in-a-lifetime curatorial opportunity to avoid setting a dangerous example to the public be rejected? Or can the public be persuaded to understand that the birds' eggs are, in effect, a scientific fossil collection, never to be repeated? It cannot be stressed too often that curators must realize the effect of what they do on those who look to them to protect the natural heritage, and that it is not only the truth of what prevails, but the public's perception of it, that must be considered. (Again, in terms of another ethical principle, should curators take up the offer themselves, to swell their private collections? Should they own such a private collection?)

Curators are under great pressure to increase the numbers of visitors to museums. (In my view this is an arbitrary and capricious yardstick by which to measure the worth of a museum, but it is not for debate in this chapter.) With the willing co-operation of local antique dealers a forum is set up in the museum where they will identify and comment on objects brought to them by the public *at no fee*. (The overtones of sponsorship emanate again, although that is not the point here.) It is an ingenious arrangement, and the public will attend in numbers. But they will not come simply to be told that their chairs are Chippendales – they will want to know their monetary value. The Code proscribes curators from giving valuations, and it is in their interests that valuations shall not be given either by them or their staff or by anyone else in the museum which they control. Is there a compromise solution, or must an otherwise exciting public-relations exercise come to nothing?

A curator in charge of a museum (or, in the case of a large museum, a keeper of a department) has authority to lend items to other museums and educational and cultural institutions. This is a time-honoured and valued practice and, although it is an operation which presents difficulties and demands safeguards, it is one within the competence of every professional curator. When a curator is requested to provide this facility to a commercial sponsoring body, the ethical problems multiply at once. The curatorial machinery would make it simple to provide *objets d'art*, ephemera, scientific instruments and the like to decorate boardrooms and reception areas for aesthetic and conversational purposes. But at what risk would the objects lie? Was that the purpose for which the objects were donated or purchased by public subscription? Who would have free access to view those objects? Would they be withdrawn from the sphere of legitimate research workers? Unless the Museums Association is to be set the impossible task of devising a code for sponsoring organizations, only individual curators can answer those questions, if necessary with ethical advice.

The reader may observe that I have not provided answers to these problems. In the context of this chapter they simply illusrate that the answers can be discovered only by a panel of experienced curators after the examination of circumstantial detail in each individual case. The reader may find some diversion in attempting to solve the problems single-handed and to express each of the answers in a few sentences.

Legal aspects

All curators are bound by the law and should be thoroughly acquainted with the legislation that governs their professional activities. This includes subsidiary legislation such as Acts relating to malicious damage, copyright, firearms, data protection and safety at work.

Numerous legal obligations are placed on curators by virtue of their employment, and these include Acts relating to contractual obligations on both employer and employee. The so-called 'Purple Book' ('Blue Book' in Scotland) lays down the conditions of service relating to county (region in Scotland) and district councils. This book also includes important guidelines to an employee's rights and restrictions in various fields, including the assurance that he may distance himself from the political activity of his governing body.

Conclusion

Students who wishes to acquaint themselves further with this difficult subject are referred to the References and Bibliography given at the end of this chapter. They should realize, however, that the most detailed of codes can never supply clear-cut answers to every problem. No amount of reading can make them an ethical curator. The summing-up by David Clarke said it all: 'No code can be a substitute for the highest personal standards of integrity and dedication'. To which I can only reply 'So be it'.'

Notes

A copy of the *Code of Conduct for Museum Curators* as adopted by the Museums Association in 1983 and amended in 1987 is included as an Appendix to this book. This chapter seeks to outline the historical reasons for the Code, and to describe its development and its mode of operation. In writing this chapter I have expressed opinions and given examples of ethical problems, and have indicated courses of action which, in my view, are sound. On no account should this chapter be interpreted as over-riding the Code or as being a substitute for it, or as an alternative interpretation of the commitments which it implies.

References

BOYLAN, P. J. (1977), 'Museum ethics: Museum Association policies, *Museums Journal*, **77**(3), 106–111

BOYLAN, P. J. (1985), *First Working Draft*, ICOM Subcommittee on Museum Ethics, ICOM, Paris

BRUNTON, C. G. C., BESTERMAN, T. P. AND COOPER, J. A. (Eds) (1983), *Guidelines for the Curation of Geological Materials. Geological Society, Miscellaneous Paper No. 17*, vii, 14, Geological Society, London

INTERNATIONAL COUNCIL OF MUSEUMS (1987), *ICOM Statutes, Code of Professional Ethics*, ICOM, Paris

MUSEUM PROFESSIONALS GROUP (1981), 'Towards a code of ethics in museums', *Museum Professionals Transactions*, **16**, Museum Professionals Group, London

Bibliography

AMERICAN ASSOCIATION OF MUSEUMS (1978), *Museum Ethics*, American Association of Museums, New York

AMERICAN ASSOCIATION OF MUSEUMS (1980), 'A code of ethics for conservators', *Museum News*, **58**(4), 27–34

ART GALLERY AND MUSEUM ASSOCIATION OF NEW ZEALAND (1978), 'Art gallery and museum officers' code of ethics', *AGMANZ News*, **9**(3)

BARSOOK, B. (1982), 'A code of ethics for museum stores', *Museum News*, **60**(3), 50–52

BOSTICK, W. A. (1974), 'The ethics of museum organization', *Museum*, **26**(1), 26–33

BOYLAN, P. J. (1976), 'The ethics of acquisition: the Leicestershire code', *Museums Journal*, **75**(4), 169–170

CANADIAN MUSEUMS ASSOCIATION (1979), *A Guide to Museum Positions including a Statement on the Ethical Behaviour of Museum Professionals*, CMA, Ottawa

COOKE, G. R. (1982), 'Should curators collect? Some considerations for a code of ethics', *Curator,* **25**(3), 161–172

DOUGLAS, R. A. (1967), 'Museum ethics: practice and policy', *Museum News,* **45**(5), 18–21

GREEN, E. L. (Ed.) (1984), *Ethics and Values in Archaeology,* MacMillan, London

LESTER, J. (1983), 'A code of ethics for curators', *Museum News,* **61**(3), 36–40

MERRYMAN, J. H. and ELSEN, A. E. (1987), *Law, Ethics and the Visual Arts,* 2nd edition, 2 Vols, xxiv + 756, University of Pennsylvania Press, Philadelphia

MUSEUMS ASSOCIATION OF AUSTRALIA INCORPORATED (1982), *Museum Ethics and Practice* (Interim document), 22, MAAI, Melbourne, Australia

ROSE, C. (1985), 'A code of ethics for registrars', *Museum News,* **63**(3)

ROYAL ONTARIO MUSEUM (1981), *Statement of Principles and Policies on Ethics and Conduct,* 102, Royal Ontario Museum, Ontario

SOUTHERN AFRICAN MUSEUMS ASSOCIATION (1979), *Code of Ethics of the Southern African Museums Association,* SAMA, Capetown

ULLBERG, P. (1979), 'Naked in the garden: museum practices after "Museum Ethics"', *Museum News,* **57**(6), 33–36

ULLBERG, P. (1981), 'What happened in Greenville: the need for museum codes of ethics', *Museum News,* **60**(2), 26–29

SECTION TWO

MANAGEMENT AND ADMINISTRATION

Section Editor

John Thompson

13

The role of the director

John Thompson

Introduction

Alone amongst the many cultural organizations in the modern world museums challenge a clear definition. The reasons lie in the diversity of museums from monolithic, multi-subject institutions to small museums associated with specific sites or subjects. There is some agreement that museums are essentially educational in nature and purpose, and that the services they provide are usually based on the collections and associated documentation.

At one end of the spectrum the museum will meet the needs of researchers and scholars whose projects require access to the collections and the records associated with them. At the other end, the museum will display selections for the general visitor supported by information to describe the exhibits and place them in context. Policies relating to public access to collections depend on the perceived purpose of the museum by its staff and governing body, and it is not uncommon for differing views to co-exist within large institutions with policies by heads of departments with responsibility for the collections. At the same time, other aspects of access such as decisions relating to charging, hours of opening, loan exhibitions and services for different user groups vary, partly through financial constraints but more through the established policy of the museums and its governing body. This implies that the views about the purposes of museums also, differ depending on factors such as the nature of the collections, the history and traditions of the institutions, the needs of the population served and the concerns and views of the governing body. The latter may be tempered in the case of local authority services, the backbone of the museums service in the British Isles, by overall policies relating to education, leisure, recreation, tourism or economic regeneration or any combination of these.

The present definition of museums seeks to identify the common characteristics of museums with the professional and institutional codes providing guidelines on important matters relating to the acquisition and disposal of collections and associated ethical issues, but is inadequate as a definition of required standards of service provision. The recently introduced Registration Scheme for museums in the UK and the British Isles marks an important stage in defining basic standards for museums, but hardly addresses the question of resources and structures appropriate to the various types and sizes of museums. Initiatives taken by the specialist groups of curators, such as the recently published report on biological collections, are more important in helping museums to define the level of resources required to manage collections of varying size and importance and the services that should be properly based on them for the benefit of the user groups. In the short-term, and until similar surveys can be undertaken within other subject areas such as the applied arts or science and technology, a balanced view of the needs of the multi-subject museums will be difficult, if not impossible, to arrive at and judgments will need to be made taking into account the demands on the collections, both from the general public and the specialist, as well as the conditions of the collections and the state of their documentation. All of this points to the lack of an assessment related to the resources of staffing and revenue and capital funding for core services of museums as well as what these are. For some the core service relates exclusively to the collections and their requirements in terms of storage, display, conservation and documentation. For others the core service would include educational provision at a basic level as well as information and interpretative services. Much will depend on the perception of the staff and governing body of the purpose of the museum and its relationship with the museum users.

In addition to these internal factors relating to the purposes of museums and their perceived responsibilities to the public, there are new external factors which, to a large degree, directly impinge on the way museum services are presented and which exercise an influence on the direction of museums. The first of these relates to the funding policies of Government and the way resources are allocated. In general, block allocations to museums have, either directly or indirectly, been replaced by targeted allocations related to particular requirements such as the conservation of collections or marketing projects. Whilst provision for existing services has remained at a similar level in recent years (and reduced in real terms), funds are available for new services on a challenge basis and usually over a limited time period. In this way, the museums are required to raise matching funds from their own resources, which implies raising income through charges and other means, the basic premise being that a limited amount of public finance applied to a new project shall be used as an incentive to attract private funding either through donors, charities or corporate organizations. In this way, Government can fulfil its own policy objectives of reducing the cost to the public in general and replacing it by a form of private patronage. As a result, the museum must direct an increasing proportion of its resources into attracting and securing corporate donations, charitable giving and company sponsorship. The result is often that the most prestigious museums attract the largest sums which, in turn, tend to be applied to projects which best meet the donor's or sponsor's interests rather than the priorities of the museum.

The foregoing briefly describes some of the internal and external factors which impinge on the provision and development of museum services in the modern age. The combination of these factors has created a complex environment in which the Director of a museum must operate and construct strategies to enable services to continue to meet public needs and expectations.

The role of the Director

The role of the Director in the modern period is probably the least well-defined role in the museum, carrying executive responsibility for the whole range of museum services as well as its public profile and answerable only to the appointed or elected governing body whether this comprises Trustee or Committee members. At the same time, the work carried out by the Director in securing essential resources for the museum is rarely specified in job descriptions even when implied in more general

terms. The traditional preparation of the Director as scholar and administrator is hardly adequate to meet the tasks arising from the general expansion and broadening of the museum's role in society and the increasing professionalism of curatorship and how this is applied to the whole spectrum of museum services. This needs to be coupled with new skills, techniques and, above all, attitudes required to lead museums in an increasingly uncertain and at the same time competitive climate. An examination of the work carried out by Directors would suggest not only a wide experience in curatorship with a grounding in a subject relevant to the museum, but also highly developed skills in administration, management, finance, personnel management, public relations and marketing, to which would be added the less definable qualities of leadership and decisiveness in managing an institution composed of many separate and semi-autonomous sections, departments and services each with their own developed sense of purpose, not necessarily consistent with the overall requirements of the institution.

Belatedly, there is a recognition by Directors that their roles each share a combination of duties and responsibilities which sets them apart from other staff in the museum who are, in general, more closely identified with the collections and the services based on them. In the same way that specialist staff in the museums have combined into groups active locally, nationally and internationally, Directors through organizations like Group of Directors of Museums in the British Isles (GODS) recognize a need to exchange information and prepare policy papers in order to establish agreements over best practice with governing bodies and funding agencies and within the working structure of the museum. The specialist sections within museums whether biologist, art historian or designer have assembled considerable data about their own operation and how their interests can be protected and fostered. Directors in general have been slower to respond, partly because they have identified with certain specialist groups representing their own subject interest and partly because the lack of definition implicit in the Director's post, which requires that the Director takes whatever steps are required to determine the direction of the museum and to ensure the continuity of services to the public, thereby suggesting that each museum faces a unique range of challenges with little in common with other institutions except perhaps in the need for resources. This ignores and dismisses the critical fact that the Director alone with the governing body represents the totality of the museum operation, for it is the services in combination rather than separately which sets the museum apart from other educational services such as universities, where separateness of departments is fully accepted and desirable. Essentially the museum is demonstrating the totality of the artistic and historical experience or of scientific and natural phenomena where the value lies in a multi-disciplinary approach towards the presentation of collections and the educational and interpretative services based on them.

The mission statement, aims and objectives

Given that the terms of reference for the Director embrace the entirety of the museums operation, the management of collections, the maintenance of public services based on them and responsibilities for the personnel employed, it is the primary task of the Director to define or redefine the purpose of the museum and to clarify the aims and objectives later to be expressed in tangible forms in programmes and actions. This requires an exhaustive examination of how the museum operates and the assumptions that have grown up by staff and the public and whether or not these have contemporary validity. A full assessment should be made of the services provided by the museum, its strengths as well as its shortcomings and taking into account any previous reports and the views of the users of the museum, staff and governing bodies alike. This can then be distilled into the 'mission' statement.

A clear and unambiguous statement of aims and objectives is a necessary prerequisite for preparing the programmes which will make up the corporate plan. The Statement will cover the work of the institution in its entirety but will not simply be a list of the main functions which would then be no different from museums sharing similar characteristics, rather it should reflect the unique situation of the museum within a particular environment likely to have an inherited tradition which may imply both constraints and opportunities for development. Most would accept the important premise that museums are provided in the public interest and as a service and this may then be stated at the outset. All too frequently statements are prepared which are almost exclusively based on the development of the collections or the organization of exhibitions as though the museum existed for this purpose rather than in meeting public needs, whereby the museum strives to become an important agent of communication and understanding of the natural and cultural worlds.

Policy formulation

It will be the task of the Director to formulate the policy of the museum with the governing body and to ensure that the policy is understood by all concerned, especially the staff. Following this, to organize the resources in programmes to meet the objectives of the policy over an agreed time-scale, and to monitor the effectiveness of the programmes in meeting the objectives and to consider any adjustments and changes required. This process leads to the policy review to be undertaken on an annual basis, or at other agreed intervals.

In order to formulate policy, an initial period of detailed research and investigation is required. This may involve discussions with staff and users, the latter expressed through visitor surveys of various kinds together with the views of client and user groups. An assessment would also be made of the constraints on the museum together with any inherited requirements and a record of past performance. The policy plan itself would need to have a very clear time perspective, either short, medium or long-term and would take into account the constraints likely to apply including the financial ones. The policy would be based on the aims and objectives of the service which may have evolved over many years in the case of established museums. The agreed policy then enables resources and ideas to be channelled purposefully and avoids the emergence of several conflicting courses of action which can divert an organization from the main task. To reach a policy objective might require sacrificing other programmes to save scarce resources.

Once the policies have been determined with the governing body, it is the task of the Director to ensure that these are communicated to all those concerned, with explanations where necessary and accepted. Organizations fail when there is insufficient commitment by staff of an organization to the policies that have been agreed. Good communication as a way of understanding is, therefore, a fundamental requirement of the museum. Hierarchies of staff can sometimes result in a modification or a distortion of policy. Unless the Director can sample opinion at various levels in the hierarchy, there is the risk that the message could become distorted. Minutes and notes of meetings are useful, as are broadsheets for staff. The outcome will be more effective if staff have been involved in the planning process and can, therefore, see the results of their own contribution to policy, even though the final outcome may differ from their own convictions. Through whatever means chosen, there needs to be general acceptance of the policy which will in turn be expressed in tangible form through the annual budget, and the work programmes defined for every section of the service. It will be the Director's task to see that progress is being maintained throughout the service in working towards the agreed programmes and to take whatever remedial action is required. A system of delegation and reporting back is essential, otherwise the Director could spend a disproportionate amount of time tracking the work of the organization rather than leading and by taking a direct responsibility for one or several of the key programmes. To carry out the programmes of the policy, there will be financial consequences which will need to be carefully monitored.

Preparation of a corporate plan

Corporate planning in Local Authorities and industry has been common practice for several years and has come to prominence in museums with the requirement of the National Museums to produce forward plans for financial-planning purposes. This has become one of the main tasks of the Director requiring a detailed survey of the operation of the institution and the setting of financial targets covering the entire operation of the service. This requires the Director to take an objective view of the service which traditionally is contrary to the prevailing idea of the role of the Director in taking a subjective view of the requirements of the museum and imposing a personal philosophy, hence the differing styles and achievements of Directors as cult figures known for the quality of exhibitions, purchases or other manifestations. The Director as 'star' projects a strong personal vision which may or may not be relevant to the needs of the organization or the public served. In contrast, the institution may be better served by an individual who can ensure the total resources of the museum, its staff, collections and revenues are fully utilized in the programmes and agreed each year to meet defined needs. The Director can then pursue the programmes which have key importance to the museum, such as a new museum extension, a major exhibition or a major purchase, where the extra experience of the Director can work to the advantage of the project awarding it a priority status amongst the other programmes.

Managerial responsibilities

The idea of the head of the museum as a manager has not been accepted easily by the museum profession. For many years the managerial side was associated with the administration and financial departments of the museum, responsible for the many non-academic, non-technical aspects of the work as well as management of the buildings. The role of Director as manager is now of paramount importance and is parallel to the other professional responsibilities. Obviously the Director with a professional basis will take management decisions in the light of the necessity to maintain standards and, therefore, the decisions taken, whilst sometimes unpalatable, will preserve this 'professionalism'. For example, the decision not to go ahead with a new permanent gallery on financial grounds in favour of a different development, perhaps the introduction of much needed new technology for registration and docu-

mentation, will be taken with regard to the need to maintain the stored collection with the attendant revenue consequences. A management decision taken without the professional dimension may lead logically to an alternative option for the collection, perhaps as a source of revenue for supporting the chosen action, by way of the saleroom?

The position of the Director is analogous to a chief executive in business or industry and, like a chief executive, support for the central management task will be provided by specialist members of the management team, each bringing essential skills to the task. The size of the Director's team may vary, but will certainly include specialist financial expertise, as well as marketing and personnel-management skills. In addition, the two main divisions of the museum's activities will be represented, broadly the collection management and public services functions. The teams will be presenting an interpretation of the performance of the museum in all aspects of its mission, on the basis of the information available, and relating it to the museum's budget. At the same time, the team will be initiating and commissioning new projects throughout the museum as necessary, as well as encouraging and supporting the efforts of others. It is vital that the management processes of the Director's team are mirrored at the various operational levels of the museums, and that the processes of planning, producing and evaluating projects and activities take place on a continuing basis, and are seen as a normal part of the work of all staff. This is expected to lead to improved services through a process not dissimilar to the practices of the best industrial and manufacturing companies.

Preparation of the annual budget

Whilst the Director will oversee the preparation of the annual budget and the forward financial plan as appropriate, the detailed compilation will usually be the responsibility of the head of financial services. The budget should not be a separate issue from the corporate plan which after defining the aims and objectives of the museum and the programmes to meet them, will simply be an indication in some detail of the financial consequences of carrying out those programmes in the forthcoming financial year and over a three- or five-year term. If the planning processes have been carried out thoroughly, the budget is the logical outcome and enables the Director and governing body to progress the corporate plan in relation to the available resources. Depending on the latter, it may mean extending programmes over a longer time-scale or reducing the programme and adjudicating between essential and discretionary areas of expenditure.

If the budget has been prepared in this way, the only decision which should be required is in relation to the income required to fulfil the plan. In the public sector it is likely that the target income figure will be pre-ordained and will be related to the previous year's net actual expenditure expressed as a percentage increase, reduction, or standstill. In the private sector, income from admissions remains the key, with prices adjusted according to the spending requirement. Here the Director and Trustees will need to make decisions about the level of admission charge and other income if the spending plans involve additional finance over and above the 'base' requirement. Both types of organization may, therefore, have to face cuts in expenditure arising from the availability of public-sector finance on the one hand and the likely income from visitors on the other.

Research, development and change

A vital responsibility of the Director is to further the work of the museum by improving its service for the public benefit and extending its influence. At any one time the museum will have a range of developments in progress ranging from major exhibitions, extensions and new buildings to the introduction of new services to the public. The Director cannot lead each project team in person, but should be able to monitor the rate of progress through regular reports and discussion with team leaders and, where necessary, to take remedial action. In many instances it will be the actions of the Director that will initiate major projects through reports to the Committee or Trustees and by presentation to interested parties. A paragraph in the planning document will not reveal the efforts of diplomacy and advocacy required in winning support at the conceptual stage of projects and securing the inclusion of the scheme in a spending programme.

The Director will also indicate from amongst many proposals the projects which most clearly meet the museum's objectives as agreed by the governing body. These should then be strongly supported by the Director from concept to completion.

From time to time major changes will be required in the organization of the museum and in the way in which the various services are provided. If the management processes previously described are an integral part of the work of the museum, drastic changes may never be required, except as a result of catastrophes and disasters such as the loss of premises or collections, or the rapid erosion of the museum's finances. In each of these cases the Director will take the lead in coping with the disaster, whether natural or man-made and in formulating the responsive actions.

Relationships

The success of the museum throughout its range of services depends greatly on the positive and beneficial relationship established between staff and the public (including specialist users of the service) and between staff and the supporting groups and organizations providing services and/or grants to the museum. Staff at all levels in the organization will have responsibility for contributing to some or all of these relationships and the Director will play a key role in this process. The particular relationships which the Director will normally need to maintain and develop include those with the staff and staff representatives (trades unions), the governing body (Committee) and, in some cases, senior officers of related services.

In addition, relations will be forged and maintained with professional and related organizations. In the UK, the Museums Association and government and grant-giving organizations including Museums & Galleries Commission, the Area Museums Service and the Arts Council. The realities of plural funding of museums and art galleries, with the consequential need to present financial plans and expenditure reviews, requires the Director to be personally involved in establishing and maintaining these funding partnerships.

In recent years, largely as a result of Government policies expressed through the Office of Arts and Libraries (England), and the general fiscal policy towards the arts, income generation in its various guises has become a preoccupation of Directors. This has led to a corresponding increase in the responsibilities of the Director in the work required to secure funds from the private sector and charitable Trusts, to complement the existing public-sector finance which can no longer match the developmental needs of the museum, as well as its continuing services to the public. As a consequence, the Director's range of contacts and relationships will extend to include representatives at a Board or senior level, of companies and grant-giving bodies. The credits on museum posters, leaflets and plaques are testimony to the results of efforts made by Directors and their senior staff to secure support for projects.

Personnel

It has been said of organizations that the staff resources are the most valuable asset and, in the case of museums, the incoming Director may find that the largest part of the annual recurring revenue budget is accounted for by the workforce. The staff are the means by which the tasks of the organization are carried out, and a primary responsibility of the Director is to establish a system through the organization to enable this to happen. The Director will need to ensure that staff are employed in the right numbers and have the right skills to meet the requirements of the organization and that the management structure is appropriate to the organization. The incoming Director will usually be faced with an established management structure and will need to judge where changes need to be made and how these can be carried out. Specialist help in this task is almost certain to be needed in both the projection of the new structure and the means of achieving it. The carrying through of a staffing review is a complex task, involving the interrelated issues of gradings, redeployment and training and often must be done in a climate of financial constraint. The process assumes formal and informal consultation with staff and their representatives and is usually carried out within an agreed industrial-relations framework. A staffing review will not normally be undertaken in isolation and is a natural consequence of a policy review. The reviews will be undertaken at regular intervals for one of several reasons, such as reductions in planned expenditure or the taking on of substantial new responsibilities.

The results of a personnel review will be changes in either the organizational structure, the duties and responsibilities of staff, redeployment or redundancies, or a combination of all of these in varying proportions. The Director is certainly bound to be directly involved in bringing about the changes, often with the painful or rewarding tasks of communicating bad or good news, respectively, to the members of staff concerned. In most cases the issues are straightforward and self-evident. When this is not the case, the Director will need to make difficult judgements based on the best evidence available, especially when choices need to be made concerning the future of staff members arising from the review. Judgements will need to have been sharpened by some training in personnel matters or, failing this, access to specialist advice from personnel professionals.

The Director and the governing body

The Director will normally be responsible to a governing body for the museum and its services and the extent of his or her responsibilities will be set out in the formal Contract of Employment and specific delegations to the Director within the Standing Orders and Financial Regulations adopted by the governing body. Whilst the extent of delegation to the Director varies according to the status of the organization, whether a company, a trust or a department of the Local Authority, it will usually be the case that the Director carries out the decisions taken by the governing body on the basis of recommendations that he or she will make in prepared reports considered at regular meetings.

The relationship established between the Director and the governing body, especially its Chair, is crucial to the success of the museum and will need to be fused into a search for common objectives. Whilst the Director will assist in the shaping of policy and, thereafter, its implementation, the Chair will seek to ensure that the policy of the governing body is consistent and is known to the funding organization and that requests for resources and other support will be accompanied by evidence, both written and verbal from the Director and the committee.

The Chair and the governing body, to be effective, will exercise a powerful campaigning lobby, especially amongst decision-makers in areas which may be less accessible to the Director as employee.

Members of the governing body are likely to have widely differing views on major matters facing the organization such as the approach to a new extension or the necessity for the acquisition of certain new exhibits referred for consideration. It will fall to the Chair to provide an opportunity for debate and discussion, to summarize, and to end with a decision. Clearly the advice given by the Director on all professional matters will carry the most weight and the Chair will generally support the case made unless there are major political or public difficulties and where support for the governing body as a whole may not be forthcoming.

Staff and staff representatives

The Director will seek to maintain a positive and constructive relationship with the staff of the organization throughout the entire management structure. A hierarchical system of management will usually be expressed through a senior management group of staff forming a team with the Director to plan, direct and monitor all aspects of the work of the organization with each member of the team having responsbility for a subgroup or range of services or a support service. Regular meetings will maintain continuity and ensure that actions agreed are taken positively and the necessary results achieved. This system depends to a large extent on the effective communication of decisions and agreed actions by each member of the team. The senior management team will also need to establish special teams or project groups to advise on areas of interest and concern such as a corporate storage or documentation plan and these, in turn, will present recommendations supported by facts to the senior management team for decision. Several of these groups will be established to carry out a finite task, others will have a standing role to deal with ongoing topics in order to maintain corporate standards in publishing or research, etc. The Director will need to review the effectiveness of the activity of the groups and the individuals involved against the express task to be carried out.

Training and development

The investment in the training of staff throughout the workforce is vital to the success of the museum, as well as keeping staff abreast of innovation and change in their own areas of responsibility. Changes in legislation need to be monitored regularly and suitable training and induction services designed to respond to the implications are essential, if only to ensure that museum personnel are not in fact breaking the law in carrying out their duties. Training and retraining of staff will be the constant concern of the Director to ensure that skills and professionalism are updated to meet ever-changing circumstances. The central importance of training in museums has recently been recognized by the establishment in the UK of the Museums Training Institute, following a major report on training by Sir John Hale in 1987. The purpose of the Institute will be to respond to the training needs of museums, and assist in providing training for all categories of staff either directly or through accredited courses arranged by others.

The Director of the museum will prepare a training policy for the institution and will play a key role in the recruitment, training and management of staff to ensure that these are meeting clearly defined needs and to achieve the objectives of the museum. Through these means the Director will seek to achieve the following:

(1) maintain the quality of the services provided;
(2) improve the performance of the museum;
(3) respond to change throughout the workforce;
(4) achieve equal-opportunities policies;
(5) maintain health and safety standards and related legislation; and
(6) improve communication between staff and between the museum and its users.

In this area of activity the Director will set the standards and ensure that staff at every level with responsibilities for recruitment, training and management will themselves have adequate training to enable them to fulfil these tasks.

Health, safety and welfare

The Director will be familiar with the relevant Acts and Statutory provisions relating to public and staff in the workplace and the resulting responsibilities that the Director and other staff will bear. The details of the Acts and their interpretation in the context of the museum will almost certainly involve other specialists familiar with personnel and safety matters, either on the staff of the museum or acting as agents or advisers to the museum. It is important that all staff are aware of their obligations under the Acts and the serious consequences of noncompliance. The Director will need to be assured that these requirements under the Acts are understood by the staff and that the procedures and practices throughout the museum are drawn up in a comprehensible manner for the attention of all staff together with a statement of safety policy. The latter is an integral part of sound industrial-relations practice and implies a commitment by the Director and the staff of the museum to high standards throughout the workplace. A Health and Safety Committee with representatives from the various trade unions and senior staff of the museum will keep standards under review and assess the safety implications of developments and changes within the museum such as working exhibits and their maintenance requirements, or the operation of visual display units. Each museum, section or department as appropriate will nominate safety representatives to monitor practices and to report on situations of potential risk. The Director will take whatever steps are required to maintain a safe working environment and to foster and encourage a positive attitude by the staff to personal safety and to concern for the safety of visitors.

Professionalism

The maintenance of the professionalism of the museum is a major task and the Director will ensure that the standards of the museum throughout its range of work are maintained to the highest levels and in accordance with the current ethical codes as well as requirements to comply with registration standards in force. The former will cover the standard of work carried out by the staff in all sections and departments, from the academic to the technical and manual; the latter the constitutional, legal and financial requirements of museums. The Director will need to define the standards required and ensure that these are communicated to the staff and reaffirmed at regular intervals, taking into account any professional developments. This assumes a full understanding and appreciation of the purposes of museums and the standards required throughout the organization.

Presenting the case

In the increasingly competitive environment, as far as public finance is concerned, it is important that the Director can present the case for investment in the museums from both the public sector and other sources. This requires the Director to distil the corporate plan into a believable vision for the museum and its service which can convince investors of the viability of the projects that make up the vision as well as firing their imagination.

As far as new projects are concerned, it is generally accepted that a project champion is essential at an early stage, not only as a co-ordinator of complex technical matters, but also, and more importantly, to keep the vision fresh and in the minds of sponsors and investors. The means of doing this include the regular meetings of Trustees and Committee and presentations to a wide range of organizations essential for the support of the project. The presentation will depend on the Director's chosen style but will almost certainly include the technical support of overhead projectors, slides and possibly video presentation. Conviction and authority are clearly the personal attributes required to convince investors to support the project. Evidence for potential investors in a museum project, as for others in the leisure and recreation sector, must be supported by feasibility studies and later by the detailed business plan. Investors will require objective assessments and, in response to this, the use of consultants has become a regular feature for the appraisal of certain aspects of museum operation, particularly for new museums, commercial operations, catering and technical operations including computerization. Whilst the final outcome of the report will depend on the expert assessment of the consulting team, it is important that the Director is involved in the process, especially at the briefing stage and at the time of the interim- and final-report preparations.

Public relations

The Director has an important responsibility in representing the Service to related organizations and the outside world. The personal style of the Director is clearly an important factor in establishing and maintaining confidence in the museum and its services, a prerequisite for making the case for investment from public and private sources. The Director alone can hardly shoulder the requirements of the normal day-to-day public-relations exercise, but can both establish the philosophy and practice of public relations as well as being the leader of specific projects and interests and acting as spokesperson, by agreement with the governing body, on matters of policy. The press and public-relations (or information) section of the museum will present information about the museum and its service in a form to suit the requirements of the museum's various publics and will establish machinery through which all sections of the museum can present information about their work to the outside world. At the same time, the section will assist in providing the environment in which the Director's view can be transmitted. The

Director and, perhaps, more importantly, the curatorial staff will appreciate that the public-relations and information section has its own professionalism of practice and may need to present complex information about aspects of the work of the Service in ways that may be interpreted by the curatorial departments as superficial or simplistic. This argues for a mutual understanding and sympathy between the originator of material and its translators and an understanding of the purposes of the information released and its target audience.

Personal qualities

In addition to the learned and transferable skills in communication, management and curatorial practice, the Director will possess personal qualities essential to the post of which leadership is the most important. This is generally the ability to motivate staff to achieve the goals that have been set. There is no specific formula; different styles of leadership will be employed, only the absence will be apparent. Leadership is in evidence when the Director shows an awareness and understanding of the goals of the organization and the needs of staff in carrying out the tasks that lead to the goals. The most obvious models of leadership come from military action, conjuring up an image of decisions communicated and orders given requiring obedience. Leadership in the museum requires a more subtle range of qualities, including an understanding of the ways in which the tasks have to be performed and an appreciation that performance will be more effective when external pressures to complete tasks are replaced by an internal drive to achieve the tasks and the will to achieve. A team of self-motivated individuals working to common goals is preferable to an organization waiting for instructions to be passed down.

Conclusion

The rapid expansion of museums and their services in the modern period coupled with the continuing pressure on public sector resources, the mainstay of most museums, has demanded a clear vision for the future of museums and a clarification of their purposes. The Director occupies the key position in defining the purposes of the museum and establishing the resulting policies and programmes throughout the organization.

It has not been easy for the museum profession to accept that the primary responsibilities of the Director do not include daily involvement with collections, displays or exhibitions. At the same time, the need for clear aims and objectives has not been easy to achieve, when the notion of museums being all things to all people has been in common currency for too long. Perhaps a certain impatience with the museums community for not always displaying firm and positive management has contributed to the suggestions that managers from a different background, e.g. in industry, commerce, or other professions, would have more success in leading the larger museums than existing Directors. It is, however, glaringly obvious that 'management' in a museums context can only be successful when the fundamentals of purpose and aims have been agreed. The intellectual challenge for the Director is to clarify the theoretical and philosophical basis of the museum and construct a managerial structure which can deliver services which are consistent with the aims of the organization and relevant to the needs of the public. This calls for the application of skills of a very high order coupled with a comprehensive understanding of the museums operation and its underlying philosophy. The training and development of Directors to assume these responsibilities which are central to the continued vitality of museums remains a high priority of the museums community in the years ahead.

Bibliography

ARTHUR YOUNG ORGANIZATION (1986), *The manager's Handbook*, Sphere, London

AUDIT COMMISSION (1991), *The Road to Wigan Pier? Managing Local Authority Museums and Art Galleries*, HMSO, London

COMPTROLLER AND AUDITOR GENERAL, NATIONAL AUDIT OFFICE (1988), *Management of the Collections of the English National Museums and Galleries*, HMSO, London

INTERNATIONAL COUNCIL OF MUSEUMS (1974), *Definition of a Museum*, Eleventh General Assembly, 3rd Statute, Paris

LAST, J. (1991), *Museums and Local Authorities*, Museums & Galleries Commission, London

LOCAL GOVERNMENT TRAINING BOARD/AUDIT COMMISSION (1985), *Good Management in Local Government*, Luton

MUSEUMS & GALLERIES COMMISSION (1987), *Museum Professional Training and Career Structure*, Report of Working Party, London

MUSEUMS & GALLERIES COMMISSION (1991), *Forward Planning. A Handbook of Business, Corporate and Development Planning for Museums and Galleries* Ambrose, T. and Runyard, S. (Eds), Routledge, London and New York

PETERS, T. and AUSTIN, N. (1985), *A Passion for Excellence. The Leadership Difference*, Collins, Glasgow

STORER, J. (1989), *The Conservation of Industrial Collections. A Survey*, The Conservation Unit, Museums and Galleries Commission

STRONG, R. (1988), *Scholar or Salesman? The Curator of the Future*, MUSE, Ottawa, Canada

THE MUSEUMS ASSOCIATION (1987), *Museums U.K. The Findings of the Museum Data Base Project*, The Museums Association, London

THE MUSEUMS ASSOCIATION (1989), *Code of Practice for Museum Authorities*, 1987 Museums Yearbook, The Museums Association, London

TRUDEL, J. (1988), *The Power of Place and Places of Power*, MUSE, Ottawa, Canada

WILSON, D. (1989), *The British Museum. Power and Politics*, British Museum Publications, London

14

Financial management

Frank Atkinson

This is not an essay on financial techniques: there are many books available on this subject which, in any case, is better operated by appropriately qualified staff. The management of a museum's finances, on the other hand, is an essential skill which should be in the hands of every senior museum officer.

It is generally accepted that finance may be divided into revenue (which covers day-to-day or repetitive matters) and capital, or 'one-off' items, which do not recur each year. Bear in mind, however, that capital spending usually carries with it the implication of subsequent revenue expenditure: one has not finished with motoring costs when the car has been bought.

Each of these two components of finance has to be studied from the opposing points of view of income and expenditure. Until relatively recently, many members of museums staffs concerned themselves only with expenditure, because the source of their funding was regular and simply understood to be the Local Authority or the Treasury. Spending these funds required the general oversight of a budget which was frequently adequate for the perceived needs. Today nothing is so simple and, just as one has to watch one's budget, so much more carefully and responsibly may one also be involved in seeking new sources of funding.

Revenue funding

Publicly funded museums still generally see their annual subvention as the main source of their funding and those so-called independent museums which nevertheless also benefit from regular grants from similar sources are equally fortunate. Two other sources which may have a part to play are earned income, such as admission charges, and sponsorship.

Earned income

Leaving aside the ethical question of charging admission, there is no doubt that admission receipts have helped many museums and made possible the very existence of others. However, from a purely economic point of view, levying an admission charge generally necessitates the use of marketing. The product has to be of a type which an audience desires, at a price which that audience will bear. If it is too esoteric, badly presented, or overpriced, then no amount of agonising about 'ethics' will produce adequate finance.

At this point the precise economics of levying an admission charge must be considered, obvious though they may seem. For example, placing a ticket-seller at a doorway or gate is by no means the end of the cost. Wages, plus on-costs (National Insurance contributions, etc.) must be taken into account and the other, less obvious, items examined, such as capital charges (repayments on borrowed capital), if any, incurred in establishing the charging point. There may also be associated costs such as rates, heating, lighting and cleaning. All this could well equal the wages payment, thus doubling the costs. So is it worthwhile making an admission charge in the first place? How much of the receipts will remain after all this expenditure has been set against them?

Leaving the pros and cons of levying such a charge until later, let us take up the less controversial, though nonetheless complex, topic of running a museum shop. Is it to be entirely a major profit earner or is it to proselytize for the museum? Whichever may be the case (or probably a mid-way position), one must not overlook the concealed costs of the operation. There may be an appreciable input of time and effort by a senior member of staff, not only in establishing the shop but also in the continuing purchasing policy. Accounting work by the office staff, plus rates, heating, lighting and cleaning and the easily forgotten capital charges, must all be considered. Whether or not the museum has a cash-flow problem (and it may be accepted that a strictly local government museum generally will not), there is clearly a need for well-defined criteria and careful thought before deciding to open a museum shop.

One other technique for earning revenue receipts is worth mentioning – that of 'facility fees'. Probably more museums could earn in this way if greater thought was given to it. Charges can be made (and will be willingly paid) for special photographs which might be used for illustrating calendars, television film books, and so on. Special television filming facilities can be made available under certain conditions, although a careful distinction has to be made between educational or children's programmes and costume drama, not so much because the former is perhaps looked upon as 'more worthwhile', as that the latter has a vastly greater budget at its disposal. The *Museums Association Information Sheet on Reproduction Fees* (1975) can be helpful here, but in the end the curator may well find himself in a bargaining situation, so it will be advisable to ensure that the auditor accepts this in advance.

Annual revenue subventions or grants

These should be regarded with some care, unless there is dependable long-term commitment. Look at them carefully: what will happen if the grant is suddenly cut or severely reduced? Can the museum withstand this and, if so, by what means? On the other hand, is the museum giving good value for such a grant? Is its operation encouraging the grant giver to continue with this generosity or indeed to increase the grant? There may be justification, for example, for a revenue grant for something specific but ongoing, such as conservation or cataloguing. Equally, it may be thought that a particular visitor-oriented operation should be funded by way of the visitor.

Other grants maybe specific, such as the purchase grants administered by the Science Museum or the Victoria and Albert Museum. By careful control and planning these can effectively be seen as a means of upgrading the museum's purchase fund, even though each such grant is of course specific to the item being purchased.

The Manpower Services Commission (MSC) has been of considerable help to museums in recent years through the various community schemes, though its successor, the Employment Training project, is much more severely limited in application. Several museums suffered seriously when MSC Community Enterprise schemes ended and care should be taken against relying too heavily on projects of this kind.

Sponsorship

Although sponsorship is supposedly a potential major source of revenue funding, general museum experience does not support this belief. Small sums (ranging from say a few hundred pounds to a thousand or so) may be available for popular museum activities, but few museums are likely to move into the multi-thousand-pound situation commanded by prominent sports with their television potential.

Major exhibitions in London have been funded by Sunday newspapers; leaflets and 'trails' have been funded by oil companies and one-day events may be supported by local breweries and the like but, apart from the first, these tend to be specific and relatively limited. The 'Museum of the Year Award' was supported by a magazine for several years and is now funded by a variety of companies, but nowhere in the museum world does one find the scale of sponsorship which supports and maintains the major sports.

Nevertheless, this source of revenue funding cannot be entirely discounted, and serious thought must be given to the needs of the sponsors. Why should they provide the funds? What is in it for them? Will the publicity justify the expense? Equally importantly, is the event under consideration unique, or will they be expected to repeat the sponsorship next year? Sponsorship must not be confused with charity giving, which will be dealt with later. The former is a strictly commercial operation to be funded out of the sponsor's advertising budget. Is the museum prepared to have the sponsor's advertising banner on its building and their logo on its printed material? Is it acceptable to have the exhibition linked with the product?

As to accounting for this expenditure, the sponsor will probably be satisfied with an approximation of cash spent, but with a certainty in terms of advertising material, whereas the Treasurer or Auditor will, of course, be concerned that expenditure and receipts match, if the sponsorship takes the form of a cash payment.

Revenue expenditure

Revenue expenditure is, without doubt, the most regular and serious contender for attention. Future expansion and development may be desired but, if the operation is failing on a day-to-day or seasonal basis, then future development is better postponed unless it is seen as the only means of recouping the losses.

Without doubt, well-adjusted and closely maintained budgeting is essential. It can achieve remarkable results. Good staff relations are essential here and if members of staff, at all levels of responsibility, are brought together and given appropriate targets, then good expenditure control will result.

First the budgeting must be designed to produce necessary and achievable ends. A realistic plan for the years work must be drafted and the budget laid out to provide this. The budget should then be shared out amongst the staff, according to their functions, needs and responsibilities.

Some kind of small reward may be introduced for those who complete the year within their target. It is just as important that the 'coffee and tea kitty' is kept in balance as it is that the purchase fund is not overspent. Monthly staff meetings can be of great help if members are provided with a schedule of their latest results, set against the annual targets.

Capital funding

The word 'capital', in the sense used here, generally means 'accumulated wealth used in producing more'. Capital funds are, therefore, in practical terms, used to pay for the erection of a building or some other singular operation such as fitting out a store or constructing an exhibition.

A museum's capital funds may be received in the form of a specific grant, or may be borrowed and repaid (together with interest) over a period of time which is related to the purpose for which they have been borrowed. Such loans are best left to financial experts. Arranging the best borrowing rates and – if the museum is not under the auspices of local government – the provision of collateral security, is complex. The chief point to note is that such loans are expensive and have a bearing on the operation for many years to come. If, by so borrowing, the museum is able to carry out some work which will generate a similar or greater income, then all is well. But the burden upon the revenue estimates should otherwise be seriously considered. All this, in any case, may be a purely academic exercise in terms of local government finance, since governmental capital controls have now reduced such expenditure to a very limited commodity.

There may, however, be an alternative, for times and techniques change. Thus, while it was once common practice for a local government to cover, say, the purchase of a museum van by a fairly short-term loan, this would probably now be financed by a hire/maintenance agreement.

A similar 'grey area' can be seen in the grant made to museums through the Science Museum and the Victoria and Albert Museum. These are generally matched by the recipient museum out of a revenue purchase fund, but may be treated as additions to the capital stock of the museum. Care is required here, however, as specimens should *not* be treated as disposable capital resources.

On the other hand, most substantial grants are obviously identified as being of a capital nature. Such may be grants from the Countryside Commission (for projects like car parks or tree planting). Grants from the National Tourist Board for some addition to the 'tourist potential' of a region were once, available under Section 4 of the Tourism Act, but have now been withdrawn.

Capital grants which come by way of the area councils, from the Museums & Galleries Commission offer a useful addition to the stock-in-trade of the ambitious museum director. These grants tend, as do so many national grants, to be 50 per cent of the approved expenditure on a specific project. They may not be exceeded, though they may be underspent. At a time of fluctuating rates of inflation, it may be advisable to ascertain whether a promised grant is a specific figure or whether it is 'inflation proofed'.

Another source of grant aid, available for larger projects, is that obtained through the Department of the Environment, from the European Regional Development Fund (ERDF). Several relatively major grants have so far been made to museums, for sums from around £100,000 up to almost £1 million, in connection with 'the regional infrastructure'. These grants, needless to say, are not easy to negotiate (probably up to a year should be allowed for this procedure). They can now cover 50 per cent of the total estimated expenditure. The remaining 50 per cent has to be found, from non-national sources. It is important to note that an ERDF grant (in common with all nationally funded grants) may not be matched against another national grant.

In applying for any national or European grant the administrative processes should not be undertaken lightly. Not only is it necessary to have the full authority of one's committee or board, it is often equally necessary to have planning consent and building regulation consent in advance of making the application, as well as a certainty of being able to provide the other 50 per cent (or appropriate percentage). Good estimating is another prerequisite.

There always remains the possibility of funds being raised by application to a trust, or by an appeal to industry, commerce and individuals. Some indication of the kinds of activities supported by various trusts can be found in the *Directory of Grant-Making Trusts* (Charities Aid Foundation, 1991). This of course needs to be read with great care and an application should not be made until one is conversant with the requirements of the selected trust. It can often prove helpful to write to the Secretary of the Trust in advance of making the formal application, and indeed visiting him or her in order to discuss the problem.

The establishment of a Development Trust by the museum itself as a means of raising substantial funds is dealt with later. It will not remove every problem. As with all capital developments, the task is not ended when that capital project has been completed. For beyond all this another spectre haunts which may not be immediately apparent. It was pointed out above that 'capital' means 'accumulated wealth used in producing more'. So is your capitally funded construction work going to earn further funds? In museum terms it is more likely to cost an additional sum. What is the nature of this newly committed annual expenditure? It will include, inevitably, loan charges, rates, heating, lighting and cleaning. Probably it will also result in additional manpower costs. Are these included in future revenue estimates? And has allowance been made for any income which may be generated by this new operation?

In short, capital developments are not to be undertaken lightly. On the other hand, any organization which does not expand or diversify will eventually ossify. The choice may, therefore, be between a painful rebirth or a lingering death.

Admission charges

A good museum is not cheap to run. How are these costs to be recouped? Some may be avoided by the use of volunteers, and activities which would not otherwise have been undertaken may be supported by the temporary use of additional labour provided with the help of the Employment Training Scheme. While the former may be a reasonably satisfactory and long-term measure, the latter must be viewed with caution, for these schemes have a way of vanishing almost overnight as national policies are changed or regional emphases modified.

The possibility of volunteer help is worth examining, though its success or failure may depend on such factors as the willingness of the staff to accept the innovation, the type of surrounding population and the very nature of the museum itself. Some Art Galleries have benefitted from the help of the National Association of Decorative and Fine Art Societies (NADFAS) whose members may help in cleaning or cataloguing fine-arts material, or by acting as guides to the public galleries. Less frequently, technical and historical collections have been helped by appropriately knowledgeable volunteers, though railway museums and the like provide outstanding examples of the availability of skilled volunteer help. It may be worth noting that many museums and technical activities being aided in this way are 'independent' bodies, unaffected by the restrictions and limitations which can apply to national and local government museums and galleries.

The essential points to be observed when considering volunteer helpers include the need for a rota and its oversight, proper training and – most importantly – keeping up enthusiasm and not treating volunteers merely as 'cheap labour'.

Many museums in Britain are funded by their Local Authority and, although rarely generous, such a source has seemed reasonably secure until recent years. Now financial restrictions and accounting 'realities' have revealed the danger of assuming that Local Authority funding is an inalienable 'right'. At the same time, the number of privately funded museums has grown to a remarkable degree, culminating in the establishment of the Association of Independent Museums (AIM). So, is charging admission fees to museums the answer to these rising costs and falling revenues? The existing pressures have to be examined before we can indulge in the luxury of discussing the ethics of free admission.

It will be helpful to identify the two chief areas of expenditure required to run a museum: *preservation* and *presentation*. The former covers such operations as collecting, cataloguing and conserving, while the latter will include display and interpretation. Not only in an ideal world should these two functions be examined separately, for justification for any public support may have to be decided according to their varied merits. It may, for example, be agreed that preservation is serving a communal need, being carried out for the benefit – in cultural terms – of the whole community. Presentation, on the other hand, benefits the individual (family group, tourist, schoolchild, etc).

If this argument is upheld, then the community as a whole should support the (reasonable) costs of preservation as a matter of social responsibility, whereas the costs of presentation could be covered by admission charges to the individuals concerned. Even within this framework subsidies are still entirely possible as, for example, reduced (or free) rates for school parties and special rates to benefit local families/individuals, by reducing charges out of the tourist season. It is also possible to help the less well-off members of the community by, for example, offering reduced transport charges if the museum is sited away from the main centre of population, and free admission on certain days, or on presentation of proof of unemployment.

On the other hand, those who believe in free education and free public library services will not readily accept this argument when it is differentially applied to museums. If visiting a museum is part of one's education, then surely it must be free to all. Yet nominal charges are frequently made for 'further education' and generally for the more specialized activities of libraries such as the loan of records and tapes, or the reservation of unusual or popular books. Perhaps a more positive approach is to make the museum so exciting and stimulating that a modest charge is acceptable.

In conclusion, if pragmatism rather than passion is applied to the discussion, it may seem reasonable to anticipate that the preservation activities of the museum will be funded by the community as a whole, while the cost of maintaining a satisfactory presentation will be borne by the individuals who choose to view this, though subsidies can be selectively applied here, if so desired. In other words, instead of arguing about the 'ethics of admission charges', perhaps we should be considering the nature and degree of social benefit: what percentage of any such benefit should be subsidised, or what type of visitor should be specifically aided, or encouraged. It then follows that many institutions could reasonably consider raising a proportion of their funds directly from their visitors.

Before leaving the question of admission charges it may be helpful to stress the value of *marketing* as a discipline for museum curators. It is not good enough to dismiss this as irrelevant, nor is it intelligent to decry it. For, however much we may deplore some of the jargon such as 'maximizing one's resources', the principles of good marketing are worthy of consideration. In the words of this subject, most museums are *product-oriented* rather than *market-oriented*: they try to interest their public in what they have to offer, rather than producing something designed to satisfy a particular 'market' or group of people. They suffer accordingly. Is it not possible to go just a little further in deciding what type of visitor museums would like to entice, and then setting targets more towards this end?

As a footnote to the foregoing, and because not all museum curators are aware of the realities of commercial thought, mention may be made of the 'breakeven' graph. An example of such a graph for a theoretical museum operation is shown in *Figure 14.1*. *Fixed charges* are such things as telephone charges, rates, and staff costs; *varying costs* include, for example, cleaning and additional security necessi-

tated by increased numbers of visitors. In reality the 'varying costs' line is rarely straight, but advances in steps occasioned by, for example, the appointment of additional attendant staff. The 'receipts' line will change its angle according to the actual rate of admission charges and numbers of visitors. The breakeven point is the position achieved when receipts equal outgoings. Beyond that point lie profits or, in museum terms, the possibility of having additional funds to use for more and better activities, including those of conservation.

Fund raising

If charging for admission is a means of matching revenue expenditure, then fund raising generally permits greater capital expenditure. As indicated above, sponsorship is not the same as capital fund raising: the former is generally intended for the support of a popular activity such as a one-day event. It is a direct charge upon the publicity budget of the commercial operator, and must therefore have some commercial content, whether this lies solely in the name of the event, or in associated advertising such as banners, logos and the like.

Establishing a fund-raising or 'development' trust, however, is a long-term attempt to encourage industry, commerce and individuals to support the overall capital development of the museum. It may anticipate obtaining grants from the charity budgets of industrial and commercial concerns, or it may go further and encourage such organizations to feel directly involved in the active growth of this meritorious activity.

Commercial organizations exist to provide the advice necessary to establish a development trust and, if so desired, to direct its operation. Alternatively, an 'appeals director' may be appointed. In either case neither the museum committee nor its curator should think that their responsibilities in this matter have ceased. Active involvement by the museum staff is imperative if a lively programme of fund raising is to be achieved. Indeed, it is often the enthusiasm and obvious dedication of the staff which convinces those in business and commerce that here is something worthy of support.

Finally, one cannot stress too greatly the need for a professional approach to this matter. For, while it will be instructive to examine the brochure of successful fund-raising schemes and to identify the names of their Trustees and Appeals Committees, it must be remembered that what generally makes them successful is their activities about which little is written: that which 'goes on behind the scenes'. Add to this a close application to routine work on a large scale and it will be seen that fund-raising should not be undertaken lightly.

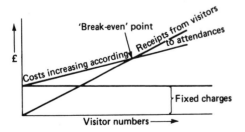

Figure 14.1 A 'breakeven' graph

References

CHARITIES AID FOUNDATION (1991), *Directory of Grant-Making Trusts* (Published annually) Charities Aid Foundation, London

MUSEUMS ASSOCIATION (1975), *Museums Association Information Sheet on Reproduction Fees*, **20,** Museums Association, London

Bibliography

ARNOLD-BAKER, C. (1989), *Local Council Administration*, 3rd edition, Longcross Press

BESTERMAN, T. AND BOTT, V. (1982), To pay or not to pay, *Museums Journal*, **82**(2), 118–119

BROWN, C. V. AND JACKSON, P. M. (1986), *Public Sector Economics*, 3rd edition, Basil Blackwell, Oxford

FARNELL, G. (1990), *The Handbook of Grants. A Guide to Sources of Public Funding for Museums, Galleries, Heritage and Visual Arts Organizations*, The Museum Development Company Ltd., Milton Keynes

HEPWORTH, N. P. (1986) *The Finance of Local Government*, 8th edition, Allen & Unwin, London

WARE, M. (1982), *Fund-Raising* (AIM Guideline 4), Publishing Association of Independent Museums, London

15

Museums and marketing

Peter Lewis

Most museum people react to the word 'marketing' with the same predictable distaste that Pavlov's dogs showed to water. The feeling that marketing equals crass commercialism equals a threat to professional standards needs to be refuted as the palpable nonsense that it is.

For many years, however, there was no reaction at all. Museums and marketing ignored each other. In the last edition of the *Manual of Curatorship* there was one reference to marketing, but one can also search academic marketing books for any theoretical or practical comments on museums. In recent years there has been a meeting, albeit an uneasy one, between marketing practitioners and museum professionals. Most of the energy and enquiry has come from the world of marketing. The museum world has remained distrustful. At the 1988 Museums Association Conference in Belfast,[1] itself devoted to marketing, a fellow delegate explained the problem to me. Imagine, he suggested, marketing as a kind of H.M. Stanley who, after lengthy travels, approaches a museological Dr Livingstone. The outstretched hand and that famous greeting is met by damnation of his presumption and chastisement for transatlantic impertinence. The simile is a seductive one. Livingstone was a venerated explorer whose journeys, inadequately funded by the state, were supported by private zeal and funding. He was a man with a strong sense of mission, possessed of the quality described by African Arabs as *baraka*, an ability to convey blessings, a capacity to explain and enhance life. Stanley was younger and brasher. He was hard, quick, egocentric and American, driven by *kudos*, the love of fame and prestige.

Historically, of course, the meeting between Livingstone and Stanley was not like this. It was marked by amiability rather than abrasion. 'When my spirits were at their lowest ebb' Livingstone recorded in his diary, 'the Good Samaritan was close

at hand. . . the flag at the head of the caravan told of the nationality of the stranger. Bales of goods, baths of tin, huge kettles, cooking pots, tents, etc., made me think this must be a luxurious traveller, and not one at his wit's end like me!' Stanley's description is equally vivid. He approached the missionary with caution and reported, 'We both grasped hands, and then I said aloud "I thank God, Doctor, I have been permitted to see you!" He answered, "I feel thankful that I am here to welcome you!"'.

I do not wish to push this parable too far. The salvation of museums does not lie solely in marketing initiatives. It is valid, however, to point out the parallels. Livingstone's mission, though worthy, was poorly equipped and had lost a sense of direction. Nor did the Government make any moves to go to his assistance. Missionaries are always an embarrassment to the establishment unless there is a direct trading profit associated with the mission. Sir Richard Burton, when approached to assist Livingstone, remarked with the semi-sardonic, semi-laconic air of a modern-day Minister of the Arts, that it was 'infra-dig to rescue a mish' (Moorehead, 1960).

The intended moral of this sermon is simple. A museum needs to combine *baraka* and *kudos*. It needs to declare and demonstrate both its integrity and its ability to confer blessings. *The Scottish Museums Council* has expressed this clearly and concisely in an important policy statement:

A museum does five main things: it preserves, documents, exhibits and interprets material evidence and associated information for the benefit of the public, and it is normally concerned to add to its collections. . . The revolutionary re-thinking in recent years. . . by professionals and public alike, imposes an obligation on existing museums, however long they have been established, to re-examine their functions, in order to determine the contributions they are making to the society that is being asked to support them. To achieve this, each museum needs to identify for itself its distinctive purpose or 'mission' and to prepare a master plan which maps out its future programme in five key areas: conservation, research, interpretation, marketing and financial planning'. (Scottish Museums Council, 1988, p. 7)

The final words are important. They emphasize the need to strengthen the continuing traditional priorities of conservation, research and interpretation with the new skills of marketing and sound financial management. The five key areas have to be given equal weight. The mark of a real 'museum professional' is not to cling to claims of curatorial primacy but to recognize the professionalism of other professionals – to 'feel thankful' that we are 'still here to welcome you'.

Why do museums need marketing?

One reason, often given, for an alliance with marketing is that museums are in crisis and must do something to survive. Faced with falling attendances, towering budgets, crumbling buildings or any combination of all three, there is perceived to be a need to achieve extra visitors and additional sources of finance. One route is for the Director, or his curatorial colleagues, to adopt selling or publicity roles; to do aggressively and officially what they have before done subconsciously. This is often performed with great energy and enthusiasm in the sure knowledge that a degree in archaeology and a diploma in museum studies fit one to do anybody else's job with total confidence. Alternatively, the museum may bring on to its staff, usually at a low level, someone to deal with publicity and advertising. Sometimes, given fair fortune and good people, these strategies can work. Usually they do not, because the theory itself is wrong. The assumption made is that the role and status of the museum is perfect and that the public and the establishment only need to be educated, cajoled or bludgeoned into recognizing this self-evident truth. This is not marketing but selling. Selling is sometimes a respectable activity, but it bears the same relationship to marketing as the banana skin does to wit. It is also self-deceptive. Success is ascribed to curatorial brilliance; failure to the fault of inefficient marketing. As in the theatre, so in museums. Success is credited to the brilliance of the director and cast, failure to poor publicity and incompetent critics.

The second argument is more subtle and one advocated by museum professionals who have attended the occasional seminar. This argument is akin to the one recognized by parents as the 'everybody else in my class is allowed to wear high heels' syndrome. Simply because the world has changed, so, it is argued, ought the museum. This

theory is lucidly expressed in the Association of Independent Museums' *The Principles of Marketing, a Guide for Museums* (Bryant, 1988):

> It is acknowledged that museums are in competition for a share of the public's time, interest, energy and support. . . Consumer goods now offer their purchasers not only function but added value 'experience' in terms of image and lifestyle. . . The pure 'experience industry', which includes sport, package holidays, theme parks, heritage centres, theatres, museums and kissograms is expanding rapidly. It has essentially only one thing to offer its customers – quality of experience. . . Added experiential value. . . is already, and will progressively become, more important.

The argument is a seductive one. The theory that 'we must adjust the way we sell ourselves in the market place' is at least one stage up the evolutionary scale from 'we should tell people about ourselves'. Bryant, the author of the Guidelines quoted above, makes the important point that marketing 'has much to do with change'. The rate of change, itself, he suggests, is speeding up at an extraordinary rate. 'If museums resist change, and do not respond to new demands, they will be left behind – out of touch with the realities, needs and demands of the day'. That is a dangerous double-ended argument. I can think of many within our profession who would argue that their precise function is to 'afford themselves the luxury of being in the past, closeted away. . . from time'! I would, intellectually, support this fundamentalist stance, if I was convinced that the decision was one that had been carefully weighed and considered. Often, however, the proclamation of allegiance to 'old values' is the noisy articulation of an inner timidity, a mindless resistance to change.

The real reason why museums need to incorporate marketing into their central core of management is a simple one – it is a sensible thing to do. Museums have become a valuable, if not always valued, part of the nation's cultural life. They are *so* important that they must be managed well if the central spiritual, educational reason for their existence is not to wither. Service institutions like charities, hospitals, theatres, orchestras and political parties have all recognized the need for such professional services as personnel recruitment, training, purchasing, accountancy and audit. So have museums. The other service institutions have also incorporated marketing and so must museums. Otherwise they will wither away.

At a critical stage of growth in any institution there comes a need to change managerial methods. In the museum world this occurs when the original collector/entrepreneur or his successor is unable to continue running the institution with the aid of helpers. A new style is required. Management change is needed. That change is possible only if 'basic concepts, basic principles and individual vision are changed radically' (Drucker, 1974, p. 8). The American writer on management matters, Peter Drucker, has compared these two kinds of institution to two distinct forms of organisms: 'the insect, which is held together by a tough hard skin, and the vertebrate animal, which has a skeleton'. He goes on to explain that land animals, supported only by a hardened skin or carapace, cannot grow beyond a few inches in size. To be larger, animals need a skeleton. The skeleton does not grow, does not evolve out of the hard skin 'for it is a different organ with different antecedents' (Drucker, 1974, p. 13). When an institution reaches a size of some complexity it needs a different form of management. That form replaces the hard-skin structure of the original entrepreneur. It is not its successor, but something new. When does a museum reach the stage when it has to shift from 'hard skin' to 'skeleton'? I would suggest that the line needs to be drawn at a level just above the smallest of museums. Peter Drucker draws an exemplary illustration of a small research laboratory employing 20 to 25 people from a variety of disciplines. Museum people will recognize the picture:

> Without management things go out of control. Plans fail to turn into action, or worse, different parts of the plans going at different speeds, different times, and with different objectives and goals. The favour of the 'boss' becomes more important than performance. At this point the product may be excellent, the people able and dedicated. . . but the enterprise will begin to founder, stagnate and soon go downhill unless it shifts to the 'skeleton' of managers and management structure. (Drucker, 1974, pp. 13, 14).

That same guru, talking of marketing within the management of an institution, has much to offer museums. He starts from the premise that marketing is 'the distinguishing, unique function' of any enterprise and that any institution which relies on support from people should 'have two – and only these two basic functions: marketing and innovation. Marketing and innovation produce results; all the rest are "costs"' (Drucker, 1974, pp. 56, 57).

In museums we claim to know a great deal about innovation. What do we make of marketing?

What is marketing?

Like 'heritage' or 'history' there is no simple definition of 'marketing'. Reading through the works of the academic marketing community, especially those textbooks used in a wide variety of university courses, is a dispiriting process. Definitions offered by academics can be mindbendingly difficult to analyse:

> Marketing is the process whereby society, to satisfy its consumption needs, evolves distributive systems com-

posed of participants, who, interacting under constraints – technical (economic) and ethical (social) – create transactions or flows which resolve market separations and result in exchanges and consumption. (Bartels, 1968)

They can also possess a deceptive simplicity that leaves a student little wiser than before:

> Marketing is the creation of time, place and possession utilities. (Converse *et al*, 1965 7th edition)
> Marketing is the set of human activities directed at facilitating and consummating exchanges. (Kotler, 1977, 2nd edition)
> The generic concept of marketing. . . is specifically concerned with how transactions are created, stimulated, facilitated and valued. (Kotler, 1977, 2nd edition)

It is easy to be cynical about the inability of the marketing profession to provide a simple explicable definition of the word 'marketing'. We should remember that our own profession is still embroiled in an attempt to provide a comprehensive and overall definition of 'museum'.[2]

The British Institute of Marketing definition can provide us perhaps with a starting point in approaching a simple definition. Marketing is, the Institute suggests, 'the management process responsible for identifying, anticipating and satisfying customer requirements profitably' (Wilmshurst, 1984). At first reading this concept would appear to be light-years away from museums. Most marketing textbooks are geared to the selling of a *product* rather than the supply of a *service*. Concepts like *customers* and *profit* are guaranteed to raise curatorial hackles. Few of our institutions make a profit unless it be at the expense of their integrity. What indeed would happen to museums and galleries if they acceded totally to customer demands? Do we in fact even know what these demands might be? We are, I would suggest, in the business (and I use the word deliberately) of giving our users what they need rather than what they demand. If we see ourselves as missionaries then we have a right to hang on to the eternal verities and not allow our congregations to fall into the modern-day heresies of heritage centres and theme parks.

My advice is that we should take a deep breath and stand back from the marketing of handbooks. We need to look 'through a glass darkly' at the terms we distrust – business, profit, product, consumer, etc. – and see what is of value to us. If we do we shall see that *marketing* has two levels of meaning. It is firstly what the textbooks refer to as a *concept* and what I would prefer to call a *philosophy*. Secondly it is a generic term that lumps together a series of practicalities, advertising, market research, public relations, publicity, etc. These latter activities are only part of the process of marketing. They are the ways by which we do things but are not in themselves the *why* of our existence. Philosophy comes first. We have to see what we do through the eyes of the people we do it for, the people who use museums and those who, directly or indirectly, fund and support our activities. Since no practical marketing manual exists for our profession I would suggest, as a starting point, a reworking of the The British Institute of Marketing's definition to read as follows:

> Marketing is the management process which confirms the mission of a museum or gallery and is then responsible for the efficient identification, anticipation and satisfaction of the needs of its users.

I have chosen words like *needs* and *users* with some care. I recall the words of John Cotton Dana, the founder of Newark Museum, who opined in 1909 that 'a museum can help people only if they use it; they will use it only if they know about it'.[3] I would add to that remark 'and if they understand its purpose'. I applaud and endorse John Cotton Dana's insistence that museums exist to *help* people and that people should be encouraged to *use* museums. I would rather welcome *consumers* than *punters*, rather have *tourists* than *consumers*, *visitors* rather than *tourists*, *users* rather than *visitors*. To invite people to consume, visit or tour what we offer in museums is to behave in an arrogant way. To invite them to participate and to use the museum is properly to behave as professionals. It forces us to rethink our philosophy.

I doubt whether any institution, including and, especially, that museum which I direct, has seriously looked at its purpose, at its articles of faith. One of the side-effects of the ongoing museum registration scheme was to force us to dust down our foundation documents. There were many museums who were forced to recognize that they had never possessed statements of purpose or that much was now irrelevant. Trustees and Boards of Management found themselves endorsing hastily rewritten statements of policy to satisfy the basic and, as yet, far from stringent requirements of the Museums and Galleries Commission. We have no cause then to stand on our dignities. The acceptance of a marketing philosophy must start with a managerial audit. We would do well to adopt and adapt the planning cycle advocated by J. Walter Thompson. It asks a series of deceptively simple questions:

> Where were we when we started?
> Where are we now?
> Where could we be?
> How could we get there?
> Are we getting there?

The cycle then begins again with the 'Where are we now?' question and the process continues. It is, as Patricia Mann has said, 'a valuable discipline for thinking. . . it can be used at a variety of levels of sophistication. . . it demands the creation and testing of hypotheses' (Mann, 1988). When the hypotheses have been tested and the mission clarified that philosophy needs to be accepted throughout the whole organization. Within the museum, from volunteers and Friends, to curators and cleaners, to technicians and teaching staff, indeed everybody from the Director upwards, have to understand and endorse the way we do things and the fundamental reasons why we do them. It is easier to understand this process if we look outside the museum world to retailing or other leisure industries. The reputation of Marks & Spencer or Sainsburys has little to do with price but everything to do with value. They have achieved customer loyalty by close attention to customer service and care. We see little if nothing of the higher management, but their company style comes through the behaviour of their visible staff. The same is true of museums. The success of some fast-food chains owes more to the courtesy of the staff and the rigidity of standards than it does to the delights of the burger. We may not wish to ape the exhibits of theme parks like Alton Towers or to send our senior staff on long trips to Disneyland but we *should* seek to emulate their day-to-day professionalism and staff training. This is not a descent into commercialism but a recognition that, if museums are as vital to the nation as we believe, they should be run to the highest standards.

This thinking process and the planning that follows does not challenge the integrity of the artefact nor the sanctity of scholarship. It strengthens them. What it does do is remind all of us that museums are not about objects but the understanding and appreciation of objects. Museums are for people not about things. A collection of objects is not a museum until staff accept professional responsibility for collections and their users.

Kenneth Hudson (1987), in his book, *Museums of Influence* neatly and with typical wit summarizes 'the recipe for survival and growth in the museums field' as:

> First the museum must be financially viable. . . Second, it must find ways of linking itself closely and actively with the local community and of satisfying real, rather than imagined tastes and needs. And third, it must never lose sight of the essential truth contained in the apparent paradox that successful popularization can only be achieved on a basis of sound scholarship. We are going to see a good many fly-by-night museums fail as a result of ignoring this maxim, and it is going to be a sad process to watch, *as sad as contemplating out-of-date museums fade away and eventually possibly die from a surfeit of learning, dullness, obstinacy and arrogance.* (Hudson, 1987, p. 194)

The practicalities of marketing

Once the painful process of defining the mission of a museum is complete, it needs to be reconsidered at least once a year and a total redefinition done every five years. The mission may not change but the recognition of the *status quo* is an important judgement.

Having identified and anticipated needs, the process of satisfying those needs can proceed with the supply of services. Business economists, concerned with *product*, generally distinguish four areas of need:

(1) analysis and forecasting, i.e. market research and post-marketing audit;
(2) product development and design;
(3) influencing of demand – design, advertising, media relations, etc.; and
(4) service, staff training, distribution, after-sales service, etc.

Economists would further suggest that successful marketing depends upon a selection of these separate ingredients to achieve a suitable mix, a recipe relevant to a particular institution. The areas listed above are those appropriate to the manufacture of a product. They can be easily adapted to the needs of a museum, in which case the ingredients would include corporate identity, market research and visitor surveys, design and interpretation, publicity, advertising, public and media relations, staff training, etc. One common system of analysis lists the variables as the 'six Ps': product, place, presentation, promotion, price and people. The Association of Independent Museums (AIM) Guidelines, quoted above, take this form of segmentation and give a useful breakdown of a typical museum mix. I have strong doubts about mnemonics of this kind which generally reinforce the image that marketing is a form of mumbo-jumbo based on slogans rather than science. It is perhaps more appropriate briefly to discuss each of the elements identified before coming to a discussion of marketing mix and the implementation of a marketing plan.

Corporate identity

I came to the museum world after time spent in teaching, retailing and the professional theatre. I was surprised and shocked to see how poorly museums identify themselves and their purpose. This reticence may be inbred or may be instilled by those self-appointed cultural historians who make judgements on us all. Despite the eminence of Robert Hewison (1987), he is wrong to suggest that museums and galleries should be 'neutral facilities for the presentation of individual acts of creation'. Neutrality or blandness is not what we are about. For good or ill, all museums have their own personalities. If they are positive they should be promoted. If they are negative they should be changed. Until the individual characteristics of the museum are understood it cannot be decided

whether its image should be preserved, modified or radically altered. I have throughout this paragraph been referring to the museum as a single unit. There is a problem when an area, perhaps that served by a Local Authority, promotes all its museums together under one Procrustean policy which makes them all seem the same. This is a waste of time, money and energy. Such authorities need to free each individual unit to express its own personality. The National Museums and Galleries on Merseyside campaign is an excellent example of such confident promotion.

Names and titles are important. They are frequently longer and more pompous than they need to be. It is better to be 'The Science Museum' than 'The National Museum of Science and Industry', better to be the 'Natural History Museum' than the 'British Museum (Natural History)' and better still to be 'Wigan Pier' than 'The South Lancashire Heritage and Field Study Centre'. There is little point in insisting on the primacy of 'The North of England Open Air Museum' if your friends and users refer to you always as 'Beamish'.

Whatever the name, however, it is important, once chosen, to test its efficiency. Play devil's advocate games and look for potential comment or jokes. Remember that fish fingers were first going to be called cod pieces by an agency with no sense of the ridiculous. The name should be incorporated into a logo and a house style that reflects the tone of the museum. You should then stick tenaciously to it, remembering the reported words of St Francis, 'Do always what you believe to be right, Brother, and if it proves to be wrong, repent later!' (Houseman, 1922). The logo and a designated typeface should appear on everything to do with the museum, stationery and signposts, posters and pamphlets, paper bags and lavatory doors. Have photographic bromides of the logo available for printers and the media; insist on your own typeface at all times. This face need not be exclusive to you but you should use no other. It takes a long time to build up a corporate identity. Do not change because it might be fun to do so this year – and ignore the bizarre or the over-fashionable (e.g. antique, medieval, gothic, playbill or computer graphics). The one factor common to all these faces is illegibility in 72 point viewed from 20 feet away.

The design of a corporate identity by a competent designer is expensive but should be afforded. The quality of the design will only be as good as the briefing you give to the designer. Museums with a miniscule budget or no budget at all should approach local colleges of further education with print or design departments. The creation of a corporate logo is a suitable project for a competent student, as is the artwork for promotional leaflets and brochures. The gain for the student is a piece of real rather than theoretical work in her or his portfolio.

Leaflets, brochures and posters

All museums need leaflets or brochures. These can be simply designed, but never use single-sided sheets giving details of opening hours and of the range of exhibitions and services. Ideally, they should be coloured brochures using a range of photographs. Do not, however, illustrate, discuss or tell all you do. Convey the quality of the experience but surprise your visitors with the excellence of the real thing. It is wise to show photographs in short shot or from angles other than those which the visitor usually gets. Brochures should be finished and folded to A5 or smaller. Other sizes are distinctive and different but will not fit standard display stands in tourist information centres, libraries or elsewhere. Distribution within your area can usually be done cheaply or free on exchange days organized at a single site by your local Tourist Authority. Distribution outside your area will cost you more. Few museums in my experience need posters. A sensible idea is to design an A5 brochure which unfolds to incorporate an A3 poster. Do not print posters larger than A3 size. Schools, libraries and information centre notice boards are too small to incorporate large posters. It is sometimes worthwhile to involve yourself in a poster campaign on bus or railway station sites. Then you need to go really large to four-sheet size.

Carefully designed, a leaflet or brochure can be made to stretch to two years, but this requires a forward discipline of well planned and agreed hours of opening, admission prices (if appropriate) and discounts. Small museums should discuss with their local Museums Service whether there are any joint marketing promotions planned. For example, in Museums Year, the North East Museums Service recently successfully designed and printed a large map which listed free of charge the address and telephone number of each museum in the area. The cost was covered by grant and paid advertising on the rear. Your Local Authority, be it County, District, or Borough will also be promoting the area which includes your museum, as will your local Tourist Board. Ensure that these institutions have bromides of your logo, coloured slides and black-and-white prints of your best features, and know your address, telephone number and opening hours. Remind them every two months or so. People change and departments are shifted and reorganized. Nothing is worse than free publicity which is inaccurate or does not reflect the reality of your museum.

Advertising

Advertising is costly and is best done with the advice of an agency. Do not automatically dismiss the use of an agency as expensive because a part of their income is derived from discounts not available to you. The agency needs from you a tight brief, a clear statement of what you want to achieve, i.e. more local visitors, more organized parties, more tourists, etc., and a stated budget beyond which they may not go. They will recommend a package of suggestions for you to approve and will themselves commission artwork and copy. Be critical if you do not feel that it represents the museum fairly. Avoid the temptation, however, to put in more and more information. Most readers or viewers can only take in three pieces of information in any message – a place, an event, a time. If you can afford it advertise on local television which is particularly advantageous at the start and midway through the season – do not advertise at peak times.

General 'puff' advertisements, statements of your excellence and worthiness are a waste of your budgets. Keep local advertising to an absolute minimum and promote events, special days, new exhibitions. Do not forget local radio advertising but keep your time slots to the important drive-in and drive-home times. Remember that local radio and newspapers, as well as national papers like *The Guardian* and *The Independent* and others run free listings for special events. Do not be afraid to use them and be brave enough always to resist cold telephone calling from publications and gazetteers. Remember that even if these agencies are honest, and many are not, the cost will not marry with any advantages to you. If your budgets are small, advertise first in some Tourist Board publications, specialist coach and driver magazines, educational heritage groups, etc. If you take advantage of your local Education Authority's distribution system to schools, send two brochures to each school, one for the headmaster and one for the staff room. Should you have no advertising budget at all, rely on your ingenuity and charm to persuade the media to give you free editorial coverage.

Publicity and editorial coverage

Contrary to common belief, all publicity is *not* good publicity. Avoid stunts, especially those suggested by professional publicists. Good publicity is often bad marketing. Consider, for example, the coverage given in recent years to the problems of the Victoria and Albert Museum and the Natural History Museum. Rarely turn down a request from radio or television but, if the image they are going to project is not positive, refuse pleasantly but firmly. From the factual basis of any story construct a scenario to suit the narrative needs of radio or the visual requirements of television or the press. The television news and current-affairs magazines need stories each day. Museum tales are often the statutory happy story to balance the bad news. Do not be afraid, however, to court regular national programmes like Blue Peter,

Any Questions, Today, Around Midnight, Down Your Way, the Sunday religious slots, etc. They are all seeking venues and topics. They provide you with a coverage that would cost a fortune to pay for. With your local press maintain a steady stream of stories and picture opportunities. Do not overdo it or they will become bored; once a fortnight is a reasonable timespan. Although it takes time, do not give everybody the same press release. Is it a local story, a possible *Guardian* feature or a television news item? It may be all three and, if so, angle the story differently. If you are asked for a spokesman or spokeswomen make sure that they have character. Serious political problems must be handled by the Chairman of Trustees or the Director. Otherwise, let your staff do the interviews. The greater the number of voices and faces, the more real the stories, the more coverage to the museum.

Marketing research

'Marketing research' is not the same as 'market research'. The first involves an enquiry into the response of the users of a museum, the second into the size, status, composition of potential markets. Both should be done but the first is more fundamental to museum work. Marketing research is 'the gathering, recording, analysing and reporting of facts relating to the transfer. . . of goods and services. . . based on statistical probability theory and always uses the scientific method' (Adler, 1969). Most museums do not know accurately how many people use their services; even more know nothing of why they are used or how people value those services. They should. Some museums, by simple observation or by intermittent visitor surveys, find out some facts. They are diligent in the gathering, recording and reporting of findings. They are still poor, and I include the institutions with which I have been associated, in the objective rather than subjective analysis of these findings. 'Research', the dictionary tells us means 'a careful search. . . endeavour to discover new facts. . . by critical investigations'. 'Scientific' means 'according to rules laid down. . . for testing soundness of conclusions, systematic, accurate'. There is no point in specifying time or money on research if you are not prepared to be surprised by the results and to react to them.

Some research will already have been done for you. The Government via HMSO, produces a mass of statistical data, though with a considerable time lapse. Similar, though more specific, information is available from national and regional Tourist Authorities, though these statistics appear to me to be often 'optimistic' in tone and should be treated with caution. Visitor surveys by other museums can also be valuable, as long as users clearly understand that this information is based on small samples of those people already using existing museums. There is some information on the wider public view of museums. The Scottish Museums Council in 1985 commissioned a survey into 'Public Attitudes to Scottish Museums'. This showed a higher level of response to museums in the A, B and C socioeconomic groupings, appearing to confirm the widely held view that museums and galleries attract the well-educated middle and upper classes. A survey of an individual museum may well show otherwise. Beamish has been interviewing users for over 15 years and our statistics show a different result to that of Scotland with a higher proportion of people at the extreme end of these groups with more A and E visitors than usual. Both Beamish and Scotland's survey highlighted, as do surveys in the performing arts, a greater interest among men than women and a higher degree of criticism in respondents between 20 and 30 years of age.

Commercial companies presented with such statistics would be inclined to narrow their selling activities into receptive areas of the market. Museums need to do the opposite. Some specialized museums will obviously cater for their own adherents, but most museums, given their missionary zeal, exist to serve all of their local, regional or international congregations. They should, therefore, use facts to correct failings and not merely to reinforce existing situations.

It is likely, given the funds available to museums, that they will give priority to questionnaires and interviews with their present users. Museums can design their own questionnaires and do their own surveys, though the process is littered with stumbling blocks and pitfalls. The questions need to be carefully chosen, to be unambiguous and be capable of statistical analysis. The list must include control questions to ensure consistency and the survey should be done on a controlled random basis to ensure that all sexes, ages, days of the week, months of the year, etc., are covered. Questioners can be members of your staff, staff specially recruited or staff from outside agencies. The first is the most difficult, but there is an emotional appeal in using curatorial staff at times. If nothing else it exposes them, in exhibitions they have themselves planned, to the views of people they rarely see or listen to.

Any survey that does not include at least 1,000 interviews is probably useless. For this reason, if no other, it is sensible to allow your own surveys to be done. Resist the attempts of schools, colleges and individuals to do their own surveys. This can lead to friction with the users of museums.

Jonathan Byrant (1988) in the AIMS Guidelines gives a long and very valuable section on visitor surveys which is worth study. He advises that competent professional advice is preferable and recommends institutions like MUSEUMSCAN or university or college departments. I have a more open mind on the subject, particularly when museums, large or small, have difficulty in raising finance. Some Area Museum Councils, Independent Trusts and Local Authorities have been known to part-fund surveys. Ask them for help. If the museum has no money at all then use existing staff.

The Museum Director should read all letters and reply to them personally within three days of receipt. She or he should not only glory in the bouquets but take seriously the brickbats. Staff at all levels should be encouraged to report comments both favourable and unfavourable. We have formal systems to report accidents or incidents. A formal reporting system of opinions is just as valuable.

Public relations

Museums are about people; the people who work in them and the people who finance and use them. Curators, and especially directors, rarely meet the public. Attendants, sales staff and demonstrators do so. It is important then that all staff should understand the mission of the museum and are given positive leadership.

Each year museums should do a customer audit and this should be followed up each and every day. The museum should open on time and all its services, (the lavatories, cafeterias and retailing areas as well as the galleries) should be cleaned and ready and should be monitored throughout the day. I have mentioned institutions like Marks & Spencer before and make no apology for doing so again. Their staff, from management to shop floor, are excellent marketeers. Their commitment to what they are doing works rather like osmosis but does not come about by accident. All staff are trained to be pleasant and helpful. They worry about the quality of the service they offer. This does not mean that museums need to develop an obsequious 'the customer is always right' attitude nor adapt the mindless 'have a nice day' kind of transatlantic jargon. Firmness and control are an important element of customer-care. Attendants are there not only to 'help the visitor' but also to deter the visitor from 'helping themselves'. It must be realized, however, that junior staff when faced with complaints should be able to refer those comments upwards, either immediately or by noting the details, and to promise a telephoned or written response from someone in greater authority. Junior staff must also be trained to be neutral in their response. A tacit agreement that all is not well, that 'I've been telling the high-ups this for months but they never listen' does irreparable harm to the museum.

Attitudes of positive help can only be achieved by thorough induction and regular systematic training.

It is every bit as important that staff with public contacts receive training in customer-care as, for example, that a conservator should receive professional training in paper conservation.

One anecdote may serve to illustrate this precept. I am fond of one large museum outside London which has superb collections, imaginatively and professionally exhibited. Its building is formidable. The frontage, a classical temple-like structure, is accessible by a high flight of steps. The large notice board proclaims only its title, gives no information, verbal or pictorial, as to its contents or opening hours. A temporary notice tells those with disabilities to go to the rear of the building and to ring at a numbered door where wheelchair access can be arranged. The entrance for able-bodied visitors is via one of a number of enormous doors, one of which is open each day. Users enter via a lobby full of quasi-military uniformed attendants and a collection of negative notices. The lobby itself is poorly lit, so it is with some trepidation that potential users even manage to penetrate the museum. Lavatories are at the rear of the building as are the catering facilities which open an hour later than the museum itself, which itself often opens late and chases away early those brave enough to attend. The staff entrance is on one side of the building so curators are probably unaware of the experience of the museum users.

A simple user audit of this museum could bring its standard of service up to the undoubted excellence of its collection and scholarship. But the marketing will is not there.

Museums of any size need to consider the messages they transmit. Never use negative notices. Thank people for *not* smoking, welcome guide dogs and, if objects must not be touched, design the exhibition to avoid that. If the museum is popular do not indulge in the intellectual arrogance that numbers must somehow be limited. Devise systems to cope with popularity. Unless a museum adopts a positive marketing approach to its users they will not come back to use the museum again.

Specialist groups and mailing lists

I have been talking throughout this brief article as if all users were individuals. Whilst museums and galleries wish to stress and hold on to their very specific roles they do have to recognize also that they are 'visitor attractions' or 'tourist spots' and that party bookings, whether educational or social, are essential elements of a museum's 'congregation'. They have to be given equal value.

Changes in educational philosophy and the management of schools have impacted on museums. In some regions there are less school visits or there has been a change in the numbers coming from junior schools as compared with secondary schools or colleges. Any museum where school children are less than 20 per cent of its total is failing in its essential mission. The days of the school pleasure trip are numbered. Teachers are now required to justify the educational value of activities outside the classroom and need detailed advice not only on specific educational gains but also the level of the project as it applies to the National Curriculum and GCSEs. Museums have to provide this and, via the distribution schemes available through educational activities, to ensure the information reaches teachers. The work of pupils, which is now predominantly project-based, has forced changes even in how children move around museums. Small groups attached to teachers and minders are becoming rarer. A freedom of access with teachers in fixed locations to welcome the children is becoming common. Museum staff need to be aware of these new systems and to react positively.

The museum also needs a policy for adults in specialized groups. Contact with local organizers, coach and tour operators, and coach-drivers clubs can all be furthered by up-to-date mailing lists, attendance at travel fairs, special seminars, etc. There needs to be a person or department within the museum that copes with these special needs and serves as an efficient point of contact. Mailing lists are difficult to build up. They can be bought or borrowed. Equally importantly they need to be kept up to date. Old information should be deleted. The records should be cross-referenced. Numbers are not everything in museums but they are some indication of success. Analysis of those museums with sophisticated party booking organizations suggests that it is this sector of the market which is growing faster than individual visits. A professional approach to these kinds of users is not a sell-out to sordid commercialism but a necessary part of a museum's mission.

The marketing plan

Museums articulate the past; they offer explanations or expositions of history. Unfortunately management techniques often have the same obsession. The average administrator or director spends too much time reviewing the past or struggling with the present. Management and marketing are dynamic situations. They have been defined in a rather 'cookie fortune cracker' way as 'making the future happen'. Though, as museum folk, we are suspicious of slick slogans, this one merits attention:

> To make the future happen one has to be willing to do something new. . . One has to be willing to say: 'This is the right thing to happen. . . we will work on making it happen. . . it is rational activity'. And it is less risky than coasting along on the comfortable assumption that

nothing is going to change, less risky than following a prediction that what is likely to happen is the most desirable. (Drucker, 1967)

The dictionary definition of the word 'plan' is 'to arrange beforehand'. Forward arrangement of priorities is the essential aspect of marketing and the prime function of management whether in museums or elsewhere. Having established the 'mission' of the museum, the consequences of that judgement have to be understood and a strategy implemented.

Plans, whether corporate or marketing, are not immutable, but it is just as well to behave, at least for the first year, as if they were. Changing needs, priorities, costs, external events will lead to adaptations, but resist the temptation to tinker with the basic precepts. Do not, however, take an unreasonably long-term view. 'Mission', to the Catholic church, may have a time-span of eternity, but in business practice 'mission' is defined more succinctly 'the paramount objective of any organization for the intermediate future'. A *Forward Planning Manual* for museums and other arts institutions, published by the Museums & Galleries Commission and HMSO in 1991, seeks to provide principles and practical guidelines. Realistically it is envisaged as a volume with a life-span of five years. That is a cool but competent professional judgement. It highlights the apparent paradox that forward planning, though the most important task, is itself transitory. It has to be done all over again, every year, every five years, every decade.

I do not propose to offer a detailed schematic marketing plan for a typical museum. A useful and intelligent one can be found in *AIMS Guideline 16* Bryant (1988), referred to above. This will need adaption by each institution. I would wish, however, to highlight some important points.

Evidence of comprehensive forward planning is now expected by grant-making bodies and Government departments. Area Museum Councils, who have themselves been through this process, can show you their scars and offer advice. Planning is as essential for small museums, even voluntary organizations. The proclamation that small is beautiful may be seductive, but the assumption that everybody in a small organization knows its plans for the future is false.

Any marketing plan should, therefore, include the following:

(1) *A definition*, i.e. a proclamation of purpose. What are the missionary aims of the museum?
(2) *An assessment*, through some sort of sound research into who is presently using the museum, how they are using it and whether their needs are being met.
(3) *A judgement*, realistically made, of the operational opportunities and constraints from outside the museum.

Are there policies of local or national Government which determine or inhibit the museum's operation? Should the museum stay within its present organizational framework, seek charitable status, go 'independent', or reinforce its local links?

(4) *A forecast* of the quantity and quality of visits by users. What numbers can we expect? How will we cope? If the museum charges for admission, what should those charges be and how can those who might not be able to afford those charges be accommodated?

(5) *A policy* of what publications, retail and catering services are appropriate. These should only be planned if they marry with the museum's image, do credit to its reputation and provide a sensible and achievable net profit, which should itself be used to improve the museum's central functions of collection, conservation and education.

(6) *A promotion* of the museum's services. This will involve a mandatory programme of all staff training and a regular update of all internal communications. It may, if affordable, involve a programme of media advertising, exhibitions, mailings, posters, pamphlets and trade shows. This should never be less than 10 per cent, including staff costs, of the museum's revenue income. If the museum, laudably, has a policy of free admission, it should calculate what its income might be if charges were made and include that same percentage in its forward plans.

(7) *A timetable* with a rational time-scale. Museums tend to take over-long views of time needed to plan exhibitions and implement schemes. 'Slippage' is an ugly word but an even uglier practice. Take shorter-term views than are currently fashionable. Long-term plans with no end-date are examples of museological lethargy.

(8) *A budget* which forecasts both income and expenditure. Set a realistic figure and keep to it. If good fortune occurs, if a sudden unexpected donation or course of finance happens, then adapt the plan. If money is short, if there is a sudden inflationary surge, keep within the budget and cut accordingly.

(9) *A dream* is always necessary. Most great museums were founded by eccentrics or entrepreneurs who defied convention. The idea that God, Government or a 'generalized good' will provide is not totally out of date. But remember, as the New Testament reminds us, that rewards go to those who use and multiply their talents, not to those who bury them in the ground in order to preserve them.

Marketing: a final thought

I made, in the preamble to these notes, a distinction between marketing as a philosophy and marketing as a set of practices. In museums we tend to be pompous about the philosophy and cynical about the practices. 'Business' is still a dirty word with us. Marketing departments like 'planning departments, personnel departments, and management development departments' can be, as Robert Townsend reminds us in his tongue-in-cheek book *Up the Organization*(1970), 'camouflages designed to cover

up for lazy or outworn chief executives'. But, marketing, as he goes on to stress, is 'in the fullest sense of the word, the name of the game. So it had better be handled by the boss of his line, not by staff hecklers!'. The museum profession sometimes seems to be a highly structured form of institutionalized heckling. It must not remain so.

Marketing is an attitude of mind, transmitted into actions, that permeates an institution from bottom to top. It starts from the premise that management is not just common sense or a collection of codified experiences but is an organized body of knowledge. The knowledge that it seeks to organize is the good of society. Each institution exists to contribute to the satisfaction of those who use it or ought to be using it. It does not exist to supply employment for staff, kudos for politicians or dividends to shareholders. Jobs, kudos and dividends are necessary means but not ends. A hospital should not exist for the sake of consultants, nurses or orderlies but for the benefit of patients. A school does not exist for the sake of teachers and administrators but for students. A museum does not exist for curators, business managers, attendants or academics but for its users.

Museum people are rightly proud of their care of objects and learning. As managers they have to be stewards of what exists. Whether they like it or not they have to be administrators. They also have to be innovators, risk-takers and entrepreneurs so that the services they offer and the artefacts they preserve survive beyond the life-span of this generation. Future users will only be able to give thanks that they, like Stanley, 'have been permitted to see you', if museums ensure, like Livingstone, that they are still 'here to welcome you'.

Notes

1. Most of the papers presented at the 1988 Museums Association Conference in Belfast are published in *Museums Journal*, (Dec. 1988 **88**(3)). Intriguingly, the keynote address, given by the then director General of the *Institute of Marketing*, was omitted. Another useful collection of articles dealing with marketing and museums can be found in *Museums Journal*, **Sep** (1988). **88**(2).
2. At the time of writing the Museums Association is considering the differences between its own definition of a museum or gallery and that of the International Council of Museums (ICOM).
3. John Cotton Dana (1909) quoted in *The Manual of Curatorship* (1984) p. 75.

References

ADLER, M. (1969), *Lectures in Market Research*, Crosby Lockwood

BARTELS, R. (1968) 'The general theory of marketing', *The Journal of Marketing*, **32**, London

BRYANT, J. (1988), *The Principles of Marketing, a Guide for Museums*, Association of Independent Museums Guideline 16, AIM, Chichester

CONVERSE, HUEGY & MITCHELL (1965), *Elements of Marketing* 7th edition, Prentice Hall, London

DRUCKER, P. (1967), *Managing for Results*, Pan, London

DRUCKER, P. (1974), *Management: Tasks, Responsibilities, Practices*, Heinemann, London

HOUSEMAN, L. (1922), *Collected Plays of St Francis*, London

HEWISON, R. (1987), *The Heritage Industry*, Methuen, London

HUDSON, K. (1987), *Museums of Influence*, 194, Cambridge University Press, Cambridge

KOTLER, P. (1977), *Marketing Management*, 1st and 2nd editions, Prentice Hall, London

MANN, P. (1988), 'Delivering the right product to the right people', *Museums Journal*, **Dec.**, 139–142, London

MOOREHEAD, A. (1960), *The White Nile*, Chap. 6, Penguin, London

SCOTTISH MUSEUMS COUNCIL (1988), *A Framework for Museums in Scotland*, Edinburgh

THOMPSON, J. (1984), *The Manual of Curatorship*, Butterworth, London

TOWNSEND, R (1970), *Up the Organization*, Hodder Fawcett, London

WILMSHURST, J. (1984), *The Fundamentals of Practice of Marketing*, Heinemann, London

16

Personnel management

Michael Diamond

Introduction

Personnel management is the process through which people are deployed for the achievement of known objectives. The larger the organization, and the more complex the demands made of it, the greater the need for a clearly understood management process through which those objectives may be achieved.

During the 1960s and early 1970s, many institutions grew, aided by a period of increasing public expenditure, and with this growth came a new range of management problems. Rapidly developing collections and the growth of 'professionalism' led to an increasing emphasis on the employment of specialist, properly trained curators and conservators. At the same time, there developed an awareness of the educational potential of the collections, and this led to the employment of specialist staff for education services and exhibition programmes. Design and publicity departments emerged during the same period, in order to ensure that the highest possible standards of presentation were applied.

During the 1980s, further pressures began to show themselves, arising from changes in the public and political perception of the museum's role in the community. The first of these concerned a need to move away from the 'palace of culture' concept towards one which engaged more directly the everyday interests and concerns of the public. This has led to more popular themes for exhibitions and displays, and a host of special events designed to explore the collections through direct contact between museum staff and their visitors. In some places, new community services have been set up, which take collections and staff into local areas to operate on a neighbourhood basis.

The second arose from the rapid growth of the tourism industry in the UK, and the realization that museums are a crucial resource for that industry.

Museums as major attractions need to demonstrate their uniqueness, the quality of their product, and their capacity to entertain as well as educate.

The effect of these changes has been to increase the complexity of the organization, and to challenge our understanding of what museums exist for. More than ever before there is a need for clear aims and objectives, and more effective management of staff time. New skills have to be developed by all staff, especially as regards the awareness of public needs and interests. Enhanced training and more formal work-programming mechanisms are needed. So too are more staff, and this need has often been met through the use of volunteer, Manpower Services Commission or Inner City Schemes, creating yet another set of management issues.

Yet, whilst there are new factors for museum management, one has always been with us. This is that most museums have to operate within much larger organizations, the structures and practices of which have been designed for purposes very different from those of museums. Central and Local Government are the obvious examples, where a welter of regulations and procedures for financial and personnel management have to be followed, regardless of their value to the museums service (though the Trustee status of National Museums protects them from much of this). Museums set up by large companies often encounter similar problems. In all such cases the museum service forms such a small part of the whole, that any attempt to make special arrangements more appropriate to its real needs is almost certainly fraught with difficulties.

A clear understanding of the context within which we work – political, economic and social – is essential to the setting of worthwhile aims and objectives. We need only compare York and Manchester to realize that museums in those cities will have very different 'markets' to deal with. The aims and objectives should reflect both that 'market' and the political aspirations of the funding body, where it has them. It is important to understand this point, as many museums have never considered their aims and objectives in these terms, preferrring to take account only of 'professional' aspirations, and it is this, at the end of the day, that has given rise to under-recognition by funding bodies. Curatorial values need not be threatened by political or marketing concerns, and a more realistic approach to the context within which we work will almost certainly yield financial rewards.

Only when our aims and objectives have been determined can we identify the employee resources required to meet them. Unless we are actually setting up a new service we will of course already have a staff complement to work with, and the nature of the next part of the exercise will be to organize and adjust that resource as effectively as possible to meet the aims and objectives defined. We do this through the staff structure.

Staff structure

It is through the staff structure that we set out the relationships between the individuals in the organization, and begin to define their responsibilities. Furthermore, the staff structure reflects the objectives of the institution through the balance it expresses between one function and another. To quote Bains (1972): 'Its objective is to influence and create an environment in which the authority can recruit and develop the employees it needs to achieve its objectives'.

The relationship between the structure and the nature of the institution is vividly illustrated by a comparison between a traditional multidisciplinary Local Authority arrangement, and one from a single-discipline Charitable Trust museum. The Local Authority has the traditional weighting in favour of the curatorial activities (see *Figure 16.1*) whereas the Charitable Trust attaches far more importance to fund raising, not so much as an objective in itself as a recognition of the facts of economic life (see *Figure 16.2*).

Charitable Trust museums have had to develop the potential of commercial, volunteer and grant-aid resources to survive, but in the process they have drawn attention to new possibilities for many publicly owned institutions. Some, as a result, now have extensive non-curatorial operations which have significantly altered the shape of their staffing structures. Things do change. Our perception of the potential of our heritage, the public's expectations of us, the collections themselves on occasion, can be transformed to the point where existing structures no longer meet the needs we have of them. So, having determined your structure, be prepared to change it.

Many structures did indeed change quite significantly at the time of Local Government reorganization in 1974. As Local Authority boundaries altered, so too did the responsibilities of many museum services. In some areas a significant geographical factor was added to the existing functional ones, as responsibility for a number of widely spread branches was added to the brief of a single existing service. One solution was to give responsibility for a branch museum to the most appropriate curatorial

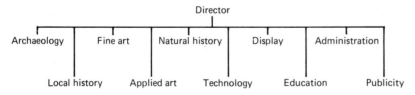

Figure 16.1 Local Authority staff structure

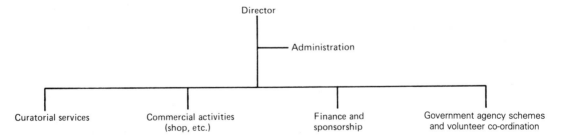

Figure 16.2 Charitable Trust staff structure

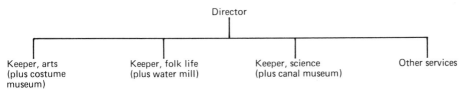

Director

Keeper, arts
(plus costume
museum)

Keeper, folk life
(plus water mill)

Keeper, science
(plus canal museum)

Other services

Figure 16.3 Responsibility for geographically dispersed branches given to the most appropriate curatorial department

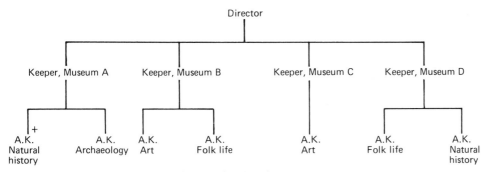

Director

Keeper, Museum A

Keeper, Museum B

Keeper, Museum C

Keeper, Museum D

A.K.
Natural
history

A.K.
Archaeology

A.K.
Art

A.K.
Folk life

A.K.
Art

A.K.
Folk life

A.K.
Natural
history

Figure 16.4 Staff structure based on buildings rather than functions

department, (see *Figure 16.3*). In others, a structure based on buildings rather than functions was adopted, (see *Figure 16.4*).

Co-ordination of subject disciplines is clearly a problem where specialists in one discipline exist in more than one museum. Equally, problems of building management arise if a discipline-based structure is applied to a series of multidisciplinary establishments.

Clearly a choice has to be made between a structure based on functions, and one based on buildings, and arrangements will have to be made to minimize the weakness of either option. A choice will in any case have to be made when determining what might be described as the philosophy of the structure. This issue was brought into sharp focus by the Bains Report (Bains 1972).

The central gospel of the Bains Report was that of 'corporate management'. Bains observed that Local Government in the 1960s consisted essentially of a 'vertical' structure of separate professional departments, each responding to the demands made of it as it saw fit. There was duplication, there were large gaps in provision, one department would be found working against the interests of another, there was little consistency in staff structure and salaries, and little sense of forward planning. In short, there was no horizontal co-ordination of policy-making or implementation; no 'corporate' identity.

The Bains solution at Authority level was to create a new management structure above the Chief Officer tier, and give that structure the job of co-ordinating and directing the development and implementation of policy.

This process was reflected in restructuring within individual departments, where a policy-making layer of management was inserted between the Director and his Section Heads. A typical post-Bains museum situation might appear as shown in *Figure 16.5*. Here a Departmental Management Team of three would be responsible for the development, co-ordination and implementation of policy for 11 separate sections.

Whilst 'corporate management' as such is not as fashionable a concept now as it was during the 1970s, the issue which it addressed remains valid. Authorities which embraced the Bains' philosophy often managed to develop a coherent sense of direction and to increase the amount of time devoted to policy issues. But the philosophy does create its own problems. Vast quantities of paper tend to be generated to support this corporate activity (though this should be offset by a reduction in the quantity of paper flowing 'vertically'), and many hours can be spent in team meetings at one level or another. These meetings, moreover, often experience the natural human difficulty of distinguishing between genuine policy issues and day-to-day administration. The creation of a new forum for debate generates unnecessary as well as worthwhile activity if it is not very strictly controlled.

There is, therefore, a fundamental choice to be made between a 'vertical' (or line management) structure and a 'horizontal' (or corporate) one. The choice itself, however, is arguably less important than an understanding of the strengths and weaknesses of the two options. If this understanding is there, then arrangements can be made to minimize the

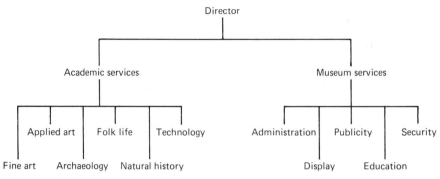

Figure 16.5 Typical museum staff structure, post-Bains

weaknesses of the structure adopted, and make the most of the strengths of the one rejected. Thus a vertical system would include arrangements for horizontal debate on matters affecting two or more sections, and a horizontal system would take care not to spend time on unnecessary communication and programming at the expense of attention to day-to-day operational issues.

From structure to action

Whatever management structure is adopted, its job is to create the mechanisms for converting aims and objectives into action, and to ensure that those mechanisms deliver. The means by which it does this will vary according to the size and nature of the institution. A small single-discipline museum, where everyone meets everyone else on a routine day-to-day basis, may well operate quite well through verbal contact, whereas a large organization will usually require formal written policies and annual action plans. The purpose of this part of the management process is to ensure that each employee understands what the institution is there for, and precisely what is expected of him or her.

There should, of course, be a policy statement covering each stated objective. In some cases more than one will be required, depending on how broadly framed the objectives are. Thus a single 'management' objective, extolling the virtues of efficient and effective management practices, may require policies on sponsorship, commercial activities and staff training, among other things. Likewise a single 'presentation' objective may generate separate policies for permanent displays, temporary exhibitions and schools services.

Responsibility for producing policy statements lies squarely with the Management Team, but it would be a foolish Team that did this without consulting staff at lower levels in the stucture. While few policies will suit everyone (the Management Team

must ultimately make the decisions), the process of consultation can make all the difference between adopting a policy which is resented and ill understood, and adopting one which is 'owned' and supported by those with the job of implementing it. It might also make the difference between arriving at a policy which is achievable rather than one which is not.

The same applies to the production of the annual Action Plan, which is the point at which all the bold declarations of intent (and that is what aims, objectives and policies really are) get translated into real action. It is here that the desirable comes hard up against the achievable, in the form of cash and manpower resources. Just how achievable the Action Plan is will emerge from the review process which should go with it. Reviews will not only show what progress has been made, but should also throw up unforeseen pressures and opportunities. These in turn will suggest targets which should be discarded from, or added to, the original Plan.

Informal structures

Many of the issues raised by the processes of policy formulation and action planning require detailed consideration across several sections of the organization. Whilst a corporate structure provides a multidisciplinary debating forum at Management Team level, it does not do so below that level, where most structures remain essentially 'vertical'. Such are the complexities of modern museum management, that a mechanism is needed which can help us to deal with variable relationships between staff groups covering a wider range of specialized disciplines than are encountered in most organizations.

Two examples might help to clarify the problem here. First, we may have three objectives covering temporary exhibitions, publicity, and schools services, and these may be quite simply expressed in the formal management structure by the appointment of specialist officers in each field. Each of these officers will then be charged with preparing a draft policy and action plan for Management Team approval, but it is self-evident that none should do so without widespread consultation. Likewise a training policy and Action Plan should involve debate across the whole organization.

In small museums this can often be dealt with on an *ad hoc* basis, provided the problem is clearly understood, but in larger institutions a more structured approach can help to ensure that all interested parties are actually involved. A simple matrix chart, plotting the structure against the policy issues, is the usual tool in such cases, and such a chart for the two examples given above is shown in *Table 16.1*.

Table 16.1 A matrix chart of structure versus policy issues for the two examples given in the text

	Finance	Administration	Personnel	Security	Curatorial	Conservation	Exhibitions	Publicity	Schools	Design	Commercial	Events
Exhibitions			★	★	★	★	★	★	★			★
Publicity				★		★	★		★			★
Education				★			★		★	★		★
Training	★	★	★	★	★	★	★	★	★	★	★	★

Further problems are immediately identified by such a chart. What, for example, do we mean by 'curators'? Do we select one to represent all of them on a working party? Or do we make some other arrangement for the full range of curatorial interest to be expressed? And how effective would a training working party be which had representatives from every section of the organization? Here it will clearly be necessary to break the process down into several consultation groups of manageable size (usually not more than six to eight people).

It is worth pointing out that informal structures like these can help not only to solve the problems they were set up for, but also to bring together staff who might not otherwise meet, and thus give rise to better co-operation as a whole.

Training

Staff training is as closely related to an institution's performance as any other aspect of personnel management. Just as the staff structure and its management arrangements should be designed to meet the needs of the institution's overall objectives, so the training programme should be designed to

meet the needs of the individual posts within the structure.

At this point the job specification (see below) becomes important, since it is in this document that the objectives of the post are, or should be, made clear. It will also make clear the qualifications required of the post holder on appointment (such as a relevant degree), and those he will be expected to acquire in post (such as the Museums Diploma).

Thus far nothing has been suggested which is not already fairly generally practised in British museums, though many still view the Museums Diploma as an 'optional extra'. At the time of writing the diploma is in the process of being replaced by new industry wide qualifications under development by the recently-founded Museums Training Institute; suffice it to say here that some form of specialist curatorial training and qualification is surely essential if our heritage is to be cared for properly, and our work taken seriously as a specialized professional activity.

Non-curatorial departments will, of course, have their own basic specialist qualifications. Thus a display officer would have a degree in fine art from a Polytechnic School of Art, an Education Officer would have a teaching degree, and an Administrator, at least at a senior level, might well have a degree in economics or business studies. At this point, however, we find that full-time higher education qualifications are shading into in-service training, as many very able administrators have worked through from day-release Polytechnic or College of Further Education courses for ONC and HNC qualifications to the Diploma in Public Administration.

The principle of in-service training extends across the whole range of museum activities, and well beyond the scope of the old Museums Diploma. All staff are subject to certain legal requirements, and must be made aware of the legal framework within which their institution operates. This will vary somewhat according to the museum's constitution, i.e. whether it is a national or a Local Authority museum, privately owned or a charitable trust. Whatever its constitution there will be a document which sets it out, and usually further papers setting out administrative rules and procedures. In Local Government, the Standing Orders are supplemented by Financial Regulations and the Scheme of Conditions of Service (Staff Handbook). These documents should be familiar to all professional staff, and senior administrators should be able to advise colleagues on their contents to a high level of detail.

Legal issues may crop up in many guises. How much physical force, for example, may be used in restraining a thief or vandal? Which hygiene regulations cover the preparation of sandwiches for a Friends' function? How do you deal with conflicting claims of ownership on a loan item, when the original lender dies? Many of these issues are best dealt with on an *ad hoc* basis by reference to the museum's legal advisers; some should be covered by short training courses given by appropriate specialist bodies; others may be covered quite adequately by making available appropriate publications, such as the *Code of Conduct for Museum Curators*, and need not be repeated here.

Even when basic training requirements have been met, substantial further needs may arise. The first group of these may be described as 'specialist' professional needs, often arising from developments elsewhere which create a requirement for some updating. Technical advances in storage, security and conservation are classic examples. Short courses of one to three days' duration, are arranged by a variety of bodies, including Federations, Area Councils, the Museums Association, specialist professional groups and the Association of Independent Museums. Advice on this complex pattern of provision will increasingly be available from the MTI.

Some of these courses will also be of value in tackling the second group of training requirements, best described as 'staff development'. In this case a comparison is made between the performance of the person in post and the job description of that post, as a result of which training needs are identified which will help to narrow any gaps which appear between objectives and achievement. Many organizations operate little in the way of formal procedures for such an assessment, and indeed it is usually a fairly simple matter for an officer to agree with his superior where any training needs may lie. Sometimes, however (the Civil Service is a case in point), formal annual assessments take place which include the examination of training needs.

Some of these needs will be 'specialist' professional ones. Thus the trainee paintings conservator attending a course on recent advances in techniques relating to the transfer of panel paintings may be developing a whole new range of skills as well as updating himself on technical advances in his craft.

However, changes in the role and complexity of museum services have led to the need for a whole new area of training which is concerned with the acquisition of administrative, management and public relations skills. Courses in marketing, receptionist skills, interview techniques, or customer care are provided, or can be arranged through, Local Authority Personnel Departments, and generally last one to three days.

Senior staff may require more advanced training of a week or more covering such things as leadership, decision-making, work programming, time management, and performance measurement. Courses are again available through Local Authorities and the Association of Independent Museums. In the latter

the quite different financial situation of private and trust museums is reflected in the time devoted to marketing and fund-raising techniques. Local authority courses are clearly not designed for this kind of institution, but it is particularly interesting to note that up to half the delegates to Association of Independent Museums' (AIM) longer courses are from Local Authorities, reflecting the increasing awareness of commercial possibilities in all quarters.

One problem which affects most of these longer courses (and some, such as one offered by Institute of Local Government Studies (INLOGOV), run for 6 weeks), is that of cost. Small museums, in particular, are frequently priced out of the market, with the result that their training opportunities are very limited.

A critical training area for any museum is that of induction training for security staff. Clearly, every new arrival should be fully briefed on the geography of the building, patrol patterns, emergency fire, theft and bomb procedures, fire fighting and legal issues relevant to his/her work. In many cases he/she may also need training in the handling of exhibits, packing, and the use of display equipment. Precise arrangements will vary according to the size and organization of the museum. Small institutions usually find it possible to handle the general induction on a one-to-one basis with the Supervisor. Larger ones will need to make more formal arrangements. The important thing is that a sound basic grounding is given immediately on arrival, and that constant supervision is provided for a period of some weeks. A written manual should be provided for all security staff, covering all basic aspects of their work.

Specific training on fire fighting and first-aid is usually organized by Local Authority personnel departments. Detailed training for security staff is arranged by many of the Area Councils though it is often difficult to release security staff for courses lasting several days. Such courses are, in any case, still very thin on the ground and most training is still carried out 'in house'. Much of the training is done on an *ad hoc* basis, involving security supervisors and curatorial staff, and it has to be said that training is still not taken very seriously by many museum managements. This is remarkable when we consider how much of the handling, packing, moving and displaying of collections is actually done by security staff.

One further training need, and one of increasing importance, is created by the developing use of volunteer and temporary staff. Volunteers work irregular hours, and temporary staff work on short-term contracts. Both present security and supervision problems, and care must be taken to ensure that their numbers do not exceeed the capacity of the permanent staff to handle these problems. They will usually have a very specfic brief, and should receive training designed to meet that brief. This may be quite informal, but must cover the basic essentials of security and fire procedures, what they can and cannot do and, in the case of curatorial helpers, how to handle collections and how to operate documentary systems. Much useful guidance on the management of volunteers is given in Volunteers in Museums and Heritage Organisations, published by HMSO in 1991.

Frequent references have been made to a number of agencies specializing in various fields of training. It must be emphasized, however, that the pattern of training provision varies greatly across the country. Universities, Polytechnics, Colleges of Further Education, Area Services, Federations, specialist professional groups, AIM and Local Authorities are all providers of training opportunities, and to these may be added the larger private-sector companies and business-management organizations. But the strength and character of provision does vary, and museum Personnel Officers will need to research the local situation carefully before constructing coherent training programmes. Assessment of the quality and content of this confusing pattern of provision will be a major responsibility of the MTI.

Personnel Officers would also do well to examine the potential within their own organizations. The gradual demise of the apprenticeship system is now affecting many museums, where the older craftsmen, often possessing time-honoured skills no longer taught on formal courses, are reaching retirement age. The problem of passing on their skills is a very real one, but with due forethought, trainees or early replacements can be arranged so as to resolve this problem, at least in part. It must also be said that in-house training is sometimes, for financial reasons, the only possible training in the less well-endowed museums.

In summary, two things must be said of training as a whole. First it is not a panacea. The business of management is to make the most of people's strengths and to minimize the effect of their weaknesses. Training can help us to do this, but it cannot convert a weakness into a strength. Second, it must serve a clearly identified purpose, and that identification should arise from the comparison of a job specification with the performance of the individual doing the job. Training, like everything else, should be designed to meet a genuine need.

The personnel function

Thus far we have looked at the overall management of human resources within the museum context. All museums should have an officer or officers whose primary role is 'personnel', and who should be a major source of advice and guidance on the management of all the processes described. His/her advice will be based on his/her knowledge and experience of the management process as such, his/her understanding of how each part relates to the others, of the human processes and resources required to move from one to another, and of options available (e.g. whether to buy in expertise or set up internal units). He/she should also be able to contribute to the definition of the context within which the museum operates through his/her knowledge of audience survey techniques, demographic data, political processes, etc.

The Personnel Officer will lead the debate on the formulation of training policy although, as we have seen, this affects every part of the organization and will require extensive consultation if all training needs are to be accurately identified and met. He/she will also be responsible for the basic employment policy of the museum, covering such matters as terms and conditions of employment, disciplinary and grievance procedures, etc. National and Local Government museums will of course work within the framework of the employing Authority.

In recent years the law relating to terms and conditions of employment, health and safety, and trades unions has become very complex. It has therefore become necessary, for legal as well as management reasons, to prepare comprehensive statements on all these matters for every employee. The current position with regard to such statements is set out in the Code of Conduct for Museum Curators.

This documentation is necessary not only to meet legal requirements but also to avoid unnecessary misunderstandings when disputes arise. Most useful in the operational context, however, is one further document, the 'Job Specification'. It is here that the fullest description of the post is set out, including formal reporting relationships, responsibilities, decision-making, a list of duties, qualifications, experience and salary. Clearly this document should be formulated in the context of the staff structure as a whole, and of related Job Specifications in particular. It should be as clear and specific as possible in order to avoid unnecessary dispute, and this can be difficult in the museum context where the success of a project often depends on a flexible approach to responsibilities on the part of staff.

It is particularly difficult to quantify the responsibilities of museum personnel, and this has led to continual problems with regard to the establishment of a proper pay structure across the country as a whole. In general, the national museums, where Civil Service scales normally apply, have developed significantly higher salaries than the Local Authority establishments. But there are also variations between Authorities, with the larger ones sometimes offering better rewards than the smaller. The Museums Association does recommend a minimum of Scale 5 (Local Government) or equivalent for holders of its Diploma, but this is difficult to enforce and only affects the bottom end of the problem. Attempts to persuade trade unions such as NALGO to exert pressure have failed, and individual Directors are effectively left to fight their own battles up and down the country. It is hard, in these circumstances, to see how things can be changed, but it is clear that the quantification of responsibilities set out in Job Specifications can only be helpful.

Precise specifications are also important when new appointments are being made. It is surprising how many appointments are made without any clear view of what is being asked of the candidates concerned, and even when there is a clear view many posts are filled by candidates who meet only a limited number of the requirements. Dealing with new appointments is itself a skilled business, and one with significant consequences when one realizes how long one may have to live with the result. Specialist short courses are now generally available, and are well worth the investment for all staff involved in making appointments.

Industrial relations

Few museums experience serious industrial-relations problems, probably because their small scale encourages a level of personal contact which defuses problems arising from poor communications. Personality clashes can, however, lead to difficulties anywhere, and it will be a continual management responsibility to watch for such problems and deal with them before they get out of hand. Some aspects of industrial relations are enshrined in law. The Health and Safety at Work Act, for example, empowers employers to appoint Safety Representatives at each place of work if employees ask for them. Safety Committees may also be set up at the employees' request.

Other formal machinery arises from the need for good communication between management and employees. Most large organizations now have a system of Joint Consultative Committees where management meets with trade union representatives on a regular basis. In Local Government Joint Consultative Committees (JCCs) generally operate at departmental and Authority level, with further committees at regional and national level for issues

transcending local significance. In the museum context, the important factor in establishing such structures is to ensure that they meet a real need for the transmission of information and the resolution of problems which it has not been possible to deal with through normal management processes.

It has to be said that most of the industrial-relations difficulties that do occur can be put down to personality clashes exacerbated by the very unusual conditions of curatorial life. The values of the curator are often a mystery to the security officer and the clerical assistant and, when lack of understanding is added to impatience on either side, trouble often ensues. There is undoubtedly room in most museums for informal discussion arrangements to reduce friction of this kind.

Conclusion

The situation outlined above in many ways mirrors the position in which museums as a whole find themselves. A misunderstanding of the role of museums by those responsible for funding them, and a misunderstanding by museum staff of the perspective of the 'world outside' are at the root of many of our problems. Better communication between the parties concerned may provide part of the answer to improving our lot. Internally, the management challenge is to apply the staff resources available to us in such a way as to make the best possible use of the considerable abilities our profession possesses.

References

BAINS, M.A. (1972), *The New Authorities*, HMSO, London

Bibliography

ATTWOOD, M. (1987), *Personnel Management*, Pan Management Guides, London

BOYLAN, P. (1986), *The Changing World of Museums and Art Galleries*, INLOGOV, Birmingham

HANDY, C.B. (1976), *Understanding Organizations*, Penguin, London

JOHNSON, R. (1984), *How to Manage People*, Sunday Telegraph/Hutchinson, London

LUCAS, H. (1978), *Companion to Management Studies*, Heinemann, London

PATERSON (1973), *The New Scottish Local Authorities: Organization and Management Structures*, HMSO, Edinburgh

17

The management of volunteers

J. Patrick Greene

Introduction

In 1991 the results of a major study on the role of volunteers in museums and heritage organizations was published (Millar, 1991). It provides a wide-ranging review of the field, with recommendations for action and examples of good practice. In this chapter I will examine aspects of the management of volunteers in museums.

Which museums use volunteers?

Volunteers play an active role in the majority of museums, as a series of studies has shown. A survey carried out by the Volunteers Centre in 1984 (Mattingly, 1984) revealed that of the 103 museums that provided information, 91 per cent benefitted from the involvement of volunteers. Whilst the sample was relatively small and was inevitably weighted towards those museums with volunteers, the striking aspect of the survey is that volunteers were found to be an integral part of the activity of every category of museum – national, Local Authority, independent and military. The only exception in the survey was university museums, but this was not a representative result, as enquiry by the writer has confirmed that here too volunteers are widely used. An important point that emerges from the survey is that volunteers are just as likely to be involved in public-sector museums as independent museums – many would have assumed that there were barriers in the former which might inhibit volunteer activity, but that is clearly not the case. The picture of widespread involvement is confirmed by a survey of museums in Surrey carried out by Ann Jones of Farnham Museum for a Museum Association seminar held in October 1987. Of the 25 museums surveyed, only five did not have volunteers. Seven of the sample were Local Author-ity museums, and of these only one had no volunteers. Ten of the sample were entirely run by volunteers. A less highly focused study, but one with near-comprehensive national information, is the Museums Database: the 1988 figures show that of 673 museums that answered the question on volunteers, 411 (61 per cent) recorded a total of 11,206 individuals involved, an average of 27 per museum.

In summary, therefore, it is clear that volunteers are an integral part of the museum community, and are found in every type of museum. It follows that the management of this resource is every bit as deserving of attention as are other aspects of the museum's operation.

What do volunteers do?

Volunteers perform an extremely wide variety of tasks. An independent museum, for example, will usually be governed by a Charitable Trust. The trustees bear ultimate responsibility for the operation of the museum (Sekers, 1987) and are usually explicitly debarred by the constitution from receiving any financial reward for their services. They are, therefore, volunteers. Elsewhere in the museum, volunteers may play a part in collecting admission fees, working in the shop and café, restoring and operating exhibits, acting as guides and room stewards, helping catalogue collections, carrying out excavations and construction work, picking up litter, organizing lecture series, and promoting the museum. Indeed, many independent museums start as entirely volunteer-run organizations, and substantial numbers stay that way. Others evolve and grow to a point where professional staff are required. That transition can be a difficult one, with a need to re-examine roles, and adapt to changing circumstances. A useful concept introduced by Stuart Smith of Ironbridge at the 1987 Management of Volunteers seminar, is of volunteers as the museum's 'pioneer corps'. Volunteers can blaze a trail for the museum by operating in new areas with innovative activities. This can often lead to the creation of jobs when their activities are particularly successful – the reverse of the frequently articulated fear that volunteers might displace paid employees.

It would be quite wrong to think that volunteers are only capable of doing routine, mundane tasks. In fact, they can assist in almost any area, including conservation. The key word here is *assist*, for as has been demonstrated by groups such as The National Association of Decorative and Fine Art Societies (NADFAS), for example, in the field of textile conservation, work of the highest standards can be achieved provided the volunteer receives appropriate training and supervision and works with professional conservators. Standards of excellence are achieved in fields as disparate as archaeological excavation, the restoration of industrial and transportation objects, and the documentation of art collections.

Who volunteers?

Stereotypes of museums volunteers exist and, like most stereotypes, individuals can usually be found who fit the mould. However, such stereotypes obscure the wide range of people who, in fact, give up their time to help museums, and who are likely to be drawn from every sector of society. This breadth of origin poses its own problems of management, for the requirements of, say, retired and unemployed people will be different to Scouts and Guides groups, or families with young children, or students on placements, or apprentices recruited through their employers, or young people on Duke of Edinburgh Award Schemes, or inmates of the local open prison (admittedly a special case, where the term 'volunteer' does not fully reflect the situation). If a museum finds it is attracting volunteers from a narrow segment of society, it would be wise to examine how it might broaden its appeal.

Why volunteer?

What is it that motivates people to sacrifice their leisure to help a museum? The reasons are various and sometimes complex; but they are likely to contain some of the following ingredients as the Volunteer Centre Survey showed (Mattingly, 1984, p. 31). In diminishing order of importance, volunteers give the following reasons:

(1) interest in subjects covered by the museum;
(2) contribution to the community;
(3) using skills that the volunteer already possesses;

(4) obtaining experience of museum work with a career in mind;
(5) filling spare time;
(6) meeting other people; and
(7) learning new skills.

A successful relationship between a museum and its volunteers is one in which the museum benefits from the presence of the volunteer who, in turn, gains satisfaction, recognition and often knowledge and expertise as well. Ideally, it will be a situation of mutual advantage, in which both parties gain from the association.

Why have volunteers?

In essence, the benefit to the museum from the presence of volunteers is that it is enabled to perform better, with improved documentation, or enhanced conservation/restoration capacity, or better service to visitors. Museums are in a situation where additional resources are difficult to obtain, so volunteers can help stretch existing ones. In addition, the museum can harness skills which are not present in its own staff. It is also important to have broad support in the community; volunteers will be valuable allies in times of difficulty. None of this would be worthwhile if supervision of volunteers became so onerous that members of staff were unable to carry out their other duties. In fact, it has been calculated (Mattingly, 1984) that for every six hours of staff supervision, 90 hours of volunteers' work can be obtained. This level of efficiency amply justifies the use of volunteers. It is a situation of partnership – a volunteer-run museum often moves into a new league when it employs its first professional staff member, and professional museum workers frequently extend their effectiveness by recruiting volunteers to assist.

Volunteers can also perform the role of an emergency task force – a pool of assistance that can be called on when the museum is stretched to the limit. Examples include popular special events, when the number of visitors exceeds the usual daily flow many times over; the sudden need to rescue the contents and fittings of a historic workshop before demolition or disposal, or (heaven forbid, but it *can* happen) the flooding of the museum store.

Another area of assistance is in fund raising. Volunteers play a part in this activity to widely different degrees in Britain, and fund raising is more likely to be an aspect of the assistance provided by art gallery volunteers than in other types of museum. In the USA fund raising often involves large numbers of volunteers, and it is tied in with the social scene. It works best if volunteers raise money towards a specific objective which can, therefore, be regarded as their pet project. However, in all cases the priority for fund raising must be agreed with the Director as part of the overall programme of the museum and, if the purpose is to acquire objects, these should become part of the museum collection rather than remain in the ownership of the volunteers.

What are the dangers of using volunteers?

It is possible for problems to arise from the use of volunteers in a number of different ways. It is important to be aware of the dangers so that matters can be arranged to minimize the chance of their occurring. This can include:

(1) Conflict between volunteers and members of staff, who may feel that their jobs are threatened by voluntary work substituting for paid employment. This is the basis of opposition from trades unions which is sometimes encountered.

(2) Strong sectional interests within the volunteer group causing tension between volunteers, or with the museum.

(3) Jealousy by volunteers of members of staff – particularly if the museum has started as a volunteer-run museum. It may not be easy for volunteers for whom this has been 'their' project to take a supporting role.

(4) A lack of appreciation by volunteers of the overall objectives of the museum, or of the pressures induced by management and development responsibilities on the staff.

(5) Activities by volunteers, such as the acquisition of objects, which do not coincide with the objectives of the museum.

(6) Exploitation of volunteers by museums as a result of creating unrealistic expectations about employment prospects that will result from voluntary activity.

(7) Damage to museum objects through the use of untrained personnel.

(8) Inability to programme work for volunteers who may not turn up when expected.

(9) The museum may take for granted the contribution made by volunteers, who in consequence feel under-valued. These, and other, problems can be minimized by good management.

How to recruit volunteers

One of the most effective ways of organizing volunteers is through a Friends of the Museum Organization. By banding volunteers together it is possible to communicate with them in an efficient manner. Furthermore, it is possible to establish a constitutional relationship with the museum's governing body (its committee or trust) which clarifies the role of each body.

It is desirable that the Friends Organization has a proper constitution, which describes its objectives and how it is to be run, and which is drawn up in such a way that it can register as a charity (England and Wales) or be recognized as charitable by the Inland Revenue (Scotland). The British Association of Friends of Museums can advise on such a constitution. Where the museum is itself a charitable trust, the objectives in the Friends constitution should mirror those in the Trust constitution. In the case of other types of museum, the governing body should be consulted when the Friends constitution is drawn up. It is worth including in the constitution the proviso mentioned previously that the Friends themselves should not acquire and own museum objects, but instead assist the museum in the collection of objects. Likewise, it is also desirable to specify that Friends should not engage in any activities without the prior approval of the museum's Director. Getting this constitutional relationship right is a vital step in ensuring that the museum and Friends are quite clear about objectives, and the role of each body. It can avoid much needless conflict.

There is a strong case for keeping the Friends closely informed of the museum's plans and for giving them a voice in the determination of strategy. This can be achieved by making the Friends chairperson a member of the governing body (e.g. a Trustee). Other mechanisms such as the Director's presence at some of the Friend's council meetings and invitations to Friends to special events can assist communication, and emphasize the value placed on their activities. Newsletters and meetings are further ways of making the Friends aware of the museum's overall objectives and activities.

Another argument for having volunteers organized as part of the Friends is that it eases the provision of insurance cover, and allows health-and-safety equipment and training to be provided, where appropriate. Most museums would wish to give volunteers free entry, and here again the Friends organization proves beneficial, with the membership card providing an easy means of identification at the till.

Overcoming staff resistance

Where volunteers have been in use in a museum for a long time there is rarely antagonism between them and members of staff. It is usually in circumstances where volunteers are an innovation that problems arise. The most straightforward solution is to adopt the principle that volunteers will *not* be used as a substitute for paid staff. The management of the museum should state that principle publicly, and should be prepared to discuss the issue fully with members of staff through, for example, a joint consultative committee.

The appointment of a volunteers co-ordinator

For volunteers to operate effectively it is important that a steady flow of tasks to be carried out is identified by the museum, and suitable people to do the work are found from amongst the pool of volunteers. There is nothing worse for morale than having an enthusiastic team of volunteers with nothing to do, or with tasks which are beyond their competence. One of the most important aspects of the management of volunteers is to overcome this problem and the selection of a volunteer co-ordinator is an effective means of doing so. In that way there is one individual to whom both museum employees and volunteers can relate, thus establishing an effective means of communication for day-to-day issues. If the museum is entirely voluntary, there is still the need for such a person to act as the bridge between the committee and other volunteers. If the museum is small, the role may be taken by one of the members of staff as part of their job. Alternatively, a volunteer with sufficient organization and communication skills – and time – may be found. This is an area in which Retired Executives Action Clearing House (REACH), which matches retired executives with charities, may help. Alternatively, it may be possible to obtain a volunteers co-ordinator through secondment by a commercial company. If a museum's volunteer activities increase beyond a certain level, then the appointment of a full-time member of staff may be necessary.

Having a volunteer co-ordinator will not absolve many other members of staff from their responsibilities for work with volunteers. The need to specify work to be done, to check progress and standards, to provide encouragement and to say 'thank you' when a task is completed all require the close attention of staff members. The volunteers co-ordinator, however, makes all this much easier. Another point needs to be stressed – that volunteers may only be available outside the standard week-day working hours. The volunteers co-ordinator needs to be available to volunteers and staff and, therefore, needs to tailor their involvement to the needs of both groups of people.

Recruitment, training and discipline

Many museums get their volunteers simply on the basis of people offering themselves as helpers. Such passive recruitment is unlikely to be satisfactory if the museum is serious about involving volunteers in a wide variety of tasks. It is far better to assess the needs of the museum, to identify those areas to which volunteers could contribute, and then to attempt to recruit appropriate people. Appropriate means matching people to tasks. Thus an individual may have a relevant skill, or be motivated to acquire skills as part of their voluntary work. A Friends Organization is an obvious source – and the availability of skills or experience can be monitored by the volunteers co-ordinator. It must not be assumed, however, that just because someone is, say, a mechanic during the week they wish to be a mechanic at the weekend too. They may want to be a guide; conversely, a bank cashier probably does not want to end up counting money at the museum, but might want to be a mechanic. Assessing the pool of voluntary skills needs to be designed so as to detect such preferences.

It may be that the volunteer force at a particular museum is very narrow in terms of social class, gender, or age. Sometimes it will be found that what was a lively group is ageing and becoming less active. In such cases the museum can try to broaden its base of support by using the local media to publicize its needs – which can make good news stories. Volunteers from ethnic minority groups are poorly represented in most museums in Britain, and it would be worthwhile encouraging people from these groups to get involved. This may be easier through the recruitment of youth organizations, schools, etc., to help the museum. Parents with young children would often offer themselves as volunteers if museums were more ready to recognize their needs.

Having recruited volunteers it is important to train them. This is, generally speaking, less well organized in Britain than in the USA. The first element of training should be an induction exercise, to acquaint them with the objectives of the museum, and what it does. This can be carried out by fellow volunteers. A Code of Practice, drawn up by the museum and its volunteers, may help clarify some of the 'do's and don'ts' at this early stage. Other training should then be tailored to the requirements of the museum, and the volunteers. Often, it will be on-the-job training. Fellow volunteers and members of staff are likely to provide the training. It may be appropriate to issue certificates of competence to people who have successfully completed certain training exercises – such as the operation of historic machinery with health-and-safety implications, or the documentation of part of the collection.

A museum should not be frightened of establishing minimum standards for the performance of volunteers. These help to determine training needs – and they are something that most people will readily accept when the underlying reasons are explained to them. If individuals are unable to achieve the minimum standards after training, alternative tasks should be found which are more suited to their aptitude or skills. If the individual is still unable to perform satisfactorily, there is no alternative but to dispense with their services. This must be handled with sensitivity.

There may be occasions when volunteers act in a way that runs counter to the objectives of the museum, or behave dishonestly. A disciplinary procedure must then be invoked, with the sanction to bar the person from the museum site. This is rarely necessary in practice, but should be held in reserve if required.

If a museum does not have volunteers it is ignoring a valuable resource that can help it to perform its tasks more effectively, and is missing out on the opportunity to strengthen its links with the community. Volunteers bring benefits to the museum, and they themselves benefit from their involvement. To maximize the advantage to both parties, however, requires a level of management as good as for any other aspect of the museum's work.

References

MATTINGLY, J. (1984), *Volunteers in Museums and Galleries*, Volunteer Centre, Berkhamsted.

MILLAR, S. (1991), *Volunteers in Museums and Heritage Organisations – Policy Planning and Management*, HMSO London

SEKERS, D (1987), *The Role of Trustees In Independent Museums* (Guideline II), Association of Independent Museums, Chichester

Bibliography

TANNER, K. (1988), *Museum Projects: A Handbook for Volunteers*, Area Museum Council for the South West, Taunton

WILSON, D. AND BUTLER, R. (1989), *Managing in Voluntary and Non-profit Organisations*, Routledge, London

A full list of its useful publications is available from:

The Volunteer Centre UK,
29 Lower King's Road,
Berkhamsted,
Hertfordshire.
HP4 2AB

18

The management of museum buildings

Max Hebditch

At some stage in a Curator's career, and not necessarily far on, he or she will become responsible for a museum building, its use and its maintenance. The principles which apply to undertaking these management tasks apply equally to small and large buildings. However, the problems of open-air museums, which involve wider issues of estate management, are not considered here. Similarly, I shall not be concerned with the commissioning of new buildings or major conversion projects. Rather, I shall look at the problem of existing buildings and historic structures which may already be, or are intended to be, used for museum purposes.

Although I shall be concerned with practical matters, it cannot be stressed too much how important is the quality of the architecture to the museum's purpose. It may be because the historic structure is itself part of the story the museum has to tell. But, even if not so directly linked, the architecture will be a powerful influence on the reactions and feelings of the visitor in his encounter with the museum. It is important that the museum manager understands this.

What are the buildings for?

In stating the requirements for a museum building, or in reconsidering the use of an existing museum, it is always necessary to keep in mind the tasks it will have to perform:

(1) to ensure the safety and accessibility of the collections and their associated data (the building itself, if historic, may be part of the collection and must be accorded proper curatorial concern);
(2) to permit collecting, research and interpretation;
(3) to welcome the public and to provide for the museum's educational role through exhibitions, teaching and other facilities; and
(4) to make money for the institution.

Museums will apply different priorities to these tasks: facilities to make money will probably be more important to an independent museum; space for research staff may be only appropriate in the largest of publicly funded institutions. In assessing a building ask some questions:

(1) Does its location permit people to get to it in sufficient numbers for the museum to be viable (assuming proper signing);
(2) Having arrived, can the visitor, including the infirm or disabled, get to the parts of the museum he or she needs to reach? Reserve collections are often inaccessible to those in wheelchairs, for instance;
(3) Are the floors strong enough?
(4) Is there enough space for all the tasks to be carried out?
(5) Can the correct environmental conditions (temperature, humidity, freedom from dust and pollution, etc.) be created to satisfy the needs of collections and public?
(6) What proportion of expenditure on the museum will be needed to maintain the fabric and services of the building? What is too high a price?
(7) Is the character of the building appropriate to the museum's purpose?
(8) Do the limitations imposed by historic buildings legislation allow the fulfilment of all the museum's tasks?
(9) Will the museum accommodate the growth of the collections?

If these questions cannot be answered satisfactorily, then the building is no good as a museum, whatever its other merits. Of all the points, that relating to the location and size of the building is very important, particularly so as nowadays museums often have to cover running costs by admission charges. If a museum costs £100 000 a year to run, and you cannot attract 100 000 visitors paying £1 because you are in the wrong place, or you cannot accommodate them because the museum is too small, then the museum is not viable.

Allocating space

All the museum's activities and administrative requirements need to be formulated into a plan for the organization of the appropriate spaces within the museum building. It is, of course, the basis of any museum operation that there should be a relationship with the public. Any thinking about space must aim to facilitate that relationship, whether with the casual visitor or the specialist user. The reception of visitors is thus the kernel of the operation. Around the kernel are grouped the resources of objects, information and expertise to which the visitor requires access. Around that are the various support services that are required to make a useful relationship between the user and the museum's resources.

Reception

The most essential requirement for the reception area is an obvious front door and an entrance hall in which visitors can orientate themselves. It may also need to serve as a security zone for checking bags. The entrance hall should include space for waiting, sitting and the assembly of parties of visitors, with clear access to other reception areas. These may include toilets, public telephones, refreshment facilities, educational facilities, lecture theatres and shops. To service these public reception areas there must be non-public offices providing information facilities, ticket-issuing arrangements and cloakrooms. These spaces together with the necessary corridors for communication within the building should take up perhaps 25% of the total space in a museum.

The museum's resources

The study should begin with an examination of spaces in which to accommodate the *main study collections*. In this it will be necessary to balance what needs to be kept centrally, and what can be accommodated in less-expensive out-of-town locations. Related to the stored collections are a number of other important areas. These comprise the archives for storing paper, photographic, sound, video and other records which relate to the collections. These may be either recently generated, such as material related to archaeological excavations, or original records, such as business records linked to objects in the collection. Both objects and records demand an adequate study area where they can be used by visitors. This space, or one closely related to it, should also accommodate the indexes to the material held, ideally in a way which permits consultation directly by the user rather than through the curatorial staff.

Other space for the museum's resources will include the main exhibition galleries, special exhibition galleries, the library and the offices of the curatorial staff; it is often forgotten that curators are supposed to be accessible to the public.

The space allocated to museum resources in a general museum as a percentage of the total might be as follows:

Storage collections, study areas and archives	25%
Permanent and special exhibitions	30%
Total	55%

The individual percentages allocated to collections and exhibitions will vary according to the scale of collections and their importance.

Support services

In order to maintain and make available the museum's resources space must be allocated to a whole range of support functions. General museum services include direction, administration, security, maintenance workshop, cleaning equipment stores, materials stores, and messing and welfare facilities. In support of the collections space must be found for conservation laboratories and studios, the reception (and decontamination if necessary) of incoming material, and facilities for staff involved in field-work, research and collecting activities. In support of the presentation of the collections must be workshops, photographic storage, information and public-relations activities. Total spaces might comprise:

General museum services	3%
Collections support facilities	7%
Presentation support facilities	10%
Total	20%

Again, the relative proportions of each element may vary substantially depending on, for instance, the extent of a museum's involvement in research or field collecting programmes.

In summary, the space allocation within a museum should be:

Reception	25%
Museum resources	55%
Support	20%
Total	100%

Instructing consultants

Any building being used as a museum should be structurally sound. The checking of this is a matter for a professional architect or surveyor. For the building requirements of each class of museum space the reader is referred to the Bibliography given at the end of this chapter. However, there are some points which should be referred to a professional adviser. The environment required for museum objects is well understood and the specifications for temperature humidity, lighting and dust can all be provided. It is necessary to decide in each instance the extent to which the ideals can be achieved in relation to available finance and the importance of the material. Buildings must be free of pests and any materials used should be unattractive to pests.

Floor loadings and ceiling heights must also be adequate to accommodate the proposed study collections or exhibitions. A height of 3–4 m and a floor loading of $4\,kNm^{-2}$ are the recommended minima for flexible galleries. Some classes of material will require higher loadings. Adequate and flexible lighting systems must be provided.

There must also be sufficient hoists and lifts to enable the collections to be handled properly from arrival in the museum, and to store and display them. Buildings must also be capable of being made secure and safe both for staff and visiting public.

Above all, in areas where collections, archives and other records are to be stored or exhibited the services for the building must be arranged in such a way that the risk of damage from water, fuel oil and other materials is reduced to the minimum. The objective is to ensure that if any part of the system fails, the collections are not placed at risk either from leaks, or from someone trying to put the matter right. It is almost certain that at some time it will.

Complying with legislation

In considering the use or alteration of an existing building, there are numerous Acts and Regulations which have to be observed. The construction of exhibitions, even temporary ones, requires compliance with legislation, e.g.

(1) *Health and Safety at Work Act.* This places upon everyone, but heads of museums and senior staff in particular, a responsibility to ensure that both those who work in a museum and those who have any reason to visit it can do so safely. Failure to do so is a criminal offence. Particular attention should be paid to machinery. Related to this are the *Factories Act* and *Offices, Shops and Railways Premises Act* and other regulations. In particular, the Control of Substances Hazardous to Health Regulations require employers to undertake comprehensive assessments and appropriate controls for every toxic, corrosive and irritant substance used or generated in the workplace. There are also numerous Codes of Practice relating to everything from safety to control of noise from intruder alarms.
(2) *Planning Regulations.* Certain sorts of work, and all those involving a change of use of premises, require planning consent. There are also the special consents required in relation to the use of Historic Buildings and Ancient Monuments under their own legislation.
(c) *Building Regulations.* There is almost nothing you can do to a building which does not require the Local Authority to give Building Regulations approval. This includes the construction of exhibitions. Related to this are the various regulations governing prevention of fire,

which are extremely rigorous and severely limit the choice of fabrics and other materials used in exhibitions.
(4) *Provision for persons who are disabled.* The *Building Act 1984* gave power to the Secretary of State for the Environment to make regulations relating to disabled access to public buildings. *British Standard 5810:1979* provides a Code of Practice for disabled access to buildings by those in wheelchairs and those whose hearing or sight is impaired. Any museum should be in the forefront of provision to enable the disabled to use its services on an equal basis with all others.

In all these matters, the museum manager will need professional advice. Although this may be available as a matter of course in the Local Government sector, independent museums and some national museums who handle this work themselves will need to appoint architects for all but the smallest project.

Keeping things going

Having decided how the building is to be used for museum purposes, it will only be a success if it is kept working and in good order. There are five points which need to be kept in mind in any institution:

(1) maintenance of the fabric and services,
(2) heat, light and water,
(3) housekeeping,
(4) security, and
(5) disaster planning.

Maintenance of the fabric and services

The importance of adequate maintenance is self-evident. Not to keep a building in good repair is to stack up trouble for the future. Leaking roofs, faulty services and defective alarms place collections at risk and Trustees will be failing in their duty if they allow it to occur. The maintenance of public areas in a safe condition is a statutory obligation for which individual members of staff can be criminally responsible under the Health and Safety at Work legislation.

Structural maintenance must include arrangements for a planned cycle of repair and cleaning of the fabric. The plan should include the frequency with which areas are done both inside and out. In areas particularly vulnerable to vandalism, such as toilets, repair must be frequent. But all areas need vandalism put right immediately. Other structural items include the replacement of carpets and floor coverings, and the resurfacing of car parks and drives. Provision must also be made for the unexpected, such as frost or gale damage.

Minor building works are often necessary. The use of buildings is always changing in response to demands placed on the museums. Doors and partitions will always need to be moved, new sinks plumbed in, or specialized equipment fitted. From time to time major maintenance will be needed, such as the complete renewal of a roof, or major attention to timber floors and roof structures. Often these costs will be met out of capital (or raised by appeal in the case of many independent museums).

The mechanical and other services of a museum require maintenance. Where fully developed and extensive air-handling systems are in operation, they may require permanent operating and engineering staff, who will carry out maintenance. Poor maintenance of air conditioning systems is a hazard to health both in the building and in adjoining areas. Prosecutions have been successful for causing death and injury through respiratory infections. In most museums, however, maintenance will take the form of contracts for the servicing of boilers, lifts, hoists, security alarms and cameras, and so forth. Again, provision has to be made for the unexpected and also for regular replacement of the plant and equipment. The life-span of equipment can be remarkably short!

These aspects of maintenance require both money and systems. The problem in Local Government is often inadequate systems. The routine regular inspection of buildings by the professional officer and the ordering of works does not happen as it should and there is too much end-of-financial-year panic. The museum manager with a good eye can to some extent compensate for this. An important aspect of these systems is, of course, the existence of standing orders relating to the appointment of consultants and the letting of contracts. Independent museums should adopt and follow such orders if they do not already have them. It is an area where corruption is not unknown.

The cost of maintenance and servicing will vary considerably. But here are some figures (at 1987 prices) as a percentage of gross revenue expenditure (but excluding any capital financing costs):

Large museum in London 9.3%
Large district (city) museum in England with nine premises 5.7%
Large district (city) museum in Scotland with many premises 7.5%
Small district museum in England 4.2%

Heat, light and water

The museum will consume energy and water. Systems for checking on the efficient use of energy are necessary, but guard against those who may not realize that the air-conditioning or other system has to operate 24 hours a day to protect the objects. It is well to keep an eye on electrical wiring, which may need regular renewal.

Housekeeping

Apart from the favourable impact on the visitor of a well cared for museum, good housekeeping is an important part of the conservation process. This is particularly true in the furnished historic building where the activities of the cleaning staff can include cleaning the collections on open display. As with maintenance of the fabric, efficient cleaning depends on having precise schedules of what needs to be done, and the methods to be employed. There must be sufficient staff to do the job. The US National Parks Service reckons that in an historic house, where some objects are cleaned, an average of 3 person-hours per year per square metre of exhibit space is required. The purpose of cleaning is to remove dust and dirt, not just push it around; and cleaning must be good enough to inhibit pests such as moths. The key to successful housekeeping will be the effectiveness of the training provided, particularly where the handling of objects is involved.

Security

This aspect of museum maintenance is dealt with more fully elsewhere. However, in managing the museum, account must be taken of the risks posed by fire (and associated threats from explosive devices) and theft. The former threatens the safety of staff and public; both affect the collection. The museum must contain systems which will:

(1) detect something is wrong,
(2) communicate that information to the appropriate people, and
(3) allow effective action to be taken.

The system will include both equipment and people. In bigger museums they may well be controlled from a permanently manned security room.

The greatest risk is fire. If detected, all subsequent action must place people first. The spread of fire is rapid. The value of damage done in non-detected fires in 5 min is 10 times that done in one min. There are three aspects to fire safety:

(1) building design (doors to prevent spread of smoke and flame; escape routes; and selection of non-combustible materials);
(2) detection systems and extinguishing systems (these may be automatic but also staff observation is needed either by routine patrols or in the ordinary course of duty); and
(3) good housekeeping (disconnection of electrical apparatus, care with chemicals, smoking restrictions, careful storage of combustible materials, and removal of rubbish).

Following detection, action to extinguish the fire may be both automatic and by people. Automatic sprinklers, carbon dioxide and Halon systems are found. Action by people includes attempts to control the fire by use of extinguishers, hose reels, etc., and also the Fire Brigade (usually called automatically).

Parallel to this are effective evacuation procedures for the staff and public and arrangements for practice drills.

In cases of theft, detection again depends on both automatic systems and observation by security and, indeed, all staff. Deterrence is important: good secure cases and exhibits, a highly visible staff, and obvious security systems such as cameras and alarms. In the event of theft you must be in a position to know what has been stolen and to be able to identify it if recovered. Good case inventories and photographs are desirable. All need, of course, to be balanced against the risk. As with fire, procedures need to be devised to deal with information that something is wrong. These procedures must not, however, violate public safety.

In summary two aspects need stressing: first, good house management will only come with training; second, there must be a clear chain of command and accountability.

Disaster planning

Although in the UK we are not subject to earthquake, other disasters both natural and man-made can befall the museum: fire, flood, wind damage, burst pipes, oil-tank leaks, leaking roofs, and accidental demolition. Obviously the museum manager seeks to eliminate as many threats as possible: water pipes should not be run over collections, for instance. Separation of the hazardous part of services from the collections themselves is an ideal to be sought. Where this cannot be done, aim to make things as fail safe as possible. If there are to be leaks from pipes try to arrange for the water to be led away and avoid sumps in which water from a leak can build up. Storage cabinets should keep collections off the floor, giving a few inches of safety.

However, even in the best regulated organization, disaster can still happen. The worst effects can be mitigated by the preparation of an action plan in advance to protect as much as possible of the collections. These arrangements will also apply to fire, which we have considered mainly from the immediate action to be taken for public safety. The person preparing the plan should study the arrangements in other museums.

The plan should include:

(1) Who is to be contacted and how they can be reached. This would include both security staff and maintenance engineers authorized to take immediate action to move collections to safety, as well as conservation and curatorial staff. Extra hands to move things should also be listed.
(2) The priorities for the movement of collections to safety. Collections should be graded as 'irreplaceable', 'important', 'inessential' or 'replaceable'. High-priority items should be so marked in stores.
(3) The location of packing materials and vehicles and other equipment necessary for moving the collections.
(4) The location of temporary stores and the security arrangements to be put in operation for their protection.
(5) The location of dehumidification and other first-aid equipment that may be necessary.
(6) The contacts for emergency building services and how they are to be supervised.

Organization

All building maintenance requires adequate financial provision and arrangements for its effective management. This means a proper chain of command and clear accountability. It is also an area where in the past much of the work in Local Authorities has been privatized, and more may take place. Architectural supervision, the execution of building works, security and cleaning can all be contracted out. If so, it is vitally important that authority to instruct a contractor, and his level of responsibility and liability are clearly spelt out. If the work is done in-house then organization is necessary.

In larger museums, these responsibilities may be grouped under the heading of administration, who may well have other functions relating to financial and personnel control and the duties of company secretary. In relation to the management of buildings, the head of administration will need to arrange for:

(1) security of the premises, including the control of staff and the overseeing of contractors;
(2) gallery staff, whose jobs combine aspects of security of collections, with public safety and assisting visitors;
(3) cleaning staff;
(4) staff to 'drive' plant and equipment for heating and ventilation; and
(5) a building supervisor (or clerk of works), to control contractors involved in the execution of works and the maintenance of mechanical and electrical services.

In a small organization, such duties will be combined – perhaps in one person. Nevertheless, they all have to be carried out. The organization for this part of a large museum may be as shown in *Figure 18.1*. Four points need to be borne in mind in arranging these duties and selecting staff for them:

(1) the lines of responsibility to the Head of Administration need to be clear, while allowing for the proper involvement of curators and conservators;
(2) these staff have a front-line responsibility for the safety of the collections and for the public; they are normally the only staff the public encounter and upon whom they will form their view of the museum;

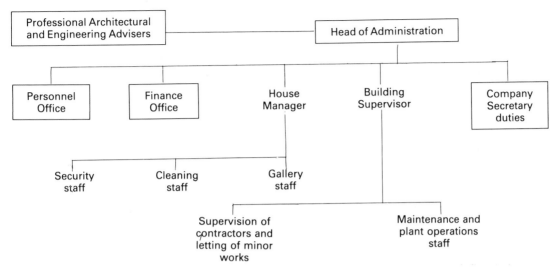

Figure 18.1 An organization chart for part of a large museum

(3) training of this group of staff is of the highest importance to the well-being of the public, the collections and the building; and

(4) if these functions are carried out by a contractor, it is essential to ensure that there are enough museum staff to supervise them.

Bibliography

The following list is selective; see also the Bibliography to Chapter 19 and the recommended Bibliography of the Department of Museum Studies, University of Leicester.

CHARTERED INSTITUTE FOR BUILDING SERVICES (1982), *Building Services for Museums and Art Galleries*, Chartered Institute for Building Services Symposium, London

CORNING MUSEUM OF GLASS (1977), *The Museum Under Water*, Corning, New York

FIELDEN, B. (1982) 'Museum management and natural disasters', *International Journal of Museum Management & Curatorship*, **1**, 231–235.

HARRIS, J.B. *et al* (1980), *Lighting of Art Galleries and Museums*, Chartered Institute of Building Services, London

HARRISON, R.O. (1966), *The Technical Requirements of Small Museums*, Canadian Museums Association, Ottawa

HUNTER, J. (1982), *Museum Emergency Preparedness Planning*, US National Parks Service, Washington

LEWIS, R.H. (1976), *Manual for Museums*, US National Parks Service, Washington

MUSEUMS OF FRANCE (1977), *Prevention et Securité dans les Museés*, Direction of the Museums of France, Paris

ROBERTSON, I.G. *et al* (1981), *Museum Security*, Information Sheet 25, Museums Association, London

THOMSON, G. (1978), *Conservation and Museum Lighting*, Information Sheet 6, Museums Association, London

THOMSON, G. (1968), *Museum Climatology*, International Institute for Conservation, London

THOMSON, G. (1978), *The Museum Environment*, Butterworths, London

TILLOTSON, R.G. (1977), *Museum Security*, International Council of Museums, Paris

UPTON, M.S. and PEARSON (1978), *Disaster Planning and Emergency Treatments in Museums* Canberra

19

Building a new museum: the roles and relationship of curator and architect in planning and project management

Richard Marks

Introduction

'Many are called but few are chosen' is an adage applicable to new purpose-built museums. Numerous ambitious schemes abound but relatively few (at least in the UK) successfully negotiate all the various obstacles, the most difficult of which is finance, and come into being. The writer is fortunate in having experience of two major projects for new museums, one of which is in the public sector, the other funded. The former is the Burrell Collection in Glasgow, opened to the public in 1983, and the latter is the Museum of Rowing at Henley, a project which at the time of writing has not progressed beyond the securing of a suitable site and selection of a consultant architect. In addition, I am closely involved in a major restoration scheme for the Royal Pavilion in Brighton, to which many of the principles of organization and curatorial involvement apply as much as in new museums. The observations made in this essay are largely based on personal experience and, therefore, concern multimillion-pound projects. Although they make no pretensions to providing a blueprint to be followed slavishly, the principles of planning and management should be generally applicable in respect of the role and responsibilities of the curator, whatever the size and complexity of the scheme.

The project team

Assuming a suitable site has been identified and the scheme to build a new museum has the consent of the relevant governing body the first stage is to establish the client project or management team to oversee and monitor the scheme from its inception through to completion of the contract, including the

Defects Liability Period and payment of final accounts.

The composition of the Project Team will probably vary according to whether the museum is under Local Authority management or is in the independent sector. It is essential to both, however, that represented on the Team is (1) a financial analyst or adviser, and (2) a professional museum curator.

In the case of a museum service operated by a Local Authority the former is likely to be drawn from within its Treasurer's Department and the latter will be a member of that museum service. In addition an officer from the Planning Department and, if the site is in parkland, a member of the Parks Section should be involved from the inception of the project. Any new museum scheme will require involvement of elected members. In some cases this could take the form of regular reports to the relevant Museums, Leisure or Amenities Committee. For the more grandiose schemes the establishment of a special subcommittee of elected members is advisable, to which the Project Team reports at regular intervals. The Subcommittee proceedings will be reported to the Finance Committee and full Council according to normal Local Government procedures. For the Burrell Collection a Steering Committee of Councillors was established and the controlling body for the restoration of the Royal Pavilion is known as the Royal Pavilion Restoration *Ad Hoc* Committee.

The organizational structure for museums in the private or independent sector should be simpler. For the Rowing Museum, it is likely that a subgroup of the present Working Committee will be formed comprising three members with expertise in curation, financial management and quantity surveying, as well as a representative from Henley Town Council. It is anticipated that this will report to the Trustees or governing body of the museum when this is formally constituted.

The architect's brief

The development of a brief for the project architect is of fundamental importance for the success of any new museum and indeed will be of great assistance in selecting the architect. Because of their knowledge of the collections and requirements for the new building, the curatorial staff must be responsible for the compilation of the brief, although the professional input of other members of the Project Team will be necessary for their own areas of expertise.

Before embarking on the exercise the curator responsible for the project is strongly advised to become acquainted with any relevant museums which have recently been completed or are still under construction. He/she should be encouraged to cast their net as widely as possible. In the case of the Burrell Collection, visits were made by the assessors responsible for selecting the architect to, amongst other museums, the Gulbenkian in Lisbon. The present writer also embarked on a tour of recent museum facilities and extensions in the USA, including the Metropolitan Museum in New York, the Mellon Centre at Yale and Washington. It is essential that, during the course of these visits, the opportunity is taken to talk to the curators and others involved in the conception, construction programme and maintenance of the new museum. In most cases the staff will be frank and keen to ensure that colleagues benefit from their experiences.

The above exercise will prove very helpful to the curator in formulating the brief. The aim of the brief is to outline for the architect the nature and scope of the artefacts to be displayed and stored and identify the conservation, accommodation, service and ancillary requirements. Any special terms and conditions attached to the collections and their presentation also need to be stated. The brief should not attempt to trespass on the architect's professional expertise or to pre-judge their concept by indicating the curator's design preference, except possibly in the case of major restoration projects, where the curator's knowledge of the building and the philosophy behind the proposed works (e.g. use of original materials and the extent to which existing features must be conserved rather than replaced) will be essential guidelines for the project architect.

The scope of the brief will vary according to the nature of the individual scheme and is likely to go through more than one draft before the final version is issued. The initial draft should be all embracing and will be revised and refined after the scheme has been costed. However, the curator should take into account from the outset not only the capital costs of construction but also the likely annual running costs; the latter are particularly important in respect of the maintenance and replacement of sophisticated environmental controls and security systems; indeed they will influence the important decision as to whether to opt for local control with low maintenance costs or to install air-conditioning.

The brief should be a lengthy document, but should contain information under the headings of the following section.

Philosophy of the new museum

This section should define the broad principles underlying the proposed presentation of the collections in the new building, e.g. whether it is intended to be a 'Temple of Art' or encourage all age groups and classes to participate in activities.

Legal restrictions

The brief shall set out clearly any mandatory requirements affecting the display and housing of the collections.

The location

If known, the proposed site of the museum should be described, including access, availability of services and (if relevant) a soil survey.

The collections

In this section the nature and scope of the items to be exhibited and stored should be outlined. An indication of the range of materials and dimensions should be given.

Display of the collections

This section should define how the collections are to be organized in the public galleries and set out the required sequence in terms of visitor circulation. The number of galleries or display areas should be indicated as should whether the galleries are to function on primary and secondary levels. The architect will need to know if the displays are to be permanent or whether the flexibility to change them radically is required. Temporary exhibition space should be identified if relevant. The range of objects in each area should be indicated, as should display requirements, e.g. showcases or wall-hanging, etc. It is particularly important to mention any architectural features which must be incorporated in the structure. It is not necessary at this stage to attempt to define the number of showcases, but an indication of floor-area requirements is esential.

Schedule of accommodation

Excluding the public galleries this will fall into two categories: visitor facilities, and administration and services.

In a large scheme visitor facilities would include:

(1) entrance area;
(2) cloakrooms and lavatories;
(3) rest room/first-aid room;
(4) restaurant and kitchen areas;
(5) lecture room/audio-visual display area;
(6) educational activities area;
(7) creche or playroom;
(8) library/study rooms;
(9) accommodation for visiting researchers;
(10) shop and sales area;
(11) public parking area;
(12) lifts; and
(13) facilities for the disabled.

With regard to administration and services, the following are applicable to a large building, but at least some of the areas will be essential in more modest schemes:

(1) storage for artefacts not on display;
(2) storage for spare parts (plant equipment, electricity);
(3) storage for publications and goods for sale;
(4) cleaners' store;
(5) offices for curatorial staff;
(6) offices for administrative staff;
(7) offices for education staff;
(8) conservation workshops and offices (NB: the activities and environmental requirements should be indicated for these areas);
(9) technicians' workshops (e.g. joiner, electrician, plumber);
(10) office and store for the Clerk of Works;
(11) office and store for handymen;
(12) darkroom, studio, and office for photographer;
(13) office for chief attendant;
(14) men's staff room;
(15) women's staff room;
(16) locker spaces for men and women;
(17) control room/security room;
(18) meeting/conference room;
(19) archive room;
(20) packing/despatch room;
(21) washroom and lavatory facilities;
(22) goods entrance with internal loading facilities;
(23) service lift;
(24) rest room;
(25) mess room;
(26) parking for official vehicles and staff; and
(27) plant room for heating/environmental control systems (see below).

Environmental requirements

The setting out of the environmental and lighting requirements of the new building will form an important section of the brief. If the building is to be fully air-conditioned the acceptable parameters of temperature and relative humidity should be stated for the galleries, conservation workshops and staff offices. The desired air changes should also be specified.

Fire and theft security, health and safety requirements, and access for the disabled

Principles governing the fire and security systems should be incorporated, e.g. water sprinklers are to be avoided for areas containing the collections. The brief should also state that the building must satisfy current statutory health-and-safety requirements and must meet the needs of the disabled.

It must be stressed that the above is not a blueprint; spaces and activities will be deleted or added in accordance with specific circumstances.

Display systems

In order to avoid future confusion the brief should define clearly whether the architect's responsibilities will extend as far as the design of mounts and display systems, information panels and labels for the artefacts. If not, the curator should identify how and by whom this very important work will be done.

Selection of architect

At the same time as the brief is being prepared the Project Team will be addressing the issue of selecting a suitable architect. The choice of architect is crucial to the success of the proposed building. The curator must be very closely involved in this selection exercise. The curator will have to work very closely with the architect and it is essential, therefore, that an individual or practice is chosen whom the museum staff consider has a good grasp of the requirements of the project and with whom harmonious and positive relations can be established.

Three basic routes can be followed in terms of choosing an architect.

Publicly or privately funded buildings

In the case of a publicly funded organization an architect may be selected from the Architect's or Technical Services Department in the case of a Local Authority, or the Department of the Environment in respect of national museums. For this course of action to be adopted the Project Team would have to be satisfied that the Architect's/Technical Services Department had the necessary expertise and experience to design very prestigious and publicity-attracting projects.

The current trend, however, is to select architects from the private sector for the larger museum schemes, with representation from the Local Authority/Civil Service architectural services on the Project Team. The Burrell Collection, the Clore Wing at the Tate Gallery and the National Gallery extension, to name three recent major schemes, have all been entrusted to private architectural practices.

These can be chosen either by open competition or from a short-list of suitably experienced architects.

Open competition

Selection by competition has its advantages in that it can produce, as in the case of the Burrell Collection, a superb design from non-established architects. On the other hand, the recent history of the National Gallery extension demonstrates that competitions can also have less happy results. Two disadvantages of the open competition method are: (1) it is not cheap to organize and administer, and (2) it is not always a speedy process.

The keys to a successful competition are a clear brief and good organization. The Royal Institute of British Architects (RIBA) provides advice on organizing architectural competitions.

A panel of assessors will be appointed, which will include members of the governing body of the museum, architects and, ideally, the curator. A brief will form the major element in the information provided to competitors. For the larger projects such as the Burrell Collection, the competition could well comprise two stages, with a short-list of architects being selected from the initial submissions. In the second stage the finalists will be requested to produce cost-estimates. The curator will be closely involved with the competition, at the very least in providing answers to questions that will arise from these submitting designs. If the curator is not an assessor, his/her views on the entries should be made known to the board.

Short-listing of suitably experienced architects

This approach is less costly than the one above, but involves more research in order to select a small number of architects with the necessary experience and record of achievement. Again, the curator has a most important role to play in this exercise. The advice of the RIBA, Museums and Galleries Commission, the Museums Association and the Area Museums Service should be sought. In addition, the curator must visit as many recent museums as possible and should not confine his/her questioning of colleagues to issues of design but should also establish the respective architect's ability to manage the construction phases and the finances. Once several likely architectural practices have expressed interest in the project they should be provided with an outline brief and invited to an interview. The panel should include the curator, a member of the museum's governing body and a quantity surveyor. This was the method of choosing an architect for the Museum of Rowing at Henley. In this case, architects were approached who had experience of building new museums or adapting existing structures to museum purposes; in addition, because of the particular nature of the museum, the panel extended an invitation to architectural practices involved in the designing of boat-houses and public amenities with water frontage. During the interviews the candidates will outline their basic design concept of the project.

Before leaving this section, reference should be made to another alternative avenue for new museums: 'design and build'. Some large construction companies retain qualified architects on their staff and offer a comprehensive service covering all aspects of design, building and project management. The present writer is not aware of this approach ever having been applied to new museums in the UK.

The curator and the architect/design team

Once the project architect has been selected, a Design Team comprising the Architect, Quantity Surveyor, Structural Engineer and Mechanical and Electrical Engineer will be formed. After the scheme has been costed a main contractor will be chosen, usually by tender. The main contractor will in turn employ a range of subcontractors and suppliers.

From this stage onwards until the building is constructed and commissioned the curator will be very closely involved with the architects on the detailed working-out of every aspect of the new museum, from the location of telephones to the environmental requirements for individual artefacts. The architect will make constant demands on the time of the curatorial staff and it is essential that a senior curator (preferably the Director or Chief Curator) is released from all other duties in order to act as the client's representative. In order to avoid the danger of giving the architect conflicting and sometimes contradictory information, the client representative should be the only member of staff authorized to brief the architect. In no circumstances should the curator give instructions to the contractor as client intervention can cause confusion and give rise to financial claims.

The principal responsibilities of the client representative are two-fold:

(1) to ensure that the architect is fully briefed on the museum's needs and provide information to the architect when requested; and
(2) to manage the work of the museum staff in order to meet the deadlines imposed by the construction and installation programme. This will involve planning a conservation programme and making arrangements for packing, moving and installing the collections.

In order to carry out these responsibilities effectively, the client representative must:

(1) develop a good working relationship with the architect;
(2) ensure that the architect has a good knowledge of the collections and understands the display philosophy;
(3) comprehend architectural drawings and service installation plans: and
(4) have from the outset a clear overall vision of the museum's requirements.

The above does not mean that the curator always has to agree with the architect or hesitate to suggest amendments. Nor should he/she be pressurized into making hasty decisions. On the other hand, time equals money/costs is an adage which applies particularly to building projects; it is equally true that changes of mind can cause delay and involve additional expenditure. Thus before requesting amendments the curator must ensure that the Quantity Surveyor has the opportunity to assess the cost implications.

The curator should work closely with the Quantity Surveyor from the outset, particularly when the latter prepares the costings and Bills of Quantity. The curator should ensure that financial provision is made for detailed photographic records to be made of construction progress for the museum archives and for packing and moving the collections into the new building. There will be a sum allocated for contingencies in respect of unexpected items of expenditure; in addition the Burrell Collection Bills of Quantity included financial provision under the heading of Assistance with Setting-up the Collections. This proved invaluable, not least because it enabled necessary amendments to display systems to be made and paid for a coherent and comprehensive system of graphic panels, labels and mounts.

The above remarks will apply while the building is under construction. The curator should spend as much time as possible on site (while remembering that the site is the legal property of the contractor)

familiarizing himself/herself with the new building as it takes shape and being available to the architect. As the museum nears completion the programme of snagging to identify and remedy defects will gather momentum. This is the architect's responsibility, but the curator should not hesitate to draw the architect's attention to any defect he/she has noted. The curator should also press the Design Team for the completion of a maintenance manual, together with an accurate and detailed set of plans and elevations of the finished building.

Summary

As has already been stated, no blueprint can be given for the role of the curator in the construction of a new museum as so much will depend on the nature of each individual project. Whatever the scheme, skills of common sense, commitment, decisiveness, communication and management will be demanded of the curator.

Bibliography

Architectural Review, **175** (Feb. 1984), 1044 (issue devoted to museum design)

BRAWNE, M. (1982), *The Museum Interior*, Thames & Hudson, London

'The Burrell Collection', *The Architects Journal*, **42** (178), (19 Oct. 1983), 56–103

The Burrell Collection Competition Brief and Documents, Glasgow

MARKS, R. (1984), 'Building the Burrell', *Scottish Art Review*, **16** (1), 3–8

NOTMAN, J. (1984), 'The new building and some conservation problems', *Scottish Art Review*, **16** (1), 21–25

SEARING, H. (1982), *New American Art Museums*, Whitney Museum of Art, New York and University of California Press, Berkeley, CA

THOMSON, G. (1978), *The Museum Environment*, Butterworth, London

20

Security

Bryan Dovey

The need

There is no doubt that the world's cultural heritage has suffered and continues to suffer loss through vandalism, misappropriation and theft. In 1987 the newspapers were reporting such diverse incidents as shotgun damage to the Leonardo Cartoon in London and the recovery in Japan of Impressionist paintings stolen from French museums.

Whilst such extraordinary events deserve and receive international media coverage, it should not be forgotten that levels of ordinary crime, which individually receive less publicity, are still on the increase. There were 3.8 million notifiable offences reported in England and Wales during 1986 which included a rise of seven per cent in burglaries and theft (Criminal Statistics: England and Wales, 1986). Against such a background of criminal activity there can be little doubt that those charged with preserving the nation's cultural heritage in museums need efficient security arrangements to enable them to fulfill that task.

The policy

Successive holders of the post of National Museums Security Adviser have devised and revised the current policy promulgated by the Museums & Galleries Commission. This provides a common standard for use in buildings housing collections which need to be protected from theft and damage and a level of security to be reached by those institutions wishing to take advantage of the Government Indemnity Scheme administered by the Commission. The policy has five essential factors dealing with physical defences, intruder and fire alarm systems, invigilation and internal security arrangements. Experience has shown that, where this policy has been used, the risk to the collection has been reduced (Museums and Galleries Commission, 1983).

Physical defences

It is recommended that the shell of the building must be of substantial construction. In general, but not always, brick, concrete or stone buildings will provide the necessary resistance to forcible attack allowing time for an alarm system to initiate a response. The openings in the building such as doors, windows and rooflights must be reduced to the minimum necessary and those remaining should be strengthened to deter and delay entry.

Intruder alarm systems

An intruder alarm system designed to initiate a signal upon a forcible attack being mounted against the security perimeter of the protected area should be installed. It is important that the system be constantly monitored and current Police policy is to refuse to accept alarm terminations in Police Stations. Efficient and secure communication with an alarm company's central monitoring station can be established by telephone line and, consequently, the Police alerted to problems within a very short period. Reliance cannot be placed on a system which depends simply on a bell or siren on an external wall to initiate a response.

Fire detector systems

It is recommended that an automatic fire detector system be installed as it is important that an early indication of fire is given to the responding force. There are a number of systems available based on the detection of heat or smoke which will provide a signal by telephone line to the Fire Brigade or an alarm company's central station as well as causing a local alarm to initiate an evacuation.

Invigilation

Many exhibits cannot be physically protected if they are to be viewed and enjoyed as the artist intended. Furthermore, many institutions provide access to collections for researchers and students and the possibility of theft or damage cannot be ignored. Security attendants must, therefore, be employed and be given the duty to ensure that fundamental rules of security are followed to prevent theft, fire and damage. Ultimate responsibility for the security of a museum will always lie with the Director and he must be given the means to protect the institution and the collection.

Internal security arrangements

These arrangements must, of course, be designed to suit the nature and use of the building. Clear and unambiguous policies and instructions should be devised to cover such matters as key security, supervision of contractors, access to non-public parts of the building, identification of accredited researchers, reception and collection of deliveries, inspection of displays, searching and closing of the building and emergency procedures in the case of theft, vandalism, fire, flood or bomb threats. In addition, some premises will need policies and instructions regarding the searching of visitors and whether to allow bags to be carried through the museum. There will always be contradictory interests, but a well thought out policy which seeks a balance between conflicting demands and that is incorporated in a training programme for all museum staff will receive support.

Building protection

Thefts from museums occur for a variety of reasons and are committed by both amateurs and professionals. Although studies have been made on the complex motives behind some thefts and acts of vandalism, not enough is known to enable decisions to be safely made as to the degree of protection to be afforded to exhibits of differing nature. What is certain is that if an article is worth displaying then it must be deserving of protection.

Whilst experience has shown that precautions are necessary to prevent incidents of theft and damage during the hours a museum is open to the public, it is the risk of a large volume loss during the closed hours that can be diminished by protecting the building. The scale of protection will depend on the nature of the collection. Factors to be considered

include value, portability and disposability, whilst not forgetting that theft may be committed to extort money or changes of policy.

New buildings

In the case of a new building responsible planning and design can ensure that basic security measures are 'built into' the premises. To achieve this satisfactory state of affairs the security requirements must be explicit in the brief to the architect. No one expects an architect to design a building not knowing the purpose to which it will be put and one element of the purpose of a museum is to preserve and protect the exhibits. It is not suggested that the effort to achieve economy and efficiency in security measures should restrict the architect's freedom to design buildings suitable to the environment and to enhance the presentation of the museum collection. Design freedom is not at issue, only the need to ensure that an explicit brief is provided.

One important benefit of a security input in the early stages of design is reduced protection and operating costs once the building is taken into use. Furthermore, it is likely that protection measures decided on after the design of the building has been finalized will mar the appearance of the museum and increase the cost. That such liaison is beneficial and necessary is instanced by the fact that eight of the fourteen Local Authorities in Kent now co-operate with the Police architect liaison officer of the County Constabulary at the design stage of new projects (Wood, 1987).

It will not fall to the lot of most directors to be involved in the choice of a site for a new museum. However, if there is some choice in the purchase of existing premises or locating a new building there are some points that should be borne in mind. The site should provide safe and easy access for the public, for deliveries and collections, for the emergency services and for safe parking of visitors' vehicles. A site which the Fire Brigade and Police can reach quickly is preferable as response time is important if criminal acts are to be frustrated. A museum should occupy an island site as buildings with joint or connecting roofs with other premises are especially vulnerable. An urban location may have advantages in the presence of 'friendly eyes' passing by as pedestrian and vehicular traffic. Isolated and remote locations may be attractive because of the countryside surrounding them but will lack some of the above advantages and may carry increased guarding costs. The possibility of natural disasters cannot be ignored since flooding from lakes or rivers or the drainage system will inevitably cause damage.

Particular attention must be paid to the strength of the shell of a new building. Museums unlike banks and jewellers shops, do not lock their valuable items in strongrooms or safes at night. The very purpose of a museum allows the criminally minded access to much of the premises and the opportunity to reconnoitre his target and the protective measures. The shell, (composed of the roof, the walls and the floor) must, therefore, be able to resist determined physical attack for at least the amount of time needed for response forces to attend.

Materials such as breeze block, foamed concrete, sheet asbestos, aluminium sheeting, plasterboard, hardboard and bitumen bonded sustances, are now used extensively in the construction of buildings. They do not offer the same resistance to attack as that afforded by the traditional materials such as stone, brickwork or reinforced concrete. It is impractical to provide here a detailed standard of building construction, but a grading system indicating quality of resistance to attack is suggested in the standard textbook used by burglary risk surveyors and is worthy of consultation (Bugg and Bridges, 1982).

As the building shell must be regarded as the security perimeter, the number of openings should be limited to the minimum necessary for access, ventilation and natural light. These openings should then be protected to offer the degree of resistance necessary to reach the required security standard.

There are a number of ways of defending doors to provide differing degrees of protection. For an exterior door the least acceptable quality is of solid hardwood or solid hardcore construction. Further strength to meet an increased risk can then be obtained by using iron or steel doors of varying thickness or laminated security doors with reinforced plastic or steel-sheet insert. Glazed doors to the exterior must be regarded as weak and must be supported by a secondary door system. Secondary systems are frequently found to be cost-effective and aesthetically acceptable and can be achieved by fitting steel roller shutters, expanding steel gates or laminated security doors inside the primary door. The weak point of any door will often prove to be the locking system. Care must be taken over the choice of system and consultation with a master locksmith will be justified for high-risk premises. Locks come in a bewildering assortment of types, sizes, qualities and descriptions, but care and consultation over choice of method will be repaid in the event of an attack.

Windows and rooflights continue to be a major problem of museum security. From the security adviser's point of view, the ideal museum would have no windows at all. Even very high windows can often be reached from roofs or ledges and this must be taken into account when deciding on a protection policy. Decisions taken at the design stage can provide some window security to meet lower category risks. The use of glass bricks set in steel or concrete frames for rooflights can be advantageous.

For windows a locked or fixed steel sash with panes not more than 23cm × 18cm or narrow windows with effective opening of no more than 18cm are beneficial. Nevertheless, despite such treatment the real defence of windows and rooflights will rest in secondary protective measures. Steel roller shutters, iron or steel bars, collapsible gates and grilles or secondary glazing using polycarbonate or laminated glass all have a useful and distinct part to play in countering a particular threat.

Consideration of security requirements at the design stage cannot be overstressed. It should be possible to avoid features that provide access, albeit unintentionally, to the openings in the shell. Thieves can, and do, take advantage of pipes, ledges and buttresses to reach windows, rooflights and doors that seem inaccessible. They can then often use an easier and quicker exit to escape at ground level taking advantage of such features as fire escape routes not secured internally during closed hours. Design should also cater for the problem of thieves who conceal themselves within premises during opening hours and break out after closing time. Careful planning can avoid unused spaces, dead ends, insecure ducts and panels which can conceal the human frame. Attention must also be paid to the exterior to eliminate conditions affording concealment such as vegetation, porches, deeply recessed doors and adjacent outbuildings. Less obvious is the risk of attack from a concealed position in a non-alarmed contiguous building. In such circumstances a case can be made for a party wall of stronger construction than the outer walls of the museum.

Existing buildings

The problem with many existing museums is the widely differing variety of premises used to house valuable collections. Many were not built for the purpose and security requirements played little part in their design and construction. The problem is exacerbated by inclusion in the lists of buildings regarded as of special architectural or historic interest, thus restricting alterations or additions unless consent is obtained. Nevertheless, some strengthening can often be achieved by co-operation with Planning Authorities and by taking advantage of maintenance and repair programmes. For example, a roof constructed of slate or tile to unlined battens can gain considerable strength if the slates are relaid to a close boarded timber covering at the time when re-roofing is necessary.

Since many existing museums are 100 or more years old, the daunting and expensive task of securing an excessive number of openings in the shell is usually the main worry of the director. Whenever possible unused doors and windows should be bricked up to the same constructional strength of the surrounding wall. It has been found possible to comply with preservation orders by leaving a door or window in place and confining the infill to the interior of the building. Rooflights should also be eliminated if unwanted, although it is recognized that severe constructional problems may prevent such treatment.

There are many ways of adding to the strength of an existing building by the use of replacement doors, steel roller shutters, iron or steel bars, expanding metal gates and the reinforcement of existing doors and wooden shutters by steel sheeting. Modern locking and bolting systems can add considerably to the defences and can often be less obtrusive than other remedies.

Nevertheless, many buildings have so many windows and doors that the owners cannot even contemplate the successful implementation of a long-term plan spread over a number of years. In such cases layout and finance may force the exclusion of some part of the building from the primary security perimeter. This may be regarded as bad practice since, although unprotected areas may contain only low-risk material, it can provide a place of concealment from which an attack can be mounted. It does, however, carry the benefit that the available funds can be spent on a smaller security perimeter drawn around the high-risk items. The excluded zone can then be used to initiate an alarm signal if an intruder progresses toward the protected area. This solution has been used in museums and galleries where the contents of some parts of the building are at less risk than borrowed temporary exhibitions.

The starting point for improvement to the security of existing buildings should be a survey by an independent person bringing a fresh pair of eyes to the problems of the building. Such a service is available from the Crime Prevention Officer of the local Police as well as from independent security consultants operating in the commercial field.

An important factor in maintaining the strength and efficiency of security measures is a programme of regular inspection and repair. Security surveys often reveal a sad litany of faults in both mechanical and electronic devices. Such faults weaken the resistance of protective measures and ease the task of the thief.

Intruder alarms

The deterrent value of an intruder alarm system depends on whether an entry and escape can be effected before the responding authority arrives on the scene. There have been numerous examples of successful theft in circumstances where the perpetrator has been able to ignore the initiation of a signal, enter and escape within the response time. In the case of museums, public access provides the thief with the opportunity to assess the nature and extent of the alarm system and the physical defences.

It is for the above reasons that emphasis has been laid on the need to provide traditional mechanical forms of security such as thick walls, strong doors, good-quality locks and barred windows. The intruder alarm system should then be regarded as a support to these defences and be used to signal an attack on them. A burglar alarm cannot prevent an intrusion nor can physical defences make burglary impossible given sufficient time and the right equipment. The correct solution is combining the alarm and the defences in such a way that a successful response can be made.

In order to achieve a balanced system it is important that a brief be drawn up setting out the requirements to be met by the alarm system. The details of the brief should be agreed between the museum Director, a representative of the museum insurance company and an independent security surveyor or the Crime Prevention Officer of the local Police force. It should not be left to an installing company's surveyor as he cannot be expected to be familiar with every aspect of the museum's needs.

There are some British Standard specifications dealing with intruder alarm systems and an industry-based regulatory body has been set up to ensure compliance with those standards and to set new standards. It may be that the museum's insurance company and/or police will insist that the installing company is approved by the National Approval Council for Security Systems (NACOSS)[1]. Seeking NACOSS approval is voluntary but it should not be assumed that an installing company which has not sought approval will ignore the relevant British Standards. Insurance company surveyors and local Police Crime Prevention Officers will often be conversant with the quality of work performed by non-member companies.

There is insufficient space here to describe the different sensing, signalling and control devices now available for use in intruder systems. There are many publications which provide the information and a good starting point is *Burglary Protection and Insurance Surveys* (Bugg and Bridges, 1982).

However, it is necessary to touch on the two main descriptions commonly used in relation to automatic detection systems. The term 'perimeter protection' is generally understood to include those devices which are activated by intrusion into, or forcible attack on, the security perimeter. 'Trap protection' is usually used to describe those devices actuated when the intruder is within the perimeter.

Experience has shown that a combination of the two systems is usually the most efficient way of providing the required standard of security. The emphasis that has already been given to the need for a physically strong perimeter, however, inevitably means that an alarm system of the 'perimeter' description will be of primary importance,

Fire detector systems

There have been many examples in recent years of the rapid spread of fire, some of which were no doubt aggravated by the age and condition of the buildings. Many museums are housed in premises built at a time when far less was known about fire precautions. It is therefore vital to detect fire at the earliest possible stage and arouse the necessary response. Furthermore, many museums are devoid of people when closed and that empty period of 12 or more hours may prove disastrous if fire breaks out and remains undetected.

Automatic systems based on the detection of heat and/or smoke which can arouse a response in a similar manner to an intruder alarm are available from many sources. In addition to specialist companies, the major intruder alarm firms operate divisions giving appropriate advice about installations. Information on UK fire authorities and private companies offering such services is printed annually.[2]

Whilst fire detector systems have become more acceptable to museum authorities as reliability has improved and the cost of providing night guards has escalated, there is still much resistance to the use of automatic repression systems – 'the sprinkler'. Understandably, directors and curators fear the consequences on collections of accidental discharge of water. The facts regarding accidental discharges are difficult to obtain but there is no reason to suppose that this equipment is so unreliable that accidents are a real problem. Many systems operate a dry pipe until the detector heads indicate a fire and even then the response is curtailed to the affected zone. Those concerned in the industry point out that, even in a real fire situation, the amount of water dispensed by a sprinkler system at the seat of the fire will be far less than that required at a later stage to control the conflagration. It was claimed in 1986 that the British Automatic Sprinkler Association records revealed 98 per cent of fires in premises equipped with sprinkler systems were extinguished by the operation of two or three sprinkler heads (Fire Protection Association, 1986).[3] In the face of such statistics it will be surprising if resistance to the use of repression systems continues for much longer.

There can be no denying the benefits of 'good housekeeping' in relation to the prevention of fire as is continually emphasized by Fire Prevention Officers in training schemes. Regular cleaning and removal of waste products coupled with an inspection system to ensure the building is safe when locking up at night are of major benefit. Many fires are caused by misuse of electrical appliances such as fires and the careless disposal of cigarette ends. These causes are amenable to discovery if daily inspections form part of a good housekeeping regime.

Invigilation

One cannot quarrel with the idea that to obtain maximum enjoyment and appreciation exhibits in a museum must be displayed in as free and unobstructed manner as possible. This policy demands the deployment of a team of guards or attendants in order to deter or detect the actions of the criminally inclined. No system has been found that will completely replace a loyal and well-trained attendant team. Of course, it is realized that the size of the institution and the financial situation will dictate the number available. Nevertheless, even one man in a small building, properly trained and briefed, with some mechanical and electrical assistance, can do much to secure the safety of the exhibits.

Having touched on the importance of an attendant force, I think it is right to say that in some places the quality and status of these employees have been inferior. Traditionally, they have been poorly paid and enjoyed few opportunities for career advancement. Nevertheless, it has often been the case that the guard force has had total responsibility for a museum at such times as weekends. Some attention given to some basic personnel matters will undoubtedly be repaid by better morale and increased efficiency.

The attendants do need to be trained and advantage should be taken of the courses offered from time to time by Area Museum Councils, the British Museum and the National Gallery in London and some security firms operating in the commercial sector. The wearing of a uniform or blazer bearing the msueum's logo assists the public when seeking help and establishes quite clearly that the building and collection is under guard. The wearing of plain clothes can be of advantage in combating particular recurring problems, but is not recommended as a regular feature. Regular briefing of attendants by curatorial staff, particularly prior to an important temporary exhibition, will enhance their knowledge, help them appreciate the qualities of the exhibits and help in identifying their role in the overall purpose of the establishment. It is most important that the attendants should be respected by other museum staff and the public and have the self-respect necessary to sustain them in their role. Experience has shown efforts devoted to building such attitudes are repaid.

The museum's rules governing security must be clearly stated, be enforceable and be published.

Certain regulations such as 'no smoking' must be exhibited for the benefit of visitors, but an attendant needs a guide in compact form that is easy to carry and study. He or she needs to be conversant with the rules and the action necessary in the event of non-compliance. A pocket guide will provide the information and the reassurance that action is being taken in accordance with the Director's wishes and that support will be forthcoming in the event of a dispute.

Many attendants are required to perform tasks that are not strictly related to security. Cleaning, portering and small repairs often fall to the lot of the attendant and, indeed, help to vary the working hours and enhance the feeling of belonging to the organization. They should however, be clearly described and set out in a Job Description issued to each employee which must emphasize the chain of command and the priorities. When on duty in a gallery during public hours the attendant must be in no doubt that his primary duty is the protection of the people and the collections in the building. Distractions from this primary task must be avoided as they have often been used as an opportunity for theft. One such distraction successfully used was the arrangement by which incoming telephone calls were switched through to a manned gallery during the lunch time of the museum switchboard operator. A genuine call which needed to be recorded in writing sufficiently distracted the gallery attendant to allow a thief to operate unobserved.

Whilst some large establishments are able to deploy attendants solely in the role of gallery invigilators, many museum authorities are obliged to use them to cover a full range of security duties. Maintaining security must include knowledge of and training in emergency procedures for incidents of theft, damage or fire. A regular inspection routine must be followed in relation to displays of exhibits, to ensure the integrity of the building and to identify fire hazards. In particular, a search of the building at closing time must be a regular task done by those entirely familiar with the layout and geography of the building. As with fire precautions, 'good housekeeping' will pay dividends.

There is no formula available by the use of which one can establish the number of attendants necessary to safeguard a particular building. Account must be taken of the nature and use of the building, the value, quality and type of the objects in the collection, the number and layout of the galleries, the number of visitors and the facilities afforded them and peripheral duties concerned with other staff, offices and storage. Having weighed these criteria and perhaps arrived at the ideal, a compromise in view of budgetary restraints will inevitably be forced on the administrator. It is then that quality, training and performance will assume particular significance and will be the only means of maintaining an acceptable standard of security.

Some of the above factors will also need to be considered when deciding on the necessity of night guarding. In addition, however, it is necessary to judge the resistance of the building to penetration, the ability of an alarm system to detect an attack and the lapse of time needed for a response to an alarm. Most buildings, treated effectively in accordance with the policy stated at the beginning of this chapter, can be left unattended, as indeed is the case in the majority of museums. Even where a night guard is employed modern practice is to monitor the building electronically and by closed-circuit television rather than by regular patrol.

In the case of a large, complex and busy establishment with a sizeable attendant force, consideration must be given to employing a head of security with the right training, background and experience. A busy director must be able to delegate authority for protection services to a properly qualified individual. In smaller institutions it may be necessary for a member of staff to take on the additional duties of security officer.

Whichever method is adopted it is necessary that someone takes on the task of planning, implementing, controlling and co-ordinating all permanent and temporary security measures. These officers must be consulted on all matters that influence security such as displays, temporary exhibitions, building works, admission of researchers and any changes that affect the use of the building. They must be able to draw up plans to cope with emergencies and institute staff training programmes to familiarize all staff with the procedures. It is particularly important that, where the task is given as an additional duty to members of the staff, adequate training is provided to enable them to function properly. There are some excellent courses provided by commercial security companies designed to train people in varying aspects of protection.

Internal security arrangements

Internal design also has a part to play and consideration must be given to the siting of galleries and displays. Benefits to security may be obtained in the choice of layouts and circulation routes, notwithstanding that initial consideration may emphasize the presentation of the collection and the control of visitor flow in normal and abnormal circumstances. Thus, galleries formed internally away from outside walls and above ground level may be regarded as being less penetrable. Conversely, it is necessary to avoid providing easy access to an intruder to circulating routes that penetrate deep within the building. Whilst some schools of thought emphasize the need to separate public routes from those areas used only by staff, some thought should be given to the benefits to be obtained of routeing staff through the galleries when they need to move. The more pairs of knowledgeable eyes that pass through the collections the better the chance of identifying problems.

Care needs to be taken at the design stage to ensure that sufficient space is available for mechanical and electrical office equipment used by the staff. Examples have been seen of such machinery housed in storerooms, thus encouraging the issue of important keys amongst too many employees. The need to give curators and keepers maximum flexibility in exhibition design will lead to changes in internal layout that will frustrate the purpose of intruder sensors and emergency routes if insufficient thought is given to the project. Whilst it is not suggested that it is for the security manager to tell an architect or designer what he can or cannot do, it is surely helpful if the consequences of his decisions are pointed out and suggestions made to find acceptable alternatives.

The rules and regulations necessary to achieve an acceptable standard of security should be regarded only as a part of the arrangements required to run the organization and building efficiently. If the operating rules for the establishment are drawn up by the director in consultation with the senior staff and security officer it is more likely they will be generally accepted by all employed in the building. Such acceptance is required, as nothing is more likely to fail than rules which are not supported by those who have to enforce and observe them. The policies must also be published to the staff with a clear indication of the result which will flow from non-compliance. The public, too, must not be left in doubt as to what is expected of them in using the museum.

It is considered important to establish in the minds of visitors as early as possible that the museum is a place of public resort deserving of respect. Whilst signs and notices have a part to play, proliferation can mar the appearance and be overwhelming. It can be achieved by creating an air of efficiency at the reception area and the visible sign in the presence of an alert attendant that the building is actively supervised. First impressions are important, particularly to those who misbehave only when an opportunity is offered rather than as a planned exercise.

There have been, and continue to be, examples of loss of exhibits when building or redecorating works are in progress. Free access to normally secure areas by outside contractors must not be allowed. If access is required and the valuable items cannot be removed to another location, supervision by staff of the museum is a necessity. It must be remembered that many companies are not too concerned about the background details of their staff and their vetting procedures may be markedly inferior to those adopted by the museum. The arrangements for such works, including contract cleaning, should include the need to work only during the hours in which a museum is manned. A daily record needs to be kept of museum workmen in the building and a pass issue system will be of considerable help. When building works are in progress the contractor must be given to understand that he must not weaken the security of the building and daily inspection by the security officer is a requirement.

People requiring access to non-public parts of the institution should be met and accompanied but, more importantly, care needs to be taken over who is to be granted such access. There have been instances of seemingly genuine persons oozing confidence who have been allowed facilities and whose motives have been later found to be less than worthy. Researchers and students must be required to identify themselves and sufficient time allowed to check references before facilities are granted. One mistake in this field can cost the museum dearly since misappropriation from reserve collections often does not come to light immediately. There are some simple precautions that can assist in avoiding disaster: an appointment system with a permanent record of dates and times; the provision of cloakroom facilities where the visitor can leave his coat and bags; providing an overall coat using the excuse of protecting against dust; separating the required specimens from the remainder of the collection and physically denying further access; constant supervision, although it is recognized that this is difficult to provide; and the checking of specimens on issue and return. Whilst such arrangements may be time consuming and costly it is certain that laxity will be taken advantage of to the detriment of the museum.

The reception and collection of deliveries deserve attention as it is without a doubt a weak point in the period of any shipment. There are criminals who specialize in striking at such moments, particularly in cities and towns. If building design permits the provision of a closed and secure loading bay locked off from the street and the rest of the building, then considerable security has been bought. Where no such facilities exist, timing the arrival and ensuring that the vehicle is quickly loaded or unloaded and never left unattended are all important factors to consider. In this connection it is also wise to restrict information about dates and times to those who genuinely need to know.

A strict policy regarding the possession of keys should be devised and enforced. The number of keys in existence should never be more than necessary and the number of people in permanent possession of them should be kept to the barest minimum. Far too often possession of keys is based on status or convenience, whereas the deciding factors should clearly be real necessity and accountability. All keys, other than the external door keys possessed by keyholders and safe keys, should remain within the building in a secure key cabinet or safe and be identified by a coding system. The issue system should operate from a secure centre, ideally the security control room, and signatures obtained as a security measure and record. A proper system will enable a visual inspection at the end of the day to confirm that all keys have been returned. Two vulnerable times of the day are at opening and closing times when advantage may be taken of a keyholder when he lacks support. Ideally, keyholders should perform this task only when accompanied, particularly if called to the premises at unusual hours. What should certainly be avoided is to allow a member of the staff such as the female cleaner to be the first to arrive and the last to leave.

Staff selection is an important and time-consuming task and, therefore, justifies some effort to check that the background of a potential employee poses no potential threat to the museum. It should not be assumed that lower grades of appointments can be treated in less depth than the higher grades. Quite low-grade employees sometimes have access to many parts of the building denied to others by reason of the nature of their duties. For example, a caretaker may possess keys to the building and have opportunities for access far in excess of the administrative or curatorial staff.

References must be checked rather than accepted at face value and care taken over applications which reveal long periods of time spent abroad or in educational establishments. Whilst it is recognized that limitations are imposed by the existence of industrial tribunals and the implementation of the Rehabilitation of Offenders Act 1974, it cannot be over-emphasized that it is easier to reject an unsatisfactory candidate than to deal with the situation once employment has started.

General

In conclusion, it must be said that the security arrangements at a museum will only work if all the staff support the idea that security is necessary. Whilst the Director will carry the ultimate responsibility it is vital that all staff take part in ensuring that the collections are secured and preserved for future generations. The willing involvement of all concerned will help to ensure that the portion of the budget spent on security does not become unduly high and detrimental to a museum's development.

Notes

1. National Approval Council for Security Systems, Queensgate House, 14 Cookham Road, Maidenhead, Berks, UK.
2. *Security and Fire Protection Yearbook* Paramount Publishing, Borehamwood, Herts.
3. Fire Protection Association, 140 Aldersgate Street, London EC1, UK. Various fire safety data sheets are available from Fire Prevention Information, Aldemary House, Queen Street, London, EC4N 1TJ, UK.

References

BUGG, D.E. and BRIDGES, C. (1982), *Burglary Protection and Insurance Surveys* Stone & Cox, London

CRIMINAL STATISTICS: ENGLAND AND WALES (1986), *CMD 233*, HMSO, London

FIRE PROTECTION ASSOCIATION (1986), *The Journal of the Fire Protection Association*, **78**, 971

MUSEUMS AND GALLERIES COMMISSION (1983), *Eleventh Report*, HMSO, London

WOOD, J. (1987), *Security Times*, **Sept**.

Bibliography

BOGGEMANN, K.A. (1987), *Fire Prevention*, International Council of Museums, Paris

HISTORIC HOUSES ASSOCIATION (1983), *Security of Works of Art and Heritage Objects*, Seminar Report, London

OLIVER, E. and WILSON, J. (1983), *Security Manual*, Gower, Aldershot, Hampshire

POYNER, B. (1983), *Design Against Crime*, Butterworths, London

ROBERTSON, I.G. *et al* (1981), *Museum Security*, Museums Association, Sheet No. 25, London

ROSOLATO, G. (1974), *Museum (USA)*, **26**

SOCIETY OF INDUSTRIAL EMERGENCY SERVICE OFFICERS (1987), *Guide to Emergency Planning* Paramount Publishing, Borehamwood, Herts

TILLOTSEN, R.G. (1982), *Building Services for Museums and Art Galleries*, Chartered Institute for Building Services, London

TILLOTSEN, R.G. (1977), *Museum Security*, International Council of Museums, Paris

21

Information technology in museums

Tim H. Pettigrew

This chapter attempts to review some of the principal applications of information technology in the context of the museum. The revolution in information technology brought about by the development of ever more powerful and sophisticated microprocessors has meant that even a small museum can, with a modest outlay, acquire a 'desk-top' computerized system with enormous data-handling capabilities. Confronted with a bewildering array of possibilities and blinded by technical jargon coupled with the rapid appearance of ever more sophisticated hardware and software it is no wonder that the average curator finds it almost impossible to decide which system to adopt. What follows is a series of basic guidelines to be considered when setting up an automated system (see Williams, 1987; Chenhall and Vance, 1988).

Assessing the museum's requirements

In carrying out the initial assessment, one member of staff should have overall responsibility for undertaking an appraisal, preferably with the support of a Working Party drawn from the departments where it is intended to introduce the new technology. If the museum is run by a Local Authority then representatives from the computing section (if there is one) should be co-opted as their expertise will be crucial. There should also be consultation with outside bodies offering an advisory service. This should include the Museum Documentation Association (MDA) and, if possible, museums which have implemented proven automated systems. It is also important to consult the relevant trade unions at an early stage to ensure that any introduction of a new system will not contravene any union/employer information technology agreements (see NALGO, 1980, 1981).

Detailed assessment as regards suitable hardware and software will very much depend on those areas of museum administration where the technology is to be introduced and whether there are any existing computer resources either within the museum or its administering Authority. The main museological areas benefitting from an automated system can be categorized as follows;

(1) documentation management;
(2) word processing;
(3) gallery displays and educational use; and
(4) museum management and financial information.

Establishing an automated documentation system

An automated documentation system facilitates the data entry of a series of records (e.g. object or site records), the editing of those records to conform to a data standard, storing them in a form for subsequent use, processing the information to produce suitably formatted catalogues and indexes, interrogating the data according to selected criteria, and exporting aspects of the data to other centres to form collective databases. Discussion of the underlying principles of information management can be found in Bearman (1987a), Orna (1987), Orna and Pettitt (1980) and Roberts (1988).

There are three main ways to obtain a computerized documentation system. The first is to have a bureau undertake the computerization and processing of the records.

Tyne and Wear Museums Service (Pettigrew and Davis, in press), and the St Albans Museum Service have adopted this approach. With the appearance of ever more powerful and cheaper microcomputer systems, the bureau option is not one of the most cost-effective options as it was a few years ago. In addition, it lacks flexibility and is long-winded in terms of updating records and in the production of up-to-date printed output. The second option is to undertake in-house computerization and processing of records, either using the facilities of a mainframe/ minicomputer (e.g. a council or university operated mini or mainframe computer could be used by the relevant Local Authority or university museums), or purchase a microcomputer system for use within the museum. The third option would be to adopt a combination of the two previous strategies and introduce microcomputers linked to either a mini or mainframe computer. (See Bearman (1987b) for a discussion of acquisition and implementation issues.)

The mainframe option

The costs of purchasing and running a mainframe computer are beyond the resources of all but the large national museums. However, in certain inst-ances a museum may be able to use the computing facilities of its umbrella organization. In this option the museum would acquire a terminal or terminals each linked to the mainframe computer. Several University Museums have adopted this strategy, e.g. The Hancock Museum (Davis and Hebron, 1982) and the Manchester Museum (Orna and Pettitt, 1980, p. 169). Brighton was one of the first Local Authority museums to implement a computerized documentation system on its Local Authority operated computer (Kirk, 1979), and the Leicester County Museum and Records Service have also adopted this strategy. One of the main advantages of this option is that the museum would not be responsible for the maintenance of the system but would normally only pay for the computer resources used.

Initial investment in establishing terminal(s) and link(s) are expensive, but thereafter the links are usually paid for on an annual rental basis. The relevant computing department may provide exper-tise either to adapt an existing database management system (DBMS) or else buy in a package suitable for museum use. If an existing DBMS package is to be adapted it is of the utmost importance that the programmers are fully briefed as to the special requirements of the museum in terms of access requirements, input format, a long-term estimate of the quantity of the data to be processed, processing requirements and format of the output. Outside specialist advice should be sought and here the advice offered by the MDA and also the National Computing Centre would be particularly useful. If the system has been used by other museums a visit should be made to see it in operation and to note any problems. Portability of data is also important. Eventually, when the computer reaches the end of its working life, it is likely that a replacement machine

will use a different operating system. It is essential that the museum data files from the old system can be imported into the new operating system. With many museums moving towards co-operative col-lective databases it is important to have the facility to export (or import) data in a form usable by other systems. Most systems can now export or import data in ASCII (American Standard Code for Information Interchange) format.

The minicomputer option

This option probably lies outside the resources of all but the national museums and the larger county museum services. Minicomputers require at least one full-time computer technician to supervise their operation. Although much cheaper to operate than a mainframe computer, minicomputers are more expensive than a microcomputer system and, as would be expected, are more powerful in their computing power and storage capabilities. If speci-fically for museum use then there is the opportunity to buy in customized software rather than relying on adapting an existing DBMS. Many of the problems discussed above in relation to setting up a mainframe system are equally pertinent to the establishment of a minicomputer system. The National Museums in Scotland have recently adopted this strategy.

The microcomputer option

As this is undoubtedly the most popular of the options currently available, and certainly the most accessible in terms of cost to the average museum, it will be considered in more detail. For a general appraisal see Avedon et al (1986) and Lewis (1986).

A microcomputer does not require a full-time computer technician to operate it and the mainte-nance is usually contracted out to an agency – often this is the supplier. The computers occupy a relatively small amount of space and are easily accommodated in an office 'desk-top' environment. Some models are portable. The disadvantages compared to a mainframe or minicomputer are slower processing and limited storage of data. The latter aspect may not be a problem if records are stored in logical groups, e.g. fine-art water-colour painting object-records could be one group whilst fine-art oil paintings could form another group. If the combined database of both groups exceeds the storage capabilities of the microcomputer they could be processed separately as required, the data being transferred to and from the computer using an appropriate secondary storage medium.

The storage capability of microcomputers is undergoing rapid development and, at the time of writing, systems with a capacity approaching

400 Mb are becoming available. See also the combined microcomputer – mainframe or mini option discussed below.

Setting up the system involves the museum purchasing a microcomputer, printer and, if possible, a tape streamer. Software is also purchased separately to process the data. The range of options of both hardware and software are enormous, but advice can be sought from the MDA and, in the case of a Local Authority museum, the Authority computing section. Advice should also be sought from the growing number of museums which have adopted relevant microcomputer systems.

Choosing a microcomputer system

The microcomputer is undergoing extremely rapid development with the introduction of ever more sophisticated hardware and operating systems. However, at the time of writing, the best option is probably an IBM PC or a PC Compatible machine. There are many different kinds with a diverse price range, although the most expensive is not necessarily the best.

Most business PC or PC Compatible microcomputers are purchased as a single unit consisting of a microprocessor, main memory, secondary storage, keyboard, screen, output and input ports and expansion slots, Such a system only needs the addition of a printer to provide a complete self-contained system. The following aspects should be considered when acquiring a system.

Random access memory

The memory of the computer is housed on special chips. The random access memory (RAM) contains the software programme being run plus the data being processed. The amount of RAM available determines the complexity of the software that can be used. For documentation purposes the available RAM should be at least 1 Mb or more (equivalent to upwards of a million characters). The contents of the RAM are lost every time the machine is switched off. To save the processed information it must be copied to a secondary storage medium.

Secondary storage

This is used for the semi-permanent storage of data. Most microcomputers have the facility to read data to and from a *diskette* (sometimes called a *floppy disk*). This consists of a disk coated with a magnetic substance held in a square plastic sleeve. Information is transferred to or from a diskette by placing it in a diskette drive usually built into the computer system unit. Diskettes are typically 5.25 inches square and, depending on their configuration, can store between 360 kb and 720 kb of data (e.g. 720 to 1440 records of

an average length of 500 characters). Newer machines have diskette drives which use more robust and reliable 3.5 inch diskettes. These can, depending on their configuration, contain up to 1.44 Mb of data (equivalent to about 2800 records of an average length of 500 characters). Cheaper microcomputers have twin diskette drives and no other form of secondary storage. Whilst adequate for documentation purposes, diskettes are limited in the amount of data that can be processed and are awkward to use as they have to be repeatedly placed in the disk drive in order to load data and software.

The more expensive microcomputers, as well as possessing a disk drive, have a much larger secondary storage medium sealed into the system unit. This is the *Winchester Disk* more familiarly referred to as the *hard disk*. The hard disk is generally not removable, although some computers are now being produced with exchangeable hard-disk units. Hard disks have a much greater storage capacity than a diskette, usually ranging between 20 Mb to 120 Mb or more (equivalent to between about 40 000 and 240 000 records of an average length of 500 characters). Such disks can easily accommodate both processing software and large quantities of data. The cost of a computer with a hard-disk drive is roughly proportional to the amount of data it can store.

If a hard disk becomes corrupted or damaged then all the data it contains may be rendered unusable. It is therefore of vital importance to archive or back-up the data on a regular basis. Traditionally this has been done by regularly backing up the entire contents of the hard disk to a series of diskettes; a tedious and time-consuming process (e.g. a 30 Mb hard disk is equivalent to about 83 diskettes of capacity 360 kb). A far better option is to invest in a *tape streamer*. This is a third type of secondary-storage medium. The tape streamer unit can be permanently connected to the computer (some computers have built-in tape drives), and can transfer the entire contents of a hard disk to a special tape cassette or cartridge containing high quality magnetic tape in as little as 15 min. The operating software is usually fairly sophisticated and can facilitate the transfer of a single file, a group of files, or the entire hard-disk contents to or from the computer.

Printers

A printer is used to output data from the computer to paper or card. There are three main types of printer; laser, daisy-wheel and dot-matrix. The price range is upwards of £50 for a dot-matrix machine to upwards of £1000 for a laser printer.

Laser printers are extremely versatile high-speed and high-quality printers which work on a similar principle to the office photocopier. They can reproduce text in a wide variety of different fonts and sizes and will also reproduce graphics to a very high standard. They are fast, quiet in operation and the more expensive machines can print in colour.

Daisy-wheel printers are similar to some electric typewriters in their mode of operation. A ribbon is struck by pre-formed metal or plastic characters arranged on spokes around a daisy-shaped wheel. The wheels are interchangeable allowing a variety of fonts and sizes of print to be selected. Output is of very high quality. The main disadvantages are slowness of operation and no ability to reproduce graphics.

Dot-matrix printers represent the cheapest option. They are fairly versatile and reproduce characters by a series of pins striking a ribbon against paper or card. Some of the more expensive models can produce document quality or even camera-ready copy, although normally the results are reasonably clear. Most will reproduce simple graphics such as graphs and maps. Many dot-matrix printers have a range of fonts which can be selected under software control. In general, printing is reasonably fast, averaging between 80–200 characters per second. One minor disadvantage is noisy operation but this can be partially overcome by means of an acoustic hood.

Microcomputer maintenance contracts

Breakdown of hardware can represent considerable problems in wasted time and expensive repairs. To minimize these inconveniences it is well worth taking out a maintenance contract to ensure that repairs are undertaken as soon as possible. Some contracts include the option of a temporary loan of replacement equipment whilst repairs are being carried out. Most reputable suppliers will provide a contract maintenance service based on an annual charge.

The combined microcomputer with mainframe or mini option

In many ways this is the ideal option for a large museum or museum service contemplating the progressive automation of their record data. It allows the system to be phased in over a period of years as finances permit and as the automation requirements expand. Hardware is progressively purchased to establish microcomputer work stations in each department or each branch museum of the service. These will be used to automate and/or process records on a subject or departmental basis. Eventually, when the automated data of a department exceeds the capacity of an individual microcomputer, or if it is required to form a collective database drawing together all the departmental databases, a mainframe or minicomputer is introduced. The departmental microcomputers can be networked to a minicompu-

ter or linked as terminals to the mainframe. The large computer would contain the collective database, but with the option of interrogation by the networked or linked microcomputers. The microcomputers would continue to be used for basic data entry and the processing of local files with the larger computer concentrating on large-scale processing and archiving of the entire database. This option is only just beginning to be explored by UK museums. The Hampshire County Museum Sevice is loading MODES- (Museum Object Data Entry System) generated data to a mainframe computer with an ORACLE DBMS (M. Norgate, personal communication) and the Leicester Museum and Records Service are considering a similar option.

Record management software

The effective manipulation of documentation records requires a sophisticated database management system (referred to as a DBMS). There are many different kinds ranging from products providing a basic record-keeping facility to sophisticated systems with many powerful data entry and retrieval facilities (for recent reviews see: Avedon *et al* 1986; Bearman, 1987b, 1988). Such systems facilitate the creation of structured records, the editing and updating of individual records and the retrieval and sorting of record data according to a variety of different user-defined criteria.

There are several options when choosing a DBMS. One of these is to purchase a standard business DBMS and adapt it in-house for museum use. However, this option usually requires considerable software programming expertise. Another option is to obtain a standard business system which has been specifically customized for museum use. The third option is to purchase a system specifically written as a museum DBMS.

The information making up museum records tends to be extremely variable according to how much is known about an object and how important it is. Categories within a record such as provenance and acquisition can vary from zero to many hundreds of characters. Such variable records do not fit in with most business database packages which tend to cater for neat fixed-length chunks of data. Records within such a system occupy a fixed amount of storage space irrespective of the amount of data within the record. Use of such a DBMS means either opting for a strategy where the framework for the records is set up to take a maximum amount of information in all categories (this is very wasteful of space particularly on a micro system where hard-disk space may be a critical factor), or the framework can be set up to limit the amount of information entered per category per record. This will mean abbreviating record data which again is not a totally satisfactory solution. In practice, the reality is a compromise between the two extremes. A better option is to adopt a system which will allow variable-length categories of information within records, the storage space occupied varying according to the size of the record.

Software applications are frequently updated and it is worthwhile to subscribe to an update facility if available. Such a scheme ensures that a user receives updates in the software (e.g. to correct any faults or 'bugs' or to receive new versions with enhanced facilities) and its documentation.

As noted previously, any DBMS shold have the facility to export and import data in ASCII format.

Data entry

A successful strategy for data entry is vital to any automation process and is, therefore, worthy of special consideration. Data entry is the most labour-intensive phase of any automation project; there are few short cuts and it is easy to underestimate the resources and time required. It is also the most crucial factor in determining how soon a system can start to operate usefully. Consequently it is of the utmost importance to allocate sufficient resources in terms of both personnel and hardware.

Data entry usually involves copy typing manual record information in at the computer's keyboard by means of a series of prompts displayed on the visual display unit (VDU) screen. In the context of museum records, strict terminology control is essential and can be partially achieved by the computer automatically checking the input data against a previously defined system of keywords and syntax written into the software programme. Deviation or errors from the system will not be accepted by the computer. Such a process is called validation. Data entry can be accelerated and accuracy further improved by the computer 'memorizing' chunks of repetitive information which can be carried forward or recalled into successive records as required without having to be retyped.

As an alternative to in-house data entry, copies of the manual records can be sent to an external bureau specializing in record automation. However, this is generally a much more expensive option than undertaking the work internally.

Staff training

It is essential that museum staff using an automated system are adequately trained it its use. The MDA currently provide a series of courses which include: 'Basic Computing', 'Introduction to PCs', 'Understanding Databases' and 'Tailoring Databases'. The courses are held at a wide range of venues throughout the UK and it is also possible for individual museums to book in-house courses for the benefit of their staff. If the computing resources of an umbrella organization such as a Local Authority are being used then it is likely that basic training may be provided internally. A supplier should be able to provide training in the general use of a software program but thereafter it may rest with the system manager to provide training in the museological application. Some software manufacturers and their agents provide a telephone 'helpline' facility to enable users to talk through operational problems whilst at the keyboard – an extremely useful service. The MDA provide this to support their MODES application.

Word processing

The main application of a word processor is to facilitate the input of a document in a format which can subsequently be edited, reformatted, stored and output on card, paper or to another software application. An ability to import and export ASCII text is particularly useful in enabling the package to be used in conjunction with a museum DBMS. Many packages have the facility to check the spelling of a document. Another useful feature is 'search and replace', e.g. to search for an incorrect word or block of text used frequently throughout a document and replace it with the correct word or text. The cost of word-processing applications varies considerably. At the cheaper end of the range it is possible to purchase a desk-top integrated hardware and software package dedicated solely to word processing. However, such packages are normally restricted in terms of importing and exporting data from other systems as regards both software and hardware compatibility. There are now a wide range of 'standard' word-processing packages which are designed to run on most of the better-known makes of business microcomputer. There is probably little to choose between such packages as MultiMate, Samna, Wordstar, Word-Perfect, and Word. The teaching documentation with these packages is generally excellent and usually includes a tutorial. Some of the larger software suppliers provide basic training in the use of the packages which they sell. Many Local Authorities using word processing offer internal training to employees including relevant museum staff.

Uses of a word-processing package in the museum

In the context of museum administration a word processor can be used in the preparation of complex committee reports and exhibition briefs. Most of the better packages have a mailmerge facility which enables a database of names and addresses to be maintained and manipulated to produce personalized letters and printed self-adhesive address labels, etc. These are useful in the context of circulating exhibition and event details to publicity outlets and other interested parties such as Friends organizations and museum-related clubs.

It is arguably from the standpoint of publication that the use of a word processor can benefit a museum most. Word processing of collection data from a DBMS can facilitate the speedy production of exhibition catalogues and labels. Many printing and publishing firms can accept word-processed text on diskette saving an enormous amount of time and cost in both typesetting and checking processes. It is now possible to purchase microcomputer-driven desk-top publishing packages which can interface graphics and word-processed data with a laser printer to produce camera-ready copy for publication.

The Data Protection Act

Any automated system which includes personal data (e.g. acquisition information with names and addresses of donors) is subject to the provisions of the UK Data Protection Act (1984). A museum planning to automate such data must be registered under the terms of the Act to comply with the law. The implications of the Act relating to museums have been fully dealt with by Jones and Roberts (1985).

Gallery displays and educational use

The scope for using computer and computer-related technology in museum exhibitions and related educational applications is almost infinite. Uses can range from a computer-controlled model-train layout where the rolling-stock movements, points, signals, etc., are operated by a computer programme, to an interactive terminal where a visitor can interrogate visual, stationary and moving images on a computer controlled videodisc player.

Management and financial information

Even a small PC or compatible microcomputer, loaded with the appropriate software, has the capability to revolutionize general and financial management procedures within the museum.

The only additional hardware requirement is a laser printer which is really essential if it is intended to produce high quality printed correspondence and reports for external and committee use. Make sure that the printer will accept and print satisfactorily on the institution's A4 headed letter-paper as well as on the envelope formats used. If it is intended to print spreadsheet graphics (or any other graphic material), ensure that the laser printer has sufficient memory; at least 2 Mb is required.

Reference has already been made to the advantages of using a word processor for producing letters and complex reports of all kinds. Similarly a business database can be used for the recording and manipulation of personnel records and mailing list names and addresses.

Potentially the most useful software for museum management is a spreadsheet package. A spreadsheet enables users to construct two-dimensional tables of numerical and textual information. The ability of the cells to store text is used to annotate the table with column headings, titles, etc. As well as entering information, the user can also embed formulas and calculations into the various cells in a table to compute column or row totals or work out variances. When fresh numerical data is entered or existing data is revised, the spreadsheet software automatically recalculates any other cells that are affected thereby saving hours of work recalculating by hand or by calculator. Spreadsheets can be used for storing, amending and displaying budgets and accounts, "what if?" financial projections, shop stocktaking, market research, museum/gallery attendance figures etc. Many spreadsheet applications can display and print data in the form of attractive graphs which is a particularly useful way of presenting, for example, monthly attendance figures or annual attendance figures related to exhibitions and/or special museum based events held throughout the year. Thus complex numeric information can be presented in a clear, concise and attractive format; a boon for museum management committee reports.

A welcome development has been the apperance of integrated modular software where, for example, a word processor, database and spreadsheet can be purchased in the form of a single package. This is generally much cheaper than purchasing separate packages for each application and confers a major advantage inasmuch as data can easily be transferred between the modules; a spreadsheet graph can be transferred and incorporated within a word processed committee report; similarly an address list held in the database can be used for a mailmerge in the word processor; database information can be transferred to the spreadsheet for analysis and so on.

Mention should also be made of Project Planning and Resource Management software. This allows the user to input data relating to project activities, the order in which they occur, deadlines for completion, available recources as regards cost, staff and materials etc. An example might be an evaluation of existing and potential resources necessary for producing a realistic timetable for the design, production and implementation of one or several exhibitions and displays over an extended period within one or several museums and galleries. The software can evaluate progress, and prepare revised schedules for any timetable deviations caused by unpredictable factors such as staff illness etc.

These are just a few of the many computer applications which have immense potential for streamlining museum management.

References

AVEDON, E.M., STEWART, T.O., GODMAN, D.S., EICHMIERER, W.E., FIJALKOWSKI, B.S. (1986), *Microcomputer Database Management Systems*, Institute for Computer Research, University of Waterloo, Ontario

BEARMAN, D. (1987a), 'Functional requirements for collections management systems', *Archival Informatics Technical Report*, Vol. 1 (3), Archives and Museum Informatics, Pittsburgh, PA

BEARMAN, D. (1987b), 'Automated systems for archives and museums: acquisition and implementation issues', *Archival Informatics Technical Report*, Vol. 1 (4), Archives and Museum Informatics, Pittsburgh, PA

BEARMAN, D. (1988), 'Directory of software for archives and museums', *Archival Informatics Technical Report*, Vol. 2 (1), Archives and Museum Informatics, Pittsburgh, PA

CHENHALL, R.G. and VANCE, D. (1988), *Museum Collections and Today's Computers*, Greenwood, London

DAVIS, P. and HEBRON, J. (1982), Computer cataloguing at the Hancock Museum, Newcastle upon Tyne: a review of progress to date, *Museum Journal*, 82(2), 82–91

JONES, S.G. and ROBERTS, D.A. (Eds) (1985), 'The Data Protection Act and Museums', *MDA Occasional Paper*, 8, Museum Documentation Association, Cambridge

KIRK, J.J. (1979), 'Using a computer in Brighton's museums', *Museums Journal*, 79(1), 17–20

LEWIS, C. (1986), *Managing with Micro's*, Blackwell, Oxford

NALGO (NATIONAL AND LOCAL GOVERNMENT OFFICERS ASSOCIATION) (1980), *New Technology, A Guide for Negotiators*, NALGO London

NALGO (1981), *The Future with New Technology*, NALGO London

ORNA, E. (1987), *Information Policies for Museums*, Museum Documentation Association, Cambridge

ORNA, E. and PETTITT, S.W. (1980), *Information Handling in Museum*, Clive Bingley, London

PETTIGREW, T. and DAVIS, P. (in press) Collection Databases in Northeast England: Their Development and Future Use, in Roberts, D. A. (Ed.), *Sharing the Information Resources of Museums* (Proceedings of the Third Annual Conference of the MDA, 1988), Museum Documentation Association

ROBERTS, D.A. (Ed.) (1988), *Collections Management for Museums*, Museum Documentation Association, Cambridge

WILLIAMS, D.W. (1987), *A Guide to Museum Computing*, American Association of State and Local History, Nashville, TN

Bibliography

FOSTER, R. and PHILLIPS, P. (1988), 'New applications for computers in the National Museums and Galleries on Merseyside', in Roberts, D.A. (Ed.), *Collections Management for Museums*, 127, Museum Documentation Association, Cambridge

SLEDGE, J. (1989), 'Successful museum computerisation: the secret ingredients', *SPECTRA* 16(4)

22

Law and legislation

Patrick Sudbury and C. K. Wilson

Introduction

Law is the set of rules made by a society to guide the conduct of its people. The law touches every aspect of the curator's work, usually lightly but sometimes with force; the curator needs to know where to find reliable legal advice at short notice. Law changes with time. This chapter will refer to the law of England and Wales as it was in 1990. The law of Scotland and of other countries contains comparable provisions to meet similar needs. Every curator should be prepared to seek legal advice about the conduct of museum business in the same way as professional advice should be sought on conservation or design.

Law and real property

Museums occupy land and buildings which are subject to the law of real property (realty = land). Lawful occupation is by freehold, leasehold or licence. Unlawful occupation by trespassers and squatters may enjoy some legal protection.

Freehold is the ownership of land and buildings in perpetuity. Leasehold creates rights of occupation for a set term, usually a period of years. Licences are used to confer temporary short-term rights, often for the hire of rooms, car parking or the use of land.

It is the occupier, rather than the owner, who is liable for mishaps within land and buildings. The curator's interest is thus to be quite clear who is in occupation at a given time. The occupier owes a common duty of care towards anyone entering his premises. Many fixtures must conform to safety regulations and may be subject to regular inspection and certification if the public is to be admitted. Certain activities are regulated by statutory licence. Examples include cinema performances; music, singing and dancing; the keeping of live animals; the storage of firearms and weapons; and the sale of intoxicating liquor.

Local Authorities, Fire Brigades and the Health and Safety Executive are generally willing to give both informal and formal guidance on the Regulations and Codes of Practice that constrain the use, maintenance and alteration of buildings. Curators should seek independent advice if they feel that the requirements are unreasonable or excessively onerous.

Law and personal property

The law recognizes two kinds of property: real property which comprises land and the fixtures upon it; and personal property which is any other thing, like goods, chattels and copyright, which a person or organization may own, possess or have rights over.

Personal property may be held by ownership, possession, custody or bailment. The owner of personal property has the right to use it in every way permitted by law and to exclude others from so doing. Possession is the physical control of property permitted by law. Custody is physical control of a temporary nature not protected by law.

Bailment occurs where one party, the bailor, delivers property into the possession of another, the bailee, upon certain conditions. The bailee is obliged to take reasonable care of the property and to return it to the bailor when required. It may be prudent to transfer the risk by insurance. The law of bailment and the law of trusteeship apply to most loans of exhibitions and museum collections and loan agreements should be checked by a lawyer.

Lost property or unclaimed items left for appraisal can be disposed of after reasonable attempts to secure their return. However, any claim to ownership by the museum would be dubious. The *Torts (Interference with Goods) Act 1977* and the *Local Government (Miscellaneous Provisions) Act 1982* apply.

Law and the collections

Museum collections are acquired through fieldwork and excavation; through purchase or exchange; by gift; by legislation; or through deposit.

In the case of public museums, there is relatively little legal restriction on what may be acquired. However, once items have been acquired and added to the museum's register of accessions there is a presumption against disposal. Such an acquisition may be regarded as held in public trust. The public are arguably the beneficial owners – not the museum. The public interest has to be served by disposal.

Acquisition by fieldwork and excavation are now closely controlled. In the UK, sites of historical, traditional, artistic or architectural interest may be scheduled and protected under the *Ancient Monuments and Archaeological Areas Act 1979*. The *Protection of Wrecks Act 1973* allows underwater sites of historic, archaeological or artistic importance to be designated. It then becomes an offence to enter the wreck area without a licence. The *Wildlife and Countryside Act 1981* makes it an offence to damage the habitat or to injure or take certain species of plants, animals and birds. Exceptions are provided by licence.

On acquisition by purchase, exchange or gift, consideration must be given to the possibility that the items have been obtained or imported illicitly. The curator will also need to check carefully if the prospective donor or vendor has breached the law relating to treasure trove (for items hidden) or droits in Admiralty (for items floating upon the sea). The museum will need to have a licence if it is to hold certain recently taken species of dead animals and birds; a zoo licence to hold certain living species; a firearms licence to hold certain weapons; and will need to be registered if it holds chemical or botanical collections which include poisons and drugs. In most purchases the curator will enjoy the protection of the *Sale of Goods Act 1979*.

The documentation of collections is important because it provides pointers to records (correspondence, contracts of sale, etc.) that give the museum legal title. If data includes personal information and is held in a computer then it may be necessary for the museum to register under the *Data Protection Act 1984*.

Law and the curator

The curator has a duty to exercise reasonable care over collections, staff and public. The standard of reasonable care is an objective one, assuming an awareness of professional standards of care and skill in comparable institutions. Ignorance or inexperience is no defence. The curator must seek advice where doubt exists or knowledge and experience is lacking. The law does not expect a curator to be an insurer against all risk, so the harm must be foreseeable.

Principles are turned into practical tests by Scott (1985) in posing six questions indicative of the standards of care to be applied by museum curators:

(1) Were premises safe for the collection, staff and visitors?
(2) Were there enough staff; were they competent and briefed on special features of their job; had the curator's delegations been reasonable; what had the curator kept as his own role?
(3) How far was the curator abreast of the shared knowledge of his profession, nationally and internationally?
(4) Was it a task where a consultant would normally be brought in?
(5) Was the mishap or the catastrophe due to an error of judgement or to negligence; was it totally unforeseeable?
(6) Was insurance cover in force and adequate?

Law and the staff

Common law regulates the relationship between employer and employee by means of a number of conditions amounting to a contract of employment. Duties are imposed by implication if not expressly stated.

Employees must obey orders and be faithful, keeping the employer's secrets. They are responsible for the consequences of lack of care in their work. They must not work on behalf of a competitor at the same time. They may not canvass their employer's customers for themselves. In short, employees must act in good faith for the period of their employment and even for a reasonable period thereafter.

An employer must provide a proper system of work, effectively supervised with competent staff and suitable materials. The duty cannot be delegated, but is not a complete assurance of safety because employees accept the reasonable risks inherent in their employment. An employer indemnifies employees against losses incurred in the reasonable performance of their duties. An employer's extensive statutory duties further regulate conditions of employment.

Statutory employment law is consolidated in the *Employment Protection (Consolidation) Act 1978,* but has been further developed in subsequent Acts. Relevant legislation includes the *Health and Safety at Work Act 1974*; the *Disabled Persons (Employment) Act 1944*; the *Race Relations Act 1976*; the *Equal Pay Act 1970*; and the *Sex Discrimination Act 1975*. Compliance with the law is evidenced by the extent to which employers have followed guidance issued by the Health and Safety Executive, the Commission for Racial Equality and the Equal Opportunities Commission.

Recruitment of an employee will normally follow advertisement, application, interview, offer and acceptance. The grounds for employment must be fitness for the job and not race, religion or sex unless these factors are essential to the performance of the job in the manner defined by equal opportunities legislation. Once appointed the employee must be provided with a contract of employment, a statement of safety policy and with the training necessary to perform the job. A probationary period with monitoring of performance should follow. Written records should be kept.

Termination of employment may be by resignation, retirement, redundancy or dismissal. Resignation is the expressed wish of the employee to cease work on a particular day. It is not possible to restrain employees from ceasing work but it may be possible to use the law to restrain them from working for a competitor or giving away information that they learned in your employment.

Retirement age is normally a condition of employment which can be varied only by mutual agreement of the employer and employee. However, the employer can impose retirement at an earlier date if there is clear evidence of incapacity through ill health or inefficiency.

Redundancy occurs when the employee's job disappears. This might arise through restructuring, changing demand or the inability of the employer to pay wages. Legally, the test would be that the job had disappeared permanently and the employee could not be redeployed. If the test cannot be met then the 'redundancy' is really dismissal.

Dismissal is the termination of employment by the employer. Dismissal is effected by giving due notice to the employee and strictly observing dismissal procedure. Severance payments may be due under the terms of the employee's contract and employment law. An employee must not be dismissed unfairly.

Fair and unfair dismissal are statutory terms. Whenever action is taken or contemplated, precise reasons for dismissal with supporting evidence must be advanced by the employer. An employer's reason for dismissal must relate to conduct, capability, qualifications, redundancy or statutory prohibition. There is special protection for those engaged in trade union activity. Fair and unfair dismissal is judged by an industrial tribunal in accordance with equity and the industrial merits of the case. Unfair dismissal is redressed by reinstatement or compensation. The employer is exempt from claims for unfair dismissal from staff employed for less than two years and those reaching normal retirement age.

Law and health, safety and welfare at work

Many items of health, safety and welfare legislation are relevant to museums. Examples include the *Factories Act 1961*; the *Offices, Shops and Railway Premises Act 1963*; and the *Fire Precautions Act 1971*. There is also much subordinate legislation: Orders, Regulations, Codes of Practice and Guidance Notes issued by Ministries or the Health and Safety Executive.

The *Health and Safety at Work Act 1974* makes the employer responsible for health and safety; requires the employer to delegate those responsibilites to employees at all levels; and imposes a general duty of care and co-operation in safety matters on everyone at work.

An employer is under a general duty to ensure the health, safety and welfare of all employees, so far as reasonably practicable. The duty covers plant and systems of work, use, storage and transport of materials; health education and work training, safe working conditions and welfare facilities. A written policy statement must be brought to the notice of all employees and should include a scheme of delegation.

Employers must discharge the responsibility for health and safety through their workforce. Curators are thus responsible for the safety of the staff, accommodation, collections and equipment under their control. They are legally and personally liable if they fail to discharge their health and safety duties.

There is provision for the appointment, or election, of safety representatives from amongst the employees. Employers must consult such representatives. However, the representatives' role is supplementary and advisory. They in no way diminish the duty or authority of the employers and their staff to organize for safety and to ensure proper communication on safety matters. Breach of an employer's duties is a criminal offence subject to a fine, but does not give rise to civil liability.

Employees are under a general duty to take such care as is reasonable for the health and safety of themselves and others and must co-operate with employers on statutory duties. Codes of Practice issued by the Health and Safety Executive are designed to assist employers and to protect employees.

Law and the public

The law places a general duty of care upon persons as to their acts and omissions towards others. The *Occupier's Liability Act 1957* codifies the duty owed by an occupier to a visitor: anyone to whom the occupier gives an invitation, express or implied, to enter or use the premises.

Public liability rests between the occupier of property and visitors. The duty is to ensure that the visitor is reasonably safe when using the premises for the purpose invited or permitted. An occupier may modify or exclude the common duty of care by contract with the visitor, usually in the form of a ticket. Terms may be set out expressly on the ticket or reference made to the place where the terms can be seen. Where the contract is silent the law restores the duty of care as an implied term. Common practice is to insure against the risk of liability. Claims for compensation will usually be based on a breach of duty. An occupier does not have any obligation with regard to risks that the visitor has willingly accepted. Regard must be had to all the circumstances and precise records are important. The automatic use of accident report forms for any incident, however minor, is a useful precaution.

Notices are commonly displayed by occupiers to limit their legal liability to visitors by means of an express warning. A warning of danger will not absolve the occupier from liability unless sufficient to enable the visitor to be reasonably safe. The *Unfair Contract Terms Act 1977* forbids the use of contract terms and warning notices to limit liability for death or personal injury due to negligence.

Special classes of visitor merit particular attention. An occupier must be prepared for children to be less careful than adults. What may be a warning to an adult may not be so to a child. Under the *Occupier's Liability Act 1984*, the occupier owes a duty to 'persons other than his visitors', e.g. trespassers. The duty is met by giving warning of the danger or taking steps to discourage persons from incurring the risk. Contractors or others entering the premises in the exercise of their calling will be expected to appreciate and guard against any special risk. A working contractor in occupation or control of premises will bear the common duty of care.

By-laws regulating the use of Local Authority museums can be made under the *Public Libraries and Museums Act 1964*. Commonly regulated are the conduct of visitors; the maintenance of good order; and the avoidance of nuisance. Model by-laws are customarily available from the confirming authority. The *Local Government Act 1972* provides a common procedure for the making and confirmation of by-laws. In cases of disorderly behaviour every effort should be made to avoid physical contact and the police should be involved. Theft from the museum, the staff or visitors should always be reported to the police.

Law and financial control

Public finance is subject to stringent control. For national museums the mechanism of control is a financial memorandum from the Government de-partment contolling their grant-in-aid. The annual accounts are audited by the Comptroller and Auditor General and made available to Parliament. Local authority museums have their expenditure control-led under the statutes which define the powers of a local authority to raise finance and incur expenditure. Accounts must be kept, scrutinized by the District Auditor and published. No expenditure may be incurred without statutory authority.

The finance of private museums is subject to a range of constraints. The most obvious is the control of the marketplace, in which operators unable to pay their way become bankrupt and cease trading. Museums registered as companies and charities are required to prepare annual accounts for their annual meeting. Copies of those accounts are subsequently lodged with the Registrar of Companies and/or the Charity Commissioners. Tax liabilities vary and up-to-date information should be sought from HM Inspector of Taxes or Customs and Excise.

Law and trusts and trustees

A trust exists where a trustee holds property for the use or enjoyment of a beneficiary. Groups of people, museums, societies, clubs and associations not having legal personality can enjoy the benefit of property held in trust for them. Trust and confidence is placed in the trustee by the creator of the trust. The law of equity will not allow trustees to depart from the obligation they have undertaken. Trusteeship can be onerous. All duties must be strictly discharged, using as much diligence as people of ordinary prudence in the management of their own affairs.

The duties of a trustee are: to administer the trust prudently; to comply strictly with the terms of the trust; not to vary the trust; not to delegate duties; to keep accounts; to invest as authorized by the trust itself or by the *Trustee Investments Act 1961*. Trustees are personally liable if they depart from those duties.

Trust property may include land, stocks and shares and money, objects and artefacts. The trustee is the legal owner and has dealings with the property, such as sale or exchange. The beneficiary enjoys the benefit of the trust property on the terms of the trust. A private trust is enforceable by the beneficiaries. A public or charitable trust is enforceable by the Crown.

Private trusts may be express trusts and implied trusts. An express trust must be made plain by three certainties: words, subject matter and objects. An implied trust arises either from a presumed intention or by operation of law. Gifts to museums often involve an implied trust.

A trust is formalized by a governing instrument and a vesting deed. A trust of land must be evidenced in writing. The trust instrument declares the terms of the trust and appoints the trustees. The vesting deed describes the trust property and vests legal ownership in the trustees. Investment is regulated by the *Trustee Investments Act 1961* or the governing instrument.

Charitable trusts are public trusts for the relief of poverty, the advancement of education, the advancement of religion, and for other purposes beneficial to the community not falling under the previous heads. No trust can be charitable unless it is for the benefit of the public. A charitable trust needs to be registered by the Charity Commission in England and Wales and recognized by the Inland Revenue in Scotland. Both bodies will offer advice.

Law and commercial activities

Museums may engage in activities ancillary to their prime museum functions, including the operation of shops, cafes, car parks and the production of publications. For museum shops there are statutory codes for the sale of goods, consumer protection and trades descriptions. For cafes there are regulations covering food storage and preparation and the sale of intoxicating liquor. Advice on these statutes and regulations may be sought from the local environmental health inspectors and trading standards officer.

A contract of sale is very simply made. All that is required is that the parties should indicate by words or actions their willingness to buy and sell, and that the goods should be identified. In a shop the display of goods, selection by the customer, presentation to the cashier and acceptance of payment meet all the requirements for a contract of sale.

The *Sale of Goods Act 1979* codifies the contract between seller and buyer. The ordinary consumer cannot reasonably be expected to know if the goods are fit for the purpose for which they were bought or if they are of good or bad quality until they are used. The Sale of Goods Act protects the consumer by providing that (unless the parties otherwise agree) there are certain implied terms and conditions and warranties which apply to every contract for the sale of goods.

If there is a breach of a condition, the buyer may treat the contract as ended and return the goods. If return is impossible, the buyer may sue for damages. A breach of warranty does not end the contract but gives the buyer the right to sue for damages.

Law and contract

A contract is an agreement intended to be legally binding and supported by consideration. It reflects a bargain from which both parties expect to benefit. A valid contract is one which the law will recognize and enforce. The courts will not enforce agreements which are illegal because they are prohibited by statute or contrary to public policy. An apparently valid contract may be rendered void or voidable by certain factors, such as mistake, misrepresentation, duress and undue influence. A void contract is a nullity; no rights can be acquired under it. A voidable contract is one which under certain conditions may be treated as ineffective by one of the parties. Contracts may be written or oral; substantial contracts may be by deed under seal to extend their limitation period.

Agents are frequently involved in making contracts. An agent acts on behalf of an organization and may be a proprietor, a partner, a director, an employee or contractor. Agents acting within the scope of their authority may make contracts without incurring personal liability for the execution of the contracts. Once the contract is made it is binding on the organization and the client but not on the agents. Even if the agents exceeded their authority, the contract may still be binding, if the clients have reasonable grounds for believing that the agents had authority. Thus a museum may be bound by the actions of staff acting outside their authority. This means that the limits of authority need to be made clear to all parties.

Law and the business community

Museums have many dealings with the business community and many museums are themselves businesses or have subsidiary business activities. Businesses may be sole proprietorships, partnerships, private companies, public companies or co-operatives.

A business is some productive activity resulting in the creation of goods and services to satisfy wants. Anyone may set up a business as a sole proprietor on their own account and under their own name. If the business trades under any other name then it must comply with the *Companies Act 1985*. A licence must be obtained for certain classes of business. Sole proprietors are self-employed and are liable to the full extent of their private wealth for the debts of the business.

Partnership is the relationship which subsists between persons carrying on a business in common with a view to profit. The responsibilities of the partners towards each other and in business were codified in the Partnership Act 1890. Each partner, acting on behalf of the firm, acts as an agent for the firm and the other partners. The partners are jointly and severally liable. Where the partnership property is insufficient to meet the firm's debts then recourse may be had to the assets of the individual partners.

Companies have a legal existence separate and distinct from the people who control them. Under the *Companies Act 1985* a Memorandum of Association defines the company's external relationships and Articles of Association control its internal affairs. Registration, incorporation and certification by the Registrar of Companies will allow operations to commence.

The liability of the people who form a company or who hold shares is limited to the amount they have agreed to contribute. Unlike sole proprietors and partners they are not personally liable to the full extent of their personal wealth. Organizations which limit their liability in this way must use the suffix 'Ltd' or 'PLC'. The former is a private limited company whose shareholders are normally the small group of people who formed the company. A PLC is a public limited company whose shares may be bought and sold by anyone through the Stock Exchange.

Museums in the private sector are generally created by individual collectors or groups of enthusiasts and for continuity are often established as a trust, charitable or otherwise. Objects and procedures are ordered in the trust instrument and property and artefacts vested in trustees by a vesting deed. Alternatively, continuity may be achieved and liability limited by the formation of a private limited company under the *Companies Act 1985* as a company limited by guarantee. A museum for public benefit may acquire charitable status.

Museum curators are frequently involved in business units, such as private museums, clubs, societies and co-operatives, which are not in business for profit. They operate generally in the same way as companies but each admitted member may have the same say in the affairs of the organization regardless of the size of individual holding or subscription. Trading surpluses are ploughed back into the business to provide a better service to members and clients rather than appearing as profits which are paid to shareholders.

Certain bodies may register as charities under the Charities Acts of 1960 and 1985. Where company profits are covenanted into the maintenance of a museum for public benefit, charitable status may be granted. This offers valuable financial advantages such as rating relief and the recovery of tax paid on covenanted gifts so that the bulk of the funds can be devoted to museum purposes. Many organizations which support museums (e.g. Friends) have charitable status.

Law and copyright

The aim of copyright law is to protect the interest of creative people in the work they create. Copyright is a branch of intellectual property law. The law applies to all literary, dramatic, artistic and musical works as well as sound recordings, films and broadcasts. In the case of literary, dramatic or musical work the law restricts the copying or publication of the text or score, public performances and broadcasts of the work in its original form or adapted. In the case of a painting, sculpture, engraving, architectural designs, or craftwork the item may not be reproduced, published or included in a television broadcast. There is a time limit of 50 years in most cases.

The *Copyright Act 1956* is being repealed and succeeded by the *Copyright, Design and Patents Act 1988*. Copyright may be held over nine categories of work listed in the Act. Unless the matter comes within these categories, no copyright can exist and there can be no copyright interests. International conventions have been established to promote international co-operation against unlawful exploitation.

Most museums will encounter copyright when they reproduce modern works in their publications, displays and activities. Many copyrights are held on behalf of their creators by copyright societies which operate collective licensing arrangements to secure the creator's claim to equitable payment for copying or broadcasting work.

Law and briefing a lawyer

At some stage in any dispute or transaction legal advice may be sought. It is generally better to seek that advice at an early stage. Matters such as premises acquisition, setting up a trading company, ownership of property or claims for injury to visitors are examples of the kind of problem where advice should be obtained as a matter of course.

Legal advice costs money. It is therefore sensible to make good use of the time of your legal adviser. Before you talk, set down your thinking on paper in as much detail as you can. If there are documents that bear on the matter then copy them and put them together in a single file. You may as well do it at the outset. The lawyer is bound to ask for them at a later date when it may be less convenient to assemble them. Discuss the matter briefly over the telephone before you send these papers. The discussion may reveal gaps in the briefing that you can readily fill. Fix the appointment and send the papers some time in advance.

In the discussion, let the lawyer take the lead. He is the professional, you are the amateur. If by the conclusion of the discussion the lawyer appears to have missed matters that you think are relevant raise them as specific issues. Keep a note of your discussion. The lawyer in the first instance will normally be a solicitor, whose role is analogous to a general practitioner in medicine. Further consultation and opinion may be sought from a barrister who operates more as a specialist.

If a matter is likely to prove contentious the lawyer may advise the briefing of counsel who will be a practising barrister. Counsel will be a specialist in the area of law the case demands. The lawyer will normally provide the brief to counsel although you may be present when it is discussed. Changes in practice envisage direct access to counsel for the professions. Counsel will normally have offices or chambers in London (or in the case of Scottish advocates, Edinburgh). Counsel will normally provide written advice on the balance of probability that your case would succeed or fail if it came to court. They may advise settlement out of court. In Scotland, the court system has marked differences from that operating in England and Wales.

The process of taking matters to court is time consuming and expensive. A range of administrative tribunals have therefore been established to provide a simple and quick way of determining cases without recourse to the courts. Matters such as disputes over employment, rent, valuation and social security may be dealt with through tribunals.

Conclusion

This paper has aimed to provide pointers to the ways the law may affect curators. The coverage is necessarily brief. The authors have, in a few lines, dealt with topics that are the subject of lengthy books. The advice given at the start should be repeated – in law, as in other matters, consult a professional.

Bibliography

There are thousands of books on the law but the authors have found the following very useful in giving simple and readable insights into a complex subject.

CROSS, C. and BAILEY, S. (1986), *Cross on Local Government Law*, Sweet and Maxwell, London

JAMES, P.S. (1979), *Introduction to English Law*, Butterworth, London

SCOTT, M. (1985), *The Law of Public Leisure Services*, Sweet and Maxwell, London

SCOTT, M. (1988), *Law and Leisure Services Management*, Longman, London

TILEY, J. and BAILEY, S. (1986), *Business Law*, Longman, London

Appendix: List of legislation and codes of practice

This list contains a number of statutes which are relevant to museums and galleries. It is by no means comprehensive but is offered as a guide. Many Acts give rise to subordinate legislation (Statutory Instruments, Regulations and Orders) to which reference should also be made. Where a statute sets in order a particular area of legislation, control is usually effected by means of Regulations published as Statutory Instruments.

Shops and Catering
1950   Shops Act
1972/1968   Trade Descriptions Act
1973   Supply of Goods (Implied Terms) Act
1977   Unfair Contract Terms Act
1978   Consumer Safety Act
1979   Sale of Goods Act
1982   Supply of Goods and Services Act
1984   Food Act
1987   Consumer Protection Act

Health and Safety
1936   Public Health Act
1961   Factories Act
1965   Offices, Shops and Railway Premises Act
1971   Fire Precautions Act
1974   Health and Safety at Work Act
1981   Zoo Licensing Act
1984/1957   Occupiers Liability Act

Employment
1958   Disabled Persons (Employment) Act
1970   Equal Pay Act
1975   Sex Descrimination Act
1976   Race Relations Act
1978   Employment Protection (Consolidation) Act
1988   Employment Act

Property
1925   Town and Country Planning Acts
1925   Law of Property Act
1949   National Parks and Access to the Countryside Act
1954   Landlord and Tenant Act
1961   Land Compensation Act
1971   Town and Country Planning Act
1973   Compulsory Purchase Act
1980   Local Government Planning and Land Act
1981   Acquisition of Land Act
1984   Building Act

Licensing
1932   Sunday Entertainment Act
1952   Cinematograph Act
1972/1963   Performers Protection Act
1964   Licensing Act
1968   Theatres Act
1972   Sunday Cinema Act
1982   Cinematograph (Amendment) Act
1982   Local Government (Miscellaneous Provisions) Act
1964   Licensing Act
1982/1902   Cinematograph Act
1984   Video Recordings Act
1984   Data Protection Act

Copyright
1988   Copyright, Design and Patents Act

Companies and charities
1961   Trustee Investment Act
1980   Partnership Act
1985   Companies Act
1985/1960   Charities Act
1989   Companies Act

Miscellaneous

1949 National Parks and Access to the Countryside Act
1953 Historic Buildings and Ancient Monuments Act
1968 Countryside Act
1969 Development of Tourism Act
1973 Protection of Wrecks Act
1977 Torts (Interference with Goods) Act
1979 Ancient Monuments and Archaeological Areas Act
1981 Wildlife and Countryside Act

1982 Local Government (Miscellaneous Provisions) Act
1982 Local Government Act
1985/1972 Local Government Act

Codes of practice

1979 Conservation Standards for Works of Art in Transit (UNESCO)
1987 Code of Practice for Museum Authorities (MA)
1987 Code of Conduct for Museums Curators (MA)

Further reading

AMBROSE, T. and RUNYARD, S. (1991), *Forward Planning: A Handbook of Business, Corporate and Development Planning for Museums and Galleries*, Museums & Galleries Commission/ Routledge, London, New York

ANON (1987), *the Clore Gallery*, Tate Gallery, London

ADVISORY, CONCILIATION AND ARBITRATION SERVICE (1980), *Industrial relations Handbook*, HMSO, London

ASSOCIATION FOR BUSINESS SPONSORSHIP OF THE ARTS (1990), *Setting Standards for the 1990s. Principles for Good Practice in Arts Sponsorship*, ABSA, London

AYKAC A. (1989), 'Elements for an Economic Analysis of Museums', *Museum*, **162**(2), 84–87

BEER, V. (1990), 'The problem and promise of museum goals', *Curator*, **33**(1), 5–18

BENNET, R. (1981), *Managing Personnel and Performance. An alternative approach*, Business Books, London

BOSTICK, L.A. (1977), *The Guarding of Cultural Property*, UNESCO, New York

BYRNE, T. (1986), *Local Government in Britain*, Penguin, London

CARNEGIE UK TRUST (1985), *Arts and Disabled People [The Attenborough Report]*, Bedford Square Press, London

CIVIL SERVICE DEPARTMENT (1974), *Health and Safety at Work Act 1974*, HMSO, London

COSSONS, N. (Ed.) (1985), *The Management of Change in Museums*, National Maritime Museum, London

DALE, E. and MICHELOW, L.C. (1986) *Modern Management Methods*, Penguin, London

DAVISON, A. (1989), *Grants from Europe*, Bedford Square Press, London

DEPARTMENT OF ENERGY (1989), *Energy efficiency in Buildings, Libraries Museums, Art Galleries, and Churches. DOE No. 1 EB58*, HMSO, London

FINDLAY, I. (1989), 'A blast for the past', *Museums Journal*, **8**, 19–22

HEBDITCH, M. (1989), 'Charging for survival?', *Museum News*, **44**(3)

HOARE, N. (1990), *Security for Museums*, Committee of Area Museum Councils/Museums Association, London

KOVACH, C. (1989), 'Strategic management for museums', *International Journal of Museum Management and Curatorship*, **8**(2), 137–48

LEVIN, M.D. (1983), *The Modern Museum – Temple or Showroom*, DVIR Publishing, Jerusalem

LORD, B. and LORD, G.D. (Eds.) (1983), *Planning our National museums*, National Museums of Canada, Ottawa

LORD, B. and LORD, G.D. (1990), *Manual of Museum Planning*, HMSO, London

MATTINGLY, J. (1984), *Volunteers in Museums and Galleries*, The Volunteer Centre, London

MIDDLETON, V. (1990), *New Visions for Independent Museums in the UK*, Association of Independent Museums in the UK, Chichester

PHILLIPS, C. (1983), 'The museum director as manager', *History News* (Nashville), **38**(3) 8–15

ROBERTSON, I. (1983), 'Financial management – publicly funded museums', *Museum Professionals Group Transactions 17.12.15*

ROBERTSON, I (1985), 'Financing museums: the view of a professional', *Museums Journal*, **85**(3), 119–124

STEPHENS, S. (Ed.) (1986), *Building the New Museum. Architectural League of New York/Princeton Architectural Press*, New York, Princeton, NJ

STEWARD, D. (1986), 'A case study of a museum thief', *Museums Journal*, **86**(2), 74–78

UPTON, M.S. and PEARSON, C. (1978), *Disaster Planning and Emergency Treatments in Museums, Art Galleries, Archives and Allied Institutions*, Institute for the Conservation of Cultural Materials, Canberra

WARE, M. (1988), *Fundraising for Museums, AIM Guidelines No. 4*, 2nd edition, Association of Independent Museums

WEST, A., BAKER, N., BOTT, V. and MIDDLETON, V. , 'Museums in the Marketplace or in the Community?', *Museums Journal*, **90**(2), 23–24

WHINCUP, M. (1984), *Modern Employment Law*, Heinnemann, London

WILSON, M. (1976), *The Effective Management of Volunteer Programmes*, Volunteer Management Associates, Colorado

YANG, M. (1990), 'Manuals for museum policy and procedures', *Curator* **33**(1), 5–18

YOUSON, F. (1987), *Employment Law Handbook*, Gower, London

WILDING, R. (1985), 'Financing museums current and future trends', *Museums Journal*, **85**(3), 119–24

Specialist Groups

Information and advice on current issues relating to the management and administration of museums is available from the following specialist groups:
(Addresses may be found in the *Yearbook* published by The Museums Association, 42, Clerkenwell Close, London, EC1R 0PA.)

GODS (Group of Directors in the British Isles)
MAGDA (Museums and Galleries Disability Group)
MPG (Museums Professionals Group)
Museums and Galleries Administrators Group
Society of County Museum Directors
Visual and Art Galleries Association
WHAM (Women, Heritage and Museums.)

SECTION THREE

CONSERVATION

Section Editor

Peter N. Lowell

23

Introduction

Peter N. Lowell

The Curator or Manager of multi-disciplinary collections is unlikely to have a comprehensive knowledge of more than one or two of the collections under his care. Despite this, the museum's management committee should reasonably expect the Curator to determine accurately priorities for the maintenance of all collections whilst making the most efficient use of the manpower, facilities and financial resources at his disposal. The chapters within the section cover a broad range of collection-management problems which it is hoped will assist the Curator in assessing a particular museum's priorities.

The museum building and its environment is the single most important aspect of collection care in preventing deterioration. The various authors of the chapters in this section, chosen for their experience and professional reputations, reinforce this view in discussing the conservation of specific collections. Where possible, evidence of deterioration is illustrated; however, this was not always possible. Some authors refer to the musty smell of damp or mould or the acid smell associated with the deterioration of photographic film. Those individuals, at all managerial levels, with a responsibility for collections, need to develop a sensitivity to situations which could lead to the deterioration of objects within their care.

All institutions, including museums, have some policies, procedures, customs or practices which are as antiquated as the objects or collections within their care. Comparisons between the guidelines and proposals within this section and the current practices of the reader's institution are inevitable. Of immediate concern should be:

(1) the museum building: environmental monitoring and control, periodic surveying of buildings and regular maintenance;
(2) the surveying of various collections, identification of

urgent problems, and determination of types of deterioration (environmental, handling, etc.);
(3) the conservation standard of display and storage facilities with particular regard to the chemical properties of fabrics and structural materials, lighting levels and storage techniques; and
(4) the techniques used to handle and transfer objects and training programmes for staff involved.

Most museums have inadequate support and yet are expected to compete with leisure activities and tourist attractions. Many museum management committees have devoted appreciable proportions of their budgets to the public face of the museum, i.e. those aspects that the general public encounter most such as exhibitions, educational activities, shops and cafe. This has often meant that there have been reductions in spending on the maintenance of collections. Such situations must be seen for what they are, a direct competition for funding between the need to attract visitors and the need to maintain the collections. It would also appear that there is increasing financial accountability within museums and there is a need to justify expenditure in all departments, including conservation. It is hoped that the chapters in this section may form the basis of a reasoned argument or justification in support of applications for funding through budgets, grants or sponsorship.

Every attempt has been made throughout this section to provide consistent advice, particularly in relation to levels of temperature and relative humidity. In some instances, it is not possible to reconcile authors knowledge/beliefs/experience and brief mention should be made of the reasons for any inconsistencies that might appear in the text.

What is the minimum relative humidity (RH) that will support mould growth? There were many figures quoted in the original text. Two specialist consultants gave slightly different answers; the following comments would probably be acceptable to both. Mould growth depends on a number of factors including the type of mould itself, the substrate (which may be a smear or stain on the artefact and not the artefact itself) the temperature and other factors in addition to relative humidity. It is therefore not possible to give an answer without taking the above into account. However, if a general guideline for a minimum relative humidity is necessary for museum collections as a whole, then the answer must be qualified by stating that it is reasonably certain that mould growth in collections will not occur below 70 per cent and that it is almost certain that it will not be encouraged below 65 per cent RH. It is commonly known that mould growth is encouraged in stagnant air; good ventilation will discourage mould growth.

The conservator's dilemma is that the objects should be in an environment which has minimal fluctuations in relative humidity and temperature (which happens when an object is placed in a storage container, box, picture frame, showcase, etc.) but that such confinements in stagnant air could lead to mould growth if the average relative humidity increases to 70% or above. The latter possibility has prompted some authors to advocate ventilation within storage units.

With regard to the treatment of mould, several different recommendations appear either in the text or the references. Mould growth will not continue once the relative humidity is below the appropriate level. Superficial cleaning may be sufficient but it will not remove all mould spores. Is the latter necessary? Since mould spores exist virtually everywhere, it might be considered more appropriate to clean superficially and concentrate on controlling the environment. Many authors would advocate this approach rather than employ sterilization techniques which could affect the artefact. Recommendations are made for any fumigation techniques considered desirable to be dealt with by responsible specialist contractors. Health and safety legislation concerning the use of fumigants is continually changing. There are several references which mention chemicals that are no longer recommended due to their toxicity or effectiveness, but the references are retained for other information they contain. As a general rule, the use of fumigants and pesticides should only be used after consultation with the relevant health-and-safety representatives. Even then, research should be undertaken to ensure the proposed materials will not affect the collections being treated.

24

Documenting collections

Sheila M. Stone

The museum has a unique role as a repository for three-dimensional objects gathered from both natural and man-made environments. The very act of collection removes objects from their context and, although many of them are inherently interesting or aesthetically appealing, it is the close inter-relationship with their environment which increases their usefulness, and the enjoyment of them by the museum public. Preserving the non-intrinsic information about an object, such as where it comes from, who found or used it, and what it was used for is the responsibility of the institution that keeps it. For this reason the documentation of museum collections is vital.

The function of documentation

Many museums have collections of poorly documented objects which have lost much of their usefulness due to the lack of associated information. Documentation is fundamental to curatorial work, and is used as a basic source of information on the collection. Comprehensive documentation is the pivot on which curatorship depends, and is essential to:

(1) enable the effective management of collections, encompassing storage, security, auditing and insurance;
(2) formulate acquisition policies by identifying the scope and limitations of the collection; and
(3) enable the collections to be researched and published – the value of publications and the presentation of the collection through displays and educational work is related to the quality of the documentation.

As stated by the Museum Documentation Association (MDA):

With an effective documentation system such activities will still involve a great deal of effort: but they will be possible. Without an effective documentation system many of them will be impossible. (Museum Documentation Association, 1980a)

The development of museum documentation

Since the 1960s, there has been a growing awareness of the need for systematic documentation of collections. The vocational, as well as academic, training of museum personnel has led to an increased professionalism and re-evaluation of the role of museums in society. Before 1960, often the only person likely to come into direct contact with the collection was the Curator, but now collections are used by a growing number of people in a variety of ways. Efficient information retrieval is essential if collections are to be utilized to the full and the information contained within them is to be exploited.

Another, less happy, aspect of late-twentieth century society which has emphasized the need for documentation, has been the increasing number of thefts from museums. The security implications of this are detailed in a Museums Association Information Sheet (Museums Association, 1981) and include the inability to trace items at district and internal audits, the apparent difficulty of museums in proving title to stolen objects in the Courts, and an increase in what are euphemistically termed 'internal losses'.

The inaugural meeting of the Museums Association in 1889 considered the possibility of producing a comprehensive index of all provincial museum collections (Plantnauer and Howarth, 1890). Its desirability was reiterated by Lewis (1965) who added a note of urgency:

However intimidating the sheer volume of the work may appear, unless a plan is formulated speedily for the completion of such an index, national specialist indexes will not come to fruition. If, however, a standardized system of indexing museum collections can be agreed by a body of expert opinion, then not only can a national index be started but curators wishing to re-catalogue their collections can do so to the standard.

To promote this objective, the Information Retrieval Group of the Museums Association (IRGMA) was formed in 1967 which in turn led to the formation of the MDA (Roberts *et al*, 1980). IRGMA was a small professional group consisting of curators active in the field of documentation and computer specialists working in museums. Through the efforts of this small group, IRGMA became the driving force behind the co-operative development of museum documentation over the next 10 years, and under its aegis a series of standardized record cards for recording museum collections was designed and produced, in conjunction with a computerized documentation system developed at Cambridge. The intention was that the cards would stand alone as part of a manual documentation system, or form a standardized data entry document for computer processing of the records. A full account of the work of IRGMA is given in a report of the IRGMA Standards Subcommittee (1977).

The MDA was set up to advise and assist member museums with the development of documentation procedures by undertaking research and systems development, by providing advice, education and training, and through the provision of services. A paper produced by the MDA Development Committee (1982) outlined the state of documentation in UK museums at that time, and summarized intended priorities for the next 5 years. In those 5 years, the MDA was, and continues to be, at the forefront of raising awareness among curators of the need for documentation by providing seminars, training courses and advisory visits to museums, backed up by a range of publications and, where required, a full consultancy service for museums wishing to review their documentation procedures and practices.

The period 1982–1987 also saw a significant increase in the number of museums using automated documentation systems. In 1982 over 30 museums in the UK had begun to computerize some aspect of their documentation, a figure which had doubled by 1984. These applications included the computing systems developed by the MDA used either independently or through a bureau service, comparable computer packages for local use on computers in their parent body or within the museum itself, and equipment acquired for in-house use. A report commissioned by the Area Museums Service for South Eastern England (AMSSEE) in 1986 provided the information that 55 museums in the AMSSEE area were using computers, with 120 museums stating an intention to acquire computer facilities

within the next few years (Roberts, 1986). Recognizing the increasing availability of low cost microcomputer systems, and the potential demand from museums, the range of MDA publications to support manual documentation systems (cards, registers, control forms, etc.) was, in April 1987 extended to computers with the release of the MODES software package for data entry of museum records. In the first 6 months over 80 copies of the package had been sold, and were in use in more than 60 museums. By the end of 1989, over 200 museums were using MODES.

In spite of the increasing awareness of the need for documentation as an essential tool in collections management, just how far there is still to go has been highlighted by the publication of two reports on current practice. The first of these was a research project funded by the Office of Arts and Libraries (OAL) and conducted by the Museums Association. Questionnaires were circulated to 2131 national and non-national museums during 1985 with an 82 per cent return rate. Although documentation was only one of the many aspects of curatorship dealt with, the returns indicated a surprisingly poor level of museum collections covered by adequate documentation. Only 44 per cent of the national museums, 46 per cent of local authority museums and 46 per cent of private sector museums could claim to have 75 per cent or more of their collections catalogued, while a figure of less than 25 per cent of collections catalogued was admitted by one-quarter of local authority museums, and approximately one-third of national and private sector museums. In terms of information retrieval, 40 per cent of public sector and 52 per cent of private sector museums had indexes to less than 25 per cent of their collections. The report states:

> From these returns . . . there appear to be serious gaps in the documentation resources of a large number of museums in all three sectors, particularly the non-public institutions, and that this tends to be concentrated in the areas of cataloguing and indexing rather than in that of the initial accession recording. (Prince and Higgins-McLoughlin, 1987).

In 1986, the report commissioned by AMSSEE into documentation practice in 900 museums in the area produced equally alarming results. Again, the survey relied on evidence from questionnaires, 600 of which were returned with over 300 providing detailed responses. Among the statistics compiled from the report is the fact that around 50 per cent of respondents had less than half of their collections covered by adequate accession records, and in the case of primary indexes such as object name, subject/classification and donor, fewer than 25 per cent of the respondents claimed to have indexes covering more than three-quarters of their collection. The report, which was prepared by the MDA, makes the following comment:

> Overall, the standard of documentation practice seems scandalous and raises serious doubts about the relative priorities of many museums in the area. It seems inconceivable that a museum can claim to be properly managing or accounting for the collections in its care when it has inadequate documentation procedures, incomplete records and superficial indexes. (Roberts, 1986).

However, there is evidence in the report that the museums were all fully aware of the problems and were planning or actively pursuing policies to improve the situation. Clearly, there is a long way to go.

Principles of documentation

Data standards

The standardized system of recording for museums referred to by Lewis (1965) is encapsulated in the Museum Documentation System (MDS), which has now been adopted throughout the UK and overseas. This multi-disciplinary system, derived from the work of IRGMA and the MDA, defines the standard form for the recording of museum data, known as the data standard. Porter (1978) describes it as follows:

> Basically, the standard supplies a format, which is a hierarchical organization of museum data concepts, and a set of recommendations for slotting pieces of museum data into the various concept headings in the format.

The data standard and data definition language is described in detail in an MDA manual (Museum Documentation Association, 1980c). A range of recording media based on the MDS data standards is available to support both manual and automated documentation systems: registers, cards, instruction books and control forms in the case of manual systems, and for automated systems the new MODES software package, which allows rapid data entry and, from May 1990, validation of museum records on PC microcomputers. This was complemented by the release of TINmus in 1988 which provides a multi-user cataloguing and retrieval system, for use on its own or in conjunction with MODES. These two software packages were, like the GOS information management package, developed by the MDA.

A full description of the Museum Documentation System is published in an MDA manual (Museum Documentation Association, 1980b). Any museum setting up a new documentation system, or redesigning an existing one, should ensure that the MDS data standards are followed, even though MDA recording media may not be employed.

Features of a documentation system

The aims of a museum documentation system are to preserve all known information about an object and to help satisfy the needs of the user, whether he be a curator, research worker or member of the public. To achieve these aims a documentation system should possess singular features, and should include three types of documentation which comprise a comprehensive museum record:

> (1) initial documentation, on the entry of the object into the museum for loan, identification, acquisition or other purposes;
> (2) item documentation, being a full record of all information about the object incorporated in the record, or cross-referenced to other files; and
> (3) control documentation, which records the movement and location of an object – this is an essential tool for collections management.

The system into which this comprehensive record fits should be capable of including any number of entries, and should not impose a limit on the size of the total record.

It is important that the system should allow for the addition of data. It should be able to accept information about a wide range of items, and allow adequate cross-referencing between the different types of record incorporated in it. There should also be safeguards to protect confidential information. It is most important that the system should be easy to use and maintain, and that documentation procedures are set down in a manual. A system that is too complex or cumbersome may serve the collection little better than no system at all.

Documentation practice

Designing the system

When considering documentation, many curators start from the 'hardware', such as cards, registers, sheets and computers, without undertaking a comprehensive analysis of the documentation problems and information retrieval requirements in their museum. Such critical assessment is known as the 'systems approach' which, as Orna and Pettit (1980) have pointed out:

> Is often thought of as being exclusively a computer technique; it is in fact a straightforward and commonsense way of looking at problems, which pays off whether the end result is computer use or not.

The diversity of documentation systems has been illustrated by Orna and Pettitt (1980) and Roberts *et al* (1986). Both publications reflect the variety of museums and their collections, and emphasize that no one system can suit all museums.

The publication of the findings of an OAL-funded research project on documentation procedures in museums provides an excellent starting point for curators thinking about systems design, and provides analysed examples of systems in a range of national, local authority and university museums in the UK (Roberts, 1985). Included in the report is a particularly useful section detailing the questions which should be asked when undertaking an internal reassessment of current documentation procedures. Orna (1982) also provides useful advice on defining information needs and analysing the existing information. The analysis should take into account the scope and extent of the collection, the likely demands to be made on it, and the staff, time and resources available for documentation. Their availability is crucial to the development of an effective system. As an absolute minimum, all non-intrinsic information about each object should be recorded. Intrinsic information may be obtained by examining the object, but for security purposes any lack of description in a record should be made good by a photograph. A new documentation system should relate not only to new acquisitions; a strategy for tackling backlog, or recataloguing old collections if necessary, should be incorporated in the system design.

When current practice and future requirements have been assessed, it is then appropriate to consider the 'hardware' for the job and decide whether a manual or automated system, or indeed a mixture of the two, can best serve the needs of the museum. The declining cost and increasing power of computer hardware, coupled with the growing availability of relevant software has brought the possibility of an automated documentation system within the reach of even the smallest museums. Curators contemplating the introduction of computer facilities are advised to contact the MDA for advice on the variety of options available, and study the literature on documentation systems employed by other museums. Roberts *et al* (1986) illustrate some of the different computer applications adopted by UK and overseas museums and Light and Roberts (1984) provides a useful guide to the role of microcomputers in museums and the variety of tasks for which they can be employed. Other useful case studies can be found in *MDA Information* sheets and the *Museums Journal*. However, as Roberts (1985) has stated:

> There is . . . a serious danger that a new automated system is viewed by a museum as the cure for all the ills of the existing procedures. In practice, the unconsidered introduction of such a system will tend to compound existing problems. It is essential that careful planning takes place before any change is implemented.

As with the range of manual systems, there is no one automated system to suit all museums, and a mixture of the two may prove to be the most effective. Thought must be given to precisely which aspects of documentation would benefit from automation, whether accessioning, full cataloguing, or control documentation as this will be relevant in the choice of computer whether in-house or bureau, mainframe or micro. Availability of finance for capital and revenue will be another consideration. In terms of the options available, the use of the MDA Computing Bureau has the advantage of involving the museum in the minimum of staff and capital investment, but the disadvantage of external expenditure. Another option could involve the museum in purchasing equipment for in-house data entry (by far the most expensive and time-consuming element of the automation process) and passing the data to an external bureau for processing. This approach provides the museum with a greater degree of control and security over its records, but requires investment in staff and equipment. There are a number of examples among the larger museums of in-house data entry and processing facilities, and several local authority and university museums use the computer systems and expertise available in their parent bodies.

There can be no doubt that a well-designed automated documentation system can serve a range of information retrieval requirements which could never be contemplated using manual techniques. However, as Roberts (1985) points out:

> In practice, the magnitude and nature of museum collections has often acted as a deterrent to their automation. . . . museums are characterized by having large numbers of detailed records to which reference is made infrequently. . . . Their relatively low acquisition and object movement rate has not encouratged a major investment in automated entry, acquisition and circulation control systems.

The range of information retrieval made possible by the use of automated documentation systems, and the ease with which it can be provided, should be judged against the actual costs of equipment and maintenance and, particularly in the case of in-house facilities, the amount of staff time involved in system and equipment 'housekeeping' should not be underestimated. The museum may be gaining a computer and losing a curator!

Putting the system into effect

The whole process of documentation ultimately depends on human resources. Documentation is costly in both staff time and money, and effective management is vital if these resources are to be utilized fully. Ideally, at least one member of staff should be responsible for the co-ordination of documentation. In a small museum the Curator is likely to assume this function, but in a large institution it may be necessary to create a separate department, headed by a Registrar, for this purpose.

The functions of a Registrar include developing the system, writing and updating procedural manuals, assigning initial and accession numbers to objects entering the museum, monitoring the movement of objects internally and externally, developing standardized terminology for general and discipline-based recording in the museum, ensuring a high standard of accuracy and neatness in documentation, and updating all catalogues and indexes at central and departmental levels. The Registrar is also involved in the security of the records of the collections, with auditing and insurance procedures, and is responsible for the training of personnel and the close supervision of the cataloguing team. Orna and Pettitt (1980) give detailed advice on the use of human resources in information management.

Finally, it is important to the success of any documentation system, especially when a large backlog is involved, that curatorial staff responsible for recording realize the direct benefits which accrue. Cataloguing may seem less of an imposition when documentation saves time in dealing with enquiries, speeds up exhibition planning, allows research which was previously impossible to conduct, and removes the frustration which may be experienced when carrying out routine maintenance on the collections.

Safeguarding the information

The establishment and maintenance of an effective documentation system represents a considerable investment, and safeguards must be introduced for the preservation of the records and the information within them. Fire, flood and theft are potential threats to security, and it is important to maintain a duplicate set of records in a separate location. Records should be stored in a secure room in lockable, fireproof cabinets, and protected from light, pollution, damp and insect infestation. The confidentiality of data can be assured by screening sensitive information from the general user. This may be achieved by keeping a separate listing of confidential information cross-referenced to the master file, or by maintaining two sets of master records, one of which is for general use and from which all sensitive information has been excluded.

Museums with automated documentation systems should familiarize themselves with the requirements of the Data Protection Act, 1984, which regulates the holding of information relating to living individuals on computers. The operation of the Act is overseen by the Data Protection Registrar, and museums storing personal data on computer files must register their holdings. An MDA Occasional Paper provides further information on the implications of the Act on collection documentation (Jones and Roberts, 1985).

Creating an object record

The essential reference works on collection recording are *Practical Museum Documentation* (Museum Documentation Association, 1980a) and *Planning the Documentation of Museum Collections* (Roberts, 1985). Both publications give a clear account of the procedures involved in documenting objects, and contain useful information on collection-related documentation such as location, bibliographical, biographical, conservation and photographic records enabling cross-reference to the collection records themselves. The 'Planning' report contains a chapter on detailed documentation procedures, and includes illustrations of entry, item and control documentation from a number of museums.

Stage 1: the object enters the museum
Initial documentation is the mechanism used to cope with every object entering the museum, whether temporarily or permanently. It ensures that information is not lost before a full, permanent record is prepared, and it acknowledges the receipt of an item by the museum. Loans, identifications and acquisitions should be assigned an initial serial number which links the object to its associated information.

The initial record should be made in a 'daybook' or initial register, a bound book with column headings for the different types of information to be recorded. Alternatively, a duplicated form such as an MDA Entry Form may be used; if this method is employed, one copy of the form is passed to the depositor as a receipt, one copy remains with the object and the third copy passes to the museum's file. Typical information included in an initial record is: date and method of receipt (for example, gift, purchase or loan); person/institution from whom received; basic identification and description (including condition); provenance and method of collection; history of the object; storage location; disposal (including permanent accession number if object is retained); and name of staff member who received the object.

Stage 2: the museum acquires title to the object
Once an object has been acquired, an accession number should be assigned to it, and marked on it in a permanent manner. (*Practical Museum Documentation* (Museum Documentation Association, 1980a) contains a useful appendix on methods of marking various types of material.) An accession number is the unique number assigned to an object or a group of objects added to the permanent collection, and the processing of the acquisition into the collection is

known as 'accessioning'. Various combinations of numbers are used for accessioning. They are usually based on a serial sequence which may be date-linked, and often, in large museums, prefixed or suffixed by a departmental letter code. An accession number should be unique and should never be re-used, even if an object is lost or disposed of. In addition to the accession number, the object may be marked with the MDA code for the institution, a five-letter abbreviation of the town and museum name. A full list of MDA codes is published by the MDA (1979) and occasional updates appear in 'MDA Information'. Even if this code is not marked on the object, it should be incorporated in the museum documentation.

At this stage a specimen (or history) file should be opened for each accession. The file should be a folder or envelope into which all supplementary information about an object is placed. Specimen files are usually arranged in accession number order. Some museums use bound accessions registers (*Figure 24.1*)

in which brief details about all acquisitions to the permanent collections are recorded for security purposes. The legal obligation to keep such a register to prove ownership of an object is now questioned, and many museums no longer use accession registers but proceed directly to the next stage.

Stage 3: a permanent record of the object is produced
This stage aims to provide, in one source, all the information known about the object, including cross-references to other files, such as conservation treatment records, photographic negative numbers and locality files.

From this record, catalogues and indexes may be produced to help staff answer enquiries about the history and contents of the collection. Many museums have adopted MDA cards (*Figure 24.2*) for recording all or part of their collections, whilst others prefer to use recording media they have designed for specific collections or, in some cases, to suit the idiosyncrasies of specific curators. Some

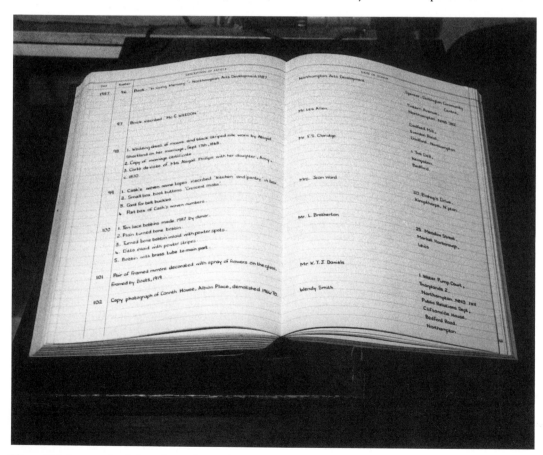

Figure 24.1 An example of a bound accessions register. Entries to a register such as this are made when the museum acquires title to the object (stage 2 in the text)

(a)

Card of	File		Institution : identity number SABMS:81.2301		Part

IDENTIFICA-TION	Simple name bowl	D	Materials keyword/detail glass		Number

C	Full name or classified identification pillar moulded bowl & form 3	System Isings	D Identifier : date Allen,D.: 6.4.1981	D

DATING	Object period or date roman & 10AD = 80AD (approx)			
C	Dating method typology	Cross reference	Researcher : date Allen,D.: 6.4.1981	D

COLLECTION OR EXCAVA-TION	Site name Ver Site B	Site number Insula XIV	Lat Long NGR	Value & units/accuracy

Place name/detail
St. Albans & Hertfordshire & U.K.

	Context B I & layers 68 and 70	Context period or date 60AD = 75AD	D 1

Locality detail

C	Collection method excavation	Collector or excavator : date Frere,S.S.: 1959	Find number D

ACQUISITION	Acquisition method donation	Acquired from : date **Verulamium Excavation Committee**	
C		D Price	Conditions D Yes/No	Valuation : date	D

DESCRIPTION	Condition keyword/detail fair	Completeness keyword/detail incomplete (base fragment only)
C		
STORE	Store : date Ver & Main Gallery & V3: 6.4.1981	Recorder : date Stone,S.M.: 6.4.1981

ARCHAEOLOGY   © IRGMA 1975   1|12|75

(b)

DESCRIPTION	Dimension measured value & units/accuracy width (of fragment) 5.5 cm length (of fragment) 5.8 cm	Dimension measured value & units/accuracy

Inscription	Method	Position
Mark		
Transcription	Detail	D
Description		

Part : aspect : description keyword/detail whole: colour: blue = green
whole: production method: cast
inner surface: finishing method: rotary ground
inner surface: decoration: horizontal wheel-incised lines above base
outer surface: decoration: ribbed
outer surface: finishing method: fire polished

PROCESS	Conservation	Other process	Method/detail : operator : date : detail	Cross reference D
C	Reproduction			
	Conservation			
	Reproduction			

DOCUMENTA-TION	L Class 1 listed	Author : date : title : journal or publisher : volume : detail Charlesworth,D. IN Frere,S.S.: 1972: Verulamium Excavations: Oxford University Press: Volume I: page 198, numbers 11 and 12	Drawing or photo

C	

NOTES	Notes
C	

Figure 24.2 A full catalogue record on an MDA
Archaeology card (stage 3 in the text). (a) Front; (b) back

museums are opting for direct data-entry to a computer running a software package such as MODES which can generate a hard copy of the records on index cards when they have been entered and validated (*Figures 24.3* to *24.5*). If staff time and

resources are limited, it may be acceptable to produce a less detailed record as a first step, ensuring that the minimum standard described earlier is attained. This may be added to as further resources become available.

Page 65

SABMS: 82.147.

identification, amphora, amphora, form 20, Dressel.

field collection: Ver Site A, St. Albans, Hertfordshire, U.K., unstratified.
excavation, Wheeler, R.E.M., 1930-1933.

acquisition: donation, Verulamium Excavation Committee, 1939.

store: Ver, Lecture Room, SC, 3.2.1982.

description: ceramic < pottery, amphora >, fair, incomplete.

length, 10 cm,
inscription: stamped, handle, I.Q.S.

dating: typology, roman, 80 AD-130 AD.

recorder: Greep, S.J., 3.2.1982.

documentation:
1: published, Callender, M.H., 1965, Roman Amphorae, Oxford University Press, (figure 1; page 164, number 922).

- - * * - -

SABMS: 82.148.

identification: amphora, amphora, form 20, Dressel.

field collection: [Ver], [St. Albans, Hertfordshire, U.K.].

store: Ver, Lecture Room, SC, 3.2.1982.

description: ceramic < pottery, amphora >, fair, incomplete.

length, 12.0 cm,
inscription: stamped, handle, L.I.T. (retrograde).

dating: typology, roman.

recorder: Greep, S.J., 3.2.1982.

documentation:
1: published, Callender, M.H., 1965, Roman Amphorae, Oxford University Press, (figure 1; page 158).

- - * * - -

Figure 24.3 Entries in a computerized catalogue of the collections, using an MDA card as the data-entry document

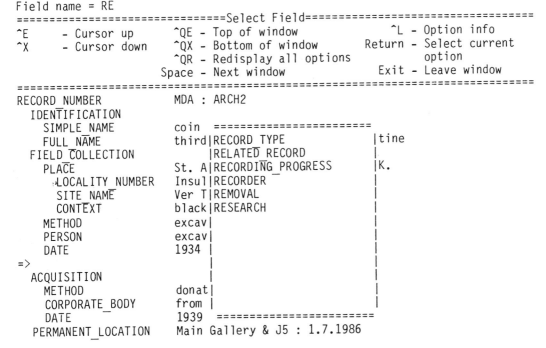

```
Field name = RE
==============================Select Field===================================
^E    - Cursor up       ^QE - Top of window        ^L - Option info
^X    - Cursor down     ^QX - Bottom of window     Return - Select current
                        ^QR - Redisplay all options          option
                      Space - Next window          Exit - Leave window
===========================================================================
RECORD_NUMBER            MDA : ARCH2
   IDENTIFICATION
      SIMPLE_NAME        coin  =========================
      FULL_NAME          third|RECORD TYPE              |tine
   FIELD COLLECTION           |RELATED RECORD           |
      PLACE              St. A|RECORDING PROGRESS        |K.
       LOCALITY_NUMBER   Insul|RECORDER                 |
       SITE_NAME         Ver T|REMOVAL                  |
       CONTEXT           black|RESEARCH                 |
      METHOD             excav|                         |
      PERSON             excav|                         |
      DATE               1934 |                         |
=>                            |                         |
   ACQUISITION                |                         |
      METHOD             donat|                         |
      CORPORATE_BODY     from |                         |
      DATE               1939 =========================
      PERMANENT_LOCATION Main Gallery & J5 : 1.7.1986
```

Figure 24.4 An example of a computer-screen format showing MODES in action. The user has requested a list of fields beginning with 'RE' that could be inserted at this point, and they appear in a window on the screen

At this stage it is important to ensure that the documentation system of which this record is to form a part contains the features described earlier, and that the record is completed accurately and neatly, duplicated (some museums produce a typed copy of the hand-written card completed by the curator), and stored with due regard to security and preservation. At least one set of these records should be filed in accession number order.

Stage 4: exploiting the records
As Roberts and Light (1980) have stated, 'The need for a wide range of entry points to a single record remains a basic problem of museum documentation'. Indexing is a complex subject; it is discussed fully by Orna and Pettitt (1980) and the MDA (1980a). An index is an ordered sequence of entries acting as a directory to one or more aspects of a catalogue. In 1973 the Wright Report on provincial museums (Department of Education and Science, 1973) recommended that a minimum standard for museum cataloguing using traditional methods should consist of a numerical catalogue of the collection, and a classified index facilitating access to specimens from

the records. The MDA (1980a) has now expanded these recommendations and advises that a museum has one or more fully descriptive catalogues about its collections, and a number of indexes to act as information directories to the catalogues. Using manual methods, the number of indexes which a museum can produce is constrained by factors such as staff time, cost and storage space. Few museums have the resources to produce more than five manual indexes, and the ones which should answer most collection enquiries are: an object name index; a subject or classified index; a collection place name index; a donor index; and a storage location index. Where museum records are stored on computer, a wide range of indexes may be generated to suit the specific needs of the museum, or appropriate to the specialized nature of a particular collection. Examples of indexes generated by computer are given in Roberts (1985) and Roberts *et al* (1986) (see *Figure 24.6*).

One of the commonest problems in indexing, whether manual or computer-based, is the lack of terminology control. This makes indexing less effective by separating objects which have similar characteristics, but have been recorded in different

```
NEWTOWN MUSEUM        FULL CATALOGUE


Record number                                    MDA : ARCH2

     Identification
       Simple name            coin
       Full name              third brass of house of Constantine


     Field collection
       Place                  St. Albans & Hertfordshire & U.K.
         Locality number      Insula XV
         Site name            Ver Theatre
         Context              black earth
       Method                 excavation
       Person                 excavator : Brown, K.M.
       Date                   1934


     Acquisition
       Method                 donation
       Corporate body         from : Excavation Committee
       Date                   1939


     Permanent location       Main Gallery & J5 : 1.7.1986


     Description
       Part:aspect:description  : material : metal
       Part:aspect:description  : condition : poor
       Part:aspect:description  : completeness : incomplete


     Process
       Type                   dating
       Method                 documentary
       Result                 roman & 346AD = 361AD


     Photography
       Person                 photographer : Lens, I.
       Date                   2.6.1986
       Result                 BW 15.2


     Recorder                 Duke, C.J. : 1.7.1986
```

Figure 24.5 A catalogue entry produced by MODES

ways. Computer-based documentation exposes inconsistencies in recording and is a salutary experience for all recorders. Guidance on terminology control should be included in the manual describing the documentation system. Aspects of terminology control and thesaurus construction are discussed in *Practical Museum Documentation* (Museum Documentation Association, 1980a) and Orna and Pettitt (1980), and a good example of a thesaurus for human history (though with a distinct North American flavour) can be found in Chenhall (1978). Another useful starting point for museums developing internal recording conventions is the Hertfordshire Simple Name list, a thesaurus of object names for use

```
ST. ALBANS MUSEUMS (SABMS)      ARCHAEOLOGY        SIMPLE NAME INDEX      Page 47


helmet
    military helmet              SABMS: 78.8

?hilt guard
    ?hilt guard                 SABMS: 81.3015

hinge
    cuirass hinge               SABMS: 79.850; 79.900; 80.423; 83.887
    decorated hinge             SABMS: 78.144 to 145; 78.147; 78.154; 78.160
    decorated hinge spacer      SABMS: 78.140
    forceps hinge               SABMS: 79.2164
    hinge                       SABMS: 78.88 to 89; 78.138; 78.141 to 143;
                                    78.151; 78.288; 79.629 to 630; 79.634;
                                    82.516; 82.531 to 533; 82.1215
    hinge rough-out             SABMS: 82.512
    loop hinge                  SABMS: 78.85
    ?loop hinge                 SABMS: 78.86

?hinge
    ?decorated hinge            SABMS: 78.155

hippo sandal
    hippo sandal                SABMS: 80.1418; 81.2767

hook
    bill hook                   SABMS: 78.539
    cuirass hook                SABMS: 82.286
    eyed hook                   SABMS: 78.286
    flesh hook                  SABMS: 78.589
    girdle-plate tie hook       SABMS: 82.1211
    hook                        SABMS: 80.1453; 81.3164; 82.74 to 75; 82.78
                                    to 79; 82.89; 82.91; 82.94; 82.191;
                                    82.1214; 82.1317 to 1318; 82.1326
    hook with tang              SABMS: 80.1454
    pruning hook                SABMS: 78.537
    reaping hook                SABMS: 78.536
    scale hook                  SABMS: 80.218; 82.76; 82.86
    ?scale hook                 SABMS: 80.219; 80.1455
    ?suspension hook from a steelyard
                                SABMS: 78.599
    wall-hook                   SABMS: 80.1471 to 1472

?hook
    ?hook                       SABMS: 82.93

horn
    ?cut horn implement         SABMS: 78.193 to 194

horn core
    cut horn core               SABMS: 78.166
```

Figure 24.6 An example of a computer-produced index, arranged by simple name and full name (stage 4 in the text). An index of this type can be used as a basic thesaurus, to guide recorders to approved terminology.

SABMS   SOCIAL HISTORY   SHIC CLASSIFICATION CHECKING INDEX   PAGE 4

(2.62)
    (jar)
                        SABMS: 86.5917 to 5918
                        SABMS: 86.5924
                        SABMS: 86.5926
                        SABMS: 86.5959
                        SABMS: 86.6117 to 6123
                        SABMS: 86.6126 to 6127
                        SABMS: 86.6198
                        SABMS: 86.6417
                        SABMS: 86.6421
    jug   SABMS: 84.3309 to 3310
                        SABMS: 86.5879 to 5880
                        SABMS: 86.5884
                        SABMS: 86.5960
                        SABMS: 86.6377 to 6398
    label   SABMS: 86.6245
    pot   SABMS: 86.5885
                        SABMS: 86.5925

2.64
    bowl   SABMS: 86.6048
    colander   SABMS: 86.6056
    mould   SABMS: 86.5891
                        SABMS: 86.6422

2.654
    warmer   SABMS: 86.5969

2.659
    pie funnel   SABMS: 86.5893 to 5894

2.661
    basin   SABMS: 86.5975
    bowl   SABMS: 86.5927
                        SABMS: 86.6049 to 6055
                        SABMS: 86.6084
                        SABMS: 86.6096
                        SABMS: 86.6208
                        SABMS: 86.6222
                        SABMS: 86.6387
    box   SABMS: 86.6343
    charger   SABMS: 78.1082
    cup   SABMS: 86.5785
    dish   SABMS: 86.5768
                        SABMS: 86.5895
                        SABMS: 86.5932
                        SABMS: 86.5971 to 5974
                        SABMS: 86.6045
                        SABMS: 86.6086
                        SABMS: 86.6145 to 6146

Figure 24.7 A computer-produced classified index
arranged by SHIC categories

```
*ident *sname flagon

*store Ver & Main Gallery & Q2 : 17.4.1981
£

*| [record 2566]
*id SABMS : 81.2566
*ident *sname flagon
*store Ver & Main Gallery & Q2 : 17.4.1981
£

*| [record 2567]
*id SABMS : 81.2567
*ident *sname beaker
*store Ver & Main Gallery & A : 17.4.1981
£

*| [record 2568]
*id SABMS : 81.2568
*ident *sname bowl
*store Ver & Main Gallery & R2 : 17.4.1981
£

*| [record 2569]
*id SABMS : 81.2569
*ident *sname bowl
*store Ver & Main Gallery & R2 : 17.4.1981
£

*| [record 2570]
*id SABMS : 81.2570
*ident *sname lid
*store Ver & Main Gallery & S2 : 17.4.1981
£

*| [record 2571]
*id SABMS : 81.2571
*ident *sname jar
*store Ver & Main Gallery & O1 : 17.4.1981
£

*| [record 2572]
*id SABMS : 81.2572
*ident *sname jar
*store Ver & Main Gallery & E : 17.4.1981
£

*| [record 2573]
*id SABMS : 81.2573
*ident *sname mortarium
*store Ver & Main Gallery & S1 : 17.4.1981
£
```

Figure 24.8 An example of control documentation (stage 5 in the text). Produced by computer, this mini-catalogue lists the storage location of objects in the collection

(VER)
(SIDE GALLERY)
(NN)

(unguent bottle, flask)		
	SABMS:	78.60

0 0

beaker	SABMS:	78.11; 78.67 to 76: 78.78 to 80
bowl	SABMS:	78.77; 78.81 to 82: 78.84
flagon	SABMS:	78.66
j a r	SABMS:	78.65

PP

bowl, fired clay	SABMS:	78.603
chisel	SABMS:	78.608
chopper	SABMS:	78.587 to 588
fired clay	SABMS:	78.605 to 607
float	SABMS:	78.610
forceps	SABMS:	78.579
hook	SABMS:	78.589; 78.599
knife	SABMS:	78.580
ligula	SABMS:	78.562; 78.573
mortarium	SABMS:	78.600 to 602
mosaic	SABMS:	78.604
needle	SABMS:	78.563; 78.576 to 578; 78.582 to 585
palette	SABMS:	78.592 to 596
probe	SABMS:	78.569; 78.571 to 572
rod	SABMS:	78.561
scales	SABMS:	78.570
shears	SABMS:	78.568
shell, pigment	SABMS:	78.597
skewer	SABMS:	78.590
skewer, pin	SABMS:	78.591
spatula	SABMS:	78.574
spindle whorl	SABMS:	78.560; 78.565; 78.586
spoon	SABMS:	79.953
spoon, probe	SABMS:	78.575
stamp	SABMS:	78.564
steelyard	SABMS:	78.581
thimble	SABMS:	78.566
tongs	SABMS:	78.567
trowel	SABMS:	78.609; 79.2001
weight	SABMS:	78.598

QQ

adze-hammer	SABMS:	78.517; 78.521
axe	SABMS:	78.520; 78.533
bar-share	SABMS:	78.532
bell	SABMS:	78.513; 78.552
bit	SABMS:	78.525; 80.1419
blade	SABMS:	78.538
chisel	SABMS:	78.515; 78.523; 78.534
crucible	SABMS:	78.555 to 559
crucible, jar	SABMS:	78.553 to 554
dolphin	SABMS:	78.548
eagle	SABMS:	78.546
figurine	SABMS:	78.549 to 550
fitting	SABMS:	78.543

Figure 24.9 An example of control documentation – an
index recording what is on display in each showcase in a
gallery

when cataloguing general social history collections, compiled by a group of curators working with a variety of social history material (Hertfordshire Curators Group Working Party, 1984). This can be used in conjunction with the Social History and Industrial Classification (SHIC) which has become the standard classification system for social and industrial history collections and their associated information (SHIC Working Party, 1983) (see *Figure 24.7*).

Stage 5: control procedures
Control procedures are vital for collections management, and should be adopted to record the movement of objects both within the museum and externally. An exit number should be assigned to all items leaving the museum, and these should be entered in a loans register, or recorded on a multi-part sheet such as an MDA Exit Form. For internal location control, a store location index should be produced for all items in the collection, arranged in numerical order (see *Figures 24.8* and *24.9*). This should be updated regularly, and used in conjunction with a storage tag which can be placed in the usual location of an item temporarily removed from store. Ideally, there should also be a register of all items stored in a particular location (simple to produce on an automated system but a time-consuming exercise to produce manually). Spot checks should be carried out from time to time to test the effectiveness of location control procedures, preferably by staff not involved in documentation. The updating of permanent records such as catalogues should be carried out methodically when store location changes for any length of time to ensure that records remain as up to date and accurate as possible.

Documentation is fundamental to the craft of curatorship, and the welcome increase in awareness and knowledge about documentation should be of immense benefit to museums. It is to be hoped that the next generation of curators will not have to face a legacy of poorly documented collections, and that those of today will ensure that the objects they collect will be of use and enjoyment to future generations.

Acknowledgements

I should like to thank the Museum Documentation Association, Northampton Museums and Art Gallery, and St Albans Museums for permission to publish the illustrations given in this chapter.

References

CHENHALL, R. G. (1978), *Nomenclature for Museum Cataloguing. A System for Classifying Man-made Objects*, American Association for State and Local History, Nashville, TN

DEPARTMENT OF EDUCATION AND SCIENCE (1973), *Provincial Museum and Galleries. A Report of a Committee Appointed by the Paymaster-General*, HMSO, London

HERTFORDSHIRE CURATORS GROUP WORKING PARTY (1984), *Hertfordshire Simple Name list*, Standing Committee for Museums in Hertfordshire, Hertford

IRGMA STANDARDS SUBCOMMITTEE (1977), 'Ten years of IRGMA, 1967–1977', *Museums Journal*, **65**(1), 11–14

JONES, S. G. and ROBERTS, D. A. (1985), 'The Data Protection Act and Museums', *MDA Occasional Paper 8*, Museum Documentation Association, Cambridge

LEWIS, G. D. (1965), 'Obtaining information from museum collections and thoughts on a national museum index', *Museums Journal*, **65**(1), 12–22

LIGHT, R. B. and ROBERTS, D. A. (Eds) (1984), *Microcomputers in Museums*, Museum Documentation Association, Cambridge

MUSEUMS ASSOCIATION (1981), 'Museum security', *Museums Association Information Sheet IS25*, Museums Association, London

MUSEUM DOCUMENTATION ASSOCIATION (1979), *MDA Museum Codes*, Museum Documentation Association, Cambridge

MUSEUM DOCUMENTATION ASSOCIATION (1980a), *Practical Museum Documentation*, Museum Documentation Association, Cambridge

MUSEUM DOCUMENTATION ASSOCIATION (1980b), *Guide to the Museum Documentation System*, Museum Documentation Association, Cambridge

MUSEUM DOCUMENTATION ASSOCIATION (1980c), *Data Definition Language and Data Standard*, Museum Documentation Association, Cambridge

MUSEUM DOCUMENTATION ASSOCIATION DEVELOPMENT COMMITTEE (1982), 'The future development of the Museum Documentation Association', *Museums Journal*, **82**(2), 71–76

ORNA, E. (1982), 'Information management in museums: there's more to it than documentation and computers', *Museums Journal*, **82**(2), 79–82

ORNA, E and PETTITT, C. (1980), *Information Handling in Museums*, Clive Bingley, Esher

PLANTNAUER, H. and HOWARTH, E. (Eds) (1890), *Reports of proceedings. Museums Association First Annual Report*, Museums Association, London

PORTER, M. F. (1978), 'Establishing a museum documentation system in the United Kingdom', *Museum*, **30**(3/4), 169–178

PRINCE, D. and HIGGINS-MCLOUGHLIN, B. (1987), *Museums UK: the Findings of the Museums Database Project*, Museums Association, London

ROBERTS, D. A. (1985), *Planning the Documentation of Museum Collections*, Museum Documentation Association, Cambridge

ROBERTS, D. A. (1986), 'The state of documentation in non-national museums in Southeast England', *MDA Occasional Paper 9*, Museum Documentation Association, Cambridge

ROBERTS, D. A. and LIGHT, R. B. (1980), 'Progress in

documentation. Museum documentation', *Journal of Documentation*, **36**(1), 42–84

ROBERTS, D. A., LIGHT, R. B. and STEWART, J. D. (1980), 'The Museum Documentation Association', *Museums Journal*, **80**(2), 81–85

ROBERTS, D. A., LIGHT, R. B. and STEWART, J. D. (Eds) *Museum Documentation Systems: Developments and Applications*, Butterworths, London

SHIC WORKING PARTY (1983), *Social History and Industrial Classification (SHIC): A Subject Classification for Museum Collections*, The Centre for English Cultural Tradition and Language, University of Sheffield, Sheffield

25

Conservation documentation

Michael Corfield

Good documentation is recognized as being an essential element of modern conservation; Conservators have always stressed the importance of keeping good records of the treatments applied to objects and the principle has been enshrined in the *Guidance for Conservation Practice* (United Kingdom Institute for Conservation, 1980). Conservation records have generally been developed in isolation, and have not been integrated into the curatorial object record other than as a possible statement that the object has received some conservation treatment. The gulf between the curatorial record and the conservation record is often exacerbated by the use by Conservators of a separate numbering system. The separation of the records is unfortunate because the conservation record will provide much information of curatorial value, particularly the condition of the object and its suitability for use in different circumstances; equally the conservation record will document the technological information gained in the course of the treatment of the object and this may be of fundamental importance to the curatorial perception of the object as a historical document.

Recently the whole concept of museum documentation has undergone a radical shift; documentation systems which have historically stood in isolation have been brought together under the concept of collections management. Conservators and conservation records are being integrated into a museum-wide documentation and collection management strategy. Miles (1988) has emphasized the importance of this integration and has described a data model for conservation and its relationship within a larger collection-management scheme.

Collection management is essential if the resources of the museum, including the collections, are to be used to their maximum effectiveness; curatorial decisions on acquisition or utilization of the collections must be viewed in relation to the ability of the museum to provide the necessary support by Conservators and others and for the museum to be able to store or exhibit the material properly in conditions conducive to its preservation. This has been fully discussed in *The Cost of Collecting* (Lord *et al*, 1989), which also considers the requirement to develop standards for condition surveys of collections.

Condition is central to any conservation documentation; indeed the aim of conservation is to maintain an object in a stable condition or to bring it into a condition considered more acceptable. Treatment records will normally include a statement of the condition of the object before treatment started and may also describe the condition after treatment so that over the years the dossier of information about a particular object will document its changing condition over time. The greater use of collections that has been brought about by loans to other museums nationally and internationally has created the need for specific condition reporting procedures. It is vital if valuable objects are to be loaned that the lender and the borrower both agree on the condition of the object at the start of the loan and again at its conclusion. Conservators will generally be required to record the condition, but occasionally the work will be done by a Registrar or a Curator; useful guidance on preparing condition reports for loans has been compiled by the South East Registrars' Association (O'Reilly and Lord, 1988).

In a climate of opinion that requires museums to maintain a proper audit of the collections, and to direct resources at those parts of the collection which are most in need, the concept of condition assumes greater importance.

Condition surveys of the collections will provide the statistical information required to identify where the greatest need lies. In condition surveys a number of parameters are chosen, not necessarily the same for each collection area, and a simple scoring system is devised. The parameters should be relevant and easily identified; they may be specific (for example, is the object in one piece?) or they may require the surveyors to apply their own judgement by assessing general condition or conservation urgency. The scoring should be limited and confined to whole numbers only. Normally the survey will be carried out on a sample of the collection only, but for small groups the whole collection may be examined. The data derived from the condition survey will enable the conservation manager to prioritize work, allocating resources to the areas of greatest need. The methodology and suggested documentation for condition surveys has been comprehensively described by Keene (1991).

Proposed acquisitions should have their condition examined and reports should indicate the extent of any work required to bring the acquisition to a condition where it can be used within the museum. Condition reporting at this time can be an aid to authentication, and will certainly help in deciding whether or not an intended acquisition is worth while; even a donation may not seem quite such a bargain if in order to bring it to a usable state a substantial element of the available resources will be absorbed. Equally, the acquisition might require special storage or display facilities not available in the museum and their provision might not be possible.

The concept of 'condition' has been proposed as a key element for measuring the effectiveness of conservation in the museum (Keene, 1990). Simple reports of numbers of objects treated provide little useful information, they are easily manipulated and do not give any indication that the objects conserved were those that required it. Using the data from condition surveys it can be demonstrated that the objects having highest priority for conservation are in fact being treated and that, as a proportion of the collection, their numbers are falling, remaining static or increasing.

Before treatment of an object begins its condition should be carefully recorded. At this level the examination should be as comprehensive as possible, identifying every aspect of the structure; techniques such as radiography should be employed to assess the condition under any surface coating or accretions, analyses of metals and pigments may be undertaken, organic materials such as binding materials or wood species may be identified. The condition of each part should be recorded, and at this stage a specification of treatment can be prepared. The specification will propose treatments and estimate costs involved which may lead to discussions with the responsible curator and possible changes to the specification. Such estimates have been routinely prepared in Area Museum Services where the museum owning the object has to pay towards its conservation; they are

now being used by some museums to indicate the extent of work to be done and its effect on planned programmes.

The treatment record itself will vary. Different institutions have different requirements and even within institutions different disciplines will not all wish to record in the same way. For routine recording of conservation treatment most records follow the same general format.

(1) *Object data:* this may include the identity of the object, its normal location, where it came from, who made it, its date and its owner. The information will be derived from the museum accession record.

(2) *Progress data:* this records the date the object is received in the laboratory or studio, the date it is required by and the date of completion. It may also include details of time of return to the person responsible for it.

(3) *Technical data:* composition and techniques of manufacture are covered in this section. The results of special examinations and analysis may be included as may the dimensions, if relevant.

(4) *Object Condition and Treatment data:* each part of the object is described, detailing the material it is made from and its condition along with a record of the treatment applied and the materials and equipment used in the treatment.

(5) *Recommendations:* the required environmental conditions for storage and display are given together with any other restrictions on use. Advice may be given on transportation or suitability for loan, and any date when the object should be re-examined can be included.

(6) *References:* any documentary information about the object or the treatment method should be noted. Cross references to photographs, X-rays and samples should also be given.

This list is neither proscriptive nor will all the information necessarily be included for every treatment.

The essential difference between conservation documentation and curatorial documentation is that the former is secondary to the basic task of conserving and maintaining the collection, while for the Curator it is a primary function.

A means must be provided of documenting simple treatments to many objects in a way which ensures that all the essential information is recorded. One way is to use an abbreviated form and a standard code for the treatment (this has proved very successful in the National Museum of Wales for dealing with the incoming material from archaeological excavations): the material is entered on a summary sheet in the excavation finds hut and then transferred to the laboratory where, following radiography and possibly investigative cleaning, the objects to be given full treatment are selected. Only these objects will have full treatment records prepared; for the remaining objects the preliminary work is recorded on the summary sheet alone. A similar sheet can be used when, for example, a large chinaware collection is washed to prepare it for display. Conversely, a conservation task of complexity may generate a vast quantity of information; detailed drawings and photographs may be included as may X-rays, micrographs, correspondence with specialists and so on.

From time to time it may be necessary to re-treat an object. In such a case it must be decided whether to continue the original record or to start a new record for a new job. There is a great deal to be said for continuing the original record so that, in effect, it becomes a record of the condition and treatment history of the object; even if an earlier record is cross-referenced, the impact of the complete record is not as great as when all the information is kept together. One of the drawbacks to conservation history files has been the use of conservation numbers where each treatment event is given a unique job number; while suitable for an agency which does not expect to have any responsibility for the long-term care of the object, this system is not really acceptable for a museum that does have such a responsibility.

The organization and use of conservation records is a matter that has been attracting ever greater attention. For many Conservators, conservation records have been an act of faith, something done because it is part of the professionalism of the discipline. Rarely until the past decade has there been close consideration of the reasons why records are kept and an appreciation of the information that can be extracted from them by a discerning retrieval system. Some ideas have been put forward for manual retrieval systems. In the 1960s and early 1970s feature cards or optical coincidence cards were used to identify particular features (e.g. Oddy and Barker, 1971). However, such systems could rapidly become unwieldy. The development of modern computer systems allowed the maximum manipulation of data contained in the record.

Computer hardware and software is still in a development stage; even 10 years ago few could have imagined the developments that have now become commercial realities. In 1978 the UK Institute devoted one volume of *The Conservator* to documentation; one paper described the system then developed by the Museum Documentation Association (MDA) to sort and index on a mainframe computer (Corfield, 1978). The tasks that then required a major computing centre at Cambridge University are now routinely undertaken with desk-top personal computers with storage capacities of many megabyte.

Nonetheless, the volume of data that can be stored and manipulated is finite; in the same volume Bradley (1978) described the system then in use in the British Museum. Here again the MDA's methods had been applied with the intention of eventual computerization. Such is the scale of the information in a major institution that full-scale computerization is only now being undertaken (Jones, 1990).

Despite the ready availability of computer systems, few Conservators are making use of them for the documentation of their work. Miles (1990) has reported a survey in which 83 per cent of respondents reported no use of computers, 7 per cent were using a computerized management system, and only 1 per cent were applying computers to practical conservation.

Administration of conservation is an obvious area for computer use, particularly when a number of client departments or museums are being served. Such a system was implemented at the Wiltshire Conservation Laboratory, the computer system replaced the conservation register allowing ready analysis of the work of the Laboratory. Over the years, the past registers have been entered into the system so that a comprehensive body of information is available about the work done on objects from the County's museums.

Conservators are still reluctant to commit their treatment records to computer, many considering that it does not provide the sensitivity to record the subtle nuances of conservation and the Conservator's observations and that these can only be described in narrative or pictorial form. Modern techniques will reduce the conflict; parallel data base and word-processing packages and direct input of images by scanner or digitized video will make automated systems even more flexible than traditional methods. Eventually we may envisage a total system in which all information is held in a machine-readable form to be retrieved at will.

For the present there are now systems in use which enable Conservators to automate all the functions of conservation. Many applications were described at a conference in Halifax in 1985 (Perkins, 1987), including the use of computers for all the purposes mentioned above. More recently, Welander (1989) has described the system in use at the Ancient Monuments Laboratory, Edinburgh. This is one of the few systems designed to handle the total record, accommodating the administrative functions as well as treatment information.

For documentation to be effective a degree of discipline is required. Computerized systems are only as good as the data that is put in; if we wish to retrieve data then we must be sure that the terms which we use for recall are those we use to input. Terminology control has been discussed at a recent conference (Roberts, 1990). Horie (1990) has pointed to the readily available industrial terminologies, particularly those of the American Society for Testing and Materials and the British Standards

Institution which give precise meaning to the words commonly and loosely used by Conservators. Jones (1990) has discussed the problems of terminology control at the British Museum observing that, on the one hand, superfluous information may be an unwelcome corollary to object treatment, but on the other hand it may be difficult to make sense of data confined to single-word statements. In the British Museum, as in most large systems, control of terminology will be achieved by means of authority lists and thesauri.

One way of ensuring standardization of input is to codify the data to be input as a mnemonic; this can also provide the means of inputting complex methods using the minimum of key strokes. For example, a standardized treatment of an archaeological iron object might be: 'Removed corrosion using an airbrasive with 53 micron alumina; desalinated in a soxhlet extractor; dried in an oven; lacquered with acrylic resin'. This could readily be reduced to a three-letter code. The danger of course is that the treatment could become subservient to the code. Such a system is in use at the Scottish Historic Buildings and Monuments Commission (Welander, 1989).

For many years Conservators have been maintaining records of the museum environment. Hitherto these records were generally in the form of spot readings taken with sling psychrometers, visual readings from hygrometers, light meters and so on, or charts from recording thermohygrographs. New systems are now available to record the data directly onto solid-state devices known as 'data loggers'. The loggers record electrical impulses created by sensors which may detect temperature and humidity, light levels or even the level of polluting gases; they can be programmed to record at pre-set intervals and may store several months worth of data. A record of the environment in a gallery may be useful; however, it would be even more informative to have a record of the environment which a particular specimen had been subjected to during its time in the museum. Such data are rarely, if ever, recorded, thus reducing the possibility of identifying deterioration resulting from a poor environment. The new generation of loggers are small self contained units having their own integral sensors and power source. The 'Stick-on' logger by Ancom Signatrol is about the size of a matchbox. The 'Hanwell' monitor made by Exeter Environmental Systems has been developed specifically for museum use, in addition to monitoring relative humidity and temperature it records visible and ultra-violet light; it has the added advantage that its stored data can be downloaded by means of an infra-red beam thus obviating the need to open the display case. These loggers can readily be attached to objects being loaned to another institution, and will provide a record of every change of environment that takes place, including changes occurring during transportation and moves between venues. The lender is thus provided with absolute proof that the conditions of loan have been met. These devices also enable records to be made of environments in display cases, in storage boxes and even those in plastic bags. Conservators have thus been provided with potent tools for documenting the collection, refined to the extent that the stresses imposed by changing environments can be kept as part of the object's condition file.

At the other extreme, environmental monitoring may be effected by a building management system (BMS) in which feedback is provided to automatically corrected deviations from present limits. Complex sensing incorporating triple redundancy has been employed at the National Gallery and the National Museum of Wales. A total BMS has been installed at the Royal Pavilion in Brighton (Rogers, 1989). This system not only monitors the temperature and humidity in the Pavilion, but also measures rainfall, sunlight and windspeed; overflow from gutters and conductivity of timber is also recorded as a guide to possible flooding.

As a general guide it should be unnecessary to keep all records of the museum environment; as long as the target conditions are maintained then the objects in the collection should not be at risk. Computerized systems can be programmed to record only when the conditions stray outside the pre-set limits; this is when the object is at risk and when a record needs to be made of the occurrence. Some loggers can be programmed to give an audible warning or to switch on other equipment such as a humidifier.

The effectiveness of any system will depend on the quality of its design. Thus it is essential that a careful analysis of the requirements of the users is undertaken before creating a documentation system. Rather than focusing on the content of the records themselves, the analyst should ask what it is that the users expect to get out of their records. This in itself will impose discipline on the users who will have to consider carefully what they record and what use is made of the information.

Conservation records represent a vast source of information which is at present largely untapped; a synthesis of the technological information gained during conservation could make a considerable contribution to the knowledge of manufacturing techniques; an analysis of objects treated by different methods would allow subjective reviews of the performance of different techniques and materials. A start has been made on this by the materials data base of the Conservation Information Network.

It would be impossible to describe conservation documentation without reference to the Network which is supported by the Getty Conservation Institute. The Network brings together information from the Art and Archaeology Technical Abstracts (AATA), the Canadian Conservation Institute (CCI), the Canadian Heritage Information Network, the Conservation Analytical Laboratory of the Smithsonian Institution (CAL), International Centre for the Study of Preservation and Restoration of Cultural Property, Rome (ICCROM), International Council for Monuments and Sites (ICOMOS), International Council of Museums (ICOM) and the Getty Conservation Institute.

The Network is organized into four main data bases:

(1) the bibliographic data base (BCIN), which contains over 130 000 literature citations derived from AATA, ICOM, ICOMOS, ICCROM, CCI and CAL;
(2) the photographic data base (PHOCUS), which contains 7000 records of publications relating to the history, permanence and conservation of photographic materials;
(3) the materials data base (MCIN), which contains over 1200 records on the use and performance of products used in conservation; and
(4) the suppliers data base (ACIN), which is a data base of mainly North American suppliers of conservation materials.

The Conservation Information Network represents a vast resource of inestimable value to the conservation profession. The bibliographic data base already contains most of the world's conservation literature; as more and more conservators begin to use and interact with the Network so its value will grow. The associated electronic mail facility allows the conservation profession to maintain international contacts in a way rarely available to other disciplines. The far-sightedness of the Getty Conservation Institute in nurturing the network deserves the support of all conservators and museums.

Documentation is a vital part of conservation; the requirement to record treatments and observations has been extended to permit the use of the information for administrative purposes, to prioritize work, to analyse work patterns and, ultimately, to provide a system interrelated to others in the museum in which the collections may be effectively managed to provide the maximum utilization of resources for their better care.

References

BRADLEY, S. (1978), 'Conservation recording in the British Museum', *The Conservator*, 7, 9–12

CORFIELD, M. (1978), 'Conservation records in the Wiltshire Library & Museum Service', *The Conservator*, 7, 5–8

HORIE, V. (1990), 'Industrial standards of terminology for conservation', in Roberts, A. (Ed.), *Terminology for Museums, Proceedings of an International Conference*, Cambridge, September 1988, Museum Documentation Association, Cambridge

JONES, L. (1990), 'Conservation terminology control in the British Museum', in Roberts, A. (Ed.), *Terminology for Museums, Proceedings of an International Conference*, Cambridge, September 1988, Museum Documentation Association, Cambridge

KEENE, S. (1990), Building a Management Information System for Conservation, in *Proceedings of the 9th Triennial Meeting of the ICOM Committee for Conservation*, Los Angeles

KEENE, S. (1991), Audits of Care: a Framework for Collections Condition Surveys, in Norman, M. and Todd, V. (Eds) *Storage, Preprints for the UKIC Conference, Restoration '91*, UKIC, London

LORD, B., LORD, G. D. and NICKS, J. (1989), *The Cost of Collecting. Collection Management in U.K. Museums*, HMSO, London

MILES, G. (1988), 'Conservation and collection management, integration or isolation', *International Journal of Museum Management and Curatorship*, 7, 159–163

MILES, G. (1990), 'Discipline developments: conservation', in Roberts, A. (Ed.), *Terminology for Museums, Proceedings of an International Conference*, Cambridge, September 1988, Museum Documentation Association, Cambridge

ODDY, A. AND BARKER, H. (1971), 'A feature card information retrieval system for the general museum laboratory', *Studies in Conservation*, 16, 89–94

O'REILLY, P. and LORD, A. (1988), *Basic Condition Reporting, A Handbook*, South East Registrars' Association, New York

PERKINS, J. (1987), *Computer Technology for Conservators, Proceedings of the 11th Annual IIC-CG Conference Workshop*, The Atlantic Regional Group of the International Institute for Conservation, Canadian Group (IIC-CG)

ROBERTS, A. (Ed.) (1990), *Terminology for Museums, Proceedings of an International Conference*, Cambridge, September 1988, Museums Documentation Association, Cambridge

ROGERS, J. (1989), 'Uses of microcomputers for monitoring and control in the Royal Pavilion, Art Gallery and Museum, Brighton', in Roberts, A. and Ingram, N. (Eds), *Computers in Museums Case Studies, 4: Computers in Conservation and Environmental Control*, Museum Documentation Association, Cambridge

UNITED KINGDOM INSTITUTE FOR CONSERVATION (1980), *Guidance for Conservation Practice*, UKIC, London

WELANDER, R. (1989), 'Computers in conservation: a microcomputer application', Roberts, A. and Ingram, N. (Eds), *Computers in Museums Case Studies, 4: Computers in Conservation and Environmental Control*, Museum Documentation Association, Cambridge

26

Control and measurement of the environment

Sarah Staniforth

Introduction

Conservation is now understood to encompass preservation as well as restoration. The majority of works of art are inherently unstable because impermanent materials are used in their making which undergo physical and chemical reactions as they age, resulting in changes of appearance, strength and other physical properties. This deterioration is accelerated by poor environmental conditions and, although changes are inevitable and irreversible, they can be slowed by controlling the environment. An understanding of the relationship between a work and its environment is needed and it has been established that works of art are most vulnerable to unsuitable levels of light, relative humidity and air pollution.

In this chapter I examine how adverse environmental conditions affect works, recommend the most suitable conditions for collections of various types, and show how the environment can be controlled by measuring conditions and adjusting them to within specified limits. It must be emphasized immediately that environmental considerations apply at all times, regardless of whether a work is on exhibition, in storage, on loan or travelling. All the care that is taken while a work is under the protective wing of its home is undone as soon as its safety is jeopardized by, for example, a journey in an unsuitable packing case to a museum with no environmental controls.

Light

The nature of light

Radiation from the sun, sky and artificial light sources can be divided into three regions according to wavelength. The human eye is sensitive to the visible region (400–700 nm) and perceives this part of the electromagnetic spectrum as violet at the short-wavelength end changing through the spectral colours blue, green, yellow, orange to red at the long-wavelength end. Infra-red (IR) radiation extends from the end of the visible spectrum to longer wavelengths; it may cause heating problems.

Ultraviolet radiation (UV) is to the short-wavelength side of visible light. Electromagnetic radiation is energy and if it is absorbed by a material it may cause photochemical change (chemical change induced by radiation). If absorbed, short wavelengths are more damaging than long wavelengths, since they are of higher energy, so UV is more damaging than an equal amount of blue light, which in turn is more damaging than an equal amount of yellow light. Red light causes a negligible amount of photochemical change. Most materials will undergo photochemical change and will therefore be damaged by UV and visible light; stone, metals and ceramics are seldom affected. However, there is less UV than visible radiation in all light sources and, in a museum with a general collection, approximately half the photochemical damage is caused by UV and half by visible light.

Dyes and pigments change colour; cellulosic materials (derived from plants) such as paper, cotton and linen, and proteinaceous materials (derived from animals) such as wool, leather and feathers are discoloured and weakened. Therefore, it is important to limit the exposure of objects that contain these materials as far as possible.

Measurement and control of ultraviolet radiation

The eye is not sensitive to UV and such radiation can therefore be eliminated without having any effect on the appearance of an object. This can be achieved using a filter that absorbs wavelengths of radiation in the UV but allows visible light to pass through. Of the forms of lighting used in museums, daylight contains the highest proportion of UV but tungsten–halogen and some fluorescent lamps also emit significant amounts. UV is most conveniently measured in units of microwatt/lumen[1] and the proportion emitted by tungsten lamps, approximately 75 μW/lumen, is considered the maximum level acceptable in a museum; there is a commercially available meter that will measure the UV proportion directly when the meter is pointed at the light source[2]. Tungsten–halogen lamps, which are increasingly used because of their high light output, emit a small amount of high energy and, therefore, dangerous, short-wavelength UV-B radiation; these lamps should always be used with a piece of glass in front of the bulb since glass absorbs the short-wavelength UV-B.

It is now possible to obtain glass-based interference filters with a vacuum coating that reduces the transmission of the longer wavelength UV-A radiation. These filters are suitable for use with tungsten–halogen lamps since, unlike plastic filters, they are not affected by the heat given off by these lamps. However, their present high cost and the small size of the glass sheets that can be vacuum coated limits their application. Plastic films containing a UV absorber laminated between two sheets of glass can be used for glazing windows. Rigid plastic acrylic sheets containing UV absorbers can be used for exhibition cases and glazing in frames. Thin acetate or polyester films and varnishes containing UV absorbers can be applied to windows and these provide a relatively cheap and simple solution. Plastic sleeves are available for slipping around fluorescent tubes. If it can be arranged for all light to be reflected off a painted wall before falling on any work then this will often provide sufficient UV absorption; most modern paints contain the white pigment titanium dioxide, which is a very effective UV absorber.

UV filtering is not permanent and should be checked periodically (say every six months). There are no reported instances of the acrylic sheets failing, but plastic films and varnishes are usually guaranteed for no more than 5 years. This is often because of failure of the film or varnish which results in its mechanical breakdown rather than a reduction in the efficiency of the UV absorber. If the windows to which these applications are made suffer from condensation then this will also reduce their lifespan. Sleeves for fluorescent tubes last for two or three changes of tubes.

Measurement and control of visible light

The rate of deterioration caused by light is proportional to both the light level and the time for which the object is exposed to that level. The damaging exposure experienced by an object illuminated at 400 lux[3] for 1 hour is the same as if it has been illuminated at 100 lux for 4 hours, in both cases the total exposure is 400 lux-hours. This is a consequence of the reciprocity law which states that the rate of photochemical change is proportional to the product of illuminance and the length of exposure. So to reduce the damage inflicted by light it is important to limit the length of time for which the works are illuminated as well as the level of illumination.

The recommended levels of illumination are listed in *Table 26.1*. These levels are already a compromise,

---

Table 26.1 Recommended levels of illuminance which should not be exceeded*,†

Material	Illuminance (lux)
Easel paintings	200
Animal and plant materials where colour is important (including undyed leather, wood, bone, ivory)	
Works of art on paper (including water-colours, drawings, prints, stamps, wallpaper, historical documents, photographs)	50
Textiles (including tapestries, costumes, upholstered furniture, carpets)	
Miniatures and manuscripts	
Dyed leather	
Natural history exhibits	

* Materials that are not light-sensitive may be lit at higher levels but it is unwise to increase the levels to above 300 lux in a museum where there are also light-sensitive exhibits because of problems with adaptation as the visitor moves from room to room.
† For photography, light levels may be increased to 1000 lux for short periods provided there is no significant heating if incandescent lamps are used, or 2500 lux for the cooler HMI lamps. Restoration may sometimes require 2000 lux.

since all exposure to light will cause deterioration; there is no minimum level below which damage will not occur. A light meter should be used to measure light levels since the eye readily adapts itself to changes in intensity and is therefore very unreliable for estimating levels of illumination. There are various pocket light meters available which are reliable and simple to use[2]. Electronic digital light meters have recently come on the market and these are more robust than their analogue predecessors.

Of the types of lighting that can be used in a museum (daylight, fluorescent lamps, tungsten and tungsten–halogen lamps) daylight is the most difficult to control since it changes through the day and throughout the year. The only satisfactory way of limiting it to within a reasonable range of 200 lux is by using motorized blinds that are controlled by photocells. The photocells sense the light falling on a surface and then open or close the blinds according to whether the surface is under- or over-illuminated.

If the blinds are fully open and there is still too little light then artificial lighting can be switched on. However, this involves the installation of complicated and expensive machinery which may be unsuitable for many collections. Manually-controlled blinds can be used, but there is always the problem of staff not being available to open and close them, and this may result in their being left open all the time. A third possibility is to apply a solar-control film (either paint or a metallized acetate or polyester sheet) to windows. These can lower the illumination to an acceptable level on the brightest days and artificial lighting can be used to supplement the lighting on duller days. Direct sunlight should never be allowed to fall on any object. In addition to the photochemical damage that it causes direct sunlight may cause local heating which will affect the relative humidity in the vicinity of the object. Sensitive objects should not be placed near windows where the light is brighter than in the centre of the room.

Fifty lux of daylight is less satisfactory than the same level of artificial light, and it is preferable to use the latter type of lighting for more sensitive exhibits. If a light meter is used when the lamps are first installed, this will ensure that no exhibit is over-illuminated. Colour temperature is a measure of the appearance of a light source. A warm or reddish light has a lower colour temperature than a cool or bluish light. There is a choice of colour temperature among fluorescent lamps. However, cool lamps require excessive light levels if they are not to appear gloomy. Lamps should also be selected for good colour rendering. The colour rendering index of a lamp compares the distortion in appearance of objects in that illumination relative to a perfect source at the same colour temperature. A lamp with good colour rendering properties will cause no distortion. The colour rendering indices of lamps are available from manufacturers. Tungsten lamps have good colour rendering properties but some fluorescent lamps can cause considerable distortion, and should not be used. There are now some 'polyphosphor' lamps available which are more efficient than fluorescent lamps and have good colour rendering properties (Thomson, 1985). Lamps with low colour temperatures (tungsten and warm fluorescent lamps) are found to be preferred by viewers for exhibits to be illuminated at 50 lux.

The phenomenon of two colours matching in one light source but not in another is called *metamerism*. This may create problems if, for example, a restoration is carried out in daylight using different dyes or pigments from the original and then exhibited in tungsten lighting. A competent restorer will, in fact, be aware of this difficulty and will choose materials accordingly. A more banal example might be if a carpet and wallpaper match in daylight but not in artificial light. The ability of viewers to discriminate between colours in certain types of lighting at low levels has been questioned. For example, is 50 lux high enough for full colour discrimination and are subtle shades of blue less discernible in tungsten lighting than daylight (tungsten light is low in blue radiation)? Experimental work indicates that colour discrimination may be reduced for older viewers at the 50-lux level (Boyce, 1987).

It is important when using relatively low light levels to ensure that the viewer's eye remains adapted to those levels. Therefore bright areas in a museum should be avoided and glare from, for example, a spotlight pointing at the viewer or the reflection of lights on glazing, should be eliminated by placing lamps in appropriate positions.

Light should be reduced to a minimum when the museum is not open to the public. Lights should be turned off and blinds drawn to exclude daylight in the early morning and in the evening. For very sensitive materials, exhibition cases can be covered with curtains which are drawn back by the viewer or they can be fitted with lights on timers. Exhibition of these objects can be alternated with periods of storage. As with all environmental control, the same principles apply when works are in store and, therefore, lights should not be left on in storage areas.

Another approach to the control of lighting is to set an exposure value for a year; 200 lux of illumination for a museum that is open from 10 am to 6 pm is equivalent to 666 000 lux hours. So light levels may be allowed to rise above 200 lux provided they are compensated for with periods of lower illumination or darkness.

Temperature

It is undoubtedly true that of all the environmental conditions mentioned in this chapter, temperature is the one of which people are most conscious and, therefore, instinctively consider most important to control. However, as far as collections are concerned, temperature is the factor to which they are least sensitive and it is therefore the least important, though rapid temperature fluctuations may cause some problems in objects comprised of different materials, such as metal inlays in timber. If the temperature is high, then the rate of chemical reactions and biological activity will increase, so lower temperatures are preferred. Its relation to relative humidity (RH) is important and this is discussed in the following section. Direct heating should be avoided since it may cause local drying. For this reason sunlight should not be allowed to fall on exhibits, powerful spotlights should be avoided, lamps should be mounted outside exhibition cases, objects should not be placed above radiators and pictures should not be hung on chimney breasts above fires.

The levels of temperature recommended (18–25°C) are usually governed by the comfort of people in museums where the exhibits are on display. In stores, or in collections that are not open to the public, the temperature may be allowed to fall to a low level provided the RH is at an acceptable level and that condensation will not occur on cold surfaces, that precautions are taken to avoid condensation on cold exhibits brought into the warmth and that warm damp air is not allowed to leak into cold areas where it might condense on cold surfaces.

Relative humidity

Definition

All materials that contain water react to the amount of water that is present in the air surrounding them. In 'dry' air they lose water and in 'damp' air they gain water. It is necessary for a scale to be defined that relates the amount of water in the air to its drying or moistening properties. One possibility is to measure the weight of water in a given volume of air (g/m³); this is called the *absolute humidity* of the air. The weight of water in a given weight of air (kg/kg) or any material is also used and is called the *moisture content*. However, neither of these is suitable since warm air can hold more water than cool air. A scale of relative humidity which relates the amount of water in a given quantity of air to the maximum amount of water that the air can hold at that temperature is the most appropriate scale to use for museum purposes. Relative humidity (RH) is expressed as a percentage and is defined as follows:

$$ RH = \frac{\text{amount of water in a given volume of air}}{\text{maximum amount of water air can hold at that temperature}} \times 100 $$

The amount of moisture that a material can hold depends approximately on the RH of the air surrounding it. If the RH of the air falls, the material will lose water. Provided the RH and temperature of the air surrounding objects is kept constant then the moisture content of the objects will also remain constant.

Damage caused by unsuitable relative humidity levels

High RH can affect objects in three ways: it can encourage biological activity; it can cause changes in physical dimensions; and it can accelerate certain chemical reactions.

Mould growth will occur on most organic materials if the RH is higher than 65–70 per cent. Its growth is also encouraged in stagnant air and warm temperatures.

Anisotropic materials such as wood which can absorb water from the atmosphere swell more across the grain than along it. An apparent contradiction of this is canvas and other twisted threads, which shrink along their length in high RH. This contraction is caused by the fibres swelling across their width, which tightens the twist in the thread. The canvases of some paintings shrink dramatically in damp conditions and since the ground and paint layers cannot shrink by the same amount, cleavage occurs between the canvas and the ground.

The corrosion of metals increases in high RH, particularly if the air is acidic. 'Bronze disease' may occur if the RH is above 70 per cent. Light damage to textiles and dyes is also accelerated by high RH. Some glasses are moisture-sensitive and become opaque and brittle if exposed to high RH.

Water-sensitive materials shrink when the RH is low. Wooden objects are particularly affected and may crack and warp. Some materials become brittle, textile fibres break and adhesives fail. Veneers may lift during periods of low humidity, partly because of adhesive failure, and partly because of dimensional changes in the thin slivers of wood.

Rapidly fluctuating conditions of RH are particularly damaging for composite objects which consist of a number of different materials all of which are affected by water in a different way. As the RH rises each material absorbs water and swells at a different rate and, similarly, as the RH falls the materials shrink at different rates. Repeated cycles of expansion and contraction (such as may occur during the winter in rooms which are centrally heated during the day but not during the night, resulting in dry air during the day alternating with damper air during the night) will cause warping and cleavage. The speed with which objects react to changes depends on the material. Paper and textiles react quickly (in minutes), whilst large pieces of wood react slowly (in months).

Further research needs to be carried out to determine the time span over which RH fluctuations occur and different materials deteriorate. An interim guideline is that the RH should not fluctuate by more than 10 per cent in any 24-hour period.

Recommended levels of relative humidity

The recommended levels of RH will depend on the nature of the collection and its location. These levels are listed in *Table 26.2*.

Table 26.2 Recommended levels of relative humidity★

Materials	Relative humidity (%)
Mixed collections in humid tropics. (Air circulation important to discourage mould growth.) Too high for metals	65
Mixed collections in Europe and North America. (May cause frosting and condensation problems in museums where winter temperatures are low)	55
Compromise for mixed collections in museums where winter temperatures are low	45–50
Metal-only collections. Local material exhibited in museums in arid regions	40–45

★ Ideally all levels should be maintained to within ±5 per cent but at any rate the danger limits of 65 per cent and 40 per cent should not be exceeded.

The humid tropics, which include large parts of the Far East, have a RH of above 65 per cent for most of the year. The major problem in these regions is mould growth. It is usually only feasible to reduce the RH to 65 per cent because the cost of running an air-conditioning plant to reduce the RH further would be high.

The major problem in European and North American museums comes from excessive dryness during the winter months when heating is used. If no humidification is available the absolute humidity of the air remains constant and the more the air is heated the lower the RH becomes. For example, air from outside at 0°C and 50 per cent RH will have an RH of 13 per cent when heated to 20°C.

The recommended level of 55 per cent RH for mixed collections may be too high in some cases during the winter months, since condensation will occur on single-glazed windows. In temperate climates, 45–50 per cent RH is an acceptable level in these circumstances.

In extremely severe climates it is possible for frost to form in the walls of the building as the water in the internal conditioned air diffuses out and freezes before it reaches the external surface of the masonry. Repeated freezing and thawing within the wall will eventually crack it. In these circumstances even lower levels of RH are necessary during the winter months. As has been said already, the most important humidity consideration is to avoid setting up daily cycles of high and low RH. For the welfare of the collection at all times, as well as for the comfort of people during the day, all humidity and heating control should operate in all areas of the museum for 24 hours a day.

Measurement of relative humidity

An instrument used to measure RH is called a *hygrometer*. Wet- and dry-bulb hygrometers (also called psychrometers), when used correctly, give accurate results against which all other hygrometers may be calibrated. The sling psychrometer (or whirling psychrometer, or sling or whirling hygrometer) is the simplest and least expensive of these instruments. It consists of two thermometers, one of which has a fabric sleeve around its bulb, which is moistened with distilled water. If air is moved past the wet-bulb thermometer by swinging the psychrometer, water will evaporate from the fabric sleeve; this cools the thermometer bulb. The amount of cooling depends on the amount of water that evaporates which in turn depends on the RH of the air. The lower the RH the greater the depression of the wet-bulb temperature will be with respect to the dry bulb. A scale is provided with the psychrometer which shows the RH for various wet- and dry-bulb temperatures. The RH can also be determined using a psychrometric chart (or hygrometric chart). Accurate results can be obtained provided care is taken when the instrument is used and the manufacturer's instructions followed.

Wet- and dry-bulb hygrometers are manufactured in which air is drawn past the thermometer bulbs by an electric fan. These are easier to use but more expensive than sling instruments.

Hair and paper hygrometers and the recording hygrograph rely on the expansion and contraction of moisture-sensitive elements with changes in RH. Hair and paper reacts quickly enough and with a large enough change in dimension to be used for this purpose. In a paper hygrometer two strips of paper which respond differently to changes in RH are glued together and coiled so that when the RH changes the coil twists and moves a pointer attached to the end of it. Hair hygrometers are used in the familiar recording thermo-hygrographs. A bundle of hairs is attached by a series of levers to a pen, as the RH changes the hairs expand or contract which makes the pen rise or fall on the chart. The temperature is recorded using a pen that is moved by the twisting of a coiled bi-metallic strip. Neither of these hygrometers is an accurate instrument, and they require frequent calibration, using a wet- and dry-bulb or electronic instrument.

There are now electronic instruments available in which a moisture sensitive element undergoes a change in electrical property (for example, capacitance) as the RH varies. Providing they are supplied with calibration caps (usually saturated solutions of a salt which give a known RH at a particular temperature) these hygrometers are as accurate as wet- and dry-bulb instruments. Dew-point hygrometers are made in which a gold mirror is cooled until moisture is deposited on it at the dew-point temperature of the air. The change in reflectance of the metal when condensation occurs is detected and the RH is calculated from tables. These instruments are accurate, but expensive. Even with electronic instruments more than one reading should be taken to ensure that the instrument has stabilized and reproducible readings are obtained. Humidity-indicating papers which change colour as the RH changes are available and these are useful if a large number of areas is to be monitored.

Humidistats are essential for the automatic operation of RH-controlling equipment. The most common type consists of a bundle of hairs connected to electrical relays which switch the instrument on and off. Humidistats require frequent calibration to ensure that the RH is at the correct level. Electronic humidistats are now made which are very reliable and require less frequent recalibration.

Control of relative humidity

Complete control of RH is possible using air-conditioning. However, the installation and running costs of an air-conditioning plant are beyond the means of many museums. RH control may be achieved within a room using free-standing humidifier and dehumidifier units that are automatically controlled by humidistats. For many museums, these units provide an inexpensive and satisfactory method of keeping RH within acceptable limits. They may not allow the fine control that a satisfactorily maintained air-conditioning plant is capable of, but they are quite adequate for avoiding dangerous conditions.

It is extremely unlikely that both humidification and dehumidification will be necessary in one room.

Humidifiers will probably be required to combat dryness caused by winter heating and dehumidifiers for damp basements, cellars or unheated areas. Their successful operation depends entirely on adequate draught-proofing of the area that they are to control.

Humidifiers

Humidifiers are designed to add water quickly to the air in a controlled manner. Unfortunately, bowls of water standing around the room and water containers on radiators are quite inadequate because they are unable to evaporate sufficient quantities of water. There are three types of humidifier that may be used. Atomising humidifiers draw water onto rapidly rotating blades which disperse particles into fine droplets which vaporize near the machine. Unless distilled or de-ionized water is used the minerals that are present in tap water will also be carried into the air and a film of salts will be deposited on all surfaces. A further problem is that if the humidistat fails and the machine does not switch off, water will continue to be added until the air is saturated and water condenses. Steam humidifiers heat water (like a kettle) so that it evaporates into the air. The steam may be injected into a ventilation duct or may be provided by a fan-assisted wall unit, these units are extremely efficient at generating the required moisture. As with the atomizer, if the humidistat fails serious high humidity problems may result and, therefore, a double humidistat is recommended. The most suitable humidifier for museum use is the unheated evaporative humidifier. A drum which carries a sponge belt slowly revolves, dipping the sponge into a reservoir filled with water. A fan blows room air through the wet sponge. Unlike the atomizing humidifier, if the humidistat fails in the 'on' position the RH will not rise to much above 70 per cent since the damp air can only absorb a certain amount of water from a damp material. The minerals are left behind on the sponge, so tap water may be used in evaporative humidifiers.

There is concern over the transmittance of Legionnaire's Disease through humidification equipment. This problem does not occur in steam humidifiers or with properly cleaned evaporative dehumidifiers.

Dehumidifiers

There are two types of room dehumidifier: dessicant and refrigerant. Which is more suitable depends on the temperature. In a dessicant dehumidifier room air is passed over a salt which absorbs water from the air. A drum which contains the dessicant slowly rotates passing in turn a region where hot air drives moisture from the dessicant through an exhaust and out of the room, and then a region where room air is passed through the dessicant. Refrigerant dehumidifiers work on a similar principle to a domestic refrigerator. They contain refrigerant gases (usually fluorinated hydrocarbons) which liquify when compressed. This occurs in the 'condensing' coils which are warm because of the heat which is given off when a gas turns into a liquid. In the 'cooling' coils the liquid expands and vaporizes, absorbing heat from its surroundings. Room air is passed over the cooling coils where it is cooled below its dew-point and deposits moisture. It is reheated by passing over the warm condensing coils. Refrigerant dehumidifiers are preferred for ordinary temperatures but frost up too readily in temperatures approaching freezing. For these conditions dessicant dehumidifiers are preferred.

Dehumidification can be achieved by heating alone, and this is a possible solution where the damp air is also cold; however, heating consumes more energy than either of the other dehumidifier types.

Silica gel and other humidity buffers
It is possible to control the relative humidity of small enclosed volumes using materials that are conditioned to maintain the RH at a predetermined level. When the RH drops below that level they will give off water and when it rises they will absorb water. Any moisture-containing material such as wood, paper or natural textiles has this property, but the amount of water a material can hold and the speed with which it reacts will often not be adequate for conditioning purposes. Silica gel is a suitable buffering agent because it holds sufficient water, responds rapidly to changes in RH and it is chemically inert. Before being used in an exhibition case the silica gel is preconditioned to the required RH by allowing it to stand in a room or environmental chamber at this level for at least 2 weeks. Further information on the use of silica gel is given in the section on exhibition cases and packing cases.

Air circulation and the capacity of humidity controllers
It is important to ensure that once the humidity controllers are installed, the conditioned air that they supply is circulated around the room. A hygrometer should be used to check that there are no pockets of stagnant air in the corners of rooms. Fans can be used to improve air circulation. The size of humidity controllers and the numbers of units depends on such factors as the size of the room, the speed with which the air changes in the room (this will be determined by the number of doors and windows), the difference between internal and external conditions and the number of people to pass through the room. Manufacturers will be able to help with these calculations.

Air pollution

Nature of air pollution

Museums and galleries in cities and industrial towns are likely to suffer from the damaging effects of pollution since it is a product of the burning of fossil fuels and the exhaust from motor-cars. Unfortunately today there are few pockets of 'clean' air in the world, so no collection can be considered free from air pollution. Pollutants may be classified into two types: particulate and gaseous.

The diameter of particulates (suspended solid particles in the air) range from approximately 0.01 to 100 μm (microns). In some cases up to 30 per cent of the particulate mass has a diameter of less than 1 μm and this will influence the choice of air filters. Particles may be generated by mechanical processes, occur naturally (pollen) or be formed by chemical processes in the air.

There are two main types of gaseous pollutant: acidic and oxidant. Acidic sulphur dioxide is produced in biological processes but it is also a product of the burning of fossil fuels, all of which contain sulphur. Sulphur dioxide reacts with oxygen and water in the air to form sulphuric acid. Sulphuric acid is very involatile so once it is on a surface it will remain there. Ozone is an oxidizing pollutant which is produced naturally in the upper atmosphere. It is also generated by the action of sunlight on car exhaust fumes and in certain types of electrical equipment (for example, photocopying machines). Nitric oxide and nitrogen dioxide are both produced in car exhaust fumes. Nitrogen dioxide is converted to nitric acid by water and oxygen. Nitric acid is an oxidizing agent as well as an acid. It is less damaging than sulphuric acid because it is more volatile.

Damaging effects of pollution

Particulates attach themselves to all surfaces in a museum, and will eventually form an unsightly layer, particularly if they contain a high proportion of sooty material from the incomplete burning of fuels. This surface dirt will need removing periodically and the cleaning operation can be dangerous for the objects. In addition the particles are often acidic due to adsorbed sulphur dioxide.

Acids attack calcium carbonate. Sulphuric acid will convert calcium carbonate to calcium sulphate. Marble and limestone are both forms of calcium carbonate and buildings or statues made of these materials that are exposed to the 'acid' rain that results from industrial air pollution are badly affected. The calcium sulphate that is formed is washed away by the rain, thereby exposing a fresh surface of calcium carbonate to attack. Frescoes, in which the pigment particles are trapped in a matrix of calcium carbonate crystals, are also vulnerable to sulphuric acid attack. Cellulosic materials (paper and cotton) and proteinaceous materials (wool, silk and leather) are embrittled and discoloured after sulphur dioxide attack. The rusting of iron is accelerated in the presence of sulphur dioxide.

Ozone is an extremely powerful oxidizing agent and will react with most organic materials, degrading their chemical structure. It weakens cellulosic materials, discolours dyes and deteriorates varnish and oil-paint films. Because of its extremely high reactivity the concentration of ozone in the air by the time it has diffused indoors is likely to be low.

Levels of pollution

The unit commonly used to measure the concentration of pollutants (both particulate and gaseous) in air is micrograms per cubic metre ($\mu g/m^3$). Particulate levels in Western Europe are lower now than they were earlier this century. Sulphur dioxide levels in cities are also improving. Ozone and nitrogen dioxide levels are highest where there are many cars and much sunshine. Los Angeles was the first city suffering from dangerous levels of oxidant pollution to be studied. Now there are many such cities throughout the world.

Recommended levels and preventive measures

There is no minimum acceptable level of pollution. Like ultraviolet radiation, pollution should be eliminated as far as possible. The complete answer for the control of pollution is air-conditioning. Air from outside is drawn into the ducted system through filters. It is circulated around the building several times, on each occasion it passes through further filters to remove any pollutants that may have been introduced. A fuller explanation of air-conditioning is given in the following section. It is impractical to try to eliminate all the particles in the air using filters since high pressures are necessary to force the air through these absolute filters and particles are introduced into the museum by visitors. 'Viscous' filters which use a liquid such as oil to trap coarse particles are suitable for rough filters when the air first enters the building. 'Fabric' filters which are bags made of layers of fibres are used for more efficient particle-filtering. Acceptable efficiencies for these filters are shown in *Table 26.3*.

The filters must be changed periodically. As they remove particles they become more resistant to the passage of air through them. This results in a pressure difference across the filter and when this reaches a level specified by the manufacturer the filters should be changed. It is possible to remove particles using electrostatic precipitators. The air

Table 26.3 Acceptable efficiencies for filters used in air-conditioning plants

Filter	Efficiency Eurovent 4/5★ (%)
Viscous†	<20
Fabric	25–90
Absolute‡	99

★ Eurovent 4/5 is a new standard for testing air filters which is being adopted by all European manufacturers. It replaces the various national standards (until now British Standard 2831 was widely used in the UK).
† Viscous filters are suitable for use as pre-filters; they remove coarser particles and extend the life of the main filters which will generally be of the fabric type.
‡ Absolute filters are not recommended for use in museums, they are mentioned here for information only.

passes positively charged wires, the particles acquire a positive charge and are held on negatively charged collector plates downstream. As these precipitators produce small quantities of ozone they should *not* be used in museums.

Gaseous pollutants may be removed by water sprays and activated carbon filters. Sulphur dioxide and nitrogen dioxide are soluble in water and they are mostly removed by water sprays. These are not effective against ozone. Activated carbon filters adsorb pollutant gases. As with the particle filters they need periodic replacement. Suggested maximum acceptable levels of pollutant gases are shown in *Table 26.4* and these levels are attainable if air-conditioning with recirculation is used.

Table 26.4 Maximum acceptable gaseous pollutant levels in a museum using air-conditioning★

Pollutant gas	Concentration ($\mu g/m^3$)
Sulphur dioxide	<10
Nitrogen dioxide	<10
Ozone	0–2

★ It is not necessary to monitor the level of pollutants continuously in museums, but there are tests available that can record pollution levels over a period of time.

The only alternative to air-conditioning is to use exhibition cases and this is discussed in one of the following sections.

Air-conditioning

An air-conditioning installation consists of a central plant which distributes air from which particulates and pollutant gases have been removed at a required RH and temperature. The air is distributed to all parts of the building through a system of ducts. It is the most effective way of controlling environmental conditions available at the moment. A typical specification for a museum air-conditioning system controlling conditions in exhibition areas is:

Temperature: summer 22 ± 1°C; winter 19 ± 1°C

Relative humidity: 55 ± 5%

Particles filtered to an efficiency of 85% to Eurovent 4/5

Sulphur dioxide and nitrogen dioxide filtered to reduce the concentration to below $10 \, \mu g/m^3$.

These requirements to be met 24 hours/day, every day of the year.

(Specification used in competition for Hampton site extension to the National Gallery, 1982).

The successful operation of an air-conditioning system relies on a competent maintenance team and adequate monitoring. It is vital that the temperature and humidity sensors located in the ducting and near the outlets to the rooms are correctly calibrated and maintained since these sensors control the system. It is also important to monitor the conditions in the exhibition rooms. This can be done by hand (using wet- and dry-bulb instruments or electronic sensors) or using a data-logging scheme (see section on monitoring).

Exhibition cases and packing cases

The control of the environment in a whole room has been discussed. In circumstances where this is impractical for one reason or another (e.g. due to size of room, impossibility of introducing ducting into a building, or expense) conditions can be controlled on a small scale in an exhibition case. The technology of environmental control in exhibition cases applies equally well to packing cases and so these are discussed together.

Construction

Since the aim of the exhibition case (or the packing case) is to isolate the objects (as far as possible) from external conditions, the cases should be as efficiently sealed as possible. If the RH outside the case changes then the RH within the case will also change but at a slower rate and to a lesser extent depending on the rate at which air leaks into the case from the outside and the amount of moisture-buffering material within the case. Experiments suggest a typical leak rate of about one air change per day. In a sealed case without buffering, if the temperature changes then this will affect the RH within the case, since (provided the water content remains the same) the RH increases as the temperature falls (and vice versa).

These effects can be minimized by using materials with good thermal-insulation properties in the construction of packing cases which may experience extreme temperature conditions in unheated aircraft luggage holds or on loading bays in winter or summer. If a case is likely to travel in these conditions then it should be lined with a highly insulating material such as polystyrene or poly-ethylene foam.

Material

Cases should be constructed using 'safe' materials which do not give off vapours likely to damage the objects in them. This is also an important point to consider when objects are stored. In the microclimate within any poorly ventilated space, pollutants can rapidly accumulate to damaging levels. For example, woods give off acids such as acetic and formic acid, wool releases volatile sulphides, polyvinyl chloride releases hydrogen chloride. These pollutants can have dangerously damaging effects on objects. A discussion of 'safe materials is given in chapter 45.

Silica gel and humidity buffering

One of the most active fields of development in environmental conservation is the control of RH in small areas using materials such as silica gel. This is a particularly popular form of control for temporary exhibitions and for museums where there is no possibility of installing large-scale conditioning schemes. It has already been mentioned that silica gel gives off water when the RH falls and absorbs it when the RH rises in such a way as to maintain the RH at a level to which the silica gel has been previously conditioned. It is recommended that 20 kg of silica gel be used per cubic metre of exhibition case. Depending on the leak rate of the case, this amount efficiently buffers RH changes over the yearly cycle. Conditions within the case should be monitored using a hygrometer. Over the year, although stability will be maintained, the RH in the case will drift towards the average room RH. In temperate climates with winter heating this level will be too low. Therefore, either some form of simple humidifier will have to be used in the room or the silica gel will have to be reconditioned if the hygrometer shows too large a drop. The case should be constructed in such a way that air can circulate around the case with easy access to the silica gel which should be laid out exposing as large a surface area as possible.

Air-conditioning units for exhibition cases

An ingenious design for a home-made air-conditioning unit to be used to control the environment (RH and pollution) within exhibition cases has been proposed by Michalski (1982). The prototype supplies pollutant-free air at a specified RH and temperature to a number of exhibition cases. It is not a forced ventilation system, and merely introduces the air at a slight excess pressure. The air is lost through natural leakage from the cases. If a large number of exhibition cases are to be conditioned, then this system has distinct advantages over silica gel buffering because of its low cost. However, it is unable to compensate for RH changes induced by sudden temperature changes. Development of this idea could provide further possibilities for RH and pollution control on a small scale (Staniforth and Hayes, 1987).

Design of packing cases

Packing cases fulfil two functions: they protect their contents from mechanical damage, vibration and shock and provide a stable environment around the object. A typical specification for a case might consist of a solid outer case made from plywood or aluminium, lined with foam to provide cushioning and insulation and with a sheet of polythene wrapping the object. The case should also be shower-proof, fire-proof, or at least constructed from flame-resistant materials, and, obviously, secure. Any device that increases ease of handling should be used, such as extra handles or light materials. Accidents are more likely to occur if the case is particularly heavy or awkward to lift.

Monitoring

It might be tempting when systems for environmental control have been installed to become complacent and to assume that they are doing their jobs efficiently and maintaining conditions to within specifications. Unfortunately this is seldom the case. No machinery can be immune from malfunction or miscalibration and only constant vigilance can ensure that all is operating well. This responsibility must lie

with the museum staff, the Curators and Conservators. Surveys of conditions within the museum must be performed whether by hand (using hygrometers and light meters) or by data logger (a central computer linked to a number of environmental sensors around the museum). This check should be made frequently and the results passed on to those responsible for the maintenance of the systems.

Conclusions

The level of environmental control achieved will be governed to a major extent by the resources of the museum. The complete answer would be to install air-conditioning, to use UV screening on all windows and light sources, and to control daylight using automatically controlled motorized blinds. This has been called Class I environmental control. Class II uses free-standing RH-controlling units, UV screening and lighting control with manually operated blinds or only artificial lighting.

There is a developing trend towards control on a smaller scale through the use of exhibition cases, and this has distinct advantages over the complicated and elaborate machinery required for air-conditioning.

Light levels generate far more controversy than RH. Is the 200 lux level adequate? Is daylight essential for viewing works of art? Surely it loses much of its 'changeable' quality when restricted to 200 lux in a system using motorized blinds? Might it be as acceptable to use artificial lights that simulate daylight? But, if we wish to retain the 'changeable' quality, is an annual exposure then a possible alternative?

Many of these questions were answered at a Lighting Seminar held in April 1987 at Bristol. (See preprints cited in suggestions for further reading.)

Environmental questions must always be asked when a new museum building is designed or rooms are renovated. The curator and conservator should write a specification for environmental controls to be installed.

In this chapter I have given the present recommended specifications for environmental control. One or two points may provoke controversy, but hopefully we are beyond the time of, on the one hand, the museum curator and designer exposing collections to high light levels with complete disregard of RH and pollutants for maximum impact in an exhibition, and on the other, the Conservator who appears to endeavour to closet objects in poorly lit exhibition cases. The Curator and Conservator should be prepared to work together to achieve the far-from-impossible goal of exhibiting collections in an attractive, stimulating and, above all, safe environment.

Notes

[1] UV is measured as the amount of UV energy per unit of visible radiation. It should be noted that cutting down the total amount of daylight radiation by, for example, installing blinds will not reduce the proportion of UV. It is still necessary to use UV screening.

[2] No reference is made in this chapter to commercially available products. This is deliberate since there is a tendency for companies to change their products or to go into liquidation, which will render any specific recommendations made here useless in the future. However, The Museums Association publishes Information Sheets which contain details of equipment and products with the names and addresses of suppliers. There are two which are particularly relevant to this chapter: THOMSON, G. and STANIFORTH, S. (1985), 'Conservation and museum lighting', *Museums Information Sheet No. 6*, 4th revised edition; THOMSON, G. and STANIFORTH, S. (1985), 'Simple control and measurement of relative humidity in museums', *Museums Information Sheet No. 24*, 2nd revised edition.

[3] The lux is a unit of illumination. 1 lux equals 1 lumen per square metre and is approximately equal to 0.1 foot candle (the old unit of illumination). It is a measurement of energy that takes into account the spectral sensitivity of the human eye.

References

BOYCE, P. (1987), 'Visual acuity, colour discrimination and light level', *United Kingdom Institute for Conservation and the Group of Designers and Interpreters in Museums Seminar on Lighting in Museums, Galleries and Historic Houses*, Bristol, 9–10 April, 50–57, Museums Association

MICHALSKI, S. (1982), A relative humidity control module for display cases, *Proceedings of the IIC Washington conference, Science and Technology in the Service of Conservation*, 28–31

STANIFORTH, S. and HAYES, B. (1987), 'Temperature and relative humidity measurement and control in National Trust houses', *8th Triennial Meeting of ICOM Committee for Conservation*, 915–916

THOMSON, G. (1985), 'Colour under some new fluorescent lamps', *National Gallery Technical Bulletin*, 9, 5–11

Bibliography

Lighting

BROMELLE, N. S. and HARRIS, J. B. (1961, 1962), 'Museum lighting, Parts 1–4', *Museums Journal*, **61,** 169–176; **61,** 259–267; **63,** 337–346; **62,** 176–186

FELLER, R. L. (1964), 'Control of deteriorating effects of light upon museum objects', *Museum*, **xvii**, 57–98

LOE, D. L., ROWLANDS, E. and WATSON, N. F. (1982), 'Preferred lighting conditions for the display of oil and watercolour paintings', *Lighting Research and Technology*, **14,** 173–192

MICHALSKI, S. (1987), Damage to museum objects by visible radiation (light) and ultraviolet radiation (UV), *United Kingdom Institute for Conservation and the Group of Designers and Interpreters in Museums Seminar on Lighting in Museums, Galleries and Historic Houses*, Bristol, 9–10 April, 3–16, Museums Association

STANIFORTH, S. (1987), Problems with ultraviolet filters, *United Kingdom Institute for Conservation and the Group of Designers and Interpreters in Museums Seminar on Lighting in Museums, Galleries and Historic Houses*, Bristol, 9–10 April, 25–30, Museums Association

THOMSON, G. (1961), 'A new look at colour rendering, level of illumination and protection from ultraviolet radiation in museum lighting', *Studies in Conservation*, **6**, 49–70

Relative humidity

ANTOMARCHI, C. and DE GUICHEN, G. (1987), 'Pour une nouvelle approche des normes climatiques dans les musees', *Triennial Meeting of ICOM Committee for Conservation*, 847–851

LAFONTAINE, R. H. and MICHALSKI, S. (1984), 'The control of relative humidity – recent developments', *7th Triennial Meeting of ICOM Committee for Conservation*, 84.17.33–84.17.37

MARSTEIN, N. and STEIN, M. (1987), 'Advanced measuring of the climatic conditions in the medieval wooden churches in Norway', *8th Triennial Meeting of ICOM Committee for Conservation*, 889–895

Air pollution

HACKNEY, S. (1984), 'The distribution of gaseous air pollution within museums', *Studies in Conservation*, **29,** 105–116

THOMSON, G. (1965), 'Air pollution – a review for conservation chemists', *Studies in Conservation*, **10,** 147–168

Exhibition cases and packing cases

BLACKSHAW, S. M. and DANIELS, V. D. (1979), 'The testing of materials for use in storage and display in museums', *The Conservator*, **3**, 16–19

PADFIELD, T., ERHARDT, D. and HOPWOOD, W. (1982), 'Trouble in store', *Proceedings of the IIC Washington Conference, Science and Technology in the Service of Conservation*, 24–27

STANIFORTH, S. (Ed.) (1985), 'Packing cases – safer transport for museum objects', *UKIC One Day Meeting*, 21 June 1985

STOLOW, N. (1987), *Conservation and Exhibitions*, Butterworths, London

THOMSON, G. (1977), 'Stabilisation of RH in exhibition cases, hygrometric half-time', *Studies in Conservation*, **22**, 85–102

Monitoring

THOMSON, G. (1981), 'Control of the environment for good or ill? Monitoring', *National Gallery Technical Bulletin*, **5**, 3–13

Further reading

THOMSON, G. (1986), *The Museum Environment*, 2nd edition, Butterworths, London. This book is indispensable. It contains sections on light, relative humidity and air pollution. It is written in two parts, the first part at a less technical level than the second. It has an extensive bibliography and I refer readers to this for all articles published before 1985. I have not repeated those references here except for articles or books of great importance.

ICOM COMMITTEE FOR CONSERVATION, WORKING GROUP 17, LIGHTING AND CLIMATE CONTROL. There are many articles of relevance published in the preprints of the Triennial Meetings.

MUSEUMS ASSOCIATION, UNITED KINGDOM INSTITUTE FOR CONSERVATION and GROUP OF DESIGNERS AND INTERPRETERS IN MUSEUMS, Preprints of *Seminar on Lighting in Museums, Galleries and Historic Houses*, Bristol, 9–10 April 1987. There are 18 papers which address many of the conservation, curatorial and design considerations encountered when dealing with lighting schemes.

27

Buildings, environment and artefacts

Trevor Skempton

Liability, asset, resource – a museum building can be any of these and is probably all three. The response to each, through the design and management of the building, can make or break a project. A building is an *asset* in that it has a market value. Good design and careful improvement can add to this value, even if that is not the prime objective. A building is a *liability* in that it requires continuous servicing and maintenance if it is to retain its value. The museum building can be a *resource*, not just containing space for exhibitions, and related functions, but also making a positive contribution to the visitor's experience as an interesting or historic structure in its own right. This opportunity may be a variable component, realized through short-term flexibility, longer term adaptability, or the sharing of facilities with other activities.

The design and management of buildings requires many specialist skills. However, the particular skill of diagnosing overall problems, recognizing other opportunities and co-ordinating specialist support, is that of the Architect. The Architect is an agent of the Client, employed to design and procure building work and, sometimes, retained to advise on the continuous monitoring and management of the building. The Client, as holder of the purse strings, is the prime mover but is not all powerful; the Architect is at the centre of many conflicting interests and has, at certain times, to adopt a quasi-judicial role (*Figure 27.1*), in particular while administering the contract between Client and Contractor.

Building design and modification

In considering a building project, the Architect should be selected as soon as possible. If a large private practice is chosen, or a public design agency

(such as a City or County Architect's Department), an individual 'Project Architect' should be identified within the organization; good design is not a bureaucratic or committee-based activity. It is also important that the Client, whilst representing a wider project team, is able to speak with a single clear voice. In Britain, and many other countries, equivalent expertise may be found in both private and public sectors (ranging in both sectors from the excellent to the mediocre). Most public offices, but only a few of the larger private practices, are organized on a multi-disciplinary basis giving the advantages of a 'one-stop shop'. However, the individual Architect can be expected to give fair and objective advice on the selection of appropriate specialist consultants to form the overall design team for the project.

Following appointment, the Architect will expect to receive a brief from the Client. Many design problems contain conflicting demands. For example, visitor comfort may conflict with 'ideal' environmental conditions, and requirements for environmental control may conflict with demands for energy conservation. The Architect may be asked to provide a report to aid the briefing process; this could involve an appraisal of an existing building, possible floor loadings, maintenance and energy requirements and costs. A building problem or opportunity may require the design of a new building or substantial structural alterations; alternatively, an Architect may be able to recommend a solution based on more efficient use and management of existing premises. A particular purpose of this chapter is to consider those areas of museum building that affect the preservation of collections, notably those incorporating display and storage. The basic questions to be answered include: What collections are to be stored and displayed? What environmental conditions are required? What type of

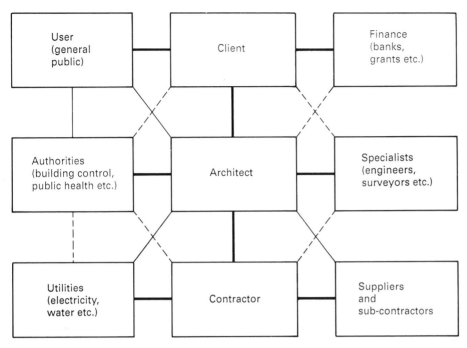

Figure 27.1 A simplified diagram illustrating the relationship between the Client (e.g. Curator), Architect and Contractor, during a building contract

display and storage facilities are envisaged? What materials are acceptable in the construction, decoration and furnishing of the building? What are the constraints on the budget, both capital spending and long-term running costs.

The brief should concentrate on the Client's overall objectives and requirements and not anticipate a particular design solution. It may include specific spatial and technical requirements and cost limitations. It may incorporate the recommendations of museum curators, conservators, 'friends', amenity societies, and those concerned with finance and 'marketing'. The brief does not need to be inclusive, but should provide an agreed starting point for the complex design process, accepting that new ideas and constraints will emerge. The Architect's work is broken down into recognized stages from inception and feasibility studies to sketch proposals, production information (working drawings and specification) and contract control. Of these stages, production information is the most labour intensive and, as far as possible, design principles and cost limits should be fixed before this stage, so that expensive abortive work can be avoided. The lateral thinking and wide involvement that is so essential in the early stages must be replaced by firm discipline later on, if the project is to be realized on time and within budget.

Management, maintenance and energy

Single problems and solutions, those which involve the mobilization of special resources and provide opportunities for promotion and dramatic change, attract most attention. However, during the life of a building, the most significant design decisions may be those relating to the continuous preoccupations of environmental control, energy use, security and building maintenance.

The environment required for the exhibition and storage of collections will be established at the briefing stage. The desired levels of temperature, relative humidity, ventilation and light (natural and artificial) must be agreed. Beyond these general principles, the complexity of the museum environment must be recognized; the microclimate can vary within a single gallery, within display cabinets or alongside a cold wall. There is also the problem of the live hazard; roof lagging can harbour golden spider beetle, proximity to kitchens can encourage rodents; infestation can be introduced via incoming material or the packing cases for travelling exhibitions. Storage areas, if infrequently surveyed and carelessly designed, are particularly vulnerable.

There is no such thing as a completely stable environment, and frequent or continous monitoring is necessary. In the previous chapter environmental monitoring techniques were discussed, but some mention should be made of combined systems. Building automation systems exist for monitoring and control of energy use, fuel efficiency and temperature. Similar systems exist for security. It is not difficult to extend these to include the measurement of relative humidity. The type of overall control suitable to a museum or art gallery is illustrated, in simple form, in *Figure 27.2*. It must be emphasized that such a system is dependent on the ability of the operator to understand and react to the data being presented. For example, a wide range of buildings in Newcastle upon Tyne are monitored within the City Architect's Department. However, if an individual client, such as a large museum, had the appropriate expertise, monitoring could be de-centralized to an individual building or group of buildings. A further option is for the monitoring and the control to be carried out by the Architect's Department and for a separate terminal to be installed within the museum building to display daily information for the benefit of curatorial and conservation staff.

In the Introduction, mention was made of solutions to problems which evolve during the development of new buildings or the adaptation of older buildings. The following three examples

illustrate the solving of a specific environmental problem in an existing gallery, the conversion of an historic building into a museum and the first steps in the design of a major new building.

A problem within a gallery

The Museum of Science and Engineering in Newcastle is housed in a large building, built by the Co-operative Society in 1901. The Maritime Gallery is on an upper floor with a high ceiling and a large area of glazing. In the absence of air-conditioning (which can impose its own problems) the gallery is subject to both daily and seasonal temperature fluctuations, with corresponding effects on relative humidity.

In 1989, the City Architect was approached to find a solution to an environmental problem within the gallery. This had three apparent components: high condensation arising from the humidification system, over-heating caused by inefficient display lighting, and a continuous unpleasant odour.

Temperature and relative humidity levels were monitored and recorded, both in the main gallery area and inside a display case, first with the

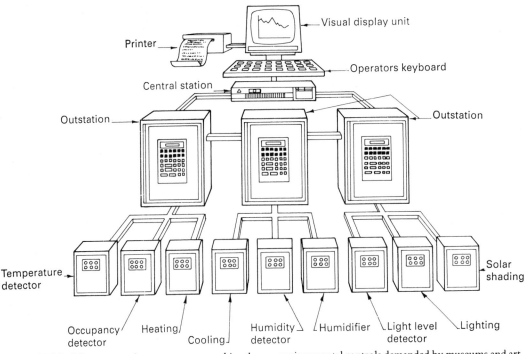

Figure 27.2 Building automation systems can combine the monitoring and control techniques developed for energy conservation and security with the sophisticated environmental controls demanded by museums and art galleries

humidifier on for 8 days, and then with it off for 6 days. From the results, it was apparent that the display cases were acting as a buffer, and that the operation of the humidifiers could be substantially reduced with little effect on the relative humidity within the display cases. Although the odour problem could have had many possible causes, it was suspected that it was linked to temperature and humidity.

New controls were added to enable humidifiers to operate on an intermittent cycle, a new efficient low-voltage lighting system was installed and the heating controls were checked and recalibrated. The condensation problem has been reduced, and humidifier operating cost reduced by one-third. The over-heating problem has been reduced with a 50 per cent saving on electricity used for lighting. The odour problem seems to have been solved. The cost of the new installations will be recovered through savings made over a 3-year 'pay-back' period. This was a specific solution which would not have been applicable if, for example, significant exhibits were not housed within display cases, but it illustrates the variable factors which exist in the everyday problems affecting museums.

New museum, old landmark

Some museums are housed in purpose-designed new buildings, but the adaptation of older buildings to a new museum use is more common. Sometimes the museum building is as worthy of conservation as the museum collection. The existing character of the building and the distortions that it will impose on the museum arrangement must be accepted as positive opportunities, as illustrated by the example of the Ceredigion Museum in Aberystwyth.

In 1980 an opportunity was taken to re-house a small county museum into a former Edwardian Music Hall (*Figure 27.3*). The building offered much greater space, as well as the potential for displaying the collections in a more interesting way. Although not an outstanding piece of architecture, the theatre was a popular local landmark and an object of

Figure 27.3 The Ceredigion Museum, Aberystwyth, Wales. An opportunity was taken to re-house a County Museum within a redundant Music Hall. The practical success of the project depended on close liaison between Curator and Architect at every stage, from the initial idea and down to the smallest detail

interest in its own right. A balance was struck between preserving the theatre in a form that was instantly recognizable (with the implied possibility of a future reconversion), while arranging the exhibits in a sufficiently positive manner to ensure that not all attention was focussed on the restored stage and scenery.

A close working relationship between the curatorial team and the Architect's team maintained this balance through the extensive building restoration and conversion work, as well as in the reconstruction within the auditorium of exhibits such as a pharmacy and a Cardiganshire farmhouse. Full-size mock-ups were made, at the design stage, to assess the impact of the more controversial structures. Consultation extended to the smallest details of presentation and graphic design, and to the range of technical issues such as environmental control and workshop and storage facilities. If the full potential of a project is to be realized, the importance of an early close relationship between Curator and Architect cannot be overstated.

Ideas competition

The building project, at all levels, depends on an alliance between technical skill and imagination. However strong the former, any scheme is constrained by the quality of the overall vision. Design competitions can allow full rein to the imagination; they have produced many successful buildings as well as much argument and heartache. They can produce great wasted effort and consequent disillusion; they require the suspension of Client–Architect contact at a critical phase in the project development. However, they can also provide a focus for public interest and debate; they can act as a showcase for new talent; they can allow unusual and adventurous

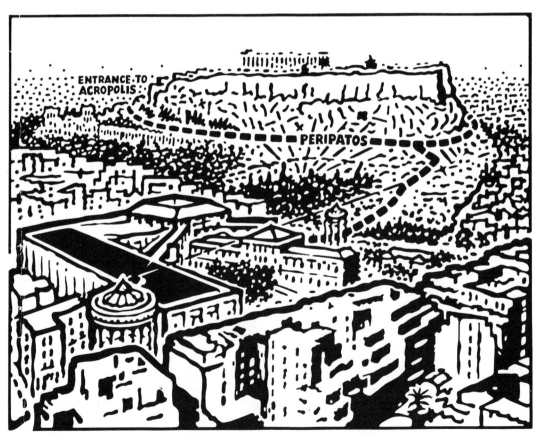

Figure 27.4 The Acropolis Museum, Athens. An international design competition produced a wealth of ideas for several potential sites. This sketch shows a proposal to re-open an ancient route around the citadel – the 'peripatos'

– to allow easy access from a new museum within the built-up area to the east, away from the sensitive archaeological zone

ideas to be tested. Design competitions have been a popular means of selecting an Architect over the centuries, and a recent example is the competition for the design for a new Acropolis Museum in Athens (*Figure 27.4*).

Controversy surrounds the restoration and exhibition of the Acropolis Sculptures (not least over the home of the 'Elgin Marbles'). The existing museum is clearly inadequate – it provides no protection from the City's polluted air, and has limited potential due to its site in a hollow on the citadel itself.

An international design competition was organized in 1990 in which entrants were encouraged to explore a wide range of possibilities. Three potential sites were offered, one at the base of the Acropolis opposite the entrance, a second some distance away but still within the open archaeological area and a third also at the base of the Acropolis, but at the east end, away from the entrance and within the crowded residential quarter of Makryanni. More than 400 Architects entered, and produced a wealth of ideas and a range of technical proposals which could then be subjected to detailed analysis and feasibility studies.

Many of these ideas could not have surfaced through a closed quantitative and analytical approach to the problem. An essential part of the design process is the conceptual stage at which imaginative leaps and lateral thinking utilize the ingenuity and speed of the human mind in ways that we do not fully understand.

28

Conservation and storage: archival paper

Michael Bottomley

Introduction

This chapter deals mostly with paper documents that become archives: that is, non-current records selected for permanent preservation. The chapter concentrates on the environment and equipment needed to promote the physical survival of such records. The techniques of repair of damaged documents are not discussed, as this should be left to competent and qualified archive conservators.

Because the chapter aims to introduce aspects of the archive profession to Curators, it may be useful to consider briefly how archives may usefully relate to the world of museums. Museums, archives and libraries are the three areas which comprise the information industry, dealing with objects, unpublished texts and published texts, respectively. Archivists are trained to deal with unique and irreplaceable documents in quantity (e.g. my own repository holds about 10,000 linear metres of documents) and quality ranging from the priceless to the barely worth keeping. They rescue records from festering cellars, attics, etc., have them repaired when necessary, sort and catalogue them and make them available to the public. Their first concern is the physical survival of records; and their second concern is the principle of provenance, whereby the arrangement of archives must not be disrupted without very good reason. Documents separated from their context lose most of their evidential value. Such documents may be interesting curiosities to display but, like finds looted from an unknown archaeological site, they represent lost opportunities rather than significant information. Therefore Curators are urged to preserve each accession of archives as a separate entity and to preserve the original arrangement of documents within each archive accession.

Most archive services include Conservators, who combine craft skills with the theoretical knowledge to organize the proper physical care of documents. It is a normal part of an archive service's work to provide advice and practical assistance (although the latter may not always be free of charge) to owners and custodians of records: Archivists have a moral duty to concern themselves with the well-being of all records, whether in private hands, a record office or in another institution such as a museum. Therefore no Curator who lacks in-house archive conservation facilities should suffer in silence when faced with problems of conserving documents. He or she should waste no time in consulting an Archivist.

The first part of this chapter summarizes the theory behind good conservation practice, the second describes the environmental conditions considered good for paper, the third considers harmful agents and how they may be countered, while the fourth looks at the equipment that is necessary or useful. Although this chapter concentrates on the care of paper documents, it should be noted that archives increasingly include documents in other media such as sound and video tapes, photographs and computer-generated records. The newer media require specialized storage and treatment, for which the relevant British Standards should be consulted in the first instance.

General principles and procedures

Active conservation

The first priority of an institution should be the physical preservation of its holdings. Archival conservation encompasses proper storage, proper repair methods and proper use of documents. Traditionally, archive conservation was called 'document repair', and attention was focused on the craft of mending damaged documents. More recently, repair has been regarded as an expensive last resort with no prospect of achieving, on its own, a total solution to the problems of preserving a repository's archival holdings.

The physical well-being of archives cannot be guaranteed by repair facilities, however lavishly funded. Most archive repositories have enough damaged documents to occupy their Conservators for at least 50 years, and the queues of casualties needing treatment tend to lengthen due to damaged items amongst fresh accessions, damage occurring to documents already in a repository, and the self-destructive tendencies of most twentieth-century documents which make up an increasing proportion of archive holdings.

To identify those documents that need active conservation, custodians should organize conservation surveys of their archive holdings. Trained staff should select documents in which the damage needs to be halted or reversed. The cause of damage should be established, which may indicate the best treatment (e.g. if documents are damaged by over-use, they should be copied and the copies used instead).

The demand for document-repair facilities is much greater than the supply, so custodians must allocate priorities to their damaged documents based on the severity of damage, the historical, legal and commercial value of the documents, their likely future use as items for display and consultation, and so on.

Documents selected for repair should be placed in the care of a professional Archive Conservator who should be given some indication of the value of each document, and told whether it merits an expensive state-of-the-art treatment, or a sound but minimal holding operation. Conservators should also be told the likely level and type of use of a document, which may affect the choice of treatment. There may also need to be discussion on how the documents were stored previously because, for instance, a Conservator may quite rightly change a folded document to a flat or rolled format which could not be returned to its exact original location. It is important that the custodian's written views and requirements accompany the documents: Conservators cannot be expected to memorize verbal comments on a piece of work that may not be started until days or weeks later.

Custodians who send work to archive conservators should be aware that the latter work to a set of principles which may not be entirely familiar to museum staff. In archive repair, every treatment should be reversible, only the minimum necessary intervention should take place, only methods and substances that the test of time has proved effective and harmless should be allowed, no text should be obscured, and repair must not be confused with restoration (a repaired section must be clearly distinguishable from the original document, and no attempt made to replace missing text). The last two points reflect the archive profession's links with the legal profession, and consequent concern for the evidential integrity of documents, which over-rides aesthetic considerations.

It must be emphasized that active conservation should be carried out by professional archive conservators. Amateur conservators often damage documents by unsound practices and treatments. Custodians who lack professional conservation staff, and who have records in need of repair, should consult their local record office in the first instance: most are listed by the Royal Commission on Historical Manuscripts (1991).

Custodians should consider photocopying or photographing important documents before sending them for repair. This preserves the text in case something should go disastrously wrong, and also provides a record of the documents' appearance before the changes caused by conservation treatment.

Passive conservation

Prevention is better and cheaper than cure, and custodians should therefore organize their premises, equipment and procedures in such a way that records are, as much as possible, saved from the need to enter a conservation workshop.

Premises and equipment are discussed later. Procedures need to be worked out, agreed and rehearsed with the aim of preventing damage to documents, and limiting the damage if disaster should strike. To prevent damage, it should be made clear to all staff that conservation is everybody's concern, and includes duties such as preventing unauthorized access, clearing leaves from drains to prevent flooding and controlling public consultation of archives (by limiting numbers of documents issued, insisting on no pens, bags, food, etc., in reading rooms and careful invigilation).

All staff should be trained to handle documents with a proper respect, and to make sure that the public do likewise. Staff should also be trained to react correctly to fires, floods or other calamities, e.g. they should know how to cut off the building's gas, water and electricity, and how to contact plumbers, glaziers, builders, etc., during and outside normal working times. Keyholders and 'disaster co-ordinators' need to be appointed, and a store of equipment should be ready to cope with disasters. The Bibliography given at the end of this chapter includes texts on disaster planning.

An unpleasant but useful preparation for disaster is the allocation of salvage priorities. No custodian likes to classify any holdings as expendable, but after a fire or flood it may be necessary to decide quickly which items should be saved first. Therefore

Curators should identify the most precious documents, mark their containers accordingly and train staff in the location and recognition of such items.

The ideal climate

Temperature

Inappropriate environmental conditions are the primary cause of damage to records. Low temperatures should be maintained to reduce chemical deterioration of documents of which items of nineteenth- and twentieth-century origin are particularly sensitive. Paper may look 'healthy' when stored initially, but over the years it can waste away as the organic dyes in the ink slowly oxidize, and the fibres of paper gradually break down, attacked by atmospheric acid. Such changes, like all chemical reactions, are accelerated by heat, and it has been suggested that every 10°F rise in temperature can halve the life of paper (Briggs, 1980). Therefore, paper is preserved by keeping it cold. However, three pitfalls need to be avoided. First, a cold repository may cause discomfort to staff. Second, archives may be damaged by moving them from a very cold strong-room to a warm reading room and back again, unless they are given plenty of time to adjust to the changes. Third, a fall in the strong-room temperature tends to cause a rise in relative humidity, and a high relative humidity encourages mould. The ideal temperature is thus a compromise between the need to keep archives as cool as possible, and the need to avoid the problems associated with cold strong-rooms. A temperature between 13 and 18°C is considered correct, without large or sudden fluctuations.

Relative humidity

The relative humidity (RH) of a document storage area is even more crucial than its temperature. If the air is too dry, paper becomes brittle and leather bindings may crack. If the air is too moist, documents may be damaged by fungi or bacteria. Paper documents should be stored at a RH of between 50 and 65 per cent. If the archive includes parchment or vellum documents, the RH should be kept between 55 and 65 per cent, since those materials are less tolerant of dry air than is paper.

Paper documents are damaged even more by fluctuations in RH than by fluctuations in temperature, because the documents themselves contain moisture, and their moisture content varies according to how moist or dry the surrounding air is. Paper, being mostly cellulose, readily absorbs moisture, and expands in the process. As it dries out, it contracts. Variations in RH therefore impose strains on the structure of paper, and the RH should not be allowed to move up or down by more than 5 per cent.

Air movement and purity

The air itself should be encouraged to move, since moving air discourages mould, and creates a more even distribution of heat and moisture within a room. The recommended rate of air circulation is six changes of air every hour. In addition, the air should be clean, with the maximum possible exclusion of dust particles greater than $2\,\mu m$, and with no less than $10\,\mu g/m^3$ of sulphur dioxide.

The enemies of paper

Incorrect temperature and humidity

Controlling the temperature of a repository is usually a simple matter, but the RH, which is more important, is more difficult both to monitor and to regulate. If the air is too dry, the cheapest way to raise the RH is usually to lower the temperature. However, this course of action may not be acceptable, especially if the same heating system warms the staff as well as the records. In such a case, a humidifier is needed to put moisture into the atmosphere.

If the air is too moist, ways of lowering the RH need to be considered. The simplest method may be to raise the temperature, since each rise of 1°C will lower the RH by about 4 per cent, but this in turn presents problems. Heating is expensive. Raising the temperature (lowering the RH) causes brittleness and shortens the life of paper. Unless the heat is distributed evenly throughout the strongroom, variations in RH will exist and this should be avoided. A simple remedy would be to use fans to keep the air circulating. A more cost-effective method, without the use of heat, would be dehumidification, which extracts water from moist air without an unacceptable rise in temperature.

Windows in strong-rooms present problems. They cause fluctuations in temperature and RH, with areas near windows becoming hot and dry, especially in summer, or cold and moist, especially in winter. If there must be windows, they should be double- or triple-glazed.

Light

The damaging effects of light on paper, together with recommendations for its reduction or elimination are listed in Chapter 5. If archival documents are exhibited, this should be done in accordance with BS 5454 (British Standards Institution, 1989). Ultraviolet lamps are often used to decipher faded documents, but should be used only when absolutely necessary and then only for short periods.

Atmospheric pollution

Polluted air may be harder both to diagnose and to rectify than incorrect temperature and humidity. Dust is bad for records, but it does at least show itself on flat surfaces. Sulphur dioxide, on the other hand, is more insidious, and more dangerous to paper. Cheap modern paper, made with mechanically ground wood pulp contains lignin which readily absorbs sulphur dioxide and the lignin thus becomes acid. The acid attacks the fibres of the paper, which becomes brittle and eventually disintegrates. This kind of attack is most severe against nineteenth- and twentieth-century paper, but even earlier, high-quality paper is at risk (Hudson and Milner, 1961). The danger is not just confined to repositories in large cities: it has been shown that a small town with practically no industry has an atmosphere which attacks paper.

The atmosphere can be tested for sulphur dioxide with strips of paper (the preparation of which is described in the *Society of Archivists' Repairers' News Sheet*, 16 February 1970) or custodians may prefer simply to assume that the air is polluted. Options include the installation of an air-conditioning system which washes out sulphur dioxide from incoming air or, more simply, windows (if any) should be closed and records wrapped in acid-free paper or packed in acid-free boxes, or both. Such wrappings and boxes will gradually absorb atmospheric acid and so to prevent them from transmitting acidity to their contents they may need to be discarded before they have obviously worn out. Containers and records can be tested with a pH meter or, less accurately but more easily, with pH indicator strips. Ideally paper should have a pH between 7 and 8.5 (that is, it should be neutral or slightly alkaline, to counter future acid attack). If the pH reading is below 5.5 remedial action is required, and expert advice should be sought.

Microbes, insects and people

Several life forms pose a threat to archives. At the microscopic level, fungi and bacteria need to be controlled by keeping the RH below 70 per cent. Documents that have been attacked by micro-organisms and are not fragile can be carefully cleaned out of doors with a soft brush, preferably on a warm summer day, and they may be stored in the correct environment. This first-aid approach will reduce the number of spores brought into the archive. For seriously damaged documents, an expert conservator should be consulted. Insects and insecticides used to be dealt with by the custodian or Curator, but today a more professional approach is advocated. The prevention of infestation needs to play a more important role in archive care, reducing the reliance on pesticides. Undoubtedly certain pesticides will have an adverse effect on the artefacts themselves; their current use is also the subject of continuous health-and-safety legislation. A further discussion of insect pests can be found in Chapter 24.

People can be a greater menace than both micro-organisms and insects, and both the staff and the public must be made to treat records with great care. Handling should be minimized. Records subject to frequent use should be made available in the form of transcripts, photocopies or microfilm. Further discussion of this topic can be found in Chapter 43.

Flooding

Should a flood occur, custodians need a contingency plan to deal with documents soaked by water (Gibson and Reay, 1980). Loose papers can be spread out to dry naturally but books take too long to dry out in this way and the pages may grow mould or become a soggy pulp. If ovens or fan-heaters are used to accelerate the drying of books, the outsides become parched while the insides remain wet. The best solution appears to be vacuum or freeze drying: each book is wrapped and frozen. Wrapping material may be release or archival paper or polythene bags, all of which have been used successfully. To remove moisture the books are put in a vacuum chamber together with a large dish of silica gel (to absorb moisture), together with an approved mould inhibitor. A vacuum of about 745 mmHg is maintained until the books are dry (which takes between 80 and 200 hours, depending on size). In certain situations the freeze-drying process may be more appropriate because it eliminates mould growth during the drying stage. When the dry books reach room temperature, repair can begin. Custodians should therefore be able to acquire plastic bags or wrapping paper in a hurry, and have rapid access to freezers, for example, by keeping up-to-date information on the nearest cold-storage company. Once the wet books are frozen they will not deteriorate further, and the rest of the procedure is less urgent.

Fire

To protect archives from fire, the repository should be separate from other buildings, and the floors, doors and ceilings should have at least 4 hours fire-resistance. Fire officers and building departments will advise on fire precautions, electrical safety, flame-retardant paints and ceiling tiles. Common sense will suggest policies such as no gas appliances and no smoking near records. There should be a fire-alarm system based on smoke detectors (which tend to react to fires sooner than heat detectors), and a direct link to the Fire Brigade (which should be advised in advance of the special needs of the repository so that, for example, water is not used unnecessarily). An automatic extinguisher is worth considering, especially to protect strong-rooms, which firemen might not be able to enter quickly. Gas extinguishers cause less damage to records than water or foam, and halon gas appears increasingly to be preferred to carbon dioxide although concern for the ozone layer may reverse this trend. Halon is less dangerous to people, and requires less storage space. Carbon dioxide, on the other hand, is said to deal more effectively with deep-seated fires. The repository should also be equipped with hand-operated carbon dioxide or powder extinguishers for small fires.

Inherent enemies

A further group of enemies of documents consists of poor ingredients in the documents themselves. Most modern records are created with built-in self-destructive devices such as alum size or lignin which promote acid attack, and ink made with organic dye that fades. This problem is not confined to twentieth-century records. For example, Victorian tracing paper was treated with oil which hardens and darkens, rendering many architectural and engineering drawings brittle and indecipherable, and volumes of damp-press copy letters consist of tissue paper bearing a thin trace of watery ink which in thousands of cases is fading towards invisibility. In addition, many records eventually suffer from rust caused by staples, pins and paper clips. Such items should, of course, be removed and custodians should consider, with the help of expert advice, how to deal with the other forms of archival self-destruction, deciding which of such records should be saved by proper (and expensive) treatment, and which should be 'preserved' by copying on to a more permanent medium. Silver halide microfilm (processed and stored in accordance with BS 1153 British Standards Institution, 1975) is the cheapest way of making long-lasting copies. Better and more user-friendly copies can be made (albeit more expensively) with a photocopier, using high-quality paper and dry toner powder with a high carbon content.

Accommodation and equipment

Premises

The archive building, as has been noted, should be separate from other buildings, on well-drained ground, and record strong-rooms are best built of reinforced concrete insulated on the inside to prevent condensation. Windows are good for staff but bad for records and, in archive strong-rooms, should be eschewed. If windows are provided, they should be unopenable, double-glazed with strengthened glass and screened against ultraviolet light.

Shelves

It is cheaper to shelve a few large rooms than to install the same amount of shelving in a number of small rooms. Also, it is cheaper to erect stacks of shelving 4 m or more high in a single-storey building than to divide the same amount of shelving between the different floors of a building. Shelves are usually about 1 m long and, if they are made deep enough from front to back, they can hold twice as many boxes by double-banking. Double-banking the boxes can save some capital outlay because only about half as many uprights are needed to support a given number of boxes. The main saving, however, is in space, because fewer gangways are needed. Double-banking is a useful step towards the kind of high-density storage that mobile shelving achieves. Triple-banking of records has been suggested as a way of saving even more space, but in such an arrangement the boxes at the back of each shelf are virtually inaccessible.

Mobile shelving is limited to a height of about 2.5 to 3 m. It is expensive compared with static shelves and it does not allow air to circulate as freely as in static shelving. Only one gangway in a stack can be opened at a time, which may slow down the production of records. Also, any records which project beyond the end of a shelf are liable to be crushed. On the other hand, mobile shelving can hold almost twice as many records as static shelving of the same height and floor area, and it gives better protection against fire, water and polluted air because, apart from a single open gangway, the shelves form a compact block of records which is more resistant to damage than are records which are more thinly distributed (in the same way that a bound volume is harder to damage than separate sheets of paper). Therefore, mobile shelving makes sense in strong-rooms with ceilings of normal height (2.5–3 m), where each square metre of floor space is costly, where the atmosphere may be polluted, and where documents are not often needed in such a hurry that simultaneous access to different parts of the strong-room is vital. Thus, mobile shelving is worth considering for archives in a repository in a city centre. With static shelving, a typical repository will run out of storage space almost twice as quickly.

If mobile shelving is chosen, there is the choice of power-operated, mechanically assisted systems or hand-operated ones. The choice depends on the funding available, on the weight of records to be moved and on the fitness of staff. Most people can move a couple of tons of records with a hand-operated system. About 5 tons can be moved without too much effort by mechanically assisted systems. Beyond such weights, a powered system is necessary. Whatever system is used, the tracks on which the racks run should not project above floor level. It is dangerous, and inconvenient, for staff to have to step over obstacles, especially when carrying heavy items or when using kick-steps.

Shelving is normally constructed of either steel or wood. A common choice is steel shelving of the angle-post type made to BS 826 (British Standards Institution, 1978); and this is preferable in many ways to wooden shelving. The latter is inflammable, it can rot, harbour insect pests, produce splinters and, because of its lignin content, it soaks up atmospheric acid. There is little difference in cost. Whatever material is used, the bottom shelf should be about 150 mm above floor level, to avoid immediate inundation and to allow air movement.

Non-standard storage

Outsize documents, especially maps and drawings, present problems. Maps should be stored flat if possible, not folded or rolled. Large, shallow drawers work well if repository staff are careful about producing and replacing the maps, if the pile of maps in each drawer is not too high, and if the map on top of each pile does not curl and get caught whenever the drawer is opened. If maps are consulted frequently, vertical storage may be better. This is said to cause distortion of scale, but in fact worse damage can be caused by pulling a map out of a heap of horizontally stored maps and subsequently ramming it back again.

Outsize maps usually have to be rolled. Rolling causes some distortion, but this is minimal if the map is rolled around the outside of a cylinder of large diameter. The map should then be wrapped in acid-free paper, or buckram. Alternatively, maps can be sandwiched between sheets of clear melinex film and rolled to form cylinders of large diameter, fastened with cotton tape. The melinex protects the maps during use. Rolled maps should be shelved horizontally, supported for their full length, and not project into corridors.

Loose papers

If papers need to be clipped together, brass paper clips should be used. If they are to be bundled, the bundles should be tied with unbleached cotton tape about 10 mm wide (string cuts into paper, and rubber bands decompose).

Boxes

Where possible, papers and books should be placed in boxes. Most record offices use boxes made of a single piece of container board of 2 mm caliper, having a pH value around 7, lined with kraft paper and stitched with brass or stainless-steel staples. The lids should be made in the same way. Lids that are 50–75 mm deep are cheaper than full-depth lids, and can be removed and replaced more easily. Full-depth lids, on the other hand, strengthen the box and make it harder for dusty or polluted air to enter it. If the repository is sited in a place where the air is exceptionally clean, or if it has air-conditioning, the records may benefit from ventilation holes in the boxes. In most buildings, however, the air is not so pure, and ventilation holes are merely another hazard. Unboxed volumes should be packed vertically, just tightly enough on the shelf to support each other. Very large volumes should be laid flat on their sides.

Labels indicating the contents of each box should be attached to the boxes rather than the lids, unless the boxes have permanently attached hinged lids. Boxes with detachable full-depth lids need labels on both boxes and lids to prevent them from being mis-matched, resulting in boxes being misplaced. Labels should be attached firmly. Rolls of self-adhesive labels are not expensive and they can be typed to produce neat box labels at speed.

Monitoring the atmosphere

To maintain the correct atmosphere in record stores, regular monitoring and control are needed. Monitoring requires easily read thermometers with good, large divisions for each degree. Hygrometers are also necessary, and three types can be considered. First, electrical-resistance hygrometers which tend to be temperamental, especially if the air is polluted, and need regular recalibration. Second, there are direct-reading dial hygrometers in which treated paper or bundles of hair absorb atmospheric moisture, and expand and contract as they become more or less moist. These also need regular recalibration. Third, wet- and dry-bulb thermometers indicate the rate at which water on the wet bulb evaporates. This type of hygrometer is available in three forms. Static models are simply hung up in strong-rooms; these can be unreliable because air movement accelerates evaporation so that readings are affected by draughts and by people moving about. Whirling hygrometers can be more accurate because rotating the thermometers is supposed to accelerate the air movement to a constant speed. This should eliminate the inaccuracy of static hygrometers but, in fact, the readings can vary, depending on who uses the instrument, and how vigorously. Thirdly, there are Assman-type hygrometers, which cost about five times as much as whirling ones. They have motor-driven fans to draw air over the bulbs at the correct speed.

The direct-reading dial type hygrometer is very easy for respository staff to use and, although its calibration gradually drifts out of true, this seems better than the unpredictable fluctuations to which whirling hygrometers are subject. It makes sense, therefore, to install dial hygrometers in record stores, and to check their accuracy periodically against an Assman hygrometer. The positioning of hygrometers needs a little thought: readings should not only be taken in the main gangways, but also in parts of the strong-rooms where cold, stagnant air is suspected. Thermohygrographs should be considered if rapid fluctuations of temperature and humidity are suspected, or if stores are rarely visited by staff.

Controlling the atmosphere

The strong-room climate (if it is not naturally suitable) is best controlled by an air-conditioning system. If this is not possible, humidifiers or dehumidifiers need to be installed. Humidifiers are most likely to be needed in winter when central heating tends to dry out the air. The best kind of humidifier appears to be the steam humidifier, though a second limiting humidistat should be installed. Other types are more complicated mechanically, and tend to cool the air. Dehumidifiers are more likely to be needed in the summer; the refrigerant type is preferred by most record offices.

Conclusion

It is apparent that records, and especially modern papers, need carefully controlled conditions to ensure their long-term survival. Custodians should aim for the conditions specified in BS 5454 (British Standards Institution, 1989) and, in addition to routine consultations with fire protection, crime prevention and health and safety officers, custodians should liaise with archivists.

References

BRIGGS, J. R. (1980), 'Environmental control for modern records', in Peterbridge, G. (Ed.), *Cambridge 1980: International Conference on the Conservation of Library and Archive Materials and the Graphic Arts*, Institute of Paper Conservation, London

BRITISH STANDARDS INSTITUTION (1989), *BS 5454, Recommendations for the storage and exhibition of documents*, British Standards Institution, Milton Keynes

GIBSON, J. A. and REAY, D. (1980), Drying rare old books soaked by flood water, *Museums Journal*, 80(3), 147–148

HUDSON, F. L. and MILNER, W. D. (1961), Atmospheric sulphur and the durability of paper, *Journal of the Society of Archivists*, 2(4), 166–167

ROYAL COMMISSION ON HISTORICAL MANUSCRIPTS (1991), *Record Repositories in the United Kingdom*, HMSO, London

Bibliography

ANDERSON, H. and MCINTYRE, J. E. (1985), *Planning Manual for Disaster Control*, National Library of Scotland, Edinburgh

BAYNES-COPE, A. D. (1981), *Caring for Books and Documents*, British Museum, London

BAYNES-COPE, A. D. and COLLINGS, T. J. (1980), 'Some specifications for materials and techniques used in the conservation of archives', *Journal of the Society of Archivists*, 6(6), 384–386

BRITISH STANDARDS INSTITUTION (1988 and 1980), *Recommendations for repair and allied processes for the treatment of documents, BS 4971: Parts 1 and 2*, British Standards Institution, London

CHAPMAN, P. (1990), *Guidelines on Preservation and Conservation Policies in the Archives and Library Heritage*, UNESCO, Paris

CUNHA, G. D. M. (1967), *Conservation of Library Materials*, Scarecrow Press, Methuen, New Jersey

JENKIN, I. T. (1987), 'Disaster planning and preparedness: an outline disaster control plan', *British Library Information Guide 5*, The British Library, London

PETERBRIDGE, G. (Ed.) (1980), *Cambridge 1980: International Conference on the Conservation of Library and Archive Materials and the Graphic Arts*, Institute of Paper Conservation, London

RITZENTHALER, M. L. (1983), *Archives and Manuscripts: Conservation*, Society of American Archivists, Chicago, IL

THOMSON, G. and BULLOCK, L. (1980), 'Simple control and measurement of relative humidity in museums', *Information Sheet No. 24*, Museums Association, London

29

Conservation and storage: prints, drawings and water-colours

Jane McAusland

Introduction

Museums inevitably house quantities of paper-supported works of art such as drawings, prints and water-colours. To be aware of the conservation problems of preserving them, the Curator needs to be familiar with, and vigilant over, mainly simple routine procedures and tasks.

Agents harmful to paper: the damage likely to be rendered

Light

The survival of many paper artefacts has been aided by proper storage, either in bound volumes or mounted and boxed away from exposure to visible light and ultraviolet (UV) radiation.

Preventive measures

(1) Use of UV filters in frames, on lamps, windows and show-cases.
(2) Careful choice of background colours in exhibition areas and the use of reflected light. Dark, light-absorbing backgrounds necessitate more highly illuminated areas and reducing this level to 50 lux makes for gloomy exhibition of prints and drawings. Lighter walls surrounding exhibited works reflect the light, making for ease of viewing while keeping to the specified light level.
(3) Careful choice of light-source colour. Warm rather than cool light sources are best for viewing.
(4) Rotation of the collection.
(5) Elimination of heat from light sources by means of fans and reflectors.
(6) Use of facsimile prints and drawings. This is not a popular solution, but may be a last resort, especially when valuable works are involved.
(7) Time switches in rooms or on show-cases. Blinds to cut down direct light. Night security lights of 10 lux.

Relative humidity

Paper is hygroscopic because cellulose fibres readily absorb water vapour from the atmosphere, and it is therefore likely to be adversely affected by extremes of relative humidity as its moisture content adjusts to reach equilibrium with the relative humidity of its environment. Below 40 per cent relative humidity (RH) the cellulose fibres of paper become dehydrated and embrittled, shrinking takes place causing buckling and distortion, tension builds up between pigments, gums and inks on the dehydrated paper, and flaking is likely. Above 70 per cent RH, the increased moisture content of the paper is likely to attract mould growth from spores in the atmosphere attracted by moisture-activated impurities in the paper. Even without mould growth, these impurities will be activated and cause chemical destruction of the paper support of the print or drawing. Damage will certainly occur when the RH is below 30 per cent or above 70 per cent, while acute fluctuations are extremely damaging to prints and drawings, as they expand and contract, leading to physical breakdown.

Preventive measures

Both temperature and RH must be controlled to obtain the optimum RH, that is, between 50 and 60 per cent. Ideally, air-conditioning should be installed and maintained to keep this balance. If this is too costly, a Curator may nevertheless take various steps to guard the collection. The storage area should be selected carefully; there should be no direct sunlight, plenty of ventilation and no damp, and minimal atmospheric pollution and dust. Prints and drawings stored in Solander boxes[1] or drawers will automatically acquire microclimates of their own, leaving changes in the environmental RH of the rooms to fluctuate more widely. Further bolstering against RH fluctuation may be achieved by the use of moisture-absorbing agents such as silica gel which may be incorporated into the boxes in small bags. However, the Curator must realize that when the storage environment is not controlled the silica gel will have to be continually conditioned – a very labour-intensive business.

Humidifiers and dehumidifiers may be necessary. On the whole, these are cheap to buy and run, and most small museums should be able to afford them.

Pollution

Paper may become chemically unstable through contact with materials that leach acids and other pollutants, or absorb impurities from the atmosphere. The purity of the materials of paper-making, and the lengths to which the manufacturers go to purify them further build a life-span into paper. For example, linen is very pure, and therefore, has an advantage over wood-based paper. Although, with the right chemical treatments, the latter can be made as pure as linen, it needs much more processing at the pulping stage of paper-making to eliminate harmful residual bleaches, lignin and other acidic materials. Acid sizes are particularly damaging (McAusland and Stevens, 1979). As paper degrades, it changes and darkens in colour, becoming brown and brittle.

Some inks, pigments and dyes in works of art on paper may chemically break down its cellulose. Copper pigments and iron gall inks are the most common offenders. On the other hand, alkaline pigments such as pastels prolong the life of the paper. It is clear, therefore, that all storage materials should be as pure as possible, chemically stable, and free from damaging agents, to protect not only the paper support, but also the pigments, inks and dyes that may be chemically altered by an unstable environment. Gums, pastes, and glues, in contact with or close to prints, drawing and water-colours should also be considered potentially damaging pollutants; if impure, they may introduce more chemical instability.

Because paper is naturally highly hygroscopic, atmospheric hydrogen sulphide, nitrogen dioxide and other gases with water vapour, will be converted to sulphuric and nitric acids along with other damaging chemicals, and taken into the hollow paper fibres causing them to break down. Ozone is harmful to organic materials, including paper. Oils, fats, and minute suspended particles from the atmosphere settle on exposed prints and drawings and find their way into the crevices between the paper fibres.

Preventive measures

(1) With inherently unstable paper, the conservation treatment of de-acidification or alkaline buffering may be implemented. However, as many of the pigments and inks of prints and drawings may be pH sensitive, it is *not* a recommended treatment for such works (Daniels, 1982). Also, a slight deposit is always apparent after this treatment and some de-acidificants may discolour the paper. Only in extreme cases should this treatment be used, and then only by a conservator who may also decide to rinse works to rid them of their pollutants.

(2) Mounts and storage boxes, drawers and other housings should be as acid-free as possible. A pH of 8 is ideal for these materials as it has a built-in margin against future absorbed pollutants (see Bradley, Chapter 45).

(3) The air should be filtered by an air-conditioner. If one is not available, the rooms chosen for storage should be clean and as pollution-free as possible.

Monitoring equipment

Acidity in paper may be tested with a pH meter, but complete accuracy is difficult to achieve as only the surface can be tested. Colour-change indicators as well as full pH testing may be used on storage materials. There are other tests for damaging agents such as ground wood, alum and rosin (Harding, 1972).

Moulds

Moulds are saprophytic fungi and grow on any material that provides moisture and organic nutrients. Even fingerprints offer enough substrate for their growth. Paper and sizing solutions in paper, animal glue, adhesives, starch pastes and acquired dust particles are all attractive to moulds. However, the right conditions must prevail for moulds to thrive, moisture and heat being the necessary factors. Spores may lie dormant for years and become activated only when the RH rises above 70 per cent.

The most common mould or fungal attack on prints and drawings is known as 'foxing' and is seen as brown spots of varying size and intensity. This type of damage is not only disfiguring but changes chemically the paper fibres in the vicinity of the spots, making the paper acidic and, therefore, weak. Little research has been done on this extensively damaging problem (books suffer badly too), but opinion generally holds that minerals inherent in the paper, especially iron and its salts, are attractive to fungi which release acids in reaction to these impurities (Meynell and Newcombe, 1978). Mould and foxing damage to prints and drawings can often be removed from the paper by various means (usually chemical), but the conservator is limited by the materials that comprise the work and the ethics of the conservation of artefacts which demand reversibility, i.e. pigments cannot be applied directly to the paper surface as they sink in and cannot readily be removed.

Preventive measures

(1) The RH should be kept between 50 and 60 per cent.
(2) Regular inspection of the collection should be carried out to look for signs of fungal attack.
(3) Any infected materials should be separated from the collection. Superfluous materials such as old mounts, which host contamination, must be removed. These will have a nostalgic, musty smell due to acidity and other pollution, which provides clear warning that remedial action is necessary.
(4) Fumigation may be required, but this should be left to professional fumigators (Dennis, Chapter 46). However, no fumigation treatment has long-lasting properties. Treatment is pointless, however, if the environmental conditions supporting the mould are allowed to persist.
(5) As with the preventive measures against pollution, controlled environments and microlimates should be organized to keep the moisture content of the air correct and stable.

Insects and other pests

In the UK, species of insect do considerable harm to prints and drawings. The larvae of furniture beetles (*Anobium punctatum*) eat the soft wood of frame backings and boxes, leaving frass in their wake along with a sticky deposit. They find paper even more attractive. This damage is evident in the common 'wormage' to be seen as holes in paper supports, upsetting the visual image of the work. Booklice (*Psocoptera*) feed on moulds. Silver-fish (*Lepisma saccharina*) find the sizing agents in paper particularly attractive and can ruin the surface of a print or drawing over considerable areas by nibbling the size-coated fibres. Better quality papers and those with glazed surfaces appear to suffer most. Earwigs (*Dermaptera*), leave stains from their excrement, as do house flies. In country areas, thrips (*Thysanoptera*) enter framed prints and drawings. No breeding appears to take place, but they die *in situ*, often leaving small brown stains.

The enormous damage that mice do to paper artefacts is well known. Besides chewing prints and drawings, their excrement can stain and irreversibly damage such works.

Although the pests listed above are the most common in the UK, the Curator must be on the alert for unusual and immigrant species.

Preventive measures

(1) Drawers, shelves, boxes and storage areas should be regularly inspected and cleaned. A vacuum cleaner that can reach corners should be used.
(2) Appropriate insecticides should be put down. Baits for mice should be strategically positioned. If infestation is severe, professional advice should be sought (see Dennis, Chapter 46).
(3) New additions to the collection must be isolated until they are determined to be pest free.

Examination analysis

Inspection

The conservation priorities of the collection can only be established by a thorough inspection of each print or drawing.

Recording forms

It is important to keep a record of the condition of the works in the collection as well as all treatments that have been carried out. This is best organized to complement the general indexing system already in use. It may be necessary to develop a system of special forms for recording. The form should be as practical as possible, simple to complete, and concise. If the museum has the use of a central computer system, the forms should comply with this amenity.

Photography

As a further aid to recording, good photographs should be taken. If colour slides are preferred, these should be reviewed for tonality every 10 years, as all colour photographs are unstable, even in the dark. Good black-and-white prints on non-resin-coated paper should be chosen if colour is not a priority. Shots should be taken in flat and raking light. Photographs should be stored in containers that will not affect the silver emulsion. It would help curators to have a good copy stand and a single-lens reflex camera for immediate use.

Unframing

Great damage can result from the clumsy removal of works of art on paper from their frames. The following steps should be taken carefully to reduce the chance of such damage.

It is wise to have a bench covered in felt, securely tacked or stuck down. The tools needed are a duster, a small vacuum cleaner, a selection of small pliers and pincers, a screwdriver (medium), a knife, a palette-knife, a scalpel and blotting paper. Prints and drawings are secured in their frames by many methods, so initially the framed 'package' should be examined closely. Obviously, until the backboard is removed, the interior cannot be revealed and has to be dealt with step by step. First, the frame should be dusted or vacuumed. Any paper, or paper tape, should be removed from the back with a knife, together with any important labels or other documentation. The latter may be removed by placing wet blotting paper over them which should release them after a short soaking. If this is not sufficient, or if the adhesive appears to be other than animal glue or starch paste, a professional conservator should be consulted. Any wires and their anchor screws should be removed.

After all the pins securing the backing board to the moulding of the frame have been revealed, the frame should be held firmly with the side to be tackled 'pulled parallel to the body'. The top of the pin should be grasped firmly with pliers or pincers and gently pulled out. In early frames, the pins had no heads, but contemporary framing pins have small ones. Pins may be difficult to remove if they have rusted into their holes. A modern invention is the small diamond or U-shaped pin, shot from a gun to secure the backing board to the moulding of the frame. These may be removed gently with a screwdriver by pushing them sideways. The frame should be turned so each side assumes a correct position in turn, until all the pins have been pulled. The backing board can then be lifted out. It may be necessary to repeat the vacuum treatment at this stage to remove debris caused by the operation. The interior of the frame should then be scrutinized carefully and the mounted print or drawing lifted out. It is sound practice to tilt the frame gently to allow the 'package' to drop back onto the supporting palm of the hand. Commonly, the contents will have been bound together with tape at the edges including the glass. If so, any tapes should be slit with a knife to separate the sections. At all times during the dismantling process, a keen eye should search for traces of pests such as silver-fish, beetles and their larvae.

After the work has been removed from the frame, the backing board may be returned and pinned into place for storage. Even if the board has to be replaced, it will support and protect the glass temporarily.

De-mounting

Deciding what should be discarded: the warning signs

Further close inspection should be carried out to determine how the work is attached to its mounting and whether any of the materials show signs of breakdown. Discoloration, especially the orange/brown bevel of a mount will indicate immediately the presence of an acid. This may not always be in contact with the front of the print or drawing, but more often than not the backing mount will be made of the same board and will be in full contact with the work. Adhesives may have discoloured the paper support of the print or drawing. Mould growth and insect attack will be obvious.

Many different practices, some good, but mostly bad, have been used to mount works of art on paper. The following are some common problems that will be encountered, together with the suggested methods of dismantling on a clean flat surface.

Hinges

If, by good fortune, the work has been hinged simply with paper into its overlay mount, then these may be slit easily with a palette-knife and the work lifted out.

Edge adhesion to backing board

To determine whether this is the method of attachment, the board should be very slightly flexed and the print or drawing will show slight cockling across the flex. If the original paper is thick it may be possible to insert a palette-knife between this and the board releasing it. However, if there are any immediate problems the operation should be left to a conservator.

Spot adhesion to backing board

A certain amount of wrinkling will be apparent if the work is secured in this way. If the work is mounted on paper this may be torn away, leaving a small amount on the adhered points. Only a skilled conservator will be able to slice the work off the board under the adhered areas.

Adhered overmount

Extreme care should be exercised in determining whether overmounts are stuck to the original, or to the backing mount. It is always inadvisable for unskilled hands to attempt to remove overmounts adhered to the surface of prints or drawings.

Total adhesion to the backing board

The work may have been totally laid down on poor-quality board, and the problems that arise will not only stem from the latter, because adhesives also play havoc with the mounted work. A good-quality board with a layer of damaging adhesive will be a continuing problem as this can be an attractive layer for mould growth, or itself be chemically unstable and cause severe discoloration. Original artists' mounts, if they have to be detached, should be kept. Also, mounts supporting works from important collections should be preserved. These often have specific designs and collection marks. Curators should *never* attempt to delaminate the original from its board or mount, but should consult an experienced conservator.

Dry-mountings

Dry-mounting has been in use since the 1930s, and the early tissues, being based on shellac, are completely insoluble. Even the use of soluble modern products is inadvisable. Yet this bad practice continues to be used by framers, and it is by no means uncommon to find beautiful prints and drawings hot-pressed onto boards. The curator should consult a conservator when this method has been used, the tell-tale signs being a shiny layer protruding beyond the edge of the print or drawing.

Textile stretcher and panel supports

An eighteenth- and nineteenth-century practice was to secure a print or drawing with starch paste or animal glue to an open textile stretcher of linen or cotton or a wooden panel (McAusland and Stevens, 1979). The former allowed dust and atmospheric pollution to penetrate the paper and, combined with the differences in expansion and contraction of the linen and paper, resulted in a break-up of the paper. Only a conservator should handle works mounted by this method as they are often extremely delicate and brittle.

When a print or drawing is totally adhered to a wooden panel, many problems will have arisen and damage to the work will continue. Discoloration and extreme brittleness will be apparent. Only when the medium of the work contains carbonate, as in pastel or gouache, will this have served to give it some protection. Conservators face enormous, sometimes insoluble, problems with prints or drawings mounted in this way. Curators should *never* attempt to remove them from the panels.

Adhesion to glass

If a print or drawing has been pressed against the glazing, gums or other thick pigments may have become stuck to it. Removal should *not* be attempted by the Curator.

Note: if, at this stage, demounted prints and drawings are to be catalogued, any marking of them should be made only in pencil. Inks, and felt-tipped or ball-point pens should *never* be used.

Special problems

Old master drawings

Although old master drawings are created in many different media, those executed in iron gall inks are the most problematic. The ink is made from gall nuts, iron sulphate and gum arabic (Watrous, 1957). It is extremely acidic and therefore likely to attack the paper fibres and break them completely causing cracks and fissures. It is especially important to keep iron gall ink drawings in conditions of near 50 per cent RH and away from light, as both moisture and UVR cause quick deterioration, accelerating the chemical instability of the ink. When originally executed, these drawings were dark black – their creators would scarcely recognize them today.

Prints

Unless executed on laid India paper (*Chine appliqué*), all prints should be free of backings unless they need such support for conservation purposes. Their natural undulations should be understood and tolerated. Colour prints can fade in light as much as water-colours. Japanese prints are usually delicate and should never be subjected to light for any length of time.

Water-colours

Photo-oxidation is the greatest danger to water-colours. Many beautiful works have been ruined by the combination of light and atmospheric oxygen. If the colours are not uniformly affected, this will produce an imbalance in the design. Often, old mountings have partially obscured the edge, where the original freshness may be seen. Collections mounted in volumes have often fared best and the splitting up of such books may ring the death knell for the water-colours. It is helpful to understand that inorganic pigments or dyes are much less susceptible to alteration by light than organic ones. However, vermilion may blacken, and verdigris, red lead, the chromates and lead white react with oxygen and other gases in the atmosphere, and darken. Other fugitive pigments and dyes include yellow lake, all the red lakes, cadmium yellow, gamboge, Van Dyke brown and indigo.[2] If storage areas are too dry, gums on water-colours dry out and crack further, and pigment may be lifted from the support surface.

Drawings: graphite, charcoal, Conté crayon, inks and coloured chalks and crayons

These categories of drawings may easily be damaged by handling or by light. Loose particles of graphite, charcoal, chalk and crayon may offset or smudge, while inks and coloured crayons may fade in light. Deeper overlay mounts may be necessary to reduce the likelihood of contact with the glass or the mount when stored in Solander boxes. Double mounts may be more suitable, these could have a Melinex window or plain card protection. There is a lot to be said for the vertical storage of such works.

Pastels

The loose and delicate surface of a pastel drawing calls for extreme care in handling and storage. No modern fixative should be used on these works. The hygroscopic gums that bind the coarse pigment attract fungal growth. Apart from keeping these drawings in an RH of between 50 and 60 per cent, unframed pastels should be stored horizontally in conservation boxes with a gap between the lid and the surface of the pastel sufficient to minimize any risk of offset. Pastels, like water-colours, and coloured chalks and crayons, may fade in light.

Practical first-aid conservation procedures: recommended treatments

The Curator should attempt very little practical conservation. Prints and drawings may be totally ruined by injudicious intervention. It is much more important that the Curator understands the preventive conservation methods and practices that should be exercised on such collections. In a supervisory capacity the Curator should be aware of basic conservation techniques.

Dry-cleaning

Acrued dust on the surface of the print or drawing when the medium is not itself loose may be dislodged with a very soft brush of sable or other equally soft hair. Some nylon brushes are fine enough for this purpose. Areas where more stubborn dust and dirt adhere to the surface (where the medium allows) may be removed with a plastic eraser. A range of fine (2 mm) and large, soft erasers is required. Careful judgement must be exercised over this practice as a great deal of damage may be caused. The work should be placed on a large white blotter on a very even surface and it is important that the work does not slip. A small piece of blotting paper should rest beneath a small but heavy weight on an area of the work that balances the pull on the paper when the rubber is in action (*Figure 29.1*). Care must be taken not to raise the paper fibres during the

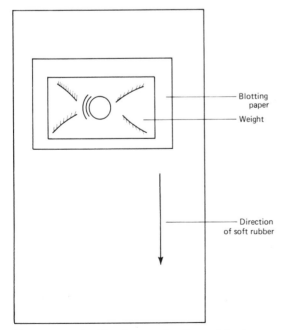

Figure 29.1 Soft rubber cleaning of surface: weighted area

operation. Dirt on a mount may be treated in the same way.

No attempt at surface cleaning should be made on soft European, long-fibred oriental or Chinese papers. Surface cleaning should not be carried out if only partial cleaning is possible or if the works are delicate, that is, pencil, graphite, pastel or any other medium that is likely to life off. Brittle papers may be further damaged by surface cleaning.

Mending edge tears

This first-aid action is a case of a 'a stitch in time' and a kit of the following equipment should be at hand. No torn print or drawing should be handled, and damage should be reported to the Curator by researchers. A notice to this effect should be displayed in the print room.

Equipment needed
Medium weight *kozo* paper.
Small scalpel with disposable blades (Swan Morton No. 15).
Pure starch paste (with preservative).[3]
White blotting paper.
Small flat pieces of plate glass.
Small paste brushes.
Scissors.
Small sable brush
Wet cutting brush.
Melinex.
Silicone release paper.
Tweezers.
Burnisher.
Small heavy weight.

Method
A clean, smooth laminate or glass table top should be utilized. First, examine the tear for dirt and dust, which may then be lightly brushed away with a small sable brush, then a plastic eraser (providing the paper is not too soft) may be drawn down and across each edge, from both the front and verso with extreme care so that no paper fibre is lost. A small piece of Melinex may be inserted in the tear to facilitate this action (*Figure 29.2*).

Next, a piece of Japanese paper should be cut out with a scalpel, scissors or a wet brush. This latter method may be the best as the edge will be frayed and lie very flat, causing no ridge. This repair patch will be no larger than 1 mm on each side of the tear. The patch is laid out on a piece of glass and pasted. It is very important that the paste be as dry as possible to avoid any movement of water into the paper, which might result in staining. Any overlapping areas of the tear may be pasted together in the correct position. The remaining length of tear should be aligned correctly. Using tweezers, the patch should be lifted gently: the work is held firmly in place with

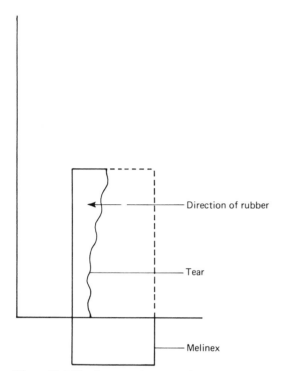

Figure 29.2 Cleaning a tear: insertion of Melinex

the left hand, and the patch is then placed evenly along the tear, and gently patted to secure it. A piece of blotting paper is then placed beneath the tear, and a piece of silicone release paper above. The patch should then be gently burnished through this to secure adhesion. The silicone release paper should be discarded, then replaced with blotting paper topped with the glass and a weight. The sheet is then left for at least 5 min the longer the better. Long tears may be dealt with in the same manner, but in stages, as they are difficult to manipulate. Abutting patches should be made.

Hinge removal

In order to stop bulking of old hinges on the verso of a drawing or print, some parts of these may be pulled away with tweezers. Great care must be taken not to 'thin' the original support. If this is likely, the hinges should await the attention of a professional, as should any self-adhesive tapes. If the work is backed, then more of the old hinges may be taken away as the original is not at risk.

Preventive conservation of prints and drawings

The way in which a collection may be mounted and stored depends ultimately on the demands that are to

be made on it and the space available. However, a number of factors must be considered.

(1) Size of collection, amount of space available, organization of that space.
(2) Mounts and frames: use of conservation materials.
(3) Amount of use and, therefore, handling which the collection will have.
(4) Security against fire, flood and theft.
(5) Aesthetic considerations, important historical evidence, and so on.
(6) Future increase in size of collection.

Allocation of available space

The size and shape of the storage area designated for the collection will determine how the store will be organized. First, a survey of the different sizes of prints and drawings, together with the sizes of likely additions (if possible) should be made. This survey should also embrace the number, size and shape of framed items. After this has been completed, the available space should be apportioned to the various types of item to be housed. The mount sizes needed for the collection should be determined. There is no uniform mount size in the UK, but the British Museum mount sizes are as follows: 22 × 26 inches (Royal); 27 × 20 inches (Imperial); 32 × 24 inches (Atlas); and 45 × 29.75 inches (Antiquarian or Double Elephant). Solander boxes or plan chests should be purchased to match the sizes chosen. These must be sturdy and made of acid-free materials.

Following these decisions, an arrangement of shelves and boxed areas should be organized, taking into account the specifics of the collection housing. There are differing opinions as to whether prints and drawings should be stored horizontally or vertically. Having seen many badly rubbed and pressed works that have been stored horizontally, I favour the vertical method, but the boxes must be completely full, otherwise the mount will fall at an angle and damage is likely to occur. If double mounts are used it is probably best to use horizontal systems, housed in felt-lined areas (Zegers, 1980).

Framed items may be stored vertically in boxed areas lined with felt to minimize scratching of glass or Perspex and damage to frames. Felt-covered separators should lie between each frame, otherwise drawers lined with felt may be used for framed item storage. This method is considerably more expensive. All stored frames should be free of wires, rings and other projections.

Various systems of sliding vertical racks are available commercially upon which framed works may be hung during storage. They have the advantage of providing easy visibility for the researchers, and from the conservation point of view any damage that has occurred can easily be seen. They have the further advantage of good air circulation. There are also systems for storing large paper artefacts in hanging chambers, bins or devices that pivot on a central column and support the works on arms extending from the centre.

Very large prints and drawings are a problem. If possible, they should be framed for full protection immediately they arrive at the museum but, if this cannot be done, they should be encapsulated (Library of Congress, 1980) and stored in plan chests, of the international standard paper size, A0 (841 × 1189 mm), or specially constructed larger units if required. These chests have a hinged bar at the front and a protection bar across the top of the rear of the drawer to keep them from lifting up and becoming damaged. Drawers must be well-ventilated, as should boxed areas: holes in the backs will allow air circulation. However, if the prints or drawings are stored in an area where the environment is controlled and forms a stable, acceptable (below 70 per cent RH, say 60 per cent for safety) micro-climate, no ventilation in the storage units is necessary.

An area should be selected for framing and unframing, preferably outside the storage area, with space to house all necessary equipment.

Mounts

Curators and conservators are not always able to determine whether all the materials of a print or drawing are chemically stable. More often they are not stable and it may not be possible to resort to full conservation treatment because of lack of funds or equipment. However, placing these works in close proximity to a chemically stable environment will help. In this instance, conservation mounting and framing seem to be the best practical method of preventive conservation; many high-quality conservation materials are now available.

The types of mount available are listed below.

(1) A simple overlay mount (*Figure 29.3*) may be constructed in varying thickness to suit the collection.
(2) A double overlay mount with Melinex protection (*Figure 29.4*) is particularly useful if the collection is to be handled frequently. The Melinex makes for easy viewing and the overmount protects the undermount from dirt, thereby cutting long-term costs. The overmount 'may simply be folded back to show the clean undermount when the works are needed for exhibition. The disadvantages of this method are that it is bulky, more costly initially, and Melinex attracts dust, as it has a static charge and it may also pull pigments off paper. If this is the case, a protective card should replace the open Melinex mount.
(3) The inlaid Perspex double-sided mount (*Figure 29.5*) is useful for double-sided drawings or works of great value. It is not suitable for works that have loose pigments or prints with plate-marks or other natural undulations such as wood-cuts. As long as conservation

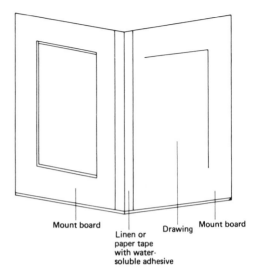

Mount board   Drawing   Mount board

Linen or
paper tape
with water-
soluble adhesive

Figure 29.3 Simple overlay mount

materials are used, mounts may be decorated to suit the aesthetic interpretation of the print or drawing or its historical background.

Hinges

How the print or drawing is secured to its mount to protect it from damage or theft will depend on the above considerations. The following are examples of various methods of hinging works to their mounts:

(1) A simple L hinge (*Figure 29.6*) is quite suitable for most small prints and drawings, as the entire image may be displayed. If the collection is housed horizontally, and not to be displayed in frames, the hinges should be on the left-hand side of the print or drawing, to make for easy lifting by the researcher. On the other hand, vertically stored works and collections that are to be displayed should be hinged on the top. Two hinges at each corner (either left side or top) are required. More than two hinges will cause buckling. This method of hinging is a poor safeguard against theft. If the object is only just covered by the edges of the window, this method of hinging may allow it to become buckled and caught between the sides of the mount.
(2) A drop hinge with securing strip (*Figure 29.7*) is suitable and physically secure if it is not necessary to show the whole sheet of paper, that is, when there are large margins.
(3) Hinges supported through backing board (*Figure 29.8*) give firm hiden support when prints or drawings are very large and heavy.
(4) Corners (*Figure 29.9*) make strong supports when the work should not have hinge attachments, or has large margins that lie under the overlay of the mount.
(5) Melinex strips (*Figure 29.10*) secured with PVA adhesive are a method of holding down works for display or storage.

Double-sided self-adhesive tape

Melinex

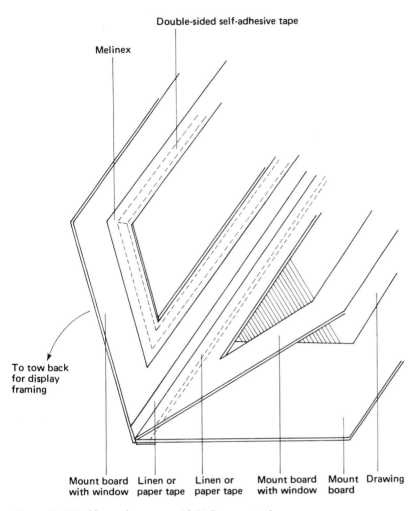

To tow back
for display
framing

| Mount board | Linen or | Linen or | Mount board | Mount | Drawing |
| with window | paper tape | paper tape | with window | board | |

Figure 29.4 Double-overlay mount with Melinex protection

Hinges should be made from either Japanese paper or thin, acid-free European paper. With the former it is possible to feather the edges by 'wet-cutting' and, therefore, to achieve neat, flat hinge. The advantages of the latter are that it is slightly more firm and less likely to drop. The only suitable adhesive for hinging is pure starch paste. Carboxymethylcellulose is a little too wet. No commercially available paste or glue is sufficiently pure or reversible. All the available 'conservation' tapes are irreversible after a time and should not be used. Self-adhesive tape should *never* be considered.

Finally, when a drawing needs the greater support of a solid panel, a conservator – never a framer – should undertake this extremely delicate operation.

Inlays

An inlay is a piece of additional paper attached to the edge of a drawing on its verso, bevelled and adhered to the original to a depth of approximately 1 mm on all sides. Prints should never be inlayed as plate-marks and other natural undulations will be restricted or drummed out.

When a suitable paper for inlaying is being chosen it must be remembered that this additional edging will put a new stress on the original drawing, so it is important that a paper of similar weight is selected. If a lighter paper is attached, wrinkling will occur along the adhered edge of the inlay. However, it is possible to make an inlay with lens tissue in order to

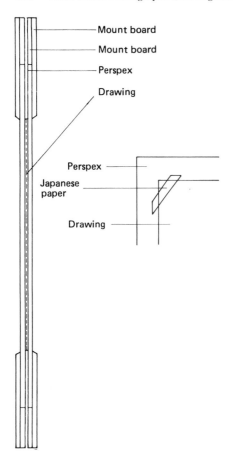

Figure 29.5 Inlaid UV Perspex double-sided mount (the Japanese paper is adhered to the Perspex with PVA)

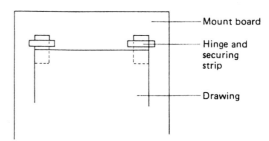

Figure 29.7 Drop hinge with securing strip

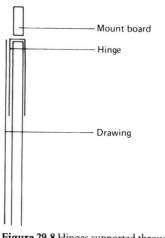

Figure 29.8 Hinges supported through backing board

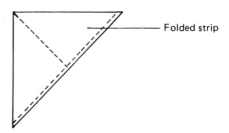

Figure 29.9 Corners

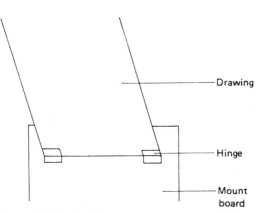

Figure 29.6 Simple L hinge

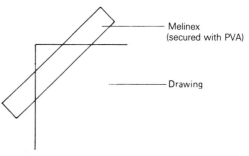

Figure 29.10 Melinex strips

display the work fully and control any inclination to curl or distort, although this would not be suitable for a collection that is handled a great deal, as the tissue is too fragile.

It is the current practice of some institutions to paste inlays down, both to the backing mount as well as to the overlay of the mount. From a security point of view this is helpful, but it obscures the verso for research purposes and also makes watermarks and other historical evidence unavailable.

Folders

If the curator is faced with extreme limitations of budget or a very large collection, a good simple method of storage is by means of folders. These should be made of strong, acid-free conservation card. Prints and drawings may be hinged to them as on a mount, or may be left free. Researchers should be warned of the likelihood of lifting the artefact on opening the folder. Sheets of tissue or Melinex (if suitable from the static point of view), will help hold down and protect the works.

Encapsulation

Full physical protection of prints and drawings may be achieved by encapsulation in Melinex sheeting. Machines are available for welding the edges. A sewing machine may also be used. Double-sided tapes were once advocated, but the adhesive was found to migrate into the encapsulated area. Aesthetically, this method may not suit the collection (it is considered an archive treatment), but there might be occasions when it could be useful.

Framing

Permanent framing

Apart from its aesthetic appeal, the moulding of a frame is the support for the entire 'packing', glazing mount and backing-board. It must be deep enough to house these integral parts, and sturdy enough to support them.

A glazing may be of glass or a polymethylmethacrylate sheet that cuts out a high proportion of UV light. The former is likely to shatter and is unsuitable for frames used for transportation. The latter attracts electricity and is not suitable for works like pastels that may be lifted by this property. It scratches easily, but it gives much better protection from UV light, and is much lighter in weight.

The backing board both stabilizes the frame and protects the back of the mounted artefact. Hardboard or marine plywood are suitable for backing boards but they should be coated with varnish to hinder migration of impurities from the wood into the

mount and eventually into the artefact. Self-adhesive tapes are not suitable for sealing the backing board into the frame, because the adhesive will migrate, dry out and eventually lose its power. Pasted kraft paper or gummed brown tapes are the most suitable, although the latter may dry out and become loose.

Temporary framing

It may suit a collection better to have a system of framing that will enable the Curator to rotate the collection on view with ease. A number of frames should be made to fit the mount sizes of the collection. These should have pivoting braces to secure the backing boards, which may be sealed with pasted or gummed tapes.

Collection marking and information recording: stamping, embossing and perforation

If information must be recorded on a print or drawing, it should be done in pencil only, and with light pressure. However, this practice should be avoided if possible, and information should normally be recorded on cards.

Items must be permanently identified as being part of the collection. Ink stamps, embossed stamps, perforated marks and UVR-sensitive stamps that are invisible without a UV light are all available. It is important that marks should be impossible to remove without damaging the item, although such action can be skilfully concealed by an expert paper restorer. Ink stamps are conspicuous, but the ink must be chosen carefully. Pure black carbon printing ink is the most stable, but inks should be tested before use to make sure that they are completely stable and able to withstand conservation treatments. Ink stamps should be carefully positioned.

Embossed stamps are aesthetically pleasing, but may be unsuitable as they press through the print or drawing. If the artefact has no margins it is impossible to use such a mark.

Perforated marks remove part of the paper and for this reason may be considered unsuitable. They are, of course, impossible to remove, but could be expertly repaired. UVR-sensitive inks might appear to be a neat solution, but a thief would not necessarily be deterred by them.

Transportation

Before transportation, preventive conservation measures in the form of correct crating, handling, storage and labelling should be taken (Stolow, 1979).

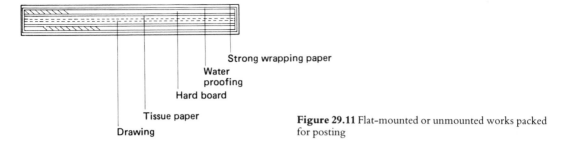

Strong wrapping paper

Water
proofing

Hard board

Tissue paper

Drawing

Figure 29.11 Flat-mounted or unmounted works packed
for posting

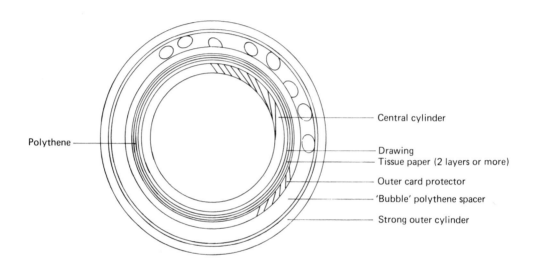

Central cylinder

Drawing
Tissue paper (2 layers or more)

Outer card protector

'Bubble' polythene spacer

Strong outer cylinder

Polythene

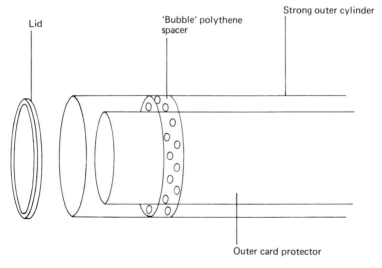

Lid

'Bubble' polythene
spacer

Strong outer cylinder

Outer card protector

Figure 29.12 Rolled prints and drawings packed for
transportation (masking tape may be used to secure outer
card and 'bubble' Polythene spacer)

Framed prints and drawings

The following steps should be taken in the case of framed prints and drawings.

(1) A condition report on each artefact should be made (if it does not already exist), and it should checked carefully.
(2) Hinges, mounts and frames should be inspected.
(3) Glass should be criss-crossed with self-adhesive tape. It is better to send works framed with acrylic sheeting and a UVR-absorbent filter as this will not shatter.

The following types of artefact should *not* be sent:

(1) very brittle works;
(2) works that are extremely sensitive to light; or
(3) pastels and drawings with unfixed surfaces should be handled separately and be sent by special courier.

Crates should be constructed to protect framed prints and drawings against vibration and shock, and should have a certain degree of temperature insulation and humidity-buffering capacity, such as that provided by silica gel. The design of the crate should accommodate the frames when held firmly in position and they should be protected further with corner padding. Ornate mouldings require specially designed packaging. For uniformly sized frames, slots to hold them vergically may be constructed, or a tray system may be utilized. It is very important that the orientation of the crates be clearly marked on the outside, in more than one language if necessary. Wood is probably the best material to use for packing cases and crates.

Prints and drawings sent through the post

Whether these works are sent mounted or un-mounted, they should be packed in the manner illustrated in *Figure 29.11*. It is very important that the recipient is informed precisely as to the packing arrangements, which should also be indicated on the outside of the package.

Rolled prints and drawings
Rolling a print or drawing for transportation would seem the last resort as a great deal of damage can result from using this method, and it leaves the work curled, even if it has not suffered in other ways. However, contemporary screen prints and original works of art are often very large and it is often not practical to send these in any other way than rolled. There are various ways to pack rolled works, but a safe method is illustrated in *Figure 29.12*.

There is a risk of condensation when polythene sheeting is wrapped immediately next to the framed print or drawing, so it is advisable to separate any waterproofing from the object with a layer or two of tissue paper or other padding. This also applies to protective, 'bubbled' polythene.

Flood damage
If flooding soaks a collection of prints and drawings there are several ways to tackle the problem, depending on the size of the collection and the nature of the flood. The works must be dried out quickly, though not so quickly as to cause distortion and this can only be accomplished by removing the prints and drawings from their frames and laying out on white blotting paper on a flat surface. If the collection is large and it is impossible to dry it may be frozen (Gratton, 1982).

Notes

[1] Designed by Dr Solander of the British Museum between 1776 and 1782, these boxes consist of a case with hinged lid and side that fold out to a horizontal position when the box is opened so that the mounted original may easily be slid in and out.
[2] Thomson, G. (1978), *The Museum Environment*, IIC and Butterworths, p. 11. The table here lists light-fast categories for some common pigments, old and new.
[3] Pure starch paste made up to the following formula:
   90 g pure starch (arrowroot, wheat or rice),
   10 g potato starch,
   700 ml pure water,
   100 ml saturated calcium hydroxide solution (2% in H_2O).

References

DANIELS, V. (1982), 'Colour changes of watercolour pigments during deacidification', *Science and Technology in the Service of Conservation*, Preprints of the Contributions to the Washington Congress of the IIC 1982, (available from the IIC, 6 Buckingham Street, London EC2N 6BA)

HARDING, E. G. (1972), 'The mounting of prints and drawings', revised edn. 1980, *Museum Association Information Sheet No. 12*, p. 1

LIBRARY OF CONGRESS (1980), *Polyester Film Encapsulation*, Publication on Conservation of Library Materials, Preservation Office Research Science, Library of Congress, Washington DC

MCAUSLAND, P. and STEVENS, P. (1979), Techniques of lining for the support of fragile works of art on paper, *The Paper Conservator*, 4, 34

MEYNELL, G. G. and NEWCOMBE, R. J. (1978), 'Foxing a fungal infection of paper', *Nature*, 274, 466–468; 'Foxed paper and its problems', *New Scientist*, 17 May 1979, p. 567

STOLOW, N. (1979), *Conservation Standards for Works of Art in Transit and on Exhibition*, UNESCO, Paris, 1979

THOMSON, G. (1978), *The Museum Environment*, IIC and Butterworths, London, p. 15

WATROUS, J. (1957), *The Craft of Old-Master Drawings*, University of Wisconsin, pp. 69–74

ZEGERS, P. (1980), 'Mounting and storage of the graphic arts collection at the National Gallery of Canada', *Cambridge 1980: The Conservation of Library and Archive Materials and the Graphic Arts*, Institute of Paper Conservation and the Society of Archivists, pp. 135–140

Bibliography

Books on conservation

BRILL, T. D. (1980), *Light: Its Interaction with Art and Antiquities*, Plenum Press, New York. The inspiration for this book came from lectures the author gave to students on the conservation course at Winterthur Museum, University of Delaware, and is concerned with the nature of light, its properties, and its good and bad effects on materials.

BROMMELLE, N. and SMITH, P. (Eds) (1976), *Conservation and Restoration of Pictorial Art*, IIC and Butterworths, London. This volume consists substantially of papers presented at a congress in Lisbon of the International Institute for Conservation of Historic and Artistic Works in October 1972, entitled 'Conservation of paintings and the graphic arts'.

CLAPP, A. (1974), *Curatorial Care of Works of Art on Paper*, 2nd edn, Intermuseum Conservation Association, Oberlin, OH. This is the only comprehensive guide for curators which deals with this subject. Most of the advice is sound, although most of the 'do it yourself' information should be disregarded.

DOLLOFF, F. and PERKINSON, R. (1972), *How to Care for Works of Art on Paper*, Museum of Fine Arts, Boston, MA. This is a helpful small publication that every Curator should acquire.

FLIEDER, F. (1969), *La Conservation des Documents Graphiques*, Eyrolles, Paris, 1969, in French and now somewhat out of date, Flieder continues her research in her laboratory in Paris and publishes regularly new information helpful to conservators of papers and books.

PLENDERLEITH, H. J. and WERNER, A. E. A. (1971), *The Conservation of Antiquities and Works of Art*, (2nd edn), Oxford University Press, London. For long considered the best handbook covering the spectrum of objects conservation; however, Dr Plenderleith's book is now out of date for art-on-paper conservation, in the light of all the mass of new research that has been done since it was first published. This second edition is not a great improvement on the first.

STOLOW, N. (1979), *Conservation Standards for Works of Art in Transit and on Exhibition*, UNESCO, Parts. Dr Stolow has consistently concerned himself with packaging works of art for transit and should be always the first person to turn to when faced with the problems that inevitably arise with travelling exhibitions and general transportation. Apart from the structure of packing cases he is also most concerned with changes in RH and fluctuations in temperature during transportation, by land, sea or air.

ZIGROSSER, C. and GAEHDE, C. M. (1969), *A Guide to the Collecting and Care of Original Prints*, Print Council of America, Crown Publishers Inc., New York. Mrs Gaehde's section on the conservation of fine prints gives sound useful information.

CASH, M. S. (Ed.) (1980), AIC, Washington. Available from: the ATC, Klingle Mansion, 3345 Williamsburg Lane, Washington, DC, 20008. This is the only full bibliography available on the subject and is a most useful guide.

THOMSON, C. (1978), *The Museum Environment*, Butterworths and The International Institute for Conservation of Historic and Artistic Works, London. An invaluable guide for every curator.

Books concerned with materials and techniques

BIEGELEISEN, J. I., *The Complete Book on Silk Screen Printing – Production*, Dover Publications, New York. A well-illustrated guide to the subject.

BRUNNER, F. (1962), *A Handbook of Graphic Reproduction Processes*, Arthur Teufen, Switzerland (reprinted 1983). This volume is an invaluable aid to determining the different methods of graphic reproduction in English, German and French. Well illustrated.

CENNINI, C. (1953), *The Craftsman's Handbook*, Dover Publications, New York. Translated by Daniel V. Thompson, from the Italian *Il Libro Dell'Arte*, this early treatise is fascinating reading giving general information on sixteenth-century craftsmen, even mentioning an 'ideal' (fish) glue for paper mending'.

COHN, M. B. (1977), *Wash and Coutache: A Study in the Development of the Materials of Watercolour*, Center for Conservation and Technical Studies, Cambridge, MA, for the Fogg Art Museum and the foundation of the American Institute for Conservation on the occasion of an exhibition of water-colours at the Fogg Art Museum. Although this publication was of more use during the exhibition at the Fogg Art Museum, it nevertheless stands in its own right as a fund of useful and interesting information on the subject.

GASCOIGNE, B. (1986), *How to Identify Prints*, Thames and Hudson, London. This book is well laid out and is a thoughtful and thorough investigation of the processes.

GEITENS, R. and STOUT, C. (1966), *Painting Materials: A Short Encyclopedia*, Dover Publications, New York. Designed as a reference work for museum curators and conservators it is most helpful as a guide and aid to the mutual understanding of the terminology of conservation as well as techniques used by artists and craftsmen. An essential reference book.

HARLEY, R. (1970), *Artists' Pigments, 1600–1835* (reprinted 1982), IIC and Butterworths, London. The second edition of this work is more fully illustrated with some colour plates, it is better laid out and therefore easier to read. Another essential work to have at hand for general interest in this subject.

HIND, A. (1963), *A History of Engraving and Etching from the 15th Century to the Year 1914*, Dover Publications, New York. The introduction to the book deals with processes and materials and proffers a short guide.

HIND, A. M. (1963), *An Introduction to a History of Woodcut*, Vols I and II, Dover Publications, New York, Arthur Hind was a Keeper of Prints and Drawings in the British Museum. These two volumes on the history of the woodcut covers Western woodcuts with a detailed survey of work donw in the fifteenth century.

IVINS, JR, W. M. (1943), *How Prints Look*, Boston, MA. Revised in 1987 by Marjorie B. Cohen and published in Great Britain by John Murray (Publishers) Ltd, 50 Albemarle Street, London W1X 4BD. Useful for determining the type of printing processes used in the manufacture of a print. Covers copies, facsimiles and other 'bothersome matters'.

JONES, S. (1967), *Lithography for Artists*, Oxford University Press, Oxford. A short concise guide.

LUMSDEN, F. (1962), *The Art of Etching*, Dover Publications, New York. The etcher, Prof Lumsden, carefully and clearly explains each step in the creation of an etching from essential materials to completed proof. This is well illustrated.

MAYER, R. (1969), *A Dictionary of Art Terms and Techniques*, Thomas T. Crowell Co., New York. This volume presents in succinct form the explanation of terms encountered in the study and practice of the visual arts and in their literature.

MAYER, R. (1970), *The Artist's Handbook of Materials and Techniques*, Viking Press, New York. Although of more use to the artist, this book gives a lot of interesting and helpful information on pigments. The conservation section should be omitted as the information is so scanty as to be positively dangerous.

WATROUS, J. (1967), *The Craft of Old Master Drawing*, University of Wisconsin Press, Madison, WI. A comprehensive and useful guide to the subject.

Periodicals containing articles on conservation

Abbey Newsletter: Bookbinding and Conservation, c/o School of Library Service, 516 Butler Library, Columbia University, New York, NY 10027, USA.

AIC Newsletter, published quarterly by the American Institute for Conservation of Historic and Artistic Works.

Conservation News, quarterly newsletter of the United Kingdom Institute for Conservation.

Conservator, annual journal of the United Kingdom Institute for Conservation. Available from the Publication Officer, UKIC, c/o Conservation Department, Tate Gallery, Millbank, London SW1P 4RG, UK.

Journal of the American Institute for Conservation, biannual journal of the American Institute for Conservation of Historic and Artistic Works, 3545 Williamsburg Lane, NW, Washington, DC 20008, USA.

Paper Conservation News, quarterly newsletter of the Institute of Paper Conservation.

Paper Conservator, annual journal of the Institute of Paper Conservation, Leigh Lodge, Leigh, Worcestershire WR6 5L13.

Restaurator, international journal for the preservation of library and archival material. Published by Munksgaard International Publishers, 35 Norre Sogade, DK–1370 Copenhagen K, Denmark.

Studies in Conservation, quarterly journal of the International Institute for Conservation of Historic and Artistic Works, for the International Institute for Conservation of Historic and Artistic Works, London, UK.

30

Conservation and storage: easel paintings

David Bomford and James Dimond

The structure of easel paintings

European easel paintings between the fourteenth and twentieth centuries display a huge range of styles and techniques, but all have comparable laminar structures. This allows a closely similar approach, in terms of classification, examination and treatment, to most easel paintings found in museum collections.

The main structural layer, the *support*, is most commonly of wood or of stretched fabric. A wide variety of wood types has been used for panel paintings, and often the species are indigenous to the geographical origin of the painting. At its simplest, a panel is made of a single piece of wood; at its most complex it may have many members, with wood-grain running in contrary directions, and secondary reinforcements such as battens or cradles. The peculiarly sensitive and unpredictable nature of wood panels necessitates precisely controlled conditions of storage and hanging. Canvas supports, usually made of linen stretched over a wooden frame, are less susceptible to environmental fluctuations but, at the same time, their lack of resilience makes them much more vulnerable to physical damage. This inherent weakness in old fabric paintings almost inevitably leads to the application of a secondary support of some kind, usually a lining. Other supports have been used for easel paintings: vellum, stone, copper, millboard and even glass, for example, may be encountered.

Usually, the support was prepared for painting by application of a *ground* or *priming*, although sometimes this layer is absent. The importance of the ground in the overall structure of a painting is often overlooked. Imperfectly prepared or deteriorating grounds can endanger an entire painting, with rather limited scope for treatment. The nature of grounds on canvas pictures is especially significant when the suitability of various lining processes is being considered. Moreover, the influence of coloured or dark grounds in pictures that are worn or have become more transparent can be profoundly disturbing.

The *paint*, composed of coloured *pigments* dispersed in a *binding medium* (such as egg or a drying oil), may be a single layer, or many layers thick. There can be considerable complexity in terms of pigment mixtures and layer structure, and the possibility of added elements such as metal leaf in old pictures and collage in modern works may compound it. The state of preservation of the paint layers is often dependent more on the condition of the support and ground layers than on internal properties of pigments and media. Movement of supports and unsatisfactory adhesion to the ground are the most common causes of cracking and paint loss. Paint defects caused by pigment change or the drying mechanism of the medium are occasionally significant, but usually accepted as characteristic of the ageing of the picture.

When the paint was quite dry, it was usual to *varnish* the picture, to protect and make the colours properly visible. Traditional varnishes used to be natural resins in an appropriate solvent, sometimes combined with drying oils. All these resins discolour with time, some very badly. In addition, some oil varnishes become almost insoluble in normal cleaning solvents and, therefore, the cleaning of paintings is made more hazardous. Modern synthetic resin varnishes have largely replaced traditional types.

Each of the layers described above can have a marked effect on the appearance of a painting. In a deteriorating structure, it is not only their interaction with each other, but also *cleavage* between layers which becomes significant. It is customary when describing the condition of an easel painting and when proposing modes of treatment, to consider the layers one by one. This is done in the following sections.

It is hardly necessary to point out that even the most routine methods of treatment applied to paintings by unskilled hands or in the wrong circumstances can have disastrous consequences. Examination of condition and treatment of defects should be carried out only by those properly trained in the conservation of easel paintings.

Conservation records

Ideally, every painting in a collection should have a detailed record of condition and treatment. Each time a painting is examined or treated, notes should be added to the records, together with photographs if necessary.

The nature of conservation records is a matter of convenience and personal preference. Some conservators favour a folder or loose-leaf system which allows expansion and flexibility of arrangement; a possible disadvantage of this is that, even with the most honourable intentions, photographs and reports may be extracted, borrowed and ultimately lost. An alternative system, somewhat more laborious but less likely to be abused, is to have blank volumes in which photographs and reports are mounted permanently. In due course, computerized records will undoubtedly become standard in many museums.

A description of the condition of a painting in terms of its various layers forms the basis of any conservation record. Again, there are different approaches against which the needs of a particular collection must be balanced. It is wise to have some sort of printed examination report form to provide a formal framework around which an assessment of condition may be constructed. At its simplest, it would merely have sections corresponding to the principal layers of the painting in which features of those layers could be noted. At its most comprehensive, it might have boxes to be ticked for every possible variation in condition for every component of the picture. Detailed forms of this kind are recommended if an examination is to be made by someone other than an experienced conservator: if every section is completed correctly, then no vital feature is likely to be overlooked. As well as written records, a conservation dossier should have at least one photograph of the painting for identification, together with as many detailed technical photographs as is feasible. Where relevant, cross-reference should be made to material filed elsewhere such as colour transparencies, scientific examination reports, historical archives and so on.

If compilation of detailed conservation records is not possible, a card index containing an essential summary of condition and treatment should be maintained. Even if full records are kept, a parallel card index summarizing the main points can be most useful for quick reference.

Wood supports

The warping of wood panels

The behaviour of panel painting is complex, not least because of the anisotropic nature of wood: although the properties of the various woods used for painting supports vary widely, generalization can be made. Wood has a cellular structure, the cells, for the most part, being formed like hollow straws parallel to the axis of the tree. The alternation of dense cells of summer wood and the lighter cells of spring wood as the tree grows outwards leads to the formation of annual growth rings and produces the visible grain in a piece of cut timber.

This cellular structure is hygroscopic and, in conditions of low or high relative humidity, will shrink or swell by an amount which varies directionally within the wood. In a log, swelling or shrinkage in a longitudinal direction (along the grain) is minimal, while in a transverse direction it is significant, the tangential change (along the arc of the growth rings) being about twice as great as the radial.

The manner in which a board was originally cut from a log is, therefore, significant in predicting its stability. A tangentially cut board, as it loses its natural moisture content, will have a tendency to shrink more at the outer face than the inner, and a warp will result. A radially cut board is more or less symmetrical, both faces will shrink by the same amount and there is no tendency to warp.

In the case of panel paintings, the situation is further complicated by the presence of an impervious layer of paint on one side and the possibility of panel constructions involving several boards. A paint layer effectively seals one face of the panel so that shrinkage and swelling caused by humidity changes occur only at the other face. Under conditions of high relative humidity (RH) one would expect the wood cells at the back to expand and therefore the painted side to be concave; under low RH, the painted side should be convex. This simple type of warping is reversible, simply by altering the humidity.

However, repeated cycles of expansion and contraction of the wood at the unprotected face can lead to permanent compression of the cells, which results in the characteristic convex warp seen in many panel paintings. With the aim of eliminating this warp, many misguided and damaging treatments have been carried out in the past.

Prevention and treatment of warping in panel paintings

Clearly, the most desirable factor in the conservation of panel paintings is precise environmental control since it is fluctuations in RH which lead to movement and, if violent enough, to the destabilization of the entire structure of the picture. No museum can control its climate with total precision, however, and so it becomes important that the natural movement of wood panels in conditions of varying humidity should not be restrained in any way, or else deformation and eventual splitting may result. Restraints such as attached bars of wood or metal, cradles, small mahogany buttons reinforcing old splits and even tightly fitting picture frames can all lead to permanent damage and should be removed if there is any indication of stress.

The theory of *cradling* appears sound, but frequently it creates more distortion than the warp it is designed to eliminate. In a traditional cradle, fixed bars are glued to the reverse of the panel, parallel to the wood grain, and free-running cross-members pass through slots cut into them. In theory, the warp is controlled while natural movement across the grain is allowed, but in practice the cross-members usually become jammed as the panel tries to warp. In addition, the fixed bars act as individual restraints and many cradled panels exhibit the corrugated 'washboard' effect, which may be even more pronounced if the panel was thinned before cradling (as was often the case).

Cradling of panels is now considered an unnecessary and potentially harmful treatment and should be avoided. Existing cradles that still function properly can be left alone, but those that are thought to be acting as restraints should be removed in small sections by carefully sawing and chiselling the fixed members. Similarly, rigid bars of wood or metal fixed across the wood grain should be removed if necessary. Frequently, such bars are tapered and dovetailed into grooves in the back of the panel and removal may be possible by sliding them laterally.

After removal of restraints, most panels assume a gentle convex warp, indicating the amount of stress that has been relieved. Many unrestrained panels also exhibit a convex warp due to development of permanent set. There is nothing inherently wrong with leaving a panel in a convex conformation – indeed, if the warp is visually acceptable it is the safest course. Once the panel has stabilized in the museum environment, it can be returned to its frame which should be adapted with slips of balsa wood within the rebate, shaped to the curvature of the panel. If the panel is structurally weak it can be held gently but firmly by shaped slips, just capping the frong edges, against a rigid background on which are rubber or cork pads reflecting the correct curvature – a construction known as a 'tray'.

If a warp is considered unacceptable, then steps may be taken to eliminate it and maintain the panel in a flattened state. By exposing the back to high humidity (over, but not touching, moistened pads) for a period of some hours, the panel will flatten under its own weight. To prevent the warp recurring, a semi-rigid backing of balsa wood blocks may be applied using a wax–resin cement, while the panel is still in its humidified state. The overall restraint of the balsa backing, together with the trapped moisture, induces plastic deformation within the wood cells which allows the attainment of a new, flatter equilibrium state. This does not happen with the traditional cradle, because the wood dries out before plastic deformation occurs. A certain degree of permanent flattening may also be achieved simply by brushing a *moisture barrier* of wax–resin onto the back of the flattened humidified panel.

Occasionally a panel is encountered exhibiting a concave warp. This is a potentially dangerous state, and may be caused by a number of factors. Remedial treatment should be undertaken at once by an experienced conservator.

Other defects of panel paintings

More frequently, panel paintings may have to be treated for a number of other defects. Flaking or blistering of the ground and paint layers, caused by movement of the support and consequent breakdown of adhesion, is frequently encountered. Prominent craquelure, although perhaps arising from the same cause, is not in itself an indication of potential paint loss. Indeed, some of the most serious cleavages, often unnoticed and invariably difficult to treat, occur in apparently well-preserved parts with little or no cracking: this is so-called *blind cleavage*. Treatment of this and of straightforward flaking is described on p. 282.

Treatment of splits or loose joins in wood panels is carried out using standard cabinet makers' methods involving cash-clamps, G-clamps and woodworking adhesives. Purpose-built apparatus incorporating longitudinal and vertical clamping has been devised for gluing split and loose panel members, but since problems can vary so much in size and complexity many conservators prefer a simpler and more empirical approach. Often, the joining of panels forms only part of a more extended treatment of removals of restraints, flattening and reinforcement and it is important that the entire operation should be carefully planned in advance so that the correct sequence can be followed. Splits or joins should be glued simply edge-to-edge, if possible, without additional reinforcement of battens, buttons, 'butterfly' inlays, fabric and so on. Sometimes hardwood V-shaped inserts are let into the back of a split if reinforcement is necessary. Weak panels may be supported in a tray or by a balsa wood backing, as described already.

Panel paintings are often attacked by wood-boring insects. Where the insects are still found to be active, the pictures should be isolated and treated either by fumigation or by injecting with a suitable insecticide: the choice of insecticide is critical, since some oil-based liquids have a disastrous softening effect on paint films. Advice should be sought before treatment is attempted. The panel should be inspected at 6-month intervals for evidence of continued activity: if existing holes are filled with wax, new ones will be easily detected.

Dry-rot, where it occurs, can also be treated with proprietary fungicides, but the same caution is necessary as with insecticides. Where wood panels are badly eaten or eroded, from whatever cause, they can be consolidated by impregnation with a wax–resin mixture or with a suitable wood-hardening compound. Wax–resin is an excellent consolidant, but it must be remembered that its water-repellant properties preclude the subsequent use of normal woodworking adhesives.

The most extreme form of treatment that can be applied to panel painting is *transfer*, in which the paint film, with or without the ground, is mounted on another support after removal of the original wood. It is only attempted when all other forms of treatment have proved ineffective. Circumstances in which it might be carried out are, for example, when the support is totally decayed, or when adhesion between the support, ground and paint layers has irreversibly broken down. Transfer is an extremely long and difficult operation with many hazardous stages: it should only be attempted by a very experienced conservator.

Finally, a word should be said about the *thinning* of panels – a sort of partial transfer in which the wood is drastically reduced in thickness before application of some secondary support. The practice is based on the belief, largely fallacious, that a thin veneer of wood is somehow less troublesome and easier to manipulate than a panel of normal thickness. Often, in fact, the reverse is true, and the potential for cracking and warping may actually be increased. As a general rule, the thinning of panels should be discouraged.

Canvas supports

Defects of canvas paintings

Many fabrics have been used for painting supports which are grouped under the traditional description of 'canvas'; linen, in a variety of different weaves (which may have a distinct effect on the appearance of a picture) has been most widely used, but cotton, hemp and even silk are sometimes found. The suitability of a fabric for use as a painting canvas

depends on its ability to be stretched taut and to maintain tension. If tension is lost, the stability of the more brittle paint and ground layers is threatened.

Tension is maintained by the wooden *strainer* or *stretcher* upon which the fabric is mounted. A strainer has rigidly jointed corners and cannot be expanded, whereas a stretcher has mitred or tongue-grooved corners which can be tapped-out by means of wooden *keys* or *wedges*. Other mechanisms for expansion can involve turn-bolts or springs and are preferred by some conservators: these can be perfectly satisfactory, but in view of their potential mechanical strength great care should be exercised when tightening, especially with fabrics whose fibres tend to *creep* or deform irreversibly.

Rigid strainers should be replaced if the opportunity arises, since retensioning of a canvas painting may be necessary in, for example, conditions of fluctuating relative humidity. Although they are not as unstable as wood panels in these circumstances, the behaviour of canvas paintings is, nevertheless, complex, because the response of fabrics to varying RH depends both on the tension within them and on coatings which have been applied to them. A stretched yarn behaves differently to an unstretched one, in which factors such as twist or crimp become significant. Moreover, a sized fabric behaves differently to an unsized one. Given the conditions usually present in canvas paintings (principally due to their traditional preparation with animal glue size) higher RH will generally result in slackening or sagging. Expansion of the stretcher to take up the slack should be carried out with caution, since a subsequent fall in RH may mean that the canvas becomes too taut. However, if a canvas is allowed to sag for too long it can deform permanently.

From the mid-fifteenth century when canvas supports were introduced into European painting, their advantage over wood was seen to be principally one of lightness relative to size. They were portable and could even, if necessary, be rolled up. If a large painting has to be rolled for transport today (and it is always best to avoid it if possible), certain elementary principles should be observed. A cylindrical roller of the largest possible diameter should be used, one end of the canvas attached to it with tape, and the painting rolled around it with the painted side *outwards* (paint will stretch more successfully than it will compress). In addition, tissue or non-stick film should be placed between each successive layer, and the whole assembly wrapped and taped around.

Although they have the advantage of portability, canvas paintings possess an inherent and ever-increasing lack of strength. This is largely due to materials used in the sizing and painting processes. Animal glues, both in the original size layer and from subsequent support treatments such as lining, encourage the growth of micro-organisms and moulds which attack and weaken the fabric; also drying oils not only embrittle the whole structure but, through their own oxidation processes, promote oxidation and degradation of the fibres.

The natural consequences of these processes is that canvases are vulnerable to all kinds of physical impact and stress. Holes, tears and dents are commonplace. Canvas can be distorted by a label or patch stuck on the back, or by resting slackly against its stretcher. Repeated tapping-out can cause it to tear away from the tacks fastening it in place (a problem often worsened by rust from the tacks themselves) or to tear at the front edge of the stretcher. In association with the cracking of thick ground and paint layers, it can be distorted into a series of saucer shapes known as *cupping*. Often, cupping is absent in an area where the back of the canvas has been protected by the stretcher; this is the *stretcher image* and is usually bounded by continuous straight cracks corresponding to the edges of the stretcher bars.

Methods of treatment, minor and major, have been devised appropriate to all the many ways in which canvas paintings can deteriorate. All are specific to particular circumstnaces, some are ill-advised under any circumstances. Treatment other than the major process of *lining* will be considered first.

Minor repairs to canvas paintings

Many of the defects of canvas paintings can be dealt with relatively simply, or avoided altogether by observing simple precautions. Clearly, all risks of impact or contact with sharp or rigid objects must be eliminated.

Stacking pictures in store-rooms is a particular area of hazard: corners of other pictures or of frames must not be allowed to rest aginst a canvas. Parts of the structure of the picture itself can represent a danger. For example, untrimmed ends of picture wires can easily pierce a canvas; loose wedges and other foreign bodies can often fall between the bottom stretcher bar and the canvas, causing bulges on the surface of a painting. In the latter case, such bodies can be removed, with great care, by means of a flat palette-knife, and the problem avoided in future by securing the wedges with cord.

Dents or bulges can vary greatly in severity before the canvas is actually punctured. If caused by a blow on the reverse side, characteristic circular crack patterns in the paint and ground layers are often formed around the point of impact and there may be associated paint losses. It is possible to treat dents and bulges, and also localized wrinkles in a canvas, by careful damping of the reverse side of the area followed by tapping-out or flattening under weights on a flat surface. However, the utmost caution should be exercised, since some fabrics shrink excessively with moisture and throw off the paint.

Small holes in a canvas can be *patched* with thin material attached by a suitable adhesive. The danger with patching (as with attaching paper labels) is that the outlines of the patch (or labels) frequently become visible as distortions on the front of the picture. This is especially true if an aqueous adhesive is used. More satisfactory results can be obtained if a thermoplastic adhesive, such as wax–resin, is used and if the edges of the patch are *feathered*, or frayed, by removing some lateral threads. The repair is completed by filling and inpainting.

If the hole is larger, it can be filled by inserting a piece of canvas similar to the original, aligned correctly and held in place by patching. However, if the hole is more than a few centimetres across, lining is probably necessary. Tears, similarly, are usually too large to be satisfactorily treated by patching.

Sometimes the tacking edges of a canvas painting deteriorate, either at the tacks themselves or at the front edge of the stretcher, while the main picture area remains sound. In order to enable secure attachment to the stretcher, the edges may be reinforced by *strip-lining*; in this process, strips of new canvas are stuck behind the tacking margins (or in place of them if they are missing) and overlap the reverse of the main picture area by a centimetre or two. Various adhesives have been used. As with patching, there is a danger of the edges of the canvas strip showing as a ridge on the front of the painting, and so feathering and the use of a non-aqueous adhesive are advisable. Reattachment to the stretcher should be carried out with non-rusting tacks, either tinned or of copper.

Occasionally, under conditions of high humidity, canvas paintings are afflicted by mould which may feed off original size or lining materials. Mould may be treated by physical removal followed by spraying the reverse side with a suitable fungicide. Any mould on the paint surface may be removed by normal cleaning methods.

Lining and relining – traditional techniques

The usual cure for the maladies of paintings on canvas is *lining*. Very nearly all canvas pictures older than, say, the middle of the nineteenth century have been lined at least once and possibly several times. An old, unlined painting is something of a rarity and merits special consideration and treatment.

To *line* a painting is to reinforce it by attaching a second support to the back of the original canvas using a suitable adhesive. To *reline* a painting is to remove an existing lining and repeat the process. The purposes of lining are, traditionally, three-fold:

(1) to strengthen a canvas support which may be weak, torn or incapable of being attached to its stretcher;
(2) to correct deformations of the support, ground and paint layers by application of heat, pressure or moisture, or combinations of those three; and
(3) to ensure firm attachment of the paint and ground layers to the support by penetration and impregnation with the chosen adhesive.

The lining process was originally devised to achieve these three objectives in a single operation. Impregnation and lining of canvas paintings have been carried out using glue and drying oils since the seventeenth century. The use of beeswax and, later, beeswax–resin mixtures became widespread in the late nineteenth century and continues to the present day.

Traditionally, lining techniques are based on the use of fine linen for the secondary support and infusion with either a glue/flour paste or a hot-melt beeswax–resin adhesive; both types may have other additives designed to impart desirable properties. These remain standard techniques and, applied in the correct circumstances, produce excellent results. Indeed, without them, many paintings would not have survived. There are clear advantages and disadvantages in both techniques; it cannot be stressed too strongly that a painting can be ruined and even destroyed by injudicious application of an unsuitable method. Of all conservation procedures, lining is perhaps the most difficult to do well and requires great experience in a conservator.

Badly cupped paintings, which will relax and flatten with moisture, may be successfully lined with aqueous, glue-based adhesives. However, certain canvases in combination with particular grounds shrink disastrously under the action of moisture and heat, throwing off the paint. Shrinking does not occur with non-aqueous beeswax–resin adhesives but, on the other hand, they are ineffective in treating cupping: some sort of pretreatment with moisture is required if cupping is to be eliminated (pp. 280 and 286–7).

The refractive index of lining adhesives is important, since it has a direct bearing on any possible darkening of a painting. Where ground and paint layers are poorly bound, or where the original canvas plays a visible role, infusion with certain adhesives can result in darkening and colour change. In a general way, the reflective index of wax–resin is such that it is more likely to cause darkening than an aqueous adhesive. In most old pictures, painted in oil and repeatedly varnished, the change is not significant: however, it is a factor that should always be considered.

One of the most common reasons for lining is the repair of tears or holes. It is obviously desirable that the chosen adhesive should be strong enough and stiff enough to maintain the edges of a tear in a flat state. Beeswax–resin adhesvies are rather poor in this respect and tears may begin to curl and sag after a period of time. As well as using a different adhesive, the problem of badly torn paintings is often best dealt with by *marouflage*, in which the painting is mounted on a rigid panel, preferably of inert materials, or by *double lining*, in which a second lining confers additional stiffness. In double lining, different adhesives can be used for the two stages – perhaps an aqueous adhesive followed by wax–resin.

The practical procedures involved in different lining methods are also of importance in deciding their suitability. Glue-paste lining is usually done with hand irons, which should be thermostatically controlled. Paintings of high impasto can present a problem and many are seen today with their texture crushed during previous hand linings. Although there are ways in which the problem can be overcome, it is probably better to avoid hand lining such paintings. Wax–resin linings may also be carried out with hand irons, but they are particularly suited to *hot-table* methods. A hot-table, usually of polished metal, provides uniform control of heating and cooling over its whole surface. In combination with a membrane fastened to the edges of the table and a vacuum pump, paintings may be held under constant pressure during the entire lining process. Such methods are only suitable for thermoplastic lining adhesives and cannot be used for adhesives which involve evaporation of water or solvents.

Lining of paintings on the vacuum hot-table is usually carried out face-up, with the adhesive and lining canvas underneath. It is therefore a suitable method for paintings with impasto; even so, a combination of heat and the pressure of the membrane can soften and flatten paint texture. The lining of paintings face down on the hot-table should be discouraged for obvious reasons.

Although the introduction of the vacuum hot-table represented a major advance in lining techniques, possible limitations and disadvantages become apparent. The technique will not, by itself, eliminate cupping in paintings; neither will it permit the use of adhesives other than thermoplastic ones. Moreover, there is a possibility of unwelcome texture changes in paintings lined under vacuum pressure: sometimes the texture of the original canvas or the lining canvas may influence the paint surface by *weave emphasis* or *weave interference*. Such effects can be reduced by interposing a non-woven *interleaf* between the two canvases.

Marouflage can be carried out on a hot-table, provided that the panel is heat conducting, as modern aluminium honeycomb constructions are. Otherwise hand ironing is necessary, or use of a cold-setting adhesive.

The final criterion by which a lining should be judged is how it behaves subsequently. Here again, traditional techniques differ. Wax–resin linings are not affected by changes in RH; glue linings are, and may sag or contract if conditions alter. In order to combat this, they may have a moisture barrier of wax or wax–resin applied to the back of the lining canvas as a final stage. Wax–resin linings do not maintain tension wholly successfully and may slacken over a period of time: it has already been mentioned that repaired tears may curl and distort.

Lining is only a temporary measure, carried out in the full expectation that it will have to be repeated within 50–100 years. It therefore becomes vital that current treatment be *reversible* in the broadest sense. In the strictest sence, impregnation of a painting with any adhesive is fundamentally irreversible but, in practical terms, reversibility implies only the possibility of physical removal of the old lining. The compatibility of adhesive within the original fabric with any future lining adhesive is important, however. Glue formulations tend to be compatible, both with the materials of the painting itself and with most other adhesives. Traditional beeswax–resin mixtures, on the whole, are not: it should always be borne in mind that once a canvas painting has been impregnated with wax–resin, treatment with other adhesives is inhibited.

Lining and related treatments – new directions

Until recent years, the choice of lining methods was limited, with minor variations, to one of the traditional techniques described above. Currently, investigation of alternative methods is a major area of research and any account must inevitably become out of date fairly rapidly; nevertheless certain trends may be identified.

Emphasis is moving away from impregnation techniques. The different objectives of the lining process – fixing of flaking paint, reinforcement of support and elimination of deformations – can be achieved in separate operations which do not necessarily require overall impregnation. Where possible, lining is avoided altogether.

Where lining is required merely as reinforcement, it is unnecessary and, indeed, undesirable to infuse the whole structure of a painting with adhesives, with possible consequences such as darkening and colour change. All that is required is a bond between the lining and the surface fibres on the reverse of the original canvas – a so-called *nap bond*. This is very difficult to achieve using traditional adhesives, which penetrate and flow uncontrollably, and so a range of synthetic adhesives of more suitable properties has emerged.

A major advance has been the development of *heat-seal* adhesives, applied in solution (unlike conventional wax–resin mixtures which are applied molten) and heat activated after drying. Heat-seal adhesives consist of, or contain, mixtures of resins of high and low molecualr weight, which combine high viscosity with powerful adhesion. They will bond two pieces of fabric together without flowing into them. Formulations containing different grades of polyvinyl acetate (PVA) have been found especially suitable for the lining process.

By adding other components such as synthetic waxes, further useful properties such as increased flow and decreased heat-seal temperature can be incorporated. The versatile Beva adhesives, developed specifically for use in lining, are based on ethylene vinyl acetate copolymers and microcrystalline waxes. They can be used either as heat-seal adhesives or, by increasing the temperature, as impregnating adhesives with flow properties analogous to conventional hot melts. Even when used for impregnation, the risk of darkening is less than with beeswax–resin mixtures, since the refractive indices of the components are lower.

The new generation of heat-activated adhesives can be used in conjunction with hand irons, vacuum hot-tables or with the *vacuum envelope* technique, in which the canvases are held between two membranes stretched over a framework. The disadvantages of the rigid hot-table are overcome by this method, and heating and cooling can be more or less instantaneous.

Another development in lining adhesives is the use of water-based emulsions containing acrylic or vinyl resins. These are cold setting and act by evaporation of water and solvent. Conventional vacuum hot-tables are unsuitable for the technique, and specially designed low pressure lining tables ('cold' tables) have been devised for it. These have metal surfaces with regularly spaced small perforations; a powerful down-draught of air not only holds the canvases in close contact but also carries away the evaporating water or solvents. With water-based emulsions such as these, the possible danger of shrinking in the picture canvas should always be considered.

The heat-seal and low-pressure methods will not, in themselves, fix flaking painting or eliminate cupping. When necessary, these are carried out before the lining stage. Fixing of flaking paint is described on page 282. Cupping may be reduced by exposing the picture canvas to water and solvent vapours and pressing out the deformations with or without heat, after the canvas has relaxed. The necessary conditions are present in traditional glue-paste linings, which is why they are successful in this respect. Treatment of cupping as a separate stage before lining may be carried out by damping and hand ironing (somewhat dangerous), by vapour treatment under warmth and pressure on the vacuum hot-table, or by repeated exposure to moisture and drying out on the low-pressure table. The most effective apparatus is a low-pressure table with heating and humidifying facilities, the multi-purpose, low-pressure table described in 'Moisture treatments', pp. 286–7.

As an adjunct to the treatment of distortions such as cupping, it is often necessary to place the picture canvas under tension, in order to encourage it to return to its former flat state. Various techniques combining vapour treatment and stretching have been devised, with or without additional pressure and heat, which are described by the general term *pre-stretching*. The subsequent lining may then be performed with the painting held in its pre-stretched condition.

As well as lining adhesives, lining fabrics have been the subject of research in recent years. Although fine linen remains the most widely used secondary support, other materials such as fibreglass, polyester fabrics and polyvinyl alcohol fabrics can have advantages in certain respects, such as permanence, stiffness, creep and so on. Fibreglass can result in a semi-transparent lining, if inscriptions on the back of the picture canvas are required to remain visible.

Lining, in the sense of permanent attachment of a secondary fabric, may sometimes be unnecessary, when the original canvas merely requires support. It can be enough to fasten a second canvas over the stretcher before stretching the picture canvas – this is so-called *loose lining* – in which the two canvases simply rest against each other. As a compromise between loose lining and full attachment, a recent development utilizes a fabric coated with a tacky silicone adhesive, which holds the picture canvas firmly, but which may be peeled of if and when this becomes necessary.

Other supports

Supports other than wood panel or canvas are sometimes encountered. Treatment of defects must necessarily be empirical, but a few specific problems may be mentioned.

The principal problem with supports of metal, stone, slate, marble and similar materials is one of poor adhesion between their smooth, unabsorbent surfaces and applied paint layers. Painters are well aware of the problem and would often etch or roughen surfaces to provide a key. However, flaking paint is the most common defect in such paintings, and may be treated by methods outlined below.

Copper, the most usual metal plate used for painting, is a reactive metal and this should be remembered when selecting adhesives for securing loose paint. Certain components of traditional wax–resin mixtures will react with copper, in time forming salts which will undermine and force off paint adjacent to treated areas. For this reason, wax–resin adhesives should never be used on copper

pictures. Inert synthetic formulations are suitable and have been used with success.

Unsupported copper plates may be in danger of flexing, bending and creasing with consequent paint loss. A copper painting, once bent, is almost impossible to straighten satisfactorily. It is therefore important to remove this risk by backing it with a rigid panel of some kind. It should not be laid down with adhesives, but held against its back board by capping the edges or with adhesive tape on the reverse side.

One other unusual support material should be mentioned, as it poses unique problems to the conservator of easel paintings. This is *vellum*, encountered only rarely, and perhaps difficult to distinguish from fabric – especially if it has been lined with canvas. The particular danger with vellum is that a combination of heat and moisture causes it to shrink markedly. Distortions and tears in a vellum picture may require treatment with controlled amounts of moisture, but it should be carried out only by an expert.

Ground, paint and varnish layers
Defects of paint and ground: treatment

Defects of paint layers arise from a number of causes. Inherent instability of materials, techniques of application, natural ageing processes, interaction with other layers and external influences, such as heat, light, humidity and physical damage, can all contribute to their deterioration.

A combination of processes is therefore operating, which manifests itself most clearly in the *craquelure* observed on the surface. Cracking of paint films is of two main types: *drying cracks*, initiated during the drying process, and *age* (or *mechanical*) cracks which occur after paint and ground have ceased to be flexible. On a microscopic scale, drying cracks tend to have rounded edges, since they are formed while the paint is still plastic, but their overall pattern is unpredictable. Whether or not they develop depends on the properties of both the paint and the ground or underlayer to which it was applied. Considerable shrinkage and cracking of a paint film can result from its own drying mechanism, especially when bituminous pigments are present which retard drying in particular areas. Also, if the ground or underlayer is still plastic, or its surface is glossy and rich in medium, then adhesive forces between layers are insufficient to counteract the contraction of the paint film. Many eighteenth- and nineteenth-century paintings show this phenomenon, resulting from the use of insufficiently aged or unsuitable commercially prepared grounds, and from the unwise use of certain paint formulations.

Whether or not drying cracks are present, most paintings of any period have a network of age cracks usually initiated by movement of the support. These are formed when the paint and ground have hardened and become brittle, and therefore penetrate both layers. Some tension remains in the paint and ground layers even when dry and this may result in the formation of concavities (*cupping*) between the age cracks. This tension can be strong enough to set up distortions throughout the entire structure of a picture and might lead ultimately to deformation of the support (in canvas paintings) or to cleavage from it. Cleavage is also caused by constant movement of the support weakening the bond between layers.

No treatment is required for craquelure as such: it is regarded as a normal ageing characteristic of a painting. If it is especially disfiguring (for example, drying cracks in dark areas which reveal a white ground) it may be inpainted using a fine brush.

However, associated cleavage leading to *blistering* and *flaking* must be treated before paint loss occurs – although, too often, loss of paint is the first indication that cleavage is present. It is important that paintings should be regularly inspected for signs of raised paint and blisters. Curators and conservators alike should resist the temptation to test raised paint with a thumbnail: a paint blister is very brittle and can shatter and be lost very easily.

Treatment of blistering and flaking is straightforward but requires much patience: it is a routine but vital operation in the maintenance of any picture collection. Canvas paintings, of course, may be treated by lining or relining and panel paintings by transfer, but for local areas on canvases, and for the vast majority of panel paintings, treatment is carried out using thermostatically controlled heated spatulas.

The principle is to introduce adhesive into points of cleavage and to flatten and hold the paint in position until the adhesive sets. Traditional adhesives are hot melts of the wax–resin type and weak animal glue solutions such as gelatine. More recently, synthetic adhesives have been widely used, as hot melts, or in solution, or as water-based emulsions. The adhesive is usually introduced through a tissue *facing* which protects the surface of the paint and holds any loose flakes in place. Aqueous adhesives or those in solution may be brushed on; hot-melts can be picked up directly on the hot spatula. With practice, it is usually possible to persuade the adhesive to flow into blisters or under raised paint through the existing craquelure. If there is no craquelure – in cases of blind cleavage perhaps – it may be necessary to allow the adhesive to penetrate. This can be done quite unobtrusively and there is no need for the excessive pricking sometimes encountered on old panel paintings.

As with lining, aqueous adhesives are more successful at dealing with cupped paint and ground, but the combination of heat and moisture can cause *blanching* of the varnish, which then has to be reformed using suitable solvents (see page 283). With an aqueous adhesive, ironing with warm spatula is continued until it is set; with a hot-melt adhesive setting is achieved by substituting a cold spatula for the hot one.

If a painting is found to be flaking and immediate treatment is not possible, then a *facing* of tissue should be applied to the affected area with a standard facing adhesive. This may be a starch paste, wax–resin based or synthetic; when dry, the tissue holds the paint firmly in place until remedial treatment can be carried out. Facing is a routine preliminary operation which precedes many conservation treatments: in support treatment, where there is a danger of paint becoming detached through movement, facing is essential.

Examples of inherent instability in paint and ground materials are the occasional chemical alterations undergone by a few pigments. The blue ultramarine may become a mottled grey colour under acid conditions; green copper resinate may become dark brown under alkaline conditions. Both processes may be accelerated by the use of unsuitable reagents during cleaning, and both are irreversible. Another pigment change identified in recent years is the discolouration of the blue smalt in oil media to a greenish-grey. In general, chemical interaction between pigments, such as the blackening of lead white by sulphides (not infrequently observed in watercolours and murals) does not occur in oil and egg-tempera paintings.

The medium, too, sometimes undergoes optical changes. The most common example of this is the increased transparency of paint layers caused by a rise in the refractive index of drying oils as they age. *Pentimenti* and dark grounds that were not originally apparent, may, in time, show through.

Less predictable are the occasional cases of *blanching* in the paint film: two distinct types may be identified. The first is caused directly by exposure to moisture (flood-damaged paintings for example) but it is important to distinguish it from the far more common blanching of the varnish layers (see above). To a degree, it may be reversed by exposure to solvents and solvent vapours. The second type of blanching is more mysterious: it tends to occur with particular painters such as Claude or Cuyp, in passages such as landscapes and foliage. Whether it is caused by deterioration of pigment or medium or both has not yet been ascertained: it is reduced slightly by solvent treatment, but is largely irreversible.

The varnish layer: cleaning of paintings

An ideal picture varnish should be transparent, without colour and of a refractive index compatible with the dried paint film it is to protect; it should be tough and resist moisture and pollutants, and yet should also be readily removable in mild solvents. Most importantly, it should retain these properties for as long as it remains on the painting.

No varnish corresponding to this ideal has yet been produced. Traditional varnishes containing drying oils and hard resins discolour badly and become quite insoluble with time. Even the best of the natural resin varnishes – dammar and mastic, which have excellent handling properties and are still widely used – discolour appreciably and become less soluble. Most of the newer synthetic resins used for picture varnishes are reasonable in terms of reversibility and colour, but fall down on other considerations – surface appearance or handling, for example.

The relatively rapid deterioration of varnishes becomes evident in a number of ways. Discolouration, opacity and blanching all impair their optical properties. They can shrivel and contract and develop independent craquelures of their own, which attract dust and dirt. A thick varnish may also exert considerable traction forces as it ages and may actually endanger a weak paint film below.

For a variety of reasons paintings are cleaned. *Cleaning* implies removal of dirt, varnishes and other surface coatings, and also any non-original paint that may conceal damage or cover original paint. The technique of cleaning is simple, but much skill and experience is necessary to interpret and to deal with problems if they arise. Varnish removal is carried out with appropriate solvents on small cotton-wool swabs; as the swabs become saturated with dissolved residues they are changed.

Cleaning (in the sense of varnish removal); has been practised for centuries and has always been an inexact and empirical operation, relying on the skill of the restorer rather than on any precise application of scientific principles. Within reason, the choice of solvent was less critical than the dexterity of its user. More recently, it has been possible to quantify and classify materials used in cleaning and to relate them directly to the coatings that are being removed. This is done in terms of *solubility parameters* which have been calculated for a wide variety of solvents and resins. Solvent mixtures may be selected whose parameters fall within the range calculated for a particular resin. Equally importantly, solvents whose parameters correspond to the swelling region of the paint medium (and which, therefore, might endanger the paint film during cleaning) can be avoided.

A technique which is closely allied to varnish removal, either as a preliminary to it or as an alternative, is *reforming*. A refined version of a nineteenth-century practice known as the *Pettenkofer* method (after its inventor) in which varnishes were rejuvenated by suspending pictures over solvent vapours, it consists of spraying or brushing controlled amounts of selected solvents on to the picture surface. Where varnishes have become opaque or cracked or blanched, reforming will greatly improve their clarity, although it will have no effect on discolouration as such. It will also render varnishes more readily soluble in relatively mild solvents in any subsequent cleaning.

A form of varnish removal sometimes used is that of *frictioning* the surface. A small crystal of resin is rubbed on the existing varnish with the fingertips, causing it to break down into white powder which can be dusted off. This operation appears more alarming than it actually is. It is an extremely inefficient method of removing varnish, but it could be used if a paint film was soluble in normal cleaning solvents. It is more often used to even up an old, patchy varnish, followed by application of a new coating.

An occasional problem with some varnishes is *bloom*, a dull bluish cloudiness which appears intermittently. Its cause is uncertain, but humid conditions seem to encourage it. It can usually be removed with a damp cloth followed by polishing with a dry one. Application of a suitable wax polish will eliminate it, but the advantage of that must be balanced against the fact that wax coatings attract dirt appreciably more than varnishes alone.

Removal of surface dirt from paintings is carried out using water, or dilute solutions of appropriate soaps on cotton wool swabs. This is an operation that must be carried out with particular care, since both water and soap might have deleterious effects if allowed to penetrate the structure of the picture. If a painting has been varnished several times over an extended period, each time trapping a layer of dirt beneath the new coating, cleaning may require repeated alternation of solvents with aqueous agents.

Removal of overpaint and retouching during the cleaning process is often achieved with the same solvents used for varnish removal. This, of course, depends on differential solubility between later and original paint. Where the two cannot be separated by solvents or reagents, physical methods such as scrapping with scalpels must be employed. Criteria for distinguishing original paint from later additions are well-established in the literature. If there is any doubt about the status of a particular passage, it must be left alone.

Some new developments in the cleaning of paintings are described on p. 285.

Restoration of paintings: filling, inpainting and revarnishing

When cleaning is completed, a painting is given a thin brush-coat of a suitable picture varnish, in preparation for *filling* and *inpainting*.

Where old damage has been revealed by cleaning, or new repairs are being carried out, the last stages of treatment are the filling of lacunae, inpainting (retouching) and the application of a final varnish.

There are many recipes for filling materials, some traditional, some synthetic. Most conservators have particular preferences, and as long as the filler satisfies certain basic conditions, the choice is not critical. Filling materials should be capable of being textured, in order to imitate the surface of the surrounding paint, either by carving or moulding in some way; they should not shrink or curl or fall out; and they should not become so hard that they cannot be removed without endangering adjacent paint (as some oil putties do). The success of a passage of inpainting depends largely on the skill with which the filling has been carried out. A check on the matching of texture may be made with the picture in raking light.

The criteria by which retouching paints should be judged are similar to those described above for an ideal varnish. Whether commercially prepared formulations are used or whether pure pigments are ground in a medium by the conservator himself, a retouching paint should retain its colour, not darken and should remain permanently removable in mild solvents. Oil paints are almost totally unsuitable for retouching, since they darken and become insoluble: even removal of excess oil with blotting paper (as some restorers do) does not render them suitable. Commerical artists' paints based on synthetic resins might be satisfactory, but the conservator may have no idea of the properties of permanence of the manufacturer's ingredients.

The most satisfactory inpainting materials appear to be pure pigments of known permanence, either ground in a range of synthetic resins of known and tested properties, or used as water-colours, or in pure egg-tempera. Suitable synthetic resins that are widely used are particular grades of polyvinyl acetate and acrylic copolymers of the Paraloid (Acryloid) range: their optical properties, permanence and reversibility appear to be excellent. Retouching using water-colour or egg-tempera is more difficult (especially in terms of colour-matching, since they change tone on varnishing) but, skilfully done, they can achieve unique luminosity and texture. It might appear that egg-tempera, which becomes insoluble in time, disobeys the principle of reversibility: but, provided it is applied over an isolating varnish that remains soluble, it can always be removed.

The degree and nature of any inpainting is a matter for consultation between curator and conservator. There are many possible compromises between leaving a hole in the fabric of a painting and 'complete' or 'deceptive' retouching. Any decision has to take into account the type of painting and the nature, size and position of the damage. But, whatever that decision, it does not affect the basic ethics of restoration, which are that: materials should be reversible, no original paint that was intended to be seen should be covered, and a photographic record of the picture in its unretouched state should, if possible, be made.

The desirable properties in a final varnish have been discussed. Retouchings are usually varnished individually with a small brush before the last coating is applied by brush or spray. Variation in gloss and mattness can be achieved by incorporating additives such as synthetic waxes in the varnish formulation. Alternatively, gloss can be regulated by judicious manipulation of the spray gun, if that method of application is used.

Handling, storage and display

The importance of environmental control for easel paintings cannot be overstated and, while full air-conditioning is beyond the range of many museums, installation of blinds, humidifiers and so on can markedly improve conditions. Ideal values for temperature and RH are 20°C and 55 per cent, respectively; a range of 10 per cent RH can be tolerated. Visible light and UV radiation levels should also be controlled since photochemical changes do occur in easel painting materials, although phenomena such as fading are less pronounced than in water-colours or textiles, for example. A value of 200 lux at the picture surface is considered to be a reasonable compromise between the need to see the painting and the need to protect it.

If climate control is impossible, then serious consideration should be given to placing fragile paintings in a sealed case of some kind, either free-standing or fastened to the wall of the room. Conditions inside are more or less isolated from environmental changes outside, and a *microclimate* is established. Such cases can vary enormously in sophistication. The simplest are merely transparent boxes which serve to delay and suppress the transmittance of atmospheric fluctuations to the space around the painting. More elaborate designs have chambers incorporated within them, containing salts conditioned to maintain the air at a particular RH level.

Handling and storage of easel paintings is, above all, a matter of common sense. Accidents occur when staff have not been shown how to handle pictures, when economies are made in time and personnel and when space is limited. In most museums, storage areas are cramped and invariably become used for other purposes as well. If it is within the museum budget, a system of mesh screens to which pictures (with or without their frames) may be fixed on both sides, is ideal for storage. These may be fixed, in which case enough space must be left between them for access, or mounted close together on a series of parallel bearings so that a single screen can be pulled out of the stack; the latter system allows much more efficient use of available space.

Often, however, there is no alternative to stacking pictures against a wall, leaning them one against another. Clearly there are dangers involved, with paintings of different sizes, sharp corners, frame mouldings and so on. If possible, rigid boards should be placed between pictures so that they do not rest directly against each other, and a weight placed against the foot of the outermost picture to prevent it sliding forward. In a basement storage area, the possibility of damp, or even flooding, should not be discounted.

For pictures without frames, especially large modern ones, it is often sound practice to construct a temporary frame which will protect the edges and by which the picture may be carried.

The permanent framing and display of pictures are areas in which correct preparation and some forethought can have markedly beneficial effects on the paintings themselves. A frame should be deep enough to contain the thickness of the picture: if not, then the back should be built up until it is. A backboard of masonite or similar material can then be fixed to the frame, covering and protecting the back of the painting. For canvas pictures, this prevents dust and foreign bodies collecting behind the lower stretcher bar. For panel paintings it can act as a rudimentary buffer against atmospheric fluctuations.

The rebates of frames should be lined with material such as velvet ribbon so that varnish around the edges of a painting is not scuffed. For warped panels, shaped slips should be incorporated within the rebate (see page 276). The fastening of pictures into frames should be carried out using mirror plates screwed to the back of the frame and overlapping the back of the picture. Rubber pads may be placed between the plates and the picture to allow for movement in the support. The traditional practice of attaching pictures to their frames with bent nails should be discouraged. Spaces around the edges of the pictures should be packed with a relatively soft material like balsa wood.

Whether paintings should be glazed is usually a curatorial decision. It is undeniable that glass or perspex protects a picture surface from physical impact, dust and pollutants and, to a degree, from atmospheric changes, but against that must be weighed the undoubted aesthetic limitations imposed.

The problem of transporting pictures and of travelling exhibitions is discussed elsewhere, in terms of packing-case design and administrative considerations. Deciding whether a painting is fit to travel should be left to an experienced conservator, who will judge its present condition and any likely consequences. Some museums refuse on principle to lend any wood panels: although this is a commendably cautious attitude, it is probably better to consider each case on its merits. Indeed, many panel paintings will actually travel more successfully than some canvas paintings, in which constant vibration of the stretched fabric may play a major role in deterioration.

Perhaps the most vital aspect of maintaining any collection of easel paintings is regular inspection. Constant vigilance will detect many minor problems before they become major ones. A routine examination programme should be instituted and repeated periodically, although its frequency will obviously depend on the size of the collection.

Recent developments in paintings conservation

James Dimond

New methods in the cleaning of paintings

A biochemical approach to the cleaning of paintings utilizing aqueous solutions of resin soaps, enzymes and solvent gels departs from the traditional techniques of solvent removal of varnish layers (American Institute for Conservation, 1988; Wolbers, 1989).

Resin soaps

The varnish remover is an aqueous solution of 'resin soap' which is basically a detergent but in molecular terms has one portion which is miscible with water and another portion which is miscible with fats or oils (Wolbers, 1989). The latter hydrophobic section mimics the shape of the 'triterpene' fraction of dammar resin, one of the most common resins used in picture varnishes. Two resin soaps so far researched, abietic acid and deoxycholic acid, have proved successful in removing varnishes, though it has proved necessary to control the pH to maintain the solution and also to add cellulose based material to produce a gel for improved control of application.

Use of enzymes

Enzymes are naturally occurring large protein molecules used by living organisms to catalyse specific chemical reactions. In water the enzyme molecules spontaneously fold into a formation that contains a region of particular geometry called an 'active site'. This formation allows only preferred molecules involved in the reaction to be catalysed.

Optimum conditions of pH (using buffers) and temperature must be created for effective activity and to avoid denaturing the enzymes. A 'wetting agent' ensures adequate contact with the substrate surface and the components are gelled in a cellulose base.

If a damaged painting has been retouched with oil medium on top of a resin varnish layer and darkening of the retouching disfigures the image, the enzyme lipase could break down the triglyceride structure of the overpaint and effect removal. On some paintings, dark and disfiguring proteinaceous material can be found in the troughs of brush marks on the painting surface due to incomplete clearance after a paste lining. Solvent can have little effect upon the residue, but a protease enzyme may be more successful.

Solvent gels

Where a coating or overpaint is extremely insoluble, the traditional conservator's approach is to resort to solvents of increasingly polar character and low evaporation rate, posing a much greater risk to the original paint layer and to the conservator due to the toxicity of the materials. Solvent gels can reduce both risks, providing a more controllable technique and reduced chemical exposure. There are two main types of solvent gel, immiscible solvents emulsified in a high concentration of detergent, and miscible solvents thickened with a gelling agent (Wolbers, 1989).

The resin soap, enzyme and gel solutions are, to some degree interchangeable, so that one system can be adapted by adding a component from another to solve a particular problem. Identification of the nature of each layer of a painting's structure plays an important part in the technique, enabling a specific cleaning system to be constructed that is appropriate to the layer targetted for removal (Wolbers and Landrey, 1987). The term 'unpacking' is used to describe the sequential removal of dirt and varnish layers and highlights the accuracy of this method compared with a conventional cleaning approach in which conventional solvents may burst through several layers at once.

Under UV radiation, materials such as dammar and mastic resins fluoresce, that is re-emit energy as visible light. A number of fluorescent dyes or 'fluorochromes' can be used to 'tag' the material structure of the various layers of a painting and examination of a cross-section with a UV microscope allows an interpretation of the structure.

Chelating agents

Some unvarnished paintings have a greyish brown layer that is very difficult to remove. Elemental analysis has shown lead to be a major component of the layer and 'fluorochrome tagging' of a cross-section sample indicates a high concentration of lipids or fatty acids. The presence of the surface layer may be due to the deposition of air-borne pollutants onto fatty acids exuded from the paint film or onto a medium-rich surface produced by the artists practice of 'oiling out'. Alternatively, atmospheric hydrogen sulphide might also react with lead soaps present in the paint formulations. Irrespective of the mechanism responsible for formation, chelating agents may be used to scavenge metal ions such as the lead present in the surface layer, thereby breaking up the darkened coating. Triammonium citrate and similar chelating agents have been used with some success to remove such intractable layers (Carlyle *et al*, 1990).

Most cleaning of paintings will continue to be done skilfully and safely using well-established methods. These new developments may be effective for a small number of cleaning problems, and add to the range of techniques available to the conservator.

Moisture treatments: new developments

Damage caused to paintings by excessive moisture is well documented, and many of the advances made in conservation treatments over the last 30 years have avoided exposing the painting to high levels of humidity. Nevertheless, there are advantages to be gained by the use of moisture treatment for some paintings on canvas in terms of relaxation, regeneration and consolidation of the paint layers, provided that the support has not previously been impregnated with non-aqueous adhesives such as waxes or resins.

As humidity levels change, the pattern of behaviour of the glue size and paint layers of the painting is different from that of the canvas; the former become stiffer and more stressed in dry conditions while the canvas becomes more flexible. The reverse occurs under moist conditions. Below a RH of around 80 per cent, paintings gain tension during desorption as the RH is lowered, and lose tension during absorption as the RH is raised. These effects are almost entirely due to the hygroscopic nature of the size layer. Above 80 per cent RH, the opposite effects are observed to a greater or lesser degree, as the fabric support shrinks creating much more powerful stresses than those caused by the size or paint layer (Hedley, 1988a).

Certain types of canvas have long been recognized as being vulnerable to moisture damage. Fine-weave Victorian canvases are notorious. When moisture damaged, the largest amount of shrinkage is a product of the structure of the fabric itself, and is termed 'weave interchange' (Hedley, 1988b) defined as the increase in crimp or the in-built winding of warp fibres around the weft. Tightening of the twist and overall shortenings of the yarn threads plays a smaller part in the shrinking process. The finer the fabric (Victorian canvases are often quite fine), the greater will be the 'weave interchange' effect or increase in crimp when water damaged. Victorian canvas suppliers' practice of applying the size layer cold, leaving a discrete size layer between the fabric and the paint layer increases the susceptibility to moisture damage. Excess moisture will swell or dissolve the size layer leaving little adhesion to a shrinking support.

Research is being carried out into the plasticizing effect of humidity on oil paint (Husband, 1990). The research shows that below 90 per cent RH there is little relaxation of the paint layers but above this level the paint becomes increasingly more relaxed or plastic. This introduces the possibility that cupping, the basin-like formation between age cracking may be permanently corrected by moisture treatment above 90 per cent RH.

A traditional paste lining can create extreme conditions of humidity and temperature that will successfully treat both planar deformations in the support and cupping in the paint layer. Moisture treatments discussed here isolate each function to gain greater control and minimize risks. Armed with a knowledge of the moisture response of each component of a painting structure, attempts can be made to introduce the appropriate temperature and RH for a particular treatment and control those conditions within set parameters.

Moisture relaxation treatments to flatten deformations in a canvas support and reduce cupping in a paint layer have been carried out on ordinary hot-tables using porous non-hygroscopic interleaves to carry water and alcohol mixtures. The system is sometimes unsuccessful because the amount of moisture introduced into the system is not easily controlled.

The multi-purpose, low-pressure table allows the conservator to carry out most forms of lining and pre-lining treatments with a much greater control over heat, moisture and temperature than has been previously possible. A tubular-steel frame supports a top of interchangeable, perforated and solid aluminium sheets, rebated into the surround. A humidifier introduces moisture into a ducting system beneath the perforated sheet, and the air is circulated evenly by a variable-speed fan. RH is controlled by wet- and dry-bulb sensors. Heated elements situated within the ducting, and extra edge heaters around the perimeter to compensate for heat loss, are thermostatically controlled. Pressure can be evenly applied by a membrane held over the table surface by the suction generated by a separate variable-speed fan.

The humidity chamber is being researched as another alternative to provide more controllable treatments for structural disorders in the layers of a painting (Goddard, 1989). A transparent chamber containing moisture at equilibrium at a prescribed level has the advantage over the multi-purpose table that the presence of water vapour above the painting encourages a gradual development of plasticity in all layers. This raises the possibility of treating the cupping as well as removing planar distortions in the support.

The chamber is constructed from cheap and widely available materials and can be adapted to different sizes of painting. A frame structure supports a polyethylene membrane to form a chamber that is as air tight as is practicable. Trays containing saturated salt solutions can be used to provide stable RH levels (e.g. at 20°C, sodium chloride produces an RH of 75.4 per cent and potassium nitrate produces an RH of 94.6 per cent). A fan circulates air to ensure more or less constant RH throughout the chamber. A dew-point sensor and a temperature probe are used to monitor the humidity and temperature. While being treated using the chamber, a painting is put under tension by attaching it to a keyable loom with paper or fabric margins. Looming makes the painting easier to handle and also may inhibit shrinkage of the support should the conditions become too extreme.

The disadvantages of the chamber are that equilibrium takes a long time to establish and is easily disturbed when access to the painting is required. Both the multi-purpose table and humidity chamber have been used to great effect in the treatment of planar distortions in the painting support using a RH below 80 per cent. While research suggests that RH levels between 90 and 100 per cent could be used to induce plasticity in a paint layer to treat cupping, the risk of shrinkage of support remains high for many canvases. Further research may provide a solution to this problem.

Conservation and contemporary art

In some cases contemporary art incorporates the use of non-proven materials and techniques, where the artist is developing ideas and creative forms that do not involve concern for durability. Experimentation with materials is not a phenomenon unique to the twentieth century. Leonardo, Reynolds and Stubbs are well-documented experimenters, and perhaps notions of the permanence of previous centuries and the evanescence of contemporary work are spurious. The most obvious factors that characterize twentieth-century work are the more dramatic effects of decay, and if the artist is still alive his or her intentions regarding that degeneration.

Examples of severe breakdown of an object are rare but, where the materials that carry or are the symbolic form deteriorate at a rapid and unpredictable rate, the conservator or curator has an enormous number of considerations to take into account.

The occurrence of the accelerated decay of materials could be accounted for by:

(1) the artist's lack of knowledge about the physical and chemical stability of materials used in construction;
(2) the search for a form of creativity at the expense of concern for the stability of materials; or even
(3) the inclusion of decay as part of the content of the work.

An example of the first category, are the colour field paintings produced by Mark Rothko for Harvard, displayed in the penthouse room of the Holyoke Centre in 1963. By 1968 they were described as 'a major mess' and were taken off display in 1979. The environmental conditions of their display area may not have been ideal and Rothko certainly was aware that his paints were not of the best quality, but the main cause of their demise was the fading of the fugitive red pigment (lithol red).

In an example such as this, the aesthetic balance of the object is irreversibly altered from the artist's original intention, but tampering with altered material would deny the integrity of the piece as a unique art work, and deny its history of ageing.

The second category is typified by a number of Naum Gabo's maquets from the 1920s onwards which were constructed from the then recently developed cellulose acetate plastic sheeting. His original 'Two Cones' (*Figure 30.1*) was made in 1927 and subsequently deteriorated so badly that Gabo reconstructed the piece in 1968 from an old stock of the same cellulose acetate material. By the early 1980s the replacement was removed from the Tate Gallery display after cracking and breakdown of structure made exhibition pointless.

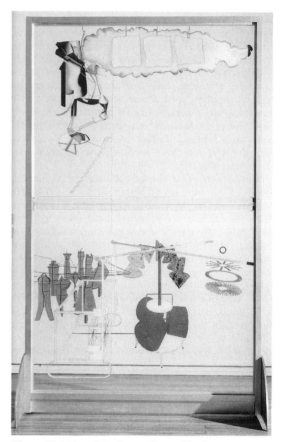

Figure 30.2 Marcel Duchamp, 'Large Glass'

Marcel Duchamp worked on 'Large Glass' (*Figure 30.2*) between 1915 and 1923, seeking permanence and durability through his selection of materials. Two occurrences denied him the desired effect: oil colours sealed between lead foil and glass reacted with the lead and altered colour irreversibly and much more destructively. In 1926 the glasses were shattered in transit. Duchamp both repaired his own work which is on display in Philadelphia and signed a reconstruction created by Richard Hamilton from Duchamp's original notes. In 1984 the lower panel of Hamilton's reconstruction suffered a similar fate, the glass shattering spontaneously on this occasion, possibly from internal stresses. After considering all the alternatives open to them, that is displaying the shattered remains, transferring the remains of the image onto a new glass, or making a complete reconstruction, the custodians of the Tate Gallery found in favour of making a technical copy of the lower panel. On completion the lead backing bearing Duchamps inscription ratifying Hamilton's work was transferred to the replica panel to maintain some sort of historical continuity.

Figure 30.1 Naum Gabo, 'Two Cones'

What makes a reconstruction possible or even desirable?

Both the above examples, 'Two Cones' and 'Large Glass', are designed pieces of an almost mechanical nature, more or less devoid of the element of chance often present in an expressive use of materials. These reconstructions satisfactorily communicate the form intended by the artists, but if there had been an expressive use of texture or colour to convey meaning, duplication would have been impossible. To give any meaningful authenticity to the reconstruction, the artists must have been either directly involved in the process or have given complete approval to the construction and to the completed article. Finally, only the careful storage and conservation of the original fragments can give the piece any relevance.

A great deal of art made in the later part of the twentieth century has not been concerned with creating lasting art objects in any identifiable form. Environments or installations have been established as relatively commonplace art statements, whereby the artist communicates subject matter and content through an assemblage of materials that are taken apart after the allotted time in the gallery space. Artist Carl Plackman's 'Relationships and the Way in Which the World Defeats Us' (Smith, 1980) exhibited (1977) in the Felicity Samuel Gallery, London, confronts us with a range of abstract forms and recognizable objects; a broom, a basin, pillows, light bulbs, drinking glasses. To keep such an ephemeral concoction would seem to break the rules of an installation, and yet the dividing line between this and an 'art object' of complicated and perhaps short-lived material construction is very grey indeed. In the Royal Academy exhibition 'A New Spirit in Painting' (Royal Academy, 1981), Pier Calzolari exhibited 'Untitled' with material construction listed as wax and tempera on board, gas cylinder and heater, aluminium bowl with water and footstool. Mario Merz exhibited three 'paintings' each constructed from oil, metallic paint and charcoal on canvas with neon lance. Clearly it is the artist's intention that defines his or her work as art object or installation. Calzolari's pieces are similar to installations in the complexity of their material construction but are, in fact, art objects. Merz's paintings are objects that incorporate neon lances of limited life-span and a technology that will become obsolete.

With an installation, environment, happening, etc., there is no question of prolonging the life of the piece other than in photographic or film documentation. As important art objects, Merz's paintings will be conserved, but what happens when the neon-tube technology becomes obsolete? Should the technology be recreated at great expense?

As for the third category, examples of work created as an art object that include decay as part of the content of the piece are rare. Artists have made statements about the very nature of the art object by painting on canvas with acid with predictable results, but these owe more to a performance than to the creation of an exhibitable work. While conscious production of disappearing art is rare, there are examples of artists who make objects where decay is inherent in the choice of materials.

The so-called Neo Dada artist Robert Rauschenberg often explored the idea of the unstable and ephemeral in what he created. 'Bed' 1955 would appear to be just that, a mattress and sheets modified by paint for expressive purpose.

Dieter Rot used a decollage technique in the creation of ironic statements about our consumer society (Red). 'Self Portrait by a Table' (Tate Gallery) (*Figure 30.3*) includes chocolate used as paint.

Anthony Gormley 'Bed', 1980–1981 (artist's own collection), is a large double-mattress-shaped piece made entirely out of wax-coated white sliced bread. Two concave figure shapes have been literally eaten out of the bread by the artist, as though sleeping within the mattress. Before exhibition at the Tate in Liverpool, the piece posed a health risk due to infestation with mould and insect life, and had to be fumigated.

The Conservation Guidelines of the United Kingdom Institute of Conservators (UKIC, 1981) suggest that 'all professional actions of the conservator are governed by total respect for the physical, historical and aesthetic integrity of the object'. 'Concern for its future should include protection against damage and loss', and that 'it is unethical to modify or conceal the original nature of the object through restoration'. Similar guidelines are to be found internationally which merely serves to magnify the potential conflict between an artist's intention and the apparent need to conserve a work of art. What rights does the artist have to prevent a conservator intervening in a decay process that he or she condones or even welcomes?

Speaking about the development of drying cracks in 'Three Dancers' of 1925, Picasso said 'some people might want to touch them out, but I think they add to the painting. On the face you see how they reveal the eye that was painted underneath'.

Dieter Rot expected his painting in the Tate to deteriorate and did not want it to be restored, any cracks in the medium leading to flaking should be allowed to occur.

Original artistic works are given the possibility of protection under the 1988 Copyrights, Design and Patents Act (Current Statutes Service, 1988), which enable the UK to ratify the latest text of the Berne Convention for the Protection of Literary and Artistic Works; Chapter IV of the Act deals with

Figure 30.3 Dieter Rot, 'Self Portrait by a Table' (Tate Gallery)

Moral Rights whereby an artist has the right to object to derogatory treatment of work. A treatment may mean deletion from, alteration to, or adaptation of the work, and treatment is derogatory if it amounts to distortion, mutilization or is otherwise prejudicial to the honour or reputation of the creator. These rights subsist as long as copyright subsists, i.e. 50 years after the death of the artist, which a conservator may need to take into account before any treatment is started.

Where does the conservator's or curator's responsibility lie?

Abdicating control of the destiny of an art object to the wishes of the artist calls into question the whole premise upon which collections are made. A gallery collects the best examples of work considered culturally important at that time. Dieter Rot wanted to destroy an earlier piece of work owned by the Tate because he considered it unresolved, an action that makes no sense to the Gallery. Artists may state an intention to allow their work in a gallery's hands to decay, but the possibility is there, that on returning some years later to see their work exhibited they may be dismayed by the work's appearance.

Artists may have the possibility of protecting the original intention of their work through copyright laws, but a custodian of a public collection may also be under some legal obligation to conserve the material of objects entrusted to his care. This conflict does not have any easy solution, but in the future could be avoided by two approaches to buying contemporary work for public collections:

(1) a conservator's condition report should assess the likelihood of any accelerated decay in the object's construction and be considered prior to the institution's decision to purchase; or
(2) a Contract of Purchase should be drawn up to the satisfaction of both artist and gallery, which permits conservation when absolutely necessary but also protects the artist's original intention.

In the future, artistic concerns may bear little relationship to our own, and a different set of sensibilities may be prized from those used as currency by present-day artists. The remnants of Greek sculpture grasp our imaginations as expressions of pure form, far removed from the full-colour and complete-limbed representations they were created to be. Perhaps a future generation may still appreciate Harvard's 'Rothkos' despite loss of colour.

Acknowledgements

Many thanks to Roy Perry, Deputy Keeper of Conservation, Tate Gallery, for his time and for allowing me to borrow heavily from his Royal College of Art Lecture, 'Conserving Change'.

References

AMERICAN INSTITUTE FOR CONSERVATION JOURNAL (1988), *Aspects of the Examination and Cleaning of Two Portraits by Richard and William Jennys*, AIC Preprints, Washington DC, p. 251

CARLYLE, L., TOWNSEND, J. H. and HACKNEY, S. (1990), 'Triammonium citrate: an investigation into its application for surface cleaning', *Dirt and Pictures Separated –* UKIC London 1990

CURRENT STATUTES SERVICE (1988), 'Moral rights Halsbury statutes', in *Copyright, Design and Patents Act 1988*, 4th edition, Chap. 4, Butterworths, London

GODDARD, P. (1989), 'Humidity chambers and their application to the treatment of deformations in fabric supported paintings', *The Conservator*, **13**

HEDLEY, G. (1988a), 'Relative humidity and the stress/strain response of canvas painting: uniaxial measurements of naturally aged samples', *Studies in Conservation*, **33**, 133–148

HEDLEY, G. (1988b), Unpublished research, and lecture given at Conference on Moisture Treatments and Related Problems, Edinburgh

HUSBAND, C. (1990), *The Plasticising Effects of Humidity on Oil Paint and its Applications in Conservation*, Student Conservation Conference, Courtauld Institute, London

ROYAL ACADEMY (1981), *A New Spirit in Painting*, Catalogue, Royal Academy, London

SMITH, E. L. (1980), *Art in the Seventies*, Phaidon, Oxford, p. 101

UKIC (1981), *Guidance for Conservators Practice*, UKIC, London

WOLBERS, R. and LANDREY, E. (1987), *The Use of Direct Reactive Fluorescent Dyes for the Characterisation of Binding Media in Cross-Sectional Examinations*, AIC Preprints, Washington DC, pp. 168–202

WOLBERS, R. (1988), *Cast History: Still Life with Parrots*, Unattributed AIC Preprints, Washington DC, p. 251

WOLBERS, R. (1989), *Notes for the Workshop on New Methods in Cleaning Paintings* (London)

Dictionary of 20th Century Art, Phaidon

Bibliography

The literature of paintings conservation is so extensive that no attempt has been made in the foregoing text to refer to specific papers. Neither is it feasible here to compile a complete bibliography of the subject, since some of the published work is repetitive or is now seen to be outdated.

The starting point for any literature survey of this subject is the massive annotated bibliography assembled by Joyce Plesters for *The Cleaning of Paintings* by Helmut Ruhemann (London, 1968). Everything of any importance published up to 1966 is listed, and the reader is referred there for works appearing before that date. The bibliography below only attempts to identify subsequent key publications and omission of a particular work does not necessarily imply unworthiness. Books of a general kind are listed first, followed by papers arranged by topic.

Abbreviations

SIC: Studies in Conservation

ICOM: ICOM Committee for Conservation, Triennial meetings (year, location and paper number given in each case)

IIC: International Institute for Conservation, Pre-prints of International congresses (year and location given in each case)

Books

BROMMELLE, N. and SMITH, P. (Ed.) (1976), *Conservation and Restoration of Pictorial Art*, Butterworths, London

EMILE-MALE, G. (1976), *The Restorer's Handbook of Easel Painting*, Van Nostrand Reinhold, Wokingham

FELLER, R., STOLOW, N. and JONES, E. H. (1971), *On Picture Varnishes and their Solvents*, 2nd edition, Cse Western Reserve, Cleveland

GETTENS, R. J. and STOUT, G. (1966), *Painting Materials: a Short Encyclopedia*, Dover, New York

KECK, C. (1967), *A Handbook on the Care of Paintings*, American Association for State and Local History, Nashville

MAYER, R. (1969), *A Dictionary of Art Terms and Techniques*, A. and C. Black, London

MAYER, R. (1973), *The Artist's Handbook*, 3rd edition, Faber, London

PLENDERLEITH, H. J. and WERNER, A. E. A. (1971), *The Conservation of Antiquities and Works of Art*, 2nd edition, University Press, Oxford

RUHEMANN, H. (1968), *The Cleaning of Paintings*, Faber, London (reprinted by Hacker Art Books, New York, 1983)

STOUT, G. L. (1975), *The Care of Pictures*, 2nd edition, Dover, New York

THOMSON, G. (1978), *The Museum Environment*, IIC and Butterworths, London

TORRACA, G. (1975), *Solubility and Solvents for Conservation Problems*, International Centre for the Study of the Preservation and the Restoration of Cultural Property, Rome

Wood supports

BEARDSLEY, B. (1978), 'A flexible balsa back for the stabilization of a Botticelli panel painting', *IIC, Oxford*, 153–156

BUCK, R. D. (1972), 'Some applications of rheology to the treatment of panel paintings', *SIC*, **17**, 1–11

CORNELIUS, F. DU PONT (1967), 'Movement of wood and canvas for paintings in response to high and low RH cycles', *SIC*, **12**, 76–80

HICKIN, N. (1970), 'Wood-destroying insects and works of art', *IIC, New York*, 75–80

HORNS, J. (1978), 'Induced strain in panel paintings undergoing conformational changes', *IIC, Oxford*, 123–130

JESSELL, B. and PRICE, G. (1978), 'Some methods of repair and conservation of easel paintings on wooden supports', *IIC, Oxford*, 169–174

LENNON, T. (1978), 'The transfer of a sixteenth century panel painting: use of a lightweight paper honeycomb material as a support', *IIC, Oxford*, 185–190

MARTIN, M. and REISMAN, S. N. (1978), 'The surface and structural treatment of a Payum portrait', *IIC, Oxford*, 191–198

MONCRIEFF, A. (1968), 'Review of recent literature on wood', *SIC*, **13**, 186–212

REIMOLD, F. (1972), 'Transferring an altarpiece by Konrad Witz, *IIC, Lisbon*, 813–830

SMITH, A., REEVE, A. and ROY, A. (1981), 'Francesco del Cossa's S. Vincent Ferrer', *National Gallery Technical Bulletin*, **5**, 45–57

SPURLOCK, D. (1978), 'The application of balsa blocks as a stabilizing auxiliary for panel paintings', *IIC, Oxford*, 149–152

Canvas supports

BERGER, G. A. (1966), 'Weave interference in vacuum lining of pictures', *SIC*, **11**, 170–180

BERGER, G. A. (1970), 'A new adhesive for the consolidation of paintings, drawings and textiles', *Bulletin of the American Group*, **11**(1), 36–38

BERGER, G. A. (1971), 'Application of heat-activated adhesives for the consolidation of paintings', *Bulletin of the American Group IIC*, **11**(2), 124–128

BERGER, G. A. (1972a), 'Testing adhesives for the consolidation of paintings', *SIC*, **17**, 173–194

BERGER, G. A. (1972b), 'Some effects of impregnating adhesives on paint films', *Bulletin of the American Group IIC*, **12**(2), 35–45

BERGER, G. A. (1972c), 'Formulating adhesives for the conservation of paintings', *IIC, Lisbon*, 613–630

BERGER, G. A. (1975), 'Heat-seal lining of a torn painting with Beva 371', *SIC*, **20**, 126–151

BERGER, G. A. (1976), 'Unconventional treatments for unconventional paintings, *SIC*, **21**, 115–128

BERGER, G. A. (1978), 'Consolidation of delaminating paintings', *ICOM, Zagreb* 78/2/1

BERGER, G. D. and ZELIGER, H. I. (1975), 'Detrimental and irreversible effects of wax impregnation on easel paintings', *ICOM, Venice*, 75/11/2

BOMFORD, D. (1979), 'Moroni's 'Canon Ludovico di Terzi': an unlined sixteenth century painting', *National Gallery Technical Bulletin*, **3**, 34–42

BOMFORD, D. and STANIFORTH, S. (1981), 'Wax-resin lining and colour change: an evaluation', *National Gallery Technical Bulletin*, **5**, 58–65

FIEUX, R. E. (1973), 'Teflon-coated fiberglass as a support for relining paintings', *Bulletin of the American Group IIC*, **14**(1), 73–74

FIEUX, R. E. (1978), 'Electrostatic hold: a new technique of lining', *ICOM, Zagreb*, 78/2/7

GREENWICH CONFERENCE ON COMPARATIVE LINING TECHNIQUES (1974), various papers, not formally published; similar material subsequently published elsewhere by some of the authors concerned. See also Percival-Prescott, W. W. (1974) and Percival-Prescott, W. W. and Lewis, G. M. (1974)

HACKE, B. (1978), 'A low-pressure apparatus for the treatment of paintings', *ICOM, Zagreb*, 78/2/12

HACKE, B. (1981), 'Low pressure, heat, moisture, stretching. Notes on further developments', *ICOM, Ottawa*, 81/2/8

HACKNEY, S. and HEDLEY, G. A. (1982), 'Measurements of the ageing of linen canvas', *SIC*, **26**, 1–14

HEDLEY, G. A. (1975), 'Some empirical determinations of the strain distribution in stretched canvases', *ICOM, Venice*, 75/11/4

HEDLEY, G. A. (1975), 'The effect of beeswax/resin impregnation on the tensile properties of canvas', *ICOM, Venice*, 75/11/7

HEDLEY, G. A. (1981), 'The stiffness of lining fabrics: theoretical and practical considerations', *ICOM, Ottawa*, 81/2/2

HEDLEY, G. A. and VILLIERS, C. (1982), 'Polyester sailcloth fabric: a high-stiffness lining support', *IIC, Washington*, 154–158

KECK, C. K. (1977), 'Lining adhesives: their history, uses and abuses', *Journal of the AIC*, **17**(1), 45–52

LEVENSON, R. (1978), 'A new method for strip-lining easel paintings', *ICOM, Zagreb*, 75/2/8

LEWIS, G. M. (1975), 'Preparatory treatment of paintings for lining' and 'A vacuum envelope lining method', *ICOM, Venice*, 75/11/6

MAKES, F. (1981), 'Enzymatic consolidation of paintings', *ICOM, Ottawa*, 78/2/7

MAKES, F. and HALLSTROM, B. (1972), 'Remarks on relining', Stockholm

MECKLENBURG, M. F. and WEBSTER, J. E. (1977), 'Aluminium honeycomb supports: their fabrication and use in painting conservation', *SIC*, **22**, 177–189

MEHRA, V. R. (1975), 'Further developments in cold-lining', *ICOM, Venice*, 75/11/5

MEHRA, V. R. (1978), 'Cold-lining and the care of the paint layer ina triple-stretcher system' and 'Answers to some questions and doubts about the cold-lining system', *ICOM, Zagreb*, 78/2/5

MEHRA, V. R. (1981), 'The cold lining of paintings', *The Conservator*, **5**, 12–14

PERCIVAL-PRESCOTT, W. W. (1974), 'The lining cycle', *Conference of Comparative Lining Techniques, Greenwich.* See also Greenwich Conference (1974)

PERCIVAL-PRESCOTT, W. W. (1975), 'Conservation of paintings: the Greenwich lining conference', *Museums Journal*, **74**, 169–171

PERCIVAL-PRESCOTT, W. W. and LEWIS, G. M. (Eds), (1974), 'Handbook of terms used in the lining of paintings', *Conference on Comparative Lining Techniques, Greenwich*

RABIN, B. (1972), 'A poly(vinyl acetate) heat seal adhesive for lining', *IIC, Lisbon*, 631–635

VILLERS, C. (1981), 'Artists canvases: a history', *ICOM, Ottawa*, 81/2/1

WALES, C. (1968), 'Lining torn paintings on aluminium panel', *Bulletin of the American Group IIC*, **8**(2), 15–17

Paint and ground

BOISSONNAS, P. B. (1977), 'A treatment for blanching in paintings', *SIC*, **22**, 43

GOIST, D. C. (1977), 'Treatment of a flood-damaged oil painting', *Journal of the AIC*, **16**(2), 21–26

GREEN, J. and SEDDON, J. (1981), 'A study of materials for filling losses in easel paintings, and their receptiveness to casting of textures', *ICOM, Ottawa*, 81/2/12

KECK, S. (1969), 'Mechanical alteration of the paint film', *SIC*, **14**, 9–30

KETNATH, A. (1978), 'The treatment of a fire-damaged picture painted on amasonite board', *SIC*, 168–173

LANK, H. (1972), 'The use of dimethylformamide vapour in reforming blanched oil paintings', *IIC, Lisbon*, 809–814

PLESTERS, J. (1969), 'A preliminary note on the discolouration of smalt in oil media', *SIC*, **14**, 62–74

WATHERSTON, M. (1976), 'Treatment of cupped and cracked paint films using organic solvents and water', in Brommelle, N. and Smith, P. (Eds.), *Conservation and Restoration of Pictorial Art*, Butterworths, London, pp. 110–125

WELSH, E. C. (1980), 'A consolidation treatment for powdery matte paint', *Preprints of the AIC 8th Annual Meeting, San Francisco*

WYLD, M., MILLS, L. and PLESTERS, J. (1980), 'Some observations on blanching, with special reference to the paintings of Claude', *National Gallery Technical Bulletin*, **4**, 49–63

Varnishes and cleaning

DE WITTE, E. (1975), 'The influence of light on the gloss of matt varnishes', *ICOM, Venice*, 75/11/6

FELLER, R. L. (1972), 'Problems in the investigation of picture varnishes', *IIC, Lisbon*, 201–207

FELLER, R. L. (1975), 'Studies on the photochemical stability of thermoplastic resins', *ICOM, Venice*, 75/11/4

FELLER, R. L. (1976), 'The relative solvent power needed to remove various aged solvent-type coatings', in Brommelle, N. and Smith, P. (Eds.), *Conservation and Restoration of Pictorial Art*, Butterworths, London, pp. 158–161

FELLER, R. L. and BAILIE, C. W. (1972), 'Solubility of aged coatings based on dammar, mastic and resin AW2', *Bulletin of the American Group IIC*, **12**(2), 72–81

FELLER, R. L. and CURRAN, M. (1970), 'Solubility and cross-linking characteristics of ethylene-vinylacetate co-polymers', *Bulletin of the American Group IIC*, **11**(1), 42–45

FELLER, R. L. and CURRAN, M. (1975), 'Changes in solubility and removability of varnish resins with age', *Bulletin of the AIC*, **15**(2), 17–26

HEDLEY, G. (1980), 'Solubility parameters and varnish removal: a survey', *The Conservator*, **4**, 12–18

HULMER, E. C. (1971), 'Notes on the formulation and application of acrylic coating', *Bulletin of the American Group IIC*, **11**(2), 132–139

LAFONTAINE, R. H. (1979a), 'Decreasing the yellowing rate of dammar varnish using antioxidants', *SIC*, **24**, 14–22

LAFONTAINE, R. H. (1979b), 'Effect of Irganox 565 on the removability of dammar films', *SIC*, 179–181

LAFONTAINE, R. H. (1981), 'Use of stabilizers in varnish formulations', *ICOM, Ottawa*, 81/2/5

LANK, H. (1972), 'Picture varnishes formulated with resin MS2A', *IIC, Lisbon*, 215–216

RAT, K. (1980), 'An examination of the value of the reforming technique in practice', *SIC*, **25**, 137–140

STOLOW, N. (1976), 'Solvent action', in Brommelle, N. and Smith, P. (Eds.), *Conservation and Restoration of Pictorial Art*, Butterworths, London, 153–157

WATHERSTON, M. (1972), 'Problems presented by colour field paintings' *and* 'Cleaning of colour field paintings', *IIC, Lisbon*, 831–845

Storage, handling, etc.

CANNON-BROOKES, P. (1978), 'Museums and fine art transporters', *Museums Journal*, **77**, 174–176

HOLDEN, C. (1979), 'Notes on the protection of modern art works during handling, packing and storage', *The Conservator*, **3**, 20–24

PERRY, R. and BOOTH, P. (1978), 'Some notes on the framing of paintings', *The Conservator*, **2**,. 41–44

SACK, S. P. and STOLOW, N. (1978), 'A microclimate for a Fayum portrait', *SIC*, **23**, 47–56

STOLOW, N. (1977), 'The conservation of works of art and exhibitions', *Museums Journal*, **77**, 61–62

31

Conservation and storage: photographic materials

Anne Fleming and Elizabeth Martin

The very title of this chapter, embracing as it does both cinematographic film and still photographs under the general heading of 'photographic materials', is in itself a distillation of the multiplicity of problems confronting those Curators concerned with the conservation of either type of photographic image.

While the motives for archiving both film and photographs are very similar, whether as works of art, historical records or social evidence, the techniques required for handling, storing and conserving the two media are not identical and should be viewed as two distinct, specialist fields, although there are a considerable number of overlapping areas.

Recognizing this, the present chapter can do no more than outline the main procedures necessary to protect film and photographic collections, and wherever possible direct Curators to publications which provide more detailed information. Nor will it be possible to discuss the conservation of photographs made by processes that were in use before negatives and prints were made on gelatin chloride or gelatin bromide materials, since the care of photographic images produced by nineteenth-century processes such as daguerreotype, calotype, ambrotype, collodion wet plate, tintype, albumen paper and platinum prints, requires individual consideration beyond the scope of this article. For similar reasons, magnetic materials are not dealt with here but these should be handled and stored in accordance with the manufacturer's specifications.

The fundamental conservation problem is the same for both film and photographs, since it is in the nature of the photographic process which presupposes that multiple copies can and will be struck from a single negative and that it will be used and re-used. Even where the only existing original is a positive print of some sort, the same assumption is made.

The Curator of any collection of photographic material will, therefore, inevitably be approached by individuals and companies wanting copies of the material for which he is responsible. Clearly, the Curator must try to provide access to the material since this is part of the purpose of any archival collection. However, because the medium is both fragile and chemically unstable, there is an inherent conflict between a policy of access and a policy of conservation. Any frequently used negative will show signs of wear, and the quality of image it is possible to reproduce from it will gradually deteriorate. Where the original is a positive print, excessive handling or, in the case of motion picture film, projection, will likewise cause damage to the image.

Therefore, the Curator's first duty is to ensure that original negatives and master prints are used and handled as little as possible and that they are stored in conditions that will at least promote, if not ensure, their long-term survival. If conservation is to be combined with access this means producing dupe negatives and positives from which users of the collection can work. Not only does this necessitate spending considerable sums of money on a duplicating programme, but it also means doubling, and sometimes tripling, the amount of storage space needed to house the collection. As Eugene Ostroff (1976), the Curator of Photography at the Smithsonian Institute has written:

> A long range financial obligation is incurred when photographs are collected; they require storage space equipment and staff.

This statement is even more true of cine filme because of its greater bulk.

The Curator who embarks on a policy of duplication is immediately faced with the problem of where to begin. A systematic approach is clearly desirable but the choice of system must depend on the type of collection which should be given priority. Apart from considerations of subject content and artistic value, the base materials on which the collection is held are also relevant. Nitrate based film or photographs should probably go to the head of the programme because they are inherently unstable and doomed to destruction sooner or later. In this case, copying is not merely an adjunct to conservation, done to provide access and protect the originals, it is the *only* means of ensuring the survival of the image. Glass plates are another obvious priority area since, despite their stability, their extreme fragility makes frequent handling particularly undesirable.

Demands for access may also affect the structure of the duplicating programme. While in an ideal world such demands should not be allowed to interfere with an established schedule of copying, the Curator of a collection in constant use will probably have to adopt a more pragmatic approach, identifying those negatives which are most in demand and making these a priority area for duplication. An institution with restricted funds for copying may even be able to turn demands for access to financial advantage by making the production of an archival negative or print at the applicant's expense one of the conditions for use of the material. Each Curator, therefore, must tailor his duplicating programme to the nature of his collection.

Having relieved the strain on original negatives and prints by producing working copies, the Curator must then ensure that the originals are stored adequately. Different base materials require different handling and storage conditions and these are perhaps best explained by a consideration of the basic structure of photographic materials.

Both cinematographic film and photographs comprise multi-layered materials. They consist of a base support and a very thin adhesive substratum upon which an emulsion layer is coated for the optical recording of the image and, in the case of motion pictures of sound as well. Black-and-white film and photographs have only one emulsion layer consisting of light-sensitive silver halides in gelatin, whereas modern colour materials have three such layers for each of the basic subtractive colours (yellow, magenta and cyan) and one or more filter layers. Since most older collections are black and white, these will be considered first.

Tables 31.1 and *31.2* show the principal materials concerned in black-and-white photography.

Gelatin

Since a substratum of gelatin is common to all forms of photographic materials considered here, it is worth stating its basic properties before discussing the various bases and how it interacts with them.

Gelatin is a highly purified animal protein (animal albumen) that is very stable as long as it is kept dry. If it becomes moist, however, it will swell, spread and become sticky, thereby endangering the image. The hazard is increased by warmth. As an organic substance, gelatin is also an excellent nutrient for bacteria and fungi and promotes their growth at high levels of relative humidity (RH). These can penetrate the emulsion layer and attack the image. To prevent this, RH levels should never exceed 60 per cent, whatever the photographic base.

Gelatin is also attacked by strong acids and acidic gases that may be present in the environment or produced by deterioration of the film base and it is therefore at its most vulnerable when in contact with the inherently unstable base nitrocellulose, or nitrate film.

Nitrate based materials

Nitrate based film, whether cinematographic or still, deteriorates even under favourable storage conditions and, in any considerable quantity, constitutes a fire hazard.

This hazard is proportionately greater for cinematographic film because of its greater bulk. While safety-based material has always been used for 16 mm and 8 mm film from the introduction of these gauges, professional 35 mm cinematographic film was produced on nitrocellulose (nitrate) up to 1951. Photographic sheet negatives were also produced on nitrate based material for much of this period, although acetate based stock was phased in during the 1930s and early 1940s for certain kinds of photography.

Table 31.1 Cinametographic film

Film base	Gauge (mm)	Substratum	Emulsion layer
Nitrate	35		
Acetate	35–16, 9.5–8	Gelatin	Silver halides
Polyester	16–8		

Table 31.2 Photographs

Film base	Substratum	Emulsion layer
Nitrate		
Acetate		
Polyester	Gelatin	Silver halides
Glass		
Paper		

How long any piece of nitrate film can survive depends on the purity of the original film stock, how well it was processed and how it has subsequently been stored, because while deterioration can be retarded it cannot be prevented. In the process of deterioration, nitrate film gives off harmful gases, in particular nitrogen dioxide (NO_2). These gases combine with the moisture in the gelatin to form nitric or nitrous acid and these bleach the silver (or colour) image in the emulsion and accelerate the decomposition of the base (Bowser and Kuiper, 1980).

The visible signs of nitrate decomposition occur in the order shown below.

(1) The silver image becomes faded and there is a brownish yellow discolouration of the emulsion. (In colour film the colours fade and a loss of balance between the colours occurs.)
(2) The emulsion becomes sticky.
(3) The emulsion softens and becomes blistered, bubbles rising as it separates from the base, and a pungent odour is given off.
(4) Cinematographic film congeals into a solid mass, or a group of single photographic negatives may weld together.
(5) The base disintegrates into a brownish powder giving off an acrid smell.

Only in the first and second stages of decomposition is rescue possible by immediate treatment and copying.

Decomposition is speeded up by storage at high temperatures, particularly when accompanied by high RH. While awaiting copying, nitrate film materials should therefore be stored at around 4°C with the RH controlled at about 50 per cent. Every endeavour should be made to keep climatic conditions constant since if they are allowed to fluctuate the emulsion can become detached from the base.

At high temperatures nitrate film can self-ignite. Most nitrate materials in existence today are of an age where the ignition point may be as low as 38–40°C. Such film burns with the force of an explosion and, since a nitrate fire cannot be extinguished, great care must be exercised by all personnel handling nitrate based material, particularly cinematographic film.

Ventilation of storage areas is crucial since the gases produced must be allowed to escape. Cine film, even in an unsealed can, gives off larger quantities of gas because of its bulk. The cans must be opened regularly and the films wound through to disperse accumulated gas and slow the rate of deterioration. Similarly, large photographic negatives stored in enclosed packages are at high risk since the damaging gases can escape only slowly and the archivist would be well-advised to make such packages a starting point in checking his nitrate holdings.

Since the gases given off by deteriorating nitrate are powerful oxidizing agents, they have a damaging effect on any other photographic material stored in proximity to them. Acetate based negatives stored in contact with nitrate materials will exhibit a yellowing and fading of the silver image and a softening of the gelatin. It is therefore essential to identify any nitrate elements in a collection and ensure that they are segregated as soon as possible.

Identification of nitrate film may in itself be a problem. Any 35-mm negatives produced before 1951 are suspect, although acetate based stock was also in use for both film and photographs for a considerable time before that. Cinematographic film often has the word 'nitrate' or 'safety' printed along both edges outside the perforations, and sheet negatives may also be identified in the same way along one edge near the code match. However, not all stock manufacturers used these forms of identification. If in doubt there are two standard tests which may be used to determine the presence of nitrate.

(1) Cut a very small segment from the edge of the photograph or film negative and drop it into a test tube containing trichlorethylene and shake it to immerse it completely. If it floats, it is safety film. If it sinks, it is nitrate (Eastman Kodak Co., 1957).
(2) One frame of cinematographic film or a thin strip from the edge of a photographic negative may be submitted to a combustion test. The frame or strip should be taken to a spot well away from any combustible materials, placed upright on a flat, non-inflammable surface and lit at the top using a long match or taper. If it ignites easily and burns rapidly, it is nitrate. If it is difficult to ignite and either keeps going out or burns very slowly then it is safety film.

Clearly it is also desirable to check the stage of deterioration of any nitrate item in a collection, since a nitrate based film or photograph apparently in good condition may reach a point where copying is impossible only 6 months later.

For cinematograph film the most common method is the alizarin red heat test (Ashmore *et al*, 1957). A film punching approximately 6 mm in diameter is dropped into a test tube closed by a glass stopper, around which is wrapped a piece of filter paper impregnated with alizarin red indicator dye and moistened with a mixture of glycerin and water. The tube is then heated in an air bath to 134°C and the time taken for acid vapours to develop is revealed by the bleaching of the lower edge of the paper. A range of times from 60 down to 10 min may be obtained. If the alizarin red test paper reacts in 30–60 min the film may be stored and retested after 1 year; if it reacts in 10–30 min, retesting is recommended within 6 months; under 10 min the film should be copied and destroyed.

This test is unsuitable for single photograph negatives since it involves taking punchings from the film which would damage the image. Kodak, therefore, recommend the following test for photographic negatives (Eastman Kodak Co., 1979). Cut a small strip from the clear margin of the negative, fold it to check for brittleness, and then soak the strip in water for a minute. Scrape the gelatin from the surface and place it on a sheet of white paper so that the degree of discolouration can be observed. The discolouration will range from faintly yellowish through to amber, and the darker the colour the more advanced the deterioration. Extreme brittleness also indicates an advanced stage of deterioration.

Acetate based film

The first 'safety base' was produced before World War I. This was cellulose diacetate and, although it proved inadequate as a professional motion picture film base because of poor geometrical stability, tensile strength and flexibility, it was used from 1922 onwards as a base for 16 mm amateur film. The search for a safety base with improved physical and chemical properties led next to the production in 1931 of a base type made from mixed cellulose esters and, although this was an improvement on diacetate, it was still not tough enough to withstand 35 mm theatrical use. Research therefore continued and in the early 1940s cellulose triacetate was developed. In its earliest form its application was limited because it proved only of limited solubility in conventional solvents, but by 1948 a slightly less esterified form of cellulose triacetate (high acetyl) was manufactured. This overcame the solubility problem and it rapidly became the preferred base for theatrical production and exhibition as well as for photographic sheet negatives.

Acetate based film is comparatively stable under good storage conditions. These depend on a balance between temperature and RH, but of the two humidity is the more critical. Prolonged dry storage conditions cause the acetate base to shrink and become brittle and the gelatin may also begin to flake away from the base. High RH, on the other hand, promotes the growth of fungi and, under such conditions the plasticizer in the base tends to form crystals. Moreover, the gelatin layer becomes soft and its capacity to absorb moisture can result in linear expansion as well as distortion of the image (Sargent, 1974). Sudden, swift temperature fluctuations may also encourage the detachment of the emulsion from the base. The most damaging conditions of all are temperatures above 24°C coupled with RH exceeding 60 per cent. Ideally, the RH should be held between 35 and 40 per cent with temperatures between 10 and 12°C, but higher or lower temperatures can be tolerated as long as humidity is controlled.

High RH may also cause the release of acetic acid, which can be detected by a smell of vinegar. Inhalation should be avoided and the material segregated. Expert advice should then be sought as this is indicative of the first stage of degradation.

Polyester based film

Polymers of the polyester type have been introduced to replace acetate base in a number of film stocks. The chemical name for this material is polyethylene terephthalate. Super 8 mm and 16 mm magnetic tracks are now routinely produced on this base and it is gradually replacing acetate as a support for both amateur and professional photographic sheet negatives.

Accelerated ageing tests indicate that polyester is equal to, or better than, acetate. It has great tensile strength, high dimensional stability and greater resistance to extremes of temperature. Unfortunately, there still appear to be unresolved problems in binding the emulsion firmly to the polyester base.

Glasss-based photographic material

Glass (an inert transparent material) is an ideal support for negative emulsions, but it is also bulky, heavy and extremely fragile. While it is no longer used for most photography, except for certain technical applications where dimensional stability is very important, many earlier photographs exist as glass negatives. Handling must be kept to a minimum and temperature and humidity held at levels similar to those for acetate film.

Cleaning of glass plate negatives should only be undertaken by a professional.

If finances allow, such negatives should be stored in a Melinex envelope and that in turn placed in a 'silversafe' paper[1] envelope for additional protection and ease of labelling. Avoid 'frosted' Melinex or plastic enclosures as these emit substances damaging to the image-carrying layer. All such storage materials should be tested periodically as batches may vary and this will require the assistance of scientific experts.

Paper-based gelatin prints

The paper used for early paper prints was produced from linen and cotton rags, but as the demand for paper increased it became difficult for manufacturers of photographic material to find rags of sufficient purity since dyes and other additives were being used in the making of cloth. The purity of the base is important since it affects the keeping properties of the emulsion coated on it. This problem led to the development of paper made from purified wood pulp and today's paper bases are made from high α-cellulose wood-fibre containing additives to provide wet strength and water and chemical resistance.

More recently, resin-coated (RC) paper has been developed. The paper base is coated on both sides with synthetic resins and the gelatin and emulsion layers are coated on top. RC paper is water resistant, washes more thoroughly and has a shorter drying and fixing time than ordinary paper base. Its use for archival prints should, however, be avoided since it is a recent development and its keeping properties are not fully understood. In an article on print conservation, Alice Swann (1981) noted that RC paper had 'already shown oxidation problems, and should be expected to suffer worse emulsion difficulties than conventional papers'.

As with other types of photographic base, RH is the crucial environmental factor for RC paper. The different layers expand and contract with fluctuations in humidity, with the paper base being affected least and the emulsion and supercoat layers reacting most. This causes the print to curl with the image inside the curve when RH levels are low, and the reverse when humidity is high. If the RH can be held fairly constant at around 40 per cent, this problem is greatly reduced. Temperature is much less crucial, but for long-term archival storage temperatures of between 10 and 16°C are recommended, although a temperature as high as 20°C can be tolerated if humidity is controlled.

Only very generalized recommendatiosn regarding storage can be given here. Methods of storage will vary and will depend on many factors including usage and access and, of course, financial resources. As stated elsewhere, however, handling of unique prints should be kept to a minimum.

Close-contact materials employed for mounts, hinges, enclosures, boxes or interleaving should be free from reducible sulphur which will tarnish silver in the image. All paper-based products used should also be unbuffered as compounds used in the buffering process may damage the image. Buffered papers may, however, be used with platinum prints as they absorb ferrotyping more readily. One should not accept that phrases such as 'archivally sound' or 'museum standard' are a guarantee of quality and all materials used should be tested periodically as batches can vary (Daniels and Ward, 1988). Never use self-adhesive tape or petroleum based adhesives as irreversible staining will occur. Adhesives should be water soluble and reversible.

Deterioration of the black-and-white silver image

The photographic silver image is extremely susceptible to chemical change, since the silver of photographic images is very finely divided, occurring in very small particles and clusters of fine filaments. Therefore, it has a very large surface area in relation to its mass, making it far more vulnerable to chemical reaction than bulk silver. The two major chemical reactions in the silver image are oxidization and the formation of silver sulphide, both caused by a combination of atmospheric pollutants in the environment and residual processing chemicals in the image itself. Both chemical reactions are accelerated by heat, particularly in the presence of high humidity.

The main visible sign of oxidization is the appearance of spots on the image. In cinematographic film these appear first in the outer layers of the reel, while on photographs they are likely to appear first as yellowing of the highlights, spreading to the mid-tones or areas of middle silver density as oxidization increases.

Oxidizing factors include pollutants in the air such as hydrogen sulphide, ammonia, sulphur dioxide, ozone and nitrogen oxides. Where there is a wide variety of industrial processes producing such pollutants, for example, areas of dense population, it is desirable to introduce an air-filtering system into the archival storage area. It should also be noted that no photograph or film should be stored near an electrostatic copying machine since this gives off ozone (Collings and Young, 1977).

Other oxidizing agents include peroxides given off by deteriorating paper and cardboard storage materials, paint fumes, some plastics and bleached woods. Wooden storage cabinets and shelving should therefore be avoided and if they are already in use, should be replaced by metal ones as soon as possible. Deteriorating paper or cardboard storage materials should also be replaced with clean acid-free papers or polyester sleeves which are chemically inert. If polyester or mylar sleeves are used to store gelatin prints, however, it is essential that humidity is controlled since at high RH the gelatin will swell, become sticky and adhere to the smooth waterproof polyester surface with disastrous results.

The formation of silver sulphide on photographic images is closely connected to oxidization since it occurs whenever oxidized silver contacts a source of active sulphide. Silver sulphide is the layer of tarnish which appears on all silverware, and on photographic prints it is usually first seen along the edges where oxidization has occurred. The image turns brownish yellow, begins to fade and may in time disappear completely.

Although active sulphur is present in polluted air

and in some storage materials, the major source is unfortunately frequently contained in the film or photograph itself.

Residual traces of sulphur containing chemicals (sodium thiosulphate or ammonium thiosulphate) used in fixing the image and silver compounds formed by the fixing reaction are often left behind after poor processing and washing. These residual chemicals and silver compounds react with the silver of the image to form silver sulphide. Paper prints are particularly susceptible to this problem because the fibrous construction of the paper base does not wash free of residual chemicals as easily as the comparatively impenetrable film bases. Collections containing many news photographs are certain to contain many examples of yellowing and fading due to residual chemicals, since such prints are likely to have had quick and poor processing.

The problem is compounded by the fact that it is impossible to tell simply by inspection which prints contain harmful residual chemicals, since a print in apparently good condition may much later begin to stain and fade.

Two tests are commonly recommended to determine whether residual silver thiosulphate complex or thiosulphate itself are present in a print: 'Kodak Hypo Test Solution ST-1' and 'Kodak Hypo Test Solution HT-2' (Eastman Kodak Co., 1979). Unfortunately, these tests are not suitable for archival prints since they involve dropping the solutions onto the margin or highlight area of a print to see whether a stain is formed. If a stain is produced residual chemicals are present, but as this stain is permanent, the print itself has been irretrievably damaged.

In a collection where there are many prints whose processing is suspect, it may be best to treat the prints against residual chemicals by reprocessing. This involves refixing and treating with a washing aid such as Kodak Hypo Clearing Agent followed by immersion in a hypoeliminating agent and, finally, rewashing very thoroughly. Unfortunately, reprocessing of older prints in this way may present some problems, since the wet strength of some early paper bases is very poor and these prints will require very gentle and careful handling if they are to survive the treatment.

Colour materials

The deterioration of colour in film and photographs is a chemical process in which the colour dyes of all three layers are destroyed. Discolouration or fading does not usually take place uniformly since the different pigments react differently to destructive agents in the atmosphere which may destroy the colour balance in a remarkably short space of time under adverse conditions. The process of deterioration in colour film and photographs is, therefore,

more complex than for silver based monochrome prints, and there are many areas of uncertainty in its archival preservation. It is, however, clear that high temperatures and high RH greatly increase the rate of fading and that storage at low temperatures with correspondingly low RH will lengthen the life of any colour film. The International Federation of Film Archives recommends storage of archival cinematographic film at −5°C with RH between 20 and 30 per cent; the film being preconditioned to the required level of humidity and placed in a sealed container before going into the cold store. Moreover, they stress that the temperature must not rise much above −5°C while in store since it has been observed that between −2 and +2°C the adhesive substratum between the base and emulsion deteriorates, causing detachment of the emulsion layer. Clearly, few archives can afford to operate such strict controls and most institutions are forced to compromise, storing their colour materials, whether film or photographs, at +2°C to +5°C with the RH between 15 and 30 per cent for acetate and 25 and 30 per cent for polyester based materials.

It has also been found that the slower the film used to make a colour film or photograph, the better its resistance to fading. Therefore, new archival prints and negatives should be produced using the slowest film available.

Due to the inherent instability of the dyes used in colour film and photographs and the difficulties in maintaining the storage conditions required to prevent fading, it has been traditionally held that the best method of ensuring archival permanence is to produce three colour separations on black-and-white stock. This is probably still the best long-term solution and it should certainly be considered for any important item in a collection. However, this method produces other problems for the archivist. It automatically increases the cost of storage since three reels of film or three photographic negatives must be stored instead of one, and the greatest care must be taken to ensure that all three separation masters are stored in identical conditions to prevent varying amounts of expansion, shrinkage or curl between the different copies, which would make the exact registration essential to reconstituting the full colour image impossible.

Thus, there is no simple solution to the conservation and storage of colour film and this is an area in which a great deal of work remains to be done.

In conclusion, it must be stressed that the chemical reactions described above, whether one is dealing with black-and-white or colour images, are greatly slowed if temperature and humidity are controlled. These are the two most crucial environmental factors in the storage of film and photographs, whether from the point of view of the base, the gelatin substratum or the image-bearing emulsion layer.

Thus, the control of these factors must be a major priority for any archive storing photographic material.

Acknowledgements

We should like to thank the following for help and advice given during the preparation of this chapter: Jame Carmichael, Keeper, Department of Photographs, Imperial War Museum. Michelle Aubert, Conservateur, Service des Archive du Film, CNC, Bois d'Arcy, and David Walsh, Department of Film, Imperial War Museum.

Notes

[1] A technical specification for suitable 'silversafe' paper can be obtained from the Atlantis Paper Company, 2 St Andrews Way, Bow, London E3 3PA, UK.

References

ASHMORE, S. A., ELLIS, L. and HUTCHINSON, A. L. (1957), *Surveillance of Cinematograph Record Film During Storage*, British Government Chemical Research and Development Establishment and the Department of the Government Chemist Report No. 2/R/48 (reproduced in summarized form in *Eastman Kodak Co. Data Book*)

BOWSER, E. and KUIPER, J. (Eds) (1980), *A Handbook for Film Archives*, FIAF Secretariat, Brussels (based on the experiences of members of the International Federation of Film Archives (FIAF))

DANIELS, V. and WARD, S. (1988), 'A rapid test for the detection of substances which will tarnish silver', *Studies in Conservation*, 2, 58–60

COLLINGS, T. J. and YOUNG, F. J. (1977), *The Care of Photographic Collections*, Area Museums Service for South East England, Milton Keynes

EASTMAN KODAK CO. (1957), 'Storage and preservation of motion picture film', *Kodak Data Book*. Eastman Kodak Co., Rochester, NY

EASTMAN KODAK CO. (1979), *Preservation of Photographs*, Kodak Publication No. P. 30, Eastman Kodak, Rochester, NY

OSTROFF, E. (1976), *Conserving and Restoring Photographic Collections*, American Association of Museums, Washington, DC (an updated and revised version of four technical reports first published in the May, September, November and December 1974 issues of *Museum News*)

SARGENT, R. M. (1974), *Preserving the Moving Image*, Corporation for Public Broadcasting and the National Endowment for the Arts, Washington DC.

SWANN, A. (1981), *The Care and Conservation of Photographic Materials*, Crafts Council, London

Bibliography

Identification of processes

COE, B. and HAWORTH-BOOTH, M. (1983), *A Guide to Early Photographic Processes*, Victoria and Albert Museum, London

GILL, A. T. (1978), 'Photographic processes – a glossary and chart for recognition', *Information sheet No. 21*, Museum Association, London

REILLY, J. M. (1986), *Care and identification of Nineteenth-Century Photographic Prints*, Kodak Publications, New York

History

COE, B. (1976), *The Birth of Photography*, Ash and Grant, London

CRAWFORD, W. (1979), *The Keepers of Light: A History and Working Guide to Early Photographic Processes*, Morgan and Morgan, new York

EDER, M. J. (1978), *History of Photography*, Dover Publications, New York

GERNSHEIM, H. and GERNSHEIM, A. (1969), *The History of Photography*, Thames and Hudson McGraw Hill, London, New York

JEFFREY, I. (1981), *Photography – A Concise History*, Oxford University Press, New York

SONTAG, S. (1979), *On Photography*, Penguin Books, London

Conservation

COLLINGS, T. J. (1983), 'Archival care of still photographs', *Information Leaflet No. 2*, Society of Archivists, London

COLLINGS, T. J. and YOUNG, F. J. (1976), 'Improvements in some tests and techniques in photograph conservation', *Studies in Conservation*, 21, 79–84

DANIELS, V. and WARD, S. (1982), 'A rapid test for the detection of substances which will tarnish silver', *Studies in Conservation*, 27, 58–60

EASTMAN KODAK CO. (1979), 'Preservation of Photographs', *Kodak Publication No. F-30*, Rochester, NY

HENDRIKS, K. B. (1984), *The Preservation and Restoration and Photographic Materials in Archives and Libraries – A RAMP Study with Guidelines*, General Information Programme and UNISIST/UNESCO, Paris

HENDRIKS, K. B. and WHITEHURST, A. (1988), *Conservation of Photographic Materials. A Basic Reading List*, available free from: National Archives of Canada, 395 Wellington Street, Ottawa, Ontario, Canada K1A ON3

MARTIN, E. (1988), *Collecting and Preserving Old Photographs*, Collins, London

REILLY, J. M. (1980), *The Albumen and Salted Paper Book*, Light Impressions Corporation, Rochester, NY

REMPEL, S. (1987), *The Care of Photographs*, Nick Lyons Books, New York

Standards

British, American and International Standards are established through seminars, research and recommendations from authorities in specific fields. They are continually updated.

AMERICAN NATIONAL STANDARDS INSTITUTE, 1430 Broadway, New York, NY 10018, USA

BRITISH STANDARDS INSTITUTION, Sales Department, Linford Wood, Milton Keynes MK14 6LE, UK

Bibliographic searches

These are available to individuals or institutions, via:

The Conservation Unit, Museums & Galleries Commission, 7 St James' Square, London SW1Y 4JU, UK

Useful addresses

AMERICAN INSTITUTE FOR CONSERVATION OF HISTORIC AND ARTISTIC WORKS (AIC), 1400, 16th St, N.W., Suite 340, Washington, DC 20036, USA (Photographic materials subgroup)

INSTITUTE OF PAPER CONSERVATION, Leigh Lodge, Leigh, Worcestershire WR6 5LB, UK

MUSEUM BOOKSHOP LTD, 36 Great Russell Street, London WC1B 3PP, UK (new and out of print books on conservation)

NATIONAL MUSEUM OF PHOTOGRAPHY, FILM AND TELEVISION, Prince's View, Bradford, West Yorkshire BD5 0TR, UK

PHOTOGRAPHER'S GALLERY, 5–8 Great Newport Street, London WC2 7HY, UK

ROYAL PHOTOGRAPHIC SOCIETY, Milsom Street, The Octagon, Bath BA1 1DN, UK

Conservation advice

For specific conservation advice or help in choosing a conservator, the following can be contacted.

CONSERVATION UNIT, Museums & Galleries Commission, 7 St James' Square, London SW1Y 4JU, UK

AREA MUSEUM SERVICES: see local telephone directories.

Conservation departments of national museums

Scientific advice

Most major institutions (i.e. museums and universities) have scientific support units who can be approached for advice on specific problems, e.g. measurement of air-borne or other pollutants.

32

Conservation and storage: textiles

Jean M. Glover

Definition of a textile collection

A textile can be defined simply as 'a woven structure produced by the interlacing of two sets of threads' but, interpreted in its broadest sense, and within the museum context, the term 'textiles' embraces three categories of objects:

(1) 'flat' items which can be either hung, laid, or rolled, such as tapestries, carpets, church and domestic furnishings, banners, fabric samples, shawls, embroideries, lace, etc.;
(2) 'shaped' items, usually costumes and costume accessories, which require three-dimensional support'; and
(3) miscellaneous items, including screens, fans, caskets, seat and bed furniture, dolls, soft toys, etc.

Frequently, textiles are closely associated with other substances and, therefore, an understanding of the properties and behaviour of paint, paper, leather, metals, wood, wax, ivory, plastics, adhesives, etc., and of their possible effects on textiles, is also essential. These non-textile materials are found as embellishments and surface decoration, fastenings, components of composite objects and substrates of mounted textiles. Alternatively, they may be incorporated in the fabric structure, as are metal threads, or be added during the finishing of the cloth to impart stiffness or lustre. Their presence may not always be detected immediately but they will almost certainly affect the life of the textile and the ways in which the object is handled during examination, storage, exhibition and remedial conservation.

Identification of fibres, yarns and fabrics

Despite the development of synthetic materials, it is with natural fibres – principally wool, silk, linen and cotton – that most Curators are primarily concerned, and which present the greatest problems of care and conservation.

Natural fibres have distinct characteristics which influence the properties and behaviour of fabrics made from them, and greatly assist their identification. Conversely, textiles composed of man-made fibres, such as rayons, polyamides (nylons), polyesters and acrylics, can be difficult to recognize, particularly if they have been made to resemble natural materials. The date of manufacture will be a guide since, with the exception of rayon or artificial silk, man-made fibres began to appear in quantity only after World War II.

Every Curator and Conservator of a textile collection should have access to two items of equipment – a hand-held or binocular magnifier, giving ×10 magnification, for the examination of yarns and fabric structures, and an optical microscope, giving magnifications of ×40 upwards, for fibre identification. The basic techniques of fibre microscopy are easily learned and, used in conjunction with a well-illustrated manual (The Textile Institute, 1970), enable all but the most degraded or uncommon fibres to be identified.[1]

Caring for a textile collection

Preventive conservation, remedial conservation, and restoration

The care of museum textiles involves the Curator in two forms of conservation – preventive (or passive) and remedial (or active).

Preventive conservation aims to delay deterioration by providing a favourable environment for every object. Remedial conservation, by removing destructive elements and introducing unobtrusive support for degraded material, aims to prolong the

(a)

(b)

Figure 32.1 Excavated tenth century wool sock. (a) Before conservation. (b) After conservation and mounting for exhibition

(a)

(b)

Figure 32.2 (a) Orphrey or apparel from a mid-sixteenth century Spanish funeral cope before conservation. Much of the linear embroidery and applied satin has fallen away, destroying the balance of the immediate and overall design. (b) The partly conserved orphrey with the balance of the design restored. Missing motifs and embroidery have been reconstructed from compatible modern materials. The work was fully documented and undertaken with the approval of the Curator/Textile Historian

life of objects, and to present them in a form which enables their original purpose and qualities to be understood and appreciated (*Figure 32.1*).

Responsible remedial conservation requires that nothing which is an original part of, or a significant addition to, an object will be taken away, and that nothing will be added which could either deceive the observer or be confused with the original. Furthermore, it is a generally accepted principle that remedial conservation should also be reversible, enabling the object to be retruned to its preconserved state if the need arises. Whereas this is usually possible it is not always practicable, as the removal of some forms of supplementary support

from severely degraded textiles could result in their destruction.

Restoration allows for a measure of repair which, in the treatment of some objects, is a necessary aspect of preservation or aid to interpretation (*Figure 32.2*) but it should never obscure, dominate, or attempt to improve upon original craftsmanship. Moreover, restoration which is preceded by the unpicking of original stitching and the removal of degraded material, from textiles which have been preserved as historic documents, is unethical, and unacceptable in the museum context (*Figure 32.3*).

Both forms of conservation should be the concern of the Curator, although it is to be expected that,

Figure 32.3 Unethical restoration of sixteenth-century embroidery. The shiny gold threads are contemporary with the linen ground but the black silk is a twentieth-century replacement, passed off as sixteenth-century work. The effect is uncharacteristically heavy and imprecise and the original fine stitch holes can still be detected around the edges of the motifs

except in an emergency, his responsibilities will lie more directly with preventive than with remedial conservation, the latter being the province of the qualified textile conservator. Nevertheless, the Curator should co-operate closely with the Conservator in caring for the collection. He should study the Conservator's reports and recommendations, visit the conservation studio, and familiarize himself with the specialized vocabulary of textile conservation. As custodian of the collection, the Curator is accountable for its safe keeping, and should understand how this can best be achieved.

Causes of deterioration in textiles and methods of control

It is a matter for concern that irreplaceable textiles have perished in museums through neglect, misuse, or ignorance of the factors which accelerate decay, whilst many which survive have deteriorated more quickly since their acquisition than during their previous history.

Textiles, especially those made from natural fibres, respond to the quality of their environment more readily than many other materials and, under unfavourable conditions, deteriorate with disturbing rapidity, and with consequent disfigurement and loss of strength. Whilst this deterioration is rarely attributable to a single factor, the most damaging elements of an unsatisfactory environment are light (especially ultraviolet (UV) radiation), unsuitable levels of relative humidity (RH) and temperature, and all forms of dirt. These, combined with biodeterioration and the mishandling arising from ill-chosen methods of storage, display and transportation, are responsible for most of the problems which confront the textile conservator. The importance, therefore, of a *controlled* museum environment, in which all these elements are kept within acceptable limits, cannot be overstated.

(a)

(b)

Figure 32.4 (a) Set of mid–nineteenth-century doll's clothing showing the short-term effect on textiles of open display in a museum atmosphere polluted by a defective central-heating boiler. (b) Doll's clothing after cleaning and support of degraded cotton fabrics

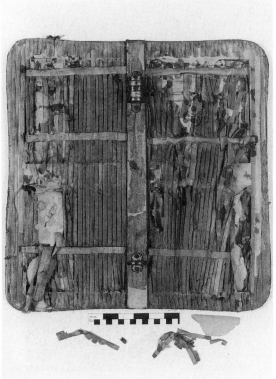

(a)

(b)

Figure 32.5 (a) Pleated silk back of a nineteenth century pole screen following long-term exposure to unfiltered natural light. The severely tendered and brittle silk is held together with strips of gummed paper and daubs of glue.

(b) The screen after conservation. The shattered silk has been replaced with modern fabric dyed to the same colour and pleated in the same manner as the original

In some instances, a remarkable improvement in the appearance of soiled and disintegrated textiles can be effected by remedial conservation (*Figure 32.4*) but this is not always the case (*Figure 32.5*). Even when the conservation and consolidation of severely degraded material can be justified, it cannot erase completely the marks of previous maltreatment (*Figure 32.6*). Furthermore, remedial conservation subjects the object to additional stress and handling which, under more favourable circumstances, might have been avoided.

In a museum, the repeated treatment of conserved specimens should rarely be necessary. If a defective environment has contributed to their initial deterioration, it is essential that the defects be identified and improvements made without delay. Until this has been done, conserved objects should be held in safe custody elsewhere.

Light

All light is damaging to textiles and all fibres are affected to a greater or lesser degree. The visible and tangible effects of exposure are progressive loss of colour, strength and flexibility, a process which may be accelerated by a damp or over-heated atmosphere and intensified by the presence of certain dyes and finishing treatments.

Of the common natural fibres, silk is the most readily affected by photo-degradation and wool the least but all textiles suffer some degree of damage and require protection from both ultraviolet and visible radiation (*Figures 32.5* and *32.7*). The surest method of providing complete protection is to keep textiles in total darkness but as this is feasible only during periods of storage, every effort should be made to restrict the amount of light which falls on them at other times.

The above examples support the need for both the elimination of ultraviolet radiation (UV) from the 300–400 nm waveband and the reduction of visible light levels to the recommended *maximum* of 50 lux, wherever textiles or other light-sensitive materials are displayed. The methods by which these ideals may be achieved are discussed in Chapter 26 (Staniforth).

Figure 32.6 Painted silk Volunteer Regiment Colour damaged by previous repairs employing coarse needles and heavy linen thread (shown after conservation)

In galleries designed for the exhibition of textiles, daylight should be excluded, since natural light is the strongest emitter of UV and is subject to seasonal and other variations which make the maintenance of a uniformly low level of illumination difficult. If, because the museum is housed in a historic building, or one of architectural interest, daylight cannot be excluded completely, a compromise can be achieved by the use of blinds or curtains, in conjunction with UV filters, but greater care will be needed in positioning display cases so that exhibits are shielded from all except supplementary lighting. To control the low-level artificial illumination of rare and particularly light-sensitive material, visitor-operated time switches can be provided, although in popular museums the switches tend to be depressed so frequently that the light is rarely extinguished during opening hours. Spotlights should not be trained directly on textiles, either from inside or outside the show-case, but effective use can be made of indirect light, reflected from other surfaces.

A further danger, which is increased where the volume of air inside an illuminated display case has been reduced substantially by the quantity of material shown, is that of over-heating, particularly when tungsten lighting is used. In a confined space

this may be coupled with localized fading and tendering of fabric placed too close to the source of light. If, in a standard display case, the lighting is concentrated above the exhibits, it should be separated from them by a translucent panel which serves the dual purpose of absorbing UV and diffusing visible radiation.

Humidity, temperature, and ventilation

The property of natural fibres to absorb moisture, thereby swelling on wetting and contracting on drying, is utilized by Conservators to straighten distorted textiles and to eliminate creases. However, these operations are controlled and infrequently applied. The permanent shrinkage of cellulosic fibres, under damp conditions, and the repeated expansion and contraction of all natural fibres with fluctuating RH (Landi and Marko, 1980) is detrimental, and creates stresses which weaken the fabric. The problem is compounded in textiles which incorporate highly twisted yarns, or mixtures of fibres which have different absorption rates. Furthermore, during periods of high RH, biodeterioration (the destruction of objects by micro-organisms and insects) is more likely to occur (*Figure 32.8*), the

(a)

(b)

Figure 32.7 Destruction of textiles and overheating of wax in a glazed show-case exposed to direct sunlight. (a) The front of the doll's magenta-coloured silk dress has faded, shattered and fallen away, exposing the tendered white cotton lining and petticoat. Wax from the doll has melted, absorbed supercial dirt and impregnated the clothing. (b) Back of doll, showing a small area of the magenta-coloured silk dress which has been shielded from the sun's rays and has escaped destruction

tendency for fugitive dyes to migrate is increased (*Figure 32.9*), and the degradation of textiles by light is accelerated. It is essential, therefore, that these hazards should be eliminated or reduced by maintaining 55 per cent RH in stores, exhibition areas and show-cases.

While the upper limits of safety must be emphasized, there are also lower limits. The flexibility of natural textile fibres is dependent on their retaining a certain percentage of moisture. If kept in an atmosphere which is too dry, they become dehydrated and embrittled, and for this reason an RH below 40 per cent should be avoided.

The unsatisfactory micro-climates and high levels of RH which sometimes develop in poorly-ventilated stores, storage containers and showcases, are hazardous. Their stagnant atmospheres encourage mould-growth which, if unchecked, can cause widespread damage amongst textiles. Good ventilation inhibits mould-growth therefore it may be advisable that wardrobes, chests and boxes be ventilated and sufficient space left inside them for the circulation of air. It is important that the collection should be inspected at fairly frequent and regular intervals, for signs of deterioration, especially if it is

unavoidable that textiles are stored in a basement or other high-risk area.

With regard to show-cases and storage cases there are two alternative views. The first is that cases should be well sealed to buffer the temperature and RH fluctuations of the surrounding area, and that if the RH needs adjustment this can be accomplished by the use of dessicants or mechanical plant. The alternative view is that the cases should be well ventilated to prevent any adverse micro-climates occurring which could support mould growth. They receive more detailed consideration in Chapter 26 (Staniforth).

Dirt and atmospheric pollution

Occasionally, a dirty or stained textile holds more interest for historians than the same item when cleaned, but soiled textiles not only look, feel, and smell unpleasant, they are also at risk from the pollutants which have impregnated them – they act as a focus for destructive organisms and can, in extreme circumstances, be a health hazard.

Ideally, all newly-acquired material should be isolated in a 'transit room' until it has been

Figure 32.8 Lining and underside of embroidery worked with metal threads on linen, following a period of damp storage, showing the destruction of cellulosic fibres by micro-organisms

thoroughly scrutinized for signs of infestation and types of soiling which could constitute a danger to the rest of the collection. Dirty textiles should then be cleaned by a qualified textile conservator before being packed for storage or mounted for exhibition. Thereafter, it is the Curator's responsibility to ensure that they remain clean and safe from further deterioration.

The more common forms of soiling result from the combustion of fossil fuels. These residues are still sufficient to cause concern in urban and industrial areas.

If allowed to accumulate on textiles, airborne dust and grit not only obscure and disfigure the surface, they ultimately destroy the structure by abrading the fibres. Moreover, ultra-fine particulate dirt penetrates twists of yarn and convolutions of individual fibres, making cleaning a hazardous and not wholly successful operation. Simultaneously, cellulosic fibres, silk and, to a lesser degree, wool, are degraded by sulphuric acid, which is produced in the fabric when sulphur dioxide (SO_2), which is present in the atmosphere, combines with water vapour.

Nitrogen dioxide (NO_2) also combines with water, forming nitric acid, which attacks cotton, wool, and some dyes, but NO_2 is less of an immediate problem.

The most satisfactory form of protection is afforded by a ducted air-cleaning system which eliminates solid and gaseous pollutants, although most museums in older premises still rely on less sophisticated measures to control dirt and provide ventilation.

For example, overlapping curtains, on runners inside wardrobes, and individual garment bags (both closely-woven and washable) will protect hanging costumes from air-borne dirt and excessive handling. If ventilation is deemed necessary, storage and display furniture should be fitted with ventilators which incorporate air-filters, to combat the restriction on movement of air resulting from dust proofing.

Where boxed storage is used, full-depth lids, combined with generous loose wrappings of acid-free tissue paper, offer the best protection from atmospheric dirt.

(a)

(b)

Figure 32.9 (a) Migration of fugitive black dye into the linen ground of an embroidered sampler during a period of high RH. (b) Embroidered sampler after conservation, mounting, framing and glazing

Polythene bags, whether sealed or not, *should be avoided*, because they are electrostatic and attract, rather than repel, dust. *Sealed* bags are hazardous

Figure 32.10 Disfiguring effects on white cotton and silk of dust-laden air entering through the floor of a defective show-case. The soft cotton netting has acted as a filter, absorbing dirt, but the smoother silk embroidery and satin trimming have resisted heavy soiling

because of the absence of ventilation, the risk of high RH and condensation within the packages, or the enclosure of destructive organisms.

Even when all reasonable precautions have been taken, some dirt will enter show-cases in heavily polluted districts, so displays should be changed frequently and the exhibition of particularly rare or vulnerable material limited to short periods.

Although it is never advisable to display textiles in the open, the problem of caring effectively for large tapestries, carpets and unholstered furniture is unlikely to be resolved satisfactorily in buildings without air-cleaning systems. Similar difficulties have been encountered with military colours, and some civil banners, which, traditionally, have been hung without protection, although this situation is improving. Certain older and rarer examples are now being preserved behind glass, following reme-dial conservation.

Pests: insects and micro-organisms

The larvae of moths (especially the common clothes moth) and carpet beetles are the insects most likely to infest textiles, and they are of roughly equal importance, in terms of numbers and the amount of damage caused. Occasionally, wood-boring beetles, and silver-fish in search of paper, will penetrate textiles closely associated with these materials

(Hueck, 1972). The materials most likely to be attacked are those containing keratin (wool, hair, fur, feathers and pelts), although evidence of moth infestation is found quite frequently on silk and cellulosic materials. Articles of soiled clothing, and composite objects which are difficult to clean, are particularly at risk and, in the museum, ethnographic and natural history specimens are as likely to be attacked as textiles. Wool felt, popular with exhibition designers as a background fabric in show-cases, is also a hazard and, if infested, can become the source of widespread damage.

Favoured locations for adult female insects to lay their eggs are the folds of hems and seams, particularly armhole and crutch seams of garments, pockets, underneath collars, cuffs and hatbands, etc., but infestation occurs almost anywhere on vulnerable objects (*Figure 32.11*).

Clothes moth larvae are about 6 mm long, and are creamy white in colour with dark heads. Their activities can be detected by irregularly shaped holes, and trails of superficial grazing on napped wool, accompanied by silky deposits, cocoons and accumulations of granular excrement, resembling sand.

Carpet beetle larvae usually make clean holes which tend to be widely dispersed over a much greater area of cloth. They deposit no silken trail, but moult several times during the larval stage, leaving transparent cast skins as evidence.

Control of insect pests begins with good housekeeping and constant vigilance; by the removal of all potential sources of infestation; by regular cleaning of the museum premises; and by *immediate*, thorough, examination of *all* newly acquired material (not only textiles).[2] It should be followed by fumigation and cleaning whenever possible, by a period of several-months isolation from the rest of the collection, and by inspection at frequent intervals of stores and displays incorporating high-risk material. If live insect larvae are found, they should be destroyed immediately and the infested articles isolated. Small outbreaks can usually be contained if treated promptly, and in this respect rapid freezing to a temperature of −20°C for 48 h has been found to be effective in killing insect pests (Florian, 1986). More widespread infestation should be referred without delay to pest-control specialists (see Chapter 46).

Micro-organic deterioration of textiles, by colonies of mould or bacteria, occurs as a result of high RH (above 70 per cent), usually caused either by a

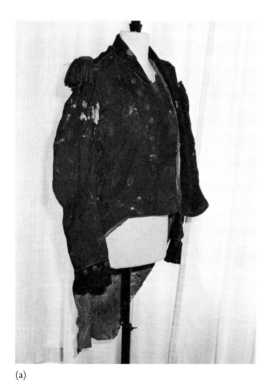

(a)

(b)

Figure 32.11 (a) Effects of long-term neglect on a Volunteer Field Officer's scarlet uniform coatee of *c*. 1804–1808: heavy soiling; leaching of dyes; destruction by clothes moth larvae, micro-organisms and rats; overall creasing. (b) White wool breeches following long-term neglect and extensive damage by clothes moth larvae

(a)

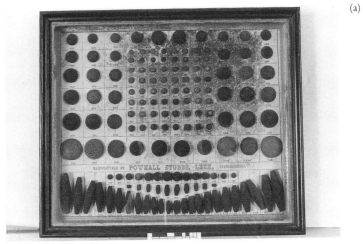

(b)

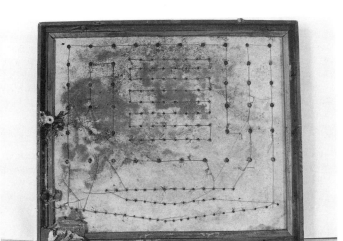

(c)

Figure 32.12 Results of undetected flood-water damge in a wall-mounted case of silk-thread- covered buttons.
(a) Infestation of textiles, paper and wood by black mould and paper mites.
(b) Green mould and weakened linen threads on underside of display card.
(c) Re-encased sample card after fumigation, cleaning and remounting of the components by specialists in the conservation of textiles and paper

poorly controlled environment or by the siting of stores in unsuitable premises. The materials most rapidly affected are those made from cellulosic fibres (for example, cotton, linen, hemp, jute and viscose rayon) but, if the damp conditions persist, and particularly if the temperature rises, all fibres and their dyes will deteriorate, sometimes within a matter of days. The onset of trouble is usually detectable by an unpleasant musty odour, but in severe cases colonies of mould will appear on damp fabric and gradually destroy its structure (*Figures 32.8* and *32.12*).

In the event of a flood in the museum, or on the discovery of damp and decaying textiles, a textile conservator's help should be enlisted *immediately*, in order to minimize the long-term damage. Otherwise, the items should be set apart, in a well-ventilated room, padded out loosely with plenty of clean, white acid-free tissue paper or rolls of soft nylon netting, to assist drying and reduce the transference of fugitive dyes. They should be dried thoroughly, but not too rapidly, in a current of warm air or with a dehumidifier. The dry textiles should be wrapped securely, to contain the mould spores, in fresh acid-free paper, and isolated. Emergency treatment other than drying should be undertaken by a qualified textile conservator and carried out in a room well away from undamaged specimens.

The control of biodeterioration is receiving urgent consideration by organizations concerned with the preservation of textiles and other organic materials (Child, 1991). Increased knowledge of chemicals, and of their effect on people, has, since the passing of the *Health and Safety at Work Act 1974*, and the *Control of Substances Hazardous to Health Regulations* (COSHH), 1988, resulted in the withdrawal of many pesticides and the imposition of stricter controls on the use of fumigants and insect repellants. Less toxic substances are being sought, but it is important that their effects on textiles, dyes and associated substances should also be thoroughly investigated before they are used in museums. Curators needing up-to-date information are advised, therefore, to consult the specialist manufacturers, suppliers and contractors.

Handling

Much of the damage sustained by textiles arises from mishandling and can be prevented, given forethought and greater understanding. Frequently it is overlooked that, even before entering the museum, most historic textiles have lost a proportion of their former strength and elasticity. Moreover, many may have concealed weaknesses which will be revealed only when the objects are subjected to a certain degree of stress. They are therefore at risk from forms of handling which subject them to tension or pressure (*Figure 32.13*) and are more vulnerable than modern textiles to the degrading effects of an unsatisfactory museum environment. Whilst an intuitive sense of strengths and weaknesses can develop with experience, fragility is not always apparent. As a precaution *all* textiles should be regarded as potentially fragile objects requiring continual underlaid support and a steady, gentle hand. They should never be moved without the aid of a box, board, or roller, nor stored or displayed under tension or so that the full weight of the object is borne by only a few threads. Neither should they be crushed, or folded unnecessarily, or subjected to rough or excessive manipulation. Costumes should never be tried on, or upholstered furniture used, or dolls and soft toys fondled and treated as playthings. It should be a rule that, after its acceptance by a museum, no object should be made to fulfill its original function, except, with the advice of a Conservator, under strictly controlled conditions. As a precaution, all persons likely to handle textiles (including exhibition designers and ancillary and voluntary workers) should be shown how to do so safely. However, handling is essentially a task which should be undertaken, or supervised, by the Conservator or Curator.

Anything which is abrasive, sharp, or otherwise potentially disfiguring, should be kept away from textiles. For this reason, it is advisable to remove watches and personal jewellery (especially rings and bracelets) and to wear clean, white cotton gloves, when handling unprotected objects. Gloves should *always* be worn when handling textiles which incorporate metal threads or trimmings, because the metal can be discoloured by perspiration on the skin.

Smoking, eating, drinking and the use of ink or ball-point pens, and artists' colours should be prohibited in workrooms and stores. Pencils can be used for recording details of textile design, cut and construction. Flash photography, if permitted, should be infrequent and restricted to the more robust specimens.

Surfaces on which specimens are laid for examination, should be smooth, easily cleaned, and entirely free from projections which could catch threads or elongate existing tears. Until unsuitable furniture can be replaced, it must be covered. For this purpose, it is useful to have several large clean sheets, or lengths of calico, which can also be used to cover the floor during the examination or conservation of large items.

Adhesive identification labels and sharp-pronged tickets of the type illustrated in *Figure 32.14* should *never be used*, nor should registration numbers be inscribed directly onto specimens. These should be written with indelible, waterproof ink on white tape, which can be sewn neatly and securely to the object,

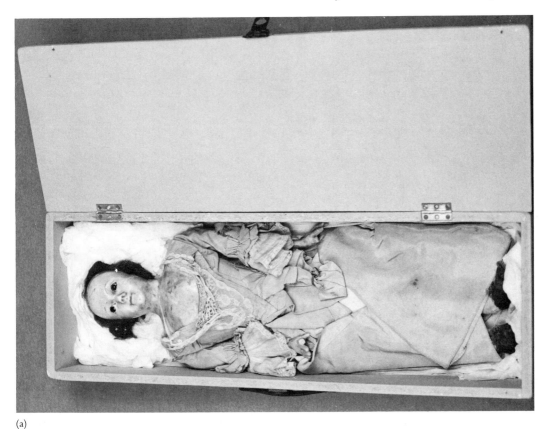

(a)

(b)

Figure 32.13 (a) Mid-eighteenth-century doll photographed on arrival at the conservation studio. The wooden box is too small, the clothing crushed and the wax head, shoulder plate and right fore-finger broken by pressure from the box lid on hard, compacted wads of tissue paper placed over and around the doll. (b) The doll after conservation of the clothing and repair of the damaged wax. The frilled triangular stomacher and wig are reproductions, copied from contemporary portraits

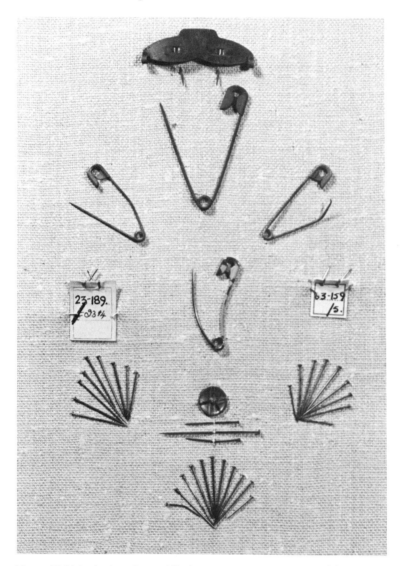

Figure 32.14 A selection of potentially dangerous items recovered from textiles during conservation treatment.

None of the pins is an original feature of the object concerned

in a position which is easily located, but which can be hidden from view when the object is displayed (*Figure 32.15*).

Inherent weaknesses

The structure of some textiles, particular combinations of materials, and processes used during dyeing and finishing, can accelerate deterioration. Silk damask, for example, first shows signs of weakness by splitting along the outlines of the woven design, while nineteenth-century challis, a plain-woven fabric with a fine silk warp and thicker wool weft,

begins to disintegrate when the silk threads weaken and can no longer support the heavier weft.

Tapestries have several characteristics which make them vulnerable. Their structure almost always dictates that they should be hung from a warp edge, so that the weight is borne by the weaker weft threads, which form the design. Frequently, in the upper part of a tapestry, these threads are almost entirely of silk, which is more susceptible than wool to tendering by light, yet is required to take more strain. As the silk deteriorates, splits will often appear near the top of the tapestry where, being above eye level, they are less easily detected. If splits

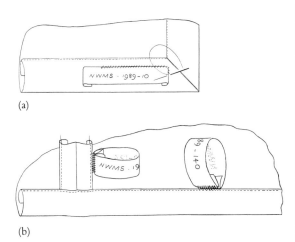

(a)

(b)

Figure 32.15 Methods of attaching woven tape identification labels. (a) Flat tape label. Label is positioned over a double thickness of fabric on the underside of the object and hemmed around all four sides. Stitches penetrate one layer of textile only; they should not be visible from the right side. (b) Looped tape labels oversewn to the inner fold of either a seam or a hem. Stitches should be securely fastened on and off and should not penetrate underlying fabric

Figure 32.16 Geometrical pattern of stitch holes in an early-seventeenth-century linen cap, indicating the former position of black silk embroidery. Only the elements of the design worked in metal threads have survived

pass unnoticed until a tapestry is moved, extensive damage may occur. Therefore, regular, thorough scrutiny is advisable, coupled with professional advice when repairs become necessary. One of the techniques of tapestry weaving creates deliberate slits in the weft, which should be distinguishable from accidental tears. These slits are usually sewn up when the weaving is finished, but where old thread has rotted and the stitching broken, the slits reopen, weakening the general structure. They should be repaired as soon as they are noticed (Finch, 1980).

Another cause of deterioration, evident in Gothic tapestries of the sixteenth century and in embroideries of earlier and later periods, is the rotting, by oxidation, of dark-coloured threads (usually black or brown wool and silk) which have been mordanted with iron salts during dyeing. These tendered threads fall away long before other colours, often leaving only traces on the underside, or stitch holes, to indicate their former position (*Figures 32.3* and *32.16*).

A contributory factor in the deterioration of some woven silks is the effect of 'weighting', a process whereby light-weight silks are impregnated with a solution of iron salts or of stannic chloride, a tin salt, which improves the draping quality and acts as a mordant for dyes. Excessive weighting damages the silk fibres, causing treated fabrics to crack along sharp creases and to shatter uncontrollably. Degrada-

tion is accelerated in silks exposed to light and heat, or stained by perspiration. Although the use of this treatment persisted well into the twentieth century, the fabrics most commonly affected date from the late-Victorian and Edwardian periods, when tin weighted silk was much used for women's clothing, especially bodice linings, petticoats and trimmings (*Figures 32.17* and *32.18*).

Concealed hazards

Loose pins, and sometimes nails, which could tear the fabric, may be concealed in garments and along the edges of any textile which has been mounted on a wooden substructure (*Figure 32.14*). With the exception of early coiled-headed pins, which could be an original feature of a garment or accessory, they should be removed, taking care (if they are corroded) to ease them out gently.

Stretcher frames of the type used for easel paintings are a hazard if used as mounts for embroidered pictures and samplers. They hold the fabric unnaturally taut, offer no support in the

Figure 32.17 Edwardian evening dress bodice, *c.* 1905, showing typical appearance of shattered tin-weighted silk (after conservation and mounting for support on fine nylon netting)

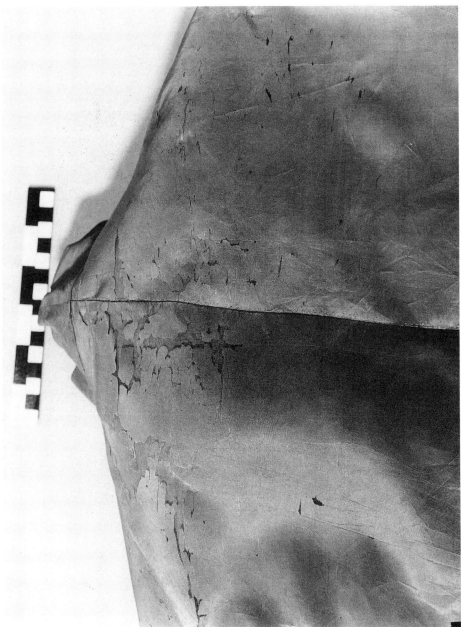

Figure 32.18 Jockey's tin–weighted silk shirt degraded by light and perspiration (after mounting for support on transparent silk Crêpeline)

centre, and no protection from atmospheric pollution. Some light-weight stretchers have weak, glued joints, which fracture when handled, with consequent damage to the textile. Seen from the outside of a glazed frame, stretcher-mounted textiles usually show a firm, broad outline which may be cleaner than the centre where dirt has penetrated. Since they are inclined to split along the unsupported inner edge of the stretcher, they should be detached and remounted, by a textile conservator, on fabric-covered, acid-free board.

Some stored costumes are a potential hazard, both to themselves and to others, because of pronged or hooked metal fastenings or abrasive trimmings, especially if these are combined with flimsy or degraded fabrics. They should be enclosed separately, with their fastenings closed, in washable cotton garment bags (not polythene), or enshrouded in washed muslin, or packed carefully with plenty of acid-free tissue paper if horizontal or boxed storage is used. Other costumes, especially if they are close fitting and made from silk, may be at risk because their cut, and the way in which they were worn, has created areas of stress and consequent weakness. They should be handled with utmost care and *never* be tried on or shown on live models.

Storage of textiles

Essential requirements for the safe storage of textiles are sufficient space for the collection, absence of light, controlled humidity and temperature, good ventilation, protection from air-borne dirt, and freedom from pests. Added to these should be ease of access.

The choice of fittings and furniture is dependent on factors which, though too numerous to be discussed individually here, have received detailed consideration by other authors (Buck, 1958; Thurman, 1978; Lambert, 1983). It is important that, when the choice has been made, storage furniture should be strongly constructed from materials which are chemically stable and can be easily maintained (see also section on show-case construction).

Materials needed for packing and support should include a plentiful supply of white, acid-free tissue paper, cardboard tubes of various lengths and diameters, custom-made cardboard boxes, plain wooden coat-hangers (including some of shorter length, and others with extra-long hooks), polyester wadding, cotton muslin and calico, and rolls of white cotton tape in several breadths. Acid-free chemically stable board should be specified for tubes and boxes but, as an added precaution, it is advisable to cover rollers and to line boxes with acid-free paper before use. The use of self-adhesive tape, pins and wire staples, which can be damaging if they come in direct contact with textiles, should be avoided.

Coat-hangers should be strong and generously padded, particular attention being paid to thick cushioning of the upper edge and ends. In the past, resilient polyurethane foam has been used as padding, but it is *no longer recommended* because it degrades and needs replacing within 5 to 10 years; also, in the event of fire, it generates dangerously toxic fumes. Polyester wadding (as sold for interlining quilted garments), covered with muslin and either tissue paper or washable cotton slip-covers, is suggested as an alternative. Coat-hangers made from cheap plastic or wire should be avoided, as they are thin, sharp and cannot provide effective support.

For the purposes of storage, the needs of 'flat' (category 1) and shaped (category 2) textiles, only, are considered. These characteristics influence the ways in which most objects are handled, and the recommended procedures can be adapted to meet most requirements.

Flat textiles

In this group are included all category 1 textiles – tapestries, carpets, church and domestic furnishings, flags and banners, shawls, embroideries, fabric samples and excavated fragments.

Flat textiles of moderate size and larger pieces which have painted or raised surface decoration, or which incorporate metal threads in their construction, should be stored flat, if space permits, separated from each other and from contact with the container, by sheets of acid-free paper. They may be placed in separate folders made from acid-free board (*Figure 32.19*), or in individual trays, or in shallow boxes, provided that the containers are not over-packed,

Figure 32.19 Folder of acid-free card, incorporating a light birch frame and a leaf of Eltoline tissue, for storage of fragile archaeological textiles. The linen mount, to which the fragments are sewn, is secured at each corner by removable thread ties

thereby causing pressure on the lower layers, impeding ventilation, and encouraging excessive handling. Small and irregularly shaped pieces will be safer if they are sewn neatly (never glued or stapled) to carefully-made individual woven supports, which leave part of the underside of the mounted textile visible, and from which the specimens need not be removed if they are required for exhibition (*Figures 32.19* and *32.20*). A fine needle, fine soft thread, such as silk, and only sufficient stitching to secure the textile safely, should be used, passing the needle between (never through) the woven threads.

Larger flat textiles, and long narrow strips, which are too large to be stored flat, should be rolled, never folded. They should be laid face downwards on a clean surface, then covered with sheets of white acid-free paper and rolled firmly and evenly onto hollow cylinders of relatively broad diameter (*Figure 32.20*). Keeping the topside of the textile outermost, during rolling, enables a lined textile to remain smooth, as the lining takes up the wrinkles which develop when two or more combined layers of fabric are rolled together.

If textiles incorporating metal threads, painted or raised surface decoration must be rolled, a cylinder of a much greater diameter than usual should be used. Additionally, as protection for bulky items, a thick layer of polyester wadding should be laid between the interleaved sheets of tissue paper, to absorb variations in thickness and reduce uneven pressure within the roll. (It is not advisable to substitute polythene 'bubble wrap' for this purpose.)

Tapestries, also, should be rolled face outermost and with the more prominent and stronger warp ends passing round the roller. Usually this requires that the textile be rolled from side to side. A tapestry should never be rolled for storage or transportation with the ridges parallel to the length of the roller, as this puts great strain on the weaker weft threads.

All rolled textiles should be secured with broad tapes fastened over soft pads, or held with 'Velcro', a nylon contact fastener; they should never be bound with cords. Unless the store is air-conditioned, the rolls should then be wrapped in acid-free paper, or washed calico (not polythene) to exclude dust but permit the unimpeded movement of air. Alternatively, large rolls can be provided with cylindrical drawstring bags made from calico or closely woven canvas. The rolls should be identified clearly on the outside, ideally with a photograph or drawing, as

Figure 32.20 Coptic textile mounted on linen and rolled for storage between sheets of acid-free tissue paper, on a cardboard tube. Note 'window' in linen mount (protected by transparent crêpeline) for viewing underside of coptic weaving

well as the reference number. Pressure on the rolled textiles should be relieved by supporting the ends of the cylinders, or by passing rods through them into some form of rack.

Shaped textiles

Costumes (category ii textiles) make up this group. Because of their cut and construction, shaped textiles require proportionately more storage space than flat textiles and even greater care in packing if they are not to suffer the effects of tension and pressure. The choice of storage method for full-length garments lies between horizontal and vertical support. Factors such as size, scope and condition of the collection, its relative importance, space and finance may influence the Curator's choice, but a combination of storage methods is usually an appropriate solution.

Manually-operated, mobile, compact storage units which roll on tracks set into the floor are not recommended, primarily because of the damage which can be caused to hanging costumes and fragile

boxed items by the momentum of repeated movement, but also because, when full and compacted, the units increase the difficulty of controlling RH and providing adequate ventilation. Horizontal storage is essential for costumes which could be damaged by hanging, for example, those which are are bias-cut, knitted, heavily ornamented or in a weakened condition.

Boxes are a convenient method of storing costumes made from soft, light-weight fabrics, children's clothing, baby linen and accessories, but are less satisfactory for heavy and bulky items, particularly those made from stiff silks. The boxes should be of a size which can be controlled by one person, and be lined with acid-free tissue paper before use. Dresses and other outer garments should be boxed singly, each garment being packed (with minimum folding) to fit the box. Every fold should be softened with a plump roll or concertina folds of tissue paper, and bodices, sleeves, breeches, and looped ribbon trimmings filled with crushed (not compacted) tissue paper. Any remaining space

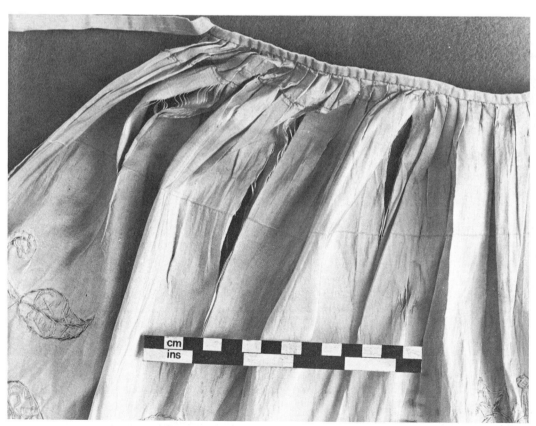

Figure 32.21 Pressure-induced creases and tears in silk. Part of the pleated waistline of an eighteenth-century embroidered apron seen from the underside. Additional well-defined vertical and horizontal creases show how the apron has been folded and compressed during long-term storage

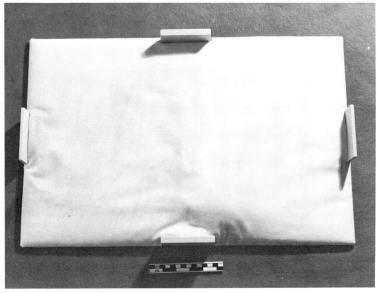

(a)

(b)

Figure 32.22 (a) Storage board for a fan. The padding, of polyester wadding covered with washed soft cotton fabric, increases in depth from left to right so that both fan-guards and all the sticks receive equal support. (b) Storage board with nineteenth century fan of Maltese lace and inlaid mother-of-pearl. Blocks attached to the edges act as handles and enable several boards to be stacked without pressure on the fans

around the garment should also be filled with crushed tissue, to minimize movement within the box.

Pressure on folded textiles and on intentionally sharp creases must be avoided, as creases eventually become permanent and, if the fabric is brittle, will crack under pressure (*Figure 32.21*). All degraded textiles are subject to this kind of damage, but it is most common among silks and cellulosic fabrics which have been exposed to a heavily polluted atmosphere. When pleats and sharp folds are a necessary feature of objects such as parasols and fans, pressure should be reduced by storing the objects partly open, with the fabric supported (*Figures 32.22 and 32.23*).

Figure 32.23 An easily fitted detachable restraint for a partly furled umbrella or parasol, made from matching tape worked with stitched loops which slip over the rib-tips

Tray-drawers are ideal for horizontal storage of costumes, for they give overall support and easy access, provided that they are wide enough (approximately 1.5 m) to accommodate a full-length garment without cross-wise folds, and that only one item is laid in each tray. Enclosed wardrobes and padded hangers are required for hanging costumes, with an individual, washable cotton garment bag for each of the most rare and vulnerable items. Standard coat-hangers may have to be adapted, or special supports made for some garments, to provide adequate support across the shoulders and at the neckline. They must not be too long since, if the ends of a hanger protrude too far into the sleeves of a garment, they can cause damage, even when padded. Coats and dresses which have high collars need hangers with extra-long hooks but, as a short-term measure, a standard hook can be suspended from the garment rail with string. A supplementary 'collar' of folded tissue paper, slipped over the hook will prevent contact of the sharp metal with the garment.

The garment rail should be fixed as high above the wardrobe floor as can be reached easily, to allow long dresses to hang freely. Trains should be raised by tapes sewn to the underside, and tied around the stems of the hangers. Dresses with wide necklines need loops of tape, sewn like shoulder-straps to the front and back bodice linings, to hold them securely on their hangers. Skirts require similar long loops, sewn (like braces) to the front and back of the waistband. Heavy, one-piece dresses can be relieved of strain in the same way, by attaching broad tapes to the inside of the waist seam, adjusting their length so that the weight of the skirt is borne by the padded hanger, and not by the bodice.

Wardrobes should not be so full that garments are compressed. Nevertheless, puffed sleeves and trimmings should be filled with lightly crushed tissue paper, or balls of polyester wadding, to preserve their shape. Whatever the size of the collection, it is advisable to separate women's from men's clothing, since the latter, being usually heavier and more robust, could abrade more fragile items.

Accessories, which are classified as 'shaped' textiles, should be stored by the method most appropriate to their particular needs. Some, such as hats, bonnets and fans, may also need specially devised supports, which can double as exhibition mounts (*Figures 32.24, 32.25 and 32.26*).

The mounting of textiles for exhibition

Ideally, the Curator, Textile Conservator and Exhibition Designer should collaborate in the planning, designing and mounting of the exhibition. All possible causes of deterioration should be considered, and measures taken to eliminate them, while the Conservator's opinions should be sought, especially with regard to the exhibition of fragile or rare objects.

Experience has shown that certain varieties of timber, composite boards, adhesives and paints emit vapours which have an adverse effect on textiles and other organic substances, dyes and some metals

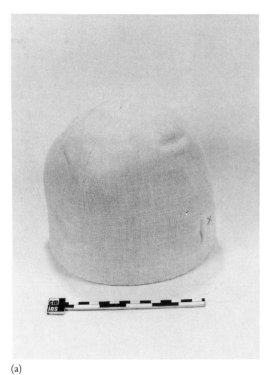

(a)

(b)

Figure 32.24 (a) Resilient support for an embroidered cap. The soft dome with filling of polyester fibre and firm base of acid-free rag-board, are covered with washed linen which has been shaped to fit the lining of the cap.

(b) Embroidered nightcap after remedial conservation, mounted for exhibition or storage. (Shown before conservation in *Figure 32.16*)

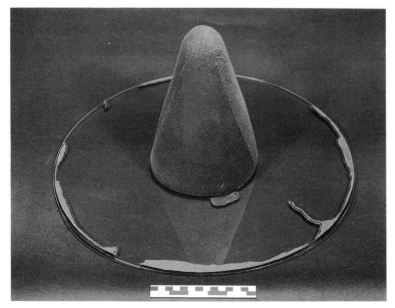

Figure 32.25 Storage and display mount for a frail seventeenth-century felt hat with conical crown and partially decayed brim. The resilient crown support, covered with dyed cotton stockinette, is attached to a disc of Perspex which has been built up at the edge with dyed non-woven Vilene, to fill gaps in the felt

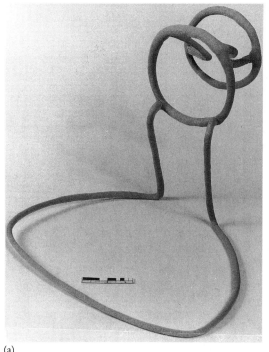

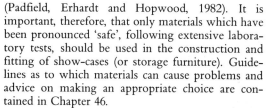

(a)

(b)

Figure 32.26 (a) Display mount for a bonnet, shaped from mild steel wire, padded and covered with fine polyester stockinette.

(b) Bonnet, *c.* 1828, mounted for exhibition

(Padfield, Erhardt and Hopwood, 1982). It is important, therefore, that only materials which have been pronounced 'safe', following extensive laboratory tests, should be used in the construction and fitting of show-cases (or storage furniture). Guidelines as to which materials can cause problems and advice on making an appropriate choice are contained in Chapter 46.

If a coloured background or mount is required, only fast-dyed fabrics should be used, so that there is no risk of the dyes staining displayed objects during periods of high RH. Dyes can be tested by wetting scraps of fabric and pressing them between damp, white absorbant paper, for several hours.

Sufficient preparation time should be allowed for any remedial conservation or the construction of special supports, and each item should be mounted in the way which is least liable to cause distortion, stress or damage. The use of pins, wire staples, self-adhesive tape and other forms of makeshift support should be forbidden.

Flat textiles

Whenever possible, flat textiles should be displayed against a horizontal or slightly inclined surface. This support may be a simple board or a three-dimensional structure. Before use, the support should be covered closely with fabric to which the object can be sewn for exhibition (*Figure 32.27*). Its fibre, texture and colour should be in sympathy with those of the object, and should provide the right degree of contrast for comfortable viewing. If a light-weight fabric is chosen, a thicker soft underlay, such as cotton 'bump' interlining, may also be needed. It is inadvisable to use felt or other wool fabric for the hidden underlay, because of the danger of attracting moths.

Before covering a board for use as an exhibition mount, ensure that all surfaces are smooth and free from fine abrasive dust. The covering should be stretched taut over the surface and fastened securely to the underside only. The woven threads should lie parallel to the edges of the board, and between 10 and 20 cm of extra fabric should be allowed on each side for turning under. Polyvinyl acetate emulsion is a suitable adhesive for securing the fabric to the board. It can be augmented with wire staples if the board is large, heavy and intended to support a substantial weight of textile, but the staples must not penetrate the upper surface, and neither they nor the adhesive should come into contact with the exhibit.

The displayed textile, also aligned with the edges

Figure 32.27 Painted silk Militia Colour, *c.* 1856, after conservation, mounted on a fabric-covered board, to which it has been sewn, in preparation for exhibiton in a glazed frame. Pieces of specially dyed fabric laid behind holes in the silk create an illusion of completeness

of the prepared board, should be secured *temporarily* with fine stainless-steel pins, set at right angles to the outer edges, before being sewn to the board covering. A fine curved needle should be used for the stitching with fine softly spun thread. Monofilament nylon ('invisible thread') is not suitable.

Frames for textiles should be made in the same way as for pictures, but with an extra-deep rebate, to accommodate a wooden fillet, or subframe, placed between the mounted textile and the glass, or acrylic sheet. The fillet should be thick enough to prevent contact between the underside of the 'glass' and the surface of the textile, but for semi-three-dimensional subjects such as stump-work and thickly padded embroidery, a shallow box frame may be more suitable (*Figure 32.12(c)*). In either instance, the back should be sealed with adhesive paper to exclude dust when the mounted textile has been secured in its frame.

It is not usually advisable to display historic textiles by draping them, because of the distortion and creasing which occurs, but it is sometimes necessary when furnishings or costume accessories are shown in the manner in which they would have been used. They should be given as much support as possible, their folds softened unobtrusively with polyester wadding, and they should not be left on view for so long that the prominent exposed surfaces become more noticeably soiled, tendered or faded than the parts of the textiles which are concealed.

Tapestries, and other textiles which are used as wall-hangings, should always be lined to protect them from the dust and grime which usually accumulates on the underside. They should hang from a continuous length of 'Velcro' nylon contact fastener to distribute the weight evenly across the full width of the textile (*Figure 32.28*). This method of hanging is secure, yet allows the textile to be pressed into position, adjusted or removed, with equal ease.

An alternative method depends on the provision of a sleeve, made from strong linen or webbing, which should be stitched to the underside, just below the top edge of the textile, and through which a rod or batten can be slotted, this being supported at each end by brackets or suspended by chains or cords.

Banners and military colours should always hang smoothly from horizontal poles or pikes, *never* in diagonal folds from acutely angled staves. Being intended to be seen from both sides they are not usually lined, but may need less obtrusive forms of support to withstand being hung. This work should be carried out by a qualified textile conservator.

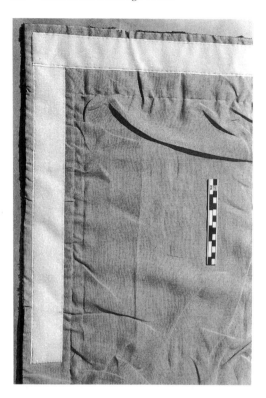

Figure 32.28 Detail of underside of a lined wall-hanging showing strips of looped–pile Velcro contact fastener. Companion strips of hooked–pile Velcro are attached to wooden batons, screwed to the wall

Figure 32.29 (a) Display dummy for a dress, *c.* 1875–1880, based on a mass-produced, slender-cast polyurethane torso, supported on a height-adjustable stand. The fabric-covered form has been built up with polyester fibre wadding to fit the dress-lining then provided with an outer covering of cotton stockinette and silk. (b) Dress, *c.* 1875–1880, after conservation and mounting for exhibition on the prepared dummy

(a)

(b)

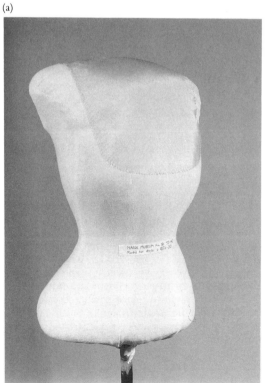

Shaped textiles

Exhibitions of historic costumes are popular with the visiting public, but clothes, which are intended to be seen in the round, and in movement, lose some of their character and appeal when separated from their original wearers. Both skill and imagination are needed in their presentation, if they are to succeed in static exhibition.

Ideally, costumes should be displayed three-dimensionally. Outer garments, in particular, should be provided with a 'body' of the correct size and proportions, shaped to portray the fashionable silhouette and deportment of the period represented (*Figures 32.29* to *32.31*). A costume which is stretched onto an unsuitable figure will not only look incongruous, it could be severely damaged. For the same reasons, historic costumes should never be worn, even for static photography.

Costume display dummies can be specially commissioned, but the expense is beyond the means of most museums. The choice lies, more usually, between mass-produced dummies and those con-structed in the museum. Whichever type is used, it is essential that the dummy should be made to fit the garment, and not *vice versa*, with sufficient soft padding inserted between the shell of a rigid dummy and its outer covering to provide a resilient support for the costume (*Figures 32.29* to *32.31*).

Museum-made dummies are generally better suited to the display of female than male attire, because the majority are based on a torso only, the absence of legs being concealed by petticoats and a long skirt. A variation on the museum-made torso is the adapted home-dressmaker's dummy, which can be reduced in girth, if necessary, before being padded and covered with stockinette.

Except when fairly recent fashions are being shown, modern shop-display dummies, in adult sizes, have only limited usefulness in the museum because, unless they are subjected to ruthless alteration, proportions and measurements rarely suit costumes of previous generations. Boys' and youths' figures, from certain ranges, can be more useful and are adaptable for either male or female clothing.

In addition to bodies, costumes need the support

Figure 32.30 Dresses of different periods and dimensions mounted on identical slender-cast polyurethane torsos supported on height-adjustable stands. Padding and appropriate underclothing have been added, including reproductions of a 1770s corset and silk petticoat for the open robe (far left)

(a)

(b)

Figure 32.31 (a) Hand-sewn modern copy of an underdress for a silk gauze ball dress, *c.* 1820. (b) Ball dress, *c.* 1820, after conservation, displayed over the modern satin underdress on a specially adapted polyurethane dummy

of appropriate foundation garments and underclothing, to enable them to hang correctly, and if the collection cannot supply genuine examples, reproductions should be made. In the same context, if part of an outfit, or an essential accessory is missing, without which the costume would appear incomplete, a reproduction should be made (*Figures 32.31* and *32.32*), using as a guide another costume of the same date, contemporary portraits and other primary sources, aided by one of the well-researched books on costume construction (Arnold, 1964, 1965, 1973, 1985; Anonymous, 1840; Waugh, 1954, 1964, 1968). It is advisable to understate colour in reproductions and, if necessary, to dye the fabric specially to a slightly duller tone than the original, if combining new fabric with old. The presence of reproductions should always be stated on the exhibition label.

Generally, the exhibition of costumes against a flat surface should be avoided because of creasing and the strain imposed on heavy garments. Exceptions might be accessories and light-weight cotton garments such as underwear, children's and babies' clothing, which can be mounted on boards, using similar techniques to those suggested for flat textiles,

provided that all folds are padded lightly, and that sufficient stitching is used to provide firm but unobtrusive support (*Figure 32.33*).

Finally, costumes need accessories to bring them to life. Unless the collection is very small it should be possible to find suitable items, but they must be chosen carefully, with reference to contemporary illustrations, to ensure that they are correct, not only in period, but also for the occasions on which the costumes would have been worn.

Caring for a textile collection: remedial conservation

Staff involvement with conservation: Curator and Conservator

Until comparatively recently, it was the custom for Curators or Technicians to carry out collection maintenance, or to entrust the care of textiles to an accomplished needle-woman, but such practices led to unintentional damage through the use of unsuitable methods and materials (*Figures 32.6* and *32.34*).

The number of fully-trained and qualified Textile Conservators is still relatively small but, ideally,

Figure 32.32 Volunteer Field Officer's uniform, *c.* 1804–1808, after conservation and mounting for exhibition. The difficulty of obtaining a suitably proportioned male dummy for this uniform (shown before conservation in *Figure 32.11*) led to the use of the flocked foam-covered figure, which has undergone extensive 'surgery' and adaptation. The gaiters, boots and stock are reproductions, copied from contemporary illustrations

every museum which houses a notable textile collection should employ at least one, whose job is to advise on all aspects of textile care and, in consultation with the Curator, to carry out remedial conservation. Where financial or other restraints preclude such an appointment, advice and practical help must be sought from Area Museum Services, independent conservation agencies and reputable freelance textile conservators. At present these resources are unevenly distributed and, even in the better-served areas, their number is rarely sufficient to meet the demand from potential clients. Nevertheless, textiles which require remedial conservation should not be entrusted to unqualified practitioners. They should be stored carefully until they can receive expert attention.

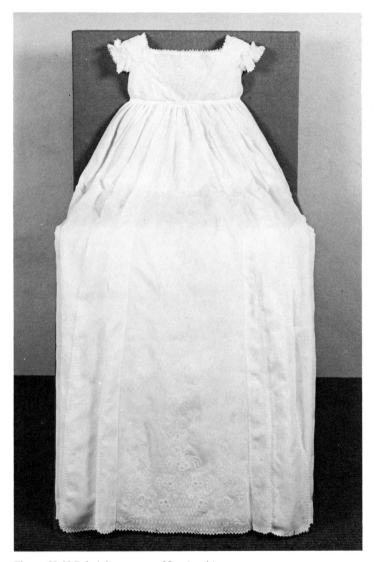

Figure 32.33 Baby's long gown of fine Ayrshire embroidered cotton, lightly padded and mounted for exhibition on a fabric-covered inclined and stepped support

Internal conservation resources

The textile conservation studio–workshop–laboratory
If specialist conservation is to be carried out in the museum, it is preferable to appoint the Conservator before planning the studio in detail.

It is difficult to generalize about space requirements for textile conservation, but approximately $50\,m^2$ would be the minimum for small-scale work. Essentially, the furnished area must be sufficient to enable the largest items in the collection to be extended fully and to be handled safely and easily. One large room, or two (for wet and dry work),

connected by a wide archway to allow for the unhindered movement of large objects and textiles supported on boards, is preferable to a series of smaller rooms. If carpets, tapestries, or flags are collected, planning will need to be on a grander scale than for costumes, and, if the collection is large, provision should be made for expansion of the conservation facilities, as the workforce is increased.

Ideally, the conservation studio should be in a clean area near the textile store, and separated from the public part of the museum. It must comply in every way with legislation imposed by the *Health and Safety at Work Act, 1974, Control of Substances*

Figure 32.34 Detail of painted Silk Volunteer Regiment Colour before conservation (shown also in *Figure 32.6* after treatment). Destructive previous repairs utilizing coarse needles and threads, extensive close darning into dense silk netting and heat-sealed dry-mounting tissue

Hazardous to Health Regulations, 1988, and the requirements of Fire Prevention and Security Officers. It should be easily accessible, well lit by natural and artificial light, comfortably warm, and have good general ventilation augmented by apparatus for efficient fume and vapour extraction. An unlimited supply of hot, cold, and deionized water, good drainage and a generous allocation of power-points (which should be of the water-proof type in 'wet' areas and spark-proof wherever flammable solvents are used).

The basic equipment need not be elaborate but should be of the best quality. It should include at least one stainless steel sink, approximately 200 × 50 × 20 cm with adjacent workbenches; a mobile textile-washing table, 300–400 × 120 cm; several large work tables (or adjustable trestle supports with loose tops) having water-repellent surfaces, and dimensions which allow them to be used either singly, in groups, or in conjunction with the washing table; a microscope; a binocular magnifier; a camera; dyeing equipment; enclosed storage for conservation materials and work in progress; a steel cabinet for small quantities of chemicals; and for each Conservator an adjustable chair, an adjustable magnifying lamp and a small mobile cabinet or trolley, for personal possessions and small equipment. A wide selection of portable equipment will also be required as well as reference books and the means to record and store conservation data. Eventually, there may also be a need for textile dry-cleaning equipment and a vacuum table. However, since requirements vary, and some of the larger equipment may have to be specially made, it is advisable to study published descriptions of conservation laboratories, and, where possible, to visit several established textile conservation workshops,[3] before purchasing the equipment.

Briefing the Conservator

While the ultimate responsibility for consigning an object to remedial conservation rests with the Curator, ideally he will be guided in his decision by the Textile Conservator, following a thorough examination of the object and an assessment of its condition.

The Conservator needs information about the object, and about the conditions to which it will be returned. She should have access to associated documentation, particularly if previous conservation treatment is recorded, and her attention should be drawn to features of special interest which, if they are to be preserved and remain accessible for study, might influence her choice of cleaning media or method of supporting the textile. It is not a Textile Conservator's usual practice to unpick original stitching but, when it is unavoidable that details of construction are disturbed or partly obscured, the Conservator will also appreciate guidance from the Curator concerning the permitted extent of the treatment.

During the initial examination, the Conservator will note the type and degree of soiling, the nature and position of damage, and the extent to which the textile as a whole has deteriorated. Using all this information the Conservator will devise a programme of treatment, for discussion with the Curator, before the work is put in hand.

External conservation resources

Area Museum Services

The principal external conservation resources used by museums in the UK are provided by the Area Museum Services (or Councils), whose role is to assist museums (other than the national institutions) in maintaining satisfactory standards of conservation and presentation of their collections.[4]

In some regions, Area Museum Councils have established their own textile conservation workshops. Elsewhere, textile conservation is carried out for the Area Museum Services on an agency basis, either at independent conservation centres or by Conservators working in the larger museums or by private Conservators.

Independent conservation agencies

There are, in the United Kingdom, a small but growing number of independent conservation agencies specializing in textiles. Most, but not all, employ professionally trained Textile Conservators, and some also offer in-service training to apprentices.

Commissions are accepted from museums, historic houses, churches and other sources, and the largest, in Surrey, are amongst the minority of workshops with facilities for handling large tapestries.

Private Conservators

Among the Textile Conservators who practice privately are many who are also employed in museums, or are respected former museum Conservators of long experience who are accustomed to working to very exacting standards. It is advisable, nevertheless, for Curators to be cautious, and to consult their Area Museum Service, before sending work to a Conservator who lacks appropriate professional qualifications or a well-founded reputation for high-class work.

The procedure when working with external Conservators differs in some respects from that followed with in-house staff. Initially, the Conservator's preliminary report and recommended programme of treatment should be accompanied by estimates of the time required to carry out the work, and the approximate cost. On completion of the commission, the Conservator should provide a final report, recording the conservation treatment and materials used, together with copies of 'before' and 'after' photographs and recommendations for future care of the object. Documentation, an essential element of all remedial conservation, assumes an even greater importance if the work is undertaken externally, and should always be preserved, preferably with other records relating to the object concerned.

Volunteers and textile conservation

From time to time museums receive offers of voluntary assistance with textile conservation, from individuals, or local branches of national organizations, which specialize in the cleaning and repair of church furnishings and material from historic houses. The prospect of supplementary help is often welcomed, initially, for some museums, and organizations such as the National Trust, have used volunteers with considerable success, but any such proposal should receive the most careful consideration before it is accepted (Finch and Putnam, 1985).

It is generally inadvisable to involve volunteers with remedial conservation, unless a qualified Textile Conservator is also employed, who can organize and exert strict control over their work, but small groups can assist with less specialized aspects of textile care, which emphasize the need for prevention of damage, rather than cure. For example, they can make curtains to exclude light from stores and dust from wardrobes; construct covers for stored furniture; cover coat-hangers and sew garment bags; or devise supports for fans, millinery and footwear. It is essential, however, that volunteers should be instructed and supervised by a responsible and suitably qualified member of the museum staff; that the limits of their duties should be clearly defined; and that the museum security and safety measures should be strictly observed. If this takes up more of the professional's time than can be justified, the museum may benefit little from the project.

Conclusion

The successful management of a textile collection requires specialized knowledge and imposes considerable demands on the Curator, the Conservator, and on the museum's other resources. Only if these demands can be met consistently should a museum begin collecting textiles (including costume) or add to existing holdings.

Acknowledgements

The author is grateful to the North West Museums Service and to the numerous authorities whose textiles are illustrated, for permission to publish photographs taken during the conservation of these items. Remedial conservation and exhibition mounting were carried out in the Textile Conservation Studios of the North West Museums Service by Jean Glover, Vivian Lochhead, Nanette Muir, and Eleanor Palmer.

Notes

[1] Readers who require instruction in the use of the microscope and in fibre microscopy are advised to enquire about tuition at the nearest College of Technology.
[2] It is essential that specimens are scrutinized *before* being put aside for cataloguing or conservation. Infested textiles should *never* be despatched to an external conservation agency without prior warning and the consent of the agency staff.
[3] Institutions in Great Britain with studios/laboratories equipped to carry out remedial conservation of textiles:

Bath Area Museum Council for the South West
Birmingham Birmingham Museum and Art Gallery
Blackburn North West Museums Service
Bristol Blaise Castle House Museum
Cardiff Welsh Folk Museum, St Fagans
East Molesey Historic Royal Palaces Agency Textile Conservation Studios at Hampton Court Palace
East Molesey The Textile Conservation Centre, Hampton Court Palace
Edinburgh National Museums of Scotland
Edinburgh The Scottish Museums Council
Glasgow The Burrell Collection
Liverpool National Museums and Galleries on Merseyside
London Museum of London
London The National Maritime Museum
London The Victoria and Albert Museum
Manchester City Art Galleries, Queen's Park Conservation Studios
Manchester The National Museum of Labour History

[4] Information and advice can be obtained on application to the nearest Area Museum Service headquarters. (For addresses and telephone numbers see *Museums Yearbook*, Museums Association, London.)

References

ARNOLD, J. (1964) (reprinted 1972), *Patterns of Fashion 1: Englishwomen's Dresses and their Construction c. 1660–1860*, Macmillan, London

ARNOLD, J. (1965) (reprinted 1972), *Patterns of Fashion 2: Englishwomen's Dresses and their Construction c. 1860–1940*, Macmillan, London

ARNOLD, J. (1985), *Patterns of Fashion, 3: The Cut and Construction of Clothes for Men and Women 1560–1620*, Macmillan, London

ARNOLD, J. (1973), *A Handbook of Costume*, Macmillan, London

ANONYMOUS (1840) (reprinted 1975), *The Workwoman's Guide*, Bloomfield Books, Owston Ferry, Doncaster

BUCK, A. M. (1958), *Handbook for Museums Curators – Costume*, The Museums Association, London

CHILD, R. E. (Ed.) (1991), *Detection, Monitoring and Control of Insect Pests*, Conference papers. Welsh Folk Museum, Cardiff

FINCH, K. (1980), 'Some notes on the care of tapestries', *Museums Journal*, **80**(1), 40–41

FINCH, K. and PUTNAM, G. (1985), *The Care and Preservation of Textiles*, Batsford, London

FLORIAN, M.-L.-E. (1986), 'The freezing process – effects on insects and artifact materials: recommended procedures for eradication of insect infestation of museum artifacts by low temperature freezing', *Leather Conservation News*, **3**(1), pp. 1–13

HUECK, H. J. (1972), 'Textile pests and their control', in Leene, J. E, (Ed.), *Textile Conservation*, Butterworths, London

LAMBERT, A. M. (1983), *Storage of Textiles and Costumes: Guidelines for Decision-making*, University of British Columbia Museum of Anthropology

LANDI, S. and MARKO, K. (1980), 'The maintenance *in situ* of architecturally related textiles', in Brommelle, N. S., Thomson, G. and Smith, P. (Eds), *Conservation within Historic Buildings*, pp. 151–154, International Institute for Conservation of Historic and Artistic Works (IIC), London

PADFIELD, T., ERHARDT, D. and HOPWOOD, W. (1982), Trouble in Store, in Brommelle, N. S. and Thomson, G. (Eds), *Science and Technology in the Service of Conservation*, pp. 24–27, IIC, London

TEXTILE INSTITUTE (1970), *The Identification of Textile Materials*, 6th edition, The Textile Institute, Manchester

THURMAN, C. C. M. (1978), 'The Department of Textiles at the Art Institute of Chicago', *Museum*, 30, 122–126, UNESCO, Paris

WAUGH, N. (1954) (reprinted 1987), *Corsets and Crinolines*, Batsford, London

WAUGH, N. (1964), *The Cut of Men's Clothes*, Faber, London

WAUGH, N. (1968), *The Cut of Women's Clothes*, Faber, London

Bibliography

Among the publications listed are some which contain descriptions of remedial conservation procedures. For reasons of their own and others' safety, as well as that of the museum objects in their care, readers are advised against practising these procedures unless they have had considerable experience of conserving textiles and of handling chemicals.

Technical analysis

General

LEENE, J. E. (Ed.) (1972), 'Textiles', in *Textile Conservation*, pp. 4–22, Butterworths, London

Idenfication of fibres

APPLEYARD, H. M. (1978), *Guide to the Identification of Animal Fibres*, Wool Industry Research Association, Leeds

CATLING, D. (1981), 'Guidance for the inexperienced microscopist', *The Conservator*, 5, 15–19

CATLING, D. and GRAYSON, J. (1982), *Vegetable Fibres: Identification*, Chapman and Hall, London

SAWBRIDGE, M. and FORD, J. E. (1987), *Textile Fibres under the Microscope*, Shirley Institute, Didsbury, Manchester

THE TEXTILE INSTITUTE (1970), *The Identification of Textile Materials*, The Textile Institute, Manchester

Identification of textile techniques

ASHLEY, C. W. (1944), *The Ashley Book of Knots*, Mariner's Museum, Newport News, VA

BARKER, A. D. (1980), *Gold Lace and Embroidery – A Brief Survey of the Manufacture and Use of Precious Metal Wires and Threads for Weaving and Embroidery*, Northern Society for Costume and Textiles, Bolling Hall Museum, Bradford

BEUTLICH, T. (1967), *The Technique of Woven Tapestry*, Batsford, London

BURNHAM, D. K. (1980), *Warp and Weft: a Textile Terminology*, Royal Ontario Museum, Toronto

CLARKE, L. J. (1968), *The Craftsman in Textiles*, Bell, London

COLLINGWOOD, P. (1968), *The Techniques of Rug Weaving*, Faber, London

COLLINGWOOD, P. (1977), *The Techniques of Sprang*, Faber, London

COLLINGWOOD, P. (1982), *The Techniques of Tablet Weaving*, Faber, London

D'HARCOURT, R. (1968), *Textiles of Ancient Peru and their Techniques*, University of Washington, Seattle

DILLMONT, T. DE (1891), *Encyclopedia of Needlework – Detailed Illustrated Explanation of the Techniques of Plain Sewing, Mending, Embroidery, Knitting, Crochet, Tatting, Macramé, Netting, Pillow and Needle Laces, etc.*, numerous editions, Dollfus-Mieg et Cie., Société Anonyme (DMC), France

EARNSHAW, P. (1980), *The Identification of Lace*, Shire, Aylesbury

EMERY, I. (1966), *The Primary Structures of Fabrics – An Illustrated Classification*, The Textile Museum, Washington, DC

GRAYSON, M. (1984), *Encyclopedia of Textiles, Fibres and Non-woven Fabrics*, Wiley, New York

HALD, M. (1980), *Ancient Danish Textiles from Bogs and Burials*, National Museum of Denmark, Copenhagen

HALLS, Z. (1973), *Machine-made Lace in Nottingham*, 2nd edition, City of Nottingham Museums and Libraries, Nottingham

HALSEY, M. and YOUNGMARK, D. (1975), *Foundations of Weaving*, David and Charles, Newton Abbot

LEVEY, S. M. (1983), *Lace: A History*, Victoria and Albert Museum/W. S. Maney, London

LEADBETTER, E. (1976), *Handspinning*, Studio Vista, London

MISCELLANEOUS (1937–1975), *CIBA Review – a Series of Monographs by Experts on all Aspects of textile History and Technology*, Chemical Industry of Basel, Switzerland

MILLER, E. (1968), *Textile Properties and Behaviour*, Batsford, London

O'CONNOR, S. A. and BROOKS, M. M. (Eds) (1990), *Archaeological Textiles*, UKIC, London

PICTON, J. and MACK, J. (1979), *African Textiles*, The British Museum, London

RUTT, R. (1987), *A History of Hand Knitting*, Batsford, London

SEAGROATT, M. (c. 1977), *Coptic Weaves*, Liverpool Museum, National Museums and Galleries on Merseyside

STRAUB, M. (1977), *Hand Weaving and Cloth Design*, Pelham, London

SUTTON, A. and HOLTON, P. (1975), *Tablet Weaving*, Batsford, London

SWAIN, M. (1982), *Ayrshire and Other Whitework*, Shire, Aylesbury

TATTERSALL, C. E. C. (1920), *Notes on Carpet Knotting and Weaving*, numerous editions, Victoria and Albert Museum, London

WEIR, S. (1970), *Spinning and Weaving in Palestine*, The British Museum, London

Introduction to conservation

ASHLEY-SMITH, J. (1978), 'Why conserve collections?', *Transactions 15*, Museum Professionals' Group, Leicester

CONSTABLE, W. G. (1954), 'Curators and conservation', *Studies in Conservation*, 1, 97

FLURY-LEMBERG, M. (1988), *Textile Conservation and Research*, Abegg-Stiftung, Bern

GLOVER, J. M. (1986), 'Preserving a textile heritage', *Textiles*, 15(2), 48–52, The Shirley (Textile Research) Institute, Manchester

LANDI, S. M. (1985), *The Textile Conservator's Manual*, Butterworths, London

SANDWITH, H. and STAINTON, S. (1984), *The National Trust Manual of Housekeeping*, Allen Lane/National Trust, London

WARD, P. (1987), *The Nature of Conservation: a Race against Time*, Getty Conservation Institute, Marina del Rey, CA

WILD, J. P. (1990), 'An introduction to archaeological textile studies', *Archaeological Textiles*, Occasional Papers, 10, United Kingdom Institute for Conservation, London

The museum environment

General

THOMSON, G. (1986), *The Museum Environment*, 2nd edition, Butterworths, London

Light

BETTS, K., CRAFT, M., DIRKS, K., FIKIORIS, M. and THOMSEN, F. (Eds) (1980), *Textiles and Museum Lighting*, Harper's Ferry Regional Textile Group, Washington, DC

BOGLE, M. (1980), Textile mounting and framing with an internally-incorporated thin-film ultra-violet light barrier, *Conservation and Restoration of Textiles, Como*, pp. 56–51, CISST, Lombardy Section, Milan

DAVID, J. (1986), 'Light in museums', *Museums Journal*, **85**(4), 203–215

DAVID, J. (Ed.) (1987), 'Lighting: papers presented at a seminar organised by the Museums Association' The United Kingdom Institute for Conservation, and the Group of Designers and Interpreters in Museums', *Museums Journal*, **87**(3), 141–154

RIDGWAY, B. (1985), 'Lighting for museums and galleries: a review of recent developments', *The Architectural Review*, **178**(1065), 92–111

STANIFORTH, S. (1982), 'Unsuitable lighting', *Museum*, **34**(1), 53–54

THOMSON, G. and STANIFORTH, S. (1985), *Conservation and Museum Lighting, Information Sheet No. 6*, 4th edition, Museums Association and Area Museum Councils, London

TURNER, J. (Ed.) (1985), *Light in Museums and Galleries*, Concord Lighting Ltd, London

Humidity, heating and ventilation

CASSAR, M. (1985), 'Case design and climate control: a typological analysis', *Museum*, **146**, 104–107

MICHALSKI, S. (1982), 'A control module for relative humidity in display cases', Brommelle, N. S. and Thomson, G. (Eds), *Science and Technology in the Service of Conservation*, 28–31, IIC, London

THOMSON, G. and STANIFORTH, S. (1985), *Simple Control and Measurement of Relative Humidity in Museums, Information Sheet No. 24*, Museums Association and Area Museum Councils, London

TYMCHUK, M. P. (1983), 'Environmental monitoring of museum collections', *Curator*, **26**(4), 265–274

Atmospheric pollution

BEECHER, R. (1970), 'Apparatus for keeping a showcase free of dust', *Museums Journal*, **70**(2), 69

BLACKSHAW, S. and DANIELS, V. D. (1979), 'Materials for use in storage and display in museums', *The Conservator*, **3**, 16–19

BLACKSHAW, S. and DANIELS, V. D. (1984), 'Safe fabrics for permanent exhibitions', *Conservation News*, **23**, 16–18

HARVEY, J. (1973), 'Air conditioning for museums', *Museums Journal*, **73**(1), 11

HODGES, H. (1982), 'Showcases made of chemically unstable materials', *Museum*, **34**(1), 56–58

MILES, C. E. (1986), 'Wood coatings for display and storage cases', *Studies in Conservation*, **31**(3), 114–124

PADFIELD, T., ERHARDT, D. and HOPWOOD, W. (1982), Trouble in Store, in Brommelle, N. S. and Thompson, G. (Eds), *Science and Technology in the Service of Conservation*, pp. 24–27, IIC, London

Textile pests and their control

CHILD, R. E. and PINNIGER, D. B. (1987), 'Insect pest control in UK museums', *Recent advances in the conservation and analysis of artefacts*, University of London, Institute of Archaeology, Summer Schools Press, London

EDWARDS, S. R., BELL, B. M. and KING, M. E. (Eds) (1980), *Pest Control in Museums*, Museum of Natural History, University of Kansas, OH

FLORIAN, M.-L.-E. (1986), 'The Freezing process – effects on insects and artifact materials. Recommended procedures for eradication of insect infestation in museum objects by low-temperature freezing', *Leather Conservation News*, **3**(1), pp. 1–13, British Columbia Provincial Museum

GRADIDGE, J. M. G., AITKEN, A. D., WHALLEY, P. E. S. and SHAFFER, M. (1967), *Clothes Moths and Carpet Beetles: their Life History, Habits and Control*, British Museum (Natural History), London

GROUP FOR COSTUME AND TEXTILE STAFF IN MUSEUMS (1982), *Pest Problems and their Control in Costume and Textile Collections*, Museum of London Symposium, November 1982

HAMLYN, P. F. (1983), 'Microbiological deterioration of textiles', *Textiles*, **12**(3), 73–76, The Shirley Institute, Manchester

HUEK, H. J. (1972), 'Textile pests and their control', in *Textile Conservation*, pp. 76–97, Butterworths, London

MOURIER, H. and WINDING, O. (1975) (revised 1977), *Collins Guide to Wild Life in House and Home: a practical guide to pests, parasites and other domestic wild life*, Collins, London

STANSFIELD, G. (1985), 'Pest control: a collection and management problem', *Museums Journal*, **85**(2), 97–99

TOWNSEND, M. W. (1983), 'Moths and wool', *Textiles*, **12**(1), 8–12, The Shirley Institute, Manchester

VIGO, T. L. (1980), 'Protection of textiles from biodeterioration', *Conservation and Restoration of Textiles, Comp, 1980*, pp. 18–26, CISST Lombardy Section, Milan

ZYCHERMAN, L. A. and SCHROCK, J. R. (Eds) (1988), *A guide to museum pest control*, Foundation of the American Institute for Conservation & Association of Systematics Collections, Washington DC, USA

Handling: movement, storage and exhibition of textiles

BLYTHE, A. R. (1974), 'Anti-static treatment of 'Perspex' for use in picture (and textile) frames', *Studies in Conservation*, **19**, IIC, London

BUCK, A. M. (1958), *Handbook for Museum Curators – Costume*, The Museums Association, London

BUCK, A. M. (1972), 'Storage and display', in *Textile Conservation*, pp. 113–127, Butterworths, London

DORÉ, J. (1985), 'Packing costumes for transport and display', *Packing Cases – Safer Transport for Museum Objects*, preprints of meeting, UKIC, London

EKSTRAND, G. (1980), 'Display: problems and methods', *Conservation and Restoration of Textiles, Como, 1980*, pp. 32–37,. CISST Lombardy, Milan

EWLES, R. (1982), 'Storing embroideries', *Embroidery*, **33**(3), 68–69, Embroiderers' Guild, East Molesey, KT8 9BB

FINCH, K. and PUTNAM, G. (1985), *The Care and Preservation of Textiles*, Batsford, London

FLURY-LEMBERG, M. (1980), 'Examples of storage and display of historic textiles – textiles at the Abegg-Stiftung, Bern', *Conservation and Restoration of Textiles, Como, 1980*, pp. 27–31, CISST, Milan

GINSBURG, M. (1973), 'The mounting and display of fashion and dress', *Museums Journal*, **73**(2), 50

GLOVER, J. M. (1973), *Textiles: Their Care and Protection in Museums, Information Sheet No. 18*, Museums Association, London

GRÖNWOLDT, R. (1980), 'Textile display and textile exhibiton at the Würtembergische Landesmuseum, Stuttgart', *Conservation and Restoration of Textiles, Como, 1980*, pp. 215–218, CISST, Milan

GOLDTHORPE, C. (1985), 'The Herbert Druitt Gallery of Costume', *Museums Journal*, **84**(4), 189–191

JACOBI, K., KRAGELUND, M. and ØSTERGÅRD, E. (1978), *Bevaring af gamle tekstiler*, The National Museum of Denmark (Danish text with English summary. Excellent illustrations)

KRAHN, A. H. (1982), 'Numbers on objects: damaging errors', *Museum*, **34**(1), 58–60, UNESCO, Paris

LAMBERT, A. M. (1983), *Storage of Textiles and Costumes: Guidelines for Decision-making*, University of British Columbia Museum of Anthropology

PRICE, M. J. and MARKO, K. (1976), 'The storage of museum textiles in Switzerland, West Germany and Holland', *Museums Journal*, **76**(1), 25

PUGH, F. (1978), *Packing and Handling Works of Art*, Arts Council of Great Britain, London

SANDWITH, H. and STAINTON, S. (1984), *The National Trust Manual of Housekeeping*, Allen Lane/National Trust, London

STANIFORTH, S. (Ed.) (1985), *Packing Cases – Safter Transport for Museum Objects*, UKIC, London

STOLOW, N. (1986), *Conservation and Exhibitions*, Butterworths, London

SUMMERFIELD, P. M. (1980), 'Guidelines for curating a costume and textiles collection', *Curator*, **23**(4), 287–291

SYKAS, P. (1987), 'Caring or wearing? – The case against the showing of costume on live models', *Museums Journal*, **87**(3), 155–157

TARRANT, N. E. A. (1983), *Collecting Costume: the Care and Display of Clothes and Accessories*, Allen and Unwin, London

WARD, P. R. (1984), 'Poor support: the forgotten factor', *Museum*, **34**(1), 54–56, UNESCO, Paris

The textile conservation studio/workshop/laboratory

LANDI, S. B. (1977), 'A textile conservation workshop at Osterley', *The Conservator*, **1**, 28–30, UKIC, London

LANDI, S. B. (1980), 'Setting up a workshop: professional training, *Conservation and Restoration of Textiles, Como, 1980*, CISST, Milan

LANDI, S. B. (1985), *The Textile Conservator's Manual*, Butterworths, London

MEREDITH, C. (1974), 'Design of conservation and general laboratories', *Transactions*, **13**, 10, Museum Professionals' Group

THURMAN, C. C. M. (1978), 'The department of textiles at the Art Institute of Chicargo', *Museum*, **30**, 122–126, UNESCO, Paris

THURMAN, C. C. M. (1980), 'Setting up a workshop: technical equipment', *Conservation and Restoration of Textiles, Como, 1980*, 116–121, CISST, Milan

Health and safety in laboratories and textile stores

ANON (1982–1983), 'Manufacturers and suppliers of protective clothing and equipment', *The Paper Conservator*, **7**, 56–72, IPC, Leigh, Worcester

CLYDESDALE, A. (1990, second, revised edition), *Chemicals in Conservation: a Guide to Possible Hazards and Safe Use*, Conservation Bureau, Scottish Development Agency and SSCR, Edinburgh

HMSO, *Health and Safety at Work Act, 1974*, Chap. 37, London

HEALTH AND SAFETY EXECUTIVE (1989), *Control of substances hazardous to health Regulations 1988* (COSHH), HSE, London

HOWIE, F. M. P. (Ed.) (1987), *Safety in Museums and Galleries*, Butterworths, London

PASCOE, M. (1980), 'Toxic hazards from solvents in conservation', *The Conservator*, **4**, 25–28, UKIC, London

SCOTTISH SOCIETY FOR CONSERVATION & RESTORATION (1986), *Proceedings of Health and Safety meeting*, Bulletin 6, SSCR, Glasgow

Conservation resources

COMMITTEE OF AREA MUSEUM COUNCILS (1991), *Museums Working Together*, Committee of Area Museum Councils, Cirencester

THE CONSERVATION UNIT (1990 – revised at two-year intervals), *The Conservation Register*. Computerised database only. Access on completion of application form and payment of modest fee. The Conservation Unit, Museums and Galleries Commission, 16 Queen Anne's Gate, London, SW1H 9AA

CORFIELD, M., HACKNEY, S. and KEENE, S. (Eds) (1989), *The Survey: Conservation Facilities in Museums and Galleries*, United Kingdom Institute for Conservation, London

CORR, S. and MCPARLAND, M. (Eds) (1988), *Irish Conservation Directory*, Irish Professional Conservators' and Restorers' Association, Dublin

TAIT, G. (1991), *Scottish Conservation Directory*. A guide to businesses in Scotland working in the conservation and restoration of historic artefacts and buildings. Scottish Conservation Bureau (Historic Scotland), Edinburgh

Ethics in conservation

AMERICAN INSTITUTE OF CONSERVATION (1980), 'Code of ethics and standards of practice', *American Institute of Conservation Directory, 1980*, pp. 9–22, AIC, Washington, DC

ASHLEY-SMITH, J. (1982), 'The ethics of conservation', *The Conservator*, **6**, 1–5, UKIC, London

JEDRZEJEWSKA, H. (1980), 'Problems of ethics in the conservation of textiles', *Conservation and Restoration of Textiles, Como, 1980*, pp. 99–103, CISST, Milan

MUSEUMS ASSOCIATION (1987), *Code of Practice for Museum Authorities*, 3rd edition, Museums Association, London

MUSEUMS ASSOCIATION (1987), *Code of Conduct for Museum Curators*, 2nd edition, Museums Association, London

PASCOE, M. W. (1980), 'Science and ethics in textile conservation', *Conservation and Restoration of Textiles, Como, 1980*, pp. 104–106, CISST, Milan

UNITED KINGDOM INSTITUTE FOR CONSERVATION (1983), *Guidance for Conservation Practice*, UKIC, London

Periodicals concerned with textiles and/or textile conservation

Studies in Conservation (1952 onwards), quarterly journal of The International Institute for Conservation of Historic and Artistic Works (IIC), 6 Buckingham Street, London WC2N 6BA, UK

AATA Abstracts (Art and Archaeology Technical Abstracts), biannual publication, IIC/Getty Conservation Institute

Conservator (1977 onwards), annual journal of the United Kingdom Institute for Conservation (UKIC), 37 Upper Addison Gardens, London W14 8AJ, UK

Conservation News (November 1976 onwards), triannual newsletter of UKIC, London, UK

SSCR Journal (1990 onwards), quarterly news magazine of the Scottish Society for Conservation and Restoration (SSCR), The Glasite Meeting House, 33 Barony Street, Edinburgh, EH3 6NX.

AIC Bulletin, journal of the American Institute of Conservation, Washington DC, USA

CCI Journal (1976 onwards), journal of the Canadian Conservation Institute, Ottawa

Conservation, The GCI Newsletter, triannual publication of the Getty Conservation Institute, 4503 Glencoe Avenue, Marina del Rey, CA, 90292-6537, USA

Textile Museum Journal, annual publication of The Textile Museum, 2320 S Street Northwest, Washington, DC 2008, USA

Textile History (1968 onwards), biannual journal containing scholarly articles on textile and costume history and conservation, The Pasold Research Fund, London School of Economics, Houghton Street, London WC2A 2AE, UK

Costume (1967 onwards), annual journal of the Costume Society, c/o Publications Secretary, Birtle Edge House, Birtle, Bury, Lancashire BL9 6UW, UK

Museum, quarterly review of the United Nations Educational, Scientific and Cultural Organisation, UNESCO, Paris

33

Conservation and storage: leather objects

C. V. Horie

Introduction

The outer surface of animals (Bereiter-Hahn *et al*, 1984) provides protection and much else for the living animal and its subsequent human user. Vertebrate-derived materials, such as leather and wool, are most commonly used, other types of animal such as molluscs and insects provide various, mostly decorative, products. The outer covering, or integument, of a vertebrate is composed of two different structures:

(1) the dermis, which is the fibrous material forming the bulk of the skin (and leather) and consists of fibres of the protein collagen; and
(2) the epidermis which is the protective surface of an animal, the top layer of skin, hair, balleen, horn and feathers composed of the protein keratin.

Leather (Douglas, 1956; Thomas *et al*, 1983) and similar products are prepared from skin from which the epidermis and much of the non-collagenous components have been removed, using chemicals, enzymes and mechanical working. The collagen network is strong but liable to chemical and microbial deterioration. The purpose of the tanning process is to stabilize the collagen network which is thus chemicall bound and cross-linked to the tanning agents. Resistance to heat is also increased by tanning. The degree of tanning, and thus the state of the collagen network, is often expressed in terms of the shrinkage temperature, i.e. the temperature at which the collagen network breaks down and shrinks (Haines, 1987). There are many types of the three main categories of oil, vegetable and mineral tannages. The oil tannages (e.g. chamois leather) were probably the first developed. By working fatty materials such as brain or fish oil into the skin to provide flexibility, the oils react with the collagen and each other to create a waterproof and flexible leather. The vegetable tans were mostly derived from tree bark and these react with and bulk out the collagen network. The process involves prolonged soaking in bark extracts producing a brown leather. The first mineral tans used aluminium (tawing) to create white, flexible, leathers. Since the late nineteenth century, chrome tanning has expanded greatly, as it provides a lightweight, chemically stable, leather. After tanning, oils are worked into the leather (dressing) in order to introduce flexibility. It may then be finished, mechanically or by a coating. The qualities of the final leather are thus the result of many variables: the species of animal from which the skin was derived, its variety and age, methods of scouring and cleansing the skin, the tanning agent and its use, the dressing material and the extent of physical manipulation. The leather may be made into rigid objects, like 'black jack' jugs or armour, be strong and flexible, like saddles and straps, or be delicate and attractive like book bindings. In addition, whole skins (with hair intact) can be tanned to create durable clothing.

There are a large number of untanned or barely tanned skins that are easily mistaken for leather and include parchment, vellum and rawhide. In all these, the collagen structure remains extremely sensitive to water and variations in humidity. Although white when new, they can be coloured to resemble leather.

Leather and skin

There are many specimens from archaeological (e.g. bog bodies) and natural history, decorative art (e.g. mounted birds) collections in which all the components of the original skin must be preserved intact. In other objects, the components have been separated, for example in leather shoes, rawhide shields, horn spoons, or tortoise-shells. These are easier to conserve than the whole skin.

Leather and skin products (Reed, 1972) were extremely important materials before the introduction of plastics and synthetic fibres, and were used for many of the purposes which are now the preserve of modern polymers (for example shatter-proof mugs, flexible hinges and waterproof upholstery). Although some of the applications of leather are obsolete, others have been redeveloped, e.g. wall hangings. The term 'leather' applies strictly to tanned skin, but, due to the non-specialist's difficulty in distinguishing tanned from untanned skin, it will be used here to cover both categories. The complexities in dealing with actual objects, and the near impossibility of recommending treatment without examining them, is exemplified by leather. Waterer (1972) describes 21 major categories of leather, subdivides them and discusses the choice of treatments applicable to each subdivision. Unfortunately, it can be very difficult (even for a specialist conservator) to decide which category a piece falls into, especially when the leather has deteriorated or is obscured by decoration. Each object should, therefore, be treated extremely carefully until its strengths and weaknesses have been clearly established.

Deterioration

Leather is a fibrous and flexible material which distorts and flows when subjected to stresses induced by, for example, folding or hanging under its own weight. Once stretching or creasing has occurred, visual or dimensional changes are unlikely to be reversed. Consequently, leather objects, particularly those made of flexible leather, should always be fully supported and never forced into unfamiliar positions. Purpose-built stands will frequently be necessary for both display and storage purposes. During storage, many objects can be wrapped in acid-free tissue paper and stored in boxes.

Observation shows that leather becomes increasingly stiff over time. This has been attributed (C. Calnan, personal communication, 1987) to high or varying humidity. Therefore, leather should be maintained at 60±5 per cent relative humidity (RH) which should prevent mould growth. Cosmetic cleaning alone may be sufficient following mould attack. Low humidity causes damaging shrinkage.

Radiation, both visible and ultraviolet, is a potent source of damage to organic materials. On exposure to daylight, the shrinkage temperature of leather drops, demonstrating that deterioration has occurred (S. Michalski, personal communication, 1987). Eventually, the shrinkage temperature may drop to temperatures met with in normal conditions (Reed, 1972) which may account for the bubbled and fluid appearance of some old leather objects. These usually show signs of shrinkage. Leather (and skin) should

be kept in the dark except when displayed, when the illumination should be low, around the 50 lux limit (Thomson, 1986). The surface colour of leather is often altered, before gross physical changes occur.

Leather and other skin products should be protected from pollution by both particulate matter and gases. The grime in city air pollution is made up of very small black particles. These frequently contain both oils and carbon from combustion. Very small particles are impossible to remove from fibrous materials, so the surface will become permanently dirty. In addition, leather is one of the most active scavengers of sulphur dioxide, an abundant pollutant even in smokeless zones (Spedding, 1974).

Although many workaday leathers were made to be washed and 'fed' with oils and polishes, they usually do not benefit from continuing this treatment. For instance, vegetable-tanned leathers accumulate deterioration products of the tanning agents which are water soluble. These will migrate in wetted leather to cause severe staining and hardening. Application of oils to flexible leathers has resulted in stiffening and the gradual agglomeration of dust and grime on the surface. Not infrequently, leathers develop a white 'bloom' or deposit on the surface, termed 'spue'. These deposits probably arise from one of two causes. First, oils and other leather dressings can migrate to the surface where, if they solidify below the ambient temperature, they will form white crystals that create the spue. Alternatively, if they do not crystallize they may form small globules called 'gummy spues'. The source is possibly low quality neat's foot or other dressing oil. A second cause of a bloom may be soluble salts absorbed from animals or humans during wear, or during use with a soluble material such as salt. The reason for its migration to the surface and crystallization there is fluctuating RH.

Some leathers disintegrate, eventually to powder. 'Red rot' occurs first as a pinking of the surface combined with a severe weakening of the structure. This leads progressively to a dark redness, cracking, powdering of the surface and, finally, disappearance. Not all leathers suffer this rot, but only those vegetable-tanned leathers which are insufficiently stabilized against acid-catalysed oxidation. Sulphuric acid, which creates the rot, may have been introduced during processing or by exposing the leather to polluted atmospheres. Leathers from the latter half of the nineteenth century are commonly affected, though inadequate leather was produced well into the twentieth century. This leather was widely used for book bindings, decorative art and utilitarian objects. Apart from a slight pinkish tone, frequently not apparent in a dyed or coated leather, nothing visible will indicate the deterioration. However, the leather may be fragile and held together only by the coating. Severe and startling damage can be caused by bending or rubbing the surface. All leather objects should be handled as if they are just about to break – some do. A less common rot is 'black rot' which is the result of contamination of the leather with iron during processing or in later use. The leather becomes darker, eventually black, as the iron diffuses through the structure. Presumably both tannins and relatively moist conditions are required, though the leather does not become excessively acid. The leather structure breaks down to a powder by iron catalysed oxidation. Leather objects that have been constructed with iron nails frequently suffer 'black rot' around the points of attachment, leading to severe weakness and the likelihood of detachment. Processes of degradation of leather, both the more serious 'rots' or the slower general oxidation, lowers the shrinkage temperature of the skin, especially if there is an increase in acidity. The shrinkage temperature is also reduced by water, and is lowest when the leather is saturated. Care should be taken never to expose skins to damp or hot conditions. Except for its extreme sensitivity to water, untanned skin is usually more stable chemically than leather, though degradation, weakening and lowering of shrinkage temperature still occurs.

Pests

Various pests will eat the rich food provided by the protein in leather. Mice and rats will eat and nest in skin products, particularly untanned materials. They can destroy or deface an enormous amount of material in a short time. Common insect pests of skin are the ominously named hide beetles (*Dermestes*) and museum beetles (*Anthrenus*) as well as others of the Dermestid family. The beetles are oval, dark and 3–6 mm long. The larvae which cause much of the damage are hairy ('woolly bears'). Clothes and house moths and larvae also cause damage to hair, especially at higher humidities. Dichlorvos strips hung in well-sealed rooms or storage cabinets can be used to kill infestations of moth, though its use should only be considered after consideration of relevant health-and-safety regulations. Fumigants may damage objects; for example cyanide fumigation is thought to increase the chance of hair slippage.

Treatment

If doubt exists as to whether the object should be treated at all, it is wiser to refrain.

Leather often forms only part of an object, joined to materials which react differently to the environment. Physical weaknesses may arise from differential movement, such as the contraction and tearing of a leather covering to a wooden box. Chemical changes such as the deterioration of leather by iron or corrosion of brass and glass by leather dressings are also common. Each of the components of an object needs separate consideration. The choice of storage or treatment method will then be a compromise, usually in favour of the most vulnerable component. Frequently the most fragile item is the thread or nail joining different parts. The reasoned conservation of leather is in its early stages of development. It is very difficult to formulate a treatment and extremely unwise to rely on any formulations, even recently published ones (Jackman, 1982; Waterer, 1986). Some advances are being made (Fogle, 1985; Hallebeek, 1986; Calnan, 1991), though many are contentious, as can be seen from the pages of *Leather Conservation News*. The UK has the benefit of a conservation consultancy specifically for leather, namely the Leather Conservation Centre.

Dust may be cleaned off most robust objects with a soft brush, drawing the dust away with a vacuum-cleaner nozzle held away from the surface and covered with a fine net (Area Museums Service for South East England, 1984). Rubbing can cause severe damage, as explained above, necessitating considerable care in handling and packing. Equally, bending can cause collapse. Surface cleaning on smooth robust surfaces can be carried out by rolling powdered art rubber, e.g. Draft Clean, over the surface. It is difficult, if not impossible, to remove the powder from porous surfaces such as the raised grain of suede. As the rubber deteriorates badly over time, it should be used only on smooth surfaces. No attempt should be made to wipe down or reshape a leather object until its condition is understood. Neither water nor other solvents should be used until the possibility of staining has been assessed. Many surface finishes are water sensitive (e.g. casein) or solvent soluble (e.g. cellulose nitrate). Saddle soap should not be used. If a liquid cleaner is used it should be applied with a cloth or a cotton-wool bud that is barely damp. The cleaning effect of water can be improved by adding a small quantity of a non-ionic detergent such as Synperonic N, adding a couple of drops to 1 litre of water. No alkaline solution should be used. Fragile or broken leather on a larger object should be bound with soft bandages to prevent further tearing or loss. If there is no other alternative, the parts may be stuck into place with the minimum of a permanently soluble adhesive (Horie, 1987), such as apolyvinyl acetate soluble material (e.g. UHU). Dispersions ('white glues') should not be used, nor should rubbery materials such as contact adhesives.

It is rare for the original flexibility of a leather object to be required in a museum object. Exceptions include book bindings and working machinery. For book bindings, the problem should be referred (unopened) to an appropriate conservator. Leather components in working machinery can be replaced and retained as evidence of the original state. Temporary flexibility can frequently be achieved by gentle humidification, so allowing reshaping. The leather will revert to its previous stiffness on drying. Reshaping should be attempted only by those who appreciate both the physical consequences and possible historical distortions of the treatment. Considerable damage can be caused to untanned skins such as vellum by this process.

Imitations of leather have been produced over many years. Cellulose nitrate coated fabric (leather cloth) or cardboard is usually easy to detect, especially in the usually highly degraded condition. Recent imitations, such as polyvinyl chloride (PVC), coated fabric or polyurethane elastomers, are far more successful and have been further disguised using leather scent. Counterfeit leathers may be made by using reconstituted leather powder or by coating and embossing a less exotic leather. The identification of the real material may require chemical tests and histological examination.

Whole skins

The junction between the surface epidermis and the underlying dermis provides many of the difficulties in preserving and conserving whole skin. There is no supporting structure that crosses the junction. The junction is corrugated giving rise to the grain pattern of leather when the epidermis is removed. The outer surface of the skin is composed of 'soft' keratin (see below) with different properties from that of the collagen structure. During flaying and later, the material of the junction is easily damaged with consequent loss of adhesion. The epidermis separates and the hair falls out ('hair slippage'). The separation will be encouraged by low humidity as the keratin becomes stiff and less responsive to movements of the underlying dermis. Other reasons for the loss of hair are hair breakage and insect attack. With degradation of the hair it becomes weaker, especially at its narrowest point where it enters the skin. Broken hairs may be distinguished from slipped hair which retains the remains of the hair follicle. Insects frequently graze over the surface of the skin, eating the base of the hair shafts and excreting silk and frass which binds the hair shafts together. Hair is lost from the skin in felted mats. There is as yet no approved method of conserving skins suffering from hair loss, of whatever cause. Considerable care is needed in handling and storage of these specimens from which the hair may fall in a slow or catastrophic shower. Effects of pollutants on hair are worse than those on leather, partly because the open fibres act as an efficient filter for particles and have a large surface area for absorbing sulphur dioxide. Wool is even more efficient than hair as an absorbent. The hairs therefore become covered with black pollutants and dust while being degraded so that the hairs break at the slightest touch. Reptile (e.g. crocodile) skin retains the scaly keratin outer layer when used by man. This is also subject to detachment from the underlying dermis. With these cautions, care of whole skins should be a compromise between the requirements of each component.

Horn and other keratinous materials

Keratins, of different but closely related proteins (Frazer and MacRae, 1980), make up the bulk of hair, horn, hoof, claws, quills, feathers, beaks and tortoise-shell. Keratin is largely insoluble in most chemicals. These are termed 'hard' keratins, which are a major constituent of baleen. A slightly different, 'soft', keratin makes up the surface of skin (see above). In addition to the main structural protein, there are small but important proportions of water, oils (e.g. neat's foot oil) and other components. In contrast to the dermis of skin, the keratinous structures are dead appendages to the living animal formed in layers from underneath. The keratins provide an expendable and renewable protection for the skin below. They are both strong and resilient. They were thus widely used where such properties were required by man. Hair and wool are important industrially and within museum collections (see Chapter 32). Other keratin products have declined in importance.

The product may be used unmodified, as in medieval Japanese feather armour and quill armour, or may require processing before use. Hoof and horn (MacGregor, 1985) are well attached to the underlying bone and flesh and are frequently removed after softening in hot water. When soft, the keratins can be bent or moulded into shapes that are maintained when cooled. In addition, keratins can be 'welded' by pressure in hot, wet conditions. A large number of products are therefore possible (O'Connor, 1987); simply adapted drinking horns (using the inate shape), spoons (after moulding), lanthorn windows (after splitting and flattening, making use of the transparency), bows and arrow components (using the flexibility and great strength of horn) (Latham and Paterson, 1970; Tan-Chiung, 1981) 'boule' tortoise-shell inlay (making use of thin transparent, well coloured sheets) as well as a range of counters, buttons, etc. Ballen requires more processing but was widely used where strips of flexible material were required, e.g. nineteenth century dress hoops.

Like all organic materials, keratins are sensitive to moisture and its variations. With decreasing moisture content, keratinous material becomes increasingly inflexible and strong. It also shrinks. The material will therefore exert considerable forces in responding to changes in RH, which must be kept to a minimum.

Horn should be kept above 65 per cent RH in order to maintain its resilience (Frazer and MacRae, 1980). While this may not be practical, efforts should be made to prevent exposure to low humidities, especially for composite objects. Keratin should never be flexed when it is or has been in dry conditions. Movements of the structure may also disturb the distribution of oils and so constribute to an irreversible change in physical properties. Heating, with consequent drying, should be avoided.

Exposure to radiation, visible and ultraviolet, will cause oxidation and other changes to the various components, proteins, oils and colouring materials. The fading of birds' feathers and dulling of tortoise-shell inlay is avoidable. Low light levels, certainly below 150 lux and probably 50 lux, should be used for objects whose surface colour has to be preserved. It has been shown (Horie, 1990) that feathers suffer a large and very rapid initial change in colour on exposure to light, followed by a less rapid fading depending on the pigments present in the feathers. Structural damage to the keratin itself occurs on prolonged exposure which is usually apparent as a loss of gloss or lustre at the surface. Horn has frequently been dyed to imitate tortoise-shell. The dyes would be expected to be fugitive.

The fibrous keratins, hair, feathers, and balleen, are excellent scavengers of pollution, causing soiling and degradation. The objects may become too weak to withstand cleaning. Keratins are subject to similar insect pests as skin. Some keratin structures such as balleen and claws, incorporate calcareous components to increase hardness. These materials will be attacked by organic acids from wood and other packaging materials.

Keratins, particularly old specimens, have a soft, easily marred surface. No abrasives should be used in cleaning, and care must be exercised in handling. Simple horn objects such as spoons and handles may be cleaned by wiping with a fine, clean cloth barely dampened with water. Composite objects hold too many snares for the unwary and should be left, appropriately packed for the professional conservator.

Degradation (O'Connor, 1987) of horn and similar materials leads not only to surface damage but also to lamination of the structure along lines of natural weakness or along manufactured welds. Where the natural layers have been cut through during shaping for an object, lines of weakness develop as small cracks visible to the eye or as smaller imperfections appearing as loss of gloss. Both hold dirt. Further degradation, e.g. in archaeological objects, can lead to weakening and disintegration. The identification of horn, tortoise-shell and similar materials can be difficult as they can be mistaken for wood, and vice versa. Distinguishing between modern imitations, such as celluloid, and the real thing may require scientific investigation.

Invertebrate products

Shells from molluscs, such as mother of pearl or nautilus, are made of particles of calcium carbonate bound together by a small amount of a protein similar to keratin. The surface is covered with a thin layer of protein. The organic material is susceptible to degradation by light, oxygen, pollutants, etc., and will respond to changes in humidity. This gives rise initially to loss and dulling of the surface followed by separation and lamination of the inorganic layers. The calcium carbonates are susceptible to attack by acids from wood used in packaging (Bryne's disease) (Tennent and Baird, 1985). The colouring materials fade on exposure to light and oxygen.

Insect skins are based on two components: chitin (a polysaccharide) is embedded in a protein. Both these components are susceptible to damage by radiation. Colours may be produced by physical means (metallic and iridescent finishes are obtained by diffraction at the surface or interference within the structure) or by pigments. In general, physical colours are far more resistant to handling and degradation than pigment colours which should not be exposed to light. The colours in butterfly and moth wings are derived from scales very loosely held to the wings. These should never be touched.

References

AREA MUSEUMS SERVICE FOR SOUTH EAST ENGLAND (AMSSEE) (1984), *Taken into Care, The Conservation of Social and Industrial History Items*, AMSSEE, England, London

BEREITER-HAHN, J., MATOLTSY, A. G. and RICHARDS, K. S. (Eds) (1984), *Biology of the Integument*, Vols 1 and 2, Springer-Verlag, Berlin

CALNAN, C. (Ed.) (1991), 'Leather, its composition and changes with time', *Seminar Proceedings*, Northampton 1986, Leather Conservation Centre, Northampton

DOUGLAS, G. W. (1956), *Survey of the Production of Hides, Skins, and Rough-tanned Leathers in India, Pakistan, Ceylon, and Africa*, British Leather Manufacturers' Research Association, London

FOGLE, S. (Ed.) (1985), *Recent Advances in Leather Conservation*, Foundation of American Institute for Conservation, Washington DC

FRAZER and MACRAE (1980), Molecular Structure and Mechanical Properties of Keratin, Symposium Soc. Experimental Biology, 34 (1980), pp. 211–246

HAINES, B. M. (1987), 'Shrinkage temperature in collagen fibres', *Leather Conservation News*, **3**(2), 1–5

HALLEBEEK, P. B. (Ed.) (1986), 'On ethnographical and waterlogged leather', Symposium Proceedings, Amsterdam 1986, Central Research Laboratory, Amsterdam (with ICOM Committee for Conservation)

HORIE, C. V. (1987), *Materials for Conservation, Organic Consolidants, Adhesives and Coatings*, Butterworths, London

HORIE, C. V. (1990), *Fading of Feathers by Light*, Reprints 9th Triennial Meeting of ICOM-CC, Dresden, 1990, pp. 431–436, International Council of Museums Conservation Committee, Los Angeles

JACKMAN, J. (Ed.) (1982), *Leather Conservation – A Current Survey*, Leather Conservation Centre, Northampton

LATHAM, J. D. and PATERSON, W. F. (1970), *Saracen Archery*, Holland Press, London

MACGREGOR, A. (1985), *Bone, Antler, Ivory and Horn*, Croom Helm, London

O'CONNOR, S. (1987), 'The identification of osseous and keratinaceous materials from York', in Starling, K and Watkinson, D. (Eds), *Archaeological Bone, Antler and Ivory, Occasional Paper No. 5*, pp. 9–21, United Kingdom Institute for Conservation, London

REED, R. (1972), *Ancient Skins, Parchments and Leathers*, Seminar, London

SPEDDING, D. J. (1974), *Air Pollution*, Clarendon Press, Oxford

TAN-CHIUNG, T. (1981), 'Investigative report on bow and arrow construction in Chengtu', *Soochow University Journal of Art History*, **11**, 143–216

TENNENT, N. H. and BAIRD, T. (1985), 'The deterioration of Mollusca collections: identification of shell efflorescence', *Studies in Conservation*, **30**, 73–86

THOMAS, S., CLARKSON, L. A. and THOMSON, R. (1983), *Leather Manufacture through the Ages, Proceedings of the 27th East Midlands Industrial Archaeology Conference*, October 1983

THOMSON, G. (1986), *The Museum Environment*, IIC and Butterworths, London

WATERER, J. W. (1972), *A Guide to Conservation and Restoration of Objects made Wholly or in Part of Leather*, Bell, London

WATERER, J. (1986), *John Waterer's Guide to Leather Conservation and Restoration*, Museum of Leathercraft, Northampton (a heavily edited version of the 1972 edition, some of whose recommendations are now known to be dangerous)

Bibliography

HAINES, B. M. (1981), *The Fibre Structure of Leather*, Leather Conservation Centre, Northampton

HAINES, B. M. (1987), Bookbinding Leather, *The New Bookbinder* 7 (1987), pp. 63–82

HARDWICK, P. (1981), *Discovering Horn*, Butterworths, Guildford

MIDDLETON, B. C. (1984), *Restoration of Leather Bindings*, 2nd edition, American Library Association, Chicago

WATERER, J. W. (1946), *Leather in Life, Art and Industry*, Faber & Faber, London

WATERER, J. W. (1957), 'Leather', in Singer, C., Holmyard, E. J., Hall, A. R. and Williams, T. I. (Eds), *History of Technology*, Vol. 2, pp. 147–190, Clarendon Press, Oxford

34

Conservation and storage: wood

John Kitchin

The aim of this chapter is to draw the attention of the reader to the variations of wood, its uses, the behaviour of wood and the factors that lead to its deterioration. Wood is a material which virtually everybody recognizes. There are relatively few people who know how it behaves and how it should be cared for. Therefore a brief description of it may help the Curator to appreciate its needs and varied nature.

Trees have evolved over millions of years to fill a particular environmental niche within the flora and fauna of their region. To do this they have developed features unique to each species that enable them to take maximum advantage of the prevailing conditions. Hence trees can provide us with a very wide range of timber from which to choose. There are about 30,000 species of 'tree' of which about 5000 are in common use (Corkmill, 1978). Trees also produce resin, oil, wax, latex (rubber) and lacquer, all of which have been used in or on wood in some form at some time.

Trees are divided into two groups (Artist House, 1982). *Conifiers*, the cone-bearing needle-leaf trees, are classified for botanical reasons as *softwoods*. With a few major exceptions, such as the sound boards of musical instruments, quality work with yew wood and timber for carving, the softwoods are used where cost and weight are important, e.g. less expensive furniture, furniture intended to be veneered, packing cases, building timbers, etc. *Deciduous* trees, the broad-leafed trees, have been classified in botanical terms as *hardwoods*. These have a much wider range of uses both in the solid and veneer form. Uses include ships' planking and decking, high-class furniture, decorative panelling, bentwood furniture, sculpture and coffins.

Mankind has recognized certain qualities in wood that make it ideal for the purpose in hand (Artist House, 1982). Because of its low weight-to-strength

ratio, oak is suited for construction such as in houses, churches and ships; cedar is light and resists decay and, therefore, is ideal for roofing shingles; apple resists abrasion; willow resists bruising; sandalwood has an attractive scent, etc. Add to these factors the range of colours found in different species: purpleheart (*Peltogyne* spp.) can be purple, padauk (*Pterocarpus* from the Andaman islands) is a deep crimson, ebony (*Diospyros* spp.) is generally black, holly (*Ilex* spp.) is almost white and between them is a wide choice of browns which verge into the greys, greens, yellows and pinks.

Health and safety

In both groups of tree there are trees the wood dust from which can be dangerous to health when the work involves the use of machinery or some hand tools and, therefore, a dust mask must be worn by the operative. There is no danger from this aspect when just handling the wood; however, care should always be taken against getting splinters which, if not removed quickly, invariably cause septic wounds (Artist House, 1982).

Structure of wood

Wood is primarily composed of cellulose from which cells are made. These are the basic units from which the tree is built. The cells are adapted to perform different functions within the tree and incorporate lignin and hemicellulose which add strengthening qualities to the cells and other chemicals provide durability, smell and colour.

The configuration of the cells dictates the quality of the timber (hard, soft, springy, brittle, tough, etc.) and, observed under a micrscope, enables us to identify accurately the family, genus and often, but not always, the species. For instance the family

Fagaceae encompasses beeches, chestnuts, oaks and Tasmanian myrtles. Each of these can easily be recognized as being in the group Fagus, Castanea, Quercus and Nothfagus, respectively. The individual types (species) of, say, oak of which there are several, can prove difficult to tell apart.

Seasoning

Much of the weight of a living tree is water and, before we can use its timber, most of this has to be removed. Most of the liquid is lost from the cavities in the cells (free water). Further water is removed from the cell walls (imbibed water). The cells both lose and gain imbibed water from their tissue and, as they do so, either shrink or swell. Thus the dimensions of wood, both in thickness and width (across the grain), shrink or swell with changes in the relative humidity (RH). The length of timber (along the grain) does not change appreciably.

There are many examples in timber constructions whether in buildings, furniture or small boxes where the wood has shrunk and suffered damage. It is probable that there are similar numbers of objects where damage has been caused by expansion of the wooden member. In these cases the damage is less obvious, being internal, and it is the cell walls that are damaged through having their movement prevented by the construction of the object.

The seasoning of wood (Johnston, 1983) is a highly controlled process, and when carried out correctly provides the woodworker with fine, straight timber ready for processing. However, the environment into which the finished article is placed more often than not lacks this control. The results of this are all too apparent, and can be seen in the ill-fitting floorboards of houses and the massive timbers from early church doors and lychgates with their innumerable small surface splits. In items of furniture with large surfaces it is common to find split and warped, or additional wood applied to compensate for shrinkage. Turned work when it leaves the lathe is perfectly circular, yet within a few weeks the measurement of diameters will probably reveal imperfections. Painted, gilded and lacquered surfaces whether furniture, sculpture, panel pictures or picture frames are particularly vulnerable to the movement of their timber support.

To avoid this damage, the finished article would ideally be kept in an environment the same as that of the conditioned timber prior to its being worked. This is naturally seldom possible. It is, however, very important to minimize fluctuations in the RH. This will slow down the inevitable dimensional changes so that the wood can adjust, one component to another in the case of furniture, or thick to thin parts in the case of sculpture.

Controlling the RH and temperature of the environment is not easy but certain basic rules can help. No artefacts should be exposed to direct sunlight and this is particularly important with wooden objects and other organic artefacts that respond to changes in RH. Sunlight cast on an object will create a heated area about that object, which will cause a drying of that part and stresses are built up that will ultimately reveal themselves in the form of failure of adhesives, lifting veneers, warping or splitting of the wood or damage to the surface finish. Reducing the light with thin blinds controls the heating factor and this will also reduce the level of ultraviolet light which is very damaging to the colours in fabrics and natural and dyed wood. The subject of the environment is discussed more fully in Chapter 5.

Case history

To demonstrate movement, part of a record of the case history of an oak sideboard designed by Hoffmeister and exhibited in the Great Exhibition of 1851 is used.

During the restoration of this piece, reassembly of many of the Gothic pierced panels was necessary (*Figure 34.1*). The panels were broken because they were fixed in place with several small nails, denying them their natural movement. The section referred to here, is one similar to that shown in *Figure 34.1* but, instead of two 'windows', it has four.

The panel was designed to fill a space 1378 mm × 432 mm high. The height was unchanged but the width was 21 mm too short. The weather conditions were dry and had been for several days. Since the gaps at the ends of the centrally fixed panel were unsightly, two slips of oak were made to fill them. The weather changed to a damp rainy period and over a period of about 50 h the panel had swollen to almost fill its intended space. The slips were discarded but had they been used would have caused the sort of damage to the cells mentioned above. The thickness of the panels is about 9 mm and, while the face side is coated with varnish, there is a lot of end grain exposed and this makes absorption/desorption of moisture during changes in the RH quite rapid.

Making the best use of wood

With very few exceptions trees have periods of accelerated growth and these can be seen in the cross-section of their trunk and branches as a series of concentric ringss (*growth rings*). In temperate regions the age of the tree can be recorded by counting these rings. At right angles to the growth rings, radiating around the centre are *rays*. Rays are a configuration of cells found in all trees. In some trees they are large while in others they are invisible to the naked eye. Where the rays are large, e.g. in oaks, they have great decorative value. To take advantage of this, the timber must be cut on the *quarter* or *radially* (see *Figure 34.2*).

Figure 34.1 A Gothic panel

Radially cut timber has another advantage. Its dimensional changes are less than other cuts. Most woods have the potential of looking plain or attractive, subject to the way they are cut. Walnut figure for instance is best seen when cut on the tangent. See *Figure 34.2.*

Factors leading to deterioration

Wood changes with time. Its colour is affected not only by light but also by some of the gases that are constituent parts of the air. Oak darkens, purple heart becomes a grey brown and padauk loses its crimson colour and becomes a rich brown. Many dark woods will become lighter, primarily due to light; while many light woods will darken, probably due to the effects of oxygen. Its qualities of strength and resilience are affected by its moisture content (MC), which, as stated above, is affected by the RH. If allowed to become too dry the wood becomes brittle, and if too wet (20 per cent MC) fungal spores can germinate.

Wood can become excessively damp in buildings through being confined in a poorly ventilated room or area which is not fitted with a damp course or where the building has a faulty roof or guttering.

Rotten wood in buildings

Rotten wood in buildings (Feilden, 1982) can, broadly speaking, be of two kinds: *wet rot* (Building Research Establishment) and *dry rot* (Building Research Establishment). Neither can happen without damp conditions to start them off. However, while wet rot will become dormant by curing the source of the dampness, dry rot may not. Dry rot may be controlled by drying out the affected area, but it is wise to treat it very much more seriously than wet rot.

Dry rot transmits moisture, once established, and will demolish timbers in a building, if not professionally treated.

Wet-rot affected wood, if the member has not been rendered structurally weak, can be treated and saved. Wood that has had wet rot and has not been treated is vulnerable to infestation from the death-watch beetle. The presence of these fungi can sometimes be detected by a typical fungal smell, and such smells should be treated seriously and their source found.

Wood-boring 'beetles'

It is in fact the grubs from wood-boring beetles that are largely responsible for the damage to wooden objects (Feilden, 1982). The pupated larvae, the beetles, emerge from the wood from their flight holes and these flight holes may be the first indication of the activity within. Most such damage in the UK is done by the common furniture beetle (*Anobium punctatum*). The deathwatch (*Xestobium rufovillosum*) and the house longhorn (*Hylotrupes*

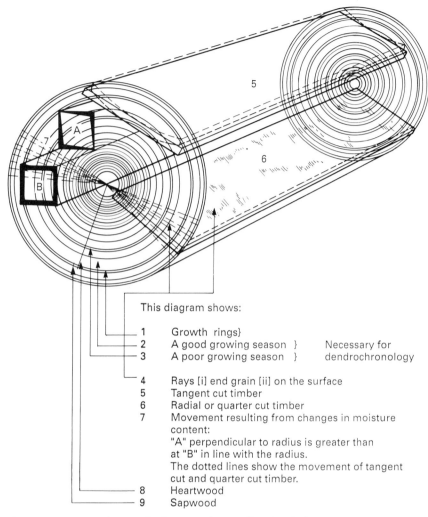

This diagram shows:

1   Growth rings}
2   A good growing season }   Necessary for
3   A poor growing season }   dendrochronology

4   Rays [i] end grain [ii] on the surface
5   Tangent cut timber
6   Radial or quarter cut timber
7   Movement resulting from changes in moisture
    content:
    "A" perpendicular to radius is greater than
    at "B" in line with the radius.
    The dotted lines show the movement of tangent
    cut and quarter cut timber.
8   Heartwood
9   Sapwood

Figure 34.2 Diagram showing the features and ways of cutting timber

bajulus) beetles are attracted to the climate of southern England, though the deathwatch beetle is occasionally found in Scotland. The deathwatch beetle is commonly found in hardwoods but may infest softwoods, while the house longhorn feeds exclusively on softwoods. The house longhorn is found almost exclusively in Surrey and Hampshire and if an outbreak is found it should be reported to the Ministry of Agriculture. The sapwood of trees is commonly devoured and in oak it is often seen that the damage stops at the border between the sapwood and heartwood. Some woods are almost immune to attack (e.g. mahogany, teak and cedar), while others (e.g. walnut and lime) can be completely 'honey-combed'.

There are many other wood-boring animals that attack only specific woods. Those like the gribble (*Limnoria lignorum*) and shipworm (*Teredo navalis*) are under-water wood feeders in the sea. The powder post (Lyctidae) beetles favour the sapwood of freshly seasoned timber. For this reason it is unlikely that antiques will suffer damage from this group. However, recent acquisitions of new wooden objects should be inspected regularly. If all the flight holes are old, close inspection may reveal dust and wax lodged inside and it may be assumed, but not guaranteed, that the infestation has died out.

Light coloured dust under an object may be 'frass'. In the case of the furniture beetle this is granular, while the residue from the powder post beetle is a fine dust. Before jumping to conclusions the object should be examined to see whether it is the moving parts that are making the dust. It could be that a drawer is wearing out its runners or some other moving joint is wearing. In either case the solution is candle wax rubbed over the wearing parts. If just one new hole is seen prompt action should be taken.

Subject to the size and nature of the object, there are two basic courses of action available. The object can be exposed to toxic gas or it can be impregnated with a proprietary woodworm-killing fluid. The choice of method depends on the possibility of re-infestation, the size of the object and what other materials such as leather or upholstery are part of the affected unit. At this stage the appropriate specialist should be contacted.

It is important that the Curator should know that processes used for the eradication of woodworm can be harmful to certain types of object material. Methyl bromide (Dow Chemical Co.), the gas generally used for this purpose may weaken the sulphur bonds in keratin, a substance found in hair, horn and tortoise-shell and in rubber and some leathers. One exposure of these materials to the gas will not be totally destructive, but it may lead to their shortened use in the collection. This is likely to be true if the gas is not continually circulated in the gassing enclosure; otherwise, the gas, which is heavy, will expose the lowest parts of the object to excessive concentrations, and damage will be far more likely to occur. Rentokil, a firm specializing in timber preservation, are experimenting with ever-increasing success with carbon dioxide for insect eradication; with this gas there would be no risk to these materials. Some liquid woodworm killers will leave a stain and if the object has a painted surface there may be a risk of changes in the pigments or the bonding of them to the wood beneath. The long-term effects of any of these substances may be small, even negligible, but are not known.

Care of wooden objects

The above is an insight into the natural causes and the effects of phenomena that most Curators will be confronted with and are essentially 'hands off' situations.

Duties within the museum will inevitably necessitate the moving and handling of objects, and the reader is referred to Chapter 43 for further detail on this subject. However, if certain factors and conditions can be observed about wooden objects, the Curator will have greater confidence and lessen the risk to the object.

The surface of wood will acquire a patina which may be smooth, shiny and relatively permanent or, subject to the ravages of conditions and time, it could be soft and very unstable. Between these extremes there are innumerable conditions both in the unadorned solid wood and that which has been coated with pigments or has veneers of other woods and other materials applied to its surface. Each object will have individual characteristics which must be assessed visually and by gentle handling before the hazards of moving it can be properly understood.

Once the adhesive at the joints or the adhesion of the surface weakens or fails, problems of handling must be considered. It is wise always to assume that antique wooden objects are frail. An example will clarify this point.

An object, unless carved out of solid wood, is constructed of members joined, into or onto one another. However, if construction is not understood, any movement may result in damage. *Figure 34.3(a)* shows two areas of weakness that are common to almost all chairs with arms of this type. (The lower detachment would be quite unexpected.) The joint of the arm rest to the arm support at its forward end is a mortise and tenon joint and is designed, in this situation, to take a downward force only. The joint of the arm to the back is achieved with an iron screw (*Figure 34.3(b)*), preventing an up-and-down force. The damage occurred due to lifting the settee by the most convenient part (the arm). It should have been lifted by the seat rails when the damage, predictable or not, would not have happened.

Many decorative features on furniture are created with veneers and often these are applied with the grain at right angles to the carcass wood. Because timber shrinks in its thickness, it is common on antiques to find that the veneers extend fractionally beyond the edge of the carcass, because they have not shrunk in line with their grain structure. In such cases great care must be taken not to break the veneers when handling this type of furniture.

Most wooden items have applied to their surface a protective coating. This may simply be to help keep them clean. For houses and boats, paint protects the wood from insect, and fungal attack. Furniture is enhanced with a coat of 'varnish' and/or wax. These coatings cannot improve the condition of the wood, nor do they prevent the article from drying out, although a thick hard coating (e.g. lacquer) will markedly retard the rate of adjustment to changes in RH. A cared-for look gets the respect of the observer and this is good preventive conservation.

Wood is perhaps the most important raw material we have on earth. In a controlled environment a wooden article will last indefinitely. Unless people who are responsible for wooden artefacts seek the knowledge necessary to protect and handle them correctly, these objects will always be at risk.

(a)

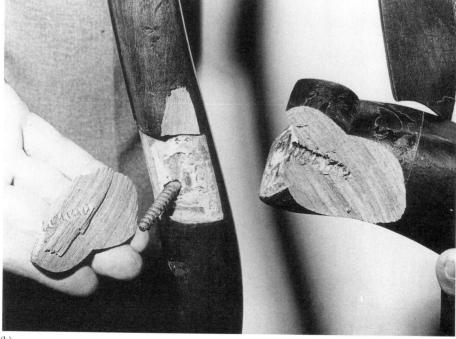

(b)

Figure 34.3 (a) Areas of weakness common to chair arms
of this type. (b) The joint of the arm to the back is achieved
by means of an iron screw

References

ARTIST HOUSE (1982), *The International Book of Wood*, Artist House, London

BUILDING RESEARCH ESTABLISHMENT, *BRE Digest No. 299, Dry Rot, Recognition and Control*, Watford

CORKHILL, T. (1978), *A Glossary of Wood*, Stobart, London

DOW CHEMICAL CO., *Methyl Bromide. Fact Sheet*, Dow Chemical Co.

FEILDEN, B. M. (1982), *Conservation of Historic Buildings*, Butterworths, London

JOHNSTON, D. (1983), *The Wood Handbook for Craftsmen*, Batsford, London

Bibliography

ALWYN, J. B. (1937), *Timber: An Outline of the Structure*, HMSO, London

COTE, W. A. (1967), *Wood Ultrastructure*, Washington

DESCH, H. E. (1938), *Timber its Structure & Properties*, 3rd edition, Macmillan, London

FARMER, R. H. (1972), *Handbook of Hardwoods*, 2nd edition, HMSO, London

FEDERATION OF NIGERIA, *Hardwoods of Nigeria*, Federation of Nigeria, UK

FINDLAY, W. P. K. (1975), *Timber: Properties & Uses*, Granada, London

HOADLEY, R. B. (1980), *Understanding Wood*, Bell & Hyman, London

INTERNATIONAL UNION OF FOREST RESEARCH (1963), *Forestry Research*, IUFR, Rome

PANSHIN, A. J. and ZEEUW, C. (1964), *Textbook of Wood Technology*, McGraw Hill, New York

RECORD, S. J. and HESS, R. W. (1943), *Timber of the New World*, Yale University, London

STAMM, A. J. (1964), *Wood & Cellulose Science*, Ronald Press, New York

WILK, C. (1980), *Thonet Bentwood and Other Furniture*, Dover Publications, New York

WISE, L. E. and JAHN, E. C. (1944), *Wood Chemistry*, 2nd edition, Heinhold, New York

WOOD, A. D. and LINN, T. G. (1942), *Plywoods: Their Development, Manufacture and Application*, Johnson, Edinburgh

35

Conservation and storage: ceramics

Christine Daintith

An object defined as ceramic is manufactured of clay which has been heated to a temperature of at least 500°C. At this temperature the effects of heating are irreversible and the clay has become ceramic. The porosity of the ceramic body may be used as a criterion for the simplest division into earthenware and stoneware, where a porosity of more than 5 per cent indicates an earthenware. Further divisions may be made according to the type of clay used and the temperature at which it is fired:

500– 900°C	Low-fired earthenware
900–1150°C	Earthenware
1150–1300°C	Stoneware
1300–1450°C	Porcelain

The term *biscuit firing* refers to the preliminary firing of a clay vessel which transforms it into the biscuit state. This is followed by glazing and decoration and a second firing, unless the vessel is to be left unglazed.

Under-glaze colours are applied to the biscuit ware and the glaze applied subsequently and the vessel fired. Decoration is, therefore, covered and protected by the glaze.

On-glaze or over-glaze colours are applied on top of the glaze. They are, therefore, not so resistant to wear and abrasion as the glaze itself, and are less durable than under-glaze decoration. However, a greater variety of colours can be used at the lower temperatures used for firing on-glaze decoration.

Sun-dried mud artefacts such as bricks, figures and cuneiform tablets will be considered as forming part of the ceramic collection, but are unfired. If left in water for a period of time, such objects will disintegrate.

Earthenware

The term 'earthenware' denotes pottery, ranging from coarse to fine, usually utilitarian, which may have incised or painted decoration. Other surface finishes may have been carried out to increase impermeability or to decorate the vessel. Burnishing may have been carried out at the leather-hard stage, prior to firing, to give a lustrous finish and increased impermeability (e.g. certain Villanovan objects). A thin coat of diluted clay known as a 'slip' may have been applied to the surface at the leather-hard stage, prior to firing. Such a finish is more fragile than a glaze (e.g. red and black Attic ware and Arretine and Samian ware). White slips are particularly fragile and stain readily (e.g. Greek white-ground lekythoi).

Terracotta

Terracotta (literally 'baked earth') objects are fired at approximately 950°C. Terracotta can be used for small figurines, but also for very large objects such as cinerary urns, architectural reliefs and decorations. They are moulded, and often hollow, usually unglazed but with a 'fire skin' formed during wet modelling of the clay prior to firing.

White slip is sometimes applied before firing at the leather-hard stage and pigment decoration may be applied before and after firing (e.g. Greek Tanagra figurines). Sometimes the fired terracotta is covered with lime plaster or gesso, then decorated with pigments and/or gilded (e.g. Etruscan cinerary urns). Such surfaces may be very fragile.

Glazed earthenware

Glazed earthenware objects are grouped according to the manner of glazing and decoration. Glaze is made of the same constituents as glass and bonds to the body of the object during the second firing. Glazed earthenwares include white earthenwares, cream wares, pearl wares and all the Staffordshire wares. Tin glazed earthenwares include Delft, Faience and Maiolica.

Lustreware

Lustreware is produced using a technique which gives a metallic appearance to a glazed earthenware vessel, either completely covering the vessel, or in a pattern. (It is occasionally used on porcelain also.)

Stoneware

Midway between earthenware and porcelain, stoneware is made of clay and a fusible stone. It is hard, strong and almost vitrified; the body and glaze mature at the same time and form an integrated body–glaze layer. A salt-glaze is sometimes used for decorative purposes. The body colour may be yellowish to dark brown, grey or bluish (e.g. salt-glazed Rhenish and English stonewares, Wedgwood's unglazed basalt and jasper wares, and Chinese celadon ware).

Porcelain

There are three main kinds of porcelain: hard paste porcelain, soft paste porcelain and bone china. Hard paste and soft paste porcelain are fired at temperatures between 1200°C and 1450°C. 'Hard' refers to the high firing temperature of about 1450°C, and 'soft' to the lower firing temperature of about 1200°C.

Hard paste porcelain
Hard paste porcelain is also known as 'true' porcelain or *grand feu* porcelain. It is manufactured from a refractory white clay (kaolin) and a feldspathic rock, is vitrified and usually white in colour. When thin it is translucent. The body and the glaze mature together to create a very thick body–glaze layer which gives the whole piece strength. First made in China in *c*. 900 AD it was not successfully made in Europe until soon after 1700 when the method was perfected at Meissen. Examples of such porcelain are Chinese and Japanese porcelains, and porcelain ware from Meissen, Vienna, Sèvres, Plymouth, Bristol.

Soft paste porcelain
Soft paste porcelain is also known as 'artificial' porcelain, or *petit feu* porcelain. It was made in an attempt to imitate the true Chinese porcelain and recipes vary, but all contain glass or 'frit'. Examples of such porcelain are Medici, Capodimonte, Rouen, Vincennes, Bow, Chelsea and Worcester.

Bone china
Bone china is a true porcelain modified by the addition of bone ash to china clay (kaolin) of the highest quality and feldspathic rock. Bone ash was added to artificial porcelains in England and added to true porcelain about 1800, and has rarely been used outside England. The firing of bone china is different from that used in porcelain manufacture. The biscuit firing of the unglazed ware is carried out at a temperature of about 1300°C; the ware is then glazed at a lower temperature of about 1100°C.

Conservation problems

The different ceramic types pose different conservation problems depending on a variety of factors which include not only the constituents and the method of manufacture but also their origin.

Archaeological ceramics

The term 'archaeological ceramics' refers to any excavated ceramic material from an archaeological environment. Archaeological ceramic material of an early date is often coarse, porous and low fired. Problems associated with burial or entombment are soluble and insoluble salts, encrustations, staining and the growth of mould. On excavated glazed earthenware an apparent encrustation could be badly decayed glaze. Stains may be organic (e.g. food residues) or inorganic, resulting from old repair materials such as rivets.

Signs of metal corrosion have been noted on the surface of partly gilded objects and may denote the presence of copper or bronze in the gilding layer, or proximity to corroding metal objects during burial or entombment.

Ceramics from an archaeological or an historical context may have problems related to poor construction and faults of composition, and these may mean that handles, feet, applied decoration, etc., are not well attached. Pigment decoration may be poorly bound to the surface of objects and easily abraded or lost, or hidden by dirt. Ceramics which have not been buried or entombed may still have some of the problems outlined for archaeological ceramics if storage conditions over the years have not been ideal. If objects have been kept outside in the past (cinerary urns, decorative architectural objects) surface spalling (when water absorbed freezes and expands, forcing off surface layers of the ceramic) or deeper cracking may have occurred. Objects such as drug jars or other objects used as containers may have staining and encrustations related to the former contents. Sampling and analysis of such material may be required before a decision is made with regard to its removal or retention. Old repairs may be antique, and should be examined with care;

plaster, bitumen, resin and metal clamps, often of lead, were used in antiquity. Dried mud covering an archaeological object may have been deliberately placed there in order to obscure material which is not original.

Ethnographical ceramics

Ethnographical ceramic material is similar· to that described above for archaeological ceramics, i.e. it is often coarse, porous, low-fired or unevenly fired, and sometimes there are problems relating to poor manufacture. Problems may be associated with organic materials such as feathers, dried grass, or leather. Careful attention must be paid to surface accretions, organic residues, sealing treatments and all signs of domestic or ritual use, and these should not be removed. Any repairs noted may date from the period of manufacture or use of the object. Surface treatments are similar to those found on archaeological ceramics. Pigments which are applied in organic mediums such as gums, resins and oils do not always bind well to the earthenware. Objects of recent manufacture may be decorated with commercial paints. Poor manufacture and faults of composition may mean that the ceramic fabric is weak, and handles, feet and decorative features are poorly applied. Pigments may be highly fugitive and handling of such objects should be severely restricted.

Stonewares

Stonewares may have some of the problems outlined for the above categories, such as staining, and old repairs may cause particular problems.

Porcelains

The porcelains are very much stronger than non-vitreous wares, but their glass-like quality means that they are brittle and sensitive to sudden changes in temperature. A slight knock can cause cracking and even shattering of an object, and the consequent release of tension can lead to fragments being 'sprung' and difficult to align correctly during conservation. When on-glaze colours have been applied at a lower temperature they may be removed by washing and abrasion. Gold decoration is often delicate and easily removed. Soft-paste porcelain can be slightly porous and brittle and old repairs with rivets and adhesives may leave stains on all porcelain types. Biscuit ware is readily penetrated by dust, dirt and grease, and handling should be restricted.

Porcelain may be found in an archaeological context and suffer staining. Association with rusting iron objects or piping on an urban site can lead to severe staining.

General stability of ceramics

Ceramic objects have a reputation for stability but, as has been seen, objects in collections may have problems which will lead to their deterioration unless the problem is dealt with. Display or storage in the correct environment can halt or retard the process of deterioration until the object can be conserved correctly. Specific problems are dealt with under the heading 'Preventive and interim measures'. Ideal exhibition conditions for perfect or conserved ceramic objects would allow for 50–65 per cent relative humidity (RH) and a temperature of 18–20°C, whilst storage conditions should be 55–60 per cent RH and a temperature of 18–20°C. The area should be dust free and spotlights and direct sunlight should be avoided. The deleterious effects of dust should not be underestimated; it is abrasive and in an urban environment can carry pollutants. Storage and display areas must be kept dust free; if this is not possible in storage areas, objects should be covered with tissue paper.

Handling

Always examine the object *before* handling, and note cracks, breaks and deterioration of old repairs. Never lift an object by the handle, foot or rim, but lift with both hands around the object. Ideally gloves should be worn, as bare hands can deposit grease, moisture and salts. Disposable surgical gloves are suitable, and cotton gloves with non-slip palms should be chosen when working with glazed, slippery objects. During examination the object may be supported on a cork ring or pad, and a padded container should be used for carrying. Lids and other movable components should be removed before carrying the object. Less obvious movable components are to be found at times on figures and groups. The head and hands of a figure may be removable or the different figures in a group may each be removed from the base. Acid-free tissue paper is the ideal covering, padding or wrapping material. Do not use cotton wool, cellulose wadding or polymer foam, as these can catch on projections and rough or damaged surfaces. Do not use newspaper as the newsprint can deposit ink onto the object, or clingfilm which can attract dust and also become statically charged with electricity and lift friable or damaged surfaces.

Display

This subject is dealt with fully elsewhere, but it should be noted that the use of reusable adhesive putty or modelling clay to hold objects onto a shelf is not recommended as these products can stain porous or damaged ceramics. Metal devices for the suspension of ceramic dishes or chargers may abrade fragile surfaces, and the metal itself may corrode. Certain components of an object may have to be independently supported after conservation work, e.g. the conserved lid of a terracotta sarcophagus. Uneven distribution of weight could cause stress to joined fragments and filled areas.

Surveys

When carrying out a general survey of a ceramics collection, conservation problems can be identified as objects are examined, and classified as urgent or otherwise. For example, a survey of vessels of recent manufacture purchased in Papua New Guinea for an ethnographic collection would have as its conservation objective the identification of any inherent problems which would lead to deterioration and a visual change, e.g. cracks or breaks due to poor manufacture, powdering and possible loss of unfired pigment deterioration. Note would also be made of all surface accretions or libations as these should not be removed by any conservation processes. Any repair work noted would have been carried out by the original maker or user and, again, should not be removed by any conservation process.

However, the main objective of a survey of a collection of Egyptian ostraca would be an assessment of the legibility of the writing on the surface of the sherds, and note would be taken of the factors adversely affecting legibility, e.g. salt growth, or early consolidation treatments to the surface which may have darkened over time and now obscure the script. Each ostracon would be classified according to its conservation requirements.

Old repairs

When carrying out a survey or caring for a ceramics collection a knowledge of repair methods used in the past is helpful. The study of any records may be useful, although the recording of early conservation work is, unfortunately, rare. Rivets (or, more correctly, staples, as they are U shaped) may be visible, but metal dowels, sealing wax, wire and solder (*Figure 35.1*), horsehair and paper may escape notice. Ancient repairs can be of great interest in themselves and a part of the object's history, and any repair that is stable and visually acceptable, and not endangering or altering the object in any way, may be left untouched. However, old adhesives do

Figure 35.1 Fragments of an Attic cup, 490 BC. Dismantling of the old repair revealed metal wires running through the filled areas and embedded in the clay body with shellac adhesive

become brittle and weak, and iron dowels and staples may corrode and stain the ceramic body. Early consolidation treatments of porous ceramic bodies with wax, resinous materials or soluble nylon may now have darkened, and altered the appearance of the vessel to an unacceptable degree. Cement-like materials poured into the interiors of fragile vessels may have ensured their survival to the present day, but make them unacceptably heavy and unsightly. The use of acids to remove encrustations may not have been followed by sufficient rinsing, and acids remaining in the ceramic body may lead to salt activity. Plaster of Paris may have been used as a fill material on unsealed break edges and water from the plaster may be drawn into the body of the ceramic and cause salt growth and staining. The fact that a repaired vessel appears to be made entirely of ceramic fragments does not mean that it is necessarily a complete vessel, as repairs may have been carried out by making and firing clay sherds of the required shape and inserting them, or by using sherds from another broken vessel. Dismantled vessels have sometimes been found to be made up of sherds from several similar vessels. Pigment decoration may have been considerably touched up and 'improved' in the past, and some pottery was polished with French chalk which can leave a white deposit in incised decoration.

An old repair may consist of an object in two or three fragments only which has been repaired with adhesive and rivets or staples. If the old repair is good, the rivets barely visible and not corroded, there is no need to remove them. However, if there is movement of the join and of the rivets which could abrade the ceramic, and any sign of corrosion of iron rivets or iron staining of the rivet area, the object should be reconserved.

Preventive and interim measures

When problems have been identified, either as a result of a survey, or after examination of a new acquisition, certain useful steps may be taken by the curator. These steps will ensure the safety of the object, either in storage or on display, until it reaches a conservator. The identification of problems which are already affecting an object, such as soluble salts or mould growth, enable the correct environment for display or storage to be chosen pending the availability of conservation.

Soluble salts

These may be clearly visible as a whitish bloom on the surface, as a white powdery substance or as white needles (*Figure 35.2*). Their presence may be suspected, for instance, where surfaces are flaking and lifting off (*Figure 35.3*). Fluctuating relative

Figure 35.2 An Egyptian ostracon destroyed by the growth of soluble salts

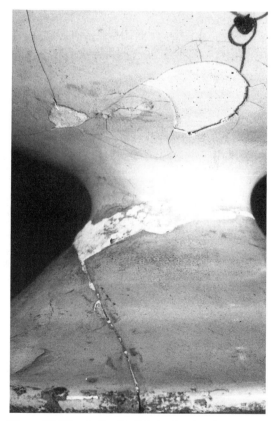

Figure 35.3 Detail of an English tin glazed earthenware drug jar, mid-seventeenth century. Soluble salts have cracked and lifted the glaze

humidity and temperature are conducive to salt growth and, therefore, these factors should be controlled.

Mould and bacterial growth

Certain stains believed to be caused by bacteria (e.g. black spots on excavated terracotta figurines) appear to be stable, and are not affected by their environment. Mould growth on animal glues used in an old repair may also feed on other organic materials used to repair the object. Such objects should be handled with caution and the mould gently brushed off in a fume cupboard while wearing gloves and a suitable mask. The object should be transported from place to place in a sealed container, and examined by a conservator as soon as possible. Storage should be at a RH of 50 per cent or lower.

Old repair materials

Animal glues and wax consolidants will be affected by adverse climatic conditions and should be stored or displayed at 55–60 per cent RH and a temperature of 18°C. Direct sunlight or a strong spotlight may cause softening of certain adhesives and fill materials, and drying of others, and cause discoloration of restored and painted areas.

General care

Objects may arrive from elsewhere with movable components held on to the body with adhesive tape, or with adhesive paper labels. Sherds may arrive from excavation sites partially assembled with adhesive tape inside and out. The adhesive on tape and paper labels can very quickly deteriorate and stain the surface of the ceramic, especially in a warm climate, and they are best removed, but with great care. Careless removal of adhesive tape can remove the friable surface from a low-fired vessel, the on-glaze decoration from a Chinese jar or the applied gold leaf from a piece of porcelain. Warm water, colourless industrial methylated spirits or acetone may be applied with a small, soft brush to the surface of the tape or label until the adhesive softens and the tape can be gently removed.

If an unglazed object has to be re-numbered after removal of a paper label, or numbered on arrival at the museum, a small area of the surface should be sealed with a 20 per cent solution of Paraloid B72 in acetone, and the number inked in on this area once the Paraloid has dried.

Cleaning

After examination of the object to locate fragile areas, loose components, metal or ormolu mounts or other non-ceramic materials, and the presence of encrustations or remains of possible archaeological or historical interest, gentle cleaning may be undertaken. Removal of surface dust is best carried out with soft paint-brushes of a suitable size and a blower brush; dusters or cotton wool may catch on deteriorated glaze or rough pottery. Further cleaning may be required, but even in cases where an object appears to be in perfect condition complete immersion in water should be avoided; low-fired objets, terracottas and glazed ware could suffer irreparable harm if immersed. Poorly bound slip, pigments or gold decoration could be lost and staining under the glaze diffused. Immersion may also mobilize soluble salts. An object which has been repaired could come apart if immersed in water, as the adhesives used could weaken, and iron rivets or dowels would be affected by water penetration.

Sound glazed surfaces may be cleaned with soft cloth pads dampened in warm water; if a non-ionic detergent such as Synperonic N is added to assist with the removal of ingrained dirt or grease the object must be rinsed several times with clean pads dampened in clean water. The addition of acetone or colourless industrial methylated spirits to the water in the ratio of 25/75 or 50/50 would hasten the drying process, but work must be carried out in a well-ventilated room. Metal and ormolu mounts and organic materials must not get wet.

Damaged objects

These should be stored carefully until they can be examined by a conservator. In the case of a cracked vessel, padding may be used to support the weak areas, woven tape can be tied around the vessel or, if a badly cracked vessel is to be transported, the whole can be bandaged with crêpe bandage and the interior well padded with tissue paper, or filled with beads of expanded polystyrene. When packing components or fragments for transport to a conservator avoid abrasion of the fragments by other fragments or by the packing material. Wrap each fragment in clean, preferably acid-free, tissue paper and avoid getting dirt and dust onto the edges of a freshly broken vessel. Small chips and fragments can be placed in a closed box or container. Do not use self-adhesive tape to secure the fragments.

Conservation

An object is conserved in order to prevent or slow down further deterioration, and thus stabilize the object. The degree to which cleaning and reassembly of an object is carried out depends on whether it is to be stored in a reserve collection, put on public display and/or be published.

Conservation becomes restoration when an attempt is made to regain the original appearance of an object, but at no stage should archaeological and historical evidence of use, breakage, repair or burial be obscured by the conservator. Complete reversibility of any conservation or restoration work carried out on an object is the ideal aimed for by the conservator, but it has to be accepted that certain processes are unlikely to be completely reversible, e.g. the consolidation of powdery surfaces which would otherwise be lost. Objects which need the intervention of a conservator could have some or all of the following conservation requirements:

(1) Dismantling of a previous repair.
(2) Removal of soluble salts.
(3) Removal of mould.
(4) Removal of disfiguring encrustations.
(5) Removal of dirt, dust, or overpaint from a previous repair.
(6) Stain removal.
(7) Consolidation of fragile surfaces.
(8) Sticking of cracks and new breaks, or complete reassembly.
(9) Replacement of chips, missing areas and missing components.
(10) In-painting.

A written record of the object's condition prior to any conservation treatment should be made and detailed notes taken as treatment proceeds. If an object is to be dismantled it should be photographed before this is undertaken.

Dismantling of a previous repair

A previous repair may have to be dismantled because of deteriorating adhesive. A repaired object may appear to be in good condition but, if old adhesive has become brittle and therefore weak, the object's condition will in fact be dangerous.

Identification of the adhesive used will facilitate the choice of method. Methods include the use of steam, placing the object in solvent vapour, immersion in solvent, or in water, or a combination of these methods. The dismantling process becomes a cleaning process as all old repair materials are removed and break edges are cleaned of all traces of old adhesives and fill material.

A new approach being used at the Musée Nationale de Céramique at Sèvres, when dealing with iron rivets or staples, is to stabilize the rivet or staple *in situ*, or remove and stabilize it, conserving it as of inherent interest alongside the object or, in certain cases, stabilize and replace it. This last approach could perhaps be considered when the rivets in question are almost contemporaneous with the object itself.

Removal of soluble salts

The removal of soluble salts by total immersion in water is the most efficacious method of desalination. Partial consolidation of fragile surfaces may be necessary before immersion. Some objects may be too large for treatment by immersion and in such cases poultices of absorbent paper will be applied to the surface in an attempt to draw out the soluble salts. It is uncertain whether this method can remove more than the surface soluble salts, and objects so treated must be surveyed regularly to check for the reappearance of salts on the surface, and kept in a suitable environment on completion of conservation treatment.

Removal of mould and bacterial staining

The cause of active mould growth on animal glues and organic repair materials will have been removed when the object was dismantled and cleaned. Stains caused by mould or bacteria, possibly during burial, may, in certain cases, be removed by a complex acid treatment. This treatment should only be carried out by a trained conservator.

Removal of disfiguring encrustations

Examples of encrustations are hardened dirt and insoluble salts. Certain encrustations may be softened and removed mechanically without damaging the surface of the ceramic. In some cases encrustations may be removed from undecorated and robust ceramic surfaces with very weak and dilute acid. The object must first be impregnated with water in order to prevent absorption of the acid by the fabric, and thoroughly rinsed after treatment.

Removal of dirt, dust or overpaint from a previous repair

After removal of loose dust and dirt using a soft paint brush, blower-brush or controlled vacuum cleaning, a surface may be dry-cleaned using Draft-clean (soya bean fibre and calcium hydroxide powder), steam cleaned, cleaned by the application of paper or wood-pulp poultices, or Sepiolite (hydrated magnesium silicate powder), or with water or solvent on cotton wool swabs. In certain cases the object will be cleaned by immersion in water, usually with the addition of a surfactant such as Symperonic N. A water softener such as Calgon (sodium hexametaphosphate) may be added when glazed objects are being cleaned, but *never* for lustreware. Other cleaning agents may be added to the water but the extensive use of chemicals may weaken or alter the ceramic.

Figure 35.4 An eighteenth-century English lead glazed earthenware mug. Overpaint from a previous repair is now peeling and disintegrating

Overpaint from a previous repair (*Figure 35.4*), may by this stage have been completely or partially removed by one of the described cleaning treatments. If not, it is normally possible to soften and remove overpaints and lacquers with the correct solvent; removal may reveal a damaged or abraded surface, but it is preferable to reveal original surfaces.

Stain removal

Certain stains may be of archaeological or historical interest and will not be removed. Stains caused by recent repairs, old adhesives, rust corrosion and dirt may be removed using some of the cleaning methods already described. Complete removal or some improvement usually results (*Figure 35.5*), but in rare cases a stain may become worse. Household bleach should never be used. A solution of hydrogen peroxide, water and ammonia is used to remove stains from hard paste porcelain only, and even this limited use should be approached with caution. It is

possible that hydrogen peroxide remains active within the body of certain ceramics for a considerable period of time, and its presence may affect any adhesive used. Rust stains on excavated objects or caused by a previous repair with dowels or rivets which have corroded can be reduced or removed by various methods (sodium dithionite treatment or electrolytic reduction treatment).

Consolidation of fragile surfaces

Earthenware objects may require consolidation at some stage during conservation treatment in order to strengthen fragile surfaces or fix fugitive pigments. Tests are first carried out on a small area of the object to check for darkening of the fabric or glossiness resulting from the application of consolidant. The ethylmethacrylate methylacrylate Paraloid B-72 or polyvinyl butyral (Mowilith B30H) in a suitable solvent are considered to be the most suitable consolidants for use on ceramic fabrics.

Sticking of cracks and new breaks or complete reassembly

Assembly of an object is always worthwhile even if complete restoration is not possible, as it reduces the likelihood of damage to or loss of fragments. New breaks can quickly become impregnated with dirt and dust and should be suitably protected. When sticking *cracks* a distinction must be made between firing cracks and cracks which have occurred because of a knock, or careless handling. A *firing crack* will have been formed during firing or soon afterwards, and is the result of unequal stresses within the ceramic body or between the body and the glaze. A firing crack should not be stuck or obscured.

A crack which is the result of a knock or other damage should be stuck, as even a hairline crack becomes visible once dirt penetrates. The injection of adhesive into a crack strengthens the object and prevents dirt penetration. Distortion may occur when an object cracks or breaks, and the innate tension in the object is released; this phenomenon is known as 'springing'. Joins may not align correctly in such a case, but it is usually preferable to fill the crack to prevent further movement and dirt penetration.

Adhesives

It is essential that the adhesive chosen be compatible with the ceramic to be repaired and be readily reversible. For example, when assembling earthenware the use of too strong an adhesive would result in thin slivers of ceramic being pulled away from the break edges if the joins made in a pot failed, and too strong an adhesive used for the assembly of a high-fired object could result in the object's cracking

(a)

(b)

Figure 35.5 (a) Detail of the rim of a late-seventeenth-century Iranian glazed earthenware disch showing staining in the area of a previous repair. (b) Detail of the rim after stain removal and filling

Figure 35.6 Detail of the interior of a fifth century BC Attic lekythos showing old fill material which has shrunk and is tearing away fragments of the clay body

or breaking in a new area, rather than at the existing joins, if the object were dropped.

Testing of both well-known and new adhesives is continually carried out in the conservation field and comparisons are made of stability, light and dark ageing, reversibility, etc. Optically clear and high-quality resins are now available. Some recommended adhesives are listed below.

Earthenware:
HMG heat and waterproof plasticized cellulose nitrate adhesive; HMG Paraloid B72 adhesive.
Stonewares and porcelains:
HXTAL NYL-1 epoxy resin (low viscosity, colourless, does not yellow); super-epoxy glue (clear two-part epoxy resin. This adhesive does yellow over time).

Note: additions to adhesives are not normally recommended as they weaken the adhesive properties.

Replacement of chips, missing areas and missing components

If it is decided to replace missing components by copying originals, and to fill gaps for reasons of stability or aesthetics, the material chosen for filling should be weaker than the body of the ceramic (*Figure 35.6*). The traditional use of fine casting plaster for earthenware remains suitable for a variety of reasons; it is weaker, it is readily shaped and moulded, it can be sealed and painted, and it is easily removed. The diffusion of plaster dust must be controlled, however, and the wet plaster must not be drawn into the ceramic body as this can cause staining and salt growth. Prewetting of the edges to be filled may prevent penetration, but it is preferable to seal the edges with a 20 per cent solution of Paraloid in acetone. It is possible in some cases to make detachable fills and components such as handles, or feet, and this may have advantages. Fine Surface Polyfilla and ICI White Cellulose Stopper (cellulose nitrate filler) are used to perfect the plaster surface which is then sealed with Rustin's bleached shellac.

Stone and porcelain need a stronger fill material which will bond well to the break edges; uncoloured polyester pastes are suitable, and HEX4 NYL-1 made into a gel with the addition of Cab-O-Sil, a fumed silica, is suitable for filling or moulding in certain cases. Pliacre 900 603 is a two-part epoxy putty suitable for filling and moulding, but some epoxy putties contain additives which react with other materials used in conservation and can cause staining. Care must be taken not to scratch or abrade the original fabric when working on the restoration. Fill and moulding materials are left uncoloured in order that they may be easily distinguished from the original vessel in any future conservation treatment. If inpainting of the surface is carried out, the paint may discolour over time, but it is a relatively simple matter to remove it and repaint the surface only.

Table 35.1 Pigments and media used for in-painting

Fill material	Sealant	Pigments and medium
Fine casting plaster	Rustin's white polish, bleached shellac	Fine-ground dry pigments mixed with Rustin's white polish, bleached shellac. Matting agent if needed. Solvent: IMS
Polyester resins and epoxy resins	Not necessary	Fine-ground dry pigments or Maimeri restoration colours mixed with Rustin's plastic coating, white or clear (urea formaldehyde type resin). Solvent: Rustin's thinners

In-painting

New components and filled areas of objects would be in-painted if this was required by the curator, with the paint confined strictly to the newly applied material and visible as a repaired area on close inspection. If the filled area is inset fractionally, in-painting to match the original may be carried out and original decoration imitated on the repaired areas if this is deemed necessary from an aesthetic point of view. The 'tratteggio' technique as used in painting conservation has been used successfully on large terracotta objects where there are large filled areas. The required colour is built up with a multitude of paint strokes using the individual colours which make up the colour required, and these strokes are readily visible from close to the object but appear as solid colour from a distance. The paints used for in-painting must retain their colour over time and remain reversible in the appropriate solvent. The use of fine-ground dry pigments in a suitable medium is the most straightforward method (*Table 35.1*).

Acknowledgement

The British Museum's advice and permission to publish photographs is gratefully acknowledged.

Bibliography

CRONYN, J. M. (1990), *The Elements of Archaeological Conservation*, Routledge, London

DANIELS, V. (1981), 'Manganese-containing stains on excavated pottery sherds', *MASCA Journal*, **1**(3), 230–231

HAMER, F. (1975), *The Potter's Dictionery of Materials and Techniques*, Pitman Publishing, London

HEMPEL, K. F. B. (1968), 'Notes on conservation of sculpture, stone, marble and terracotta', *Studies in Conservation*, **13**, 34–44

HIGGINS, R. A. (1970), 'The polychrome decoration of Greek terracottas', *Studies in Conservation*, **15**, 272–277

JAESCHKE, H. and JAESCHKE, R. (1987), 'Early conservation techniques in the Petrie Museum', in Watkins, S. C. and Brown, C. E. (Eds), *Conservation of Ancient Egyptian Materials*, pp. 17–23, UKIC Archaeology Section, London

JOHNS, C. (1977), *Arretine and Samian Pottery*, British Museum Publications Ltd, London

KOOB, S. (1987), 'Detachable plaster restorations for archaeological ceramics', in Black, J. (Ed.), *Recent Advances in Conservation and Analysis of Artifacts*, pp. 63–65, Summer Schools Press, London

LACOUDRE, N. and DUBUS, M. (1988), Nettoyage et dégagement des agrafes au Musée National de Céramique à Sevres', *Studies in Conservation*, **33**, pp. 23–28

LARSON, J. (1980), 'The conservation of terracotta sculpture', *The Conservator*, **4**, 38–45

NOBLE, J. V. (1988), *The Techniques of Painted Attic Pottery*, Thames and Hudson, London

PATERAKIS, A. (1987), 'The deterioration of ceramics by soluble salts and methods for monitoring their removal', in Black, J. (Ed.), *Recent Advances in Conservation and Analysis of Artifacts*, pp. 67–72, London

RHODES, D. (1975), *Clay and Glazes for the Potter*, Pitman Publishing, London

ROBSON, M. (1988), 'Methods of restoration and conservation of Bronze Age pottery urns in the BM', in Daniels, V. (Ed.), *Early Advances in Conservation*, British Museum Occasional Paper No. 65, pp. 141–146, British Museum, London

ROSENTHAL, E. (1975), *Pottery and Ceramics*, Penguin Books, London

RYE, O. S. (1981), *Pottery Technology*, Tamaxacum, Washington, DC

SANDWITH, H. and STAINTON, S. (1984), *The National Trust Manual of Housekeeping*, Allen Lane/National Trust, London

SAVAGE, G. and NEWMAN, H. (1976), *An Illustrated Dictionary of Ceramics*, Thames and Hudson, London

THOMSON, G. (1978), *The Museum Environment*, IIC and Butterworths, London

THOMPSON, J. M. A. (Ed.) (1984), *Manual of Curatorship*, Butterworths, London

WILLIAMS, N. (1983), *Porcelain Repair and Restoration*, British Museum Publications Ltd, London

WILLIAMS, N. (1988), 'Ancient methods of repairing pottery and porcelain, in Daniels, V. (Ed.), *Early Advances in Conservation*, British Museum Occasional Paper No. 65, pp. 147–149, British Museum, London

36

Conservation and storage: stone

Jennifer K. Dinsmore

Introduction

Stone, composed of a mixture of minerals, is distributed universally at or below the earth's surface and has been worked continuously since prehistoric times; hence virtually any type of stone could be found in a museum collection. Pure minerals may also be found in geological and gemological collections. Buildings, sculpture, inscriptions, utilitarian objects, etc., were generally made from one of the three rock types, classified according to origin as igneous, sedimentary and metamorphic.

Igneous rocks arise from the crystallization of magma formed beneath the earth's crust. The rate and conditions of cooling determine the variety of rock produced: volcanic events produce basalt, obsidian and pumice; hypabyssal rocks such as porphyry occur through injection of magma into surrounding stone; intrusive rocks such as granite and diorite solidify slowly under the earth's crust.

Sedimentary rocks are formed through the alteration of pre-existing (generally igneous) rocks. Sandstones derive from the weathering, transportation, deposition and consolidation of quartz-rich materials. The precipitation of minerals and/or the fossilization of living organisms including shells and plant matter, produce rocks such as limestone, shale and coal. Sedimentary rocks generally have a banded or 'bedded' structure resulting from the laying down of sediments.

Metamorphic rocks are produced by the action of heat and/or pressure on either igneous or sedimentary rock. Examples of these are marble (derived from limestone), quartzite (from sandstone) and schists (from either volcanic rock or from clays) (Read and Watson, 1968).

The range in scale of stone objects in museum collections is as broad as the diversity of stone types. It extends from fragile talc inscriptions to colossal sculpture, substantial architectural elements and even whole buildings, such as the Egyptian temple of Dendor at the Metropolitan Museum of Art.

Loss of original polish on stone

Dense, hard stone such as granite, diorite, quartzite and marble were often finished with a high polish; frequently this was done selectively to create a contrast in textures. Original polish may be partially or completely lost through weathering, atmospheric pollution, abrasion and/or inappropriate cleaning techniques. The practice of cleaning marble with acids, prevalent in the nineteenth century and early twentieth century, was responsible for the loss of polish on many classical and neo-classical sculptures. Alabaster, which was generally highly polished, is slightly water soluble. Its polish can thus be lost through cleaning with water alone or from water condensing on the surface (Larson, 1979).

A surface which has lost its polish can only be restored by re-polishing. As this involves the removal of a small amount of stone it is not appropriate for sculpture or ancient stonework, although it may be suitable for modern hard stone flooring.

In some instances it is possible to reproduce the appearance of a high polish by applying a thin layer of microcrystalline wax. It is essential to use a hard wax such as this because softer waxes will imbibe air-borne dirt. The wax should be applied sparingly and any excess removed with tissue. The wax coating can be buffed, as desired, with a lint-free cloth (Plowden and Halahan, 1987).

Decay

Causes

A common perception of stone is that it is strong and immutable. This notion is erroneous and even seemingly highly durable materials such as granite will decay in unfavourable conditions. There are a number of agents and mechanisms of stone deterioration. In external situations these include: weathering, such as wind erosion; freeze–thaw cycles; atmospheric pollution; soluble salts; micro-biological attack and inappropriate treatments such as the use of high alkali cements (Feilden, 1982). An object removed from its original external position and placed in a museum may show signs of decay resulting from these factors.

Within museums the most common and pernicious form of decay affecting limestones and sandstones results from soluble salt activity. Stone may contain salts at the time of quarrying and/or may become contaminated with salts during burial, from contact with saline water or from the use of inappropriate mortars. In the presence of high relative humidity salts will go into solution and travel by capillary action through the pores of the stone. As the humidity drops the salts crystallize on the surface, where they appear as small whitish particles or needle-like structures (*Figure 36.1*) or just

Figure 36.1 Detail of limestone stele (EA 1332) illustrating needle-like salt efflorescence (Trustees of The British Museum)

sealants and acid-catalysed varnishes. The acid vapours can react with salts present in the stone to form damaging efflorescences and hence these materials should not be used in close proximity to stone; where this cannot be avoided, buffering materials should be incorporated in show-case design (Fitzhugh and Gettens, 1971; Blackshaw and Daniels, 1979).

Decaying objects which have been in a museum for some time may have undergone a number of putative stabilizing treatments which have exacerbated the deterioration. Oils, waxes, adhesives and resins have all been used to preserve stone, often with deleterious consequences (Hanna and Lee, 1988). Their removal should only be attempted by a Conservator.

Effects of decay

Stone decay is manifested in a number of ways, but for convenience may be grouped into two categories: textural and structural. In the former the surface may contain areas of friability, crumbling or spalling (*Figure 36.2*). Any paint or gilding present may be

Figure 36.2 A limestone head of a divine figure (EA 1476) displaying severe textural decay (Trustees of The British Museum)

below the surface where their increased volume in crystal form may cause the loss of small fragments of stone. This can lead to weakening of the fabric of the stone and, in extreme cases, the complete loss of carved detail (Torraca, 1988).

Other factors which can contribute to the decay of museum objects include high levels of relative humidity, which can cause swelling of clay minerals, and pollution from both external and internal sources. Wood, wood composites and some adhesives give off formic acid vapour, while acetic acid vapour is emitted by wood, some paints, silicone

affected. Structural decay involves the loss of structural integrity. In limestones this is evident in delamination along the bedding planes (*Figure 36.3*). This can equally occur in sandstones which are also susceptible to large-scale spalling. In granitic stones the cementing material may be lost, resulting in disaggregation of the mineral particles (Winkler, 1975). Although both forms of decay can arise from the same cause, the effects are related to the type and origin of the stone, as research into the decay of Egyptian limestones has shown (Bradley and Middleton, 1988). Structural decay is generally deemed

Figure 36.3 Limestone stele (EA 1314) showing massive structural decay (Trustees of The British Museum)

more severe than trextural decay, although the significance of the latter should not be underestimated as it can result in carved detail being lost and inscriptions becoming illegible.

On external stonework the pollutant sulphur dioxide reacts with calcium carbonate in limestones and marbles to form a thick crust of calcium sulphate; this process is known as 'sulphation'. In sheltered areas the calcium sulphate rapidly blackens through absorption of dirt. Thin sulphation films may occur on museum objects, particularly where coal-fired heating was used in the past.

Treatment

Although the treatment of decayed stone should only be undertaken by a conservator, there are a number of valuable remedial measures which will help slow deterioration; these conditions should also be observed following treatment. The object should be isolated from all sources of acid vapours and soluble salts. It should be stored in a dry, stable and clean environment (relative humidity 40 ± 5 per cent, temperature 20 ± 1°C) (Hanna, 1984). Handling should be kept to a minimum.

Treatment may involve the use of acid-free tissue paper and a water-soluble adhesive to temporarily protect areas of spalling. Textural decay may be treated with low concentrations of an acrylic resin in a slow-evaporating solvent. This must be done judiciously to avoid staining. Treatment of structural decay may involve the use of a deeply penetrating consolidant based on organo-silane compounds. These materials restore strength to stone by reacting with atmospheric moisture to form strong, inert silicon–oxygen molecules which line the pores of the stone (Bradley, 1987). Silane consolidants are not reversible and should only be considered as a last resort. There are also risks associated with their use on stones of a high clay content or where adhesives, waxes, coating materials or certain paint media are present as these may be solubilized by silane. Additional treatment with acrylic resin and inert fillers may be necessary to secure delaminations or spalling surfaces (Dinsmore, 1987).

Desalination, or soluble salt removal, has in the past been carried out by soaking in or poulticing with water. The former method can cause loss of decayed surface as well as paint and gilding and should not be used (Larson, 1980). Recent experience at the British Museum with the poultice technique has indicated that, whilst this method will remove salts from the surface, it mobilizes those at depth in the stone. This can lead to further damaging cycles of salt activity in the future. Careful mechanical removal of the superficial salts followed by the placement of the object in controlled conditions (see above) may constitute a safer, long-term option.

Metal pins

Large sculpture, monuments and architectural elements were often constructed using metal pins or cramps; most commonly these were of ferrous material. Even in antiquity the dangers of using iron were known and the pins were set in molten lead to isolate them from air and from the stone.

Later methods of construction and restoration were not as conscientious and frequently iron was placed in direct contact with the stone or was set in plaster of Paris or mortar. In the presence of moisture and oxygen iron will corrode and the corrosion products can cause staining and, in extreme cases, fracturing of the stone due to their increased volume (Proudfoot, 1986). Copper and its alloys will corrode in the same circumstances, producing a bluish-green stain. The corrosion of copper can be exacerbated by the presence of soluble salts. Both types of corrosion are difficult to remove safely and effectively.

Breaks and their repair

Old repairs

The removal of old repairs should only be attempted by a conservator. If a conservator is not available and a repair appears to be unstable the object should be removed from exhibition and positioned in such a way as to take weight off the break.

Ferrous pins not sheathed with lead should be removed for the reasons described above. Copper pins which show no signs of corrosion may be left in place if the object is housed in stable conditions. Removal generally involves separating the joined elements and then drilling out any adhesive or plaster holding the pin or, if this is not possible, drilling through the pin itself.

Old adhesives such as shellac, animal glue and cellulose nitrate may become unstable through ageing, potentially resulting in the disintegration of a repair and further damage to the object. Epoxies, polyester and cellulose nitrate tend to yellow with time which may make a repair unsightly (Horie, 1987). These materials are removed by controlled application of an appropriate solvent. Plaster of Paris and Portland cement can contaminate stone with soluble salts and may be harder than the stone, potentially inducing mechanical stresses (Torraca, 1988).

Before a repair is removed, several questions should be considered. Could the repair be ancient or even original? Is any damage or decay occurring or likely to occur? Is the repair unsightly? Removal is frequently time consuming and may pose some risk to the object.

Dry repairs

Some broken objects may be mounted in such a way that joining the fragments is not necessary. This is most appropriate to objects consisting of a few large pieces. They should be firmly held and supported by the mounting system, although the break surfaces should not be in direct contact with each other as any vibration could cause abrasion. An Egyptian schist battlefield palette in the British Museum, composed of four fragments, two of which are restoration, is mounted on a polymethylmethacrylate backing plate and held in place with clips of the same material. This arrangement permits easy removal of the restorations if desired.

Adhesive and dowel repairs

Dowels or pins are required to support a load-bearing join or to re-attach large, heavy fragments. The use of dowels can be damaging in areas where there is the potential for future damage such as the outstretched fingers of a sculpture's hand. A blow to a dowelled repair in this area could cause it to shatter. In some instances it is possible to re-use existing dowel holes, obviating the need to remove more original material, although this may limit the size of the new dowel.

Drilling should only be carried out by a conservator and the area should be examined first for the presence of old repairs, fissures or delaminations. A power drill with appropriate masonry bits should be used. New dowels should be of sufficient diameter to prevent flexing and should be made from a machining quality stainless steel; polymethylmethacrylate rod may be used for translucent stones such as alabaster. The ends of the dowel should be secured with an adhesive, such as polyester mastic; all surfaces should be clean and grease free before its application.

Adhesive repairs

Adhesive may be used to join small fragments or in cases where dowelling is undesirable. For lightweight fragments acrylic adhesives may be used; larger pieces will require a polyester mastic. All break surfaces should be dry and grease free.

Losses and replacement

Losses may require filling for conservation reasons, to help hold an object together and to lend strength to fragile areas. Such fillings may be recessed to be unobtrusive yet clearly differentiated from the object. Alternatively, missing areas may be completely restored. The choice of approach depends on how the museum wishes to present its objects. Equally, fillings and replacements may be removed from an object which is considered to be inaccurately or overly restored. Before any action is taken the historical value, if any, of the replacements as well as the risk of damage during removal should be considered. If materials such as plaster of Paris or Portland cement are causing decay they should be removed.

Fillings may be made with acrylic or polyester resins mixed with an appropriate aggregate to match the colour and texture of the stone. To avoid creating mechanical stresses the filling should be softer than the stone. Larger replacements may be either modelled and then cast in polyester or epoxy resin or carved from stone. Both operations require considerable specialist skill and sufficient physical or documentary evidence to reconstruct the missing area.

Cleaning

The cleaning of stone should only be undertaken by a conservator as considerable damage such as abrasion, loss of original paint, activation of soluble salts and the production of intractable stains may result from unsuitable treatments. Sound, dense stone such as granite and marble which does not contain paint traces may, however, be safely dusted by a non-specialist by using a soft, clean brush to direct the dust into the nozzle of a vacuum cleaner held just above the surface.

Before cleaning, the object should be examined for signs of decay and for traces of paint or gilding which might be disturbed. Discrete cleaning tests should be conducted to find the most effective solvent and technique. The following materials should not be used: abrasives, acids, unbuffered strongly alkaline materials such as ammonia, chlorine bleaches, proprietary stone cleaners and soap. (Non-ionic detergents are safe.) Tap water should be avoided, and water should never be used on alabaster because it is slightly soluble. Steam cleaning and poulticing can be highly effective but they must be used in a careful and controlled manner to avoid damage and staining.

Transport

The movement of heavy stone objects within the museum should only be carried out by specialist staff who know how to lift without injuring themselves or damaging the objects. Movement must not rely solely on the strength of those carrying out the operation and equipment such as platform trucks, hydraulic stackers, fork-lift trucks, hoists and slings should be provided. It may be possible to hire infrequently used items. Lifting equipment is generally rated to a particular weight and should be inspected regularly to ensure that the rating is maintained. It is useful to know the weight of an object before moving it and if a weighing scale is not available this can be estimated by gauging its approximate volume and then multiplying this figure by the density of the stone. Tables of density can be found in some geology textbooks (Hatch and Rastall, 1913).

Clean padding materials should be provided to protect the object from chipping or scratching during transport. Gloves will protect against transference of dirt from the hands but may also prevent getting a secure grip.

The same considerations apply to the transport of stone objects outside the museum but, in addition, a strong wooden packing case is required. Padded, internal supports are useful for holding the object in place, provided that they do not exert pressure on fragile areas.

Health and safety precautions

Some of the materials used for stone conservation, notably silane-based consolidants, are toxic. Consolidation should, therefore, normally be carried out in a fume cupboard. If this is impossible, a full-face respirator, with suitable canister filtration should be used. Disposable gloves and overalls should be worn. Normal safety precautions should be observed when using polyester and acrylic resins (Clydesdale, 1990).

References

BLACKSHAW, S. and DANIELS, V. (1979), 'The testing of materials for use in storage and display in museums', *The Conservator*, **3**, 16–19

BRADLEY, S. M. (1987), 'An introduction to the use of silanes in stone conservation', *The Conservation of Geological Material, The Geological Curator*, **4**(7), 427–432

BRADLEY, S. M. and MIDDLETON, A. P. (1988), 'A study of the deterioration of limestone sculpture', *Journal of the American Institute for Conservation*, **27**, 64–68

CLYDESDALE, A. (1990), *Chemicals in Conservation*, Scottissh Society for Conservation and Restoration, Edinburgh

DINSMORE, J. K. (1987), 'Considerations of adhesion in the use of silane-based consolidants', *The Conservator*, **11**, 26–29

FEILDEN, B. (1982), *Conservation of Historic Buildings*, Butterworth Scientific, London

FITZHUGH, E. W. and GETTENS, R. J. (1971), 'Calcacite and efflorescent salts on objects stored in wooden museum cases', in *Science and Archaeology*, MIT Press, Cambridge, MA

HANNA, S. B. (1984), 'The use of organo-silanes for the treatment of limestone in an advanced state of deterioration', in Brommelle, N. S., Pye, E. M., Smith, P and Thomson, G. (Eds), *Adhesives and Consolidants*, International Institute for Conservation of Historic and Artistic Works, London

HANNA, S. B. and LEE, N. J. (1988), 'The consequences of previous adhesives and consolidants used for stone conservation at the British Museum', in Daniels, V. (Ed.), *Early Advances in Conservation*, British Museum Publications, London

HATCH, F. H. and RASTALL, R. H. (1913), *The Petrology of the Sedimentary Rocks*, George Allen and Company Ltd, London

HORIE, C. V. (1987), *Materials for Conservation*, Butterworths, London

LARSON, J. H. (1979), 'The conservation of alabaster monuments in churches', *The Conservator*, **3**, 28–33

LARSON, J. H. (1980), 'The conservation of stone sculpture in historic buildings', in Brommelle, N. S. and Smith, P. (Eds), *Conservation Within Historic Buildings*, International Institute for Conservation of Historic and Artistic Works, London

PLOWDEN, A. and HALAHAN, F. (1987), *Looking After Antiques*, Pan Books, London

PROUDFOOT, T. (1986), 'An outline of the repair and maintenance of statuary in the care of the National Trust', in Brommelle, N. S. and Smith, P. (Eds), *Case Studies in the Conservation of Stone and Wall Paintings*, International Institute for Conservation of Historic and Artistic Works, London

READ, H. H. and WATSON, J. (1968), *Introduction to Geology, Vol. 1, Principles*, 2nd edition, MacMillan Press, London

TORRACA, G. (1988), *Porous Building Materials*, 3rd edition, International Centre for the Study of the Preservation and the Restoration of Cultural Property, Rome

WINKLER, E. M. (1975), *Stone: Properties, Durability in Man's Environment*, 2nd edition, Springer-Verlag, Vienna

37

Conservation and storage: metals

Hazel Newey

The majority of metalwork that is found in museum collections can be divided into two broad categories: historical and archaeological. The former has remained above ground for most of its life and the latter has been buried for a long period of time and then dug up.

The care and conservation of archaeological metalwork is dealt with elsewhere (see Chapter 34) and so in this chapter I consider historical metalwork up to modern day. It is not intended to look at problems associated with specific types of objects that are made of metal, for example arms and armour or clocks and watches, but to outline general principles of conservation and care. The attitude of Conservators towards historic metalwork has changed to some extent over recent years, resulting in a general policy of minimal cleaning and restricted restoration.

After the general discussion of deterioration, conservation and restoration there is a section describing the principal corrosion products found on the most common metals and alloys found in museums and some illustrations of problems that can arise, followed by a short bibliography.

Deterioration

There are two types of deterioration that can occur in a museum: chemical and physical. Both can be minimized by following some basic guidelines which are explained below. Information is also included on how to recognize that corrosion is taking place.

Chemical deterioration

Chemical deterioration, i.e. corrosion, takes place because the metallic state is an unstable one. The majority of metals are derived from mineral ores by smelting, producing a high-energy state which will then react with its environment to form a variety of oxides, carbonates and other compounds. These are often identical with the original ore. The rate at which this reaction occurs depends upon the particular metal and the amount of moisture, chemicals and gases in the atmosphere around it.

The metals can be arranged in order of stability to give the electrochemical series, beginning with platinum and gold, the most stable, to zinc and aluminium, the most reactive of the common metals. This will give an indication of how the metals will behave when they are in contact with each other. When two metals are in close association the presence of moisture can set up a reaction causing the baser one in the series to corrode.

As knowledge and experience of metalworking increased, it became apparent that the properties of individual metals could be enhanced or altered by the addition of one or more other metals to form alloys. Base metals could be decorated with noble ones and, in some cases, deterioration could be slowed down by applying a coating of a more stable metal, or of an inert substance like resin.

In some cases the method of manufacture can lead to problems. For example, impurities in the alloy or soldering flux left by poor-quality workmanship can act as centres for corrosion. Breaks in lacquer, paint or other surface layers allow penetration of moisture and gases to the metal surface.

In a museum, chemical deterioration can be accelerated by reaction with moisture and pollutants in the air or from the immediate storage or display environment. While it is difficult and expensive to remove all chemicals from the atmosphere, it is relatively simple to ensure that the materials used in exhibition construction and storage are safe for metal objects and that they remain dust and moisture free. This aspect is covered elsewhere (see Chapter 26).

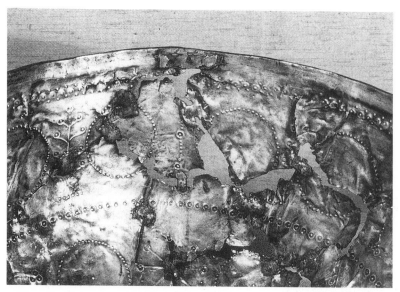

Figure 37.1 The area adjacent to the rim of a thin silver bowl has been repaired in the past with lead solder. The fragments were not straightened before soldering and, consequently, the joins were misaligned, producing an incorrect overall shape as well as an unsightly appearance. More importantly the use of lead solder could lead to damage to the object. If heat is applied to remove the solder the lead will combine with the silver to form a low-melting-point alloy and a hole will result

Corrosion can also occur if the wrong conservation method is selected or if cleaning materials are not thoroughly removed from the object. Grease and acids from human skin will cause etching on polished metal surfaces if objects are handled without wearing gloves. The fingerprints left behind can only be removed by abrasive cleaning (*Figure 37.2*).

Conservation and cleaning

Ideally, all cleaning of museum objects should be carried out by Conservators. However, removal of surface dust and dirt by careful brushing, or washing with water and non-ionic detergent, followed by thorough rinsing and drying could, in some cases, be carried out by non-conservators on sound objects, provided that a thorough examination is undertaken first to check on the object's suitability. Removal of corrosion usually involves the use of chemicals and should only be undertaken by a trained Conservator.

Physical damage

Physical damage to metal objects is usually caused by poor handling techniques or storage conditions. Although apparently less fragile than glass or ceramic, some alloys will shatter if dropped on the floor. Even if the object does not break, it may become misshapen or a piece may detach from the main body.

Physical handling should be reduced to a minimum and efforts made not to manipulate movable parts, otherwise joints will weaken. Objects should always be handled over a padded surface using two hands to support the whole shape. Objects should never be picked up by handles or necks as these are often points of weakness in old objects.

One of the other great causes of physical damage is over-zealous cleaning and polishing. Any cleaning method will remove some of the metal surface by removing the corrosion, leading to blurring of inscribed designs. In the case of silver gilt, Sheffield plate or electroplate, the base metal may be revealed.

Restoration

The term 'restoration' when applied to metal, has come to mean the repair and reshaping of the object to bring its appearance as close to its original condition as possible. This can involve heating the object, either as part of a soldering or welding process or to assist in the reshaping. It can also mean repatinating the surface with a chemical solution to produce the correct colour or, perhaps, replacing

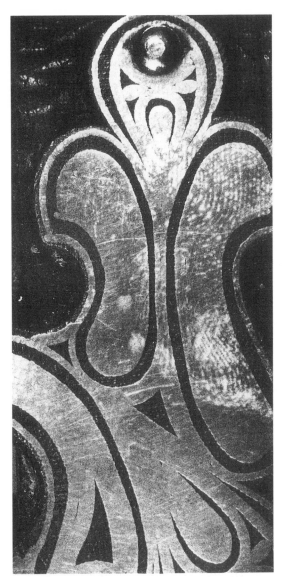

Figure 37.2 Detail of a Russian horse trapping decorated with applied steel encrusted with thin silver strips hammered into the keyed surface. The photograph clearly shows a fingerprint which has etched the surface, resulting from handling the polished object without wearing gloves

missing areas or parts with modern pieces made from a similar alloy to the original.

The restoration of a museum object should only be carried out by a Conservator experienced in such work. Furthermore, restoration should only be undertaken after discussion and agreement between the Curator and the Conservator so that the ethical implications are understood by all concerned.

Accurate records must be kept of the object before and after treatment.

Characteristic properties of the metals commonly found in museums

This section lists the metals that are most common in museum collections, together with information on their alloys and how they corrode in the museum environment. Specialized scientific and industrial collections may contain other metals but, owing to lack of space, these are not dealt with here. With the exception of gold and copper and its alloys, metals in their pure, polished state can be described as 'white' or 'silvery' coloured. It is possible to distinguish between metals by careful visual examination, because each metal has a distinctive colour cast or tone. The ability do to this usually comes with experience derived from studying a range of objects. It is important to stress at this stage, however, that the only accurate way of identifying the composition of an artefact is by chemical analysis.

Gold

Unless the museum possesses objects made of platinum, gold is the most precious and stable metal found in collections. Yellow in colour, gold is soft and easily worked and is usually alloyed with either copper or silver to increase its hardness. It can be beaten into thin sheets and used to decorate other metals and materials. Alternatively, baser metals could be gilded or electroplated, forming a chemical bond between them and the gold. In the pure state gold does not corrode, but will become covered with the corrosion products of associated metals.

Silver

Silver is a white, lustrous metal that can be polished to a highly reflective surface. Like gold it is a soft metal, easily worked and is usually alloyed with copper for hardness to produce Sterling silver (92.5 per cent silver) or Britannia silver (95.8 per cent). In the UK these can be identified by the hallmarks stamped into the finished object. Silver was combined with baser metals in the form of Sheffield plate (a silver–copper–silver sandwich formed by heat and pressure) and, from the 1840s, more commonly electroplate. Plated ware can also be identified by maker's marks stamped onto the objects.

Silver is extremely susceptible to the presence of sulphur in the atmosphere. Minimal quantities will react with the metal to form silver sulphide or tarnish. This starts off as a thin yellow–brown iridescent layer over the surface and, if left, will gradually become black and obscure any decorative features. It is not chemically damaging to the object, merely cosmetically disfiguring. The previous comments about excessive cleaning and polishing apply, especially to objects made of silver and silver plate.

To prevent the formation of tarnish all exhibition and storage materials should be checked before use. It is also possible to coat the cleaned surface of the object with a clear synthetic lacquer. If, however, the lacquer is damaged in any way, tarnishing will begin at this point.

Copper

In the pure state copper is a pink-coloured metal that is easily worked. It is added to both gold and silver to produce more durable alloys, and is itself alloyed with other metals to modify its properties.

Copper is relatively corrosion resistant but, like silver, reacts with sulphide fumes in the atmosphere forming a thin layer of tarnish. It will also react with acetic acid vapour given off by paints and wood, producing verdigris (basic copper acetate). Like all copper compounds, this green waxy substance is poisonous, so great care should be taken when handling objects in this state.

Brass

Zinc, in varying proportions is added to copper to produce a series of brasses. These yellow alloys can then be gilded to produce ormulu, used for furniture fittings. Alternatively, they can be coated with a shellac-based lacquer to simulate gilding and protect it from corrosion. As with any protective coating, once this is damaged enhanced corrosion takes place.

Bronze

Bronze is an alloy of copper and tin with other metals added in small proportions. Objects made of bronze are usually cast and the surface treated chemically to produce a brown or green artificial patina or corrosion layer for decorative purposes. If the chemicals used for artificial patination are not totally removed they can subsequently react with moisture in the atmosphere and begin a true corrosion process.

Nickel silver

The colour of this alloy of copper, nickel and zinc can vary from silvery to yellow. It was often used as a cheap substitute for silver and as a base for silver plating.

Lead

An object made of lead can usually be recognized by its weight. Pure lead is a grey, soft, malleable metal which turns dull grey on exposure to air and will mark paper with a grey line. It is often alloyed with

tin to produce a harder metal, pewter. Lead reacts readily with carbon dioxide in the presence of organic acid vapours to form basic lead carbonate, which appears as a white powder on the metal surface. Once this is seen, the object must be removed from the source of the vapour, possibly unseasoned wood, to prevent further corrosion taking place. It is important to note that lead and its compounds are poisonous and so care must be taken when handling the objects. Lead corrosion should only be treated by experienced Conservators.

Tin

Tin is rarely used to make objects but is more likely to be found alloyed with lead, as pewter, or with antimony, as Britannia Metal. It also occurs as tin plate, iron sheets covered with a protective layer of tin.

The 'warty' corrosion found sometimes on pewter is typical of tin alloys and is seen on the photograph of the Chinese mirror described below. Removal of these 'warts', either chemically or mechanically, will result in a pit or a hole in the metal (*Figure 37.3*).

Figure 37.3 Mirrors like this Chinese example were often made of bronze containing a high proportion of tin, because it would take a high polish to produce a reflective surface. The stresses within the alloy mean that, if dropped, the object would shatter. If there is enough metal present it may be possible to solder the fragments together. There is the problem however, of heat affecting the surface patina and altering the colour. Thus it is often preferable to repair such an object using an adhesive. The characteristic 'warty' corrosion that indicates a high percentage of tin in the alloy can be seen as pale lumps on the surface of the metal

Figure 37.4 A polished-steel plaquette with eruptions of rust disfiguring the surface. Cleaning with a proprietary rust-removing solution could result in pitting of the metal and blurring of fine detail. Faint traces of a fingerprint can be seen on the right-hand side

Iron

Iron is mixed with carbon to form one of three different alloys; cast iron ($c.$ 4 per cent carbon), wrought iron ($c.$ 0.5 per cent) and steel (0.1–1.3 per cent) whose strength and workability vary accordingly.

Iron and steel corrode readily in the presence of moisture to form a layer of red–orange–brown rust on the metal surface. If the object is not protected in some way corrosion will continue leading to surface pitting and eventually to total disintegration.

In the past, the metal surface was tinned, painted or galvanized to try to prevent rusting. Steel was 'blued' (by heating to a certain temperature) or 'browned' chemically, both as decorative and protective methods. Like all such layers, however, once punctured corrosion occurs; with any iron or steel object it is important to keep it in a dry condition.

Zinc

Zinc is usually associated with galvanizing, that is the formation of a protective coating on iron, or as a component of the copper/zinc alloy, brass. Zinc can also be found as the base metal on bidri-ware, a decorative type of metalwork from India which is inlaid with silver. Ethnographic collections may contain small objects made entirely from zinc, again usually from India. The surface layer of white zinc oxide formed on exposure to air looks like lead oxide, but analysis should confirm the presence of zinc.

In conclusion, it is essential to consult a trained, experienced Conservator before attempting the cleaning or restoration of any piece of metalwork. The Conservator will be able to assess the condition of the object and advise on a suitable treatment. Furthermore, conservation treatments are subject to the recently introduced Control of Substances Hazardous to Health (COSHH) regulations where each process must be assessed and subsequently carried out in the approved manner. Advice on this would also form part of the professional Conservator's role in relation to the Curator and the museum.

Acknowledgements

I would like to thank W. A. Oddy, Keeper of Conservation, for reading the text and my colleagues, M. Hockey and I. McIntyre for their assistance with the descriptions of the photographs.

Bibliography

SANDWITH, H. and STAINTON, S. (1984), *National Trust Manual of Housekeeping*, Allan Lane/National Trust, London

PLOWDEN, A. and HALAHAN, F. (1987), *Looking After Antiques*, Pan, London

CHILD, R. E. and TOWNSEND, J. M. (Ed.) (1988), *Modern Metals in Museums*, proceedings of a one-day meeting organized jointly by National Museum of Wales, Scottish Society for Conservation and Restoration and United Kingdom Institute of Conservation, Institute of Archaeology Press, London

38

Conservation and storage: machinery

John Hallam

Technology may be defined as the application of science and the useful arts to the apparatus/machines and processes used in the conversion of natural raw material into finished articles. A technology exhibit may be found within many museum disciplines such as archaeology, social history, transport or applied art. Although the materials from which they are made are generally familiar to Curators and Conservators, large or working technological exhibits are considered to pose difficult problems for non-specialist museums. This chapter looks at many of the problems associated with large static or working exhibits, (principally made of metal), which have been or are to be removed from their working environment and received into museums. The technical problems include dismantling, transport, conservation or restoration, and storage and display. Depending on the object, it should be obvious that these aspects are not necessarily carried out in the order presented in this chapter.

Conservation of science and engineering collections has lagged behind other fields of conservation for which training courses have been established and ethical practices or standards determined. Many of the conservation problems in this field have yet to be indentified. At the current rate of training, it is likely that it will be at least a decade before there are sufficient trained Technicians and Conservators to make any recognizable impact on the extent of the problem as outlined in the Storer Report (Storer, 1989).

Because of the nature and size of some of the objects in the collections and the possibility of operating exhibits, museums' Management Committees may develop policies and make decisions which are not in the interest of the long-term preservation of the collections. Walter Brownlee, Historian to the Warrior Project identified a dilemma for the Conservator/Restorer of historic artefacts

such as ships or aeroplanes (and buildings?) being restored as a public attraction. 'There is a clash of interests and in most cases the money making restoration takes precedence over conservation. The primary task . . .is to face the inevitable and to minimize any of the destructive effects of restoration on the original material'. 'The aim to have hundreds of tourists aboard. . .caused the destruction of . . .probably the only remaining intact example (of an armoured bulkhead) in the world. . .It was a case of either cut through, or no visitors allowed' (Brownlee, W., private communication).

Similar problems occur with working exhibits or the perceived need for display material to be in 'as new' condition. It may be unreasonable to insist on the restoration of an exhibit to its original condition as first manufactured, particularly if the object has been modified or repaired during its working life. Such repairs or modifications, and even the 'wear and tear' are part of the historical evidence, and often part of the attraction of an exhibit.

With any large, complex conservation or restoration project involving a number of individuals or groups, communication is often a problem. It is essential to define various terms to avoid costly misunderstandings.

Artefact: machine, structure instrument or other piece of man-made equipment.
Conservation: all the processes of preserving *artefacts* of historic importance, such as preservation, restoration, repair, maintenance and, where of an acceptable standard, reconstruction and adaptation.
Preservation: maintaining the material of an artefact in its existing state and halting deterioration.
Restoration or repair: returning the existing materials of an artefact to a known earlier state with the minimum introduction of new material.
Maintenance: the continuous care of an artefact without alteration of its materials. (Note that this is not the same

as the generally accepted run of industrial maintenance.)
Reconstruction: returning the existing materials of an artefact to a known earlier state involving more than the minimum amount of new material.
Adaptation: modification of an artefact to fulfil a new compatible use. (Wallis, 1988)

To these definitions should be added

Replica: strictly an exact facsimile of an artefact but usually extended to include a representation of the external appearance of the artefact, using traditional or modern materials and techniques as appropriate.

The fundamental aim should be the long-term preservation of the historically significant artefact and ideally the conservation process should be limited to stabilization of the whole object and preventing further deterioration. Important elements are:

(1) improvement of environment, including conditions causing deterioration;
(2) protection of surfaces;
(3) consolidation of the original materials and possible removal of reactive componenets and replacement by inert materials;
(4) minimizing the risk of mechanical damage caused by improper handling; and
(5) provision of support to weak or loaded elements (e.g. crutches under aircraft wings).

All the above are standard conservation techniques, to which should be added in the case of working exhibits:

(6) reduction in the duty, loading, pressures, frequency of operation, etc.; and
(7) use of replicas, demonstration apparatus or 'consumable' artefacts.

Restoration

The decision to go beyond the basic conservation processes and restore the object would ideally ensure minimal intervention. Often this involves considerable research and ethical considerations of the treatment of individual components and the object as a whole.

The construction methods used in technological exhibits are too diverse to be described in this short survey. The whole range of techniques from crude handwork to high-precision engineering will be encountered. Since the availability of new materials and the development of machine tools played such a key role in the design or development of any particular machine or technological artefact, it is not unreasonable to expect the artefact to display evidence of contemporary methods, together with later techniques used during maintenance, repair or modification. However, the varying rates of diffusion of techniques and availability of new methods and materials can give rise to the retention of outmoded or archiac features. Fortunately, there is a considerable body of information from extant drawings (such as the Watt Papers held by Birmingham Reference Library or the many technical and works records still held by long-established companies) coupled with 'engineer's handbooks', design manuals and technical journals and treatises available in many libraries or held by enthusiast or learned societies. It is, therefore, not an impossible task for the Curator or Restorer to ensure the historical accuracy of a technological exhibit, including reconstructed parts and, for machinery after the introduction of standardization (from the 1850s), even to arrive at the correct screw threads.

Practical considerations

Some of the practical aspects of conservation or restoration of large or working mechanical objects are set out below. In general, the final result must be the product of careful research, judgement and continual dialogue between Curator and Conservator or restorer. It may be necessary to modify specifications as the work progresses; nevertheless, all aspects of the project should be recorded meticulously.

Preparation work

The ideal situation would be to see the machine working on site, discuss the operation and maintenance of the machine with operators, fitters or millwrights, noting any 'alarming' sounds such as belt slap, creaks, or knocking sounds which may be perfectly innocuous. Often, however, the machine is unused awaiting removal from site, in a half-derelict state and without any information regarding its potential as a working exhibit. Following an initial survey, the first job is to arrange removal and transport of the object into museum premises, although in certain instances this might be proceeded by cleaning if facilities are available. Arrangements with contractors, plant hire specialists, and transporters need to be co-ordinated with any museum staff involved. Insurance arrangements for the period of transfer need to be finalized after discussing liabilities with contractors. The object may be heavy or awkwardly shaped; partial dismantling may be required. Obviously this work will need to be put in hand sufficiently in advance of the removal date to allow for any difficulties that might arise.

During the actual move a member of the museum staff should be present as co-ordinator or director of operations. It is a point worth considering whether museum staff actually direct the operation. In the

Figure 38.1 Machinery was dismantled into components to be lifted by the original erecting crane, recommissioned for the purpose. As work proceeded, significant safety hazards were presented by large voids under the motor bedplate and surfaces indurated by 50 years of oil drips

Recovery of a heavy electric 'mill engine' (*c.* 1935) from the seventh floor of this flour mill required careful planning and co-operation between museum curatorial and technical staff, the mill engineer and specialized cranage and transport contractors.

Figure 38.2 Some jobs were best left to other professionals. Access problems for the mobile crane were increased by the limited room between the mill building and the River Tyne

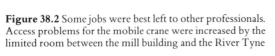

event of any accident occurring the contractor's liability may be greatly reduced if a museum staff member has assumed responsibility for directing the work of professional contractors. The safety aspects of dismantling and removal cannot be overstated and the potential danger to the object, staff and general public are numerous, as illustrated in *Figures 38.1* and *38.2*.

Cleaning

Some machinery may be caked with dirt, oil and grease to the extent that neither the bare nor painted metal surfaces are apparent. In this case superficial dirt must be removed to allow a thorough examination of the object. Some information of historical importance may be gleaned from sampling the accumulated debris on the machine. But there are also potential hazards. Machinery, products or product residues of a given industry may represent health hazards. The process may require heating pipes, perhaps with asbestos lagging. Some investigation is therefore necessary before undertaking restoration, and in some instances specialist contractors may need to be employed before general cleaning can begin.

The methods of cleaning will obviously vary depending upon the complexity of the artefact, its material composition, finish, size and condition. As in all conservation procedures, the most gentle procedure possible to accomplish the task should be used. Power washers with either cold, warm or hot water are effective and, if necessary, detergents may be added. Steam cleaning may be appropriate to some transport vehicles. However, consideration must be given to the possibility that water will be forced into flanges or fittings, initiating further corrosion. Hand cleaning of particular components might be considered, using minimal amounts of water. Some components may be handled in a solvent cleaning unit, after testing the effects of solvent on the object and its finish.

The term 'cleaning' is also used to describe the removal of surface finishes to reveal bright metal in preparation for repair and refinishing. This was traditionally done by burning and scraping or application of chemical paint strippers. The toxicity of the paints and the chemical strippers have led away from such stripping operations and dry stripping techniques are often considered more appropriate in terms of efficiency and safety. Abrasive blasting machines, with nozzle sizes varying from 0.5 mm to 6 mm are capable of operating pressures between 10 and 120 p.s.i. A variety of abrasives including glass and plastic beads are very effective in many stripping operations. The operation of such machines is, however, a highly skilled task and should be left to trained operatives,

with appropriate safety apparatus. If done indoors, the area should be completely sealed to prevent airborne abrasive or toxic paint dust from entering the general museum or workshop environment. Following operations, the object should be immediately cleaned, preferably vacuumed together with the blasting area and if the surface is to be painted priming should begin immediately.

Dismantling

Some machines may contain hundreds, if not thousands, of parts which may need to be assembled in a particular sequence. It is possible that the Conservator or Restorer may not be a specialist in the type of machine or object being worked on and it is common to find that all engineering records, drawings or operating details have been destroyed. It is therefore imperative that a systematic approach to the dismantling, storage and restoration of any technological item be adopted.

The greatest danger to an object is when it is lying in pieces, possibly awaiting spare parts, with all the information on how the object was dismantled being entrusted to the fallible memory of an individual. Unfortunately this is not uncommon, particularly as many objects are dismantled in haste during urgent rescue operations. The stages of dismantling are essentially as follows.

(1) Before touching the object all existing records and information should be available. Photographs and sketches of the whole machine plus individual assemblies, should be prepared. This recording procedure should continue throughout the whole of the job. At this stage too much information is better than too little — the superflous information can later be ignored.

(2) The object should be cleaned sufficiently for examination to establish whether parts are numbered or otherwise marked up, as illustrated in *Figures 38.3* and *38.4*.

(3) Mark up the components and assemblies. The extent of marking-up must be jointly decided between Curator and Conservator, bearing in mind that the object may have been previously assembled incorrectly or marked in error.

Major parts which appear identical, and even nuts and bolts, may not necessarily be interchangeable. This can apply to machinery made after engineering standards were introduced, as a result of original manufacturing tolerances, later wear or repairs. Marks should be recorded, together with any additional numbers applied by the museum.

The method of numbering should exceed expected storage or process times and should not be readily removable. Wired-on tags, paints, special machinery markers, stamped, engraved, incised or simple 'pop'

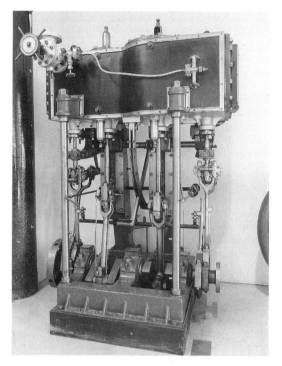

Figure 38.3 Compound marine engine by Smulders (Werf Gusto), Schiedam for the TITAN II floating crane, 1922

marks have all been used. It is important to mark the fitting joints, otherwise it is likely that parts will be fitted upside-down. Care must be taken to ensure that marks cannot be confused and that each part removed can be identified and replaced.

(4) The object should be broken down into the minimum number of loose parts or assemblies, each of which should be labelled with the job or accession number as well as a part number. Loose parts should be wired on to relevant assembles.

Although components may be recognized by the actual person doing the dismantling, unless labelled properly there is no guarantee that they will be identified when found in store, perhaps years later, by a different person.

(5) The records of work should be written up regularly and copies retained in a form suitable for archival storage. The shop logbook or fitter's notes, however grimy and oil stained, should be kept, although their condition may require a separate location from the process file. It is not uncommon to find that the shop log is the only form of record for a significant period of time.

(6) Be patient. Less damage will ensue to the object and the dismantler if time is allowed for dismantling fluids to act. The application of gentle heat or pressure over a period of perhaps several days

is better than resorting to the unskilled use of large hammers, lengths of pipe to extend the leverage applied by spanners or attack with thermal lances.

(7) At each stage the parts should be re-examined and original cost and time estimates revised. If there is likely to be any major delay in restoration it is advisable in many cases that the machine is built up again, after first applying suitable treatment against existing or possible deterioration.

Repairs and replacement

With regard to essential missing parts, the decision is between replacement or fabrication. It is common commercial practice to fit 'spare parts' from another machine. There are many Conservators and Curators who find this practice of 'cannibalization' ethically unacceptable. An alternative view is that many of the objects being restored have been subjected in the past to many previous replacements in their working life and, therefore, cannot be considered to be totally original. It might further be argued that such 'cannibalized' parts may be more historically accurate than modern replacements.

Fabrication of many components may be straightforward, though it might not be prudent or even possible always to follow the original material or manufacturing specifications.

There is little excuse for drilling out contemporary threads, and replacing with modern off-the-shelf parts. Still less is there an excuse for modern fastenings with 'Posidrive' heads or 'pop' rivets to be used – unless they were original fittings or 'in-service' replacements.

The repair or 'recovery' of worn or damaged parts is well beyond the scope of this chapter. For example, fractured castings could be welded (there were problems with wrought iron from which many pressure vessels and stressed machine components are made). Similarly, electroplating, metal spraying and welding may be used to build up worn parts. It is feasible to apply layers of different materials, for example a final coat of chromium on a piston rod to reduce maintenance costs, but at the expense of absolute authenticity.

Modifications and improvements

In many cases contemporary replacements may not be available for missing parts. For working exhibits, safety regulations may not favour the use of traditional materials for repairs or replacements, or the re-use of components such as stressed bolts from engine crankpin bearing caps.

Decisions to use fabrications instead of castings, or to join metal by welding instead of rivetting, may be

Figure 38.4 Close up of part of the valve gear of the engine shown in Fig 38.3 showing several methods of marking-up, including a confusing series of '9s' on the left-hand split bearing. Excluding nuts and split pins there are at least 60 parts in this assembly

made on grounds of expediency, but traditional techniques are still used by specialist contractors.

The question of correcting existing defects caused by earlier misassembly or serious faults in the original design needs to be carefully considered. It is not uncommon to find excessive clearances in moving parts which compensate for errors in design in eighteenth- and early nineteenth-century machines or more modern artefacts. It is also not uncommon to find poor workmanship in the original manufacture or in a previous repair. Consideration should be given to the need for rectifying such work. Defects may be perfectly acceptable in the static exhibit but unsafe in the working exhibit. For example, the replacement of manufactured coal gas by natural gas in the 1970s required alterations to burners and gas engines because of the different air-gas ratio required for complete combustion of the different fuel. Modifications may be necessary to fit devices to prevent unauthorized operations. Some modifications may not require additions to, or alteration of, an artefact's structure but may alter the relationship of its parts. For example, the resetting of steam engine valve gear for running on light loads or on compressed air.

The choice of material for replacement parts may pose questions, which are illustrated by two common examples.

A large number of treadle-operated machines such as small platen printing presses have thin cast iron footplates. Under repeated bending stress this component often fractured and many machines have been repaired by fitting a steel plate splint. Replacement of the complete footplate in cast steel could provide a much stronger part with an appearance similar to the original manufactured item.

Wrought iron ignition tubes in gas engines are rapidly converted to brittle iron carbide, which has a very short life under the shock of the explosions in the engine cylinder. The danger of showering staff and visitor alike with red-hot fragments can be minimized by fitting tubes made from nickel or stainless steel.

If modifications are to be made then they should be reversible. Replacement or new parts should be identified as such (perhaps by a standard punch mark) and significant original material must be retained and entered into the records. Many parts removed during restoration make ideal exhibits in their own right or help to interpret the original object if displayed alongside. This also minimizes the chance of such parts being misplaced.

Any component which is to be discarded, in accordance with the institution's guidelines, could be considered for re-use in the restoration of other objects – perhaps as material for the manufacture of new parts. For example wrought iron is now virtually unobtainable.

In the case of a unique object of specific technological or historic importance, or those objects which are substantially in original condition, it must be argued that such exhibits should neither be operated nor 'restored' but 'preserved'. If it is necessary to demonstrate how such an item is worked it is feasible to construct a 'replica' using modern materials (*Figure 35.5*).

A case in point involving an important historic exhibit is the 1875 Hornsby portable steam engine owned by the Museum of Science and Engineering, Newcastle-upon-Tyne. It was initially decided that the restoration of this exhibit would be limited to cleaning, setting up the motion, replacement of decayed timbers in the forecarriage and cosmetic repairs to the badly corroded base of the smokebox. Following dismantling (including removal of corroded fire-tubes and descaling of the boiler plates) it was reported that it might be possible to put the engine back into steam if new tubes were fitted, minor repairs to blotched (pitted) tubeplates were carried out and the corroded longitudal stays were replaced. Since none of this work would affect those parts of the original structure which were sound, it was decided to go ahead and the boiler was eventually inspected, hydraulically tested and passed to steam at 40 lb pressure – half its original working pressure. Because the engine would happily run for demonstration purposes at 5 p.s.i. steam pressure, the spring safety valve was reset to 20 p.s.i.g. so that the boiler would not be unnecessarily stressed. During the second operating season one of the original cylinder head bolts fractured due to crystallization of the wrought iron.

During preparation for the next annual safety inspection the foundation ring of the wrought iron boiler was found to be excessively grooved at the corners. Repairs would have significantly altered the structure of what was probably the only boiler of this type still extant in substantially original condition

Figure 38.5 A stage in the building of an electrically powered 'replica' of Ericsson's 'Novelty' locomotive for the Rainhill Trials of 1829. This was being built in the workshops of the Greater Manchester Museum of Science and Industry using parts from an earlier, non-working, full size model

with a 'Z-iron' foundation ring and bearing the stamped legend 'J Brown & Sons Best Iron' plainly visible on the steam side of the wrapper plate. It was decided that the firebox would not be repaired. It is interested to note that if the main requirement had been merely to show a working portable engine or to provide steam then a more modern example could have been purchased at half the cost of firebox repairs to the historic exhibit.

Surface finishes

The principal function of an applied surface finish is to provide a protective coating against deterioration of bare metals or organic materials exposed to attack by chemical or biological agents in the environment. The choice of finish is usually dictated by the environment to which an object is exposed. For example, an iron surface could be painted with a drying oil containing inert filler or pigment, covered with grease or tar, be vitreous-enamelled or be subjected to controlled corrosion as in the browning of gun barrels. In some technological and scientific exhibits the choice of a coating may reflect an essential physical property, such as the use of varnish for electrical insulation. Where an existing, but not necessarily original, finish is sound, consideration must be given to conserving it, but this will depend on a number of factors.

The treatment of the surface finish begs certain questions.

(1) Is the object rare or unique with the original finish, or with the original finish overpainted? Or is the object a representative sample of many similar objects still in existence?
(2) Is the finish sound and still adequately protecting the metal beneath from corrosion?

Obviously, if the object is partially corroded beneath the otherwise sound paint layers then corrosion might be environmentally controlled. Often this cannot be done and it is of paramount importance to protect the structure. As a last resort, the paint is stripped and the object repainted. Samples of the original paint should be retained for later analysis; it is unlikely, however, that precise formulations of the paints used even in the early twentieth century are available today. Therefore, consideration must be given to using the best primers, undercoats and colour-matched top finishes to protect the object. When an original finish, even overpainted, it to be retained it is sometimes desirable to remove some of the old paint layers revealing an earlier stage of restoration or perhaps even the original finish. Except on small objects, the solvent-cleaning approach of art restorers is too lengthy a process for this. It is reported that carbon dioxide blasting techniques when expertly used can result in layer by layer removal of old paint, assuming the layers have differing coefficients of thermal expansion. Before embarking on such treatments a sample area should be tried to ensure that the technique is satisfactory and to determine, at an early stage, whether the original finish is worth recovering as it may have been damaged or abraided prior to repainting.

Invariably on large objects there will be paint losses and in some instances it may be deemed worthwhile to effect local repairs. This obviously will include the cleaning and removal of corrosion products from the area of the paint loss, priming, and perhaps filling and rubbing down before repainting. The removal of the corrosion products can be accomplished chemically, mechanically or efficiently with small abrasive blasting machines. One report suggests that portable techniques may be applicable.

The paint used for the repair may well fade and weather at a different rate from the old paint. A varnish may be considered to cover the old paint and the repair. Before embarking on a large programme for the replacement of paint losses, some research would be prudent. For instance, is a new paint (possibly slightly oversprayed onto the old paint) compatible, or is it likely to flake off? Are the fillers, if any, likely to key to the old paint and, if not, are cracks likely to develop? Will any fillers be affected by vibrations in a working exhibit or by heat?

Bare metal is often found in engineering exhibits, for example on shafts, name plates, castings, etc. Obviously these may need to be treated immediately following cleaning to prevent corrosion. Bare iron and steel can be waxed, oiled or lacquered, depending on the usage and the environment in which the component is maintained.

Traditionally, copper and brass components such as casting, pipework and nameplates were often polished in service. The continuance of such procedures in the museum may lead to an unacceptable degree of wear, or accumulation of polish deposits which are unsightly but, more importantly, may be introduced into the moving parts of a working exhibit. Polishing never seems to be confined solely to the metalwork and often extends onto the painted surfaces rendering these surfaces more highly polished than the rest of the paintwork. It may be more appropriate for such metalwork to be cleaned and, where necessary, polished followed by lacquer treatment. This would also reduce maintenance time for static exhibits and may be appropriate to working exhibits subject to the action of heat, steam and pollutants present. There are obviously problems with any surface treatments including polishing, lacquering and oiling where these materials may inadvertently transfer to adjacent materials.

Re-assembly and installation

Provided that records have been kept and correct procedures for dismantling and repair have been followed, the reassembly and finishing of an exhibit should present few problems. With all exhibits, particularly complex or working machines, erection should not be rushed. It is easy to skimp a repair on the grounds of economy. Even skilled fitters may leave a tool or spare bolt inside a machine or forget to cut the hole in a valve joint unless they work methodically. At best, careless work could lead to the expense of opening up a machine and starting again; at worst it could lead to a serious accident.

Before assembly of a large object is commenced its eventual location or the design of foundations should be settled, particularly with respect to floor loadings, suitability of foundation (especially in relation to vibration and noise), availability of services and access for maintenance.

During erection, each stage should be tested and adjustments carried out. In the case of working exhibits final testing may have to be supervised by the relevant authority, for example an Insurance Company Engineer/Surveyor. The question of adequate and suitable insurance must not be forgotten, together with the necessary licences or tax payable. Similarly, the statutory requirements of the Health and Safety Executive should be sought, particularly where semi-skilled operators may be required to demonstrate working machinery.

Management of conservation restoration projects

The curator has a duty of continuing care for the artefact when it passes into the hands of a third party.

Large, complex and lengthy conservation projects will require considerable administrative and managerial skill in dealing with such matters as budget forecasting, control of expenditure, tendering procedure, work programming and securing of financial support. The success of such projects is ensured by:

(1) The provision of a proper specification for the project, which may be on a single page or the length of a book; it is as long as required to describe adequately the work processes to be carried out. This will undoubtedly need to be continuously revised during the dismantling procedure and as the work is progressed. Greater detail may be necessary if the work is to be carried out by unskilled or semi-skilled staff.
(2) Maintaining effective two-way communication with all staff involved to ensure that there is adequate co-ordination among the various groups involved. It is essential that there be sufficient liason to ensure the work carried out meets the written specifications.
(3) Selection of a suitable contractor, which might be the institution's own staff, volunteer organizations or professional contractors. The specifications will determine the groups that have the necessary skills, knowledge and equipment to complete the project satisfactorily.

In selecting a professional contractor, it is often necessary for the work to go out to tender and, if the written specifications are fairly detailed, the completed tenders will reflect costs for similar work to be carried out. Quality is another matter; it is advisable to check on the contractor's track record, including security and their compatibility with the museum's conservation philosophy.

Costs

Estimating the costs

Even with a detailed brief, an accurate estimate of time and costs of the job may only be possible after dismantling. It is advisable to allocate a budget for preliminary investigations, including dismantling and reassembly plus, if a working object, the necessary safety, structural and operational aspects. The various technical possibilities and ethical considerations will obviously be influenced by financial considerations. The requirement to set an object in motion could increase the costs of restoration by a factor of 10 or more, as illustrated by the following example.

A case history

The Museum of Science and Engineering, Newcastle upon Tyne, acquired a 1948 Aveling-Barford steam-roller, the last design of steamroller built in England under contract by the Scotswood Works of Vickers Armstrong Limited (*Figure 38.6*). A prominent feature of the machine was the safety valves contained in a cast-iron housing bolted to the engine steam chest, with a vertical pipe to lead the steam away.

This design was faulty and often led, as in the case of the museum's engine, to a flange on the casing fracturing. The last owner had replaced the assembly with a crude fabrication using parts from a standard Aveling & Porter steamroller. The original casing and baseplate (*Figure 38.7*) were found by museum staff searching the scrap-heap. Copies of Aveling-Barford drawings were obtained from the company but no spare parts were available.

Several options were open to the Museum:

(1) leave the unit 'as found';
(2) replace with the original (broken) casing omitting all of the missing original internal parts;
(3) as (2) but make a cosmetic repair for the missing section of flange, with cost depending upon whether plaster, metallic fillers or metal was used; or

Figure 38.6 Maker's photograph of Aveling–Barford 'R' type steamroller (from Vickers Armstrong (Scotswood) works album, July 1946). This actual machine shows minor differences from the museum's roller, as it was a model built for Cumberland County Council

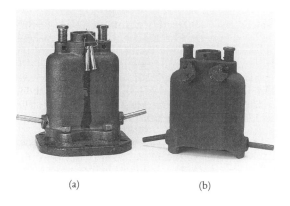

(a)	(b)

Figure 38.7 Aveling–Barford safety valve.
(a) Reproduction safety valve assembly. Newly machined casting complete with valve discs, springs, spring spindles, easing (testing) levers, spring adjusting screw caps mounted on the original baseplate with refurbished valve-seats. The wired-on retaining pins (with new small padlocks) will be fitted into holes drilled in the spring adjusting screw caps *after* the valves have been set at the correct steam pressure, to meet the legal requirements of a tamper-proof means of setting the 'blowing-off' pressure. (b) Original valve casing showing fractured flange

(4) replace with a wooden (or other material) model. This could later cause problems if shrinkage occurred but has the advantage of possibly forming the basis for a pattern (see below).

All of the above are unsatisfactory if the roller is to be put into steam again, in which case further options must be considered.

(5) Retain the existing replacement assembly (there is no guarantee that this would be acceptable to the Engineer/ Surveyor of the insurance company without extensive rebuilding).
(6) 'Re-manufacture' the original part, if it is repairable, with missing parts replaced or reconstructed.
(7) Replicate a standard Aveling–Barford safety-valve assembly as originally designed or modified to eliminate the design fault.

The estimated relative costs of the various options are shown in *Table 38.1*. As a matter of record, it was eventually decided to adopt option (7) while retaining the original. A new casing (with a distinctive '88' added to its pattern number) was cast in 'spheriodal graphite' instead of 'grey' cast iron, on advice from the foundry.

Table 38.1 Estimated costs for various options: Aveling Barford steamroller safety valve

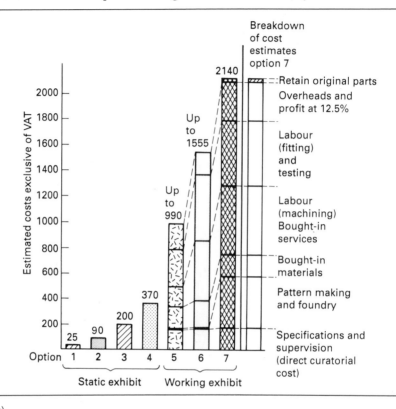

(January 1990 prices)

The true cost of the job

Until recently, the market value of most objects found in industrial collections has, with very few exceptions, been related to their intrinsic or 'scrap' value. Conservation or restoration of these objects is expensive in terms of labour costs, economic use of capital equipment and the floor area occupied during the process. It is not uncommon for labour costs to be in the order of 75–80 per cent.

Whereas 30 years ago a machine in use would have been discarded if it needed extensive repairs – such as a new firebox in a steam locomotive – museum (and private owners) now consider such repairs as entirely practicable. With many classes of object, particularly transport items, much of the restoration work has been undertaken by unpaid volunteers whose labour has been freely contributed. If this labour element and hidden costs such as supervision and occupation of workshop space for an extended period were to be costed out many more Curators and Management Committees would realize the true cost of restoration projects.

The scale of the operation may be illustrated, in its crudest terms, by considering an extreme case,

namely heavy repairs to a steam locomotive carried out by volunteers working one day and one evening per week over a 6-year period (see *Table 38.2*). Of course, this illustration is simplistic and should not be taken to suggest that properly supervised, resourced and accountable volunteers are not an excellent means of progressing museum work. The arguments for and against volunteers will not be rehearsed here.

The costs of restoration can be further broken down in terms of the materials and labour input for the various elements required in a given project. An illustration of the cost elements for the restoration of a Dennis Motor Fire Engine is given in *Figure 38.8*. Such a breakdown is useful in determining the total resource implications, including hidden costs such as staff time, which should enable the financial resources to be linked to a work programme allowing a continuous project. Often with large projects a fairly substantial amount of time and resources is needed even to provide the necessary estimates. The time spent is usually justified if it results in a continuous work programme which maintains the enthusiasm of staff involved.

Table 38.2 The cost of heavy repairs to a steam locomotive

Item	Own staff or contractor (full time)	Volunteers (part time)★
Time taken (years)	1.2	6
Cost of premises and plant	£18,000	£72,000 (assuming non-availability for other work)
Haulage subcontractor Materials	For this argument, these factors are considered approximately equal and left unquantified	
'Supervision'	£5000	£18,000
Labour at £12 per hour	£60,000	'Free'
'Profit'	£10,000	–
Total	£93,000	£90,000

Assuming volunteers work one day and one evening a week over a 6-year period.

Working exhibits

There is persistent and perhaps increasing pressure from enthusiasts, teachers, the general public and Management Committees to make exhibits more accessible, entertaining or easier to understand by demonstrating them. This may compromise the integrity of objects by exposing them to unnecessary wear and tear or risk from accidental damage or misuse.

The Curator must explore the ethical and logistic arguments before deciding to operate any exhibit. For example, what level of deterioration is likely to occur as a result of the object being operated (see *Figure 38.9*)? What modifications, both temporary and permanent, are necessary to provide a working exhibit? What risks will the museum staff and the general public be exposed to as a result of the operation of the exhibit (see *Figure 38.10*)? What effect will the operation of the artefact have on other exhibits due to, for example, the problems of noise, vibration, omission of heat, water vapour or dust? What statutory regulations exist relating to the operation of the exhibit? Can the requirement for a working exhibit be met without compromising the original artefact, i.e. can a replica or model be used?

Apart from the costs of restoration, and associated capital costs (e.g. building work, services) it is essential to forecast and secure the continuing resources for maintenance and operation. This includes the availability of qualified staff who the museum may have to train. It may be possible to reduce the initial and recurring costs and also make a working exhibit easier to start and stop – an important safety feature – by providing a different means of operation, such as an electric motor, although at the cost of authenticity and 'atmosphere'.

Safety requirements

It can only be a matter of time before a serious accident will occur in a museum as a result of unforeseen and undetected deterioration, metal fatigue, inadequate restoration techniques or faulty operational methods.

Spectacular failures of preserved machinery have already occurred. On at least two occasions, metal fatigue has led to flywheels (and the end of the crankshaft) dropping off an engine travelling on the road. On another occasion a flywheel from a stationary engine worked loose and bowled across a rally field simply because the owner had forgotten to fit the retaining 'key'.

The highest standards must be demanded of the restoration engineer and a 'fail safe' approach be adopted. Similarly, machinery must only be operated by qualified and experienced personnel. Both machines and staff must be subject to regular review, whether or not such inspection is required by law.

Before putting any exhibit into motion, the Curator must determine whether he has done everything reasonably practicable to protect visitors, staff and the exhibit from each other. It must be remembered that many old machines will be below modern safety standards. The requirements of the Health and Safety at Work Act or other legislation do not distinguish between different grades of safety, although the Construction and Use Regulations for Motor Vehicles take the age of a vehicle into account and the Civil Aviation Authority maintenance checks for aircraft take usage into account.

In the writer's experience, Officers of the Health and Safety Executive, Railway Inspectorate, or other statutory bodies, are able to assist museums greatly in these matters. It is rare to find a safety official who

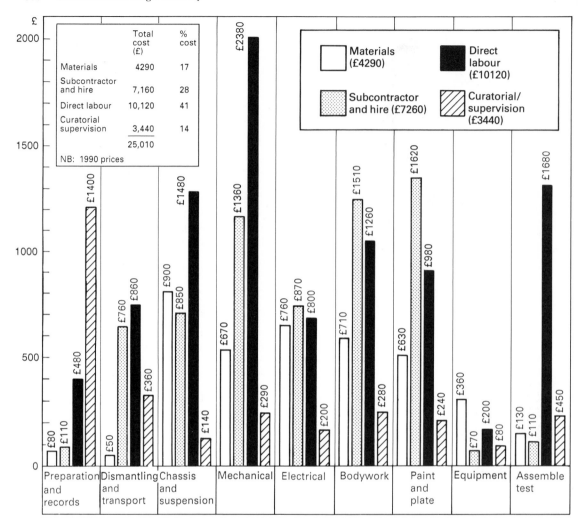

Figure 38.8 Illustration of a breakdown of total costs for restoration, in this case of a Dennis Motor (Fire) Pump, 1941, show variable proportions of costs for individual elements. The proportions will vary for other types of exhibit or restoration project but *Figure 38.8* serves to demonstrate the high cost of 'labour' to 'materials'. The overall cost (£25110) exceeds the current market value of the vehicle

is unwilling to advise on the best designs for unobtrusive guards and barriers. The Curator will ignore such advice at his peril.

Code of operating practice

The safe operation of machinery is generally the subject of statutory legislation or local regulations. Museums with working exhibits should draw up an overall Code of Practice for the operation of working exhibits both within the museum premises and at public events. Separate 'descriptions and working instructions' should be drawn up for individual exhibits. These should provide descriptions of the object, its methods of operation, routine maintenance instructions, a log of maintenance work carried out, together with details of regular inspections.

Operating staff, whether employee or volunteer, must be selected carefully and given thorough training, particularly in safety procedures. A formal test of their competence should be instituted; if necessary, this should be repeated periodically. Ideally, a log-book should be provided in which necessary authority to operate can be recorded and the operator can record relevant information. The

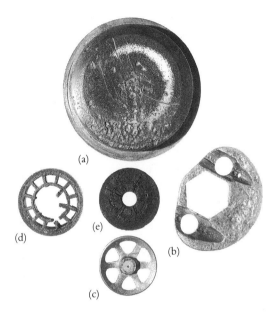

(a)

(d) (e) (b)

(c)

Figure 38.9 Original parts removed from a Steam Fire Engine. (a) Pump end cover showing severe battering due to stones sucked into the pump. Replaced. (b) Locking plate for pump rod nut, showing pitting. There were several fractures. The result if this plate fell into the body of the pump during operation can be left to the reader's imagination. It was replaced for safety reasons. (c) Valve guard – original part with threaded central hole temporarily filled with plaster for use as a pattern to cast replacement parts. (d) Valve seat with central part of grid fractured. A new part was turned and drilled from gunmetal bar. This performs the same function as the original but is obviously a replacement. (e) Rubber valve disc, age hardened. New discs were cut from flexible vulcanized sheet rubber

Figure 38.10 (enlargement) Defective cast gunmetal boiler mounting (the top of a pair for water gauge) which fractured without warning while the boiler was under steam at 8 atmospheres pressure. This fitting had recently been stripped to bare metal for visual examination, tested hydraulically to 12 atmospheres and had been under steam for a total of less than 30 hours. There was no evidence of having received a blow, but the casting (dated 1942 if contemporary with the boiler) had an eccentric steam passage which left one wall very thin. Some insurance companies are now insisting on replacement of boiler mountings that are more than 20 years old

(a)   (b)

Figure 38.11 Pair of defective bolts. (a) Modern cheap steel bolt showing threaded portion separated from the head which was swaged on during manufacture and probably supposed to have been welded. A most unsuitable bolt for any application requiring it to be pulled up to a high torque. (b) Wrought iron nut and bolt *c.* 1898, showing (i) crystalline fracture of the threaded portion of the bolt, and (ii) excessive tension which has caused the thread in the nut to deform so that the whole of the pressure is applied on a thin ring of metal instead of being spread over the whole area of the nut. Apart from this, rounding of the corners of the hexagon is obviously due to the use of an ill-fitting spanner

Curator and person responsible for maintenance must be informed of any variation from normal, such as unusual noises, defects or vibrations.

The instructions (Standing Orders) must be clear and concise, leaving no room for misinterpretation, and be available to all persons concerned.

It is important for the museum to preserve the skills related to operation or maintenance of exhibits, but is impractical to hope that all skills no longer required by our fast-changing industrial society will be enshrined in the museum. On the simplest level, this may be possible. It takes comparatively little retraining for a modern driver to become accustomed to a pre-1940 car or lorry, or to move a traction engine around a rally field. I would question whether this is a reliable indicator of that person's ability to do the real work demanded of the original driver. How much more difficult is it for today's 'demonstrator' to acquire a lifetime's experience of more unusual trades.

Maintenance of working exhibits

It must be recognized that displays involving working exhibits should allow for ease of maintenance, a point often forgotten until a whole display has to be dismantled in order to replace a minor part.

It is an advantage to divide working exhibits into groups using different methods of motive power so that failure in one system need not affect all exhibits.

A planned maintenance programme is a much neglected element of the technical support for museum displays. Such programmes are often considered to be subservient to the 'immediate' needs of an exhibition programme with agreed opening dates. Often routine work is afforded an even lower priority, with an attendant increase in the rate of wear of unoiled or unadjusted machinery and, at worst, a risk of injury due to undetected defects.

Some museums have reduced this problem by dedicating staff solely to the maintenance function or by employing semi-skilled demonstrators specially trained in routine tasks such as cleaning, oiling, minor adjustments and the systematic examination of machines in their charge.

Museum induced deterioration

In museums the most common, unrecognized cause of deterioration of original finishes, or wear on 'brightwork' is improper or over-enthusiastic cleaning and polishing. Highly polished metal surfaces are only achieved by deliberate abrasion. The rate of such damage can be assessed readily by observing the worn surfaces of nameplates on engines or the brass showing through tops of plated car radiators lovingly touched by a generation or two of visitors and attendants.

Large technological exhibits are frequently uncased and, therefore, are subject to mechanical and chemical damage during the daily housekeeping operations in the galleries. Attendants or others entrusted with keeping exhibits and the galleries clean should be instructed in correct methods. The frequent use of wire wool or abrasive papers on brightwork – often the wearing surfaces of machines – is to be deprecated.

Other forms of museum-induced deterioration caused by unstable storage conditions or careless handling should be more readily indentifiable. Much of this deterioration can be minimized by regular inspections.

Storage

A major problem in the storage of museum collections relates to the wide variations in physical dimensions and mass of the objects, together with their environmental requirements. The essential difference between museum stores and commercial warehouses is simply that the latter are set up for the rapid turnover of a limited amount of stock, generally in a limited number of unit sizes.

It is generally agreed that purpose-built stores are more convenient and efficient in terms of security and environmental control. Except in the case of large numbers of objects of similar size, it is difficult

(a)

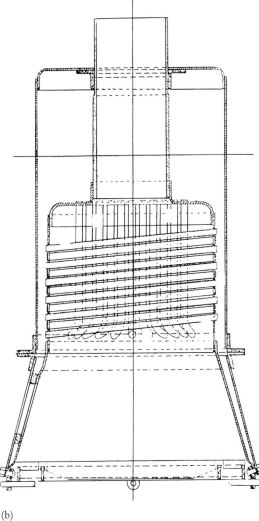

(b)

(c)

Figure 38.12 (a) Merryweather boiler split for annual boiler inspection, showing (i) flanges for steam-tight bolted joints, (ii) bell-mouthed ends of water tubes, and (iii) scale and blotching corrosion of steel boiler plates. (b) Vertical section from maker's patent specification. (c) View of firebox and water tubes coated with soot. Note the many rivet heads and the very narrow spaces between the inner and outer plates of the firebox 'petticoat' where scale, dirt and rust lodge; it is difficult to dry out these spaces completely.

The minimum annual cost, including labour, for dismantling reassembly, materials, survey fees and Public Liability Insurance is estimated at £600 (1992) – even if the boiler is only required to be used once

to devise a single cost-effective museum storage system. Therefore it is advisable for museums to divide the collection into different storage categories and to provide different types of facility for each store. A large object store is not simply a scaled-up version of a small store because distinct advantages may accrue from adopting palletization and providing mechanical handling equipment. This can maximize access and facilitate the safe handling of exhibits while reducing both staff and unit storage costs.

The principles of industrial storage are generally adaptable for museum use. Advice should be sought from independent specialists (such as the Institute of Purchasing and Supply, and the National Materials Handling Centre) rather than the individual manufacturers of equipment. Proper specifications for parking bays, pallet loadings or capacities for pallet, fork-lift and stacker trucks are vital as overloading is dangerous and excess capacity is expensive.

For new buildings consideration should be given to incorporating the workshops adjacent to the store. This has advantages in economic use of plant and may indeed permit the installation of travelling cranes. Also the proximity of conservation and technical staff will predispose to regular reviews of the condition of artefacts in store.

Most of the storage requirements for large exhibits can be met with a minimum headroom of 16 feet (5 m) with an access door of 16 feet × 13 feet (5 m × 4 m). Greater height is needed for large transport objects such as double-decker buses or where mobile cranes may need to be employed within the building. Ground-level premises offer greater floor loadings and convenience of operation. The nature of the floor surfaces will have a great influence on the employment of certain types of handling equipment.

In large exhibit stores the capital cost of installing heavy-duty, adjustable pallet racking together with a fork-lift truck to enable loads to be stored in several tiers, must be balanced against the gain in available floor space and savings in staff costs or plant hire. The careful choice of module size and loading will reduce costs. It should be recognized, however, that without adequate records and the marking of parts it is likely that even large parts may be mislaid during long-term storage through failure to later recognize what they are.

It is unlikely that the environment within a 'large exhibit' store will be satisfactory for all materials. Metal objects need to be kept in an atmosphere of low humidity. Condensate dripping from roofs or joists may fall on the uppermost surface of the objects, usually those most difficult to inspect. Highly polished surfaces (the brightwork or paintwork) on machines are likely to suffer from condensation problems because they may cause local chilling of the air below the dewpoint. Similarly, a microclimate may develop within a machine (or packing case) due to moisture being left in tanks and boilers or collecting in undrained cavities.

Wooden objects suffer shrinkage cracks or glue joints may fail if kept in a dry (or varying humidity) atmosphere. Textiles, such as upholstery and leather are also sensitive to low humidity.

Excessive moisture may cause fungus or mould growth. The environmental conditions for these materials are referred to in the various specialist chapters in this book. However, it should be noted that where these materials are incorporated in a large exhibit it is unlikely that the 'ideal' storage conditions for each material can be achieved. It might be possible to create a suitable microclimate within part of the exhibit, or to set apart an area within the store for more accurate, and costly, environmental control for the more susceptible objects.

If 'waterproof' coverings are used, their manner of use should allow for the full circulation of air. Objects stored on the ground should be raised on waterproof battens to prevent damage by rising damp from concrete floors.

The preparation of exhibits for long-term storage requires expert advice. At the very least an attempt should be made to protect bare metal with grease or commercially available protective barriers (usually varnishes or waxes dissolved in volatile organic solvents). Engine sumps should be drained and filled with appropriate fresh oil. Lubricated parts should be cleaned and relubricated.

Road grit and mud should be cleaned off road vehicles using copious quantities of water and a *small* quantity of detergent before rinsing. After thorough drying, a surface coating such as microcrystalline wax may be thinly applied. Preparations of silicone waxes are to be avoided as they are difficult to remove.

To limit corrosion boilers, pipework, pump chambers and other parts containing water must be emptied thoroughly (see *Figure 38.12*) – including often-forgotten pockets in valve boxes and the like and the space opened to allow free circulation of air. Motor vehicle cooling systems should be drained and refilled with water plus a rust inhibitor. Fireboxes and smokeboxes should be cleaned thoroughly of soot and ashes (which form a corrosive paste when damp) and left open, Packing should be removed from the glands of steam engines.

Wheeled exhibits should ideally be supported to relieve the weight on bearings and springs. If this cannot be done, vehicles should be moved to avoid damage to bearings and also tyres. Rubber tyres cause particular problems due to light energy and oxygen breaking chemical bonds. Similar problems exist for rubber tubing (e.g. in medical or laboratory equipment). An easy solution has yet to be found.

Hydraulic fluid and battery electroyte should be drained; fuel tanks should be drained and flushed to prevent the formation of explosive mixtures.

In the case of heavy machinery displayed or stored in the open air, particular care has to be taken during preparation, even for large machines which spent their working lives in a relatively unprotected environment. They did, of course, receive regular maintenance and daily inspection during use. A simple canopy with roll-down canvas sides is a great advantage for protection against rain, snow and direct sunlight. If this is not possible, it is important to investigate all the means by which water, dirt, birds etc can gain access to partially closed cavities and stop them up or provide a convenient means of cleaning or drainage. These few examples serve to highlight the necessity of obtaining advice on individual objects.

Stored exhibits need to be inspected regularly to detect corrosion or other deterioration and, ideally, machinery should be turned over to assist in preventing seizure of mating components.

Acknowledgements

The Author would like to thank the many Curators, Restorers and Conservators who have made useful suggestions and given help or advice in rewriting this paper. In particular, Dr K. A. Barlow, formerly of the Greater Manchester Museum of Science and Industry, and Mr G. J. Wallis of Dorothea Restorations. All photographs are reproduced by permission of Tyne and Wear Museums Service except for *Figure 38.5*, which is reproduced courtesy of The Greater Manchester Museum of Science and Industry.

References

STORER, J. D. (1989), *The Conservation of Industrial Collections: A Survey*, Science Museum/Museums & Galleries Commission, London

WALLIS, G. (1988) Minutes of Conservation Forum, Science Museum, London

Bibliography

COMPTON, H. K. *Storehouse and Stockyard Management*, Macdonald & Evans, Plymouth

CRANE, F. A. and CHARLES, J. (1984), *Selection and Use of Engineering Materials*, Butterworths, London

HEALTH & SAFETY EXECUTIVE, *Guidelines* (e.g. Locomotive Boilers), HMSO, London

HORIE, C. V. (1989), *Materials for Conservation*, Butterworths, London

MCCONNELL, A. (1976), *Preservation of Technological Material*, Proceedings of a symposium, Science Museum, London

MUNDY, J. and HARRISON (Eds) (1978), *Material Handling, an Introduction*, HMSO, London

NATIONAL PHYSICAL LABORATORY (NATIONAL CORROSION SERVICE), *Guides to Practice*

SCULLY, J. C. (1975), *Fundamentals of Corrosion*, Pergamon Press, Oxford

SHARP, C. (Ed.) (1988), *Kemps Engineers Yearbook*, Morgan Grampian

UKIC/AREA MUSEUMS SERIVCE FOR SOUTH EAST ENGLAND (1984), *Taken into Care*, proceedings of symposium, 26 October 1984, Area Museums Service for South Eastern England

VAN THOOR, T. (1968) *Materials and Technology* (8 vols), Longman/de Bussy

Early works

A great number of important and essential out of print volumes are available from major technical libraries and specialized museums. A few are mentioned below:

BYRNE and SPON (1874), *Dictionary of Engineering*, E & FN Spon, London

CLARK, D. K. (1889), *The Steam Engine* (also *Railway Machinery; Tramways; Gas, Petrol and Oil Engine*), Blackie & Son, Glasgow

FAREY, J. (1827), *Treatise on the Steam Engine*, (reprint by David & Charles), London

FAREY, J. (1914), *Cyclopaedia of Applied Electricity*, American Technical Society

I.C.S. REFERENCE LIBRARY (c. 1920), Many volumes covering technical aspects of industrial technology (e.g. draughting, design, steam engines, mill work, blacksmithing). I.C.S. Ltd, London

KELEHER, T. J. (1941), *Naval Machinery*, US Naval Institute, Annapolis

LINEHAM, W. J. (1894), *Mechanical Engineering*, Chapman & Hall, London

REYNOLDS, M. (1882), *Stationary Engine Driving* (also *Locomotive Engine Driving*), Crosby, Lockwood and Son, London

UNWIN, W. C. and MELLANBY, A. L. (1912), *Elements of Machine Design*, Longmans Green & Son, London

Also the following journals: *Engineering; The Engineer; The Autocar*.

39

Conservation and storage: archaeological material

Elizabeth Pye

The adjective 'archaeological' is often used to describe material of early date, but for the purposes of conservation and storage the significant fact is that archaeological material has been buried or entombed at some time. In this sense the word 'archaeological' may be applied to a wide range of artefacts from all cultures and periods up to the quite recent past.

The effects of burial and excavation

In normal burial conditions – in the presence of oxygen, moisture and micro-organisms – all material will deteriorate to some extent and most organic materials will ultimately deteriorate completely. In certain conditions, however (for example where oxygen is excluded, as in waterlogged contexts), material may be well, or even exceptionally well, preserved. During burial, artefacts tend to achieve an equilibrium with their environment and the deterioration rate, which may have been fast at first, may slow down appreciably.

Unfortunately, however, the effect of excavation is to change the environment suddenly and completely, with the result that the deterioration rate speeds up considerably. Not only is the chemical and biological environment changed, but the physical support provided by the surrounding soil is removed. Many objects are too weak to bear their own weight and cannot survive normal handling. Unless proper conservation measures are taken on the site, excavation can be a very damaging process.

Although it is not alway possible for a conservator to be present on site at all times, planning and liaison between archaeologist, curator and conservator should ensure that all fragile, fragmentary or particularly sensitive material is prepared correctly for, and given adequate support during excavation. It should then be packed in a way which minimizes the 'shock' caused by excavation and removal from

the site. In some cases this may be achieved by packing which simulates the burial environment.

The condition of excavated material

The condition of excavated material is dependent on many factors including handling during and after excavation. Unnecessary touching, and on-site cleaning may be very damaging to artefacts and may result in the loss of valuable evidence. Condition is also dependent on the conservation care the material has received and whether it has been continuous or was undertaken some time after excavation as a 'rescue' measure. Condition also depends on where and when the material was excavated. Archaeological material in British museums comes either from this country or from overseas: for example, Egyptian artefacts are likely to include a high proportion of dry organic materials and exhibit problems unlike those of many British assemblages.

Material excavated in the past

Unconserved, excavated material will eventually achieve some equilibrium with its environment: it may survive reasonably intact or may disintegrate in the process of achieving this equilibrium. Material which has been excavated and treated in the past may be in a worse condition than similar untreated material, since many early conservation treatments involved the use of substances or methods now known to be unsatisfactory.

Recently excavated material

Some recently excavated objects reach the museum after receiving only 'first aid' in the field and unless promptly treated, they will deteriorate very quickly. If a fragile artefact is encased in plaster of Paris or polyurethane foam to give it support during excavation and simply left in store, it is likely to disintegrate inside the jacket. Waterlogged material may reach the museum after temporary wet packing. If it cannot be treated immediately it will need constant monitoring and possibly repacking to ensure that it does not dry out or give rise to the growth of algae or micro-organisms. Untreated material may arrive in unsuitable packaging such as tobacco tins, brown paper envelopes and cotton wool and will need examination and repacking as soon as possible.

Ideally, where liaison between archaeologist, conservator and curator is effective, recently excavated material should have been properly conserved to an agreed level, packed in suitable containers and should arrive with full instructions for storage.

Once a museum accepts a collection of archaeological material, provision must be made for controlled storage and long-term conservation. In whatever condition the objects reach the museum, they should be received, assessed and thereafter monitored by a qualified conservator who will advise on conservation and storage and carry out treatment.

Conservation Part I: aims, records, examination, selection

Aims of conservation

The aim of conservation is to prolong the life of the material. Two factors are particularly important: first, action at the time of excavation, or as soon as possible afterwards, to counter the likely increase in deterioration, and second, meticulous examination before and during treatment to establish the function of the objects, how they were made, and how they were affected by burial and excavation.

Objects are prepared for handling, drawing, study, publication and display. These different requirements involve different levels of conservation including the removal of accretions and/or chemical and physical stabilization. Correct storage is essential, and is sometimes referred to as 'passive conservation'. This is, in fact, the main type of conservation which much archaeological material receives.

The limitations of conservation treatment

Although methods of treatment are improving all the time, many of the substances employed, such as adhesives and consolidants, do not possess all the properties desirable for conservation use or the ultimate survival of the object. Conservators agree that, ideally, all treatments should be reversible. This is sometimes difficult to achieve because some substances may not remain reversible, and the artefacts may be endangered by attempts to remove them. Accelerated ageing tests can provide some indication of the likely long-term behaviour of conservation materials, but all treatments need monitoring to assess their effectiveness on the artefacts themselves. For these reasons conservators also agree that the minimum of treatment should be undertaken, in other words objects should be changed as little as possible.

The role of the conservator

On site and in the museum, the informed archaeologist or curator can deal with most preliminary conservation care, and may also undertake first-aid procedures when a conservator is not available or after an emergency such as flood or fire. However, it is essential that a conservator should be consulted, and should undertake any full conservation treatment. Intervention by the more inexperienced in conservation can cause irreparable damage or the loss of valuable information.

Records

Full records are essential. Recording should begin on site and the record should accompany the object or be readily accessible at all times. All necessary information should accompany the object from site to store or laboratory. The record should provide concise information about the object in the ground, including archaeological context, soil conditions and associated material, its condition when excavated, the method of lifting it, and first-aid procedures. The complete record should include methods and results of examination, reasons for level of treatment chosen, unambiguous information on treatments themselves and recommendations for handling, packaging, storage and display. The written record should be augmented with drawings, photographs, radiographs and analytical reports.

Precise details of all substances used must be recorded. These should include both chemical and trade names, and any distinguishing numbers which indicate a particular property such as grade or molecular weight. Other information about solution strengths and duration of treatment should be equally precise.

The use of records

There are two major uses for conservation records. Firstly, the information yielded during microscopic examination and cleaning is vital for the understanding of the artefacts and is therefore of great importance to archaeologist, curators and students. Secondly, the information enables conservators to assess the effectiveness of treatments and provides a basis for the choice of further treatment. Where an early treatment has failed, the record may help to avoid unnecessry investigation before further treatment. Good records are important aids in archaeological and conservation research, and ensure the safety of the object.

Methods of keeping records
Records should be standardized and should cover all aspects of the information (including photographs and radiographs).

Information retrieval
It is desirable to retrieve the information under a number of headings so that the conservator can, for example, find the treatment already given to an object, or its storage conditions. Conservation and curatorial records should be cross-referenced so that *all* the information on an object is accessible to both conservator and curator. The increasing use of computerized record systems is very helpful here.

Examination

Examination is part of the care of an object. It is essential in deciding on the level of conservation to employ; and it must take place at every stage of treatment. Much archaeological material is in fact subject to closer scrutiny during conservation than at any other time and this is why the conservation record contains much essential technological and archaeological information.

When dealing with a complex object on site the conservator may use simple visual examination and cautious investigative cleaning to establish its type and condition and to decide on lifting and handling methods. Inspection for shape, size, colour, surface texture and accretions can be useful and, if the object can be handled safely, an estimation of its weight can sometimes give information on its condition. A small magnet may be used to estimate the extent of metallic iron remaining in an object. This type of examination will be repeated during the selection process, but once an object is in the conservation laboratory, more sophisticated examination methods can be used. During examination, handling should be minimized by packaging methods which allow a large part of the object to be seen without touching or removing it from the container.

The binocular microscope
A binocular microscope providing magnifications of × 10 to × 30 allows the conservator to examine in detail the surface of an object and small fragments of associated material, such as textile fibres, which are not clearly distinguishable with the naked eye. The microscope is also used during investigative cleaning, particularly of metal objects. Here, the partial

removal of accretions may reveal information not only about the accretions themselves but also about the surface of the object.

Radiography
In some cases the object, or group of objects, may be an amorphous mass or may reveal insufficient information about its structural components. Radiography, may provide some of the answers. Normally, industrial equipment in the 80–110 kV range is the most suitable, but medical equipment can give reasonable results if skillfully used. Careful selection of position and exposure will increase the amount of information gained but further cleaning and further use of radiography may be necessary before the maximum possible detail is revealed.

Radiographs of iron objects are essential (they are extremely useful in the case of other metal objects) before selection for treatment. They may reveal the extent of deterioration and clarify the shape of the object (*Figure 39.1*). They may also provide other very important information about metal objects such as the surface detail on coins, evidence of organic materials preserved in corrosion products, and indication of methods of construction or repair. They may be equally useful on non-metallic or composite objects in revealing, for example, structural details of wooden objects, traces of metallic or other ornaments on organic materials and the remains of cores in cast metal objects. Radiographs have proved to be essential guides for the cleaning and elucidation of intricate objects such as inlaid buckles or strap ornaments.

Chemical and physical analysis
The conservator may employ simple chemical tests to establish, for example, the nature of a white metal decoration or of the salts on ceramics or stone, or of pigments or other coloured deposits. Whenever possible the help of the archaeological scientist will be enlisted in the application of X-ray fluorescence or other physical methods to provide further information on corrosion products and similar substances, or to confirm the results of the chemical tests.

Results and limitations of examination
Detailed examination produces useful technological evidence and provides essential information without which it is not safe to start a treatment. There are, however, limitations on the sensitivity of all the examination methods, and interpretation of results relies heavily on the training and experience of the conservator.

Selection and levels of conservation

Many archaeological sites yield large amounts of material from which a selection must be made for

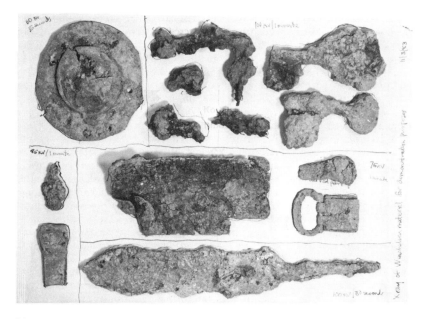

(a)

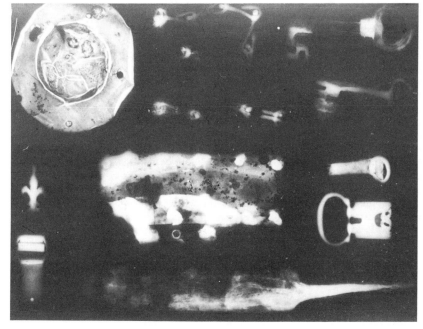

(b)

Figure 39.1 (a) A group of corroded iron objects laid out in preparation for routine radiography. (b) The radiograph revealing details of form and construction. (By courtesy of the Institute of Archaeology, University College, London)

treatment. Different objects will recieve different levels of conservation. The selection is governed by the needs of the objects themselves and the requirements of the archaeologist, curator and conservator.

In most cases only a small proportion of the objects will be fully treated and only a very few will go on display. However, much of the material will be studied and drawn for publication and as it will form part of the site archive, it is necessary for each distinguishable item to be given at least the basic conservation care of examination, recording and proper storage.

Criteria used in selection
The criteria used for selection may be archaeological, curatorial or conservation ones. Some objects such as coins are of particular significance to the site, and need prompt attention. Some objects may be needed for immediate display to promote local interest in the site, and other may be so sensitive to environmental change that they must be treated immediately. Large quantities of similar material must be sorted into various categories, and here radiography should be routine, particularly for iron.

Levels of conservation
Some material will simply be stored, some will need clarification before drawing, and some will need full treatment possibly including restoration. In *Conservation Guidelines No. 1: Excavated Artefacts for Publication: UK Sites*, the Archaeology Section of the United Kingdom Institute for Conservation distinguishes five possible levels of treatment from *no conservation* (merely involving handling and checking) through *minimal, partial,* and *full* conservation to *display-standard conservation* which includes photography, radiography, examination, investigation, cleaning, stabilization, reconstruction and restoration, including cosmetic treatment.

Selection of material excavated in the past
In the case of large amounts of material from past excavations, a similar selection, undertaken by curator and conservator, will be necessary, but may be complicated by the effects of early treatments or the absence of records. Some material will require priority treatment because the earlier treatment has failed or become actively damaging or because storage or display conditions have been unsuitable.

Conservation Part II: handling, packaging and storage

Introduction

The following section deals with the packaging and storage of material from land sites. Material from marine sites is considered to be a separate and special category which is covered in *First Aid for Marine Finds* (Robinson, 1981). Further details on packaging and storage methods can be found in the *Guidelines* (Nos. 2 and 3) prepared by the Archaeology Section of the United Kingdom Institute for Conservation (UKIC).

Handling

Handling during examination, selection and in preparation for packing should be kept to a minimum. Apart from the physical dangers, fingers may deposit moisture and salts which encourage corrosion on metals. Unnecessary exposure to the air and to micro-organisms may lead to deterioration of organic materials. The ideal is to pack objects so that they are easily visible without handling.

Small objects are sometimes more safely handled with delicate flexible forceps (or vacuum tweezers) than with the fingers. Large objects should be cradled with both hands, wearing protective cotton or surgical plastic gloves when necessary, and should be carried on a padded tray or trolley after enlisting aid in opening doors. Objects on the conservation bench should not be touched or lifted without first ascertaining from the conservator that it is safe to do so.

Packaging

Packaging should provide physical, chemical and biological protection, should allow the object to be examined easily, and should be informative and durable. Packaging materials should be, as far as possible, inert and should not cause physical damage.

Containers
Each object should be in a container which provides physical protection and supported by firm shock-absorbing padding. If more than one object are packed together each should be clearly separated from the next, and padding should prevent damage caused by knocking or rolling together. Small objects may be packed in individual boxes or bags which are then grouped in larger boxes.

Padding should be positioned below and around the object and a final pad placed above (*Figure 39.2(a)–(c)*). This provides complete support while allowing the object(s) to be examined easily by lifting off the final pad. Wrapping or winding in paper is unsuitable as it obscures artefacts and may cause damage or loss during unpacking.

Where necessary, a purpose-built container should be used with a well made in the padding of exactly the size and shape to hold the object (*Figure 39.2(d)* and (*e*)). A large object in a deep container may be provided with a sling which passes

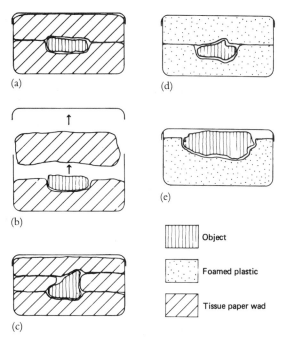

(a)

(b)

(c)

(d)

(e)

	Object
	Foamed plastic
	Tissue paper wad

Figure 39.2 Padding. (a) Use of a tissue-paper wad beneath and another above an object. The wads can be 'moulded' into the shape of the object. (b) The wad above can be lifted off, allowing easy access to the object. (c) An awkwardly shaped object can rest on one wad and be surrounded by others with a final wad placed above. (d) A well, made in the padding, of exactly the shape to take the object. In this case, foamed plastic is used, and a second piece, also cut to shape, is used to cover the object. (e) An object resting in a well cut into foamed plastic and held securely in position by the lid of the box. Where a clear plastic box is used, this method allows viewing of the object without opening the box

underneath it and helps to take its weight when lifting it out. This is safer than grasping part of the object. Otherwise, a container should be designed with one side that folds down or lifts off, exposing the full height of the object.

Packaging materials
Clear plastic boxes (which are better then even good-quality cardboard boxes) with inert foamed plastic sheet or acid-free tissue paper padding should be used to provide maximum protection. Some foamed plastics degrade easily and may give off undesirable breakdown products. Most low-grade paper, including newspaper, coloured tissue and toilet paper, may give off acids. Cotton wool may catch in, and damage, fragile surfaces. It is safer to use wads made of acid-free tissue paper (*Figure 39.3*) unless a reliable foamed plastic is available. Cotton wool may be used provided it is separated from the object, e.g. by acid-free tissue paper.

Boxes, bags
The following could be used:

> small clear polystyrene snap-shut boxes,
> polythene boxes with self-seal lids (various sizes), or
> polythene bags (self-sealing).

'Tailor-made' bags may be made from polythene tube or sheet with the aid of a heat sealer.

Padding
Acid-free tissue paper wads may be used for dry packaging. The following types of inert foamed plastic sheet may be used with both wet and dry material:

> polyethylene (Polythene) foam,
> polyether foam, or
> expanded polystyrene.

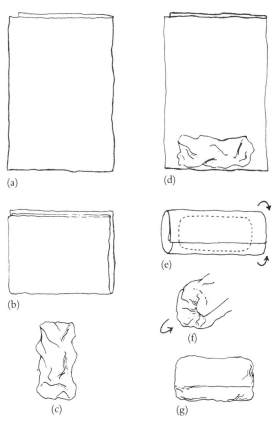

(a)

(b)

(c)

(d)

(e)

(f)

(g)

Figure 39.3 How to make a tissue paper wad. (a) and (b) A sheet of tissue paper of the required size is doubled and then folded again. (c) The folded tissue is rolled and very slightly compressed to form a crumpled pad. (d) and (e) The pad is then rolled in a single or double sheet of tissue. (f) The ends of the outer sheet are tucked in neatly around the pad. (g) A smooth and resilient cushion of tissue paper results

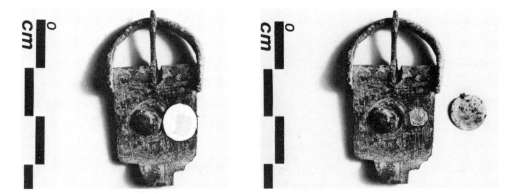

Figure 39.4 (a) A copper alloy buckle to which a self-adhesive label has been attached. (b) After removal of the label, a patch of corrosion is revealed beneath, indicating that chemical damage has been caused or exacerbated (such labels will also endanger fragile surfaces) (Copyright, Velson Horie)

Labelling

Clear and efficient labelling is necessary. Objects should be labelled with an identifying number. Methods of labelling should be agreed by archaeologist, curator and conservator since they depend on the type and condition of the objects.

Robust objects may have a label attached loosely in an appropriate position, but the knot should be firm. On no account should the string cut into the surface of a fragile object; wide strips of lightweight polythene sheet may be used as a less damaging alternative. Labels should not be stuck directly onto objects and self-adhesive labels should never be used as the adhesive may stain or damage the object (*Figure 39.4*) and be difficult to remove.

The best way to guarantee that the label does not become detached is to write the relevant information directly onto the object in Indian ink. This method is suitable only for certain materials and should be fully discussed with the conservator.

Packaging should be labelled durably both inside and out, giving an identifying number, an indication of which way up the container should be held and stored, the number and description of objects or parts of objects, type of material, instructions for unpacking, and instructions for storage and monitoring of conditions.

Wet material stored in a sealed polythene bag may have an inert label sealed in with it together with a second label sealed into a separate compartment (*Figure 39.5*).

Labelling materials

All materials used including labels, string and ink should be durable. Labels of spun bonded polyethylene (polythene) which looks like paper are particularly suitable because they can be used successfully with wet materials. Ideally, the label attached in the field should be large enough to allow

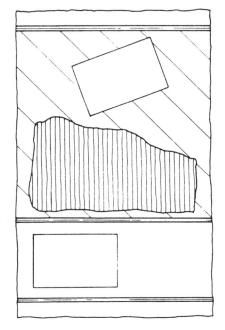

Water

Object

Figure 39.5 A waterlogged object sealed in a polythene bag. An inert label is sealed in the bag with the object. As a safeguard against water damage a second label is sealed in a separate dry section of the bag (this two-compartment system provides a useful means of holding a label in position on any polythene packaging; it also protects the label from dirt)

the later addition of museum and laboratory information. String should be durable (for example made of terylene, such as blind cord), strips of polythene sheet are a useful alternative, rubber bands should not be used. Ink should be resistant to water and the effects of light. Good quality, spirit-based waterproof permanent markers or good quality ball-point pens should be used.

Packaging to control the environment
If packaging is judiciously chosen it can be used to prevent decay of material. The climate within the package may be dry, desiccated, damp or wet.

Dry or desiccated packaging
Because of the danger of condensation, sealed containers cannot be used for dry packaging unless the object is thoroughly dry before enclosure. Some sensitive materials must be desiccated rather than just dry, and in this case a desiccant such as silica gel must

be included in the package. Silica gel absorbs moisture efficiently until it is saturated, after which it is no longer effective and must be dried out (regenerated). Self-indicating silica gel has a colour indicator which shows when the gel is dry (bright blue) and when it is saturated (pink). The gel is regenerated by heating gently at 120–130°C until the blue colour returns.

The amount of silica gel included should equal one-fifth to one-tenth of the volume of the object(s). It should be placed in the package in a perforated bag or container so that it can be removed easily for regeneration (*Figure 39.6(a)* and *(b)*): it should never be used loose or in direct contact with objects. If the bag is placed at one end of a polythene box any colour change should be clearly visible even if several boxes are stacked together (*Figure 39.6(e)*). Where several polythene bags containing objects are to be packed inside a large box each bag should be perforated with holes of 2 mm or more in diameter

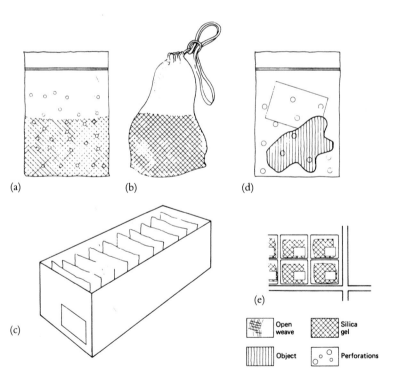

(a)   (b)   (d)

(c)   (e)

| Open weave | Silica gel |
| Object | Perforations |

Figure 39.6 The use of silica gel in packaging. (a) A perforated Polythene bag containing silica gel, probably the simplest way to include the gel in a package. (b) An open-weave bag containing silica gel; the weave must be open enough to allow adequate air circulation. If the bag is made of heat-resistant material there is no need to remove the gel from the bag for regeneration. (c) A box containing several objects each in a polythene bag. A single bag of

silica gel may be used, provided that the bags within the main box are perforated (see (d)). (d) An individual object housed in a perforated polythene bag. To ensure adequate air circulation there should be plenty of large holes, preferably larger than 2 mm diameter. (e) Self-indicating silica gel visible through the ends of plastic boxes stacked in a storage area and one batch of silica gel placed in the sealed box (*Figure 39.6(c)* and (*d*)). Alternatively, it is possible to use relative humidity indicator cards or strips in conjunction with non-indicating silica gel, but the strips can be difficult to read accurately.

This type of desiccation is possible for long-term packaging only if it is monitored regularly.

Damp or wet packaging

Different methods must be adopted when storing damp or wet materials. Not only must the damp conditions be maintained, but microbiological growth and other undesirable changes, for example in the degree of acidity or alkalinity of the storage water, must be prevented. This type of packaging is suitable for short-term duration.

Well-sealed polythene boxes or several layers of sealed polythene bags will help to maintain wet conditions. Flexible foamed plastic may be used as a 'reservoir' by thoroughly wetting it before including it as padding in the package. The exclusion of oxygen will also reduce the rate of deterioration.

Low temperatures, the exclusion of light and the use of a biocide when absolutely necessary, will deter microbiological growth. As an alternative to the use of biocides, material may be refrigerated (*not* frozen), and this will slow down other changes.

The efficiency of packing methods depends on storage in controlled conditions. This needs constant monitoring by trained personnel.

Storage

The importance of protection from physical, chemical and biological deterioration has been mentioned. Well-designed packaging methods provide a great deal of protection but will fail if storage conditions are unsuitable. One of the difficulties in storing archaeological material is the large volume of space needed, and many museums have been forced to make use of unsuitable areas. Poor storage conditions may cause valuable archaeological evidence to be lost from some objects while others may deteriorate completely.

The storage area

Storage areas should be designed or modified to maintain desired conservation conditions. The room should be structurally sound, dry and clean. Lifts, passages and doors should be of reasonable size and situated so that trolleys and large containers can be brought in easily. If should be possible to restrict access, and the stores should not be used as a through-route. It should not be near a heating system since this may bring fluctuating temperatures, undesirable fumes, and flooding. It should also be remote from sources of vibration.

Storage conditions

Well-designed storage areas and good packaging will prolong the life of many objects. The standard store should be used for materials such as ceramics and stone which do not need stringently regulated conditions. Each object is well packed but the climate within the package is not individually controlled. The sensitive store should be used for materials such as certain metals, glass and dry organic material, which require more strictly controlled conditions.

Some materials, such as many metals, and ivory require special microclimates and here the conditions in the individual packages are controlled; for example iron can be kept very dry using silica gel.

Where there are large quantities of material such as iron which need precisely the same special conditions, separate cabinets or sealed tents (or separate storage areas) may be controlled to the right humidity levels using equipment such as dehumidifiers, thus obviating the need for individually controlled packages. In this case the objects must be packed in a way which allows the air to reach them.

The standard store

To attain a suitable climate for general storage, certain factors must be controlled. The factors which are most crucial are relative humidity (RH), temperature, light (considered also as a source of heat), micro-organisms, dust, dirt and pollutant gases.

Relative humidity

Relative humidity levels in the store and in the packages are dependent on temperature and this will be affected not only by the heating but also by the lighting system and the impact of sunlight. Fluctuations and extremes of RH are damaging, and it should not rise above 70 per cent for more than 10 per cent of the time. A stable level of 65 per cent RH is preferable. Generous amounts of acid-free tissue paper padding help to buffer objects against rapid fluctuations in RH.

Temperature

Temperature is chiefly important for its effect on the relative humidity and to some extent on micro-organism growth. Again, extremes and fluctuations may be damaging and in the standard store the temperature should never be outside the range 4–30°C and should lie preferably between 10°C and 25°C with no more than a daily movement of ±5°C.

Light

Sunlight should be screened out completely. Visible and ultraviolet light can cause breakdown of organic materials and fading of some paints, dyes and inks. Objects which are covered or enclosed in opaque packing will be protected from light but the packing materials and labels may suffer. Ultraviolet filters should be used on fluorescent lamps.

Insects, fungi, micro-organisms

Airborne micro-organisms are difficult to control without an efficient filtering system but they (and insects and fungi) will be deterred by clean, dry (below 65 per cent RH), well-ventilated conditions. Where there is a particular danger of algal or fungal growth cool, dark, dry and well-ventilated conditions are deterrent. Infestations such as furniture beetle or dry rot affecting the building spread readily to shelving, packing and objects.

Dust, dirt and pollutant gases

Dust and dirt are undesirable because they give rise to, or encourage, deterioration and because the repeated cleaning of objects is damaging. Filtering systems can be used to exclude much such pollution, but proper packaging provides good protection. Pollutant gases are difficult to exclude from storage areas.

The sensitive store

Sensitive material should be stored in more stringently controlled conditions. The relative humidity should lie between 45 and 60 per cent, preferably between 50 and 60 per cent, with very little variation. The temperature should be between 15°C and 25°C with a gradual daily movement of only ±5°C. All daylight should be excluded and ultraviolet filters used on fluorescent lamps. All objects should be boxed; open storage is permissible only if dust filters are in use.

It should be noted that, ideally, the conditions in both the standard store and the sensitive store should be even more closely controlled than is suggested here. The figures given above represent levels and ranges which it should be possible to achieve and maintain in museum storage.

Monitoring of storage conditions

The regular monitoring and recording of conditions and the cleaning and inspection of storage areas are essential. The stored objects should be examined regularly by a conservator who can then advise on any necessary changes of the storage arrangements.

Conservation Part III: treatment

Cleaning

Almost all objects will be at least partially cleaned during initial investigation and further cleaning will depend on the level of conservation chosen.

The term 'cleaning' covers a number of different processes including the removal of accretions from corroded metals, the removal of dirt and stains from poorly stored material, the washing of archaeological textiles or of waterlogged wooden artefacts. Cleaning is an essential part of conservation as it can help not only to reveal evidence but also to preserve it. For example, the removal of salts from some metals or ceramics may halt rapid deterioration, and the removal of dust, dirt and spores from organic objects may minimize the development or spread of mould or fungal attack. On the other hand, cleaning destroys some types of evidence (the nature of corrosion, or adhering soils or organic substances) and all such materials must be thoroughly investigated and fully recorded. Details of the cleaning method used and observations made in the process must be included in the conservation record.

Cleaning is a highly skilled part of the Archaeological conservator's job, calling for careful judgement in the selection and manipulation of tools or chemicals. It is not a simple process. Indiscriminate cleaning, or over-cleaning, can result in loss of evidence and in damage to the objects. Part of the skill is knowing when to stop. Sometimes objects which have been cleaned by an experienced conservator may appear 'unfinished' to the lay eye but the conservator has stopped at a certain point, knowing that further cleaning could be damaging. In short, cleaning should *reveal* evidence, not remove it.

Almost all conservation techniques can be harmful if used incorrectly or applied inappropriately. Simple washing may remove slips or paint from pottery or cause low-fired or unfired material to disintegrate. Washing, particularly if it involves the use of unsuitable detergents or other cleaning agents, can remove or obscure evidence of tannins and dyes in leathers and textiles; unskilled mechanical cleaning may remove the surface and detail from a coin. Only a trained, experienced conservator should undertake the cleaning of archaeological material.

Stabilization

The conservator uses particular treatments and makes recommendations in order to keep archaeological material stable. Stabilization is not a 'one-off' process, although certain individual treatments may be called stabilization treatments. Correct handling, packaging and storage or display methods are – in general – more important than any other aspect of stabilization and are essential before, during and after laboratory treatment. In most cases, the treatment used by the conservator is not fully effective unless supported by good storage or display conditions.

Most laboratory stabilization can be divided into four categories:

(1) The strengthening of weakened objects, such as the consolidation of fragile ceramics, or the joining and backing of wall-plaster fragments.

(2) Removal of substances or organisms in the objects which cause deterioration. This includes the removal of water-soluble salts from ceramics, or salts causing corrosion of metals or micro-organisms in organic materials.

(3) Inhibition or prevention of certain chemical or other reactions by the use of corrosion inhibitors, insect or fungal repellants.

(4) Control of one or more environmental factors such as by lacquering metals to limit access of oxygen, moisture or pollutant gases.

There are considerable variations in the methods used within these categories, and some methods cannot be fitted into them at all. The treatment of waterlogged organic materials such as wood and leather must effect the removal of the water without the structural collapse of the object. It can also involve the introduction of an agent which bonds chemically with the deteriorated structure and gives mechanical strength. The treatment of composite objects is also difficult to categorize. Where both inorganic and organic parts of an object survive it is difficult to choose a suitable treatment.

As far as possible, stabilization treatments should be reversible. Sometimes, however, the condition of the object or the limitations of the treatment mean that a method cannot be considered reversible.

Restoration

Restoration, in the sense of reinstatement, may be considered part of the process of revealing archaeological and technological evidence. Restoration, in the sense of repairing or replacing missing parts in an attempt to regain the original state of an object, may increase its strength but may go further than conservation in the strict sense.

Restoration is often necessary to prepare an object for use in teaching or display. Where the original shape or purpose of an object is not clear, the conservator will discuss the problem with the curator before attempting restoration.

A restored feature should be shaped or modelled as accurately as possible, but a restoration should be neither invisible nor glaringly obvious. Archaeological evidence of use, breakage, repair and burial should not be obscured by producing too perfect a restoration. The colour and texture of restored areas should approximate to those of the original, but not match them. It should be possible for anyone at a distance of 10–15 cm to see which parts are original and which are restored. Yet it should be possible to appreciate the object as a whole at a distance of 1 m.

The methods and materials used in restoration must be just as carefully chosen by the conservator as those used in stabilization treatments as they can also be potentially damaging. They should be reversible as far as possible. This is important for the welfare of the object and because the interpretation of shape and form in archaeological objects changes. The methods and materials used and the evidence on which the restoration is based, must be included in the conservation record. Where a large amount of restoration is necessary to make an object 'presentable', it is sometimes preferable to make a facsimile for display rather than to endanger the original.

Display

Archaeological objects which have been conserved, restored and prepared for display must still be considered to be fragile and potentially unstable. The conservator should advise on suitable conditions for displaying archaeological material and should be fully involved at the earliest stages and throughout the process of exhibition design. Failure to make suitable provision for the well-being of the objects from the start may necessitate extensive modification of the exhibition design at a later (and expensive) stage.

Environmental conditions in display cases should be as rigorously controlled as those in storage areas and particular regard should be given to the effects of both light and heat within the display case. Methods of mounting should be carefully chosen so that no stress is placed on potentially fragile objects; for example suspension from nylon thread can be very damaging. Materials used in the construction of display cases such as woods, adhesives and sealing strips and in the display itself, such as textile backings or paints, should be thoroughly tested in order to avoid those which may be chemically harmful. The condition of the object on display should be monitored regularly by the conservator.

The care of archaeological materials

Introduction

The care of archaeological materials falls into four main groups:

(1) porous materials (ceramics, stone, plaster, mosaics);
(2) glass;
(3) metals; and
(4) organic materials (wood, leather, bone and ivory, and textiles).

Emphasis is placed on monitoring and care of archaeological material in display or in store. Each section concludes with a brief summary of the changes or signs that indicate active deterioration and urgent need for conservation treatment. Although the special problems of marine material are not discussed specifically most of what is said here is applicable. Before conservation treatment, all such material must be stored *wet*. For further information see *First Aid for Marine Finds* (Robinson, 1981).

Porous materials: ceramics

In general, ceramics, including brick and tile, are considered to be reasonably stable and not to need special conditions of storage or display. However, many archaeological ceramics, particularly pots, are highly porous, fragile and affected by burial conditions.

Handling of ceramics

Pots which appear to be whole should be handled carefully using both hands to encircle the body. They should not be picked up by the rim or by a handle as the fabric may be weak or earlier repairs may have failed. Adhesives and gap-filling materials can become brittle and shrink away from the pot. Plaster of Paris, often used as a gap filler can be broken or chipped. When an object is dirty it is often difficult to distinguish areas of weakness or early repairs.

Ceramics after long-term storage or display

Archaeological ceramics which have been stored or exhibited for some time may be badly affected by greasy dirt and dust which are easily absorbed into their porous surfaces. They may even show signs of mould growth (which can cause particularly resistant stains). Ordinary washing is not advisable as it can cause stains to spread and deepen, and water soluble adhesives to dissolve. Adhesives can become unsightly with age and may even be damaging (an unsuitably strong adhesive can cause considerable damage to the edges of porous sherds) (*Figure 39.7*).

Much early material, for example Neolithic or Bronze Age pots, was fired at low temperatures and is thus likely to be weak, friable and badly affected by water. On material fired at a higher temperature paint, slips or glazes may be flaking or coming away from the surface of the ceramic either because of faults in composition or manufacture or because of the effects of burial. In the case of ceramics from marine sites or from arid areas this type of damage is particularly likely to be caused by the presence of water-soluble salts (which may be visible in the form of fine crystals) (*Figures 39.8* and *39.9*). Occasionally, apparently similar damage may be caused by an earlier treatment which has failed (*Figure 39.10*). All such material should be handled very carefully, should not be washed and should be conserved as soon as possible. Where water-soluble salts are suspected, carefully controlled storage conditions help to prevent further damage before treatment can be undertaken.

Recently excavated ceramics

Recently excavated ceramics may be sent to the museum after washing, marking and packing on site. It is as well to make sure that the material is properly dry (any further drying should take place in cool,

Figure 39.7 The adhesive applied to these sherds is stronger than the pot itself, the failure of the joins has resulted in thin slivers of ceramic being pulled away from the break-edges. (Courtesy of Institute of Archaeology, University College London)

Figure 39.8 Damage in the form of loosened flakes and pitted surface caused by water-soluble salts. The salt crystals are visible only as patches of whitish 'bloom' (approximately ×2 reduced by ⅗ in reproduction), (Courtesy of Institute of Archaeology, University College London)

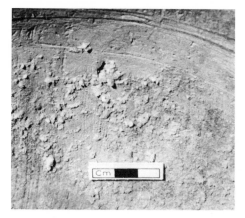

Figure 39.9 Large salt crystals and consequent damage on the inside of a pot. (Copyright Kathryn Tubb)

well-ventilated conditions; heat should never be used) and that the packaging is durable, protective and well-labelled. Paper bags, used for packing loose sherds, are not suitable for long-term storage. Sherds may be packed in linen bags or in well-perforated polythene bags; fragile sherds should be packed between pads of acid-free tissue paper, or foamed plastic sheet, in strong cardboard or polythene boxes.

If necessary, well-fired robust sherds can be washed carefully in regular changes of clean tapwater plus one or two drops of non-ionic detergent and using soft brushes (those with nylon bristles should be avoided). Care should be taken not to scrub the surfaces or edges too vigorously; detergent (if used) should be rinsed off and drying should again take place in cool, well-ventilated conditions.

Storage of ceramics
Treated ceramics, and those showing no active deterioration, can be housed in the standard store. Material which is suffering from the effects of water-soluble salts should be conserved as soon as possible; in the meantime it should be maintained at the relative humidity it has become 'used to'. Fluctuations in relative humidity are most likely to cause further damage. Early or low-fired ceramics (normally excavated in a block of surrounding soil) must be kept damp. All such material should be stored only temporarily and conserved as soon as possible as should any object which has been consolidated in the field or provided with a polyurethane foam or plaster jacket.

Figure 39.10 Extensive damage on a pot probably caused by a combination of water-soluble salts and the application of a coating. Rather than halting the damage, the coating has made the situation much worse (approximately ×1.5, reduced by ⅘ in reproduction). (Courtesy of Institute of Archaeology, University College London)

Porous materials: stone

Porous stone such as some limestones, sandstone and marbles may exhibit many of the same problems as porous ceramics. The stone may be friable, dirty, affected by water-soluble salts or mould growth and suffering from the effects of earlier treatment. Non-porous stones such as flint or granite develop fewer problems.

Handling

Stone artefacts should be fully supported and handled with care as cracks and weak areas may not be immediately apparent. Large and heavy items may be much weaker then they appear and may be difficult and dangerous to lift without proper equipment and experience. Protective padding (for example foamed plastic sheet) may be necessary when lifting or carrying an awkward-shaped object as may a purpose-built container for transport.

Stone after long-term storage or display

The surface of stone artefacts may be dirty and flaking and such objects should be touched as little as possible (*Figure 37.11*). They should be examined for signs of water-soluble salts, moulds and for traces of paint, gilding and so on. A small soft brush (for example a squirrel or sable hair water-colour brush) and a magnifying glass (× 10 magnification) can be useful when examining the surface, but great care

Figure 39.11 Dust and dirt on a stone object, which may conceal both traces of paint and a very fragile surface. (Courtesy of Institute of Archaeology, University College London)

must be taken not to dislodge flakes of paint or stone (*Figure 39.12*).

General cleaning should be avoided, particularly if paint or other decoration is visible or if the surface is deteriorating. Stone artefacts should not be wetted or washed. It is particularly important not to wet translucent stone as this may be alabaster and slightly water soluble.

Objects which are displayed in the open gallery, such as statuary, will inevitably become dusty. The

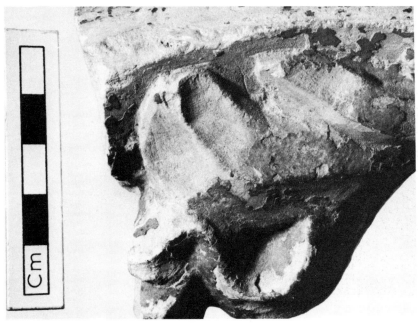

Figure 39.12 Traces of paint on stone, which may be removed all too easily by injudious handling or treatment.

(Courtesy of Institute of Archaeology, University College London)

best solution is to filter the dust and dirt particles from the museum atmosphere. Where this is not possible, routine cleaning should be carefully controlled. Objects should *not* be rubbed over with cloth dusters (these may drive dirt into the surface of the stone) but gently brushed with a *clean*, very soft brush (the dust being collected with a vacuum cleaner). Where objects are on open display, the conservator's advice should be sought over the suitability of cleaning methods and improvement of display arrangements.

Occasionally, archaeological stonework is displayed in the open air. Moisture and pollutant gases in the atmosphere may cause the formation of a dirty and damaging crust on the surface of the stone, which may come away in flakes or sheets causing much loss of detail. Iron dowels inserted as part of a repair can corrode in these conditions and cause stains and disruption of the stonework. Deterioration will continue unless the objects are removed, fully conserved and housed indoors.

Recently excavated stone

Such stone should be examined carefully for signs of deterioration and for traces of decoration. Shale, which is normally recognized by its dark colour, fine grain and highly laminated structure, may need special treatment, particularly if it comes from a waterlogged site. If it is allowed to dry out the laminae will separate and the object disintegrate

(*Figure 39.13*). It must be packed and kept wet until it is conserved.

Storage of stone

Stonework showing no signs of deterioration can be housed in the standard store. It should be covered with light cloth rather than polythene (to avoid problems of condensation on the surface), or packed in boxes, to exclude dust. Material suffering from the presence of water-soluble salts should be conserved as soon as possible and, in the mean time, housed at a constant level of relative humidity. Wet or waterlogged material should be given special provision in the sensitive store.

Porous materials: painted wall-plaster

This usually consists of lime plaster with a painted surface. It is porous and suffers from problems simular to those of porous ceramics and stone. The paint surface may be relatively strong (in some cases of true *fresco*) or very fragile (where *tempera* has been used). Any unevenness in the surface such as isolated areas of thickly applied pigment may be very vulnerable and liable to flake (*Figure 39.14*).

Handling of wall plaster

Plaster should always be fully supported when being moved. Suitably sized padded trays should be used and individual fragments handled as little as possible.

Figure 39.13 Shale from a waterlogged site, which has been allowed to dry out causing separation of the laminae.

(Courtesy of Institute of Archaeology, University College London)

Figure 39.14 Two fragments of wall-plaster showing the fragile painted surface and vulnerable break edges.

(Courtesy of Institute of Archaeology, University College London)

Where several fragments are stored together they should be packed so as to prevent shifting or touching.

Wall plaster after long-term storage or display
Material which has been stored or displayed for some years may be adversely affected by water-soluble salts, by early attempts at consolidating the paint layer, by accumulated dirt and by methods of support and display now considered unsuitable. In such cases the painted surface may be very delicate and should not be touched. No attempt should be made to clean untreated, excavated fragments which have been stored for some time; the obscuring dirt may be more firmly attached to the paint than the paint to the plaster and cleaning may simply remove the paint layer. All such material should have specialist conservation treatment.

Recently excavated wall plaster
Freshly excavated fragments which have been packed and brought into the museum damp should be kept damp because, once the surface dries, the adhering soil and dirt may become very difficult to remove. Large sections of plaster which have been removed from a standing wall by means of adhesive and cloth facing should be stored only for a short time in case the adhesive becomes difficult to remove. Both types of recently excavated wall plaster should be conserved as soon as possible.

Storage of wall plaster
Controlled storage is the best care much of this material can be given while awaiting conservation. In general, the same conditions of storage apply as for stone. Freshly excavated plaster which has been deliberately packed damp can be stored only temporarily; it should be inspected regularly and sent for conservation treatment as soon as possible.

Porous materials: mosaics

Mosaics normally consist of predominantly porous tesserae such as stone, ceramic, and occasionally glass set in lime mortar. The mortar may deteriorate and the tesserae become loose; the surface may be dirty and affected by water-soluble salts or by earlier treatment. Sometimes, however, the problem is of a different kind. A complete mosaic may have been excavated in the past and placed on the floor or wall of a public building. Such mosaics were often set in concrete which makes them very difficult to reposition or remove.

Mosaics after long-term storage or display
Small mosaics and fragments should be handled, examined and stored in a similar manner to wall plaster or stone. Large areas of mosaic, or complete floors, need specialist advice and treatment. They should not be washed or wetted unnecessarily for example to 'bring up' the colours for photography,

and they should be carefully examined for damage which might be caused by water-soluble salts and damp coming through the floor or through the wall. They should also be examined for other signs of deterioration such as the corrosion of iron rods or bolts which may have been inserted when the mosaics were placed in position.

Recently excavated mosaics
Fragments of mosaic recently removed from a site with the use of adhesive and cloth facing should be fully conserved as soon as possible. Although the mosaic is unlikely to be as fragile as painted wall paper it is advisable not to leave a temporary adhesive on the surface for longer than is absolutely necessary. Ideally, no large area of mosaic floor should be stored for any length of time before treatment. If the decision is taken to lift such a floor from a site, a team of experienced conservators or a specialist firm should be called in and provision should be made for immediate and complete conservation.

Indications of active deterioration on porous materials
When any signs of the presence of water-soluble salts or of flaking and loss of surface are found, the conservator's advice should be sought.

Glass

Depending on the way they were made, some types of glass are more stable than others. The less stable glasses may simply not have survived the effects of burial or occasionally may be discovered in an extremely deteriorated and fragile state. Some Roman glass is in very good condition, much Medieval glass less so.

Handling of glass
Much archaeological glass consists of small fragments which should be handled with care both because they are fragile and because of their sharp edges. In many cases sherds and vessels are extremely thin. They may also have flaking and vulnerable surfaces which should, as far as possible, not be touched or disturbed. Glass vessels should be handled by cradling them carefully with both hands and carrying them in padded trays or boxes. As it is very difficult to make durable repairs in glass (many adhesives are not effective), all objects which may have been repaired or gap-filled should be handled with particular care.

Glass after long-term storage or display
Glass which has been in a museum for some time may show varying degrees of surface deterioration.

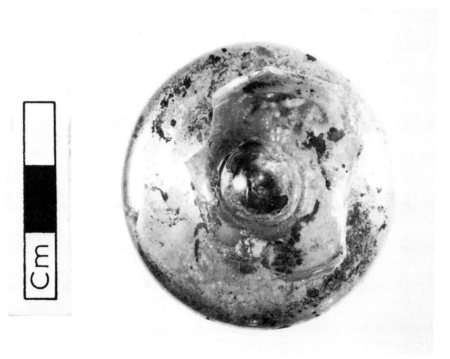

Figure 39.15 The base of a glass vessel with an iridescent surface. When handled thin iridescent flakes 'float' off the surface. (Courtesy of Institute of Archaeology, University College London)

Figure 39.16 A fragment of dark-coloured glass showing patches of opaque whitish crust on the surface. A thick crust of this type may obscure the surface and colour of the glass totally. (Courtesy of Institute of Archaeology, University College London)

There may be a slight iridescence or a series of iridescent skins (*Figure 39.15*), or a thick opaque crust which may be whitish (*Figure 39.16*) or discoloured (often dark). There may be remains of a thick crust which has flaked off in places revealing a pitted glass surface beneath. In all cases, deterioration may continue. Moisture is the chief cause of changes in glass but heat or extreme dryness can also be damaging. When a deteriorated surface dries out it can craze, become opaque and flake off, thus damaging the glass and changing its appearance considerably.

Glass may have been repaired in the past with unsuitable adhesives which have yellowed with age or begun to break down. Decorated glass should be handled with great care. The decorative paints or enamels may be thick and can flake easily and gilding can be easily abraded.

Crusts and iridescent flakes must not be cleaned off (*Figure 39.17*) and none of this material should be washed. It should be kept away from direct heat, preferably at a constant relative humidity of 45–55 per cent. Conditions in the sensitive store (50–60 per cent RH) may be adequate, but the conservator's advice should be sought.

Adhesives and gap-filling materials may not only fail but often become yellow and discoloured through exposure to light. Although some modern adhesives and fillers appear to be more resistant than earlier ones it may be worth using a filter to exclude ultraviolet light when displaying a collection of recently restored glass objects.

Figure 39.17 Removal of the crust from this glass would result in loss of the original smooth surface and would reveal an unsightly pitting (already visible in the damaged areas on the right). (Courtesy of Institute of Archaeology, University College London)

Display of glass
When displaying glass, all forms of heat (including lights) should be carefully screened or controlled; the use of filters to exclude ultraviolet light may prolong the life of adhesives and gap-filling materials.

Recently excavated glass
One of the main difficulties with recently excavated glass is that the exposure to a new environment can cause rapid and irreversible changes to take place (the deteriorated surface can dry out quickly, the crust may fall off or adhering soil may become impossible to remove). Methods of packing and storage should be designed to prevent – or minimize – these changes until conservation takes place.

Storage of damp or wet glass
It is difficult to prevent changes taking place under damp conditions. Leaching of materials from the glass may make the storage conditions increasingly alkaline, and this can be very damaging. Mould may grow on packing materials, and many biocides may be unsuitable because they are alkaline. Refrigeration slows the rate of chemical change and prevents mould growth. This can be a useful storage method but is not often feasible on a large scale. Hence, freshly excavated, damp glass should be stored *temporarily* in cool, dark conditions and conserved as soon as possible. It should not be unpacked for examination although, if necessary, the packaging can be checked to make sure it is still damp.

Storage of dry glass
Dry glass objects should be stored in boxes with shaped supportive padding. Sherds may be packed in horizontal layers between sheets of foamed plastic or pads of acid-free tissue paper. Normally, all glass may be housed in the sensitive store but all decisions about storage (and display) conditions should be taken with the advice of the conservator.

Indications of active deterioration on archaeological glass
Flaking, or shedding of the surface (often seen as very fine iridescent skins 'floating off') or a change from a glassy to a more or less opaque appearance indicate that the glass is fragile and highly deteriorated. It should not be handled, and immediate conservation should be arranged. Damp or wet glass which has been allowed to dry out in storage should also be sent for immediate treatment.

Metals

The condition of archaeological metal artefacts

A number of metals were used in antiquity, both pure and as alloys. Some were applied to others as a coating or decoration and many objects were made of combined metal and non-metals. Many metals are considerably changed by burial and corrode rapidly on excavation. The colour and texture of corrosion products may obscure both the nature of the metal and the shape of the artefact. In certain conditions such as waterlogging, metals may appear almost unaffected.

Non-metallic materials – such as enamel, niello (a black sulphide), glass (*millefiori*), gemstone, bone, ivory and horn – were used to decorate metals. Some of these may be highly deteriorated. Enamel often remains only as a discoloured granular substance. They may be covered by the corrosion products of the metal.

Any organic feature such as a wooden handle, may have deteriorated completely. In some cases evidence of the feature or of associated material may remain as small traces, wholly or partly replaced by metal salts in the corrosion products of the metal (*Figure 39.18*).

Figure 39.18 Traces of wood preserved in association with iron. The direction of the grain of the wood is clearly visible; the species may also be identified from traces of this kind. Injudicious cleaning could therefore result in considerable loss of evidence. (Courtesy of Institute of Archaeology, University College London)

Such fragments of textile, compact or fibrous layers of leather, and slivers of wood are sometimes clearly recognizable. Often, however, this type of evidence is not detected or is lost if corroded objects are mishandled.

No attempt should be made to clean archaeological metal artefacts, however robust they may appear.

Removal of corrosion products by picking or abrasion, polishing of any metal (particularly silver or gold), can be extremely damaging and will result in loss of evidence.

Details are given below of the main types of metal found in archaeological contexts and of how they appear when they are excavated.

Gold

If relatively pure, gold may appear to be in more or less perfect condition but in this form it is fairly soft and the surface may be easily damaged. In some cases, what looks like a gold artefact is in fact gilded; the underlying metal may be very fragile and such objects should be handled with great care. Gold may be alloyed with other metals such as silver or copper in which case the corrosion products of the alloying metal may be visible. It may also be decorated, for example, with enamels or gemstones.

Silver

Silver may be fairly pure or alloyed with other metals, notably copper. It can be covered with black or mauve corrosion products or completely obscured by the green corrosion products of copper. It can be extremely fragile and the slightest pressure may cause it to crack or break. Silver can be decorated. It can be used as a thin decorative coating (for example, on copper alloys), or an inlay (for example, on iron).

Copper and its alloys

Copper is often alloyed with other metals, particularly tin to form bronze, and zinc to form brass. It is usually covered with green corrosion products which may be either compact (*Figure 39.19*) or powdery (*Figure 39.20*) and can incorporate soil particles. Bright green spots of 'bronze disease' may be apparent (*Figure 39.21*). It may be very fragile and cracks and fissures may not be immediately visible.

Objects should be examined carefully for traces of decoration (*Figure 39.22*). Small amounts of organic materials may be preserved in contact with copper alloys. These may be largely unchanged, being protected against micro-organisms by the copper, or the physical structure may be replaced and preserved by copper salts (*Figure 39.23*).

Iron

Iron objects may be covered with dark- or rust-coloured corrosion products which are often massive and incorporate soil, stones and other debris (*Figure 39.24* and *39.25*). The shape of the artefacts may be completely concealed as may other features such as

Figure 39.19 Compact and stable corrosion products on a copper alloy object. (Courtesy of Institute of Archaeology, University College London)

Figure 39.20 Active corrosion on a copper alloy, indicated by loose, powdery (bright green) products. (Courtesy of Institute of Archaeology, University College London)

Figure 39.21 Patch of bright green powdery active 'bronze disease' on a copper alloy object. Such patches may vary in size and number, sometimes a 'rash' of small bright green spots may be seen. (Courtesy of Institute of Archaeology, University College London)

pattern–welding, inlay, or associated organic materials such as bone handles, traces of wood, skin, or textiles which may have been completely replaced by iron salts (*Figure 39.18* and *39.30*). Iron may be very fragile, cracked and laminated and very often little actual metal remains, the shape being retained in the corrosion products. Visual examination provides only minimal information and the use of radiography is essential (*Figure 39.1*).

Lead and its alloys
Lead may be used in more or less pure form or alloyed with tin to form pewter. It may be recognized by its considerable weight and its whitish or grey corrosion products (*Figure 39.26*). When heavily corroded, it may be cracked and very fragile. When apparently little-corroded, the surface may be easily scratched and objects made of sheet lead may deform under their own weight. Lead should be handled with care since the corrosion products are toxic.

General handling of metals
It is as well to assume that all archaeological metal work is fragile and that it needs particular care in handling. Moisture and salts may be introduced from the hands if the objects are touched. Clumsy handling, such as dropping or banging, may result in physical damage and renewed corrosion. As far as possible, important objects should be examined and handled in purpose-built containers.

Figure 39.22 The gilding on the brooch on the left is almost totally obscured by copper corrosion products. The brooch on the right was in similar condition before treatment. (Courtesy of Institute of Archaeology, University College London)

Metals after long-term storage or display

Treatments, both past and recent, may have removed or inactivated potentially damaging corrosion products on archaeological metalwork. Some material may have been stripped of all corrosion. Copper alloys may appear coppery or brassy and may show pitted surfaces where the corrosion has been removed (*Figure 39.27*); ironwork may appear thin, pitted and even 'lacy'. More recent treatments have aimed at conserving the corrosion products where they have preserved the shape or form of the object or have been otherwise informative. In this case, copper alloys may retain a greenish surface and iron may retain a layer of dark or brownish corrosion over the remains of the metal. On most objects, protective layers of wax or lacquer have been applied to the surface after treatment in order to exclude moisture. These may have collected dust or have been injudiciously applied in thick layers or with an incorporated tint.

The most important consideration when caring for such metalwork is to examine it for any signs of change which may indicate that active deterioration is taking place. However carefully the original treatment was undertaken, it may not have successfully removed or inactivated all harmful products. In addition, the protective coating or lacquer may have deteriorated or been scratched or punctured, thus allowing moisture and pollutants to reach the metal.

Figure 39.23 Traces of textile preserved in association with a copper alloy object. (Courtesy of Institute of Archaeology, University College London)

Figure 39.24 An iron shield boss covered in massive corrosion products incorporating soil. (Courtesy of Institute of Archaeology, University College London)

Figure 39.25 An iron object completely obscured by corrosion incorporating stones and other debris. (Courtesy of Institute of Archaeology, University College London)

Figure 39.26 Lead alloy showing typical pitting and whitish corrosion products. (Courtesy of Intitute of Archaeology, University College London)

Figure 39.27 The shiny pitted surface which may result from the complete removal of the corrosion products from a copper alloy object (approximately ×2, reduced by ⅘ in reproduction); (Courtesy of Institute of Archaeology, University College London)

The effects of the museum environment on metals

Moisture

Different factors can be responsible for renewed corrosion of archaeological metalwork. In many cases, moisture reacts with the corrosion products formed during burial to cause further damaging changes. In general, therefore, if metal objects are kept in dry conditions (below 40 per cent RH) deterioration will at least be slowed down.

A sudden and widespread outbreak of corrosion (for example, 'bronze disease') may indicate an unexpected, and possibly undetected, change in the normal climate of the museum or store. Lowering the central heating temperature as an economy measure may have unforseen effects on the climate and thus on metal objects.

Pollutants

Some metals should be protected from pollutants. Tarnishing on silver is caused by hydrogen sulphide, sulphur dioxide and other sulphur containing compounds which occur in some textiles, paints and rubber products. Corrosion on lead is caused by organic acids which may be given off by adhesives, woods, papers and cardboards. The advicee of a conservator should be sought over the suitability of storage or display materials. Tests may be necessary before deciding which materials can be safely used.

Physical damage

Archaeological metal should be protected from physical damage. Well-designed and supportive packing methods provide good protection during storage. Soft metals (for example, gold and lead), brittle metals (for example, corroded silver) and generally fragile objects should be fully supported during display. Stresses caused by support at one or two points only can be very damaging. Metal items such as wire and nails should not be used in display. In contact with a metal antiquity, they may corrode readily themselves or cause local corrosion on the object.

Storage

Metal objects should be packed individually and stored in the sensitive store. In most instances silica gel should be used to maintain the relative humidity in the package to below 40 per cent. Where suitable, several small boxes containing artefacts of the same metal or alloy may be packed inside one large box.

Storage conditions for recently excavated metals

Recently excavated metals should be conserved as soon as possible. They must be stored carefully while awaiting treatment and in most cases they will need individually controlled conditions.

Gold, gilded objects, silver, copper alloys

These should be packed individually in polystyrene boxes grouped in larger polythene boxes and stored in the sensitive store at a relative humidity of below 40 per cent. The material should be inspected regularly to make sure that conditions are properly maintained and to check the state of the artefacts. Copper alloy objects with decorative enamels or evidence of organic materials in their corrosion products should be kept damp and sent for immediate conservation.

Lead and its alloys

These should be stored in similar conditions but all sources of organic acids, such as cardboard, must be avoided.

Iron

Iron is more difficult to deal with. Such large quantities may be found that only a proportion can be conserved fully and the selection of artefacts for treatment must depend on thorough radiographic examination. Both before and after examination, iron objects need to be stored in conditions which as far as possible prevent further deterioration. They should be dried thoroughly and thereafter kept very dry (below 15 per cent RH) by storing in well-sealed polythene containers with silica gel. The storage conditions should be monitored to make sure that the low relative humidity is maintained. Conservation of important artefacts should be undertaken as soon as possible. An alternative storage method is to store wet in an alkaline solution (sodium sulphite), but this should be undertaken only with guidance from a conservator.

Metal with associated organics

Particular care should be taken of any metal object with an organic feature attached, or with evidence of organic remains preserved in its corrosion products. Such objects should be sent for immediate conservation.

Indications of active corrosion on archaeological metals (treated and untreated)

A powdery, loose or voluminous corrosion (which may appear in isolated spots), is likely to indicate that undesirable changes are taking place.

Gold

If it is alloyed with copper, the appearance of cracks or green copper corrosion products may indicate active corrosion. If it is alloyed or decorated with silver, a purple–brown staining is an indication of active corrosion. Gilded objects may show signs that the gilding is becoming detached due to active corrosion of the underlying metal.

Silver

On relatively pure silver, rapid tarnishing (producing a blackish or brownish colour) is particularly damaging. When alloyed with copper, spots of green corrosion products may appear and such alloys may become brittle.

Copper and its alloys

Spots of bright green powdery corrosion indicate the presence of active and highly damaging 'bronze disease' (*Figure 39.28*; see also *Figure 39.21*). Black, mildew-like spots should also be reported to the conservator as they may indicate another form of active corrosion.

Figure 39.28 A bright green patch of powdery 'bronze disease' showing clearly on a corroded copper alloy. (Courtesy of Institute of Archaeology, University College London)

Iron

Patches or spots of bright rust-coloured products which may sometimes be seen as dampish 'pustules' indicate the changes sometimes referred to as 'weeping iron' (*Figure 39.29*). Cracks and laminae are also found in corroded archaeological iron.

Lead

A whitish powdery deposit may indicate active corrosion.

Organic materials

The condition of archaeological organic materials

Most organic materials used in antiquity do not survive in the archaeological record. As they are

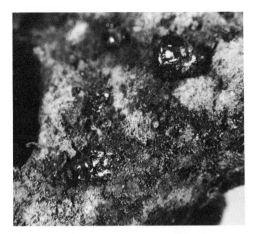

Figure 39.29 Damp rusty coloured 'pustules' typical of 'weeping iron' (approximately ×5). (Courtesy of Institute of Archaeology, University College London)

Figure 39.30 Traces of textile preserved in the corrosion products of an iron object. Although the form of the textile has been replaced by iron salts and no organic substance remains, extremely valuable evidence of the type of fibre and textile is retained. (Courtesy of Institute of Archaeology, University College London)

particularly susceptible to deterioration during burial reasonably complete artefacts will be found only in areas or 'pockets' (mircroenvironments) where conditions for preservation are exceptional, as for example where conditions are extremely dry or where oxygen has been excluded by waterlogging.

On some sites, evidence of organic materials may be preserved only as small traces in the corrosion products of metal artefacts. In this case the substance is often wholly or partly replaced by the metal salts and is no longer really organic (*Figure 39.30*). Other organic materials survive because they contain appreciable amounts of inorganic material such as bone, or shell, or because they are resistant to biodeterioration, as is the case with amber and jet. Organic materials also survive in forms which hitherto may have been undetected, such as ancient organic adhesives or coatings on objects.

There are two main problems in caring for archaeological organic materials. Although the form of an artefact may have been almost perfectly preserved, the material will have lost the greater part of its mechanical strength and, on excavation, is likely to deteriorate more quickly than almost any other substance. Secondly, traces of organic materials on artefacts may not be recognized and may therefore fail to be recorded or sent for immediate conservation.

Organic materials after long-term storage and display (dry organic materials)

Most of the archaeological organic material housed in museums is now in a dry state irrespective of the way it was originally preserved, and is likely to have lost much of its original strength. Artefacts from dry sites may be desiccated and consequently fragile. Previously wet objects which have been allowed to dry out are likely to be shrunken, brittle and distorted. Both these types will need care in handling and may need complete physical support before they can be safely lifted or carried.

Conserved objects from wet sites may display some of their normal characteristics, such as flexibility in leather. However, most conservation treatments stabilize the object rather then increase its strength, so this material should also be handled carefully. Where treatments have failed the material is likely to be particularly fragile.

The effects of the museum environment on dry organics

Relative humidity

Deterioration may continue in the museum, particularly if the environment fluctuates. All organic materials contain moisture and during use and even after some deterioration they continue to take up and lose moisture in response to humidity changes. This leads to changes in dimension and so to stresses, causing physical damage which is often seen as distortion and cracking. Repeated environmental changes are particularly damaging. It follows that one of the most important factors in the care of these materials is the maintenance of a constant level of relative humidity (45–60 per cent, preferably 50–60 per cent) but material can acclimatize and remain stable in steady conditions outside this range. Too low a RH may lead to further desiccation, too high a RH (above 68 per cent) can lead to mould and fungal growth.

Light

Light, particularly ultraviolet light, is very damaging to many organic substances and can cause considerable chemical breakdown. Although the effects on already very degraded and discoloured material may not be apparent, all organic materials should be protected from ultraviolet light. Moreover, textiles should be displayed at a suitably low light level, even where there is little remaining visible evidence of the use of dyes.

Insects, fungi, micro-organisms

In favourable conditions, insect and fungal pests may attack these materials. Insect frass or flight holes, whitish patches of mould, and strands (fungal hyphae) are danger signs. These are usually seen where RH is above 68 per cent and conditions are somewhat dirty and poorly ventilated. Careful examination will be needed to establish whether the infestation is active or not. Whatever measures are taken by the conservator, improving the climate, the ventilation and the general cleanliness of the storage or display area will greatly decrease the chances of reinfestation. Specialist advice should be sought when dealing with an infestation of any size, particularly if it is affecting the structure of the building and furnishings as well as the artefacts.

Dust and dirt

Dust and dirt can be unsightly and can encourage further deterioration such as mould growth. Particles may adhere to consolidants on treated objects such as leather, and may become enmeshed in textile fibres where they can be particularly damaging. Repeated cleaning of dirty objects can in itself be harmful.

General care of dry organics

General care, therefore, should include monitoring of the climate and where necessary, improvement of the conditions. It should also include careful and regular examination.

Storage of dry organics

Most dry organic materials should be stored in the sensitive store, a relative humidity of between 50 and 60 per cent being particularly suitable. They should be packed individually using acid-free tissue paper as padding. This will act as a buffer against slight humidity fluctuations. Some materials may need individually controlled packaging.

Care of individual dry organic materials

Wood

Wood from dry sites may be extremely desiccated, pale in colour and light in weight. Cracks may run along the grain but their presence across the grain, as also seen in charred wood, is a particular sign of weakness (*Figure 39.31*). Painted or decorated

Figure 39.31 Cracks across the grain of a piece of wood, indicating considerable deterioration and loss of strength. (Courtesy of Institute of Archaeology, University College London)

surfaces may be flaking, powdery and dirty. They may have been treated at some earlier date with a coating which has subsequently become brittle or yellow. Some varnishes, such as those on Egyptian mummy cases, may be original and care must be taken to distinguish the 'old' from the 'new' before deciding on conservation treatment. Occasionally, dry material is consolidated at the time of excavation and may show the presence of, for example, paraffin wax.

Previously wet wood which has simply dried out is likely to be distorted and shrivelled severely with pronounced cracks or breaks across the grain. Depending on the original state of the timber, it may be relatively tough or extremely fragile. Treated waterlogged wood may appear substantial but is either light and fragile, or heavier but lacking in resilience (*Figure 39.32*). The surface, including valuable evidence such as tool-marks, may be readily damaged and is sometimes clogged with absorbed dirt which cannot be simply or safely removed.

The effect of fluctuating relative humidity may be particularly serious on wood since the resulting changes in dimensions are greater across the grain than along it (wood is anisotropic). Considerable warping, or cracking parallel to the grain can result; the effects can be worse in an artefact made of more than one piece of timber since the stresses set up will almost certainly run in difference directions.

Figure 39.32 Pieces of treated waterlogged wood showing cracks and breaks typical of the brittle nature of such material. (Courtesy of Institute of Archaeology, University College London)

Danger signs are sudden warping, fresh cracks, insect or fungal attack, and surface deterioration such as paint flaking.

Bone, antler and ivory

Bone, antler and ivory are more widely preserved than other organic materials on archaeological sites. Excavated material may include human and animal skeletal remains as well as artefacts or parts of artefacts which may have been stained, painted or gilded and should be carefully examined for evidence of such decoration. It may be discoloured, desiccated, 'chalky' (*Figure 39.33*) and fragile or splitting as a result of drying out from a damp or wet state (*Figure 39.34*). Where attached to metal (particularly iron) it may be damaged by the disruptive action of the corroding metal. In cases where, for example, an object has been consolidated in the field, the consolidant may have failed to restrain subsequent warping and cracking as the material has dried slowly. Consolidants suitable for use on damp material may work well initially but may deteriorate or change with age. These materials are anisotropic and sensitive to changes in relative humidity; deterioration is often seen in the form of splits along the length of the bone or antler.

Ivory is particularly sensitive but it has a different physical structure and deterioration takes the form of splitting and lamination following the orginal circumference of the tusk (rather like onion rings; *Figure 39.35*). Even when highly degraded (or even fossilized) it can react in this way. Storage conditions for ivory should be particularly carefully controlled. Silica gel should be used to maintain a constant relative humidity of between 50 and 55 per cent, together with acid-free tissue paper padding to minimize any fluctuations in RH. If ivory has acclimatized to dry conditions (i.e. below 50 per cent RH), it should be left in these conditions. The main danger signs are fresh cracking or lamination and flaking of the surface.

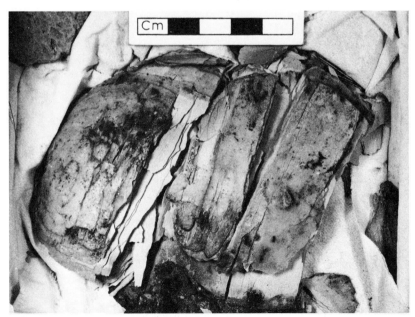

Figure 39.33 Highly deteriorated and 'chalky' ivory. (Courtesy of Institute of Archaeology, University College London)

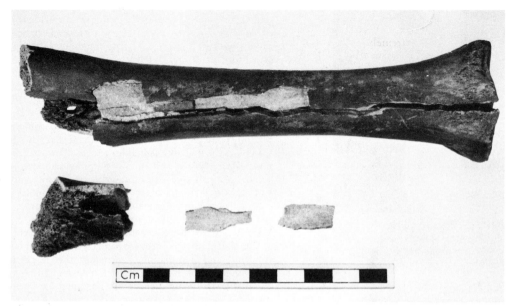

Figure 39.34 Splitting and flaking resulting from allowing
a waterlogged bone to dry out. (Courtesy of Institute of
Archaeology, University College London)

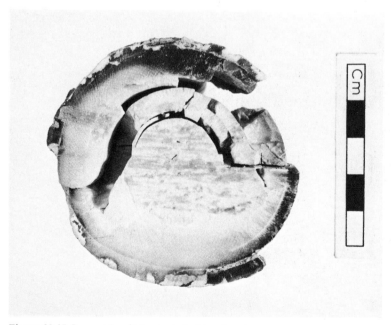

Figure 39.35 Concentric splitting typical of deteriorating
ivory. (Courtesy of Institute of Archaeology, University
College London)

Skin and leather

Skin and leather from dry contexts are often crumpled, shrunken and extremely brittle (*Figure 39.36*). They may show traces of decoration, such as paint. Fragments from a wet site may be dark, cracked and very hard or brittle if allowed to dry without treatment (*Figure 39.37*). All such material will need careful handling and no attempt should be made to unroll or flatten artefacts in this state as they may crumble or shatter. Treated waterlogged material is usually dark in colour and should retain some flexibility. In some cases, however, the dressings or consolidants used may be 'sweating' or

Figure 39.37 Leather from a waterlogged site; uncontrolled drying has resulted in distortion and rigidity. (Courtesy of Institute of Archaeology, University College London)

Figure 39.36 Cracking typical of leather weakened either by desiccation or by allowing it to dry out from a waterlogged state. (Courtesy of Institute of Archaeology, University College London)

leaching out of the leather making the surface sticky and attractive to dust. Occasionally, the treatment has failed to stabilize the leather which may be becoming hard and cracked. Increased brittleness and the appearance of cracks, and patches of mould-growth (*Figure 39.38*) are signs of further deterioration.

Textiles

Archaeological textiles may vary from complete garments found on dry sites with their original

Figure 39.38 White spots and patches on treated leather, indicative of mould growth. (Courtesy of Institute of Archaeology, University College London)

colour well preserved, to small, highly discoloured scraps from waterlogged sites. They may be folded crumpled and brittle. No attempt should be made to unfold or spread them out, or to wash them; when wetted, degraded textiles of this kind can disintegrate.

Conserved textiles which have been provided with a backing should nevertheless be considered very fragile, and should be fully supported in storage or on display by, for example, lying flat or on a slightly sloping flat support. Garments should be padded out with acid-free tissue paper during storage to avoid folds and should be given the support of a purpose-made dummy figure for display.

Fluctuating relative humidity may be very damaging causing the textile fibres to expand and contract. Dirt present in the textile may act as an abrasive when the fibres expand and contract against each other. At points of stress such as folds, the textile may be weakened considerably. They should be displayed and stored in dust-free conditions.

Light may be particularly damaging to textiles especially cotton and linen, and to vegetable dyes (and the effects are cumulative). It is therefore necessary to exclude ultraviolet light and to display textiles at a low light level.

Powdering of fibres or breaking of threads during gentle handling indicates that the textile is in a very fragile state (*Figure 39.39*). Whitish patches or dark spots on the surface may indicate mould growth.

Recently excavated organic materials

Recently excavated organic material is likely to fall into two main categories, bone and antler, both of which may survive in several types of burial environment, and waterlogged organic materials. In many cases, unworked damp bone (and antler) can be allowed to dry slowly and be dealt with as dry material. Such material can be housed in the standard store. (Traces of organic materials preserved in the corrosion products of metals are considered under metals.)

Waterlogged organic material

Although apparently well-preserved, waterlogged artefacts are often degraded considerably. They may be heavily stained, swollen, and soft or spongy in texture. The degraded structure is filled with water and if the water is allowed to evaporate the structure will collapse irreversibly. It is therefore extremely important to keep such material wet (*Figure 39.40* and *39.41(a)–(c)*).

Figure 39.39 Fine powder (visible in the centre of this plate) produced by handling the highly degraded textile fibres. (Courtesy of Institute of Archaeology, University College London)

Figure 39.40 Pieces of waterlogged wood being stored in water. Although fragile, the structure and surface detail are well preserved. (Courtesy of Institute of Archaeology, University College London)

Water logged materials need special storage conditions and prompt conservation treatment. It is difficult to provide adequate facilities for large objects such as timbers. After consultation with all concerned, it may be better to record and sample them rather than lift and conserve them.

General care of waterlogged material

All waterlogged material must be kept thoroughly wet when being examined or photographed (photographic lights can cause considerable drying). A fine garden spray can be very useful. Once exposed to oxygen, micro-organisms may grow readily on the material and storage conditions should be designed to minimize this growth. Waterlogged objects should be handled carefully. Washing should not be undertaken without the advice of a conservator; the use of anything but the softest tools or fingers can damage the surface. Leaving an object under running water may be harmful, and in some cases washing may remove valuable evidence.

Storage

Small quantites can be stored in part of the sensitive store provided the containers are well sealed. Large quantities should be provided with a separate storage area.

Containers

Small objects may be firmly sealed inside polythene bags filled with water and immersed, in groups, in large sealed boxes full of water. Larger objects can be housed in individually sealed boxes. Very large objects should be stored in tanks which may have to be purpose built, although containers such as plastic dustbins can be useful. Objects can be sealed in bags and suspended in a tank from a horizontal bar, with an identifying label attached to the suspending cord to avoid 'fishing around'.

Labels

A label should be placed inside each package, and another outside. Spun-bonded polyethylene (polythene) labels are suitable, using ball-point pens or spirit-based markers. To label individual timbers stainless steel embossing tape can be attached directly to the timber with stainless steel pins or wire bent into a staple shape. These labels withstand the effects of later treatment, including heat. It is important that all metals used should be rust-proof.

Prevention of microbiological growth

To minimize growth of aerobic micro-organisms, oxygen should be excluded as far as possible. This can be done in two ways. First, objects can be closely wrapped in thin polythene sheet, enclosed in heavier grade sheet and kept wet. Large timbers can be stored at least temporarily, by wrapping in thin polythene, then wrapping in thoroughly wet foamed-plastic sheet and sealing the whole in heavy-grade polythene. Second, objects can be sealed in bags or boxes that are completely filled with water, leaving little or no space for air. Cool, dark storage conditions also help to prevent algal and some microbiological growth. Tanks should be opaque and may be covered with black polythene sheet; stacks of sealed boxes may also be covered with black sheet, but arrangements should always allow for easy inspection. Refrigeration also inhibits micro-organism growth but, in general, objects should not be frozen.

Biocides can be used as a preventive measure, but if material is needed for, for example ^{14}C dating they should be avoided. Panacide (dichlorophen) can be added to produce a concentration of 0.20 per cent in the storage water, but the conservator should be consulted about selection and use of biocides and about safe methods of use. Large quantities of storage water containing biocide should be disposed of in accordance with Health and Safety Regulations.

Wood

Wood may be difficult to store because of its size. It may appear misleadingly robust, and particular care should be taken to support long thin timbers along their length. Care should also be taken not to damage the surface.

(a)

(b)

(c)

Figure 39.41 (a) Part of a large piece of waterlogged timber which had dried out slowly in inadequate storage conditions. The apparently flat area presented to the viewer is in fact two sides of a split along the grain, which can be seen more clearly in (b). The short score-mark seen on the upper left has been made with a thumbnail in order to indicate the softness of the wood. (b) View of the end of the same piece of timber showing position and extent of the split. (c) The same piece of timber after allowing it to dry freely for a further 2 weeks. The resulting collapse and distortion are extensive. (Courtesy of Institute of Archaeology, University College London)

Bone and antler

From 'dry' or damp sites bone or antler may be allowed to dry out slowly while partially enclosed in polythene bags or boxes. It may be advisable to dry a sample bone in order to assess how well the material withstands this treatment. If it appears not to stand it well, then the material should be stored damp and conserved as soon as possible. Waterlogged material should be stored as outlined above.

Ivory

Ivory should not be allowed to dry out, but should be stored damp with foamed-plastic support, and sent for immediate conservation.

Leather

When handling waterlogged leather, care must be taken not to damage the grain surface which provides evidence of the animal source. Prolonged washing should be avoided as it may remove tannins and the remains of dyes. Complete objects such as shoes and purses should not be washed or handled more than is absolutely necessary as the stitching is likely to be very fragile.

Unlike most other organic materials, it is possible to freeze leather artefacts during storage as the fibrous structure of leather is not damaged appreciably by the formation of ice crystals. Objects should be wrapped in two polythene bags from which the air has been excluded and then placed in a freezer. It is preferable to avoid the use of biocides as they tend to be alkaline and damaging to leather.

Textiles

Textiles should be handled as little as possible and particular care should be taken where seams or stitching remain. They should not be washed as evidence of dyes may be removed. They can be stored wet or frozen but fungicides should not be used in case they affect traces of dyes.

Other organic material

Materials such as amber, or jet should be kept damp or wet depending on the condition in the ground and sent for conservation treatment as soon as possible.

Composite objects

It is particularly difficult to decide on suitable storage for composite objects. Where the object is predominantly metal, it should be dealt with as a metal, where predominantly wood, as wood, and so on. Where suitable freezing may be used, but all such objects should be given priority conservation treatment.

Indications of active deterioration of waterlogged organic materials

It is important to inspect all stored waterlogged material carefully for signs of micro-organism growth (usually indicated by a foul smell and the presence of slime), and for signs of drying out.

Acknowledgements

This paper was prepared with the advice of members of the Archaeology Section of the United Kingdom Institute for Conservation amongst whom I would like to thank Louise Bacon, Michael Corfield, Janey Cronyn, Kate Foley, Velson Horie, Susanne Keene, Barry Knight, Sonia O'Connor, Wendy Robinson and Sylvia Turner. I am particularly grateful for being able to draw on the work on storage undertaken by members of the Section.

I would also like to thank my colleagues Sandra Davidson, Stuart Laidlaw, David Scott and Kevin Reeves and, especially, Nicholas Balaam for very useful comment, and help in preparation of the text and illustrations.

I am particularly grateful to my colleague Kathryn Tubb for help with revision of the original text for this edition.

Further reading

Archaeological conservation

CRONYN, J. (1990), *The Elements of Archaeological Conservation*, Routledge, London

ROBINSON, W. S. (1981), *First Aid for Marine Finds, Handbooks in Maritime Archaeology No. 2*, National Maritime Museum, London

SEASE, C. (1987), *A Conservation Manual for the Field Archaeologist. Archaeological Research Tools*, Vol. 4, UCLA, Institute of Archaeology, Los Angeles, CA

TUBB, K. (1985), 'Preparation for Field Conservation in the Near East', *The Conservator*, **9**, 17–21

WATKINSON, D. (1986), *First Aid For Finds* Rescue & UK Institute for Conservation, Hertford

Examination and evidence

CORFIELD, M. (1982), 'Radiography of archaeological ironwork', in Clarke, R. W. and Blackshaw, S. M. (Eds), *Conservation of Iron, Maritime Monographs and Reports No. 53*, 8–14

CORFIELD, M. and FOLEY, K. (Eds), (1982), *Microscopy in Archaeological Conservation*, United Kindom Institute for Conservation Occasional Paper No. 2

JANAWAY, R. (1983), 'Textile fibre characteristics preserved by metal corrosion: the potential of S.E.M. studies', *The Conservator*, **7**, 48–32

KEEPAX, C. (1975), 'Scanning electron microscopy of wood replaced by iron corrosion products', *Journal of Archaeological Science*, **2**, 143–150

Records

BRADLEY, S. (1983), 'Conservation recording in the British Museum', *The Conservator*, **7**, 9–12

CORFIELD, M. (1983), 'Conservation records in the Wiltshire Library and Museum Service', *The Conservator*, **7**, 5–8

KEENE, S. (1983), 'Conservation records – editorial introduction', *The Conservator*, **7**, 4

Storage

ARCHAEOLOGY SECTION, UK INSTITUTE FOR CONSERVATION, (1982), 'Excavated artefacts for publication: UK sites', *Archaeological Artefacts, Conservation Guidelines No. 1*, London UKIC Archaeology Section, London

ARCHAEOLOGY SECTION, UK INSTITUTE FOR CONSERVATION (1983), 'Packaging and storage of freshly excavated artefacts from archaeological sites', *Archaeological Artefacts, Conservation Guidelines No. 2*, UKIC Archaeology Section, London

ARCHAEOLOGY SECTION, UK INSTITUTE FOR CONSERVATION (1984), 'Environmental standards for the permanent storage of excavated material from archaeological sites', *Archaeological Artefacts, Conservation Guidelines No. 3*, UKIC Archaeology Section, London

KEENE, S. (1977), 'An approach to the sampling and storage of waterlogged timbers from excavations', *The Conservator*, **1**, 8–11

KNIGHT, B. (1982), 'Why do some iron objects break up in store?', in Clarke. R. W. and Blackshaw, S. M. (Eds), *Conservation of Iron, Maritime Monographs and Reports No. 53*, 50–55

SPRIGGS, J. (1980), 'The recovery and storage of materials from waterlogged deposits at York', *The Conservator*, **4**, 19–24

WHITE, A. J. and PARTINGTON-OMAR, A. (Eds), (1981), *Archaeolgical Storage*, Society of Museum Archaeologists and Yorkshire and Humberside Federation of Museums and Art Galleries

Monitoring and control of the storage/display environment

BOFF, R., DANIELS, V. D. and WARD, S. E. (November 1981), 'Humidial Corporation humidity indicating card 6203-BB: A note on its use', *Conservation News*, **16**, 11

RAMER, B. L. (1981), 'Stabilising relative humidity variation within display cases: the role of silica gel and case design', *ICOM Committee for Conservation, 6th Triennial Meeting, Ottawa, 81/18/6*

RAMER, B. L. (November 1981), 'The use of colour-change relative humidity indicator cards', *Conservation News*, **16**, 10

THOMSON, G. (1978), *The Museum Environment*, Butterworths/IIC, London

WEINTRAUB, S. (1981), 'Studies on the behaviour of RH within an exhibition case. Part 1 Measuring the effectiveness of sorbents for use in an enclosed showcase', *ICOM Committee for Conservation, 6th Triennial Meeting, Ottawa, 81/18/6*

Testing materials for use in display

BLACKSHAW. S. M. and DANIELS, V. D. (1979), 'The testing of materials for use in storage and display in museums', *The Conservator*, **3**, 16–19

DANIELS, V. and WARD, S. (1982), 'A rapid test for the detection of substances which will tarnish silver', *Studies in Conservation*, **27**, 58–60

ODDY, W. A. (1973), 'An unsuspected danger in display', *Museum Journal*, **73**, 27–28

ODDY, W. A. (1975), 'The corrosion of metals on display', in Leigh, D. *et al* (Eds), *Conservation in Archaeology and the Applied Arts*, International Institute for Conservation (IIC) Stockholm Congress, 1975, 233–237

Periodical conservation literature

Conservation News, newsletter of the UK Institute for Conservation'

The Conservator, the journal of the UK Institute for Conservation

Studies in Conservation, the journal of the International Institute for Conservation

40

Conservation and storage: geological material

Francis M. P. Howie

Introduction

Geological material, whether rock, fossil or mineral, is composed ultimately of one or more mineral species. A single, crystalline and generally inorganic phase constitutes what is usually defined as a mineral specimen. The mineral kingdom, however, encompasses a wide variety of naturally occurring substances ranging from native metals to complex organic compounds (Hey, 1962). Rocks and fossils are, for the most part, composed of assemblages of minerals, which may be simple aggregates possessing integrity only through weak cohesive forces between particles or grains (as, for example, clays or lignite), or they may be complex intergrowths of crystalline and amorphous phases possessing great inherent strength (as, for example, granite or mineralized fossil bone). Single minerals, as crystalline, cryptocrystalline or amorphous phases, do however make up a variety of rock types and fossils. Marble and quartzite are well-known examples of single phase or mono-mineralic rocks, and fossils replaced wholly by calcite or pyrite are abundant in sediments.

At the present time, more than 3500 minerals of terrestrial and extra-terrestrial origin are known. Of these it have been estimated by Waller (1980) that some 300 are unstable to varying degrees in museum and other collections. A small minority are extremely reactive and may rapidly deteriorate on exposure to light and air. The majority are, however, metastable, being chiefly affected by variations in storage or exhibition environment over relatively long time periods. While the proportion of unstable to stable minerals is comparatively small, it should be borne in mind that, in terms of numbers of geological specimens, the proportion in many collections is very much larger. This is because a small number of unstable minerals occur commonly in a wide variety of fossils, rocks and mineral assemblages.

It is uncommon to find two or more unstable phases in close association within a single specimen, but where this does occur it is often the case that the phases require differing treatments or storage. In general, however, the problems encountered with the conservation and storage of geological material may be greatly minimized by taking simple measures for their safe handling and transport, and steps to moderate or exclude damaging environmental influences in their surroundings.

Published information on techniques used for preserving, conserving and storing geological material remains comparatively scarce. The palaeontological field has perhaps been best covered by the useful bibliographies in Kummel and Raup (1965) (covering the period 1900–1955) and Rixon (1976), and a series of bibliographies published in *Der Praparator* (1974–1976). Bannister (1937) and Waller (1980) have provided comprehensive articles on conservation problems in mineralogy and *Table 40.1* is largely based on these two authors findings. Sharpe (1983) has produced a comprehensive bibliography on museum geology which includes many references on conservation; see also Howie (in press) and Collins and Howie (in press). Further articles on these subject areas are published from time to time in *Curator*, *Studies in Conservation*, *The Geological Curator*, *Bulletin of the American Institute for Conservation*, *Mineralogical Record*, *Der Praparator*, *The Conservator*, *Museums Journal* and *The Journal of the Russell Society*.

The basic principles of, and approach towards, conserving geological specimens differ little from those adopted by practitioners in other disciplines. Although written for the antiquities and arts conservator, Plenderleith and Werner's (1971) standard reference work on conservation has much to offer those engaged in preserving geological material. However, as Feller (1974) has suggested, the long-term usefulness and advisability of many consolidative techniques should be questioned. In the past great numbers of geological specimens have been treated with an alarming range of natural and synthetic products in the name of preservation, many of which now cause considerable problems for the conservator attempting restabilization. There is considerable need for future research to be directed towards improving methods for the long-term preservation of unstable geological material, both through a better understanding of its deterioration and through a more thorough assessment of contemporary conservation technology.

The general care of minerals

In general, physical methods for conserving minerals, other than those necessary to preserve the original form, either in the field or during and after laboratory preparation or development, are not recommended. Applied resins and lacquers may react directly with a mineral and their removal for scientific examination is always attended by considerable risk to the specimen. Useful guidance on field collection, initial cleaning and processing is given by Croucher and Woolley (1982) and King (1982). Of great importance is the preservation of sometimes extremely delicate original assemblages and cleaning methods must allow for this.

Carrying by hand is usually the best way to transport highly delicate mineral specimens. However, many minerals will tarnish on contact with unprotected skin and everyday handling should in general be kept to a minimum. The transport of large or unwieldy specimens requires specialist assistance and methods applied to the movement of large, fragile antiquities may be appropriate (Stolow, 1981).

Minerals are classified and normally stored or exhibited primarily on a chemical basis commencing with the native elements and finishing with organic compounds. To some degree, this classification reflects the reactivity shown by unstable members of different groups but is not to be taken as a guide. *Table 40.1* is organized on the generally accepted mineralogical classification as an aid to the Curator looking for potential problem areas. Of the 300 or so unstable minerals known, the majority are comparatively rare and specific information on their physical, chemical and mineralogical properties may be found in Dana (1944) or by reference to *Mineralogical Abstracts*. Detailed data on their stability fields within collections has been reviewed by Waller (1980, in press). The data given in *Table 40.1* provide information on the environmental behaviour of some common unstable minerals.

Effects of light on mineral specimens

Some 90 minerals are known to be altered or decomposed by the action of light (*Table 40.1*). A minority, including varieties of some precious and semi-precious stones, suffer colour change only. Bannister (1937) describes varieties of topaz, sodalite, nepheline, fluorite, barytes, apatite and anhydrite which will fade if exposed to strong sunlight. With some of these, for example nepheline, the colour change is reversed when the specimens are replaced in the dark.

Although this problem was recognized by many early workers, little work on evaluating those wavelengths which may lead to colour change in specific mineral types has been undertaken (Nassau, in press). Observations made in modern mineral exhibitions suggest that low-level and ultraviolet (UV) filtered artificial light may be used with care. In general, however, it is recommended that photosensitive minerals be stored in light-proof cabinets wherever possible. This should certainly apply to fine and important specimens.

More serious for the curator is the effect of light and (usually) oxygen on a large number of sulphides, sulphosalts, halides, chromates and phosphates (*Table 40.1*). Many of the minerals listed will decompose through dissociation or oxidation reactions, or both, which are photochemically initiated or sustained. Some will decompose instantaneously upon exposure to light, for example certain silver halides, others such as realgar, stibnite and vivianite may take days or months to degrade, depending to some extent on crystal size. Vaughan and Stanley (1987), Buckley *et al* (1988) and others have shown that the surface reactions which sulphides undergo on exposure to light and/or oxygen are complex and usually involve molecular reconstruction of the mineral's surface, formation of unstable, transient phases and migration of constituent elements to the surface. All light-sensitive materials should be stored in light-proof cabinets or boxes, preferably constructed from materials which are unlikely to emit acid vapours. Some organic compounds will react with sulphides and other minerals, causing either surface contamination or, over the long term, degradation.

Vibration

Many minerals are highly sensitive to slight vibrations or jarring because of their extremely delicate crystalline nature. Examples are certain zeolites, native metals such as crystalline iron, and acicular or fibrous forms of common minerals such as halite. The individual crystals may adhere to a weak substrate or they may themselves be inherently brittle and fragile. Where the substrate or matrix can

Table 40.1 Effects on mineral of variations in environmental conditions: C, corrodes; Ch, colour change; D, decomposes; Dh, dehydrates; Dl, deliquesces; E, effloresces; Hl, hydrolyses; Hy, hydrates; O, oxidizes; T, tarnishes

High RH

Elements and alloys
- Copper — C
- Iron — C
- Iron/nickel alloys — C
- Lead — T
- Nickel — C

Sulphides and sulpho salts
- Arsenopyrite — O
- Blende — O
- Bravoite — O
- Chalcocite — O
- Daubréclite — O
- Enargite — O
- Ferroselite — O
- Galena — O
- Gersdorffite — O
- Hessite — O
- Mackinawite — O
- Marcasite — O
- Oldhamite — O
- Plenargyrite — O
- Proustite — O
- Pyrite — O
- Pyrrhotine — O
- Realgan — O
- Smaltite — O
- Smythite — O
- Stannite — O
- Stibnite — O
- Volynskite — O

Oxides and hydroxides
- Opal — Hy

Halides and oxyhalides
- Albrittonite — Dl
- Antarcticite — Dl
- Bischofite — Dl
- Carobbiite — Dl
- Carnallite — Dl
- Chloraluminite — Hl

Low RH

Sulphides and sulpho salts
- Daubréclite — O
- Oldhamite — O

Halides and oxyhalides
- Albrittonite — E
- Antarcticite — E
- Bischolite — E
- Carnallite — E
- Chloromanganokalite — E
- Chloromanganesite — E
- Douglasite — E
- Eriochalcite — E
- Erythrosiderite — E
- Kremersite — E
- Nickel-bischofite — E

Borates
- Boracite — E
- Borax — E
- Kernite — E
- Larderellite — ?E
- Probertite — E

Carbonates
- Gaylussite — E
- Hanksite — E
- Natron — E
- Pentahydrocalcite — E
- Spurrite — E

Nitrates
- Nitrocalcite — E
- Nitromagnesite — E

Silicates and aluminosilicates
- Chloropal — Dh
- Chrysocolla — Dh
- Clay minerals, e.g. allophane — Dh
- Montmorillonite — Dh
- Sepiolote — Dh
- Vermiculite — Dh

Temperature change

Elements and alloys
- Sulphur — D

Halides and oxyhalides
- Hydrohalite — D, −5°C
- Fluorite — D

Borates
- Tinca'conite — D, 60°C

Carbonates
- Gaylussite — D
- Pirssonite — D

Phosphates
- Autunite — Dh
- Metaautonite — Dh
- Variscite — Dh

High light levels

Oxides and hydroxides
- Cuprite — D
- Opal — Ch
- Quartz — Ch
- Quartz (amethyst) — Ch
- Quartz (rose) — Ch
- Quartz (smokey) — Ch
- Rutile — Ch
- Corundum — Ch

Halides and oxyhalides
- Bideauxite — Ch
- Bromargyrite — D
- Calomel — Ch
- Chlorargyrite — D
- Egelstonite — D
- Embolite — D
- Fluorite — Ch
- Huantajayite — Ch
- Lodyrite — Ch
- Lodembolite — D
- Kleinite — D
- Marshite — D
- Miersite — D
- Terlinguaite — D

Silicates and aluminosilicates
- Beryl — Ch
- Hackmanite — Ch
- Nepheline — Ch
- Serpentine — Ch
- Sodalite — Ch
- Topaz — Ch
- Zircon — Ch

Phosphates
- Apatite — Ch
- Turquoise — Ch

Light and/or oxygen

Elements and alloys
- Copper — T
- Lead — T

Sulphides, sulpho salts and sulphates
- Acanthite — T
- Aguilarite — T
- Alabandine — T
- Alaskaite — T
- Andorite — T
- Antimonpearcite — O
- Aramayoite — T
- Argentite — O
- Argyrodite — T
- Arsenpolybasite — O
- Baumhauerite — O
- Berzelianite — T
- Canfieldite — O
- Chalcocite — O
- Chloanthite — T
- Cinnabar — O
- Daubréclite — T
- Daiphorite — T
- Dufrenoysite — T
- Fizelyite — T
- Freieslenbenite — T
- Hessite — O
- Hodrushite — O
- Hutchinsonite — T
- Jordanite — T
- Lengenbachite — T
- Limacite — O
- Lorandite — T
- Matildite — T
- Miagyrite — O
- Mekinstryite — T
- Naumannite — O
- Oldhamite — O
- Pavonite — T

Pollutants

Elements and alloys
- Copper — C
- Iron — C
- Iron/nickel alloys — C
- Lead — C
- Meteorites (iron/nickel) — C
- Nickel — C
- Silver — T
- Tin — C

Carbonates
- Calcite — C

High RH	Low RH	Temperature change	High light levels	Light and/or oxygen	Pollutants
Chlormanganokalite Dl	*Zeolites, e.g.*		*Arsenates*	Pearceite T	
Chlorocalcite Dl	analcime Dh		Erythrite O	Penroscite O	
Chloromanganesite Dl	Chabazite Dh		Symplesite O	Plenargyrite O	
Douglasite Dl	Laumonite EDh			Polybasite T	
Eriochalcite Dl	Natrolite Dh			Polydymite O	
Halite Dl	*Phosphates*			Prousite O	
Huantajayite Dl	Autunite Dh			Pyragyrite Ch	
Kremersite Dl	Brushite Dh			Pyrostilprite T	
Lawerencite Dl	Metaautunite Dh			Rathite T	
Molysite Dl	Variscite Dh			Realgar O	
Nantokite Hl	Vivianite Dh			Samsonite T	
Nickel-bischofite Dl	*Vanadates and uranates*			Sanjunite T	
Rinncite Dl	Metavanuralite E			Smaltite T	
Sal-ammoniac Dl	Tyuyamunite E			Smithite Ch	
Scacchite Dl	*Arsenates*			Stephanite T	
Sylvine Dl	Annabergite E			Stibnote O	
Tachydrite Dl	Erythrite ?E			Stromeyerite T	
Borates	Symplesite ?E			Sylvanite T	
Borax Dl	*Sulphates*			Trechmannite O	
Metakernite Dl	Bianchite E			Violarite O	
Carbonates	Bieberite E			Volynskite O	
Cerrusite	Bonattite E			Vibaite O	
Teschemacherite	Boothite E			Xanthoconite T	
Thermonatrite Dl	Boussingaulite E			*Oxides and hydroxides*	
Trona Dl	Chalcanthite E			Cuprite T	
Nitrates	Coquimbite E			*Phosphates*	
Nitratine Dl	Cyamochroite E			Anapaite O	
Nitre Dl	Epsomite E			Grafonite O	
Nitrobarite Dl	Etringite E			Hureaulite O	
Nitrocalcite Dl	Goslarite E			Koninekite O	
Nitromagnesite Dl	Gunningite E			Vivianite O	
Silicates and aluminosilicates	Halotrichite E			*Vanadates and uranates*	
Clay minerals e.g. allophane Hy	Hexahydrite E			Tyuyamunite Ch	
Montmorillonite Hy	Hydrocyanite E			*Chromates*	
Sepiolite Hy	Jokouite E			Crocoite D	
Vermiculite Hy	Kainite E			Dietzite D	
Zeolites (e.g.): analcime Hy	Kiersite E			Phoenicochroite D	
Chabazite Hy	Mallardite E			*Organic compounds*	
Laumonite Hy	Melanterite E			Amber D	
Natrolite Hy	Mirabilite E			Copal D	
	Morenosite E				
	Nickel-hexahydrite E				

Vanadates and mafiates		Pentahydrite	
Metatyuyamunite	Hy	Pieromerite	E
Metavamuralite	Hy	Portevinite	E
Vamuralite	Hy	Rhomboclase	E
Vanuranilite	Hy	Sanderite	E
Sulphates		Starkeyite	E
Breberite	Dl	Szmikite	E
Bonattite	Hy	Szomolnokite	E
Boussingaulite	Dl	Tschermigite	E
Chalcanthite	Dl	Voltaite	E
Chalcocyanite	Hy	Zinc-melanterite	E
Coquimbite	Hy	*Organic compounds*	
Cyanochroite	Dl	Amber	Dh
Goslarite	Dl	Retinite	Dh
Gunningite	Hy	Copal	Dh
Hanksite	Dl	Fusain	Dh
Hexahydrite	Hy	Vitrain	Dh
Hydrocyanite	Hy	Protein degradation	Dh
Jokoknite	Hy	products	
Kainite	Dl	Lignite	Dh
Kierserite	Hy		
Leonite	Hy		
Mallardite	Dl		
Mascagnite	Dl		
Matteuccite	Dl		
Melanterite	Dl		
Mercallite	Dl		
Mirabilite	Dl		
Moorhousite	Hy		
Morenosite	Dl		
Nickel-hexahydrate	Hy		
Pentahydrite	Hy		
Pictromerite	Dl		
Pontevmite	Hy		
Retgersite	Hy		
Sanderite	Hy		
Starkeyite	Hy		
Szmikite	Hy		
Szmolnokite	Hy		
Thenardite	Hy		
Zinc-melanerite	Dl		
Organic compounds			
Amber (some)	Hy		
Retinite	Hy		
Copal	Hy		
Fusain	Hy		
Vitrain	Hy		
Protein degradation products			

be strengthened, the use of various consolidants, both of reversible and irreversible type, has been recommended. Waller (1980) suggests that weak, thin matrices can be adequately supported using polyester or epoxy resin bases provided these are applied to the matrix over a separator or film of readily removable adhesive. Where extremely fragile acicular crystals have been damaged or require direct support, the use of lacquers or synthetic polymers should not be considered except as a last resort. Where, for example, it is necessary to restore or repair a specimen for exhibition, the task should be referred to a specialist conservator, as any mistake made in the application, or later attempted removal, of consolidants will lead to damage.

Mineral specimens should be stored in cupboards or cabinets which are adequately damped to prevent vibration affecting drawers or shelves. Drawers should always run freely and remain level, Compactor units require especially careful vetting before they are used for mineral collections, to ensure that the travel mechanism is jolt free. Especially delicate or weak specimens may be further cushioned by setting on a slip or block of a stable expanded polyethylene foam with lint-free tissue paper or other non-fibrous material as a separator between the mineral and acid-free foam. Mineral specimens, like other categories of fragile geological material, should be stored in areas not subject to continuous or intermittent noise or vibration. Situations to avoid include proximity to air conditioning and ventilation plants and major roads and railways.

Effects of temperature

Contrary to popular belief, there are few minerals which are significantly altered by exposure to the temperature variations experienced in normal storage or exhibition environments. There are, however, many hydrated minerals which, if exposed to temperatures in excess of 30°C, will melt in their own water of crystallization. There are also many minerals which contain aqueous inclusions which, if subjected to freezing and thawing, would undoubtedly crack. Of the few minerals which are damaged by rapid but slight temperature changes, native sulphur crystals are the most sensitive and hand heat is enough to cause these to decrepitate. According to Waller (1980), some fluorites are damaged when washed in water which is not at room temperature or when transferred from a cold to a warm environment. It is recommended that minerals should be stored and exhibited at temperatures maintained between 10°C and 25°C with steps taken to prevent rapid fluctuations of more than ±5°C in this range. However, with moisture-sensitive materials (as described in the next section) it

is necessary to further restrict temperature changes in enclosed cases to ±2°C to prevent gross changes in relative humidity.

Relative humidity

Of all the factors influencing the stability of minerals, variation in ambient relative humidity (RH) is considered to be potentially the most damaging. The changes brought about fall into four major categories:

(1) Corrosion – generally of native metals and alloys.
(2) Oxidation – decay of sulphide minerals.
(3) Dimensional instability – distortion of hydrated silicates.
(4) Deliquescence, efflorscence, hydrolysis and hydration.

The measurement and monitoring of RH in storage and exhibition areas requires the use of calibrated instrumentation and should be entrusted to a trained conservator or competent ventilation engineer. Thomson (1985) describes in detail both theoretical and practical approaches to this subject and his book is essential reading for those whose duties include the care and management of mineral collections.

Corrosion

Native metals such as copper, silver, lead and iron, and some meteoritic iron–nickel alloys are highly susceptible to humidity-enhanced corrosion. This may be limited to surface tarnishing or may be more serious through corrosion and etching reactions brought about by hygroscopic salts present on the surface or within interstices of the specimen. One of the most notable corrosion problems ever recorded was caused by the presence of lawrencite, a hygroscopic iron–nickel chloride, within the body of the Cranbourne Meteorite. In an attempt to enhance its stability this specimen was exhibited for many years at the British Museum (Natural History) under an atmosphere of dry nitrogen in a sealed exhibition case (Bannister, 1937).

Oxidation

It is now known that a significant number of sulphides, arsendies and sulphosalts will oxidize when exposed to high relative humidities at normal temperatures. The mechanisms involved in the oxidation of iron pyrites have been investigated by Howie (1977, 1979a), and those of pyrite, chalcopyrite and pyrrhotite by Steger and Desjardins (1978) and those of galena, sphalerite and chalcocite by Steger and Desjardins (1980).

For many years it had been considered that thiobacteria were responsible for the oxidation of many museum sulphides, in particular pyrite, and treatments based on bactericides were advocated by Broadhurst and Duffy (1970) and Booth and Sefton (1970). Howie (1978a), however, demonstrated that the complicity of thiobacteria in the oxidation of pyrite under museum conditions was most unlikely.

The oxidation reactions of pyrite, marcasite, chalcopyrite, galena, sphalerite, arsenopyrite, bravoite and pyrrhotite probably all proceed through purely chemical mechanisms initiated by high relative humidity. Above 50–60 per cent RH, many of these minerals will react with oxygen and water to form hydrated metallic sulphates and free sulphuric acid. For pyrite it is now known that an important factor influencing rate of oxidation is crystal size, with microcrystalline pyrite being most susceptible to oxidation. This is undoubtedly an important consideration in the stability of other sulphides, arsenides and sulphosalts as well.

The effects of pyrite oxidation can be diminished by storing specimens at RH levels below 50 per cent, and methods for treating decayed pyritic material are detailed by Howie (1979a, b) and Waller (1987). These involve drying, removal of oxidation products by mechanical or chemical methods, neutralization and consolidation. The techniques involved require trained conservators and laboratory facilities.

Work by Thomson (1985), Stolow (1981), Kenjo (1981) and others has shown that optimum storage and exhibition microclimates may be achieved by using conditioned silica gel or other moisture buffering agents. The application of these techniques to the long-term preservation of unstable sulphides and other humidity-sensitive minerals is worthy of much wider consideration than has hitherto been accorded to it.

Dimensional stability

Certain hydrated aluminosilicate clay minerals, such as montmorillonite, have considerable capacity for moisture absorption and desorption, accompanied by significant swelling and subsequent shrinkage. This behaviour, which can be triggered off by changes in relative humidity, can cause extensive damage to specimens contained in shales. Swelling and shrinkage will cause shale delamination and shattering. Observations of stored shales suggest that below about 40 per cent RH rapid shrinkage can occur. An upper limit of 70 per cent RH is recommended, above which swelling may occur. Impregnation of particular types of shale using polyethylene glycol has been recommended by Oddy and Lane (1976) and polyvinyl acetate by Rixon (1976) and Waller (1980).

Other minerals affected by changes in RH are opal, chrysocolla, autunite and probably various types of amber. All develop shrinkage cracks through decrease in water content following lowering of ambient relative humidity. Critical humidity limits for these phenomena have not been determined.

Deliquescence, efflorescence, hydrolysis and hydration

A water-soluble mineral tends to draw moisture from the air, or deliquesce, when the ambient RH is higher than the water vapour pressure which would be exerted by a saturated solution of the same mineral at the same temperature. Deliquescence may occur with or without decomposition. The former occurs with some minerals containing multiple cations or anions or both. The latter is in evidence either where crusts of original mineral reform on the initial mineral's surface or where crystal corrosion and etching has occurred.

Hydrolysis is a chemical reaction between the mineral phase and water vapour with the formation of products. This occurs with several halide materials. The products are generally basic salts and hydrogen chloride, the latter being potentially corrosive to many other minerals.

Efflorescence is the loss of water from a hydrated mineral caused by a decrease in ambient RH to a level below the water vapour pressure of the hydrate at that temperature. Such water loss usually results in a change in hydration state and hence in crystal structure. Specimens often decompose physically during efflorescence.

Hydration is the uptake of water from air to form a higher hydrate. The new hydrate generally appears as a crust on the original mineral.

The long-term preservation of minerals subject to these processes can only be accomplished by storage in sealed containers over suitable dessicants or materials preconditioned to hold RH levels within the known limits of stability. Detailed information on this aspect of mineral conservation is given in Waller (1980, in press).

Effects of atmospheric pollutants

The effects of the major atmospheric pollutants on mineral specimens has received little attention. It is wise to avoid exposing carbonates, oxides and hydroxides to atmospheres containing more than trace quantities of acid gases such as sulphur dioxide. The detection and activity of atmospheric pollutants in museum collections is discussed in considerable detail by Thomson (1985).

An often ignored aspect of storage and conservation is the potential danger of the build-up of corrosive vapours within exhibition or storage cases. This can be brought about by the presence of certain timbers such as oak and through the slow deterioration of a variety of natural synthetic materials. Blackshaw and Daniels (1978) showed that metals such as silver and lead suffered considerable corrosion through the activity of many commonly used materials under accelerated ageing test conditions. Fitzhugh and Gettens (1971), Howie (1978a). and Tennent and Baird (1985) describe the damaging effect of organic acid vapours on calcareous material stored in cabinets containing oak components. Argyrakis (1981) provides a useful review of atmospheric pollutants and their activity in museum collections.

Fossils

Over the past century the conservation of fossil material in collections has tended to become synonymous with the use of a range of natural or synthetic resins, glues and waxes for the repair, impregnation and protective coating of specimens (Howie, 1985). However, during the past two decades, considerable advances have been made in understanding both the properties and long-term stability of many of the materials used in conservation, and there is now some knowledge about the factors governing the stability of certain categories of palaeontological material. It is perhaps in the wider field of technology that an increased awareness of the effects of processing palaeontological material, over both the long and short term, is required.

Processing fossil material

The active conservation of fossil specimens should begin at the time of collection or excavation. Damage caused by faulty procedure or through the use of unsuitable materials in the field can be extremely difficult to rectify later. The excavation of fragile fossil material from wet or loose sediments often necessitates the application of a consolidant or other supporting medium to exposed surfaces. The treatments used must be reversible during later processing without undue risk of damage to the specimen.

The excavation of unstable fossil material may present problems. For example, partly fossilized bone or tusk, lignitic or organic-rich fossil plant remains or specimens in paper shales often occur preserved in wet or waterlogged sediments. To prevent warping or even complete collapse it is essential to ensure that drying out does not occur during excavation, transport or pre-treatment storage. Simple measures such as enclosure in field cocoons or wrapping in sealed plastic bags, with a fungicide to prevent mould growth, are often all that is required. On the other hand, pyritic material will inevitably deteriorate in a damp cocoon, and the sooner it is processed the better.

A variety of techniques has been developed for safely collecting and transporting fossil material and these are described in Kummel and Raup (1965), Rixon, (1976) and Croucher and Wooley (1982).

Useful information on conservation-oriented excavation is provided by Downman (1971), Leigh (1978) and Brothwell (1981). These publications, although written mainly for the field archaeologist, contain much of value to the palaeontological collector.

During specimen preparation or development, one or other of a variety of processes or substances may be used which, without special precautions, could lead to damage or deterioration. Time and effort should be spent in protecting delicate material during mechanical preparation with percussive, rotary or vibratory equipment. Rixon (1976) describes the general use of a variety of shock-absorbing and supporting media, for specimens undergoing preparation, and Whybrow (1982) details, as a case study, the techniques used and precautions taken during the mechanical preparation of the delicate cranium of the holotype of *Archaeopteryx lithographica*.

With the increased use of chemical techniques for the development of fossil material there is greater risk of specimen damage during both the processing stage and in subsequent storage. Problems arise through a number of factors including the use of chemicals incompatible with the specimen, poorly applied or inadequate supporting resins and insufficient washing-out of applied chemicals. The importance of a thorough knowledge of the properties of the material to be treated, the substances to be used and the precautions required cannot be stressed enough. The use of any chemcial process should be followed up by periodic examination of treated material in storage.

Storage and handling of fossils

The range of specimens in even a modest palaeontological collection can be extremely diverse. Handling and storing specimens as different as slide-mounted microfossils and multi-element fossil vertebrate skeletons present problems that require carefully considered solutions. Systematic or stratigaphic constraints usually dictate that collections be housed on a flexible basis with allowance made in storage areas and individual storage units for specimens of greatly differing size, fragility and stability. Doughty (1981) describes many of the shortcomings found in geological collections and has highlighted the poor state of conservation which results from inadequate storage. Rickards (1979) describes the basis for the development of the effective storage of fossil material and Owen *et al.,* (1981) detail the arrangements for storing the national collection of fossils at the (Natural History Museum). Useful guidance on the handling and storage of large and fragile vertebrate material is provided by Gentry (1979) and Fitzgerald (in press).

Delicate fossil material such as acid-developed specimens should be treated in the same way as fragile minerals and stored in shock-absorbent protective packing. The use of cotton wool for packing should be avoided at all costs as extensive damage and loss of material easily results.

Consolidation and repair

Fossils, whether large or small, robust or delicate, can be damaged through neglect, mishandling, inherent instability or the deterioration of aged glues and consolidants. Repair and consolidation, except for the most basic type, should be entrusted to a conservator for a number of reasons. The type of consolidant required and its application may have to be varied depending on, for example, the permeability of the specimen; specific adhesives may be required for durable results with certain types of material; old consolidants and glues may, if not thoroughly removed, interfere with or inhibit retreatment with modern synthetic materials. In addition, details of treatments should be recorded, and the records stored safely, for the guidance of future workers.

The amount of literature on this subject is extensive and for specific information on particular applications reference should be made to standard texts such as Horie (1987) and to conservation journals. Rixon (1976) and Howie (1979b) describe various methods developed for the repair, consolidation and restoration of several types of fossils, including old and salvaged specimens. Of importance to the storage and exhibition of treated material is the long-term stability of modern synthetic resins. Many of the standard conservation materials, for example polyvinyl acetate, polyvinyl butyral, and polybutyl and polymethyl methacrylate, have been used in conservation for only a realtively short period. The limited data available from ageing tests and observations of behaviour under storage and exhibition conditions suggest that many polymers slowly degrade through exposure to ultraviolet radiation in the 250–500 nm band, and that high relative humidity and the presence of trace quantities of oxidizing agents in air can lead to accelerated scission, cross-linking and reduced resolubility (see also Grassie and Bejuki, 1966; Carlick, 1976; von Fraunhofer and Boxall, 1976; Howie, 1985). As a general rule the use of consolidants should be kept to a minimum and, as with repair or restoration, undertaken only where necessary to support or impregnate material or render it transportable.

Relative humidity

Variations in RH give rise to four main problems with the storage and exhibition of fossil material. At high RH pyritic fossils deteriorate. Low RH causes shrinkage of hygroscopic materials and warping or distortion occurs in certain types of shale, sub-fossil bone and enamel and in lignitic or partially carbonized fossil plant remains.

Pyritic fossil material

In fossils, pyrite occurs in a number of forms and its oxidation causes considerable damage, both through the destruction of bone or calcareous minerals present, and by destroying labels and containers. Howie (1979a) describes the occurrence of reactive and stable pyrite in fossil material, outlines the mechanisms proposed for the oxidation of reactive pyrite and shows that the use of conventional consolidants for specimen coatings gives little protection when the RH rises above about 60 per cent. The treatment of decayed pyrite specimens is delt with by Rixon (1976) and Howie (1979a, b), and because of the special technical facilities required, should be referred to conservation staff. The long-term prevention of pyrite oxidation should be achievable through control or modification of the storage environment. In older buildings the use of well-constructed timber cabinets generally provides a fair degree of protection, but in newer buildings, or where climate dictates, it may be necessary to have recourse, to air-conditioning (Owen *et al*, 1981; Thomson, 1985). The use of moisture buffering agents, such as preconditioned silica gel in individual storage units or exhibition cases, offers a low cost, low maintenance alternative (Howie, 1979a; Thomson, 1985).

Hygroscopic shales

Many types of shale, most notably those containing montmorillonite, will respond to decreases in RH by delaminating and splitting, as with the notorious paper shales. Hard shales will, however, also degrade when exposed to low RH by shrinking and shattering. Limiting conditions of humidity for their storage has not been determined. Conservation treatments suggested include: the use of water-soluble waxes where pyrite oxidation is not a problem (Oddy and Lane, 1976); impregnation using polyvinyl acetate (Rixon, 1976); and, in suitable cases, removal of as much shale as possible (Howie, 1979b).

Sub-fossil bone

Much sub-fossil bone contains collagen or its protein-rich breakdown products. Little research has been carried out into the deterioration of aged proteinaceous material. What data are available suggests that exposure to low humidities can cause temporary or permanent alterations in protein amino acids, (Karpowicz, 1981). The effects of lowering the RH around sub-fossil bone have been reported by

Howie (1978b) and it is recommended that such material be stored at 45–55 per cent RH. The treatment for warped and split sub-fossil bone, detailed by Rixon (1976) and Howie (1979a, b), should be carried out by conservation staff.

Moisture-sensitive palaeobotanical material

Partially carbonized fossil plant material, including leaves, wood, seeds and roots, is perhaps the most difficult type of material to treat satisfactorily. When it contains pyrite, one partly successful method is storage immersed in an inert silicone fluid (Howie, 1979a). When pyrite is not present, the use of polyethene glycol has sometimes been successful (Rixon, 1976). Palaeobotanists, however, do not generally work with immersed or coated material and the increasing use of scanning electron microscopy dictates that type specimens may be on stubs, thus precluding the use of any coatings or liquids in their conservation. Collinson (1987) suggests the use of specially constructed desiccated units in which such specimens could be stored at an optimum RH.

Acknowledgements

I thank numerous colleagues in the Departments of Mineralogy and Paleontology of the Natural History Museum London and elsewhere for useful comments on the manuscript. I also thank Rob Waller at the Mineral Sciences Division of the Museum of Nature in Ottawa for advice and guidance.

References

ARGYRAKIS, A (1981), *Conservation Problems in Museum Displays*, Area Museums Service for South Eastern England, Milton Keynes

BANNISTER, F. A. (1937), 'The preservation of minerals and meteorites', *Museums Journal*, **36**(11), 465–476

BLACKSHAW, S. M. and DANIELS, V. D. (1978), 'Selecting safe materials for use in the display and storage of antiquities', *Preprint 5th Triennial Meeting ICOM Committee for Conservation, Zegreb*, 23 February 1978, pp. 1–9

BOOTH, G. H. and SEFTON, G. V. (1970), 'Vapour phase inhibition of thiobacilli and ferrobacilli: a potential preservative for pyritic museum specimens', *Nature*, **226**, 185–186

BRAODHURST, F. M. and DUFFY, L. (1970), 'A plesiosaur in the Geology Department, University of Manchester', *Museums Journal*, **70**(1), 30–31

BROTHWELL, D. R. (1981), *Digging up Bones*, British Museum (Natural History), London

BUCKLEY, A. N., HAMILTON, I. C. and WOODS, R. (1988), 'Studies of the surface oxidation of pyrite and pyrrhotine using X-ray photoelectron spectroscopy and linear sweep voltametry', *Proceedings of the International Symposium of Electrochemical, Minerological and Metallurgical Processes*, **2**, 234–246

CARLICK, D. J. (1976), 'Photodegradation, Controlled', *Encyclopedia of Polymer Science and Technology, Supplement 1*, 378–401, Interscience, New York

COLLINS, C. and HOWIE, F. M. P. (Eds) (in press), *Conservation of Geological Material, Vol. 2: Palaeontological and Palaeo-anthropological material*, Butterworths, London

COLLINSON, M.E. (1987), 'Special problems in the conservation of palaeobotanical material', *The Conservation of Geological Material, Geological Curator*, **4**, 439–445

CROUCHER, R. and WOOLLEY, A. W. (1982), *Fossils, Minerals and Rocks: Collection and Preservation*, British Museum (Natural History), London and University of Cambridge, Cambridge

DANA, J. D. (1944), *A System of Mineralogy*, Wiley, New York

DOUGHTY, P. S. (1981), *The State and Status of Geology in UK Museums. Miscellaneous paper No. 13*, Geological Society, London

DOWMAN, E. (1971), *Conservation in Field Archaeology*, Methuen, London

FELLER, R. L. (1974), 'Fundamentals of conservation science: induction time and the auto-oxidation of organic compounds', *Bulletin of the American Institute of Conservation*, **14**, 142–151

FITZGERALD, G. R. (in press), 'Storage and transport', in Collins, C. and Howie, F. (Eds), *Conservation of Geological Material: Volume 2: Palaeontological and Palaeonthropological Material*, Butterworths, London

FITZHUGH, F. W. and GETTENS, R. J. (1971), 'Calcacite and other efflorescent salts on objects stored in wooden museum cases', in Brill, R. H. (Ed), *Science and Archaeology*, Massachusetts Institute of Technology Press, Cambridge, MA, pp. 91–102

GENTRY, A. W. (1979), 'Curation of fossil vertebrates', in Bassett, M.G. (Ed.), *Curation of Palaeontological Collections, Special Papers in Palaeontology No. 22*, 87–95 The Palaeontological Association, London

GRASSIE, N and BEJUKI, N. W. (1966), 'Degradation', *Encyclopedia of Polymer Science and Technology*, **4**, 647–735 Interscience, New York

HEY, M. H. (1962) *Index of Mineral Species and Varieties arranged Chemically*, British Museum (Natural History), London

HORIE, C. W. (1987), *Materials for Conservation*, Butterworths, London

HOWIE, F. M. P. (1977), Pyrite and conservation. Parts 1 and 2: historical aspects, *Geological Curator*, **1**, 457–465, 497–512

HOWIE, F. M. P. (1978a), 'Storage environment and the conservation of geological material', *Conservator*, **2**, 13–19

HOWIE, F. M. P. (1978b), 'Storage and exhibition environment and the conservation of fossil material', *Preprint Museums Conservation Climate Conference JCCROM*, November 1978, Rome

HOWIE, F. M. P. (1979a), 'Museums climatology and the conservation of palaeontological material', in Bassett, M. G. (Ed.), *Curation of Palaeontological Collections, Special Papers in Palaeontology No. 22*, 103–25, The Palaeontological Association, London

HOWIE, F. M. P. (1979b), 'Physical conservation of fossils in existing collections', *Geological Curator*, **2**(5), 269–280

HOWIE, F. M. P. (1985), 'Minerals used for conserving fossil specimens since 1930: a review', *Preprint 10th International Congress ICC, Paris*, September 1984

HOWIE, F. M. P. (Ed.), (in press), *Conservation of Geological Material, Vol. 1: Minerals, Rocks and Lunar Finds*, Butterworths, London

KARPOWICZ, A. (1981), 'Ageing and deterioration of proteinaceous media', *Studies in Conservation*, **26**(4), 153–160

KENJO, T. (1981), 'A rapid-response humidity buffer composed of Nikka pellets and Japanese tissue', *Studies in Conservation*, **27**, 19–24

KING. R. J. (1982), 'Section one – the cleaning of minerals', *Journal of the Russell Society*, **1**(1), 42–53

KUMMEL, B. and RAUP, D. (1965), *Handbook of Palaeontological Techniques*, Freeman, San Francisco, CA

LEIGH, D. (1978), *First aid for Finds: a Practical Guide for Archaeologists*, Rescue, Hertford

NASSAU, K. (in press), 'Conserving light sensitive minerals and gems, in Howie, F. (Ed.), *Conservation of Geological Material Volume 1: Minerals, Rocks and Lunar Finds*, Butterworths London

ODDY, W. A. and LANE, H. (1976), 'The conservation of waterlogged shale', *Studies in Conservation*, **21**, 63–66

OWEN, H. G., PARSONS, E. and PATERNOSTER, R. (1981), 'Rationalized storage of fossils in the British Museum (Natural History)', *Curator*, **24**(2), 77–88

PLENDERLEITH, H. J. and WERNER, E.A.E. (1971), *The Conservation of Antiquities and Works of Art*, Oxford University Press, Oxford

RICKARDS, R. B. (1979), 'The physical basis of palaeontological curating', in Bassett, M.G. (Ed.), *Curation of Palaeontological Collections. Special Papers in Palaeontology, No. 22*, 75–86, The Palaeontological Association, London

RIXON, A. E. (1976), *Fossil Animal Remains: Their Preparation and Conservation*, Athlone Press, London

SHARPE, T. (1983), *Geology in Museums: a Bibliography and Index, Geological Series No. 6*, National Museum of Wales, Cardiff

STEGER, H. F. and DESJARDINS, L. E. (1978), 'Oxidation of sulphide minerals, 4, Pyrite, chalcopyrite and pyrhotite', *Chemical Geology*, **23**, 225–237

STEGER, F. H. and DESJARDINS, L. E. (1980), Oxidation of sulphide minerals, 5, Galiena, sphalerite and chalcocite', *Canadian Mineralogist*, **18**, 365–372

STOLOW, N. (1981), *Procedures and Conservation Standards for Museum Collections in Transit and on Exhibition*, UNESCO, Paris

TENNENT, N. H. and BAIRD, T. (1985), 'The deterioration of mollusca collections: identification of shell efflorescence', *Studies in Conservation*, **30**, 73–85

THOMPSON, G. (1986), *The Museum Environment*, Butterworths/IIC, London

VAUGHAN, D. J. and STANLEY, C. J. (1987), 'The surface properties of bornite', *Mineralogical Magazine*, **51**, 285–293

VON FRAUNHOFER, J. A. and BOXALL, J. (1976), *Protective Paint Coatings for Metals*, Portcullis Press, Redhill, Surrey

WALLER, R. (1980), 'The preservation of mineral specimens', *Preprint 8th Annual Meeting AIC*, pp. 166–178

WALLER, R. (1987), 'An experimental ammonia treatment method for oxidized pyrite mineral specimens', *Preprints 8th Triennial Meeting, ICOM Committee for Conservation*, 623–630

WALLER, R. (in press), 'Temperature and humidity sensitive mineralogical and petrological specimens', in Howie, F. (Ed.), *Conservation of Geological Material Volume 1: Minerals, Rocks and Lunar Finds*, Butterworths, London

WHYBROW, R. J. (1982), 'Preparation of the cranium of the holotype of *Archaeopteryx lithographica* from the collection of the British Museum (Natural History)', *Neus Jahrbuch fur Geologie und Palaontologie, Monatshefte*, **3**, 184–192

41

Conservation and storage: zoological collections

Geoffrey Stansfield

The conservation of biological collections differs from the conservation of objects of art and antiquity in a number of respects. First, animals and plants are usually collected live and the process of preparing them for the museum is termed 'preservation' rather than 'conservation'. This often involves several stages, including collecting, narcotization, killing, fixing and preserving. In the natural sciences the term 'conservation' is used normally to describe treatment after preservation, made necessary by either shortcomings in the preservation process or damage caused by inappropriate conditions of storage and inadequate maintenance. Second, the preservation method employed often depends on whether a specimen is destined to be used for exhibition or research. In mounting a specimen for exhibition, much of its scientific value might be lost, due to the preservation method employed. Third, in many instances parts of the object are discarded, retaining only those parts which are easily preserved and which embody diagnostic features.

Collecting

Although there are circumstances in which biological specimens are collected by amateurs, in most cases it is preferable that specialists undertake collecting. Failing this, collectors should be provided with detailed instructions and training. Without such training, there is a danger that significant data will not be recorded, that appropriate techniques will not be used, and that significant specimens will escape attention.

As a general principle, material should be processed as soon as possible after collection. Biological decomposition begins to take place as soon as the animal or plant dies and, under warm conditions, irreparable damage can take place within hours. If it is not possible to process the specimen immediately,

interim steps should be taken to prevent deterioration until such time as a complete preservation can be undertaken. Such general measures include keeping the material as cool as possible, and placing specimens in insect-proof containers to guard against damage by scavenging insects and other animals which might regard the freshly collected specimens as a source of food.

General works or reference on collecting include the British Museum (Natural History) *Instructions for Collectors* series (particularly Lincoln and Sheals (1979)), Wagstaffe and Fidler (1955, 1968), Knudsen (1975) and Steedman (1976).

Collecting policies and restrictions

The collecting of zoological specimens should take place within the parameters of a clearly defined collecting policy which reflects the museum's research and education needs. Particular restrictions apply in the case of biological specimens, arising from the need to comply with national and international wildlife laws, treaties and conventions.

In Britain the operative law is the *Wildlife and Countryside Act* HMSO, (1981) which repeals and re-enacts with amendments earlier legislation. The Act prohibits the collecting or disturbance of certain species of vertebrates, invertebrates and plants; it prohibits specific collecting methods; and it prohibits the sale or trading in listed species. Protected species are listed in Schedules which may be updated by the Secretary of State as needed. The current operative Schedules are included in *The Wildlife and Countryside Act 1981 (variation of Schedules) Order 1988* (HMSO, 1988a). There are provisions for the granting of licences to collect for scientific purposes.

The Act also amends the *Endangered Species (Import and Export Act) (1976)* which makes it an offence to export or import certain animals and plants (listed in Schedules) without a licence. The Schedules are prepared by the *Convention on International Trade in Endangered Species* (CITES) and they are updated periodically. Details may be obtained from the CITES Secretariat, 6 Rue du Maupas, P.O. Box 78, 1000 Lausanne 9, Switzerland.

International Wildlife Law (Lyster, 1982), is a valuable reference work for museums which plan to import or export specimens of protected species. Museums may obtain a licence relating to an individual transaction, or museums which are involved in large numbers of exchanges (e.g. National Museums) may obtain open licences which cover multiple transactions, subject to the keeping of detailed records. The *CITES Identification Manual* in five volumes – *Mamals, Aves, Amphibia Reptiles and Pisces, Parts and Derivatives 1* and *Parts and Derivatives 2* – facilitates the identification of animals and plants and derivatives. Details of trade in endangered species are given in the periodical *Traffic* published by The Wildlife Trade and Monitoring Unit of the International Union for the Conservation of Nature.

Dry preservation

Preservation by drying may be used for whole organisms in the case of small animals and most plants. It may also be used for parts of organisms such as the shells of molluscs, the tests of echinoderms, the skins of mammals and birds and the bones of vertebrates. Drying may be carried out in air if the relative humidity is low enough but may be assisted by heat.

Wet preservation

Wet preservation is more appropriate for the preservation of the whole bodies of vertebrates (except for the largest animals), for soft-bodied invertebrates and for immature stages of animals. Wet preservation is most appropriate for specimens required for reference or research, and is less suitable for material required for exhibition (although there are exceptions). Wet preservation is a complex process involving a number of stages which can include narcotization, killing, fixing and preservation. If in doubt about the procedure to be followed, it is best to consult a specialist in the group concerned.

The report of a one-day course held at the Manchester Museum in 1989 (Horie, 1989), includes a number of useful papers on the conservation of spirit collections.

Narcotization

Narcotization is a necessary stage in the preservation of many invertebrates where killing methods cause the animal to contract and to withdraw organs and appendages which carry characters essential for indentification. Some narcotization techniques are described by Wagstaffe and Fidler (1955, 1968). Smaldon and Lee (1979) have produced an extensive list of methods for the narcotization of marine invertebrates.

Killing

Killing may be accomplished by depriving animals of oxygen or by the use of poisons. If poison is used, it is imperative that the Curator is thoroughly familiar with health hazards and safety procedures, and regulations and laws governing their use.

Fixing

Fixing is the process by which the protein constituents of tissue are stabilized. For some types of specimen, fixing and preservation may be carried out in the same medium, while for others two stages and two media are necessary.

Preservation

A wide range of preservatives are in use, together with mixtures favoured for particular groups of specimens. The most common preservatives are formaldehyde, alcohol (in various forms) and phenoxetol.

Commercial formalin is readily obtainable as a 40 per cent aqueous solution of the gas formaldehyde. To make formaldehyde solution suitable for use as a fixative and preservative, commercial formalin is usually diluted with water to between 3 and 10 per cent. To make 10 per cent formaldehyde, it is necessary to add 3.5 parts of water to one part of commercial formalin. Although a good fixative, it is less favoured as a preservative because of its pungent and irritating odour and possible health hazards. Formaldehyde solutions almost always have an acid reaction, due to the presence of formic and other acids, and are thus unsuitable for treating calcareous animals. Solutions may be neutralized in several ways. For example, formalin may be buffered with the organic base hexamine (hexamethylenetetramine), the appropriate concentration being 200 g of hexamine per litre of undiluted commercial formalin (see Lincoln and Sheals, 1979).

Ethyl alcohol (ethanol) diluted with water to a concentration of approximately 70 per cent by volume is one of the most widely used preservatives. In Britain, and many other countries, pure ethyl alcohol is very expensive owing to the high tax it carries. As an alternative to pure ethyl alcohol, industrial methylated spirit (IMS) is used. IMS is available in several forms and that suitable for preserving biological material consists of 95 parts by volume of ethyl alcohol and 5 parts per volume of either crude or pure methyl alcohol, depending on the grade. To purchase any quantity of IMS in Britain, a permit must be obtained from the Commissioners of Customs and Excise. Disadvantages of ethyl alcohol and IMS are that they are volatile and inflammable. If containers are not sealed they may need to be topped up periodically with preservative, and care must be taken to maintain the concentration of the preservative. It is also advisable to take the advice of a Fire Officer in planning a store in which a significant amount of material is to be stored in alcohol.

Propylene phenoxetol is a widely recommended post-fixation preservative. Its main advantages are that the specimens stored in it retain their colour and remain pliable. It is also non-flammable, may be transported as a concentrated solution, and is a relatively inexpensive preservative. Several workers, including Steedman (1976), recommend procedures for transferring material from alcohol to propylene phenoxetol. Recently, doubt has been expressed about its suitability as a long-term preservative, particularly for fish (Crimmen, 1989) and for some insects.

There are health hazards in using most preservatives, particularly formaldehyde, and their future use may well be determined by health-and-safety regulations. In Britain, use may be restricted by the provisions of the *Control of Substances Hazardous to Health Regulations (1988)*, discussed below. Details of toxicity and precautions to be taken are given in Sax (1988).

Containers for spirit collections present a number of problems. Ideally, museums should adopt a standard range of containers but, as they are obtained from commercial sources, suitable containers often go out of production. In general, flat-bottomed glass tubes are most suitable for the smallest specimens, wide-mouthed glass jars for larger ones, and fibreglass or stainless steel tanks for the largest. Jars need to be well-sealed, particularly if alcohols are used. Evaporation may be reduced, however, if the temperature in the store is maintained at a low level. In Britain 'Copenhagen' jars are widely used. Although there is a strong case for transferring specimens into standard jars, it is important to note that there are circumstances in which the jar itself can provide information about the origin of the specimen. For a recent paper on containers see Horie (1989).

For the labelling of material stored in liquid preservatives, it is recommended that labels should be placed *inside* the containers, but be visible from the outside. Lables attached to the outsides of containers may become detached or may be eaten by insects. Label paper should be good-quality, non-sized, rag paper free from starch and mineral matter and with a high wet tensile strength. An alternative to paper is a spun-bonded, high-density polythene fibre (see Pettit, 1975). Data should be written in waterproof ink or pencil. If there is any doubt about the permanence of the ink, tests should be carried out to ensure that labels and ink do not fade and are not dissolved by the preservative.

Freeze-drying

Freeze-drying is the process by which water is removed from frozen specimens by sublimation. That is, the water vapour passes directly from the solid phase (ice) to the gaseous phase without passing through the liquid phase. This has the advantage that shrinkage which often accompanies drying is reduced or eliminated. The application of freeze-drying to the preservation of natural history specimens dates from the early 1960s, and follows experimental work carried out at the Smithsonian Institution in Washington (Meryman, 1960, 1961). Although the technique was originally used for the preservation of animals for exhibitions (and has been used successfully for quite large mammals), freeze-drying is most suitable for smaller animals. Its main potential lies in the preservation of soft-bodied animals for which the previous alternative was preservation in liquid. It should be noted, however, that when used to preserve specimens for exhibition, considerable skill is required to pose the animals in life-like attitudes and, for example, to replace the eyes in vertebrates.

Early equipment for freeze-drying was purpose built, but a number of manufacturers have produced more or less standard equipment suitable for museum use. Larger units still have to be custom built.

Doubts have been expressed about the long-term stability of freeze-dried specimens, and research is needed to monitor stability and into the biological, chemical and physical changes which take place during the process. It should also be noted that some insect larvae have been shown to be able to survive the process. Freeze-dried specimens provide an attractive source of food for many animals (including carnivores) and care is needed to prevent infestation by insect pests.

The manufacturers Edwards High Vacuum have issued a warning that explosions may occur in freeze-drying equipment if azides are present in the specimens or have been used in preservation. The present consensus of opinion suggests that there is no danger from naturally occurring azides but that freeze-drying should not be used for specimens which have been preserved with azides.

Freezing

Biological research is now carried out more and more at the molecular level. Such work may be performed on fresh material or frozen material. Frozen tissues have served as the primary source material for basic research in evolutionary biology, systematics, genetics, biochemistry and immunology focused at the molecular level. Frozen material has also been used in breeding programmes in zoological parks, by researchers monitoring levels of pollutants and in the identification of material involving endangered species.

A report by Dessauer and Hafner (1984), *Collections of frozen tissues; value, management, field and laboratory procedures, and directory of existing collections,* presents a strong case for the establishment of collections of frozen material. In the USA a number of museums have now initiated such collections, but in Britain the only collections appear to be at the University of Salford and the University of Loughborough.

Documenting zoological collections

Standard documentation procedures for museum specimens are described elsewhere in this book and in other works of reference. For natural science collections the reader is referred to *Natural History Specimen Card Instructions* (Museum Documentation Association, 1980), For natural science collections it is important to stress the need to record the scientific name (together with the author and the date) according to the rules of the International Code of Zoological Nomenclature and the International Code of Botanical Nomenclature. It is also important to record the name of the collector, the method of collection, cause of death and any preservatives used. As well as recording the locality from which the specimen is collected it is necessary to record the habitat. Many museums in Britain use *Habitat Mapping Manual (Phase 1)* (Nature Conservancy Council, no date), but there is no universally accepted convention. It is important to remember that the 'habitat' can refer to a particular location on a plant or to the host of a parasite. It is particularly important to record full acquisition details for specimens of any species which are subject to conservation laws, in order to be able to show that the museum has not contravened these laws.

Vertebrate specimens

Some general comments about vertebrate collections are appropriate. For most vertebrates it is usual to employ quite different preservation methods for animals being preserved for exhibition and animals being preserved for reference or research. Whereas most competent museum workers should be able to master the skills in preparing specimens for the reference collections, including cabinet skins of mammals and birds, the mounting of specimens for exhibition requires the skills of a trained taxidermist. The acquisition of such skills demands a long period of training and a great deal of experience. Taxidermy is a subject in its own right with its own training courses and literature and is outside the scope of this chapter.

The report of a one-day course held at Manchester Museum in 1988 (Horie and Murphy, 1988) includes useful and authoritative up-to-date papers on the conservation of vertebrate collections.

Osteology collections

The preparation of oesteological material merits special note. For larger vertebrates, the traditional method when collecting in the field at some distance from the museum has been to 'rough skin' the animal and remove the contents of the body cavities, allowing the specimen to dry before transportation. Once in the laboratory, the remaining flesh is removed mechanically after boiling in water. This method is still employed for large species, although the drying stage can be omitted if specimens are taken to the museum promptly.

The cleaning process can be facilitated in a number of ways. Enzymes have been used by some museums, although this method is not now widely used. Smaller specimens are most conveniently cleaned in a dermestarium (a colony of dermestid beetles) as described by Sommer and Anderson (1974). Great care should be taken to ensure that beetles and larvae from the dermestarium are not allowed to infest the stored collections. Sodium perborate has also been used, particularly by archaeozoologists to clean specimens. Very large specimens (marine mammals) have been treated successfully by burying in silver sand. Some bones may need to be degreased.

Mammal collections

Mammal collections consist largely of mounted specimens, mounted heads, flat and round skins, articulated and disarticulated skeletons, specimens in liquid preservatives, specimens showing evidence of mammal feeding or damage, film and tape. Collecting methods are discussed in the standard works of reference cited below. It should be noted that the collecting of many mammal species is controlled by wildlife conservation laws.

Most specimens intended for research and

documentation are preserved by removing the skin from the carcass, retaining only the dried skin, the skull and some of the limb bones. In the case of a larger species, the skin has to be pickled or tanned after removing any remaining fat or flesh. For smaller species, the skin may be preserved by drying, often with the addition of a preservative as a precaution against decay or insect attack. The standard reference works are Anderson (1965), British Museum (Natural History) (1968), and Nargorsen and Peterson (1980). The preparation of skeletons and skeletal material has already been discussed.

There are no specific conservation problems peculiar to mammals, but normal precautions must be taken against attack by insect pests. If the fat has not been completely removed during preservation, it will decompose and cause damage known as 'fat burn'. Skeletal material may crack if the relative humidity is too low.

The storage of mammals does not present particular problems. Mounted heads are best stored on vertical racks, skins in trays or drawers, and spirit collections in accordance with normal wet-storage procedures. Some North American museums have low-temperature stores for mammal skins.

For further information on the management of mammal collections see particularly Genoways *et al* (1987).

Bird collections

Bird collections consist largely of mounted specimens, skins, articulated and disarticulated skeletons, specimens stores in liquid preservatives, eggs, nests, specimens showing examples of feeding and damage, photographs, film and tape. Collecting procedures and mounting techniques are described in the literature cited below. Many species are covered by wildlife conservation laws and agreements.

The mounting of skins for research and study is described by Harrison *et al* (1970). It is usual to leave the major part of the skull attached to the skin as well as the radius, ulna, tibia and tarsus. In most cases, the skin may be preserved by drying with the addition of a preservative as a precaution against deterioration. There are some exceptions, including water birds which must be treated with solvents to remove grease and fat. A recent paper (Johnson *et al.*, 1984) describes how research of systematic ornithology is carried out by electrophoresis techniques carried out on tissue samples. The paper also describes the preparation of 'skin-skeletons' which allow all routine skin and skeletal measurements to be taken from the same individual. The latter preparations are used at the Royal Ontario Museum in Toronto.

Egg-shells are usually preserved by drying after removing the contents through a drilled hole or holes

(Prynne, 1963; Harrison *et al.*, 1970). Nests may need to be fumigated to destroy any insects or other pests (e.g. dermestid and other pest beetles) which might pose a threat to the collections. Storage of bird specimens in liquid preservatives should follow standard procedures for wet preservation, and skeletal material should follow normal osteological management procedures.

The conservation problems affecting bird skins and skeletons are similar to those described for mammals. Bird eggs may be damaged by fungi and mould if the relative humidity is too high. Also, bird eggs may deteriorate if stored in wooden drawers made of oak and other woods in which organic acids are present and interact with the calcium salts in the shell (Tennent and Baird, 1985). Bird eggs are stored on soft supports such as cotton wool or rayon wool which should be acid free and periodically tested. If in doubt seek the advice of a Conservator.

Amphibia, reptile and fish collections

Amphibia, reptile and fish collections largely consist of mounted specimens, skeletal material, specimens preserved in liquid preservatives, casts and photographs. Nearly all research and study collections are preserved in liquid preservatives. In cases where specimens are too large to preserve in their entirety it has been the practice to make casts. The traditional method of mounting specimens for exhibition has been to skin the animal and to preserve the skin. Because this technique has its limitations, however, casting techniques using plaster and, more recently, fibreglass have been preferred by many preparators. Mounting techniques are described by Migdalski (1960). McGonigal (1970) describes a technique for making fish mounts by vacuum forming from a plaster mould. Gardner (1984) describes how casts can be made from living amphibia and reptiles. Mounted specimens of amphibia, reptiles and fish, particularly the fins, are susceptible to physical damage.

Collecting techniques are described in British Museum (Natural History) (1953) and in Wagstaffe and Fidler (1955). Collecting is controlled by wildlife conservation laws.

Herpetological collecting and collections management is the subject of *Herpetological Circular No. 16* (Simmons, 1987).

Insect collections

Insect collections consist largely of mounted specimens, specimens preserved in liquid preservatives, microscopical preparations and insect structures such as nests and galls, specimens showing evidence of insect attack, photographs and audio tapes.

There is a wide variety of collecting methods for insects many of which are peculiar to a particular insect group. General reference works include Oldroyd (1970), British Museum (Natural History) (1974) and Walker and Crosby (1988). More specific methods are described in the publications of the Royal Entomological Society.

The collecting of some insects is subject to wildlife conservation laws.

Most small insects are prepared by drying. There are many conventions for mounting and the general principle is to mount the insect in such a way as to expose the diagnostic identification features. In some cases this entails dissection (for example, genitalia), and the mounting of these separately, but with the insect (with pinned insects, on the same pin). Larger insects may need to have the contents of the body cavity removed and some insects may need to be degreased. In cases where the diagnostic features are within the body it may by necessary to clear the integument of the insect. (In making microscope mounts of fleas, for example, this is done in a solution of potassium hydroxide.)

Most insects are mounted on pins, or on pieces of card or other material which are themselves mounted on pins. The pinned insects are then stored in trays, storage boxes or drawers. There are few standard storage systems, although details of suppliers may usually be obtained from the various societies of Natural History Curators. Drawers have traditionally been fitted with a layer of cork and with a glass lid but polyethylene foam is now used in preference to cork. In the USA it is more common for drawers to be fitted with removable small trays. This facilitates handling in that insects may be examined by removing trays from the drawers without removing individual pins. This system also facilitates the addition of new material or the rearrangement of the collection. In Britain, this system is used by the National Museum of Wales, and the British Museum (Natural History).

The labelling of insects presents a problem because of their small size. For pinned insects it is usual to keep basic information with the insect in the form of one or more labels mounted on the pin. To identify insects from a particular collection or from a particular locality it is advantageous to have labels specially printed. Most labels are written by hand but some museums now use a typewriter with a very small typeface and laser printers offer another alternative. There are also methods by which typewriting can be reduced photographically to produce small labels. Good-quality paper, such as goatskin parchment, should be used.

Insect collections are particularly vulnerable to attack from pests including mites and the larvae of moth and beetle. For this reason it is usual to anchor a small quantity of insect repellant within the drawer

or storage box. A great deal of attention has been given in the past to close fitting lids to prevent access by insect pests. Recent research has shown that the newly hatched, and very small larvae of some species of *anthrenus* beetles are very mobile and are able to penetrate close fitting lids.

Insects are very fragile and some training is advisable in handling techniques. Conservation problems can arise with old pinned insects if the pins corrode, and it is recommended that stainless steel pins be used.

Mollusc collections

Mollusc collections consist largely of dried shells, whole animals in liquid preservative, specimens showing evidence of molluscan activity and feeding, and photographs. Molluscs present a problem common to many invertebrate groups in that collections largely consist of the dried exoskeletons which alone do not carry sufficient characters to permit identification. Collecting methods are described by Lincoln and Sheals (1979). A few species are governed by wildlife conservation laws.

Mollusc shells may be labelled by marking the shells (in the case of the largest species), by placing a label within the shell (gastropods) or by placing the shell with its label in a tray, box or tube. It is advisable to place very small specimens in tubes. Molluscs preserved in liquid preservatives should follow normal procedures.

Most mollusc shells are fragile and need to be handled carefully. Calcareous shells are susceptible to damage if they are stored in an acid environment (which might result from the use of unsuitable woods in the construction of storage cabinets). Chitinous shells may dry out and distort if the relative humidity of the environment in which they are stored is too low.

Other invertebrate collections

Other invertebrate collections include protozoa, arthropoda other than insects, echinodermata and coelenterata. Although these groups are very extensive in the wild, and may also be represented by extensive collections in museums, relatively few Curators have specific responsibilities for these groups and there is very little in the way of established practices for their curation other than those described in the general works relating to invertebrates such as Wagstaffe and Fidler (1968) and Lincoln and Sheals (1979). Most of the general procedures relating to specimens stored in liquid preservatives, for dried specimens or for microscopic preparations are appropriate for these groups.

Types and voucher specimens

A voucher specimen has been defined as one which physically and permanently documents data in an archive report by:

> verifying the identity of the organism(s) used in the study; and, by so doing, ensures that a study which otherwise could not be repeated can be accurately reviewed or reassessed.

The Association of Systematics Collections identifies three categories of voucher specimens:

> (1) type specimens, upon which the names of taxonomic units are based;
> (2) taxonomic support specimens – specimens of primary importance in taxonomic studies other than nomenclatural studies, such as range extensions, life-history studies and morphological variability; and
> (3) biological documentation specimens – representative organisms derived from studies or projects other than primarily taxonomic.

Because of their importance, some notes on their care and use are appropriate. In the first place, type and voucher specimens need to be clearly identified as such in any documentation and, in the case of types, by marking the specimen in some way. It is helpful to have a separate list of type specimens in the collection.

Some museums find it convenient to segregate all type specimens into special storage areas where they can be given special care. It is generally agreed that type specimens should be deposited in museums which have the necessary facilities to care for them and to make them available to researchers. In practice this usually means the national, university and the larger Local Authority museums.

Particular care needs to be taken for the security of type specimens, particularly in respect of loans and transport. See also Swinton (1948), Owen (1964), Jeffrey (1976) and the International Commission for Botanical Nomenclature (ICBN).

The storage of zoological collections

The general requirements for zoological collections are similar to those for most museum collections described in Chapter 45. These requirements are that stores should be secure from theft and accidental damage. Temperature should be stable and within the range 15–18°C. Relative humidity should be maintained as near as possible to 55 per cent with as little fluctuation as possible, ideally not more than ±5 per cent. Light should be excluded from storage areas wherever possible and should be restriced to 50 lux. Ultraviolet light should be excluded by the use of filters. Ideally there should be air conditioning to remove gaseous pollution and dust.

As will have been noted, some categories of zoological collections require special storage fittings.

Zoological collections are particularly susceptible to biological deterioration. Maintaining the level of relative humidity at the above levels will prevent mould and reduce the danger of insect infestation. Special precautions however may have to be taken to prevent infestation by insects (see below).

In general, it will be found convenient to house similar collections together. However, as a general rule it is advisable to store collections in liquid preservatives separately, particularly if alcohols are widely used. Because of the difficulties in upgrading existing buildings, some museums are now constructing purpose-built stores in which optimal conditions can be maintained. An example is the store at Tring in Hertfordshire which was built to house the ornithological collections of the British Museum (Natural History). A more elaborate building, the Museum Support Centre, has been commissioned by the Smithsonian Institution in which it is planned to house a large proportion of the collections of the National Museum of Natural History (Duckworth, 1984).

Handling zoological collections

When handling zoological collections, direct skin contact with specimens should be avoided. Perspiration on hands can soil specimens, and older specimens which might have been preserved with toxic chemicals can present a health hazard. Specimens which are susceptible to such damage should be stored in polythene bags and handled, wherever possible in their bags. Bird skins mounted on a piece of dowel should be handled by the dowel. Pinned insect collections should be handled in their trays or with entomological forceps, and specimens preserved in liquid preservatives should also be handled by means of forceps or using gloves.

Specimens which might be contaminated with chemical insect deterrents and preservatives, including specimens stored in liquid preservatives should be handled in a well ventilated room, or preferably a fume cupboard, using neoprene or nitrile gloves, and, where appropriate, anti-splash goggles. Where large numbers of collections (e.g. insect collections) stored in high levels of insecticides are being worked upon consideration should be given to the installation of an air purifier.

Control of pests

Insect pests have been responsible for the destruction of vast numbers of historically important collections and they remain one of the main hazards for zoological collections. The main danger is from beetles and moths, particularly in their larval stages, but mites and even rodents can be a problem.

Prevention should be the main element of any strategy, and the key to prevention is good housekeeping which should ensure that buildings are insect proof (elimination of bird nests), that insects are not introduced accidently through open windows, through food used in cafeterias and restaurants, with new material and with loans. Storage units and exhibition cases should as far as possible be insect proof and it is a good principle to have several barriers by keeping specimens in closed containers. Frequent inspections should be made making use of traps. By this means it should be possible to isolate any infestation and to take appropriate measures to deal with an infestation.

Detection is usually by finding live or dead insects or their larvae, by the appearance of exit holes made by the adult insects, by the characteristic frass made by beetles or the webbing by moths.

Some preservation methods reduce the danger of infestation, for example, material stored in liquid preservatives. Historically 'poisons' were used to protect specimens including arsenic trioxide for treating bird and mammal skins and mercuric chloride for herbarium specimens. Health-and-safety considerations are persuading museums to use less-toxic chemcials and to investigate non-chemical methods of control.

Many museums make use of deterrents in the form of chemicals in the storage drawers. Such chemicals have included DDT, *p*-dichlorobenzene and naphthalene. Only the latter is now recommended, although it should be remembered that substantial amounts of other chemicals may still be present in the collections. Safe working limits of deterrents are given in Sax (1988).

The treatment of infestations will depend upon the scale of the problem. For large and well-established infestations it may be necessary to fumigate an entire store or building and this practice is common in the USA. For collections which are transportable, it may be possible to have the collection fumigated in one of the commercial or museum operated methyl bromide, ethylene oxide or phosphine fumigation chambers. There are problems with this treatment, however, in that the treatment itself may affect the specimens. For local infestations it may be possible to use a chemical like Vapona, placed with the specimens in a closed container for a specified period (2 weeks) or placed in insect drawers (see Scoble, 1983). Many museums are adopting the procedure of deep-freezing all incoming material to control insect pests. At the Royal Botanic Gardens at Kew, herbarium specimens are subjected to a temperature of below −18°C for a minimum of 48 h and this has been found effective in controlling pest insects at all stages of the life-cycle (for further details see Foreman and Bridson (1990)).

A Guide to Museum Pest Control (Zycherman and Schrock, 1988) surveys pest control procedures in the USA. Although legislation controlling the use of insecticides in Britain differs from that in the USA and other countries, many of the recommendations and procedures described in the report are appropriate to all countries.

Health hazards in handling biological history collections

Health hazards in natural history museums arise from a number of cources. Live animals may be capable of inflicting injury, and should be handled with caution, particularly if the species is unknown. Gloves should be worn where appropriate. Recently killed vertebrates (and some invertebrates) present a risk of infection by dangerous pathogens. Detailed accounts of these dangers are described in McDiarmid (1966) and Irvin *et al* (1972). The dangers are greater in handling animals in poor condition or which have died through transmissible disease. (It should be remembered that a larger number of animals which find their way into museums have not died from natural causes.) Some infectious organisms, such as anthrax, may persist for long periods after death. Vertebrates which have recently died may be carrying blood-sucking ectoparasites including fleas, flies, lice, ticks and mites which are capable of biting and spreading infection.

Each country will have its own health-and-safety laws and regulations. In the UK the provisions of *Control of Substances Hazardous to Health Regulations 1988* (COSHH) came into force on 1 October 1989 (HMSO, 1988b). These regulations require the assessment of any risk exposure to any substance that is harmful to health and the control of exposure to hazardous substances and require that detailed records are kept. The implications of the regulations are likely to have far-reaching effects on practices in natural history collection management.

The following simple rules apply:

(1) use plastic bags for collecting and handling dead specimens;
(2) work in a well-ventilated room;
(3) fumigate new specimens;
(4) immerse whole bodies of animals in disinfectant where possible, particularly rats and farm stock;
(5) wear protective clothing including overalls, gloves, face masks and goggles where appropriate;
(6) make sure that instruments and worksurfaces are clean and sterilized; and
(7) maintain high standards of personal hygiene.

Other hazards may arise from the use of preservatives. In the past, arsenic trioxide was widely used to poison skins of vertebrates, and mercuric chloride is still used in some herbaria to poison new specimens. If such practices are still in operation, specimens should be handled with care, protective clothing worn, and hands washed frequently. Specimens treated with toxic chemicals should be clearly labelled to this effect. The use of insecticides and pesticides in museums is now covered by the COSHH regulations referred to above. It has been common practice in museums to use naphthalene, vapona, thymol and formaldehyde, but such practices will now have to be re-examined. Staff should not be exposed to high concentrations of any of these substances or for any protracted period. It is a good principle for museum staff to avoid working in stores where insecticides are or have been used.

A further hazard may arise from the use of plastics and resins in making moulds and casts. The manufacturer's instructions must be closely followed.

References

ANDERSON, R. M. (1965), *Methods of Collecting and Preserving Vertebrate Animals*, National Museums of Canada, Ottawa

BRITISH MUSEUM (NATURAL HISTORY) (1953), *Instructions for Collectors, No. 3 Reptiles, Amphibia and Fish*, British Museum (Natural History), London

BRITISH MUSEUM (NATURAL HISTORY) (1968), *Instructions for Collectors, No. 1 Mammals*, British Museum (Natural History), London

BRITISH MUSEUM (NATURAL HISTORY) (1974), *Instructions for Collectors, No. 4a Insects*, British Museum (Natural History), London

CRIMMEN, O. A. (1989), 'Phenoxetol: an unsatisfactory preservative for fishes', *Biology Curators Group Newsletter*, 5(3), 26–27

DESSAUER, H. C. and HAFNER, M. S. (EDS) (1984), *Collections of Frozen Tissues*, Association of Systematics Collections, Lawrence, KA

DUCKWORTH, W. D. (1964), 'The Smithsonian new Support Centre', *Museum News*, 62(4), 32–35

FOREMAN, L. and BRIDSON, D. (EDS) (1989), *The Herbarium Handbook*, Royal Botanic Garden, London

GARDNER, G. S. (1984), 'Casting lifelike models from living animals', *Curator*, 17, pp10–15

GENOWAYS, H. H., JONES, C. and ROSSOLIMO, O. L. (1987) *Mammal Collection Management*, Texas Technical University, Lubbock, Texas

HARRISON, C. J. O., COWLES, G. S. and DAHL, A. L. (1970), *Instructions for Collectors, No. 2 Birds*, British Museum (Natural History), London

HMSO (1981), *The Wildlife and Countryside Act*, HMSO, London

HMSO (1988a), *The Wildlife and Countryside Act 1981 (Variation of Schedule) Order 1988*, HMSO London

HMSO (1988b), *The Control of Substances Hazardous to Health Regulations 1988*, HMSO, London

HORIE, C. V. (ED.) (1989), *Conservation of Natural History Specimens – Spirit Collections*, University of Manchester, Manchester

HORIE, C. V. and MURPHY, R. G. (EDS) (1988), *Conservation of Natural History Specimens – Vertebrates*, University of Manchester, Manchester

IRVIN, A. D., COOPER, J. E. and HEDGES, S. R. (1972), 'Possible health hazards associated with the collection and handling of post-mortem zoological material', *Mammal Review*, 2, 43–54

JEFFREY, C. (1976), *Biological Nomenclature*, Systematics Association, London

JOHNSON, N. K., ZWINK, R. M., BARROUCLOUGH, G. F. and MARTEN, J. A. (1984), 'Suggested techniques for modern avian systematics', *Willson Bulletin* 96(4), 543–560

KNUDSEN, J. W. (1975), *Collecting and Preserving Animals and Plants*, Harper and Row, London

LINCOLN, R. J. and SHEALS, J. G. (1979), *Invertebrate Animals – Collection and Preservation*, British Museum (Natural History)/Cambridge University Press, London/Cambridge

LYSTER, S. (1982), *International Wildlife Law*, Grotius Publications, Cambridge

McDIARMID, A. (1966), 'Safety precautions at post-mortem examinations', *Mammal Society Bulletin*, 26, 17–18

McGONIGAL, S. (1970), 'Transparent fish casts for museum displays', *Museum Journal*, 69(4), 169–172

MERYMAN, H. T. (1960), The preparation of biological specimens by freeze-drying, *Curator*, 3, 5–19

MERYMAN, H. T. (1961), The preparation of biological specimens by freeze-drying-instrumentation, *Curator*, 4, 153–174

MIGDASKI, E. C. (1960), *How to Make Fish Mounts and other Trophies*, Ronald Press, Rochester, NY

MUSEUM DOCUMENTATION ASSOCIATION (1980), *Natural History Specimen Card Instructions*, Museum Documentation Association, Cambridge

NATURE CONSERVANCY COUNCIL (no date), *Habitat Mapping Manual (Phase 1)*, Nature Conservancy Council, Peterborough

NARGORSEN, D. W. and PETERSON, R. L. (1980), *Mammal Collectors Manual*, Royal Ontario Museum, Toronto

OLDROYD, H. (1970), *Collecting, Preserving and Studying Insects*, Hutchinson, London

OWEN, D. (1964), 'Care of type specimens', *Museums Journal*, 63, 288–291

PETTIT, C. (1975), 'Label materials for wet-preserved biological specimens', *Museums Journal*, 75(4), 175–176

PRYNNE, M. (1963), *Egg Shells*, Barrie and Rockcliffe, London

SAVILLE, D. B. O. (1973), *Collection and Care of Botanical Specimens*, Canada Department of Agriculture, Ottawa

SAX, N. I. (1988), *Dangerous Properties of Industrial Materials*, Van Nostrand, New York

SCOBLE, M. J. (1983), 'A pest control strategy for insect collections', *Biology Curators Group Newsletter*, 3(6), 339–342

SIMMONS, J. E. (1987), *Herpetological Collecting and Collections Management*, Society for the Study of Amphibians and Reptiles, Lubbock, Texas

SMALDON, G. and LEE, E. W. (1979), *A Synopsis of Methods of Narcotization of Marine Invertebrates*, Royal Scottish Museum, Edinburgh

SOMMER, H. G. and ANDERSON, S. (1974), 'Cleaning skeletons with dermestid beetles – two refinements in the method', *Curator*, 17, 290–298

STEEDMAN, H. F. (ED) (1976), *Zooplankton Fixation and Preservation*, UNESCO, Paris

SWINTON, W. E. (1948), *Type Specimens in Botany and Zoology – Recommendations for their Conservation in Natural*

History and General Museums, International Council of Museums, Paris

TENNENT, N. C. and BAIRD, T. (1985), 'The deterioration of mollusca collections: identification of shell efflorescence', *Studies in Conservation*, **30**(2), 73–86

WAGSTAFFE, R. and FIDLER, J. H. (1955), reprinted 1970, *The Preservation of Natural History Specimens, Vol. 1 Zoology – Invertebrates*, Witherby, London

WAGSTAFFE, R. and FIDLER, J. H. (1968), *The Preservation of Natural History Specimens, Vol. 2 Zoology – Vertebrates, Botany, Geology*, Witherby, London

WALKER, A. K. and CROSBY, T. K. (1988), *The Preparation and Curation of Insects*, revised edition, Department of Scientific and Industrial Research, Wellington, New Zealand

ZYCHERMAN, L. A. and SCHROCK, J. R. (1988), *A Guide to Museum Pest Control*, Asociation of Systematics Collections, Washington, DC

Bibliography

ANON. (1982), *Report – Workshops on Frozen Tissue Collections in Museums*, South Australian Museum, Adelaide

BRITISH MUSEUM (NATURAL HISTORY) (1965a), *Instructions for Collectors, N.3, Fishes*, British Museum (Natural History), London

BRITISH MUSEUM (NATURAL HISTORY) (1965b), *Instructions for Collectors, No. 10 Plants*, British Museum (Natural History), London

CHAPMAN, D. E. (1969), 'The use of sodium perborate tetrahydrate in the preparation of mammals skeletons', *Proceeding of the Zoological Society*, **159**, 522–523

CLYDESDALE, A. (1982), *Chemicals in Conservation*, Conservation Bureau Scottish Development Agency, Scottish Society for Conservation and Restoration, Edinburgh

EDWARDS, S. R., BELL, B. M. and KING, M. E. (EDS.), (1981), *Pest Control in Museums*, Association of Systematics Collections, Lawrence, Kansas, USA

FABER, S. (ED.) (1983), *Proceedings of 1981 Workshop on the Care and Maintenance of Natural History Collections*, National Museum of Natural Sciences, Ottawa

FABER, S. (1977). 'The development of taxidermy and the history of ornithology', *Isis*, **68**(244), 550–566

FINK, W. L., HARTEL, K. E., SOUL, W. G., MOON, E. M. and WILEY, E. O. (1977), *A Report on Current Supplies and Practices used in Curation of Ichthyology Collections*, American Society of Ichthyologists and Herpetologists, Washington, DC

FRANK, P. G. (1982), *Some Techniques for Narcotizing and Preserving Invertebrate Animals, Except Insects*, National Museum of Natural Sciences, Ottawa

FRANKS, J. W. (1965), *A Guide to Herbarium Practice*, Museums Association, London

HANGAY, G. and DINGLEY, M. (1986), *Biological Museum Methods*, Academic Press, London

HARRIS, R. H. (1984), *A Selective Bibliography in Preservation*, Biology Curators Group, Leicester

HAWKS, C. A., WILLIAMS, S. L. and GARDNER, J. S. (1984), *The Care of Tanned Skins in Mammal Research Collections, Texas*: Texas Technical University, Lubbock, Texas

HOEBEKE, E. R., LIEBHERR, J. K. and WHEELER, Q. D. (1985), 'A unit storage system for fluid-preserved specimens', *Curator*, **28**(2), 77–84

HOWER, R. O. (1979), *Freeze Drying Biological Specimens – A Laboratory Manual*, Smithsonian Instiution Press, Washington DC

JANNETT, F. J. (1989), 'Some tests of synthetic paper and polythene sacks for specimens preserved in fluids', *Curator*, **32**(1), 24–25

JEWETT, S. (1987), 'Paper specifications for spirit labels', *Biology curators Group Newsletter*, **4**(8), 157

LEE, W. L. *et al.* (1982), *Guidelines for the Acquisition and Management of Biological Collections*, Association of Systematics Collections, Lawrence, Kansas, USA

MUIR, D., LOVELL, M. and PEARCE, C. P. (1981), 'Health hazards and natural history museum work', *Museums Journal*, **80**, 205–206

PEDEN, A. E. (1976), *Collecting and Preserving Fishes*, British Columbia Provincial Museum, Victoria, BC

PETTIT, C. (1989), 'The new zoology storage at Manchester Museum: a new curatorial strategy', *Journal of Biological Curation*, **1**(1), 27–40

PINNIGER, D. (1989), *Insect Pests in Museums*, Institute of Archaeology Publications, London

ROGERS, S. P., SCHMIDT, M. A. and GÜTEBIER, T. (1989), *An Annotated Bibliography on Preparation, Taxidermy and Collections Management of Vertebrates*, Carnegie Museum, Pittsburgh, PA

ROGERS, S. P. and WOOD, D. S. (1989), *Notes from a Workshop on Bird Specimen Preservation*, Carnegie Museum of Natural History, Pittsburgh, PA

ROMERA-SIERRA, C., WEBB, J. C., LANE, P. and LYONS, G. W. (1988), 'Improvements in techniques for freeze-drying vertebrate specimens', *Collection Forum*, **4**(1), 10–11

STANSFIELD, G. (ED.) (1983), *The Wildlife and Countryside Act (1981) and its Implications for Museums*, Biology Curators Group, Leicester

WADDINGTON, J. and RUDKIN, D. M. (1986), *Proceedings of the 1985 Workshop on Care and Maintenance of Natural History Collections*, Royal Ontario Museum, Toronto

WILLIAMS, B. (1987), *Biological Collections UK*, Museums Association, London

WILLIAMS, S. L., LAUBACK, R. and GENOWAYS, H. H. (1977), *A Guide to the Management of Recent Mammal Collections*, Carnegie Museum of Natural History, Pittsburgh, PA

Addresses

Association of Systematics Collections, 730 11th St. NW, 3rd Floor, Washington DC 20001, USA

Biology Curators' Group, Derek Whiteley, (Secretary), c/o Sheffield City Museum, Western Park, Sheffield S10 2TP, UK

Geology Curators Group, Simon Knell, (Secretary), c/o Scunthorpe Museum and Art Gallery, Oswald Road, Scunthorpe DN15 7BD, UK

NIPA Laboratories Ltd, Llantwit Fardre, Pontypridd, Mid Glamorgan CF38 2SN, UK

Society for the Preservation of Natural History Collections, 5800 Baum Blvd., Pittsburgh, Pennsylvania 15206, USA

Wildlife Trade Monitoring Unit of the Interantional Union for the Conservation of Nature, 219c Huntingdon Road, Cambridge CB3 0DL, UK

42

Herbarium practice

Roy Perry and Barry A. Thomas

Introduction

One herbarium specimen may be a single plant, several plants, or portions of a plant or plants, that have been dried or otherwise preserved. Such specimens are kept for future reference in some form of storage units which are usually constructed specially and housed in a special room or building set aside for the purpose (herbarium). For further general remarks on herbaria see Fosberg and Sachet (1965).

Acquisition of specimens

Collecting

This subject is thoroughly covered by Savile (1962) and by Womersley (1981). It must be remembered, however, that there are many national and international regulations which must be observed when making collections. Countries may have their own laws concerning the picking of wild plants. For example, in Britain the *Wildlife and Countryside Act 1981* lists plant species for special protection, there is the *Endangered Species Act 1973* (as amended in 1983) in the USA, while in Canada there are many complex laws protecting plants, although they are mainly at the Provincial level. Davis *et al* (1986) give a great deal of information, country by country, on threatened plant species and the laws protecting plants. The exporting and importing of dried herbarium specimens usually pose no problems, although the international trafficking of many species is regulated under the CITES regulations. National customs authorities will probably give detailed advice on request.

Donations, bequests and purchases

It may be worthwhile to purchase specimens for several reasons: they may fill gaps in existing collections, they may contain specimens that provide valuable data, or they may be of historic value. With donations and bequests, the herbarium manager may have no idea of the scientific value of the collections donated or bequested until they arrive in the preparation room. It is thus important that the herbarium receiving such collections is able to exercise the right, if necessary, to discard or redistribute all or part of the collection thus received (see Chapter 1). The object should always be to build up an elite collection containing well-documented material of scientific worth.

Driers and drying

Vascular plants are often dried through pressing procedures initiated in the field. Each collection is placed between a folded light-weight sheet of paper ('flimsy') and labelled. Newspapers may be used for this purpose. Specimens are laid out so that foliage and flowers are separated from each other as far as possible and not overlapping, and so that all parts of the collected plant, for example upper and lower leaf surfaces, are visible from one aspect. At this stage of the drying process it is useful to have in mind the size of the herbarium sheet to which the specimen will eventually be attached to ensure that the specimens being pressed will fit directly onto the herbarium sheet (a suitable size is 260 mm × 412 mm) without modification. Specimens that are too large for a single herbarium sheet should either be folded before pressing or cut into pieces. The size and nature of the specimen will determine which action should be taken. Flowering plants and some fern fronds could be folded once without harm, but larger specimens would be better cut and pressed as single pieces prior to mounting on several sheets. Careful labelling is necessary for cut specimens.

The flimsies, each containing a laid-out specimen, are separated from each other by sheets of absorbent drying paper (e.g. high-quality blotting paper, 300 g). Flimsies allow papers to be changed more easily as the specimens themselves do not need to be handled, but if flimsies are not used specimens can be placed directly between sheets of drying paper. Occasional interleaved corrugated cardboard sheets acting as ventilators help to speed the drying process. The pile of prepared specimens is then pressed between slatted plywood or wire-mesh frames using weights (such as bricks or stones) or canvas straps. Book presses may be used for plants, although care must be taken to avoid overtightening the press and subsequently crushing the specimens.

The press must be held tight continuously, either by tightening the straps or applying a weight, otherwise wrinkling may occur as the plants lose water and become flaccid. In the herbarium this process can be facilitated through the use of controlled heating. This can be done either in a dedicated room or in a specially constructed cabinet. Such a cabinet must have slatted or grilled shelves to allow a free upward flow of air and can be heated with either a small electric heater or light bulbs.

The drying papers need to be regularly changed (daily for 5 days, then every 2 or 3 days for about a fortnight or until the specimens and their flimsies are dry). Care must be taken to ensure that the label is never separated from the specimen. The specimens can be repositioned during the earlier changes of papers to give a more presentable finish to the specimen prior to mounting. When they are dry, flimsies containing specimens are removed and stored together for future curation.

A microwave oven (preferably a large industrial model) can be used if specimens need immediate drying or where only a few specimens are dried at infrequent intervals (Sauleda and Adams, 1981). Plants being pressed in the usual way can be dried by maximum power in 1–2 min. However, it is advised that preliminary testing be undertaken to ensure that specimen burning does not occur through over radiation. There is also a danger that too rapid drying can create brittle specimens. Succulents, which are notoriously difficult to dry by conventional means, can often putrefy before drying out and microwaving is an effective way of preventing this.

Preparation of specimens for the herbarium

General

For easy handling all parts needed for identification/description should be visible after mounting. A good-quality acid-free paper of 220 g weight and standard size (260 mm × 412 mm) should be used.

For those specimens to be preserved in paper packets it is recommended that the paper used be 100 per cent rag paper. The folded herbarium packet should be a standard size, for ease of storage, usually folded A4 which makes a packet approximately 140 mm × 100 mm, and should have a herbarium label incorporated on its front flap for the data.

Many Curators rubber stamp or emboss their herbarium sheets with their herbarium title or its abbreviation; waterproof ink is recommended. This procedure is useful for identifying the herbarium to which a specimen belongs if it is sent on loan to another institution.

Flowering plants – Angiosperms

The specimens should be attractively laid out on the paper prior to mounting to ensure the visibility of diagnostic parts. Several small plants can be arranged on one sheet, while large specimens may have to split between several sheets that can be taped together.

Specimens can be mounted in a number of ways. The preferred technique is to strap them in position using narrow strips of acid-free gummed linen tape. An advantage of this method is that specimens may be easily removed from the sheet if it is necessary to do so, for example for re-mounting or in order to examine the undersurface. It is recommended that heavy specimens such as woody stems, or specimens with bulky parts, e.g. seed pods, are first sewn into position using a needle and linen thread before final strapping. Plastic or water-based glues such as Unibond or white wood-workers' glue can be used as an alternative method for mounting; the specimen is either brushed with adhesive on the underside and then laid down on the mounting sheet or, if rigid enough, may be laid down on a sheet of glass previously coated with the glue and then transferred to the mounting sheet. Delicate specimens are not easily dealt with by using this method and for them strapping is recommended. Under no circumstances should self-adhesive tape be used because the glue will sometimes creep causing several of the herbarium sheets to stick together. Peeling off the tape can, however, damage the specimen or leave it equally as sticky. 'Sellotape', however, does eventually dry and become loose, so it is better to wait until this happens rather than run the risk of damaging the specimen.

Fragments of specimens that have become detached during processing, for example flower buds, seeds, etc., may be placed in small folded paper packets ('fragment packets') which are attached to the sheet with the specimen. The label for the specimen should be glued to the bottom right-hand corner of the sheet, with space being left elsewhere on the sheet for additional labels or comments or determinations by specialists. Specimens that have been cut and mounted on several sheets should be clearly labelled as such, e.g. '1 of 3 sheets', and accompanied by notes and/or diagrams showing how the pieces relate to each other.

Pteridophytes

Pteridophytes, being vascular plants, can be treated for herbarium purposes as though they were angiosperms. Ferns, however, need special care in mounting as the distinctive reproductive sori are usually on the underside of their fronds. If the collection consists of one fertile frond only its rachis should be broken half way and the two parts of the frond mounted with different surfaces uppermost.

Spores are often shed in vast numbers as the fronds dry and an opportunity to examine them might be of great value in the future. Spores can be gathered into fragment packets which can be attached to the herbarium sheet. Spores from different specimens must be kept separate, so care must be taken to prevent these very light objects from becoming mixed.

Conifers

Coniferous material often disintegrates on drying. Shoots, especially those of *Picea* and *Tsuga*, shed leaves, the female cones of *Abies*, *Araucaria* and *Cedrus* self-destruct, and most male cones disintegrate. Cones can be tightly bound to prevent their disintegration, although Page (1979) suggests the following chemical pretreatment for such specimens. Completely immerse them for 10 minutes in 95 per cent ethanol. Gently shake off the excess liquid before immersing them in 50 per cent aqueous glycerine solution for 4 days. The excess glycerine should then be removed by a brief rinse in water, then the plant material should be dried in the usual way. Shoots can be pressed and mounted on standard herbarium sheets, and cones are dried whole and usually kept with other carpological collections in individually labelled boxes. Cross-referencing of such material should be carried out.

Fungi

Many fungi putrefy rapidly after collection, especially mushrooms and toadstools, so they should be dealt with as soon as possible. Freshly collected material of this type, however, may be kept reasonably intact for a day or two if placed in the lower part of a refrigerator (*not* a freezer). Traditionally, specimens are preserved by air drying over circulated heat, either whole, or as sections taken longitudinally through the fruiting body. Domestic radiators can be used for this purposes, but driers based on a heating element and a fan to circulate the heated air through mesh shelves on which the specimens are placed are likely to produce better results. Specimens processed by air drying frequently shrivel and become discoloured. Colours are of great importance in the study of higher fungi, especially agarics, and should be noted carefully from the fresh fruiting bodies prior to their preservation. Reference to a colour standard is important for critical work. Recommended standards are listed by Hawksworth *et al.* (1983). Accurate notes on the colour of the fresh fungus, together with notes on other features which are likely to change on drying, need to be incorporated if the specimen is to be of maximum value. Freeze drying is a more recent technique for toadstool preservation and has the advantage of producing a herbarium specimen which very nearly retains the original appearance of the collected specimen. Air-dried specimens are usually kept in paper packets. Freeze-dried material, because of its greater bulk, and often fragile nature, is best kept in specially made cardboard boxes of a size that can be stacked or placed together in herbarium drawers.

Species of fungi parasitic on the non-woody parts of plants (e.g. moulds, rusts and smuts) are usually pressed in a herbarium press then placed in packets. Other non-fleshy fungi such as saprophytes on dead wood are air-dried and then packeted.

Lichens

These are usually collected into bags or envelopes. Foliose and fruticose types are collected with or without part of the substrate. Crustose types need to be collected together with their substrate, either rock (removed using a hammer and small chisel), bark (removed using a stout knife) or soil (skimmed up with a knife). All types are placed in packets and are air-dried. For the herbarium they are repacketed. Specimens of some larger foliose types (such as *Peltigera*) may be very lightly pressed to avoid damage within the herbarium packet. Because of the friable nature of soily substrata, specimens collected on soil may be advantageously treated with a soil binder to prevent fragmentation in the packet (Hitch, 1983). Matt acrylic copolymer emulsion (Spectrum Oil Colours, Richmond Road, Horsham, Sussex RH12 2EG, UK) is suitable when diluted with a little water. The solution is painted onto the back of the soil specimen and allowed to dry overnight. Fragments of rock, bark or soil supporting crustose species may be glued to a piece of card very slightly smaller than the internal dimensions of the packet. This practice protects the specimen from disintegration and abrasion within the packet. Fragile specimens may be further protected by being covered within the packet by several layers of tissue paper. Very small specimens should be placed within a small packet within the larger packet.

Freshwater algae and marine plankton

Filamentous forms may be collected directly with forceps, but the vast majority are microscopic. Algae are best examined fresh, when the cell contents can be observed and described, but collections may be fixed in Lugol's iodine and preserved in 2–4 per cent formaldehyde or 1:3:6 formalin:alcohol:water in glass vials. A number of groups require special techniques for preparation (e.g. see Barber and Haworth (1981) for diatoms).

Seaweeds and charophytes

Seaweeds and charophytes need to be kept cool and wet until ready for mounting. Large brown seaweeds can be dried directly in a press, but the smaller browns and the reds and greens need a more delicate mounting procedure. They and charophytes should be spread out on a mounting sheet held under water which is then gently eased out of the water so that the specimen remains spread out evenly in the centre of the sheet. A large photographic tray is ideal for this procedure. Practice is needed to prevent the plant becoming displaced through water flowing off the paper, and several attempts at the floating-out process may be required before a reasonable result is achieved. Forceps may be used during the floating-out process to disentangle the fronds. Cheese cloth or washed muslin is then laid over the specimen before the sheet is put between drying papers into a press. The cloth can be peeled off later. If it sticks to the specimen it may be necessary to wet it and start again. Under these circumstances wax paper may be used as a cover, although this may greatly increase the drying time. It is best not to mount the smaller seaweeds directly onto herbarium sheets as they can be difficult to handle under water. Instead, they can be floated on to small pieces of paper which can then be attached to herbarium sheets with strips of gummed linen tape. Care must be taken to avoid any mix up of specimens during the floating stages. Pencil notes on the paper to be immersed is one way of ensuring this.

It may be advantageous to preserve at least part of each charophyte specimen in 60 per cent ethanol or 4 per cent formaldehyde, because pressed specimens may be unsuitable for accurate interpretation of some features. For coralline red algae Woelkerling (1988) recommended 7:2:1 ethanol:water:glycerol.

Mosses and liverworts

Almost without exception specimens on collection are placed loose into paper bags or envelopes and then air dried with or without slight pressure. Epiphyllous species collected on leaves are best pressed lightly in the herbarium press. Bryophytes are repacketed for the herbarium. If the collected specimen is minute it should be placed in a small paper packet within the herbarium packet. A soil binder may be advantageously used on specimens collected on friable substrata (Hitch, 1983).

Wood

Collections of wood can be used to supplement other herbarium specimens in providing taxonomic information on trees. Wood samples are, therefore, most useful when supported by voucher specimens of herbarium material. They should be cut to a standard size and stored in drawers. Microscopic slides with the wood cut as tranverse, radial longitudinal and tangential longitudinal sections are usually necessary for detailed anatomical studies. Stern (1967) refers to the main centres of wood studies where help may be obtained for identification.

A collection of timber planks can be maintained to show their appearance for use in building and joinery. Planks can be hung on special swivel wall brackets for reference display. Wood-boring beetles are the most likely source of any damage to wood collections, so wood collections should be regularly examined. Single specimens can be deep-frozen at about −22°C for several days to kill any eggs or larvae. If there are signs of a major infestation a specialist firm should be consulted.

Carpological and economic collections

Large dried specimens such as fruits, rhizomes, tubers, bark samples and galls are best kept in individual boxes. Woody or fibrous specimens can be dried naturally, but soft specimens need to be freeze-dried (see under 'Sterilization') to retain their original shape.

Economic plant products, such as small seeds, oil and powder extracts, are best kept in tubes. They can either be maintained as a separate collection or merged with the carpological collection if there are few specimens overall.

All of these collections should be accompanied whenever possible by herbarium voucher specimens on sheets.

Liquid collections

Some specimens are not suitable for drying. For example, the flowers of some orchids which may be needed for identification purposes are destroyed by pressing and specimens of *Salicornia* cannot be identified satisfactorily from pressed material. Such plants or parts of plants are best preserved in a mixture of 70 per cent alcohol (ethanol or ethanol and a trace of methanol), 29 per cent water and 1 per cent glycerol. The containers need to have tightly fitting lids to minimize liquid evaporation, and regular examination should reveal any need to top up the preservative. The containers should be labelled, but second labels must be included in the container with the specimen (written in either pencil or indelible ink). Containers with alcohol must be treated as flammable and should be stored on secure shelving either in metal cupboards or in dedicated rooms. They should not be stored in compactor units as movement could cause breakage.

Herbarium storage

Herbarium cupboards/cabinets

Various types of storage are in use, but pigeonhole shelving in cupboards with dust-proof doors is one of the most satisfactory systems for the storage of herbarium sheets. Cupboards may be metal or wooden. Pigeonhole size is of great importance as its width and depth must take the size of herbarium sheet being used. The space between successive shelves is critical because if it is too large too many sheets, with little or no support between them, may cause some specimens to be crushed. The optimum space between shelves is 120–150 mm. Cupboard height will partly be determined by ceiling height, but should not be so high that reaching the top shelves is inconvenient or dangerous. A set of herbarium steps may be required. Sheets are usually kept together in species or genus folders. In the larger herbaria a system of different coloured folders enables specimens from different parts of the world to be housed together.

Packets of specimens may be glued to herbarium sheets which are then stacked in cupboards as before, or packets may be kept separated in drawers made for the purpose in dust-proof cupboards.

Compactors

This subject is dealt with by Touw and Kores (1984).

Filing systems in the herbarium

Specimens need to be kept in the herbarium in a predetermined order so that they can be found and incorporated with minimum effort. Several filing systems are in use. Herbaria of British vascular plants may have been arranged using a systematic arrangement based on Druce (1928) or on Dandy (1958), but a sequence following *Flora Europaea* (Halliday and Beadle, 1983) is now distinctly preferable for all European vascular plants. Non-European flowering plants are often arranged according to the systematic order of Durand (1888). This work divides the world

into 18 zones which allows specimens to be kept in zone folders if required, each zone being allocated a different-colour folder. Cultivated plants can be kept separate from the main collections, but can be arranged in a similar way.

Various systematic lists exist for various parts of the world for other groups of plants, for example mosses and liverworts, and lichens, and these can be used for arranging specimens in the herbarium. However, it is now common practice to keep specimens in alphabetical order by genus and species. If specimens are kept in card-index fashion in drawers, the alphabetically arranged genera and species can be separated by coloured cards showing accepted names. Other cards (possibly of a different colour) with synonyms which cross-refer to accepted names, can also be inserted in alphabetical position. This procedure makes it unnecessary to refer to manuals for the name under which the species is filed and thus saves time.

Sterilization and pest control in the herbarium

Herbaria should give permanent protection to the specimens housed in them while providing a safe and pleasant working space for users. The methods of protection should never endanger the working environment.

A primary aim must be to exclude all insects from the herbarium. However, insects that eat dried plants, paper or mountants can be found in protected herbaria throughout the world. Common pests are biscuit and spider beetles. In warmer regions, termites might prove a problem.

Keeping pests at bay

Fumigants can be avoided if all incoming material is sterilized. The storage cupboards should instead be sprayed with an insecticide such as pyrethrum.

There should be limited entry of extraneous personnel into the herbarium.

Processing of specimens should be done in a separate room.

Accumulations of dust or rubbish could encourage pests, so thorough cleanliness should be exercised at all times and the herbarium regularly cleaned.

New material (including loans) should be deep frozen on arrival in the herbarium to ensure that no infestation is introduced from outside.

Live plants should not be kept in the herbarium because of the insect pests they may harbour.

Controlling pests in the herbarium

Insect attack may be recognized by the presence of chewed or grazed specimens and mounting papers, by holes in specimens and by droppings on the sheets or in the cabinets. Fumigation and chemical means have been traditionally used to kill insects, the most frequently used chemicals being carbon disulphide, phosphine ethylene dioxide, methyl bromide and mercuric chloride (very poisonous and its use now widely discontinued). Extreme care should be taken with all these chemcials and they must be used only in properly constructed fumigating chambers. Hall (1988) gives a good review of pest control methods. See also Chapter 26.

Two relatively safe methods are avilable for sterilizing specimens; deep-freezing and microwaving. Deep-freezing at $-20°C$ for 48 h kills both insect and fungal infestations. In order to prevent condensation on the specimens when they are removed from the freezer they must be enclosed in polythene bags (bin liners are suitable) which are sealed before entering the freezer. They should remain sealed after removal from the freezer until room temperature is reached. Routine recycling of herbarium material through the deep freeze is one way of ensuring continued sterilization of the herbarium.

Spraying the cupboards with Permethrin while they are empty ensures that no insects remain to reinfest the sterilized specimens on their return.

Industrial microwaves occupy little space, but offer a quick, safe and practical method of treating specimens (Hall, 1981). This is especially useful in disinfecting specimens that will be in the herbarium for a short while before being sent out again; for example, it is a method of ensuring that dried material being brought in for identification will not become a source of contamination. It must be remembered that microwaving will kill not only animals and fungi but the plant material itself including seeds and other propagules. Specimens cannot then be used as sources for propagation or to test the longevity of spores or seeds.

Environmental control

Herbarium specimens, books and documents need to be kept in a controlled environment if deterioration and the effects of any unnoticed infestations are to be kept to a minimum. Optimum conditions are those for all organic materials. The effects of increasing temperature and relative humidity (RH) can be quite dramatic (Thomson, 1986). For example, the life-cycle of the common booklouse, *Liposcelis bostrychophilus*, is about 1 month at 20°C but 3 weeks at 27°C though they can live for 5–6 months. They breed most actively at high humidity (80–90 per cent RH) but not at all in dry conditions (40–50 per cent RH). Other texts such as Busvine (1980) and Edwards *et al.* (1981) give accounts of the biology and control of insects likely to be encountered in museums.

Remedial action

Sometimes herbaria are acquired or inherited in a very bad condition. Specimens may be broken, badly mounted, or detached from the paper and the label lost, illegible, faded or with little or no worthwhile information on it. The Curator is then faced with a difficult task. The first decision is to decide whether the specimens are worth saving. If there are type or voucher specimens, then every effort should be made to salvage as many of them and as much of the individual specimens as possible. If they are old, they may provide valuable information on the former distribution of the species so again they may be worth salvaging. Once a decision has been made to keep the specimens, some simple immediate conservation should halt, or at least slow down, further deterioration until further time can be spent on them. Deep freezing, possible repackaging and storing in a safe environment should be the least that is done. However, if the specimens are common species from well-known localities and there are better specimens in the herbarium then it might be better not to waste time on them. If the Curator is unsure of the specimens' scientific value, they should receive at least minimal remedial conservation to keep them in a stable condition until advice can be sought.

Public displays

Most herbarium specimens are often not considered sufficiently appealing for public display and their scientific value is likely to decrease if they are put on exhibition for any length of time in daylight. Thus, only suitably rigid plants should be used that have been slowly dried while buried in fine sand or freeze dried especially for the purpose. Material on display in closed show-cases can be kept dry most easily by the use of silica gel which has relatively simple maintenance requirements. It must be said, however, that on the whole displays are more attractive if constructed of life-like models.

Outdoor collections of living plants can be attractive features especially if there are sufficient funds for a greenhouse. Then it may be possible to stage collections of living plants in public galleries. Enclosed 'greenhouses', especially if they are maintained by natural light, can be a valuable asset. On a smaller scale, terraria or wardian cases can be used to show mosses, pteridophytes and smaller angiosperms. Collections of cut plants or pot plants are equally valuable providing they are fully and accurately labelled. Simple physiological experiments can be a major attraction for the public, providing sufficient explanations are given. The major drawback to all of these, of course, is that they require very regular maintenance and are thus time consuming. Depending on locality and climate, the introduction of living plants into the general museum environment may introduce unwanted insect pests to the detriment of several collections.

References

BARBER, H. G. and HAWORTH, E. Y. (1981), *A Guide to the Morphology of the Diatom Frustule, Scientific Publication No. 44*, Freshwater Biological Association, Ambleside

BUSVINE, J. R. (1980), *Insects and Hygiene*, 3rd ed. Chapman and Hall, London, UK and New York, USA

DANDY, J. E. (1958), *List of British Vascular Plants*, British Museum (Natural History), London

DAVIS, S. D., DROOP, S. J. M., GREGERSON, P., HENSON, L., LEAON, C. J., VILLA-LOBOS, J. L., SYNGE, H. and ZANTOVSKA, J. (1986), *Plants in Danger. What do we know?*, International Union for Conservation of Nature and Natural Resources, Gland, Switzerland and Cambridge

DRUCE, G. C. (1928), *British Plant List*, 2nd ed., T. Buncle & Co., Abroath

DURAND, T. (1888), *Index Generum Phanerogamorum*, Becquart-Arien, Brussels

EDWARDS, S. R., BELL, B. M. and KING, M. E. (1981), *Pest control in Museums: A Status Report (1980)*, Association of Systematics Collections, Lawrence, Kansas, USA

FOSBERG, F. R. and SACHET, M.-H. (1965), 'Manual for tropical herbaria', *Regnum Vegetabile*, **39**, 1–132

HALL, A. V. (1988), 'Pest control in herbaria', *Taxon*, **37**, 885–907

HALL, D. W. (1981), 'Microwave: a method to control herbarium insects', *Taxon*, **30**, 818–819

HALLIDAY, G. and BEADLE, M. (1983), *Flora Europaea: Consolidated Index*, Cambridge University Press, Cambridge

HAWKSWORTH, D. L., SUTTON, B. C. and AINSWORTH, G. C. (1983), *Ainsworth and Bisby's Dictionary of the Fungi*, 7th edition, Commonwealth Mycological Institute, Kew

HITCH, C. J. B. (1983), 'Soil binder for lichens', *Bulletin British Lichen Society*, **53**, 18

PAGE, C. N. (1979), 'The herbarium preservation of conifer specimens', *Taxon*, **28**, 375–379

SAULEDA, R. P. and ADAMS, R. M. (1981), 'Drying herbarium specimens by microwave radiation', *Taxon*, **30**, 561

SAVILE, D. B. O. (1962), *Collection and Care of Botanical Specimens, Publication No. 1113*, Department of Agriculture, Canada

STERN, W. L. (1967), 'Index Xylariorum: institutional wood collections of the world', *Regnum Vegetabile*, **49**, 1–36

THOMSON, G. (1986), *The Museum Environment*, 2nd edition, Butterworths/IIC, London

TOUW, M. and KORES, P. (1984), 'Compactorization in herbaria: planning factors and four case studies', *Taxon*, **33**, 276–287

WOELKERLING, W. J. (1988), *The Coralline Red Algae*, British Museum (Natural History), Oxford University Press, London/Oxford

WOMERSLEY, J. S. (1981), *Plant Collecting and Herbarium Development, FAO Plant Production and Protection Paper 33*, Food and Agriculture Organization, Rome.

43

Object handling

Gwyn Miles

Introduction

Anyone who comes into contact with museum objects during their work must appreciate that there is a real need for care when objects are handled. Damage to objects occurs in all museums. However, with forethought much of the damage caused by poor handling or transporation can be avoided.

All staff who work in a museum may need to handle objects at some point in their career; handling is not simply the prerogative of the Curator and Conservator. In a large museum there will be other specialist groups: technicians dealing with object handling and installation, designers, photographers and object cleaners who will come into contact with objects as part of their normal duties. However, in the event of unforeseen circumstances such as fire or flood, staff from other areas may be asked to assist. In smaller museums where roles are less specialized the attendant staff may assist the Curator to move or even clean ojects. Whether it is part of the normal routine or only in exceptional circumstances, anyone working in a museum should understand the nature of the collection and the principles governing the handling of objects.

Most objects within a museum are inherently vulnerable. This may be due to their nature: their structure, size or shape; to the materials from which they are made; or they may become fragile as they age. The value of an object is immaterial, the same standards of care should be shown to all objects, which need to be handled in a safe way that is appropriate for their physical make-up and construction.

Failure to understand the nature of museum objects can lead to irreparable damage. The object in a museum is not simply a thing of beauty, it is also a piece of evidence. Often this evidence lies on the surface of the object – patination on the surface of a bronze, gilding on the frame of a painting, gesso and paint on the surface of a medieval sculpture.

The simple answer would seem to be not to handle the objects, but no museum can run without object movement. Objects enter a museum where they will be inspected and registered. They will then be moved into store before being photographed, conserved and displayed. Once in display they may be required for loan. Displays change. Objects that are never displayed will still be required for study. All these activities are part of the normal life of a museum. We do not simply preserve objects in museums, we preserve them in order to make them available to the public through display and study. The duty of the museum profession is to preserve objects for future generations while making them accessible to this one. We cannot stop deterioration of objects, but we can take all possible steps to slow it down and prevent careless damage.

When an object is moved it is at risk:

(1) from direct impact, e.g. dropping a pot;
(2) from pressure on its surface, e.g. lifting flakes on a painting; and
(3) from unnatural stresses, e.g. lifting a chair by its arms.

To minimize the risks from these factors an object should never be carried unprotected, but should be placed within a container. To guard against any damage being caused through friction or vibration the object should be protected by padding or packing.

Preparation

The key to successful object handling is preparation. This includes preparation of the handler, the object, the route and the destination. The basic principle of all object movement is to think through every stage involved in the move before you start; then the move itself should be undertaken calmly and smoothly. Object movement should not be ill prepared and hurried – that way mistakes are much more likely.

The first step is to inspect the object. Ask yourself the following questions.

(1) What is it made of?
(2) Will it stand lifting?
(3) By which part should the object be lifted?
(4) Are there any loose parts which could become detached?
(5) How heavy is the object?
(6) How many people will be needed?
(7) What equipment is required?
(8) How heavy is the equipment needed?

If any of these questions are difficult to answer, get help from someone with more experience.

The second step is to decide how to move the object from A to B. Check the route and ask these questions.

(1) Will the object go through the doors?
(2) Will the object be able to make all the turns?
(3) Are there stairs, ramps or lifts to negotiate?
(4) What are the floor loadings permissible?
(5) Is the floor level, smooth, etc.?
(6) Will you damage the floor?
(7) How will you transport it?
(8) Does it need supporting, padding or tying?
(9) Will you clash with the public?
(10) Is the destination suitable and prepared?

The next step is to prepare yourself and the team who will move the object. It is wise to ensure that two people are always present when an object is moved. Thus one person can concentrate on the object while a second can make sure that the path is clear. If several people are needed to handle a given object the team must be disciplined. There can only be one team leader who will give instructions to the rest of the team. The responsibility for a safe move always rests with the team leader, who must ensure that everyone involved in the move understands exactly what is expected of them.

There should be no eating, drinking or smoking in the vicinity of the object. All handlers must have clean, dry hands and jewellery that could cause damage to an object must be removed. Ink or felt-tip pens should not be used near to objects, any notes that need to be made during a move should be taken in pencil. Any equipment to be used during the move, whether a pair of gloves, a basket or trolley, must also be clean and dry.

The use of gloves when handling objects is not as simple as might appear at first sight. It depends on the nature of the object to be handled.

Gloves must be worn:

(1) where acids from the hands can accelerate corrosion – this applies to metalwork, sick glass, lacquer and fine bindings and manuscripts;
(2) where heat from the hands can damage a surface – this applies to gilding; and
(3) where the health of staff is involved – this applies to dealing with soiled material for any reason such as a flood.

Gloves are optional:

(1) where staining or marking from fingerprints is a possibility; this may apply to unglazed ceramics, including terracotta, and the card mounts for prints, drawings, photographs or textiles.

Gloves should not be worn:

(1) where snagging may result – this is the case with paintings, fine jewellery, polychrome surfaces, un-mounted textiles and paper;
(2) where direct contact is essential for a secure grip – this is the case with stained glass panels, books and large furniture and sculpture.

The move

Once prepared and properly equipped, the object handlers must decide how to make contact with the object. Again you may find it useful to ask a series of questions:

Where do you grab hold of the object?

(1) Not at the top – to pick up any object such as a painting, pot or sculpture by the top is inviting disaster. The tension caused by the weight of the object can easily open up cracks and cause damage. Always lift from as low down on an object as possible and preferably with most of the weight balanced above the point of contact. To avoid this type of stress it is important not to drag an object – always push it.
(2) Not by any protrusions. All protrusions from an object are potential weak points and must be avoided at all costs. Never pick up a pot by its handle or a figure by its arms. Look for the most solid, stable area and use that as the point of contact.
(3) Maximize the area of contact. If you are manually lifting an object use the widest area of your hands possible as pressure increases if the area of contact is small. If moving a table try not to use only fingertip pressure, but lay your fingers along their length.
(4) Be aware of the centre of gravity. Remember that a high centre of gravity or a narrow base means that a small tilt could make the object unstable. If you are putting pots into a basket, it may be better to lay certain items on their sides, otherwise they could easily fall over. The centre of gravity of a supported object must be

vertically over its base. If an object is suspended it will slip until its centre of gravity is vertically under the point of suspension.

How much force?

(1) The more force you use, the faster the object will move, or the quicker you may damage it.
(2) A weak force at the end of a long lever can do as much work (and, therefore, damage) as a strong force at the end of a short lever.
(3) If the speed of an object doubles, the amount of damage that could occur in the event of collision quadruples.

How do you transport the object?

(1) Never simply carry an object in your arms, it should be *in* something (e.g. a box or basket) or *on* something (e.g. a tray or trolley).
(2) Never overload a container or vehicles and make sure that the object fits properly within it without overhanging the sides.
(3) Never move objects of the same general type but of vastly different sizes or weights together.

Where do you put the object down?

(1) In a clean, stable environment, similar to the one from which the object was moved.
(2) Never leave an object sitting directly on the floor or in any kind of vulnerable position.
(3) Changes of environment should take place slowly, if an object is to move outside the museum the packing must provide reasonable insulation from outside conditions.

Safe lifting

It is important to remember that the law demands that we pay constant attention to health and safety at work, this is of particular relevance to the movement of objects. It should be seen as an area of mutual concern for both employers and employees. The employer is responsible for providing safe conditions of work, training and instruction and to make available all necessary safety and protective equipment for the tasks. The employee is responsible for using the equipment provided and to assist in making any improvement necessary to conform with safety standards.

Manual handling

Organize the work to minimize the amount of lifting necessary using mechanical means or other aids. When help is needed for lifting heavy or awkward loads, get everyone to work together, but make sure only one person gives clear and unhurried instruc-

tions. Provide protective clothing for hands and feet where necessary.

Make sure that everyone knows the correct lifting techniques.

(1) Do not jerk and shove, twisting the body may cause injury.
(2) Lift in easy stages, floor to knee, then from knee to carrying position. Reverse this lifting method when setting the load down.
(3) Hold weights close to the body. Lift with the legs and keep the back straight.
(4) Grip loads with palms, not fingertips and do not change your grip while carrying.
(5) Do not let the load obstruct your view, make sure the route is clear as you move.

When using equipment:

(1) always have a competent person operating any machinery or lifting gear;
(2) obey all instructions and procedures for using equipment, do not take short-cuts and never exceed safe working loads;
(3) never use make-shift, damaged or badly worn equipment; and
(4) always check even the simplest piece of equipment regularly to see that nothing is loose or dangerous (e.g. check that the tyres are firmly in position on a truck)

With regard to orderly placement of the object:

(1) do not allow items to protrude from stacks or bins into gangways;
(2) never climb racks to reach upper shelves, always use a ladder or steps;
(3) do not lean heavy stacks against structural walls; and
(4) never exceed the safe loading of racks, shelves or floors.

Once a move has been completed it is essential that the object's new resting place is recorded and that the personnel who will be responsible for the object are informed of its arrival. Check that no damage has occurred to the object, remember not to discard any packing material before searching it thoroughly for fragments which may have become detached in transit. If any damage has occurred it must be reported thoroughly and the cause of the damage investigated.

Policy on object handling

It is expected practice for museums to develop a Collections Management Policy, to provide guidelines for the body of museum practices and procedures which allow the sensible acquisition and disposal, care and preservation, security and accountability for objects, their movement (including loans) and documentation. The systems and procedures used for the handling of objects, both during routine operations and in 'disastrous' circumstances, should be established for any museums so that all staff understand what is expected of them.

Staff should be trained in the proper handling of objects so that they have an appreciation of the need for care and an understanding of the many dangers that face objects within the collections. Knowledge of the general principles of planning moves and handling objects is essential as is the thorough grounding in the procedures for safeguarding objects and the welfare of the people who work with them.

Recognition of the need for training in this area has been growing in the last few years as some museums (e.g. Tate Gallery and Victoria and Albert Museum) have developed in-house training manuals. The National Trust, with its large number of volunteer staff, have taken an active lead in this area with the production of their *Manual of Housekeeping* and, more recently, a number of training videos. However, as yet there are no national training courses for this important topic, staff are more often than not expected to pick it up as they go along. Safe handling of museum objects is easy if you apply good common sense; all that is needed is a sound knowledge of the material to be moved and good planning. Nevertheless, experience shows that if staff are provided with clear rules to be followed as they move objects the risk to those objects is reduced. The compilation of such rules depend on the nature of the museum.

44

Storage systems

James Tate and Theo Skinner

Introduction

The storage of objects can be greatly improved by the use of suitable storage systems. Such systems aid efficient object retrieval and help to eliminate physical damage to the objects. The implementation and use of good quality storage systems can be one of the most significant steps forward in the passive conservation of a museum collection.

For the storage of museum objects, it is necessary to identify, and perhaps design, the correct style of storage unit and system appropriate to the particular type of object, and to determine the space required using that system to house the collection. While this process is determined by factors general to all museums, the degree of variation and the constraints which apply are such that it is impossible to produce more than general guidelines. This chapter therefore gives examples of two aspects, a method of assessing storage requirements of a particular collection, and some of the successful storage systems which have been developed. No attempt is made to give a complete review of the types of storage system available, nor a comprehensive bibliography. Readers requiring such information are referred to Johnson and Horgan (1979) and the references therein.

Factors affecting the choice of storage system

Obviously, overall cost will be a prime consideration, and the availability and cost of space will be a major determining factor as to which systems can be considered and eventually chosen. Storage facilities are not glamorous and are unlikely to attract sponsorship, but grants may be available to up-grade and provide facilities; for example, in England, funding for archaeological site collection storage may be provided by English Heritage.

The choice of storage system will be affected by:

(1) The type and kind of use to which the collection will be put. How often will staff, both internal and external to the museum, wish to examine the various groups of objects in store?

(2) Can the objects be segregated by size/material/ environmental requirements, or must they be kept in some sort of imposed order, e.g. chronological or typological, for curatorial reasons? (This is closely linked to the useage above.)

(3) Can the objects be boxed or otherwise enclosed, or must they be available to constant inspection? Boxes can be used to provide microclimate conditions for sensitive objects.

(4) Is the available space adequate, or will high density mobile storage units have to be used to maximize space utilization? Space can be very expensive, and high density storage units are often cost-effective, especially as they may also offer savings in travel, security, and environmental control costs, They may, however, require higher floor loadings.

(5) Would mechanical handling be an advantage? There may be savings in manpower costs within the store.

(6) How much will the collections increase in size or range over the probable lifetime of the store and/or of the storage units?

(7) Are there objects with unusual storage problems, e.g. extraordinary length, height, weight, or fragility which will require special consideration?

(8) Will there be sufficient access to the store and within the store for the type of object intended?

(9) Must a particularly high level of security be provided for all or parts of the collection, e.g. coins or precious stones?

(10) Are the objects likely to be adversely effected by the materials of the storage system? Tarnishing of silver and corrosion of lead are well known examples. If possible the construction and finishing materials should be tested. Where known inert materials cannot be used, it may help to seal the surfaces: we currently use a vapour barrier produced for the buiding trade consisting of aluminium foil supported on a thin plastic backing.

(11) Are the storage systems able to give some primary protection against disaster, especially flooding? (Precautions against common damage, such as raising the storage units off the floor, are not covered here.)

By addressing basic questions such as these it should be possible to determine the precise type of system which best suits the overall needs of the collections.

Assessment of space requirement

One of the most difficult questions to answer, especially where large and diverse collections are held in inadequate storage conditions (a situation not unfamiliar to most museum Curators!) is just how much storage space is needed.

The storage needs of a particular collection should ideally be investigated quantitatively. In large collections, it may be possible to do this only by measuring the attributes of a sample of the objects, this technique being especially suitable for large collections of small objects. For large objects, particularly those of a fixed size, it may be more satisfactory to survey the whole collection, although if the collection is large this may prove an impossible objective in terms of available staff time. Very large objects will probable require individual consideration in any case.

For the purposes of surveying, the use of standard forms to record the required information is essential, prompting recording of the relevant information and allowing easy collation of the results. Collation is readily carried out on paper, or with fairly basic data base or spreadsheet facilities, and should aim to provide information about the total areas required for each of the various classes of object previously decided upon.

The final choice of particular storage systems will be based on the type of object and the homogeneity of the collection, as well as the financial and use considerations outlined above. Some storage systems are more flexible than others with regard to the size and weight of objects they will house, and it is usually important to maximize efficient use of the available space.

Case studies

Assessment of the storage systems required for the reserve archaeological collections

In 1988, a rationalization of central storage provision within the National Museums of Scotland necessitated the rehousing of the reserve archaeological collections. At the start of this project the objects were stored in a number of locations, primarily in undercase cupboards in the display gallery. A survey of the material was instigated to determine storage requirements and, simultaneously, to assess the conservation needs.

Early consideration was given to the use of the material, essentially a study collection. It was decided not to enclose the objects individually, but to segregate objects according to their environmental requirements. The basic type of storage unit required for the different types and sizes of object were also decided on at this stage. For the smaller objects, (flints, stone axes, metalwork, leather and other organic materials) drawers were considered to be the best storage system, whilst shelved cabinets were thought preferable for complete pottery vessels. Steel pallets were chosen to house the collection of large sculptured stones, allowing them to be easily moved within the store and thus be inspected from most sides by visiting scholars.

Examination of a range of different manufactured products led to the conclusion that the most useful units for this purpose were those made of metal rather than wood construction. These, whilst expensive, are made from conservationaly sound materials, have a long lifetime, would allow a degree of flexibility in specifying the size of drawer combinations in each cabinet, have high weight-loading capacity in each drawer, and could be moved as complete units by a pallet truck if necessary.

The large size of the collections (estimated as 23,000 objects), the limited resources available, and the short time-scale made it necessary to undertake the survey by sampling. For this purpose, the collections to be rehoused were divided into categories expected to have similar properties and requirements, for example size and environment, as far as appeared possible from examination of the cataloguing system. This was intended to have the effect of reducing variations within the samples, thus increasing the efficiency of the sampling technique.

Standard forms were designed to record the relevant information, together with guidelines for recording data to ensure consistency between surveyors. Arrangements were made to obtain access to the objects chosen in the samples, and the survey carried out over a period of 3 weeks, by a team of four Conservators. A total of 784 objects were examined, that is some 3 per cent of the collection. The data relevant to storage were entered on a computer, and analysed using suitable software (largely Lotus 1-2-3).

The analysis consisted of calculating the height distribution of objects in each category and then determining the total storage area required for each of a selected series of height categories, chosen to fit in with the type of storage units envisaged for that category and size of object (*Figures 44.1 and 44.2*).

An allowance of 20 per cent of the storage area was made for space between the objects, to allow access. This is a somewhat arbitrary figure, and it is hoped that it will be possible to calculate a more exact one when the units are filled with objects. Similarly, a

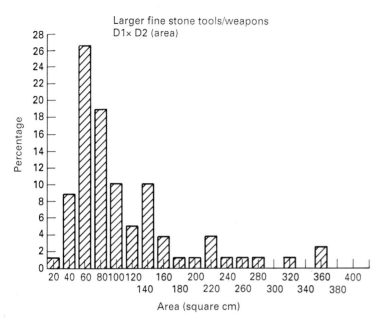

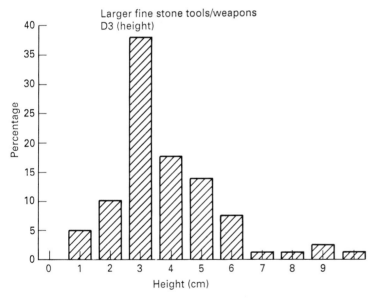

Figure 44.1 Size distribution of the sample of larger fine-stone tools/weapons

factor was included to allow for the probable growth of the collection over the next 20 years. The figures were then used to itemize a series of cabinets and drawer combinations for the small metal, stone, organic objects and pottery sherds, as well as a series of shelved cupboards for the pottery collection and metal pallets to house the collection of large sculptured stones.

The itemized list of units was used as the basis for a quotation for fitting out the store and, eventually, the units were purchased, although it was not possible to purchase them all in one financial year. This turned out not to be a serious problem, as the time and manpower required to rehouse the material meant that the process took a very long time, indeed it has not yet been completed. The location of each

AREAS

Total number of registrations:	1905
Sample size:	79
Total area of sample:	7808 sq cm
mean:	98 sq cm
Calculated total area for whole population:	10.82 sq m

BOXES

		%	Approx number	% (cumulative)
Optimal box sizes (areas)	20 cm	1	20	1
	40	9	180	10
	80	45	900	55
	160	29	600	84
	320	10	200	94
Optimal ratios, (D2:D1)	1:1.5	2	40	
	1:2	16	320	
	1:3	45	900	
	1:4	13	260	
	1:4+	5	100	
Optimal heights	1 cm	5	100	5
	2	10	200	15
	3	38	760	53
	4	17	340	70
	5	13	260	83
	10	17	340	99

DRAWERS
83% of population can be stored in drawers 5 cm high.
A further 16% of population can be stored in drawers 10 cm high.
1% of population requires drawers of a greater height, say 18 cm.

Thus require 2 cabinets:
   1 with 20 drawers at 54 mm (catalogue 101.02.703)
   1 with   9 drawers at 104 mm (catalogue 101.02.705)
   and   2 drawers at 179 mm (catalogue 101.02.707)

ENVIRONMENT
As for lithic assemblages

SHELF AREA
Zero.

Figure 44.2 Estimation of storage system needed for the sample shown in *Figure 44.1*

item within the store will be logged on the National Museum of Scotland computer database, and retrieval of objects should then be a simple matter once the object registration number has been identified.

Storage of the ethnographic collection

Information about the storage of the ethnographic collections of the Royal Museums of Scotland has been published previously (Idiens, 1973). Here the intention is to provide more detailed examples of the types of storage system used for particular aspects of the collection.

Weapons store
One room of the general store and all of the spear store, have been fitted with sliding vertical panels, made of 50 mm expanded steel mesh within mahogany frames, 1930 mm × 1450 mm (larger frames in the spear store). There are 7 cupboards, each containing 7 such frames which hang from sliding channels similar to those used for garage doors. Each frame is separated by 160 mm, and can be slid out individually to examine the objects on it which are fixed to the mesh with string or (preferably) cotton tape. Some of the panes have mesh made from unfinished metal and fairly sharp edges. Although

this has not caused any problems since the system was installed our preference now is for plastic covered 50 mm square wire mesh.

Obviously this type of storage is only suitable for objects which have sufficient strength to be supported hanging and which are not liable to have component parts detach. Although the panels are fairly close together, and care has to be taken to ensure there is no danger of objects in adjacent panels rubbing or catching against each other, the system has proved very satisfactory in use since its installation in the 1970s (see *Figures 44.3* and *44.4.*) Similar systems are used for other items both here and elsewhere in the museum, for example for firearms in the Scottish United Services Museum.

Figure 44.3 General view of the spear store

General small objects

The bulk of small items are kept in plastic trays within internally adjustable dust-proof cupboards. The trays are commercially available bakers' trays with perforated bottoms, (731 mm long × 426 mm wide × 76 mm deep) (Idiens, 1973). The trays are sufficiently rigid to support a fairly wide range of items, and are supported within the storage cupboards from side rails, that is they do not require individual shelves. An alternative type of tray has

Figure 44.4 An open panel showing spears

been tried, consisting of an upper part of plastic of similar dimensions, but mounted on a sheet of plywood to provide adequate support from the shelf runners. There are two problems: firstly the introduction of plywood into the sealed cupboards may cause undesirable environmental factors; and secondly, the tray plus plywood support are heavy and awkward to use.

Among the advantages of the system which is in use are: flexibility – the trays can be left out to provide space for larger items, or the central upright of the cupboad can be removed to allow the trays to be put in sideways; the trays can be drawn out to see all items on that 'shelf' without having to handle or disturb them; in an emergency trays can be rapidly removed to an alternative location and the cupboard can be emptied without having to repack or handle individual objects; the consistency of storage units means that reorganization between cupboards is simplified; and absence or movement of trays from the store can easily be recorded or noticed. (See *Figures 44.5* to *44.7.*) Objects can be stored individually within the trays or within specially cut-out shapes in polyethylene foam lining the tray.

Skin and textile clothing

At present, part of the collections of skin and other costumes are stored in cupboards with the items hung on individually padded coat hangers. This system was introduced some years ago and we would not now recommend it, the aim now being to

Figure 44.5 General view of cupboards used to store small objects

Figure 44.6 View of open cupboards with one tray pulled out containing medium sized objects

Figure 44.7 View of open cupboards for storing irregularly shaped objects

Figure 44.8 Present hanging system for skin and textile clothing

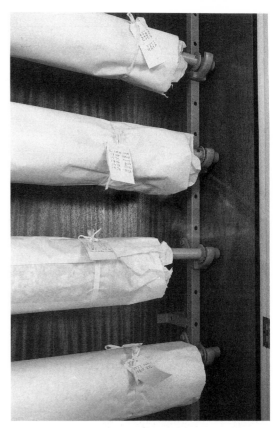

Figure 44.9 General view of rollers and cupboards for storing large textiles

store all such costumes flat on large shelving, since it is felt that this gives far better support to items which may be fairly fragile and subject to damage when hanging side by side. There are disadvantages in storing the costumes flat, particularly the fact that some have to be laid on top of each other where individual shelving cannot be provided, so that examination of one has to involve moving other items. However, the benefits of improved support to the costumes are considered to outweigh this. Acid-free tissue paper is of course placed between individual items of costume with additional padding if needed. (See *Figure 44.8*).

Large textiles, etc.
Large flat textile, bark cloth and similar items are stored efficiently on large padded rollers, similar to those used for the storage and display of flooring materials in carpet warehouses. The rollers rest on adjustable side supports within shallow cupboards, and each can be individually removed (by two people) to be unrolled on a central table. Lack of space has meant that some rollers have to contain more than one item, protected by acid-free tissue paper and padding where necessary. The rolled textiles are held in place on the roller by suitably placed cotton ties. (See *Figures 44.9* and *44.10*.)

Figure 44.10 Removal of a textile roller to a table

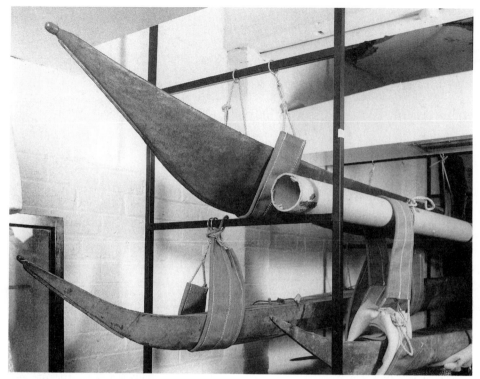

Figure 44.11 Padded slings used to store canoes

Figure 44.12 High density picture storage

Fragile and heavier large items pose other problems, particularly in terms of removing them from shelving without subjecting them to stress and without mechanical lifting aids. In the same cellar as the canoes, Egyptian sarcophagi are stored on simple racking, with each piece being placed on a rigid board with attached handles so that the whole unit can be slid forward and lifted out in one piece for study.

Other examples

Picture storage
Widely used systems for picture storage consist of wire mesh covering walls or other vertical surfaces, the pictures being suspended from the mesh. Such systems are simple but allow considerable flexibility. Higher packing density can be achieved by the use of mobile racking, or by the use of compactor storage (*Figure 44.12*). As with all mobile racking the space between racks must be adequate to clear adjacent paintings, frames etc, while the effectiveness of sealing against dust must also be checked (see also Chapter 30.)

Geological specimens
Storage of geological specimens using efficient packing systems may raise a serious problem of weight, both in terms of floor loading and within the storage system itself. This may need specially constructed racking, such as the system illustrated in *Figure 44.13* where specimens are housed in wooden boxes with hinged lids, each box sitting on a shelf in a frame made from 1 inch welded steel tubing. (See also Chapter 40.)

Acknowledgements

Thanks are due to Maureen Barrie and Dale Idiens for comments on the ethnography storage and to Ian Larner for taking the photographs.

References

IDIENS, D. (1973), 'New ethnographical storage in the Royal Scottish Museum', *Museums Journal* **73**(2), 61–62

JOHNSON, E. V. and HORGAN, J. C. (1979), 'Museum collection storage', *UNESCO Technical Handbooks for Museums and Monuments*, 2, 34–56

Figure 44.13 Example of storage of small specimens

Large ethnographic items
The storage of large and irregularly shaped objects is generally an exercise in ingenuity for the Curator. Open shelving and storage bays are, of course, standard and broadly useful solutions. In our ethnographic store we have found the use of padded slings particularly suitable for large but light objects, especially the undisplayed collection of skin canoes (*Figure 44.11*), both model and full size. The number of slings depends on the rigidity and fragility of the object, but could clearly be adapted in many ways.

45

Conservation aspects of storage and display

Susan M. Bradley

Introduction

There should be no difference between the quality of storage and exhibition facilities as both provide the same functions for a collection. These functions are security and preservation and are the primary responsibilities of a museum towards its collection. Storage facilities are built to house a large number of objects as efficiently as possible. As a result objects can be on shelves, in cupboards, boxes, trays or drawers in fixed or movable racking. However, the storage is arranged the objects should be separated so they are not touching or piled on top of one another. They should be protected from dust, insects and pests, mould growth and corrosive gases and the relative humidity and temperature should be stable and in a range which does not cause deterioration. Objects should be ordered so that they can be readily located and are easily observable so that the presence or absence of individual items is instantly recognized. The store-room must also be secure. The purpose of an exhibition is to show the objects in such a way that the public has full appreciation of them. As a result a considerable amount of thought is given to the layout of the show-cases and to the positioning of free-standing objects in the gallery. The requirements for the objects in the gallery are the same as in storage and galleries should be kept free of dust, mould, insects and corrosive gases. The relative humidity, temperature and light levels should be such as are required for the type of object being exhibited.

Security, handling and mounting and environmental considerations are discussed in more detail below.

Security

Free-standing objects in exhibition galleries are insecure since it is easy for the public to come into contact with them. Unfortunately, graffiti and other acts of vandalism are difficult to prevent. Barriers can be positioned to prevent people leaning over and writing on objects but spray paint can still be directed onto objects from a distance. Serious vandalism can only be prevented by searching the public on their way into the museum. It is therefore better to display objects inside show-cases if this is possible. However, in certain circumstances, such as for large three dismensional objects and oil paintings, a better appreciation of the objects is gained if they are not in show-cases.

Storage areas, show-cases and galleries should have secure locks and an alarm system. To ensure that the security is itself secure access to keys should be limited to named members of staff and keys should not be taken off museum property. Advice on the selection of a good system can be obtained from the Police, the Area Museum Service, the National Museums Security Advisor and Security Officers in other museums. However, regardless of how much money is available it is better to seek the advice of museum professional rather than to select a security firm without having first obtained good references.

Handling and mounting

The most common cause of damage to objects in museums is handling. In order to limit this cause of damage some general rules on handling should be observed. Before handling an object all rings and heavy jewellery should be removed. Hands should be washed to remove dirt and salts and, if possible, cotton gloves should be worn. Objects should not be carried unsupported but should be placed in a box, basket or trolley with suitable padding material and covered before moving. Objects should not be lifted by protrubances such as handles as these may be insecurely fixed and break.

In storage areas there should be good access to objects with wide unobstructed gangways between racking or cupboards. The position of objects should be clearly identified for ease of location. They should not be piled high on shelves as they might be knocked off when other objects are removed. If shelving is higher than can be reached by an average-height person, adequate step ladders should be available and two people will be needed to take objects from the high shelves, one to lift the object from the shelf and one to receive the object at ground level. If objects are stored in individual boxes or drawers the boxes or drawers should be lined with an inert material such as polyethylene foam in which shapes are cut to hold the objects so that they do not bump against the sides of the container or each other. Large flat objects such as tapestries and other textiles require special storage facilities and should be stored flat or rolled and not folded.

Objects may need mounting for both safe storage and display. For instance, fragmentary swords will be safer if they are supported on a mount which has been moulded to support the whole of the length. When objects are mounted for exhibition the mount should be designed to support the object so that all points of stress are relieved and there is no abrasion of the object by the mount. Thus there should be no sharp edges and the mount should be padded with cushioning material such as a polyester wadding covered with a suitable fabric where is comes into contact with the object. There is a tendency to display some objects by suspending them in show-cases. This can lead to damage if the suspension thread, wire or chain chosen is not strong enough to support the load of the object and breaks. The suspension material should be chosen to have a breaking load well in excess of the weight of the object. All knots or joins should be doubly secured, for instance by glueing. The suspension material should be checked regularly for signs of strain and renewed at regular intervals even if no deterioration is detected. Nylon fishing line is used for this purpose in the British Museum and it is recommended that it is changed at intervals of 3 years.

Objects may be damaged by vibration which can arise from springy floors, adjacent lift shafts or building work. The effects of vibration may be dampened by use of absorbent materials placed between objects and shelves or walls if they are wall mounted. The most popular way of mounting small objects such as jewellery is to pin it onto boards. Base-metal pins can corrode onto metal objects when the metal of the pin is in direct contact with the object. This can occur even if the relative humidity is below 45 per cent. Pins can also cause damage to objects by scratching them. For these reasons all pins should be sheathed in polyethylene tubing. The pins should be bent first and the tubing slid on. Some types of tubing can be shrunk onto the pins using a hot-air blower. This makes the tubing less obtrusive and does not greatly increase the time involved in pinning.

Environmental considerations

The main environmental requirements for the storage and display of museum collections are that areas should be free of dust, insects and other biological pests and pollutant gases and should be capable of sustaining appropriate levels of relative humidity, temperature and light.

Dealing with dust and insects

Keeping areas free of dust, insects and rodents is mostly a matter of good housekeeping. Air from venitilation and air-conditioning systems should be filtered to remove dust, but visitors and museum staff will create dust. As a result, storage areas and galleries should be cleaned regularly taking particular care that dead spots such as the tops of show-cases, high shelves, awkward corners and underneath units are also cleaned. Vacuum cleaners should be of the type that contain dust totally. Foodstuffs should not be taken into storage and display areas because food debris attracts insects and rodents and can, therefore, be the cause of an infestation. Mould and fungal growth normally arise when the relative humidity and temperature are high, although they also need a nutrient medium and dust and food debris can fulfil this need as can artefacts made from organic materials.

If insect, fungal or mould infestations occur, pesticides or fungicides can be used. However, the use of these materials is controlled by the *Control of Pesticides Regulations 1986*, and only perscribed commodity chemicals and trade-name materials can be used. Before using any materials the health and safety risks for staff who are working constantly in storage areas or who will be handling objects should be assessed in accordance with the *Control of Substances Hazardous to Health* (COSHH) regulations.

Insect infestations can be started when objects which harbour insects are added to a collection. In order to avoid this problem some museums undertake fumigation of new artefacts before they are put into stores or on display. This most often occurs with ethnographic collections. Methods for fumigation in museums are at present under review because the new pesticide legislation has restricted the use of some of the materials which have been used in the past such as ethylene oxide. Methods using freezing and carbon dioxide may become more widely used. Freezing has been used with considerable success in the USA, Canada and Denmark. If it is not possible to fumigate suspect objects then they should be separated from the rest of the collection for a period to allow any infestation to become apparent. The object can then be dealt with on an individual basis before being returned to the appropriate storage area.

Pollutant gases

Pollutant gases such as sulphur dioxide, nitrogen oxides and hydrogen sulphide are always present in the atmosphere. They can be removed from the air in the museum by filtration in ventilation and air conditioning systems. However, many museums do not have such sophisticated systems and even if these systems are installed they often do not function as well as might be expected. It is therefore often true that the museum air is potentially corrosive to some objects in the collection.

Materials used in the construction and decoration of storage and display areas can also give off corrosive vapours adding to the problem, especially in areas where air flow is restricted. There are three ways of dealing with this problem. These are using scavengers to remove the gases from the air, using inhibitors to prevent the reaction of the gases at the surface of the objects or selecting materials which do not give off gases. The later approach is the most satisfactory.

Hydrogen sulphide which causes silver to tarnish is naturally present in the museum air and, although selecting materials which do not give off this gas will help to protect silver, the background levels in the air will still cause tarnishing. To reduce the background level of hydrogen sulphide scavengers and inhibitors can be used. The use of zinc oxide catalyst and charcoal cloth in show-cases as scavengers of hydrogen sulphide are being investigated. Both show promising results. Inhibitors to prevent the tarnishing reaction occurring on the surface of silver, such as are present in some proprietary silver polish preparations, do have a good effect and increase the length of time before the tarnish layer begins to reform. Lacquers also have this effect, but each time the silver is cleaned the lacquer has to be removed. Vapour-phase inhibitors can also be used, but the health-and-safety implications for staff must be considered. These inhibitors are only effective in a very well-sealed space. For the storage of silver all of the methods for the prevention of tarnishing described can be used as long as the silver is stored in boxes with well-fitting lids. Another material, an impregnated cloth which is made into bags can also be used. This material is impregnated with a chemical which reacts with hydrogen sulphide. The bags also have the advantage of preventing the silver from being scratched.

Because of its commercial value, there has been a lot of work done on inhibiting the tarnishing of silver. However, other metals found in museums collections are prone to corrosion. Charcoal cloth can be used to absorb organic acids and, possibly, formaldehyde. These gases are involved in the corrosion of lead to basic lead carbonate or lead formate. Unfortunately there are no polishes which will inhibit this reaction, although lacquers may be of some help. Copper based alloys can be corroded to green copper corrosion products. The most common corrosion seen on polished copper alloy artefacts are green copper acetate and red cuprite. There are polish formulations available for copper based alloys that contain an inhibitor which can lengthen the time taken for corrosion to occur.

Selection of materials for the storage and display of artefacts

The most effective way to prevent corrosion of metals is to select construction, storage and display materials which do not give off corrosive gases. Very acid or alkaline materials will cause the deterioration of organic based artefacts made of materials such as paper, leather and textiles. Materials suitable for use with organic artefacts should also be carefully selected to be within the archival standard of pH 5.5–8.5 and dyes should not be fugitive.

At the British Museum a series of simple tests to screen materials for their potential to give off corrosive gases were devised and have been in use since 1973. Accelerated corrosion tests are carried out in which a polished metal test piece and a sample of the material of interest are placed in a quickfit test tube with a small test tube packed with cotton wool wetted with distilled water. The sealed test tube is placed in an oven at 60°C for 28 days after which time the surface of the metal test piece is examined for signs of corrosion. If any corrosion is present the material is rejected for use in the permanent storage or display of the metal. These tests are normally carried out using copper, silver and lead test pieces. A spot test to detect the presence of reducible sulphur in a material which is based on the catalytic decomposition of sodium azide solution is also used on fabrics. The Beilstein test is used to detect the presence of chlorine in a material because the evolution of hydrogen chloride gas or chlorides can cause the corrosion of copper and silver. To test that the acidity of a material is within the archival limits the pH of an aqueous extract is measured. The fastness of dyes becomes apparent during the preparation of the aqueous extract. The use of these tests has resulted in a reduction of instances of metal artefacts corroding on exhibition. Over 3000 materials have been tested for use with the museum collection since 1973. These materials include fabrics for dressing show-cases, construction materials such as wood and plastics, adhesives, sealants, paints and peat, sand and cork shavings. The Museum offers a testing service and access to the files of materials tested to other institutions and exhibition designers. Information on the service and costs can be obtained from the Department of Conservation. Area museum services may also provide a similar service. The corrosion tests are relatively easy to carry out and many Conservators who have the appropriate laboratory facilities do this.

There is considerable debate about the use of wood in museums. Wood is a very easy material to use for the construction of show-cases and storage units. Composite boards such as Sundeala board make very good mounting boards on which to pin objects. However, woods give off acidic vapours such as acetic acid which initiates the corrosion of lead. Special provision should be made for the storage of lead using plastic boxes and metal cabinets rather than cardboard or wood, although acid-free cardboard boxes could be used. Because of cost factors and because no suitable replacement has been found, it is often only practical to use wood in the construction of show-cases. In these circumstances vulnerable objects can be protected by laminating acid-free board onto Sundeala mounting boards or covering boards with an inert polyester film or displaying objects inside separate perspex boxes within the showcase. If the whole display is to be of lead based objects it would be best to use aluminium or steel and glass showcases.

Control of relative humidity, temperature and light levels

Relative humidity, temperature and light play a very important part in the deterioration of artefacts in museum collections. It is fluctuation in relative humidity which causes deterioration of many types or organic materials. It does not matter what relative humidity is chosen as long as it is stable. The fluctuation of temperature within a small range, e.g. 3–4°C causes much less damage. It is therefore acceptable to control the relative humidity without controlling the temperature. Both parameters can be controlled if an air-conditioning system is installed. However, full air-conditioning is probably beyond the budget of many museums. Humidifiers, dehumidifiers or both can be used together with thermostatically controlled heating to control the environment in an exhibition gallery or storage room. However, high external temperatures in the summer can raise the temperature inside the building to an unacceptable level. The desired environment can only be maintained if there are interlocking doors to contain the conditioned air and all windows and other potential air leaks are sealed.

Another approach is to control the environment in a discrete space such as a show-case or sealed area in a store room. For show-cases which are opened infrequently two approaches can be taken. One is to install a humidifier, dehumidifier, or both, beneath or adjacent to the show-case and duct the wet or dry air into the area of the case where the objects are displayed. The other is to use conditioned silica gel to maintain the required relative humidity. If the show-case is reasonably well sealed the amount of water needed to keep the humidifier topped up will be minimal since, having obtained the required relative humidity, little water will be needed to keep the level constant. Similarly, having reduced the relative humidity to that requird, a dehumidifier will need to remove little moisture from the air of a sealed show-case to maintain the required level. If the dehumidifier is of the condensation type, water will have to be emptied from the dehumidifier infrequently. However, to maintain a required relative humidity using conditioned silica gel the show-case must be very well sealed. If it is not well sealed the moisture from the silica gel will be lost into the surrounding atmosphere and the gel will not be able to maintain the required relative humidity within the case. The amount of silica gel required is 25 kg per cubic meter of show-case space. This is a large volume of silica gel and special provision, for instance silica gel trays, must be made to hold the gel and for direct exchange with the air in the display case. A facility for conditioning the silica gel to the required relative humidity is also needed. This will involve an oven to dry the silica gel and a large space humidified to the required relative humidity for conditioning the silica gel.

Problems can occur in completely sealed show-cases since if any corrosive gases are given off they build up in the show-case instead of being diluted by the surrounding air leaking into the case and the show-case air leaking out. Thus the requirements of the objects, the control mechanisms available and the staff time available should all be considered. Both approaches need the use of staff time in setting up the system and in maintenance. Getting silica gel to work can be very time consuming because all leaks in the show-case must be sealed and all organic show-case parts must be conditioned to the required relative humidity before the silica gel can begin to condition the air space and hence the objects.

For controlling the relative humidity in a store-room the use of a humidifier or a dehumidifier is necessary because there are likely to be many staff movements into and out of the room.

Light has a deleterious effect on most organic materials and on some inorganic materials. The most commonly observed effect of light is the fading of organic pigments and dyes, although structural deterioration of substrates also occurs. Inorganic pigments undergo changes which affect their colour. Cinnibar turns from vermillion to black on exposure to light. The silver chloride patina which is commonly seen as a compact purple–black layer on excavated silver can break down to give a powdery white layer on exposure to strong light such as sunlight.

High-energy ultraviolet (UV) light is the most damaging, but visible light can also have adverse effects. In order to prevent adverse reactions, lighting in museums should be filtered to remove UV light to a level of less than 70 mw/lumen. This can be achieved by putting UV absorbing film on all windows if natural light is being used as a source of lighting galleries and store rooms and by using UV filters on fluorescent tubes or using low UV tubes or tungsten lamps when artificial lighting is used. The lux level should also be lowered to 50–80 lux for very sensitive material and to 150–200 lux for oil paintings and less-sensitive organic material such as wood. These levels can be achieved by using light-density films on windows and dimmer switches to control artificial lighting.

Lighting in show-cases can be filtered using UV absorbing plastic sheet in the base of the light box or light absorbing films laminated on to glass.

By taking into account all the factors discussed above the storage and display areas can be used to play a part in the conservation and hence continued preservation of the collection. If the conditions in storage and display areas are bad, the collection will continue to actively deteriorate no matter how high the standard of conservation work carried out on individual objects.

Bibliography

Handling and monitoring

BRADLEY, S. M., UPRICHARD, K. and MUNDAY, V. (1990), 'General guidelines on the handling of objects', in Bradley, S. (Ed.), *A Guide to the Storage, Exhibition and Handling of Antiquities, Ethnographia and Pictorial Art*, British Museum Occasional Paper No. 66, pp. 15–17 British Museum Publications, London

PLOWDEN, A. and HALAHAN, D. (1987), *Looking after Antiques*, Pan, London

STOLOW, N. (1987), *Conservation and Exhibitions*, Butterworths, London

Insects and other pests

MINISTRY OF AGRICULTURE, FISHERIES AND FOOD AND THE HEALTH AND SAFETY EXECUTIVE (1990), *Pesticides 1990, Pesticides Approved under the Control of Pesticides Regulations 1986*, HMSO, London

STORY, K.O. (1985), *Pest Management in Museums*, Conservation Analytical laboratory, Smithsonian Institution, Virginia

Pollutant gases and selection of materials for storage and display

BAER, N. S. and BANKS, P. N. (1985), 'Indoor air pollution: effects on cultural and historical materials', *The International Journal of Museum Management and Curatorship*, **4**, 9–20

BLACKSHAW, S. M. and DANIELS, V. D. (1979), 'The testing of material for use in storage and display in museums', *The Conservator*, **3**, 16–19

BRIMBLECOMBE, P. (1989), 'A theoretical approach to the pollution of air volumes within museums', *The Conservator*, **13**, 15–19

DANIELS, V. D. and WARD, S. E. (1982), 'A rapid test for the detection of substances which will tarnish silver', *Studies in Conservation*, **27**, 58–60

GREEN, L. R. (1990), 'Selection of materials and methods for display', Preprints of a one day meeting on *Practical Museum Display and Conservation*, February 1990, Area Museum Council for the South West, Taunton

HACKNEY, S. (1984), 'The distribution of gaseous air pollution within museums', *Studies in Conservation*, **29**, 105–116

ODDY, W. A. (1973), 'An unsuspected danger in display', *Museums Journal*, **1**, 27–28

PADFIELD, T., ERHARDT, D. and HOPWOOD, W. (1982), 'Trouble in store', in *Science and Technology in the Service of Conservation*, Washington Congress preprints, International Institute for Conservation of Historical and Artistic Works 24–27

Relative humidity and temperature

BRADLEY, S. M. (1989), 'Environmental monitoring and control in the galleries of The British Museum', in Scott, G. (Ed.), *Environmental Monitoring and Control*, preprints of the symposium held in Dundee, 15–16 March 1989, Scottish Society for Conservation and Restoration, Edinburgh

CASSAR, M. (1985), 'Checklist for the establishment of a microclimate', *The Conservator*, **9**, pp. 14–16

NEWEY, H. (1987), '17 years of dehumidified showcases in The British Museum', in preprints of the 8th triennial meeting of the ICOM Committee for Conservation 901–907

ORGAN, R. M. (1957), 'The safe storage of unstable glass', *Museums Journal*, **56**

THOMSON, G. (1977), 'Stabilisation of RH in exhibition cases: hygrometic half time', *Studies in Conservation*, **22**, 85–102

THOMSON, G. (1984), 'Specification and logging of the museum environment', *The International Journal of Museum Management and Curatorship*, **3**, 317–326

THOMSON, G. (1986), *The Museum Environment*, 2nd edition, Butterworths/IIC, London

THOMSON, G. and STANIFORTH, S. (1985), 'Simple control and measurement of relative humidity in museums', *Museum Information Sheet No. 24*, British Museum, London

Light

BRADLEY, S. M. (Ed.), *British Museum Occasional Paper No. 66*, British Museum, London

CHARTERED INSTITUTE OF BUILDING SURVEYORS (1968), *CIBS Lighting Guide: Museums and Galleries*, The Chartered Institute of Building Surveyors, London

CHARTERED INSTITUTION OF BUILDING SERVICES ENGINEERS (1984), *CIBSE Code for Interior Lighting*, CIBSE, London

FELLER, R. L. (1964), 'The deteriorating effect of light on museum objects', *Museum News Technical Supplement No. 3*

HARRISON, L. S. (1954), An investigation of the damage hazard in spectral energy, Illuminating Engineering

46

Pest control in museums

Richard Dennis

Over the course of their evolutionary history, insects have become adapted to exploit a wide variety of environmental features, often in ways that bring them into direct conflict with man. While mankind seeks to preserve certain artefacts for cultural reasons, insects seek to utilize them as alternatives to the natural habitats to which they are adapted.

There has been a tendency in the past to view insect infestations in stored collections as isolated incidents. This view is incorrect since many of the pest problems encountered in museums have direct parallels in industry and public hygiene. Insects have the ability to utilize almost all fibres and tissues of plant or animal origin, and hence have the capacity to damage almost any stored product or artefact. One consequence of this is that many of the pest-control techniques used in industry and public hygiene can be adapted to deal with pest problems in museums.

Museum pests

Not all insects are pests. Of the world's several million insect species only a few hundred have evolved the body design and feeding habits to exploit the habitats found in stored collections. Nevertheless, given the warm, undisturbed conditions found in a majority of collections, an abundant supply of food and suitable egg-laying sites, population explosions of just a single species may occur quickly and dramatically. Over the course of its 3-month life-cycle, for instance, a single female hide beetle (*Dermestes maculatus*) can produce up to 800 eggs, each of which may, under favourable conditions, become reproductively viable in 7 weeks (Busvine, 1980).

Collections can harbour a vast array of insect species. A description of museum pests must, therefore, be brief. In *Table 46.1* only species representive of the major pest types are included.

The table is far from complete. In addition to those listed are numerous other species, some of which, e.g. the oriental and German cockroaches (*Blatta orientalis* and *Blattella germanica*, respectively) and silver-fish (*Lepisma* species), cause a range of problems and can infest a wide variety of materials. Others, such as spiders, do little or no harm to collections.

Where do pests come from?

Insects have various methods of dispersal. Very often the principal damage is caused by the relatively sedentary, feeding larval stage, while dispersion and reproduction are achieved by winged adults. The wood-boring insects such as the furniture beetle are prime examples. An open doorway or window often provides a route of insect attack: insects can simply fly or walk in.

Birds' nests and dead animals in a roof void or gutter are also associated with invasions of various species, particularly spider beetles and carpet beetles.

Artefacts are very often lent out to other collections for exhibition or research pruposes. In this way insect infestations can be transported between collections.

Infestations can go unnoticed in a building for considerable periods of time. It is often many years before an infestation becomes apparent. This is a particular problem with wood-boring insects, the larvae of which often take several years to develop. However, adopting a flexible and comprehensive approach to the management of collections can keep pest problems down to a minimum.

Pest management

Pest-management programmes have been in use within the food industry for several years, and are gaining increasing popularlity in the museum world. An integrated approach is adopted whereby a variety of pest-control techniques is used in conjunction with good management practices to monitor and treat pest problems only as they occur. There is an emphasis on exclusion of pests from premises, with minimum application of pesticides.

To initiate and maintain a pest-management programme, it is necessary to inspect every aspect of the collection, including the building's exterior. The inspection should take into account all current pest problems, their location, and the environmental conditions that support them. An assessment should be made of all potential routes of invasion. This last point is of great importance, since by preventing access of pests to collections future problems can be avoided.

The inspection procedure should be performed on a regular basis. A routine of inspection, with all aspects of the collection monitored in strict rotation,

Table 46.1 Materials damaged by insect pests and evidence of infestation

Wood

Furniture beetle (Anobium punctatum)
Found mainly in old softwood, including furniture, structural woodwork and accidentally in books bindings. Larvae bore in the wood for 3 or 4 years before changing into pupae. In summer, adult beetles gnaw circular exit holes 1.5–2 mm across, powdered excreta and wood dust may fall out of the hole leaving characteristic evidence of infestation.

Death watch beetle (Xestobium refovillosum)
Usually confined to very old oak timbers in buildings. Adults make characteristic tapping sound in warm weather in spring

Powder post beetles (Families Bostrychidae and Lyctidae)
Infest hardwoods, including oak, tropical hardwoods and bamboo. Exit holes 1–1.5 mm. Fine, talc-like powder falling from holes in damaged objects indicates an active infestation

Dry vegetable materials

The following are the most important pests of dry vegetable materials (herbaria, plants and displays, corn dollies, etc.)

Biscuit beetle (Stegobium paniceum)
Oval body and silky hairs on the thorax and wing cases distinguish it from furniture beetle. Breeds in stored tobacco, spices, and other plant materials

Australian spider beetle (Ptinus tectus)
Often associated with birds' nests. Globular body and long legs account for the name

Golden spider beetle (Niptus hololeucus)
Often associated with birds' nests. Body more rounded than the Australian spider beetle and covered with silky golden hairs

Textiles

The following are some of the most important textile pests, all feeding exclusively on the keratin of animal fibres (wool, fur, hair and feathers)

Varied carpet beetle (Anthrenus verbasci)
Adults sham death with legs and antennae withdrawn into grooves in the body and barely visible. Body covered with scale-like hairs which produce variegated patterns. Adults feed on pollen and nectar of flowering plants. Larvae feed on fur and woolen materials such as carpets. Important museum pest. Larvae have long spear-head-shaped hairs on the abdomen which accounts for their popular name, 'woolly bears'

Common clothes moth (Tineola bisselliella)
12–17 mm wingspan. Uniformerly golden buff or yellowish grey in colour. Larvae sometimes, but not always, spin a silken tube in which to pupate. Larvae most liable to attack areas stained with sweat or urine

Case-bearing clothes moth (Tinea pellionella)
Dusky brown colour with three dark spots on the fore-wings. Larvae spins silk case in which to pupate, sometimes including shreds of cloth fibre. Feeds on wool and hair

Artefacts of animal origin

Hide and leather beetles (Dermestes species)
Basic colour black or dark brown, with sprinklings or patches of whitish or yellowish hairs. The larvae feed on animal and plant proteins, dead insects, animal carcasses, lather, skins, etc. Have been used for cleaning skeletons of small mammals and birds for museum collections

Carpets beetles (Anthrenus spp.)
Larvae feed as above

House mite (Glycerophagus domesticus)
A pest of animal skins and feathers. Very small size. Requires damp conditions and feeds on moulds growing on surfaces

Moths (Tinea, Trichophaga spp.)
Larvae devour animal and plant material, including carcasses, leather, skins, etc.

Books

Booklice (Psocids)
Small insects, 1–2 mm, which run rapidly, with soft bodies, cream to light brown. Feed on microscopic moulds that grow on glue and paste used in old book bindings

Hide beetles (Dermestes spp.)
Feed on leather and parchment

Biscuit beetle (Stegobium paniceum)
Might attack leather bindings

is more profitable than the infrequent, reactive inspection performed in response to pest problems.

The pest-management programme is best achieved with the close co-operation of an experienced pest-control contractor.

Inspecting the building exterior

Are doors and windows tight fitting? Where ventilation is required, windows can be fitted with mesh screens which allow air to circulate while keeping insects out.

Is the air-conditioning system, if present, both clean and in a good state of repair? Poorly maintained it can circulate pests (insects, bacteria and mould spores) throughout a building.

Are there any birds' nests present on cornices or ledges of the building, or in the roof void? Birds' nests are potential sources of insect pests and should be removed.

Inspecting the building interior

Is there evidence of insect infestation of structural timbers? Such an infestation, as well as threatening the structure of the building, may provide a source of insects to infest the collection (*Figures 46.1* and *46.2*).

Is there a problem with dampness? If so, the source should be eliminated. Many museum pests depend on high humidities for survival, and sometimes on the mould and fungal growth associated with damp conditions.

Is the general level of hygiene adequate? Accumulations of dirt and grime in kitchens, attics, between floor boards and on skirting boards, etc., can provide food and harbourage for pests. All areas where bad hygiene and accumulated rubbish prevail should be searched for cockroaches and evidence of rodents (droppings and greasy smear marks along runs). A good torch and hand lens are essential equipment for all inspections.

Inspecting the collection

Most objects of an organic nature in a collection can harbour pest insects. Care and diligence are required to ensure that no evidence of infestation goes unnoticed.

Surfaces of wooden objects should be examined for the characteristic exit holes of wood boring insects. Radiography can be useful for detecting larvae hidden deep within woodwork (*Figure 46.3*).

Books and manuscripts should be carefully inspected, with attention paid to the gum along the spines of binders for booklice damage. The insects themselves, if present, will probably be visible (*Figure 46.4*). Pockets and seams of textiles and

Figure 46.1 Adult furniture beetle (*Anobium punctatum*) and exit holes in infested timber

Figure 46.2 Adult death watch beetle (*Xestobium rufovillosum*), a major pest of structural timbers in old buildings

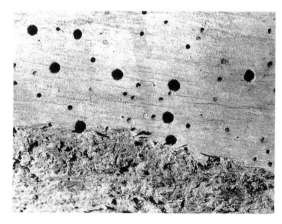

Figure 46.3 Exit holes of furniture beetles (*Anobium punctatum*) and death watch beetles (*Xestobium rufovillosum*), the larger holes belonging to the latter species

Figure 46.4 Booklouse (*Psocidae*), a pest that can cause havoc in library materials

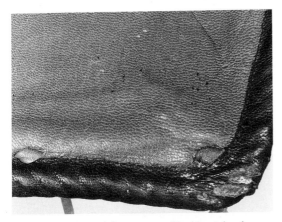

Figure 46.5 Unusual damage caused by biscuit beetles (*Stegobium paniceum*) in a camel-hide saddle. Detecting such damage requires very careful inspection. Time spent inspecting is worthwhile, to prevent more serious damage occurring

clothing should be investigated for beetle damage, and the webbing of textile moths (*Figure 46.5*).

Any evidence of past infestation, e.g. dead insects or cast skins of larvae, should be removed to avoid possible confusion in the future.

The search should not be restricted only to the collection, but should also cover display cases and items brought into the museum that could harbour pests, such as potted plants.

Inspecting the store

Most museums have stores where artefacts are kept prior to restoration. The store-room, which is not always at the same location as the museum, is very often infested with pests. Items are frequently destroyed before any restorative work is started. The crowded conditions common to many stores often inhibit the inspection process: however, if possible, inspection should be performed. Wherever possible artefacts should be treated against pests before being placed in storage.

A pest-control contractor will have available a variety of items to assist in inspections, for example sticky traps with attractant to capture cockroaches and tracking dusts to detect rodents. All findings, pest free or otherwise, must be recorded in a log book. The log should also include details of new arrivals to the collection and movement of artefacts within the collection.

The inspection process is not in itself a measure that will prevent pest problems, although by ensuring early detection it will mitigate the damage that pests can do. Inspections should be followed by all necessary proofing and improved housekeeping measures identified. Any pest problems encountered will have to be dealt with using an established technique, that may or may not involve use of toxic chemicals.

Methods of pest control

There will always be situations that demand the use of chemical treatments. By their nature pesticides are toxic compounds and should be treated with appropriate caution. Moreover, pesticides vary in their effect on different species of insect, and the active ingredient together with the solvent or carrier, can exert an adverse effect on certain types of material. There is always a possibility of unwanted side-efects from a treatment that was previously regarded as acceptable.

Insecticides

The majority of insecticidal formulations have a residual effect that will protect treated objects for some time after application. A vast array of formulations are available for treating different problems, including space sprays, dusts, emulsions and lacquers. More recently, compounds with very low mammalian toxicity have appeared, i.e. juvenile hormone analogues such as methoprene for Pharaoh ant control, which interfere with the insect's moulting process.

Fumigation

Of particular interest to Curators are the fumigant gases such as methyl bromide that do away with some (but not all) of the problems associated with insecticide treatments. The principle of fumigation is that a toxic gas is introduced into the air space around infested objects, which are held in a chamber or outdoors under a sealed sheet. The gas must be maintained for a sufficient period of time to penetrate the material and kill all insects and eggs present. Following exposure the gas must be safely vented to the atmosphere or absorbed through filters.

The commonly used fumigants in the UK for insect control are methyl bromide and phosphine. Among other gases used in some countries are ethylene oxide, sulphuryl fluoride and hydrogen cyanide. All these chemicals are very toxic and must only be used by people trained and certified in the techniques of fumigation.

Fumigation has a particular value for the control of wood-boring insects hidden deep within timbers and protected from conventional insecticides, resulting in a rapid destruction of both larvae and eggs.

Fumigant gases have no residual efficacy and following treatment objects are susceptible to reinfestation. It may be advisable to treat the cabinets and boxes in which the artefacts are stored with a residual insecticide, to prevent this occurrence. Moreover, if used incorrectly, fumigant gases can have an adverse effect on certain materials. Methyl bromide, for example, is not recommended for use on library materials, i.e. leather and vellum, or on wool or animal hairs, and photographic film or prints, and surface reactions may occur with zinc, tin and iron in the presence of impurities such as alcohol (Zycherman and Schrock, 1988). Subsequent retreatment tends to increase residue levels and the chances of spoilage.

Fumigation with phosphine may tarnish precious metals such as gold, silver and copper.

The two conventional methods of fumigating objects are sheet (stack) fumigation and fumigation chambers.

Sheet fumigation
Objects to be treated are placed under gas-impermeable sheets with the edges sealed to the floor by sand snakes and chains. Methods of sealing the sheet are often less than 100 per cent effective; gas leaks occur even under the best conditions. Also, it can be difficult to achieve an even distribution of gas around objects. This may result in greater than necesary concentrations at the base of the stack, increasing the likelihood of tainting or damaging goods. The smaller than necessary concentrations at the top of the stack may allow some insects to survive.

Fumigation chambers

Fumigations carried out in specially designed chambers can proceed safely and efficiently, particularly when a vacuum cycle is incorporated into the process. The effectiveness of the technique, however, must be balanced against very high purchase and installation costs. Chambers are permanent fixtures

which occupy valuable space when not in use. Fumigations can only be carried out by personnel holding a fumigation certificate.

The Rentokil 'bubble'
The development of a portable fumigation 'bubble' (*Figure 46.6*) offers museums a new technique of fumigation. Objects to be treated are placed indoors inside an inflatable chamber which is filled with a fumigant/air mixture. Complete mixing of fumigant with air is assured. Following treatment the fumigant can be safely discharged into the atmosphere via a hose. If there is no safe way of venting the gas to the atmosphere it can be absorbed through an activated carbon filter. If required, treated items can remain in the bubble, which then acts as a 'quarantine' store. When not in use the system packs away into a small space. Bubbles can be made to any size and large, permanent models up to 300 m^3 can be made to order. The bubble offers all the benefits of a fumigation chamber, but with more flexibility and without any high installation costs.

Figure 46.6 The Rentokil 'bubble', a revolutionary technique for fumigation

The store-room as a fumigation chamber

New store-rooms can be designed, and existing store-rooms can sometimes be adapted, so that they are capable of retaining fumigant gases. This is an excellent way of treating entire collections, although care is required to ensure that the fumigant does not exert an adverse effect on different kinds of artefact present. The technique is, however, fraught with difficulties, not least the safe disposal of fumigant following treatment. A permanent bubble offers a useful alternative.

Atmospheric gases as fumigants
Cabon dioxide has been used as a fumigant since Roman times. The chief advantage of this gas is that it leaves no residues and presents no risk to valuable or sensitive items. Unlike other gases, it poses little

health hazard to man. However, until the advent of fumigation chambers and bubbles it proved difficult to hold sufficiently high concentrations of the gas around treated objects for the extended periods required. It is often necessary to maintain a 60 per cent concentration of carbon dioxide for up to 21 days to kill all life stages of certain pest species. Nevertheless, the gas is effective against most pests of collections, including mites, booklice, moths and even wood-boring beetles.

Carbon dioxide has been extensively used in the Rentokil 'bubble' to treat infestations in valuable artefacts, with good result. Tapestries, clothing, dolls, furniture, wooden artefacts, furs and stuffed animals have all been successfully treated. Work is in progress to reduce exposure times by raising the temperature during fumigation, and good results are now achieved against certain pest species after less than 4 days exposure. The 'bubble' is the only portable system available that can hold this useful gas for sufficiently long periods of time.

It may be possible to treat the entire store-room with carbon dioxide, although very large store-rooms may need to be divided by partitions into a number of gas tight 'rooms' which are treated independently. As with other fumigants, fans may be required to ensure an even distribution of gas.

Environmental control

There is an increasing concern about the release of toxic chemicals into the environment. This has meant a growing interest into alternative techniques of pest control. Manipulation of the environment has been applied successfully in many museums and stores, and often is the only viable method of controlling pests without incurring any risk of damage to artefacts.

Temperature

Insect species can exist only within certain environmental parameters, of which a suitable temperature regime is one example. Although many species can survive at temperatures over 40°C, temperatures higher than this may cause them to die and their eggs to fail. Occasionally, therefore, it may be possbile to destroy insect pests by heating the infested material in an oven.

Temperatures below −18°C will kill pest insects provided these conditions are maintained at least 7 days (2 weeks is often more appropriate). Freeze drying, or even placing objects in a conventional freezer, may achieve the required effect. Holy relics infested with pests have been treated in this manner. However, meticulous care is required to prevent damage from condensation.

Prolonged low temperatures below 5°C will prevent most insects developing, and will certainly prevent them breeding.

Humidity

Pest insects vary in their requirement for water. Flour beetles can survive in the most arid conditions, whereas booklice require a relative humidity in excess of 70 per cent. Controlling humidities at less than the 70 per cent level can often confer a protective value on manuscripts and books in storage.

The Rentokil 'bubble' offers potential for such methods of environmental control. An insulating material can be fitted to a normal bubble so that it retains hot or cold air, and dehumidifiers can be linked to the system, thereby turning it into a dehumidification chamber.

Ideally, the storage facilities in the museum would be completely air-conditioned, allowing temperatures and humidities to be adjusted at the press of a button to the detriment of insect pests. However, vigilance and careful measurement are always required to check for the presence of microclimates within artefacts, where pest populations might flourish.

Effective pest management depends foremost on an awareness of potential pest problems plus the availability of resources to deal with them. The long-term benefits of employing an integrated approach to pest management result in a collection preserved for the benefit of future generations.

References

BUSVINE, J. R. (1980), *Insects and Hygiene*, (3rd edition), Chapman and Hall, London

ZYCHERMAN, L. A. and SCHROCK, J. R. (1988), A Guide to Museum Pest Control, American Institute for Conservation of Historic and Artistic Works and the Association of Systematics Collections, Washington, DC

Bibliography

CHINERY, M. (1986), *Insects of Britain and Western Europe*, Collins, London

HICKIN, N. (1974), *Household Insect Pests*, Rentokil Library, East Grinstead

HICKIN, N. (1975), *The Insect Factor in Wood Decay*, Rentokil Library, East Grinstead

HICKIN, N. (1985), *Bookworms, The Insect Pests of Books*, Sheppard Press, London

LINNIE, M. J. (1987), 'Pest control, a survey of natural history museums in Great Britain and Ireland', *The International Journal of Museum Management and Curatorship*, **6**, 277–290

McCOMB, R. E. (1983), 'Three gaseous fumigants', *Abbey Newsletters* **7**, 12

PINNIGER, D. (1989), *Insect Pests and Museums*, Institute of Archeology Publications, London

RENTOKIL LTD., 'Rentokil fumigation system ('bubble')', *Rentokil Technical Release No. 101*, Rentokil Ltd, East Grinstead

SMITH, C. P. (1988), A New Concept in Fumigation, BPCA Conference

47

Scientific examination of artefacts

Andrew Oddy

Introduction

A thorough examination of an artefact may be required for two reasons: to describe it fully for cataloguing purposes or to evaluate its condition from the point of view of its future preservation. Any examination will start with a thorough visual inspection, aided by a good hand lens or, preferably, a binocular microscope with variable magnification up to $c. \times 50$. The abilities of the eye can then be further extended in three ways, depending on the type of object being examined: radiography, ultra-violet fluorescence and infra-red photography.

The 'visual' inspection should provide much of the data required for writing either catalogue entries or condition reports, but in many cases it will need to be amplified by scientific analysis to refine the descriptions of the objects. Thus, for instance: 'Copper alloy inlaid with white and yellow metal wires' can become 'bronze (7 per cent tin with traces of other elements) inlaid with silver and brass wires'; 'limestone statue with traces of red paint on the face' may become 'magnesian limestone statue with traces of red pigment (haematite) on the face'; 'wooden box with metal hinges and ivory inlay' may become 'wooden box made of willow (*Salix* sp.) with brass hinges and walrus ivory inlays'.

The list of possible identifications is endless and includes the analysis of metals and alloys, the analysis of glass and ceramics, the petrological examination of ceramics and stone, the analysis of pigments, binding media and dyes, the identification of timber species, the identification of fibres, etc.

Having answered the fundamental questions of what the artefact is made of and how was it made, there is the equally important question of how old the object is and whether it is authentic? These questions depend first and foremost on curatorial expertise, but the scientist can contribute to dating in

those cases where dendrochronology, ^{14}C dating or thermoluminscent dating are applicable, and to the study of authenticity by means of numerous examination and analysis techniques. In fact, in recent years, the forensic aspect of the scientific examination of historical artefacts has become increasingly important as a result of the ever-increasing numbers of sophisticated fakes appearing on the antiquities market.

The examination of metals

At the start of the present era, seven metals were known in a reasonably pure elemental form – gold, silver, copper, iron, lead, tin and mercury. Zinc was the next to be discovered, and it has been followed by numerous others in relatively recent times. These elemental metals are easily distinguishable from one another by eye, but they can be mixed together to form innumerable alloys which require chemical analysis for their full characterization.

The characterization of metals by chemical analysis in not, however, as simple as it may seem as most 'pure' metals contain trace impurities of other metals. The addition, therefore, of a few per cent of a second metal to make an alloy will create a 'cocktail' of elements present in different quantities, which are conventionally described as 'major', 'minor' or 'trace'. There is usually no difficulty in identifying the (single) major element present, but the distinction between minor and trace elements can be a problem. Minor elements are deliberately added, but trace elements arise naturally either because ores are never pure or because they have been introduced from the fuel, flux or furnace materials used in the extraction process. Thus Medieval brass often contains a few per cent of iron, as well as zinc and copper, but the iron is present accidentally and actually meant that the brass could not be used for making compass cases because it was magnetic. Similarly, bronze consists of copper (major), tin and sometimes lead (minor), and traces of a host of elements such as arsenic, antimony, bismuth, gold, silver and iron. It is, however, not always easy to tell whether lead is a deliberate addition or an accidental contaminant when it is only present at a level of 0.5–2.0 per cent.

Analysis can be carried out qualitatively and/or quantitatively, although qualitative techniques will sometimes also give an approximate idea of how much of each element is present, and may be subject to calibration so that the technique becomes quantitative.

Simple qualitative techniques include colour, hardness, chemical spot tests, and the use of a magnet to detect iron and some iron containing alloys. More scientific techniques include X-ray fluorescence, variations on emission or absorption spectrometry, and nuclear acitivation methods.

When analysing the metal or alloy of an artefact it is important also to characterize secondary components, such as plating of a second metal onto the surface or inlaying of differently coloured metals into the surface. This cannot always be done by eye as, for instance, traces of tinning on an excavated metal object can be mistaken for silvering (and, less commonly, *vice versa*) or inlays of yellow brass may be assumed to be gold.

Having established what a metal artefact is made of, the next stage in the process of description is to determine how it was made. There are two basic processes which can be applied to metals – casting and working – and these can often be distinguished by eye. Castings are, however, often finished by various working processes, such as hammering, filing, engraving, or turning on a lathe, and these processes should be borne in mind during the initial microscopic inspection.

The standard way of determining how a metal object, or component of a larger object, was made is to carry out a metallographic examination of a small sample of the metal removed from an inconspicuous position, or of a polished area on the underside of the object. The composition of the alloy itself may also be a clue as to whether the component was cast or worked.

Where metal objects are made of more than one component it is important to establish how the separate parts were fastened together. Were they soft soldered, hard soldered, forged, welded, rivetted or stuck together with an organic adhesive? And is the method of attachment original or the result of a subsequent repair, and, if so, is the repair ancient or modern?

Finally, there is the question of dating. This must normally be done by the curator/art historian as there are no scientific techniques which can be applied to metals as such, although ^{14}C dating can, in theory, be applied to the carbon in steel and cast iron if it can be assumed that the original smelting was carried out with freshly made charcoal and not with fossil fuel such as coal or peat.

As far as determining the authenticity of metals is concerned, however, scientific techniques can be useful, and both the analysis of the alloys and a study of the methods of manufacture may be indicative of a date 'inconsistent with that assigned on stylistic grounds'. It is, however, an examination and analysis of the corrosion products which can be most indicative. The first point to establish is whether the corrosion products have grown naturally on the surface or whether they have been made by attaching pigments or coarsely ground minerals to the surface with an adhesive. If the corrosion products are genuine, the scientist must then determine whether they have grown slowly over a long period of time or whether they have been induced rapidly in the workshop/laboratory. This will depend on identification of the composition of the corrosion products (usually by X-ray diffraction analysis) and on a study of their morphology (usually by metallographic examination of a cross- or taper-section through the corrosion layers and into the metal).

The examination of ceramics

To most people the word 'ceramics' conjures up pictures of pottery vessels used in the storage, preparation and eating of food, but sculpture, ornaments, architectural components and floor and wall coverings (e.g. tiles) can also be ceramic. Ceramics are made from wet clay which is allowed to dry when the artefact has been formed, and is then heated ('fired') to bring about chemical and physical changes to the structure. According to the temperature of firing the ceramic is known as terracotta, earthenware, stoneware, or porcelain. Unfired clay objects, such as many cuneiform tablets, are not ceramics.

The analysis of the major elements in ceramics is not, on the whole, meaningful as most of the structure consists of silicon, aluminium and oxygen, the exact ratios of which are not particularly useful for diagnostic purposes. However, clays also contain traces of numerous metals, and the quantification of these by chemical analysis can sometimes be used to identifiy the kiln site.

Because of the use of trace-elements analysis requires the building up of a data bank of analyses of wasters from all possible kiln sites, it is never possible to say with absolute certainty that a pot is from a particular site, as there may be an as yet undiscovered kiln site using clay from the same geological source. Thus analysis can be used to show that two ceramic artefacts are from different sites, but it can never be used to prove with absolute certainty that they are from the same site. (The same principle applies to the analysis of metals. Thus two associated bronzes with the same composition might well be cast from the same crucible load of alloy, but this can never be stated as an absolute certainty.)

Clay is sometimes mixed with an inert material called 'grog', such as sand or ground-up pot sherds, the presence of which diminishes the diagnostic value of the trace element analysis of a drilling. In these cases, more information is obtained from a petrological examination of a thin section of the ceramic body to identify the minerals which are present. These may contribute towards localizing the source of the raw materials.

An indication of firing temperature can be obtained in three ways, by measuring hardness with a scatch test on an inconspicuous unglazed area of surface, by thermal dilatometry or by examining a fractured surface in a scanning electron microscope.

Glazes, or other forms of decoration such as paint, are more susceptible to characterization by chemical analyses than is the body of the ceramic. Glazes are essentially a special type of glass, for the analysis of which see below. Paint requires the separate analysis of pigments (by either X-ray diffraction or polarizing microscopy) and of the binding medium by chemical tests, infra-red spectroscopy and/or chromatography.

Ceramics are made by hand forming (from slabs, coils or lumps of clay), by throwing on a wheel or by casting in a mould. The technique used will usually be obvious, although radiography is sometimes a useful aid for determining whether the artefact has been made in several sections which have been luted together. However, the fact that a ceramic has been radiographed should always be recorded as it may have affected the thermoluminescence (TL) of the fabric, so rendering subsequent TL dating impossible.

Dating of pottery is done on stylistic grounds, although TL dating of ceramics from early cultures is a useful tool in certain instances. However, TL is more commonly used for authenticity examination, where it has proved invaluable. Since the technique was introduced in the 1960s it has shown just how extensive the forging of ceramics artefacts is now, and has been for at least a century.

The authenticity testing of ceramics is bedevilled by the fact that large areas of a pot may have been restored, so that date of a sample from one of the original fragments may be used to give the impression that the pot is original and undamaged if it has been expertly (invisibly) restored. A visual examination by an experienced consevator will often reveal the extent of restored areas, and suspect areas of overpaint may be detected by the judicious use of various organic solvents. However, radiography, examination under ultraviolet light or photography on infra-red sensitive film will provide a permanent record of whether a ceramic object has been restored.

The examination of glass

Glass is made by heating together lime, sand and an alkali (soda or potash). It may also include metal oxides (or similar compounds). Glass is non-crystalline and it technically a super-cooled liquid.

The full characterization of glass requires a complete chemical analysis of the metal oxides, lime and silica, and of any other components. It is important to identify those additions which are responsible for the colour and opacity of decorative glass.

Glass can be shaped by blowing free, blowing into a mould, casting, forming round a core, carving from a block and fusing together cut fragments of glass (often glass mosaics) within a mould or former. Glass was decorated by trailing different coloured glass on the surface and by enamelling, gilding, painting, cutting and engraving. These techniques can invariably be identified upon a close inspection.

Glass was also used to glaze ceramics, both to decorate them and to make the lower fired ones watertight, and for the enamelling of metals. It was also used to imitate precious stones as an inlay, when it can usually be distinguished under the microscope by looking for the presence of small round bubbles with the glass, which are not present in minerals. In these cases, sampling for a full chemical analysis is not always possible, but the examination of a small fragment with a freshly fractured surface in a microprobe will give sufficient information for cataloguing purposes.

The composition of glass and of the metal compounds used to colour it may be characteristic of the place and date of manufacture, and hence analysis may be of more use when questioning authenticity that a study of the methods of manufacture, which are relatively easy to copy. However, the styles of applied decoration may also be diagnostic, as may the analysis of surface alteration layers by X-ray diffraction.

The examination of stone and minerals

Stone, in the context of a cultural history museum, occurs as a material of architecture and sculpture, and less frequently for making useful objects such as grindstones, whetstones and containers. Minerals are also used for sculpture and as jewels. Both stone and minerals are part of most natural history collections.

Stone is very rarely transformed by man, although some primitive societies may have 'anointed' their religious sculpture, and traces of the anointing materials may await analysis. On the whole, however, the characterization of stone is limited to the scientific description of a thin section. For some types of stone, however, which consist of essentially only one mineral (e.g. limestone or marble), a chemical analysis or X-ray diffraction analysis will be equally useful.

Careful examination of stone sculpture, especially in the case of unfinished objects, will often reveal information about the techniques used to carve the stone. Until very recent times, many tools and the methods of using them have been almost universal over a long period of time, so that an understanding of post-Renaissance technique, which is well described in the contemporarty literature, can be used as a basis for trying to work out how stone was worked and carved in antiquity. Apart from the working of the actual stone, any description of a composite stone artefact must also consider how the separate pieces were fitted together and how they were then joined securely.

Minerals are identified by the use of a combination of colour, hardness tests, polarizing light microscopy, density, reflective index, chemical analysis and X-ray diffraction analysis. Minerals which have been fashioned into gemstones can often reveal significant information about their origins if examined by an expert gemnologist, and these days it is important to bear in mind that many minerals can be made synthetically.

Sculpture was frequently painted in Antiquity and the Middle Ages, so any scientific examination of a stone artefact should include a microscopic search for traces of colour. These can then be subject to the normal methods of analysis for pigments, binding medium and ground.

The only cases where stone is transformed by man is in the manufacture of lime and cement, the former by burning limestone alone and the latter by burning limestone and clay together, and in the manufacture of plaster of Paris by heating gypsum. Lime was often mixed with inert fillers and so the examination of thin sections is a useful form of characterization.

Microfossils from the limestone will often survive the burning process sufficiently to be recognized in the lime, where they may give information about the source of the limestone. The identification of the inert fillers is also important, especially when the lime has been used for the manufacture of floors, the lining of walls as a support for frescos or wall-painting, or for making architectural stucco reliefs.

Stone and minerals are not susceptible to scientific dating as the date of the actual raw material is irrelevant. It is the date when it was converted into an artefact which is important. Hence it is only the technology of carving, the nature and extent of weathering crusts, and the identification of added decoration which can be used as complementary data for the stylistic dating of stone and mineral objects. The same criteria can be used for studies of authenticity when, as with metals, ceramics and glass, it is the inappropriate use of materials and methods for the supposed date of the piece which can lead to the unmasking of a modern forgery.

The examination of organic materials

Materials of plant and animal origin (leaves, bark, wood, seeds, vegetable fibre, shell, leather, fur, wool, feathers, intestine, bone ivory, horn and claw) have been widely used to make artefacts. These materials may be used as found (e.g. wood and ivory for carving) or modified by a manufacturing process (e.g. the making of bark cloth and leather). A very special case of modification is the manufacture of yarn from animal or vegetable fibre and the working of the yarn into textiles by either weaving or knitting.

For materials which are used unmodified it is only the species of plant or animal which needs to be identified (i.e. tree or plant, animal, bird or insect) and this will have to be carried out by an appropriate specialist. In the case of wood and fibres a microscopic examination of a thin section or of a single fibre is usually diagnostic, but ivory, bone, horn, leaves and insect remains usually depend on comparisons of the remains with a reference collection of natural history specimens. If the original shape of the material (e.g. bone) has been retained, the identification of the species will usually be possible, but where carving or other forms of working have destroyed the natural shape then identification may be difficult or impossible. Only ivory usually retains sufficient evidence when carved to enable the different ivory producing species to be distinguished (elephant, hippopotamus, walrus, sperm whale, etc.).

For materials which are modified before use, the scientific examination should aim not only to identify the species of plant or animal, but also to characterize the manufacturing process. Which of the numerous tanning processes was used on a piece of leather or how was a textile woven from its constituent yarn are obvious questions to ask. Even horn, which has been delaminated to produce a translucent rigid sheet, or wood, which has been shaped by steaming, require comment in a full technological description.

Chemical analysis has no place in the description for cataloguing purposes of organic objects themselves, although it must be employed in order to fully describe the methods and materials which were used to process them (e.g. tanning of leather) or to decorate them. The materials of decoration usually consist of dyes and/or paints and inlays, or possibly special surface finishes in the case of furniture.

Organic objects have one advantage when it comes to dating in that art historical opinion may be backed up by ^{14}C dating. For many years this has only been applicable to large or expendable objects because of the relatively large size of the sample which was required, but recently new methodology has been introduced which enables dates to be obtained from very small samples. [14]C dating is also applicable to questions of authenticity, although the characterization of the techniques and materials of construction and decoration will also play their part in some cases.

It must be remembered, however, that the ^{14}C dating of a piece of wood, ivory or bone does not date the manufacture of the artefact, it only dates the death of the plant or animal. Thus this technique must be used with caution as it is relatively easy to obtain supplies of old timber (from demolished buildings) which can be used for faking furniture or other objects made of wood. There is also the problem, encountered with the dating of ceramics, that an object may be heavily restored, but so long as the ^{14}C sample is taken from an 'original' component, the date may be passed off as that of the object as a whole.

The examination of paper

Paper is usually present in museums as books or archives and as the support for prints, drawings and water-colours. The full characterization of a piece of paper involves determining whether it is hand or machine made, identifying whether it is made of wood pulp, linen or cotton rags or a mixture of two or more, and identifying fillers and sizing materials. In fact, a full description is rarely given for paper, and it is usually only relevant when there is a question of date or authenticity.

The technique of manufature can be determined by holding the paper up to the light or examining a β-radiograph of the sheet. The materials of manufacture are investigated by pulping a sample in water, separating out the fibres and fillers and water-soluble components and applying appropriate techniques of identification or analysis (microscopy for fibres, and X-ray diffraction and/or chemical analysis for fillers and water soluble components).

The conversion of a paper into an artefact, be it a book, manuscript, print, drawing or water-colour, introduces other materials which may need to be identified. Pigments and media used in drawing, printing or painting are obvious candidates for analysis, but there is frequently the problem of being able to remove sufficient sample to enable the analysis to be carried out, and the cataloguing of paper artefacts is rarely accompanied by a scientific examination.

Paper is the most common support for photographic images, but a discussion of the identification of the different photographic processes is beyond the scope of this short chapter.

Nowadays, with the introduction of the new small-sample methods of ^{14}C dating, it is possible to contemplate the use of this technique for authenticity work. However, again it must be remembered that dating the paper does not date the work of art. Determined forgers can still get hold of old paper (by removing the fly leaves from old books for example), So the interpretation of ^{14}C dates must be handled with care, as it is only one aspect of the authenticity of a problem object.

The examination of easel paintings

Easel paintings are layered structures consisting of a support (canvas or wood), a prepared ground (an inert white substance mixed with an adhesive), a paint layer (pigments mixed with a binding medium) and a varnish layer (natural or synthetic resin). All of these components of a painting are susceptible to scientific examination.

Wooden panels must be identified as to the species of tree(s) involved, and it is important to describe their method of construction in terms of the number of separate pieces of wood involved and how they have been joined together. Radiography is the most useful technique for studying the structure of a panel. Canvas supports are made of vegetable fibre (cotton, linen or hemp) which should be identified by microscopy, together with the type of weave.

The prepared ground usually consists of white lead, chalk or gypsum, and these can be distinguished readily by X-ray diffraction analysis of a minute sample. The binding medium will be identified by a combination of chemical tests, infra-red spectroscopy and various types of chromatography.

The pigments can be identified by polarising microscopy, microscopic spot tests and/or X-ray diffraction analysis, but it is important not only to identify pigments but also to determine the sequence of their application. This is done by taking minute samples of the whole layered sequence and making a cross-section of this for examination in a high-powered reflected-light microscope. Further information can be obtained by analysis of the cross-section by X-ray emission in a scanning electron microscope.

The binding medium for the pigments (traditionally egg or a natural drying oil) and the varnish layer are subjected to the same types of organic analysis used for the binding medium of the ground. There is, however, the problems of distinguishing the organic components of the ground, the paint layer and the varnish layer as it may be very difficult to separate these for sampling purposes. Furthermore, it should be remembered that varnish layers have often been removed and replaced on one or more occasions.

Dating is largely a question of art-historical opinion, but this can be amplified by ^{14}C dating of wood or canvas if a sample can be obtained which is free from contamination by the organic components of the superimposed ground, paint and varnish layers. For wooden panels, dendrochronology has proved to be very useful on numerous occasions.

As usual, however, the dating of the wooden panel does not date the painting of the picture, and when questions of authenticity have been raised it must be remembered that timber cut in Medieval times is relatively easy to obtain.

One other aspect of the scientific examination of an easel painting is the characterization of the painter's brush technique, and the elucidation of the sequence in which the various parts of the image were painted. These aspects of technology are often visible in a radiograph, which is particularly useful for 'seeing' changes in composition. Infra-red techniques of imaging are also very useful, and are a relatively recent addition to the methods for the scientific examination of paintings.

Condition reports

The examination of an artefact to determine its 'state of preservation' may be carried out for a number of reasons, but the most common are:

(1) to evaluate the condition (and value) of a prospective purchase;
(2) to quantify the amount of conservation which is required; and
(3) to evaluate whether it is safe for the artefact to be loaned to another venue for an exhibition.

The questions to be answered are whether the object is stable (assuming acceptable environmental conditions), whether the object is all original or whether it has areas of modern restoration, and whether it will withstand the rigours of packing and transportation to another institution.

In addition, for insurance purposes for a loan, it may be necessary to list every chip, crack or other blemish, although this aspect of condition reports can often be covered by making a high-definition negative, which can be enlarged and printed if the need arises.

Condition reports are usually carried out by eye alone (or with the aid of a hand lens or binocular microscope), although radiography, infra-red imaging techniques and ultravoiolet fluorescence may be very useful. However, in most instances, an experienced conservator will be able to evaluate the condition of an object and estimate the amount of conservation time required for its treatment by eye alone, amplified by touching, tapping and discrete probing with hand-held tools. For looking inside hollow objects with small openings (bottles, narrow necked vessels, statuary, etc), an endoscope (a light and a lens at one end of a flexible glass-fibre 'cable' with an eyepiece at the other end) is very useful.

Where a large collection of similar objects is being examined the process of ducumenting the findings may be speeded up by designing a standard *pro forma* involving ticking of boxes and writing in of minimal descriptions. This same aid to recording may be useful when examining prospective loans.

As far as loans are concerned, however, it is becoming increasingly common for the loaning institution to provide a very full description of every object, concentrating on the visible signs of wear and tear, which the borrowing institution must initial when the object is unpacked. It is then assumed that any additional damage has occurred during the course of the loan – usually during transit between venues or when the loan is on its way back to its home institution. Because the writing of very full descriptions and the repeated checking of the objects against these descriptions are very time-consuming processes, there is a natural reluctance on the part of both curators and conservators to get involved, and any director who believes that a full written description of an object is an essential prerequisite to a loan should ask himself whether it is really necessary, or whether a set of photographs taken from several angles would not be equally effective.

The same principles apply to the making of a condition report, whether the artefact is an easel painting or an excavated bronze, an African mask or a Medieval sword, and the results of the examination should be preserved as part of the file on that object. This is particularly important for those objects which are likely to be the subject of repeated loan requests, when an accessible archive of condition reports may save the labour of repeated examinations.

Sources of expertise

The scienific examination of artefacts is best carried out by trained and experienced in-house scientists and/or conservators, with the exception of the full listing of visible signs of wear and tear which can equally be done by a curator.

The evaluation of conservation requirements, and of the extent of previous conservation, can only be done by an experienced practising conservator, preferably one who is familiar with the collection as a whole and who will, therefore, be knowledgeable about previous conservation practices.

Similarly, the use of many diagnostic and of all quantitative scientific methods of examination and analysis should normally be restricted to trained scientists who are familiar with the limitations of the techniques and who are familiar with the problems associated with the examination of artefacts and the interpretation of the resulting data. However, there are a number of diagnostic techniques (such as radiography and ultraviolet fluorescence) and qualitative analytical techniques (such as chemical spot tests and fibre and wood identification) which may equally be used by experienced conservators, or those with appropriate training. In fact, in the absence of an appropriate scientist, the training of conservators in particular analytical techniques is a viable proposition, provided that the problems of interpreting the scientific data are taught at the same time as the methods of obtaining the data. For instance, the identification of traces of zinc on an iron artefact may be the remains of galvanization, but it might also be the residue left by cleaning by electrochemical reduction, or the detection of a tin-rich surface on a bronze may be the result of deliberate tinning, or of segregation of the tin during the casting process, or of preferential corrosion of the copper rich phase during burial.

The advantages of an in-house scientific examination service are that an archive of information will be accumulated which is then available as comparative data for new examinations. Equally as important as the archive of data is the accumulated experience of the scientists/conservators who carry out the work.

It is for these reasons that the use of service analysis by university based or industrial scientists is regarded as very much second best, unless these scientists have the time and inclination to build up their own expertise in the scientific examination of historical artefacts. Too often university or commercial scientists will take unnecessarily large samples, or take samples (from alteration layers) which are unrepresentative. They will not be aware of the skill of conservators so that samples have even been taken from areas of restoration and the results unwittingly presented to the curator. But it is not only the taking of a meaningful and representative sample which may be a problem for an inexperienced analyst; the interpretation of the results may also cause concern. The identification of pigments on a polychrome sculpture for instance, presupposes a knowledge of those pigments which might have been used and those pigments which could not have been used. Dyes on textiles, colourants in glazes and enamels, elements in alloys and organic components in binding media are all examples of where a straight

analysis should be accompanied by an interpretation. Thus for instance, the reporting of 40 per cent zinc in a Renaissance brass object calls for little comment, but the same composition of a 'Roman' object requires it to be described as a 'fake'.

Radiography (in its various forms) is one technique of examination which can often be successfully carried out by a skilled commercial operator. Hospitals have traditionally often provided this expertise for museums in the past, although it is usual for the radiographer and the curator or conservator to work together on obtaining the radiographs in order to maximize their usefulness.

Curators who require scientific examinations on their objects would be well advised to consult with the in-house scientists in the major national museums, the English Heritage Ancient Monuments Laboratory, those few universities with appropriate specialists, or with one of the small number of independent scientists who have built up a practice of examining museum objects, before commissioning analytical work from an otherwise untried scientist. The names of those who have built up a reputation in these fields can be obtained from their publications in international journals like *Archaeometry*, the *Journal of Archaeological Science* and *Studies in Conservation*, as well as from various national conservation and museology journals and conference proceedings.

Bibliography

The results of scientific investigations of antiquities can be found in journals such as *Archaeometry, Archaeomaterials, Journal of Archaeological Science* and *Historical Metallurgy*.

AITKIN, M. J. (1990), *Science-based Dating in Archeology*, Longman, London

AITKIN, M. J. (1985), *Thermoluminiscence Dating*, Academic Press, London

BOWMAN, S. (1990), *Radiocarbon Dating*, British Museum, London

CALEY, E. R. (1964), *Analysis of Ancient Metals*, Pergamon Press, Oxford

FLEMING, S. J. (1975), *Authenticity in Art: The Scientific Detection of Forgery*, Institute of Physics, London

FLEMING, S. J. (1976), *Dating in Archeology: A Guide to Scientific Techniques*, Dent, London

FLEMING, S. J. (1979), *Thermoluminscence Techniques in Arhcaeology*, Clarendon Press, Oxford

LEUTE, U. (1987), *Archaeometry: An Introduction to Physical Methods in Archaeology and the History of Art*, VCH, Weinheim

PYDDOKE, E. (1963), *The Scientist and Archaeology*, Phoenix House, London

TAYLOR, R. E. (1987), *Radiocarbon Dating*, Academic Press, London

TITE, M. S. (1972), *Methods of Physical Examination in Archaeology*, Seminar Press, London

48

Disaster planning

Sue Cackett

Introduction

Disaster is, by its very nature, unpredictable and unexpected. The ability of a museum to cope depends on the existence of a plan. It is only possible here to offer guidelines as a disaster plan must be tailored to suit individual needs. Any plan must be adaptable and capable of intelligent interpretation for any set of circumstances.

In the course of the preparation of a plan, it will become obvious that the plan is only the beginning. There is much preparation and training to be done and many preventive measures will be identified. Do not expect to do it quickly!

No plan will ever be complete, it will need to be kept up-to-date and modified in the light of changing circumstances and experience.

Prevention

A few minutes thought will probably bring to light an alarming range of potential disasters, but in many instances quite simple precautions which would alleviate the possibility or minimize the effect will also be evident. In helping to prevent disaster, there is no substitute for good housekeeping and curatorial care. The following ideas might be a good starting point.

Have a good look at the building and its surroundings. Is it vulnerable to flood? How efficient are the gutters and drains? Does the roof leak anywhere? Is the building well maintained? How recently has it been re-wired? Are all electrical installations to an approved standard and does this extend to exhibition wiring and audiovisual displays? Is the museum store in the basement and, if so, are objects kept off the floor? Where is discarded packaging stored?

Look carefully too at exhibition design. Make sure that shelves and plinths are adequately fixed and that the bases of show-cases are secured. In the flood at the Corning Museum of Glass, an object was 'lost' only to be discovered underneath the base of the case. The base had risen with the flood water and dislodged the object which came to rest under the baseboard as the water receded. The same can happen with shelves in storage cabinets.

It is almost too obvious to state that museum documentation must be of the highest order. If starting from scratch on a programme of documentation, begin with the most significant items in the collection. Ensure that the records of such objects are complete in every detail and consider storing a copy in another building. Should the original be destroyed, the information contained in the records should be sufficiently detailed to enable a replica to be made. Take regular back-up copies of computer records and store them elsewhere.

In considering all aspects of disaster planning, talk to the local Fire Service and other advisers, possibly in association with the insurance company. The fire service may well be willing to co-operate in staging the occasional practice.

Look at the possibility of installing smoke and flood detectors. If a full system is beyond the means of the museum, a range of do-it-yourself equipment is available and should be considered for vulnerable areas which are little used. Keep an open mind on the thought of installing a sprinkler system. The amount of water from two or three sprinkler heads which extinguish the fire and then shut off is far less than would be applied by the fire brigade's hoses and which may still be too late to save the museum's collections.

Outline of a disaster plan

The actual document is likely to be a loose-leaf folder, possibly divided into two sections; the first to cover the procedure to be followed at the moment disaster strikes, and the second a compendium of information for immediate needs.

Procedures

Evacuation of the public and staff must be the first priority and the plan must include clear instructions for this, it will incorporate the museum's normal evacuation procedure with which all staff should be familiar. Keep lists of staff at the exit nearest their designated assembly point so that a roll can be called quickly and accurately. Include written instructions for calling the emergency services.

Advice for the public in the event of an emergency evacuation should be posted in strategic places, be included in any simple guide to the museum, and given over the public-address system if one is available. It maybe possible to designate an area outside the museum for family or other groups who become separated to be reunited.

In all but a very minor emergency, a senior member of staff should assume the role of Incident Controller to liaise with the emergency services and co-ordinate all other activities. This person should not get involved with the detail.

In the event of a fire, a senior officer of the Fire Service has the sole responsibility for the building and no one should enter until it has been declared safe and permission is given for people to enter. In other circumstances, access may be restricted until forensic evidence has been obtained.

For an emergency outside the opening hours of the museum, the disaster plan should include a call-out chart for key staff so that the Incident Controller can call in those who will be needed depending on the circumstances. The senior member of staff who will act as Incident Controller should keep a copy of the plan at home and the museum should ensure that someone to act in this capacity is always available. For museums which are not warded 24 hours a day, a mechanism for contacting key staff should be established.

In areas which are especially vulnerable to disaster and where warning systems operate, the plan should include the strategy to be adopted depending on the severity of the warning.

Information

The information section of the plan should include contacts for the public utilities, for building mainte-nance, transport, crane hire, freezer facilities, legal and welfare services, etc. Think through what might be needed on the assumption that access to offices will be impossible and compile the information accordingly. Add 24-hour-contact telephone num-bers where possible.

Instructions for emergency conservation treatment should also be included.

No matter how confident you are that you would remember the plumber's telephone number or know instinctively which sodden objects had priority, none of us knows how we would react in the event of a disaster and even the most obvious information should be written down.

Preparation and training

The degree of preparation any museum can afford will obviously vary and will need to be considered in the light of the likely risk. It is worth spending time to give some thought to a whole range of possible situations, and see if simple (and inexpensive) solutions can be found.

It is almost inevitable that a disaster will mean groping around in the dark. What provision can be made for emergency lighting? Is a full emergency system with back-up battery power feasible, or would a small generator suffice? In any case, it would be sensible to keep torches (with spare batteries) at strategic places.

Is there easy access to another telephone? Might a line operated by another network be an advantage or is it adequate to make arrangements with the neighbours or to use the nearest public telephone box (and make sure the necessary coins or card are always available).

Is there a building separate from the museum which could be used in an emergency, for casualties, for an office, for a press conference? Does this building have its own power supply and telephone, is it easily accessible from the road? One could go on, but attention must be turned to the collections.

In the event of damage to show-cases or storage areas it is vital to have lists immediately to hand of what is displayed or stored in each location. 'Snatch lists' should be prepared listing all objects case by case (or storage area) giving the accession number and a brief description. Arrange for all cases to be photographed and keep all this information in a safe and accessible place.

Add to this the location of especially important or vulnerable items. This really must be a very short list and will include objects which are unique and of outstanding international or national significance and valuable loan items.

A salvage squad should be set up and trained so that they are thoroughly familiar with the museum and have some knowledge of emergency conserva-tion treatment relating to the objects in the collections. Ideally, members of the squad should have a telephone contact, live quite close to the museum, be young and fit, and be able to work under pressure and as part of a team. Technical staff and those able to lift heavy objects should be included. The salvage squad will need to know what has top priority and what can be left. This will probably be adequate until specialist help is available. A list of specialist Conservators should be included in the plan. This might be compiled on a local basis or kept by an Area Museum Service or simply be a list of colleagues in the profession who could be called upon for advice.

In addition to the objects of great significance noted on the snatch lists, the salvage squad will need to know which materials are the most vulnerable and how each should be treated in the immediate aftermath of the disaster. The first priority is to ensure the area is safe to work in and that there is no danger of physical damage to the objects. If objects are dry then, unless there is a pressing need to move them, they can be left.

It is important to do nothing in the early stage of rescue that might be detrimental to the eventual restoration of the object. If books and manuscripts have become water-logged it is often better to freeze them, if suitable facilities are available, to be dealt with later. This will allow time to concentrate on other vulnerable objects. Take care to record what is done to each item and its location.

The recommended immediate treatment for a range of materials is given in *Table 48.1*. Specialist museums would include more detailed information on some materials, a small museum might be able to include instructions for treating specific objects. It must be stressed that immediate treatment implies undertaking treatment the first 2 days after the disaster, after which time it is hoped specialist help would be available.

In a fire, it is important to remember that items which escape water damage may still be vulnerable to damage from smoke or volatile substances which might be given off in the heat. Porous materials such as stone should be removed from the polluted environment as quickly as possible in order to prevent further damage and hence minimize the difficulty (and cost) of treatment.

In order to carry out emergency conservation, it will be necessary to set up emergency stores or disaster boxes. Ideally some of the equipment should be in the gallery, with a larger store in another building. Again, the contents will reflect the needs and means of each museum; a possible list is shown in *Table 48.2*.

Table 48.1 Procedure for the immediate treatment of different materials which have suffered water damage

Material	Procedure
Books and manuscripts	Wrap in polythene and freeze
Paintings	Oils on fabric – remove from frame, but not stretchers and leave to dry face down on pad of tissue or paper Oils on card, etc. – leave in frame and dry face up Watercolours – freeze and leave to an expert
Wood and leather	Dry slowly. If dirty, rinse and cover with polythene sheeting to dry. Do not apply heat. Do not rinse if surface coating is flaking
Textiles	If robust, clothing can be hung to dry. Dry delicate fabrics flat, avoid sunlight. Can be frozen
Organic materials	Dry slowly. Do not rinse ethnographic material. Do not touch wax items
Metals	Dry quickly. If dirty, rinse in clean water, blot off excess liquid. Dry in air
Electrical items	Rinse if necessary, dry quickly, do not heat. Open cladding to assist drying
Photographic film, etc.	Immerse films, etc., in water and seek expert advice; air dry prints – emulsion side up
Stone, ceramics, glass	Do nothing unless exposed to risk of physical damage

Table 48.2 Suggested list of emergency supplies

Building services	Generator, emergency lighting, extension leads, water supply, heating, tarpaulins, pumps
Health and safety	Safety helmets, protective clothing, goggles, face masks, overalls, wellington boots, gloves. First aid
Cleaning equipment	Mops, buckets, shovels, wet vacuum cleaner. Brushes, sponges, cloths, paper towels, etc.
Conservation	High-pressure washer, fans, hairdryers, dehumidifier, whirling hydrometer, humidity indicator cards
Packaging	Polythene bags (various), 'Tyvek' bags and labels, string, adhesive tape, boxes and trays (freezer quality)
Documentation	Stationery – waterproof markers, pens, notepads, clipboards, camera and film
Staff requirements	Toilet facilities, food/drink, torches (keep batteries separately)

For museums whose collections are insured, it would be wise to discuss arrangements for emergency treatment when agreeing the terms of the policy. To be effective, rescue conservation must be carried out quickly and cannot wait for a lengthy period of assessment and the provision of estimates. Be sure that the insurance cover is adequate.

Specialist firms of disaster-control contractors offer comprehensive clean-up services, although these are likely to be expensive.

Conclusion

The preparation of a disaster plan will not only be a salutary experience, but a valuable and even enjoyable one. No time spent planning will be wasted and it might save your museum.

Bibliography

AMERICAN SOCIETY FOR TESTING AND MATERIALS (1987), *NFPA 911 Protection of Museums and Museum Collections*

ANDERSON, H. *(1985), Planning Manual for Disaster Control*, National Library of Scotland, Edinburgh

CORNING, N. Y. (1977), *The Corning Flood: Museum under Water*, Corning Museum of Glass, Corning

HUTCHINS, J. and ROBERTS, B. (1990), 'Flood cyclone – Is your museum ready? *Museum*, **167/3**

NATIONAL PRESERVATION OFFICE (1988), *If Disaster Strikes* (video), National Preservation Office, London

UPTON, M. S. (1978), *Disaster Planning and Emergency Treatment in Museums, Art Galleries, Libraries, Archives and Allied Institutions*, Institute for the Conservation of Cultural Material Inc., Canberra

SECTION FOUR

COLLECTIONS RESEARCH

Section Editor

Alexander Fenton

49

Collections research: local, national and international pespectives

Alexander Fenton

Since collections are basic to the existence of museums and galleries, it follows that without them museums could not exist. Existence is one thing, however, and purposeful use another. Everyone knows the usual ways of using collections. We conserve them, store them, display them, and write about them, but in general we do not really apply the concept of collections research which illuminates the objects, and give perspectives which, on the one hand, can guide us towards selectivity rather than random ingathering and, on the other hand, opens up new paths of knowledge.

Collections research has often been regarded as something a Curator did if he found time. It was thought to be a luxury in which smaller museums could not indulge ('unless one can call on a really big staff, provincial galleries are not for research', said one Curator (Ogborn, 1978)), although times are changing as trained professionals increase in numbers and spread more into general-purpose, smaller museums. It has been stated, with some degree of truth, that the major museums had the concentrations of subject-related expertise that allowed real research to proceed, and the supporting range of services that both helped staff research, and could be offered to the scholarly world (see Longworth, 1987). Indeed, some museums, like the British Museum (Natural History), amount to research institutions in themselves, in this case devoted to a single coherent discipline, taxonomy (Greenway. 1983).

All the same, the large museums are not perfect. A well-based research policy is not something that can be worked out casually and few large museums have tackled the subject. They have taken research for granted, without establishing a policy and firm programme, though some do at least pay lip service to a research policy. The *British Museum Act 1963*, for example, observed that a 'substantial research effort is needed to sustain the essential purpose of any great museum'. A recent policy statement from Nordiska Museet, Stockholm, emphasized that research was the nerve centre of the Museum's work and should be coupled to all its basic tasks. The National Museums of Canada put the undertaking or sponsoring of relevant forms of research second only to the collection, classification, preservation and display of objects in their list of purposes. Nevertheless, attempts to work out specific research policies have nowhere been made.

That there is a need for collections research policies within which research outlets in the form of well-labelled displays, publications and the like, can be promulgated with greater accuracy, economy and efficiency, in line with a museum's overall broad policy, is beyond question, especially in view of the present-day place of museums in the world of learning. A large museum with important collections forms a link with university expertise, with archaeologists and historians involved with artefacts, with geologists and natural historians. It also is or should be a transmitter and mediator of knowledge and expertise to other museums and museum staff, in fulfilment of an important pastoral role which relates to them and to 'heritage' in general, as part of a broad educational thrust. It has potential for making directly a strong impact on the educational system, not just through facilities like handling collections, teachers' aids and the taking of classes, but also at national curriculum development level. Because a large museum's range of professional expertise constitutes a kind of 'mini-university', there is an opportunity to take initiatives to fill gaps in the processes of research that institutes of higher learning are increasingly forced to ignore, especially in relation to the collections which give museums a unique cultural and educational role.

Defining museum-based research

Museum-based research is not, in practice, different from other kinds of reearch except in its collection-based, three-dimensional emphases (which document-orientated historians sometimes find hard to grasp). There is no such thing as abstract research; nor is research something rare and special.

In many respects research is a process, building on the Curator's personal interests and training, a constant reasoned accumulation of knowledge in the course of experience, a transformation of raw data in archives, computers and notebooks into vehicles of thought about the collections and their significance in terms of the development of the physical world and of humanity in general. It moves from the amassing of data through sorting and analysis to interpretation and understanding, the last sometimes flowing from a kind of inspiration, but it is inspiration for which step-by-step processes have prepared the ground.

A number of views about research have been put forward. One writer sought to distinguish between research and connoisseurship, which he regarded as 'the mature judgement of the nature origins, relationships and significance of a wide range of objects of some common character' (Greenaway, 1984). Another writer thought it imprecise to apply the term 'research' both to collecting and ordering of data as well as to sorting it into meaningful conclusions, often to test hypotheses (Davies, 1984). There have been attempts to distinguish between research on collections for academic use and research done to help the interested but non-specialist visitor (Farr, 1984). But the fact remains that research is a multilevel concept with many facets at each level. The *co-ordination* of these levels, within individual museums, between local and national museums, with other centres of learning, and internationally, is more important than any long-winded discussion about the niceties of the concept of research. And we should not think that research is anyone's special prerogative. We all do it as soon as we start to go beyond the mechanics of compiling lists.

Research policy and perspectives

An attempt to work out a research policy with good perspectives in a large institution with a set of departments that covers all of human, natural and inanimate history from the beginning of time and for much of the world is not a simple matter. It must take account of collections built up over long periods, in some cases over two centuries; of departmental structures and of profiles of staff expertise; and of lines of development in the shorter or longer term. Fashions in research must be acknowledged also, and outside pressures may for a time dictate (or inhibit) research directions. There will be a strong bearing on the 'essential purpose' and general policy of the museum, and on the 'heritage' as represented in its own collections and in the collections and archives of other museums and bodies with related interests. Research may lead to a transcending of traditional bounds and point to an increasingly missionary role in education and in the community. It should contribute substantially to museological studies at practical and theoretical levels also, as part of the infrastructure of museum work within a country.

To be fully effective, research based on such criteria will stand on well-organized collections, archives and support facilities, including automation of documentation; on staff selected for skills in developing points of strength and identifying and filling gaps; and implicit in the whole must be the means of implementation for the benefit of the public and of specialists alike.

For a smoothly and purposefully working institution, the broad policy and research policy with its accompanying programme will march hand in hand. Research can provide a basic means of guiding museums into meaningfully functional development. It is at the centre of a two-way process or even multi-channel set of processes in a major museum. Management, through the provision of finance, space, staff and facilities related to the collections and to the activities of 'partners' with like interests, develops and facilitates a research programme leading to displays, publications, teaching and the like. Out of this programme should come, through analysis of feedback, fresh ideas and possibilities for management to take into account, fresh knowledge of gaps in collections that can then be filled or – even more importantly in view of the high cost of storage space – knowledge that allows for greater selectivity in collection.[1] *Figure 49.1* provides in digested form a sample of what is appropriate to the work of a 'research museum', a major museum with a wide range of collections and facilities.

But what of the wider perspectives, particularly the relationships between national and general-purpose local museums that comprise the majority of the museums in most countries?

In this context, the Museums Association is in Britain playing an increasing role. Its Corporate Plan includes a research programme that lays emphasis on four strands: 'museum statistics and trends; social statistics and trends which impact on museums; case studies of excellent museum practice; and facilitating the development of collections surveys' (Museums Association, 1988–1992). This is not collections research directly, but the kind of data produced by such activity could help to give shape to museum

COLLECTIONS RESEARCH FLOW DIAGRAM

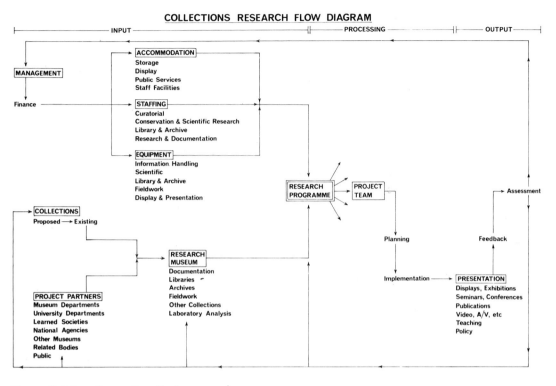

Figure 49.1 Flow diagram for collections research

research policies, and to facilitate collections research. The *Manual of Curatorship* is itself relevant in this context, as will be other elements of the Association's future publication plans, such as the manuals for Social History Curators, Heritage Management and Biological Curators.

Perspectives flowing from such effort will inevitably open up discussion about national collecting policies. This should not simply relate to who collects what and where, nor to the rising standards in non-national museums, including professional expertise and research capabilities (see Schadla-Hall, 1987), but should take fully into account the pressures of the present time (tight budgets, limited specialist staff numbers, overflowing storage, etc.) and consider how a basically more economic approach can be achieved by striving for an overview of the totality of our collections, which may be construed as the 'national heritage'. Within such a broad overview there will, of course, be different levels (district and region as well as 'national' units) but, somehow or other, the effort to see the heritage as a whole should be made, and tasks identified in the light of research-based knowledge. Economic considerations are not the prime factor, however, but

rather the effort to harness and control the enormous educational potential of museum collections, through coordinated approaches.

Common gooals: SAMDOK, SHIC, interpretation

This point can be exemplified by two approaches, one period based and the other subject based: SAMDOK and SHIC. SAMDOK is the more significant example, at least in its Swedish practice. The word is an acronym from Swedish *samtids dokumentation*, 'contemporary documentation', though we must remember that to a Swede 'documentation' implies a full process covering fieldwork, recording, acquisition and cataloguing, and is not simply the paperwork associated with collected objects. SAMDOK is a concept that relates to the modern world, stemming from a sense of social responsibility in collecting that seeks to find the identity of modern communities and transmit it for the future. It depends heavily on research as a prelude to the selection of items for presentation, acknowledging that blind collection is a poor investment.

SAMDOK, in Sweden, is a voluntary organization that enables co-operation between all cultural historical museums. It was formed with the support of the Swedish Government in 1977. It sees the country's museums as an overall resource, for which responsibility must be divided. Participating museums work in 'pools' each accepting responsibility for specific areas of research and collection. The approach is valid enough for modern, mass-produced, centrally distributed material that has little or no specific local significance. It is, perhaps, less easy to apply for earlier material that does have such local significance, but the principle of approach, based on collaboration between museums of all levels of status, is an important one, as is the way in which the system uses research into social and economic characteristics as a means of avoiding *ad hoc* acquisition. One point should be stressed again: investment in research can lead to economies based on reasoned selection of items. It is a feature of the SAMDOK approach in Scandinavia that it has led to a fundamental questioning of museum roles and functions and to a reassessment of what they are about, and of the what and why of object collection.[2]

SHIC (Social History and Industrial Classification), is related in some degree; in some ways it represents the equivalent British way of going about things. It grew out of the work of the Group for Regional Studies in Museums (founded 1971), which changed its name to the Social History Curator's Group (SHCG) in 1982. The aim is to improve standards in social history curating – and, after all, social history collections are common to almost every museum in the country – through publication, seminars, training and campaigning. One whole issue of the *Museums Journal* was devoted to 17 articles relating to the SHCG in 1985. These show much concern for the concept of twentieth-century collecting, and mark the anxiety that social history curators are feeling about the role of museums in the modern world.[3]

Inevitably, this quite strong movement is reflected in research orientations. There is what many would describe as a marked move to the left, an effort to explore topics such as the working life of working men, labour history in general, ethnic minorities, women's history, and the like. The group called Women, Heritage and Museums (WHAM) came into existence after a conference under that heading in 1984,[4] as a subgroup of the SHCG.

These activities mark nearly two decades of enthusiasm for social history in modern terms, partly in reaction to, but also flowing out of, the 'folk-life' tradition. They include entirely laudable efforts to integrate museums more closely with their communities (especially urban industrial) and much research has been directed accordingly to record areas of life such as housing, food and drink (including fast foods), education, religion, women's lives, sport and leisure, health, crime, death, etc. (see O'Neill, 1987; Jenkinson, 1987), i.e., to a great degree, all the things with which Local Authorities are concerned.

Such work is building up useful archives of data for the future, but the major research tool to come out of the work of the SHCG is the SHIC, covering the primary areas of community life, domestic and family life, personal life and working life. This subject classification was said to be in use in over 350 museums and in 22 countries by 1987 (SHIC Working Party, 1983); the implications for comparative research are great. SHIC, of course, complements the work of the Museum Documentation Association (MDA), whose remit is as wide as the range of items held anywhere by museums and galleries.[5]

These means of, and guides to, the accumulation of data on collections over a wide field are complemented by specific projects like Natural Science Collections Research, carried out from 1982 as a joint exercise between the Scottish Museums Council and the National Museums of Scotland. This followed similar activity in England where the North West Collections Research Unit (formed 1977) led to the publication of a Register of Natural Science Collections in North West England in 1981. The Scottish work is now in print also; it covers 3338 collections and was built up as a data base managed by the Manchester Museum Computer Cataloguing Unit (Ambrose and Stace, 1984). Such projects, exemplifying co-operation between national and local museums and Area Councils, set important patterns for the topic-by-topic accumulation of research data to a level that can eventually constitute a national overview.

The twentieth-century-collecting issue with its accompanying aspects of labour history, urban history, industrial/working life history, women's emancipation history and the like has been one strong force in research approaches. Another has been the rise of interpretation, which has sparked off much thinking and led to much publication. In its original essence, the science of interpretation came to this country in the 1960s from the USA. It grew out of the perceived need in National Parks to explain to visitors what they saw around them, whether it related to past, present or future, and implicit in it also was the fostering of understanding and awareness that would encourage visitors to be more caring and conservation conscious. It was site specific to a large extent, with a main concern for the things of nature and for the effects on these of the activities of man.[6] Those who led in translating the concept of interpretation from the National Parks of the USA to Britain maintained a comparable approach (notably Aldridge (1975)).

However, a shift in emphasis quickly appeared. Thinking began to embrace not only the natural environment but also the 'built' environment and the man-made heritage in general. This often amounted to little more than the application of interpretive media and facilities to the elucidation of these matters.[7]

However, the important point for us is that the movement had a substantial effect on museums. In some cases it made them more outward looking, as in the case of the guided walks which Cardiff and other museums have seen as good ways of linking collections (especially geological) with the environment (Sharpe and Howe, 1982). It also made museums begin to rethink their presentations of objects in galleries, most obviously in the case of interpretive displays of geological and natural history specimens, recreating, as it were, site interpretation indoors. But there is in reality a great difference between site interpretation where all the objects and data relate to that site, and general museum collections, however strongly grouped thematically, that have been removed from their original context. Though the concept of interpretation has been taken up by museums, and has been much discussed in the pages of the *Museums Journal*, the main thrust of the movement has been through countryside bodies, including a number of mainly independent countryside museums which have sought to weld artefacts, sites, buildings, archives and oral history into a single, integrated interpretation strategy (Stansfield, 1983 pp. 47, 50). Such interpretation is, of course, heavily dependent on detailed research and the search for interrelationships.

Site interpretation is directional or manipulative, to the extent that it aims at modifying human behaviour towards conservationist ends through the progression: interpretation→understanding→appreciation→protection. The interpretation of objects within a museum context – and in this case it might be preferable to stick to the word 'explanation' – normally aims at education in the broadest sense, with no essential propagandist intention beyond the enhancement of knowledge,[8] though the various technical devices of site interpretation might well be employed to sharpen up communication and achieve readier assimilation of fresh knowledge. Thus, David Wright's discussion in the *Museums Journal* of interpretation in museums of general technology, even with his analyses of nominal, functional and contextual levels of interpretation, is basically an examination of device-aided explanation organized in logical sequences (Wright, 1983).

There has been a flood of writing on interpretation (Barclay, 1983), and it has undoubtedly given museum folk new perspectives, both in the integration of research data and in the technical presentation of information, but museum work still remains different, with a potential level of wide comparative exploration that site interpretation will normally lack or is not suitable for.

Material culture

Museum collections are about objects and specimens. With regard to natural history and geology, research is a tight ship sailing through seas of disciplined international codes of practice and precision of nomenclature. Stress is laid on a dispassionate study of specimens for what they have to say in their own right. Accumulated data in the form of taxonomic lists and classifications gain wider scientific value because they are compiled under conditions of particular control. Artefact research may also have elements of science in that it can take advantage of laboratory techniques such as thermoluminescence, X-ray fluorescence, neutron activation, dye and chemical analysis, and so on. To such scientific analysis can be added relevant factors like the historical setting in time, place and social milieu. Nevertheless, an element of subjective interpretation is often unavoidable and, though the aim is to reduce the subjective element, research into historical and aesthetic objects remains an art to a greater degree than a science.

It has been said that there is as yet no real theoretical basis for the study of material culture (Paine, 1985). Perhaps museum people have a habit of looking too narrowly at their own artefact collections. The fact is that a substantial body of theory exists. Geologists and natural historians are obliged by the nature of their discipline to work internationally. Those concerned with artefacts must learn to do so also. As the SAMDOK 'movement' shows, the British museum world is not immune to outside influences, but we must learn to be more outward looking still.

America is often a rich source of inspiration. Schlereth's thought-provoking *Material Culture Studies in America* reviews the history of material culture studies in America from 1876 onwards, and examines theory, method and practice (Schlereth, 1982). There is also Stocking's *Objects and Others. Essays on Museums and Material Culture* which is more patchy and discursive but, nevertheless, shows that people in the USA are thinking about collections in museums. Britain is catching up, however, as a recent publication on material culture shows (Pearce, 1989).

In Europe there is an enormous literature on the subject, though often in languages other than English. The journal *Ethnologia Europaea* is much concerned with theoretical bases. There are innumerable books on specific aspects of material culture, often including theoretical introductions, and some take broad approaches to the subject, like D.W.H.

Schwarz's *Sachgüter und Lebensformen. Einführung in die materielle Kulturgeschichte des Mittelalters und der Neuzeit* (Schwarz, 1970).

There is no shortage of material. The real question is, what are we to make of it, how are we to use it, in looking afresh at our own collections? Few of us have consistent research policies in relation to our collections, at least of artefacts, and we tend to be blown about by winds of fashion like the twentieth-century collecting concept and the interpretation concept. But, in the end, we have to come down to the hard bit, and face ourselves with the meaning of our collecting activities in terms of our locality, region and nation, and with questions of co-ordinating activity on aspects of the 'national heritage' between museums of different levels of capability. If we can honestly try to do this, and in so doing begin to understand what characterizes one area rather than another, and how the life and culture of one area affects and is affected by that of others, close at hand or far away, then perhaps we can also begin to wield our collections more positively in adding our respective bits to the elucidation of the story of mankind, the begetter of the artefacts we curate.

Notes

[1] See *SHCG News* (1984), **7**, 5, which comments specifically on research and documentation as a means of selection in the collecting of countryside material, but the comment is generally valid.

[2] Much has been written about SAMDOK in Britain, though it has not caught on here as it has in the countries of Scandinavia, perhaps because we still have to learn to apply the full 'documentation' technique. There is also some confusion with the concept of 'twentieth-century collecting', which is in itself not clear, referring on the one hand to art objects and on the other to the paraphernalia of working life, whether domestic or in the workplace. See, for example Kavanagh (1983, 1987), Cedrenius (1987), Shaw (1987) and Rosander (1977).

[3] See, for example, *GRSM Newsletter* (1971–1981); *Museums Journal*, **85**(1) and Davies (1985).

[4] *Women, Heritage and Museums*, report of the conference, 7–8 April 1984, Woolton Hall, Fallowfield, Manchester.

[5] See Roberts *et al.* (1980) and several articles marking Information Technology Year in *Museums* (1982), **82**(2); also Stewart (1983), Stone (1984) and Roberts (1984).

[6] Among the 'bibles' of interpretation in the primary sense are Tilden (1957) and Brown (1971).

[7] See Pennyfather (1975) and Percival (1979). For a review of the development of the concept and its relationship to statutory Government provision through a variety of Acts and countryside bodies see Stansfield (1983).

[8] Though a modern view, entirely valid provided it is not one-sided, is that 'Museums ... share with other educational and cultural institutions a responsibility for the forming of historical consciousness' (*SHCG News* (Winter 1985–1986), **10**, 4, in a comment on a seminar on labour history in museums).

[9] A recent paper by Mohrmann (1987) also raises the problem of relating the study of 'things' too closely to an absolute chronology. See also Meiners (1990).

References

ALDRIDGE, D. (1975), *Principles of Countryside Interpretation and Interpretive Planning*, HMSO, Edinburgh.

AMBROSE, T. and STACE, H. (1984), 'National science collections research in Scotland', in *Museums Journal*, **83**(4), 230–233.

BARCLAY, D. (1983), *Interpretation of the Environment, A Bibliography*, Carnegie United Kingdom Trust, Dunfermline

BROWN, W. E. (1971), *Islands of Hope. Parks and Recreation in Environmental Crisis*, National Recreation and Park Association, Washington, DC

CEDRENIUS, G. (1987), 'Collecting today for today and tomorrow', *Recording Society Today*, pp. 15–19, Scottish Museums Council, Edinburgh

DAVIES, D. G. (1984) 'Research: archaeological collections', in Thompson, J. M. A. (Ed.), *Manual of Curatorship*, p. 164, Museums Association/Butterworths, London

DAVIES, S. (1985), 'Social History Curators' Group', *Museums*, **85**(3) 153–155

FARR, D. (1984), 'Research: fine art collections', in Thompson, J. M. A. (Ed.), *Manual of Curatorship*, p. 187, Museums Association/Butterworths, London

GREENAWAY, F. (1983), 'National museums', *Museums Journal*, **83**(1), 8

GREENAWAY, F. (1984), 'Research: science collections', in Thompson, J. M. A. (Ed.), *Manual of Curatorship*, p. 142, Museums Association/Butterworths, London

JENKINSON, P. (1987), 'A taste of change – contemporary documentation in inner city Birmingham, *Recording Society Today*, pp. 33–39, Scottish Museums Council, Edinburgh

KAVANAGH, G. (1983), 'SAMDOK in Sweden: some observations and impressions', *Museum Journal*, **83**(1), 85–88

KAVANAGH, G. (1987), 'Recording society today', *Recording Society Today*, pp. 5–13, Scottish Museums Council

LONGWORTH, I. (1987), 'The British Museum: a case study', *Museums Journal*, **87**(2), 93

MEINERS, U. (1990), 'Research into the history of material culture. Between interpretation and statistics', *Ethnologia Europaea*, **XX**(1), (1990), pp. 15–34

MOHRMANN, R. E. (1987), 'Anmerkungen zur Geschichte der Dinge. Die Form der Zeit' als Instrument der Periodisierung', in Wiegelmann, G. (ed.), *Wandel der Alltagskultur seit dem Mittelalter (Beiträge zur Volkskultur in Nordwestdeutschland 55*). 103–116

MUSEUMS ASSOCIATION (1988–1992), *Museums Association Corporate Plan 1988–92 (typescript)*, **8**, 15–16, Museums Association, London

OGBORN, E.A. (1978), 'Researching your collections – fine art', *Museum Assistants Group Transactions*, **15**, 7

O'NEILL, M. (1987), 'Recording modern Springburn', *Recording Society Today*, pp. 28–32, Scottish Museums Council, Edinburgh

PAINE, C. (1985), Report on SHCG Weekend, D. Hopkin *SHCG News*, **9**, 4

PEARCE, S. M. (Ed.), (1989), *Museum Studies in Material Culture*, Leicester University Press, London

PENNYFATHER, K. (1975), *Interpretive Media and Facilities*, HMSO, Edinburgh

PERCIVAL, A. (1979), *Understanding our Surroundings. A Manual of Urban Interpretation*, Civil Trust, London

ROBERTS, D. A. (1984), 'The development of computer-based documentation', in Thompson, J. M. A. (Ed.), *Manual of Curatorship*, pp. 136–141, Museums Association/Butterworth, London

ROBERTS, D. A., LIGHT, R. B. and STEWART, J. D. (1980), 'The Museum Documentation Association', *Museums Journal*, **80**(2), 81–85

ROSANDER, G. (Ed.) (1977), *Slutrapport rorande Samtids Dokumentation genom foremålsinsamling vid kulturhistoriska museer*, Nordiska Museet Stockholm

SCHADLA-HALL, T. (1987), 'Regional and national collections of archaeology', *Museums Journal*, **87**(2), 90

SCHLERETH, T. H. (1982), *Material Culture Studies in America*, The American Association for State and Local History, Nashville, TN

SCHWARZ, D. W. H. (1970), *Sachgüter und Lebensformen. Einführung in die Materielle Kulturgeschichte des Mittelalters und der Neuzeit*, Berlin

SHARPE, T. and HOWE, S. R. (1982), 'Family expeditions – the museum outdoors', *Museums Journal*, **82**(3), 143–147

SHAW, J. (1987), 'Recording society today, a postscript', *Recording Society Today*, pp. 40–43, Scottish Museums Council, Edinburgh

SHIC WORKING PARTY (1983), *Social History and Industrial Classification. A Subject Classification for Museum Collections; Vol. I, The Classification; Vol. II, Index*, The Centre for English Cultural Tradition and Language, Sheffield

STANSFIELD, G. (1983), 'Heritage and interpretation', *Museums Journal*, **83**(1), 47–51

STEWART, J. (1983), 'Museum documentation in Britain – a review of some recent developments', *Museums Journal*, **83**(1), 61–62

STOCKING, JR., G. W. (1985), *Objects and Others. Essays on Museums and Material Culture, History of Anthropology Vol. 3*, University of Wisconsin Press, Madison, WI

STONE, S. M. (1984), 'Documenting collections', in Thompson, J. M. A. (Ed.), *Manual of Curatorship*, pp. 127–135, Museums Association/Butterworths, London

TILDEN, F. (1957), *Interpreting our Heritage*, revised edition University of North Carolina Press, Chapel Hill

WRIGHT, D. W. (1983), 'Idealised structures in museums of general technology', *Museums Journal*, **83**,(2/3), 111–119

50

The nature of museum collections

Peter Cannon-Brookes

Collecting is a very basic activity, in that food-gathering is a characteristic of all animals, but, setting aside the activities of certain species of birds, the systematic collecting of objects which fulfil a cerebral, as against bodily, function is confined to a limited number of cultures and societies of man. In the evolution of this phenomenon certain, but not all, societies in Western Europe, together with those springing from them, have played a crucial role. However, the identifying characteristics of museum collections – objects assembled and maintained within a specific intellectual environment – separate them from accumulations of household objects, no matter how princely, originally brought together under different criteria, or collections of votive objects given in response to favours sought or received from a deity, church or temple treasuries etc., though by means of a subsequent conscious decision, such accumulations may be converted into museum collections. Art collections existed as such in sixth century B.C. Greece, and Pausanias has provided us with descriptions of the collections in Athens in the second century A.D., but according to Pliny the Roman emperors did not wish Rome to be seen to dominate the world through military force alone and they were thus determined to make Rome the metropolis of world civilization as well as its political capital. Subsequent rulers patronized the arts in order to provide a visible expression of their spiritual power, as against their temporal authority, but loot (including artistic) has always been a visible symbol of superiority, and, for example, the entry of the captured works of art into Paris for the Musée Napoleon was modelled on a Roman triumph. The intellectual environment which has provided the essential framework for the assembly of museum collections is Renaissance Humanism and although the first organized collections were formed in the Greek and Roman world, the fundamental Humanist concept that Man could be understood through his creations and Nature through the systematic study of Her manifestations, positively demanded, for the first time, the formation of collections for study purposes.

For the fifteenth-century Humanist the collecting of the surviving remains of Classical antiquity – sculpture, coins, architectural fragments and so on, as well as the texts of the ancient authors – fulfilled an important function and these objects provided a potent insight into the vanished civilization which they sought to emulate and became a powerful stimulus to scholars and creative artists alike. Thus, the formation of collections for study purposes was a concomitant of both the rebirth of Classical rationalism and of experimental science, after the arid philosophical speculations of the Middle Ages, and it is only too easy to underestimate the intellectual basis of the formation of the Renaissance *Kunst– und Wunderkammern* which are the immediate forerunners of modern museum collections. Consequently, the process of collecting cannot be considered separately from the cultural characteristics of the society undertaking it and the widely differing pattern of distribution of museum collections world wide is by no means accidental.

Seen in a historical context, the vast majority of societies, past and present, are 'concept-centered' and for these the individual object is of very limited significance. For these societies the process of collecting/preserving objects is limited to fetishes, totems and so on which perform an ongoing functional role and the transmission of cultural traditions is overwhelmingly oral. However, for the minority – the 'object-centered' societies – the accumulation of objects is of crucial importance in the transmission of the cultural traditions, and the curiosity manifested by them in the artefacts created by the 'concept-centered' societies is not reciprocated. Consequently, the relevance today of museum collections to any particular society, and the significance accorded by it to them, varies widely and although museum collections are relevant to most Western societies, they are not equally important and may indeed be irrelevant to many other societies in the world. Unfortunately. within the 'object-centered' societies the possession of great collections of artefacts and natural history specimens became, during the nineteenth century, a manifestation of nationalism and the concept of the *Musée Napoleon* ultimately reached an apogee of megalomania in Hitler's plans for Linz. On the other hand certain societies, such as the Australian aboriginals and Bushmen, are fundamentally opposed to the collecting of objects because of the danger of interfering with the spiritual dimensions of all objects, and thus the concept of the museum collection is totally unacceptable to them.

Consequently, the process of collecting not only cannot be considered separately from the cultural characteristics of the society undertaking it, but also must take into account the cultural characteristics of the society being collected. Mercifully, the impact of collecting on 'concept-centred' societies has generally been relatively limited, as might be expected from their characteristics, and much less than is sometimes claimed for them today. But the historical consequence has been that for many living societies the only artefacts of any age to survive are those which have been collected by the 'object-centred' societies. This state of affairs remained acceptable to all the parties concerned until the materialistic values of the 'object-centred' societies began to be adopted by all other societies, more as a political manifestation of national cultural identity, cast in an alien mould, than as a newly-developed fundamental need, and the growing demands of previously 'concept-centred' societies for the outward trappings represented by museum collections present formidable problems. Indeed, one of the major museum problems in the last decades of the twentieth century is that posed by the ambitions of societies which were 'concept-centred' and have subsequently adopted the priorities of an 'object-centred' society, and their rights as against those of the long-term 'object-centred' societies through whose collecting activities the artefacts of the former have survived.

Collecting policy

The fundamental role of the museum, of assembling objects and maintaining them within a specific intellectual environment, emphasizes that museums are storehouses of knowledge as well as storehouses of objects, and that the whole exercise is liable to be futile unless the accumulation of objects is strictly rational. This does not mean that selection of the objects is to be limited to any one single cultural or other theory, unless the museum's stated function is limited to the documentation of that theory, and thus great catholicity in the processes of selection is to be desired so that the collections will be able subsequently to support many interpretations. The process of selection is dependent upon the knowledge which has been accumulated and new acquisitions cast new light on previous acquisitions leading to a constant revision of ideas. This feedback process is not only the intellectual lifeblood of the institution, it is also one of the basic elements in the formulation and evolution of an institution's collecting policy. For static collections, such as the Wallace Collection, London, or the Isabella Stewart Gardner Museum, Boston, the processes of selection have been undertaken initially by the private collector who formed them, but these processes have been confirmed by the community in accepting responsibility for those collections as entities, in perpetuity.

For collecting museums there are as many collecting policies as there are museums, but within the general parameters already established by the terms of reference of the institution *per se*, the collecting policy adopted will almost invariably be a matter of reducing rather than increasing the collecting options (that is, a natural history museum is unlikely to consider the acquisition of a Raphael altarpiece as central to its collecting policy, notwithstanding the considerable botanical interest of the plants depicted around the feet of the Virgin!). Collecting policy will be, in most institutions, heavily circumscribed if not dictated by much more mundane considerations, such as financial constraints and limitations on space, before the strategic plan for the future development of the collections can be formulated.

Given those constraints, and the legal and moral limitations imposed upon the freedom of action of the institution in its collecting activities, the main questions in formulating a collecting policy will revolve around the present and future balance of the collections and the services which are to be based on them. In evolving that policy within the resources available the first strategic objective to be clarified is whether the collection is intended to be representative of a broad spectrum of possible material, or comprehensive within a much narrower field, or what compromise between the two. Although the desirability of concentrating a high proportion of rare or unique material into relatively few collections is hotly disputed. The advantages for scholars and scientists of such concentrations are self-evident, but by their very nature they increase the risks of catastrophic loss in the event of a disaster and they tend to negate the fundamental strategy of museum collections in providing comparative material over a wide geographical area. The same arguments can also be put forward in respect of temporary concentrations, as represented by temporary exhibitions. An important factor in the formulation of collecting policy all too often neglected is the capacity of the institution to curate and conserve both its existing collections and the objects it is seeking to acquire.

The formulation of collecting policy and its operation are likely to be two different matters since it can be justly argued that a too tightly defined and operated collecting policy ignores the realities of collecting and may bar the institution from benefiting from the unexpected. On the other hand, windfalls accepted more out of opportunism than as the product of a rational analysis can be extremely detrimental to the future development of the institution. Nevertheless, the fundamental function of museums is the acquisition of objects (a museum without a permanent collection of authentic objects, not manufactured exhibits or replicas, is a misnomer) and in this process there is the act of deliberate selection. The exercise of judgement can only be undertaken on the basis of a sound knowledge of the object, the group to which it belongs and its interrelationships; the geologist taking a specimen from one bed in a cliff face is as much exercising a process of rational selection as an art gallery director bidding for a Rembrandt at an auction. Furthermore, apart from being able to obtain good title for any new acquisition and to conserve it, the museum should be able to preserve it under conditions which will ensure its availability for museum purposes and should make the acquisition with the intention of retaining it within the collection in perpetuity. If there is any doubt about the latter it should be clearly stated in the documents recording the decision to acquire it.

Perpetuity is not accepted by a number of museums, such as the Metropolitan Museum, New York, which as early as 1885 decided that 'the Museum could in all propriety exchange duplicates of which it had no use, for others which would prove important and valuable additions to the collection'. In the Metropolitan Museum's *Annual Report*, published in October 1970, the Trustees announced formally the renewed emphasis on the upgrading of its holdings, rather than on simple accumulation, with the statement that;

> The Metropolitan has begun a determined effort to refine the quality of its numerous collections. From now on the various funds restricted for the purchase of works of art given to the Museum will be utilized to pursue the rare masterpiece of the highest quality. It is an important part of our policy to reach out for the few works of art of exceptional importance and to reject the temptation to purchase large numbers of objects of secondary or tertiary significance. Refinement of the collections also involves the disposal, whenever legally and professional-

ly permissible, of those objects that for any one of a variety of reasons are no longer appropriate for the Museum. Objects selected for deaccessioning are examined with care every bit as stringent as that brought to bear upon a work of art proposed for addition to the collections.

The provisions for exhibition and storage space in the Comprehensive Architectural Plan were based on this stabilization of the extent of the collections; indeed, the Museum's firmly stated commitment to stay within the boundaries provided in the Plan was a major reason that the Plan was approved.

Thomas P.F. Hoving, the then Director of the Metropolitan Museum, reissued the relevant sections of the Annual Report in a statement made in 1973 (*Museums News*, May 1973) and added 'It is important to emphasize that it is aesthetic gain, not financial gain, that ultimately determines the Metropolitan Museum's programme of deaccessioning and acquisition. In such transactions, the aesthetic factor must be weighed as well as economic ones. But the economic factors concerning works of art are extremely complex and open to many interpretations'. The evolution of the Metropolitan Museum's collecting policy illustrates excellently the pitfalls as well as the advantages of accepting disposals deaccessioning as an integral part of a museum's collecting policy, and no hard and fast rules can be proposed. On the other hand the culling of natural history collections, for example, fortunately does not often have the same economic overtones and can be undertaken that much more dispassionately.

More than any other great museum, the Metropolitan Museum has been in recent years prepared to explain both its philosophy and its techniques of collection in great detail, and in *The Chase, the Capture* (1975) a wide range of collecting activity has been discussed by the then Director, Thomas Hoving, and his staff. In that account there is an exhaustive description of the processes leading to an acquisition, and although other museums have been less willing to make public their own processes of acquisition, few will differ greatly in their fundamentals. The Metropolitan Museum 'Recommended Purchase Blank' and 'Recommended Purchase – Curator's Report' are models of their kind.

An additional constraint placed upon the collecting activites of art museums is concerned with the moral and legal rights of the creative artist (the 'Droit Morale'), and this is a particular problem in the acquisition of three-dimensional works of art. Apart from aesthetic objections to the pernicious practice of surmoulage (the casting of bronzes from a finished bronze and not the original plaster prepared by the artist) such casts, when not specifically authorized by the sculptor, should not be acquired by museums, and similarly museums should avoid the acquisition of unauthorized enlargements and unauthorized transfers into new materials (in particular post-humous bronze casts from welded or carved original sculptures) unless they be clearly identified at all times as unauthorized reproductions. However, when a sculptor has created a model with the specific intention of casting it in bronze such casts, be they contemporary or posthumous, are legitimate and it is for the curator to satisfy himself that the aesthetic standard is appropriate to his collection. Further problems are posed by the rights claimed by artists to have their works displayed only in conditions which do not distort their artistic intentions. What constitutes a significant distortion will all too often be the subject of sharp differences of opinion between artists and their heirs or curators, but the museum must consider carefully the implications of acquiring damaged or modified works of art if the intention is to display them to the public, and these constraints are over and above the normal critical judgement exercised by the curator.

Sources of specimens

There are almost as many sources of specimens as there are specimens themselves and in pursuing its collecting activities the museum has a very wide range of opportunities within its collecting policy. However, the museum is not alone in the world, and in obtaining its specimens, directly or vicariously, it must respect the need to conserve both the world's natural resources and its cultural heritage. Consequently, the deliberate killing of an individual with breeding potential belonging to a threatened species, in order to obtain a specimen, is contrary to the spirit of conserving natural resources and the museum seeking to acquire such a specimen should approach a zoo or obtain a specimen from an earlier collection, which for extinct species, such as the Great Auk, is the only possible course. All collecting activities should seek to inflict a minimum of damage on the ecology of the area in which the collecting takes place and indiscriminate techniques (such as moth lamps) should only be employed when more specific techniques are unavailable. The role of the museum is that of the active conserver and passive connivance at, or financial encouragement of, the flouting of conservation measures is unacceptable. Similarly, the museum must actively discourage illicit excavations and avoid purchasing archaeological and related material which is inadequately documented. Indeed the *sine qua non* of all museum acquisitions is that no laws and regulations have been contravened en route to the museum.

The relationship between museums and ancient monuments is a great deal more fraught and the responsibility of museums to co-operate in the conservation of ancient monuments and historic buildings has all too often been ignored. Art museums are, in a sense, at the top of the art food chain, in as much as virtually nothing now housed in them was in fact created specifically for them, and little, once it has entered, will leave them in the future.

It is convenient to divide the accommodation of works of art into primary, secondary and tertiary environments in order to clarify that chain. Primary environments house works of art specifically created for them, such as the monumental sculpture and frescoes which form an integral part of the structure of buildings and also the suites of furnishings, etc., created for a specific room. Unfortunately, the scruples of most museums in not removing the sculpture or frescoes does not extend to the furnishings or, for that matter, the framed paintings hanging on the walls even if they were painted specifically for that location. This lack of consistency, encouraged by the fiscal policies of governments, results all too often in the finest objects being torn from a primary environment and the remainder being broken up on the grounds that it has been irretrievably compromised. The museum should only acquire objects from primary environments as a last resort and only after every effort has been made to preserve the environment intact. However, with archaeological specimens it is often impossible to conserve them *in situ* and the removal of them to the museum is the only means of ensuring their continued survival after excavation.

Secondary environments are those accommodating works of art created for other locations but brought together by later collectors exercising discrimination, so that the totality of the assemblages are more significant than merely the sum totals of their component parts. In such a secondary environment there may be major works of art which are less closely linked to the accommodation than those in the primary environment, but the totality is worthy of conservation and, although the removal of specific items might be marginally less compromising, the future conservation of the ensemble is likely to be hazarded. In contrast to the primary and secondary environment the tertiary environment, which includes all museums and art galleries, is deliberately depersonalized and the context in which the works are displayed is totally artificial. Consequently, there are moral arguments to support the view that, contrary to the *laissez faire* attitude of allowing museums to use historic buildings as a convenient source of raw materials for their displays, the museums should have a specific responsibility for the conservation of primary and secondary environments and only acquire works of art removed from them as a last resort when it is for their protection. Consequently, art museums should exercise great discretion as to their sources of specimens and, like the natural history and archaeological museums, seek to avoid hazarding, by their own actions, the

RECOMMENDED PURCHASE BLANK

TO THE DIRECTOR AND THE ACQUISITIONS COMMITTEE: cc: Vice-Director for
Curatorial and
Educational Affairs (2
copies of this blank and 2
copies of Curator's
Report) Registrar (this
blank only) Secretary
(this blank only)

I recommend the purchase of the object(s) fully described in the attached report and briefly cap-
tioned below.

Classification _____

Artist. title. date:

Vendor: Recommended loan class:

Price:

Additional expenses: Transportation $ _____ Insurance $ _____
                              Sender to pay   Sender to pay
                              M.M.A. to pay   M.M.A. to pay

                    Installation $_____ Restoration $ _____

                    Other $_____

Recommendation approved: Submitted by:

_____   _____

Director: Curator of _____

                                           Date _____

FOR USE OF SECRETARY'S OFFICE ONLY

ACTION BY ACQUISITIONS COMMITTEE To be charged against income from the

        (authorized)   _____ Fund. 19

Purchase (not authorized) _____   Authorized at: $_____

Reported to Board _____   Secured for: $_____

Reported to   Purchase authorization no._____

Acquisitions Committee _____   Accession no. _____

RECOMMENDED PURCHASE – CURATOR'S REPORT

Classification

Attach at least one photograph of the object(s) to the Director's and Vice-Director, copies.

I. Name the title, artist, nationality or school, period, material, dimensions in inches and centimetres.

II. Full description of the object. Provide a complete visual account, including the description of all parts. Transcribe any inscriptions, describe marks and mention any added attachments or missing parts, etc.

III. Describe the condition of the piece, indicating any repairs and attempting a prognosis for future condition. Name the results obtained from scientific investigations, whether of microscopy, chemical tests, X-ray, infra-red, ultra-violet, spectrographic analysis, thermo-luminescence, etc.

IV. State the function of the piece, and whether anything about the object indicates its function as part of a greater whole or as an independent work.

V. Describe the iconography of the object. Does it follow traditional iconography, or is there something unusual in its iconography?

VI. Stylistic considerations

A. State briefly your initial reaction to the object.

B. Describe the style and relate the style of the piece to the appropriate artist, school, period, etc.

C. Discuss and illustrate the two or three pieces that make the best stylistic comparisons with this piece. Indicate what distinctive qualities this piece has in relation to them in terms of style, technique, condition, documentation, etc.

D. Provide a list of all relevant works of art, whether copies, variants or other closely similar compositions, pointing out the relationship to each work named.

VII. State how the work of art complements the existing Museum collections or how it fills a gap.

VIII. Explain your plans for exhibiting and publishing the piece.

IX. Give the history of the piece, all known provenance with traditional documentation, when available. Include any hearsay evidence or traditional provenance, with source.

Recommended Purchase—Curator's Report—*cont*.

X. Give any significant archaeological information.

XI. List all published references, pointing out those of greatest importance. Also include any expert advice sought or volunteered from outside the Museum.

XII. Give a resume of your reasons for deciding to recommend the piece, being candid as to its strengths and weaknesses, its rarity of quality, technique, type, etc. Mention any problem outstanding that could affect the decision to buy.

XIII. Tell how long you have known of the piece and give a history of negotiations.

XIV. If possible give recent market prices for comparable works of art.

XV. Financial considerations

    A. If the object is to be purchased, state the price _____

    B. State the name of the fund if you recommend that a specific fund be used.

    C. If the object is to be acquired by exchange, specify M.M.A. object(s) involved, including accession number(s), valuation and status of de-accessioning.

    D. Specify any anticipated additional expenses:

Transportation $ _____ Insurance $ _____
  Sender to pay _____ Sender to pay _____
  M.M.A. to pay _____ M.M.A. to pay _____

Installation $ _____ Restoration $ _____

Other $ _____
    E. State any conditions attached to the purchase. State chances for bargaining.

conservation of the resources on which they draw. Similarly, the collecting of technological artefacts should not, where possible, lead to the destruction of the site and related material of significance, when other means for their conservation *in situ* are practicable.

Acquisition of specimens

Having formulated its collecting policy and agreed the acceptable sources of specimens, the next task is to clarify the means by which the acquisition of specimens may be achieved. The principal mechanisms by which museums acquire artefacts are gift, purchase or bequest, while for natural history specimens it is more often by direct or indirect collection. All can present increasingly formidable legal and moral problems, but despite the tendency for UNESCO to include natural history specimens in the category of cultural property, the problems posed by them are at present the least intractable. Indeed, the main difficulties experienced in the collecting of natural history specimens are those concerned with the legitimacy of the authority under which the collecting is, or was, undertaken. One view, albeit extreme, is that any specimen collected during a period of Colonial rule has been acquired illegally and that neither the museum nor a private collector seeking to sell such a specimen possesses 'good title'. Other problems stem from the increasingly complex laws intended to conserve threatened species and the need for the vendor/donor to prove to the Curator that the material offered to the museum has been obtained before the introduction of the relevant legislation, or had been acquired legally since then. To take an example, for birds' eggs this is often well-nigh impossible and the temptation to fence eggs which have been illegally acquired, by a process of 'topping up' a genuine private collection formed shortly before the regulations came into force, is self-evident. Indeed the 'topping up' of ancestral collections of works of art is not unheard of and provenances cannot always be accepted at their face value. The museum has to take all reasonable precautions to ensure that the specimens which it is acquiring have been obtained by the owner legally, and that its own collecting activities do not contravene either individual property rights or relevant legislation in the country of origin.

Similarly, the acquisition of 'good title' is of crucial importance in acquiring artefacts and the museum can only make acquisitions on this basis, exercising the utmost good faith. Thus the vendor/donor must himself not only possess good title but the transfer of ownership must not contravene any legislation or statutory controls. Both of these factors will vary from country to country, as do the limitations on their effective lives, so that materials stolen during the Napoleonic Wars do not present any legal problems today when bought and sold, while the status of material stolen during World War II will depend upon which country it was stolen from and the country in which it is located today. It is for the vendor to establish that he has good title

---

Dear

1. The Metropolitan Museum of Art in New York is considering the purchase of the following work of art which, to the best of our knowledge, is unpublished (photograph attached as Appendix I).

    a) Subject _____

    b) Material _____

    c) Dimensions _____

    d) Condition _____

2. In this form letter we should like to ask whether you, your ministry or service, have any information concerning the provenance or previous ownership of the described work of art.

3. We would appreciate hearing from you at your earliest convenience. If after 45 days we have received no reply from you, we shall assume you have no information concerning the above mentioned work of art.

4. At your early convenience, we would appreciate the return of the enclosed photograph.

Very truly yours,

Ashton Hawkins
Secretary

before entering into a contract of sale, but *caveat emptor* applies and the wise museum, when making major purchases, will seek specific assurances from the vendor, backed if necessary with documentary evidence, and will enter into a formal contract with him. The moral problems posed by the acquisition of artefacts which have, at some time in their history, been the subjects of illegal acts must be assessed by the museum in accordance with the particular merits of the case in hand if the vendor can nevertheless prove good title. The limitations will depend upon the laws effective at each stage and it can be argued that as the guardian of the public interest the museum must behave strictly in accordance with the law as it is, no more and no less, and not, perhaps, as the over-scrupulous Curator might wish it to be. The question of balancing legality and morality when the passage of legislation is so much slower than the rate of development of informed opinion remains highly controversial, and it is always essential that governing bodies are fully aware of all contingent facts when deciding upon all acquisition.

The Metropolitan Museum, like the J. Paul Getty Museum and an increasing number of museums with dynamic collecting programmes, has, in the last decade, become particularly sensitive to the problems posed by illicit exports and when an object is offered to it without a clear provenance or plausible history, a formal letter is sent to the appropriate bodies in the possible country (countries) of origin. If no objections are raised, or after at least 45 days, no reply is received, the Metropolitan Museum assumes that all is well and it proceeds with the purchase.

On the other hand, there is a growing body of legal precedents in the USA for the intervention of the Courts in cases of maladministration of musem collections and unwise financial operations by trustees. Furthermore, the tax status of a 'not-for-profit' museum will ultimately depend upon the faithfulness with which it carries out its approved mission statement. In this context the Museums & Galleries Commission, in its Museum Registration Scheme, makes it a condition of registration that the collections may not be mortgaged, but the question of those collections without special protection being already *de facto* part of the general assests and thus collateral for the borrowings of local authorities, universities, hospitals, orphanages, almshouses and other similar museum authorities, for which their museum functions are secondary, remains. Indeed, the problem of collections vested in trustees whose prime responsibilities are not the holding of musem collections in kind has not been adequately addressed within the UK.

Additional problems are posed by copyright and *droits de suite* which some would wish to be made inalienable. In making an acquisition the museum should always seek to acquire the copyright but if this is not owned by the vendor/donor the governing body should be informed of the limitations placed upon the museum's freedom of action by making such an acquisition. *Droits de suite* (resale royalty rights) are only applicable if a work of art subject to them is deaccessioned/sold in a country or state of the USA subject to the relevant legislation, and this may influence the place and means of disposal selected. Once again the museum acquiring a work of art subject to this liability should seek either to acquire the rights from the artist or his heirs at the time of acquisition or seek a waiver of his rights, whilst the attentions of his heirs, who under French and certain other legal systems have considerable authority, can present serious difficulties. The unfortunate truth is that a considerable proportion of modern materials, as used by twentieth-century artists for creating works of art, are highly susceptible to light damage and severe chemical changes, and when making an acquisition of a potentially unstable work of art, a legal disclaimer should, whenever possible be obtained from the artist or his estate. Furthermore, the lighting conditions created by certain types of fluorescent tubes can have a devasting impact on the aesthetic effect of works of art and, apart from the specific problems of metamerism, the artistic intentions of the creator cannot but be compromised. The legal implications have only begun to be explored, but the ethical and moral implications are obvious.

Collection ethics

Collection ethics, as against collecting ethics, have been the subject of much less detailed scrutiny in recent decades, although the ethics of conservation have attracted considerable attention and are discussed elsewhere. The holding of a collection is the acceptance of a trust on behalf of mankind, though the more immediate beneficiaries are those defined in legal terms. However, the legal rights of the community with regard to collections held on trust for its benefit vary enormously between different countries and they do not always correspond closely to the moral rights claimed for them. This is again in part due to the more rapid rate at which moral rights become accepted to their becoming enshrined in legislation. Consequently, the legal rights of the community remain often minimal, when sought in respect of specific problems, and its moral rights are closely limited to the extent to which it is prepared to carry out the trust. In other words, the whole community is, through its political representatives, a trustee and it has in this respect no more rights than its degree of commitment allows. In other words, the community, once it has taken on the responsibility for the housing and maintenance of an object in perpetuity is morally not at liberty to change its priorities and neglect that object at will, and the legal constraints placed upon trustees under British and British-based law are clear, but few legal precedents exist for the courts to enforce them.

Much more controversial are the rights of the creator of the object (*droit morale*), notwithstanding its acquisition by the museum, and not only to continue to enjoy the fruits of copyright. The artistic rights of the creator are claimed to be that his creation may not be willfully destroyed, mutilated or exhibited in such a condition or manner as to distort seriously his artistic intentions, without his specific consent, and the constraints which they impose upon the museum's collecting policy have been noted above. However, the ethical problems posed by the display of works of art which have been damaged and/or restored while in the possession of the museum are of great significance, since the maintenance of the integrity of the object is a fundamental objective of all museums. The problem becomes particularly acute with certain types of contemporary art, not least paintings with large areas of undifferentiated colour, when the creator can claim that a single scratch has distorted his artistic intentions beyond redemption. The artist is, unfortunately, not always the most dispassionate and disinterested of judges.

Disposals

Museums are archives of objects and, unless specific provision has otherwise been made in the formal act of acquisition (deed of gift, committee minute, etc.), the normal presumption is that the object has been acquired in perpetuity. The Cottesloe Committee Report (*Report of the Committee of Enquiry into the Sale of Works of Art by Public Bodies*, 1964) states:

'The basic principle upon which the law rests is that when private persons give property for public purposes the Crown undertakes to see that it is devoted to the purposes intended by the donor and to no others. When a work of art is given to a museum . . . the public thereby acquires rights in the object concerned and these rights cannot be set aside. The authorities of the museum are not the owners of such an object . . . they are merely responsible under the authority of the Courts, for carrying out the intentions of the donor. They cannot sell the object unless authorized to do so by the Courts, Charity Commissioners or the Minister of Education on behalf of the Courts.'

The Museums Association's *Code of Conduct for Museum Curators* is founded on this summary of the law and lays down:

There must always be a strong presumption against the disposal of specimens to which a museum has assumed formal title. Any form of disposal, whether by donation,

exchange, sale or destruction, requires the exercise of a high order of curatorial judgement and should be recommended to a curator's governing body only after full expert and legal advice has been taken.

This position is reinforced by the *Museums Association Code of Practice for Museum Authorities*:

. . .there must be a strong presumption against the disposal of any items in the collections of a museum. A number of the most important national museums and galleries are governed under Acts of Parliament which specifically prohibit the disposal of items in the collections, and, even where this is not the case, various severe restrictions are placed on the powers of dispose of items.

Disposals, or deaccessions, from a museum collection require a higher standard of care than that accorded to acquisitions. A school of thought, in opposition to that represented by the Metropolitan Museum, holds that museums must live with their mistakes as well as their successes, and the disposal of objects thought to be mistakes constitutes an attempt to falsify the historical record the museum was set up to document dispassionately.

However, setting aside these fundamental objections to disposals, the first question must be whether the museum has the legal right to do so. Many art museums do not have the legal power to dispose of items from their collections, no matter what were the particular conditions under which the individual acquisition was made.

Consequently some boards of trustees view the acceptance of a gift or bequest as an act of 'utmost good faith' and they see retrospective changes in the basis on which past gifts or bequests have been received as deeply offensive and inconsistent with the principles of 'utmost good faith'. Others allow only the disposal of purchases, not gifts or bequests, while others treat their collections as stock with the quality to be upgraded by a balanced programme of acquisitions and disposals as the opportunity arises ('trading up'). The arguments for employing the latter approach are perhaps easier to justify in the field of contemporary art than, for instance, in the Old Master field, and there is justification for the proposal to make such acquisitions into a holding collection for a period of say 20 years and then for the board to reconsider the acquisition before recommending its inclusion in the permanent collection. More recently the technique of deferred decision has been proposed for the collecting of technological artefacts when the relative importance of any particular item cannot be known until many years later when the overall pattern of technological innovation can be seen more clearly and the vast majority of examples will have been scrapped. For this purpose large warehouses are proposed, with the contents protected from the weather and little else, so that large quantities of specimens in good condition are always available for incorporation into the permanent collection, and surplus material, also in good condition and by then scarce, is available for sale at good prices, thereby funding the operation.

If the institution has the legal power to dispose of objects from its permanent collection much will depend upon the precise wording of the decision previously taken to acquire it and any conditions laid down by the vendor/donor. Unless there are overwhelming reasons for acting otherwise, it is always understood that any pecuniary gain stemming from a disposal is reserved for the acquisition of further material and no other purposes, and this principle is enshrined in the Museums & Galleries Commission Museum Registration Scheme. However, the mechanisms which have been evolved to enable disposals vary enormously and can take the form of gifts (appropriate, for example, in respect of natural history and archaeological material of little or no pecuniary value), exchange or part-exchange (particularly useful for study collections, but, more questionably, also used by some museums in the USA for the acquisition of works of art from the fine-art trade) or sale. In any such disposals the residual rights of the donor/vendor/creative artist must be safeguarded, as well as those of the institution as a legally constituted body and those of the community which it serves.

The recommendation in the *Code of Practice for Museum Authorities*, that 'objects should be offered first by exchange, gift or private treaty sale, to other museums before sale by public auction is considered' is flawed in that when Trustees dispose of an asset by sale, unless released from so doing by the terms of the trust, they are legally obliged to use their best endeavours to obtain the highest price. The difficulties often experienced by museums in the past in obtaining satisfactory valuations for private treaty sales have been highlighted by the sale of the Chatsworth drawings and paintings from the collection of the British Rail Pension Fund. The *prix d'ami*, even if agreed by both sides as not representing a true market price, is a dangerous course of action and could leave the Trustees open to legal action at a later date. Sale by auction, particularly of natural history, archaeological and ethnographical material, can also have the disastrous effect of separating objects from their documentation, but for museums and responsible private collectors bidding at an auction, proper documentation greatly increases the desirability and thus the value of the items, and it is in the best interests of the purchasers to maintain that documentation. Furthermore, sale by public auction – with the full identity of the vendor clearly stated in the catalogue and accompanying publicity – has the double advantage of making a potential museum vendor think twice about the adverse publicity likely to accrue, and of making the entire transaction public. Furthermore, charitable bodies raising money to assist museums in making acquisitions have every right to know when those museums have abrogated the trust placed in them, by selling items from their collections, just as it is a confidence trick to vire money from the funds set aside for purchasing specimens while at the same time seeking charitable grants to assist in making further purchases.

The public scandals which have stemmed from the disposal in the past of individual objects and collections have encouraged museums either to cloak their disposals in great secrecy (an approach likely to increase the risk of abuse, as well as the public outcry if or when they are made public) or to undertake the drafting of detailed policy documents well in advance of any specific disposals. One of the most recent and most thorough documents of this nature is the *Deaccessioning Policy* prepared by the Art Gallery of Ontario and its accompanying *Disposal Policy*, and the separation of deaccessioning (a curatorial decision) from disposal (an administrative function) is particularly valuable and is quoted below. Due to the high pecuniary values involved, and the public interest often created, the deaccessioning of works of art has attracted more attention than other fields. However, the increasingly high pecuniary values of many ethnographical, archaeological and natural history specimens invites caution and adoption of the control mechanisms evolved for works of art. The problem remains of the disposal and dispersal of museum collections which are uncurated, or have been poorly curated, so that the documentation is minimal or has been lost. All disposals from registered museums in the UK will in the future have to be referred to the Museums and Galleries Commission for advice and, presumably, after inspection, the neglect of a collection will be a factor taken into account by the Commission in formulating its advice and in seeking to protect the public interest. One of the most difficult decisions is the deaccessioning of an object and its transfer to those by whom it will be destroyed, in particular cult objects and human remains, and a consensus concerning the moral and ethical considerations has not yet been reached.

Deaccessioning policy

Introduction

The Art Gallery of Ontario has disposed of works of art in the past. The most significant recent instance was the sale of Pissarro's *Printemps, Temps Gris, Eragny* (1890) in 1972. Such deaccessioning was done in an orderly and responsible fashion with the full participation of staff, respective Collection Committees and the Board. Nevertheless, practice and procedure for deaccessioning have heretofore not been defined in a formal way as policy.

Deaccessioning

It should be understood that the term 'deaccession' as used by the Gallery does not necessarily mean sale. It does mean that the appropriate persons at the Gallery, that is the relevant collection committee and the Board, have concluded, with the aid of staff recommendations, that a work of art may be removed from the collection and be further considered for disposal by sale, exchange, etc. Before proceeding to deaccession a work of art, the Gallery should consider the alternative of offering the work on extended loan to a sister institution, preferably in Ontario. A work of art may be removed from the collection for a number of reasons.

(1) The work has no relevant place or useful purpose within the collecting, exhibiting, or research programmes of the Gallery.
(2) The work does not add significantly to the Gallery's holdings in its historical period or in its representation of a specific and could be disposed of in order to acquire another work which would add to the depth or scope of the collection.
(3) The work is truly a duplicate, as may be possible in the case of prints or so-called multiples.
(4) The work for some reason has deteriorated beyond usefulness.

It is important, however, that procedures for deaccessioning include a system of checks and balances to ensure that a proposal for deaccessioning be discussed from all points of view. While such a system must not be so extensive as to deter proposals, its purpose is to allow a review of all pertinent considerations such as:

(1) *Changing taste.* Deaccessioning must not be governed by current fashion or the individual taste of curators. Consideration must be given to the temporal nature of aesthetic judgements and changing taste in art historical and aesthetic evaluations.
(2) *Presentation/installation.* The presence of a pair of, or even several, similar works in the collection may not be a justification for deaccessioning. Such concentration may make not only a stronger statement for the artists, but allow a more handsome and telling installation.
(3) *Research use.* It is sometimes a rule of thumb referred to by collection committees when considering gifts that if we would exhibit a work of art we should accept it. The reverse – that if we do not use a work of art we should deaccession it – is not so clearly applied. The usefulness of a work may also be gauged in relation to the research function of a museum. While there can be no question regarding the importance of acquiring exhibitable and significant works of art, it would be a mistake to assume that works not on display are not important to the collection. A collection becomes increasingly important to scholars and other museums when it holds a group of significant works by a given artist, or that are representative of a period school, even if many of these are viewed only in the vaults. Building in depth should never be undermined by a deaccessioning policy which assumes that exhibition is the primary function, and those works which appear to be less important or unexhibitable should be disposed of. Such works might better be sent on loan to sister institutions until they are needed.
(4) *The fabric of the collection.* The collection has a character, it is made up of many separate collections and collection minds, and reflects the changing taste of different periods and individuals. It is, as a whole, an entity reflecting the community, curators, private collectors (Walker, Presgrave, Wood, etc.) and other organizations the Canadian National Endowment (CNE), who have contributed to its growth. The pictures acquired, both 'good' and 'bad', all document the history of collecting in Toronto and the influence of these collections is an important part of the history of the development of art in Canada. The fabric of the collection should be respected as having integrity and importance in its own right.
(5) *Historical perspective.* This is not unrelated to the question of taste but is specifically concerned with the problem of how long it takes for a work of art to find its proper place within the history of art. For the gallery this is a consideration which might apply to such modern non-Canadian works which fall outside the Paris–New York mainstream tradition (for example, the English paintings acquired in the 1950s). That such works may currently be little exhibited is in itself not a sufficient criterion for deciding their future.

Steps for deaccessioning

The steps taken in deaccessioning are as follows:

(1) A proposal for deaccessioning can originate only with the Curator responsible for the area of the collection in question.
(2) The Curator recommends the deaccessioning to the Chief Curator and the Director. If all three decide that the matter should be considered further the following steps are taken:
  (a) The Gallery ascertains that there are no legal or time restrictions against disposal of the work and that the disposal will not contravene cultural property legislation. Where there are no legal restrictions to deaccessioning, the Gallery will consult with the donor or, if the donor is not living, the donor's heirs or legal representatives.
  (b) The recommendations for deaccessioning by the appropriate Curator is presented to a committee comprised of the Director, Chief Curator and all curators.
  (c) Only upon receiving unanimous approval by the above committee is the recommendation for deaccessioning presented to the appropriate Collection Committee.
  (d) The Curator makes a presentation to the appropriate Collection Committee. The presentation

must include an evaluation of the work. If the Curator estimates the work to be worth more than $2000, two outside appraisals should be presented.
(e) The Collection Committee decides on the basis of the preceding presentation whether to forward the recommendation for approval by the Board.
(f) The Chairman of the Collection Committee, with the participation of the responsible Curator, presents the recommendation for deaccessioning to the Board. Approval by the Board requires a two-thirds majority vote of members present.

Disposal policy

Methods of disposal are: outright sale, credit against future purchase, gift and destruction. If disposal is by outright sale, sale by public auction is preferable, but other recipients may be another institution, a private individual or a dealer. If disposal is not by public auction, sister institutions, especially in Canada, should be given preference over private individuals or dealers. Only public institutions may be the recipients of gifts of deaccessioned works. Given the range of options, the responsible Curator would seem to be in the best position to explore possibilities and to undertake negotiations.

At no time should a staff member, Board member, or anyone connected with the Gallery in any formal way, including membership of a committee or under a contract, etc., be permitted to acquire directly from the Gallery a deaccessioned work of art.

Steps of disposal
The steps taken in disposal are as follows:

(1) In order to protect the Gallery from criticism, authority for the method of disposal of the work of art be granted by the Director, the Chief Curator and the appropriate Collection Committee.
(2) If the method of disposal is other than auction (or destruction) the negotiated terms of disposal (sales, exchange, etc.) must be approved by the Chief Curator and the Director.
(a) If the work of art is valued at less than $25 000 and the negotiated terms fall below the evaluation as determined by the two outside and disinterested appraisals as provided in step (d) of the deaccessioning policy, further approval is required from the appropriate Collection Committee.

(b) If the work of art is appraised above $25 000 and the negotiated terms fall below the appraisal as provided in step (d) of the deaccessioning policy, approval of the Board is required.
(3) After the proposal for disposal has been approved as per the appropriate preceding steps the Corporate Secretary reviews and approves the exact terms of the sale or exchange, and in the case of a consignment sale such terms are then set forth in a letter of agreement signed by the Corporate Secretary on behalf of the Gallery.

All proceeds realized from an act of deaccessioning and disposal must be credited to the art purchase fund. Prior consideration should be given to allocate such proceeds to the collection area from which the deaccessioning proposal originated.

All acts of deaccessioning and disposal will be reported at the meeting immediately following the General Meeting of the Art Gallery of Ontario.

Bibliography

AMERICAN ASSOCIATION OF MUSEUMS (1978), *Museum Ethics*, American Association of Museums, Washington, DC

ART GALLERY OF ONTARIO (June 1983), 'Deaccessioning and disposal policies of the art gallery of Ontario', *The International Journal of Museum Management and Curatorship*, **2**(2), 204–208

ASSOCIATION OF ART MUSEUM DIRECTORS (1981), *Professional Practices in Art Museums – Report of the Ethics and Standards Committee*, AAMD, Savannah

DETROIT INSTITUTE OF ARTS (1979), *Guidelines for Professional Practices* The Detroit Institute of Arts, Detroit

ELSON, A. *et al.*, *Statement on Standards for Sculptural Reproduction and Preventive Measures to Combat Unethical Casting in Bronze*

HOVING, T. P. F. (May 1973), 'A policy statement from the Met', *Museum News*, **51**(9), 43–45

HOVING, T. P. F. (1975), *The Chase, the Capture: Collecting at the Metropolitan*, New York, approved by the College Art Association of America, 27 April 1974

MERYMAN, J. H. (1977), *Legal Aspects of Museum Operations: Principles and Code of Curatorial Conduct*, Stanford

TABORSKY, E. (December 1982), 'The socio-structural role of the museum'. *The International Journal of Museum Management and Curatorship*, **1**(4), 339–345

51

Researching geological collections

Philip S. Doughty

This chapter is about the curatorial method as it applies to geological collections as entities. It is not a review of the scientific method and its various research applications to museum material – that is the basic stuff of scientific advance, and not an exclusive museum preserve.

Philosophical considerations

The whole area of collection management is aimless without some founding principles; most museums have written collecting policies but no equivalent statement on their philosophy, though one can not exist without the other.

Collections can be viewed in a variety of ways: as a finite number of specimens, allocated to stated taxa, derived from defined areas, and rocks of given age, collected by a stated collector, at a given time, worth a specified price for insurance or replacement purposes and used by academics to develop geological thinking in academic papers. Such concepts are readily embraced by recording formats (Museum Documentation Association, 1980a,b) and can be digested in computing systems. Such records are basic management tools for museums in structured, routine work. Standard curatorial practices essential to good collection management of geological materials are now stated authoritatively (Brunton *et al*, 1985) and the inexperienced geological curator has a growing body of guidance to hand (Knell and Taylor, 1989).

Curatorial expertise lies outside these highly structured systems. Hunches, intuition and other supposedly indefinable qualities come into play. In reality they synthesize a large mass of detail and derive from the refinement of skills and practice by generations of talented geological curators. Quality of collections management testifies their skills, but these have never been discussed in detail, perhaps because they are considered too specialized a brand of common sense or too mundane to be worthy of statement. But even curators with the most highly developed skills in large museums, where long-term continuity of curation has obviated the need for written analysis of procedures, are now making invaluable statements of role and giving reminders that procedures have evolved for sound reasons (Embrey, 1987).

The difference between the experienced curator and the competent practitioner is his concept of collections, the adoption of a more metaphysical approach. Geological specimens are not mere caches of natural objects. They represent ideas, concepts, hypotheses, expressions of interest, trophies of the search and reflections of the development of precepts which required some material expression. A collection is part of the life of an individual or like-minded group, an enthusiasm, a passion, an intellectual quest of which objects are an essential part. Collectors prize their specimens highly and a good curator will endeavour to discover the nature of that acquisitive compulsion. If a collection is not seen as the product of some process and motivation then much of what it represents is lost or never sought. Whether museums like it or not, their geological collections are also part of the history of ideas (Waterston, 1979; Medawar, 1979, pp. 29–30).

The way in which a collection or specimen is perceived conditions the kind of information gathered about it. A limited perception confines observation and almost always qualifies the future uses of material. Yet no curator can foresee the full long-term potential of his collections; concepts crucial to coming generations of users will be missed or imperfectly grasped. A good curator will try to minimize such omissions by being constantly aware of cultural and technological developments and alert to the latent possibilities of a collection. Such awareness gives collections strength and character.

Receiving the collection

In accepting a collection, the transfer process should become the responsibility of the curator who will take it into his care. The suggested course of action combines the experience of curators of a number of large collections, and is a protection against loss of information during the transfer.

Where possible the collection should move in its original furniture without disturbance. The furniture may have permanent labels on doors, drawers, liners or side panels. It may be of a standard pattern for its period or it may be custom-built. It may be expensive or cheap. What appears to be trivial detail may ultimately prove to be important.

The arrangement of the collection should be carefully examined and maintained undisturbed through the initial period of inspection. If it has to be disturbed, as when specimens are in packing cases and cardboard boxes, keep as accurate a record as possible. Even when it is known that someone other than the collector did the packing, follow the procedure because the packing is likely to be systematic and will have retained elements of a former arrangement. From such information the collector's views on taxonomy and classification may emerge, or his preferred arrangement for his method of working or collection management, both useful factors in assessing him. Geographical or stratigraphical arrangements in early collections, particularly if they are unpublished, might indicate early pioneering research. Collectors tend to isolate material of special interest, material on loan, and incorporated collections, all revealed in arrangement. The keeping of duplicate collections may suggest exchange arrangements which might be sought in documentation.

The nature of the wrappings is important and may help in fixing the earliest date of packing and something of the intellectual and academic environment of the collector. Note titles of newspapers, but pay particular attention if pages from notebooks, discarded drawings, pages of learned journals, outside correspondence, page proofs or even unpaid bills are used. Notes and markings should be elevated to the status of labels. Unwrap carefully so that loose slips enclosed with specimens are kept with them; it may be difficult or impossible to match them up later. If wrapping has been poor or disturbed in storage so that labels have become dissociated, identification sometimes allows re-matching, as do label shapes and corresponding marks or the nature of an adhesive and its failure. If there is no immediate relationship store the specimens and labels from the one container together for a time. Information from undisturbed parts of a collection often gives new insight, making at least a partial rescue possible.

The specimen

Geological specimens differ from most others in natural history. Unlike biological specimens they are not merely a convenient but poor substitute for the living organism, but the ideal expression of its nature. Only the context of its finding is absent in the cabinet specimen, and the good collector ensures that those details are known, or the expert geologist can infer them. The scope for individuality of specimens in collection terms may appear limited, but this is rarely true and the treatment of specimens by some collectors is highly idiosyncratic.

First look for surface data: numbers, letter/number combinations, identification labels, paper pointers, colour-coded stickers, even newspaper clippings. The mechanics of data association are important. Information may be engraved into the specimen or written on its surface, or on a prepared area such as a ground flat or painted panel or a label stuck to the specimen. Collectors have strong preferences in these matters and vary them only when the nature of the material is unsuitable for their favoured method. Numbers and letter/number combinations indicate the existence of notebooks, registers, ledgers, catalogues or indexes which must be found to give the specimens meaning and value. Handwriting is treated with labels in the following section. Newspaper cuttings may relate specimens to specific events or indicate the breadth of the collector's reading. The complexity of marking is a measure of the degree to which a collection was worked.

The style of preparation of specimens in matrix is useful, sometimes unique. If the matrix has been trimmed, note whether it has been done with hammer and chisel, pliers, vice, saw or some other means. There is often a favoured 'finished' form of a specimen such as a rectangle, a rectangle with rounded corners, a tendency to follow the outline of form, or a preference for total extraction or as near as can be achieved, bearing in mind the nature of the material. Some results are highly distinctive, particularly in thoroughly developed specimens with marks such as chisel courses, needle courses, picked surfaces, etched surfaces and those left in deliberate patterns or textures.

Methods and materials of repair are also informative. The adhesive used must be recorded: brown organic glue, shellac, celluloid, coloured sealing wax, tallow, paraffin wax, beeswax and even bituminous compounds were used by early collectors as adhesives. Wax, plaster, glue-soaked cotton wadding and other absorbent and pliable materials were, with plaster of Paris, popular fillers. Shields (1984) and Rixon (1976) give information on more recent adhesives and a valuable summary statement is given by Brunton *et al* (1985)

Since the middle of the present century, materials

and equipment used in geological technology have become more standardized nationally and, to some measure, internationally. This has not resulted in standardized presentation because materials science has produced so many new products that the possible variations and permutations are now greater than ever. Laboratories now keep records of treatments, so documentation exists to assist the curator. In the case of amateurs, limited access to technical facilities imposes many of the constraints common to the nineteenth and first half of the twentieth century.

Museums already keep other geological media such as microscope thin sections, other microscope mounts, peels, casts, moulds, electron microscopy stubs, specimen preparations used in analytical procedures such as X-ray diffraction and fluorescence, and many more. All these methods lend themselves to variations, and individuality can still emerge when the same principles of examination are applied. Other technical treatments are still used on a rule-of-thumb basis for want of thorough research into conservation of geological materials (Howie, 1979), although there are some indications of a changing climate (Crowther and Collins, 1987). Personal preferences show clearly, particularly in old collections, and most treatment was limited to the consolidation of fragile and friable specimens with thin solutions of familiar adhesives such as organic glues, gelatin, shellac and size. Waxes (North *et al.,* 1941) and various varnishes were sometimes used in special circumstances.

There is still no formal history of geological techniques, although Whybrow (1985) has made a first attempt. There is a need to fill this gap. The creation of chronologies of materials, processes and methods will in turn be applied to new work on collections.

The label

Original labels are the most fruitful single source of information about collections; most collections in the UK have most data in the form of original labels (Doughty, 1981). Regardless of kind, all labels should be kept.

Label materials, form and presentation should be examined minutely. Pay particular attention to the paper of plain labels noting such matters as type, weight, tint, watermarks, dimensions and any other characteristics that might be useful features of recognition (Higham, 1968; Britt, 1970). Printed labels should be photocopied and a file of types established. Dimensions, the nature of printed lines and decorations, printed titles, and print fount are all important. For large collections, second and subsequent printings of labels are often subtly, but recognizably, different due to changes of paper, line

detail, print weight or slight variations in fount size or face. Often there are several versions of the label for a single specimen, indicating events such as the supplanting of a field label by a cabinet label, and both may be accompanied by display labels. Display labels are a study in themselves (North *et al.,* 1941).

Handwriting is of the greatest importance. It requires careful analysis where fine judgements may require expert opinion, but most handwriting is identifiable (Hilton, 1956; Harrison, 1981; Cleevely, 1982). The style of most individuals is variable and writing on the confined area of a label usually differs significantly from that of the same individual in, say, correspondence. Hand printing on labels is normally very different from the writing of the same person, although key construction habits often betray the source. Specimens of writing and printing for each collector, preferably dated and showing the range of variation, should be photocopied and a file for individual collectors compiled. Files should also be compiled for unidentified collectors whose identity may eventually be established and the lead back to the specimens secured.

Frequently, labels and specimens are related by a system other than the ubiquitous card tray, as when card, glass or wooden tablets are used, or closed boxes of a variety of kinds. Tablets are frequently hand made by or for the collector and many made their own individual boxes. If space permits, there is much to be said for retaining specimens and labels on their tablets and for keeping containers.

Labels were primarily used as identification markers and reference to other information is normally slight. Locality is the next most common item, followed by a period or formation name, and sometimes a date. Some modern curators discount early identifications which are 'wrong', but to appraise a collection properly it is worth establishing whether a name was wrong by the standards of the day, perhaps indicating a naive or inexperienced collector, or whether it was accurate or justifiable by contemporary standards. If an experienced collector consistently misnames relatively small numbers of his specimens, his identification media may have been misleading, or his judgement was contrary to that of his peers. In that case it must be respected and his material examined in this light.

A collector's command of identification is important. It reveals his concept of names, access to literature, association with other collectors and ability to critically blend opinions. Many early names were drawn from rapidly advancing concepts of classification which were later modified or abandoned. To determine an acceptable modern interpretation of these names, not merely a modern name of the specimen, is mainly a curatorial preoccupation often without a ready solution, although there is a limited literature to help.

Minerals

Many names on minerals in old collections have been abandoned or have slipped from usage. The second edition of Hey's *An Index of Mineral Species and Varieties arranged Chemically* (Hey, 1962) and its subsequent appendices (Hey, 1963; Hey and Embrey, 1974) is an invaluable source for obsolete names. Other useful references are Dana's *System of Mineralogy* (Dana, 1892), Chester's dictionary (Chester 1896), English's *Descriptive List of the New Minerals 1892–1938* (English, 1939), largely a compilation from other handy sources, and most recently Embrey and Fuller's manual (Embrey and Fuller, 1980). A useful current source of name derivations covering all the common species is given by Duda and Rejl (1986) and a more limited source is Mitchell (1979).

Rocks

Until recently there has been less interest in compilations of rock names. The Wernerian system was widely applied in the eighteenth and early nineteenth centuries. Jameson's account (Jameson, 1808) gives all Werner's German terms and his own English equivalents. Most of the rock names survived into the post-Wernerian age but there is no useful summary. Early primers such as Phillips *A Guide to Geology* (1835) gave neat outlines of classifications then current, and Jukes' *Students' Manual of Geology* (1862) gives more names and insight into development over the intervening quarter century. The failure of petrologists to adopt any single classification provoked Kinahan (1873) to write *A Handy Book of Rock Names*, valuable but not fully indexed. Better indexed, including a locality listing, is Von Cotta's *Rocks Classified and Described* (Von Cotta, 1893) which includes French, German and English synonyms for rock names with reference to roots and name sources, but it omits some of the earliest names.

One recent geological dictionary. Tomkeieff's *Dictionary of Petrology* (Tomkeieff, 1983), is as near comprehensive as such a work can be with an impressive citation list of first uses. This and *English Rock Terms* (Arkell and Tomkeieff, 1953) which describes the legacy of names from miners, masons and quarrymen, resolve most rock-name problems.

Fossils

There are 50 times more fossil than mineral names and most museum collections are dominated by fossils (Doughty, 1981). By 1825, fewer than 1000 names had been applied to British fossils and by 1850 around 4000 species had been described. All early names applied to fossils collected during or before this time are interesting and a proportion is important. With new names appearing rapidly from about 1840 synonymies could not hope to keep palaeontologists abreast of developments and a number of summaries appeared, now of value to the curator: e.g. Morris (1845), Bronn (1848–1849), Sedgwick and M'Coy (1854) and Ethridge (1888). Sherborn's *Index Animalium* (1902–1933) for names to 1850 is excellent and Neave's *Nomenclator Zoologicus* (Neave, 1939 onwards) is an extremely useful names checklist. Huge summaries became less relevant from 1870 when the *Zoological Record* met the need. The last great summary of genera was by Zittel (1895) before the massive redescription of invertebrates now substantially completed in the various volumes of the *Treatise on Invertebrate Paleontology* (Moore and Teichert, 1953 onwards). But, for many taxa, the only recourse for the curator is to the systematic study of material and literature.

Stratigraphy

Stratigraphic terminology is the most untidy area of geological nomenclature. Good editors now require the precise definition of stratigraphic boundaries in contributions to geological journals in an attempt to establish some fixed points in the terminological chaos. Lack of definition of lithostratigraphy and the mixing of chronostratigraphic and biostratigraphic concepts by many early authors have left a legacy of insoluble problems. Practising stratigraphers have made valiant efforts to provide standards. The *International Stratigraphic Guide* (Hedberg, 1976) and *A Guide to Stratigraphic Procedure* (Holland et al, 1978) by the Geological Society of London are the basis of most current practice. The problem for curators, however, remains the curation of the mass of early material. Original literature, vast in extent, is summarized in the *Stratigraphic Correlation Charts* of the Geological Society of London (1971–1980) for the British Isles and the *Lexique Stratigraphique International* (CNRS, 1956 onwards) on the world scale. For other useful literature see Brunton *et al.*, (1985).

Misidentifications of strata have some curatorial uses; many of the local problems were resolved by known dates, so that collections from wrongly designated strata can be time defined.

Important errors can arise from misinterpretation of some labels, particularly those of the nineteenth and early twentieth centuries stating 'type' or 'type specimen'. Curators have published specimens to which such labels adhere as having type status. The typology of animal specimens including fossil material has been defined by rules only since 1901 when the *International Code of Zoological Nomenclature*

(International Commission on Zoological Nomenclature, 1985) was first adopted. A useful summary statement on primary and secondary types can be found in Brunton *et al.* (1985). For some insight into the establishing and operation of the code, see Heppel (1981). The naming of fossil plants falls within the rules of the *International Code of Botanical Nomenclature* (Stafleu and Voss, 1978), itself not without operational problems (Tjaden, 1981). All subsequent specimens with type markings should be thoroughly investigated against original literature.

There are, of course, hazards in type recognition when original drawings or photographs are poor, text numbers for plates wrongly given, images reversed, drawings idealized or prints retouched to eliminate imperfections in the original material, or the wrong registration number quoted for the figured specimen (Edmonds, 1977). Coloured stickers on specimens can also indicate special status. It is worth assembling similarly marked specimens to see if a common factor emerges, and checking literature if the collector has left no notes.

Much of the work on the housing of specimens, their appearance and treatment and their associated labels is an attempt to establish a unique identity for a collection. The combination of details discussed give a particular 'style', often sufficiently distinctive for specimens to be recognized outside their usual context. Seasoned curators often distinguish elements of collections familiar to them in other museums and such judgement can often be corroborated. The recognition of collections, collectors, their competence, significance, dates, balances of interest, contacts and publications are the fundamentals of curation and of research based on collections.

Associations of collections

Many collectors store information on specimens in a catalogue or register kept remotely from the collection, employing a unique notation on the specimen to link it to its catalogue entry. For a geological collection treated in this way to have any scientific worth, the catalogue must accompany it. This is one example of data linking and data security, important aspects of curation treated fully by Palmer (1977). There may also be notebooks describing the sections from which specimens were collected with dates and further details. Diaries of serious collectors are invaluable, as are their commonplace books. Nebulous verbal geography can become exact landscape features from marked maps, and annotations of books in collectors' working libraries can assert an attitude otherwise elusive. Inscriptions on papers and books indicate correspondents, associates, collaborators and friends, while sketches, diagrams and correspondence may all relate to

collecting activities. Portraits of the collectors, and their geological photographs, negatives or transparencies are becoming increasingly important. How far to press for associated material to be included in a donation is up to the curator and interested archival organizations. Papers which are meaningless without the collection should obviously accompany it. Display potential must also be considered and personalia from working materials and equipment to items of clothing, suitably presented, can mutely state what a dozen labels never can.

The acquisition and allocation of material associated with collections is not simply a passive activity. When the collector is giving or selling material in his lifetime the good curator should actively seek associated non-specimen material through personal contact and detailed discussion. The curator must always bear the personal sensitivities of the donor in mind but, since the serious collector has a vested interest in ensuring the status of his collection, he is likely to readily identify and deposit associated materials.

The biography

For a rounded view of a collector, to help to measure his achievements, the basic information on file should include: full name; dates of birth and death; names of parents (with dates); full list of brothers and sisters; education (including all schools and other institutions); qualifications; marriage date; full name of partner and offspring; residence (particularly that for the period of active collecting); socio-economic status; personal, career, institutional and society memberships; honours; lectures and papers given and published; professional associations and friends (geological associates for amateurs); travels (including all formative influences as well as collecting excursions); collections (with the history of dispersals); whereabouts of other material (for example books and manuscripts); eponymy; obituaries, biographies, and assessments; and portraits. If the collector is alive or recently dead, this kind of information is relatively easy to gather but when researching old collections obituaries may have to be sought in journals or newpapers.

The best compilation of biographical information on the better known collectors is Sarjeant's *Geologists and the History of Geology* (Sarjeant, 1980, 1987). The work of Lambrecht and Quenstedt (1938) still remains useful as does that of Thackray (1972) on collectors who died between 1850 and 1900. The *World Directory of Mineralogists* (Cesbron, 1962) is also a useful source and any collectors with botanical interests might be sought in Desmond (1977). Prominent scientists may have entries in the *Dictionary of National Biography* (Stephen and Lee) and *Dictionary of Scientific Biography* (Gillispie, 1981). Otherwise, registry documents are a starting point from which other leads can be pursued. The genealogist and local historian can often be allies. When collections were the property of institutions, histories are harder to compile but sources are more plentiful.

Locating collections

Many museums and other type repositories have fulfilled their obligations under the international codes and published catalogues and lists of their type holdings. But these catalogues appear in such different forms and are so diversely published that many are difficult to trace. Bassett's (1975) bibliography indexes such catalogues for Britain. Cleevely (1983) expanded the list, and a supplement by Bassett of his original work is imminent.

Until recently, the problems of locating collections or elements of dispersed collections of named collectors or institutions have been substantial. Sherborn's (1940) compilation was useful, but small and isolated. This paucity of key information was recognized as a major barrier to professional progress and an initiative taken by the Geological Curator's Group in the 1970s spawned major curatorial efforts. The most important single product is *World Palaeontological Collections* by Cleevely (1983), an index of over 5000 collections. Of UK interest is Appendix 2 of Doughty (1981), a listing of 800 UK geological collections, and other collections have parts of their transfer histories in Chalmers-Hunt (1976). A collections' research movement in UK museums has been an enduring legacy of this work and information on natural science collections including geology is being steadily published. The *Register of Natural Science Collections in North-west England* (Hancock and Pettitt, 1981) appeared first and has been followed by collections information from north-east England (Davis and Brewer, 1986), Yorkshire and Humberside (Hartley *et al.*, 1987) and Scotland (Stace *et al.*, 1988). Other projects are in progress. Embrey and Symes' (1987) *tour de force* on the *Minerals of Cornwall and Devon* includes a model account of collectors and underlines the importance of commercial dealers, a group often overlooked.

Of the two UK seminal collections the *History of Collections of the British Museum* (1904) mentions the major collections up to its publication and subsequent reports refer to important later additions, but there is no equivalent statement for the British Geological Survey collections.

For Europe, Burchard's (1986) *Mineral Museums of Europe* breaks new ground but omits the smaller museums, and on the world stage there is the *World Directory of Mineral Collections* (Zwann and Paterson, 1977).

Elusive collections often yield to an enquiry in the *Geological curator*, a Geological curators' Group publication full of collection information. For the principles underlying the location of collections, by far the most useful statement is that of Torrens (1974). But a collection described in the literature as 'lost' may not actually be so unless its complete destruction was witnessed. Edmonds' (1977) cautionary tale of John Phillips' collection and Hill's (1938–1941) account of James Thomson's collection relate how collections were described by authors as lost when they had largely survived.

The scope of collection research

The caricaturish view that curatorial research involves human trivia in the recording of antiquarian trivia is difficult to sustain. The importance of apparent trifles is readily illustrated by Torrens (1979) and Forbes (1979) in a case presented to the International Commission on Zoological Nomenclature in 1974 for the designation of a particular specimen as the lectotype for a species of fossil ammonite. The identification of the original specimen as that seen by an earlier authority depended on an unbroken chain of evidence involving the recognition and dating of a mounting tablet, the survival of an original label and the verification of the handwriting on it, the survival of a paper note added to the tablet, a note on the reverse of the specimen indicating that it was the specimen seen by the original authority, and an annotation of a printed book by a subsequent owner of the collection whose handwriting was recognized. A knowledge of transfer history of the specimen and a knowledge of the glue patterns helped. On the basis of evidence presented by the curator, the specimen he identified, and not the one originally proposed for designation, was accepted by the Commission in their ruling. This case is unusual only in the length of the chain of evidence; there are many similar examples involving a greater diversity of material evidence. It illustrates forcefully the range of skills essential to the curators of significant, well used, collections.

Almost all curators in the study and evaluation of collections and collection information uncover strong potential leads. Good documentation may indicate a last known residence for an unlocated collection and many examples have been discovered in attics, garages, outhouses, garden rockeries and walls. Relatives may help in locating documentation and bibliographical information for collections accepted in the absence of a specialist curator. Material with unexpected locality data collected by a reputable geologist positively demands investigation. Collections occasionally yield rare or fine specimens subsequently shown to be of great research or aesthetic potential, requiring a thorough check of the original site. Loosely stated locality data for mines, quarries, cuttings, and drainage schemes that later prove to have yielded interesting or valuable material need more precise definition. Collections, on investigation, often prove to be incomplete in the sense that the collector was unable to complete an intended project and where such collections are accepted further work and development are required. Thus many of the curatorial aspects of collection research are not simply cabinet, bench or laboratory pursuits, but require structured programmes of fieldwork to establish or re-establish.

The thorough researching of collections makes their academic, cultural and social significance clear, and their importance emerges often quite startlingly. The wealth of the collection tradition and its contribution to our cultural life is now giving rise to revealing social histories which still struggle with the generalized view (Allen 1976; Barber, 1980), but undoubtedly the collection movement has changed our perception of the world we inhabit in important, sometimes radical, ways. Writing about the individual careers of geologist collectors is an established tradition, but the erudite and great, the Lyells, Darwins and Murchisons have been favoured. There are now signs that other ranks are being deemed worthy of notice (Fountaine, 1980).

The collections themselves rarely appear in any detail in such writing. This is a major flaw, for specimens are not merely a product of scientific exploration but part of the essential fabric of the science of geology (Doughty, 1981, p. 3). A collector can make a major contribution without ever writing a paper of note (James, 1986). The bias of historians to written sources, a condition described as 'papyrophilia' by Torrens (1988), has already produced such omissions (Laudan, 1976, 1987). Faced with this situation curators should never be mere guardians of collections but should champion the concepts they present.

There have been notable contributions, however, based firmly on the significance of specimens (Colbert, 1968; Desmond 1975; Stearn, 1981) and in the case of the Piltdown forgery a complete text is based on a handful of specimens and their implications (Weiner, 1955). Occasionally geological memoirs and autobiographies transmit something of the thrill of discovery of significant specimens (Sternberg, 1930; Simpson, 1934; Colbert, 1980) but they are rare, though Embrey and Symes (1987) *Minerals of Cornwall and Devon* revels in specimens, collectors and collections. It is a model of readable scholarship, unique in its field. The palaeontologist curator Stephen Gould's inspiration is firmly in the field of material geology. His three collections (Gould, 1977, 1980, 1983) and the range of topics clearly indicate the vast potential of specimens in popular writing.

A single work that has shifted the palaeontologist's view of his science and demonstrated the supremacy of collections and individual specimens in the founding of palaeontology and its subsequent development is Rudwick's (1972) *The Meaning of Fossils*, a text unashamedly and confidently centred on specimens and their impact on scientific thought. It points many clear paths of research and some of the complexities are now under examination (Porter, 1977). Some realities of collection research can be examined in journals treating the history of science, particularly the *Archives of Natural History*, the *Geological curator*, *Annals of Science* and occasional papers in a wide range of other journals.

Pooled research findings point to major movements in collecting, reflecting a changing and evolving pattern of specimen use. The curiosity collection was followed by the show collection around which philosophical discussions revolved in the seventeeth and eighteenth centuries. The investigation of variety is reflected in early-nineteenth-century collections and the relationships and groupings of specimens became a major preoccupation later. The use of fossils for dating rocks still goes on, with emphasis turning from macrofossils to microfossils.

There are collections of all periods that are regionally centred, local responses to national movements; there are teaching collections, investment collections, obsession collections and, in the second half of this century, collections based around hypotheses of geology, the product of State sponsorship of higher education. Analyses along these lines are rare, but should prove rewarding, offering possibilities for research in all sizes of museums.

Anyone who has traced a research course through a major collection is constantly confronted with a bewildering choice of routes and must learn to select carefully. The assembling and reading of such collections requires many skills, and entails responsibilities that are awesome but bracing and exacting but essential to curatorial perception. The experienced curator mentioned at the outset is an expression of these qualities: the achievement of the curator, whilst taxing, is both exhilarating and inspirational.

Acknowledgements

Many colleagues have provided comment and suggestions for this chapter. I would particularly like to thank Hugh Torrens, and Tom Sharpe, author of *Geology in Museums* (1983), an invaluable bibliography and index of such widespread use that I have found it difficult to place it sensibly in the text. To all others who provided comment, my grateful thanks.

References

ALLEN, D. E. (1976), *The Naturalist in Britain*, Allen Lane, London

ARKELL, W. J. and TOMKEIEFF, S. I. (1953), *English Rock Terms*, Oxford University Press, Oxford

BARBER, L. (1980), *The Heyday of Natural History 1820–1870*, Jonathan Cape London

BASSETT, M. G. (1975), 'Bibliography and indexes of catalogues of type, figured and cited fossils in museums in the British Isles', *Palaeontology*, **18**, 753–773

BRITISH MUSEUM (NATURAL HISTORY) (1904), *History of the Collections, contained in the Natural History Departments of the British Museum*, Vol. 1, British Museum, London

BRITT, K. W. (1970), *Handbook of Pulp and Paper Technology*, Van Nostrand Reinhold, Wokingham

BRONN, H. G. (1848–1849), *Index Palaeontologicus*, E. Schweizerbart, Stuttgart

BRUNTON, H. H., BESTERMAN, T. P. and COOPER, J. A. (Eds) (1985), *Guidelines for the Curation of Geological Materials*, Geological Curators Group, Geological Society, London

BURCHARD, U. (1986), *Mineral Museums of Europe*, Walnut Hill, Lalling, Germany

CESBRON, F. (ED.) (1962), *World Directory of Mineralogists*, International Mineralogical Association, Marburg

CHALMERS-HUNT, J. M. (1976), *Natural History Auctions 1700–1972*, Sotheby Parke Bernet, London

CHESTER, A. H. (1896), *A Dictionary of the Names of Minerals Including their History and Etymology*, Wiley, Chichester

CLEEVELY, R. J. (1982), 'Some thought on methods of classifying and cataloguing hand-writing collections', *The Geological Curator*, **3**(4), 189–194

CLEEVELY, R. J. (1983), *World Palaeontological Collections*, British Museum (Natural History)/Mansell Publishing, London

COLBERT, E. H. (1968), *Evolution of the Vertebrates*, Wiley, Chichester

COLBERT, E. H. (1980), *A Fossil-Hunter's Notebook*, Dutton, New York

CNRS (1956), *Lexique Stratigraphique International*, CNRS, Paris

CROWTHER, P. R. and COLLINS, C. J. (EDS) (1987), 'The conservation of geological material', *Geological Curator*, **4**, 375–474

DANA, E. S. (1892), *System of Mineralogy*, 6th edition, Wiley, Chichester

DAVIS, P. and BREWER, C. (EDS) (1986) *A Catalogue of Natural Science Collections in North-east England*, North of England Museum Service, Durham

DESMOND, A. J. (1975), *The Hot-blooded Dinosaurs*, Blond and Briggs, London

DESMOND, R. (1977), *Dictionary of British and Irish Botanists and Horticulturists including Plant Collectors and Botanical Artists*, Taylor & Francis, London

DOUGHTY, P. S. (1981), *The State and Status of Geology in United Kingdom Museums, Miscellaneous Paper No. 13*, Geological Society, London

DUDA, R. and REJL, L. (1986), *Minerals of the World*, Spring Books, Twickenham

EDMONDS, J. M. (1977), 'The legend of John Phillips's "lost fossil collection"', *Journal of the Society for the Bibliography of Natural History*, **8**, 169–175

EMBREY, P. G. (1987), 'Mineral Curators, their appointment and duties,' *The Mineralogical record*, **18**, 389–390

EMBREY, P. G. and FULLER, J. P. (1980), *A Manual of New Mineral Names 1892–1978*, British Museum (Natural History) Oxford University Press, London/Oxford

EMBREY, P. G. and SYMES, R. F. (1987), *Minerals of Cornwall and Devon*, British Museum (Natural History) Mineralogical Record Inc., London/Tucson

ENGLISH, G. L. (1939), *Descriptive List of the New Minerals 1892–1938*, McGraw-Hill, Maidenhead

ETHRIDGE, R. (1888), *Fossils of the British Islands Stratigraphically and Zoologically Arranged*, Vol. 1, Oxford University Press, Oxford

FORBES, C. L. (1979), 'Credit where it is due', *Newsletter of the Geological Curators' Group*, **2**, 404

FOUNTAINE, M. (1980), *Love among the Butterflies*, Collins, Glasgow

GEOLOGICAL SOCIETY OF LONDON (1971–1980), *Stratigraphic Correlation Charts, Special Reports 1–15*, Geological Society of London, London

GILLISPIE, C. C. (Ed.) (1981), *Dictionary of Scientific Biography*, Scribner, New York

GOULD, S. (1977), *Ever Since Darwin*, Morton, New York

GOULD, S. (1980), *The Panda's Thumb*, Morton, New York

GOULD, S. (1983), *Hen's Teeth and Horse's Toes*, Morton, New York

HANCOCK, E. G. and PETTITT, C. W. (EDS.) (1981), *Register of Natural Science Collections in North West England*, p. 178, Manchester Museum, Manchester

HARRISON, W. R. (1981), *Suspect Documents – Their Scientific Examination*, Nelson-Hall, Chicago, IL

HARTLEY, M. M., NORRIS, A., PETTITT, C. W., RILEY, T. H. and STIER, M. A. (1987), *Register of Natural Science Collections in Yorkshire and Humberside*, Area Museum and Art Gallery Service for Yorkshire and Humberside, Leeds

HEDBERG, H. D. (1976), *International Stratigraphic Guide: A Guide to Stratigraphic Classification, Terminology and Procedure*, Wiley, New York

HEPPELL, D. (1981), 'The evolution of the Code of Zoological Nomenclature', in *History in the Service of Systematics*, Wheeler, A. and Price, J.M. (Eds.), pp. 135–141. Society for the Bibliography of Natural History, London

HEY, M. H. (1962), *An index of Mineral Species and Varieties Arranged Chemically*, Trustees of the British Museum, London

HEY, M. H. (1963), *Appendix to the Second Edition of an Index of Mineral Species and Varieties arranged Chemically*, Trustees of the British Museum (Natural History), London

HEY, M. H. and EMBREY, P. G. (1974), *A second Appendix to the Second Edition of an Index of Mineral Species and Varieties arranged Chemcially*, Trustees of the British Museum (Natural History), London

HIGHAM, R. A. (1968), *Handbook of Papermaking*, Business Books, London

HILL, D. (1938–1941), *A Monograph on the Carboniferous Rugose Corals of Scotland*, Palaeontographical Society, reprinted, 1966, Johnson Reprint Corporation, London

HILTON, O. (1956), *Scientific Examination of Questioned Documents*, Callaghan

HOLLAND, C. H. *et al.*, (1978), *A Guide to Stratigraphic Procedure, Geological Society of London Special Report No. 10*, Geological Society, London

HOWIE, F. M. P. (1979), 'Museum climatology and the conservation of palaeontological material', in M.G.

Bassett (Ed.), *Curation of Palaeontological Collections, Special Papers in Palaeontology No. 22*, pp. 103–125, Palaeontological Association, London

INTERNATIONAL COMMISSION ON ZOOLOGICAL NOMENCLA-TURE (1985), *International Code of Zoological Nomenclature*, 3rd edition, Ride, W. D. L., Zabrosky, C. W., Bernardi, G., Melville, R. V., (Eds.), International Trust for Zoological Nomenclature, London

JAMES, W. K. (1986), *'Damned Nonsense!' – The Geological Career of the Third Earl of Enniskillen*, Ulster Museum and National Trust Belfast

JAMESON, R. (1808), *System of Mineralogy*, Vol. iii, Blackwood, Edinburgh (Facsimile reprint Hafner Press, New York 1976)

JUKES, J. B. (1962), *The Student's Manual of Geology*, 2nd edition A. and C. Black, London

KINAHAN, G. H. (1873), *The Handy Book of Rock Names*, Hardwicke London

KNELL, S. J. and TAYLOR, M. A. (1989), *Geology and the Local Museum*, Area Museum Service for South Eastern England and Area Museum Council for the South West HMSO, London

LAMBRECHT, K. and QUENSTEDT, A. (1938), *Palaeontologi. Fossilium Catalogus. I: Animalia*, Junk, W. (Ed.), reprint edition (1978), Arno Press, New York

LAUDAN, R. (1976), 'William Smith. Stratigraphy without palaeontology', *Centaurus*, **20**

LAUDAN, R. (1987), *From Mineralogy to Geology: The Foundations of a Science, 1650–1830*, Chicago University Press, Chicago, IL

MEDAWAR, P. B. (1979), *Advice to a Young Scientist*, Harper and Row, London

MITCHELL, R. S. (1979), *Mineral Names. What do they Mean?*, Van Nostrand Reinhold, Wokingham

MOORE, R. C. and TEICHERT, C. (Eds.), (1953–), *Treatise on Invertebrate Paleontology*, Geological Society of America, Kansas

MORRIS, J. (1845), *A Catalogue of British Fossils*, J. Van Voorst, London

MUSEUM DOCUMENTATION ASSOCIATION (1980a), *Geology Specimen Card Instructions*, Museum Documentation Association, Duxford

MUSEUM DOCUMENTATION ASSOCIATION (1980b), *Mineral Specimen Card Instructions*, Museum Documentation Association, Duxford

NEAVE, S. A. (1939–), *Nomenclator Zoologicus*, Zoological Society of London, London

NORTH, F. J., DAVIDSON, C.F. and SWINTON, W. E. (1941), *Geology in Museums*, Oxford University Press, Oxford

PALMER, C. P. (1977), 'Data security in scientific objects', *Newsletter of the Geological Curators' Group*, **9**, 446–449

PHILLIPS, J. (1835), *A Guide to Geology*, 2nd edition, Longman Rees, London

PORTER, R. (1977), *The Making of Geology*, Cambridge University Press, Cambridge

RIXON, A. E. (1976), *Fossil Animal Remains: their Preservation and Conservation*, Athlone Press, London

RUDWICK, M. J. S. (1972), *The Meaning of Fossils: Episodes in the History of Palaeontology*, Elsevier, Amsterdam

SARJEANT, W. A. S. (1980), *Geologists and the History of Geology*, 5 Vols, Macmillan, London

SARJEANT, W. A. S. (1987), *Geologists and the History of Geology, Supplement 1979–1984 and additions*, 2 Vols, Kreiger, Malabar, FL

SEDGWICK, A and M'COY, F. (1854), *A Synopsis of Classification of the British Palaeozoic Rocks, with the Systematic Description of the British Palaeozoic Fossils in the Geological Museum of the University of Cambridge*, Cambridge University Press, Cambridge

SHARPE, T. (1983), *Geology in Museums: A Bibliography and Index*, National Museum of Wales, Cardiff

SHERBORN, C. D. (1902–1933), *Index Animalian*, Cambridge

SHERBORN, C. D. (1940), *Where is the. . .Collection?*, Cambridge University Press, Cambridge

SHIELDS, J. (1984), *Adhesive Handbook*, 3rd edition, Butterworths, London

SIMPSON, G. G. (1934), *Attending Marvels*, University of Chicago Press, Chicago, IL

STACE, H. E., PETTITT, C. W. A., WATERSON, C. D., HEPPELL, D. and DAVIDSON, K. J. (eds.), (1988), *Natural Science Collections in Scotland*, National Museums of Scotland, Edinburgh

STAFLEU, F. A. and VOSS, E. G. (Eds), (1978), *International Code of Botanical Nomenclature*, (adopted Leningrad 1975), Regnum Vegetabile, 97 Bohn, Scheltema and Holkema, Utrecht

STEARN, W. T. (1981), *The Natural History Museum at South Kensington*, Heinemann, London

STEPHEN, L. and LEE, S. (eds) *Dictionary of National Biography*, 1900 onwards Oxford University Press, (1885–1900, Smith Elder and Co., London)

STERNBERG, G. F. (1930), *Thrills in Fossil Hunting*, Aerend, Hays, Kansas

THACKRAY, S. (1972), *A Bio-Bibliography of British Geologists who Died between 1850 and 1900*, Science Museum Library Bibliography, Gen 801, London

TJADEN, W. L. (1981), 'Botanical nomenclature and pitfalls in relevant history', in *History in the Service of Systematics*, Wheeler, A. and Price, J. H. (Eds), pp. 129–133, Society of the Bibliography of Natural History, London

TOMKEIEFF, S. I. (1983), *Dictionary of Petrology*, Walton, E. K., Randall, B. A. O., Battey, M. H., Tomkeieff, O. (Eds) Wiley, Chichester

TORRENS, H. S. (1974), 'Locating and identifying collections of palaeontological material', *Newsletter of the Geological Curators' Group*, **1**, 12–17

TORRENS, H.S. (1979), 'Detection at the Sedgwick: an illustration of the importance of data retention', *Newsletter of the Geological Curators' Group*, **2**, 333–340

TORRENS, H. S. (1988), 'Hawking history – a vital future for geology's past', *Modern Geology*, pp. 83–93

VON COTTA, B. (1893), *Rocks Classified and Described*, Lawrence, P. H. (trans.), Longmans, Green and Co., London

WATERSTON, C. D. (1979), 'The unique role of the curator in palaeontology', M. G. Bassett (Ed.), in *Curation of Palaeontology Collections, Special Papers in Palaeontology No. 22*, pp. 7–15, Palaeontological Association, London

WEINER, J. S. (1955), *The Piltdown Forgery*, Oxford University Press, London

WHYBROW, P. J. (1985), 'A history of fossil collecting and preparation techniques', *Curator*, **28**, 5–26

WILSON, R. H. (1981), *Suspect Documents – their scientific examination*, Nelson Hall, London

ZITTELL, K. S. VON (1895), *Grundzuge der Palaeontologie*, R. Oldenbourg *Textbook of Palaeontology*, 2 Vols, English revised edition (1900), Eastman, C. R. (trans and Ed.) Macmillan, London

ZWANN, P. C. and PATERSON, O. V. (1977), *World Directory of Mineral Collections*, 2nd edition, Commission on Museums of the Mineralogical Association, Marburg

52

Archaeological research collections: prehistoric and Roman

Ian. H. Longworth

It would be unwise to think of archaeological collections as being divisible into two categories: those capable of sustaining research and those which are not. All archaeological artefacts convey a degree of information. In some the information yield may be small, while for others the yield can be proportional to the amount of time invested in their study. The bulk will fall between the two extremes. Research collections might be seen, therefore, as including all material whether on display or in store, the realization of their research potential depending largely on those who come to study them.

At the lowest level of enquiry, all artefacts can yield information about their basic technology – how they were made and from what materials; the more elaborate give evidence of the technical achievement, expertise and artistry of those who fashioned them. The majority will also convey some idea of the needs which led to their manufacture, while others will go beyond this simple function giving insight into taste and socially dictated forms. More accurate and a greater range of data can be gathered from groups rather than individual pieces, particularly when these are well-documented as to provenance and association. The greatest scope will be offered by artefacts recovered through scientific excavation which bring with them all the ancillary data gleaned during their extraction by modern archaeological techniques.

The artefactual evidence which comes to us from the past is itself but a small part of what must once have existed. With the exception of bone, much of the organic component rarely survives. The wood and leather, skin, rope, cloth and baskets have usually decayed, though these must once have figured large in the material culture of the time. Prehistoric pottery too, often poorly fired, shows variable rates of survival and once brought to the surface through modern disturbance can rapidly disintegrate. Of the metals, iron in particular is frequently recovered in a poor state. In short, the artefacts which come down to us are often simply those most resistant to decay or those which, through some peculiarity of context, have escaped the processes of natural destruction. It is a Curator's task to ensure that as much as possible of what survives is preserved for the future.

Once the Curator has agreed to accept archaeological material, that material must be preserved in its entirety. This is particularly important with regard to excavated assemblages where the decision as to what should or should not form part of the excavation archive must be agreed between the Director of the excavation and the Curator before acceptance. Once accepted the archive should not be subjected to further personal selections made by successive curators (see Longworth, 1982). Future generations will then be assured of a less biased sample from which to research the past. Like all subjects, archaeology is prone to fashion but while displays may fairly be expected to reflect something of the thinking of the age, collections should be formed against future needs, not all of which may yet be apparent. If recent experience is any guide, however, we can be sure that the range and quantity of questions likely to be posed will rapidly increase as new methods and new techniques are brought to bear on the material.

Over the past three decades, museum archaeology has come a long way. The desire to preserve only the rare and the fine has been superceded by an understanding that to gain a wider knowledge of society it is necessary also to study the common and the everyday. As studies progress, questions of what is it, how was it made and how was it used are joined by others: how often was it used, how widespread was its use. If these questions are to be answered with conviction they require the preservation of the artefacts themselves, for few areas of the subject have reached such a state of taxonomic refinement as to make the object itself redundant once initial recording has taken place. Clearly not all museums should attempt or be encouraged to undertake the unglamorous (but expensive!) task of amassing and curating large quantities of sometimes repetitive material. Since archaeology remains largely a comparative study there are strong arguments for limiting the number to a few large collections rather than an array of smaller ones. In Scotland, Wales and Northern Ireland, the National Museums already serve this function, while in England the formation of large regional collections would offer the most cost-effective solution. In this field the British Museum has a major role to play. By building up fully representative collections, the museum can offer the research worker a unique opportunity for direct inter-regional comparisons as well as a chance to set those collections alongside contemporary material from Europe and beyond. The British Museum also provides a safety net for collections which, for one reason or another, cannot be safely curated elsewhere.

Some conflict of interest is perhaps inevitable where local pride seeks to dictate that all objects should remain in the immediate locality. Research collections, however, require facilities beyond the financial reach of small museums. These museums have a different but no less important role to play in archaeology, as foci for the stimulation of local interest and for provoking in the local community an awareness of our common past.

Facilities

To ensure the long-term survival of antiquities, certain facilities are essential and many of the basic requirements have been set out by the Museums & Galleries Commission. Amongst these, adequate storage conditions and ongoing conservation facilities are of prime importance. Staffing levels must be of an order to allow not only a prompt service to be offered but permit security and supervision of the collections to be maintained so that archives are neither depleted nor allowed to become confused. From time to time new and sometimes more costly requirements may well emerge from new forms of research. The study of micro-wear, for example, on bone and flint implements, is greatly assisted if the implements to be studied have survived in the same state as when extracted from the ground without the addition of subsequent 'museum wear'. The latter may well be a subject entirely suitable for research in its own right, but is an obvious distraction to those primarily interested in prehistoric utilization. Here the rigorous separation of individual artefacts, hopefully already initiated by the excavator, must be maintained in the museum.

It is equally important to offer research workers adequate facilities to undertake their work within the museum. A sloping desk top hurriedly cleared in a corner of the Curator's office may be a friendly gesture, but is no substitute for adequate, clear, flat table space, well lit by *natural* light. Research workers should also be able to expect to find at their disposal a low-powered binocular microscope and scales (preferably digital) together with basic facilities for taking photographs, e.g. lights and camera stand. Last, but by no means least, research workers should find available a Curator who knows the collections well and is able to talk with authority about them. If research workers are not led to relevant parts of the collections, particularly those which have not already received full publication, much that should have been studied will be missed and they will go away happy in the misconceived belief that another collection has been fully analysed. Only those museums, therefore, that have adequate storage and study facilities to cater for those who wish to study the collections should seek to extend their holdings beyond the needs of display and their education services.

Active or passive collecting?

A museum may choose to adopt a purely passive role, electing to receive archaeological collections if and when they became available through chance discovery or from excavations funded by outside bodies. In this way, over time, gaps in the collections may or may not be filled but the museum will have little or no control over the timetable or be able to set priorities. A more active approach is to be preferred if the needs of the collections and posterity are to be satisfied fully. It is sometimes unwise to wait. Museums have been slow, for example, to promote the recovery of just those objects made of soft organic substances like wood and leather which are so lacking in almost all collections, yet without these a view of the life of any period is bound to be highly distorted. Time is not on our side in this as the few remaining sources fall to the constant threat of drainage or peat extraction. Here the passive role serves us ill, for opportunities missed are lost for ever.

The ability to respond quickly and effectively to chance discovery is often equally vital. In how many cases can we say of hoards, almost invariably discovered by chance and by the untrained, that either the entirety of the find has been recovered, or the circumstance of deposition fully explored? Prompt evaluation by the museum, which often will be the first to have knowledge of the find, can fill out the evidence for a find which otherwise will remain of interest but of uncertain research value. Of equal importance to secure are selected examples of those minor structures which cannot be preserved in the ground but which will often provide not only key display material but also the source of much on-going future research: kilns, well frames, pit-linings, surviving fragments of walls and roofs. Here the excavator's descriptions, no matter how precise they now appear, are no substitute for the ability to re-examine the actual evidence in the future. An awareness of what the collections lack, coupled with an ability to respond to the unexpected, offer the best hope of ensuring that the research needs of the future will be met in full.

Publication

Research without publication is not only selfish but a profound waste of a rare resource. It is the duty of all research workers to report their knowledge to others and it is important for Curators to impress this moral duty upon those who come to study the collections they curate. The task is made less difficult if the museum itself can document its own ability in this field. In many instances the resident curatorial staff are in fact best placed to undertake the research themselves (Stead, 1985, p. 7) and this is particularly the case where objects have enjoyed a complex history. Published catalogues provide the most flexible form of information dissemination for categories of object, offering many of the basic facts and allowing the researcher to gain a fair impression of the work which needs to be undertaken (e.g. Annable and Simpson, 1964; Bailey, 1975, 1980 and 1988; Kinnes and Longworth, 1985; Lynch, 1986; Maaskant-Kleibrink, 1986; Manning, 1985; Platz-Horster, 1984; Savory, 1980; Sieveking, 1987) and corpora (e.g. Clarke, 1969; Longworth, 1984; Menzel, 1986). Check-lists, while less informative, at least provide some indication of extent of holding and the likely length of time which will be needed to make a study of them. Many of these can be generated cheaply as collections become computerized.

With praiseworthy exceptions (e.g. Stead and Rigby, 1986, 1989), the finds-catalogue element of many excavation reports following the recommendations of the Cunliffe Report (Cunliffe, 1982) have become considerably less exhaustive. For large assemblages a strategy to study only a sample of the finds may have been adopted. The consequence for museums is that many excavated assemblages arrive in need of further study and provide an ever-increasing field for future research. The future then is likely to see much greater use made of the Prehistoric and Roman collections for research and the museums concerned will need to adjust their resources to cope with this predicted need. It is for this future need, rather than the present, that the Curator needs to plan.

References

ANNABLE, F. K and SIMPSON, D. D. A. (1964), *Guide Catalogue of the Neolithic and Bronze Age Collections in Devizes Museum*, Wiltshire Archaeological and Natural History Society, Devizes

BAILEY, D. M. (1975), (1980) and (1988) *Catalogue of Lamps in the British Museum*, vols I–III, British Museum Publications, London

CLARKE, D. L. (1969) *Beaker Pottery of Great Britain and Ireland*, Cambridge University Press, Cambridge

CUNLIFFE, B. W. (1982), *The Publication of Archaeological Excavations*, report of a joint working party of the Council for British Archaeology and Department of the Environment, London

KINNES, I. A. and LONGWORTH, I. H. (1985) *Catalogue of the Excavated Prehistoric and Romano-British Material in the Greenwell Collection*, British Museum Publications, London

LONGWORTH, I. H. (1982), *Selection and Retention of Environmental and Artefactual Material from Excavations*, report by a working party of the British Museum, London

LONGWORTH, I. H. (1984) *Collared Urns of the Bronze Age in Great Britain and Ireland*, Cambridge University Press, Cambridge

LYNCH, F. (1986), *Catalogue of Archaeological Material*, Museum of Welsh Antiquities, Bangor

MAASKANT-KLEIBRINK, M. (1986) *Catalogue of the Engraved Gems in the Rijksmuseum G M Kam, Nijmegen*, Ministry of Welfare, Health and Cultural Affairs, Nijmegen

MANNING, W. H. (1985), *Catalogue of the Romano-British Iron Tools, Fittings and Weapons in the British Museum*, British Museum Publications, London

MENZEL, H. (1986) *Die Römischen Bronzen aus Deutschland III – Bonn*, Verlag Philipp von Zabern, Mainz am Rhein

PLATZ-HORSTER, G. (1984) *Die Antiken Gemmen in Rheinischen Landesmuseum Bonn*, Rheinland-Verlag, Köln & Rudolf Hablet, Bonn

SAVORY, H. N. (1980), *Guide Catalogue of the Bronze Age Collections*, National Museum of Wales, Cardiff

SIEVEKING, A. (1987), *A Catalogue of Palaeolithic Art in the British Museum*, British Museum Publications, London

STEAD, I. M. (1985), *The Battersea Shield*, British Museum Publications, London

STEAD, I. M. and RIGBY, V. (1986), *Baldock. The Excavation of a Roman and Pre-Roman Settlement, 1968–1972*, Britannia Monograph Series No. 7, Society for the Promotion of Roman Studies, London

STEAD, I. M. and RIGBY, V. (1989) *Verulamium: The King Harry Lane Site*, English Heritage/British Museum Publications, London

53

Archaeological research collections: medieval and post-medieval

John Cherry

Research may be said to begin with the ordering of collections and end with the enlightenment of the mind. It may also be argued that research begins with a question based on previous conceptions and, passing through an ordered analysis of the evidence, ends in an answer which itself forms the conceptual basis for the next question. In either view the way in which collections are known and ordered can affect the conceptual basis of questions and the type of questions may affect the ordering of the material. It is the intention of this article to introduce the particular nature of archaeological questions, to indicate how the enquirer can find out what is in museums, to draw attention to the bibliographical aids for research and to indicate some of the attempts at the synthetic understanding of the problems of medieval and post-medieval archaeology.

Archaeological collections

Archaeological collections in this period may be divided into three types. Firstly there are the old collections in museums of objects of archaeological interest. These were generally discovered in the eighteenth and nineteenth centuries and preserved because of their attractiveness or their curiosity. This category might include modern chance finds. The second category of collection comprises finds from properly conducted excavations, the finds having been preserved in their entirety without selection and the context from which they came can be determined. Lastly there are the reference collections which have been created on a typological or geographical basis to illustrate a particular purpose.

There needs to be much greater study of the old collections of museums and in the ways in which they have been collected. Many important archaeological finds have been discovered in the past 200 years and both these and the records of early

finds, which may now have been lost, deserve much greater research than they have hitherto received. Two of the main sources for information about such collections are the catalogues of museums and early archaeological journals. *The Gentleman's Magazine* and the Minutes of the Society of Antiquaries are a most important source for discoveries made in the eighteenth and nineteenth centuries. From the 1840s the national archaeological periodicals, the *Archaeological Journal* and *Journal of British Archaeological Associations*, as well as the range of local archaeological periodicals founded in their period, provide details of such early finds. A most useful guide to the manuscript sources for early antiquarian discoveries and records of comments is the *Guide to British Topographical Collections* published by the Council for British Archaeology (Barley, 1974). Two examples of the value of the study of old collections is the work on the Roach Smith collection (Kidd, 1977) and that on the Meols collection (Merseyside Museums, unpublished).

It is, however, the enormous growth in excavation over the last 30 years that has vastly increased the quantity of the medieval and post-medieval archaeological collections and created both problems of storage and ordering and also greater opportunities for research. The problems of storage have been discussed in *Archaeological Storage* (Society of Museum Archaeologists, 1981) and the problems of selection and retention of environmental and artefactual material in the report by a working party of the British Museum (Longworth, 1982). There are two major divisions between the old collections and the new collections derived from archaeological excavations. The first is that the objects are not preserved in a selective manner according either to aesthetic considerations or to a particular view of their importance, and secondly, however they are stored, the context and contextual relationships of the objects should be discoverable in order that conclusions may be drawn concerning the relationship of the object to the site. It is research on objects in context that provides the basis for the setting of objects in the context of the social, economic, or religious life of the period. This particular point has been well illustrated recently in a discussion of the pottery and metalwork from the ditch of Penhow Castle, Gwent (Wrathmell, 1987).

A considerable amount of money devoted to rescue archaeology is now spent on post-excavation work. In the period 1987–1988, 180 grants totalling £2 525 065 were spent by the Historic Buildings and Monuments Commission for England (English Heritage, 1987). Although not all is directed to finds research, a considerable proportion is devoted to research on finds which subsequently enter museum collections. In many cases this is the only serious research that the finds will receive. It is therefore worth setting out the principles on which that research is based and the implications for museum collections. The principles are set out in the *Cunliffe Report* (Cunliffe, 1982), which distinguishes between three types of research. Firstly there is processing and primary research which is that work necessary to prepare the excavation archive for preservation in a usable form, and to produce a synthesis for publication. Secondary research is the analysis of classes of data well presented on the site which are not essential to a direct description of the site but which contribute to an understanding of systems at work within the society. Lastly there is ancillary research, i.e. detailed analyses and comparative studies facilitated, or directly inspired, by new data from the site. This distinction is essential to ensure that the extent of post-excavation research design is limited to the primary research of those classes of data essential to a direct description of the site. It does not envisage full research on the entire archive of finds from the site. It is therefore possible that there is a considerable quantity of research that can still be carried out on material from excavations after the post-excavation research design has been completed and the completed archive passed to the museum for storage.

Although the post-excavation primary research, publication, and storage grant are met by English Heritage, when the archive is transferred to the museum it is the museum authority which will bear the responsibility and, therefore, the cost of curation and research. This has many implications for museums in terms both of space and finance, but it is the implications for research that concern us most. Since it is possible that primary research will not have extracted the full significance of the finds on site and that there is a need for further research, then the museum staff must be of sufficient archaeological and academic calibre either to service such research

by others or possibly, in certain cases, to undertake such research themselves. This emphasis on the need for museum staff to be of high archaeological calibre is all the more important if an increasing distinction is seen between publication and the ordering of the archive. Increasing costs of publication are likely to limit publication to conveying a general picture of the site, its features and finds rather than providing a detailed key to the original site archive.

The reference collection provides a means of classifying artefacts by types, geography or fabric. It is particularly suitable for pottery where large-scale and repetitive production creates both difficulties of handling a large bulk of material and opportunities of classifying according to kiln source. Medieval pottery reference collections have been established both at the British Museum and the Museum of London (Rhodes, 1977; Cherry, 1986). Reference collections may be either national or local. As it is dealing with much newly excavated material the type series of pottery evolved in a local archaeological unit is often a focal point in developing the understanding of a local pottery sequence. The essential problem of a reference collection for both organizer and user is how effectively it can respond to developments in research which create changing attitudes in pottery classification and nomenclature.

Museum collections: how does the enquirer discover the content?

One of the problems for the researcher is to find the relevant material in any particular museum. In the future the researcher may be able to carry out a computer search of all museum archaeological collections. Such a search can only be as good as the quality of the original identification. This may be rendered less worthwhile by the way in which the entries have to be written and the way in which the information has to be classified. Such searches may be made more difficult in the future by incompatibility of systems.

For the next few years the researcher will have to rely on more traditional methods: looking at the published material, writing personal or circular letters, and visiting the museums themselves. It is still important to stress the value of the printed catalogue or survey, which not only indicates the nature of collections but often provides significant steps forward in the study of a subject. Notable examples in the last 20 years have been studies of late Saxon ornamental metalwork (Wilson, 1964; Hinton, 1974) and medieval tiles (Eames, 1980). There have been major achievements in the publication of finds from excavations, notably those from medieval and post-medieval excavations in Exeter (Allan, 1984) as well as the volume on knives and scabbards, the first in the series of studies devoted to finds from excavations in the City of London (Cowgill *et al.*, 1987). It is clear that the increasing cost of publication for a limited market may lead to large published catalogues being superseded by computer print-outs. However, it must be remembered that one essential advantage of the printed publication over the computer print-out is that it is far easier to make an accurate bibliographical reference to a printed publication than to a computer print-out.

One of the greatest gaps in most museums' publications is the provision of a guide to the collections. Such a guide could indicate the general strengths and weaknesses of any particular collection. *The London Museum Medieval Catalogue* (London Museum, 1940) provided not only an important classification of finds but also a guide to the collections of that museum – it is unfortunate that it has never been revised and is now out of print. Again the series of *Guides* to various collections in the British Museum published in the early part of this century have never been replaced. *The Guide to Medieval Antiquities* (1924) is the most useful for this period. Many local museums in the second half of the nineteenth century such as those at Salisbury, Devizes, Maidstone and Norwich, provided most useful lists of the objects in their collections. There is an important need for lists, guides and catalogues to be available at a series of different levels. In 1969, John Eames bewailed the lack of such publications (Eames, 1969). I doubt very much whether the situation in 1999 will really be very different.

The publication of excavation reports often provides an indication to researchers of the archaeological contents of a museum, particularly if it is clearly stated where the material is deposited. Publication of finds from excavations is often incomplete for reasons outlined above. It is also true that publication of finds in microfiche, which is perhaps better than no publication at all, is more restrictive than printed publications. There have been some notable achievements in the publication of finds from excavations which are now museum collections, notably from Southampton, York, Exeter and Norwich (Platt and Coleman-Smith, 1975; MacGregor, 1982; Allan, 1984; Atkin *et al.*, 1985; Tweddle, 1986). The assemblage of information from smaller archaeological reports ranging from larger county journals to more obscure local journals is much more difficult and is considered later.

It is worth making the point that sometimes the only way to discover what is in a museum is to see what is on display in the galleries. This is increasingly less satisfactory as museum displays are more frequently designed with eye-catching displays to enhance the imagination rather than educate the mind.

Bibliographical aids to research

There is no published annual survey of research in medieval or post-medieval collections. The basic bibliographical device for British Archaeology is the *British Archaeological Abstracts* published by the Council for British Archaeology. So far 20 volumes (1967–1987) have been published. Its purpose is to indicate the most significant material currently being published and to provide a research source for consultation in future years. The 1987 volume is the result of scanning 350 British and Irish periodicals and the most important of the Continental scanning list of 360 serials and periodicals. Finds are only rarely mentioned in abstracts of excavation reports, although section PF (Artefacts and Art History) is extremely useful. However, it is clear from recent studies that museum archaeologists are indifferent to the provision of a bibliographic abstracting service (Lavell, 1984, p. 2). Archaeologists apparently acquire knowledge either by using a grapevine of contacts, by browsing, by individual researchers searching back issues of likely journals, or by assuming that no previous work is relevant. Lavell comments 'a little familiarity with past published work would save a lot of New Archaeological ink' (Lavell, 1984, p. 5). It is this indifference that has led to the failure to implement, through lack of funding, any of the recommendations of the Fircroft seminar held in 1976 (British Library, 1977) which called for an extension, deepening and computerization of both Abstracts and the Archaeological Bibliography, which could then be integrated as far as possible with other types of record such as the Ordnance Survey indexes.

A useful research tool for those with access to London is the subject index at the Society of Antiquaries of London. This provides a comprehensive coverage of all books in the Antiquaries' Library and selected articles in periodical literature. The present policy is to provide a comprehensive coverage of all major periodical literature on a fairly comprehensive scale. The subject index is basically a dictionary catalogue into which a topographical index is inserted. If one wishes to find out the current work carried out on different types of sites in different parts of the country with occasional reference to finds, the annual surveys of medieval Britain that have been published in *Medieval Archaeology* since 1957 and of post-medieval Britain published in *Post-Medieval Archaeology* since 1967 are of great value. More specialized bibliographies are available for particular types of sites, notably for castles (Kenyon, 1978, 1983), in the annual reports of the Medieval Landscape Group (the amalgamation of the Medieval Village Research Group and the Moated Sites Research Group). For artefacts alone, *Medieval Ceramics*, the annual publication of the

Medieval Pottery Research Group, has included a bibliography from 1984, while the *Census of Medieval Tiles* has produced Bulletins (1985, 1986) containing a bibliography of medieval tile publications bringing up to date the bibliography given in Eames (1980). For groups of finds examined by the Ancient Monuments Laboratory for the purposes of archaeological science and conservation a 6-monthly list of reports is circulated and microfiche copies can be obtained on request from the Historic Buildings and Monuments Commission. Finally, the report of the Council for British Archaeology conference on medieval industry (Crossley, 1981) contains a good range of bibliographical references related to the production processes for artefacts.

Research: its contribution to our understanding of the past

The philosophy of medieval and post-medieval archaeological research has not yet received the same attention as the philosophy of the study of history. Any such philosophical approach will have to comprehend the considerable contributions that can be made in their periods by a study of the documentary evidence not as a source for history alone but also as a source for the very problems that archaeologists are trying to solve. There is a good general guide to historical sources for medieval and post-medieval archaeology in England (Platt, 1969). The way in which historical sources may be used to illuminate a direct archaeological problem is well illustrated by recent work on medieval pottery (Moorhouse, 1978, 1983). A general survey in which the recent work in medieval archaeology has been incorporated into a study of the social history of England, indicated by the subtitle of the book *A Social History and Archaeology from the Conquest to 16 AD*, has been produced by Platt (1975). Two other surveys have been written from different view points: Clarke's survey (Clarke, 1984) concentrates on analysing the contribution of excavation in different areas, while that of Steane (Steane, 1985) is essentially a survey for the field archaeologist concerned with the impact of man on the urban and rural landscape.

A synthetic view of archaeology in the medieval and post-medieval period cannot simply be based on objects. It must be based not only on landscape and architectural evidence but also on the recovery of environmental evidence of plants and animals and the skeletal evidence of the people of the period. In museum terms this means that archaeological research must spread beyond the artefactual to encompass a wider vision of society. Even so, the essential contribution that can be made either by the museum Curator or the researcher in a museum is likely to focus on the analysis of the nature of the artefacts and what can be learnt from them. Research may be sometimes a matter of precise detail – for instance the identification of heraldry on an object, whilst at other times it may construct an entirely new classification for a type of artefact, and in some instances in may involve the relationship between an artefact and the whole structure of society such as, for instance, the study of the diffusion of the stirrup and the rise of heavy cavalry in the post-Roman period (White, 1962). It is only systematic research based on well-ordered collections that will enable a vision of the past to be created which can then be passed on to the museum visitor through publication and display.

References

ALLAN, J. P. (1984), *Medieval and Post-Medieval Finds from Exeter, 1971–80*

ATKIN, M., CARTER, A. and EVANS, D. H. (1985), 'Excavations in Norwich 1971–8 Part II', *East Anglian Archaeology* **26**

BARLEY, M. W. (1974), *A Guide to British Topographical Collections*

BRITISH LIBRARY (1977), 'Problems of information handling in British archaeology: report of a seminar', *British Library Research and Development Report 5239*, British Library, London

BRITISH MUSEUM (1924), *A Guide to the Medieval Antiquities and Objects of Later Date*, British Museum, London

CHERRY, J. (1986), 'The National Reference collection of Medieval Pottery', *Medieval Ceramics*, **10**, 125–130

CLARKE, H. (1984), *The Archaeology of Medieval England*

COWGILL, J., DE NEERGAARD, M. and GRIFFITHS, N. (1987), *Knives and Scabbards*

CROSSLEY, D. W. (1981) *Medieval Industry*

CUNLIFFE, B. (1982), *Publication of Archaeological Excavations*, Council for British Archaeology and Department of the Environment, HMSO, London

EAMES, E. S. (1980), *Catalogue of Medieval Lead-glazed Earthenware Tiles in the British Museum*, British Museum, London

EAMES, J. V. H. (1969), 'Museums and Scholarship', *Museums Journal*, **69**(3), 103–105

ENGLISH HERITAGE (1987), *Rescue Archaeology Funding in 1987–8*

HINTON, D. (1974), *A Catalogue of the Anglo Saxon Ornamental Metalwork 700–1100, in the Department of Antiquities, Ashmolean Museum*, Ashmolean Museum, Oxford

KENYON, J. R. (1978), *Castles, Town Defences and Artillery Fortifications in Britain: a Bibliography 1945–1974*

KENYON, J. R. (1983), *Castles Town Defences, and Artillery Fortifications in Britain: a Bibliography 1977–82*

KIDD, D. (1977), 'Charles Roach Smith and his Museum of London Antiquities', *British Museum Yearbook*, **2**, 105–136

LAVELL, C. (1984), 'Why don't you want to know? – Information and the archaeologist' *Scottish Archaeological Review*, **3**

LONDON MUSEUM (1940), *Medieval Catalogue*, London Museum, London

LONGWORTH, I. H. (1982), 'Selection and retention of environmental and artefactual material from excavations', unpublished

LONGWORTH, I and CHERRY, J. (1986), *Archaeology in Britain since 1945*

MACGREGOR, A. (1982), 'Anglo Scandinavian finds from Lloyds Bank, pavement, and other sites', *Archaeology of York*, **17**(2)

MOORHOUSE, S. (1978), 'Documentary evidence for the uses of medieval pottery: an interim statement', *Medieval Ceramics*, **2**, 3–22

MOORHOUSE, S. (1983), 'Potential for understanding the inland movement of medieval pottery', *Medieval Ceramics*, **7**, 45–87

PLATT, C. (1969), *Medieval Archaeology in England*

PLATT, C. and COLEMAN-SMITH, R. (1975), *Excavations in Medieval Southampton 1953–1969*

RHODES, M. (1977), 'A pottery and fabric type series for London', *Museums Journal*, **76**(4), 150–152

RODWELL, W. J. (1981), *The Archaeology of the English Church*

SOCIETY OF MUSEUM ARCHAEOLOGISTS (1981), *Archaeological Storage*

STEANE, J. M. (1985), *The Archaeology of Medieval England and Wales*

TWEDDLE, D. (1986), 'Finds from Parliament Street and other sites in the city centre', *Archaeology of York*, **17**(4)

WHITE, L. (1962), *Medieval Technology and Social Change*

WILSON, D. M. (1964), *Catalogue of Anglo Saxon Ornamental Metalwork 700–1100 in the British Museum*, British Museum, London

WILSON, D. M. (1976), *The Archaeology of Anglo Saxon England*

WILSON, D. M. (1981), *The Anglo Saxons*

WRATHMELL, S. (1987), 'Observations on artefacts from ditch deposits', in *Studies in Medieval and Later Pottery in Wales presented to J. M. Lewis* Vyner, B. and Wrathmell, S. (Eds)

54

The hardware of science

John Burnett

There are two kinds of knowledge:
Knowing about things and knowing things,
Scientific data and aesthetic realization,
And I seek their perfect fusion in my work.

Hugh MacDiarmid

Introduction

The role of science in the history of the Western world has been immense. However, with the exception of specialist institutions, the history of science is inadequately represented in museums. We live in a web of technology: public utilities, transport, and the food and drink industry all involve technologies which depend on the discoveries of science. (I am here defining science loosely as a systematic knowledge of the natural world.) Science has always been important. At the beginning of the twelfth century Abelard and Heloise named their child Astrolabe. Yet to many Curators science seems to fit Churchill's description of the attitude of Russia in 1939: a riddle wrapped in a mystery inside an enigma.

Since the seventeenth century the literature of science has expanded (and continues to expand) at a remarkable rate. The consequence is that research in the history of science is dependent on libraries with collections of older scientific material – in the UK this amounts to little more than the Science Museum Library, the Science Reference Library and the libraries of the older universities. There is hope for the future in that twentieth-century science is so expensive that it is beginning to attract economic historians. Larger museums, with their greater resources of staff, collections and libraries, have a responsibility towards smaller institutions to help them understand their holdings in the history of science.

One might expect the history of scientific instruments to be a subdivision of the history of science, but this is not usually perceived to be the case. There is no historical justification for this situation, and it appears to be a product of the divergent interests of museum Curators and academic historians of science. There is distressingly little contact between the two, and academic historians have contributed little to the history of the hardware of science.

It must also be recognized that the concept of the scientific instrument is modern, and has no role in history. In the seventeenth and eighteenth centuries there were mathematical, optical or philosophical instrument makers, each of whom had different skills. A barometer might have been more of a piece of furniture than a precision instrument.

Four approaches to scientific instruments

The first consideration in handling any scientific instrument is to establish what it is, i.e. to identify it. The range of instruments in use in the Middle Ages was very small indeed, but the number began to grow in the sixteenth century, and novel devices proliferated during the Scientific Revolution of the seventeenth century. The trade in instruments grew in the eighteenth century, and in the nineteenth century there was an explosion in interest in, and institutionalization of, science. The number of types of instrument which have to be considered is, therefore, very large indeed. Two sources are of particular importance for identifying items: contemporary scientific textbooks, such as George Adams' *Geometrical and Graphical Essays* (1791) or Deschanel's *Elements of Natural Philosophy* (1870–1872, in English), and the trade catalogues of instrument makers. Both these sources are often well illustrated,

530

and there is access to trade catalogues (see *Figure 54.1*) through the hand-list of Anderson *et al.*, (1990).

The questions of dating and authenticity are most pressing for older instruments, for which recondite skills are required to establish their provenance. For this type of instrument more than any other it is necessary for Curators to cultivate their visual memory: there is no substitute for hours spent poring over surfaces of engraved and stamped brass, ivory or wood, turning over each instrument in the hand and every detail in the mind.

Next, we may ask who made the instruments, and what was the history of the trade in scientific instruments? The secondary literature is particularly rich in this area, as the bibliography given at the end of this chapter indicates. It should be noted that Taylor's two books (which are now difficult to obtain) are not entirely accurate. The structure of the trade in instruments has always been complex: various parts of an object might be made by different men, whilst the item might have been sold by a specialist vendor or by a trader with other interests, such as a bookseller.

The manufacture of instruments did not exist in isolation from other trades such as metalworking, glassworking, and precision engineering. For example, from the middle of the eighteenth century the Italian glassworkers who spread over Europe produced not only thermometers and barometers, but also other kinds of blown glass, and they were closely linked to sellers of mirrors, particularly carvers and gilders. In nineteenth-century England, R. and W. Munro of London made banknote printing presses for the Bank of England, and machines for cutting glass photographic plates for Ilford Ltd; in addition, they constructed scientific instruments, specializing in seismographs.

Particular mention should be made of the project administered by the Museum of the History of Science, Oxford, called SIMON (Scientific Instrument Makers: Observations and Notes). The aim of SIMON is to create a data base listing all the traders in scientific instruments who have worked in the British Isles between 1500 and 1900. It is far more than a list of names, covering the relationships between makers such as apprenticeships and partnerships, the dates when individuals worked and the addresses they traded at, and the types of instruments made by each craftsman. It draws heavily on guild records. SIMON exists as a data base, and is continually being updated and expanded.

Finally, we reach the most difficult and interesting question: Why were scientific instruments made? What function were they to perform in society? This is the history of the market for instruments, and of the relationship between the makers and the market. Some Renaissance instruments were made purely to demonstrate the inventive genius of the man who devised them, and some were intended to do little more than illustrate the skill of the maker.

From the middle of the eighteenth century, and perhaps earlier, scientific instruments began to be used by people other than scientists, and their industrial and social role became more conspicuous. Hydrometers were employed to measure the specific gravity of liquids in the chemical industry. Brewers, for example, tested their wort with hydrometers in the 1750s, and about the same time began to use thermometers to follow the course of their processes. The development of navigational instruments was crucial to the growth of world trade in the eighteenth century. Surveying instruments were of economic importance because they gave a method of determining the quantity of land in an era when land was regarded as the synonym of wealth. Above ground such instruments were used to measure fields: the Scots novelist John Galt describes 'the land surveyor, wi' brazen wheels within wheels, and [the laird] directing one o' his flunkies here wi' the chain, and there wi' the mark'. What was presumably a simple theodolite is also noticed as a 'brazen whirligig'. Similar instruments were used underground in the mining industry. Further varieties were invented to ease the parcelling out of land in the Colonies. At least as important was the use of precision instruments (particularly Garvatt's dumpy level) in laying out railways.

JOHN J. GRIFFIN AND SONS,

CHEMICAL AND PHILOSOPHICAL INSTRUMENT MAKERS,

22, Garrick Street, Covent Garden, W.C.

FIVE MINUTES' WALK FROM CHARING CROSS.

REMOVED FROM

119, BUNHILL ROW, FINSBURY.

London, January, 1866.

Figure 54.1 Title page of Griffin's catalogue of 1866

Modern science requires a fundamentally different approach. Today it is impossible for a scientist to remain abreast of the full sweep of the discoveries and applications of science. It is quite unrealistic to suppose that a Curator can possibly approach the level of understanding of a professional scientist.

Research into the artefacts of modern science is often conducted less in the spirit of the groves of academe, and more in the manner of a barrister mugging up a brief. Important instruments frequently come to the Curator's attention only a few days before the arrival of the scrap-merchant's lorry, and the possible acquisition has to be assessed and recorded *in situ*, dismantled, and all or part of it transported to a museum store. At this stage there are opportunities to collect documentation (technical manuals and log books) associated with the instrument, and to interview staff who worked with it – and who will be the only people who can set it in a human context.

Finally, we may ask: How well did the instrument perform its function? This question is often unanswerable. Sometimes it can only be answered with access to a university research laboratory, and the expertise of professional scientists. Where investigation is possible, as in the case of the optical performance of telescopes, the results can be revealing, and can affect one's judgement on the points raised in the preceding paragraphs.

History of medicine

The history of medicine is obviously allied to social history, and is a particularly appealing subject of study. Sanitation and sewage, diet and disease, Medical Officers of Health and the evolution of hospitals are all topics with a large human element. Materials for research are plentiful. Newspapers, for example, can reveal much about a cholera epidemic. Many hospitals had a stable institutional history from the middle of the nineteenth century until recent years, and Record Offices contain their notable and unexploited archives.

The centre for the history of medicine in Britain is the Wellcome Institute for the History of Medicine in London. Its enormous library (over 400 000 volumes) is open to anyone carrying out research, and it maintains a subject index of books and articles published on the history of medicine. Additions to it are published quarterly as *Current Work in the History of Medicine*. The collections of objects which were formerly displayed in the Institute are now on permanent loan to the Science Museum, and constitute by far the largest and most wide-ranging museum of the history of medicine in the UK. It is arguably the most important collection of its kind in the world. Its catalogue (over 100 000 items), has been automated.

There are a number of books on this history of medical artefacts which are more or less satisfactory. The area of medical technology is perhaps the best served, thanks to Davis (1981) and Reiser (1978). The decorative nature of drug jars has generated a literature in most European languages, and Drey's book is the most reliable English source. Crellin's (1969, 1972) two catalogues are particularly valuable since they cover useful objects as well as beautiful ones, and include a range of Continental material.

Research and curatorship

Research, since it is time-consuming, is expensive, but it must also be recognized that it saves money. Many instruments dating from the seventeenth century or earlier are now very expensive, and fakes are not unknown. Modern instruments such as early computers can be difficult to transport, require high-quality storage, and may potentially place exceptional demands on Conservators. Acquisitions must be selected with great care: expertise is at a premium.

The concern of funding bodies that museums should be accountable for their collections indicates also that Curators should identifiy correctly the items for which they are responsible, and part of the value of an object lies in the knowledge of its provenance and historical context. Research should be seen as contributing to this aspect of accountability.

It is a truism that an understanding of the content of a collection can only be gained by working with it over an extended period of time, and that a high level of understanding can only be attained by intensive study. The reality of curatorial life, however, does not allow research to be the end of curatorial existence, or the beginning of it, but rather something shuffled off to one side. Scholarship is always time consuming, and is often unrewarding for the institution, no matter how much it pleases the Curator.

Collections research on scientific instruments cannot be carried out solely by the Curator of each collection. The expertise of other Curators, and the historical knowledge of specialists and enthusiasts outside the museum community must be involved. Collections must, therefore, be made accessible. The requirements are well-organized galleries and stores, good basic documentation, and publication of summaries of that documentation.

Information handling is at the heart of curatorship. Museums are distinguished from other institutions because they hold large quantities of objects in perpetuity. Curators, however, spend little time handling objects. Instead, they handle information relating directly or indirectly to their collections.

It cannot be emphasized too strongly that good documentation lies at the base of all collections research activity (and at the base of most other aspects of curatorship too). The documentation need not be complex or particularly detailed but, unless the basic facts about the objects in a collection are listed (and preferably indexed), only a Curator who has worked on a collection for a number of years can have a grasp of what it contains. Poor documentation may be the product of selfishness, as well as of overwork or incompetence. Furthermore, a method is required for editing the catalogue records as more information becomes available. Too many ledgers and card indexes remain static as the years pass and Curators change, whilst the knowledge which each individual has built up is lost on their departure. This is gross waste. Where a museum maintains a hard-copy file associated with each object, conjecture as well as knowledge should be placed in the file. In an automated documentation system, each record can contain a 'scratch pad' which can be used by Curators or outside researchers to note ideas which are not sufficiently certain to be placed in the more formal part of the record.

Collections, institutions and publications

There are five museums in the UK which have large collections of international importance: the Science Museum, the National Maritime Museum, The Whipple Museum of the History of Science (Cambridge), the Museum of the History of Science (Oxford), and the National Museums of Scotland. Among the larger collections abroad are those in: Paris, France; Leyden, Utrecht and Haarlem in the Netherlands; Munich, Germany; Florence, Italy; and Washington, DC. There are many smaller collections of great significance, such as the Faraday material at the Royal Institution in London.

Before World War II the Science Museum had a good record of publishing catalogues of its collections. These catalogues included an extended description of each object, and a discussion of its technical importance. If they had a fault, it was that they rarely related the instrument to the wider history of science, or to the history of society. Since then there have been regrettably far fewer catalogues produced, although those written by Chaldecott (1955) and McConnell (1986) demonstrate the standard which is required. More basic catalogues, which provide no commentary on the objects, but

merely identify and describe them, have in recent years been produced by the Whipple Museum, and they admirably fulfil their intended function. They are produced at very low cost, to ensure that they are available to as many institutions as possible. Two catalogues have also been produced, in manner only slightly more lavish, by the Museum of the History of Science, Oxford. At the other extreme are the highly scholarly catalogues of Teyler's Museum, Haarlem (Turner, 1973), of the Playfair Collection of chemical apparatus (Anderson, 1978), and of the former Time Museum at Rockford, Illinois (Turner, 1987).

Another approach is to write longer entries on the more important items in a collection, and supplement them with brief listings of the less interesting items. The astronomical and navigational collections at the National Maritime Museum have been treated in this way, with great success. *Sic itur ad astra.*

Jayawardene has produced an admirable guide to the bibliography of the history of science: few other disciplines are so well served. It contains over 1000 items, and its coverage – like science itself – is international. It includes basic works of reference which are of wider use than to historians of science; and it includes some highly recondite volumes. It is, therefore, valuable both to the student and to the scholar. Any museum which has the least pretension of having an interest in the history of science should have this book. Annual bibliographies are published in *Isis*, typically running to over 3000 items, and the *Isis Cumulative Bibliography* is of great value.

Certain specialist journals carry articles on the history of scientific instruments, or on their background. Most specific are the *Bulletin of the Scientific Instrument Society*, and its American equivalent *Rittenhouse*. Among more general periodicals, *Annals of Science* must be mentioned for its coverage of instrumentation. Links between instrumentation and the wider history of technology are discussed from time to time in *Technology and Culture*. Relevant material may also be found in the *British Journal of the History of Science*, *Isis*, *Revue de l'Histoire des Sciences*, *Nuncius* (particularly on Italian subjects), and *Ambix* (on the history of chemistry). An annual bibliography published by the Scientific Instrument Commission of the International Union for the History and Philosophy of Science has very good coverage of publications relating to hardware.

Research into the history of science in Britain is focused on the British Society for the History of Science: the equivalent international body is the International Union for the History and Philosophy of Science. Included under the aegis of the IUHPS are a number of subject-orientated commissions, of which the Scientific Instrument Commission is one of the most active. Its annual bibliography is an extremely useful document. The membership of the

Scientific Instrument Society includes dealers and collectors as well as Curators, and its interests are by no means confined to the UK. It publishes a quarterly *Bulletin*. A more curatorial approach to the history of science and technology is fostered by the Science and Industry Curators' Group (SICG). The SICG can be particularly useful for making contact with Curators with specialist interests. A number of scientific societies, such as the Institute of Physics, the Royal Institute of Chemistry and the Royal Meteorological Society, have historical groups whose chief function is to organize meetings.

Acknowledgements

The author is greatly indebted to D.J. Bryden for his advice on a draft of the text. Any remaining eccentricities of opinion are the author's sole responsibility.

Notes

At the time writing SIMON can be contacted through the Department of the History of Science and Technology, Imperial College, London, SW7.

References

Items marked with an asterisk are of particular importance either for their content, or as exemplars.

*ANDERSON, R. G. W. (1978), *The Playfair Collection and the Teaching of Chemistry at the University of Edinburgh 1713–1858*, Royal Scottish Museum, Edinburgh

ANDERSON, R. G. W., BURNETT, J. and GEE, B. (1990), *A Handlist of Scientific Instrument-Makers' Trade Catalogues up to 1914*, Science Museum, London

CHALDECOTT, J. A. (1955), *Handbook of the [Science Museum] Collection Illustrating Temperature Measurement and Control: Part II: Catalogue*, HMSO, London

CRELLIN, J. K. (1969), *Medical Ceramics: Catalogue of Collections in the Museum of the Wellcome Institute*, Wellcome Institute for the History of Medicine, London

CRELLIN, J. K. (1972), *Glass and British Pharmacy 1600–1900*, Wellcome Institute for the History of Medicine, London

DAVIS, A. B. (1981), *Medicine and its Technology*, Greenwood Press, Westport, CT

DREY, R. E. A. (1978), *Apothecary Jars*, Faber, London

*JAYAWARDENE, S. A. (1982), *Reference Books for the Historians of Science*, Science Museum, London

McCONNELL, A. (1986), *Geophysics and Geomagnetism: Catalogue of the Science Museum Collection*, HMSO, London

REISER, S. J. (1978), *Medicine and the Reign of Technology*, Cambridge University Press, Cambridge

TURNER, A. J. (1987), *Early Scientific Instruments: Europe 1400–1800*, Philip Wilson, London

*TURNER, G. L'E. (1973), 'Descriptive catalogue of Van Marum's scientific instruments', in Turner G.L'E and Levere, T.H. (Eds.), *Van Marum's Scientific Instruments in Teyler's Museum*, Part II Leiden H. D. Tjeenk Willink (*Martinus van Marum: Life and Work*, vol. 4)

Bibliography

Items marked with an asterisk are of particular importance either for their content, or as exemplars.

*BENNETT, J. A. (1987), *The Divided Circle: a History of Instruments for Astronomy, Navigation and Surveying*, Phaidon, Oxford

*BENNETT, J. A. *et al.*, (1982–), [Catalogues of the Whipple Museum, Cambridge]

BRITISH OPTICAL INSTRUMENT MANUFACTURERS ASSOCIATION (1921), *Dictionary of British Scientific Instruments*, London (reprinted Schiedam, Interbock International 1976)

BROWN, J. (1979), *Mathematical Instrument-Makers in the Grocers' Company 1688–1800, with Some Notes on Earlier Makers*, Science Museum, London

BRYDEN, D. J. (1972), *Scottish Scientific Instrument-Makers, 1600–1900*, Royal Scottish Museum, Edinburgh

BURNETT, J. and MORRISON-LOW, A. D. (1989), *Vulgar and Mechanik: A History of the Trade in Scientific Instruments in Ireland, 1660–1921*, Royal Dublin Society, Dublin

CATTERMOLE, M. J. G. and WOLFE, A. F. (1987), *Horace Darwin's Shop: a History of the Cambridge Scientific Instrument Company 1878 to 1968*, Adam Hilger, Bristol

CONNOR, R. D. (1987), *The Weights and Measures of England*, HMSO, London

CRAWFORTH, M. A. (1979), *Weighing Coins: English Folding Gold Balances of the 18th and 19th Centuries*, Cape Horn Trading Co., London

CRAWFORTH, M. A. (1984), 'Evidence from trade cards for the scientific instrument industry', *Annals of Science*, **42**, 453–554

DE CLERCQ, P. R. (Ed.), (1985), *Nineteenth-Century Scientific Instruments and their Makers*, Leiden Museum Boerhaave (Contains papers on the trade in Britain, Italy, Germany, France and the Netherlands)

FERGUSON, E. S. (1968), *Bibliography of the History of Technology*, Society for the History of Technology, Cambridge, Ma

GILLESPIE, C. C. (Ed.), (1970–1980), *Dictionary of Scientific Biography*, 16 vols, Scribners', New York

INTERNATIONAL UNION OF THE HISTORY AND PHILOSOPHY OF SCIENCE. SCIENTIFIC INSTRUMENT COMMISSION (1983–) *Bibliography of Books, Pamphlets, Catalogues and Articles on or Connected with Historical Studies on Scientific Instruments*, (published annually; available from the Secretary of the Scientific Instrument Commission)

KITSON CLARK, G. (1968), *Guide for Research Students Working on Historical Subjects*, 2nd edition, Cambridge University Press, Cambridge

MADDISON, F. R. (1963), 'Early mathematical and astronomical instruments', *History of Science*, **2**, 17–50, (a survey of the sources)

MULTHAUF, R. P. (1960), 'The research museum in the physical sciences', *Curator*, **3**, 355–360

NATIONAL MARITIME MUSEUM (1970), *An Inventory of the Navigation and Astronomy Collections in the National Maritime Museum*, 3 Vols, National Maritime Museum, London

POGGENDORFF, J. C. (1863–), *Biographisch-literarisches Handwörterbuch (zur Gecshichte) der exakten Wissenschaften*, Barth Leipzig, (in press)

RUSSO, F. (1969), *Elements de Bibliographie de l'Histoire des Sciences et Techniques*, 2nd edition, Paris

SINGER, C., HOLMYARD, E. J. and HALL, A. R. (Eds.) (1954–1978), *A History of Technology*, 7 vols., Clarendon Press, Oxford

TAYLOR, E. G. R. (1954), *The Mathematical Practitioners of Tudor and Stuart England*, Cambridge University Press, Cambridge

TAYLOR, E. G. R. (1966), *The Mathematical Practitioners of Hanoverian England 1714–1840*, Cambridge University Press, Cambridge

TURNER, G. L'E. (1969), 'The history of optical instruments: a brief survey of sources and modern studies', *History of Science*, **8**, 53–93

TURNER, G. L'E. (1983), *Nineteenth-Century Scientific Instruments*, Sotheby Publications, London

WATERS, D. W. (1958), *The Art of Navigation in England in Elizabethan and Early Stuart Times*, London

WELLCOME MUSEUM OF THE HISTORY OF MEDICINE (1980), *Subject Catalogue of the History of Medicine and Related Sciences*, 18 vols, Kraus, Munich

WHITROW, M. (1971–1984), *Isis Cumulative Bibliography*, 6 vols, Mansell, London

55

Research: natural science collections

M. V. Hounsome

Museums have many functions, but natural history museums, or departments, have one fundamental and necessary imperative which is laid upon them by the scientific community. The absence, or insufficiency, of certain services may render a museum inadequate, but the absence of attention to its fundamental taxonomic function denies it the title 'museum' and makes it 'an exhibition' or 'an educational centre' or whatever title describes its remaining functions.

The philosophy of the scientific method ensures that it should never be necessary to believe the statements of other scientists; observations by one authority must always be repeatable, or verifiable by others. In practice, it is not possible to verify for oneself every conclusion drawn by every other scientist, so one is obliged to believe eminent authorities. Nevertheless, for observations to be called scientific they should be verifiable. In the physical sciences, this means that experiments must be repeatable before they are accepted. One should understand the difference between observations and the conclusions which may be drawn from them. The same observations may be susceptible to more than one set of conclusions, and it is in this field that debate and logical argument find their place.

In the fields of taxonomy and distributional biology the scientific observations are seldom the result of experimentation, but rather of accurate observation. The only way in which such observations can be rendered scientific is for the material observed by one person to be available for observation by others. The presence of a specimen in a museum is (duplicity excepted) proof of its existence, and its identity can be checked by all subsequent investigators.

Living things are named according to the Linnaean system, as administered by two professional bodies, one botanical and the other zoological. The rules are,

for the most part, similar. An organism is identified as belonging to a species which was given a name in a certain year by a certain author. That species is regarded as a member of a group of species, or a genus. Thus the components of the name are: **Genus** (always with a capital initial letter), **species** (never with a capital letter), **author, date**. Both names must be in Latin, or in Latinised forms of non-Latin words, and they must obey the normal rules of Latin grammar. For plants the word after the generic name is termed the 'specific epithet' or the 'trivial' name, so that the 'specific' name consists of both the generic and trivial names. A similar rule has been proposed for animals, but at present the rule is that the first name is the 'Generic' name, the second is the 'specific', and the complete binomen is the 'scientific' name.

It may be that some populations of a species are distinct, but not distinct enough to be regarded as separate species; in such cases a subspecific name can be added after the specific name, in which the author and date refer to the description of the subspecies. For example, in 1758 Linnaeus gave the European sparrowhawk the name:

> *Falco nisus* Linnaeus, 1758
> i.e. *Falco.* . . . .generic name
> *nisus.* . . . .specific name
> *Falco nisus.* . . . .scientific name

The tenth edition of Linnaeus' *Systema Naturae*, dated 1758, is taken as the start of the Linnaean system; names given before this date have no status under the rules of nomenclature. The sparrowhawk has now been taken out of the genus *Falco* and put into the genus *Accipiter*, and several subspecies are now recognized, two of which are:

> *Accipiter nisus nisus* (L, 1758). . . . most of the palaearctic
> *Accipiter nisus granti* Sharpe, 1890. . . . Madeira and the Canaries

These two examples illustrate several points.

(1) The use of trinominal names for subspecies.
(2) The abbreviation of well-known authors' names (e.g. L. for Linnaeus).
(3) The use of italics (underlined in typescript) for Latin names.
(4) The use of parentheses around the authors' names when their species have been taken from the original genus and put into another. Sharpe originally described his bird as being in the genus *Accipiter*, so his name is not in parentheses, but Linnaeus' species has been transferred, so his name and date (separated by a comma) are enclosed.
(5) The nominate subspecies is that which bears the same subspecific name as its specific name; thus the type of the species is also the type of the nominate subspecies.

Sometimes names are abbreviated on museum labels, and it is common to omit the date, and even the author; both practices are to be deprecated for all but the most common species. Abbreviation of the Latin names and the authors' names are justifiable where ambiguity can be avoided. Thus '*A.n.nisus*(L.)' is acceptable, especially in a collection where one expects to find only European species. Where space permits, and especially with types, abbreviations should be avoided.

Taxonomy is the process of recognizing, defining and naming taxa; in biology this involves identifying specimens as to which taxon (or named group) they belong, and devising new names for those which cannot be allocated to any existing taxon. The description and definition of new taxa is the work of the taxonomist. Nomenclature is the branch of taxonomy concerned with the legalistic rules governing the giving of names. Most taxonomists also regard themselves as systematists, as it is not sufficient simply to describe a new taxon, but one must comment on its relationship to other taxa. A systematist is concerned with not only the naming of taxa but also their arrangement into a classificatory system which illustrates the relationships between them. Systematics, therefore, has been not as precise a science as taxonomy, because supposed relationships are seldom, if ever, scientifically verifiable. In recent years there has been an increase in interest in systematics, especially in phylogenetic systems which illustrate the supposed evolutionary history of taxa.

Central to the international functioning of taxonomy is the Type System. The word 'type' has been used in more than one context, one of which is synonymous with 'typical', or 'representative'. This is not acceptable in biology, as the type concept is rigidly embodied in The International Codes of Nomenclature. Zoological nomenclature is governed by the International Code of Zoological Nomenclature (1985), devised by The International Commission on Zoological Nomenclature. The corresponding botanical code is The International Code of Botanical Nomenclature (1988) and the nomenclature of cultivated plants is governed by the International Code of Nomenclature for Cultivated Plants (1980).

A brief discussion of the zoological type system will serve to illustrate the main points relating to types, which is the area most likely to concern museum curators. The rules governing the naming of animals are couched in a legalistic framework, and can be correspondingly difficult to understand, but the central rule is that of priority. This states that the name of the species shall be the earliest valid name that was used for it; the date of publication (and page number in the same publication) determines which is the earliest description. This appears to be perfectly straightforward, but there may be considerable difficulty with early publications because the descriptions may be so poor as to cast doubt on which taxon is being described. The value of museum specimens, particularly types, in such cases is clear. A type specimen is the actual specimen that the taxonomist described as a new species, and is the ultimate arbiter of the definition of that species. This is true even if, subsequently, that species is deemed to be a synonym of an earlier-described species. Thus it is the duty of every name-giver to ensure that types of his new taxa are deposited in places that, as far as one may tell, are permanent, which will care for them, and make them available to taxonomists throughout the world in perpetuity.

The intricacies of taxonomic argument are sometimes so complex as to baffle the mind, but most changes of name have their origin in one of two situations: synonymy, and homonymy. In the first, an earlier name may be found, or what was thought to be two or more different species is considered to be a single species, which must, therefore, bear the earliest name. In the second, a name is found to refer to more than one species, so that new names must be devised for portions of the original taxon. In both these cases examination of the types is necessary, and it is their absence which opens the way to doubt and dissension.

Types come in several guises, from the rigorously defined holotype, down to the less important topotype. The more important categories are:

Holotype: a single specimen, chosen by the author to be the physical embodiment of the concept of his species. Once chosen, this specimen takes precedence over any abstract concept of the species, whether the author's or anyone else's. Colonial animals, such as corals, complicate the issue, but generally there is only one holotype.

Paratype: all the remaining specimens in the sample from which a holotype was chosen. There may be many of these, and they are often deposited in several museums for safety and availability for consultation. They will all have been collected at the same place at the same time. New species based upon only one specimen (the holotype) will have no paratypes.

Allotype: a special paratype, in that it is a single specimen chosen from the paratypes, that is of the opposite sex to the holotype. Allotypes have no more status than other paratypes, but it is sometimes useful to designate such specimens.

Syntype: authors have not always chosen holotypes, and have distributed 'types' to museums or friends; members of such a type series with no holotype are termed 'syntypes'. They are not encouraged in modern taxonomy, but museums may contain specimens labelled as such, or simply as 'type'.

Cotype: an outmoded and imprecise term for either paratype or syntype.

Lectotype: a holotype subsequently chosen from a syntypic series. The remaining syntypes are paralectotypes.

Neotype: a new holotype, usually chosen from a paratype series from which the original type has been lost or destroyed.

Topotype: a specimen collected from the same site as the original types. One of a range of so-called types which have no taxonomic status.

The object of taxonomy is to present the agreed framework of names that is necessary for the unambiguous exchange of information between biologists. Such a framework is essential to all ecological and distributional biology, and responsible museums are a vital part of the system. Type specimens are not the only scientifically important elements of a collection: they are of primary importance, but it is possible to distinguish two further groups of secondary and tertiary status. Specimens which have been figured or described in publications have a special value, particularly if the author was the author of the species or of a major taxonomic review or monograph. Specimens commented upon, in print or otherwise, by eminent specialists are similarly valuable. In the former case, the original description may not be sufficient to settle a particular point, and reference may have to be made to the actual specimens, to examine parts not figured or described, or to dissect the gonads, for example. Specimens authoritatively commented upon can greatly clarify one's view of the attitudes and intentions of such eminent commentators and can, for example, help in the selection of lectotypes.

Museum specimens can also act in confirmation of new or interesting records. New county or national records are put beyond question by the presence of the specimen in a museum, with the reservation that even this will not rule out deliberate deception. Subsequent workers may call into question the identity of a species claimed to have occured for the

first time in, say, a county, but a specimen in a museum will allow anyone to confirm its identify for themselves. Whenever it is legal and ethical to do so, such new records should be collected and preserved in a museum as voucher specimens for posterity. It is impossible for future workers to repeat once-and-for-all events, so that first records cannot be regarded as scientific in the absence of specimens. For sensitive groups, such as birds, where it is neither legal nor, most would say, ethical to kill unusual individuals, the acceptance of records is governed by a panel of experts. These experts sometimes have recourse to museum collections to compare written descriptions or photographs with authenticated specimens. Much acrimonious debate would have been avoided if previous generations of biologists had implemented either a voucher or a panel system for the verification of new records.

Of tertiary scientific importance are collections made locally, even of common plants or animals; or collections of single groups made over any area; or collections of unusual forms or aberrations; or, most elementary of all, collections showing as wide a range of specimens as possible. Modern biometrical studies demand large numbers of specimens from which it is possible to determine the range of variation. Indeed, some workers regard the type system as outdated, and prefer to consider populations rather than single representatives. Even within the traditional system it is essential to determine the variability within a species before establishing criteria to distinguish it from others.

There are many other reasons why a collection, or specimens within it, may be considered important, from interest in the taxidermal or preservation technique, to historical associations with people or events. The possibilities are legion; indeed, if no point of interest, actual or potential, can be found in a specimen or collection, then its place in a museum is questionable. The practical problem for curators in deciding what does or does not have a place in their collection is carried by the word 'potential', for they must make decisions based upon what work they *think* future workers will regard as important. Considerable experience in museum work is necessary to develop a 'feel' for what is potentially important and what is not. It is possible to lay down guidelines for the assessment of the current value of specimens, but inexperienced curators should not be called upon to make, unaided, decisions on their potential importance.

Most of the research on a collection will be either taxonomic or distributional. Taxonomic research involves the examination of types or specimens authoritatively commented upon, and the examination of a series of specimens to determine the degree of variation to be found within a single taxon. Distributional research also uses large series of specimens, both to establish the limits of occurrence in time and space, and to assess the degree of geographical variability. Biometrical studies involve the measuring of large numbers of specimens, and researchers may well travel the world to visit several museums in order to measure, or otherwise assess, as large a sample as possible.

Research may not always be directly related to specimens, as bibliographers may want to consult manuscripts, diaries and letter-books pertaining to people who were, perhaps incidentally, collectors. The cost of objects or services, such as taxidermy, can be of interest to historians and bibliographers. The collecting details themselves are proof of a person's presence at a certain place on a certain date, and the course of an expedition can be traced onto a map using the dates and localities on museum labels. Of more biological relevance is the plotting of past avian breeding distributions using museum egg collections. Museum collections are almost never random samples so that research demanding numbers or proportions is ruled out, but the presence of a clutch of eggs in a collection is proof of at least an attempt to breed at the recorded locality. It is thus vital that all documentary evidence should be preserved no less assiduously than the specimens themselves, and that such documentation is effectively related to the material or to the collector. The advice of conservators should be sought for the preservation of documents as well as for the specimens. It is clear that there is little point in keeping specimens, important or otherwise, if they are not stored effectively. This involves the proper initial preservation, careful conservation, and the use of suitable containers. These are discussed elsewhere in this volume.

Just as there is little point in having collections if they are not adequately looked after, they are of little use if nobody knows where they are or what they contain. It is necessary to maintain adequate catalogues, or at a bare minimum, to arrange the collection systematically so that it acts as its own catalogue. Ideally, all collections should be catalogued, and should have cross-referencing facilities from, for example, taxon to locality, and from taxon to collector. Such catalogues should be published so that they are available throughout the world. In practice, no museum does this for all its specimens, although type catalogues have been published for many collections, and many more are likely to be published in the future. The advent of computer cataloguing and the willing hands supplied by the Manpower Services Commission has put many museums on the road leading to this ideal, but it remains to be seen whether it is ever achieved. Certainly, it is within the powers of most museums to make available to scholars a catalogue of their types and specimens of primary importance.

An adequate library is the aid to research which many museums find most difficult to provide. Only very large museums have libraries adequate for all researchers. Others should content themselves with supplying key works which relate to the strengths in their collections. Even this objective may be impossible to achieve within the limited budgets available to many museums. It sometimes happens that a collection comes to the museum complete with the collector's library: in this case it is vital that the library is not split up or irrevocably disassociated from the collection as it is likely to contain all the important references relating to the material. Further value is added to the library if the books are annotated by the collector, or the author.

Both taxonomic and curatorial research involve a considerable amount of detective work, and clues found in manuscripts and annotated books may form vital links in a chain of reasoning. It is also important that original labels, in whatever state, are preserved; apart from explicit information, such as dates and field-book numbers, such labels may contain valuable handwriting clues which the experienced researcher can interpret.

Visiting researchers usually require some kind of workspace in which to lay out their books and equipment, and to examine the specimens. They may need to use the museum's equipment. Most researchers make contact initially by post, and in reply any deficiencies in the available equipment should be made clear, so that alternative arrangements can be made.

The question of who is allowed access to the collection and under what circumstances is a delicate one to be decided by individual curators in the light of local conditions. Clearly, collections should be available for as wide a range of users as possible, but frivolous demands should be rejected and impossible demands on the curator's time should be firmly discouraged. The major problem is that of security; unknown and unvouched for visitors should not be given the run of the collection. Ideally, there should be a visitor's room to which the material is brought, but some people may want to examine a large amount of material, so that is more practical for them to work in the storeroom. If they are unknown to the curator and are unvouched for, then they must be accompanied by a staff member at all times. This can place heavy demands on the staff, and it can be insulting to the visitor.

The circumstances in which loans are made are similarly fraught with problems. Monographs and extensive revisions of the systematics of a group may demand the examination of hundreds of types and authoritatively named specimens from all over the world. It may be impossible to visit all the museums which hold the relevant specimens, so requests are made to borrow material. Museum curators should have a clear policy on the loan of specimens, particularly types. Clearly, it is pointless for a museum to preserve specimens if their use is denied to scholars; on the other hand, holotypes are unique and priceless, and perhaps should not be entrusted to the postal system of certain parts of the world.

Restrictions on a loan of specimens usually centre on three factors: what can be loaned; the mode of transport of the specimens; and to whom a loan may be made. It may be decided, for example, that anything other than holotypes may be loaned, and that types must be collected by hand but other specimens can be sent by registered post. It is quite usual for loans to be made only to professional biologists at an institutional address, but such restrictions may be waived for certain persons known to the curator. A wide range of conditions may be enforced, and each museum, or museum department should have a clear policy on these conditions. One is never certain of attaining the correct balance between caution and imprudence, and individual curators' views tend to be determined by whether they have ever lost an important specimen. curators should be encouraged to be as liberal as their consciences, or their superiors, will allow them; loss is then regarded as a rare occurrence to be accepted philosophically.

A related problem is the treatment that some scholars may wish to give to type specimens. Clearly, destructive treatments must not be used, but what about dissection, or change in storage medium or form? One can never be certain of the correct procedure in these cases, as we cannot be expected to predict all the possible future uses of our specimens. Nevertheless, two main principles can be laid down: first, all the described characters must be preserved, in particular those mentioned by the author of the species, but also those that subsequent scholars have found to be of use; and secondly, the proposed treatment should not destroy other characters which may be of use in the future. It is this latter requirement that presents the problem, and curators must decide each case on its merits. If one feels incompetent to judge, then the advice of experts must be sought.

One of the privileges, and duties, of a museum curator is to carry out research on the collection in his care. Not all museum authorities encourage this activity, but besides bringing a good reputation to the museum, it is one of the best ways of obtaining a thorough knowledge of the collection. Being an active researcher gives greater insight into the needs of visiting scholars, and enables the curator to meet them as equals and to discuss matters relating to the collection with authority. The choice of research topic may be predetermined by the curator's experience, but is often related to a particular strength in the collection. In the course of reorganiz-

ing a major collection the curator will become a specialist in the taxonomy of the group, and may feel that he should let others know of his discoveries. This process is a natural one and should be encouraged, even though there may be no immediate and obvious advantage to the museum. The long-term benefit is found in the extra attention the collection receives, the use made of the collection by other experts throughout the world, and the job satisfaction derived by the curator.

Publication of results is an essential part of research, and curators should be encouraged to publish freely. The museum will gain in reputation, and the collections will be publicized and hence more frequently consulted. Some Directors or Governing Bodies reserve the right to approve or disapprove of proposed publications by their staff. This is not an unreasonable restriction, provided it is impartial and the criticisms are fair. Some authorities may restrict curatorial research to topics directly related to the collections, rather than to the wider aspects of taxonomy. In some cases this may be reasonable, but it is usually unjustified and short-sighted. It should always be made clear to visiting researchers and people receiving loans that the museum should be acknowledged in any publications which may result, and that reprints or copies of books should be sent to the museum.

Research in museums is usually specimen oriented. The fundamental duty of the curator is to safeguard the collection and to make it available to the world's scholars in the most useful manner possible. If resources allow, then the collection should be brought to the attention of potential researchers by the publication of catalogues and research. The role of research in museums is fundamental, and its neglect often results in institutional stagnation.

Bibliography

The following bibliography is intended as a source of further reading largely on the subject of systematics and taxonomic procedure. References to museum procedures and philosophy are given elsewhere in this volume.

BLACKWELDER, R. E. (1967), *Taxonomy*, Wiley, New York

BRICKELL, C.D. *et al.*, (Ed.) (1980), *International Code of Nomeclature for Cultivated Plants*, formulated and adopted by the International Commission for the Nomenclature of Cultivated Plants of the IUBS, Bohn, Scheltema and Holkema, Utrecht, pp. 32

CROWSON, R. A. (1970), *Classification and Biology*, Heinemann, London

DAVIS, P. H. and HEYWOOD, V. H. (1963), *Principles of Angiosperm Taxonomy*, Oliver and Boyd, Edinburgh

FERNALD, H. T. (1939), 'On type nomenclature', *Annals of the Entomological Society of America*, **32**, 689–702

FRIZZEL, D. L. (1933), 'Terminology of type', *American Midland Naturalist*, **14**, 637–638

GOTO, H. E., (1982), *Animal Taxonomy, Studies in Biology No. 143*, Edward Arnold, London

GREUTER, W. *et al.*, (Ed.) (1988), *International Code of Botanical Nomenclature*, adopted by the Fourteenth Botanical Congress, Berlin, July-August 1987, Koeltz Scientific Books, Koenigstein, xiv, 328pp.

HAWKSWORTH, D. L. (1974), *Mycologists Handbook. An Introduction to the Principles of Taxonomy and Nomenclature in the Fungi and Lichens*, Commonwealth Mycological Institute, Kew

HENNIG, W. (1978, in English: 1966 in German), *Phylogenetic Systematics*, University of Illinois Press, Urbana, IL

HEYWOOD, V. H. (1976), *Plant Taxonomy*, 2nd edition, Edward Arnold, London

HUXLEY, J. (Ed.) (1940), *The New Systematics*, Clarendon Press, Oxford

INTERNATIONAL COMMITTEE OF MUSEOLOGY (1978), *Possibilities and Limits in Scientific Research Typical for Museums*, ICOM, Brno, Czechoslovakia

JEFFREY, C. (1977), *Biological Nomenclature*, Systematics Association Edward Arnold, London

JEFFREY, C. (1982), *An Introduction to Plant Taxonomy* 2nd edition Cambridge University Press, Cambridge

JONES, S. B. and LUCHSINGER, A. E. (1979), *Plant Systematics*, McGraw Hill, New York

LEENHOUTS, P. W. (1968), *A Guide to the Practice of Herbarium Taxonomy*, International Bureau for Plant Taxonomy and Nomenclature of the International Association for Plant Taxonomy, Utrecht

MAYR, E. *Principles of Systematic Zoology*, McGraw Hill, New York

NASH, R. and ROSS, H. (1978), 'The type method and the species', *Porcupine Newsletter*, **1**(5), reprinted in *BCG Newsletter*, **9**, June 1978 29–33

PANKHURST, R. J. (1978), *Biological Identification, the Principles and Practice of Identification Methods in Biology*, Edward Arnold, London

PARR, A. E. (1959), *Mostly about Museums*, American Museum of Natural History, New York

RIDE, W. D. L. *et al.*, (Ed.) (1985), *International Code of Zoological Nomenclature*, third edition, adopted by the XX General Asembly of the International Union of Biological Sciences, International Trust for Zoological Nomenclature and the British Museum (Natural History), University of California Press, Berkeley and Los Angeles, xx, 338pp.

SAVORY, T. (1962), *Naming the Living World*, English Universities Press, London

SIMPSON, G. G. (1945), 'The principles of classification and a classification of mammals', *Bulletin of the American Museum of Natural History*, **85**, 350

SIMPSON, G. G. (1961), *Principles of Animal Taxonomy*, Colombia University Press, Colombia, NY

STACE, C. A. (1980), *Plant Taxonomy and Biosystematics*, *Contemporary Biology Series*, Edward Arnold, London

ZUSI, R. L. (1969), 'The role of museum collections in ornithological research', in Chen, D.M. and Cressey, R. F. (Eds.), Natural history collections. Past. Present. Future, *Proceedings of the Biological Society, Washington*, **82**, 651–661

56

Research: fine-art collections

Dennis Farr

Research on art collections, in this context, includes paintings, sculpture, prints, drawing, watercolours and applied arts – glass, furniture, textiles, ceramics, metalwork; and *objets d'art* – a term used here to describe small items in precious or semi-precious metals, and/or other precious or semi-precious materials (such as snuff boxes, paperweights, and inkstands, or artistic curiosities), which may have no practical use, but are simply beautiful ornaments or ingenious toys (Fabergé mechanical toys are an example).

An implied distinction is made between research on collections which is intended for academic use, and that performed for the benefit of the interested, but non-specialist, visitor. This does not mean there is a fundamental difference in the type of research involved in serving these two categories but rather there is a difference in the use that is made of the information and in its presentation. In practice, basic information about a work of art, its physical shape and size, the material(s) from which it is made, its subject matter or function, and data about the artist or craftsman who is thought to have made it, are of prime interest to both the scholar and the layman. The next stage for the specialist will be to establish its provenance (that is, where it came from, who commissioned it, and who has owned it at various times during its existence), its purpose, and its historical significance in relation to what is known about the wider cultural context of the country, or region, or city of origin at the time of its creation.

To summarize, the methodology of research in this, as in other fields, must start with a thorough physical examination of the object; next comes a review of all available documentary and photographic evidence (see below), including works which appear to be related in use, style or authorship to the object under examination; then comes the interpretation of this evidence, which may well lead the

Curator into many diverse areas of knowledge. It can be the most difficult (and most exciting) part of his work.

The knowledge thus accumulated by the specialist historian can then be presented in a variety of ways, depending on the type of public to be catered for. It is essential for Art Curators, who are now usually by training academic art historians in museum employment, to establish clearly in their own minds for whom the information is intended before deciding on the format to be used for its presentation. It is a truism that it is often more difficult to write an intelligible and interesting popular introduction to a specialist subject than to prepare a learned dissertation. If we need proof that an academic historian and a museum Curator can write popular introductions to the history of art, we have only to refer to Ernst Gombrich (1950) *The Story of Art,* or Michael Levey (1962) *From Giotto to Cezanne: A Concise History of Painting.*

Both these authors draw on their own very wide knowledge of the subject, and work within a carefully considered framework, so as to present a coherent, simplified narrative unencumbered by excessive detail or too many names and dates. They select the important developments in the evolution of art, and illustrate their story by examples accepted as key works. That is, works which can stand as the epitome of an aspect of the civilization which produced them, or which point the way to new developments, either technical, artistic, or both.

These books are general in their scope, and are not directly related to the collections of one museum or gallery. Consideration must now be given to the research that should be undertaken for specific collections and an attempt made to categorize the stages by which the basic physical information about a work of art is recorded, the use to which this is put, the problems which may be posed by physical evidence, the use and interpretation of data gained from scientific examination (for example, radiography, ultraviolet and infra-red photography, pigment analysis, and spectrometry), and the retrieval of information.

Having established a dossier of information about the object itself, the task of linking this with known facts about other similar objects or works by the same artist/craftsman, either already in the museum collection or known first-hand or from documents and printed sources, should be begun. The physical evidence can be considered as a *primary* historical source, in the same way as contemporary documentation (contract notes, letters (published or unpublished), and other archive material) can be regarded as primary. *Secondary* sources include accounts written either some years after the work was completed (assuming its approximate date is known), or which have only indirect bearing on the work and its creator. Biographies of artists written by contemporaries, or near-contemporaries, are primary sources, but need to be used with special care, as they may contain legends about the artist's career which he had wished to have perpetuated, or be written by those who were prejudiced against their subject. The same caveat must be entered for tape-recorded interviews with living artists, valuable though these are. *Tertiary* sources would include recent historical research and commentaries about an artist or craftsman, or a school or movement. This information may be published as a book, monograph, conference paper, or be accessible to scholars as unpublished dissertations held by university libraries. (A regular publication, *Dissertation Abstracts International*, covers universities in North America, with a small selection of European universities; but for more detailed, world-wide coverage, the researcher is advised to look elsewhere. The University of London Library, Senate House, London, WC1, produces a guide to sources of this kind.)

For the museum Curator, there are many ways of presenting the material evidence about his collections, and it is proposed to deal with the principal types of publication by which information may be disseminated, starting with the simplest. For ease of reference, attention is confined to UK publications, but the reader is reminded of the wealth of publications now available from North-West Europe and North America.

Brief guides

The size of the museum and the variety and range of its collections will determine the scope of a brief guide. As well as essential information (location, opening hours, etc.), the guide should present a concise history of the museum's development and purpose, its principal masterpieces, and so on.

Illustrations, with some in colour, will add to the usefulness and enjoyment of the guide. *Labels* to the exhibits should be legible and well-designed, with basic information, supplemented by *information sheets* in each gallery where this is practicable. If some form of house style and typographical linkage between the brief guide and the labels can be achieved, so much the better.

The brief guide which acts as a room-by-room survey of the permanent collections has obvious advantages, but many require constant revision if the permanent displays are altered frequently. *Prerecorded sound tapes* are another form of guide, providing a form of spoken running commentary for the visitor by means of portable cassettes and headphones. These recordings, like the printed brief guides, can be provided in different languages, but these too will require updating if the displays are changed frequently.

The character of a museum should be conveyed in the guide, and the *Victoria and Albert Museum: Brief Guide* (c 1970) serves this purpose. Somewhat more discursive, and more of a concise history, is the *British Museum Guide* (Pope-Hennessy, 1976), which gives a very clear picture of this august institution's history, of its departments, and its principal treasures.

The National Gallery, London, has produced *100 Great Paintings: Duccio to Picasso* (Gordon, 1981) which admirably conveys to the general reader an idea of the range and quality of the collections. Each of the 100 masterpieces is reproduced in colour, with a page of explanatory text, and there is an introduction in which the history of the National Gallery is outlined.

Where a museum authority has charge of a country house it is highly desirable to provide an illustrated guide with an accurate account of the history of the building, and of its previous owners. Original research can be incorporated in such publications, as, for example, in the revised guide to Aston Hall, Birmingham (1981) (Fairclough, 1981).

Handlists

These usually deal with specific collections, and are intended to convey basic information. Those for collections of paintings and drawings will list the artists represented and the individual works by each artist held in the collection. Title, accession number, medium, size and date (also whether and how signed or inscribed, and where) are given, and sometimes, how acquired. All this information can be computer coded and printed, with updating or corrections incorporated for subsequent editions. An example of this type of publication is *The Collections of the Tate Gallery: British Paintings; Modern Paintings and Sculpture* (Tate Gallery, 1967). Handlists can be illustrated, often by small-scale photographs of each work, which are intended for reference purposes, such as the recent concise catalogues prepared by the Manchester City Art Gallery (Treuherz, 1976, 1978, 1980).

Summary catalogues

Similar in format to a handlist, a summary catalogue contains additional information about provenance, previous collections, and essential documentary references (such as oeuvre catalogues), with a brief account of the history of the object and/or any iconographical or stylistic feature of particular significance to an understanding of the content or subject matter of the work. The catalogue of *Paintings in the Ashmolean Museum*, University of Oxford (1962), the *Katalog der Alten Meister der Hamburger Kunsthalle* (1956), the *Catalogue of 170 Paintings and Drawings of Vincent Van Gogh belonging to the Collection of the State Museum Kröller-Muller* (1952), and *The Museum of Fine Art, Houston. A Guide to the Collection* (1981) are excellent examples of four different types of summary catalogue (Hammacher, 1952; Hentzen, 1956; Parker, 1962; Agee, 1981).

Catalogues raisonnés

The catalogue raisonné, as its title implies, is the vehicle for presenting all the relevant data about a work of art, its history, iconography, and where the attribution may be in question, the arguments for and against its authorship by a particular artist. The writer will also be expected to indicate his own view of matters open to discussion. The material to be presented is often complex, and ranges over a wide field of scholarship. The compiler may have to familiarize himself with points of erudition culled from, say, the writings of the Early Fathers of the Church, obscure aspects of Greek mythology, of medieval legend, or of the now vanished topography of a *quartier* in nineteenth-century Paris. In the history of art, new standards of scholarship have been set by the late Sir Martin Davies and his successors in the series of catalogues of the major schools of painting represented in the National Gallery, London.

Davies' *Early Netherlandish School* (1945), was the first of the genre to be published after World War II, the format of which has been followed, with typographical improvements introduced to facilitate the cross-referencing within, and legibility of, the individual entries. While Davies did not invent the catalogue raisonné, he introduced new subtleties and refinements which like all good scholarship, made his catalogues raisonnés into works of art in their own right. Davies' catalogues of the *French School*, of

the *British School* and of the *Earlier Italian Schools*, followed in quick succession, he having had a unique opportunity to examine the paintings closely during their war-time sojourn in the slate quarries of Wales, to which they had been transferred for safe-keeping. His catalogues were complemented by those on the German, the seventeenth- and eighteenth-century Italian, the Spanish, and the Dutch schools, compiled by his colleagues Michael Levey and Neil MacLaren, and further catalogues for other parts of the collection have also now been published (Davies, 1945, 1946a and b, 1951; Levey, 1959; MacLaren, 1952, 1960).

In the highly specialized field of Old Master drawings, the Department of Prints and Drawings of the British Museum has long been pre-eminent; and Freeman O'Donoghue and Henry M. Hake's six-volume *Catalogue of Engraved British Portraits. . . in the British Museum* (1908–1925), is an invaluable source of historical material in this field (O'Donoghue and Hake, 1908–1925). Recourse to this compilation has often enabled the historian or interested layman to identify the sitter and, sometimes, the artist of what might otherwise have been yet another anonymous seventeenth- or eighteenth-century portrait painting. The catalogue raisonné may also be devoted to the work of one artist represented in a collection, such as Johannes Wilde's *Italian Drawings in the Department of Prints and Drawings in the British Museum: Michelangelo and his Studio* (1953), which while published as one of a series of catalogues under A. E. Popham's editorship, stands as a fundamental and authoritative contribution to our knowledge of Michelangelo, (Wilde, 1953). The catalogues raisonnés of the Royal Collection, which are divided into two series comprising many volumes, *Drawings in the Royal Library at Windsor Castle* and *Pictures in the Collection of Her Majesty the Queen*, draw on the expertise of many authors who provide in these catalogues most valuable scholarly contributions on the collections (*see* for example, Clark and Pedretti, 1969; Millar, 1963). Another series has been begun to deal with the furniture and *objets d'art* in the Royal Collection.

Sir John Pope-Hennessy's exemplary three-volume catalogue of *Italian Sculpture in the Victoria and Albert Museum* (1955, 1958, 1963) and his many other publications and catalogues on Italian sculpture, perform the same service for this specialism as the National Gallery catalogues do for Old Master paintings.

Pope-Hennessy's *Italian Sculpture* catalogue represents the distillation of many years of study, and this type of catalogue appears to be an endangered species. All too often nowadays, museum Curators are under pressure to produce ephemeral catalogues for spectacular temporary exhibitions, for which commercial sponsorship is available, but fundamental work on the permanent collections either has to be forgone or remain unpublished. The British Museum is able to finance its scholarly publications from the profits of its museum shop, as do a few other national institutions.

In the field of contemporary art, the catalogues raisonnés of the modern foreign and modern British collections at the Tate Gallery have introduced an interesting principle (Chamot *et al.*, 1964; Alley, 1981). Wherever possible, the artist, or his close relatives and friends, have been approached for first-hand information, not only about the works acquired for the collections, but also biographical data not always readily available elsewhere. In this way, unique primary sources have been tapped, and the results edited and published. The *Annual Reports* of the Tate Gallery from 1953 to 1967, and *Biennial Reports* since 1968, contain detailed information about new acquisitions and provide a running record for the use of the public. The documentation thus acquired is preserved in the Tate Gallery archives, along with much other source material such as dealers' records and annotated exhibition catalogues and press cuttings.

Scholarly research on collections particularly rich in the work of individual artists has also been published as catalogues raisonnés, notably the collections of painting by J.M.W. Turner and of William Blake's paintings and drawings at the Tate Gallery, by Martin Butlin, who has subsequently enlarged the scope of his Blake catalogue (first published 1957) of the Tate holdings to provide a catalogue raisonné of the complete works of William Blake (Butlin, 1981). Similarly, the late Professor Andrew McLaren Young's catalogue of the complete works of J. McNeill Whistler, which was completed and edited by three of his former colleagues and published in 1980, has as one of its starting points the rich collections of paintings, drawings, prints and memorabilia at the University of Glasgow (Young *et al.*, 1980).

Exhibition catalogues

Much new research on specific aspects of art history or of the work of individual artists is incorporated in the catalogues of major thematic or retrospective loan exhibitions. Such temporary exhibitions may often be related to the permanent collections of the museum and include items from those permanent collections which, because they are seen in a new context, may deepen understanding of their place in the history of art and shed light on the culture of which they are a part. The important series of Council of Europe exhibitions held in various European cities over the past 40 years, fall into this category, examples being *The Age of Humanism* (Palais Royal, Brussels, 1951), *The Age of Rococo*

(Residenz, Munich, 1958), *The Romantic Movement* (Tate Gallery and Arts Council of Great Britain, 1959), *Les Sources du XXe Siècle; les Arts en Europe de 1884 à 1914* (Musée Nationale d'art Moderne, Paris, 1960), and *The Age of Neo-Classicism* (Royal Academy of Arts and Victoria and Albert Museum, London 1972). Each of these international exhibitions surveyed a major artistic movement which transcended national frontiers.

There has also been a number of detailed investigations into particular aspects of the modern movement, of which the *Paris–Moscou 1900–1930* exhibition (Centre Georges Pompidou, Paris, 1979) and *Art of the Avant-Garde in Russia: Selections from the George Costakis Collection* (The Solomon R. Guggenheim Museum, New York, 1981), are important recent examples (Hulten, 1979; Rudenstein and Rowell, 1981). In this connection, tribute must be paid to the pioneering work of the Museum of Modern Art, New York, which, since 1937, has produced many important exhibitions of the art of our time, the published catalogues for which have often become standard books on the subject (Barr, 1937; Selz and Constantine, 1963).

An important new bequest or acquisition may provide an opportunity for publishing a scholarly exhibition catalogue which will serve as a permanent record of the collection. This was done for the Princes Gate Collection, bequeathed to the University of London, Courtauld Institute Galleries, and first exhibited to the public in July 1981 (Braham, 1981). The historical growth of a gallery collection, or the pattern of taste and patronage over a given period can also be charted, thus adding to our knowledge in a particularly graphic manner. Two recent exhibitions of this type were Colin Thompson's *Pictures for Scotland: the National Gallery of Scotland and its Collections*, (Edinburgh, 1972), and Allan Braham's *El Greco to Goya: The Taste for Spanish Paintings in Britain and Ireland*, (National Gallery, London, 1981).

In recent year, several major commemorative exhibitions for individual artists have been held which have advanced scholarship. A few may be noted here: *Rembrandt* (Rijksmuseum, Amsterdam and Boymans Museum, Rotterdam, 1955), *Poussin* (Musée du Louvre, Paris 1960), *Dürer* (Germanisches National Museum, Nuremberg, 1971), *Rubens* (Musée Royal des Beaux-Arts, Antwerp, 1977) and *El Greco* (Museo del Prado, Madrid, 1982). In London, *Turner* (Royal Academy, 1975), *Constable* (Tate Gallery, 1976, and 1991), and *Landseer* (Tate Gallery, 1982), have been honoured.

The decorative arts have been well served by the work of specialists at the Victoria and Albert Museum, London, and the staffs of some major British provincial museums. Floud's *Victorian and Edwardian Decorative Arts* (1952) set the standard for the series of major exhibitions which have done much to re-awaken the public's interest in, and knowledge of, this aspect of our heritage (Floud, 1952; Pope-Hennessy, 1971; Jervis, 1972; Wild *et al.*, 1973).

References

AGEE, W. C. (Ed.) (1981), *The Museum of Fine Arts, Houston. A Guide to the Collection*, The Museum of Fine Arts, Houston, TX

ALLEY, R. (1981), *Tate Gallery Catalogues: the Foreign Paintings, Drawings and Sculpture*, 2nd edition, Tate Gallery, London

BARR, A. H. (Ed.) (1937), *Fantastic Art, Dada, Surrealism*, The Museum of Modern Art, New York

BRAHAM, H. (1981), *The Princes Gate Collection*, Courtauld Institute of Art/University of London, London

BUTLIN, M. (1981), *The Paintings and Drawings of William Blake*, 2 vols, Yale University/The Paul Mellon Centre for Studies in British Art, New Haven/London

CHAMOT, M., FARR, D. and BUTLIN, M. (1964), *Tate Gallery Catalogues: the Modern British Paintings, Drawings and Sculpture*, 2 vols, Oldbourne Press/Tate Gallery, London

CLARKE, K. and PEDRETTI, C. (1969), *A Catalogue of the Drawings of Leonardo da Vinci in the collection of Her Majesty the Queen at Windsor Castle*, 3 vols. 2nd edition, Phaidon Press, London

DAVIES, M. (1945), *Early Netherlandish Schools* (revised 1955), Publications Department, National Gallery, London

DAVIES, M. (1946a), *French School*, Publications Department, National Gallery, London

DAVIES, M. (1946b), *The British School* (revised 1959), Publications Department, National Gallery, London

DAVIES, M. (1951), *The Earlier Italian School*, (revised 1961), Publications Department, National Gallery, London

FAIRCLOUGH, O. (1981), *Aston Hall. A General Guide*, Publications Unit, Birmingham Museums and Art Gallery, Birmingham.

FLOUD, P. (Ed.), (1952), *Victorian and Edwardian Decorative Arts*, Victoria and Albert Museum, London

GOMBRICH, E. H. (1950), (and many subsequent editions). *The Story of Art*, The Phaidon Press Ltd., London

GORDON, D. (1981), *100 Great Paintings: Duccio to Picasso. European Paintings from the 14th to the 20th Century*, Publications Department, National Gallery, London.

HAMMACHER, A. M. (Ed.), (1952), *Catalogue of 270 Paintings and Drawings of Vincent van Gogh belonging to the Collection of the State Museum Kröller-Müller*, Rijksmuseum Kröller-Müller, Otterlo-Gelderland

HENTZEN, A. (1956), *Katalog der Alten Meister der Hamburger Kunsthalle*, 4th edition, Kunsthalle, Hamburg

HULTEN, P. (Ed.), (1979), *Paris–Moscou 1900–1930*, Centre Georges Pompidou, Paris

JERVIS, S. (Ed.), (1972), *Victoria and Edwardian Decorative Arts. The Handley Read Collection*, Royal Academy of Arts in collaboration with the Victoria and Albert Museum, London

LEVEY, M. (1959), *The German School*, Publications Department, National Gallery, London

LEVEY, M. (1962), (and later editions), *From Giotto to Cézanne. A Concise History of Painting*, Thames and Hudson, London

LEVEY, M. (1971), *The 17th and 18th Century Italian Schools*, Publications Department, National Gallery, London

MACLAREN, N. (1952), *The Spanish School*, Publications Department, National Gallery, London

MACLAREN, N. (1960), *The Dutch School*, Publications Department, National Gallery, London

MILLAR, O. (1963), *The Tudor, Stuart, and Early Georgian Pictures in the Collection of Her Majesty the Queen*, 2 vols, Phaidon Press, London

O'DONOGHUE, F. and HAKE, H. M. (1908–1925), *Catalogue of Engraved British Portraits . . . in the British Museum*, British Museum, London

PARKER, K. T. (Ed.), (1962), *Paintings in the Ashmolean Museum, Illustrated Catalogue*, for the Visitors of the Ashmolean Museum, University Press, Oxford

POPE-HENNESSY, SIR J. (1955. 1958, 1963 and reprints) *Italian Gothic Sculpture; Italian Renaissance Sculpture; Italian High Renaissance and Baroque Sculpture*, Phaidon Press, London and New York

POPE-HENNESSY, SIR J. (Ed.) (1971), *Victorian Church Art*, Victoria and Albert Museum, London

POPE-HENNESSY, SIR J. (Ed.) (1976), *British Museum Guide*, British Museum Publications Ltd., London

RUDENSTEIN, A. and ROWELL, M. (1981), *Art of the Avant-Garde in Russia: Selections from the George Costakis Collection*, The Solomon R. Guggenheim Museum, New York

SELZ, P. and CONSTANTINE, M. (1963), *Art Nouveau: Art and Design at the Turn of the Century*, Museum of Modern Art, New York

TATE GALLERY (1967), *The Collections of the Tate Gallery: British Paintings; Modern Painting and Sculpture*, Publications Department, Tate Gallery, London

TREUHERZ, J. (Ed.) (1976), *Concise Catalogue of British Painting. Artists Born Before 1850*, City Art Gallery, Manchester

TREUHERZ, J. (1978), *Concise Catalogue of British paintings. Artists Born in or after 1850*, City Art Gallery, Manchester

TREUHERZ, J. (Ed.) (1980), *Concise Catalogue of Foreign paintings*, City Art Gallery, Manchester

V & A MUSEUM (*c* 1970), *Victoria and Albert Museum: Brief Guide*, Victoria and Albert Museum, London

WILD, G., LATTA, C. and POW, V. (1973), *Gold and Silver 1777–1977. An Exhibition to Celebrate the Bicentenary of the Assay Office*, Birmingham Museum and Art Gallery, Birmingham

WILDE, J. (1953), *Italian Drawings in the Department of Prints and Drawings in the British Museum: Michelangelo and his Studio*, British Museum London

YOUNG, A. M., MACDONALD, M., SPENCER, R. and MILES, H. (1980), *The Paintings of James McNeill Whistler*, 2 vols, Yale University Press for the Paul Mellon Centre for Studies in British Art, New Haven and London

57

Research — social history

Roy Brigden

Perspectives

Social history collections are reflections of the everyday lives of people and their communities. They are the product of a society where rapid social change has created, and is counterbalanced by, a heightened awareness of the past and a deep-seated need to hold on to what has gone before. The faster the change the greater this need grows and the more absorbed we become in collecting and interpreting. Over the course of time, the collections develop their own historical interest encapsulating as they do the perspectives of those that nurtured them and the prevailing cultural environment in which they worked. For many of the more venerable museums operating in the field of social history this evolutionary element in the acquisition of material provides an additional illuminating insight into the collection (see Kavanagh, 1987).

It began with the concept of the bygone, a blanket term applied to any utilitarian object of historical interest but no financial value. Bygones were quaint curiosities: relics of a more primitive time that had a certain emotional appeal 50 and more years ago to a middle class flush with its own sense of progress but also wistful for that lost 'age of innocence' before World War I. Conventional wisdom today is quick to dismiss the sentimentality, the patronizing overtone and the unprofessionalism of these pioneer collectors, but countless museums now would be immeasurably poorer without the fruits of their labour. Dr. Kirk, the founding father of the collection that now forms the basis of the York Castle Museum in England, is the most illustrious member of a generation (Brears, 1982), that included many others collecting and recording on a smaller scale. Take, for example, Lavinia Smith who in the 1920s and 1930s collected redundant household and other objects from the inhabitants of East Hendred, her native Berkshire village, and documented them with extensive notes and sketches.[1] There was no deep philosophical background to her approach: just a love of the subject and of a job well done.

Today we tend to agonize a great deal more about the theoretical justification of what we do: about what we should collect and why. This is not surprising considering the progress that has been made in professional staffing and training. Furthermore, ideas about the nature of a museum's function and the material in its care inevitably change over the years so that what once appeared to be a balanced working framework may now appear to be less appropriate. We have also been able to draw on the efforts to codify material culture studies that have been made by colleagues overseas, notably in Western Europe and the USA (Pearce, 1985–1986). Meanwhile, museums of social history in the broadest sense have been expanding faster than most over the last decade at the leading edge of what has become known as the heritage industry. Their Curators, often now in the guise of leisure managers, have to weigh the finer points of collection management against over-riding demands to service and extend the visitor experience. Although most recent advances, and the application of most resources, have therefore been in the field of presentation, it is still the theory and practice of collecting that is the fundamental aspect and arouses most internal debate.

At the heart of the problem, if in fact it is a problem, is that social history curatorship in the UK now appears to spring from two different schools of thought. The first is what might be termed the 'folk life' school which had the field to itself throughout the 1950s and 1960s and was able to establish a commanding influence on curatorial thinking at that time. It was a natural translation into British terms of North European ideas concerning the study and interpretion of folk culture which had first come to notice here earlier in the century and in the immediate post-World War II years furnished the principles upon which a new phase of museum growth was based. As a subject discipline, it has become most closely associated over the years with the life and work of rural communities and it is here that its greatest contributions have been made.[2] There has been a tendency also to concentrate on surviving traditional forms, such as particular crafts or customs, that have evolved over a long period and are to a degree anachronistic in the modern, industrialized world. Here the comparative study of object material is a major source of evidence and a key element in the research process.

The Society for Folk Life Studies, founded in 1961, is of international stature and remains the principal focus of communication for this group. Although drawing considerable support from strongholds in the Celtic heartland, its annual publication *Folk Life* (with the significant subtitle, *A Journal of Ethnological Studies*) attracts contributions from authors in all parts of Britain, only a proportion of whom are museum prefessionals. Essays in recent issues on flails, wooden harvest bottles and one-way ploughs (North, 1985; Newman, 1986; Harris, 1987) are all the result of object–centred studies that have drawn extensively also upon documentary, linguistic and other sources. As such they follow on directly from the work begun in the 1950s and are a reminder of just how much scope still remains for primary research on object collections of this sort.

Since the early 1970s, the continuing growth of museums of social history has brought forward a new generation of Curators born in a different time and with a freshness of approach that is consolidating now into what might be called the 'contemporary' school. The distinguishing feature here is a mission to track and interpret the evolution of our essentially urban and suburban society through the twentieth century. In particular, the recent past encompassing the decades since World War II is seen as presenting the greatest opportunity and the greatest challenge to the conventional folk life orthodoxy. Here we are dealing with a quick-fire succession of eras, each one the result of a complex interplay between technology and fashion on the one hand and social, economic and political change on the other. We are dealing, moreover, not with individually crafted objects to be studied as unique specimens but with the mass produced consumer goods of a throw-away society. The most mundane, the least considered items now gather new significance, because in aggregate they are touchstones evoking the style, flavour and the spirit of the time.

Central to this movement is the Social History Curators Group (SHCG) which was created in 1983 out of what had been known since 1974 as the Group for Regional Studies in Museums. The change of name was significant; the original implied too much of the ethnological root and no longer projected adequately the interests of the majority of members. Since 1984 and the first Women, Heritage and Museum (WHAM) Conference in Manchester, there has also been a growing circle of special interest in the role of women in history and in museums.[3] Contemporary collecting has dominated the SHCG's activities and its journal in recent years,[4] partly because the respectability of the concept had to be established within the museum world as a whole but also because the practical implications of a contemporary collecting policy begged many questions that required examination.

While the first of these has been largely overcome there is still some way to go on the second. Once it has been accepted that all contemporary material is fair game in collecting terms, then the matter of selection begins to take over. With each passing year, the modern world bequeaths an image of itself to the future through a multiplicity of media. The museum may choose to collect material with which to reinforce that image or it may prefer to go off in search of a different world that lies beyond the glossy magazine photographs and film clips. Questions of how and what to select are not new but they do become rather more pronounced when dealing with the very recent past for, although more material may be available, the museum's capacity to house it professionally is an obvious constraint. It is no accident that the current interest in contemporary collecting has brought into the open another debate on collections disposal.[5]

The ground rules for these new trends in social history curatorship are still emerging, helped by a body of experience that is being gathered and reported on around the country.[6] Further assistance is available from abroad. In the late 1970s, a programme for the recording of contemporary life was put together by Swedish museums, led by the Nordiska Museet, as a means of widening the scope of museum-based research beyond its otherwise heavy Scandinavian concentration on traditional cultural and peasant studies.[7] The purpose, therefore, was to promote the concept of contemporary recording and to create a structured approach that would make sense of the subject and put the available resources in museums to the most effective use without duplication.

The collective effort of the museums concerned is divided into categories that cover the principal elements of social and economic activity from the major industries, to food, public administration and the home. Within each section the changing face of contemporary life is recorded through the appropriate media. Objects are collected in the course of this recording process and some attempt has been made to define the criteria upon which selection is made. Now known by its Swedish acronym, SAMDOK, the scheme has aroused British interest from some quarters in recent years, but as yet nothing comparable has been proposed here.[8] No doubt one of the reasons is that, in England at any rate, there is no national museum in the social history field and, therefore, no central co-ordinating body that could realistically launch and sustain such a programme.

A major step toward greater collaboration amongst museums did occur in 1983 with the introduction of the Social History and Industrial Classification (SHIC). This was developed by a working party that first came together under the auspices of the Group for Regional Studies in Museums and is currently operated in a reputed 350 museums both in Britain and abroad. The essential need was for a unified system of codifying material drawn from the whole spectrum of human economic and social activity and one that would be equally applicable to the many different kinds of museum that operate within this area. By demonstrating that objects from whatever source can be subject to the same cataloguing discipline, SHIC has lowered some of the otherwise irrelevant demarcation barriers between social and technological history. It is beginning to work the same process now on the folk life and contemporary schools of social history curatorship: the schools might have a different approach that springs from different philosophical foundations, but the basic purpose and the methods by which it is achieved are common to both. It cannot be long before the two are fully aligned.

Procedures

The central idea that distinguishes the social history museum from just a collection of objects is that of context – historical, geographical and cultural (see, for example, Jenkins (1969)). Once formulated and defined by research, the context can be projected through an exhibition to create a suitable medium of interpretation. The context makes the object speak: characteristics that divide one period from another emerge together with the threads of continuity that inextricably link our present way of life to its roots.

Within this overall historical framework, the objects possess their own context, for behind each there is a human element. The object itself is the clearest tangible link with the people who made it, the people who used it and the era to which it belonged. Research brings us closer to an understanding of these people, and separates each item individually; for even with mass-produced goods, the story of ownership and use is different in each case.

Systematic object-based research depends on locating sufficient examples to provide the data base.

Variations between the objects, their manufacture, design and use, can suggest distinct cultural regions whose boundaries encompass common streams of material. This concept is particularly suited to objects that were either home-produced or emanated from local craftsmen in districts where clear expression was given to regional traditions and influences.[9]

The plough is a good example of an implement adapted for use in different parts of the country under the combined pressures of external influences and local agricultural conditions and prejudices. However, during the last century, specialist agricultural engineering firms captured national markets and complicated the picture by sending factory-built versions of traditional plough designs to compete alongside the products of smaller, regional workshops. Consequently, this aspect of farming history presents a number of uncertainties worthy of nationwide research. By studying in detail the surviving type specimens and adding to that study the fruits of field work and documentary research, it is likely that the regional nature of the plough would be more clearly understood.

Where data are plentiful, distribution can be mapped to reveal the extent of the cultural regions. The *Atlas of Swedish Folk Culture* (two volumes of which appeared in 1957 and 1977) assimilates information collected from a network of informants on a range of cultural features including objects, customs and dialect.[10]

Although trends can usefully be established in this way, there are limitations to a method that tends to remove inconsistencies and classify social development into neatly defined segments. The Atlas can identify different regions but cannot, in isolation, account for the differences between them. As this must be the ultimate objective, the Atlas is a means to an end rather than an end in itself.

In Britain, object research of this kind may be hampered by the absorption of original material into private collections where, in many cases, haphazard restoration and disregard of provenance have undermined its value by destroying the context. Furthermore, the method is not always so relevant for later twentieth-century material. In the case of the plough, the last 60 years have seen manufacture concentrated in a small number of national and multi-national organizations. Modern technology produces many different types of plough, and while these have been designed to match varying specifications of tractor, and to cater for different working conditions, the regional element is no longer applicable in the same way.

This principle applies to other goods manufactured in the twentieth century. It is not easy, for example, to think in terms of regional variations in television sets or refrigerators. However, while the technological design features exist on a general level, there is still a local story to be told particularly from the usage point of view. The part paid by local distributors and the social impact of such products upon a family or a community are but two of the aspects that a social history museum can usefully investigate.[11]

Rather than concentrate on one type of artefact, research projects often seek to analyse the evolution and development of one occupation, industry or aspect of social life.[12] This can flow naturally from the existence of a particular collection in the museum, and the desire to extend the known background information. Alternatively, the research project can begin with the intention of adding to existing collections. A temporary exhibition, especially when accompanied by a publication, is a useful focus for presenting the fruits of such work by promoting a wider understanding of the museum's function and, by arousing public interest, may lead to the discovery of further relevant material.[13]

Once the subject has been chosen, the results of preparatory work in libraries and record offices will often suggest the pattern of subsequent field work.[14] Appeals through the local press may cause people associated with the activity to come forward. The forthcoming clearance of a site, the closure of a business, or the retirement of a traditional craftsman may have been the initial stimulus for the project. In such cases, all the varied sources of information – from the building,[15] the business records, the tools of the trade, and the people involved – must be fully researched and synthesized.[16]

In its other main form, museum-based research is not confined to a single category, but works through a spectrum of social material in order to study a particular community from the present back into the past.[17] This, in effect, is the role of the social history museum in creating a sense of local identity by giving the community an insight into its historical development. Here the Curator requires the skills of the local historian[18] to correlate the information embodied in his collection with that derived from documentary evidence, buildings and other landscape features, and from the memories of the inhabitants. This type of research establishes and enriches the link between the museum and its environment.

Site and open-air museums (Atkinson and Holton, 1973) extend this concept by arranging their material in order to immerse the visitor in the cultural atmosphere of the past. Authenticity can only be achieved through sustained preparatory research and field work;[19] the research may also reveal gaps in the collections to be filled by further investigations or through public appeals.

Other evidence of value unfolds in the course of creating the museum itself. The work of reconstructing or restoring the building implies a mastery of architectural developments and building techniques that in some cases can only be acquired through detailed examination of previously hidden parts of surviving structures (Lowe, 1972). Similarly, the operation of machinery in the museum requires a knowledge of how that machine works, and perhaps an ability to reconstruct missing or broken parts. Furthermore, by operating the machinery, more can be learned by the Curator, as well as the visitor, about the working conditions of the original operators. Hence research is not only inseparable from the conservation function of a museum, but is also closely linked with the display and interpretation function.

All these forms of research depend on the accurate recording of the information associated with the objects. This is a basic requirement of the accessioning procedure and one aspect of the discipline of research that allows for further work. Computerization allied to the SHIC classification have made sophisticated cataloguing and information-retrieval systems widely available. Even so many collections suffer from the weight of unprovenanced material not properly recorded at the time of acceptance.

Levels of information

The information associated with museum collections may be separated into three tiers. The first contains the *physical details* of the object and includes, for example, the material it is made from, the process of manufacture, and any recognizable period features. This level can reveal clues about its working life: whether the original form has been altered or converted, and whether any repairs that have been made to it are authentic or the result of later restoration. Many agricultural implements bear the marks of adaptation. It was not uncommon, for example, for old scythe blades to be fashioned into a variety of small edge tools for general-purpose use. A field mower or binder initially built to be horsedrawn will often have been converted, sometimes crudely, for tractor draught. Careful recording of such characteristics outlines a unique profile for each object and suggests questions for further research.

The second tier covers *oral information* about the object. The donor may have been responsible for its manufacture and so be able to describe the techniques employed. Further probing may reveal the tools and equipment used and the history of the business. If the firm is still trading, or at least if the premises have survived, then an accompanied tour may result in further material for the notebook, tape recorder and camera. The donor's colleagues and employees may also provide information. By asking them for the names of past and present business associates, before long a research project on a trade or occupation has developed and begun to generate its own momentum.

Oral information does not come solely from donors. A museum may possess an extensive collection of objects, but only a moderate degree of accompanying background material. An appeal through the press, local associations, and other groups may suggest contacts able to supply a local context for the collection. The popularity of reminiscence therapy amongst organizations caring for the elderly has in recent years opened up further possibilities. As Ewart Evans (1976) has said:

> What oral history does admirably in this respect is to supplement, supplying extra resources for conventional history by salvaging the sort of material that tends to slip between the meshes of print or documentation.

Context enhances the exhibition potential of museum material as well as increasing understanding and appreciation of the objects. The emergence of oral history as a discipline in its own right has over the last decade served to 'affect the presentation of history in museums, record offices and libraries. These all now have a means of infusing life into their collections, and through this of bringing themselves into a more active relationship with their community' (Thompson, 1978).

Recordings have been incorporated into social history exhibitions, particularly temporary exhibitions, to allow the human voice to heighten the atmosphere and the personal sense of contact with the past.[20]

Not all museums are in a position to afford the considerable labour input required for an extensive programme of oral history research. Very often a worthwhile recording is possible only after two or three meetings – when the informant is completely at ease – and the subsequent production of transcripts may burden secretarial resources (Fitzpatrick and Reid, 1987). While, therefore, it is important that the Curator should take detailed notes of conversations, a tape recorder should also be used.[21] Some Curators have overcome manpower limitations by enlisting the help of volunteers, thereby involving other sections of the community in the research work. This has the added advantage of widening the museum's circle of contacts and extending the range of potential informants.

The questionnaire is another survey tool that complements the methods already described. When composed around a research theme and actively distributed through local organizations, the net is cast widely in search of otherwise untapped data. The drawbacks of questionnaires include the preconceived and contrived nature of the questions and their tendency to invite short, standard answers, while leaving unsaid many of the more colourful and idiosyncratic details of the informant's experiences. A questionnaire, however, is useful in locating people willing to co-operate with research. They may then be visited so that information from the questionnaire is supplemented by that obtained in conversation.

The third tier includes *two-dimensional background information*. Primary sources, contemporary in date with the object, include manufacturer's catalogues, instruction manuals, advertising material and photographs. The Institute of Agricultural History at the University of Reading has extensive collections of trade material produced by over 2000 manufacturers of agricultural equipment. From these records, machinery can be dated, colour schemes identified, and a great deal learned about operation in the field. A business archive has a serious research function: production figures, with the names and geographical distribution of agents and individual customers, enable theories on the introduction and diffusion of new equipment to be tested. Other papers may show how the business was managed, how many men were employed, what the conditions of work were like, and what form of housing or recreation, if any, was provided. Business records, particularly advertising material, have an immediate visual appeal and a graphic style evocative of the period that gives them outstanding exhibition potential. Similarly, contemporary photographs not only supply vital information about how something was used or what a building, since demolished, looked like: they also create an atmosphere, providing the human context that allows associated objects to be viewed sympathetically.

However, danger lies in accepting at face value the visual image that such material provides. Would an early twentieth-century photograph of corn being mown by the scythe imply that this method was the norm in the area, or was the photograph taken because hand harvesting was by then a rarity? The print cannot supply the answer so again the importance of background research into contemporary agricultural reports, journals and farm records is obvious. Similarly, we may all have a mental picture of the furnishings in an eighteenth-century cottage, but how much is accurate and how much arises from commonly held romantic notions? The checking of inventories is one way of going back to the basic data on which to build a more informed and authentic portrait.[22]

Historical context depends not only upon the consultation of all these sources but also on a sound environmental awareness. Evidence of the interaction between man and his environment over the centuries is all around in the form of buildings, landscape features and people. It cannot be confined within the walls of a museum. It can, however, be recorded and interpreted so that, in matters of environmental conservation, the museum becomes a source of informed opinion. Furthermore, the museum may be involved actively in external interpretation by, for example, organizing a town or country trail around features of historic interest. The underlying principle is to harmonize what is inside the museum with what is outside. This link is forged through field work, the process that takes the Curator out to discover and study the raw material of his subject. As a simultaneous research and public relations operation, organized field work utilizes all the curatorial skills in concentrated form. Not surprisingly, it is one of the most important and enjoyable activities of the social history museum.

Notes

[1] The Lavinia Smith collection was an important acquisition of the Museum of English Rural Life in 1951.

[2] The published work of J. G. Jenkins has been particularly influential in this respect: e.g. *The English Farm Wagon* (1961a) and *Traditional Country Craftsmen* (1965).

[3] A report of the WHAM Conference, 7–8 April 1984, was published by the Social History Curators Group.

[4] See *Social History Curators Group Journal*, 13, (1985–1986), and *Museums Journal*, 85(1), most of which are given over to discussion of contemporary collecting.

[5] See papers on disposal of collections in *Museums Journal*, 87(3).

[6] See, for example, Mastoris (1987). Much of the *Social History Curators Group Journal* (1989–1990), 17, is given over to the interpretation of popular culture in museums.

[7] For a full description of SAMDOK see Kavanagh (1984).

[8] Some individual projects do, however, have much in common with SAMDOK: e.g. the kitchen recording project at Gunnersbury Park Museum described in Griffiths (1987b).

[9] Jenkins (1961b) records nearly 600 wagons around the country. See also Fenton (1974).

[10] An analysis of 'classical' Nordic ethnology is provided by Owen (1977).

[11] For comment on the social history content that should be evident in a motor car, see Green (1981).

[12] For an example of a survey combining historical material and oral evidence see Porter (1969) and also the trade bibliographies in 'sources for the social historian', *Social History Curators Group Journal*, 12 (1984).

[13] For example, the 'Cap and Apron' and 'Shops and Shopkeepers' projects at the Harborough Museum, described by Mullins (1987).

[14] See Jenkins (1974) for a description with case studies of how a research project is set in motion.

[15] For information on the recording of buildings see Major (1975).

[16] See Hayhurst (1987) which is based on work recording the last bottle-brush-making workshop in Nottingham.

[17] In Glasgow, current collecting reflects issues that concern the city and its people, see King (1986). See also Birmingham Museum's 'Change in the Inner City' project described in *Social History Curators Group Journal*, 11.

[18] Here the works of W. G. Hoskins are inspirational e.g. Hoskins (1967).

[19] This point is most clearly pursued through recent developments in the heritage industry in Jenkins (1987).

[20] See Griffiths (1987a). For a case study using the Maritime Museum in Lancaster see Whincop (1986). The whole volume 14 of *Oral History* is devoted to museums and oral history.

[21] For advice on the use of tape recorders seen Winstanley (1977) and Cheape (1978).

[22] For the value of inventories in research see Trinder and Cox (1981).

References

ATKINSON, F. and HOLTON, M. (1973), 'Open air and folk museums', *Museums Journal*, **72**(4)

BREARS, P. (1982), 'Kirk of the castle', *Museums Journal*, **82**(2)

CHEAPE, H. (1978), 'Some technical means for higher quality recording in oral history', *Oral History*, **6**,(1)

EVANS, G. E. (1976), *From Mouths Of Men*, Faber and Faber, London

FENTON, A. (1974), 'The Cas-chrom. A review of Scottish evidence', *Tools and Tillage*, **11**(3)

FITZPATRICK, J. and REID, S. (1987), 'Indexing a large scale oral history project', *Oral History*, **15**(1)

GREEN, O. (1981), 'Museum of British road transport: a review', *Museum Journal*, **81**(3)

GRIFFITHS, G. (1987a), 'Memory lane: museums and the practice of oral history', *Social History Curators Group Journal*, **14**

GRIFFITHS, G. (1987b), 'In the kitchen', *Social History Curators Group Journal*, **14**

HARLEY, J. B. (1972), *Maps for the Local Historian*, Standing Conference for Local History, National Council for Social Service, London

HARRIS, S. C. L. (1987), 'The wooden harvest bottle, 1700–1900', *Folk Life*, **25**

HAYHURST, Y. (1987), 'Recording a workshop', *Social History Curators Group Journal*, **14**

HOSKINS, W. G. (1967), *Fieldwork in Local History*, Faber and Faber, London

JENKINS, J. G. (1961a), *The English Farm Wagon*, Oakwood Press for Reading University

JENKINS, J. G. (1961b), *The English Farm Wagon*, Oakwood Press for Reading University

JENKINS, J. G. (1961c), 'Folk life studies and the museum', *Museums Journal*, **61**(3)

JENKINS, J. G. (1965), *Traditional Country Craftsmen*, Routledge & Kegan Paul, London

JENKINS, J. G. (1969), 'Folk museums – some aims and purposes', *Museums Journal*, **69**(1)

JENKINS, J. G. (1974), 'The collection of ethnological material', *Museums Journal*, **74**(1)

JENKINS, J. G. (1987), 'Interpreting the heritage of Wales', *Folk Life*, **25**

KAVANAGH, G. (1984), 'Folklife: present and future tenses', *Folk Life*, **22**

KAVANAGH, G. (1987), 'Beyond folk life', *Social History Curators Group Journal*, **14**

KING, E. (1986), 'The cream of the dross: collecting Glasgow's past for the future', *Social History Curators Group Journal*, **13**

LOWE, J. (1972), 'The Weald and Downland Open Air Museum', *Museums Journal*, **72**(1)

MAJOR, J. K. (1975), *Fieldwork in Industrial Archaeology*, Batsford, London

MASTORIS, S. (1987), 'Pre-empting the dustbin: collecting contemporary domestic packaging', *Social History Curators Group Journal*, **14**

MULLINS, S. (1987), 'Beyond a collecting policy: projects as policy at the Harborough Museum', *Social History Curators Group Journal*, **14**,

NEWMAN, P. R. (1986), 'The flail, the harvest and rural life', *Folk Life*, **24**

NORTH, D. (1985), 'The one-way plough in south eastern England', *Folk Life*, **23**

OWEN, T. (1977), 'Folk life studies: some problems and perspectives', *Folk Life*, **19**

PEARCE, S. (1985–1986), 'Thinking about things' a series of four articles in *Museums Journal* **85**(4), **86**(2), **86**(3), **86**(4)

PORTER, E. (1969), 'Fen skating', *Folk Life*, **7**

THOMPSON, P. (1978), *The Voice of the Past*, Oxford University Press, Oxford

TRINDER, B. and COX, J. (1981), *Yeoman to Collier*, Phillimore, Chichester

WHINCOP, A. (1986), 'Using oral history in museum displays', *Oral History*, **14**

WINSTANLEY, M. (1977), 'Some practical hints on oral history interviewing', *Oral History*, **51**(1)

58

Research: social-history sources

Peter Brears

The documentary research sources for the social historian are extremely rich, ranging from formal archival material to a wealth of oral, literary and pictorial evidence. By using a combination of these, it is possible to establish, with a fair degree of accuracy, the life-style, attitudes and working practices of the societies under consideration.

However, it should always be remembered that the author of any document had a definite purpose for compiling it, a purpose which might well cause it to have a particular bias. Topographical artists were frequently liable to move or change features in order to compose a pleasing view, while the authors of Government reports, etc., could select their evidence to promote a particular course of action. It is therefore necessary to verify one source against another, or at least to take the very nature of the evidence into account, before drawing conclusions from it.

Research sources (documentary)

Standard archival sources

It is assumed that standard archival sources held in national and local record offices are sufficiently well known not to require detailed description. In brief, they include records of land ownership and management (manorial court rolls and custumals, estate papers and lease books, enclosure and tithe awards), maps and plans (including ordnance survey and earlier material), judicial records, (such as those from manorial, quarter-session and ecclesiastical courts), testamentary records (including wills, inventories and administrations), ecclesiastical records (established, and other churches' visitations and parish registers), business records, household accounts, directories, census returns and local government records.[1]

Museum records

Every museum should be able to provide documentation of its collections in the form of accession registers, correspondence and information files. It is particularly important that the information gained from such records is verified from external sources wherever possible. The name and address of the donor, as recorded in accession registers, need bear no relationship to the original provenance of a specimen, for example, while the reaccessioning of museum specimens may cause sound provenances to be lost.

When dealing with individual collections, it is important that every effort should be made to trace any notes or catalogues prepared by the collector. Frequently, these have become separated from the collection itself, perhaps remaining in the possession of the collector's family, or passing into the hands of local societies or records offices.

Museum catalogues

Few worthwhile catalogues of social history collections have been published to date, and much remains to be done in this field. In 1903, the Guildhall Museum published its *Catalogue of London Antiquities* which remains the only published source to that most important of collections. New standards were set by Dr Iorwerth Peate of the National Museum of Wales, in his *Guide to the Collection of Welsh Bygones* of 1929 and *Guide to the Collection – Illustrating Welsh Folk Crafts and Industries* of 1935. Since this time, very little activity has taken place in this important field (see Curtis and Warmer, 1979; Brears, 1979).

Collectors' publications

As social history material was already being collected by the late nineteenth century, a number of important seminal articles have appeared in a variety of collectors' publications from that time. The pages of periodicals such as *The Reliquary, The Connoisseur, Country Home,* or *The Bazaar, Exchange and Mart* contain a wealth of relevant information, as do the individual volumes of *Collectors' Guides*.

Descriptive sources

One of the most important and easily accessible sources of information for the social historian is provided by the great wealth of both printed and manuscript descriptions of this country, provided over the past three centuries. Works such as Camden's *Britannia* (English edition, 1695) and Plot's histories of Oxfordshire (1677) and of Staffordshire (1686) established a form of topographical writing which combined historical evidence with current accounts of manufactures, domestic and social life and customs which has continued unabated to the present day.[2] Most districts possess their sequences of local histories, providing unique evidence of the development of their particular communities.

Further descriptive accounts are given in the travelogues of Celia Fiennes (1888) or Daniel Defoe (1748), and in the reports of the Boards of Agriculture, the Factories Inspectorate, or the Sanitary Commissioners. For customs and beliefs, ample material has been published in the pages of the *Gentleman's Magazine*, and in such works as W. Hone's *Everyday Book* (1826).

Evidence of a more personal nature may be gained from diaries, autobiographies, and commonplace books, many works of this type now being available in printed form.

Literary sources

From the early nineteenth century a number of major novelists and poets have tended to lay claim to different regions and social strata of this country. Thomas Hardy is inseparable from rural Wessex, Jane Austen from middle-class Southern England, the Bronte sisters from the South Pennines or, more recently, James Herriot from the Yorkshire Dales.[3] Although such works were intended to serve literary ends, they contain many unique and illuminating passages referring to most aspects of human activity within their region. Where available, the source notes and manuscripts, biographies, memoirs and personalia of such writers may also provide further information.

The works of other, more general writers may provide sources of a different kind. Dickens' account of Christmas celebrations, or school life at 'Dotheboys Hall', or Kinglsey's description of the life of climbing boys, provide classic examples of this type of source. It should be remembered, however, that these sources are essentially of a secondary nature and should be verified from other primary, contemporary material wherever possible.

Dialect publications

From the late seventeenth century, poetry, prose and plays were composed in dialect, and this movement expanded rapidly in the third quarter of the nineteenth century due to the increasing literacy of the working classes and the respectability given to dialect composition by such poets as Robert Burns. These works are often based on early memories, or on events of local significance, and throw considerable light on the practices and attitudes in the writers environment. In addition to documenting practical details, they also possess an 'atmospheric' quality, giving a unique impression of 'what it was like'.

Dialect dictionaries and glossaries can provide similar information, but usually of a more practical nature. Here, the main interest lies not only in the derivation or distribution of the word itself, but more particularly in the definition of the operation or artefact described. Wright's *English Dialect Dictionary* (Wright, 1898) is still the standard work of this type, its bibliography providing sources for further work. It may also be worthwhile to examine entries in the *Oxford English Dictionary*, drawing on its depth of etymological research in order to obtain the earliest references and quotations to the widest variety of artefacts and practices.

Oral evidence

The personal reminiscences of individuals provide one of the richest sources for the social historian, and museums working in this field should undertake taperecording in the field as a matter of course. The tapes should be transcribed, indexed, and placed in suitable storage conditions as soon as possible, in order to ensure their ready availability and the permanence of their content.

Pictorial evidence

The vast range of pictorial sources available to the social historian includes paintings, sketch books and topographical prints (these frequently being housed in separate art gallery collections, due to their aesthetic quality); photographs (in local collections, newspapers, libraries, and in commercial picture libraries largely serving the publishing trade); illustrated books (including volumes on regional costume, street cries, or various books of trades, such as Pyne's *Microcosm* of 1806) and political, satirical, and humorous prints, such as those by Hogarth and Rowlandson.

In addition to this original material, much relevant information may be extracted from the reproductions printed in sale catalogues, advertisements and on greetings and postcards.

Comparative studies

As museum studies are primarily concerned with actual specimens, it is important that any research into collections should consider every aspect of their physical qualities. This practice is already well established in most other disciplines, but is only slowly being adopted by social history departments within museums. It should be recognized that comparative studies of material culture between one region and another is just as valid and important in the post-medieval period as it is for those earlier periods considered by the archaeologist. Such studies might be based on the design, manufacture, decoration, use and provenance of any group of artefacts:

(1) Manufacturing and decorative techniques – on general themes, such as blacksmithing, domestic rug and quilt making, and horse decoration, or on more specialized subjects, such as the use of pewter inlay or coloured wax inlay in aspects of folk art.
(2) Design of tools and working practices – such as the design of hedging implements and their relationship in different landscapes, the distribution of certain culinary artefacts in relation to their local environment and cultural tradition.
(3) Decorative motifs, which may include survivals from the pre-historic periods, such as rosettes, 'x' motifs, or 'Celtic' heads, or survivals from more recent political and social events, such as the 'Bonny Bunch of Roses' commemorating the 1801 Act of Union. The use of distinctive decorative motifs may also be used to trace the distribution of products from a particular workshop or craftsman.

Work of this type can be successfully completed only by following detailed surveys of the collections of many museums. Due to the present state of documentation and information retrieval, comparative studies may have to be undertaken by making personal visits to many separate collections. The adoption of common classification systems and the increasing use of computers should enable the scattered knowledge to be brought together and assimilated.

Exposition

All research work undertaken in the museum should be publicized in one form or another, both to disseminate the results, and to leave a permanent record for the use of future scholars and other institutions holding comparable material. In addition, educationalists, academics, designers, and craftsmen, may wish to make use of the knowledge accumulated by the museum.

The dissemination of the results of museum research may be achieved in a number of ways:

Museum catalogues

Catalogues of museum collections, including descriptions of physical characteristics, dimensions and provenance, should be published, line drawings or photographs being used as fully as possible. Where the details of provenance are weak (this being a common feature of collections acquired from private collectors), comparative studies of soundly provenanced specimens in other collections should be made in order to suggest a region or date of origin. Where such suggestions are made, the catalogue entry must make it clear that they are suggestions, and not documented facts.

It is important that catalogues should not be mere lists of the museum's holdings but that they should be accompanied by a reasoned introduction, providing details of the background of the collection, relevant details of the subject gathered from documentary and comparative research, and a description of the location and availability of the collection itself.

Exhibition catalogues

Exhibitions featuring particular aspects of social history provide a valuable opportunity for the publication of catalogues, particularly when the specimens are being drawn from a number of separate, and perhaps disparate institutions. The above approach is recommended.

Academic articles

Where museum-based research contributes to the development of fresh concepts, it is often preferable to publish the results in the appropriate academic journal. The *Journal of Folk-Life Studies* serves most aspects of social history in the British Isles, in addition to which there are a large number of more specialized journals dealing with costume, numismatics, agriculture, military history, industrial history and post-medieval archaeology.

For more general distribution, such well-established periodicals as *Country Life* and *The Countryman*, or various county magazines, can provide an excellent avenue of publication.

Books and booklets

Where there is sufficient commercial interest, curatorial staff may be able to work with publishing houses on preparing books and booklets for general sale. This is perhaps the most effective way of making widely available the museum's collections and academic standards, frequently permitting many copies of a good-quality publication to be printed, while attracting income to the museum concerned.

Notes

[1] For national records, see Guiseppe, M.S., *Guide to the Contents of the Public Record Office*, 3 vols. (1963–1968), HMSO, London

[2] E.g., Howitt, W. (1840), and the works of Gertrude Jekyll, George Sturt, Flora Thompson, Marie Hartley and Joan Ingilby, George Ewart Evans, etc

[3] See *Oxford Literary Guide to the British Isles*, Oxford University Press, Oxford (1977)

References

BREARS, P. C. D. (1979), *The Kitchen Catalogue*, York Castle Museum, York

CURTIS, W. H. and WARNER, S. A. (1916), *An Illustrated and Descriptive List of the Smaller Implements etc. formerly (or still) in use on Farms*. Curtis Museum, Alton, Hampshire

DEFOE, D. (1748), *A Tour Through the Whole Island of Great Britain*, G. Strahan, London

FIENNES, C. (1888), *Through England on a Side Saddle*, Field and Tuer, London

HOWITT, W. (1840), *The Rural Life in England*, Longman, Orme, Browne, Green and Longmans, London

WRIGHT, J. (1898), *English Dialect Dictionary*, Oxford University Press, Oxford

59

Classical antiquities: forgeries and reproductions

Donald M. Bailey

There has been, since the Renaissance, a greater demand for the artefacts of Greece and Rome than finds of actual antiquities could supply. Engraved gems and cameos, in particular, were highly prized by collectors, and many of the finest 'Greek' and 'Roman' gems in museum collections today are products of the sixteenth to nineteenth centuries. Indeed, although the antiquity of many an ancient gem is easily determined with a little experience, and while many non-ancient gems are readily recognized, there is a whole middle ground, mostly of engraved gems and cameos of the highest quality, where even the most expert student of the subject can have no certainty, but can only guess. Gems and cameos both ancient and more recent come occasionally onto the market, but there can be few artisans these days skilful enough to produce forgeries of really fine gems. However, more and more interest is being shown of late by collectors, and good forgeries might well start to be made again.

Gold jewellery is another fruitful field for forgers as it can command a high price; gold normally bears no sign of ageing, and style is the main visual criterion for accepting or condemning a particular piece. However, it is worth while examining the composition of the gold, as the metal used in most Greek and Roman jewellery is almost pure, while most modern gold is considerably alloyed with base metals. Nondestructive methods of analysis are now extremely accurate. A forger could, however, use broken pieces of ancient jewellery as his raw material. It has been argued that poor workmanship is a bad sign, but there is just as much badly made jewellery of the classical period as there are other low quality artefacts from antiquity. Over the past 20 years or so, a large quantity of 'Etruscan' jewellery has emanated from Italy. It is often on a much larger scale than is ancient jewellery, and sometimes exhibits lowgrade granulation work. For really fine modern granulation (but not the finest dust-like globules on some Etruscan pieces) one has to go back to the products of the Castellani family, working in Italy in the middle years of the nineteenth century. They made unequivocal modern jewellery copying ancient forms, but as dealers in antiquities they often repaired and made good ancient but broken articles before selling them.

Sculpture in marble and other stones has always attracted collectors, landowners with country houses to embellish, and museums, and forgers have readily produced statues and busts for this lucrative trade. The only portrait of Caesar and the best portrait of Nero in the collections of the British Museum were both probably made as early as the seventeenth century. As most collectors preferred complete pieces, the restorers' workshops in eighteenth-century Rome were adept at completing even the most truncated ancient fragment, so one gets, for example, the torso of a Roman marble copy of Myron's bronze Discobolus, transfigured into a rather contorted Diomedes stealing the Palladium by the addition of all four limbs, a head and a small figure of Minerva, all modern. To determine what is ancient, what is broken and replaced, what is ancient but alien and what is restoration, is not always easy, and analysis of the marbles of such a pastiche is often helpful, as is the use of ultraviolet light to distinguish patching and recent overworking. In more recent times, the master forger Dossena (1878–1937) made superb examples of Greek archaic statuary which convinced many scholars, and there are pieces of sculpture whose antiquity is still not proven to everyone's satisfaction: the Boston Throne, for example.

At the lower end of the market, peasants with a little imagination, less skill and a sharp knife have, throughout the Mediterranean, carved small pieces of limestone into extraordinarily inept human figures and sold them to travellers as antiquities. From the so-called Baphomets of the mid-eighteenth century, to the 'Siculan' figures of the 1860s (examples of both groups are in the British Museum), to the works of modern Turkish Cypriots and inhabitants of Tunisia, these figures, bearing a family likeness imposed by the material and the ignorance of the makers, are legion and they may well be brought to museums for identification.

There is always a market for fine bronze and brass figures of Greek, Etruscan and Roman origin, both small and large, and forgers have not failed to make good its deficiencies. Most forgeries tend to be of small-scale objects, as the casting of life-size sculpture is a formidable task, particularly in these days of high technology. But heads 'broken' from statues are not beyond the modern forger. The difficulty with copper alloys is to build up a convincing series of corrosion products in the induced patination, which many of the forgeries effect. It is not easy, perhaps impossible, to reproduce the copper alloy/red cuprite/green malachite sequence, with natural adhesion between layers, of a well-patinated ancient bronze. However, ancient bronzes sometimes lack these features, depending upon the conditions of burial: Roman objects from the mud of the Walbrook in London, for instance, can appear no different from the day they were lost. Thus, the lack of a patination is no firm objection to the antiquity of an object.

Some collectors in the past have cleaned all such corrosion products from the bronzes. Richard Payne Knight, despite deploring the restoration of marble sculpture, had something very odd done to the bronzes in his superb collection, bequeathed to the British Museum in 1824. The majority appear to have been stripped of their patination and given a polished brown surface. The compositions of ancient bronzes and brasses are now being actively analysed, and the examination of a small drilling is often conclusive in determining whether an object is likely to have been made in antiquity.

Until fairly recently, when the work of Schumann, Bimson and Noble showed the materials and processes involved, the production of a convincing Greek vase was not really possible. Science and archaeology are in their debt but so, unfortunately, is the forger. But to suggest that such technical information should not be published, as has been done, is to argue against the very real contributions of the scientist to the study of the past, and these results just cannot be hidden. Although fired-on ceramic colourings of different compositions have been used in the past, these normally produced results which were unlike Greek black glaze. The only way to make a realistic vase was to fire the pot and paint it afterwards, and such colouring matter can be removed with solvents. Many a vase made in

this fashion has found its way into museums and private collections. Nowadays, such is the accuracy with which forgers can emulate Greek glazing techniques that it is only lapses in painting styles and the shaping of the pots which indicate their falsity. One has to fall back on subjective art-historical criteria. Fortunately, most forgers do give themselves away in this manner, but there must be highly skilled practitioners against whom the only weapons are clay analysis and thermoluminescence examination (and even here it is said that irradiation methods can circumvent the latter). Most good forgeries of Greek vases are made in Italy, and some in France; some are sold openly as reproductions. Samian ware, which employed the same production techniques as Greek black glaze, except for a reduction-firing phase, is also being produced. Other aspects of vase falsifying to watch for include the extensive replacement of missing portions combined with complete over-painting to give the effect of an unbroken vessel, the scratching away of the glaze of undecorated vases to produce 'red-figured' scenes, and the cutting of inscriptions to add interest to ancient plain pots.

In the 1870s the cemeteries of the Greek city of Tanagra in Boeotia were discovered, the tombs of which often contained exquisite terracotta statuettes, many of these being attractive figures of draped women. These, together with terracottas from Myrina in Asia Minor, discovered a few years later, were much prized by collectors and connoisseurs. When the supply dried up as the cemeteries were worked out, enterprising forgers continued to supply the market. Not only Tanagra ladies were made, but many complex mythological groups, alleged to be from Asia Minor, were produced, often in a romantic prettified style owing more to nineteenth-century concepts of decorative art than to anything conceived of by Hellenistic Greeks. Although giving the impression of being mould-produced objects, many of these figures and groups were hand-modelled one-off pieces; they commanded very high prices indeed in the sale-rooms of Europe. They were eventually exposed by the savant Salomon Reinach (who himself was deceived decades later by the forgeries of Glozel). The output of the more spectacular of these groups was probably not very great, but examples survive in the collections of museums, and others may well be brought into museums from time to time. Other terracotta forgeries include the large-scale Etruscan warriors in the Metropolitan Museum of Art in New York, made by the Riccardi family at Orvieto during and immediately after the First World War. Comparable to these is the Penelli Sarcophagus in the British Museum, sold to that institution in 1873 by Alessandro Castellani, and made a few years prior to that by the Penelli brothers. The difficulties of firing such a large object are such that, like the New York Etruscan Warriors, it was probably modelled, broken up, the fragments fired in small kilns, and then was pieced together.

Probably one of the most forgery-beset fields of small antiquities is that of pottery lamps. At least as early as the beginning of the eighteenth century false lamps have been made for hapless collectors. Between 1739 and 1754 Cardinal Passeri published his lamp collection in three sumptuous volumes: a very large proportion of these are false. Since then false lamps have been made in large numbers, principally in Italy in the nineteenth century, but now everywhere the tourist treads in Mediterranean lands, forgeries or reproductions of lamps are offered him. In Turkey, Egypt, Petra, Cyprus and Carthage false lamps are for sale to the unwary, and these are brought back to Britain. Unlike the eighteenth- and nineteenth-century examples, most of these are of appallingly bad workmanship, much worse than the poorest of Roman products.

Ancient glass, in the main the product of illicit tomb robbings, is possibly the most frequent class of classical artefact to be seen in sale-room catalogues in recent years, and is very popular with collectors. Even here, where the supply seems adequate to meet the demand, forgeries are found. In most cases because of the difficulties of producing glass vessels both ancient in shape and in physical appearance, the majority of forgeries are easy to recognize, but there are some convincing specimens which are hard to detect.

The Curator must also be aware of the presence of reproductions, not made to deceive, but sold legitimately as souvenirs. These can be very fine pieces of work, although the majority of souvenirs are trashy objects with only a superficial resemblance to the originals they purport to copy. But decorative bronzes made in the eighteenth and early nineteenth centuries for neo-classical interiors are often of high-class workmanship and are often difficult to recognize as not ancient. In the second half of the nineteenth century and the early part of the twentieth, there were many foundries in Naples making very close copies of ancient artefacts in bronze, and also in marble and terracotta. Such firms as de Angelis, Sommer and Chiurazzi were very prolific, and it is fortunate that many issued illustrated catalogues from which their products can nowadays be recognized. Once such souvenirs change hands or are even thrown away and found again, their origin is forgotten and they are brought to museums for identification or are sold as ancient in sale-rooms. For example, about 20 years ago a bronze was found buried deep in the earth and was described in a national newspaper by an unwary museum Curator as one of the finest bronzes from Roman Britain yet found. The response was immediate: several readers wrote to say that they had one just like it, as a garden ornament in one case. The bronze turned out to be a copy of the so-called Narcissus found at Pompeii in 1862, examples of which were made in various sizes by Naples foundaries.

Forgeries have been made in every culture where collecting the products of the past becomes fashionable or is regarded as an investment. The range of classical forgeries is much wider than has been described briefly above, and embraces such things as wall-paintings, mosaics, sarcophagi, Minoan objects, and, recently, those popular and pricey objects, marble Cycladic idols. Scientific analysis of the composition of the substances of which an object is made is becoming more and more useful, but forgers are constantly seeking to counteract this work, using the very results of the scientists to aid them. Thus, present-day forgeries can be among the most diffcult to detect, much more so than counterfeit objects of the past. Museums must beware of out-and-out forgeries, fine-quality reproductions and highly restored objects. With most of the objects discussed here, years of experience, working with and constantly handling the material is the main defence, and this expertise is not easily acquired by the Curator of a small museum with a non-specialized collection; it is here that national Museums may be of use to provincial institutions.

Bibliography

General

ANDREN, A. (1986), *Deeds and Misdeeds in Classical Art and Antiquities*, Paul Åström, Partille

HELLMAN, M. C. *et al.*, (1988), *Vrai ou Faux? Copier, imiter, falsifier* Bibliothèque Nationale, Paris

JONES, M. (Ed.) (1990), *Fake? The Art of Deception*, British Museum Publications, London

KURZ, O. (1948), *Fakes*, Faber & Faber, London

OST, H. (1984), *Falsche Frauen*, Walter König, Cologne

PAUL, E. (1962), *Die Falsche Göttin*, Koehler and Amelang, Leipzig

PAUL, E. (1981), *Gefälschte Antike*, Koehler and Amelang, Leipzig

TÜRR, K. (1984), *Fälschungen antiker Plastik seit 1800*, Gehr Mann, Berlin

Particular

ASHMOLE, B. (1962), *Forgeries of Ancient Sculpture: Creation and Detection*, Oxford University Press, Oxford

BAILEY, D. M. (1974), 'Taormina forgeries in the British Museum', *Κωκαλοσ* 20, 172–183

GUARDUCCI, M. (1984), 'La cosiddetta fibula prenestina: elementi nuovi? *Atti della Accademia Nazionale dei Lincei, Memorie, Series 8*, **28**, 127–177

LUSETTI, W. (1955), *Alceo Dossena, Scultore*, de Luca Rome

MUNN, G. C. (1984), Castellani and Giuliano, Trefoil Books, London

SOX, D. (1987), *Unmasking the Forger: the Dossena Deception*, Unwin Hyman, London

VON BOTHMER, D. and NOBLE, J. V. (1961), *An Inquiry into the Forgery of the Etruscan Terracotta Warriors*, Metropolitan Museum of Art, New York

Reproductions

CHIURAZZI, J. ET FILS and DE ANGELIS, S. ET FILS, (1914), *Fonderie Artistiche Riunite, Bronzes, Marbres, Argenterie*, Ferruccio Lazzavi, Naples

SOMMER, G. (1914), *Fonderie Artistique en Bronze, Atelier de Sculpture en Marbre*, Sommer, Naples

60

Coins: fakes and forgeries

John Kent

The recognition of the very competent coin forgeries which have been produced in modern times will generally be beyond the powers of Curators without specialist training and interest. There remain, however, many forgeries that can be detected with greater facility, and Curators with access to a well-arranged general collection should not despair of becoming competent judges of authenticity.

General principles

Most coins are (relatively) mass-produced objects, and even if individually rare, will conform to the norms of *style, form* (fabric), *metrology* and *technique* of their series. The detection of forgeries is, therefore, essentially a matter of comparison, and objects of undoubted authenticity provide the essential basis of reference. Forgeries are of two kinds: those made contemporaneously with the genuine prototypes, and designed to enter circulation; and those made in order to deceive collectors. The two categories are mainly, but not totally, mutually exclusive. For instance, certain false silver half-crowns made early in this century for currency bore dates never found on authentic pieces and some have been sold in recent years to collectors as genuine rarities. Such contemporary forgeries for currency have an evidential value related to that of the prototypes, and are 'false' in a different sense to those of the second category, to which the ensuing remarks will be largely restricted.

How forgeries are made

The identification of the way in which a piece has been made will often suffice, on its own, to condemn a fake. Most coins were produced by striking a prepared blank between two engraved dies. The dies were produced by freehand engraving or by the use of a master punch or (earlier) punches. The resulting

design, however crude, possesses a characteristic *style*, that a modern engraver working with modern tools finds difficult to reproduce. Most coins down to the later seventeenth century were either struck by hammer-blows on the upper die, or by machinery that has become entirely obsolete; these methods produced coins of characteristic *fabric* (outline, thickness, edge and flatness), which are almost impossible to recreate in modern workshops. Since, on the whole, style betrays his hand more readily than fabric, the forger has sometimes sought to reproduce designs onto dies by some facsimile process, such as spark-erosion.

Metrology – correct weight and dimension – is the characteristic most easily achieved by the forger, and one can only be surprised and gratified at how often he has failed to pay attention to these details. With the development of non-destructive techniques of analysis, metrology now has a new dimension – metallic composition. The coinage alloys of antiquity were often of some complexity, and their composition is now known to have varied in a systematic way. It requires unusual knowledge and skill to reproduce the correct alloy. This can be achieved to some extent by melting down genuine contemporary pieces in poor condition, a practice which has unfortunately greatly increased in recent years. Early Anglo-Saxon and, to a lesser extent, Ancient British silver coins have suffered in this way; both are series in which large-scale recovery by treasure hunters has rendered all but the best pieces of comparatively little commercial value, and whose apparent crudity and randomness of design tempt even the maladroit forger.

Many false coins are *cast* rather than struck. Style remains, of course, that of the original, and certain details can, if desired, be altered on the mould before use; but the other characteristics invariably suffer, to an extent dependent on the skill of the forger.

Casting a two-piece mould, despite its relative crudity, is employed surprisingly often, no doubt on account of its technical simplicity. It relies, often with success, on the collector's unfamiliarity with authentic material. More refined methods can, however, give a dangerously convincing finish to the cast. In recent times, the flow of metal in stationary moulds has been accelerated by electromagnetic and vacuum processes, or by centrifugal action in rotating moulds.

Forgeries can be made by electrotyping, although it is usually the case that the electrotypes themselves were originally made for study or exhibition, and have subsequently fallen into dishonest hands. The abuse of authentic coins is also to be guarded against. Examples include the numerous 'double-headed' pennies, and rarities such as the 1933 penny. A variety of tools and skills, which should not be underestimated, have been employed to achieve these results.

Probabilities

It would obviously be wrong for the Curator to assume that everything that is brought to him is false. On the other hand, he would be unwise to lend too credulous an ear to the circumstantial tales which may be told in justification of the piece almost, if not quite, too good to be true. Many a fake has been accepted because it 'had a provenance' or because the person showing it 'could not have known enough to make up such a story, unless it were true'.

Always reserve judgement until the suspect object can be examined unhurriedly and dispassionately, and away from the urgent representations of the owner or would-be vendor. Under no circumstances write a 'certificate of authenticity' for a specific piece. Even if the object *is* genuine, the authentication may eventually be attached to a fake of similar type. When it is necessary, a formula such as 'the object (coin and so on) I have examined is, *in my opinion*, authentic', should satisfy the genuine enquirer; always write the identification itself on a separate sheet of paper, such as the envelope in which the coin is placed.

Some forgeries and their characteristics

Casts

The product of the two-piece mould is generally recognizable by its blurred appearance; details are much less distinct than the apparent state of wear warrants. For instance, the enclosed portions of letters such as ABP and R may be largely filled in. Lines in the design may show unaccountable weaknesses or breaks, while the extremities of details are often deformed or missing. The design does not meet the field at a sharp angle, but at a curve. Pock-marks on the surface are due to air-bubbles; sometimes the surface has been tooled over to remove these, but there remains a scraped and soapy finish. The edge of a cast sometimes shows traces of a raised line, marking the junction between the two halves of the mould. Generally, however, this line will have been tooled off, leaving a smooth and vertical edge unusual in an authentic coin. Large ancient coins sometimes split at the edge in striking; look out for such 'splits' that appear on each face, but that do not go right through the flan, or are incorrectly positioned with regard to each other – sure sign of a cast copy. Such casts may show every sign of age. Not only were they made by counterfeiters in antiquity, but they have been produced for unwary collectors at least from the seventeenth century down to the present day. Casts of this character are not necessarily of rare coins. Early casts often appear to be very small; this is due to shrinkage of the mould.

Pressure-cast pieces are all recent, and are generally of silver or gold coins. They can be difficult to recognize, but may sometimes be distinguished by a tendency for the relief of the lettering and outer border to fail to match that of the centre of the design. The surface, too, may appear lifeless and slightly soft. These fakes are usually very clean and 'new' in appearance; any toning will have been artificially induced, and will have a shallow and chemical look.

A cast, when balanced on the finger and tapped with a coin, will not 'ring' in the same way as a struck piece. Absence of a 'ring', however, may also result from cracks or degradation of metal structure, and is not in itself proof of falseness.

Struck forgeries

Some of the best-struck forgeries were produced more than a century ago. They are, therefore, well known and well-published – but also widely disseminated. The products of Becker (mainly Greek and Roman) and Emery (mainly medieval and Tudor) are still dangerous because of the skill of the forgers in reproducing the styles and fabrics of their chosen periods. Older struck pieces often copied the engraved plates of books rather than originals, and have a correspondingly unconvincing style and finish. Modern strikings may be made by machinery exerting greater pressure than was available in earlier times, and such forgeries often show greater and more even definition, particularly at the circumference, and higher relief, than the genuine article. Almost all large ancient and medieval coins show traces of double-striking – evidence of the 'jumping' of the upper die under repeated blows. The total absence of this feature gives grounds for suspicion.

Curators are recommended not to attempt the authentication of modern gold coins; the recognition of such as forgeries is a very difficult and technical process that should be referred to the Royal Mint.

Electrotypes

These are formed by two thin shells of copper, appropriately coloured on the surface, backed and joined together by another metal, often lead. Electrotypes may therefore show signs of a junction running around the edge, though this can easily be plated over. Look on the edge for the small impressed letters BM or RR, showing the piece to have been produced long ago as a British Museum replica. Electrotypes never 'ring' and, due to their composition, their weights are almost always wrong.

Replicas

The British Museum ceased many years ago to supply electrotypes of coins to the public. However, numerous replica coins of all periods have been produced in recent years for a variety of purposes in this country and abroad. An *'as of Antoninus Pius'* was made some 30 years ago as a button for ladies' raincoats; with its shank filed away it becomes simply a cast forgery. Many museums themselves sell commercially produced replicas or even encourage visitors to strike their own. It is a depressing reflection on human nature that such objects are regularly shown to unwary Curators as having been found at specific sites and at great depth. Not even production in the wrong metal, to the wrong scale and by the wrong technique prevents these replicas becoming the object of mischievous deceit, and Curators should be constantly aware of their existence and of the problems created by their sale.

Alterations to authentic coins

The purpose is usually to make a rare coin out of a common one, or to 'improve' the design or inscription of a poor specimen. In the case of altered dates, two techniques are used. The appropriate digit may be altered by the skilful use of the engraver's tool; or it may be completely cut away from the surface and replaced by the required figure which has been moulded from some other source. The new digit will generally lack the sharp outline of a genuine figure, and under high magnification traces of the solder with which it has been fixed may be seen. 'Double-headed' coins, or other incompatible combinations of head and tail, are sometimes produced by grinding away one face up to the rim, and inserting in the hollow thus created the required portion cut from some other piece. The join should be sought just inside the raised rim of one face, where there will generally be found a slight deformation of the beaded border. Such a composite piece will, of course, not 'ring' correctly.

A suggested procedure

If one is asked to authenticate a coin, it is useful to give some thought to the possible motivation and technique of a potential forger. If the piece appears to be a rare (or documentarily impossible) variant of a common coin – for example, the 1933 penny – then alteration of an authentic object should be suspected. Great rarities in the classical series, particularly if they are Greek, often turn out to be electrotype copies. Try to decide how a piece has been made, and if it looks 'new'. Ring it, examine its edge and surface, look at the definition of the detail of the lettering and design, and compare it, if possible, with material already in the collection, as well as with catalogue illustrations. Weigh it, and see if the weight is plausible.

Do not be discouraged by the failure of a piece to appear in a standard work. Unrecorded varieties and even types are constantly turning up, and the forger is more likely to reproduce a known rarity than to attempt a novelty. But, if in real doubt, it is better to refer the enquiry to a specialist rather than to accept – or condemn – a piece on unsure grounds.

Bibliography

BOON, G. C. (1988), 'Counterfeit coins in Roman Britain', in Casey, J. and Reece, R. (Eds), *Coins and the Archaeologist*, 2nd edition, London, pp. 102–108

HILL, G. F. (1924–1925), *Becker the Counterfeiter*, Spink and Son, London

KLAWANS, Z. H. (1977), *Imitations and Inventions of Roman coins*, Society for International Numismatics, Santa Monica

LAWRENCE, L. A. (1904), 'Forgery in relation to numismatics', *British Numismatic Journal*, **2**, 397–410

NEWMAN, E. V. G. (Ed), (1976 onwards), *Bulletin on Counterfeits*, International Bureau for the Suppression of Counterfeit Coins, London

PAGAN, H. E. (1971), 'Mr Emery's mint', *British Numismatic Journal*, **40**, 139–170

61

Collections research: industry

William D. Jones

During the last three decades there has been a dramatic awakening of interest in Britain's industrial past. It has been reflected in the growing number of industrial museums in both the public and independent sectors, and of industrial archaeology and preservation societies. Behind this phenomenon lies a remarkable change of attitude towards our industrial past from one of neglect and even distaste to one which recognizes the importance of the heritage of the world's first industrial nation and the need to preserve it. The virtual disappearance of many old, familiar industries has been the spur and possibly the cause of such new concern, while in more recent years the industrial heritage itself has been viewed as a resource for regenerating declining or derelict industrial areas.

Traditional museums have concentrated on prime movers and items of transport when collecting industrial material and industry was regarded solely as the preserve of technology. Nowadays, however, former industrial buildings, often with their machinery intact, are being preserved and have become working museums. Preservation has also been extended to include the buildings of industrial communities, either *in situ* or re-erected at other sites. These developments have been stimulated by a combination of heritage tourism and the growth of interest in the history of work and in social and labour history, aided by the use of oral history and video as recording media.[1]

The new perspectives emphasize the human element, the social and work experience of people, and are in part a reaction to a dehumanized view of the development of industry and technology. There is much discussion about a need for wider interpretation of the term 'industrial history'.[2] A broader definition is that it is multidisciplinary in scope and comprises many integral elements. The elements involved include the industrial activity itself, buildings and equipment; the products from the extractive and manufacturing industries and the transport systems associated with them. These comprise what might be termed the anatomy of a particular industry. All these elements have their human dimension and their social consequences, touching on the experiences of men, women and even children at work; the impact of industry's products on people's lives and the impact of industry on the environment in which people lived and on the landscape. Industrialization created industrial communities which could prosper or could suffer the anguish of slump and unemployment. In short, industry is inseparable from a much wider phenomenon – the growth, development and consequences of industrial society, which has been the dominant motif in the history of Britain for the last two centuries. Thus, many disciplines overlap in the study of industry: technology, engineering and social, labour, economic, business and architectural history. All such areas are of crucial importance and are needed to establish the full context.

The wide parameters demanded by the study of industry entail that its proper contextualization cannot be achieved solely by the building up of a library of objects. In this field there is a close relationship between the museum's function and the subject. Museums of industry should not concern themselves only with the material culture, though it is, of course, a basic element, but must take the subject as a starting point and view their collections as one aspect of the record of human experience and endeavour and as reflections of communities at both local and regional levels. This overall context can only emerge from detailed and vigorous research into a wide variety of sources which is of as high a standard as possible.

The nature and importance of research

Collections research is just as essential and integral to the work of a Curator of industrial material as it is for other museum disciplines. It is the process that enables the Curator to increase knowledge of, and levels of familiarity with, the phenomenon of industry and industrialization in all its various dimensions and the sources of evidence from which information can be acquired. Research is an overriding function which is needed to accomplish effectively a number of other museum activities: collecting, conservation, interpretation and presentation, whether in the form of permanent displays or of temporary exhibitions. Research is also inextricably related to the museum's function as a public service, in making the collections available for the use of the scholar and the visitor. Equally, it is not only a case of studying the collections already in the Curator's keeping. It is essential preparatory work for future musuem activities and also for the contemporary collecting of material from industries which are still active and the new modern industries. An up-to-date general knowledge of the latest developments in the subject area of the Curator's remit – whether a specific industry or industrial activity in a particular locality or region – is a necessary preliminary to documentation and collecting and this cannot be done effectively without research.

The objective of research, however, is not only to accumulate the 'facts' – the nuts and bolts as it were – about an item or group of items in the collections. It is also to evaluate their significance and establish the inter-relationships between them, leading to a greater understanding of the general context into which the diverse individual industrial artefacts in the collection should be located to reveal their meaning. There are many sources of evidence and techniques which Curators of industry can use to acquire information and gain a more comprehensive insight into their area of study. The objects themselves are obviously one major source of evidence, but the Curator should be aware of the possible limitations of the surviving material culture which have direct implications for the research process. Using objects in research depends on locating sufficient examples to form a comprehensive data base. This can present a major problem in the case of industrial equipment since its size and scale and the consequent difficulties of storage have often prevented preservation or collection. Contemporary documentation or the results of recording through plans, diagrams and photographs may be all that remain. The Curator must, therefore, seek out and examine similar material in other museums and rely more heavily on other sources of information. Furthermore, there are fundamental areas of the histories of various industries where the material culture may not even have existed in the first place, e.g. in relation to attitudes towards work and working conditions, labour relations and the like.

Research into industrial collections thus presents the opportunity not only of investigating the surviving physical material and consulting documentary and archival sources but also of adopting techniques of oral history and industrial archaeological fieldwork. Each of these forms of research requires specific skills and the Curator should acquire competence in all of them since they are essential components of a combined study. The Curator should develop an enquiring mind, for a narrow or even antiquarian approach will inhibit a broader interpretation and wider perspectives, and at the same time a discerning one. Above all, when embarking on research the Curator, like the historian, should treat all historical sources with circumspection and be aware of their limitations for they are often biased and selective in nature. The information gleaned from the sources has to be corroborated and interpreted.

Research, then, is no trivial pursuit. It is a time-consuming and sometimes frustrating process but at the same time one which is immensely enjoyable and rewarding. Yet, despite its importance it is too often the aspect of curatorial activity which is neglected and relegated to odd quiet moments because of other pressures. Time for research should be built in from the start as a recognized and valuable part of the curator's working week.

Preliminary procedures

These lay the groundwork for subsequent, more detailed study and involve two key, inter-related elements: choosing and planning the research project and background reading.

Choosing and planning the research project includes identifying and locating likely helpful sources of evidence and personal contacts, and drawing up a programme of work, however rudimentary. Planning, rather than unsystematic approach, is essential and at all costs the Curator should resist the temptation to plunge into the primary sources or approach organizations, institutions and individuals prematurely.

The types of research project usually conducted in museums with industry collections are:

(1) the history and development of specific items of industrial equipment, forms of motive power or processes;

(2) the past and present industrial activity of a specific locality or region or, more specifically, an important local industry, company or business;

(3) the work experience of a single occupational group, e.g. miners; and

(4) in on-site museums, the history of the preserved site, equipment, buildings, etc.; research is essential here for authenticity and interpretation.

Whether focusing on a similar group of artefacts or a wide variety of objects, the research project can arise from the existence of a particular collection and the desire to extend existing knowledge, or be aimed at adding to existing collections or creating new ones. In some cases it will be desirable to take a completely holistic approach, using the subject as a whole and not the objects as the starting point. This is, in other words, a SAMDOK type approach.[3]

Choosing and planning the research project cannot be done satisfactorily without the other element in the preliminary stage. Before embarking on a more detailed investigation of the sources of evidence, as it were the raw materials, much background reading will often be needed to acquire a basic knowledge and to assimilate and synthesize the findings of previous researchers in the same field. Curators will accumulate knowledge with experience but this step is essential when starting out for the first time, since a firm grasp of the subject is needed to understand and evaluate the significance of new information. The Curator will need access to libraries and record offices and, first, conduct a literature search for bibliographies and published secondary sources, i.e. books and articles in relevant journals and periodicals. Depending on the subject, the list of appropriate books and articles can be quite long.

The findings of previous researchers in the same or allied fields are valuable not only for the information they contain. Their bibliographies and references will provide guides to primary sources, especially documentary ones, as well as suggest possible guidelines for the Curator's own research project. A useful exercise at this preliminary stage is the drawing up of a bibliography which can be added to as the project progresses and, later, can aid in the preparation of publications.

As well as reading, it is also important to contact other researchers in the field – fellow Curators, academics, local historians, industrial archaeologists, etc. This activity goes hand in hand with the examination of written sources and may involve appeals in museum journals, etc., and in local newspapers.

Having acquired a basic knowledge and drawn up a programme of work, the Curator will be in a position to carry out more detailed research. The types of sources available and the techniques to be adopted are now looked at in more detail.

Sources of information and evidence

Published secondary sources

Bibliographies

There are published bibliographies of literature on some individual industries, e.g. Benson *et al.* (1981) on the coal industry, whilst literature on the technological aspects of various industries is compiled in the annual *British Technology Index*. Shorter bibliographies or reading lists are occasionally published in museum and other relevant journals.

Books and monographs
These consist of both historical studies and contemporary works. They include studies of various industries and on social and industrial history; local and regional histories (the publisher David and Charles has a series of books on the industrial archaeology of various regions); travelogues; autobiographies of entrepreneurs, government officials involved in industry, and workers; encyclopaedias and treatises. Other valuable contemporary publications are textbooks of industrial processes and practices, and instruction manuals and catalogues issued by companies.

Periodicals and Journals
For articles on industrial subjects relevant museum journals are *Museums Journal, Curator, Museum, Social History Curators Group Journal* and the *Newsletter* of the Science and Industry Curators Group. Relevant non-museum journals are, e.g. *Transactions of the Newcomen Society, Industrial Archaeology, Industrial Archaeology Review, Technology and Culture, Oral History, Labour History*, and more specialized journals such as *Transport History, Textile History*, etc. Company and street directories, and the trade journals and newspapers relating to specific industries such as, e.g. *Colliery Guardian* and *Iron and Steel Trades Review*, can be very useful, as are the Proceedings of professional bodies such as the Institute of Civil Engineers, etc. Reports of specific events in local newspapers also usually contain helpful information.

Published primary sources

These cover Government publications such as Commissions of Enquiry, the Annual Reports of the various Inspectorates, Acts of Parliament and the Census returns.

Archival and documentary sources

Business records
Business records, relating to both public and private industrial and commercial enterprises. If extant these

may be housed in public repositories or remain in private hands. Orbell (1987) provides a useful guide to the types of source material involved and their location.

Trade Union records
Trade Union records of national and regional unions and of local branches and lodges.

Local Government records
Local Government records including those touching on public health, highways and transport.

Wills and inventories for sale, etc.
Wills and inventories for sales, auctions, etc., can be useful sources.

Maps and plans
These are invaluable aids for locating former industrial activity and establishing the layout of sites and they can be used to trace changes over a period to point to the industrial development of an area. They

are essential for the interpretation of sites during fieldwork and are also good visual appeal material for interpretive displays.

Pictorial evidence
The wide variety of pictorial sources of industrial scenes and material available include not only contemporary photographs but also paintings, sketches and topographical prints and even reproductions in advertisements and catalogues (see *Figures 61.1 to 61.4*). Illustrations can supply vital information regarding a number of aspects of industrial activity and development, e.g. industrial processes and methods of work, the layout of industrial enterprises and changes in buildings and in the landscape in general. They enable objects to be located in their wider context and often illuminate the human dimension by showing workers at work, their styles of dress, etc.

The images contained in photographs or works of art should not, however, be accepted at face value. Their accuracy must be corroborated by other

Figure 61.1 Coal mining in South Wales and the landscape it created. Glamorgan Colliery, Llwynypia, Rhondda, *c.* 1920. Welsh Industrial and Maritime Museum

Figure 61.2 'Holing' the coal, Sirhowy No. 7 Pit, Tredegar, Gwent, 1898. Welsh Industrial and Maritime Museum

evidence to ensure that information they contain is typical and not the exception. Such sources can be biased and it is important that the Curator should consider pertinent questions such as who took the photographs and why were they taken, or in the case of works of art, what were the motives of the artists in making the depiction. If such details are unknown then pictorial images can still provide an extra dimension of information for their very existence is historical. Companies often photograph their enterprises not only to record equipment but also to celebrate their achievements, so this may well result in romantic cosy images at times.

Paintings, sketches and topographical prints have usually been preserved in art galleries whilst there are a number of locations where relevant photographs, if extant, can be found: in local collections, e.g. in museum and library archives; in newspaper libraries, and in commercial picture libraries largely servicing the publishing trade (such as the Radio Times Hulton Library).

Such is the present-day interest in photographs, reflected in the almost innumerable collections of old photographs and similar publications now appearing, that most areas have amateur or professional collectors who can be contacted. For general guides see Wall (1977), and West (1983). In addition the Curator should be aware of illustrations in encyclopaedias (such as Rees' encyclopaedia), in historical works such as Agricola's *De Re Metallica*, in advertisements or in textbooks of practices in various industries. For photogaphs of industrial sites and

Figure 61.3 Puddlers, Cwmbran Ironworks. Painting by P. Curral Price, 1880s. Welsh Industrial and Maritime Museum

Figure 61.4 Women 'openers' at work, Clayton Tin Plate
Works, Pontarddulais, West Glamorgan. Early 1960s.
Welsh Industrial and Maritime Museum

buildings which may not have survived, there are
often records held by the relevant Ancient Monuments Boards.

Obviously, if no visual evidence can be found, a
newspaper appeal is likely to be helpful.

The material remains

The material remains of industrial activity comprise
the artefacts and equipment in museum collections,
the surviving buildings (which may themselves
house museums), industrial sites and the landscape
itself.

The physical details of the objects in the collection
should be examined closely in order to analyse and
record their intrinsic features, e.g. the materials they
are made of and their dimensions, variations in type,
aspects of technological innovation and improvement, etc. Other basic information should also be
sought, such as when, where and by whom an item
of equipment was built, when it was installed, its

function and how it worked, and the duration of its
working life.

This data should be available in accession registers,
but it must be corroborated. It is often the case that
such detail has not been recorded so that physical
examination is a necessity. Research does depend on
the accurate recording of information associated with
the objects at the accessioning stage, otherwise much
of the potential of researching and exhibiting
material is lost.

Industrial archaeology

The physical remains of industry, however, do not
only consist of items in museum displays and stores.
Much of the history we seek remains on site. There
has been a marked growth in the concern for
industrial archaeology in recent years and this has
entailed the development of appropriate fieldwork
techniques in order to acquire further information.
Use of such techniques can be of much value in

securing an understanding of our industrial past through corroborating, and giving an extra dimension to, findings from other sources. Fieldwork is also a useful source of evidence in itself in areas where no documentation exists.

A concern for industrial archaeology also ensures that the impact of industry on the landscape, and vice versa, are not forgotten. The visiting of sites gives the Curator a greater empathy for his subject, allowing him to gain a greater understanding than documentary sources alone would provide.

Work in industrial archaeology requires not only the use of museum resources but is often undertaken with groups and societies involved in the same discipline. Such activities should be fostered since they can help to provide not only a record of industrial work in a certain area but much additional information besides. Pannell (1973) and Cossons (1987) provide approaches to the procedures dictated by the subject, and the various relevant journals provide banks of information on particular subjects as well as useful guidance on procedures.

Oral history

The personal reminiscences of individuals are one of the richest primary sources for industrial historians, as for social historians. The value of oral history is that it allows the Curator to create his or her own sources of information on the subjects under study and acquire data and insights from a broad spectrum of society. It gives a voice to the mass of the population who have left few records behind them and who have rarely had anyone speaking on their behalf. Oral history is ideally suited to viewing industry and society through the eyes of those who lived through their particular experiences. It can also uncover a wealth of technological and other forms of detail about the operation of industrial processes. Yet oral history, too, has its limitations and as with all source material it should be treated circumspectly and the accuracy of the information checked against other sources.

Curators of industry should be encouraged to undertake tape-recordings, and questionnaires and newpaper appeals will often help in the hunt for contacts. Tapes should be transcribed, indexed and stored in suitable conditions as soon as possible after the interviews. For introductions to oral history and guidance on techniques and procedures see Thompson (1978) and Lummis (1987).

Publication

The dissemination of the results of research is an important follow-up activity, as is the need to leave a permanent record of the Curator's findings. Such activity is for the benefit of the museum visitors as well as of fellow curators and of scholars in general.

The results of research can be made available in detailed catalogues or, if the project is geared to a temporary exhibition, to a specialized catalogue or handlist. Articles in museum publications and journals relating to industrial history often lead in the research field by being first to present the results of the research activities carried out by curators.

Notes

[1] For general surveys of trends in the preservation and interpretation of industrial history see Cossons (1987) and Stratton (1987).

[2] The new perspectives are suggested in Schirmbeck (1981) and Greene (1985). See also the various opinions expressed in Mansfield and Jones (1987), Fitzgerald (1987), Kavanagh (1987), Nuttall (1987), King (1988) and Porter (1988).

[3] Kavanagh (1983); see also Fenton (1988) for a Norwegian approach to contemporary documentation.

References

BENSON, J., NEVILLE, R. G. and THOMPSON, C. H. (1981), *Bibliography of the British Coal Industry*, Oxford University Press, Oxford

COSSONS, N. (1987), *The BP Book of Industrial Archaeology*, 2nd edition, David & Charles, London

FENTON, A. (1988), 'Industrial heritage and contemporary documentation: considerations from Norway', *Museums Journal*, **88**(ii) pp81–83

FITZGERALD, R. (1987), 'Industrial history in museums: a reply', *SHCG News*, **15** pp 5–6

GREENE, J. P. (1985), 'Machines, manufactures and people: social history at the Greater Manchester Museum of Science and Technology', *Social History Curators Group Journal*, **13**, pp 29–33

KAVANAGH, G. (1987), 'Ah yes but . . . Some thoughts on the object vs people debate', *SHCG News*, **16**

KAVANAGH, G. (1983), 'Samdok in Sweden: some observations and impressions', *Museums Journal*, **83**(i) pp 85–88

KING A. (1988), 'Andy Capp and industrial museums', *Science & Industry Curators Group Newsletter*, **2**, pp 2–5

LUMMIS, T. (1987), *Listening to History*, Century Hutchison, London

MANSFIELD, N. and JONES, B. (1987), 'Industrial history in museums', *SHCG News*, **14** p 4

NUTTALL, A. (1987), 'What about the workers: an industrial archaeologists' view', *SHCG News*, **16**

ORBELL, J. (1987), *A Guide to Tracing the History of a Business*, Business Archives Council, London

PANNELL, J. P. M. (1973), *The Techniques of Industrial Archaeology*, David & Charles, London, (new edition J.K. Major)

PORTER G. (1988) 'What about the workers?', *SICG Newsletter*, **2** pp 7–8

SCHIRMBECK, P. (1981), 'The Museum of the City of Russelheim', *Museum*, **23**(i) pp 35-50

STRATTON, M. (Ed) (1987), 'Interpreting the industrial past', *Ironbridge Institute Research Paper, No. 19*, Ironbridge

THOMPSON, P. (1978), *The Voice of the Past*, Oxford University Press, Oxford

WALL, J. (1977), *Directory of British Photographic Collections*, Heinemann and Royal Photographic Society, London

WEST, J. (1983), *Town Records*, Phillimore, Chichester

Bibliography

BOTT, V. (Ed) (1987), *Labour History in Museums: Papers from a Joint Seminar*, Social History Curators Group – Society for the Study of Labour History, Manchester

BURNETT, J., VINCENT, D. and MAYALL, D. (1987), *the Autobiography of the Working Class: An Annotated Critical Bibliography*, Vol. II *1900–1945*, Harvester, Brighton

BUTLER, S. (1989), *Information Sheet 3*, 'Bibliography of information concerning science and industry museums and their collections', *Information sheet No. 3*, Science and Industry Curators Group

DERRY, T. K. and WILLIAMS, T. I. (1960), *A Short History of Technology*, Oxford University Press, Oxford

FERGUSON, E. S. (1968), *Bibliography of the History of Technology*, Cambridge, MA

GORMAN, J. (1973), *Banner Bright: An Illustrated History of the Banners of the British Trade Union Movement*, Allen Lane, London

GORMAN, J. (1985), *Images of Labour*, Scorpion, London

HARLEY, J. B. (1972), 'Maps for the local historian', *Standing Conference for Local History*, National Council of Social Services, London

HAYHURST, Y. (1986), 'Recording a workshop', *SHCG Journal*, **14**

HOBSBAWM, E. J. (1968), *Industry and Empire*, Penguin, London

HUDSON, K. (1983), *The Archaeology of the Consumer Society: The Second Industrial Revolution in Britain*, Heinemann, London

KITSON CLARK, G. (1969), *Guide for Research Students Working on Historical Subjects*, 2nd edition, University Press, Cambridge

KLINGENDER, F. D. (1968), *Art and the Industrial Revolution*, Elton, A. (Ed.), Adams & Mackay, London

McCONNELL, A. (Ed.) (1976), *Preservation of Technological Material. Proceedings of a Symposium held at the Science Museum*, Science Museum, London

McCOY, F. M. (1974), *Researching and Writing History, A Practical Handbook for Students*, University of California Press, Berkely, CA

RICHARDSON, P. (1983), *Making Hitory 1/The Factory*, Television History Centre, London

ROYAL COMMISSION ON HISTORICAL MANUSCRIPTS (1990), *Records of British Business and Industry 1760–1914: Textiles and Leather*, HMSO, London

SCOTT, A. (1989), 'What are we here for?', *Science and Industry Curators Group Newsletter*, **2** pp 5–7

SMART, T. E. (1978), *Museums in Great Britain, with Scientific and Technological Collections – A List*, 2nd edition, Science Museum, London

SMITH, C. S. (1970), 'Art technology and science: notes on their historical interaction', *Technology and Culture*, **11** pp 493–549

STANDING COMMISSION ON MUSEUMS AND GALLERIES (1971), 'The preservation of technological material', *Report and Recommendations: Standing Commission on Museums and Galleries*, HMSO, London

STORER, J. D. (1989), *The Conservation of Industrial Collections: A Survey*, Science Museum – the Conservation Unit of the Museum and Galleries Commission, London

TRINDER, B. (1982). *The Making of the Industrial Landscape*, Dent, London

SECTION FIVE

USER SERVICES

Section Editor
Douglas A. Bassett

62

Introduction

Douglas A. Bassett

Museums have been booming in popularity both in Britain and elsewhere in an unprecedented fashion since the 1960s. The kind of phrases and sentences used to describe the phenomenon are: 'public visibility and popularity have never been greater' (Bloom and Powell, 1984); 'a time of unprecedented growth and interest in museums and exhibitions but also at a time when the museum world is facing an apparent crisis' (Vergo, 1989); 'more visited, more venerated and more criticized than ever before' (Hudson, 1985); and 'one of our few growth industries' (Hewison, 1986). According to a national survey carried out in 1989 for the Museums Association by Touche Ross Management Consultants, around half the adults in Britain had visited a museum or an art gallery in the previous two years.

Some of the reasons suggested for this growth have been – the increase in mobility, leisure and tourism, the increase in the concern for conserving both the natural and man-made heritage, as well as that of nostalgia, the revolution in teaching methods in schools, the influence of television and the greater and more effective promotion, advocacy and advertising on the part of the museums themselves as well as a change of attitude on the part of many members of museum staff.

Information on trends in leisure along with a range of other social indicators, for example, are now provided on a regular basis by the annual government publication *Social Trends* (Central Statistical Office). The most persistent message is that time spent at work is decreasing, time available for leisure increasing, and there are significant related changes in family life and the role of women. See also the detailed diary studies of Gershuny and Jones (1987).

One reflection of the growing interest in museums is the number of books published by people from outside the profession about the development and problems faced by museums and museum staff. *The Museum Time-machine. Putting Cultures on Display* (Lumley, 1988), for example, is a set of essays designed to identify some of the major changes currently taking place in the museum world, to present them in a way that they can be discussed, and to follow up the criticisms with instructive proposals. Two sections of the book ('The landscape of nostalgia' and 'Sociology of the museum public') are by 'outsiders' and the third ('Museums in a changing world') by museum professionals. Most of the contributors from museums were members of what are described as 'radical pressure groups inside the museum world' – the Museum Professionals Group, Social History Curators Group and Women, Heritage and Museums. Three broad areas of concern in the essays are the commercialization of museums, the pursuit of 'realism' and the impact of the media.

Other examples are: *Palaces of Discovery. The Changing World of Britain's Museums* (Tait, 1989), *The Heritage Industry* (Hewison, 1987), *The New Museology* (Vergo, 1989) and *On Living in an Old Country* (Wright, 1985).

A different kind of change in the museum world in Britain is reflected in the statistics gathered for the Museums Association's Museum Data-base in the mid 1980s (Prince and Higgins-McLaughlin, 1987). Of the 2000 museums which replied, three-quarters were established after the Second World War and nearly a half since 1971.

The museum visitor

As far as the nature of the museum public is concerned, few generalizations are possible because it differs from country to country, from region to region and even from museum to museum. It is possible to state, however, that almost any museum public is extremely heterogeneous in its make-up, that it is composed of people from a wide range of age-levels and with varying economic, ethnic, social and educational backgrounds, and with a diversity of interests, attitudes, pre-conceptions and motivations.

In spite of the diversity of the museum public, it is helpful to try and group them so that, if possible, various 'models' of visitor behaviour can be constructed. The following examples are characteristic.

First, visitors have widely varying levels of literacy, numeracy and graphicacy (or visual–spacial understanding) and that they include representatives of the four main types of personality which correspond to the four major modes of mental activity (thinking, feeling, sensation and intuition) and to four distinct modes of perception. Individuals are also motivated to visit museums for different reasons. The Director of the National Museum of Ethnology at Leiden in the Netherlands, for example, distinguished three motives amongst visitors, each of which he considered made particular demands on the way in which the museum displays its material. He isolated the aesthetic, the romantic (or escapist) and the intellectual (or the wish to satisfy a thirst for knowledge) (Pott, 1963).

Second, in considering exhibitions and museums, three main audiences can be recognised – actual, potential and target – and Roger S. Miles (1986) considers them from a theoretical point of view. In addition he looks at two different perceptions of the public galleries of a museum as systems in which the visitor and the exhibits interact – 'the 'scholarly' and the 'visitor' perception.

Third, a quotation from Paul Perrot's chapter in *The Smithsonian Experience* (1977) provides a useful starting point and underlines the fact that the major services provided by museums are based on the collections:

> Collections are the essential raison d'être of museums. They are the source from which the museum's unique role in the cultural fabric of society emanates. They are the basis of its contribution to scholarship, the instruments of its educational role, and the cause of its public enlightenment. (p. 76)

Such a grouping identifies three groups of people which, although not mutually exclusive, are readily distinguishable:

(1) The person involved in the advancement of knowledge in a particular discipline – the scholar or research worker (and it may be appropriate to include the professional man and 'the collector' in this category).
(2) The person involved in the formal education system – the pupil and the teacher; at primary, secondary and tertiary level.
(3) The person with little, if any, systematic knowledge of a particular subject – a member of the so-called 'public'.

From the standpoint of the visitors' expectations, it has been suggested that the following are representative: (Middleton, 1985).

- 'Value for money' and effort – even when an admission fee is not charged
- To plan a visit
- To find a visit rewarding – i.e. stimulating, entertaining and, to some extent, presenting an opportunity to learn
- Not to know much about the collections
- To be guided – bearing in mind that most visitors will not buy a guidebook
- To find high standards of service
- Not to stay too long but to queue, if necessary
- To pay, if necessary
- To have an opportunity to spend money
- To go away satisfied.

The various expectations are clearly not mutually exclusive. See also Mann (1988).

Expectations of a totally different order are expressed by Neil Postman (1990) who expects a museum to conduct an argument with society and to direct attention to what is difficult to contemplate. He discusses his ideas by comparing the message of the conventional museum with that of the Experimental Prototype Community of Tomorrow (EPCOT) at Orlando, Florida.

Museum-goers may, equally and legitimately, be 'seeking frivolous diversion, consolation, social status, companionship or solitude' (Weil, 1989), or innumerable other group or individual goals.

Museum-going, therefore, 'is neither tidy nor predictable' (Weil, 1989). In the circumstances, Glanmor Williams was right to conclude that 'the moral, perhaps, is that the Museum is like the sower in the parable. Its seed is uniformly good and wholesome; but a lot of what it scatters will fall on the stony ground of apathy and much of it will be choked by the thistles of more frivolous attractions. Yet a great deal of its falls on soil far more potentially receptive than we often suppose' (1983, p. 13).

The case for the primacy of the user of the museum was proposed in a novel and effective way by the Chairman of the Museums & Galleries Commission to the General Assembly of ICOM in London in 1983 (Morris, 1984). By metaphorically donning Moses' cloak and by comparing his audience to the unruly Israelites, he offered them ('on behalf of your god, the user of the museum') the 'Ten Commandments' of the museum user.

Different authorities use different terms for the museum's public and these include: visitors, clients (clientele), users, customers and community. The word 'customer', for example, is usually used in order to stress the contention that 'any museum . . . . is essentially a business' (Hudson, 1985). See also Loomis (1987), Miles (1986) and Morris (1984).

In using the term public it is useful to remember that it can be considered as representing an 'internal public', including Trustees and staff, a 'supporting public', including financial sponsors and supporters, volunteers and 'Friends' of the museum, and the group of 'intermediary agents' which includes the officers and staff of associated or co-operating societies and Trusts of nearby colleges, universities or tourist boards, and of newspapers and the media (Van Vleuten, 1986).

The range of visitor characteristics provides a continuing challenge to the educationalist, the psychologist and the sociologist who study behaviour in order that the museum can provide better services. The Members of the American 'Commission on Museums for a New Century', for example, urged a high priority for research into the ways people learn in museums, underlining the fact that 'continuing systematic research into these unique processes and mechanisms is the key to the success of the museum as an environment for learning' (Bloom and Powell, 1984), and pointed to the need of research in order to guide the introduction of computers and other electronic technology into museum learning. (See also Loomis, 1987.)

The range of public services

Most museums and galleries provide a wide range of services for its public, both within its premises and elsewhere. The internal services include: the mounting of exhibitions, both permanent and temporary; the provision of advice and information on an individual basis regarding the collections and exhibitions and on matters related to them; organizing guided tours, gallery talks and demonstrations (often by artists, writers or craftsmen in residence), activities for children and families and various special events; arranging lunchtime and evening lectures, films, recitals and concerts, poetry readings, theatrical and dance performance by visiting groups and personalities; providing accommodation for meetings, seminars, conferences and receptions for other bodies; providing snack-bars, restaurants and shops, as well as such practical facilities as the provision of cloakrooms, toilets and rest-rooms. When considering the questions asked most frequently by teachers planning school visits to museums, for example, the top three have to be practical ones: 'Is there anywhere to eat packed lunches?'; 'Do you have a place to leave coats and bags?'; and 'Where are the toilets?' (Middleton, 1990). See also, for example, Dimondstein and Getzler (1984), Gibbs-Smith (1975), Kaminski (1976), Sharpe and Rolfe (1979) and Siliprandi (1987).

The external, extra-mural or outreach services include: organising travelling exhibitions, workshops, lectures, guided walks and 'family expeditions'; and arranging travel programmes (including overseas travel). The variety of meanings of the word outreach are considered in a section on 'The role of outreach programmes' in *Sharing Science* (Quin, 1989, pp. 20–33). Among seven meanings considered by Anthony Wilson of the Science Museum, London, is '. . . realising how many and how varied are the effects we have, as providers of experiences, on the minds of our visitors, and how little we know of what these effects really are' (p. 30). See also, for example, Coulter (1987), Craig (1987), McCullough (1984) and Sharpe and Howe (1982).

Almost without exception members of a museum staff are active participants for local conservation and heritage bodies, historical, archaeological, art or natural history societies, and co-operate with educational bodies, local government, commercial and industrial concerns, and also with radio and television in the preparation of programmes. The range of the partnership was clearly demonstrated at the annual conference of the Museums Association in 1983, devoted to the theme 'Museums in partnership' (Jenkins, 1984; Bassett, 1984).

The museum is, therefore, a combination of repository, exhibition centre, information centre, classroom and centre for informal learning, an establishment of learning or research centre, reference library, theatre, activity centre, meeting-place and side-show, as well as being home to a wide-ranging group of professional museum staff. While it cannot be all things to all men, it aims to provide something for everybody (see Fosdyke, 1949). The challenge is to provide access, orientation, information and understanding, draw attention to standards and values, and, at the same time, provide the setting for important experiences that may be wholly beyond the museum's control or intention.

The major museum services (provided in one way or another by every museum) are: the preparation and mounting of exhibitions; the publication of books, catalogues, etc.; the giving of advice and information; and an educational service. Each of these is considered in the following chapters of this Manual.

The theme of Graham Carter's chapter in the first edition of this Manual (1984, pp. 435–447) is developed in his Guidelines on education for the Association of Independent Museums (Carter, 1984) and is completed in this edition by Eilean Hooper-Greenhill's contribution (Chapter 68).

The theme of Iain Bain's chapter in the first edition (1984, pp. 461–466) is developed further in his contribution to the *ICOM Handbook of Museum Public Relations* (Bain, 1986) and complemented in Chapter 70 of this edition of the Manual.

The chapters by Michael Belcher, Giles Velarde and Eilean Hooper-Greenhill should be read in conjunction with their recent books on similar themes (Belcher, 1991; Velarde, 1988; Hooper-Greenhill, 1991).

The ethical aspects of these services are detailed in Chapter 12 and the Museums Association's 'Code of Conduct for Museum Curators' (*see* Appendix).

The primary or core functions of museums, their relationships, and the different opinions regarding their respective positions in the hierarchy of museum work, are described in the chapters on the different types of museums in Section I of the Manual (Chapters 7 (pp. 86 and 87), 8, 9 (pp. 98–101), 10 (pp. 110 and 111), 11).

Many efforts have been made over the years to reduce the functions of a museum to a description of epigrammatic proportions. Francis Bather of the British Museum (Natural History), for example, suggested that the essential functions of a museum were threefold – 'Investigation, Instruction and Inspiration', appealing respectively to the Specialist, the Student and the Man in the Street (1903). John Henry Merryman of the Stamford University Law School, in his recent studies of public policy with respect to cultural property, on the other hand, maintains that the basic framework of any such policy must be based on 'the ordered triad of preservation, truth and access' (see Weil, 1989, p. 58). The Science Museum, London (Bud, Cave and Hanney, 1991) adopts Enlightenment, Preservation and Scholarship and Stephen Weil, of the Hirshorn Museum and Sculpture Garden, Washington, DC, simplifies Joseph Veach Noble's five-point analysis of museum functions – his 'Museum manifesto' of 1970 – by adopting the Dutch museologist Peter van Mensch's threefold 'preservation, study and communication'. Weil's analysis is of particular interest because he assesses the suitability of the words used in these various exercises bearing in mind that 'At its final, least calculable, and most magical moments, the museum can be more than merely a communicator or a stimulant. Museum-going can be a deeply affective experience' (p. 64). It can be and must remain a place of wonder. Weil underlines the need to define the purposes for which a museum deals with its public in far finer and more precise ways than have so far been achieved.

Museum problems and museum trends

In the penultimate and ultimate decades of a century it is to be expected that attempts will be made to draw attention to the lessons of the past and anticipate the problems of the forthcoming century.

Two of the most prolific of contemporary writers on museums and museology have surveyed the most influential museums and galleries and the most innovative and influential directors of the past. The one (Alexander, 1983) confines his international survey to the period up to the First World War, providing analyses of the work of 12 'masters' in five countries; the other (Hudson, 1985) covers the period up to the 1980s. He not only includes a 'corps d'elite' of 37 museums in 13 separate countries, but also groups 'all twenty-seven of the French eco-museums' which together 'represent one of the most important museological developments of the past fifty years (p. 163).

The American Association of Museums' 'Commission on Museums for a New Century' started work in 1982. In spite of its title, however, the Commission's report (Bloom and Powell, 1984) is not a statement of specific needs or a 'wish-list' for the future, but a clear statement about what museums are, why they are important to our culture and what they contribute to the quality of life.

Of the seven conditions considered by the Commission to require study from a new perspective and with new insights, two are relevant to this section of the Manual. They are: first, that 'Museums have not realized their full potential as educational institutions'. Despite a long-standing and serious commitment to their function as institutions of informal learning, there is a troublesome gap between reality and potential that must be addressed by policy makers in education and museums' (p. 28). And, second, that 'The diversity of the community of museums is not fully representative of the diversity of the society it seeks to serve'. In their governance and staffing museums have much to gain by making a commitment to greater diversity.' (p. 24).

In 1988 the Association of Independent Museums commissioned Victor Middleton, a consultant in travel and tourism, to review the present state and potential of independent museums in this country following the first formal review in the Annual Report of the Museums & Galleries Commission in 1988.

The report, presented to a special committee of the AIM, was designed, a) to define and classify the key dimensions of change in the external environment expected to influence the demand for museums in the next decade (economic, social, environmental and governmental), b) to assess, and as far as possible measure, the significance, direction and speed of change in the identified directions, c) to identify the strengths and weaknesses of independent museums and the strategic implication for their future management (Middleton, 1990).

The 1980s also witnessed the publication of the first volume devoted exclusively to providing guidance for museum staff about their relations to or with the public. A selection of essays in a limited edition was published by ICOM on the occasion of the ICOM General Conference in Mexico in 1980, and this was superceded in 1986 by a completely revised, and substantially enlarged version, available for a much wider audience – *Public View: The ICOM Handbook of Museum Public Relations* (Bellow, 1986). The tone of the volume is set by the title of the first section: 'A warm welcome'.

It is clear from this and from other studies that certain categories of the general public are not adequately represented in the museum public. This applies particularly to the disabled (those who are visually handicapped, have hearing disability or are retarded or emotionally disturbed), the ethnic minorities and older visitors.

Access to museums and to their collections

The importance of access in the museum context is stated clearly in the Centennial Policy Statement of the Museums Association (1989, p. 37) – 'The strength of any museum and its value to the public is . . . only as great as the quality of the curatorship of its collections: that is, the conservation, preservation, interpretation and accessibility of the collections to the public, students and researchers'.

There are a number of aspects to the question of access in the museum context. For example, the accessibility of a museum (or museums) to the population of an area or region is commonly a problem. This was a matter considered during the consideration of the role and nature of national museums in Scotland during the mid 1980s. Concern was expressed, for example, that the national museums should develop 'outreach programmes for the whole of Scotland'.

Secondly, the accessibility of the objects or specimens or information in a particular museum to the public is a wide-ranging matter which has been extensively considered. The importance of direct access to a specimen or object in a museum's collection was, of course, stated clearly by the eminent continental naturalist Conrad Gesner (1516– 1565) as long ago as 1565. He demonstrated that both description and illustration of specimens, although extremely useful because they could be duplicated in large numbers by printing, were, nevertheless merely a convenient substitute for the material itself. Both descriptions and illustrations could be misleading and ambiguous, whereas objects, in Dillon Ripley's favoured phrase, 'cannot lie'. Despite many important advances in the technical aspects of illustration, Gesner's contention remains true today.

The problem, for example, was (1) the subject of a recommendation (concerning the most effective means of rendering museums accessible to everyone) at the UNESCO General Conference on 14th December 1960; (2) a matter of concern during the Rayner Scrutiny of two of Britain's major national museums (Burrett, 1982); (3) the theme of a review of three projects in Canada (Ames, 1985); (4) the theme of a description of recent developments at Liverpool Museum following the rapid adoption of a policy on improving public access to collections by the Trustees of the newly created National Museums and Galleries on Merseyside (Greenwood, Phillips and Wallace, 1989; Fewster, 1990).

The most obviously controversial aspect of access to museums centres around the question of admission charges. Museums became front-page news in British newspapers in October 1971 when the Chancellor of the Exchequer announced that admission charges would be introduced to all National Museums and Galleries, and remained in the public eye for the next two years whilst the matter became the subject of parliamentary and public debate. Admission charges were finally brought in on 1 January 1974. Few people were surprised that attendances fell: many more were surprised at the extent of the fall – to about half of what they had been in the equivalent months of the previous year. With the change of Government the charges were removed on 1 April and attendances quickly returned to normal.

The issue has been revived during the second half of the 1980s and has been a matter of continuing concern. In part at least, the debate has been fuelled by the conclusion of the House of Commons Select Committee on Education, Science and the Arts that 'all national museums and galleries should consider introducing compulsory admission charges'. The practical and ethical arguments against charging for admission are outlined by David Wilson in his *The British Museum: Purpose and Politics* (1989, pp. 99–105) – a book written specifically to explain the complicated practicalities of running a major museum and the philosophy upon which it was founded. The same problems are considered from a different perspective in Chapter 14 (pp. 144, 147, 148), in a historical context in Chapter 3 (pp. 33, 43) and in a legal context in Chapter 6 (pp. 73–75).

The wider problems of access – both physical and intellectual – are considered by Duncan Cameron (1982): the paper contains a revealing anecdote on 'the Museum Brat Syndrome'. See also Stam, 1989.

Access and disability

The variety of problems of access confronted by the disabled have been considered for many years, but there is no doubt that the designation by the United Nations of 1981 as the International Year of Disabled Persons (IYDP) was of paramount importance.

One of the resolutions adopted by the International Council of Museums at its 13th General Assembly recommended that museums not only provide facilities for the disabled, but that they encourage the training and education of the handicapped, grant them free access and contribute to a better understanding of the problems involved by collecting, documenting and exhibiting material related to the handicapped.

The special issue of *Museum*, the UNESCO journal devoted to the IYDP (Anon., 1981) contains a section on 'Words and classification', in which the definitions recommended by the World Health Organisation's 'International classification of impairments, disability and handicaps' (Geneva, 1980) are given and 'The United Nations Declaration on the rightsof Disabled Persons' (9 December 1975) is quoted in full.

In an item on 'Nine varieties of handicap' (de Marez Oyens, 1981) the author chooses as the ninth handicap one that is still far too common: namely, blindness to other people's impairments.

General developments in Britain during the 1980s have included:

(1) the establishment, in 1982, of a National Committee of Inquiry by the Carnegie UK Trust under Sir Richard Attenborough as Chairman. Its report was published in 1985 and, in the same year, the Trust also published guidance on provision for disabled people (Pearson, 1985). The section on 'museums, art galleries, exhibition centres and visitor centres' in the latter publication (pp. 21–36) has 36 sub-sections, including: Access, Labels and Obstacles; Textured Paths; Sonograms; etc.
(2) the establishment, in 1989, by the Carnegie UK Trust (with financial assistance from the Office of Arts and Libraries and from a number of Charitable Trusts) of the Access for Disabled People to Arts Premises Today (ADAPT) Fund. The Fund is designed to assist in improving provision for disabled people in arts venues, museums and galleries.

Major developments in the museum world in Britain include:

(1) the establishment, in 1987, of the Museums and Galleries Disability Association (MAGDA), a voluntary body which aims to provide a focus for all concerned with making museums, their services and staffing opportunities accessible to all in the community.

One of MAGDA's most successful early conferences was that organised in conjunction with the Royal National Institute for the Blind in 1988. Called *Talking Touch*, the subject of the conference was 'touch exhibitions' and their implications for museum professionals. (See Royal National Institute for the Blind, 1988; see also Pearson, 1991.)

(2) the appointment (albeit temporary), in 1989, of a Disability Adviser at the Museums & Galleries Commission. Since that time the Adviser has been responsible for maintaining a monthly column on 'Access and Disability' in the *Museums Journal*, and co-ordinating the Commission's work in preparing a Code of Practice for Disabled People, a Disability Resource Pack and a Bibliography and List of relevant organisations. A draft version of the Code of Practice has already been circulated and the final version will be issued in 1992. See also Keen, 1991.

Examples of recent American literature include: the museum directory available in large print, cassette and Braille editions – published jointly by the Museum of Folk Art, New York and the American Foundation for the Blind (New York), released in conjunction with an exhibition 'Access to art: bringing folk art closer' (Shore and Jacinto, 1989); and the volume designed specifically to help museum guides to greet and help blind and visually impaired visitors (Groff and Gardner, 1989), published by the American Foundation for the Blind and available in cassette and Braille editions as well as in the standard edition.

Helpful continental comparisons are provided in the papers read at a European conference on 'Museums and the disabled' held in Paris in 1988 (Fondation de France/International Council of Museums, 1991).

Probably the only quantitative progress report on the reactions of museums generally to one aspect of the problem is that provided in the last update of the Museums Association's Data-base questionnaire. Thirty-six questions, commissioned by the Royal National Institute for the Blind were included and the response was as follows: Some 1400 museums responded, of which only 2.5 per cent provided a Braille guide, 3.9 per cent a large print guide, 4.6 per cent a cassette guide, 1 per cent Braille labels and 9.9 per cent large print labels. In addition, 6.9 per cent had equipped permanent exhibitions with lighting which might enhance the use of low vision.

The use made of museums by students with special needs has been carried out as part of the general survey of work in schools by Her Majesty's Inspectors (Department of Education and Science, 1987). Two valuable complementary sources to those already described are the very appropriately titled weekly BBC Radio 4 programmes 'In touch' and 'Does he take sugar?'.

Access and ethnic minorities

The Deputy Chairman of the Commission for Racial Equality, Professor Bikhu Parekh, argued, at a Conference on 'Presenting Ethnic Heritage' in

London in 1989 (Hasted, 1989a), that: 'British society has not yet come to terms with the need to recognise and accommodate legitimate minority differences' and that 'The realities of minority experience, rather than stereotyped images of "immigrant" groups, must be recognised'.

Professor Parekh's criticism applies equally to British museums as it does to British society generally. Among positive steps taken to improve the situation, however, the following examples can be cited.

A special issue of the *Journal of Education in Museums* (volume 7, 1987) was devoted to multi-cultural education and two issues of the *Museums Journal* have contained groups of papers providing news of developments in certain museums, and also discussion of the problems involved.

The earlier of the two issues of the *Museums Journal* (**90**(9), 1990) considered 'representations of Black history'. The four items were introduced by the guest editor, Anandi Ramamurthy (p. 23). The items included a description of the background and impact of *The Black Contribution to History* (Fraser and Visram, 1988). This was a report, commissioned by the Geffrye Museum and the Inner London Education Authority on the presentation of Black (meaning Afro-Caribbean and Asian) history at the Museum. The report was compiled by two historians well known for their work on this theme. Responses to the contributions were given in the succeeding issue of the *Journal* (**90**(10), 1990, pp. 20 and 21). The second issue considered cultural inclusion and exclusion in museums. The six items were introduced by Amina Dickerson of the Chicago Historical Society in a contribution which included a checklist of 'action steps' towards achieving greater pluralism in museum institutions.

A useful section on multi-cultural education is provided in the GEM Bibliography on museum education (Bosdêt and Durbin, 1989) and a more widely-based inventory in a resource-list for anti-racist social history museums by Rachel Hasted (1989b).

Equivalent developments in the USA are reflected in an issue of *Museum News* (March/April 1989) which contains three articles on the theme 'Cultural diversity: museums explore a topical terrain' and in which four museum professionals consider some of the difficult issues that arise as museums become more sensitive in their representation of cultural diversity.

Various aspects of the problem of reflecting a plural society are considered by the Chief Rabbi, Jonathan Sacks, in his 1990 Reith Lectures 'The persistence of faith', and particularly in the fourth lecture 'Paradoxes of pluralism'. He refers to pluralism in theory in America in the early decades of this century (drawing attention in particular to the new model of a culturally distinct model prepared by Horace Kallen in 1915) and then to pluralism in practice from the 1960s onwards. The Arts Council of Great Britain and the Museums & Galleries Commission have also considered aspects of the problem (Francis, 1990).

Women and museums

The related problem of equal opportunities in museum employment is the theme of another issue of the *Museums Journal* (**90**(11), 1990). The theme is introduced by Gaby Porter, convenor of The Museums Association Equal Opportunities Working Party. Her contribution includes three brief guides prepared by the Equal Opportunities Commission. The overlapping issue of 'Women and museums' is the main theme of the *Museums Journal* for September 1988 (**88**(2), pp. 55–72), which contains five separate items. This includes a comparison of the statistics from the Museums Data-Base to national statistics obtained by the Office of Population Censuses and Surveys (OPCS) and others on women in employment (Prince, 1988). American experiences are outlined in an issue of *Museum News* (July/August 1990) which contains four articles on the theme 'Making a difference: women in museums'.

The voluntary group Women, Heritage and Museums (WHAM) which offers an information exchange for all who are interested in the portrayal of women through museum collections, exhibitions and activities, also works to promote equal opportunities.

References

ALEXANDER, E. P. (1983), *Museum Masters: Their Museums and Their Influence*, American Association of State and Local History, Nashville, Tennessee

AMBROSE, T. (Ed.) (1987), *Education in Museums. Museums in Education*, Scottish Museums Council/HMSO, Edinburgh

AMES, M. M. (1985), De-schooling the museums: a proposal to increase public access to museums and their resources, *Museum*, **145**, 25–31

ANON. (1981), Museums and disabled persons, *Museum* [Special IYDP issue], **33**(3), 126–196

ATTENBOROUGH, R. (1985), *Arts and Disabled People. Report of a Committee of Inquiry under the Chairmanship of Sir Richard Attenborough*, Carnegie UK Trust/Bedford Square Press, London

BAIN, I. (1986), Publishing for the museum shop and beyond, pp. 55–64 in Bellow, C. (Ed.), *Public View. The ICOM Handbook of Museum Public Relations*, International Council of Museums, Paris

BASSETT, D. A. (1984), The relationship of museums with national and local government, and with other bodies, in Wales: a retrospective view [1907–1983], pp. 13–17 in Jenkins, J. (Ed.), Museums in partnership, *Museums Journal*, **83**(4), Supplement

BATHER, F. A. (1903), (Presidential Address to the Museums Association at Aberdeen in September 1901), *Museums Journal*, **3**, 71–94 and 110–132

BELCHER, M. (1991), *Exhibitions in Museums*, Leicester University Press, Leicester and London [Leicester Museum Studies Series: General Editor, Susan M. Pearce]

BELLOW, C. (Ed.) (1986), *Public View. The ICOM Handbook of Museum Public Relations*, International Council of Museums, Paris

BLOOM, J. N. and POWELL, E. A. (Eds) (1984), *Museums for a New Century. A Report of the Commission on Museums for a New Century*, American Association of Museums, Washington

BOSDÊT, M. and DURBIN, G. (1989), *Museum Education Bibliography 1978–1988*, Group for Education in Museums. [Supplement 1, 1988–1989. *Journal of Education in Museums*, **11**, 1990, Supplement]

BOWN, L. (1987), New needs in adult and community education, 7–17 in Ambrose, T. (Ed.), *Education in Museums, Museums in Education*, Scottish Museums Council/HMSO, Edinburgh

BUD, R., CAVE, M. and HANNEY, S. (1991), Measuring a museum's output [Science Museum], *Museums Journal*, **91**(1), 39–31

BURRETT, F. G. (1982), *Rayner Scrutiny of the Departmental Museums: Science Museum and Victoria and Albert Museum*, HMSO, London (Cyclostyled Report)

CAMERON, D. F. (1982), Museums and public access: the Glenbow approach, *International Journal of Museum Management and Curatorship*, **1**(3), 177–196

CARTER, P. G. (1984), AIM Guidelines No. 6. *Education in Independent Museums*, Association of Independent Museums, Chichester, West Sussex

COULTOR, S. (1987), Cables of communication, *Journal of Education in Museums*, **8**, 2, 3

CRAIG, T. L. (1987), Around the world in eighty ways. A guide to museum travel programs, *Museum News*, **65**(3), 57–62

DAVIES, J. H. and THOMAS, J. E. (1988), *A Select Bibliography of Adult Continuing Education*, 5th edition (revised), National Institute of Adult and Continuing Education, Leicester. [Includes section on Museums and Galleries]

DAVIES, M. (1989), Half population visits museums, *Museums Journal*, **89**(7), 8

DE MAREZ OYENS, J. (1981), Nine varieties of handicap, *Museum*, **33**(3), 158–159

DEPARTMENT OF EDUCATION AND SCIENCE (1987a), *A Survey of the Use Schools make of Museums for Learning about Ethnic and Cultural Diversity*, HMI Report 163/89, HMSO, London

DEPARTMENT OF EDUCATION AND SCIENCE (1987b), *Report by HM Inspectors on a Survey of the Use some Pupils and Students with Special Education Needs make of Museums and Historic Buildings, carried out Summer 1987*, HMI Report 4/88, HMSO, London

DICKERSON, A. (1991), Redressing the balance [Cultural inclusion and exclusion], *Museums Journal*, **91**(2), 21–23

DIMONDSTEIN, G. and GETZLER, A. (1984), Poetry in the gallery, *Museum Studies Journal*, **1**(4), 32–42

FEWSTER, C. (1990), Beyond the show case [at the Liverpool Museum], *Museums Journal*, **90**(6), 24–27

FONDATION DE FRANCE and INTERNATIONAL COUNCIL OF MUSEUMS (1991), *Museums without Barriers: A New Deal for Disabled People*, Fondation de France, International Council of Museums and Routledge, London and New York. [The Heritage Care Preservation Management Series: General Editor, A. Wheatcroft]

FOSDYKE, J. (1949), The function of a national museum, in *Museums in Modern Life*, Royal Society of Arts, London

FRANCIS, J. (1990), *Attitudes among Britain's Black Community towards Attendance at Arts, Cultural and Entertainment Events*, Arts Council of Great Britain, London

FRASER, P. and VISRAM, R. (1988), *The Black Contribution to History*, Geffrye Museum/Centre for Urban and Environmental Studies/Inner London Education Authority, London

GERSHUNY, J. and JONES, S. (1987), The changing work/leisure balance in Britain: 1961–1984, 9–50 in Horne, J., Jary, D. and Tomlinson, A. (Eds), *Sport, Leisure and Social Relations*, Routledge & Kegan Paul, London

GESNER, C. (1565), *De Rerum Fossilium, . . .* [On Fossil Objects], Tiguri

GIBBS-SMITH, C. H. (1975), *The Arranging of Lectures*, Museums Association Information Sheet 8, Museums Association, London

GOMBRICH, E. H. (1979), The tradition of general knowledge, 9–23 in Gombrich, E. H. *Ideals and Idols. Essays on Values in History and in Art*, Phaidon, Oxford

GREENE, J. P. (1989), Museums for the year 2000 – a case for continuous revolution, *Museums Journal*, **88**(4), 179, 180

GREENWOOD, E. F., PHILLIPS, P. W. and WALLACE, I. D. (1989), The Natural History Centre at the Liverpool Museum, *International Journal of Museum Management and Curatorship*, **8**, 215–225

GROFF, G. and GARDNER, L. (1989), *What Museum Guides Need to Know: Access for Blind and Visually Impaired Visitors*, American Foundation for the Blind, New York

HASTED, R. (1989a), Mirror images [Report of a Conference 'Presenting ethnic heritage or breaking the hall of mirrors' St Mary's College, Twickenham, 1989], *Museums Journal*, **89**(2), 17

HASTED, R. (1989b), Suggestions towards a resource for an anti-racial social history museum, *Social History Curators Group Journal*, **16**(1988–89), 44, 45

HEWISON, R. (1986), Museums are one of our few growth industries, *Listener*, **115**, (1986), 11, 12

HEWISON, R. (1987), *The Heritage Industry: Britain in a Climate of Decline*, Methuen Paperback, London

HOOPER-GREENHILL, E. (Ed.) (1989), *Initiatives in Museum Edcuation*, Department of Museum Studies, University of Leicester, Leicester

HOOPER-GREENHILL, E. (1991), *Museum and Gallery Education*, Leicester University Press, Leicester and London [Leicester Museum Studies Series: General Editor, Susan M. Pearce]

HORNE, D. (1984), *The Great Museum: The Re-presentation of History*, Pluto Press, London

HORNE, D. (1986), *The Public Culture*. Pluto Press, London

HUDSON, K. (1985), Museums and their customers, 7–15 in *Museums are for People*, Scottish Museums Council/HMSO, Edinburgh

HUDSON, K. (1987), *Museums of Influence*, Cambridge University Press

INTERNATIONAL COUNCIL OF MUSEUMS (1984), *ICOM 83. Museums for a Developing World. Proceedings of the 13th General Conference and 14th General Assembly of the International Council of Museums, London, 24 July–2 August 1983*, ICOM, Paris

JENKINS, J. (Ed.) (1984), Museums in Partnership. [Proceedings of the 54th Annual General Meeting of the Museums Association, Swansea 1983], *Museums Journal*, **83**(4), Supplement

KAMINSKI, W. (1976), Music in the museum, *Icom Education*, No. 7, 23–33 [bilingual]

KEEN, C. (1991), Provision for disabled people, 106–110 in Ambrose, T. and Runyard, S. (Eds), *Forward Planning. A Handbook of Business, Corporate and Development Planning for Museums and Galleries*, Museums & Galleries Commission/Routledge, London

LEGGETT, J. (1984), Women in museums – past, present and future, in *Women, Heritage and Museums. Report of a Conference held in Manchester, 7 and 8 April 1984*, Social History Curators Group

LOOMIS, R. J. (1987), *Museum Visitor Evaluation: New Tool for Management*, American Association for State and Local History, Nashville, Tennessee (Management Series No. 3)

LUMLEY, R. (Ed.) (1988), *The Museum Time-machine. Putting Cultures on Display*, Routledge, London and New York. [A Comedia Book]

MCCULLOUGH, D. (1984), The making of the *Smithsonian World* [TV Series]: a journey into space and time, *Smithsonian*, February 1984, 67–74

MANN, P. (1988), Delivering the right product to the right people, *Museums Journal*, **88**(3), 139–142

MERRIMAN, N. (1989), Museum visiting as a cultural phenomenon, 149–171 in Vergo, P. (Ed.), *The New Museology*, Reaktion Books, London

MIDDLETON, J. (1990), [The Education Column], *Museums Journal*, **90**(4), 16

MIDDLETON, V. T. C. (1985), Visitor expectations of museums, 17–26 in *Museums are for People*, Scottish Museums Council/HMSO, Edinburgh

MIDDLETON, V. T. C. (1990), *New Visions for Independent Museums in the UK*, Association of Independent Museums, Chichester, West Sussex

MILES, R. S. (1986), Museum audiences, *International Journal of Museum Management and Curatorship*, **5**(1), 73–80

MOODY, E. (1989), Education or entertainment? The museum and gallery business, *British Book News*, May 1989, 312–316

MORRIS, B. (1984), The demand placed upon museums and their uses, 14–18 in International Council of Museums, *ICOM 83. Museums for a Developing World. Proceedings of the 13th General Conference and 14th General Assembly of the International Council of Museums, London 24 July–2 August 1983*, ICOM, Paris; and *The Yearbook of the British Association of Museum Friends*

MUSEUMS & GALLERIES COMMISSION (In Press), *Code of Practice on Disability, Disability Resource Pack, Bibliography and List of Organisations*, Museums & Galleries Commission, London

MUSEUMS ASSOCIATION (1989), Museums – a national resource, a national responsibility [Centennial Policy Statement], *Museums Journal*, **89**(8), 36, 37

MUSEUMS ASSOCIATION WORKING PARTY ON EQUAL OPPORTUNITIES (1990), Interim Report, *Museums Journal*, **90**(7), 38

PEARSON, A. (n.d. [1985]), *Arts for Everyone. Guidance on Provision for Disabled People*, Carnegie UK Trust/Centre on Environment for the Handicapped, London

PEARSON, A. (1991), Touch exhibitions in the United Kingdom, 122–126 in Fondation de France and International Council of Museums, *Museums without Barriers. A New Deal for Disabled People*, Fondation de France/International Council of Museums/Routledge, London and New York

PERROT, P. N. (1977), Taking care of things, 76–83 in *The Smithsonian Experience. Science–History–The Arts . . . The Treasures of the Nation*, Smithsonian Institution, Washington, DC

POLICY STUDY INSTITUTE (1989), Museums, the visual arts and crafts, *Cultural Trends*, No. 4

PORTER, G. (1990), Are you sitting comfortably? [Equality in employment], *Museums Journal*, **90**(11), 25–27

POSTMAN, N. (1990), Museum as dialogue [in feature entitled, 'Considering the Public: Impact of Popular Opinion'], *Museum News*, Sept./Oct. 1990, 55–58

POTT, P. H. (1963). The Role of Museums of History and Folklore in a Changing World, pp. 157–170 in *Curator*, **6**(2)

POTTER, M. G. (1986), The care of the museum visitor, 35–39 in Bellow, Corrine (Ed.), *Public View. The ICOM Handbook of Museum Public Relations*, International Council of Museums, Paris

PRINCE, D. R. (1988), Women in museums, *Museums Journal*, **88**(2), 55–65

PRINCE, D. R. and HIGGINS-MCLAUGHLIN, B. (1987), *Museums UK: The Findings of the Museums' Data-Base Project*, Museums Association, London

PROCKAK, M. (1990), Multimedia is the message, *Museums Journal*, **90**(8), 25–37

QUIN, M. (Ed.) (1989), *Sharing Science: A Collection of Reports and Discussion Articles to Inform the Debate on Hands-on Education*, Nuffield Foundation/Committee on the Public Understanding of Science, London

RAMAMURTHY, A. (1990), Museums and the representation of Black history [An introduction], *Museums Journal*, **90**(9), 23

RIVIÈRE, G. H. (1975), *The Museum of Negro Civilization at Dakar*, United Nations Educational, Scientific and Cultural Organization, Paris

ROYAL NATIONAL INSTITUTE FOR THE BLIND (1988), *Talking Touch: Report of a Seminar on the Use of Touch in Museums and Galleries held at the RNIB on 19th February 1988*, Royal National Institute for the Blind, London

SACKS, J. (1990), Paradoxes of pluralism, *Listener*, 4 December 1990, 16–18 [1990 Reith Lecture No. 4]

SHARPE, T. and HOWE, S. R. (1982), Family expeditions – the museum outdoors, *Museums Journal*, **82**(3), 143–147

SHARPE, T. and ROLFE, W. D. (1979), Geological enquiries, *Museums Journal*, **79**(1), 61, 62

SHORE, I. and JACINTO, B. (1989), *Access to Art: A Museum Directory for Blind and Visually Impaired People*, Museum of American Folk Art and American Foundation for the Blind, New York

SILIPRANDI, KATRINA (1987), Play groups and museums, *Journal of Education in Museums*, **9**, 13 and 14

SMITHSONIAN INSTITUTION (1977), *The Smithsonian Experience. Science-History-The Arts . . . The Treasures of the Nation*, Smithsonian Institution, Washington, DC

STAM, D. C. (1989), Public access to museum information: pressures and policies, *Curator*, **32**(3), 190–198

TAIT, S. (1989), *Palaces of Discovery. The Changing World of Britain's Museums*, Quiller Press, London

VAN VLEUTEN, R. (1986), The role of the museum public relations officer, 21–24 in Bellow, Corinne (Ed.), *Public View. The ICOM Handbook of Museum Public Relations*, International Council of Museums, Paris

VELARDE, G. (1988), *Designing Exhibitions*, Design Council, London

VERGO, P. (Ed.) (1989), *The New Museology*, Reaktion Books Ltd., London

WASHBURN, W. C. (1984), Collecting information, not objects, *Museum News*, **62**, 15

WEIL, S. E. (1989), The proper business of the museum: ideas or things, *Muse*, **7**(1), 43–56. Reprinted in Weil, S. E. (1990), *Rethinking the Museum and Other Meditations*, Smithsonian Institution Press, Washington, DC and London

WEIL, S. E. (1990), Rethinking the museum: an emerging new paradigm, *Museum News*, March/April 1990. Reprinted in Weil, S. E. (1990), *Rethinking the Museum and other Meditations*, Smithsonian Institution Press, Washington, DC and London

WILLIAMS, G. (1983), *Wales and the Past: A Consort of Voices. A 75th Anniversary Lecture by Glanmor Williams*, National Museum of Wales, Cardiff

WILSON, A. (1989), Outreach is . . . 29–30 in Quin, M. (Ed.), *Sharing Science: A Collection of Reports and Discussion Articles to Inform the Debate on Hands-on Education*, Nuffield Foundation/Committee on the Public Understanding of Science, London

WILSON, D. M. (1989), *The British Museum: Purpose and Politics*, British Museum Publications, London

WOMEN, HERITAGE AND MUSEUMS (n.d.), *Resources List*, Women, Heritage and Museums, Teddington, Middlesex

WRIGHT, P. (1985), *On Living in an Old Country. The National Past in Contemporary Britain*, Verso, London

Addresses

Among the national or international museum organizations which have contributed most to the theme of Section Five of the Manual are the following:-

American Association of Museums, 1225 Eye Street NW, Suite 200, Washington DC 20005.

International Council of Museums, Maison de l'Unesco, 1 rue Miollis, 75732 Paris Cedex 15.

The Museums Association, 42 Clerkenwell Close, London EC1R 0PA.

Among the specialist groups and associations are:-

American Association for State and Local History, 708 Berry Road, Nashville, Tennessee 37204.

Association of Independent Museums, c/o Weald and Downland Museum, Singleton, W. Sussex.

Group for Museum Publishing and Shop Management, c/o Ashmolean Museum, Oxford OX1 2PH.

Group of Designers/Interpreters in Museums, c/o Museum of Science and Industry, Liverpool Road, Manchester M3 4JP.

Group for Education in Museums, [Ms. Susan Morris] 63 Navarine Road, London E8 1AG.

Museums and Galleries Disability Association, c/o City Museum and Art Gallery, Stoke-on-Trent ST1 3DW.

Museum Professionals Group c/o Cecil Higgins Art Gallery and Museum, Castle Close, Bedford MK40 3NY.

Touring Exhibitions Group, c/o Exhibitions Department, Commonwealth Institute, Kensington High Street, London W8 6NQ.

WHAM. Women, Heritage and Museums, c/o Weybridge Museum, Church Street, Weybridge, Surrey KT13 8DE.

A body which also deserves special mention is the Museum Reference Center of the Smithsonian Institution (The Castle, The Mall, Washington DC). The Center probably houses the largest single collection of bibliographic and documentary material on all aspects of museum operations. The holdings in the education category are particularly rich, partly in that they now incorporate the material hitherto held by the Center for Museum Education at the George Washington University.

63

Museum libraries

John R. Kenyon

Introduction

In the first edition of the *Manual of Curatorship*, the only major mention of libraries occurs at the end of Bassett's chapter on museum publications, although some other chapters do refer to them ('Research: natural science collections', p. 153; 'Research: archaeological collections', pp. 166–167). That there was no section on libraries in the Manual is not altogether surprising, seeing that librarianship is a profession in its own right, with a huge range of publications serving its practitioners. Also, very little has been written on museum librarianship, and most of what has been published appears in American publications;[1] only a few key references are given in a recent book (Woodhead and Stansfield, 1989, pp. 29–30).

A perusal of the *Museums Yearbook 1989/90* shows that only about 32 of the institutions listed have professional library staff,[2] although most museums will have libraries of some kind, even if the collection is only represented by a shelf of books in a Curator's office. It is not surprising, therefore, that it is the larger museums and galleries, notably the national ones, which maintain a professionally run library, although other large institutions, such as the Ironbridge Gorge Museum and Glasgow Art Gallery and Museum, have librarians on their staff. Some of the libraries are outstanding and well known, virtually national libraries in their own right, and one thinks automatically of the collections of the British Museum (Natural History) (Sawyer, 1971; Stearn, 1981), the Science Museum (Follett, 1978, pp. 125–136), and the Victoria and Albert Museum's National Art Library (Esteve-Coll, 1986; Kaden, 1977; Somers Cocks, 1980, pp. 164–181); such libraries are departments in their own right, as opposed to what might be termed back-up sections. Nor should one forget the original collections in the British Museum which now form part of the British Library, and here again the British Museum Library was anything but an adjunct of the other departments. Other important libraries include the National Museums of Scotland (McCorry, 1987), the Tate Gallery (Symons and Houghton, 1977), the Ashmolean Museum (Ovenell, 1986), the Museum of the History of Science, Oxford (Simcock, 1987), the National Museum of Wales (Kenyon, 1989), and the Manx Museum (Harrison, 1986).

Other bodies within the museum profession may also house libraries, namely the area museum councils. These include the Area Museum and Art Gallery Service for Yorkshire and Humberside and the Scottish Museums Council (Alexander and Bass 1984–1985). The Museum Documentation Association in Cambridge has a library which visitors are able to use upon application, but it is obviously a specialized library within the profession, with the bulk of its stock relating to documentation. One of the strongest collections is, of course, in the University of Leicester, serving the students and staff in the Department of Museum Studies.

Some of these libraries may be centralized, others may have departmental libraries as well as a central collection within one building, or out-stations scattered around the country. The range in the size of some of these libraries is clearly indicated in a recent survey on biological collections in the UK (Williams, 1987). Out of the 242 responding institutions, 132 replied that they had some kind of library associated with their collections. Of this figure, between 39 and 55 per cent had less than 500 books and serial titles in the libraries, and many of them took no periodicals at all (Williams, 1987, pp. 300–322, 555–573).

There are museum libraries which have a long ancestry but, although a short paper was given on the subject at a Museums Association conference at the end of the last century (White, 1895), it has only been since 1945 that there has been an increase in museum library literature (apart from catalogues), notably in the 1950s in the pages of the American journal *Special Libraries*.[3] White stressed that the 'Museum Library should be treated by those in authority as just as necessary a part of the provision of the Museum outfit as the cases in which the specimens are shown' (White, 1895, p. 45). It is a truism, although one about which people often need to be reminded, that a library forms an essential core of any academic institution, whether university, college or museum. Without adequate facilities, which in the larger towns and cities may well be supplemented by a large central public library, the Curator is unable to fulfill his or her duties to the museum or gallery or to the public. Also, it is not just the Curator who is served by the library, but also those working in other sections, such as the Designer and Conservator.

Librarians who work in museums have not been seen as a separate branch of the library profession; nor should they be. Museum and gallery libraries form just part of a wide range of special libraries and information services, each with their own problems, their own way of curating their collections. There is not a 'Museum Libraries Group' amongst the more than 20 specialist interest groups of the Library Association. This is offset to a considerable degree by the body known as ARLIS, the Art Libraries Society. In the words of its publicity leaflet, this group was formed to 'promote all aspects of the librarianship of the visual arts', and its serial publications, *ARLIS News-Sheet* and *Art Libraries Journal* are of particular benefit to those who work in this field, the majority being outside museums and galleries. Art librarianship is also fortunate to have been the subject of various monographs, including Jones and Gibson's (1986) volume on development, organization and management and the collection of essays edited by Pacey (1985), the former chairman of ARLIS. This is not to say that museum librarianship as a whole has been neglected in monograph literature. The works by Collins and Anderson (1977), Larsen (1985) and Ratner and Monkhouse (1980) are useful, particularly Larsen, although they all have an American bias.

Library operations[4]

As with any academic institution, the instigators of the acquisition of new material for the collections will be both the librarians, based on their extensive knowledge of the range of their holdings, and the curatorial staff in the subject departments. Libraries also make use of the fact that the institutions which they serve are, to a greater or lesser extent, publishing houses, and this enables them to acquire a wide range of publications on exchange, notably from overseas museums and galleries. The profession also has its own 'manuals of curatorship' in order to process the acquisitions before they are made available to readers. Examples are the *Anglo-American Cataloguing Rules*,[5] and the Library of Congress and Dewey Decimal classification schemes, of which the latter is in its twentieth edition. Also, there are a number of guides issued to help in the processing of material (see, for example, Chapman (1990)). Special libraries are also the theme of the *Aslib Handbook* (Anthony, 1982).

Often the specialist nature of the collection means that the librarian has to devise a unique system for curation, such as the in-house classification scheme devised for the library of the Institute of Agricultural History and Museum of English Rural Life, Reading (Creasey, 1978). The Scottish Museums Council eventually found that the Dewey classification scheme was not suitable for specialised museological collections, and devised their own after alternatives could not be found (Alexander and Bass, 1984–1985, p. 172). In fact, a good expanded Dewey scheme already existed, although it has not appeared in full in recent editions (Coleman, 1927). It is this system that is used for the museum studies section of the library in the National Museum of Wales.

It is sometimes said by librarians, and not just those in the museum field, that at times they feel that their services are not exploited to the full. At times curators do not stop to think that their colleagues in the library could help over certain matters. A librarian may not know the answer, but he or she should be able to guide the enquirer to a satisfactory result, whether it is obtained from sources inside or outside the institution. Many of the library staff are appointed with a good knowledge of some of the fields covered by the museum or gallery, or they soon acquire it. It is really in the hands of the librarians to make their colleagues aware of such services.

Publications, whether in-house or more formal, are one of the best ways of exploiting library collections. The Victoria and Albert Museum used to issue and circulate to other institutions a quarterly list of accessions to its library, but this ceased in 1985 for economic reasons. In the National Museum of Wales a monthly list of 'Recent Additions' is issued for internal circulation, arranged by department and out-station, and which includes photocopies of title pages of recent annual reports and serials housed in the main library. Then there are the more important catalogues ranging from the magisterial volumes listing the contents of a complete library down to special collections within larger holdings. Examples of catalogues on a grand scale are those produced by the British Museum (Natural History) listing both monographs and serials (British Museum (Natural History) 1903–1940, 1987). A large part of the library collections of the National Maritime Museum has been published by HMSO (National Maritime Museum, 1968–1976). Catalogues of special collections within a library include the pre-1641 books in the Science Museum Library (Brody, 1979) and the Willoughby Gardner collection of early printed natural history books in the National Museum of Wales (Kenyon, 1982).

Library staff are also active authors in the various fields on which they specialize. Natural history has benefitted from this in particular; for example, the entomological source books produced by Gilbert, the entomology librarian at the British Museum (Natural History) (Gilbert, 1977; Gilbert and Hamilton, 1983). In addition, there are the volumes compiled by Root listing the artists whose works have featured in the *Proceedings* and the *Transactions* of the Zoological Society of London (Root and Johnson, 1986a,b). The extent of the library in the British Museum (Natural History) made it the obvious choice for the publication of the *Annual Bibliography of the History of Natural History*, where it is compiled by the staff of the Department of Library Services.[6] The other important bibliographic publication to note is *Museum Abstracts*, compiled by the Information Officer of the Scottish Museums Council. This service began in 1985, and is now published jointly by the Scottish Museums Council and Routledge.[7] Nor should one forget the numerous papers that have appeared in journals, such as *Archives of Natural History*, on individual books and series that have been to the benefit of Curators and Librarians alike.

Libraries and museology

It was mentioned above that various area museum councils do provide library facilities, primarily for the benefit of the staff and members of the council. The small budgets for the purchase of books for many museum libraries, particularly those without a Librarian, mean that the acquisition of a wide range of museological books does not have priority. However, a larger museum with a number of smaller institutions in the immediate hinterland might be expected to cater to some extent for the needs of professional colleagues. A museum library with what might be called a pastoral role in this field is the National Museum of Wales. The collection has grown considerably in the last decade, most of it being held in the general main library so that the key English-language monographs and periodicals are easily accessible not only for staff but also for Curators in provincial museums in the Principality. One of the aims in the development of the museology library has been as an aid for those studying for museum qualifications and, although it

is difficult for Curators in north Wales to make use of the library, except through inter-library loans, it is possible for them to study the small amount of material that is kept in one of the Museum's branches, Amgueddfa'r Gogledd, the Museum of the North in Llanberis, Gwynedd. The central collection obviously does not compare with the holdings in the University of Leicester, but with about 800 titles on curatorial matters, over 2000 general books and pamphlets on museums and galleries throughout the world,[8] and 35 periodical titles, the coverage of the collection is more than reasonable. The libraries in two other branches of the National Museum of Wales, the Welsh Folk Museum and the Welsh Industrial and Maritime Museum, house a certain amount of museological material, particularly the former which has its own Librarian.

Although the majority of the smaller museums and galleries are unlikely to be in a position to spend large sums of money on their libraries, let alone employ a professional Librarian, there are certain museological books, the *Manual of Curatorship* apart, which are often used by those from other museums who visit the National Museum of Wales's library. It is these works which museums perhaps should aim to add to their own collections of books, and this writer has made a selection in the following paragraphs, the items selected being based on the experiences of the National Museum of Wales library staff. No doubt others could list as many books again, so the books detailed below could be regarded as the bare minimum.

There are various organizations whose publications should all be on the bookshelves of the museum. One thinks of in particular the information sheets of the Museums Association, the reports of what is now the Museums and Galleries Commission, and the *AIM Guidelines* issued by the Association of Independent Museums. The publications of the Scottish Museums Council are popular, and one must also mention their *Museum Abstracts*, especially as few of the periodicals covered will be found in a small museum. A number of titles emanating from the Royal Ontario Museum and the American Association of Museums are often referred to, notably the Royal Ontario Museum's (1976) *Communicating with the Museum Visitor*, and Dudley *et al*'s (1979) *Museum Registration Methods*.

There are also the publications issued by the Museum Documentation Association, and no doubt most museums will have these; mention must also be made of Abell-Seddon (1988), *Museum Catalogues*, Chenhall and Vance (1988), *Museum Collections and Today's Computers*, and Light *et al*'s (1986) *Museum Documentation Systems*.

Butterworths, the publishers, have virtually cornered the market in the field of conservation, and many of the titles in their conservation and museology series ought to be in all major museums. However, as a set of these publications costs several hundred pounds, and certainly more than many museums spend on books, it is to major repositories of museological books that Curators have to look. Nevertheless, there are some titles which ought to be regarded as essential, for instance, Thomson's (1986) *The Museum Environment*, to name but one.

On the display side, two books of note are Hall (1987), *On Display*, and Miles (1988), *The Design of Educational Exhibits*, while in the field of security mention should be made of Fennelly (1983), *Museum, Archive, and Library Security*, and Tillotson (1977), *Museum Security*.

Conclusion

In one of the chapters of *Museum Librarianship* it is stated that 'The museum library is a hybrid of a public, research, and special library, catering to audiences with very different levels of information needs' (Larsen, 1985, p. 79). This is certainly true of the larger professionally run libraries; one has to cater for the specific needs of the curatorial staff and the support services, the under- and post-graduates who are unable to find everything in the university library, and the members of the public who might want information on anything from the history of a given area down to an opinion of a book, whether it happens to be a Victorian family Welsh Bible or a copy of the *Eikon Basilike*. Furthermore, without a strong supporting library, the effectiveness of the curatorial staff in carrying out their own duties and dealing with the public is severely curtailed. The library is one of the most important educational resources a museum can possess.

Notes

[1] The Bibliography and References given at the end of this chapter list the main references to museum libraries and librarianship, but are not intended to be an exhaustive list.

[2] This excludes those museums which form part of Local or County Authority departments and which are run by a County Public Librarian, such as the Clwyd Library and Museum Service.

[3] For example, the entire issues of volumes **42**(5) and **50**(3) for 1951 and 1959, respectively. See also articles cited in the References and Bibliography to this chapter.

[4] It is not my intention in this section to discuss library practices in detail; such coverage is not relevant to this volume. Also, some parts of the *Manual*, such as the chapter on enquiries, relate as much to the library as they do to the subject departments.

[5] Second edition (1988 revision), edited by M. Gorman and P. W. Winkler, Library Association, London

[6] The first three volumes, published in 1985–1987, cover the publications of 1982–1984. It is expected that volumes 4 and 5 will appear towards the end of 1990.

[7] However, this service does not abstract monographs. Although some recent publications would be time-consuming to prepare, the omission of even a list of recent key items is unfortunate for the museum profession.

[8] The figure of 2000 excludes the numerous catalogues of collections held by museums and art galleries.

References

ABELL-SEDDON, B. (1988), *Museum Catalogues*, Clive Bingley, London

ALEXANDER, W. and BASS, H. (1984–1985), 'Information services in Scotland and Yorkshire and Humberside', *Museums Journal*, **84**, 171–175

ANTHONY, L. J. (Ed.) (1982), *Handbook of Special Librarianship and Information Work*, Aslib, London

BRITISH MUSEUM (NATURAL HISTORY) (1903–1940), *Catalogue of the Books . . . in the British Museum (Natural History)*, 8 vols, British Museum (Natural History), London

BRITISH MUSEUM (NATURAL HISTORY) (1987), *Serial Publications in the British Museum (Natural History) Library on Mcirofiche*, British Museum (Natural History), London

BRODY, J. (1979), *A Catalogue of Books printed before 1641 in the Science Museum Library*, Science Museum, London

CHAPMAN, L. (1990), *How to Catalogue: A Practical Handbook using AACR2 and Library of Congress*, 2nd edition, Clive Bingley, London

CHENHALL, R. G. and VANCE, D. (1988), *Museum Collections and Today's Computers*, Greenwood Press, New York

COLEMAN, L. V. (1927), *Classification for Printed Matter and Notes on Museum Work*, American Association of Museums, Washington, DC

COLLINS, M. and ANDERSON, L. (1977), *Libraries for Small Museums*, 3rd edition, University of Missouri, Columbia

CREASEY, J. S. (1978), *Museum Procedure: Library*, Institute of Agricultural History and Museum of English Rural Life, University of Reading, Reading

DUDLEY, D. H., WILKINSON, I. B. *et al* (1979), *Museum Registration Methods*, 3rd edition, American Association of Museums, Washington, DC

ESTEVE-COLL, E. (1986), 'Image and reality: the National Art Library', *Art Libraries Journal*, **11**(2), 33–39

FENNELLY, L. J. (1983), *Museum, Archive, and Library Security*, Butterworth, London

FOLLETT, D. (1978), *The Rise of the Science Museum under Henry Lyons*, Science Museum, London

GILBERT, P. (1977), *A Compendium of the Biographical Literature on Deceased Entomologists*, British Museum (Natural History), London

GILBERT, P. and HAMILTON, C. J. (1983), *Entomology: a Guide to Information Sources*, Mansell, London

HALL, M. (1987), *On Display*, Lund Humphries, London

HARRISON, A. M. (1986), 'The Manx Museum Library', in Harrison, S. (Ed.), *100 Years of Heritage: the Work of the Manx Museum and National Trust*, pp. 134–167, Manx Museum and National Trust, Douglas

JONES, L. S. and GIBSON, S. S. (1986), *Art Libraries and Information Services*, Academic Press, Orlando, FL

KADEN, V. (1977), 'The National Art Library', *Library Association Record*, **79**, 310–311

KENYON, J. R. (1982), *The Willoughby Gardner Library*, National Museum of Wales, Cardiff

KENYON, J. R. (1989), 'Books and curators: the Library of the National Museum of Wales', *New Welsh Review,* **4,** 64–66

LARSEN, J. C. (Ed.) (1985), *Museum Librarianship,* Library Professional Publications, Hamden

LIGHT, R. B., ROBERTS, D. A. and STEWART, J. D. (1986), *Museum Documentation Systems,* Butterworth, London

MCCORRY, H. (1987), 'Scottish United Services Museum Library', *Scottish Libraries,* **3,** 3, 5

MILES, R. S. (1988), *The Design of Educational Exhibits,* 2nd edition, Unwin Hyman, London

NATIONAL MARITIME MUSEUM (1968–1976), *National Maritime Museum: Catalogue of the Library,* 5 vols in 7, HMSO, London

OVENELL, R. F. (1986), *The Ashmolean Museum 1683–1894,* Clarendon Press, Oxford

PACEY, P. (Ed.), (1985), *A Reader in Art Librarianship.* Saur, New York

RATNER, R. S. and MONKHOUSE, V. (Eds) (1980), *The Role of the Library in a Museum,* Smithsonian Institution, Washington, DC

ROOT, N. J. and JOHNSON, B. R. (1986a), *'Proceedings' of the Zoological Society of London: an Index to the Artists 1848–1900,* Garland, New York

ROOT, N. J. and JOHNSON, B. R. (1986b), *'Transactions' of the Zoological Society of London: an Index to the Artists 1835–1936,* Garland, New York

ROYAL ONTARIO MUSEUM (1976), *Communicating with the Museum Visitor,* Toronto, Ontario

SAWYER, F. C. (1971), 'A short history of the libraries and list of manuscripts and original drawings in the British Museum (Natural History)', *Bulletin of the British Museum (Natural History): Historical Series,* **4**(2), 77–204

SIMCOCK, A. V. (1987), 'An ark for the history of science', *IATUL Quarterly,* **1,** 196–215

SOMERS COCKS, A. (1980), *The Victoria and Albert Museum; the Making of the Collection,* Windward, Leicester

STEARN, W. T. (1981), *The Natural History Museum at South Kensington,* Heinemann, London

SYMONS, A. C. and HOUGHTON, B. (1977), 'Tate development responds to increased demands', *Library Association Record,* **79,** 311, 313

THOMSON, G. (1986), *The Museum Environment,* 2nd edition, Butterworths, London

TILLOTSON, R. G. (1977), *Museum Security,* International Council of Museums, Paris

WHITE, W. (1895), 'Museum libraries', *Museums Association: Report of Proceedings . . . Newcastle-upon Tyne,* 41–46

WILLIAMS, B. (1987), *Biological Collections UK,* Museums Association, London

WOODHEAD, P. and STANSFIELD, G. (1989), *Keyguide to Information Sources in Museum Studies,* Mansell, London

Bibliography

BIERBAUM, E. G. (1984), 'The museum library revisited', *Special Libraries,* **75,** 102–113

COOLIDGE, J. (1959), 'American art museums: past, problems and potentials', *Special Libraries,* **50,** 119–122

DANILOV, V. J. (1977), 'Libraries at science and technology museums', *Curator,* **20,** 98–101

DRAHEIM, M. W. (1976), 'Libraries in British museums', M.Lib thesis, University of Wales

EDWARDS, E. H. (1955), 'The Library of the National Museum of Wales', *Library Association Record,* **57,** 56–60

HARRISON, C. (1964), 'Education and the museum library', *Museum News,* **42**(5), 33–36

HULL, D. and FEARNLEY, H. D. (1976), 'The museum library in the United States: a sample', *Special Libraries,* **67,** 289–298

JAY, H. L. and JAY, M. E. (1984), *Developing Library-Museum Partnerships to Serve Young People,* Library Professional Publications, Hamden

KENYON, J. R. (1987–1988), 'Recent additions to the special collections of the Library of the National Museum of Wales', *National Library of Wales Journal,* **25,** 470–473

MOUNT, E. (Ed.) (1985), *Sci-Tech Libraries in Museums and Aquariums,* Haworth Press, New York

SHILLINGLAW, N. (1986), 'Public relations and museum libraries', *Mousaion,* Series 3, **4**(1), 77–84

SOMMER, F. H. (1974), 'A large museum library', *Special Libraries,* **65,** 99–103

USILTON, B. (1963), 'The museum library', *Museum News,* **42**(2), 11–14

64

Museum publications: a descriptive and bibliographic guide

Douglas A. Bassett

The purpose of this chapter – which is a completely revised, rearranged and enlarged version of the one in the first edition of this Manual (1984, pp. 467–475) – is to look in some detail at the most important types of museum publications and to provide a bibliographic guide to the literature on them. It provides, therefore, a sequel to Geoffrey Stansfield's *Sources of Museological Literature* (Information Sheet No. 9, 2nd edition, Museums Association, London, 1976) and complements his joint publication with Peter Woodhead, *Keyguide to Information Sources in Museum Studies* (Mansell, London, 1989). It also complements the seminar volumes *Museum Publishing: Problems and Potential*, edited by Jenni Calder (National Museums of Scotland, Edinburgh, 1988) and *Museum Publications in Science, Technology and Medicine*, edited by R. I. H. Charlton for two specialist museum groups (see Conference Proceedings, p. 606). To a lesser extent it complements the revised and enlarged second edition of Lois Swan Jones' *Art Research Methods and Resources. A Guide to Finding Art Information* (Kendall/Hunt Publishing Co., Dubuque, Iowa, 1984).

The *Keyguide* and *Art Research* volumes are described fully in the section on 'Tertiary publications' and the *Museum Publishing* and *Museum Publications* volumes in the section on 'Conference proceedings'. Throughout the remainder of the text these four volumes are referred to by their titles or short titles only.

The 'Short note on museum libraries' in the first edition of this chapter is superceded by the separate chapter on 'Museum libraries' by J. R. Kenyon (Chapter 63). There are, however, a number of references to both libraries and archives in this chapter because, 'Museums, archives and libraries comprise a spectrum of collecting institutions whose interests range from unique objects to published information (Homalus, P., (1990), 'Museums to libraries: a family of collecting institutions', *Art Libraries Journal*, **15**(1), pp. 11–13). See also: Lemke, A. B. (1989), 'Art archives: a common concern of archivists, librarians and museum professionals', *Art Libraries Journal*, **14**(2), pp. 5–11.

The role of publication

The relationship of publication to the research and curatorial roles of museums is clearly reflected in the Report by a working party of the Ancient Monuments Board for England, Committee for Rescue Archaeology – *Principles of Publication in Rescue Archaeology* [The Frere Report] (Department of the Environment, 1975). In the Introduction it states: 'Archaeologists and those who employ or sponsor them in undertaking excavations have an obligation to publish their work: they also have the responsibility of seeing that the significant excavated material and the full original records of the work are preserved for reference by future scholars. The two aspects of publication and preservation of the records are inter-related'.

The same emphasis is given in the chapter on 'Community and communications' in John Ziman's *Public Knowledge. An Essay Concerning the Social Dimension of Science* (Cambridge University Press, Cambridge, 1968, pp. 102ff.). The main thrust of his thesis about the nature of science is that the 'literature' of the subject is quite as important as the research work that it embodies.

The intimacy of the connections between science and printing and the distinctive roles of research articles and textbooks are emphasized in T. S. Kuhn's seminal The Structure of Scientific Revolutions (in *International Encyclopedia of Unified Science, Foundations of the Unity of Science* Vol. 1, No. 2, University of Chicago Press, Chicago, IL, 1962, 2nd edition, 1970) and neatly summarized by M.

MacDonald-Ross in 'The Role of Science Books for the Public' (in Evered, D. C. and O'Connor, M. (Eds.) (1987), *Communicating Science to the Public* [CIBA Foundation Conference], pp. 175–184, 185–189, Wiley, Chichester).

Another role is the one that professional journals play as a critical attribute of a clearly defined museum profession: they not only provide one of the most tangible pieces of evidence of professionalism, but also they are the attribute most open 'to verification by peer examination' (Griesemer, A. D. (1983), 'Publication channels for museum professionals: a professional concern', *Museum Studies Journal*, **1**(2), 60–64, 71–76). This role is also stated, implicitly or explicitly, in most of the contributions to the first issue of *Museological Working Papers* ('Museology – science or just practical museum work?', *Museological Working Paper No. 1*, 1980) (*see* 'Periodicals').

Publications policy

Aspects of publication policy are considered in two papers in *Museum Publishing: Problems and Potential* (1988), namely: 'Publications policy: the need for planning' (R. I. H. Charlton, pp. 8–13) and 'Publications policy: the need for flexibility' (Patricia Bascom, pp. 14 and 15); and in G. L'E. Turner (1982) 'Do museums of science and technology have a publications policy? A review of the current situation' (in *Museum Publications in Science, Technology and Medicine*, pp. 3–9). Turner, finding a dearth of published policy statements, attempted to infer the publications policy of a number of British and Continental museums by studying their output. He paid particular attention to the Deutsches Museum, Munich, the Museum Boerhaave, Leiden, the History of Science Museum, Oxford and the National Maritime Museum and the Science Museum in London.

More specific policy statements are made in the various Corporate Plans. The paragraph on 'Publishing' in the section 'Aims of the museum' in the *British Museum (Natural History) Corporate Plan 1986–1991* (1987), for example, states: 'To publish for sale, exchange or donation, the results of taxonomic research and to promote the sale to the general public of popular scientific works, prints, models, etc. in order to cover the overhead cost of scholarly publications and to provide a net trading for the Museum' (p. 29).

The paragraph which deals with publications in the 'Statement of Objectives . . .' for the Leicestershire Museums, Art Galleries and Records Office, states: 'The Service is responsible for the promotion and publication of research relating to the collections of the Service, and to the history and environment of Leicestershire and adjacent areas'. In the accompanying comment it states: 'The Leicester Museum has been acting as a publisher of information about the Museum collections and the locality for over a century, and this has been greatly expanded in recent years (under the provision of a special Act of Parliament, the Leicester Corporation Act, 1956). The Service has special legal powers which enable it to publish, not merely material about the Museums, etc. and their collections, but also 'any work of scholarship having reference to the City or its neighbourhood or to any museum specimen, work of art or document in the possession or under the management or control of the Service' (Boylan, P. J. (1980), *Museumleven*, No. 7–8, 132–138).

The role of publication in the wider context of information policies is considered by Elizabeth Orna in *Information Policies for Museums, Occasional Paper 10* (Museum Documentation Association, Cambridge, 1987).

The different kinds of museum publications

The range of museum publications is considerable. It stated in a recent symposium that museums 'probably produce a greater assortment of printed and/or published items than any other comparable institutions or organisations', in large measure 'because of their great range of subject materials and the diversity of different users for whom these must be interpreted' (Heppell, D. and Smith, D. (1988), 'What is a publication?', in Calder, J. (Ed.), *Museum Publishing: Problems and Potential*, p. 1).

Material published by museums and museum bodies can be categorized in a number of different ways. For example:

(1) according to the museum that issues it (as in Roulstone, M. (Ed.), 1980, *The Bibliography of Museum and Art Gallery Publications . . . 1979/80*, Chadwyck–Healey, Cambridge; 550pp.) (*see* Bibliographies);

(2) according to the organization that produces it (as in Anon, 'Just who produces museological literature?' *ICOM News*, **38**(2), 1985, p. 4);

(3) according to its subject matter, as in the usual book catalogue (and also in most of the annual or periodical catalogues of books-in-print issued by the larger national museums);

(4) according to the audience for whom it is designed, e.g. scholars, the general public or for educational purposes (as in Charlton, R. I. H., 1988, 'Publications policy: the need for planning', in *Museum Publishing: Problems and Potential*, pp. 8–13);

(5) according to the purpose which it is designed to serve (as in Gregg, R., 1959, 'Art museum publications – their nature and design', *Curator*, **11**(1), 49–67, in which the author distinguishes those publications that stimulate people to visit the museum from those that interpret the

collections and refers twelve types of publication to these two categories;

(6) according to the categories regularly used in the various published guides to literature – into 'primary', 'secondary' and 'tertiary' literature.

In this present chapter the sixth type of classification is adopted. The three cateogies – primary, secondary and tertiary – clearly are not mutually exclusive: many journals, for example, regularly include both primary and secondary material.

Primary publications

The major types of museum publications in this category are: catalogues, the majority of periodicals, separate books, scholarly or specialist monographs, theses and conference proceedings. Each of these is considered separately.

Catalogues and handbooks to permanent collections

The importance of published catalogues to permanent collections in museums is stressed and prescriptions given in a number of chapters in this and in the first edition of this Manual. At the same time, the fact that in a number of disciplines catalogues are comparatively rare and expensive to produce is also emphasized. Christopher Wright ('Curators, collections and catalogues', *International Journal of Museum Management and Curatorship*, **7**(3), 1988, pp. 269–273) identifies three factors which have resulted in the reduction of the role of research on art collections and, consequently, to the virtual elimination of the publication of collections catalogues for the non-specialist.

A survey of catalogues to permanent collections in art museums was made in the early 1970s as part of an assessment of the research information and facilities available to graduate students in 45 European and 45 American museums (Jones, L. S., 1974, 'Let your fingers do the walking', *Museum News,* **52**(5), pp. 36–39). Although 90 per cent of the 90 museums studied published some kind of check-list, catalogue or guide to their permanent collections, less than half had published a scholarly catalogue for any part of their collection. The author provides a brief critical analysis of the nature of 325 of these scholarly catalogues.

Failure to publish catalogues is not, however, universal. The Tate Gallery, for example, publishes an *Illustrated Catalogue of Acquisitions* biennially. It also maintains that the Tate is 'the only museum in the world to attempt to research and document as thoroughly as possible every object – be it painting, sculpture, drawing or print – that enters the collection at the time of its acquisition. This

labour-intensive work reflects the Gallery's belief that research and scholarship are fundamental to the life of a museum and form an essential part of the service it provides to the public'. The most recent catalogue (*Illustrated Catalogue of Acquisitions 1984–86. Including supplement to Catalogue of acquisitions 1982–84*) has individual entries of over 700 works, nearly all of which are illustrated.

Proof of the importance that other museums give to the publication of catalogues is provided in the various lists of publications-in-print. In *British Museum Publications. . . Complete catalogue 1990*, for example, each of the subheadings 'Scholarly titles' in the main subject subdivisions contains details of major catalogues. See also the Museum's triennial reports.

Lois S. Jones devotes a chapter in her *Art Research Methods and Resources* (1984, pp. 27–37) to 'Understanding specialized art references'. These are grouped into three:

(1) museum collection and exhibition catalogues;
(2) auction sales catalogues and the indices which report them; and
(3) art history books.

In the first category she divides museum collection catalogues into 'a checklist or summary catalogue' and 'a scholarly catalogue', and provides an inventory or check-list of 11 kinds of information normally included in each entry in the latter. She also describes the terminology used in entries in both exhibition and museum collection catalogues. In the third category (Art History Books), she distinguishes two groups of reference works:

(1) monographs, catalogues raisonnés and oeuvres catalogues; and
(2) *corpora, Festschriften,* and symposia papers.

The terms 'catalogues raisonnés' and 'oeuvres catalogues' are therefore used in a slightly different sense from that adopted by Dennis Farr in the first edition of this Manual (1984, pp. 188–190).

A useful checklist of the range of catalogues published in Britain and available at the end of the 1970s is provided in Roulstone, M. (Ed.) (1980), *The Bibliography of Museum and Art Gallery Publications . . .*, (Chadwyck-Healey, Cambridge). A rather similar check-list for fine- and decorative-art collections is given in Chapel, Jeannie and Gere, Charlotte (Compilers and editors) (1985), *The Fine and Decorative Art Collections of Britain and Ireland* (The National Art–Collections Fund Book of Art Galleries and Museums, Wiedenfeld and Nicolson, London). It covers 400 public museums and galleries, large and small, and lists catalogues of permanent collections and of temporary exhibitions wherever appropriate. A third check-list, for the late

1960s, is given in two consecutive editorials in the *Burlington Magazine*: the first, for June 1970 (**112**, no. 807), lists catalogues and guides to the Royal Collection and to museums and galleries in London; the second, for July 1970 (**112**, no. 808), lists 'Museum catalogues – outside London'.

A select bibliography of some of the important printed catalogues of the permanent collections of seventeen internationally famous museums (including the Bayerische Staatsgemäldesammlungen, Munich; The British Museum, London; the Frick Collection, New York; the Musée National du Louvre, Paris, etc.) is given in *Art Research Methods and Resources* (1984, pp. 187–190). Parts of the collections reprinted on microforms are noted (pp. 210–215).

An early example of the realization of the importance of well-illustrated publications in spreading knowledge of the collections to those who could not visit a museum, is outlined in Morris, B. (1986), *Inspiration for Design. The Influence of the Victoria and Albert Museum* (Victoria and Albert Museum, London). One of the first catalogues was the *Treasury of Ornamental Art*, published in 1857 with descriptive notes by the Curator, J. C. Robinson. The 46 plates, as the preface states, are examples of 'ornamental' or 'decorative' art and were selected 'on the widest possible basis, in order to respond to every phase of connoisseurship, antiquarian interest, and practical utility to the art student, in short a complete "museographic" work has been projected'.

Prints and drawings

The main collections of prints and drawings in British institutions are housed in the British Museum and in the major art museums and galleries. See, for example, Griffiths, A. and Williams, R. (1987), *The Department of Prints and Drawings in the British Museum, User's Guide*, British Museum Publications.

A major exception, however, is the collection of natural history illustrations housed in the British Museum (Natural History), part of which is described by Diment, J. A. and Newington, L. (1985), 'Botanical prints and drawings at the British Museum (Natural History)', in *Art Libraries Journal*, **10**(1), pp. 5–27.

Details of the best known individual collection – the natural history drawings commissioned by Sir Joseph Banks (1743–1820) on the Endeavour voyage (1768–1771) – are published in three parts in the Historical Series of the Museum's *Bulletin* (**11**, 1984, pp. 1–183; **12**, 1985, pp. 1–200; and **13**, 1986, pp. 1–172), and 738 of the drawings have been published by the Museum in association with Alecto Historical Editions (Diment, J. A. and Humphries, C. J. (Eds) (1980–1986), *Banks' Florilegium . . . a publication in thirty-four parts of seven hundred and thirty eight copper plate engravings of plants collected on Captain James Cook's first voyage – gathered and classified by Sir Joseph Banks . . . and Dr. Daniel Solander . . . engraved . . . after drawings by Sidney Parkinson*, London.

The project, which was started in 1960, 'may well represent the most ambitious, large-scale, fine-arts printing venture of modern or any other time (Schiff, B., 1983, 'It took more than 200 years to get *this* work finished', *Smithsonian*, **13**(12), pp. 76–85).

Maps, atlases and charts

The major collection of topographical maps in Britain is the one in the British Library, originally in the Library of the British Museum. It is recorded in *Catalogue of printed maps, charts and plans . . . in 15 volumes* (1967) – complete to the end of 1964, with a supplement for the years 1965–74 published in 1978. The major collection of marine charts is housed in the National Maritime Museum, Greenwich and recorded in Sanderson, M. (Ed.) *Catalogue of the Library. Vol. 3. Atlases and Cartography* (1971). The major collection of geological maps is housed in the Geological Museum and is partly recorded in British Geological Survey (1985), *Catalogue of Printed Maps*, Natural Environment Research Council, London.

Details of the topographical and allied map collections in libraries, museums, universities, etc. throughout Britain are given in Watt, I. (1985), *A Directory of the UK Map Collections*, 2nd edition, Map Curators Group Publication No. 3 [The British Cartographic Society, London]. See also: Hodgkiss, A. G. and Tatham, A. F. (1986), *Keyguide to Information Sources in Cartography*, Mansell Publishing Ltd., London.

Type specimens

The importance of type, figured and cited material in biology and palaeontology and the need to compile and publish lists or catalogues of such material in museums and in private collections, is stressed in a number of publications. See, for example, Swinton, W. E. (1955), *Type Specimens in Botany and Zoology. Recommendations for their conservation in natural history museums*, International Council of Museums, Paris; Swinton, W. E. (1948), 'Notes for students' [Nomenclature and Type-specimens], *Museums Journal*, **48**(2), pp. 24–27, **48**(3), pp. 49–51, **48**(4), pp. 72 and 73; Bassett, M. G. (1975), 'Bibliography and index of catalogues of type, figured and cited fossils in museums in Great Britain and Ireland', *Palaeontology*, **18**, pp. 753–773; Bassett, M. G. (1979), 'Institutional responsibility for palaeontological collections' pp. 37–47 in Bassett, M. G. (Ed.), 'Curation of palaeontological collections', *Special Papers in Palaeontology*, No. 22 (Palaeontological Association, London); and Cleevely, R. J. (1983), 'Bibliography of published catalogues of type, figured and cited material', in Cleevely, R. J., *World Palaeontological Collections*, British Museum (Natural

History) and Mansell Publishing Ltd., London, pp. 26–37.

The place of published catalogues of permanent collections in the rapidly changing field of collections management is described in such publications as: Roberts, D. A. (1985), *Planning the Documentation of Museum Collections*, Museum Documentation Association, Duxford, Cambridge. A report on a project undertaken from September 1981 to March 1983 to investigate the state and future development of documentation procedures in museums in Britain.

Exhibition catalogues, handbooks and handlists

Fine and applied art
Exhibition catalogues occupy a distinctive place among the publications of art museums and galleries. They are of particular importance because they provide a record of what is almost always a unique event and commonly one of world-wide significance. Exhibition catalogues are virtually the only means for a visitor to retain some image of the exhibition and they have been considered as the most important single category of the printed matter produced by an art museum or gallery if only because they 'are part of our responsibility to lenders' (Gregg, R. (1959), 'Art museum publications – their nature and design', *Curator*, **11**(1), pp. 49–67). They are also important records of research and commonly provide attractive introductions to specific topics. They range in subject matter from the thematic to the chronological, and may cover the work of one artist, a group of artists, a period in history, or a specific theme.

Peter Cannon-Brookes, in 'The evolution of the art exhibition catalogue and its future' (*Museumleven*, **7/8**, 1980, pp. 139–144), states that, 'considering the huge expenditure incurred every year in publishing art exhibition catalogues it is remarkable how little attention has been given to the . . . catalogue *per se*'. He provides a brief historical summary of the production of the exhibition catalogue in Europe from the sixteenth century onwards, and a framework for an understanding of recent trends and problems. He draws attention to a 'watershed' in attitudes towards their function with the publication in London of the commemorative catalogues of the Burlington Fine Arts Club from around 1900. From this time onward the catalogue could 'either be an expanded check-list intended to be used in the exhibition itself, or commemorative in function with varying numbers of illustrations to act as an *aide memoir* after the exhibition has been dispersed, or for the benefit of those who had been unable to visit it'. The author argues – citing many examples from France, Germany, Italy, the UK and the USA – that this difference of intention has been lost sight of and, 'in the resulting confusion art exhibition catalogues which endeavour to combine the two functions have become increasingly common'. He also draws attention to the growth of specialist publishers for books and catalogues in art, cites print runs and sales figures for some British catalogues and briefly mentions the politics of art publishing. See also: Cannon-Brookes, P. (1981), 'The 1980 historical exhibitions', *Museums Journal*, **81**(1), pp. 45–48 and Vaizey, Marina (1985), 'Pictures as pegs for publications', *Sunday Times*, 23 June.

A critical French view of the nature of the contemporary exhibition catalogue is given by Elisabeth Foucart-Walter (1982), 'The catalogue; favoured instrument of the art historian', which is the preface to the catalogue of seventeenth century French paintings in the museum of Le Mans, 'Inventoires des collections publique françaises (vol. 26), Réunion des Musées Nationaux. (For an English translation, see Rosenberg, P. (1983), 'Considerations inspired by French provincial museums', *International Journal of Museum Management and Curatorship*, **2**, pp. 147–152.)

Examples of various kinds of temporary exhibition catalogues, including those issued to accompany the Council of Europe exhibitions from the early 1950s onwards, are given by Dennis Farr in the first edition of this Manual (1984, p. 190). Other examples of popular series are the well-known ones at the National Gallery – the two series 'Themes and painters in the National Gallery' of the late 1970s and the more recent 'Acquisition in focus', 'The artist's eye' and 'Art in the making' series. The last mentioned presents to the non-specialist the important new information about methods and materials revealed recently by the technical investigations at the Gallery.

Naomi B. Pascal considers the potential of joint publication for both collection and exhibition catalogues ('Publishing with museums', *Scholarly Publishing*, **10**(2), 1979, pp. 147–153) and the value of museum catalogues as source material for research work is pointed out by Dianne M. Nelson in 'Methods of citation analysis in the fine arts, (*Special Libraries*, **68**(11), 1977, p. 394). See also: Burton, A. (1977), 'Exhibition catalogues', in Pacey, P. (Ed.), *Art Library Manual: a Guide to Resources and Practice*, R. R. Bowker, New York and London, pp. 71–86; and Giles, T. (1985), 'Art exhibition catalogues', *British Book News*, December, pp. 711–714.

Art librarians in this country have long been concerned that many exhibition catalogues published by British museums and art galleries are not being submitted to the Copyright Receipt Office of the British Library in accordance with the terms of legal deposit as defined by the Copyright Acts. Such publications are not, therefore, listed in the *British National Bibliography* which is an essential tool for all librarians in selecting books for their shelves (see, for example, *Museum Bulletin,* **16**(9), 1976, p. 101). Because of this, the Art Libraries Society (ARLIS UK & Eire) has set up a research project to examine the feasibility of establishing a national network of art-exhibition catalogues. As the catalogues are usually outside the normal network of commercial publishing, they are rarely listed in the standard book trade or library bibliographies and are, therefore, commonly difficult for libraries to acquire. See Houghton, Beth (1984), 'Acquisition of exhibition catalogues', *Art Libraries Journal,* **9**(3,4), pp. 67–78; and Smith, Gaye (1989), 'A wasted resource', *Museums Journal,* **89**(9), p. 37.

Natural history and archaeology
The number of temporary exhibitions in the natural sciences and in archaeology is not as great as that in the fine and decorative arts and, because of the different nature of the exhibitions, the publications produced are usually handbooks devoted to the subject of the exhibition that can be sold in the museum, and elsewhere, rather than exhibition catalogues.

Roger Miles and his colleagues, for example (Miles, R. S., Alt, M. B., Gosling, D. C., Lewis, B. N. and Tout, A. F., 1988, *The Design of Educational Exhibits,* 2nd edition, British Museum (Natural History) and Allen & Unwin, London), stress the importance of such a publication as an integral part of an exhibition but, at the same time, point to the fact that in general less effort has been allocated to the publication than to the exhibition. In the section on 'Publications', they state: 'A handbook that puts an exhibition into take-away form can play a valuable part in the learning process. As a general rule, one should be published as part of each phase of work, to be available by opening day. Apart from this, museum publications should aim to supplement commercial literature rather than replace it, so that the best use can be made of limited writing and editing capacity. Each handbook should include a comment on, or brief critical review of, the commercial literature as a guide to further reading' (pp. 123 and 124).

They also maintain that: 'In general, the rules for exhibition text apply equally to books and printed sheets', and stress that the illustrations are frequently 'so much a part of the whole that they cannot be conceived and developed in isolation. The aim should be to integrate text with design' (p. 122).

Examples of the Exhibition Companion Series (British Museum, Natural History) which illustrate this integration (all translated into three or four languages and co-published with commercial publishers) are given in Chapter 65 (p. 636).

The relationship of the published volume to the other elements in what A. W. Melton called 'museum technology' (the body of practical know-ledge produced by the maximum exploitation of resources for the visitor) (Melton, A. W., 1935, *Problems of Installation in Museums of Art. Studies in museum education,* New Series No. 14, Reprinted 1988. Publications of the American Association of Museums, Washington, DC) is outlined both in written and diagrammatic terms in the book by Miles and his colleagues (p. 122 and Fig. 14.1).

Rather surprisingly, the two complementary volumes on exhibition design *On Display: A Design Grammar for Museum Exhibitions,* by Margaret Hall (Lund Humphries, London, 1987) and *Designing Exhibitions,* by Giles Velarde (The Design Council, London, 1988) make no mention of what Miles considers an integral part of an exhibition, and calls a 'major educational element' in the whole exercise.

Periodicals

Periodical literature is probably the main avenue of publication by museums. The term 'periodical' is used here as a blanket term to include publications which are issued regularly or irregularly as part of a numbered series, i.e. serials, journals, bulletins, transactions, etc.

Periodical publications fall fairly readily into five categories: the scholarly or research journals; the more general journals concerned largely with museological and museographical subjects; the interpretive, popular or semi-popular magazines or journals; the educational journals; and the reference journals.

SCHOLARLY OR RESEARCH PERIODICALS

A varied selection of British examples of this first category includes: the *Bulletin of the British Museum (Natural History), Studies in Conservation, The National Gallery Technical Bulletin,* the *Occasional Publications of the British Museum, Review of Scottish Culture,* and the recently launched *Journal of the History of Collections.*

Bulletin of the British Museum (Natural History). The Bulletin contains five separate series – for Botany, Entomology, Geology (which now incorporates Mineralogy), History and Zoology – all initiated between 1949 and 1953. Papers in the various series are primarily the result of research carried out on the unique collections of the Museum, both by the scientific staff of the institution and by specialists from elsewhere who make use of its resources. Parts are published at irregular intervals as they become ready, each part is complete in itself, available separately and separately priced. There is, in addition, a series of supplements.

Studies in Conservation (Études de Conservation) – the journal of the International Institute for Conservation of Museum Objects (IIC, renamed International

Institute for the Conservation of Historic and Artistic Works in 1959). The Journal was launched in 1952, with texts in French and English, two years after the formation of the Institution in London. It was designed to help fulfil the purpose of IIC, to provide a 'permanent organisation to co-ordinate and improve the knowledge, methods, and working standards needed to protect and preserve precious materials of all kinds'. Cumulative indexes: **1–12** (1952–1967), 1969; and **13–22** (1968–1977), 1978. For a short note on the background to ICC (1930–1950) and the editorial arrangements of the journal see: Anon (1982), *International Journal of Museum Management and Curatorship,* **1**(2), pp. 159–161.

The National Gallery Technical Bulletin. Issued annually by the Gallery since 1977, the Bulletin reports on recent research into the history, technique and conservation of works in the Gallery's collections. The contributors are the art historians, restorers and scientists of the Gallery's staff. The contents of the volumes are listed regularly in the annual *National Gallery . . . Book Catalogue.* The 1989 issue (Vol. 13), for example, includes articles on the Leonardo Cartoon, the investigation and treatment of a complete altarpiece by Carlo Crivelli, and a technical study of Caspar David Friedrich's *Winter Landscape.*

British Museum: Occasional Papers. From January 1979 the British Museum has issued a series of *Occasional Papers.* The papers are reproduced photolithographically in order to provide a rapid, simple and comparatively cheap method of making public current research on and connected with the collections. An average of eight publications are issued every year which range in content from the proceedings of symposia to preliminary excavation reports to monographs on topics of special interest.

Review of Scottish Culture (ROSC). Inaugurated in 1984, this annual series on the material aspects of economic and social history is published jointly by John Donald Publishers Ltd., Edinburgh, and the National Museum of Antiquities of Scotland (now part of the National Museums of Scotland). The abbreviated title is more than a handy acronym, for it is the Gaelic word which signifies both the act of seeing (vision, perception and understanding) and also what is seen (the written word in prose).

Journal of the History of Collections. The Journal, inaugurated in 1989, is a by-product of the successful symposium organized as part of the tercentenary celebrations of the Ashmolean Museum at Oxford in 1983 (see the section on *History*). It is designed to include papers on every aspect of the history of collections and is published by Oxford University Press, Oxford. In the words of the editorial in the inaugural issue (Impey, O. and Macgregor, A., **1**(1), 1989, p. 2): 'No rigid editorial agenda will be found here, beyond the insistence on quality and, of course, relevance. A broad spectrum of topics may be anticipated, although entire issues may, on occasion, be given over to the investigation of a particular theme. It would be absurd to study the history of collecting in isolation or to attempt to promote it as a subject in its own right, but in these pages we may expect to see unfolding a progressively more detailed and more coherent understanding than exists today of the philosophical principles that shaped the development of collections, the mechanisms of supply that fed them, and the programmes through which – by means of display or publication – their founders and curators communicated their special characteristics to the wider world'.

Smithsonian Institution Contributions. The nearest American equivalent of the British Museum (Natural History) Bulletin is the *Contributions* series issued by the University Press of the Smithsonian Institution, Washington. Joseph Henry's formal plan for the Smithsonian contained the following statement: 'It is proposed to publish a series of reports, giving an account of the new discoveries in science, and of the changes made from year to year in all branches of knowledge'. The theme of basic research has been adhered to through the years by thousands of titles issued in series publications under the Smithsonian imprint, commencing with *Smithsonian Contributions to Knowledge* in 1848 and continuing with the following active series: Smithsonian Contributions to Anthropology, Astrophysics, Botany, Earth Sciences, Marine Sciences, Paleobiology and Zoology; as well as *Smithsonian Folklife Studies,* and Smithsonian Studies in Air and Space and in History and Technology. In these series, the Institution publishes small papers and full-scale monographs that report on the research and collections of its various museums and bureaux or of professional colleagues in the world of science and scholarship. Equivalent publications are issued by the American Museum of Natural History, New York. For example, its *Memoirs* (1893–1930), *Bulletin* (1881–) and Anthropological *Papers* (1907–).

Nomenclatorial problems A nomenclatorial problem for biological and palaeontological journals arises from the internationally accepted practice of naming animals, plants and fossils according to priority. The name first applied to a species is the valid one and this means that journals publishing descriptions of new species are expected to follow the recommendations of the *International Code of Zoological Nomenclature* (3rd edition, International Trust for Zoological Nomenclature, London and University of California Press, Berkeley, 1985) and/or the *International Code of Botanical Nomenclature: Adopted by the 13th Internation-*

al Botanical Congress (Sydney, 1981; Bonn, Scheltema and Holkema, Utrecht; W. Junk, The Hague, 1983).

The implications of these recommendations for authors, editors, librarians and publishers are considered by D. Heppell and D. Smith ('What is a publication', in *Museum Publishing: Problems and Potential*, 1988, pp. 1–7). The relevant parts of the *International Code of Zoological Nomenclature* are quoted and the limits placed by the two codes on the definition of the word 'publication' for the purposes of zoological or botanical nomenclature are cited. The role of the *Zoological Record, being the records of zoological literature relating chiefly to the year* is outlined. See also: Bridson, G. D. R. (1968), 'The Zoological Record – a centenary appraisal', *Journal of the Society for the Bibliography of Natural History*, **5** (1968–1971), pp. 23 and 34; and the chapters by M. V. Hounsome in both editions of this Manual.

Other academic journals Some academic journals, which are not officially published by a museum, are, however, edited and their preparation and publication managed by members of museum staff. Some of these journals have, therefore, long been associated in people's minds with particular museums. A well-known example is *The Journal of the Society for the Bibliography of Natural History*, initiated in 1936 and renamed *Archives of Natural History* in 1981. The Society was formed under the Natural History Museum's auspices in 1936 and has received much support from the Museum ever since. The relations of the two bodies have been 'symbiotic'. The Society changed the word 'Bibliography' in its title to 'History' in 1983 to reflect a widening interest. There is a 'Contents List' (with indexes of authors, names and institutions) for Vols 1–8 (1936–1978), published in 1979.

Another example is *Folk Life: Journal of the Society for Folk Life Studies* (later *A Journal of Ethnological Studies*), initiated in 1963 and closely associated with the National Museum of Wales' Welsh Folk Museum. (Cumulative Index Vols 1–20, published 1982.) It was the successor to *Gwerin. A Half-yearly Journal of Folk Life* (Blackwell, Oxford, 1956–1962), also very closely associated with the Museum.

MUSEOLOGICAL OR MUSEOGRAPHICAL PERIODICALS

The main British example of the second category is *Museums Journal*, the journal of the Museums Association (the world's first national association of museums) and called *Musea* during its gestation period. Initiated in 1901 as a monthly publication, it changed in 1961 to a quarterly in order to print more substantial papers. At the same time a *Monthly Bulletin* was introduced for members, becoming the *Museums Bulletin* in 1975. In 1989 the Journal and Bulletin were combined to provide a new monthly

journal. The new version has a number of aims: 'Perhaps the most important is to inform the Museum community of the latest important 'news' about museums by actually going out to look for it. The *Museums Journal* aims to present a wide range of views and opinions and to encourage debate about the major policy issues facing museums today' (*Annual Report*, 1988–89 (1989), p. 6).

Regular short items in the new journal include: 'Access and disability', 'Education' and 'MGC (Museums & Galleries Commission) News'.

There is no comprehensive cumulative index but an index (subject and author) for papers presented to the Association between 1890 and 1909 is included in Volume 9 and for items issued from 1982–1988, in Volume 88, No. 4, pp. 203–214. Technical indexes were prepared for the periods 1930–55 and 1955–66 by the Midlands Federation of Museums and Art Galleries. A comprehensive centenary index is projected in the Association's *Corporate Plan 1988–92*. Volumes 1–75 are available on microfilm.

Two complementary journals, both issued by commercial publishers, are:

International Journal of Museum Management and Curatorship has been published quarterly since 1982 by Butterworth & Co. (Publishers) Ltd., London. The Journal, in the words of the editors, 'sets out to provide an international forum for the exchange of information between museum professionals, and it seeks to encourage a continuous re-assessment of the disciplines governing the establishment, care, presentation and understanding of museum collections'. The emphasis is mainly on the arts, including architecture. It is one of the very few journals of its kind to publish articles long enough to allow detailed study of a particular subject and to include a regular, and often forthright, editorial.

Other regular features include: 'Notes and comments' and 'Publications digest' (both from 1982); 'Conservation notes' (1986–); Legal notes (1988–); 'Computer notes' (1988–); and 'World of museums' (1989–). There is a cumulative index for volumes 1–4 (1982–1985).

Museum Development, published monthly since October 1989 by Museum Development Ltd., Milton Keynes. The journal aims to help museums face new challenges, in particular 'those of increasing competition, of enhanced visitor expectations, of pressures for greater economy, efficiency and effectiveness in management; and, of course, the challenge of a new financial climate in which a plurality of fundings is likely to become the norm of the future'. The approach is practical and regular items include, 'In focus', a detailed look at a single institution and 'The museum development interview'.

Two less substantial series issued by national bodies in Britain are:

Museum News. The Journal of National Heritage. The Museum Action Group, London, issued twice a year from 1972 until 1981 and three times a year thereafter.

AIM. The Quarterly Bulletin of the Association of Independent Museums, Chichester – issued from 1977 to 1985 when it became the *Bi-monthly Bulletin* . . . .

The major American museological and museographical journals are: *Museum News, Curator* and the more recent and short-lived *Museum Studies Journal.*

Museum News is the journal of the American Association of Museums, Washington. The Association's first serial publication, the *Proceedings*, was launched in 1907, becoming *Museum News Letter* in 1917 and *Museum Work* in 1918. The present journal, *Museum News*, was launched in 1924 and adopted its present bi-monthly frequency in 1975 with the accompanying upgrading of the newsletter *Aviso* (*A Monthly Dispatch from the American Association of Museums*).

The main concern of the Journal is with museums and museum work in the USA. There is an annual index to author and subject, an index to special articles for Volumes 1–30 (Supplement, 1953) and a 'Ten-year index, 1980–1989' (1990). Two issues (**53**(5), 1975, pp. 21–43 and **62**(2), 1983, pp. 21–61) are devoted almost entirely to museum publishing. The special 60th [1924–1984] anniversary issue (**62**(3), 1984, pp. 19–74) traces the history of museums and the museum profession as reflected in the pages of the Journal. Special features include: a reprint of the first issue and excerpts from 'classic' articles, with 'afterwords' by the authors.

Curator is the quarterly publication of the American Museum of Natural History, New York. The rationale for creating the Journal, which has an editorial board drawn from science, art and historical museums, is described by the first editor in the first number in the following words: 'Museum men and women have things to say and contributions to make to the common fund of museology in all its phases. These by-products of dedication to museum techniques deserve the dignity and the value of a publication which will make them available to colleagues now too scattered and too numerous for informal or easy communication'.

A regular feature introduced in 1979 ('Recent publications in natural history') became a separate publication in 1983 (see Section on Bibliographies). The journal is one of the most comprehensively indexed of its kind. The most recent cumulative index is for the first 30 years (1958–1987). It is divided into: author, title and subject categories, the subject index being further divided into 76 sections, including one on 'Libraries/Publications'. The introduction to the index, by T. D. Nicholson ('Thirty years of *Curator*', *Curator*, **30**(4), 1987, pp. 263–265), outlines the characteristics of the journal and provides a very brief summary of the major topics discussed during the previous five-year period.

Museum Studies Journal was published twice yearly by the Center for Museum Studies, John F. Kennedy University, San Francisco, CA, from 1983 to 1988. This Journal was launched 'in recognition of the pressing need for a publication devoted to museum studies literature' ('Editorial', **1**(1), 1983). The inaugural issue introduced the journal's three main divisions: 'Perspectives', 'History'; and 'Research and methodology'. It also included the first edition of a 'Museum studies library shelf list'. The serial ceased publication with Vol. 3, No. 2, Spring–Summer 1988. (See also the section on Bibliographies).

Museum, published quarterly by UNESCO was the first truly international and multilingual museological and museographical journal. It has appeared in its present format since 1948, when it succeeded *Mouseion: Organe de l'Office International des Musées* (Publication de l'Institut International de Cooperation Intellectuelle, Paris, **1–54**, 1927–1947). It is printed in French and English and early numbers had summaries in Spanish and Russian. Its predecessor was published in French only.

The aim of the journal was 'to become a medium for the exchange of professional opinion and of technical advice, and to serve as a stimulus to museums and museum workers in the development of their service to society in all the fields of knowledge and expression in which they operate' ('Editorial', *Museum*, **1**(1), 1948, pp. 2–4). The articles are arranged thematically and address issues of topical concern. Typically, the articles are divided into three groups: first, a presentation of the subject theme; second, perspectives by different authors in various of its (sometimes controversial) aspects; and third, possible paths or resolutions for the future. A favoured editorial approach is to present a collection of articles on museums of one nation or city. The 40th anniversary issue ('Museum at forty', 163, 1989) contains an excerpt from the editorial of the inaugural issue and an assessment of the changes in eight 'great pioneer museums' over four decades.

There are no indexes to the individual issues but a cumulative index for volumes 1–25 (1948–1973) was published in 1977. It is arranged by author, subject (bilingual), country and museum category, the last-mentioned being further divided into 37 categories. Comprehensive cumulative indexes for its predecessor *Mouseion* are given in volumes 51–54 (1945).

MuWoP: Museological Working Papers. The concern for a journal dealing largely with the theory and methodology of museums – as a companion to the more 'practical' *Museum* and, in a way, an offspring of the annual Czechoslovak journal *Muzeologické Sěsity* (*Museological Papers*, 1969–) – led in 1980 to the launch of *MuWoP* (*Museological Working Papers*)/ *DoTraM* (*Documents de Travail sur la Museologie*) as a publication project of the International Committee for Museology (ICOM). The Journal's policy was: 'to be an open forum for a permanent discussion on fundamental museological problems . . . at the theoretical and methodological levels'. The theme of the first issue was: 'Museology – science or just practical museum work?', and of the second (1982), 'Interdisciplinarity in museology'. These two issues, published by The Museum of National Antiquities, Stockholm, Sweden, on behalf of the ICOM Committee, are the only ones so far published.

OTHER MUSEOLOGICAL JOURNALS

Among the other long-running national and international journals issued by museum associations are, in chronological order:

Museumkinde, the journal of the German Museums Association, launched at Bonn in 1905 (– 1924, annual) with a second series from 1927 (– 1939, quarterly) and a third from 1960 (– 1972, three times a year). The reasons why the journal was launched 12 years before the establishment of the Assocaition, as well as its relation to *Zeitschrift für Museologie . . .* (1878–1885), probably the first museum studies journal, is given in Klausewitz, W. (1984), *66 Jahre Deutscher Museumsbund*, Deutscher Museumsbund, Bonn.

History News, the monthly magazine of the American Association for State and Local History (AASLH), Nashville, TN, was inaugurated in 1940.

ICOM News (*Nouvelles d'ICOM*), the bilingual (English and French) quarterly issued by the International Council of Museums (ICOM) since 1948 which includes a directory of the members of the various ICOM committees – the territorial or National Committees, which are considered 'the fundamental units of ICOM' and 'the principal instrument between ICOM and its members'; and the functional or pragmatic International Committees which are characterized in the statutes as 'the principal instruments for the work of ICOM and for the realization of its program of activities'.

Musées et Collections Publiques de France (formerly *Bulletin Trimestriel . . .* (1948–1955), the quarterly publication of L'Association Générale des Conservateurs des Collections Publiques de France, 1955–). The supplement, Bergeon, M. (Ed.) (1985), *Les*

Musées Aujourd'hui: Musées et Collections Publiques de France (No. 168), contains 17 articles which provide an overview of the developments in French museums in the mid-1980s.

A list of a further 27 journals, mostly by national museum associations and which the compilers consider should be on the shelves of museum libraries and museological institutions, is given in *Basic Museum Bibliography* (UNESCO-ICOM, Paris, 1986). See also the section on Bibliographies.

INTERPRETIVE, POPULAR OR SEMI-POPULAR PERIODICALS

This third, or interpretive, category of periodicals is not strictly of primary publications, but it is convenient to include this section with the journals of the first two categories. Interpretive serials are published, almost without exception, by individual museums and are considered as part of their 'out-reach' programmes. Three comparatively recent British examples are: *The V & A Album, The Ashmolean* and the *Imperial War Museum Review*.

The V & A Album is a series of essays, published initially every year in time for Christmas by Templegate Publishing Limited in association with the Friends of the Victoria and Albert Museum and was initiated in 1982. The Foreword of the first issue described the contributions as 'scholarship worn lightly' and expressed the hope that the series would become as well loved an institution as *The Book of Beauty* of the 1840s or the *Saturday Book* in the post-war era. Annual publication ceased in December 1987, three issues were produced in 1988 and one in Spring 1989: the serial was then discontinued.

The Ashmolean was launched on the threshold of the Museum's 300th anniversary in 1983. Each issue contains, as its core, three or four short articles on museum topics and also features on Oxford as well as on the Ashmolean.

Imperial War Museum Review, issued on an irregular basis since 1986. The aim, as stated in the foreword to the first issue, is 'to act as a showcase for the Museum, both in terms of the expertise of its staff . . . and the richness of its collections'.

Early British examples include the following 'house magazines':

Bankfield Museum Notes (County Borough of Halifax), issued in three series from 1912 to 1939.
The Journal of the Manx Museum, issued quarterly from 1924 to 1976.
British Museum Quarterly, issued from 1926 to 1973, and *British Museum Society Bulletin*, issued since 1969.
Natural History Magazine, issued quarterly by the British Museum (Natural History) from 1927 to 1936.

Preview (City of York Art Gallery), issued quarterly from 1948 to 1978.
Scottish Art Review, initiated in 1944, published by the Glasgow Art Gallery and Museums Association (i.e. the Friends) and now issued irregularly.
The Liverpool Libraries, Museums & Arts Committee Bulletin, issued three times a year from 1951 to 1968 (from vol. 7, 1958, the three annual issues became the 'Museums', the 'Walker Art Gallery' and the 'Libraries' number, respectively, and the title simplified to *Liverpool Bulletin*);
Leeds Art Calendar (Leeds City Art Gallery), initially a quarterly and more recently issued twice a year (1947–).
The Victoria and Albert Museum Bulletin, issued quarterly from 1965 to 1968.
Victoria and Albert Museum Yearbook (1969–72), Phaidon Press, London for the V & A;
Amgueddfa, Bulletin of the National Museum of Wales, issued three times a year from Spring 1969 to Autumn 1976 (Cumulative indexes in Nos. 6, 12 and 24), second series 1985–87, third series 1988–.

The general purpose of such periodicals is stated clearly in the introductions to the first issues of the *British Museum Quarterly*, the *Natural History Magazine*, and the *Victoria and Albert Museum Bulletin*, by the Directors of the respective institutions, and, in the *Liverpool Bulletin*, by the Lord Mayor of the City.

Examples of other recently inaugurated periodicals which are concerned largely with news of activities and of work on the collections, include:

Gallery, issued bi-monthly by the Aberdeen Art Gallery & Museum since 1979.

National Galleries of Scotland Bulletin, issued six times a year since 1981.

Focus, the quarterly newsletter of the National Museums & Galleries on Merseyside, issued in 1987 following the 'upgrading' of the Merseyside County Museums.

Museum Reporter, issued six times a year by the National Museums of Scotland since 1988 as successor to the twice yearly *Royal Scottish Museum News* (1986–1988).

American examples of the third or interpretive category are the much more elaborate and much more widely distributed magazines *Natural History* and *Smithsonian*.

Natural History, issued by the American Museum of Natural History, New York. The Journal is designed to provide a medium for papers and articles on natural history generally. Initiated at the turn of the century as *The American Museum Journal*, it is devoted to natural history, exploration and the development of public education through the museum. The title

was changed in 1919 to *Natural History*. *The Journal of the American Museum of Natural History*, with the words 'For the people, for education, for science' boldly printed on the outside back cover. Even by the mid-1970s this journal was a $3 million operation which yielded an annual profit to the Museum of $185,000. The circulation at that time was around 300,000 and the print run is now just over 500,000 (400,00 of which are distributed to the Museum's Associates).

Most of the articles in the 80th anniversary issue (**89**(4)) were selected from the magazine's first half century, with brief notes and photographs of their authors. See also: Ternes, A., 'Some thoughts on reaching eighty' (Editorial), *The Journal of the American Museum of Natural History*, **89**(4) (1980), pp. 7–15.

Smithsonian is issued by the Associates of the Smithsonian Institution, Washington. Launched in 1970, this monthly magazine was conceived in order to 'record notable events at the Institution, as well as to present the kind of subjects the Smithsonian is interested in the world over: science, history and the arts – fine and folk'. The magazine was soon described as the 'second fastest-growing magazine in America': on its fifth birthday in April 1974 the circulation was more than 750,000 and on its tenth anniversary in 1979 it had a readership of over 1.6 million families. During 1981 the magazine printed 2172 pages, of which 1047 were of advertisements. In the same year the Institution published *The Best of Smithsonian*, an anthology of articles from the first decade of the magazine. See Faul, R. H. (1975), 'Nothing succeeds like success', *Museum News*, **53**(5), pp. 32–35.

EDUCATIONAL JOURNALS

The three journals devoted almost entirely to museum education and education in museums, namely *Journal of Education in Museums* (Group for Education in Museums (GEM), 1980–), *The Journal of Museum Education: Roundtable Reports* (Museum Education Roundtable (MER), Washington, 1973–) and *ICOM Education* (1969–) are described in Chapter 64. A number of subject journals concerned specifically with educational matters are also noted.

REFERENCE JOURNALS

A number of reference journals (for example, *Recent Publications in Natural History*, American Museum of Natural History, 1983–) are described in the sections on 'Bibliographies', 'Abstracts' and 'Indexes'.

SURVEYS AND INVENTORIES OF JOURNALS

An annotated inventory of 125 professional journals in the English language used by the museum and related professions is tabulated by A. D. Griesemer on the basis of a survey ('Publication channels for museum professionals: a professional concern', *Museum Studies Journal,* **1**(3), 1983, pp. 60–64, 71–76). Four characteristics of the journals are tabulated: first, the target audiences; second, the disciplines covered; third, the nature of the reviewing procedure – whether internal or external reviewing; and fourth, whether the journals accept unsolicited articles from museum professionals.

The Keyguide to Information Sources in Museum Studies (1989) includes an inventory of 86 journals – largely in the museological category – each entry including bibliographical details and a brief description. It is the only published inventory that includes details of the newsletters and journals of the various specialist groups in Britain – listing 16 publications issued by 13 groups.

The Keyguide (p. 54) categorizes journals into those published by: national and international museum organizations; regional museum associations; specialist groups including those reflecting a particular kind of museum work, and a particular subject area; individual museums and other academic institutions; different kinds of museum administration or user groups; and by commercial publishers.

A series of descriptions of important professional museum journals and periodicals was initiated in *Museum Studies Journal* in 1983 but, unfortunately, it was discontinued after only five journals had been described. These were: *Muse* (the journal of the Canadian Museums Association and formerly called *Gazette*, 1962–83), the *International Journal of Museum Management and Curatorship, Museum, Museum Quarterly* (published by the Ontario Museums Association and formerly *Ontario Museum Quarterly,* 1971–1983), and *Museums Journal* – in **1**(2), 1983, 65; **1**(2), 1983, 65, 66; **1**(3), 1984, 52, 53; **1**(3), 1984, 53; and **1**(4), 1984, 55, respectively.

Details of most current British periodicals are given in Woodworth, D. P. and Goodair, C. M., *Current British Journals 1989,* 5th edition, The British Library Document Supply Centre, Wetherby in association with the UK Serials Group. These include: current title (and previous title, if any); year of first issue; number of issues per year; price; brief subject statement; average number of pages per issue; presence of advertisements, reviews and indexes (if any); print run; additional formats (e.g. microfiche); and sources in which contents are indexed or abstracted.

Books and specialist monographs

The range of books and monographs produced by museums in this country and overseas is considerable. Most are issued as individual volumes, but there are also some well-known series. For example: 'The Ship Series' (of 10 short books) and the

'Modern Maritime Classics' of the National Maritime Museum, Greenwich; the earlier 'Themes and Painters' and the contemporary 'Schools of Painting' series of the National Gallery; the British Museum's 'Introductory Series', containing 'highly illustrated introductions to civilizations and subjects within the Museum's collections; the 'Arts & Living Series' of the Victoria and Albert Museum of the early 1980s – 'a unique series of books about the whys and wherefores of the great variety of beautiful things made for daily use from the earliest times to the present day'; the 'Economic Series' and the 'Instructions to Collectors' series of the British Museum (Natural History); and the distinctive and popular series of illustrated booklets published by the Science Museum during the 1960s and 1970s (each containing 20 colour plates of items in the collections and sold at 35 pence each!).

In this chapter, attention is concentrated on two developments which are not considered fully elsewhere in this Manual and which have become progressively more popular over the last two decades. These are the publication of works on the history of individual museums and on biographical studies of museum personnel, of donors and of collectors.

HISTORIES OF INDIVIDUAL MUSEUMS AND MUSEUM ASSOCIATIONS IN BRITAIN

The tercentenary of the Ashmolean Museum, Oxford, in 1983, was made the occasion for a week-long international symposium on the subject of sixteenth- and seventeenth-century cabinets of curiosities. The proceedings of the seminar were later published under the title *The Origins of Museums: the Cabinet of Curiosities in Sixteenth and Seventeenth Century Europe* (Impey, O. and MacGregor, A. (Eds.), Clarendon Press, Oxford, 1985) – 33 papers emended, as appropriate, in the light of discussion sessions which followed the formal presentations; and with a useful composite bibliography (pp. 281–328).

The sustained interest generated by the volume (now in its third impression) encouraged the publishers and the editors to launch a new journal – *Journal of the History of Collections* (see Periodicals) – and the tercentenary itself resulted in the publication of a number of books of historical interest on the museums in Oxford. They include: MacGregor, A. (Ed.) (1983), *Tradescant's Rarities. Essays on the Foundation of the Ashmolean Museum 1683 with a Catalogue of the Surviving Early Collections* (Essays by the Editor, Martin Welch and April London; and catalogue, pp. 107–374), Delegates of the Clarendon Press/Visitors of the Ashmolean, Oxford; MacGregor, A. (1983), *Ark to Ashmolean. The Story of the Tradescants, Ashmole and the Ashmolean Museum,* The Ashmolean Museum/Tradescant Trust, Oxford,

Ashmole, E. and Wharton, T. (1656), *Musaeum Tradescantianum, or a Collection of Rarities Preserved at South-Lambeth near London* (Grismond, London) – a facsimile, Ashmolean Museum, 1983; Harden, D. B. (1983), *Sir Arthur Evans 1851–1941. 'A Memoir'*, Ashmolean Museum Publications: Archaeology, History and Classical Studies, Oxford; Simcock, A. V. (1984), *The Ashmolean Museum and Oxford Science 1683–1983*, Museum of the History of Science, Oxford; Simcock, A. V. (Ed.) (1985), *Robert T. Gunther and the Old Ashmolean*, Museum of the History of Science, Oxford; Ovenell, R. F. (1986), *The Ashmolean Museum 1683–1894*, Clarendon Press, Oxford, (from the foundation to the move to the new building).

Other provincial museums   These volumes on Oxford reflect a growing general interest in the history of museums in Britain by both the museums themselves and by commercial publishers. Other local and provincial museums and museum bodies which have issued histories of their institutions in recent years include, in chronological order:

Walton, K.-M. (1980), *75 years of Bristol Art Gallery. The Gift of Sir William Henry Wills, Bart, to his fellow citizens, 1905. A short history.*

Lloyd, D. (1983), *The history of Ludlow Museum, 1833–1983* (Shropshire Museum Service) – a brief history of one of the oldest 'small town' museums in the country.

King, E. (1985), *The People's Palace and Glasgow Green*, Richard Drew for the Museum, Glasgow – the official history and guide. 'There is no museum, art gallery or community centre like it anywhere else in the world' (p. 82).

Durbin, G. (1984), *The Past Displayed: a Picture History of the Norwich Museums* (Norfolk Museums Service) – a series of some 120 photographs with descriptive captions.

Davies, S. (1985), *By the Gains of Industry. Birmingham Museums and Art Gallery 1885–1985* – 'not a definitive history', but 'a brief history illustrated mainly by some of the more attractive items in the collections' of, arguably, 'Britain's leading provincial museum'.

Pyrah, B. J. (1988), *The History of the Yorkshire Museum and its Geological Collections*, Wm. Sessions, York for the North Yorkshire County Council – tracing the story from the formation of the Yorkshire Philosophical Society (1822) and its Museum to the 'modern museum' (1970–1988).

Brears, P. (1989), *Of Curiosities & Rare Things. The Story of Leeds City Museums*, (with six contributions by members of the Museum staff, pp. 42–77), The Friends of Leeds City Museums – which should be read in conjunction with the author's 'Temples of the muses. The Yorkshire Philosophical Museums 1820–50', *Museums Journal, 84*(1) (1984), pp. 3–19 and Orange, A. D. (1973), *Philosophers and Provincials. The Yorkshire Philosophical Society from 1822 to 1844*, Yorkshire Philosophical Society, York.

Brears, P. and Davies, S. (1985), *Treasures for the People*, published as part of the Museums Association's Centenary celebrations by the Yorkshire and Humberside Museums Council, Leeds. Unlike the earlier volumes listed above, this work is one of the first regional histories of museums.

The provisional bibliography of histories of provincial museums (arranged alphabetically by town) in Durbin, Gail (Ed.) (1984), *Provincial Museums: a Bibliography of Some Museum Histories Compiled by Members of a Seminar on the History of Provincial Museums that met in Birmingham on 19 March 1984* (cyclostyled), contains a number of references – to booklets, pamphlets, articles in magazines and in newspapers, and the occasional thesis. Museums in 36 towns and cities are represented and there are particularly helpful lists to those in Bristol, Chester, Liverpool, Kingston-upon-Hull, Sheffield and Stoke-on-Trent as well as for the Ironbridge Gorge Museum, Telford, Shropshire.

National museums   A selection of recent histories of the national museums in Britain published by the institutions themselves and arranged in chronological order, include:

Gould, C. (1974), *Failure and Success: 150 Years of the National Gallery, 1824–1974*. A picture book, which traces success and failure in the quest for new pictures for the Gallery; and which should be read in conjunction with the series of nine articles on the history of the institution by G. Martin in the magazine *Connoisseur* for 1974 ('The founding of the National Gallery').

Follett, D. (1978), *The Rise of the Science Museum under Henry Lyons* – the key chapter of which is that which presents a general account of the main events from 1920 to 1933, describing the year-by-year development of the Museum (during Col. Lyon's directorship). It should be read in conjunction with the earlier Morrison Scott, T. C. S. (Ed.) (1957) *The Science Museum: the First Hundred Years* (HMSO, London). See also: *Science Museum Review 1987* for a striking diagram of the 'Main events in the development of the Science Museum' (p. 15).

Nesbitt, N. (1979), *A Museum in Belfast: a History of the Ulster Museum and its Predecessor* – which traces the story from the foundation of the Belfast Natural

History Society (1821) and its museum (1831) through the formation of the Belfast Municipal Museum (1890) to that of the Ulster Museum (1962) and thereafter.

Anon. (1980), *The History of the Victoria & Albert Museum*, HMSO (Small Picture Book No. 31) – first issued to commemorate the centenary of the V & A in 1952. It is now complemented and partly superceded by the Museum's *Inspiration for Design. The Influence of the Victoria & Albert Museum* (Morris, B., 1986), which has sections on the Museum's predecessors – 'The Museum of Oriental Art' (pp. 18–30) and the 'South Kensington Museum' (pp. 31–43) as well as a section on 'Publications and Photography' (pp. 43–48); and Somers Cocks, A. (1980), *The Victoria & Albert Museum. The Making of a Collection* (Windward, Leicester). There is an illustrated chronology of 'major events, acquisitions and exhibitions' for the period 1974–1987, compiled by J. Voak in the Gold Edition of the *V & A Album* (1987, edited by Hugh Casson) and a brief history of the National Art Library (which is a Department of the V & A) is given by Esteve-Coll, E. (1986), 'Image and reality: the National Art Library' (*Art Libraries Journal*, **11**(2), pp. 33–39).

Caygill, M. C. (1981), *The Story of the British Museum*, reprinted 1985 – based in large measure on more detailed earlier studies, such as Edward Miller's *That Noble Cabinet. A History of the British Museum* (Andre Deutsch, London, 1973). See also: Wilson, D. M. (1989), *The British Museum: Purpose and Politics*, which provides helpful historical information in an analysis of the Museum in the late 1980s and which clearly distinguishes the collecting policies of the major London museums.

Stearn, W. T. (1981), *The Natural History Museum at South Kensington. A History of the British Museum (Natural History) (1753–1980)* which provides a detailed account of the natural history collections and their physical separation in 1882 from the archaeological, historical and art collections of the British Museum to form the British Museum (Natural History) at South Kensington. Stearn's work is a natural complement to Edward Miller's and the dates given in the second half of the title of Stearn's volume reflect the overlap in the two volumes and in the histories of the two institutions. The fifth part of Stearn's book (written by the Secretary (A. P. Coleman) and the Keeper of Palaeontology (H. W. Ball) at the Museum) deals with 'An era of change and independence, 1950–1980' (pp. 333–385). It contains five chapters dealing, respectively, with: 'Prelude to change', 'Administering the Museum', 'In the interests of science', 'The public face of the Museum', and 'Space, the eternal problem'.

Bell, A. S. (Ed.), (1981), *The Scottish Antiquarian Tradition. Essays to Mark the Bicentenary of the Society of Antiquaries of Scotland and its Museum 1780–1980*, published for the Society by John Donald, Edinburgh. Two of the longest essays in the volume, by R. B. K. Stevenson (pp. 31–85 and 142–211) contain the history of the oldest national museum in Britain outside London, the National Museum of Antiquities of Scotland (now part of the National Museums of Scotland).

Calder, J. (n.d., [1984]), *Royal Scottish Museum: the Early Years*, Department of Education and Public Relations, Royal Scottish Museum, Edinburgh (cyclostyled) – which provides a brief survey of the development of the Museum from the 1860s (then known as the 'Museum of Science and Art') and the incorporation of the Natural History Museum at the University of Edinburgh with the national collection, to the end of the century. See also: Anderson, R. G. W. (1989), 'Museums in the making: the origins and development of the national collections', in Calder, J. (Ed.), *The Wealth of a Nation in the National Museums of Scotland*, the National Museums/Richard Drew Publishing, Glasgow, pp. 1–18 – a volume issued to accompany a major exhibiton on 'The wealth of a Nation' (1989).

De Courcy, Catherine (1985), *The Foundation of The National Gallery of Ireland*, concerned specifically with the years 1853–1864.

Smailes, Helen (1985), *A Portrait Gallery for Scotland: the Foundation, Architecture and Mural Decoration of the Scottish National Portrait Gallery, 1882–1906*, and Gow, I. and Clifford, T. (1989), *The National Gallery of Scotland. An Architectural and Decorative History* – both published by the National Galleries of Scotland, Edinburgh and together presenting a number of aspects of their history. See also: Thompson, C. (1972) [with contributions by Brigstocke, H. and Thompson, D.], *Pictures for Scotland: the National Gallery of Scotland and its Collections: a Study of the Changing Attitude to Painting since the 1820s*.

Harrison, S. (Ed.), (1986), *100 Years of Heritage. The Work of the Manx Museum and National Trust* – with chapters on the Museum, the Trust, the National Art Gallery, the Manx Museum Library, on the three outstations (Cregneash Village Folk Museum (1938–); the Nautical Museum, Castleton (1951–); the Grove Museum (1978–), and on 'Voice of the people: the work of the Folk-life Society'.

Other national organizations Recent studies of two of the most important national museum bodies in Britain are:

Lewis, G. D. (1989), *For Instruction and Recreation. A Centenary History of the Museums Association*, Quiller

Press for the Assocation, London – which traces the story from the decade of gestation (1880s) and the first conference held at York in June 1889 (at the invitation of the Yorkshire Philosophical Society) to the Association's Centenary Year 1989.

Esmé, Countess of Carlisle (1988), *A History of the Commission.* Museums & Galleries Commission, London, from its foundation in 1931, as the Standing Commission on Museums and Galleries (formed following a recommendation made by the Royal Commision on National Museums and Galleries (1928–30)) to 1981, when the name was changed and new functions added, and to 1985 when further major executive functions were acquired and more scheduled.

International organisations   There is no history of the International Council of Museums (ICOM), but the annotated chronology in 'Thirty-four years of co-operation between UNESCO and ICOM' (*Museum*, **32**(3), 1980, pp. 154–162) cites many of the important events in its development.

Other references   The historical context for all these studies is provided in the first three chapters in this Manual by G. D. Lewis, and summarized by the same author in the section on 'Museums' in Goetz, P. W. (Ed.), (1987), *The New Encyclopaedia Britannica*, 15th edition, vol. 24, pp. 478–490, Encyclopaedia Britannica Inc., Chicago. A number of references to other general studies of the history of museums are given in the bibliographies cited later in this chapter and particularly in: *Basic Museum Bibliography* (1986), *Museum Studies Shelf List* (1986) and *History-option Learning Goals and Bibliography for Museum Studies Students* (updated annually).

Details of five 'colonial' museums, in Argentina (Buenos Aires and La Plata), Australasia (Christchurch and Melbourne) and Canada (Montreal) during the 'unprecedented explosion in the creation and expansion of natural history museums all over the world' and the impact on them of metropolitan museums in Britain, continental Europe and North America, are given by Sheets-Pyenson, S. (1988), *Cathedrals of Science. The Development of Colonial Natural History Museums during the Late Nineteenth-century* (McGill–Queen's University Press, Kingston and Montreal) and summarised in 'How to "grow" a natural history museum: the building of colonial collections, 1850–1900', *Archives of Natural History*, **15**(2), 1988, pp. 121–147. The former has a comprehensive 'Note on sources', subdivided into: general surveys and histories of natural history museums; metropolitan museums; natural history dealers and collectors; colonial museums; museums in Canada, New Zealand, Australia and South America.

References to histories of particular disciplines are given in: the 'History' series of the *Bulletin of the British Museum (Natural History)*, the bibliography and index *Geology in Museums* (Sharpe, T., National Museum of Wales, 1983), and in the 25 'Papers presented at the International Conference on the history of museums and collections [of specimens and books] in natural history (London 1979)', *Journal of the Society for the Bibliography of Natural History*, **9**(4) (1980), pp. 365–670.

The influence of social change on the many natural history and archaeological societies, and their museums, formed during the nineteenth-century in mainland Britain is described in Allen, D. E. (1976), *The Naturalist in Britain: a Social History*, Allen Lane, London. (Paperback edition, 1978) – the first work of its kind.

A number of references to the history of American museums is provided by E. P. Alexander in 'The American museum chooses education', *Curator*, **31**(1) (1988), pp. 61–80), a historical review concerned mainly with the eighteenth- and nineteenth-centuries, and in 'Early American museums. From collections of curiosities to popular education' (*International Journal of Museum Management and Curatorship*, **6**, 1987, pp. 337–351).

Taxonomic archaeology   The work involved in correctly naming the species of a plant, animal or fossil is commonly described as history. It is, as David Allen has described, 'That remarkably varied delving into the past that has developed as an outgrowth of taxonomy and museum work, the identification of collections, the reconstruction of the routes of pioneer explorers, the pinpointing of type localities, the more precise annotation of specimens, the inside story of how particular institutions have come by what they have. At one extreme this work grades into biographical studies, at the other, particularly in the matter of establishing the printed dates of publications for nomenclatorial purposes, it becomes inseparable from bibliography' ('Naturalists in Britain: some tasks for the historian' (The Ramsbottom Lecture for 1976), *Journal of the Society for the Bibliography of Natural History*, **8**(2) (1977), pp. 91–107). Allen maintains that the work is more correctly classified as antiquarianism and that it deserves to be considered as a quite distinct scholarly discipline. He suggests the name 'taxonomic archaeology'.

BIOGRAPHIES AND BIOGRAPHY

The interest and importance of biographical studies for museum work has been stressed by many people. Among them is Sir William Flower, sometime Director of the British Museum (Natural History), who, in his presidential address to the British Association for the Advancement of Science (1889), stated that: 'What a museum really depends upon for its success and usefulness is not its building, not its cases, not even its specimens, but its curator. He and his staff are the soul of the institution'. See also Flower, W. H. (1898), *Essays on Museums and Other Subjects*, Macmillan, London. (Reprint, Books for Libraries Press, Freeport, NY, 1972).

Prominent among recent biographical studies is *Museum Masters: their Museums and their Influence* (American Association for State and Local History, Nashville, Tennessee, 1983) by E. P. Alexander, recognized in his own right as a 'museum master' of the twentieth-century ('Honoring a museum master. Edward P. Alexander receives Distinguished Service Award', *Museum News*, **62**(1) (1983), pp. 46–48). In it he selects 12 persons whom he considers to have been innovative and who transformed the early concepts of the museum.

The titles of the chapters, which are based on a museum studies course given by the author at the University of Delaware, are:

Sir Hans Sloane [1660–1753] and the British Museum: From collection of curiosities to national treasure (pp. 19–42);

Charles Willson Peale [1741–1827] and his Philadelphia Museum: the concept of a popular museum (pp. 43–78);

Dominique Vivant Denon [1747–1825] and the Louvre of Napoleon: The art museum as symbol of national glory (pp. 79–112);

William Jackson Hooker [1785–1865] and the Royal Botanic Gardens of Kew: The Botanical Garden (pp. 113–140);

Henry Cole [1808–1882] and the South Kensington (Victoria & Albert) Museum: The Museum of Decorative Art (pp. 141–176);

Ann Pamela Cunningham [1816–1875] and [George] Washington's Mount Vernon [Virginia]: The Historic House Museum (pp. 177–204);

Wilhelm Bode [1845–1921] and Berlin's Museum Island: The Museum of World Art (pp. 205–238);

Artur Hazelius [1833–1901] and Skansen [Stockholm]: The Open Air Museum (pp. 239–276);

George Brown Goode [1851–1896] and the Smithsonian Museum [Washington]: A national museum of cultural history (pp. 277–310);

Carl Hagenbeck [1844–1913] and his Stellingen Tierpark [Wild Animal Park, Hamburg]: The moated zoo (pp. 311–340);

Oskar von Miller [1855–1934] and the Deutsches Museum [Munich]: The Museum of Science and Technology (pp. 341–376);

John Cotton Dana [1856–1929] and the Newark Museum [New Jersey]: The Museum of Community Service (pp. 377–412).

The chapters, each of which contains a select bibliography and a portrait, reflect the author's interpretation of the word 'museum', a concept which he examines in the introduction to the book (pp. 3 and 4), and the importance he attaches to a biographical/historical study of this kind.

A complementary volume to Alexander's is Sheets-Pyenson, S. (1988), *Cathedrals of Science. The Development of Colonial Natural History Museums during the Late Nineteenth-Century*, McGill-Queen's University Press, Kingston and Montreal. It contains sketches of the work of five 'museum-builders', namely: Hermann Burmeister (1807–1892), at the Museo Publico, Buenos Aires, Argentina; Francisco Moreno (1852–1919), at the Museo General de La Plata, Argentina; Frederick McCoy (1817–1899), at the National Museum of Victoria, Melbourne, Australia; John William Dawson (1820–1899), at The Peter Redpath Museum, Montreal, Canada; Julius Haast (1822–1887), at the Canterbury Museum, Christchurch, New Zealand. It also contains information on a number of major dealers and collectors: Edward Gerrard, taxidermist of London; August Krantz, geological merchant of Bonn; the Verreaux brothers, taxidermists of Paris; and Henry Ward, 'merchant naturalist' of Rochester, New York State.

The work of 12 major and many minor collectors of natural history material, including Joachim Barrande (1799–1883), Hugh Cuming (1791–1865), Charles Darwin (1809–1882) and Alfred Wallace (1823–1913), is considered in the papers read at the International Conference on the history of museums and collections in natural history in London in 1979 (*Journal of the Society for the Bibliography of Natural History*, **9**(4) (1980, pp. 365–670).

A selection of biographical series issued by individual museums or museum associations includes:

(1) the many volumes on famous scientists in the Science Museum's illustrated booklets of the 1970s and early 1980s;
(2) the 'Recollections' series of the National Maritime Museum;
(3) the 'Personal reminiscences' series of the Imperial War Museum;
(4) the 'Collections and collectors [and museums] of note' series, initiated in 1974 and currently (1990) at No. 55, in *The Geological Curator*;
(5) the 'Uncurated [i.e. neglected] curators' series initiated in *The Geological Curator* in 1986;
(6) the series 'Pioneers in American Museums' in *Museum News* during the 1970s; and
(7) the series of publications on individual artists published by most of the main art galleries.

Wherever possible, from the late 1950s onwards, the compilers of the catalogue raisonné of the modern British collections at the Tate Gallery, approached the artist or his close relatives and friends, dealers, art historians and collectors in order to obtain first-hand information not only about his works, but also in order to collect biographical data not always readily available elsewhere. In this way unique primary sources were tapped and the results edited and published. See Robertson, J. (1989) 'The exhibition catalogue as source of artists' primary documentation', *Art Libraries Journal,* **14**(2), pp. 32–39.

The kind of biographical information gathered is also outlined by P. S. Doughty in Chapter 51 (pp. 517 and 518).

Monographs

Representative selections of the kind of scholarly monographs that are produced by major museums throughout the world are given in the respective annual reports, publications catalogues and histories of individual museums. For example: Oehser, P. H. (1970), *The Smithsonian Institution* (Praeger Publishers, New York), a selection of approximately 100 works selected for their monographic character and which have attained some reputation and importance, and as typical examples of the Smithsonian's programmes; *Filling the Gaps in Knowledge,* Parts 1, 2 and 3, The American Museum of Natural History, 84th, 85th and 86th Annual Reports, New York, 1954; Anon. (1982), *Catalogue of Early Works, Monographs, Catalogues of the Collections and Reports on Scientific Expeditions still in Limited Supplies,* British Museum (Natural History), London; *The British Museum. Report of the Trustees 1966,* British Museum, London, 1967 – which contains an inventory of the publications issued by the Trustees between 1939 and 1966; and *Catalogue of Publications,* National Maritime Museums, Greenwich, 1988 – which lists the items in the 'Maritime Monographs and Reports' series.

Theses and dissertations

Recent inventories of theses on museum studies and related subjects include:

Dockstader, F. J. (1979), 'Graduate studies relating to museums: a tentative bibliography 1919–1978', *Museum News,* **58**(1), 77, 78, 80, 81, 83, 88.

Anon. (1983), 'Museum studies thesis index', *Museum Studies Journal,* **1**(2), 66–70.

Lewis, G. D. (1983), 'List of dissertations and theses prepared for higher degrees in the Department of Museum Studies, University of Leicester', Appendix A in 'The training of museum personnel in the United Kingdom', *Museums Journal,* **83**(1), 65–70.

Anon. (1987), *Bibliography: Theses, Dissertations, Research Reports in Conservation. A Preliminary Report,* ICOM Committee for Conservation Working Group Training in Restoration and Conservation, National Centre of Museums, Budapest – the first attempt to collect, on a world-wide basis, the results of research carried out by students of major conservation institutes. There is no index.

A valuable characteristic of theses is that the authors are generally required to make a detailed survey of the literature and include a comprehensive bibliography in the thesis. The main problems associated with the use of thesis literature are those of discovery and availability.

Since 1970 the British Library Document Supply Centre has had a policy of collecting as many British theses as possible, by borrowing and microfilming them. After some initial reluctance, most universities and the Council for National Academic Awards now participate in the Centre's monthly publication *British Reports, Translations and Theses.*

Another British organization which actively promotes the use of theses as sources of information is the Association for Information Management (formerly Association of Special Libraries and Information Bureaux, Aslib). It gives details of new British theses in its *Index to Theses accepted for Higher Degrees by the Universities of Great Britain and Ireland and the Council for National Academic Awards,* first published in 1950. Since 1986 (Vol. 35) abstracts have been included and publication has been quarterly.

Conference proceedings

In spite of the importance attributed to museum publications, only two conferences have been organized to consider the many problems associated with them. They are:

Charlton, R. I. H. (Ed.), (1982), *Museum Publications in Science, Technology and Medicine. Papers from a Joint Meeting held at the National Railway Museum, York, 27 April 1981,* Group for Scientific, Technological and Medical Collections and Group for Museum Publishing and Shop Management. Science Museum/ Ashmolean Museum, London/Oxford.

Calder, J. (Ed.), (1988), *Museum Publishing: Problems and Potential. Papers given at a Seminar held by the National Museums of Scotland at the Royal Museum of Scotland, Chambers Street, Edinburgh, 15–16 October 1987,* National Museums of Scotland, Edinburgh.

The Edinburgh seminar was organized to provide an opportunity for those involved in museum publishing, as authors, editors, designers, printers and marketeers, to get together to discuss this particular aspect of communication. The aim was to highlight some of the problems, particularly for those museums whose ventures into publishing had inevitably been tentative, and to offer some solutions. The publication contains 12 papers. See also: Calder, J. (1988), 'Museum publications: problems and potential', *Scottish Museum News*, Spring, p. 12.

For details of other conference proceedings, probably the best guide is *Index of Conference Proceedings Received*, published monthly by the British Library Document Supply Centre (Boston Spa) with annual, 5-year and 10-year cumulations. There is also a 1964–1986 cumulation on microfiche. The Index is particularly useful in that it gives not only bibliographical details, but also provides locations for the items in question. Conference proceedings which are published in book form can be traced through such general bibliographic tools as the *British National Bibliography* (weekly, with cumulations, British Library National Bibliographic Service).

Secondary publications

Many secondary publications are reference books which are designed to be consulted repeatedly rather than read through. The commonest types are directories, bibliographies, abstracts, indexes, etc. Examples of each variety are outlined separately.

Directories

The term 'directory' is usually given to a published list of names and addresses of organizations or of individuals linked together by some common feature or features. In the various commercial guides to literature such compilations are commonly divided into three categories: directories of commercial organizations, or trade directories; directories of non-commercial organizations, or institutional directories; and directories of individuals, or personal directories. In a museum context it is also possible to recognize two further categories – those of collections and of key sites. The five categories are not necessarily mutually exclusive.

Examples of the first category, published by museums or museum organizations, include:

Scourfield, E. (n.d.[1979]), *A Directory of Agricultural Machinery and Implement Makers in Wales*, National Museum of Wales (Welsh Folk Museum), Cardiff. The inventory, the result of research undertaken during the preparation of a catalogue of the collection of agricultural material at the Welsh Folk Museum, deals mainly with nineteenth-century makers – agricultural foundries, leading country blacksmiths, etc.

Group for Museum Publishing and Shop Management (1986), *The Trade Directory*, Group for Museum Publishing and Shop Management, Ashmolean Museum, Oxford – divided into five sections: publishing services (editorial design, specialist printers, type-setters, etc.), shop design, design, giftware and special services.

Examples of the second or institutional category include the various regional, national and international directories of museums. Examples of the first include the series 'Exploring museums', commissioned jointly by the Museums Association and the Museums & Galleries Commission to mark Museums Year 1989.

A list of officially published national museum directories, for 42 countries, is provided in the ICOM Document Centre's regular column in *ICOM News* (**41**(2), 1988, pp. 20–24) and an equivalent inventory, with brief annotations, in the *Keyguide to Information Sources in Museum Studies* (1989).

Two well-known examples of international directories are: Hudson, K. and Nichols, A. (1985), *The Directory of Museums and Living Displays*, 3rd edition, Macmillan Publishers, Basingstoke and Stockton Press, New York; and Saur, K. G. (1981), *Museums of the World*, 3rd edition, K. G. Saur, München, London, New York and Paris (Handbook of International Documentation and Information 16). The compilers of the former, state: 'We have decided for the first time to include what we are calling, for want of a better term, Living Displays – the world's zoos, aquaria, botanical gardens and living-history farms. This has been done for two main reasons, because the International Council of Museums accepts such places as falling within its definition of a museum, and equally because we could see no logical justification for keeping them out'.

The merits and demerits of the two volumes are considered in *ICOM News*, **40**(3,4) (1987), p. 35.

Another example of the second category is: Meenan, A. (compiler) (1983), *A Directory of Natural History and Related Societies in Britain and Ireland*, British Museum (Natural History), London. The compilation of the directory, as described in the Introduction, is largely the result of work in the Acquisitions Section of the Museum's Department of Library Services, where one of the major objectives is to obtain as comprehensive a collection as possible of British natural history publications. The Museum's libraries do not benefit from deposit of British publications under the Copyrights Act and in order to keep track of the publications emanating from an ever-growing number of clubs, societies and associations, considerable research is often required.

A volume which is both an institutional and a personal directory is the Museums Yearbook of the Museums Association. Initiated in 1955 as the *Museums Calendar*, and published annually, the early volumes contain a directory of the museums and galleries of the British Isles (giving details of their principal staff) and an inventory of the Association's membership. In 1976 the publication was renamed *Museums Yearbook* and extended to include an index of the administering authorities of the museums and galleries in Britain. The Centenary Yearbook (*Museums Yearbook 1989/90*) contains a list of the Annual Conferences and the names of the Presidents of the Association from 1890 to 1989.

Examples of the third category include:

Gilbert, P. (compiler) (1977), *A Compendium of the Biographical Literature on Deceased Entomologists*, British Museum (Natural History).

Herriot, S. (Ed.), (1968), *British Taxidermists: a Historical Directory*, Leicester Museums and Art Gallery.

An annotated, classified inventory of 87 biographical dictionaries of 'historically prominent' and 'contemporary' artists, etc., and of 18 indices to biographical information is provided on pp. 141–150 of *Art Research Methods and Resources* (1984). It includes the 37-volume *Allgemeines Lexikon der bildenden Künstler von der Antike bis zur Gegenwart*, compiled by Ulrich Thieme and Felix Becker (E. A. Seemann, Leipzig, 1907–50; reprinted edition F. Allmann, Leipzig, 1964; new edition currently in progress).

An example of a directory to collections of a particular kind on a national scale is provided in: Doughty, P. S. (1981), *The State and Status of Geology in United Kingdom Museums. Report of a survey conducted on behalf of the Geological Curators' Group*, Geological Society of London Miscellaneous Paper No. 13, which includes an 'Alphabetical list of named collections' (Appendix 2, pp. 67–99), giving the name of the holding institution and a key to the 'Geographical location of named collections' (Appendix 3, pp. 101–118).

A volume which acts as a multiple directory is *World Palaeontological Collections* (1983) compiled by Cleevely, R. J. (British Museum (Natural History) in association with Mansell Publishing Ltd., London). The entries, arranged alphabetically by collector (pp. 38–232), contain references to obituaries and biographical memoirs and details of the nature and whereabouts of the collections. The index (pp. 325–364) is arranged according to institutions and gives their collection holdings.

Other inventories of collections are those issued by the various natural history collections research units. The first comprehensive survey of the natural history collections of a region took place in north-west England and the results are available as a readily accessible data base in the Manchester Computer Cataloguing Unit. It was published first as a computer list and, in 1979, as the *Register of Natural Science Collections in North West England*, compiled and edited by E. G. Hancock and C. W. Pettitt and issued by Manchester Museum. The value of this work was apparent and further collections research units were formed to cover the whole of Britain. The Federation for Natural Sciences Collection Research (FENSCORE) was constituted in 1981 to co-ordinate and facilitate the work of these units in association with the Manchester Museum Cataloguing Unit.

Recent examples of the publications produced by these regional units include:

Stace, H. E., Pettitt, C. W. and Waterston, C. D. (1987), *Natural Science Collections in Scotland (Botany, Geology, Zoology)*, Heppell, D. and Davidson, K. H. (Eds) National Museums of Scotland, Edinburgh. Like the earlier publication by Cleevely, this is another multiple directory – to collections and relevant material associated with them, in Scottish museums; to collectors, donors and readers; and to the institutions. The Directory of collectors . . . and the Indexes (Subject and Literature references) are produced on microfiche.

Hartley, M. M., Norris, A., Pettitt, C. W., Riley, T. H. and Stier, M. A. (Eds) (1987), *Register of Natural Science Collections in Yorkshire and Humberside*, prepared by the Yorkshire and Humberside Collections Research Unit (YHCRU) with financial help from the Area Museum and Art Gallery Service for Yorkshire and Humberside, Leeds.

The majority of published national directories of natural sites of special conservation, scientific and educational value, are published by the Nature Conservancy Council. The main examples are:

Ratcliffe, D. A. (Ed.), (1977), *A Nature Conservation Review: the Selection of Biological Sites of National Importance to Nature Conservation in Britain*, 2 volumes, Cambridge University Press/Nature Conservancy Council/Natural Environment Research Council, Cambridge/London.

The work contains a description of the whole range of biological conservation interest in Britain and is written with a wide and mixed audience in mind. It includes, in the first volume, a detailed analysis of the criteria for site assessment and selection. These include size, diversity, naturalness, rarity, fragility, typicalness, recorded histories, position in an ecological/geographical unit, potential value and intrinsic appeal. The descriptive directory of each of the chosen sites (in the second volume) provides what one reviewer described as a sort of 'Domesday Book of Britain's natural [biological] heritage'.

Campbell, S. and Bowen, D. Q. (1989), *Geological Conservation Review. Quaternary of Wales*, Nature

Conservancy Council, Peterborough – the first volume in the series 'Geological Conservation Review' which publishes the work carried out since 1977 on assessing and documenting the key earth science sites in Britain. It complements the survey of key biological sites described in *A Nature Conservation Review*.

Local directories of sites of special geological importance are in preparation by the Record Centres of the National Scheme for Geological Site Documentation. The background to the scheme, with details of the 41 Record Centres (almost all museums) and a comprehensive bibliography, is provided in Brunton, C. H. C., Besterman, T. P. and Cooper, J. A. (Eds) (1985), *Guidelines for the Curation of Geological Materials*, compiled by the Geological Curators' Group and published as Geological Society Miscellaneous Paper No. 17, London. See also: Cooper, J. A., Phillips, P. W., Sedman, K. W. and Stanley, M. F. (1980), *National Scheme for Geological Site Documentation, Geological Record Centre Handbook*, Museum Documentation Association/ Geological Curators' Group, Duxford, Cambridge.

The equivalent biological schemes are considered in the 15 papers read to a conference at the Leicestershire Museums, Art Galleries and Record Service in 1984 (Garland, S. P. (Ed.), (1985), 'Biological recording and the use of site based biological information', Supplement to the *Biology Curators Group Newsletter*, **4**(2), pp. 1–71). See, in particular, Lambley, P. W., 'Museums as Biological Recording Centres' (pp. 6–10); and also see the section 'The value of museums as records centres', *Museums Association: Conference Proceedings* (1976), pp. 19–24.

Bibliographies, abstracts and indexes

The proliferation of catalogues, periodicals, books, monographs, conference proceedings and theses makes the preparation of bibliographies, abstracts and indexes progressively more important.

Bibliographies
The two main periodic sources of current museological and museographical literature are the following:

International Museological Bibliography/Bibliographie Muséologique Internationale. The ICOM International Committee for Documentation decided, in 1967, to publish an annual bibliography as a supplement to the journal *ICOM News (Nouvelles d'ICOM)*. The first volumes (1967–1980) were produced annually by the Central Office of Museology (Museologický Kabinet) at Prague; and subsequent volumes from the computerised data base at the UNESCO-ICOM Museum Documentation Centre in Paris.

The Bibliography is in two parts: the main entry section, which lists references according to the UNESCO-ICOM Museum Documentation Centre's Classification scheme (given in the first issue) and which provides full bibliographic citations, including keywords and identifiers; and the indexes (subject, corporate subject, personal author, corporate author, and periodicals and serials). The two most recent issues have a helpful key to the detailed bibliographic citation. The publications listed are of world coverage in all languages. For the most part they are periodical articles, but monographs and reports are also included. References in the fields of conservation and restoration are 'rather limited' because of 'the existence of the excellent publication '"Art and Archaeology Technical Abstracts"'. (See section on Abstracts.)

Publication during the 1980s has, unfortunately, been irregular: for example, volumes 15–17 (for 1981–1983) were issued in 1986; volume 18 (for 1984) in 1987; and volume 19 (for 1985) in 1988. The composite volume 15–17 contains 5000 references, most of which are to articles from periodicals (some 300 titles).

Selected Bibliography of Museological Literature (initially, to 1975, *Bibliographical Selection of Museological Literature Per-year*). In the late 1950s, the Museological Cabinet of the Slovak National Museum in Bratislava decided to publish an annual annotated bibliography as a companion to the unannotated bibliographies contained in *ICOM News* and in order to draw particular attention to material published in the countries of Central and Eastern Europe. From 1960 onwards, therefore, an annual bibliography has been published in Slovak and Czech and from 1968(–1990) an English language version was published as well. Unlike the UNESCO-ICOM annual the bibliographic citations are not as elaborate, but the abstracts in English are particularly helpful. The Bibliography contains references to books, articles and occasional reviews. Initially the compilers scanned 89 journals: by 1989 it had increased to 128. The entries are grouped in 27 categories and include a section on 'Museological literature and bibliography'. The index is skeletal.

Three other, more selective, retrospective sources of museological and museographical literature are:

Basic Museum Bibliography: Bibliographie Muséologique de Base. Prepared by the UNESCO-ICOM Documentation Centre, Paris, 1986 (earlier versions in 1969, 1980 and 1984), as No. 14 in the 'Studies and Documents on the Cultural Heritage' series. The volume, based on the holdings of the Centre, includes references to books, manuals and proceedings as well as articles in periodicals, all of which it is considered, '*should be on the shelves of all libraries in museums and in museological institutions*' (compiler's italics). The 405 entries are grouped into 25 categories arranged within the major themes 'General resources', 'Protection of the cultural and natural heritage', 'Philosophy and history of museums', 'The museum institution', 'Collections', 'Communication and interpretation' and 'Museum categories'. There is no index.

Museum Studies Library Shelf List, 2nd edition, 1986. Compiled by Barbara Thompson and Jennifer Feeley for the Center for Museum Studies, John F. Kennedy University, San Francisco, CA. The compilation is a bibliography in the strict sense of the word because it includes references to books only. It is an enlarged and updated version of the one issued in the inaugural issue of the Center's *Museum Studies Journal* (1983) and includes two subsequent 'supplements'. The 890 entries deal directly with the history, philosophy and function of museums. They range from 1918 to 1985 with the preponderance issued in the late 1970s and 1980s. The entries are arranged in 27 categories grouped under the major themes 'general resources', 'history and philosophy of museums' and 'museum function'. There is no index.

These two compilations are complementary in the sense that 30 per cent of the entries in the UNESCO-ICOM bibliography are in languages other than English and a further 15 per cent with bilingual texts, whereas virtually all the entries in the Center for Museum Studies *Library Shelf List* are in English. The latter does provide a useful check-list of the publications of some of the major American Institutions. For example, the American Association for State and Local History (71 entries), the American Association of Museums (34 entries) and the Smithsonian Institution (37 entries). The former does the same for the publications of UNESCO (40 entries) and ICOM (32 entries).

The *Bibliography for Museum Studies Training*, a classified list of publications of all kinds on museum studies, is issued by the Department of Museum Studies, University of Leicester, compiled by the departmental staff and updated annually. The main sections are: 'The museum context: a world view'; 'Collection management'; 'Museum management'; and 'Museum services'.

The bibliography is complemented by a series of four booklets which list the learning goals and bibliographies for some of the special subject options studied as part of the courses leading to the Graduate certificate and Master's degrees at Leicester. The booklets are for archaeology, history, museum education and natural history, respectively[1].

More than 40 bibliographies on the work of museums (including one on 'Museum publications') have been published by the UNESCO-ICOM Documentation Centre (see *ICOM News*, **36**(2,3) (1983), 9) and are available on request. The Centre will also supply, at short notice, lists of bibliographical references of publications issued since 1981 (see *ICOM News*, **37**(1,2) (1984), 4).

Three bibliographies which list the publications of individual museums are:

Roulstone, M. (Ed.), (1980), *The Bibliography of Museum and Art Gallery Publications and Audio-visual Aids in Great Britain and Ireland 1979/80* (Chadwyck-Healey Ltd., Cambridge). This, the second edition of the work, lists the publications of 955 institutions. The numbered institutions (which range in size from major museums to small, sometimes private or regimental, museums and commercial art galleries) are listed alphabetically and the details of publications and audio-visual aids are given under such headings as: 'Books', 'Guides', 'Catalogues', 'Newsletters/bulletins', 'Annual reports', 'Slides', 'Postcards', 'Films/filmstrips', etc. The volume has author, geographical and subject indexes.

Brown, D. K., Jennings, G., MacFarlane, S. D. and Triarsmith, J. L. (Eds) (1982), *World Museum Publications 1982. A Directory of Art and Cultural Museums, their Publications and Audio-visual Materials* (R. R. Bowker Co., New York), including references to 21,000 publications in print at 10,000 museums; with author and title indexes. The relationship of this volume to the two massive volumes: *Art Books 1950–1979: Including an International Directory of Museum Permanent Collections Catalogs* (1980) and *Art Books 1876–1949: Including an International Index of Current Serial Publications* (1981), both published by R. R. Bowker, New York, is described in the Foreword by W. B. Walker of the Metropolitan Museum of Art.

Clapp, J. (1962), *Museum Publications [A Classified List and Index of Books, Pamphlets and Other Monographs and of Serial Reprints]: Part I. Anthropology, Archaeology and Art; Part II. Publications in Biological and Earth Sciences* (Scarecrow Press, New York). A classified bibliography of the publications available from 276 museums in the USA and Canada (with 4416 entries in Part I and 9231 in Part II).

Three other important bibliographic sources, of specific subject areas and published by museums or museum associations, are:

Rath, F. L. and O'Connell, M. R. (Eds) (1975–1984), *A Bibliography on Historical Organization*, American Association for State and Local History, Nashville,

History, Nashville, TN. The series contains six volumes: Vol. 1, *Historic Preservation* (1975); Vol. 2, *Care and Conservation of Collections* (1977); Vol. 3, *Interpretation* (1978); Vol. 4, *Documentation of Collections* (1979); Vol. 5, *Administration* (1980); and Vol. 6, *Research* (1984). The entries in each are annotated, the national, foreign and international organizations involved are described concisely, an annotated list is provided of all the journals mentioned and detailed indexes are provided. Each volume contains a 'Basic reference shelf' section.

Recent Publications in Natural History is a quarterly bibliography, issued by the Department of Library Services at the American Museum of Natural History, New York, since March 1983, and is a sequel to a regular feature in the Museum's journal *Curator*. The listings are arranged alphabetically by subject, with cross-references to those entries which deal with multiple subjects. The subjects include 'Anthropology and Archaeology' as well as those usually under 'Natural History'. There is also a section on 'museology', which is commonly the shortest in the publication. Full bibliographic citation is provided along with short annotations for those titles that do not accurately describe the contents. In addition, the serial includes some full-length reviews of books of particular interest.

Annual Bibliography of the History of Natural History is a periodical issued by the British Museum (Natural History), London, and was the first comprehensive bibliographical periodical of articles, books and monographs relating to the history of natural history. The entries are gathered from the 8000 periodicals currently held in the libraries of the Museum as well as from holdings of several other large London libraries: and the volumes are comprehensively indexed. Volume 1 (including the publications issued in 1982) was published in 1985.

Earlier bibliographic references are given in the following three works:

Borhegyi, S. F. and Dodson, E. A. (Compilers) (1960), *A Bibliography of Museums and Museum Work 1900–1960, Publications in Museology No. 1*, Milwaukee Public Museum, Milwaukee, WI; and a supplementary volume for 1960–1961, Borhegyi, S. F., Dodson, E. A., Janson, I. A. (1961), *Publications in Museology No. 2*. The coverage is largely of North American museums.

Board of Education (1938), *Illustrated Catalogue of Publications of the National Collections. Prepared Especially for the Use of Educational Institutions. Part I. Arts Subjects* (HMSO, London). A selection of the publications of 13 national museums, including the Public Record Office, in London. As the catalogue was compiled 'chiefly for the purpose of making

known the wealth of material provided by the national museums and galleries that can be used by teachers and educational institutions in the provinces where visits to the collections are impossible', many of the entries are annotated. There is an index of 'collections, main subjects and centres of life and art illustrated'.

Murray, D. (1904), *Museums: Their History and Their Use, with a Bibliography and List of Museums in the United Kingdom* (3 vols, MacLehose, Glasgow). Volumes 2 and 3 are devoted exclusively to bibliography. The entries, which include material from North America, Britain and Continental Europe, are divided into: (I) 'Literature of museums' ('Bibliography of bibliographies'; and 'Current literature') (Vol. 2, 3–14); (II) 'Museography', (Vol. 2, 15–54); (III) 'The collection, preparation and preservation; the registration and exhibition of specimens' (Vol. 2, 55–68); (IV) 'Catalogues and other works relating to particular museums' (Vol. 2, 69–363; Vol. 3, 1–289); and (V) 'Travels and general works' (Vol. 3, 290–313); 'Additions and corrections' (Vol. 3, 314–341).

The entries, which are commonly annotated, are arranged under the towns or places where they are situated and, in the case of private collections, under the name of the collector or of his residence when it is well known. The term 'museum' in the title is 'taken in its ordinary English acceptation' (Vol. 1, *ix*) and galleries of painting and sculpture are excluded. The compiler remarks that: 'The difficulty there is in getting information regarding museum catalogues will scarcely be credited'.

The Art of Bibliography The importance of bibliographic study for museums, and in particular as part of their research role, is illustrated in a number of papers in Wheeler, A. and Price, J. H. (Eds) (1981), *History in the Service of Systematics. Papers from the Conference to Celebrate the Centenary of the British Museum (Natural History), 13–16 April 1981* (Special Publication No. 1, Society for the Bibliography of Natural History, London). In his contribution to this symposium ('Bibliography in the British Museum (Natural History)', pp. 1–6) W. T. Stearn, for example, draws attention to the definition of bibliography as the 'description or knowledge of books in regard to their authors, subject, editions and history'. And he compares bibliography to some species complexes. The same author in an earlier 'keynote' address ('The use of bibliography in natural history', in Buckman, T. R. (Ed.), *Bibliography and Natural History*, pp. 1–26, University of Kansas Libraries, Lawrence, KA, 1966) presents a broad but detailed view of the uses made of bibliography in natural history ranging from a consideration of the sixteenth-century naturalists (including 'the father of bibliography', Conrad Gessner) down to modern facsimile publishing of classical floras.

Fruitful sources of analytical bibliographies and biobibliographies are the *Journal* and *Special Publications* of the Society for the Bibliography [now History] of Natural History. For example: Bridson, G. D. R. and Harvey, A. P. (1971), 'A checklist of natural history bibliographies and bibliographical scholarship, 1966–1970', **5** (1968–1971), 428–467, in which almost 1000 items are subdivided into 'Bibliographical methods and organization', 'Subject bibliographies', 'Guides to periodicals', 'Libraries and documentation centres' and 'Physical and historical bibliography'; and Sawyer, F. C. (1955), 'Books of reference in zoology, chiefly bibliographical', **3** (1953–1960), 72–91.

Practising bibliographers will enjoy the eight-page Introduction to the second edition of the *Bibliography of British Railway History* (1983). The work is compiled by G. Ottley with the co-operation of W. J. Skillern, C. R. Clinker, J. E. C. Palmer and C. E. Lee, fellows of the Railway and Canal Historical Society. It is published jointly by the Science Museum and the National Railway Museum.

Guidelines for the preparation of working bibliographies (and chronologies) in art, including a check-list of the 10 most pertinent types of art reference sources for such work, are given in *Art Research Methods and Resources* (1984, pp. 41–74).

Bibliographical citations   A check-list of the elements in the reference to a book or other separately issued publication, given in *BS 1629 Bibliographical References* (British Standards Institution, Milton Keynes, 1976) includes the following:

Name(s) of author(s) or compiler(s),
personal or corporate, if given
Title of the publication
Translation of the title
Title of the original (if the publication is itself a translation)
Edition number, or other specification of the edition, if not the first
Name(s), of editor(s), translator(s), illustrator(s), etc.
Place(s) of publication
Publisher(s)
Year(s) of publication
Number of volumes, if more than one
Pagination
Mention of any illustrations, etc., bibliography, summary, index,
Size
Title of series and number in the series
International Standard Book Number
Price

The title of a volume is that printed on the title page of the book and should normally be given in full. References consisting of essential elements only (those in italics above) are called 'minimum references'; those containing supplementary elements, 'expanded references'. Most of the entries in museum bibliographies and lists of references are minimum references: examples of expanded references are given in the UNESCO-ICOM bibliographies.

The treatment of plates in bibliographical citations receives little attention in the standard works on bibliography. It is, however, given in detail in Bridson, G. D. R. (1976). The treatment of plates in bibliographical description [with particular reference to natural history], *Journal of the Society for the Bibliography of Natural History,* **7**(4), pp. 469–488.

Abstracts
With the exception of the *Selected Bibliography of Museological Literature* (Central Administration of Museums and Art Galleries, Bratislava, Czechoslovakia), which, in spite of its title, contains abstracts for all entries, the only other regular abstracting service concentrating on museum and related topics and published by a museum body is *Museum Abstracts. A Monthly Information Service.* Inaugurated in 1985 by the Scottish Museums Council, the publication became part of the new Heritage: Care Preservation – Management Publishing Programme in 1989 and is now published jointly by the Scottish Museums Council and Routledge.

All the journals and newsletters (over 180 in number), press releases, information sheets and national newspapers received at the Scottish Museums Council's Information Centre in Edinburgh are scanned and relevant entries incorporated under such headings as: 'Arts'; 'Collecting and collection management'; 'Conservation'; 'Education'; 'Exhibit design and display'; 'Heritage management, conservation and interpretation'; 'Museum development'; etc.

Museum Abstracts is important because the periodicals scanned include the newsletters and journals of all but one of the Area Museum Councils in Britain (including the Scottish Museum Council's own *Scottish Museum News*, inaugurated in 1982 and successor to *Omnigatherum* 1978–1981) and of the many specialist groups affiliated to the Museums Association and other academic bodies. The British Library's *Current British Journals*, in comparison, lists the publications of one Area Museum Council and of two of the specialist groups only. Unfortunately, books are not included in *Museum Abstracts* and there is no index other than one to the periodicals scanned.

Two other abstracting services in regular use by museum personnel are:

Art and Archaeology Technical Abstracts, published by the Institute of Fine Arts, New York for the International Institute for Conservation and issued twice yearly. The publication was launched as *IIC Abstracts* (Abstracts of the Technical Literature on Archaeology and the Fine Arts), Volumes 1–5, 1955–1965, IIC, London. Indexes to the first 10 volumes are provided as Supplements to **11**(1) (Summer 1974), Subject index, and **12**(2) (Winter 1975), Author and abbreviated title index.

Other Supplements include:
Alexander, S. M. (1969), 'Towards a history of art materials – a survey of published technical literature in the arts. Part I. From antiquity to 1595', **7**(3), 123–161; Part II. 'From 1600 to 1750', **7**(4), 201–206.

Winter, J. (Ed.), (1977), 'ICOM Reports on Technical Studies and Conservation' (295 entries), **14**(2), 372–471.
Alexander, S. M. (Ed.), (1979), 'Information on historical techniques: Textiles. Part 1. Classical authors', **15**(2), 344–380; Part 2. 'The Medieval Period', **16**(1), 197–225.
Asher, C. G. (1979), 'Multilingual specialized dictionaries of use to conservators' (239 entries), **16**(2), 325–360.

A predecessor of the IIC serial is: Gettens, R. J. and Usilton, B. M. (1955), *Abstracts of Technical Studies in Art and Archaeology, 1843–1952*, Freer Gallery of Art, Washington, DC, and Occasional Papers, **2**(2), with a subject index in Usilton, B. M. (1964), *The Subject Index to Technical Studies in the Field of the Fine Arts*, Vols 1–10 (1932–1942), Pittsburgh, Pennsylvania.

RILA: International Repertory of the Literature of Art. Répertoire International de la littérature de l'Art, issued twice a year since 1975, with cumulative indexes for volumes 1–5 (1975–1979) and for volumes 6–10 (1980–1984). A comprehensive abstracting service covering all periods from medieval art to the twentieth century, it is the work of teams of librarians and art historians throughout the world, co-ordinated through several European regional offices and the central editorial offices in Williamstown, MA, USA. RILA is sponsored by the College of Art Association of America, the Union Académique International and the International Committee for the History of Art. See: Anon, 'RILA', *International Journal of Museum Management and Curatorship*, **3**(1984), 81, 82.

Fuller details of the abstracting indexing services in Art, the Humanities and Social Sciences – with a sample of the cumulative indexes of such journals as the *Burlington Magazine*, etc., are given on pp. 161–171 of *Art Research Methods and Resources* (1984).

Indexes
The advantages of incorporating an index in bibliographies and catalogues are regularly emphasized by professional bibliographers and information scientists. The advantages of a comprehensively indexed bibliography are clearly illustrated in *Geology in Museums: a Bibliography and Index* (T. Sharpe, National Museum of Wales, Cardiff, 1983). The material was collected partly by members of the Geological Curators' Group (in response to a request from the compilers of the first edition of this Manual (1984)) and partly by Tom Sharpe during his Museum Diploma study course.

The work is in two parts: a list of 1094 titles arranged alphabetically by author, with bibliographic citations and keywords; and a subject index (of 2930 items arranged under 266 headings) based on the keywords (see Sharpe, T. (1982), 'Geology in museums – a computerized bibliography', *MDA Information*, **6**(3), 50, 51). The index allows access to the list under individual institutions and societies, disciplines and subdisciplines, materials, functions, policies, etc. The primary data is filed on a computer at the Museum Documentation Association (where the sorting and generation of indexes took place) and the file of references is being kept up to date in order to issue supplements or revisions.

The large number of avenues of access to this bibliography underlines the fact that the total absence of indexes in the retrospective bibliographies of similar size, mentioned earlier in this section, and the absence of cumulative indexes in most of the long-running journals, is to be regretted.

Among the long-standing indexing journals of particular relevance to museum personnel are:

British Humanities Index, a quarterly subject index to about 360 publications published by the Library Association, London since 1962, when it superceded *The Subject Index to Periodicals* (1915–1961, excluding 1923–1925).

Art Index, a quarterly author–subject index published by the H. W. Wilson Co., New York, since 1929. It now covers about 200 journals.

Computerized information services

Many indexing and abstracting services are now produced by computer, and the data bases for these are being made available so that literature searches can be done using a computer terminal for online access. These developments began in the fields of science and medicine and have extended to other subject areas (see, for example, the more recent volumes in the Bowker-Saur series *Guides to Information Sources* (Foskett, D. J. and Hill, M. W.) (Eds.)), and it is now possible to perform on-line searches on various aspects of museum studies. Details are given on pp. 43 and 44 of *Keyguide to Information Sources in Museum Studies* (1989). See also: Nicholas, D., Harris, K. and Erbach, G. (1987), *Online Searching: Its Impact on Information Users* (Mansell Publishing Ltd., London), and *Art Research Methods and Resources* (1984, pp. 63–73, 161–171) for information on specialized bibliographic on-line data bases and how to use them.

On-line information services have been in widespread use in academic libraries in Britain for the last 15 years and have become available in virtually every academic library in the last 10 years. A survey of the use of these services at a time when they were no longer a novelty, was carried out by Winship, I. (1986), 'The use of online information services in the UK higher education libraries', *British Journal of Academic Librarianship*, **1**(3), 191–206.

Manuals or handbooks

The most regularly cited manuals – volumes written primarily for practitioners – for general museum work are, in chronological order:

Lewis, R. H. (1976), *Manual for Museums*, National Park Service, US Department of the Interior, Washington, DC – an outgrowth of the Burns, N. J. (1941), *Field Manual for Museums*. Although intended primarily for the staff of the museums administered by the US National Park Service, the volume has much wider application.

UNESCO (1978), *The Organisation of Museums: Practical Advice. L'Organisation des Musées. Conseils Pratiques* (Museums and Monuments Series No. 9), 4th edition, UNESCO, Paris.

Burcaw, G. E. (1983), *Introduction to Museum Work*, 2nd edition, American Association for State and Local History, Nashville, TN. An introductory text for students of museum studies and for the museum worker with no prior training; with emphasis on the USA.

Thompson, J. M. A., Bassett, D. A., Davies, D. G., Duggan, A. J., Lewis, G. D. and Prince, D. R. (Eds) (1984), *Manual of Curatorship: A Guide to Museum Practice*, Butterworths/Museums Association, London. It contains 62 chapters, by a variety of authors, which are arranged in four sections: 'The museum context'; 'Collection management'; 'Visitor services'; and 'Management and administration'. It replaces the Association's *Handbook for Museums* (general editor, D. B. Harden) 1956–1967, planned to contain 41 subject booklets grouped into seven themes: 'Administration'; 'Museum techniques'; 'Archaeology, ethnography and folk life'; 'Art'; 'Natural and applied sciences'; 'Temporary activi-

ties'; and 'Museum school services'. It also largely supercedes the Association's series of Information Sheets.

Anon. (1986), *Faire un Musée: Comment Conduire une Operation Muséographique?*, Ministere de la Culture, Direction des Musées de France, Paris – a summary of the principles for creating or renovating a museum and of the techniques for implementation. Emphasis is on effective conservation measures and the requirements of museum visitors.

The most recent manual is the singular Weis, H. (Compiler), *La Museologie Selon Georges Henri Rivière. Cours de muséologie/Texts et Témoignages* (Dunod, Paris, 1988). The work is based on Rivière's course in general museology at the University of Paris. It also contains a selection of comments by colleagues concerning museum programmes with which he was involved and a postscript, by A. Desrallées, which sets Rivière's work in the context of present-day museology.

Two smaller and less ambitious manuals are:

Paine, C. (1984), *Notes for Amateur Curators*, Area Museums Service for South Eastern England, Milton Keynes. Although intended for a British public and more specifically for museums in south-east England, the work contains basic practical advice for small museums in general.

Ambrose, T. (1987), *New Museums – A Start-up Guide*, Scottish Museums Council, Edinburgh. It is arranged in four sections – 'First steps'; 'Managing the museum'; 'Managing the collections'; and 'The museum and its users' – and is a view of the challenges faced in starting up and running a successful independent museum with answers to some of the questions commonly asked by those involved. It lists the Scottish Museums Council's 22 *Fact sheets* and the AIM *Guidelines*. It is illustrated with cartoons.

The series of *Guidelines* on topics of particular relevance to museums issued by the Association of Independent Museums (AIM), provides a composite manual designed particularly for independent museums. It includes, for example, guidelines on: 'Charitable Trust status' (No. 3, 1981); 'Fund raising' (No. 4, 1982, revised 1988); 'Museum public relations' (No. 5, 1983); 'Education' (No. 6, 1984); 'Insurance' (No. 7, 1984, revised 1988); 'Designers and the small museum' (No. 8, 1984); 'Employment practice and law for the smaller museum' (No. 9, 1985); 'Setting up and running a new museum' (No. 12, 1988); 'Museum collecting policies and loan agreements' (No. 14, 1980, revised 1988); and 'The principles of marketing' (No. 16, 1988).

A short primer on administrative manuals is provided in 'Manuals for museum policy and procedures' (Yang, M., *Curator,* **32**(4) (1989), pp. 269–274). It considers organizational function, operational procedures, and personnel policy, and provides a short bibliography of primers published in North America.

Among the very small number of museum manuals in particular subjects, the most recent is: Brunton, C. H. C., Besterman, T. P. and Cooper, J. A. (Eds) (1985), *Guidelines for the Curation of Geological Materials,* compiled by the Geological Curators' Group and published as Geological Society Miscellaneous Paper No. 17, London. It contains much that is of relevance to museum curators in general.

'Annual' reports and reviews

Most museums and galleries are required either by Act of Parliament or Charter to prepare an annual (biennial or triennial) report for the governing body, and, usually, to publish it as well. These published reports vary in size and in coverage or comprehensiveness. Most reports, however, contain an account of the developments of the museum or gallery (commonly arranged by Department), a statement of accounts (with, in many instances, a separate statement for the Publications Department), details of acquisitions to, research on and conservation and documentation of the collections, loans (inward and outward), exhibitions, publications, extra-mural work (including fieldwork and excavation), attendance figures, details of any changes to the building and, in recent years, of any sponsorship or 'alternative' funding, as well as the names of the members of the governing body and of the staff with a list of their publications. The emphasis on the different aspects of the museum's work naturally varies from year to year and from museum to museum.

Some museums issue complementary publications. The Tate Gallery, for example, publishes two volumes biennially. The first is the *Illustrated Biennial Report,* which contains general essays on the acquisitions made for the British and Modern Collections, and reports from the various departments within the Gallery. A complete list of acquisitions is included but the full annotation and illustration of each work is given in the second volume, the *Illustrated Catalogue of Acquisitions* (see section on Catalogues).

The British Museum introduced the *British Museum Quarterly* in 1926 (and later added the subtitle *A Journal Dealing with Recent Acquisitions and Research Concerning the Museum's Collections*) and when, in 1973, the Library Departments of the British Museum became the Reference Division of the British Library, replaced it by *The British Museum Yearbook* (which retains the dual role of providing short notes on acquisitions and longer items resulting from research on the collections, and still aimed at the regular museum visitor). Each of the annual volumes contains contributions around a common theme: the first four titles being, *The Classical Tradition* (1976), *Collectors and Collections* (1977); *Captain Cook and the South Pacific* (1979); and *Music and Civilisation* (1980). The series was discontinued in 1980.

The Walker Art Gallery, Liverpool, in 1970, replaced the Gallery issue of the Liverpool Museums' *Bulletin* with an *Annual Report and Bulletin,* 'in the hope it will give a fuller idea of the Gallery's acquisitions and activities'.

Some museums and galleries have experimented with both the form and the content of their reports. The National Galleries of Scotland, for example, made three substantial changes to its Annual Report between 1976 and 1984. In the period from 1981 to 1984, it changed the name to annual 'Review', its format to that of a two-colour, four-column, 16-page tabloid newspaper, and its content by introducing articles by members of staff and others and in issuing a 'Facts & figures' supplement, available on request. The 1982 issue (Incorporating the 76th Report of the Board of Trustees laid before Parliament pursuant to Section 4(6) of the National Galleries of Scotland Act, 1906), for example, contains articles with banner headlines (in 60-point type) on 'Squashed cars and bruised sensitivities' by the Director, in response to correspondence regarding a recent purchase; 'Live music, live painting', reprinted from the *Scotsman*; 'A case of over exposure' by the arts correspondent of the *Guardian*; 'Recording the face of a nation', the plans for the future of the Scottish National Portrait Gallery, by its Keeper; and illustrations and descriptions of 'The most important gifts, loans and purchases' (commonly up to 300 words in length). The complete list of acquisitions is given in the Supplement.

This almost certainly represents the most striking experiment to make an annual report or review more attractive and more interesting to its readers. Most museums and galleries have, however, made certain changes in their reports. As regards content, there is a distinct tendency to include more statements on the policies of the museum and more didactic statements about its structure. As regards presentation, there is a much greater use of graphic designers and of illustrations, commonly in colour.

Some reports or reviews issued during periods of major change can reflect the changes quite forcibly. The Victoria and Albert Museum, for example, having not issued a comprehensive published Report for over 60 years, published a quinquennial report for the period 1974–1978 (*Victoria & Albert Museum*

Review of the Years 1974–1978, London, 1981), at a time when some other museums were probably considering the discontinuation of their annual publication as an economy measure. The Report explains the reasons for the demise of the 'National Museum Loan Service' (see the *Annual Reports* of the Department of Circulation, published from 1964 to 1974) for full details of the Service (initiated in 1855) and the Purchase Grant to help non-national museums (inaugurated in 1880)).

A welcome innovation in the 'statistical' part of the Report was the linking of the exhibition catalogues and other documentation (giving bibliographical details and the nature of the publications) directly with the details of the major, minor and departmental exhibitions themselves. Unfortunately, this helpful arrangement was not continued in the next report (*Report of the Board of Trustees, October 1983–March 1986*), in which the references are separated from the exhibitions and neither bibliographic detail nor nature of publication is given. The quinquennial report also reflects the range of the Museum's publications. The following 10 types are cited in the lists of publications – V & A Brochure, Exhibition Catalogue, Large Picture Book, Library Handlist, Masterpiece Sheet, Museum Catalogue, Museum Monograph, Museum Yearbook, Small Colour Book and Wallsheet.

The first triennial report of the National Museums and Galleries on Merseyside gives details of a different kind of event. On 13 February 1986, Richard Luce, Minister for the Arts, stated that it was the Government's intention to create a trustee body to administer the Museums and Galleries on Merseyside 'which would give them National status on a par with the major institutions in London'. The first Report of the Board of Trustees of the National Museums and Galleries on Merseyside (NMGM) provides the background to the unique event of creating a national museum from the museums and galleries of an English provincial city. The summary of the objectives of the Trustees given in the Report (p. 8) does not include any reference to publications but, in the section on 'Scholarship' (p. 13) it states: 'One of the primary responsibilities of a museum or gallery is to undertake study and research on its collections and to make that knowledge available in catalogues, scientific monographs, learned journals, popular guidebooks and leaflets'.

Museum guides

This characteristic form of publication, issued in some form or other by almost every museum – either as a simple means of orientation, as a companion to the exhibits, as a keepsake or souvenir, or as a mixture of all three – varies considerably in size and shape as well as content.

Examples of a number of guides to London museums were cited in the previous edition of this chapter and a much fuller list, including many for museums outside London, was included in the compiler's article 'Museums and museum publications in Britain, 1975–85' (*British Book News* (May 1986), 263–273).

In a survey of world trends in museums during the second half of the 1970s, Kenneth Hudson (*Museums for the 1980s*, Macmillan/UNESCO, London, 1977) catagorized Curators into those who approved and those who strongly disapproved of printed museum guides and made some suggestions in support of the former (pp. 108 and 109).

Compared with the many people who have evaluated the educational content of museum exhibits, only a handful have assessed the usefulness of published guides. For example, there appear to be only five evaluations of self-guiding brochures:

Porter, M. (1938), *Behavior of the Average Visitor in the Peabody Museum of Natural History*, Yale University, new Series No. 16, American Association of Museums, Washington, DC.

Owen, D. E. (1953), 'Popular publications', *Museums Journal*, **53**, 11–14, a consideration of the responses to a questionnaire covering the usefulness of museum guidebooks and descriptive leaflets for the museum visitor.

Hill, M. (1967), 'Catalogues [Raisonné], guides and gimmicks: three aspects of gallery publications', *Museums Assistants' Group Newsletter, No.* **8**, 8–13, which advocates guides dealing with reasonably compact sections of a museum's collection, accompanied by such publications as the National Portrait Gallery's 'Five famous portraits in fifteen minutes'.

Loomis, R. J. (1982), *Evaluation of a Visitor Gallery Guide*, The Visitor and the Denver Art Museum, Working Paper No. 2.

Jones, L. S. and Ott, R. W. (1983), 'Self-study guides for school-age children', *Museum Studies Journal*, **1**(1), 36, 38–42. The self-study guide is defined as 'a published brochure, worksheet or booklet that contains materials to assist visitors, on an individual basis, to further their observations and perceptions of museum collections'. Referred to by various names (self-guides, treasure hunts, museum games, architectural or service trails, activity books, gallery tours, or questionnaires), self-study guides provide all or parts of the following elements: (1) an intriguing title differentiating the self-study guide from other museum publications; (2) a theme that unites the collection of objects to be studied; (3) brief explanation on the museum collection highlighted, including object location information; (4) a series of questions pertaining to these objects; (5) suggestions for various activities which may be done in the museum or, more often, as follow-up projects in the classroom or at home; (6) eye-catching illustrations, including photographs, reproductions, line-drawings and cartoons; (7) background material, such as bibliographies and maps; (8) supplemental information for students, teachers and parents, which helps promote a complete understanding of the self-study guide.

Korn, R. (1988), 'Self-guiding brochures: an evaluation', *Curator,* **31**(1), 9–19. Korn evaluates the effectiveness of two different styles of written interpretive self-guiding brochures. One brochure uses a traditional declarative technique, while the other uses an inquisitive approach. See also: Bain, I., 'Museum publishing and shops', in the first edition of this Manual (1984, p. 461).

Examples of unusual or innovative 'guides' include:

Adams, P. (Ed.), (1985), *With a Poet's Eye: a Tate Gallery Anthology* (Tate Gallery, London), which includes specially commissioned poems, by some 50 leading contemporary poets as well as winning entries in both the adult and children's sections of an open competition held at the Tate. The poems selected are those in which the subject (either an individual work of art or some aspect of the Gallery itself) has been the stimulus to something more than simple poetical description.

Griffiths, A. and Williams, R. (1987), *The Department of Prints and Drawings in the British Museum: User's Guide* (British Museum Publications, London). A succinct guide to one of the world's greatest collections 'aimed to provide a working tool that is as simple as possible to use, and as exhaustive as the limits of space allow', rather than the more usual historical account enlivened with illustrations of some of the major treasures.

Anon. , *Women's Work and Leisure: A Guide to the Stranger's Hall and Bridewell Museum, Norwich,* Open University/Norfolk Museums, Norwich. The text, which formed part of the Open University Course 'The Changing Experience of Women', is designed to accompany a museum trail (but can also be used by the general visitor). It shows how a museum can be used to explain some of the hidden details of women's everyday lives.

Anon. (1982), *Completing the picture. Materials and Techniques of Twenty-six Paintings in the Tate Gallery* (Tate Gallery, London), a series of essays by members of the Gallery's Conservation Department drawing attention to the materials and techniques employed by a selection of well-known artists whose work is represented in the Gallery. The publication was prompted by the exhibition of 'Paint and Painting' on the history of the artists' colourmen's trade prepared to coincide with the 150th anniversary of the firm Windsor and Newton.

Tertiary publications

One of the main categories of tertiary publications is the 'Guide to literature'. Such publications have been common in many subjects for almost a quarter of a century. The first such guide to museum studies in book form has, however, only just appeared. It is: Woodhead, P. and Stansfield, G. (1989), *Key guide to Information Sources in Museum Studies* (Mansell, London).

The work is arranged in two sections: one is 'an overview of museum studies and its literature', and the other a bibliographic listing of sources of information. The former contains chapters on: the history and scope of museum studies and its literature; the origins and utilization of museum studies information; tracing organizations, collections, individuals and research; keeping up to date with current publications, developments and events; retrospective bibliographies; the literature of museum studies; audio-visual materials; and trade suppliers. The latter contains: lists of bibliographies (of a general nature (three entries), of museum studies literature (14 entries), of publications by individual museums (6 entries), of annual bibliographies, abstracts and indexes (14 entries), periodicals (three guides and 86 journals); theses (4 entries), monographs (three of a general nature, 77 of museum context, 21 on management and 32 on services)); directories (of a general nature (10 entries), of specialized museums (8 entries), and of museums by continent and country (45 entries)); and of a selection of organizations, both international (41 entries) and national (52 entries). The index is excellent and there is a simple but effective method of cross-reference.

Another guide of particular relevance is Jones, L. S. (1984), *Art Research Methods and Resources: a Guide for Finding Information,* 2nd edition, Kendall/ Hunt Publishing Co., Dubuque, IA. The emphasis of the guide, which includes fine, decorative and graphic art, architecture, photogra-phy, printmaking, films, and some archaeology, 'is on the methods of research, the many ways reference tools can be used to find art information'.

The 26 chapters are grouped into four parts: the first ('Before research begins', pp. 1–37) provides 'definitions and discussions on how to begin research projects and how to utilize all aspects of a library'; the second ('Art research methods', pp. 38–130) has chapters that detail, step-by-step, the methods by which research projects can be conducted by utilizing the resource tools which are cited in the third part; the third ('Art research resources', pp. 131–256) consists of an annotated list of more than 1500 diverse kinds of resource tools, including microforms and online data bases; and the fourth ('Deciphering and obtaining the reference material, pp. 257–282) states where to locate and how to obtain the needed material.

In the Appendices (pp. 283–314), the compiler provides three glossaries (French–English, German–English and Italian–English) as well as a multilingual glossary of terms. The two indexes are to 'Publications and institutions' and to 'Subjects, terms and professions'.

The annotated list of references (Part III) is subdivided as follows: 'Art encyclopedias and dictionaries'; 'Biographical dictionaries of artists'; 'Catalogues of holdings of famous libraries'; 'Indexing and abstracting services and data bases'; 'Art references'; 'Information on museum catalogues of permanent collections'; 'Resources for exhibition information'; 'Resources for sales information'; 'Sources for reproductions of works of art and architecture'; 'References that assist in authenticating and preserving art'; 'Fashion and jewellery'; 'References on subjects and symbols in art'; 'Book- and review-sources'; 'Reference aids and directories'; 'Special references: for architects, Art/Museum educators, commercial designers, film researchers, photographers, and printmakers'; 'Marketing aids and suppliers of products and services'[2].

Shorter reviews of museum publications include the four contributions to the British Council's *British Book News. A Monthly review of books*. The first, by A. P. Harvey (November and December 1967), attempts to demonstrate the range of subjects. The first part deals with the scientific literature and the second with that of the fine and applied arts. The emphasis in both parts is on the publications of the provincial museums rather than on the national ones. The second and third parts, by D. K. Smurthwaite (January 1974 and January 1980), cover the material for the years 1970–1973 and 1974–1979, respectively. The fourth part, by D. A. Bassett (May 1986), partly overlaps the third and deals with 'Museums and museum publications 1975–1985'. It includes 200 or so publications on museums and by museums, and by museum bodies in general in Britain.

Other short reviews are: Grove, K. (1975), 'Museum cookbooks: for fun and profit', *Museum News*, **59**(9), 53–59, a critical survey of both the content and format of cookbooks from ten American museums (five from art museums, four from historic restorations and one from a children's science museum); the review of the publications of the Ironbridge Gorge Museum on pp. 109–110 of K. Hudson's *Museums for the 1980s: A Survey of World Trends* (UNESCO, Paris, 1977); the guide to the 10 volumes issued by the British Museum (Natural History) during its centenary year (Bassett, D. A. (1982), *Nature in Wales*, **1**(1), 68–70); the guide to the 16 volumes on biological and geological themes issued by the National Museum of Wales during its 75th anniversary (Bassett, D. A. (1984), *Nature in Wales*, **2**(1,2), 100–105); a guide to the literature relating to natural history in museums (Stansfield, G. (1985), *Curator*, **28**(3), 221–226); and 'Bells, blankets, baskets and boats', a review of 18 publications, 19 information sheets and the publications policies of Oxford Museum Services (1968–1982) (Viner, D. (1985), *Museums Journal*, **85**(2), 105–107).

A commercial perspective

The obligation to publish has almost always been one of the duties that has been readily accepted by most major, and many minor, museums. The nature and organization of this role has, however, changed quite considerably over the last quarter of a century. The commercial aspects of this change are reflected in the following works:

Dowling, C. (1980), 'The museum as publisher', *Author*, **91**(4), 48–50, a brief report on the Imperial War Museum's associations with Jane's Publishing Company.

Bain, I. (1984), 'Museum publishing and shops', in Thompson, J. M. A., Bassett, D. A., Davies, D. G., Duggan, A. J., Lewis, G. D. and Prince, D. R. (Eds), *Manual of Curatorship. A Guide to Museum Practice*, pp. 460–466, based on the author's experience at the Tate Gallery and which includes a helpful list of references.

Bain, I. (1986), 'Publishing for the museum shop and beyond', in Bellow, C. (Ed.), *Public View: The ICOM Handbook of Museum Public Relations*, pp. 55–64, ICOM, Paris, based partly on the previous item, conceived as a survey of some of the work at the Tate Gallery and subdivided into: 'Guides and leaflets', 'Exhibition publishing', 'Permanent collection catalogues and reports', 'Postcards, slides and prints', 'Copyright control', 'Design and production', 'Pricing and distribution', and 'The retail shop'.

Sheppard, R. (1988), 'Notes on commercial operations', in *Museum Publishing. Problems and Potential*, pp. 52 and 53.

Association of Independent Museums, *Publishing Guidebooks and Postcards, AIM Information Paper No. 1*, Association of Independent Museums, Singleton, West Sussex.

In addition, there are a number of short papers in the *Newsletter* of the Group for Museum Publishing and Shop Management. The Group was created in 1978 (and affiliated to the Museums Association in 1980) 'to provide a forum for discussion and exchange of ideas and information between members of the museum profession involved in any part of publishing, shop management, or related activity':

Cross, R. S. (1979), 'Museum co-publishing', No. 2.

Silvester, J. W. H. (1979 and 1980), 'The small museum's publishing function', Nos 2 and 3.

Huskinson, J. M. (1980), 'Fitzwilliam Enterprises Limited', No. 3.

Bird, N. (1980), 'Victoria & Albert Museum/Pitman Publishing Series', No. 4.

Semmens, P. W. B. (1980), 'Selling postcards at the National Railway Museum', No. 4.

Talbot-Rice, E. (1983), 'The armies of Britain, 1485–1980. A new venture in sponsored publishing [National Army Museum]', No. 8.

Anon. (1987), 'Friends, sponsorship and publishing', No. 12.

Thompson, A. (1987), 'An effective gift catalogue', No. 12.

Luyster, C. (1988), 'The British Museum connection', No. 13.

Glover, P. (1989), 'HMSO – the museum publisher', No. 14.

Anon. (1989), 'Publishing for exhibitions. Lund Humphries Publishers', No. 14.

Anon. (1989), 'The new museum store [Museum Development Unit]', No. 14.

Pittman, N. (1989), 'Setting up a trading company: experience of a national museum [National Museums of Scotland]', No. 14.

Outlines of the change in the nature of museum publishing are also given in some triennial reports. For example, in *Report of the Trustees 1978–1981* (1981, pp. 48 and 49) of the British Museum which provides the background to the creation, in 1973, of British Museum Publications Ltd. – a body 'totally owned by the Trustees, but wholly separate from government finance and the staffing limitations of the Museum'; *The National Gallery Report January 1985 – December 1987* (1988, pp. 44 and 45) which outlines the retailing and publishing roles of National Gallery Publications (the self-financing operation reporting through the Publications Committee to the Trustees of the Gallery); the appointment of distributors, resulting in the Gallery's products being on sale in Japan, the Far East, Australasia and North America; and the production of the first all-colour mail order catalogues to tap the 'lucrative direct sales market'; and the *Report of the British Museum (Natural History) 1984–1986* (1987) which, in the chapter on 'Publishing' has sections on 'Sponsorship', 'Marketing', 'Retailing' and 'Mail-order catalogue' (introduced in 1986). Details of the total sales and sales of foreign language rights of exhibition books (1972–1986) and of total sales and co-publishers of a selection of the scientific books (1950–1986) are provided in the Museum's *Corporate Plan* (1987, Tables 1 and 3).

Preparation and publication

In a few of the largest museums, the publication procedures are similar to those at major commercial publishers, but for the most part the museum Curator has to teach himself the principles of publishing. One of the very few general texts published by a museum body is: Felt, T. E. (1976), *Researching, Writing and Publishing Local History*, 2nd edition, 1981, (American Association for State and Local History, Nashville, TN).

A number of guides to research writing and publishing are analysed by B. Currier Bell in 'Maps for learning' (*Scholarly Publishing*, **14**(1) (1982), 61–78). Three types of guide (descriptive, critical and 'training') are recognized, and nine of the most useful examples are considered in detail. All have two general and related failings: they lag behind the development of new or newly important fields in their disciplines and they do not adequately cover computerized research techniques. The most useful guide is judged to be *The Modern Researcher* (3rd edition, Harcourt Brace Jovanovich, New York, 1977) by two well-known and respected historians – Jacques Barzun and H. F. Graff.

Four other manuals are considered by N. B. Pascal in 'Four more enchiridia' (*Scholarly Publishing*, **10**(4) (1979), 351–358).

Two other works, by Barzun, which are regularly cited, are: *On Writing, Editing and Publishing. Essays Explicative and Hortatory* (University of Chicago Press, Chicago, IL, 1971); and *Simple & Direct. A Rhetoric for Writers* (Harper & Row, New York, 1975). An equivalent British publication is: Graves, R. and Hodge, A. (1963), *The Reader Over Your Shoulder. A Handbook for Writers of English prose* (Jonathan Cape, London). In the first part the authors outline the principles of clear statement and, in the second, apply the principles to selected items from the writings of authors known for the quality of their writing.

R. S. Miles *et al*, the authors of *The Design of Educational Exhibits* (British Museum (Natural History)/Allen & Unwin, London, 1982; 2nd edition

1988) rightly comment that, although many books have been written on how to write, ironically many of these are poorly written. They recommend the following as the most useful:

Barrass, R. (1978, *Scientists Must Write: A Guide to Better Writing for Scientists, Engineers and Students* (Chapman & Hall, London).

Evans, H. (1972), *Newsman's English. Book 1. Editing and Design* (Heinemann, London).

Flesch, R. (1960), *How to Write, Speak and Think More Effectively* (Harper & Row, London).

Kapp, R. O. (1973), *The Presentation of Technical Information*, 2nd edition revised by A. Isaacs (Constable, London).

Other more recent guides include:

Hall, N. (Ed.), (1984), *Writing and Designing Interpretive Material for Children* (Design for Learning and Centre for Environmental Interpretation, Manchester Polytechnic).

Farr, A. D. (1985), *Science Writing for Beginners* (Blackwell Scientific Publications, Oxford).

Tinniswood, A. (1982), *Guidelines: Some Problems Encountered in Writing Guide Books to Historic Buildings* (University of Nottingham, Nottingham).

All the major publishing houses issue one or more guidebooks for the use of writers, authors or printers. Those issued by the Oxford University Press and Cambridge University Press are listed in the previous edition of this chapter. Similarly, many of the major learned societies and associations issue similar guidebooks. For example: the *MHRA Style Book. Notes for Authors, Editors and Writers of Dissertations*, edited by A. S. Maney and R. L. Smallwood, in consultation with the Committee of the Association, Modern Humanities Research Association, London, 3rd edition, 1981; the Royal Society's *General Notes on the Preparation of Scientific Papers*, 1974; and *Signposts for Archaeological Publication. A Guide to Good Practice in the Presentation and Printing of Archaeological Periodicals and Monographs*, prepared by the Publications Committee of the Council for British Archaeology, 3rd edition 1991, London.

The CBA's *Signposts*, for example, includes sections on: 'Design'; 'Production'; 'Estimates'; 'Presentation'; 'Standardization'; 'Deposit copies'; 'Sales and possible outlets'; 'Copyright law'; 'Select bibliography'; 'Glossary of printing terms in common use'; and two appendices. The 'Select bibliography', for example (pp. 20–23), contains 74 entries (considered as 'further signposts to good practice as well as theory') subdivided into the following categories: (1) archaeology and publishing; (2) technical processes in printing; (3) the editor's job; (4) directories; (5) preparation of archaeological illustrations; and (6) index preparation[3].

A similar but less comprehensive list is given in Heppell, D. and Smith, D. (1988), 'What is a publication', in *Museum Publishing: Problems and Potential*, pp. 1–7.

Relevant volumes in the British Standards Institution series (for indexes, periodical title abbreviations, transliteration, proof correction, bibliographic references, etc.) are listed in the *BSI Yearbook*.

A helpful case study of the planning, development, writing, editing and preparation for the typesetting of an actual volume is given in 'The true story of a typescript' by Jenni Calder in the symposium volume that she also edited (*Museum Publishing: Problems and Potential*, 1988, pp. 18 and 19). An unexpected and ironic twist to the story is that the two columns on page 19 were transposed during preparation so that an erratum page had to be issued with the volume!

Other useful references are:

Hunnisett, R. F. (1972), *Indexing for Editors, Archives and the user No. 2* (British Records Association, London).

Partridge, E. (1963), *The Gentle Art of Lexicography as Pursued and Experienced by an Addict* (Andre Deutsch, London).

Partridge, E. (1953), *You Have a Point There. A Guide to Punctuation and its Allies* (Hamish Hamilton, London).

Prytherch, R. (1987), *Harrod's Librarians' Glossary of Terms used in Librarianship, Documentation and the Book Crafts and Reference Book*, 6th edition (Gower Publishing Co., Aldershot).

Fowler, H. W. (1965), *A Dictionary of Modern English Usage*, 2nd edition, revised by Sir Ernest Gowers (1st edition 1926), (Clarendon Press, Oxford).

Turning to other problems of printing and publishing, the following, chosen from among the large number of relevant works, are of particular interest in the museum context:

Starks, R. (Ed.), (1984), *How to Publish a Successful Newsletter* (Communi Corp, London), written for those who are not professional newsletter editors or publishers.

'Microform museum publications', a set of six articles by leading microform publishers in Britain on the present state of microform museum publications. *International Journal of Museum Management and*

Curatorship, **2**, 1983, 79–102. The items are: 'Micro-fiche, the poor man's alternative to print' (J. Emmett, pp. 80–82); 'Conservation and cataloguing hand-in-hand with commercial or museum micro-publishing – cooperation between the parties' (P. Ashby, pp. 82–86); 'The economics of microform publishing for museums' (F. F. P. Moore, pp. 86–89); 'Art exhibition catalogues on microfiche. The development of the Chadwyck-Healey publishing programme' (C. Chadwyck-Healey, pp. 90 and 91); 'The monthly art sales index on microfiche and the ASI Data bank of picture prices' (R. Hislop, pp. 92 and 93); 'Microform v. microfiche? English architectural drawings from the Victoria & Albert Museum, London' (S. A. Cornfield, pp. 94–96); and 'The Microform Association of Great Britain' (pp. 96 and 97).

Williamson, H. (1981), *Photocomposition at the Alden Press, Oxford* (Bodley head, London), an introduction to the principal characteristics of the system of photocomposition used by the Alden Press, Oxford, and which is used to print the *International Journal of Museum Management and Curatorship* (see **1**(2) (1982), 171, 172).

Crawford, C. (1988), 'The editor and new technology: asset and liability', in *Museum Publishing: Problems and Potential*, pp. 45–49, a personal introduction to desk-top publishing and associated methods.

Macdonnell, V. (1988), 'Smithsonian Institution Press desktop publishing', *Scholarly Publishing*, **19**(4), 187–193, an outline of the entry of electronic publishing into the work of the Smithsonian Institution Press, and in particular into its 'Series' publications.

Hill, L. (1989), 'Editorial', *Journal of Museum Ethnography*, **1**, iv, a short history of the publications of the Museum Ethnographers Group from the first Roneoed sheet to a desktop publication.

See also: *Newsletter of the Group for Museum Publishing and Shop Management*, No. **13** (1988), 7 for details of other published guides to desk-top publishing.

The developments that could arise in universities as a result of the electronic revolution in printing and publishing are considered in Patricia Battin's provocative article 'The library: centre of the restructured university' (*Current issues in Higher Education*, **1** (1983–1984), 25–31; and reprinted in *Scholarly Publishing*, **17**(3) (1986), 255–267). 'The computerized library is no longer just a place to "mark and park" knowledge but the potential centre of its university – becoming interalia, the primary publisher in the process of scholarly communication'. These developments, which are probably equally relevant to the larger museums, are considered further by H. S. Bailey in an article, 'On the future of

scholarly communication' (*Scholarly Publishing*, **17**(3) (1986), 251–254), and in the report of a working party on the effects of information technology on the shape of library services in the future (Day, M. P. (1986), 'Electronic publishing and academic libraries', *British Journal of Academic Librarianship*, **1**(1), 53–70).

Design of publications

The importance of good design in museum publications is widely recognized and the role of the designer accepted. Two items in the symposium volume *Museum Publishing: Problems and Potential* (1988) consider the matter – namely, 'Publications design: fundamental or cosmetic' (P. Macdonald, pp. 25–35, with illustrations) and 'Working with the designer' (S. Hamilton, pp. 36 and 37). The different methods of typesetting and printing are illustrated in the volume: a different method is used for each paper and the method is specified at the end of the appropriate contribution.

Equivalent American essays are two contributions to one of the special issues on museum publishing of *Museum News*, namely 'When you care enough to send the very best' (G. Brown, **62**(2) (1983), 22–33) and 'Quality design: it's a matter of attitude' (P. A. Degen, **62**(2) (1983), 38–49), which has a helpful bibliography.

A particularly useful series of papers is that associated with the museum publications competition initiated by the American Association of Museums in 1982. Entries were invited in nine categories: (1) posters, (2) calendars of events and newsletters, (3) catalogues and books, (4) brochures, folders and hand-outs (up to 24 pages), (5) invitations, (6) annual reports, (7) fund-raising material, (8) magazines, and (9) scholarly journals and bulletins. The Association issues an annual brochure listing the winners of the various categories and the winning entries are considered and illustrated every year in *Museum News*. In the August 1987 issue, for example (Ligeia Z. Fontaine, 'The jurors speak', **65**(6), 40–51), the jurors are interviewed on the following subjects: cover design, typography, illustrations, binding, paper, and the impact of the budget. In 1988 the competition attracted over 2000 entries and the September/October issue of *Museum News* (Eike, C. M., 'A look at the winners', **67**(1) (1988), separately paginated 1–16, and available as a separate catalogue) contains 13 pages of illustrations of the winning entries. The one shortcoming is that all the illustrations of books are of the outside front cover only. See also: Gardner, T. (1986), 'Museums and their publications. Imprinting an identity', *Museum News*, **64**(6), 46–62 (illustrated).

The effectiveness of the variety of printed material distributed by 39 municipal art museums – both large and small – in the USA is analysed in Gregg, R. (1959), 'Art museum publications – their nature and design', *Curator,* **11**(1), 49–67. See also: Ferguson, M. D. (1978), 'Do-it-yourself design [of the publications of the Dayton Art Institute]', *Museum News,* **56**(4), 38–41.

The book *A Designer's Art* (Yale University Press, New Haven, 1985) by Paul Rand, a pre-eminent American graphic designer, is helpful for those who are not themselves designers but wish to understand the ways of the designer and his problems.

Catalogues of art exhibitions, and of art collections, are issued in every imaginable size, shape and format. Some of the unusual ones – those 'that are boxed, bagged or bundled, bound in peculiar substances, wrapped or canned; catalogues that contain objects; publications that are not printed . . .' – are considered by G. H. Marcus ('These catalogues don't stand on shelves', *Museum News,* **53**(5) (1975), 25–29), with a list of the publications discussed or illustrated.

Much helpful material is published in the following two journals:

Scholarly Publishing. A Journal for Authors and Publishers, published quarterly since 1969 by the University of Toronto Press. Examples of articles concerned mainly with writing have already been cited. Others, concerning printing and design, include:

Hartley, J. (1985), 'Current research on text design', **16**(4), 355–368, in which the author reviews recent studies of layout, 'access structures' (i.e. devices such as titles, contents pages, summaries, running heads, headings, subheadings, numbering systems, etc.) and procedures for writing instructional text.

Finney, D. J. (1986), 'On presenting tables and diagrams', **17**(4), 327–342.

Bryant, M. and Cox, S. (1983), 'The editor and the illustration', **14**(3), 213–229, a guide for authors and editors on the best use of photographs, maps, charts, graphs and other graphics in their publications. The authors maintain that editors need to be 'visually literate'. See also: Jeanneret, M. (1989), 'The origins of *Scholarly Publishing*', *Scholarly Publishing,* **20**(4), 197–202.

Visible Language, a quarterly journal inaugurated in 1967 as the *Journal of Typographical Research* and renamed in 1970. It is published by Wayne State University Press, Detroit, IL. An example of its content is 'Computer graphics: a special issue' (**19**(2) (1985)). A number of other examples of papers in the journal are listed in Hall, M. (1987), *On Display: A Design Grammar for Museum Exhibitions* (Lund Humphries, London).

Notes

1. The 10th edition (1991) has a different title (*Museum Studies Bibliography*) and is an extensively revised and re-organized edition. Edited by Susan M. Pearce, it has 22 sections.
2. The 3rd edition (1990) has a different title (*Art Information. Research Methods and Resources*) and is almost completely rewritten.
3. The 3rd edition (1991), edited by Peter Boulton for the Publications Committee, is a completely revised version.

65

Museums and education: a bibliographic guide

Douglas A. Bassett

Introduction

The growth of educational activities in museums, and particularly the growth of the schools service movement, has been described as one of the outstanding developments in the techniques of the museum profession in the last 40 or so years.

The initiative in forming school museum services and in providing educational services in general in museums in Britain, appears to have come in large measure from the institutions themselves and not from the educationalists. The growth has not, therefore, followed a set pattern as decreed, for example, by a Ministry of Education, but has evolved according to local resources and to meet local needs.

There is no comprehensive history of the growth of education in museums in either Britain or elsewhere, nor indeed is there a truly comprehensive bibliography. There is, however, an extensive literature.

The best and most accessible bibliographies are those issued by the Group for Education in Museums (1989) and the annual bibliographies of the Department of Museum Studies at the University of Leicester. The former are described in the chronological bibliography in this chapter; the latter in the chapter on 'Museum Publications'. The best source for items in languages other than English, and particularly those of mainland Europe, is the annual *Selected Bibliography of Museological Literature* (Institute of Museology, Slovak National Museum, Bratislava) which contains sections on 'Educational activities and museums' and 'Museum co-operation with schools and youth' and which provides an abstract in English for each item.

The most comprehensive coverage of reviews is that in the *Museums Journal*, the American *Museum News*, and the *International Journal of Museum Management and Curatorship*. The general standard of reviews, particularly of exhibitions, is, however, commonly criticized: for example – McManus P.M. (1986), 'Reviewing and reviewers. Towards a critical language for didactic science exhibitions', *International Journal of Museum Management and Curatorship*, **5**, pp. 213–226; Schlereth, T. (1980), 'A perspective on criticism guidelines for history museum exhibition reviews', *History News*, **35**(8), pp. 18 and 19.

For the purposes of this selective essay, references are subdivided differently from most other bibliographies in order to: give some indication of the growth of education in museums from the formation of the first museums association, in 1889; to draw attention to the long-standing commitment of certain institutions and associations to education in museums; and to try to note the links between museum education and education generally. The subdivisions are:

(1) a chronological bibliography of publications (1890–1990) on education in museums, which includes a number of items on adult education, interpretation and evaluation;
(2) publications concerned primarily with education through the medium of one subject;
(3) other perspectives;
(4) graphical;
(5) general works on education and psychology.

References to contemporary or retrospective comments on the items in the chronological bibliography are usually given in the Notes. Many of the references cited in the first issue of this chapter are not repeated here. The references and annotations complement the chapter on education in the first edition of this Manual (by P. Graham Carter, 1984, pp. 435–447) and in Chapter 68 of this edition (by Eilean Hooper-Greenhill).

A selective bibliography arranged chronologically: 1890–1990

The dearth of literature on museums in general and on museums and education in particular, prior to the 1890s, is clearly demonstrated in Greenwood, T. (1888), *Museums and Galleries*, Simpkin, Marshall & Co., London, 'The subject upon which this book treats is almost without a literature' (p.v) (see chapters on 'The place of museums in education' and on 'School and University museums'). From the last decade of the century onwards, however, the situation changed considerably following the establishment of the Museums Association (in 1889) and its publications, and that of the equivalent American and German Associations in 1906 and 1917, respectively.

1890–1920

Higgins, H.H. (1890), President's Address, pp. 18–36 in *Museums Association Report of Proceedings. . . Liverpool, 1890*. The Association's first Presidential Address contains references to 'Circulating cabinets' and 'Clinical Lectures' inaugurated at Liverpool in 1884. At the same meeting complementary papers were read 'On circulating museum cabinets for schools and other educational purposes [at Liverpool]' (Chard, J. pp. 54–59) with two Appendices: 'Circulating museum for schools and other educational purposes' (Higgins, H.H. pp. 60–64), the Memorandum distributed to schools at Liverpool in 1883; and 'From report on the progress of the circulating museum collections. . . (Liverpool Museum) 1884' (Moore, T.J. pp. 64–68).

A number of other papers on educational matters were delivered to the other conferences of the 1890s and the place of education in museum work clearly stated in the widely cited paper by G. Brown Goode, 'The principles of museum administration' (Newcastle upon Tyne, 1895, pp. 69–141).[1]

Flower, W.H. (1898), *Essays on Museums and Other Subjects Connected with Natural History*, Macmillan & Co. London; reprinted, Books for Libraries Press, Freeport, New York, 1972. A selection of addresses and essays issued between 1870 and 1897. It includes reprints of: a Presidential Address to the British Association for the Advancement of Science (Newcastle-upon-Tyne, 1889) on 'museum organisation' – the only one on museums in the 60 years of the Association's history; a Presidential Address to the Museums Association (London, 1893) on 'modern museums'; suggestions for the formation and arrangement of a Museum of Natural History in connection with a public school' (*Nature* 1889); an article on 'boys' museums' (*Chambers' Edinburgh Journal*, 1897) and 'Local museums' (an address at the opening of the Perth Museum, 1895).

Hutchinson, J. (1908), 'On museum education [Presidential Address]'[2], *Museums Journal*, **8**(1), pp. 5–23. One of a number of papers in the early volumes of the *Museums Journal* which reflected a strong sense of educational purpose. In a slightly earlier address (Hoyle, W.E., 'The education of a curator', **6**(1), pp. 4–24), the air is referred to as 'saturated with the fumes of education' and the Association described as being 'an educational factor of no common order'.[3]

Dana, J.C. (1917), *The New Museum*, Elm Tree Press, Woodstock, Vermont. This was the first of four books issued by Dana in a series called 'The Changing Museum: the new museum series' and was published at his own expense. Two other titles are *The Gloom of the Museum (with suggestions for removing it)* (1917) and *A Plan for a New Museum: the Kind of Museum it will profit a City to Maintain* (1920). 'The Director of the Newark Museum from 1909 to 1929, Dana was one of the most passionate promulgators of museums as institutions of learning. He believed education was a museum's social responsibility and should be its prime mission.'[4] The books provide a summary of Dana's thinking about museums, their past, present and future, and are widely considered as authentic classics of American museum literature and of the educational role of museums in society.

Gilman, B.I. (1918), *Museum Ideals of Purpose and Method*, Riverside Press for The Museum of Fine Arts, Cambridge, Mass., second edition, 1923, Harvard University Press. Another American work now considered a classic of museum literature. It contains a number of essays on the educational role of art museums including, 'Popular education in fine art' (pp. 45–73) (reprinted from the Report of the United States Commission of Education for the year. . .1913). 'Although Gilman advocated esthetic sensitivity rather than education *per se* as the most important function of a museum, he is considered to have invented the principle of gallery instruction at the Museum of Fine Arts, Boston in the first part of this century.'[5]

British Association for the Advancement of Science (1920), 'Museums in relation to education. Final Report of the Committee. . . appointed to examine the character, work, and maintenance of museums', *Report of the British Association for the Advancement of Science*, Cardiff, pp. 267–280. The Chairman, Prof. J.A. Green, summed up the Committee's work as follows: 'Just as the appointment of the Committee [of the BAAS] of 1886 may be regarded as crystallizing the various movements towards a museum organization based upon definite ideas of the spread of scientific instruction among the people, so this Committee may be looked upon as an endeavour to give more definite form to the various educational calls which have in recent years been made upon museums.'[6]

1921–1940

Miers, H.A. (1928), *A Report on the Public Museums of the British Isles (Other than the National Museums). . . to the Carnegie United Kingdom Trustees*, T. & A. Constable for the Trustees, Edinburgh. The title of this report is slightly misleading because its purpose was to report on 'museums as a factor in education' (p.1) and to be a survey of public museums (exclusive of the national museums) 'with special reference to their present services to education, culture, and learning, and their possibilities for the future' (p. 5). It was to be the first comprehensive survey of its kind and it involved 530 museums.

The material was presented in three main parts: a general survey; criticisms and suggestions; and a statistical index of the museums studied (which occupies well over half the volume). The public services rendered by museums were considered to be threefold – being directed to the needs of

(1) the general public,
(2) school children and adults seeking instruction;
(3) advanced students or investigators.[7]

The Report marked the very beginning of the partnership between the Museums Association and the Carnegie United Kindom Trust.[8]

Board of Education (1932), *Memorandum on the Possibility of Increased Co-operation between Public Museums and Public Educational Institutions*, Board of Education, Educational Pamphlet No. 87, HMSO, London. (Dated 1931 but issued January 1932.) A pamphlet described in an enthusiastic editorial in the *Museums Journal* **31**(11) (1932) p. 505 – and in spite of the recent publication of the Miers Report (1928) and the Reports of the Royal Commission on National Museums and Galleries (London, 1928–1930) – as 'perhaps the publication of the greatest significance to the provincial museums of this country that has appeared during the present century'. The importance of the pamphlet was considered to be 'in the fact that it was prepared and published by the Board of Education' and that it was a sign 'that the Board had definitely stepped into the arena and joined us in our long struggle towards the more effective use of museums for educational purposes'.[9]

Leicester Art Gallery and Museum (1934), *Leicester Museum and the Schools: an Illustrated Account of the Activities of the Museum in Relation to Leicester Schools*, Leicester. The account contains a brief description of the work of the Department, created in 1924 when a resident guide lecturer was appointed. In the second edition (1943) the subtitle refers to the work of the School Service Department. A report by the Education Officer of a study tour of museums in the USA and Canada sponsored by the Carnegie United Kingdom Trust is given in Weston, R. (1939), 'American museums and the child', *Museums Journal*, **39**(2), pp. 93–115, a Supplement. Ruth Weston returned to organize a loan scheme based on American practice which was to become a model for future services.[10]

Melton, A., Goldberg, N. and Mason, C.W. (1936), *Experimental Studies of the Education of Children in a Museum of Science*. Publications of the American Association of Museums, New Series, No. 15, Washington D.C. Between 1928 and 1936 Arthur Melton and his colleague and fellow psychologist at Yale University, Edward Robinson (who are generally credited with being the 'fathers' of museum evaluation studies) produced 10 important papers. The first was Robinson E.S. (1928), *The Behavior of the Museum Visitor* (No. 5 in the AAM series).[11]

Markham, S.F. (1938), *A Report on the Museums and Art Galleries of the British Isles (other than the National Museums)*, T. and A. Constable Ltd., Edinburgh, a report to the Carnegie United Kingdom Trustees. The work includes chapters on: school visits; loans to schools and school museums; and adult education – each containing details of the services available at the time.

Adam, T.R. (1939), *The Museum and Popular Culture*, American Association for Adult Education, New York (Studies in the Social Significance of Adult Education in the United States No. 14), reprinted, University Microfilms, Ann Arbor, Michigan, 1974 and 1990. The study is limited to an evaluation of the specific types of museum activities that touch on the diffusion of learning among the adult population and the author concludes that 'when the role of museums, embracing art, science, history, industry and commerce is viewed as a whole. . . the striking fact becomes apparent that organization for educational purposes is usually fortuitous and haphazard' (p. 163). Furthermore, 'Museums suffer from the lack of definiteness attached to the educational function: they stand before the public as educational institutions, but the clients they serve and the type of instruction given are not clearly defined even by the institutions themselves' (p. 31). An earlier volume by the same author and the fourth in the same series *The Civic Value of Museums*, 1937, reprinted, University Microfilms, Ann Arbor, 1974 and 1990) answers 'the question as to the educational values that may be derived by the ordinary adult citizen from the existence and functioning of our metropolitan museums' (p.v.).[12]

The combined impact of the work of T.R. Adam, P. Rea, C.R. Richards (first Director of the AAM), and particularly of J.C. Dana and H.W. Kent, was 'to place the emphasis of the American museum movement upon education and community service rather than upon traditional collecting.[13]

Winstanley, B.R. (1940), 'The Derbyshire School Museum Service', *Museums Journal*, **39**(12), pp. 472–478. In September 1936, The Carnegie United Kindom Trust offered to assist one or two experimental circulating museum schemes in country areas and invited county authorities to submit proposals. The first of these grants was given to the Derbyshire Education Committee to cover an experimental period of three years, ending in August 1939. The experiment is briefly described by the organizer.[14]

1941–1960

Low, T.L. (1942), *The Museum as a Social Instrument: a Study undertaken for the Committee of Education of the American Association of Museums*, Metropolitan Museum of Art/American Association of Museums, New York. In 1941 the AAM appointed a committee to review 'the social and educational problems which museums are now facing in a rapidly changed world'; and they hired Theodore L. Lowe to carry out the survey. The result was *The Museum as a Social Instrument*, which was immediately controversial. 'Critics found it bombastic, shrill, irritating, dangerous and just plain wrong. Admirers thought it pointed the way to a new and glorious future for museums in this country.' In view of continuing criticism, Low (after sixteen years as the Director of Education at the Walters Art Gallery, Baltimore), reviewed the book in 1964 ('The museum as a social instrument: twenty years after', *Museum News*, **10**(5), (1964) pp. 28–30).[15] Of the sixteen recommendations made in 1984 by the Commission on Museums for a New Century, eight were anticipated by Low.

Allan, D.A. (1949), 'Museums and education', pp. 86–106 (with a folding map) in *Museums in Modern Life. Seven Papers read before the Royal Society of Arts in March, April and May 1949*, Royal Society of Arts, London (Reprinted from *Journal of the Royal Society of Arts*, **97**.) This assessment of the role of education in museums and review of current development starts with the words: 'Museums and education – museums *are* education. They exist only to further it; they can be neither provided, maintained, nor utilized without it'. The map ('Museum pattern') illustrates the distribution of the different kinds of museums in the UK.[16]

Wittlin, A.S. (1949), *The Museum, its History and its Tasks in Education*, Routledge & Kegan Paul Ltd., London (International Library of Sociology and Social Reconstruction, Mannheim, K. (Ed). One of the first books to deal comprehensively with the subject. The reasons for writing were twofold: first, the conviction that the unsettled conditions in contemporary society would not find a balance until general education, both as to its content and to its method, had been radically revised and adjusted to existing reality; and second, the belief that the method of communicating information and experience by the visual means of the exhibition and the appeal of the three–dimensional object held special potentialities for the fulfilment and furtherance of educational requirements.

Harrison, M. (1950), *Museum Adventure. The Story of the Geffrye Museum*, University of London Press, London. The story of working with children at Shoreditch – 'one approach, in one small museum, in one area of London'. The service for organized visits from schools was established in 1935.[17]

Glasgow Art Gallery and Museums (1951), *Educational Experiment: 1941–1951*, Corporation of the City of Glasgow. (Foreword by T.J. Honeyman.) A description of an experiment initiated during the 'holidays at home' scheme of 1940 and carried out in the schools and museums of Glasgow. The appendices include: a list of the Schools Museum Service publications and of the staff (which included six trained teachers) of the Museum's Education Department; details of specimen lessons for primary schools, for secondary schools and for adults; and an extract from the summary of records. See also: Thompson, S. (1942), 'The school and the museum. Close co-operation at Glasgow', *Museums Journal*, **42**(4), pp. 81–84.

International Council for Museums: Committee for Education (Cart, G., Harrison, M. and Russell, C.) (1952), *Museums and Young People: Three Reports* with a Foreward by Georges-Henri Rivière and an Introduction by Peter Floud, ICOM, Paris. The book is a result of an ICOM decision in 1948 to publish a report on the problems of children and museums. Originally planned as a world-wide survey by a single author, it resolved itself into three separate reports – on conditions in continental Europe (Cart, G.), on those in Britain and the Commonwealth (Harrison, M.) and on those in America (Russell, C.). The Introduction exposes several recurring misconceptions about museum programmes for children based on experience at the Victoria and Albert Museum. The work contains an excellent annotated bibliography (pp. 107–121).[18]

United Nations Educational Scientific and Cultural Organisation (1953), 'The role of museums in education. UNESCO International Seminar, Brooklyn, 1952', *Museum*, **6**(4), pp. 213–281 (bilingual). This, a pioneer project of its kind, was followed two years later by a second seminar, at Athens, bearing the same title as the first (*Museum*, **8**(4) (1955) pp. 201–265 [bilingual]). Although the titles were identical, the four-week seminars differed considerably in a number of respects. The place chosen dictated in each case the examples considered and the methods used.[19]

John, D.D. (1955), *The Museum Schools Service. The First Five Years*, National Museum of Wales, Cardiff. An outline of the work of the first national service to schools, inaugurated in direct consequence of the *Education Act 1944* (The Butler Act), financed on a voluntary basis by all but one of the Local Education Authorities in Wales and administered by the National Museum. The Service was assessed in: Ministry of Education (1954), *A Survey of the Schools Service of the National Museum of Wales*.[20]

Tilden, F. (1957), *Interpreting our Heritage. Principles and Practice for Visitor Services in Parks, Museums and Historic Places*, University of North Carolina Press, Chapel Hill, third edition, 1977. Most modern commentaries attribute the first adequate definition of the term interpretation in a heritage or conservation context to Freeman Tilden. It is 'an educational activity which aims to reveal meanings and relationships through the use of original objects by first hand experience and by illustrative media, rather than simply to communicate factual information'. The definition was later summarized (Schultz, 1962), 'Interpreting park values', *Park Practice Guidelines*, **3**, pp. 12–16, in the mnemonic: 'through interpretation, understanding; through understanding, appreciation; through appreciation, conservation'.

Tilden maintained that he and his colleagues were clearly engaged in a new group education based upon a systematic kind of preservation and use of national cultural resources. 'The scope of this activity has no counterpart in old nations or other times.' He also maintained that his work was based on six principles:

(1) Any interpretation that does not somehow relate what is being displayed or described to something within the personality or experience of the visitor will be sterile.
(2) Information, as such, is not interpretation. Interpretation is revelation based upon information. But they are entirely different things. However, all interpretation includes information.
(3) Interpretation is an art which combines many arts, whether the materials presented are scientific, historical or architectural. Any art is in some degree teachable.
(4) The chief aim of interpretation is not instruction but provocation.
(5) Interpretation should aim to present a whole rather than a part and must address itself to the whole mass rather than any phase.
(6) Interpretation addressed to children (say, up to the age of 12) should not be dilution of the presentation to adults, but should follow a fundamentally different approach. To be at its best it will require a separate program.

Tilden, an established and successful novelist and short-story writer, became concerned and interested in conservation in the 1940s and 1950s and, at the Director's invitation, became a collaborator in the US National Park Service. The bulk of the book, prepared under the guidance of R.F. Lee, the Head of the Division of Interpretation of the Serivce, is an examination of each of the six principles in operation, an analysis which one reviewer called a 'beautifully worked-out interpretation of interpretation' (Saunders, J.R. (1958), *Curator*, **1**(4), p. 96).

D'Amico, V. (1960), *Experiments in Creative Art Teaching: a Progress Report on the Department of Education (Museum of Modern Art) 1937–1960*, Doubleday, Garden City, New York. The volume describes the work of the Department of Education at the MOMA from its inception in 1937–38 to the end of the 1950s. Included are references to a range of what the author considers as pioneer projects – among them the Young People's Gallery, the National Committee on Art Education, the People's Art Centres, the Children's Carnival of Modern Art, parent child art classes and NBS television series (e.g. 'Through the enchanted gate' and 'Art for the family').

The wider influence of MOMA on art education in general and from the inception of the Museum in 1929, is described in Russell Lynes' *Good Old Modern. An Intimate Portrait of the Museum of Modern Art, New York*, Atheneum, New York, 1972. The author states that few museums can have had such a specific, focused and burning purpose at its inauguration, and writes of the museum's 'missionary zeal' and 'missionary spirit'. He highlights the intention of the first Director, Alfred Barr, to use the Museum 'as a means of educating the public not merely in what was new in the arts but in how they had evolved and where they seem to be heading'. Figuratively speaking, according to Lynes, 'Barr was conducting a public course on the history of the modern movement and his blackboard. . . was the museum' (pp. 127, 156 and 141).

By the time of its 25th Anniversary in 1954, the Museum had been so successful in its missionary task that Paul Sachs, the highly acclaimed teacher and one of the founding trustees, could say of the men and women who had built it, 'They have made the Museum a telling instrument in the field of general education. . . Their influence and example have liberalized the policies of every one of our leading museums – even the most complacent' (quoted in Lynes, 1973).

1961–1970

Standing Commission for Museums and Galleries (1963), *Survey of Provincial Museums and Galleries* (The Rosse Report), HMSO, London. The main body of the survey contains a brief but succinct section on educational activities in which the Commission strongly recommends the extension of museum schools services all over Britain and contains an appendix, compiled by Barbara R. Winstanley, on school museum services in the British Isles.[21]

Victoria and Albert Museum, Department of Circulation (1965), *The National Museum Loan Service. The Year's Work 1964–65*, Victoria and Albert Museum, London. In 1963, the Standing Commission on Museums and Galleries recommended an increase in the staff and facilities of the Department of Circulation in order to include among the travelling exhibitions a greater proportion of material from museums other than the Victoria and Albert. The increase was effected in 1964–65 and the preliminary results given in an annual report – the first of its kind.[22]

Walden, T.A. (1967), 'The alternatives: a survey of methods of providing educational services in museums in Great Britain', *Museums Journal*, **67**(2) pp. 141–148. The author surveys the educational activities of some of the museums in this country, considers the alternatives they offer and comments upon them. He considers that 'the growth of the schools service movement in museums had been one of the outstanding developments in the technique of our profession in the last thirty years'.

Winstanley, B.R. (1967), *Children and Museums*, Blackwells, Oxford. The work contains sections on: children on their own in museums; organized group visits; school museum loan services; how to make the best use of museums where there are no school services. The book is one of the first of a group of commercially produced volumes on museum education. Others include: three by Molly Harrison (*Changing Museums: Their Use and Misuse*, Longmans, Green & Co., London, 1967; *Learning out of School: a Teacher's Guide to the Educational use of Museums*, revised edition, Ward Lock Educational, London, 1970; and *Museums and Galleries – on Location Educational Series*, Mills & Boon, 1974) and one by Anne White (*Visiting Museums*, Faber & Faber, London, and International Publications Service, New York, 1968).

Group for Educational Services in Museums (1967), *Museum Schools Services*. Prepared by the Group for Educational Services in Museums (edited by F.W. Cheetham) for the Museums Association, London.

Larabee, E. (Ed.), (1968), *Museums and Education*, Smithsonian Institution, Washington, D.C. The proceedings of a conference held at the University of Vermont in 1966. The three principal objectives of the conference were: (a) to survey the present relations between museums and education; (b) to explore possible methods of involving museums more directly and more fruitfully in the educational process at all levels; and (c) to formulate proposals for research and development activities relating to museums and education. In a broad sense the purpose was 'to learn, or at least begin to learn, ways of making more effective educational use of the more than five thousand museums that exist in the United States'.

Shettel, H. H., Butcher, M., Cotton, T. S., Northrup, J. and Slough, D. C. (1968), *Strategies for Determining Exhibit Effectiveness*, US Department of Health, Education and Welfare, Office of Education, Bureau of Research, Washington, D.C. The 1960s and 1970s are usually considered as the formative years of evaluation studies in museums and in exhibitions in the United States. It was a period when three influential movements came together 'in an exciting way' – namely, accountability, measurement and museum education. This particular study, one of the first of its kind, was undertaken 'to initiate the systematic development of research strategies that will make it possible to better evaluate the effectiveness of scientific and technical exhibits, particularly those designed to reach educational objectives'. It contains the results of an 18-month project on a travelling exhibit entitled 'The vision of man'. A summary of this work and of Shettel's views are given in his 'Exhibits: art form or education medium?', *Museum News*, **52**(1), (1973) pp. 32–41.[23]

Standing Commission on Museums and Galleries (1968), *Universities and Museums. Report on the Universities in Relation to their own and other Museums*, HMSO, London. The Report was the outcome of a full survey which included the services performed in local museums for university teaching and research. The appendices, which make up 30 of the 48 pages, contain brief descriptions of the collections in the various university museums.[24]

Zetterberg, H.L. (1968), *Museums and Adult Education*, Evelyn, Adams and Mackay for ICOM, London; A.M. Kelly/ICOM, Clifton, N.Y. The text of the first part of this publication was written in 1965 as a report to UNESCO and, in particular, to its Division of Adult Education. It was considered as the 'first time in the history of museums' that a sociologist had 'dealt with the educational role of these institutions'.[25]

[University of Leicester] (1969), 'Conference on Countryside Centres', *Museums Journal*, **69**(2), pp. 63–73 (Discussion pp. 72 and 73). The report of a conference held in Leicester in December 1968 and organized jointly by the Departments of Museum Studies and of Adult Education at the University, with sponsorship from the Carnegie United Kingdom Trust. The conference was initially called

'Conference on Field Museums and Interpretive Centres'. The Introduction to the report, by Geoffrey Stansfield, traces the growth in interest in nature trails, field museums and countryside centres and assesses the influence of the *Public Libraries and Museums Act 1964* and the *Countryside Act 1968* on these developments.

The conference resulted in the establishment of: (i) a Working Party on Countryside Centres; (ii) a second conference, also at Leicester (see Stansfield, G. (1970), 'The 1969 Countryside Centre Conference', *Museums Journal*, **70**(1), pp. 17 and 18); and (iii) a review of the use being made of interpretation (Carnegie United Kingdom Trust (1970), *A Review of Interpretation Carried out by Statutory and Non-statutory Bodies. A Report of Standards of Interpretation in the United Kingdom*, Working Party on Countryside Centres, Dunfermline).[26]

International Council of Museums (1969), *The Annual: Museums Education, Cultural Action/Annales: Musées, Education Action Culturelle*, ICOM, Paris. This, the first journal devoted entirely to museum education matters, was renamed *Museums Annual: Education, Cultural Action/Annales des Musées, Education, Action Culturelle* in 1970 and *ICOM Education* in 1976. The first issue was devoted almost entirely to a factual bibliography of national Working Parties, with lists of their publications and reports from 1964 to 1969. A selective bibliography for the years 1970–1976 is given in No. 7 (1975/76, 57–60) and for subsequent years in later issues.

Robbins, M.W. (Ed.), (1969), *America's Museums: the Belmont Report. A Report to the Federal Council on the Arts and Humanities by a Special Committee of the American Association of Museums*, Washington, D.C. The Report, on the needs and resources of America's museums, stresses the need to pay special attention to the educational role of museums – '. . . the times call for a sharp increase in the educational and cultural opportunities which museums are uniquely equipped to provide. . . A museum can stretch the mind as well as engage the emotions.' (pp. v–vii).

Museum of the City of New York (1969), *Exploration of the Ways, Means and Values of Museum Communication with the Viewing Public: A Seminar with Marshall McLuhan, Harley Parker and Jacques Barzun*, Museum of the City of New York, New York. In 1967 Marshall McLuhan (University of Toronto) and Harley Parker (Head of Exhibits Design, Royal Ontario Museum) were moderators of 'an unusual seminar' held in the Museum of the City of New York. It was, in part, concerned with non-linear communication and on 'pattern recognition'; and it was the first time that the 'controversial communications theorist' had turned his attention and attack on museums in a public exchange of ideas. The seminar is summarized in Anon (1968) 'McLu-

hanism in the museum' (*Museum News*, **46**(7), pp. 11–18) and the full text of Jacques Barzun's closing address given in 'Museum Piece, 1967' (*Museum News*, **46**(8) (1968) pp. 17–21).[27]

Council for Museums and Galleries in Scotland (1970), *Report on Museums and Education*, Edinburgh. In 1968 the Council set up a Committee to report on the educational services provided by museums and galleries in Scotland. The Committee's report was presented for consideration and action to the Scottish Education Department and to education authorities and museum authorities in Scotland.

Schools Council (1970), *School and innovation. 1870–1970*. Supplement to *Dialogue, Schools Council Newsletter*, and issued separately. The volume celebrates the centenary of *The Elementary Education Act 1870* (the Forster Act) and UNESCO's International Education Year, whose theme was 'lifelong education'. The booklet contains sixteen contribution by educationalists and teachers.

Two examples of the very small number of museum publications issued to commemorate the centenary are: Dony, J.G. (1970), *A History of Education in Luton*, County Borough of Luton Museum and Art Gallery; and Roscoe, S. (1970), *Norwich Museums. A Check-list of Books in the Museum's Collection which were Published for the Enjoyment, Edification and Instruction of Children and Young Persons up to the Year 1837, with an Index of Publishers, Printers and Booksellers*, Norwich City Museums.

Museums Association (1970), *Report of the Museums Association Working Party on Museums in Education*, Museums Association Report No. 1. (Emended edition, May 1971.) The report contains the results of the work of a Working Party established by the Association in 1970 'to examine the role of museums in education in the United Kingdom and to recommend a policy for the future'. It contains 12 recommendations (three general, two relating to informal and seven to formal education) and the text of: 'Evidence submitted by the Museums Association Working Party to the Russell Committee on Adult Education' (Appendix II).

The Working Party was established in response to three significant events – the survey carried out by a working party of the Schools Council on museums as a source of curriculum material; the establishment by the Department of Education and Science of a committee, under the chairmanship of Sir Lionel Russell, to examine non-vocational adult education; and the survey carried out by Her Majesty's Inspectorate, under the guidance of W.W. Taylor, on the educational services provided by national museums and selected provincial museums with the object of making recommendations to local authorities.

1971–1980

Department of Education and Science (1971), *Museums in Education*, Education Survey No. 12, HMSO, London. The report is the result of a survey in 1969 of a number of museums in Britain by a group of Her Majesty's Inspectors designed to examine the contribution of museums to education and to make suggestions how available resources might be better used. Five loan services to schools are described in detail.[28]

Oliver, Ruth N. (Ed.), (1971), *Museums and the Environment: a Handbook for Education – Prepared by the Environmental Committee of the Association*, Arkville Press for the American Association of Museums, Washington DC. The volume is the product of a contract awarded to the AAM by three departments and agencies of the United States Government to undertake the study of, and to prepare a report on, 'Developments of museum education techniques for human ecology'. The volume contains chapters on 'Man and the environment', 'Population', and 'Environmental Pollution' with, in each case, a section on 'exhibits and projects'. There are also chapters on 'Creating and building environmental exhibits', 'Added dimensions through the use of films', 'The emerging role of museums in environmental education', and a comprehensive bibliography.[29]

Schools Council (1972), *Pterodactyls and Old Lace: Museums in Education*, Evans Brothers Ltd/Methuen Educational Ltd, London, and Citation Press, Scholastic Magazines Inc, New York. The report describes the results of the work of a Working Party, Chairman Mrs. M. Long, set up jointly in 1967 by the Schools Council and the ICOM Committee for Education in Museums in the United Kingdom, in order to consider ways 'in which the services provided by museums, both national and local, could be more effectively exploited by teachers and to prepare a publication containing a clear statement of the philosophy of the educational use of museums'. The compilers make extensive use of quotations from a wide variety of sources. Two short films (*What I see* and *Insight*), sponsored by the Working Party as experimental exercises in visual perception, were made in the Art Gallery and Museum at Lincoln.

Department of Education and Science (1973), *Provincial Museums & Galleries. A Report of a Committee Appointed by the Paymaster General* (The Wright Report), HMSO, London. The Committee, under C.W. Wright of the DES as chairman, was established to 'review the needs of museums and galleries with particular regard to the conservation and display of their collections and to links with related activities, including educational authorities'.

A general statement in the report states that 'the increasing demands of education, national trends towards more leisure and greater mobility, the growth in cultural television programmes and the increase in tourism are putting pressure on the resources of museums to an extent that calls for a fresh initiative'. Among its recommendations was the following: that 'local education authorities should be involved to a greater extent in the planning of museum education services'.

Screven, C.G. (1974), *The Measurement and Facilitation of Learning in the Museum Environment: an Experimental Analysis*, Smithsonian Institution (Office of Museum Programs), Smithsonian Institution Press, Publications in Museum Behavior, No. 1; Smithsonian Institution Press Publication 5230), Washington, DC. The volume describes experimental studies carried out at the Milwaukee Public Museum, Milwaukee, Wisconsin, using a diversity of devices, teaching machines and interactive exhibits to measure the reactions of visitors.

Museums Association (1975), 'Museums and interpretive techniques: an interim report', *Museums Journal*, **75**(2), pp. 71–74. The interim report is based on three sources: a paper on 'Exhibition effectiveness', presented by Geoffrey Stansfield to the Symposium on Communication and Design in Museums and Galleries, held in Leicester in April 1973; a paper by Dr Warren Johnson, on 'Differences in interpretation in the United States and Britain'; and the taped discussions at the Association's seminar at West Dean College in March 1975.

Aldridge, D. (1975), *Guide to Countryside Interpretation. Part One. Principles of Countryside Interpretation and Interpretive Planning*, HMSO/Countryside Commission for Scotland/Countryside Commission. This is the first reference book on interpretation to be published in Britain and is a sequel to Tilden's volume (1957). The five sections comprise: an introduction to the subject, the philosophy behind it, the principles of interpretive planning, the assessment of the standard of the programme, and 'the future of interpretation'. Table I contains definitions of four types of interpretation (p. 4).[30]

Part Two of the work (Pennyfather, K. (1975), *Interpretive Media and Facilities*), is divided into four sections: a glossary of interpretive terms; a description and comparative evaluation of the various media, services and facilities that can be used; techniques and methods of approach to enhance or increase the effectiveness of the service provided; and a list of 136 sites in Britain where the media described in section two can be found.

Group for Educational Services in Museums (GESM) (1975), *Museums as an Influence on the Quality of Life*, London. Proceedings of an International

Conference, arranged jointly by the Group for Educational Services in Museums and the British National Committee of ICOM and held at the Victoria and Albert Museum, 6–11 April 1975. Five of the papers presented at the Conference are included in the proceedings. The contribution by G. McCabe ('Five years on – the future of museum education', pp. 16–18) considers the major effects of the *Local Government Act 1972* on museums, their staffs and services in England and Wales.[31] A second seminar, held jointly by the Group (GESM) and the Departments of Museum Studies and Adult Education at Leicester in September 1975 was, *Museums and the Handicapped*, Leicestershire Museums, Art Galleries and Record Service, Leicester, 1976.

Royal Ontario Museum (1976), *Communicating with the Museum Visitor. Guidelines for Planning*, The Communications Design Team, Royal Ontario Museum, Toronto. In the words of one commentator, this work is 'An extraordinary compendium of quotations, theory and design advice which distills the thoughts and practices of many people over many years into a single volume. Even so, it can only skim the final (and sometimes controversial) theoretical principles off the top of many more profound essays by professionals throughout the field'.[32]

The expertise gained by the Royal Ontario Museum in providing a variety of opportunities for its visitors to use all their senses in learning within a museum context is provided in one of its later publications – *Hands on. Setting up a Discovery Room in your Museum or School*, 1979.

Rath, F.L. Jr. and O'Connell, M.R. (Eds.), (1978), *Interpretation* (compiled by R.S. Reese), American Association for State and Local History, Nashville, Tennessee. This is the third volume of the Association's exemplary series 'A bibliography on historical organization practices'. The word 'interpretation' is defined by the editors as: 'The way in which a museum uses its resources to carry out its educational function.' (p. vii). The chapter on 'Role of interpretation' includes 'references which deal with such issues as the museum's responsibility to interpret, the value of interpretation in the total museum programme, the "language" of interpretation, and the status of museum educators'.

Olofsson, U.K. (Ed.), (1979), *Museums and Children* (Illustrations by Gerard Teichert), UNESCO, Paris, (Monographs on Education No. 10). This 'assemblage' of studies of educational work in 14 countries is published as a contribution to the International Year of the Child (1979). The editor provides a critical panorama of the work of museums in relation to teaching practice throughout the world. Each of the other contributors considers and discusses the themes most relevant to his or her country. The

selective bibliography is provided by the UNESCO-ICOM Documenation Centre at Paris in collaboration with Stella Westerlund.[33]

Group for Education in Museums (GEM) (1980), *Journal of Education in Museums* 1980–. The Group replaces its *Newsletter* (1972–79) with a *Journal*.[34] The annual volumes of the *Journal* deal with the following themes:

1 (1980)–History of museum education in Britain.
2 (1981)–Education in art galleries; dramatic approaches to museum education
3 (1982)–Museums and environmental education
4 (1983)–International edition (issued to mark the meeting of the ICOM 83 Conference in London)
5 (1984)–International edition II
6 (1985)–Training teachers, students and museum educators to use museums
7 (1986)–Multi-cultural education and museums
8 (1987)–Museum education today (with a GCSE Supplement)
9 (1988)–Drama and role play in museums
10 (1989)–Transport museums
11 (1990)–Museum education, interpretation and evaluation.

Chadwick, A.F. (1980), *The Role of the Museum and Art Gallery in Community Education*, Department of Adult Education, University of Nottingham/National Institute of Adult Education, Nottingham (Nottingham Studies in the Theory and Practice of the Education of Adults, No. 4). Based upon the author's PhD thesis, the study analyses the function of museums and galleries in Britain and considers possible future changes.[35]

1981–1985

Department of Education and Science (1981), *Environmental Education: a review*, HMSO, London. The review contains sections on: the concept of environmental education; current practice; the international context; future development in the United Kingdom; and a brief history of environmental education in the United Kingdom. The companion volume, *Environmental Education: Sources of Information*, is a successor to the DES booklet *The Environment: Sources of Information for Teachers* (1979). It contains notes on the resources of over 250 organizations, including a number of museums.

Commission Nationale Suisse pour l'UNESCO (1981), *L'enfant, l'art et le musée. Seminaire Européen de Cartigny* (24–27 September 1980), Swiss National Committee of UNESCO, Berne. The seminar was designed to examine the problem of the child in an art gallery and the extent to which the child allows himself or herself to be led by the *animateur*. The proceedings contain an introduction, brief summaries of the 13 papers (expressing very different approaches), together with a summing up.

Council for Museums and Galleries in Scotland (1981), *A Directory: Museum Education Scotland*, HMSO, Edinburgh. The first part of the work examines the general role of museum education and explains how to plan a visit; the second is a Directory of museums and the educational services they provide; the third, a selective annotated bibliography of books and monographs.

Collins, Z.W. (Ed.) (1981), *Museums, Adults and the Humanities: a Guide for Educational Programmes*, American Association of Museums, Washington DC, second impression, 1984. The work, based on a series of seminars sponsored by the AAM Education Committee in 1979–80, contains a section on 'Adults as learners', in which four adult educators recognise several crucial distinctions between children and adults as learners. The chapters include: a summary (by R. Hiemstra, pp. 61–72) of the key findings of recent research on adult learning, designed for museum professionals and including a number of helpful tables presenting data, principles and applications of the current adult learning theories; and a summary of the history of adult education in the USA by a pioneer in the field (M.S. Knowles, pp. 49–60) which concentrates on the development of the pedagogic and andragogic models. A third section considers the theme of 'lifelong learning and the museum' with chapters on the basic components, the implications and the future of lifelong learning.[36]

Moore, D. (1982), 'Thirty years of museum education: some reflections', *International Journal of Museum Management and Curatorship*, **1**, pp. 213–230. A review in three sections: what is museum education?; evaluation; and conclusions. In the third section the author suggests that the 1950s saw the 'introduction as it were of a Trojan horse full of teachers into a museum world which had become for the most part inward-looking or stale'; the 1960s were marked by the rise of the designer; and the 1970s, in which 'a golden age seemed to have dawned', was not to fulfil its promise.[37]

Museums Association (1982), 'Working party – museums in education', *Museums Journal*, **81**(4), pp. 236–239. The article contains the product of the work of a working party of the Association established in 1977 in order 'to review the role of museums in education bearing in mind the 1970/71 Policy Statement in order to provide further guidelines for the profession and other interested bodies'.

Miles, R.S., Alt, M.B., Gosling, D.C., Lewis, B.N. and Tout, A.F. (1982), *The Design of Educational Exhibits*, British Museum (Natural History)/George Allen & Unwin, London, Boston and Sydney, second edition 1988. A major premise of the book is that learning in the museum is quite different from learning in school. This thesis is elaborated in chapter three ('Psychological and educational aspects of exhibition design'), and in an earlier article ('The museum as an educational facility'), both by the educational consultant B.N. Lewis (*Museums Journal*, **80**(3), (1980) pp. 151–155). Lewis, in a critique of museums as educational environments, notes three reasons why museums have a much greater potential to teach than is commonly believed. These are that: (1) learning under conditions of freedom or non-coercion is qualitatively different from learning under conditions of coercion; (2) learning under conditions of freedom is also superior because it does not lead to the cognitive fixity that is induced by coercive or fear-based learning; (3) museums have the potential to become powerful environments that can potentiate in the participants a process of self-healing and self-understanding.[38]

Hansen, T.H., Anderson, K-E. and Vestergard, P. (Eds.) (1982), *Museums and Education*, Danish ICOM/CECA. Based partly on the theme of the 1981 Conference of the Committee for Education and Cultural Action (CECA), the 19 contributions in the volume are considered by the editors to provide 'a catalogue of ideas, looking at education in museums as an alternative to the common learning procedure being used in schools, universities and higher education, study groups', etc.[39]

Hooper-Greenhill, Eilean (1983), 'Some basic principles and issues relating to museum education', *Museums Journal*, **83**(2/3), pp. 127–130. Using one of B. N. Lewis' conclusions as a basis (*Museums Journal*, **80**(3), (1980) pp. 151–155) – that 'from an educational and social point of view museums can hardly be said to serve the general public well' – the author sets out six basic principles of museum education. These are that museum education should: be relevant to the museum and relevant to the museum's audience; be educationally relevant and based on objects; make the learner feel confident and competent and must be of the highest quality.

Barclay, D. [1983], *Interpretation of the Environment: a Bibliography*, edited by Lord, G. and Paterson, J., Carnegie United Kingdom Trust, Dunfermline, Fife, and the complementary bibliography, Stevens, T. R. (1985), *Environmental Interpretations: a Bibliography*, Centre for Environmental Interpretation, Manchester. In the former, approximately 200 items are divided into 'Books and Reports' and 'Articles in Journals'; each item is annotated, there is a section on 'Recommended Journals' and there is an index. In the latter, prepared as part of a doctoral thesis (University of Wales, 1982),[40] the 680 items are listed alphabetically and there is no index. In both bibliographies, although the items include references to interpretation, research and evaluation in museums, the natural heritage and the man-made heritage, the emphasis is heavily on the third of these categories.

Nichols, S.K., Alexander, M. and Yellis, K. (Eds.) (1984), *Museum Education Anthology: Perspectives on Informal Learning 1973–1983: a Decade of Roundtable Reports*. Museum Education Roundtable, Washington.[41] A selection of 39 items from the first decade of the issues of *The Journal of Museum Education: Roundtable Reports* (initially known simply as *Roundtable Reports*), along with invited 'afterwards' from some of the contributors. The items, selected to have appeal and relevance for those working in 'art, history and science', are arranged in six groups: (1) Priming the muse (concerned largely with the philosophical underpinnings of museum education); (2) A distinctive brand of education; (3) Audiences as clients (each item focusing on a special interest or client group that 'enjoys the resources of our institution in interestingly different ways'); (4) Teaching objects; (5) Towards building a profession; (6) First questions (concerned with a variety of approaches to museum evaluation). One of the most useful contents of the volume is the comprehensive 44-page classified index to the *Journal* (1973–83), divided into volume, topic, author and institution index.

Bloom, J. N. and Powell, E. A. (Eds.) (1984), *Museums for a New Century. A Report of the Commission on Museums for a New Century*, American Association of Museums, Washington, DC. The work highlights the thinking of 24 distinguished museum directors, trustees, foundation and business leaders on the state of America's museums (what museums are, why they are important to the country's culture and what they contribute to the quality of human life), and forges a number of recommendations to guide the museum community into the next century.[42]

In the preamble to the first of three recommendations in the chapter 'A new imperative for learning' (pp. 54–71), the authors state: 'If learning is to remain at the philosophical core of museums, we believe its place in the internal structure of museums must be re-examined. Placing all education efforts under the direction of a separate department may not be the best organizational structure for achieving the museum's educational role'. The significance of the recommendation is debated in Leavitt, T.W. and O'Toole, D. (1985), 'Two views on museum education', *Museum News*, **64**(2), pp. 26–31. The second recommendation urges 'a high priority for

research in the ways people learn in museums' and this matter is considered further in Miles, R.S. (1986), 'Museum audiences', *International Journal of Museum Management and Curatorship*, **5**(1), pp. 73–80. The second recommendation also highlights the need for computers and other electronic technology in museum learning. The third recommendation calls for active dialogue about the 'Mutually enriching relationships museums and schools should have'.

Frostick, E. (1985), 'Museums in education: a neglected role', *Museums Journal*, **85**(2), pp. 67–74. The author states that although a forum for developments in museum education 'was formally established [in this country] with the publication of the first issue of the *Journal of Education in Museums*' (in 1980), to suppose that the educational value of museums is a recent discovery is far wide of the mark. The main task of the article is to try to 'isolate possible explanations for the failure of museums to develop as fully as possible into the specific field of school based instruction'.

1986–1990

Screven, C.G. (1986), 'Exhibitions and information centers: some principles and approaches', *Curator*, **29**(2), pp. 109–137. The paper considers: (1) audience analysis (information about audiences needed in the earliest stages of exhibit planning); (2) visitor motivation (factors that encourage or discourage visitor attention, time and effort); (3) concept networks and learning hierarchies (conceptual framework for exhibit planning); (4) evaluation as a tool for design planning; (5) visitor orientation (spatial and conceptual organizers that prepare visitors for viewing exhibits); (6) labels (uses and misuses, motivations for reading and not reading, layering, information maps, questions); (7) computer applications. It pays particular attention to John Falk's work on informal education and summarizes the eight types of learning in Robert Gagne's suggested hierarchy of learning. See also Screven, C.G. (1984), 'Educational evaluation and research in museums and public exhibits: a bibliography', *Curator*, **27**(2), pp. 147–165.[43]

Museums & Galleries Commission (1986), *Museums in Scotland. Report by a Working Party*, HMSO. Of the three regional reports prepared by Committees or Members of the Commission (Wales – 1981; Northern Ireland – 1983) only this volume has a separate chapter on 'Museum education' (pp. 50–62). It includes a Postscript: Museum Education Officers: their functions and qualifications.[44]

Department of Education and Science (1986) *Report by H.M. Inspectors on a Survey of the Use some*

Hertfordshire Schools Make of Museum Services, carried out 1–4 July 1985. HMI Report 40/86. The results of the first of a number of regional surveys on the use made of museums by schools (including Oxfordshire, 312/87, 1987 and the North West, 20/87, 1987).[45]

Loomis, R.J. (1987), *Museum Visitor Evaluation: New Tool for Management*, (AASLH Management Series No. 3), American Association for State and Local History, Nashville, Tennessee. The volume, the first attempt to produce a comprehensive text on the subject, contains chapters on: (1) Understanding museum visitors: evaluation and management; (2) Evaluating attendances: making figures count; (3) The visitor survey; (4) The identity of museums: evaluation, marketing and audience development; (5) Welcome to the museum: evaluating visitor orientation; (6) Exhibit evaluation: making things work; (7) Using evaluation to improve programmes.

Ambrose, T. (Ed.), (1987), *Education in Museums: Museums in Education*, HMSO for the Scottish Museums Council, Edinburgh.[46] The 10 contributions (presented to a conference organized jointly by the Council and the Scottish Council for Educational Technology) are by both educationalists and museum educators. They provide a useful contribution to the debate on the structure and content of the British education system and, in particular, illustrate the many opportunities for collaboration between those working in all sections of education and those working in museums in Britain.

Museums & Galleries Commission (1987), *Museum Professional Training and Career Structure. Report by a Working Party* (The Hale Report), HMSO, London. The section on the General Certificate of Secondary Education (GCSE) clearly recognizes the demands which will be made on museums as a result of the introduction of the new examinations and particularly because of the new emphasis on child-centred learning, the assessment of course work as well as examinations and the stipulations of the national criteria.

Museums Association (1987), 'GCSE and museums', *Museums Journal* (Special Issue), **87**(1), pp. 3–43. The special issue contains an introductory note on 'GCSE for Curators' (April Whincop, pp. 3–6), 13 items on the problems regarding individual subject disciplines and 'Leicester Museum Initiatives' Avery-Gray, A. pp. 41–43). A companion volume is provided by Goodhew, E. (Ed) (1987), *Museums and the New Exams*, issued by the Area Museums Service for South Eastern England, London.

Goodhew, E. (Ed.), (1988), *Museums and the Curriculum*, Area Museums Service for South Eastern England (funded by the Office of Arts and Libraries), London. Using a format similar to that of its predecessor (*Museums and the New Exams*, 1987), the volume contains examples of how teachers in England, Northern Ireland and Scotland have successfully incorporated museum resources in the work of primary and secondary schools in a variety of subjects.

Moffat, H. (1988), 'The educational use of museums: an English case study', *History and Social Science Teacher*, **23**(3), pp. 127–131 – a description of the work of the Museum Committee of Her Majesty's Inspectorate (HMI) in England and Wales.

Hooper-Greenhill, E. (Ed.), (1989), *Initiatives in Museum Studies*, co-ordinated and produced by the Department of Museum Studies, University of Leicester. The publication, which contains 15 contributions, each accompanied by a case-study, focuses on good practice in various initiatives in museum education. It 'aims to be of interest to schools, their governing bodies, local education authorities (LEAs), teacher training institutions, local community groups and all involved in the management of museum education' (from the Introduction, by Hazel Moffat, HMI).

Museums Association (1989), 'Museum education – a new era?', *Museums Journal* (Special feature), **89**(2), pp. 21–27. Five authors consider the three features of the *Education Reform Act 1988*[47] which are of particular relevance to museums: (1) the funding of museum services to which LEAs presently make a contribution; (2) the charges for school visits; (3) on the requirements of the new National Curriculum. Relevant sections from Circulars 7/88 and 2/89 issued by the DES regarding the Act are cited and commented upon.

Department of Education and Science (1989), *National Curriculum. From Policy to Practice*, Department of Education and Science, London. The book deals with 'the curriculum for pupils of compulsory school age, and the new legal requirements for the curriculum contained in the Education Reform Act 1988 (ERA)'. The chapters aim '(1) to show how the ERA requirements relate to thinking about the curriculum over the last two decades; (2) to set the National Curriculum in the context of the whole school curriculum; (3) to describe and explain the ways in which the National Curriculum and related requirements will affect practice in schools'.

One chapter, for example, defines the four elements of the National Curriculum – (1) foundation subjects (including core subjects); (2) attainment targets; (3) programmes of study; (4) assessment arrangements. The glossary (Appendix B) summarises the definitions and deciphers the abbreviations, including those of the two statutory bodies established by the Secretary of State to assist the DES –

National Curriculum Council (NCC) and School Examinations and Assessment Council (SEAC). The section on background reading, DES circulars, etc. (Appendix D) contains a very useful inventory of the relevant publications of the DES, HM Inspectorate, the National Curriculum Council and the Training Agency.

Museums Association (1989), 'Museums – a national resource, a national responsibility', *Museums Journal*, **89**(8), 36, 37. 'A key policy statement on government responsibilities towards museums' adopted at the Association's Annual General Meeting on 22 September 1989. The problem of the relationship of schools and museums is given a prominent place.[48]

Bosdêt, M. and Durbin, G. (1989), *Museum Education Bibliography 1978–1988*, Group for Education in Museums, Aberdeen. The bibliography, with 1040 items, is over four times the size of its predecessor (1972) and it clearly demonstrates the growth in the number of publications on education in museums during the last decade. It is also much more elaborately subdivided than its predecessor, containing 36 sections grouped into eight major themes – namely: history, principles and developments, serving the community, working in specific museums, using and developing museum resources, outreach, professional development, and evaluation.[49]

Although, unfortunately, the bibliography does not have an index, it does provide a classified inventory for the decade 1978–88 of all the main items in the Group's own *Journal* (70 items), its American equivalent *Journal of Museum Education: Roundtable Reports* (54 items) and *ICOM Education* (14 items). It also lists the educational contributions to the general museographical and museological serial *Museums Journal* (62 items), its American equivalents – *Museum News* (82 items) and *Curator* (47 items), and UNESCO's *Museum* (42 items) as well as the comparatively new *Museums Studies Journal* (15 items) and the *International Journal of Museum Management and Curatorship* (20 items). Fuller details of the general journals are given in Chapter 64.

Uzzell, D.L. (Ed.), (1989), *Heritage Interpretation. Volume 1. The Natural and Built Environment, Volume 2. The Visitor Experience*, Belhaven Press/Centre of Environmental Interpretation/Society for the Interpretaton of Britain's Heritage, London. The volumes are considered not so much as the proceedings of the Second World Congress on Heritage Presentation and Interpretation held at Warwick in September 1988, but as an attempt to provide a comprehensive 'state of the art' review of interpretive philosophy, theory, practice and research. The papers included have been carefully selected from those presented at the Conference and revised for inclusion in the volumes. Volume one contains a paper, 'How the ship of interpretation was blown off course in the tempest: some philosophical thoughts' (Aldridge, D., pp. 64–87), which, among other things, emphasises the differences between 'Site interpretation' and 'Environmental education for schools' (see Table 7.1, for example) and considers the application of hermeneutical philosophy to environmental interpretation. Volume two contains 'Evaluation in museums: a short history of a short history' (Shettel, H.H., pp. 129–137).

Drysdale, L. (1990), *A World of Learning. University Collections in Scotland*, Scottish Museums Council, Edinburgh. The report contains sections on the educational services, work with schools, outreach and further educational programmes based on the university collections, and it also contains a number of recommendations concerning these services.

University of Leicester (1990–), Leicester Museum Studies Series. This series, produced by the Department of Museum Studies at Leicester and Leicester University Press, was launched in early 1990 with the publication of the volumes *Archaeological Curatorship* by Susan M. Pearce and *History Curatorship* by Gaynor Kavanagh, mentioned in the sections on 'archaeology' and 'history' respectively in the present chapter. The third volume, *Museum and Gallery Education* (1991), by Eilean Hooper-Greenhill, contains an introduction to education in museums and galleries and 17 chapters grouped into three parts – Historical Perspectives, Management and methodologies, and Audiences and approaches. The work has been written 'for all those who believe that museums and galleries are a unique source of knowledge, inspiration, enjoyment and information' (p. viii).

Publications concerned with education in specific subjects

Many museums specialise in one discipline and are subdivided or classified accordingly. For example, in Alexander, E.P. (1979), *Museums in Motion. An Introduction to the History and Functions of Museums* (American Association for State and Local History, Nashville, Tennessee,) museums are grouped into four classes – art; natural history; science and technology; and history. Botanical gardens and zoos are considered as a separate class. In *Framework for a System for Museums: Report by a Working Party 1978* [The Drew Report] (HMSO, London) on the other hand, the Standing Commission (now the Museums & Galleries Commission) subdivides collections into: (1) fine and decorative arts; (2) natural history and geology; (3) archaeology; (4) ethnology and social history; and (5) science, technology and industrial archaeology. The section 'Working in specific subject areas' in the GEM Bibliography (Bosdêt, M. and Durbin, G. 1989) is divided into eight sections:

art; history and archaeology; costume; heritage education (historic houses, sites and monuments); science and technology; natural history; zoos and aquaria; natural environment.

In this chapter the papers dealing with education through the medium of particular disciplines are divided as follows: the biological (or life) sciences – commonly referred to as 'natural history'; the geological (or earth) sciences; 'science and technology' – incorporating the physical sciences; history; archaeology; ethnography and anthropology; and the visual arts.

The term 'natural history' is currently used in at least three senses: first, to encompass botany, geology and zoology; second to include botany and zoology; and, occasionally as a synonym of zoology. For this reason a more modern terminology is adopted.

The biological (or life) sciences

The number of papers on education through the medium of biological materials in museums is unusually small. For example, eight references only are given in the GEM Bibliography (Bosdêt M. and Durbin, G. 1989). There are, in addition, three papers on education in Engström, K. and Johnels, A.G. (Eds), (1973) *Natural History Museums and the Community. Symposium held in October 1969 at the Swedish Museum of Natural History [Naturhistoriska Riksmuseet] in Stockholm.* Universitetsforlaget, Oslo. They are: on the British Museum (Natural History); the Swedish Museum of Natural History; and on the role of the natural history museum in university education. There are also short but useful papers in the special issue of *Museum* devoted to 'Museums and children' such as one by P. N. Haase ('Educational activities within the framework of the Zoological Museum of Copenhagen', *Museum*, **31**, (1979), pp. 197–199). Of the 300 000 visits at Copenhagen, approximately one half are children and for this reason 'former museum guards, or custodians. . . have been replaced by biology students, which has been especially important from the educational standpoint'.

Natural history in the examination system is covered in Elizabeth Goodhew's article in the special feature 'GCSE and museums' (*Museums Journal*, **87**(1) (1987) pp. 33–38). It includes an Appendix comparing the four national criteria themes for GCSE biology (diversity of organisms; relationships between organisms and with the environment; organization and maintenance of the individual; development of organisms and the continuity of life) in the various Examination Boards for England and Wales. It also includes a diagram of the diverse content of biology which effectively demonstrates

the overlap with other subjects, including geography and geology.

There are obvious and strong links between the biological and geological sciences in field work and with environmental studies generally. Useful references include: Greenwood, E.F. and Osler, A. (1967), 'Museums and fieldwork', *School Science Review*, **49**, pp. 56–63 – a description of two courses offered by the City of Liverpool Museums and based on the Ainsdale Sand Dunes National Nature Reserve; Walden, T. (1965), 'Museums and field studies', in *The Countryside in 1970. Second Conference*, Keele; Anon. (1976), *Environmental Awareness. A Survey of Types of Facilities used for Environmental Education and Interpretation in Europe*, Council of Europe – being the result of a survey carried out under the auspices of the European Committee for the Conservation of Nature and Natural Resources; Stansfield, G. (1969), 'Museums and environmental education', *Museum Assistants Group Transactions*, **8**, pp. 3–6; Whiting, J. (1979), 'The role of natural history museums in environmental education', *ICOM Natural History Museums Newsletter*, **5**, pp. 20–27; Sharpe, T. and Howe, S.R. (1982), 'Family expeditions – the museum outdoors', *Museums Journal*, **82**, pp. 143–147.

Another major theme common to biology and geology is the theory of evolution. The problems of presenting what has been described as a metaphysical research programme are considered in the following two papers in the Institute of Biology's *Journal of Biological Education*: Deadman, J.A. and Kelly, P.J. (1978), 'What do secondary schoolboys understand about evolution and heredity before they are taught the topics?' (**12**(1), pp. 7–15); Brumby, M. (1979), 'Problems in learning the concept of natural selection' (**13**(2), pp. 119–122); and by Dobzhansky, T. (1973), 'Nothing in biology makes sense except in the light of evolution' in *American Biology Teacher*, **35**, pp. 125–129.

A third theme common to the two disciplines is biological classification. The booklet *Classification. A Beginner's Guide to Some of the Systems of Biological Classification in Use Today* (Jones, S. and Gray, A. British Museum (Natural History), 1983) is an illustrated guide to the concept and to three methods – phenetics, cladistics and the orthodox classification. It provides a useful reading list and a helpful glossary, and forms part of the Exhibition Companion Series. Other items in the same series are *Origin of Species* (1981), *Human Biology: an Exhibition of Ourselves* (2nd edition, 1981) and [*The Feathers Fly!*] *Is Archaeopteryx a Fake?* (1987).

Lessons learnt by the design team at the British Museum (Natural History) in creating the exhibition on human biology are outlined by the team leader R.S. Miles in 'Lessons in human biology: testing a theory of exhibition design' (*International Journal of*

Museum Management and Curatorship, **5**, (1986) pp. 227–240); and an inside view of education at the Museum is provided by S. Pollock (*Journal of Biological Education*, **17**(2), (1983) pp. 119–122). See also two papers by Pauline McManus: 'Work-sheet induced behaviour in the British Museum (Natural History)' (*Journal of Biological Education*, **19**(3), (1985) pp. 237–242) and 'What people say and how they think in a science museum [British Museum (Natural History)]' (pp. 156–165 in Uzzell, D.L. (Ed.), *Heritage Interpretation*, volume 2 *The Visitor Experience*, Belhaven Press, London 1989).

A fourth theme is that of making museum collections more accessible to visitors. Over the last 15 years or so a number of attempts have been made by natural historians to make large parts of the stored collections available to the general public. This has resulted in the Naturalist or Natural History Centres in museums (see, for example, Madden, J.C. (1978), 'Bridge between research and exhibits – The Smithsonian Naturalist Center', *Curator*, **21**, 159–167). The development in general and the experiences at Liverpool in particular, are outlined in Greenwood, E.F., Phillips, P.W. and Wallace, I.D. (1989), 'The Natural History Centre at the Liverpool Museum', *International Journal of Museum Management and Curatorship*, **8**, pp. 215–225. At Liverpool, after an experimental phase in 1983 and 1984, the Centre [offering Botany, Geology and Zoology] was built and equipped during 1986 as part of the Natural History Gallery. It contains an Activity Room (including a children's area) and a Collections Room.

M.M. Ames suggests a new approach to museum education, borrowing from the concept of 'deschooling' advocated by Ivan Illich in 'The deschooling of society', pp. 103–126 in Rusk, B. (Ed) (1971), *Alternatives on Education*, Toronto General Publishing Company. See Ames, M.M. (1985), 'De-schooling the museum: a proposal to increase access to museums and their resources, *Museum*, **37**(1), pp. 25–31 (also published as Chapter 6 of the author's *Museums, the Public and Anthropology*, Concept Publishing Co., New Delhi, 1984).

The twice-yearly periodical *Seeing Things*, issued since 1986 by the Education Department at the Royal Museum of Scotland, Edinburgh, provides a guide for teachers to the variety of events and activities for children with biological and other materials carried out in its Discovery Room. The Summer 1987 issue contains 'an update on Standard Grade and Museums' and reference to the first four titles in the Museum's 'Spotlight' packs.

The geological (or earth) sciences

A number of papers on education through geology are included in *Teaching Earth Sciences, Journal of the Earth Science Teachers Association* (a journal which was initiated as *Geology, Journal of the Association of Teachers of Geology* (1969–1975) and then became *Geology Teaching* (1976–1988)) and its American equivalent *Journal of Geological Education* (1951–), issued by the National Association of Geology Teachers [USA]. Volume 3(2) (for June 1978) of *Geology Teaching* is devoted almost entirely to the theme of educational services in geology in museums and the recent issues of *Teaching Earth Sciences* have a number of papers on the earth sciences in the GCSE syllabus and in the National Curriculum for Science. The journal *Geology Today* (Blackwells, 1985–) also contains relevant items.

Twenty-four papers on education (from Britain, Germany, Canada and the USA) are listed in Sharpe, T. (1983), *Geology in Museums: a Bibliography and Index*, National Museum of Wales, Cardiff. The range of material offered on loan to schools by one of the larger services is clearly illustrated in *Catalogue of Loan Material in Geology* (8th edn., 1984), Museum Schools Service, National Museum of Wales, Cardiff – it lists handling boxes (unmounted specimens and notes), exhibition cases, framed charts, illustration boxes, filmstrip containers, slide packs, etc.

Experimental work with children on the identification of minerals, rocks and fossils was carried out by D.E. Evans in an 'activities' room (or 'do it yourself' laboratory) at the National Museum of Wales and in association with the Schools Council 5/13 project. This is described in two papers – 'Investigating minerals' (1972) and 'Investigating and indentifying rocks' (1973), both in *Amgueddfa, Bulletin of the National Museum of Wales* (**10**, pp. 9–21, 12 illus. and **14**, pp. 16–27, 13 illus., respectively). The same investigator also experimented with the use of new media (particularly polystyrene) in the making of models (topographical, crystallographic, mineralogical and geological) by children and teachers and described his results in, 'Involving the student in the study of the materials and the concepts of geology (with particular reference to an experiment at the National Museum of Wales)' (*Geology*, **3**, (1971) pp. 54–64). The concepts included the unit cell, glaciation, vulcanicity, faulting, folding and sea-floor spreading.

The Curator of the Geological Museum, South Kensington (now part of the British Museum (Natural History)) responds (F.W. Dunning, *Geology*, **6**, 1975, pp. 12–16) to the reactions of a primary and secondary school teacher to the first of the Museum's four major permanent exhibitions '*The Story of the Earth*' (designed so that visitors with IQs in the region of 115 could understand 100 per cent of it) – see [Dunning, F.W.], *The Story of the Earth*, Institute of Geological Sciences, London 2nd edition, 1981. The fourth exhibition, *Treasures of the Earth*, is analysed by Clough, P.W.L. and Mercer, I.F. (*Geology Teaching*, **13**(2), (1988) pp. 79–83) and

McManus, P.M., 'Reviewing the reviewers' (*International Journal of Museum Management and Curatorship*, **5**, (1986) pp. 213–226).

The problem of geologic time is considered from an historical standpoint by Albritton, C.C. (*Journal of Geological Education*, **32**, (1984), pp. 229–237) and from an educational standpoint in 'Time in geological explanations as perceived by elementary-school students' (Ault, C.R., *Journal of Geological Education*, **30**, (1982), pp. 304–309). The distinctive historical nature of geology is presented in an imaginative way in Toulmin, S. and Goodfield, J. (1965), *The Discovery of Time*, Hutchinson, London, Harper & Row, New York for the Nuffield Foundation Unit for the History of Ideas (Ancestry of Science series), and Harper Torchbook, 1966; and in Gould, S.J. (1987), *Time's Arrow: Time's Cycle. Myth and Metaphor in the Discovery of Geological Time*, Harvard University Press, Cambridge, Mass. and London, an elaborated and reworked version of the first series of The Jerusalem–Harvard Lectures (1985). 'Deep time [i.e. geological time] is so difficult to comprehend, so outside our ordinary experience, that it remains a major stumbling block to our understanding' (Gould, p. 2).

The paramount importance of illustration in geology is considered in two publications by M.J.S. Rudwick – *The Meaning of Fossils. Episodes in the History of Palaeontology*, Macdonald, London and American Elsevier Inc., New York [History of Science Library, Ed. M.A. Hoskins], 1972; 2nd edition, University of Chicago Press, 1976; reprinted 1985; and 'The emergence of a visual language for geological science, 1760–1840', *History of Science*, **14**, (1976), pp. 149–195. In the former the author considers fossil illustrations and maintains that 'technical advances in illustration might be said to have played a part in the history of palaeontology similar to that of improvements in instrumentation in the physical sciences' (p. 9); and this applies equally to illustrations in botany and zoology. In the latter he considers geological maps, geological sections and landscape drawings, and maintains that these forms of visual communication are not supplements to verbal description and verbal concepts; 'still less are they merely decorative in function': they are an essential part of 'an integrated visual and verbal mode of communication' (p. 152).

D. Edwards explains the innovatory nature of teaching geology in the Open University ('Teaching Earth sciences at a distance', *Geology Teaching*, **12**(4), (1987), pp. 139–145) and provides a useful bibliography, and W.T.C. Sowerbutts illustrates one role of computergraphics in geological education (*Geology Today*, **4**(2), (1988) pp. 54–56).

Geology and the Local Museum. Making the Most of your Geological Collection, by S.J. Knell and M.A. Taylor (HMSO for the Area Museums Service for South Eastern England and Area Museum Council for the South West, 1989) and 'The use and conservation of palaeontological sites', edited by P.R. Crowther and W.A. Wimbledon (*Special Papers in Palaeontology*, No. 40, 1981) are both useful resources for teachers and museum educators: the latter contains the proceedings of a two-day meeting at the Geological Society in 1987 under the auspices of the Geological Society, the Palaeontological Association and the Geological Curators' Group.

'Science and technology'

A useful introduction to the work of museums and centres of science and technology is provided by Quin, M. (Ed.), (1989), *Sharing Science: Issues in the Development of Interactive Science and Technology Centres*, produced by the Nuffield Foundation's Interactive Science and Technology Project on behalf of the Committee on the Public Understanding of Science (COPUS), London. The volume is divided into four sections: a keynote essay by R.L. Gregory and sections on the variety of hands-on centres, the role of outreach programmes, and exhibit fabrication.

Richard Gregory, founder of the Exploratory at Bristol and chairman of COPUS, considers (pp. 1–8) the nature and potential of the hands-on medium, i.e. perceptual (interactive) explorations, and introduces the allied concepts of 'Hand-waving' – intuitive (common-sense explanations) and 'Handle-turning' – formal (mathematical) computations. In the section on the variety of hands-on centres, three authors consider the respective roles of traditional exhibits with the emphasis on history and the new contemporary participatory exhibits within a museum – with reference to the Museum of Science and Industry in Manchester (J.P. Greene, pp. 11 and 12) and the University Museum at Utrecht (S. de Clercq and Pieter't Hart, pp. 12–14). This is a theme also considered by Orchiston, W. and Bhathal, R. (1984), 'Introducing the science centrum: a new type of science museum' (*Curator*, **27**(1), pp. 33–47). In the section on outreach, Anthony Wilson (pp. 29 and 30) considers the various meanings of the term in the context of his work on Launch Pad at the Science Museum, South Kensington. For example, he assesses the complementary role of the book *Launch Pad* (Wilson, A. and Watts, S. Science Museum, London 1986) to the exhibition: 'Away from the frenetic pressures of the gallery, it [the book] allows its readers to reflect on what they did there, to forge links between the exhibits and their real-world applications and to understand in more formal language what was happening at individual exhibits. It also helps its readers to step back a little and see what Launch Pad is all about – something that is not easily appreciated from within the exhibition itself.'

Among the many publications dealing with hands-on exhibits, the following are representative: Danilov, V.J. (1982), *Science and Technology Centers*, MIT Press, Cambridge, Mass, and London. A comprehensive guide to the early history of the centres (with particular reference to the USA), to the different kinds of organization and adminstration and to the exhibits and programmes. See also 'Early childhood exhibits at science centers', *Curator*, **27**(3), (1984), pp. 173–188 and 'Science exhibits for the young', *International Journal of Museum Management and Curatorship*, **5**, (1986) pp. 241–151 by the same author. 'Museums of science and technology', a special issue of *Museum*, (**38**(2), (1984) 67–136).

Gregory, R.L. (1986), *Hands-on Science: an Introduction to the Bristol Exploratory* (with contributions by J. Dalgety and F. Evans), Duckworth, London. Pizzey, S. (1987), *Interactive Science and Technology Centres*, Science Projects Publishing, London. Elliott, M. (Ed.). The first part of the volume contains brief descriptions of the various centres by their creators: Oppenheimer, F., The Exploratorium, San Francisco, 1969; Wilson, A., Launch Pad, Science Museum, London, 1986; Sudbury, P.V., Technology Testbed, Liverpool, 1986; Miles, R.S., Human Biology Gallery, British Museum (Natural History), 1977; Leto, G.K. and Chiaverina, C.J., The Science Place, Woodland School, Carpentersville, Illinois, 1981; Thomas, Gillian, The Inventorium, Paris, 1986; Carter, S., The Micrarium, Buxton, 1981; Gleason, K., Museum of Scientific Discovery, Harrisburg, Pennsylvania, 1982; Gere, M., Questacon, Canberra, Australia, 1980; Gregory, R.L., The Exploratory, Bristol, 1987; Beetlestone, J., Techniquest, Cardiff, 1986; Mueller, G., Phaenomena, Zurich and Rotterdam, 1984–1985.

The diversity of the meaning of 'science' as used in the titles of science and technology museums throughout the world prior to the development of the hands-on movement, is discussed by W.T. O'Dea in 'Science museums and education' (*Museum*, **8**, (1955), pp. 242–245).

Earlier volumes on science museums include: Greenaway, F. (1962), *Science Museums in Developing Countries* (additional chapters by Torsten Althin, W.T. O'Dea and W.S. Thomas), ICOM, Paris. Lee, B-H. (1970), *A Study of Science Museums with Special Reference to their Educational Programs*, Office of Museum Programs, Smithsonian Institution, Washington DC.

Related papers arranged in chronological order include the following:

'More than buttons, buzzers and bells', by J. Whitman (*Museum News*, **51**(1), (1978) pp. 43–50) – excerpts from interviews with selected museum directors: four from science museums and one from a children's museum with innovative science education exhibits.

'Participatory exhibits: is fun educational?', by Pam Gillies and Anthony Wilson (*Museums Journal*, **82**(3), (1982) pp. 131–134) – based on an evaluative report of an eleven-day visit by the Ontario Science Circus to the Science Museum, South Kensington.

'Exploration and culture', by K. Starr (*Museum News*, **61**, Nov./Dec. 1982 pp. 36–45) – which contains the response to the American Association of Museums' 'Distinguished Service to Museums Award' 1982 by the physicist Frank Oppenheimer. The recipient (founder of the Exploratorium at San Francisco), whose name has become synonymous with the early 'hands-on' or 'participatory' exhibits, considers museum learning and museums as places of ideas.

'Scientific literacy and informal learning', by A.M. Lucas (*Studies in Science Education*, **10**, (1983) pp. 1–36) – a review of work in these fields in museums and science centres.

'Development of scientific concepts through the use of interactive exhibits in a museum', by E. Fehrer and K. Rice (*Curator*, **28**(1), (1985) pp. 35–46) – which provides a useful key to the various categories of studying the learning process in museums – naturalistic, ethnological, etc.

'Showplace, playground or forum. Choice point for science museums', by Alice Carnes (*Museum News*, **64**(4), (1986), pp. 29–35) – which includes an analysis of the mission statements for 66 museums on the mailing list of the Association of Science Technology Centers.

'The museum as a teacher of theory: a case history of the Exploratorium [San Francisco], by Hilde Hein (*Museum Studies Journal*, **2**(4), (1987), pp. 30–40). The 'vision section' of the Exploratorium embodies and systematically expands a particular perceptual theory, essentially that explained in Gregory, R. (1970), *The Intelligent Eye*, Weidenfeld & Nicolson, London, [World University series]; reprinted 1971; McGraw Hill, New York, 1978.

The Exploratorium of San Francisco twenty years later, by V.J. Danilov (*Museum*, **41**(3), (1989), pp. 155–159).

Papers on science and technology are now widely distributed throughout the general museological and educational journals and in the more specialized serials dealing with science in education, e.g. *Journal of Research in Science Teaching* (John Wiley, London, 1963–), *International Journal of Science Education* (initially *European Journal of Science Education* (1979–1987), Taylor and Francis, London, 1988–), *School Science Review* (Association of Science Education, London 1919–), *Studies in Science Education* (Centre for Studies in Science Education, University of Leeds, 1974–) and *Science and Children* (National Science Teachers Association, Washington, DC). See also: *Teaching at a Distance* (Open University Press, Milton Keynes, 1974–).

History

The American Association for State and Local History (AASLH) – established in 1940 – which has been described as the papacy of historical organizations in the USA, issues a number of volumes of relevance to museum education as well as publishing the journal *History News* (1940–). Examples of the publications include:

Anderson, J. (1985), *Time Machines: the World of Living History*, the first book to examine comprehensively the living history movement. It is divided into three parts: (1) the living history museums, (2) living history as a research technique, (3) the recreational uses of living history. Two companion volumes by the same author are, *The Living History Sourcebook* (1985) which provides annotated lists and descriptions of items and events in the living history movement, and *A Living History Reader* (1988), a collection of over 50 essays representing both wings of the movement – re-enactment and outdoor museums.

Schlereth, T.J. (Ed.), (1982), *Material Culture Studies in America*, a selection of 23 papers compiled and edited, with introductions and bibliography, by the editor. The work is designed as an introductory Baedeker guide to the classics of the field and to contemporary research. In the main introductory essay the author attempts a synoptic historical overview of material culture studies and he defines and discusses nine different analytical approaches to the study of material culture currently in vogue – namely, the art history paradigm, the symbolist perspective, the cultural history orientation, the environmentalist pre-occupation, the functionalist rationale, the structuralist view, the behaviouralistic concept, the national character focus and the social history paradigm. A complementary volume by the same author (*Artifacts and the American Past*, 1980) is a collection of ten essays in which Schlereth probes 'learning environments' and 'enquiry pedagogy'.

Other separate publications by other publishers on historical themes are:

Department of Education and Science (1985), *History in the Primary and Secondary Years: an HMI view*, HMSO.

Lowenthal, D. (1985), *The Past is a Foreign Country*, Cambridge University Press, Cambridge – in the third part of which the author discusses the deliberate or unconscious altering of relics, not least by displaying or restoring them and the creation of additional relics. The extensive bibliography has a citation index.

Nichols, S.K. (Ed.), (1982), *Working Papers: Historians – Artifacts – Learners*, Smithsonian Institution, – presenting discussions of the theories and methodologies of teaching history using the evidence of material culture.

Kavanagh, G. (1990), *History Curatorship*, Leicester University Press. The chapter on 'Meaning, learning and education' contains sections on 'History museums and children', 'History museum education and adults' and 'Museums and messages'.

The introductory article in the special feature of the *Museums Journal* on the 'GCSE and Museums' (**87**(1), (1987), pp. 3–43) includes an Appendix on 'The national criteria: history' and another listing the GCSE history syllabuses by topic. These include the various historical periods and countries plus Transport, Agriculture, Political Reform and Policies, Population, the Poor, Welfare and Medicine, Education, Religion, Crime, Women, etc. Other journal articles include: Schlereth, T.J. (1978), 'It wasn't that simple', *Museum News*, **56**(3), pp. 36–44; Fertig, B. (1982), 'Historians, artifacts, learners: the history museum as educator', *Museum News*, **60**(6), pp. 57–61; Fry, H. (1987), 'Worksheets as museum learning devices', *Museums Journal*, **86**(4), pp. 219–225 – which contains a helpful bibliography; and Rivard, P. (1988), 'Made in Maine. A case study in history museum exhibit development', *International Journal of Museum Management and Curatorship*, **7**, pp. 327–351. An additional 30 papers in the Historical Association's journal *Teaching History* are cited in the GEM Bibliography (Bosdêt, M. and Durbin, G. 1989). See also the *Journal of the Social History Curators Group* (SHCG) – initially the Group for Regional Studies in Museums (GRSM).

Among the papers dealing with the problem of 'time' the following are noted: Lovell, K. and Slater, A. (1960), 'The growth of the concept of time', *Journal of Child Psychology and Psychiatry*, **1**, pp. 179–190; Jahoda, G. (1963), 'Children's concepts of time and history', *Educational Review*, **15**, pp. 87–104; Levin, I. (1977), 'The development of time concepts in young children: reasoning about duration', *Child Development*, **48**(2), pp. 435–444; and Vukelich, R. (1984), 'Time language for interpreting history collections to children', *Museum Studies Journal*, **1**(4), pp. 43–50. The last mentioned paper includes sections on: 'How and when do children acquire time concepts?'; 'How do children learn clock, calendar and historical time?'; 'Using time concepts in the museum'; and a table which summarizes 'age-related time findings' and provides bibliographic details of the relevant papers.

Archaeology

Education through archaeology has benefited greatly from the various publications of the Council for British Archaeology (CBA). For example:

Corbishley, M. (Ed.), (1983), *Archaeological Resources Handbook for Teachers*, second edition, replacing the previous handbook (1979), containing sections on 'books' (classified bibliographies), 'examinations' and 'museums' (including an inventory of museum education services).

Cracknell, S. and Corbishley, M. (Eds.), (1986), *Presenting Archaeology to Young People*, CBA Research Report No. 64, which contains chapters on, for example, 'the use of video', an 'educational computer package' and 'experimental archaeology' as well as one on 'The Schools Committee of the CBA, established in 1975'.

In addition, the Council issues a quarterly *Education Bulletin* (which was initiated as a *Bulletin of Archaeology in Schools* – 1977–1985, vols. 1–15). The first issue of the new *Bulletin* (1986) contains a report from the CBA's Adult Education Committee; the third (1987) is devoted to the theme of the educational role of the regional archaeology units and that of museums and the GCSE; and the sixth (1989) contains selected papers from a conference on 'Archaeology and education'. The Council also issues three series of booklets aimed at teachers. The first (1983) includes *Archaeology in the Primary School* and *Archaeology in the Classroom*; the second (1986) includes *Archaeology and Computers* and *The Archaeology of Death*; the third (of practical handbooks) includes *British Archaeology: an Introductory Booklist* (Dyer, J. (Ed), 1987),

Other references include: Pearce, S.M. (1990), *Archaeological Curatorship*, Leicester University Press – the third part of which is devoted to 'Museums, the public and the past', with chapters on 'Exhibiting archaeology' (pp. 143–169) and 'Reaching out into the community' (pp. 181–197), the latter containing a section on 'Archaeology, education and museums'; and Dyer, J. (1983), *Teaching Archaeology in Schools*, Shire Archaeology Series No. 29, Shire Publications, Market Risborough.

Relevant items in the overlapping field of heritage education are common in *Heritage Interpretation* (Journal of the Society for the Interpretation of Britain's Heritage 1983–; formerly *Interpretation*); *Environmental Education* (Journal of the National Association for Environmental Education 1974–); *Journal of Interpretation* (Association of Interpretative Naturalists, Maryland, USA 1976–); and *Remnants: Journal of the English Heritage Education Service* (1987–, Oxford).

English Heritage (Historic Buildings and Monuments Commission for England) also publishes a series of 'Teacher's Handbooks' (e.g. Totnes Castle, 1988) which have inventories of Further Reading for adults and for children and Teacher's Resource Books (e.g. Carisbrook Castle, 1988), as well as being responsible for commissioning from the Centre for Environmental Interpretation at Manchester Polytechnic the much more elaborate *Visitors Welcome: a Manual on the Presentation and Interpretation of Archaeological Excavations* (Binks, G., Dyke, J. and Dagnall, P.) HMSO, 1988. The *Manual* is a step-by-step guide to planning and setting up interpretation for visitors to excavations.

The English Heritage Education Service issues a booklet (*Information for Teachers*, 1989) which describess the Service and provides an overview of the kinds of visits and classroom activities which could be related to some historic sites. A complete list of the sites in the care of English Heritage is given as are the details of booking and support materials for school visits.

A little less than half of the Heritage Education Trust's *Heritage Education Handbook* (M. Dyer (Ed.), 1983) is concerned directly with heritage education (with chapters explaining the work of the Heritage Education Group (Lord Briggs, pp. 17–23) and Heritage Education Trust (M. Dyer, pp. 25–37); the remainder includes a section of brief descriptions on 'Heritage organizations' (pp. 181–193) and another on 'Art organizations and education' (pp. 195–203).

The *Selection of Papers on Heritage Presentation and Interpretation Given at the First World Congress* (Heritage Interpretation International and Alberta Cultural & Multiculturalism, 1988) includes a section of seven papers 'On education and the young' and another of three papers 'On training and evaluation'. The transactions of the Second World Congress (Uzzell, D.L. (Ed.), *Heritage Interpretation*, two vols., Belhaven Press, are described in the chronological section of this chapter.

Three chapters in Lumley, R. (Ed.), (1988), *The Museum Time-machine. Putting Cultures on Display*, Routledge, London and New York, are also relevant. They are (1) Hoyau, P., Heritage and 'the conserver society': the French case (pp. 27–35), which examines the process whereby the definition of heritage has been expanded; (2) West, P. The making of the English working past: a critical view of the Ironbridge Gorge Museum (pp. 36–62) (a shortened and emended version of 'Danger! History at work: a critical consumer's guide to the Ironbridge Gorge Museum', Occasional Paper, Centre for Contemporary Cultural Studies, University of Birmingham, 1985); (3) Bennett, T., Museums and 'the people' (pp. 63–85), a comparison of three history museums – North of England Open Air Museum, Beamish, County Durham; Hyde Park Barracks, Sydney, Australia; and People's Palace, Glasgow.

Ethnography and anthropology

The overlapping of many of the disciplines grouped as humanities is clear when viewed from the perspective of material culture. T.J. Schlereth, in his *Material Culture Studies in America* (American Association for State and Local History 1982), describes work in the field as including 'archaeology, anthropology, art history, cultural geography, history of technology and folklife studies' (p. 4). The diversity of the uses of ethnographic collections is reflected in Elizabeth Goodhew's contribution to the special feature on the 'GCE and museums' in the *Museums Journal* (**87**(1), (1987), pp. 21–23). Museums with such collections may usefully offer help and guidance to schools studying syllabuses such as religious studies, textiles, food, family and home, sociology, history, etc.

The anthology *Folklife and Museums: Selected Readings* (Hall, P. and Seeman, C. (Eds.), 1987, American Association for State and Local History, Nashville, Tennessee), one of the first American volumes to explore the collaboration between folklorists, historians and museologists, contains an article on 'Connecting the past with the present: reflections upon interpretation in folklife museums' (W.B. Moore), another on 'Presenting the live folk artist in the museum' (C. Seeman) and a selected bibliography compiled by the editors.

Other appropriate studies are: van Wengen, G. (1968), 'The development of educational methods in an ethnological museum', pp. 233–234 in *Role of Museums in Education and Cultural Action* ICOM; Anon (1985), 'Images of the ecomuseum', *Museum*, **37**(4), pp. 182–244; Frese, H. (1960), *Anthropology and the Public: and Role of Museums*, Brill, E.J., Leiden, *Mededlingen van Het Rijksmuseum voor Volker-Kunde*, No. 14; and two books by A.P. Sebolt, both issued by Old Sturbridge Village, Mass. – *A Guide for the Development of a Curriculum Model* (1980) and *Building Collaborative Programs: Museums and Schools* (1980); Ames, M. (1986), *Museums, the Public and Anthropology. A Study of the Anthropology of Anthropology*, University of British Columbia, Vancouver, BC.; and Melins, H. (1972). The Nordiska Museet in education. *Fataburen*, 1972, pp. 153–176.

The professional anthropologist (and 'closet folk-lorist') James Deetz in 'The link from object to person to concept' (pp. 24–34 in Collins, Z.W. (Ed), *Museums, Adults and the Humanities*, American Association of Museums, 1981) emphasises that the man-made objects in a museum's collection are expressions of the human experience and human concepts; and cites examples to show these links and the broad, humanistic themes that underly them. He 'concludes': 'If I have any conclusion, it relates to our duty as custodians of that which we, as a species, have stacked on this planet. We must not only preserve it but also find reasonably imaginative and creative ways to share it with other people. That is what the museum business is all about.' (p. 34)

A complementary and more poetic perspective is provided in the works of another American anthropologist and 'sometime fossil collector', Loren Eiseley, particularly in *The Night Country. Reflections of a Bone-hunting Man* (Garnstone Press, London, 1971) and especially in the chapter 'The mind as nature' (pp. 194–224). See also Eiseley's *Notes of an Alchemist* (Charles Scribner & Sons, New York, 1972), a volume of poems which includes the striking 'Arrowhead', 'The figure in the stone' and 'The Hand Ax'.

The Visual Arts

A fundamental distinction exists between the problems of communication in art museums and those in museums of history and natural science. The following quotation from *On Understanding Art Museums* (Lee, S.E. (Ed.), 1975, Prentice Hall, New Jersey for The American Assembly) underlines the fact that the problems in the one are only tangentially applicable to those in the other:

'In a science museum, for example, the laws governing planetary revolutions, the genetic structure of cells, or the development of lower vertebrates may not be self-evident, which is to say visually intelligible, without the support of written texts. For the sake of argument I shall assume that the development of artistic structures is much more, possibly almost wholly intelligible with a minimum of peripheral documentation.

'From this position I deduce a distinction between the kind of knowledge, usually historical, which is supplied by verbal sources and comprehended by the conscious, rational mind, and the kind of knowledge which grows from artistic experience, conveyed through the senses when confronting a work of art as a work of art. Such knowledge, irreducible to verbal formulae and not easily communicated by one individual to another, is largely nonrational; for the work of art may generate emotional responses from the preconscious and unconscious areas of psychic life'. (Hamilton, G.H. pp. 98 and 99).

One of the fullest discussions of this difference is still that in B.I. Gilman's *Museum Ideals of Purpose and Method* (Museum of Fine Arts, Boston, Mass., 1918). See also item in chronological bibliography.

There is a more extensive literature on the use of works of art in education than on any other subject. Among the most regularly quoted works is: Newsom, B.Y. and Silver, A.Z. (Eds.) (1978), *The Art Museum as Educator. A Collection of Studies as Guides to Practice and Policy*, published for the Council on Museums and Education in the Visual Arts by the University of California Press, Berkeley. This is almost certainly the most comprehensive production of its kind. It provides not only a rationale of the work but a detailed account of every institution in the USA offering facilities. The book contains conclusions, judgements and statistical evaluations. It contains two short preliminary articles on: 'Issues in art museum education: a brief history' and 'Art museums and education'; and major sections on: the art museum and its general public; the art museum and the young, their teachers and their schools; and, the art museum and its college, university, and professional audience. The sections contain chapters on; teachers' training and classroom material; the artist and the museum; training for museum education; and, cooperation among museum professionals. There is a bibliography for each chapter.

In addition to the art museums and art galleries included, there are descriptions of the Discovery Room at the National Museum of Natural History (Washington), the 'Anticostia Neighborhood Museum' and the Exploratorium, San Francisco. Two expansive Appendices contain basic information about the institutions surveyed in the study.

The role of education in art museums was given considerable prominence with the appearance in 1986 of the controversial volume: *The Uncertain Profession: Observations on the State of Museum Education in Twenty American Art Museums* by E.W. Eisner and S.M. Dobbs. The aim of the study (published by the Paul Getty Center for Education in the Arts, Los Angeles) was to identify needs in museum education that, if met, would enhance the effectiveness of the service. The study involved interviewing both the Director and the person in charge of education at each of the institutions. A summary of the study's findings and recommendations is given by the authors in *Museum News*, **65**(2), (1986), pp. 42–49 and an extract from the volume ('The mission of museum education') in *Museum Studies Journal*, **2**(3), (1986), pp. 10–15.

The strong reactions to the methods and the findings of the study are expressed in, for example, a long review article by Terry Zeller (*Museum News*, **65**(3), (1987), pp. 17–28) and 'On the ethics of museum education' by Danielle Rice, which summarises the reactions of a group of museum directors (*Museum News*, **65**(5), (1987), pp. 13–19). The authors respond in *Museum News*, **65**(5), (1987), pp. 5–10. Zeller's commentary (which contains a comprehensive bibliography) is an excellent example of constructive criticism applied to one publication.

The GEM Bibliography (Bosdêt, M. and Durbin, G., 1989) contains 62 items in the section on Art, including items from six specialist art journals – *Art Education* (National Art Education Association, USA, 1948–), *Art Journal* (College Art Association of America, New York, 1941–), *Arts Council of Great Britain Education Bulletin* (ACGB, London, 1979–), *Bullet* (Art Galleries Association, 1976–), *Oxford Art Journal* (Oxford University Press, 1978–) and, particularly, *Journal of Art and Design Education* (National Society for Art Education, 1982–).

Special Issues of *The Journal of Aesthetic Education* (University of Illinois) include: 'The International Society for Education through Art (INSEA)' (April 1978); 'INSEA 1981 – art, ideology, and aesthetic education' (April 1981); 'Defining cultural and educational relations – an international perspective' (Summer 1984); 'Art museums and education' (Summer 1985).

Works concerned with basic problems in the teaching of art include: (1) Judson, B. (1987), 'Teaching aesthetics and art criticism to school children in an art museum', *Museum Studies Journal*, **2**(4), pp. 50–58. The author takes a statement in John Dewey's *Art as Experience* (Capricorn Books, C.P. Putnam, New York, 1958) as a starting point and draws on a number of the background papers prepared for the 46th American Assembly (on *Art Museums in America*, Arden House, November 1974) published as Lee, S.E. (Ed) *On Understanding Art Museums*, The American Assembly, Columbia University, Prentice-Hall, Inc., Englewood Cliffs, New Jersey. (2) Gombrich, E.H. (1960), *Art and Illusion. A Study in the Psychology of Pictorial Representation*, [The A.W. Mellon Lectures in the Fine Arts, 1956 ('The visible world and the language of art'), National Gallery of Art, Washington, D.C.], Pantheon Books, New York and Phaidon Press, London; Fifth edition, 1977; third impression, 1983. (3) Gombrich, E.H. (1979), *The Sense of Order. A Study in the Psychology of Decorative Art* [The Wrightman Lectures delivered under the auspices of the New York Institute of Fine Arts], Phaidon Press, London.

Three other volumes of wider scope are: (1) *Art Perception and Reality*, by E.H. Gombrich, J. Hochberg and M. Black (John Hopkins University Press, Baltimore, 1972; paperback, 1973). The book consists of three essays, all concerned with the problem of understanding pictures. The problem is viewed from different stances – those of a philosopher (Black), a psychologist (Hochberg) and an art historian-cum-psychologist (Gombrich). (2) *Illusion in Nature and Art* (Duckworth, London 1973), edited by the neuro–psychologist R.L. Gregory and E.H. Gombrich, with contributions by the psychologist Colin Blakemore, the zoologist H.E. Hinton, the psychologist Jan B. Deregowski and the President of the Institute of Contemporary Arts, Roland Penrose. (3) *Art and Visual Perception: a Psychology of the Creative Eye*, by R. Arnheim (Faber, London, 1956. Expanded and revised edition, University of California Press, Berkeley, 1974) intended for the general reader but of interest to the educator because of its practical consequences for the function of art in education and, more broadly, for visual training in all fields of learning. Arnheim deals with the visual image from the point of view of Gestalt psychology.

Other perspectives

Clearly there are a number of other perspectives from which to consider education in museums. The main perspectives adopted in the GEM Bibliography (Bosdêt, M. and Durbin, G. 1989) have already been listed in the chronological bibliography. Each perspective is further subdivided. For example, 'Serving the Community' is divided into: pre-school children (seven items), school children (general/ examinations/safety and administration of visits – 99 items), families (22 items), adults (27 items), multicultural education (33 items), special educational needs (43 items) and training teachers (26 items). The section 'Using and developing museum resources' is divided into: working with objects (65 items), learning from objects and visits (36 items), drama, role play and living history (55 items), educational materials (24 items), exhibits (17 times), volunteers and docents (20 items).

In a selective guide of the kind presented here, developing each of these approaches is not possible. It is, however, appropriate to consider one theme which is not specifically considered in the GEM Bibliography (Bosdêt, M. and Durbin, G. 1989).

Graphicacy

Some psychologists (see Guildford, J.P., 'Three faces of intellect', *American Psychologist*, **14**, (1959), p. 459) have claimed that there can be as many as 120 different aspects of intelligence, but whatever the number, the range may be grouped into four basic types which are also four basic modes of communication between human beings. The names for three of these are well-known – 'literacy', to describe communication by means of written language; 'articulacy' (or 'oracy'), to describe facility with spoken language; and 'numeracy', to describe communication through (by means of) mathematical symbols (universally adopted to describe competence with numbers). There is, however, a need for a word which describes the communication of spatial relationships. The geographers W.G. Balchin and Alice M. Coleman (*Times Educational Supplement*, 11 May 1965) have suggested the term 'graphicacy' for the fourth group.

The term appears to have gained favour when it was used by Professor Balchin as the title of his presidential address to the Geographical Association in 1971 ('Graphicacy', *Geography*, **57**, (1972) pp. 185–195) and when he defined it as 'the communication of spatial information that cannot be conveyed adequately by verbal or numercial means' (using the word 'verbal' as meaning the written as distinct from the spoken word). He was later to argue (*Times*, 19 April 1977) that the Three R's should be replaced in schools by the Four Aces (using 'ace' as short for 'acies') – i.e. literacy, oracy, numeracy and graphicacy.

In 1983 David Boardman (*Graphicacy and Geography Teaching*, Croom Helm, London, repr. 1986) analysed the theoretical underpinning of the concept by using the stages of intellectual development identified in children by Jean Piaget and his associates. He also outlined some of the studies undertaken into the problems that people encounter

in reading and using maps and photographs, and discussed methods of teaching the essential concepts and skills of graphicacy to primary, secondary and advanced level children. Finally, he demonstrated the use of the computer and microcomputer in teaching the elements of visual language by drawing on such examples as those in the Schools Council's *Computers in the Curriculum: Geography* (Longman Resources Unit, 1979). See also Macfarlane-Smith, I. (1964), *Spatial Ability: its Educational and Social Significance*, University of London Press. An appendix provides tentative suggestions regarding 'the approximate ages by which children of average ability should normally be capable of acquiring various skills of graphicacy'.

The material in Boardman's book is, therefore, of relevance to any discipline concerned with understanding, representing and interpreting spatial information – with landscape drawing, ground photographs, air photographs, maps, plans and diagrams as well as with most aspects of field work.

General works on education and psychology

The best inventories of the general works on the theory and practice of education and psychology, in the books and papers cited in this bibliographic guide, are the following – arranged in chronological order:

Rath, F.L. Jr. and O'Connell, M.R. (Eds.) (1978), *Interpretation* (compiled by R.S. Reese), American Association of State and Local History, Nashville, Tennessee – particularly in the sub-section on 'Education theory' (24 items) with annotations.

Collins, Z.W. (Ed.), (1981), *Museums, Adults and the Humanities: a Guide for Educational Programming*, American Association of Museums, Washington, DC – particularly in the references to the two chapters by M.S. Knowles (pp. 60 and 143) and the one by A. Sebolt (p. 312).

Miles, R.S., Alt, M.B., Gosling, D.C., Lewis, B.N. and Tout, A.F. (1982), *The Design of Educational Exhibits*, British Musum (Natural History) and George Allen & Unwin, London second edition 1988 – particularly in the chapter 'Psychological and educational aspects of exhibition design' by B.N. Lewis.

Screven, C.G. (1984), 'Educational evaluation and research in museums and public exhibits: a bibliography' (*Curator*, **27**(2), pp. 147–165). The second part of the bibliography (73 items, published mainly between the late 1960s and 1984), dealing with studies originating outside the field of evaluation (psychology, communication and education, for example), is divided into three: (1) Learning and the design of instruction; (2) Testing, measurement and evaluation; (3) Research studies. References recommended as non–technical starting points for beginners are starred.

Gregory, R.L. (1989), (Keynote Address) 'Turning minds on to science by hands–on exploration: the nature and potential of the hands–on medium' (pp. 1–9 in Quin, M. (Ed), *Issues in the Development of Interactive Science and Technology Centres*, Nuffield Foundation for COPUS, London).

Nangeroni, S., Vukelich, R. and Vukelich, C. (1986), 'The use of learning style theory to design a co-operative school-museum program for gifted students', *Museum Studies Journal* 2(3), pp. 46–56, four tables.

Another major source is R.L. Gregory's *Mind in Science. A History of Explanations in Psychology and Physics* (Weidenfeld and Nicolson, London and Vail–Ballou Press Inc., New York, 1981), which relates theories of knowledge to theories and experiments on perception and learning.

Details of the established educational studies of the Americans J.S. Bruner, George Dennison and John Holt, as well as of the many official reports on education published in this country in the 1960s and 1970s, are given in the first edition of this chapter (1984).

Useful contemporary works of reference include: *British Education Index* (BEI) (three parts annually with annual cumulations) – established in 1954 to record bibliographic references to significant articles in educational periodical literature. Formerly produced by the Librarians of Institutes and Schools of Education (1954–1971) and the British National Bibliography and the British Library (1972–1985), the index was moved to the Brotherton Library, University of Leeds, in 1985 and the publication redesigned in 1986. Over 280 (chiefly British) journals are scanned and all significant articles indexed.

British Education Theses Index (BETI) – a subject and author index to theses accepted since 1950 on all aspects of education which have been listed in Aslib's *Index to Theses accepted for Higher Degrees by the Universities of Great Britain and Ireland and the Council for National Academic Awards*. It is produced by the Librarians of Institutes and Schools of Education (LISE) and is available in two microfiche sets: *BETI Cumulation 4*, 1950–1983; and *BETI New Series*, No. 1, 1983–1987.

British Education Thesaurus (BET) (Marder, J.V. Ed) produced for the first time in 1988 at the Brotherton Library (Leeds University Press).

Fuller descriptions of these three sources of information are given in *British Sources of Information on Education. A Brief Guide to: British Education Index*,

British Education Thesaurus, British Education Theses Index, British Education Index, University of Leeds (Brotherton Library), Leeds, 1990. See also: Marder, J.V. (1989), 'The development of the British Education Thesaurus: a personal account', *Education Libraries Journal*, **32**(1), pp. 2–8; and Johnson, J.R.V., Marder, J.V. and Sheffield, P.W. (1990), 'Educational research and educational practice: bridging the gap', *Journal of Education for Teaching*, **16**(1), pp. 83–89 – which describes the aims of the new British education data base as it has been developed under the auspices of the University of Leeds.

Notes

1. See also: Horsfall, T. C. (1892), 'The Manchester Art Museum' (Manchester 1892, pp. 51–65) – a description of the loan service of the elementary schools in Manchester.

2. Jonathan Hutchinson was the founder of a 'strongly individualistic' educational museum at Haslemere in 1895. The story is told by the first curator in Swanton, E.W. (1974), *A Country Museum. The Rise and Progress of Sir Jonathan Hutchinson's Educational Museum at Haslemere*, Educational Museum, Haslemere. See also Hutchinson, M. and Jewell, A. L. (1973) 'The museum that started in a barn', *Natural Science in Schools. Journal of the Natural Science Society*, **11**(1), pp. 12–15.

3. Other examples include: Hoyle, W. E. (1903), 'The use of museums in teaching' (2, pp. 229–239); Crowther, H. (1905), 'The museum as a teacher of nature–study' (**5**(1), pp. 5–14); Plunkett, G. T. (1906), 'Dublin museum: the circulation branch' (**5**(10), pp. 317–331); Bolton, H. (1908), 'Museums of elementary and higher grade schools' (**7**(9), pp. 299–302). In his Presidental Address in 1903 ('Functions of museums', **3**(3) pp. 71–94), F. A. Bather recognized three main museum functions – those of 'Investigation, Instruction and Inspiration' which he considered appealed respectively to the Specialist, the Student, and the 'Man in the Street'. See also: Gilman, B. I. ('On the distinctive purpose of museums of art', **3**(7), (1904), pp. 213–224) who questions 'the right. . . to conceive and manage a public treasury of art as if primarily an agency of popular instruction'.

4. The quotation is from Bloom, J. N. and Powell, E. A. (1984), *Museums for a New Century*, American Association of Museums, Washington DC. pp. 121 and 122. The books are considered in: Grove, R. (1978), 'Pioneers in American museums: John Cotton Dana', *Museum News*, **56**, pp. 32–39 and 86–88; Cushman, Karen (1985), 'Four books by John Cotton Dana', *Museum Studies Journal* [Masterworks Series], **1**(5), pp. 49–52; and the chapter on Dana in Alexander, E. P. (1983), *Museum Masters. Their Museums and their Influences*, American Association for State and Local History, Nashville, Tennessee, pp. 377–411.

5. The quotation is from Bloom, J. N. and Powell, E. A. (1984), *Museums for a New Century*, American Association of Museums, Washington DC. pp. 121 and 122. Benjamin Ives Gilman (p. 47) recognizes three uses of the term education – the loose, the broad and the

narrow. 'In the loose sense education is synonymous with influence, in the broad sense with improvement and in the narrow sense with teaching'. Furthermore (p. 49), 'These three senses. . . do not exhaust the ambiguities of the word "education". Each of the three has a primary and a secondary meaning duly set forth in the dictionary. The primary meaning is that of process; the secondary that of its product.'

6. The Committee was established in 1913, following a discussion on 'Educational use of museums' at the British Association meeting. Its remit and its methods of work were outlined to the Museums Association by the Committee Chairman (Green, J. A., 1915), 'The museums committee of the British Association (Section L)', *Museums Journal*, **14**(11), pp. 341–346) and the results of a joint discussion by the Committee and the Association by Green and others (1915), 'Discussion on museums in relation to education at the London conference, 1915', *Museums Journal*, **15**(4), pp. 129–145. See also: Kavanagh, G. (1988), 'The first world war and its impact for education in British museums', *History of Education*, **17**(2), pp. 163–176. For the reports of the BAAS Committee appointed in 1886 see Report BAAS, Manchester 1887 (John Murray, London, 1888, pp. 97–130) and Report BAAS, Bath, 1888 (John Murray, London, 1889, pp. 124–132) – 'The Committee was reappointed [in 1887] for the purpose of considering the ideal to which provincial museums should endeavour to attain, and of suggesting practical methods for approaching that ideal.' (p. 124).

7. The historical section contains a helpful discussion of the relevant legislation, from the first Act of Parliament in 1845 to the Public Libraries Act of 1919 (the word libraries being understood to include 'museums' and 'art galleries') which repealed the much cited Museums and Gymnasiums Act of 1891. It also contains a section on the equivalent legislation in Scotland. The report was considered in detail at the Museums Association Conference, Glasgow 1928 (*Museums Journal*, **28**(4–8), 1928, pp. 123–128, 153–156, 182–189, 221–225, 247–253) and summarized in a lecture by the compiler ('Museums and education', *Journal of the Royal Society of Arts*, 1929 and *Museums Journal*, **28**(10), 1928, pp. 316–320). See also the Review, by Frank Stevens in *Antiquity*, **3**, (1929), pp. 121–125.

8. See: Mitchell, J. M. (1932), 'The museum policy of the Carnegie Trust', *Museums Journal*, **31**(11), pp. 491–494; and pp. 50–57 in Lewis, G.D. (1989), *For Instruction and Recreation. A Centenary of the Museums Association*, Quiller Press, London.

9. See also: Scottish Education Department (1932), *Museums and Galleries and the Schools*, Circular No. 87, Scottish Education Department, Edinburgh, HMSO.

10. See also: Anon (1942), *Catalogue of Models, Specimens and Illustrations in Schools Service*, Leicester Museum and Art Gallery.

11. Details of the other papers are cited in Shettel, H. H. (1989), 'Evaluation in museums: a short history of a short history', pp. 129–137 in Uzzel, D. L. (Ed), *Heritage Interpretation*, vol. 2, *The Visitor Experience*, Belhaven Press, The 1936 report and Melton, A. W. (1935), *Problems of Installation in Museums of Art* (N.S.14) are reprinted as the inaugural issues of the AAM's Museum Classics series (1988).

12. The main museums studied were: the American Museum of Natural History, Brooklyn Museum, Metropolitan Museum of Art, Museum of the City of New York, Whitney Museum of American Art – all in New York.

13. The quotation is from Alexander, E. P. (1983), *Museum Masters*, American Museum for State and Local History, Nashville, Tennessee, pp. 377–411. See also: Rea, P. (1932), *The Museum and the Community*, Science Press; Kent, H.W. (1949), *What I am Pleased to Call my Education*, Grolier Club, New York, and Dobbs, S. M. (1971), 'Dana and Kent and early museum education', *Museum News*, **50**(2), pp. 38–41.

14. See also: Anon. (1949), *Museum Service*, Derbyshire Education Committee, Derby, and Good, P. (1987) *Fifty Years on. A Museum Loan Service 1936–1986*, Derbyshire Museum Service, Derbyshire County Council.

15. The review was specifically in response to Washburn, W.E. (1961), 'Scholarship and the Museum', *Museum News*, **40**(2), pp. 16–19. Twenty years later Karen Cushman reassesses the work in the 'Masterworks' section of *Museums Studies Journal*, **2**(1), (1985), pp. 60–62. See also Low, T. L. (1948), *The Educational Philosophy and Practice of Art Museums in the United States*, Columbia University, Teachers College, New York, (Contributions to Education No. 942.)

16. The volume is reviewed by Wallis, F. S. (1950), *The Journal of Education*, **82**(no. 970), pp. 280 and 281.

17. The author also describes the new educational methods in use in the museum in: *School Nature Study Journal* (October 1949, pp. 50 and 51); *National Froebel Foundation Bulletin* (No. 52, 1948, pp. 1–4); and *Museum* (**1**(3,4), 1948, pp. 188–192). See also: *Introducing the Educational Work of the Geffrye Museum*, London County Council, 1964.

18. See also: (1) Floud, P. (1952), 'Changing fashions in museum teaching', *Museums Journal*, **52**(9), pp. 215–224. The author was 'astonished' to find that the files of the Journal were so 'full of enthusiastic accounts of educational work and experiments carried out in museums, going back to well before the first World War. The sobering fact is that so many of these enthusiastic beginnings came to nothing and that so much excellent work was done and then entirely forgotten' (p. 215). The main concern of the paper is to emphasise the principles of museum education and to make a plea for further consideration of the aim and purpose of museum teaching. (2) ICOM Committee for Education (1956), *Museums and Teachers*, ICOM, Paris – an account of some of the ways in which the problems of education and museums are being approached, based on material supplied by 25 contributors

19. The first report is introduced by D. A. Allan and appraised by Ralph Lewis; the second by Grace L. McCann Morley, with some reflections of the seminar by Molly Harrison. See also: UNESCO (1954), *International Seminar on the Role of Museums in Education, 14 September – 12 October 1952, Brooklyn, New York, USA. Report by Douglas A. Allan, Director of the Seminar*, UNESCO, Paris.

20. See also: Edwards, Vesta (1969), 'Twenty years' service to schools [throughout Wales]', *Amgueddfa, Bulletin of the National Museum of Wales*, **2**, pp. 27–35, Illus., and,

for an assessment of the problems of the late 1970s, Bassett, D. A. (1980), *The Museum Schools Service: a Discussion Paper*, National Museum of Wales, Cardiff. (Cyclostyled).

21. See also: Winstanley, B. R. (1959), *School-loan Services*, Handbook for Museum Curators, Museums Association, London: and Museums Association Information Sheet No. 1, *Museum Education Services* (1969), 2nd ed. 1973.

22. The Report also contains a brief history of the Service which 'is as old as the Victoria and Albert Museum itself and was inherited with the collections of the Government School of Design, which had been circulating objects of art through the provincial schools of design in the eighteen forties'. The background to the demise of the Service in 1977 is given in the V & A's *Review of the Years 1974–1978*, (1981).

23. See also: Alt, M. B. (1977), 'Evaluating didactic exhibits: a critical look at Shettel's work', *Curator*, **20**(3), pp. 241–258 and the response, **21**(4), (1978), pp. 329–345. Shettel was later to state that 'perhaps the philosophical objections to evaluation reached their apogee' in Alt's paper ('Evaluation in museums: a short history of a short history', pp. 129–147 in Uzzel, D. (Ed) (1989), *Heritage Interpretation*, Vol. 2, Belhaven Press).

24. The later report (*Report on University Museums*, HMSO, 1977), is concerned solely with those university museums open to the public with collections which, in terms of scope, quality and size, transcend the needs of departmental teaching collections.

25. The quotation is from a letter from P. Lengrand (Head of the UNESCO Division for Adult Education) included as Appendix F, pp. 72–75.

26. See also: the published report of the second conference, University of Leicester (1969), *Countryside Centres 1969 Conference Report*, Departments of Adult Education and Museum Studies, University of Leicester; Walden, T. W. (1965), 'Museums and field studies', in *The Countryside in 1970, Second Conference*, Keele; Stansfield, G. (1967), 'Museums and the countryside', *Museums Journal*, **67**(3), pp. 212–218, which considers the involvement of museums in the growing interest in the study, use and conservation of the countryside and with particular reference to the preliminary meetings of the 'Countryside in 1970 Conference'; and Smythe, J. E. (1966), *The Educational Role of Museums and Field Centres in England 1884–1966*, Unpublished PhD Thesis, University of Sheffield.
The work and outline history of the Department of Museum Studies, established at Leicester in 1966, is described by its Director, G. D. Lewis, in, 'The training of museum personnel in the United Kingdom (*Museums Journal*, **83**(1), (1983) pp. 65–70) and 'Museum, profession and university: museum studies at Leicester' (*Museum*, **39**(4), (1987), pp. 255–258). For the significance of the 1964 Act, see Edwards, J. (1965), 'Local authority museums and the Public Libraries and Museums Act, 1964', *Museums Journal*, **65**(1), pp. 6–11.

27. See also: pp. 78 and 82 in Hudson, K. (1977), *Museums for the 1980s. A Survey of World Trends*, Macmillan/UNESCO, London.

28. See also: Taylor, W. W. (1971), 'Museums and education [in the United Kingdom]', *Museum*, **23**(2), 1970–71, pp. 125–128 (bilingual) – a review of seven representative museum schools services at a time when 'there is a ferment of activity at all levels and at all ages on the educational scene'. The author was HMI for Schools, with special responsibiltiy for education in museums.

29. The AAM (founded in 1906) is, like its British equivalent, committed to furthering education in museums. Since 1973 this has been done largely by the Standing Professional Committee on Education which represents the concerns of salaried and volunteer personnel in the field of museum education. See: Madden, Joan (1976), 'The AAM Education Committee: who, what, when, where, why?', *Roundtable Reports*, January 1976, 1–4. The 1971 report followed the passing of the '*Environmental Education Act*' in 1970 which, for the first time, specifically included United States museums as educational institutions eligible to secure grants for providing educational services on a community level on the subjects of environmental pollution.

30. See also: European Committee for the Conservation of Nature and Natural Resources [Aldridge, D., Epler, G. and Wals, H.] (1976), *Environmental Awareness. A Survey of Types of Facilities used for Environmental Education and Interpretation*, Council of Europe, Strasbourg – which considers 12 types of facility, ranging from Zoological Gardens to Museums.

31. See also: Museums Association Report No. 2, *Local Government Reorganization*, 1972.

32. The quotation is from Bergmann, E. (1977), 'Making exhibitions: a reference file', *Curator*, **20**(3), pp. 227–237. The background to the educational work at the Museum is provided in: Dickson, L. (1986), *The Museum Makers. The Story of the Royal Ontario Museum*, Royal Ontario Museum, Toronto; and in papers in the Museum's magazine *Rotunda* (eg Barnett, R. (1982), 'The cluster concept', **15**(2), pp. 24 and 25; Kinoshita, G. (1982), 'Museums are for people. The evolution of a design concept', **15**(2), pp. 18–23.

33. The special issue of *Museum* published for the International Year of the Child ('Museums and Children', **21**(3)) has sections on: 'theoretical aspects' (three papers); 'case studies' (four papers) and 'album' (six papers); and an introduction by Georges Henri Rivière. Publications issued and CECA conferences held during or in association with the Year are cited in *ICOM Education*, No. 9, 1981, pp. 36 and 37.

34. An organized museum education group was established in Britain in 1949. It became the 'Group for Children's Activities in Museums' in 1952, the 'Group for Educational Services in Museums (GESM) in 1967 and 'Group for Education in Museums' (GEM) in 1980. The Group's work is described in the pamphlet *Group for Education in Museums*, issued by the Group (1988) and in short articles in *Safety Education* (P. Divall, 1987, p. 8) and *Teaching History* (S. Winterbotham, **44**, (1986), pp. 24 and 25).

35. The investigation, which arose from the main conclusion drawn in the DES *Education Survey* No. 12 (HMSO, 1971), is based on a survey of two samples: (1) the civic museums and art galleries of Derby, Leicester and Nottingham; and (2) a random sample of adults chosen from these three areas.

36. The term and concept of 'andragogy' was introduced by Knowles to characterize educational methods that relate to adult needs and developmental stages as distinct from pedagogy, the teaching of children – see his *The Modern Practice of Adult Education*, Association Press, New York, 1970, 8th edition 1977. See also: the May/June 1981 issue of *Museum News* (**59**(5), pp. 23–35) which focuses on lifelong learning as a preview to the *Guide*. It includes the text of the chapter on 'Adults as learners' by A. B. Knox (pp. 24–29) and a section 'Resources in lifelong learning'.

37. Comments on the article are given in Hoek, G. van der (1982), 'Thirty years of museum education: some "deflections"', in the same journal (**1**, pp. 374–376).

38. Lewis's thesis is criticised in Hill, M. (1981), 'The museum as an educational facility', *Museums Journal*, **80**,(3), pp. 151–155; and the criticism answered in *Museums Journal*, **81**(1), (1981), pp. 54 and 55.

39. The Committee for Education and Cultural Action (CECA) of ICOM was established in 1965 as successor to the ICOM Committee for Education. It published an information leaflet in 1988 (in three languages) to describe how the Committee works, its activities and its conference themes.

40. The title is: *Environmental Interpretation in Wales. (An Investigation into the Status of, Attitudes Towards, and the Application of Environmental Interpretation in Wales.)*

41. *Museum Education Roundtable* (MER) was founded in Washington in 1969 as the Museum Educator's Roundtable. It changed its name on incorporation in 1971. The organization seeks to improve the educational services of museums through information exchange and all its activities are educational. For a short history see Grove, R. (1978), pp. 662–667 in Newsome, B. Y. and Silver, A. Z. (Eds.), *The Art Museum as Educator, a Collection of Studies as Guides to Practice and Policy*, University of California Press, Berkeley.

42. The major part of the August 1984 issue of *Museum News* (**62**(6), pp. 17–45) is devoted to a preview of the volume, including a copy of its first chapter.

43. The work of five of the leaders in the field of museum evaluation – Minda Borun (Franklin Institute Science Museum), Alan J. Friedman (New York Hall of Science). Roger S. Miles (British Museum (Natural History)), Harris Shettel (Independent Consultant) and Chandler G. Screven (University of Wisconsin) – is compared in Hicks, E. C. (1986), 'An artful science: a conversation about exhibit evaluation' (*Museum News*, **64**(3), pp. 32–39.

44. The Standing Commission on Museums and Galleries, created in 1931, became the Museums & Galleries Commission in 1981 with revised terms of reference and increased responsibilities. See: Drew, A (1981), 'The government and museums', *Museums Journal*, **81**(3) Supplement), pp. 3–5; and Esmé, Countess of Carlisle (1988), *A History of the Commission*. Museums & Galleries Commission, London.

45. Full details of these and other thematic surveys are given in the DES *Library Bibliography*, No. 110, 1988.

46. The Council for Museums and Galleries in Scotland became the Scottish Museums Council in 1985. See: Farnell, G. (1983), 'The Council for Museums and Galleries in Scotland: a decade of development', *Museums Journal*, **83**,(1), pp. 37–40, for the early history; and Scottish Museums Council (1986), *The American Museum Experience: in Search of Excellence*, HMSO for the Council, Edinburgh, which contains two papers on education in American museums (Carr, J. R., pp. 41–47; Glaser, J. R., pp. 85–91).

47. *Education Reform Act 1988. An Act to Amend the Law Relating to Education*, HMSO London.

48. The Association also issued a Children's Magazine for Museums Year – *Eureka. Facts and Fun for Everyone*. Special Centenary Issue, 1989. Edited by Keith Ralph, produced by CCC and published for the Museums Association by Eureka Publications, London.

49. See also Stannett, A. (1990), Supplement I 1988–1989, *Journal of Education in Museums* 11 (1990), 22–28. The Bibliography complements the group's earlier publication – McCabe, G. I. (1972), *Education through Museums: a Bibliography* [1902–1972] – with an addendum in 1975.

The problems confronting both the compilers and users of the bibliography are reflected in the fact that items from 95 separate journals are included along with 215 books. Prominent among the latter are volumes issued by the Royal Ontario Museum, the Boston Children's Museum, the Metropolitan Museum of Art, New York, the Association of Science and Technology Centres and, particularly, the American Association for State and Local History, the Smithsonian Institution and the Council for British Archaeology.

66

Communicating through museum exhibitions

Michael Belcher

The concept of the museum as a medium of communication is not new. It has long been recognized that one of its major roles is to facilitate an encounter between object and observer. This experience, for the majority of visitors, occurs through the exhibitions and, for many, the reason why museums and art galleries exist at all is to enable objects to be seen. Whilst there is an awareness of the museum's other functions the extent of its commitment to them is probably not realized. Nevertheless, effective communication by the museum with its public goes beyond the exhibition galleries to include the entire 'public interface', i.e. every point at which contact is made with the public. This is important in the context of an overall image and communications policy of which the exhibitions are only a part – albeit one of the most important.

This chapter considers the museum's communications policy. It also discusses those factors which relate to the formulation of an exhibitions policy and examines briefly how this might be implemented.

Museum policy

Many museums had, at their inception, clearly stated aims and objectives. However, regrettably few have kept them under review or have defined their function clearly, especially in relation to the public. Miers (1928) lamented the fact that, given policy and resources, 'the duty of a museum to the public had yet to be defined'. On the same theme, American museums were criticized by Theodore Low (1942), when he said: '. . .of all institutions, both public and private, which have flourished in this country, few, if any, have wandered so aimlessly toward undefined goals as have the museums'.

Today, the need for museums to clarify their aims and objectives has never been greater. In a rapidly changing economic climate, with the political emphasis on enterprise, profitability and competitiveness, the pressure to participate in this style of economy is considerable. But, to be worthy of the name, museums must not lose sight of their basic objective – the advancement of knowledge. Furthermore, whereas once the problem was to strike a balance between, as Flower (1893) put it, '. . .the two distinct objects. . . research and instruction', today, with all museum functions competing for a share of the available resources, a balance needs perhaps to be achieved between entrepreneurial and academic pursuits.

The formulation of an overall policy is the obvious starting point, but unless the policy is known, understood and implemented by the entire staff, it is unlikely to be wholly effective. Within this overall policy, consideration must be given to the museum's function as communicator. Today there is a greater awareness of the need for each museum to consider how it relates to its public, and the type of service it should provide. This is particularly important as museums increasingly find themselves part of the booming leisure industry where each attraction competes for the attention of visitors in what is a highly competitive market.

Nevertheless, regrettably few museums have, as yet, undertaken the type of study which the Royal Ontario Museum (1976) pioneered. Entitled *Communicating with the Museum Visitor*, the published document provides a comprehensive analysis of a communications strategy. It must be recognized that each museum is different, and needs to examine for itself those factors which particularly affect its role. These will include: location, size and resources, extent and quality of the collections, the basis of funding, and the proximity of other institutions and their respective functions.

For many years industry has recognized the benefits of setting targets and implementing some form of total resource management in order to achieve specific priority objectives. One way to implement a policy through management by objectives is to produce a corporate or business plan. This will specify target objectives in a work programme which covers a period of several years and indicate resource implications.

Communications policy

Among the subjects to be addressed in the policy document should be 'communications', which may well be amplifed in a separate communications policy paper. The issues any particular museum might wish to address will be peculiar to that institution and its aims and objectives. However, they may well include the following.

The nature of the museum's approach to communicating

The main issues to be considered will be the extent to which the museum should attempt to inform, educate and entertain. As a result, it may go further and specify a set of approaches with which it particularly wishes to be concerned. The medium of exhibition would be expected to feature prominently in this as the main vehicle for communicating information about the collections and for interpreting them.

A statement might therefore be made on the ratio of permanent to temporary exhibitions and the extent to which travelling exhibitions might be produced and circulated to other centres. Accessibility to the collections is fundamental to a communications policy and, therefore, such controversial issues as charges for admission will need to be addressed and considered in conjunction with other relevant sections of the overall policy. The museum's involvement with such activities as publishing and distance-learning material will also need consideration.

The image the museum wishes to project

Emanating from the museum's overall policy and the nature of its approach to the public is the *image* it wishes to project. Purposeful consideration of how the museum wishes to appear is probably one of the most important yet frequently the most neglected tasks. There is a tendency to think that one has no control over an image and that it is something which is gradually acquired. The truth is that good images have to be worked for and actively maintained. If a museum wishes to appear professional, authoritative, friendly and approachable, it will need to take positive steps in order to achieve these goals. Indeed, how dynamic, topical, controversial and concerned

with current issues the museum wishes to be will depend on the sort of image it chooses to adopt and whether it seeks a high or low public profile.

The type and content of material to be communicated

The central issue here is how the museum should use its collections. Particularly important is the nature of the main topics which the museum wishes to communicate. Since collections can be arranged in many different ways, consideration must be given as to whether the material is arranged in exhibitions which, for example, indicate taxonomy or material type, period or chronology, comparisons or some other storyline.

Indentification of the people with whom the museum wishes to communicate

Drawing up a list of the groups of people with whom the museum specifically wishes to communicate is a useful first step – to be followed by considering how best their needs might be catered for. A rationale for this approach is that the museum wants to serve a community. It recognizes that this comprises many different sections of people. It also believes that, based on the type and content of material it wishes to communicate, it has something which will be of interest to particular groups. It seeks to identify what might usefully be communicated to whom – and relates this to policy. This approach is very close to the marketing strategy which might seek to identify markets and satisfy them with suitable products.

Groups of people for whom the museum might wish to formulate specific policies include the young and those at various educational stages, specialist groups, local societies, local residents, special-needs groups, tourists, and ethnic minorities.

The levels at which communication is to take place

The levels must obviously relate to the selected groups with whom communication is to be effected. An important consideration in determining levels is the intellect and knowledge of the various groups of visitors. This will affect the style of such things as labels and audio-visual units and their content; the use of computers and other interactive devices and, indeed, all aspects of educational psychology and technology.

The importance of design

Increasingly it is being realized that design is a matter of such importance that it warrants specific commitment on the part of an institution. Design is a consideration in virtually every facet of the museum system and, in particular, it relates to its communication activities and to its image. In relation to communication, the museum will doubtless wish to develop and strengthen a concept of corporate identity and ensure that this is adhered to throughout the organization. It may also wish to associate itself with the highest standards of design.

Communication strategy and plan

If the museum's communications policy sets out the general principles and rationale for its work in this area, the strategy shall be concerned with the organizational aspects of implementing the policy. As such, it determines the system, setting out how the work is to be done and by whom. Obviously there are various models which could apply, depending on the type and size of the museum, but responsibility for the formulation and implementation of a communications plan should be clearly identified. It might be that in larger museums a committee is formed to oversee communications. However, irrespective of size, all museums should charge one person who has the relevant expertise,

commitment and managerial skills with the responsibility of implementing the plan and also provide that person with the necessary executive authority and resources to operate effectively.

The communications plan should embrace all those projects which the museum has identified as necessary in order to fulfil its aims and objectives and declared policy. In formulating the plan the museum may wish to canvass opinion from both staff and interested parties outside the museum. Certainly all senior staff and interested junior staff should be encouraged to contribute to any debate, the outcome of which could have far-reaching implications.

Once it has been formulated, and its feasibility considered, the plan may be incorporated into the museum's corporate or business plan, with a view to it being implemented within a specified period of time.

Factors which determine exhibitions policy

A museum's exhibitions policy should be a part of the wider communications policy which, in turn, should feature prominently within the overall policy.

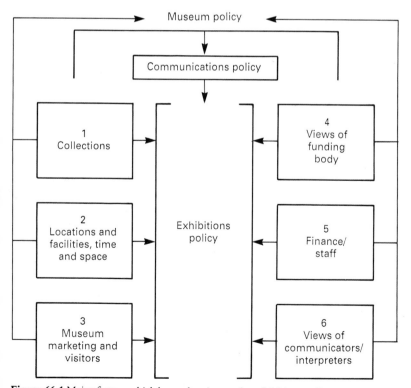

Figure 66.1 Major factors which have a bearing on the exhibitions policy

Aspects will also be embraced within the communications strategy and plan. Both museum staff and outside agencies should have access to the policy statements in order that they may have clarification of the basis on which the museum undertakes its exhibitions.

In any museum situation, a number of factors will have a bearing on the exhibitions policy. The major ones are indicated in *Figure 66.1*. However, the influence to be exerted by each factor will vary considerably both within any given museum and between different museums.

Collections

The objects in the museum's collections have traditionally formed the basis for communication. Cameron (1968) was of the opinion that the museum as a communications system 'depends on the non-verbal language of objects and observable phenomenon'. Real objects are the essence of museums (and what distinguishes them from other media) and as such must be a major influence on what is communicated. Exactly how a museum uses it collections resource for this purpose will depend on the nature and quality of its material, as well as the importance it attaches to it and its relevance to the themes it has decided to pursue. So the selection of objects in order to illustrate an idea must be done with care and exactness. Displaying the wrong objects, or the right objects but the wrong relationships to one another will only confuse the visitor, whilst displaying too many objects of similar type will lose the attention of all but the specialist.

Whilst the collections form the main resource to be used in relation to exhibitions and, therefore, are a major influence, omissions and weaknesses can be overcome if loans can be negotiated or if there is enough money available to purchase suitable material.

The richness and rarity of the material available will be a factor in determining how comprehensive the exhibitions will be and whether, within its own resources a museum can implement a series of changes. The need for change must be recognized if visitors are to be encouraged to revisit the museum. Whilst certain objects will justify permanent display, others will not and should, therefore, be identified as such and used, perhaps in temporary displays.

Location and facilities – time and space

There is clearly a need for an overview of museum and exhibition facilities at local, regional and national levels if material is to be made accessible on a geographical basis. This overview may well extend to include the increasing number of related developments such as interpretive centres, nature and town trails, historic houses, parks, gardens and zoos, demonstration farms, industrial sites and craft centres. However, at institutional level, each museum needs to determine its role as a provider of exhibitions with regard to its location and the policies and activities of other neighbouring (and possibly competing) organizations. This should help identify opportunities, encourage complementary and collaborative ventures and, at the same time, help reduce duplication.

As both time and space are limited, the use of both needs to be maximized, and the apportionment of space to permanent and temporary exhibitions is one of the most difficult decisions to be made. Having sufficient space to enable a viable temporary exhibition gallery to be created and setting aside areas within designated 'permanent' exhibitions for such things as topical displays or recent acquisitions will clearly reflect the museum's approach to exhibitions. The timing and duration of exhibitions are also reasonably complex issues and it is perhaps unwise to generalize when so much depends on the size and topic of any given exhibition, the type of museum and its visitor pattern. A large museum may well be able to maintain fairly constant visitor attendance at a 'temporary' exhibition even after several years, whereas a small local museum, especially outside the tourist season, might reach exhaustion point – when all those likely to want to visit the exhibition have done so – in a very short period. Irrespective of size, the typical attendance pattern is high at the beginning and towards the end of the exhibition period. Other major factors affecting the longevity of an exhibition are the environment it creates and the physical durability of the structure and equipment. Clearly the safety of objects must be an overriding consideration and in this conservation and security requirements must be satisfied and may well determine the period of time during which an object is exposed.

Indeed, failure to meet minimum standards for the various categories of objects may mean that an exhibition may not be mounted at all. This is particularly true of certain types of loan exhibitions. Exhibition materials and components which go to make the structure of an exhibition also vary in quality and durability and need to be specified with a particular 'life expectancy' in mind. However, irrespective of the intended duration of the exhibition, it must be adequately maintained, particularly if electrical, electronic or mechanical elements are incorporated.

Museum marketing and visitors

Marketing is a concept of business which puts the customer at the centre of the activity. It is embodied in a cyclic approach based on market research, service and product development, selling and promotion, quality control and after sales service. Put simply, it is about identifying and meeting the needs of the consumer or user group and providing the right product or service at the right price. (This is important for both consumer *and* purveyor if economic harmony is to be achieved.) In recent years museums have gradually become more interested in their customers (i.e. the visitors to their exhibitions), although they have seldom regarded them as such.

Many surveys have been undertaken to identify who visits museums and why but, interesting as this information is, of more use, perhaps, is finding out who does not visit and why, and who would like to visit the museum if it provided what they wanted, whatever that is. In a society which is rapidly moving towards free markets, with economic pressures mounting and considerable rivalry for the attention of visitors coming from many sources it is particularly important that museums look seriously at the concept of marketing.

In the studies which have been undertaken, some useful information has been obtained which can have direct application in the design of exhibitions. Most researchers agree that the visitors consist of a heterogeneous group with numerous variables. These include age and sex; intelligence and knowledge; social and economic grouping, and, particularly important, motivation. Motivated visitors derive more benefit from displays than those who casually visit the museum or wander aimlessly around the galleries.

The various studies which have been made of visitor characteristics and behaviour – notably by Melton (1935), Goins and Griffenhagen (1957), Shettal *et al* (1968), de Borhegyi and Hanson (1968) and Screven (1974) and more recently by various researchers at the British Museum (Natural History) – provide much detailed information which should be considered in relation to exhibition design and planning. However, care must always be exercised in the interpretation and application of the data. For example, it is known that the average time a visitor spends before a display is between 20 and 45 seconds (Neal, 1965; Shettel *et al*, 1968). Coles (1982) reports that people walking round a large exhibition of paintings spend on average 5 seconds in front of an individual picture. However, Alt (1982) quite rightly makes the point that the concept of an average time may not be very useful since it does not necessarily describe many people. Of more use are such facts that visitors to museums seldom come alone: this clearly has implications for the design of exhibition and supporting facilities. Observations, too, which establish whether certain exhibits attract visitors, and why, can also be helpful, as can information on circulation patterns. The salutary observation of Gardner and Heller (1960), that 'an exhibition does not in fact exist until it is crowded with people' should not be forgotten.

In the studies of the behaviour of visitors, anthropomorphic data are also important, particularly when ergonomic factors are being considered. But, in addition to this type of information, it is also useful to know what visitors are thinking, and what expectations they have. For example, visitors returning to a museum will expect to see new things, as well as renew their acquaintance with established favourites.

They also expect high standards of presentation and the use of modern technology. To deny them this may mean that they will go away feeling dissatisfied, and visitors who leave the museum in this frame of mind will do little to promote it. This is important, because one of the most effective ways of promotion remains the personal contact between visitors – actual and potential. Borun (1977) recognized the importance of knowing what visitors were thinking and in particular the need for regular channels of feedback for visitor response, 'so that the museum becomes a flexible, self-correcting institution in touch with the desires of its public'.

Many aspects of the cyclic approach of museum marketing with its concern for visitor opinion are also linked with the important topics of exhibition evaluation and effectiveness. For a more detailed discussion see the chapter on Exhibition Effectiveness in Belcher, M. (1991) *Exhibitions in Museums*.

Views of funding body

For the most part, the views of the funding body will have been considered in the overall museum policy and will, therefore, be applied to the exhibitions policy via the communications policy.

It is inevitable that the body which funds an organization, or which is charged with responsibility for it, will have a view on how the resources should be deployed. Trustees, Governors, Local Authority representatives and industrial sponsors will all need to be satisfied with the exhibition policy pursued, as will organizations such as the Arts Council of Great Britain and Regional Arts Associations if financial support from these bodies is to be successfully sought. However, in the current economic climate when commercial sponsorship is becoming commonplace, the views of the funding body may be such that they begin to influence the exhibition content in ways which are incompatible with a museum's policy. In such situations, where ethical implications need consideration, the museum will need to exercise professional integrity and adhere to truth. The museum also has an obligation to its public (as tax payers and/or admission fee payers) and, although representatives of the public are frequently elected to committees charged with the oversight of individual museums, those elected do not necessarily have a knowledge of museology, nor do their views necessarily reflect those of the public in general or the museum audience. In this context, the specialist advice and opinion of the professional museum staff is essential.

However, it should be remembered that it was this very group of professionals who, earlier this century, was responsible for isolating museums from the public. The prudent professional will therefore take note of the wishes of his governing or funding body, his staff and the public before using his professional judgement to determine the manner in which the exhibitions policy is to be implemented.

Finance/staff

Adequate finance is a prerequisite of any effective exhibition programme. Pearson (1981) makes the point that the public art galleries have suffered in the past from the ideas that exhibitions can be run on the cheap. The same can be said of museums. Money buys staff – and staff need money in order to function effectively. Materials, equipment, transport charges and insurance all have to be paid for, even if the manpower is available.

What can be achieved in any one exhibition will inevitably depend, not only on the total resources available, but also on the manner in which these resources are deployed. Money spent, for example, on creating a suitable setting in which objects can be viewed, can so heighten the experience of the visitor to the exhibition that it is money invested wisely. The most memorable exhibitions tend to be those in which special consideration has been given to the environment in which objects are seen.

Where funds are restricted, it may be that exhibitions are smaller, less well-produced and less frequent. Financial considerations may also determine whether the items displayed are two- or three-dimensional and whether the exhibition environment can be changed to relate to each successive display. A consequence of limited finance and the ensuing restrictions on exhibitions could be a falling off in visitor interest and museum attendance, particularly at a time when other branches of the leisure industry are investing heavily in order to attract visitors. In the pursuit of professional standards and the need for the museum to be respected by the public for its professionalism, it is necessary that not only is sufficient finance available, but also the right type of expertise. This will vary according to the project and the size of operation. However, suitable academic or scientific expertise must be available in respect of the exhibition content. Professional advice on conservation and design must also be sought, and educational and editorial expertise is clearly advantageous.

Where professional staff are not available, one solution could be to hire exhibitions produced by others. Pearson (1981) makes the distinction between art galleries and exhibition spaces, regarding the former as active and the latter as passive.

It is not enough for a gallery merely to receive exhibitions from others. it needs to initiate its own policy, and implement it through the exhibition programme and other organized events. It needs to fulfil a social role, stimulate and educate, and have an active relationship with an involved public.

The successful museum or gallery will carefully initiate and select exhibitions which complement and extend its activities. It will look to those bodies which prepare and circulate exhibitions – the Arts Councils, certain national museums, the Area Museums Services and commercial and industrial organizations and make a selection from that offered. It will also be aware of the grants available for the production of exhibitions, and the criteria which have to be met in order to qualify. In particular, it will be opportunist and take advantage of the benefits to be derived in participating in festivals and other promotions as well as national events.

Consideration will also need to be given to charging admission to exhibitions, and to the purchase by visitors of supplementary information in the form of guides, catalogues, leaflets or souvenirs. The issues raised by the principle of charging for access to information have been well rehearsed, and the extent to which charging will create a barrier to the museum communicating with its public and to what extent it will aid it, must be the central question to resolve.

Views of communicators/interpreters

Few should have a greater input into the debate regarding the formulation and implementation of a museum's exhibitions policy than the communicators and interpreters themselves. The subject specialists, designers and educationalists should form the nucleus of this group.

It will be the communicators/interpreters who advise on what the specific objectives of a particular exhibition will be and how and by what means they can be attained. The qualities which distinguish good communicators from the mediocre are difficult to define, but they are those which enable the attention of the intended audience to be gained, held and then satisfied. So much, therefore, will depend on the skills, experiences and preferences of those charged with the task of communicating, for communicating through exhibitions is not an exact science. Exhibitions, although designed for a purpose, nevertheless remain a plastic art form. As such, they can be fashioned by their creators to elicit certain responses from visitors, and can impart the personality of the main contributors – be they Designers or Curators.

Exhibitions policy

Those factors which have a particular bearing on a museum's exhibitions policy have been indicated above and need to be considered in relation to the communications policy. This consideration should address such issues as:

(1) the nature of the museum's approach to communicating;
(2) the type and content (i.e. subject matter) of material to be communicated;
(3) identification of the people with whom the museum wishes to communicate and for what purpose;
(4) the levels at which communication is to be effected;
(5) the modes of communication (i.e. media); and
(6) the importance of design.

Within the above topics, the museum should formulate a distinct policy in relation to its exhibition activity, which will probably include both permanent and temporary modes and possibly other forms such as circulating or mobile exhibitions. A set of aims and objectives for each mode may then be formulated, an exercise which should again be repeated at individual exhibition and indeed, display levels.

Policy implementation

The implementation of the exhibitions policy needs to be considered on three levels: first, the practical organization of staff and the deployment of resources; second the formulation of the design problem; and, finally, solving the design problem.

Practical organization of staff and deployment of resources
It cannot be overemphasized that the production of successful exhibitions is a group activity, with each member contributing specialized knowledge and skills. In implementing the policy, each individual will need to liaise closely with colleagues at all stages. And it is important that everyone concerned with an exhibition should be involved right from the start, consulting and discussing as necessary, before ideas are rigidly fixed.

Briefly, in a medium-size museum, responsibilities might be undertaken in the following way. The Directorate should initiate the project, seek and obtain the necessary approval and authorize the resources in accordance with the agreed policy and corporate plan. The Curator's role is to provide the specialist information, contribute to the writing of the design brief and identify the material from which the final selection of what to display in the exhibition will be made.

The designer should assist in the preparation of the brief and will provide design solutions. Once approved, the solutions will be translated into specifications and working drawings by the designer, who will normally supervise the contractual arrangements and production stages of the project. The conservation staff will prepare the material for exhibition and advise on the environmental conditions of the display. The overseeing of all aspects of security, both for the exhibition in preparation and once it is complete, will be the responsibility of the security officer, in conjunction with the Curator and Designer.

Education staff should also contribute to the brief and provide advice on aspects of educational technology and psychology. It may also be that, in the absence of a professional editor, the education specialist will assist in writing and editing the exhibition text. The production and maintenance staff with responsibility for producing and maintaining the exhibition will also be able to provide practical advice at the design stage on their aspects of the project.

A further activity for all concerned with the project, perhaps aided by subject specialists and representative samplings of the intended audience, will be evaluating the proposals.

Taking the industrial models of research and development, test marketing and market research and applying these to the museum situation, evaluation will be seen as a continuous process. It should be undertaken as the project is taking shape (formative evaluation) and once it is in existence (summative evaluation). Only through this approach can the museum be the flexible, self-evaluating and self-correcting institution described by Borun (1977). In order to maximize the efficiency and production capacity of staff, effective organization and management techniques with systems to determine, control and monitor the complexities of exhibition production are essential. Hall (1987) in *On Display*, her excellent design grammar for museum exhibitions, provides much useful information on the various stages in the development of exhibition concept, design and structure. Howell (1971) produced a detailed network system for the planning, designing, construction and installation of exhibits, within which he identified the individual activities which are involved in the total exhibition project and showed how certain activities are dependent on the completion of others. At its simplest, critical path analysis can be little more than a bar chart, listing activities and indicating their duration on a time scale, together with the critical points at which one activity has a bearing upon another.

It may also indicate the individuals or groups who have been charged with the responsibility of undertaking a particular activity within the programme.

For these techniques to be valid, realistic estimates of the time which a particular stage will take must be obtained from those competent to make such predictions, and ideally those responsible for the work. Once target completion dates are fixed, the system must incorporate suitable contingency factors and should be updated as new information becomes available. Its benefit is as a planning tool; to help those responsible for a project to consider all its aspects; to show all participants the importance of the part they play and essentially to bring the project to completion on time.

Formulation of the design problem

The definition of the problem should be given in the design brief. This should identify a particular need and state simply what is required and why. It should not state how things are to be done, as that constitutes the solution. Much has been written on the design problem in terms of stated objectives (Shettel *et al*, 1968; Nicol, 1969; Screven, 1974). It is generally agreed that the following are required:

(1) the need for an exhibition should first be identified;
(2) the overall aims and objectives of the exhibition should be specified;
(3) the aims and objectives of each section of each display within it need to be stated, i.e. what it is intended that the exhibit will achieve;
(4) where possible, these should be stated in measureable terms; and
(5) the purpose of exhibits is to bring about some change in the visitor, and to do this, the characteristics of the intended audience must be identified.

Every element of an exhibit – whether it be specimen or artefact, label or caption, model or diorama, audio-visual presentation or interactive device – must be related to a stated objective of the exhibit and have a considered purpose. Since each will compete for the visitor's attention, particular care must be taken over sequence and comparative emphasis. The changes which the exhibit is intended to bring about may be either affective or cognitive – changing attitudes or feelings or levels of knowledge through exposure to or interaction with the exhibit. The brief should, therefore, indicate whether the character of the exhibit is to be aesthetic (enabling the visitor to experience beauty) romantic or evocative (enabling the visitor to escape from everyday life to perhaps a different time or place) or didactic (providing information and satisfying intellectual curiosity) – or a combination of all of these! In addition to defining the problem and specifying the aims and objectives, the brief should also provide information on the constraints, i.e. all those factors which, for one reason or another will have a limiting effect on the solution. These will include such practical considerations as a budget, time schedule,

location; and may extend to such matters as security and conservation. If specialists from outside the museum staff are to be employed, terms of contract will also have to be specified and agreed by all parties at the outset.

A solution to the design problem

Design may be defined as arranging elements to some purpose or the solving of a stated problem. Exhibitions have rightly been regarded as an art form providing the opportunity for self-expression and argument, and capitalizing on the effects which space, form, light, colour and sound can have on the senses. They are also purposeful, in that an exhibition exists to communicate with the visitor in order to bring about change. This can be an increase in knowledge, greater awareness and understanding of concepts or facts previously unkown. Or it can also be an emotional change – elation, enjoyment or sadness – brought about through an aesthetic experience.

In attempting to provide a solution to the design brief, the designer will adopt a methodical, problem-solving approach and formulate his proposals in the light of previous experience and current research. While accepting that no two problems are identical, and that exhibition design is, as Gardner and Heller (1960) said 'an empirical process', there are, nevertheless, certain theories and practices which have application and relate to each element associated with an exhibition. At the centre of these is the information which exists on visitor behaviour and which relates particularly to ergonomics and psychology.

Of paramount importance must be the scientific data available on the conservation of the specimens to go on display. For this determines the environmental conditions in which the objects may be shown. Light, heat, relative humidity and other atmospheric factors must be carefully determined and monitored if the object is to be displayed safely. Similarly materials may need to be selected with conservation requirements in mind, as will such things as the methods by which certain objects are physically supported. Finally, there exists a body of knowledge which relates to exhibition components and their application. The media and materials of exhibition – dynamic models, audio-visual presentations, photographs, lighting, labels and backgrounds – have been evaluated and their strengths, weaknesses and suitability of purpose determined.

It is, then, primarily the designer's task to draw on this body of knowledge and to consult colleagues as necessary prior to proposing, testing and modifying his solutions in response to the design brief. Solutions will take the form of sketches and mock-ups or models and prototypes and ultimately a series of working drawings and specifications.

Orientation

One aspect of exhibitions which is often neglected is the need to prepare visitors for what they are about to experience. Orientation relates both to the physical location as well as the subject matter (conceptual orientation). Cohen (1974), in a survey of orientation in 12 selected institutions in the USA, defines orientation as 'the logical relationship of one situation to another already familiar' which is in accordance with the accepted educational principle of progressing from the known to the unknown. Orientation can be a gradual process, with each stage capable of standing on its own, yet building up to provide a complete coverage. It might commence through advertisements which provide awareness of an exhibition and progress through press, radio and television exposés of the subject concerned.

Detailed information leaflets might follow, and then information packs, comprising background material, lists of exhibition contents and plans, worksheets and teaching material, all of which may be particularly useful for school parties or other groups preparing for a visit, and which should help ensure that the time spent in the exhibition is used to best advantage. To this end, a plan and guide placed at the entrance to an exhibition is also important.

Sign-posting is an aspect of orientation neglected by virtually every museum in the country. Despite the reference made to them in the early reports of Miers (1928) and many other distinguished critics since, museums, to their detriment, are still not acting on the need to have the location of their premises adequately indicated. Signs should be provided for both pedestrians and motorists from a town's major arrival points – be they stations or roads, to the museums, and from other major features such as the civic centre or related educational or leisure facilities. In addition to being directionally functional, signs also serve as useful advertisements and reminders. Buildings, too, need to be clearly identifiable, with the entrance marked and hours of opening stated. Symptomatic of the times, there is now also a need to state whether admission is free or if a charge is made. Inside museums, particularly large ones, there is also a need for a plan and guide to the exhibits, plus a comprehensive sign-posting system to enable visitors to find their way.

Summary

This chapter has stressed the need for museums to consider the issues which relate to exhibitions, and within overall policies, to formulate a specific policy on communicating which will embrace communicating through exhibitions. The very process of deliberately considering policy and plans should generate the impetus to improve existing facilities and to progress with exciting new schemes. This can only be to the benefit of individual museums, the museum movement as a whole, and to the visitor.

References

ALT, M. (1982), in *Research in Illustration*, 1981 Conference at Brighton Polytechnic, Proceedings, **11**, p. 140

BELCHER, M. (1991), *Exhibitions in Museums*, Leicester University Press, Leicester/Smithsonian Institution Press, Washington, pp. 197–209

DE BORHEGYI, S. F. E. and HANSON, I. A. (Eds) (1968), *The Museum Visitor (Publications in Museology, 3)*, Milwaukee Public Museum, Milwaukee

BORUN, M. (1977), *Measuring the Immeasurable – Pilot Study of Museum Effectiveness*, Franklin Institute, Philadelphia

CAMERON, D. F. (1968), 'A viewpoint: the museum as a communications system and implications for museum education', *Curator*, **XI**(1), 33–40

COHEN, M. S. (1974), *The State of the Art of Museum Visitor Orientation*, Smithsonian Institution, Washington, DC

COLES, P. (1982), 'Eye movements and picture perception', in *Research in Illustration*, 1981 Conference Proceedings **11**, Brighton Polytechnic, pp. 123–142

FLOWER, W. (1893), 'Presidential address', *Proceedings*, Museum Association, London

GARDNER, J. and HELLER, C. (1960), *Exhibition and Display*, Batsford, London

GOINS, A. and GRIFFENHAGEN, G. (1957), 'Psychological studies of museum visitors and exhibits at the US National Museum', *The Museologist*, **64**, 1–6

HALL, M. (1987), *On Display – A Design Grammar for Museum Exhibitions*, Lund Humphries, London

HOWELL, D. B. (1971), 'A network system for the planning, designing, construction, and installation of exhibits', *Curator*, **14**(2), 100–108

LOW, T. (1942), *The Museum as a Social Instrument*, The Metropolitan Museum of Art, New York

MARKHAM, F. (1938), *The Museums and Art Galleries of the British Isles*, Carnegie United Kingdom Trust, Dunfermline

MELTON, A. W. (1935), 'Problems of installation in museums of art', *Publications of the American Association of Museums, New Series No. 14*, Washington, DC. (This article originally appeared in *Museum News*)

MELTON, A. W. (1972), 'Visitor behaviour in museums: some early research in environmental design', *Human Factors*, **14**(5), 393–403

MIERS, H. (1928), *A Report on the Public Museums of the British Isles*, Carnegie United Kingdom Trust, Edinburgh

NEAL, A. (1965), 'Function of display: regional museums', *Curator*, **8**(3), 228–234

NICOL, E. H. (1969), *The Development of Validated Museum Exhibits*, US Department of Health, Education and Welfare, Office of Education, Bureau of Research, Washington, DC, and Children's Museum, Boston

PEARSON, N. (1981), *Arts Galleries and Exhibition Spaces in Wales*, Welsh Arts Council, Cardiff

ROYAL ONTARIO MUSEUM (1976), *Communicating with the Museum Visitor*, Royal Ontario Museum, Ottawa

SCREVEN, C. G. (1974), *The Measurement and Facilitation of Learning in the Museum Environment: An Experimental Analysis*, Smithsonian Institution, Washington, DC

SHETTEL, H. H. *et al.*, (1968), *Strategies for Determining Exhibit Effectiveness (Project No. V-011; Contract No. OE-6-10. 213)* American Insitute for Research, Pittsburgh, PA

Bibliography

ALT, M. B. (1977), 'Evaluating didactic exhibits: a critical look at Shettel's work', *Curator*, **20**(3), 241–257. A thorough analysis of Shettel's paper, from which he concludes that by ignoring the fact that visitors to museums are different in make-up and intention, Shettel does not come to grips with evaluating the educational effectiveness of didactic exhibits

ALT, M. B. (1980), 'Four years of visitor surveys at the British Museum (Natural History) 1976–1979', *Museums Journal*, **80**(1), 10–19. A review of the annual surveys of visitors carried out in September each year. Visitors' profiles, expectations, interests and their most memorable exhibits are given in 20 detailed tables

ARNELL, U., HAMMER, I. and NYLOF, G. (1976), *Going to Exhibitions*, Riksutstalingar/Swedish Travelling Exhibitions, Stockholm. A critical appraisal of the work of Swedish Travelling Exhibitions and the effect of the exhibitions on knowledge and attitudes

BAYER, H. (1961), 'Aspects of design of exhibitions and museums', *Curator*, **4**(3), 257–287. Selected exhibition elements and characteristics are traced back to their nineteenth- and twentieth-century origins

BEDEKAR, V. H. (1978), *So you want Good Museum Exhibitions*, Department of Museology, Faculty of Fine Arts, MS University of Barona. A manual on exhibition preparation and design intended for trainees for the museum profession

BELCHER, M. (1991), *Exhibitions in Museums*, Leicester University Press, Leicester/Smithsonian Institution Press, Washington. A comprehensive introduction to the various factors which relate to exhibitions in museums

BERNADO, J. R. (1972), 'Museum environs for communications: a study of environmental parameters in the design of museum experiences', Ph. D. dissertation, Columbia University, Columbia CH. Considers those elements of the environment which a designer can manipulate to influence desired behavioural responses in museum audiences

BORUN, M. (1975), *Museum Effectiveness Study – a Bibliographic Review*, The Franklin Institute, Philadelphia

BRAWNE, M. (1965), *The New Museum: Architecture and Display*, Architectural Press, London. Illustrated international survey of new museums and their displays

BRAWNE, M. (1982), *The Museum Interior – Temporary and Permanent Display Techniques*, Thames and Hudson, London

BUTLER, P. M. (1970), *Temporary Exhibitions*, Museums Association, London. Suggestions of sources and checklist

BRIGHTON POLYTECHNIC(1981), *Research in Illustration, Conference Proceedings, Parts I and II*, Brighton Polytechnic, Brighton. Proceedings of the conference held on 26–27 March 1981 – possibly the first to be held in the UK on research in illustration. The aim of the Conference was to explore potential areas of investigation in relation to illustration

CANNON-BROOKES, P. (1971), 'The loan of works of art for exhibition', *Museums Journal*, **71**(3), 105–107. A discussion of draft conditions of loan, for the protection of object, lender and borrower

CARMEL, J. H. (1962), *Exhibition Techniques – Travelling and Temporary*, Reinhold, New York. A comprehensive,

well-illustrated manual related to all aspects of the design and preparation of temporary exhibitions

CORDINGLY, D. (1975), *Methods of Lettering for Museums*, Museums Association, London. A guide to production methods

COUNTRYSIDE COMMISSION(1978), *Interpretation in Visitor Centres*, Countryside Commission, Cheltenham. A study of the visitors and displays at seventeen centres in the UK

EAST, M. (1952), *Display for Learning: Making and Using Visual Materials*, Holt, Rinehart and Winston, London. A brief introduction to the theory of display for learning followed by specific examples, mainly for use in schools or small units without professional assistance

ELLIOT, P. and LOOMIS, R. J. *Studies of Visitor Behaviour in Museums and Exhibitions*, Smithsonian Institution, Washington, DC. An annotated bibliography

FAZZINI, D. (1972), 'The museum as a learning environment. A self motivating, recycling, learning system for the museum visitor', Ph. D. dissertation, University of Wisconsin, Milwaukee, WI. Meticulous study of a recycling system applied to the museum environment

FOLLIS, J. and HAMMER, D. (1979), *Architectural Signing and Graphics*, Architectural Press, London. A comprehensive, well-illustrated study of contemporary sign design practice

GARDNER, J. and HELLER, C. (1960), *Exhibition and Display*, Batsford, London. A comprehensive treatment of the subject. Although photographs are now dated, illustrations and text are very relevant today

GATACRE, E. V. (1976), 'The limits of professional design', *Museums Journal*, **76**(3), 93–99. A paper read at the Museums Association Annual Conference, 1976. Contemporary designers are taken to task for responding to fashion, and doubts are expressed on current museum design developments

GLEADOW, E. T. (1975), *Organising Exhibitions*, Arts Council of Great Britain. A manual which outlines the methods used to organize temporary exhibitions of works of art

GREEN, M. (1977), 'The museum designer: an examination of the present to anticipate the future', *Conference Proceedings for 2001. The Museum and the Canadian Public*, Canadian Museums Association, Ottowa. A brief paper expressing concern regarding commercial design as applied to museums, and stressing the need for the development of a museum's own communications technology

HALL, M. (1987), *On Display – a Design Grammar for Museum Exhibitions*, Lund Humphries, London. A comprehensive examination of designing museum exhibitions, with numerous diagrams and photographic examples

JOHNSTONE, C. (1980), 'Art museums in the communications age: a summary', *Museums Journal*, **80**(2), 72–77. Summaries of papers presented at a one-day conference in February 1980 on how art galleries should interpret their collections to the general public, including: Grote, D. A. 'Art and Information'; Macdonald-Ross, M. 'Research and development for museum exhibits'; Luckett, H. 'An experiment in interpretive design – "Landscapes" at Southampton Art Gallery'; Johnstone, C. 'A guide to interpretive techniques'

KNEZ, E. L. and WRIGHT, A. G. (1970), 'The museum as a communications system: an assessment of Cameron's viewpoint', *Curator*, **13**(3), 204–212. An alternative viewpoint: that Cameron's 'subsidiary media' (labels, photographics, etc.) are really primary and that objects are not the medium

LEWIS, B. N. (1980), 'The museum as an educational facility', *Museums Journal*, **80**(3), 151–155. A critical appraisal of museums as educators

MALIK, M. (1963), 'Principles of automation in museum exhibitions', *Curator*, **6**(3), 247–268. Account of the 'Interkamera' project which introduced automation to the museum exhibition. Brief technical details given

MANCHESTER POLYTECHNIC LIBRARY (1980), *Exhibition Design (Bibliographic Series No. 11)*, Manchester Polytechnic, Manchester. Annotated bibliography of 152 items

MILES, R. S. and ALT, M. B. (1979), 'British Museum (Natural History): a new approach to the visiting public', *Museums Journal*, **78**(3), 158–162. Article based on a paper read at the Museums Association Annual Conference 1978, in which the new approach and its use of educational technology and evaluation studies is outlined

MILES, R. S., ALT, M. B., GOSLING, D. C., LEWIS, B. N. and TOUT, A. F. (1982), *The Design of Educational Exhibits*, George Allen and Unwin, Hemel Hempstead

MORRIS, R. G. M. and ALT, M. B. (1978), 'An experiment to help design a map for a larger museum', *Museums Journal*, **77**(4), 179–181. Results of an experiment to test and compare axonometric and plan drawings of a museum map to aid visitor orientation. Both were found to be inadequate and neither better than the other

NEAL, A. (1963), 'Gallery and case exhibit design', *Curator*, **6**(1), 77–96. A brief introduction of the ergonomic factors related to exhibitions and various design proposals for cases and case layouts

NEAL, A. (1965), 'Function of display: regional museums', *Curator*, **8**(3), 228–234. Address given to the Utah Museums Conference, 1965 in which the need is stressed for regional museums to cover the local story first

PEARSON, N. (1981), *Art Galleries and Exhibition Spaces in Wales*. Welsh Arts Council, Cardiff. A report commissioned by the Welsh Arts Council to survey existing galleries and exhibition spaces in Wales, and to reappraise their activities and potential

ROBINSON, P. V. (1960), 'An experimental study of exhibit arrangement and viewing method to determine their effect upon learning of factual material', D.Ed. dissertation, University of Southern California. A comprehensive review of related literature and in depth account of experiments undertaken to determine the effect of selected exhibit installations on learning

ROYAL ONTARIO MUSEUM (1976), *Communicating with the Museum Visitor*, Royal Ontario Museum, Toronto. A most comprehensive guide to planning, bringing together the findings of previous researchers and presenting them in an accessible form. Extensive bibliographies and appendices. A major work, essential to all concerned with museum and exhibition design

SOBOL, M. G. (1980), 'Do the "blockbusters" change the audience?', *Museums Journal*, **80**(1), 25–27. A brief analysis of visitor profiles in relation to major temporary exhibitions at Dallas Museum of Fine Arts

SORBEY, B. D. and HORNE, S. D. (1980), 'The readability of museum labels', *Museums Journal*, **80**(3), 157–159. A comparison between newspaper reading habits of the general population and those of visitors to Merseyside County museums in 1975, leading to the conclusion that at least two-thirds of museum labels will not gain the full attention of the majority of visitors

SPENCER, H. (1969), *The Visible Word*, Lund Humphries, London. A brief survey of the major research undertaken in word legibility

SPENCER, H. and REYNOLDS, L. (1977), *Directional Signing and Labelling in Libraries and Museums: a Review of Current Theory and Practice*, Readability of Print Unit, Royal College of Art, London. A study of current practice and a review of relevant research findings. Twenty-seven libraries and eighteen museums were examined in detail

STANSFIELD, G. (1981), *Effective Interpretive Exhibitions*, Countryside Commission, Cheltenham. A review of the research into the effectiveness of communication achieved through exhibitions and the printed word, with particular emphasis on results and conclusions which, it is considered, have wider application

SVEDBERG, E. (1949), 'Museum display', in *Museums in Modern Life*, Royal Society of Arts, London. Much of the post-World War II museum design movement is identifiable with the concepts put forward in this paper

SZEMERE, A. (Ed.), (1978), *The Problem of Contents, Didactics and Aesthetics of Modern Museum Exhibitions*, Institute of Conservation and Methodology of Museums, Budapest. Papers read at the International Museum Seminar (July 1977)

THOM, V. M. (1980), 'Evaluating countryside interpretation: a critical look at the current situation', *Museums Journal*, **79**(4), 179–185. A review of recent studies on aspects of visitor centre operation

THOMSON, G. and BULLOCK, L. (1978), *Conservation and Museum Lighting*, 3rd edition, Museum Association, London. Identification of dangers and recommendations for protection, including product guide

TYLER, B. and DICKENSON, V. (1977), *A Handbook for the Travelling Exhibitionist*, Canadian Museums Association, D. Howa. A brief check-list for those preparing travelling exhibitions. Amusing cartoon illustrations

WEINER, G. (1963), 'Why Johnny can't read labels', *Curator*, **6**(2), 143–156. An examination of label content, legibility and form

WILLIAMS, L. A. (1960), 'Labels: writing, design and preparation', *Curator*, **3**(1), 26–42. A step-by-step account of label production

WITTEBORG, L. P. (1958), 'Design standards in museum exhibits', *Curator*, **1**(1), 29–41. A brief history of exhibition design

WITTLIN, A. S. (1971), 'Hazards of communication by exhibits', *Curator*, **14**(2), 138–150

67

Exhibition design

Giles Velarde

Had the museum curator been alive to commerce earlier, design and designers would have been brought into museums at least a quarter of a century before they were. It was, after all, in the world of commerce that the exhibition started. In the market place, the need to sell goods gave rise to the need to display them to advantage. In the museum the need to display objects to advantage is, in very simple terms, the essence of museum exhibition design.

Unknown to most curatorial staff, nearly all the display techniques now used in museums were being developed by exhibition designers working for commerce. At the same time others working mainly in the field of conferences and propaganda were developing the devices now commonplace in information and educational technology. These fields have merged within the single discipline of museum exhibition design.

Now that the bridge between mammon and museum has been built, it is in everyone's interests to maintain it. The obvious advantages include sponsorship for the museum and up-market advertising for industry. It is, however, worth remembering that no industrialist would consider any involvement with a museum exhibition unless highly professional designs were involved.

Intentions

Before starting any design project in any specialization it is essential to decide exactly what needs to be done. A specialist can help with this decision and, particularly when working with an in-house designer, it is best to make this decision together; thus guaranteeing not only mutual enthusiasm for the project but also increasing its likelihood of success.

Exhibitions have, like any other medium of expression, their own particular set of advantages and disadvantages. The danger is that the curator,

keen to express his ideals in glamorous, three-dimensional terms, will select the wrong subject to expose in this way. When examining what is a good subject, it is well to remember what museums are for. The curation and preservation of objects is fundamental; therefore any exhibition which has little to do with objects and is simply narrative has little hope of success unless objects can be made or found to form the basis of the story. After 20 years barrage with the flat image it is likely that the museum visitor is craving to see something real and round; not only to see it, but to touch it and walk around it. We are tactile three-dimensional creatures. It cannot be satisfactory to sit in the man-made twilight of television and then to make the brave step outside and through the door of a museum to see yet more of the same thing. It is essential to think in terms of giving the visitor something he cannot get at home, at school or from a library or shop; and to decide what the public should learn, feel, enjoy or believe when it leaves the exhibition.

There are many reasons for mounting an exhibition. Ideally the curatorial and design staff who form the production team should have these reasons in common. It is not possible to get a good exhibition out of tortured, mistrustful relationships. However, assuming that such harmony of intentions exists, the defined, well-articulated and mutually agreed list of intentions is an excellent platform upon which to build.

Unfortunately, at least as many effects of an exhibition can be unintended as are intended. Some are laudable: to please and excite, to give three-dimensional assistance to the process of education, to inform a specific age or social group. Some are circumstantial necessities: to draw publicity, attention or money to influence events or people. Some, especially when intended, are inexcusable: to pander to fellow professionals, to build a memorial, to isolate the learner from the learned: in other words to show off, to bore, to confuse or to irritate. Every exhibition may do a combination of these things, assuming of course that it receives any attention at all. What visitors do and how they behave in response to varied types of display is vital knowledge for all curators and designers. Unfortunately, most information sought on the subject seems to relate to the educational value of museums.

In essence, however, museums are places of what might be termed 'higher entertainment'. They are the places to which those who delight in knowledge resort. They are the havens for those who love to rootle among the clues to man's immortality. They are the repositories of tangible reality where the actual paint that Van Gogh used can be seen, the thigh that Rodin smoothed can be touched or the ring that Henry V wore can be admired. There is no way that factors like that can be quantified in statistics and, banal though they may sound when set down here, it is nothing to their banality when tabulated nebulously under 'pleasure'.

The designer, of necessity, must be open to all sources of information about his potential audience. It is of great value for the objective designer to observe for himself public reaction to his work. For one employed in a museum there is a unique opportunity to mingle, unrecognized, with the visitors, hear their comments and watch their movements. If he notes down these observations, and when and where they were made, all to the good. But he is entirely the wrong person to approach the visitor, ask him questions, declare himself and thus get involved in an inevitably subjective, and possibly offensive, confrontation. At this point the importance of the professional evaluator is manifest and there can be no doubt that recent work in Canada, the USA and London is of immense value and significance. But can anyone, either designer, evaluator or psychologist appreciate – by observations or questioning – the intensity of the relationship between the visitor and the object? Can a visitor put into words his possibly vague reasons for being in a museum? And, if asked the question 'Why did you visit this museum?' will probably respond with an answer which he knows will either please or embarrass the bright-eyed young questioner he sees before him. Like every other means of improving the work of designers and curators, professional evaluation can only be used satisfactorily with a clear eye to its limitations, and should not be regarded as the complete solution.

Types of exhibition

Consideration of the visitor is basic when discussing design, and this consideration leads logically into an assessment of the types of exhibition that can be mounted. These broad, differing types are inevitably a permutation of two factors. First, their *physical properties*: permanent, temporary, portable and mobile, all of which are separate descriptions (though 'temporary' may well be applied to both portable and mobile). Second, the exhibition's *informative characteristics*: thematic, systematic, object-oriented, interactive and responsive. Some or all of the latter can appear in the same exhibition. A definition of all these general terms is necessary as they are an important part of the language of museum exhibition production.

Permanent speaks for itself, or it should, but it really ought to be taken to mean 'for as long as curatorial policy upholds the need for the exhibition'. This, therefore, means over 20 years in a national museum and perhaps 7–10 years in a small provincial museum. It is almost inevitable that, assisted with central government funds, the permanent exhibition in a national museum will be built to far higher standards of finish, if not design, than its provincial counterpart. But it will inevitably date. Furthermore, since it is more likely to be built by in-house designers than freelance ones it has earned the former the reputation of conservativism and the latter a name for trendiness and poor attention to detail, neither necessarily deserved. 'Permanent' should mean built to last, using well-seasoned timbers and well-tried methods of construction and finish. It would be unwise, for instance, to build these structures using materials such as chipboard and hardboard, or clad them with finishes of unknown durability using untried adhesives and non-fast colours. Clearly, the information presented in these displays should be thoroughly researched, since errors are more difficult to rectify in permanent finishes and, when left uncorrected, stand as irritating memorials.

Temporary. In many museums a temporary exhibition, to be accurate, frequently means semi-permanent. It may be planned for 3 to 6 months but its popularity, or lack of funds to replace it, may result in it remaining for many years. By its ephemeral nature, a temporary exhibition has a freedom not allowed to the permanent. It is an abuse of this freedom to constrict people into tight aisles, deprive them of fresh air and make them struggle to read text and labels, but it seems, quite wrongly, to be permissible when the exhibition is only standing for a short period. This is patently bad design and can only be got away with because there is not sufficient time for a body of complaint to develop. 'Temporary' should only apply to the durability of the materials used in construction, and to the loan of valuable exhibits.

Portable quite definitely means only one thing: an exhibition which can be dismantled, carried to another place and re-erected. The main considerations for such exhibitions are evident: strong, light construction; compatibility of services, voltages and so on; and construction from easily cleaned and repaired materials. They should be designed with repackaging as an integral feature. Problems arise when exhibitions of this kind are considered in conjunction with valuable or fragile exhibits, neither of which lend themselves to constant handling. It is also necessary to keep the maintenance of such exhibitions to a minimum, since museums have differing facilities for such work. Some have none at all.

Mobile again means precisely that. It is an exhibition which has its own wheels or, in some cases, keel. In the UK the use of such a design is more common among commercial organizations or Government information services, for there is in fact a very wide distribution of museums among the population. However, in countries like Canada, where the population is more widely spread, there are many communities hundreds of miles from a museum, and this has led to the creation of a successful and continuing programme to take the museum to the public. Caravans, trains and even fishing boats have been most effectively used. There are rare occasions when this is the logical solution in this country, but before embarking on such a scheme it would be as well to consult organizations which have been involved in the production of such exhibitions.

An exhibition's informative qualities, not being practical, are more difficult to define. Many words in specialist use take on a meaning peculiar to the user and the words 'thematic', 'systematic' and so on – used in the beginning of this section – apply only to broad types of exhibition, although in a single exhibition many different types of display can be found. Work is currently being done on categorizing these display types, so it is dangerous to embark on definitions which may eventually be proved wrong.

Nevertheless, for the sake of this work an attempt must be made.

Thematic means with a theme, the theme being the original concept. The objects are found or made to support the story line. It is narrative-oriented (*Figure 67.1*).

Systematic means that it is evolved around a specific system of classification. Cases are laid out according to a classical order, or in order of the age of the objects. In broad terms, the collection exists, is classified and then the exhibition is laid out systematically around it. It is, therefore, largely object oriented (*Figure 67.2*).

Object-oriented is, however, a term often associated with one, or a collection of, fine objects not laid out in any system; it is simply the preferred order. The objects are the reasons for the display (*Figure 67.3*).

Interactive is probably the most misused word in the vernacular. It means a slightly different thing to almost every user. Does an interactive display interact with a neighbouring display or the visitor in front of it? Is it interacting or responding? Is it interactive or simply active? Those displays which depend for their effect on the visitor's contribution, whether electronic or mechanical, should be termed *interactive* (*Figure 67.4*). Those which are simply changing or oscillating constantly should be termed *active*. Those which automatically respond to the arrival of the visitor should be termed *responsive* (*Figure 67.5*). Therefore, those which respond to the visitor's arrival and depend on his presence are *responsive–interactive*.

Presentation

The museum designer must not be considered simply as an arranger, decorator or man of taste. In fact he will hate to be so considered, commonplace though it is to think of the designer in those terms, or

Figure 67.1   Story of the Earth (James Gardner, 1972)

Figure 67.2   British fossils (Geological Museum, 1980)

Figure 67.3 Apollo module (Science Museum, 1979)

even as a man of fashion. A museum designer is an *information designer* or nothing. It is the information that, in today's museum, is considered by the visitor to be integral with the object. Museums that make no effort to inform are rewarded by poor attendance, despite the public's rising interest and awareness of cultural matters. In a *narrative-oriented* exhibition it is the glamour of the story which attracts the public: for instance, the temporary bicentenary exhibition at the National Maritime Museum in 1976 or the permanent 'Story of the Earth'[1] exhibition at the Geological Museum, opened in 1972. The construction of those narratives is crucial to the story told in three-dimensional form and the presentation of the story's words is the basic design problem. The effective designer must be involved, not only in the deployment of these words, but also in their quantity, meaning and use. It is no good, for instance, choosing big, easy-to-read and eye-catching type for headings that cannot be understood. In fact the designer is, if sufficiently detached, an excellent arbiter of what is comprehensible to the

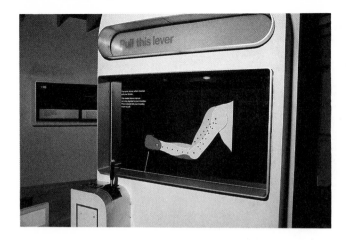

Figure 67.4   Human biology (British Museum, Natural History, 1976)

Figure 67.5   Earthquake simulation operated by pressure pad below final step and under target (Geological Museum, 1981)

ordinary visitor. If his knowledge of the subject is too specialized he ceases to be of value in this way and professional advice should be sought.

Museums, almost uniquely among exhibitions, demand a presentation of real information in clear terms. It is possible (and should happen wherever possible) to display objects in such a way that their relationship to each other is in part explanatory. A simple example might be a block of raw material, wood or clay, shown evolving into a carving or a piece of pottery. These might be presented alongside the tools or photographs or diagrams to show the production techniques at each stage. A minimum quantity of words will be required in such a display, especially when compared with the number of words needed to explain the evolution of a single artefact. The minimum quantity of words must be free of jargon unless it is aimed solely at specialists, but it takes skilled writing to produce them. It is effectively an interpretative skill. Comparatively few academics can explain their own discipline in writing without using technical terms, but such terms not only deter the possibly interested; they also exclude the actually interested.

Professional editor/writers, both staff and free-lance are increasingly being used to bridge the gap between the academic and the public but they are all too often resisted. It is hard to understand why. Nobody would dream of publishing a medical thesis in a daily paper but specialist medical correspondents often write excellent synopses for public consumption. Government Ministers can rarely understand the complex submissions of their own experts in defence or agriculture for example; again skilled writers produce effective summaries. It is difficult in a rapidly evolving profession but it is a problem which cannot be avoided.

Another aspect of the use of words is that of their position in a display or exhibition. Obviously they should be put in a position where they can be easily read, but many a designer of a contemporary exhibition has apparently ignored this basic consideration. In the Age of Chivalry exhibition at the Royal Academy (1988) for example, many presumably interesting labels were out of range for normally sighted people. When the new Clore Gallery was opened at the Tate Gallery two blocks of text, amounting to 1500 words (a 5-minute read) were placed in the 1.5 m wide access to the Watercolour Room. One or two people reading this text almost blocked the doorway and caused considerable problems of circulation. Such matters seem self-evident, but the two examples just cited demonstrate how commonsense seems to elude both designers and curators in the high drama that sometimes prevails when producing an exhibition.

Whilst discussing the presentation of information, it is relevant to consider for a moment the reception of it. Assuming that most museum visitors are literate, it is wrong to assume that they will read in the same way or with the same motivation. Certain people read everything avidly from the 'E numbers' on a sauce bottle to the health warning on a cigarette advertisement. Others resist reading almost totally, preferring to acquire information experientially or aurally. Many people, and it is possible that most curators come into this category, are so stimulated by the sight of a lot of interesting-looking words that they cannot appreciate that others are depressed or repelled by them. The writer, who has acquired the basic skills of literacy, is however, like a number of designers, far more stimulated by visual experience than anything else. In a hierarchy of preferred means of information reception, written words come fourth after visual stimuli, actual experience and spoken words; yet the writer's preferred means of communicating is the spoken word, the spoken word accompanied by visual aids (drawings, prepared or spontaneous), exhibitions, i.e. objects and pictures backed up by minimal text, text backed up by pictures in a book or article and finally written text on its own.

These are the somewhat disjointed thoughts of a non-academic. Clearly, however, there is room for further thought and research when it comes to presenting information. We take great risks when we make assumptions about our audience, even assumptions based on visitor research. There are no definitive rules; there are tests such as the Fry test (Fry, 1968) for calculating reading levels, but the test only examines readability, not the reader.

Types of designer

Consideration of the extent of involvement of the designer inevitably leads to a discussion of what type of designer is or should be involved in museum work. In such a recent discipline it is inevitable that practitioners should come from a variety of backgrounds. Interior designers, through invitation or demand, have moved into the field. Graphic designers likewise are employed in museums or design practices working on flat production or publications, some with the right experience, move across into 3D design. Now, however, Humberside Polytechnic has established a Centre for Museum and Exhibition Design Studies in Hull, this has an honours degree course. With increasing public interest in heritage matters, universities and design colleges are paying serious attention to the possibilities of the subject as a speciality. It is the selection of such a person that is clearly in need of consideration. It is vital for the curator–designer relationship to be that of equals: professional to professional. It is hopeless for the curator to see the designer as the expresser of his own ideas and fancies. He should employ someone whose work, or pictures of whose work, he has seen, understood and respected: someone who can execute the curator's policies in the designer's style. If the curator's policy leads more in one direction than another, then the designer should be selected with a similar leaning. It should be someone with an interior-design background if it is the development of the museum as a tourist attraction with increased public facilities; someone with a graphic design background if the museum's three-dimensional form is essentially unchangeable and the information presentation is paramount. If the curatorial policy is to start afresh with new exhibitions and galleries, then it is best to employ a designer with a background in exhibitions. This last type of designer is also likely to, and indeed should, along with the graphic designer, have a strong informational bias and, if not actually a graphic designer, will certainly appreciate the need to use such a designer in the production team.

The word 'team' has, until now, been avoided deliberately. Among the museum fraternity the numbers of establishments who can even think of employing teams of people is minimal. To many, even one full-time designer is out of the question. There is no doubt, however, that team production – where complementary talents are assembled in concerted effort – is an ideal to be striven for. A small museum occasionally acquires lump sums, or can find sponsors of a once-only exhibition on popular or industrially connected subjects, so that small museums would be well-advised to hire a design team on a freelance basis for the production of that one exhibition. There are many design practices in existence offering varying levels of capability, but frequently the quality, or lack of it, it as much to do with the relationship between the commissioner and the commissioned as it is to do with the abilities of the members of the practice. The curator in the position of needing such expertise should spend part of his new-found budget travelling from one newly constructed exhibition to another until he finds one that he understands and with which he is in sympathy. He should then hire the design practice responsible for it, not before talking to both the academic and the designer to sound out any possible future difficulties.

Larger museums can, of course, afford to employ teams and it is the make-up of these teams, together with the attitude of the employer towards the teams which will determine their success. There can be no set rule, but a team of four designers will undoubtedly need managing by a fifth member, preferably a specialist design manager. The other four might well be two exhibition designers, a graphic designer and an information designer – a newly emerging specialism. There is a good case for

employing a scriptwriter/editor in a museum where words are given a high priority; museums with a very strong natural science orientation for example. Perhaps that editor could assume the management, if not the leadership, of the team. The leader should be the most experienced person, and from any discipline within the team, provided he can articulate the ideals of the group. Every circumstance will make a different demand and these generalizations must be taken only as a very loose guide.

To refer back to the question 'in-house or freelance?', a big museum should have its own design team and place its confidence in it. That team's capabilities will be eroded if directors are constantly going to freelance practices for their more glamorous enterprises. A small museum is best advised to go freelance, but an in-house design post at a clearly defined level would be of great value, and act as a starting-point for a young designer.

The brief

Whether in-house or freelance, the essential link between the curator and the designer is the brief. This is a word easily used, but as easily misunderstood, being often confused with a script or a specification. A good brief *is* brief; it is the essential basic information together with a synopsis of the curator's requirements. The essential information is generally statistical (place, size, cost and so on), together with the curator's requirements of subject, purpose and duration. The best brief is evolved and written by the curator and the designer, but it is important that what is written does not take the form of a detailed specification. The ideal brief stimulates the designer. It is a catalyst. The bad brief depresses the designer. The quality of the brief will inevitably be reflected in the eventual design. There is a tendency for curators to instruct designers; to leave nothing to their initiative and to provide so many, often out-dated or impractical ideas of their own that there is no room for the designer's creativity to be fully exploited. Such curators should employ draughtsmen.

Assuming that the designer is well-chosen and capable, his creative input is of considerable value. This creative factor is rarely understood. It tends to be airily described as 'artistic' or assumed to be the ability to draw, choose materials or colours. Design is in fact the creative process allied to technical knowledge. The most easily understood expression of this alliance is the architect. The optimum effect of briefing a designer well is for that designer to find the perfect means of expressing the ideals in the brief. He must then convince the curator with drawings, models or words and then use his technical abilities to communicate that perfect solution through drawings and specifications to the craftsmen, technicians and contractors who will execute the finished exhibition.

The contractual side of the process or exhibition production is potentially less hazardous than the relationship between curators and designers. Nevertheless, the lack of business expertise of many curators can leave them at a considerable disadvantage when working with commercial organizations. It is as well to be aware of these shortcomings and to involve the museum's administrators closely in any contractual arrangements. It is well to inform such administrators at an early stage of the general intentions and to describe what is to be done in the hope of gaining their interest in, and sympathy for, the ideals. If, in fact, all contracts are placed at an informed adminstrative level, it leaves the curator and in-house designer free to maintain their necessarily amicable relationships with the various producers while any contractual or financial conflicts are ironed out by executives elsewhere. It is also advisable, where possible, to place contracts precisely where they are needed. Involvement with one company and many subcontractors means the museum will pay the main contractor's handling charges on top of the subcontractor's actual costs, while simultaneously losing control of the work done by the subcontractor. If the museum wants all the supervisory chores taken off its hands, then it can pay that price, but it should remember that if the main contractor goes bankrupt it will lose everything. The subcontracts might well be for models and special effects, photographic or screen-printed treatments, and audio-visual devices. If contracted by the museum, it will have total control of their production and also will be in a position to monitor any unforeseen developments. Obviously, basic contractual items such as electrical wiring or lighting, or decorative work can be precisely specified and, therefore, subcontracted by the main contractor if he does not hold these services, but anything which involves other designers or craftsmen with development work is best contracted and supervised by the commissioner of the exhibition. As stated earlier, an intrinsic part of the brief is the cost, and any competent designer must be able to stay within, or close to, that stated.

Publicity

There are two areas which are given very little consideration by the commissioners of exhibitions but which are, in fact, very important. The first is the publicity associated with the exhibition. This ranges from a curator's fond hope that the press might notice what he has done, to the employment of a full publicity machine drumming up an audience with which the exhibition and staff are completely unable to cope. It is not up to the designer to go out and publicize his exhibition (though if he is freelance and the exhibition is good, he will welcome the publicity). The essence is balance; good exhibitions do acquire their own audiences with very little bought publicity, but it is a slow process. A campaign of press releases, interviews, television coverage or posters which can generate media hysteria over evocative subjects such as 'gold' can produce an audience far in excess of the exhibition's capacity to cope. The publicist should be involved at the design stage of the exhibition to assess the possible traffic of visitors, and their ease and spread of movement resulting from the positioning and readability of the captions and labels. He can then at least attempt the depth of publicity coverage which will attract the right number of the right type of visitors. Unhappily, when this is not done the public is subjected to horrendous conditions never experienced or reported by journalists on press day. Simply because the public do not complain, nothing is done. It can, and should be. It is up to the curator and the designer to consider the problem with professional publicists and evaluators. On the other hand, a delightful but empty exhibition is as great – if not as offensive – a disaster. It cannot be emphasized enough that the employment of professionals (in any field) while initially costing often hard-earned money, does generally pay off in the long term; if not necessarily in countable cash, certainly in the knowledge that the enterprise which costs so much is not just there as a monument to curatorial and design expertise, but is of positive service and benefit to the community.

Maintenance

The second generally ill-considered area is that of maintenance. While this certainly applies to temporary exhibitions, especially when electronic, mechanical or live exhibits are concerned, it is a problem most associated with permanent constructions. Where galleries are fabricated on conventional, 'show-case and panel' lines, the only maintenance to be considered is that involved with the deterioration of the structure, decorative finishes and lighting, together with the regular cleaning (these comments are restricted to the exhibition, not to the exhibits or objects on display – they are a curatorial problem). In most exhibitions built today there is at least one audio-visual system involving a minimum of three projectors. There may well be other devices which will need regular attention from either their manufacturer, his agent, or staff especially employed by the museum. Again it is a question of balance. Many manufacturers will enter into service or maintenance contracts, but how quickly they can get to the ailing device is one thing and how much this service will cost when a large number of units is involved is worth taking into account when compared with the value and cost of in-house maintenance technicians. In the process of design, the designer, confronted by the too small space and too long script, will be anxious to direct the bulk of the space towards the public. So often this is done at the expense of access for service personnel. Good design will consider maintenance at the earliest planning stages and the far-sighted curator will ensure that this is so. At the same time, the curator must consider the long-term maintenance needs at the earliest point in costing. He will also balance his exhibition programme with the need to employ further maintenance and cleaning staff as new areas and galleries open to the public. Obviously if he cannot foresee the staff being available he must balance his exhibition policy accordingly. A poorly maintained exhibition with non-working display devices is worse than no exhibition at all.

Summary

Permanent exhibitions should be designed to give objects dominance or context and not be expressions of fashionable decorative ideas. Temporary exhibitions can, however, explore or exploit contemporary themes to the advantage of the display. Recessive exhibitions need not, however, be dull, grey, neutral places. Judicious complementary use of light, colour or texture can ensure that exhibitions are lively, cheerful and inviting places to visit.

It is dangerous for the curator to assume that there is always a 'scientific' solution to every problem, either of management or presentation. It is very possible to eliminate the chance of serendipity which, emerging from a harmonious team of curator, writer and designer, can give an exhibition a unique charm and pulling power. All too often over-analysis can be destructive. We all know of exhibitions that seem to break every rule and yet are highly successful; others that have been prepared with considerable thought remain lifeless and dull. In museums it is important to remember that ordinary people are the end-users. This surprisingly gives museum and automotive design something powerful in common. It is only necessary to think of the huge success of the Volkswagen Beetle – ugly, awkward to drive, tail-heavy, susceptible to side winds and uncomfortable. Human beings, no matter what the statistics say, are unpredictable. Human Biology at the British Museum (Natural History) was the first exhibition of its most recent period of modernization and, therefore, based on the least experience and yet it is the most successful.

Everything said in this chapter has been in the form of advice and generalizations, hopefully informative but in no sense didactic. Even when care has been taken to be explicit about the exact meaning of the words used, there has been only the most superficial treatment of the subject.

Design and creativity, while in no sense dependent on fashion, are undoubtedly influenced by it. Materials and techniques are continually evolving and developing. What is considered to be fundamental today may be trivial tomorrow. The concern of this section has been to help the curator and design worker together to a pre-stated, common good. It has been concerned to show that the designer, recently arrived on the museum scene, is a professional and, when treated and respected as such by the curator, is an integral part of the expression of the best museological ideals. Designers are, by and large, advocates of the theory that form follows function. If the function is clearly defined and its demands met then the form which follows from the designer will generally be satisfactory. Design is not an exclusive world wherein the visually oriented lurk, hiding their fiendish and exotic ideas from the curator lest he balk at their expression; it is a specialist field. It is unlikely that even with the aid of visuals or models, the curator will ever be able to visualize clearly what the designer intends. A large element of trust is therefore involved. The importance to the curator of knowing the designer's capabilities cannot be overstressed. The expression of confidence in the designer should encourage him to produce his best and not surprise the curator with outlandish displays or costly and unnecessary gimmicks. The ultimate aim of both must be the improvement of the visitor's mind and the enhancement of his life.

Notes

1. These exhibitions are not quoted as examples of success or failure, but as examples of type.

Bibliography

BELCHER, M. (1991) *Exhibitions in Museums*, Leicester University Press, Leicester/Smithsonian Institution Press, Washington

BORMUTH, J. R. (1966), Readability: a new approach, *Reading Research Quarterly*, **1**, 79–132

DALE, E. and CHALL, J. S. (1948), 'A formula for predicting readability', *Educational Research Bulletin*, **27**, 11–20, 37–54

FLESCH, R. (1948), 'A new readability yardstick', *Journal of Applied Psychology*, **32**(3), 221–233

FLESCH, R. (1949), *The Art of Readable Writing*, Harper and Brothers, New York

FLESCH, R. (1950), 'Measuring the level of abstraction', *Journal of Applied Psychology*, **34**, 384–390

FLESCH, R. (1951), *How to Test Readability*, Harper and Brothers, New York

FRY, E. (1968), 'A readability formula that saves time', *Journal of Reading*, **11**, 513–516

GILLILAND, J. (1972), *Readability*, University of London Press, London

HALL, M. (1987), *On Display*, Lund Humphries, London

HUNT, J. D. and BROWN, P. J. (1971), 'Who can read our writing?', *Journal of Environmental Education*, **2**(4), 27–29

KLARE, G. R. (1963), *The Measurement of Readability*, Iowa State University Press, Iowa

MATTHEWS, G. (1991), *Museums and Art Galleries*, Butterworth Architecture, Oxford

MCLAUGHLIN, H. (1969), 'Smog grading – a new readability formula', *Journal of Reading*, **22**, 639–646

TINKER, M. A. (1963), *Legibility of Print*, Iowa State University Press, Iowa

VELARDE, G. (1988), *Designing Exhibitions*, Design Council, London

68

Museum education

Eilean Hooper-Greenhill

Introduction

This chapter aims to provide a starting point in the construction of a philosophy of museum education, a philosophy which has partly emerged through a long tradition of thought and action concerned with learning and teaching with objects and specimens. The broad historical parameters of the practices of learning and teaching with objects will be outlined, although an analysis of discontinuities in these practices will not be addressed here.[1] This chapter is also written as a guide and a resource for further reading. There are, therefore, many references in the text, and an extensive bibliography.

Learning and teaching with objects has often entailed the collection of groups of related things, whether by individuals, groups, or by the state. Conversely, the existence of a collection of things has promoted and enabled the production of knowledge (Hooper–Greenhill, 1992a). In some cases collections of objects have been assembled in order to shape consciousness in the context of ruling class control (Hooper-Greenhill, 1980). In other cases a more democratic end has been paramount (Chadwick, 1983). The construction of a world view through the choice of representative objects and their arrangement in space has been an enduring function for collections, although the world view so represented has varied with time, space, individual subjectivities and the context of knowing.

This chapter also aims to emphasize the importance of this long-undervalued area of museum work (Miers, 1928; Markham, 1938; Rosse, 1963; Wright, 1973; Eisner and Dobbs, 1986), in such a way as to support those who are engaged in it or who are sympathetic towards it. It should not be forgotten that education is one of the prime functions of a museum and the reason for the existence of a museum. In the case of museums governed by charitable trusts there is a requirement in law to meet educational objectives. It should be stated very firmly at the outset that museums have clear responsibilities in their educational work both to the public (actual and potential) and to the educational workers within museums. It should also be noted that many museums fail on both counts. There is a pressing need both for more knowledge of who this public is (Hooper-Greenhill, 1988b, p. 220) and for at least adequate resources and personnel to work in the museum on behalf of this public. The General Certificate of Secondary Education (GCSE) is one area of work for a specific user-group that has been emphasized recently (Anon, 1987; Hale, 1987, p. 22; Millar, 1987; Museums Association, 1987), as has the equivalent Standard Grade in Scotland (Lawson, 1987), but this is just one area of need among many.

Curators and museum educators are often suspicious of each other. It has become clear that curators have been unaware of the training, skills, expertise, and experience of many educational personnel, despite (or perhaps because of) the fact that curators are likely to be the most under-trained section of the museum staff (Hale, 1987). Other staff members, particularly the educators, are far more likely to have had specialist training. Curators tend to experience the use of 'their' objects as a threat, and in some cases complain about 'their' galleries being used by education staff who have not first approached them to discuss how this should be done. In turn, museum educators often experience curators as distant and unhelpful, and unaware of (and uninterested in) recent educational developments and requirements.

These difficulties are sometimes more pronounced in the larger departmental museums. In smaller museums, communications are likely to be much better, and curators and educators are likely to work more closely together and to share the same goals and objectives. The possibilities of using each other as resources is acknowledged, with the educator making suggestions as to appropriate topical themes for temporary exhibitions, and for relevant and interesting ways of communicating, and the curator helping the educator develop the necessary specialist knowledge about the collections and providing selected objects to be either handled, demonstrated or simply observed more closely than is possible in a display case. It must also be said that some museum educators are unaware of the 'museum' context within which they are required to work, and do not understand the curatorial concerns of their colleagues. There is no excuse for this, and it behoves both curators and educators to move more than half way towards each other in the joint objective of improving the museum experience for their publics. Clearly the overall work of the museum, both curatorial and educational, will be greatly enhanced if various specialist staff members respect and allow for the expertise of others (Locke, 1984).

Museum educationalists work to create relationships between the museum and its public. Problems may often emerge which stem from the dual functions of museums, to preserve and to display, to keep contained and to expose. Successful educational work articulates a combination of balances – first, a balance between the internal and external needs of the museum and its actual and potential audience, educational 'cover' for the entire museum collections as far as possible, and a response to curriculum needs; second, a balance of provision for different audiences, which includes all kinds of formal and informal educational groups, pre-school, primary, secondary, tertiary, special education, open university, teacher trainers, teachers in-service, clubs, specialist groups, holiday groups, etc; and third, a balance of different forms and scales of provision both in the museum and in the community, which might include hour-long structured taught sessions, half-day discovery sessions, day-long drama-work, teachers' courses, loan services, written materials, film and video, lectures for adult groups, concerts, walks, or even a mobile museum.

The history and philosophy of museum education

Museum education is centrally concerned with teaching from and learning with objects and specimens. Epistemological interest in the use of things has emerged in different and sometimes contradictory ways in the histories of teaching and learning in Europe, but enough evidence can be identified to suggest that museum education and object-teaching, if they have not been intimate bed-fellows, have at least gone hand-in-hand.

In the early Middle Ages, Thomas Aquinas stated that 'human cognition is stronger in regard to the

sensibilia', and that 'it is natural to man to reach the *intelligibilia* through the *sensibilia* because all our knowledge has its beginnings in sense' (Yates, 1966). By *sensibilia*, Aquinas is referring to 'sense impressions' or 'data' collected through the use of the senses, in other words the processes of human relationships to objects (Hooper-Greenhill, 1988c). Later, Roger Bacon emphasized the *argumentum ex re* the observation of the things themselves rather than the exposition of doctrine (Heidegger, 1951, p. 6).

During the Renaissance, knowing consisted of endless and circular references to all that had ever been written about a particular phenomenon, with no distinction made between that which had been observed from the real thing, that which had been written about it, and those myths and fables which surrounded it (Foucault, 1970). Collections were compiled to represent the entire structure of knowledge, the theatre of the world (Kaufmann, 1978; Laurencich-Minelli, 1985).

As a reaction to the complexities of this, and as an attempt to cut away the endless proliferating words that had previously obscured the 'true' meaning of the thing itself, seventeenth-century philosophers and educationalists emphasized 'solid philosophy', the direct study of nature, and the rejection of all knowledge that could not be demonstrated through the study of objects (Hunter, 1981). Francis Bacon was instrumental in promulgating this new approach to knowing, and Comenius applied Bacon's ideas to education: 'Instruction will succeed if the method follows the course of nature. It must begin with actual inspection, not with verbal description of things. What is actually seen remains faster in the memory than description a hundred times repeated. . . It is good to use several senses in the understanding of one thing. . . Things and words should be studied together. . . The first education should be of the perceptions, then of the memory, then of the understanding, then of the judgement' (Calkins, 1880). At least one museum (the Repository of the Royal Society) was established during the late seventeenth century specifically to enable this approach to learning at the scholarly level (Purver and Bowen, 1960, p. 5; Ornstein, 1938, p. 109; Hunter, 1981, p. 65), while in 1660 'Mr John Tradescants, or the like houses or gardens, where rarities are kept' were recommended for the 'full improvement of children in their education' (Mac-Gregor, 1983, p. 23).

At the end of the eighteenth century, the Louvre in Paris was the first free public museum established as part of the state education system (Hudson, 1987, p. 42). Cheap catalogues were produced, written from the point of view of the visitor rather than the curator (Hudson, 1987, p. 186) and translated into several languages. The Louvre acted as the central museum in a country-wide network of museums which together were intended to partly enable the transformation of the still feudal peasant into a citizen of the Republic. For the first time, the Museum was constituted as an instrument of public education (Hooper-Greenhill, 1988a). This had a great influence in Europe, with new major institutions being established, particularly in Germany. In Britain, the British Museum had emerged earlier, composed of three private cabinets, and the new museum retained the features of this earlier institutional model, with lip-service only paid to the needs and rights of the public. Indeed, the British Museum was celebrated as being 'like a family' as late as 1973 (Miller, 1973, p. 17). Nonetheless, even in Britain, museums were seen during the nineteenth century as institutions with education and social objectives, along with libraries, public parks, and swimming pools (Hooper-Greenhill, 1991a).

During the nineteenth century, small collections, cabinets and museums were established in schools to furnish the required objects (Busse, 1880, p. 423; Board of Education, 1931, p. 17). Mechanics Institutes compiled small museums as an integral part of their educational work (Chadwick, 1983, pp. 50–53). Many museums were explicitly established with educational purposes. Early literary and philosophical societies at the beginning of the nineteenth century with their libraries and, later, museums, were among the media of dissemination of the radical ideas concerning the power of education to effect social change (Lawson and Silver, 1973. p. 229). The Museums at South Kensington, originally the Museum of Science and the Museum of Art, were established to exhibit the progress of scientific discovery and the best of aesthetic design, for both educational and economic purposes.

The 'object-lesson' was a major feature of nineteenth-century schooling (Lawson and Silver, 1973, p. 248) and its philosophical context is firmly set within the progressive, child-centred theories of Rousseau, Pestalozzi and Froebel, which in contemporary writing are placed in relation to the earlier ideas of Bacon and Comenius (Calkins, 1880; Busse, 1880). Although in the event much object-teaching may well have degenerated into rote learning, a process that was no doubt partly enabled by the production of endless methods textbooks, the initial aims of the object-lesson were imaginative and forward looking. The purposes of object-teaching were to develop all the child's faculties in the acquisition of knowledge, rather than to impart facts or information *per se* (Calkins, 1880). This 'development of sense-perceptions', combined with reflection and judgement, was to lead to appropriate activity based on the existing knowledge and competencies of the child. In short, in some of these late-nineteenth-century discussions of the philosophy and principles of object-teaching we are looking,

on the one hand, back towards the *sensibilia* of Aquinas, and on the other forwards towards the familiar child-centred progressive theories later to be crystallized by John Dewey (Dewey, 1979), they underlie much of the most valuable educational work in schools, particularly primary schools, during this century.

What is learning with objects? How do you do it? As Aquinas and Comenius would recommend, learning and teaching with objects starts from sense-perceptions, from the use of all five senses to accumulate as much data as possible about the object(s) under analysis. This data is then discussed, related to previous information and experience, and compared with the perceptions of others. A synthesis of material demands the input of further information, and may promote research on the part of the teacher, the learner, or both together. Hypotheses and deductions as to use and meaning over time and through space may be constructed and tested. The meaning of things is not limited to one interpretation only. Individual interpretations may hold as much weight as scholarly ones, depending on the framework of reference used. Perceptions may be extended or changed through new imput, either from other objects or other forms of information, including manuscripts, photographs, maps, letters, tapes, or through the perceptions of others.

Some objects stimulate or are discovered through practical activity, either in being recorded through drawing, writing, or photography, or through their use (or the simulation of this). Some objects stimulate interest and questioning through their oddness or attractiveness. Objects can be a lot more interesting both to teach with and to learn from, than

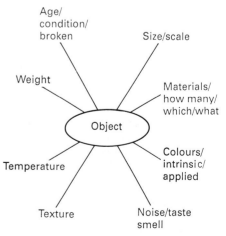

Looking, touching, feeling, listening, smelling, tasting

Figure 68.1 Sensory exploration

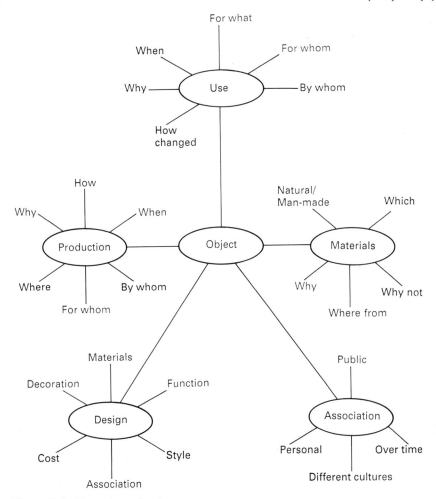

Figure 68.2   Discussion and analysis

books. All objects require other sources of data to release their full information potential. Many objects lead learning into curious unpredictable paths, and most reveal the arbitrariness both of subject boundaries in the school and of collection classification schemes in the museum. Museums objects also lead to questions about the roles and functions of the museum, which in itself is a very important aspect of museum education. Although object-teaching is unfamiliar to many teachers, practice with an open mind and in a sympathetic environment soon brings expertise. *Figures 68.1* to *68.5* suggest one methodological process that works both in the museum and in the classroom, and suggest ways in which objects cross-relate to many areas of the curriculum. Experience will soon provide other ways of working (Durbin, Morris and Wilkinson, 1990).

The object-lesson at its best was, and is, intended to enable many different approaches to the learning

of skills, including the training of the senses, the development of thinking, and the development of language (Busse, 1880; Delahaye, 1987). It underpins museum education today as it has done for a very long time.

The development of educational services in museums during the twentieth century has been sporadic and haphazard. It has followed no national plan, and specific instances have emerged as a response to local need (Hooper-Greenhill, 1992b). Some outstanding practitioners can be identified (Harrison, 1950, 1967; Winstanley, 1966), but often the work done has gone unrecorded and unremarked. The pattern outlined by Carter (1984) can be traced through reference to the major contemporary reports (British Association for the Advancement of Science, 1920; Miers, 1928; Markham, 1938; Rosse, 1963). Bassett's useful bibliographic essay should also be consulted (Bassett, 1984).

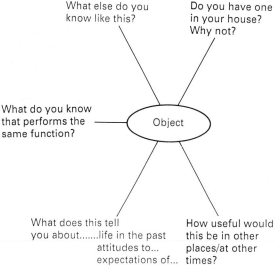

Figure 68.3   Remembering, comparing and synthesizing

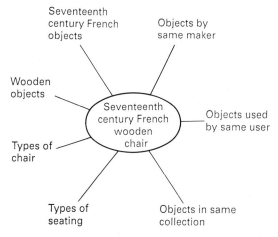

Figure 68.4   Objects can be multi-contexted: one object can lead into many different ideas; other objects will develop a specific approach theme; and related material (documents, photographs, drawings, buildings, film and people) 'thickens' the context

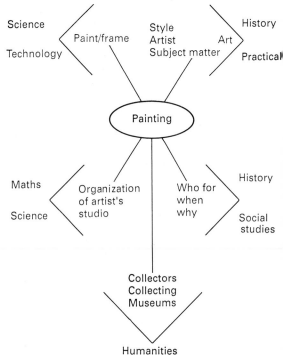

Figure 68.5   Objects are cross-curricular

The two reports on museums in Scotland (Williams, 1981; Miles, 1986) are the most useful of the recent governmental reports on museums when it comes to thinking about museum education. Williams (1981) discusses museum education in the context of the communicative function of the museum, which it sees as a 'keystone in the conduct of the whole museum' (Williams, 1981). It is further pointed out that 'the status and standard of a museum's education department are measures of that institution's commitment in the field of education'. The report goes on to deal with structural provision for education in the larger museums and stresses that education should have a properly constituted departmental structure in the same way as the other departments of the museum, with a head of department at Keeper level. Where there is the possibility to employ several staff these should represent a variety of expertise covering different subject areas and different age-related teaching experience. Strong links should be made with other departments, which include practical working together on such matters as the type of display, the 'storyline', or conceptual objectives of exhibitions, and the presentation and content of labels.

Miles (1986) deals with the matter of educational provision in the non-national museums and reiterates many of the points concerning the general educational responsibility of museums. The variety of educational work carried out by curators in museums without specialist staff is discussed.

It is clear that there are many choices to be made in deciding on the form and content of educational provision in the museum. As with other work areas of the museum, there is a need for a policy to articulate priorities in relation to objectives (Hooper-Greenhil, 1991b). This must be drawn up after reviewing the differential weightings of the following elements – the objectives of the museum, the nature of its collections, the expertise of the staff, the existing pattern of public use, potential new patterns of use, the sources and availability of resources, relationships with the Local Education Authority, the location of the museum, and evaluative practices. In addition, and perhaps most importantly, the educational philosophy of the museum, department, or members of staff concerned (Hooper-Greenhill, 1983, 1987a).

Some museums and museum authorities are now beginning to produce policy statements. This is recommended by the Museums & Galleries Commission (1991), the Audit Commission (1991) and the Museums Association (1991), as suggested by published guidelines and case studies (Hooper-Greenhill, 1991b). Hertfordshire, a County Museum Authority, has produced a thoughtful and comprehensive document that reviews the current situation in the three main museums in the county, relates it to possible extended provision and proposes a two-stage development plan over 5 years. This kind of coherent thinking is vitally needed in this (as in all other) area of museum work. Policy statements for specific educational provision such as the production of materials for teachers, or the teaching of particular groups, for example, need to be written in the context of the communicative objectives of the museum as a whole, including the display and exhibition policy, and other policies that relate to the qualitative experience of the visitors.

The current scene

The recent Museums Association study (Prince and Higgins-McLoughlin, 1987) suggests that less than 5 per cent of the total full-time staff (including security staff) are employed in each of either education, conservation or design work. Education staff make up a tiny percentage of the staff as a whole: 1.8 per cent in national museums, 3.6 per cent in Local Authority museums, and 2.1 per cent in independent and other museums. Carter (1984, p. 437) identified 362 professional museums posts in education in 154 museums. Volunteers and Manpower Services Commission workers are extensively employed in educational work in museums, particularly in private-sector museums (Prince and Higgins-McLoughlin, 1987, pp. 103–105).

Full-time specialist education staff are employed in a number of different ways, with no overall national pattern of employment, remuneration or working practice. National museum education staff have up till now been employed as Civil Servants on Civil Service pay scales along with the other museum staff. They work museum (Civil Service) hours with museum holidays. Government plans for the national museums include the employment of staff by the Trustees directly, which may have a bearing on the employment of educational workers. Education departments in the national museums generally take responsibility for the provision of service for all sections of the museum's clientèle.

Until recently Local Authority museum education staff have been employed directly through the Museum Committee budget, or have been financed through the Education Committee budget to teach in the museum, or have been employed through a combination of monies from both these sources. In Leicester, for example, the Local Education Authority paid four-fifths of the salaries of the education staff, and the museum service paid the remainder. The staff were museum officers, but tend to work exclusively with schools and teachers. Work with adult groups is covered in the main by curatorial staff. In Birmingham, a secondment system is in operation, where teachers are employed directly by the Local Education Authority, working teachers' hours and with teachers' holidays, and pay scales, and are seconded to work in the museum, again working only with schools. Many different varieties of arrangement have evolved to meet local needs and possibilities (Bateman, 1984). Section 11 (*Local Government Act 1966*) monies have been used to fund education posts in a handful of Local Authority museums. With changes in the structures of local government, much is in flux at the moment.

A new form of educational provision has made its appearance and that is the use of sponsorship monies to pay for educational staff. At the Barbican Art Gallery in London, British Petroleum PLC have sponsored an education officer to work for a period of three years. Dulwich Picture Gallery has acquired sponsorship to fund two one-day-a-week posts for specialist provision for two very particular areas of work. These are work with handicapped schools and work with deprived schools. At the Geffrye Museum in London the excellent educational work carried out by the education staff has been supplemented by a local charitable foundation and industrial sponsorship. Although sponsorship may supplement existing educational provision in the short term, it is no substitute for permanently employed education staff.

The Museums Association study showed that approximately one-third of all museum visits are made by children, and given that some museums are unable to discriminate in their figures between adults and children, this figure could in fact be substantially higher (Prince and Higgins-McLoughlin, 1987, p. 135). Although museum education is not only concerned with work with children, the mismatch between the percentage of child visits (30 per cent) and the percentage of education staff to provide for them (less than 5 per cent) is very striking. This is the kind of statistic that underlies the story one hears about a large national museum whose visitor figures were falling, but whose education department was turning away customers because they were overstretched. Most museum education workers in large and small museums *are* overstretched. With museums looking desparately for ways to demonstrate their relevance to society in the late twentieth century, this is a thoroughly ludicrous situation, and one that must be changed in the very near future.

In the past, all but the national museums have largely depended on the Local Education Authority to provide either extra money or extra staff for educational provision. This has indeed been the recommendation of nearly all the Government reports. But it has not worked. There are very few education authorities that provide anywhere near the amount of educational provision that is needed. It is now time for Local Authority and independent museums to consider museum education staff as more central to the responsibility of the museum as a whole and to consider employing education staff from the museum staffing budget as the national museums do. This would be a radical change in policy, but would avoid many of the problems that occur when there are two sets of working conditions in one institution. With recommendations currently being made that every museum should provide an Education Officer (Anon, 1987), perhaps new decisions over priority staffing need to be made? With new methods of allocating the LEA schools budget, following the *Education Reform Act 1988*, it is possible that any monies previously used to support museum education may be withdrawn. This will force museums to develop new ways of funding the delievery of educational services.

In the appointment of staff it is strongly recommended that all museum Education Officers should have successful teaching experience behind them (Miles, 1986) and that where possible this experience should span more than one age group. Museum education staff may work with all age groups from pre-school to postgraduate and adult students, and in the community with informal groups. A wide experience of communicating in different ways and at different levels is required.

The training available to museum education officers is, at present, limited (Hale, 1987). The only full-time course is at the Department of Museum Studies, where an education option is offered alongside curatorial options on the one-year postgraduate course (Hooper-Greenhill, 1985). The limited number of Government bursaries allocated to this course as a whole (13–15) which must be shared between all the different option groups, means that only a very small number are available for potential Education Officers. This course has been redesigned

and offered on a modular basis, with at least two 2-week modules of relevance to education and related staff. These are 'Museum education' and 'Communication'. These will form part of a full-time course of study but will also be available on an in-service basis.

The Ironbridge Institute offers courses on Heritage Interpretation, some of which are concerned with education and interpretation in the context of the heritage industry. The Museum Training Institute is developing standards of competence in museum education.

In some teacher-training courses there may be a museum-education component (Gooding, 1985), with perhaps the best example of this being the Museums Option in the Post Graduate Certificate in Education (PGCE) course at the Institute of Education, University of London. This has been running for a good number of years and involves work within a museum education department in London which is related to the school-based teaching practice (Paine, 1985). This is, however, designed more for the classroom teacher than for the museum teacher. The Inspectorate is currently encouraging the development of thinking among initial teacher trainers about how to use both museums and artefacts. Courses have been organized on a nationwide basis to encourage the permeation of the use of museums across the curriculum, and across the school-age range. Good practice in relation to the knowledge children should have of museums is described as follows: by the age of 7 years children should be aware of museums, have visitied at least one, and have handled artefacts; by the age of 11 children should have visited a variety of museums, understood their purposes, and have developed ciritical and discriminatory skills in relation to museums, have handled artefacts, and have undertaken sustained observation; by the age of 16 pupils should understand all the services of museums, be fluent in the skills required to work with artefacts and specimens, know what can and cannot be learnt from museums and their objects, and be familiar with the appropriate recording techniques (Moffat, 1988).

The specialist group concerned with museum education, the Group for Education in Museums (GEM),[3] offers valuable opportunities to meet colleagues, to discuss educational approaches, and to attend study sessions in museums. The annual conference has for some years taken the form of a study week. The Group produces a quarterly newsletter and an annual journal. The international committee of the International Council of Museums (ICOM) that covers museum education is the Committee for Education and Cultural Action (CECA). ICOM/CECA meet annually and publish *Education Annual* biannually.

The literature on museum education is mainly in the form of articles from journals, with very few books covering the topic, although two have recently been produced (Hooper-Greenhill, 1991a; and Berry and Mayer, 1989). GEM has produced a useful bibliography.

Museum education is currently being affected by wide social changes (Hooper-Greenhill, 1991a), by changes in the structure and financing of museums, and by educational changes. The wider social changes include the fact that the leisure learning market is increasing, and projected to increase from 5 to 10 per cent of total leisure spending by the end of this decade (Rodger, 1987, p. 35). Although the emphasis is on learning, 'learning' here must not be equated with the old chalk-and-talk school-based learning of which so many adults have negative memories, but must be seen, and marketed, as participative, exploratory, activity-based, and informal (Hood, 1983).

Changes in the structure and financing of museums include the move towards privatization and plural funding which is already identified in relation to the national museums, (Museum & Galleries Commission, 1985, p. 9–11; *The Independent*, No. 458, p. 1) and which is on the not very distant horizon for Local Authority museums. Museums are now being referred to at Government level as the 'museums industry' (Luce, 1988) and by marketing men as the 'museum business' (Rodger, 1987). The 'heritage industry' is a £30 billion marketplace and the governing bodies of museums are rapidly trying to identify their market share. Educational work in museums is increasingly being scrutinized in this context, and arguments about qualitative experience, and about different levels of educational provision must be developed and strongly argued. It is also cautionary to note the analysis and condemnation of the 'history' as mere nostalgia, or, worse, as a useless past, manufactured at rapid speed by the heritage industry and by museums in order to capitalize on this new market (Horne, 1984; Hewison, 1987; Bennett, 1988; West, 1988). New forms of relationships between the institutional form, collections and people (both user-groups and workers) need to be actively developed (Hooper-Greenhill, 1988b; Durrans, 1988).

Educational changes which are affecting museum education include the new forms of exams, with an emphasis on resource-based learning, investigation, and modular courses, (Millar, 1987; Lawson, 1987; Museums Association, 1987) and the National Curriculum. The stress on coursework, and the development of skills, concepts and understanding are leading to new opportunities for learning which will help to bring the museum and its resources into the front line (Goodhew n.d.). Museum education services are radically reviewing their practices in the light of these new possibilities and are finding new ways to make contacts in schools and to develop networks. In one example, having found ways to talk to potential users, the museum education staff designed provision that was jointly identified as necessary and relevant to the National Curriculum. This included teachers courses on the study of artefacts, support material for museum visits including videos and 'self-service' selections of artefacts for handling, and document packs that related to the collections.

Current main emphases in educational provision in museums include a shift from direct teaching to the provision of resources and training for teachers; investigation of how best to provide for the National Curriculum, including making links and networks with examiners, co-ordinators, and classroom teachers; new publishing initiatives related to new developments in museum shops; consolidation and development of the specialist group; an emphasis on community outreach work (Nicholson, 1985), and a growing concern for the museum as a really useful community resource (O'Neill, 1987).

Current problems are almost entirely related to money and to governmental policies of self-sufficiency. On the one hand governmental action in reducing public expenditure is threatening jobs in some areas of the country, and on the other hand the squeeze on museum finance and the resultant search for new sources of revenue and the move towards a 'market-led' approach is being crassly interpreted in some museums as an emphasis on quantity rather than quality. Very few museums have carried out efficient visitor needs assessment as recommended by museum planners (Lord and Lord, 1988, p. 176) and decisions are being made on visitor provision, emphasizing the visitor spend, in the time-honoured museum way, guesswork. Sensitive visitor analysis with clearly defined objectives such as that carried out at the National Portrait Gallery recently (Harvey, 1987) reveals information that can support and direct both general visitor policies and specific educational provision. For example, at the National Portrait Gallery, London, nearly half of the visitors specified that one of their hobbies (or a secondary job) was painting (Harvey. 1987, p. 10). This provides support and justification for the practical art sessions provided for adults at the gallery. It might even provide justification for restructuring and extending these sessions as a revenue-generating educational service. The development of a 'market-led' approach in the museum means researching the market, and building on the strengths of the qualitative work in which the museum is already experienced (Hooper-Greenhill, 1988d). Too often this is being dealt with at management level in a way that disregards the experience, expertise, contacts and needs of the educationalists in the museum. This is clearly neither cost-effective nor good management.

The current scene in museum education presents a crossroads of change. Clear policies and well-founded educational convictions will be required to identify ways forward that do not compromise the genuine museum learning experience.

Management, structure and organization

An ideal structure for a museum education department is a Head of Department at Keeper level assisted by officers with a variety of different subject expertise in relation to the collections and different educational experience including primary, secondary, adult and outreach work. This is, in general, only possible in the large departmental museums, and in many of the smaller museums, the work is done by one person. In some cases, staff work across a number of museums.

In the appointment of staff, the objectives of the museums are critical. At Sheffield and Dundee, for example, where outreach work in the community is a priority, officers with this kind of experience have been appointed. At Dundee, the appointment is linked to further training provision. Section 11 (*Local Government Act, 1966*) posts have been established in some Local Authority museums where multicultural work is a priority. These include Leicester, Bradford, Kirklees and Ipswich.

Clear communications are necessary both within the education department and within the museum. In all too many cases, there are large gaps in communication either within departments, or between education and curatorial workers. Clear delineations of responsibilities and tasks should be identified, and it should be clear how these interrelate within the department and the museum as a whole. Staff development should be considered and allowed for in the budget, including seminars and conferences, training or retraining to keep up with new educational methods and concerns both within the museum and in the educational world in general.

The educational work of the museum should have a clearly identified budget, which relates to the scale of the tasks identified and to the educational ambitions of the museum. Regular management meetings should be held, both within the department and with the other museum staff. These meetings should be used to review, evaluate (Hein, 1982; Otto, 1979) and develop current practice and to identify priorities. Short- and long-term objectives should be set. A booking system should be in operation, and a detailed diary kept up to date. From this useful statistics as to the type of user, the frequency of use, and the areas of non-use can be generated, as can mailing lists. Specialist accommodation (Carter, 1984, p. 439), often seen as a luxury,

is necessary, as is at least access to a library, and to administrative support. Within a large departmental structure, a specific administrative office is necessary. Where the education work includes a loan service, drivers and design staff are required.

The educationalists of the museum should be used more in the planning and production of permanent and temporary displays (Locke, 1984). This has been recommended for years by many reports (e.g. Williams, 1981, p. 122), but few museums have adopted this as part of their policies. Where this has happened, qualitative changes have emerged in the interaction of visitors with artefacts. For example, at Nottingham Castle, where the Education Officer was heavily involved with the writing of the labels, visitors can be observed spending longer than usual in front of each painting, discussing aspects of the painting that the label has suggested, such as the changes the artist made in the painting.

Education staff should always be included in management meetings where decisions are made that affect their work. (How many education officers have gone to teach in a particular gallery only to discover it closed for redecoration for 6 weeks? And I for one have had a picture removed from the walls as I was actually talking about it, although that was in the days before I learnt to shout.) Planning committees for exhibitions should include education staff. In making decisions about which exhibitions to mount, the views of the education staff should be sought. If education programmes are expected to be arranged around these exhibitions, the timing of the school year must be considered. How many exhibitions with excellent educational potential are planned to neatly straddle the summer holidays, or the Christmas carol concert bonanza? With schools encouraged to use museums and their exhibitions far more in their teaching it makes sense to inquire widely into how exhibitions can relate to consistent syllabus demands, and to plan programmes of exhibitions that, for example, show how to use museums, or how to 'read' objects, or develop a group of related objects into many different syllabus areas (see *Figure 68.5*). One example of an exhibition that explores the museum as a process is 'The Things That Time Forgot', held at the Geoffrye Museum in 1988.

In the relations outside the museum, lines of communication and networks of support to the Local Education Authority should be established and used. Other local and community groups can usefully be approached depending on the type of work that is identified as important. Multicultural work must be carried out in association with the various ethnic and religious groups, while work with special audiences such as the blind, will necessitate contact with the Royal National Institute for the Blind (RNIB) and local schools or day centres.

Networks can also be established between museums (Cox and Loftus, 1979). Joint projects can exploit the relationships between collections. Museum Countywide Consultative Committees may act as vehicles for joint ventures.

Relationships with the press are necessary. Holiday projects, specially imaginative or innovative work, or large-scale ventures can all be used to promote the image of the museum both locally and nationally. Publishing should be considered. Longmans have developed a good relationship with museums and this seems likely to develop. Ironbridge has recently published a useful series of guidelines. Accounts of work done, including photographs, descriptions of activities, educational principles, and the uses of artefacts might be turned into a saleable product now that teachers are looking for ways to use musuems. Now that museums are thinking about how to make themselves financially viable it must be said that museums hold vast resources and museum education staff are generally running very interesting projects which, if they were written up and well presented, would form interesting case studies. This is one way that sponsorship might be used, by paying for a temporary recorder and writer, and by paying for publishing costs.

Methodologies and examples

School services

The type of service for schools varies with almost each museum. It can include all or any of the following: direct teaching either in the museum or gallery itself, or in an adjoining room using demonstration and handling material, as at the National Gallery, the Horniman Museum (Mellors, 1982), and Kelvingrove Art Gallery and Museum; the provision of resources for teachers and children, as at the British Museum (Reeve, 1983) and the Natural History Museum, and the Weald and Downland Museum (Newbery, 1987); the use of drama, as at Aberdeen Maritime Museum (Keatch, 1987), Clarke Hall (Stevens, 1981, 1987) and Suffolk, (Fairclough, 1981) or reconstruction (Phelan, 1987); short-term displays can be mounted and used as a resource for a series of sessions for teachers and children, as at Leicester; and large-scale events are popular, if time consuming to organize. One or two museums have explored the possibilities of mobile museums which may tour schools or other venues (Porter, 1982). Perhaps the best resourced and most well-known is the mobile museum in Liverpool (Rees, 1981). Extended study is desirable where possible, but again can be time consuming if resources are limited. The GCSE in Museum Studies designed 10 years ago as a Certificate of Secondary Education (CSE) Mode 3 at the National Portrait Gallery provides a model (Cox and Loftus, 1979; Morris, 1985).

Almost all museums are now running courses for teachers which include museum or artefact teaching strategies. The *Journal of Education in Museums, Volume 6*, deals exclusively with this issue and includes general advice (Moffat, 1985), accounts of work with science teachers (Sorsby, 1985), art teachers (Paine, 1985), advice on how to use historic buildings (Heath, 1985), comparisons with work in America with initial teacher training (Gooding, 1985), and some cautionary remarks about the usefulness of school visits (Pond, 1985). Pond's work should be studied closely by museum educationalists as it is one of the few sustained investigations of the type of learning that is possible on museum visits (Pond, 1983, 1984). He discusses some of the potential problems of depending on a Piagetian theory of cognitive development in planning learning experiences and outcomes in relation to the history subject area and suggests other theoretical models that might be more appropriate. These emphasize directed imagination, and the use of the emotions in learning. A useful counterpart to this work on young children and the learning and teaching of history is that of Blyth (1988).

Very young children have not often been provided for in museums, although the Bethnal Green Museum of Childhood and Norwich Castle Museum (Siliprandi, 1987) are exceptions. Bristol Museum has recently run a day for children under 5 year of age in conjunction with Women's Heritage and Museum (WHAM). This attracted a fair amount of publicity including a half-page spread in *The Guardian* and an interview on *Woman's Hour* (BBC Radio 4). Ironbridge Gorge Museum have begun a series of exploratory workshops with pre-schoolers and their teachers. This work is being recorded on video with the help of Shropshire Local Educational Authority, and is forming the basis for the production of guidelines for teachers of these groups. This is seen as the beginning of a long process that will proceed in a similar fashion through the other age ranges.

Primary-school children have in the past made up approximately two-thirds of the children provided for by educational departments. This pattern may alter as priorities and demands change with the introduction of new teaching methods in schools, which emphasize the analysis of evidence and the use of primary sources. The problem of reaching older students is reviewed by O'Connell and Alexander (1979) from Old Sturbridge Village in America. Many of their comments are very relevant to the British situation, and case studies of their work are available.

The structure of the school visit to the museum needs careful thought. Guidelines have been drawn up by individual museums, Area Museum Councils (e.g. Ambrose, 1987) and by some Local Authorities. Preliminary visits by the teachers are desirable, wherever possible, as are jointly agreed objectives. Many teachers, at least when they first start to use museums, are not clear about what is possible, and so their objectives are often not completely formed. Courses explaining the potential of the museum can help here, as can discussions of the specific visit. Once the objectives and possibilities are defined, the visit to the museum can be placed within a course of study as a whole. This should include preparatory work at school, focusing on the knowledge required to best use the experience of the objects the children will experience. It should not include coaching on the specific objects and the rehearsing of apparently desired answers. The course of study might include visits to other institutions or sites, churches, record office, historic building, or park, for example. It is helpful for the museum officer to know this and often links and references can be made. Follow-up work stimulated by the museum visit should also form part of the course of study. Some follow-up work has been known to last many weeks, even a term on occasions where it is the museum as a set of processes that is the object of study (Hooper-Greenhill, 1988d).

Teachers may well need support in planning the work at the museum, or even the course of study as a whole, and this might take the form of visits to schools, phone calls, teachers' courses, or notes or other written support. Where museums or historic houses are without any form of support in terms of staff, teachers' and children's handbooks can be prepared. English Heritage have produced some good models[3]. A long-term involvement with classroom and advisory teachers, schools, and, less often, individual children or students is more likely to lead to better learning outcomes.

Many museums have traditionally prepared worksheets for use during class visits. These can lead to either very good or very bad experiences. Bad worksheets are those which are not specifically geared to the needs and abilities of the group using them, direct attention to the label rather than the artefact, do not encourage thoughtful looking and use of observation, are too long, are limited to a 'see it, tick it' approach and, all in all, prevent rather than enable learning. Good worksheets are carefully planned, tried and tested in relation to specific objectives, are age-related, encourage deductive thinking, are theme or person based, are limited to a few key objects, often use drawings and illustrations in imaginative ways, enable follow-up discussion either at school or at the museum, and enable modifications by the teacher. Some worksheets are produced in 'suites' or series, with the same approach in each, which can be successful. Worksheets and

their use are discussed by Jones and Ott (1983), Reeve (1983) and Fry (1987).

Loan services

Loan services to schools began at the end of the nineteenth century. Liverpool (1884), Sheffield, (1891), and the Ancoats Art Museum in Manchester (Chadwick, 1983) were among the first provincial museums to circulate material to schools, although the Victoria & Albert Museum had been loaning material to other museums and to art schools since 1864 (Whincop, 1983). The newly founded Museums Association had as one of its first objectives in 1889 'the preparation of small educational loan collections for circulation to schools' (Rosse, 1963, p. 288). Successive Government reports have encouraged loan services, particularly where distances between museums are great, but it is recognized that the burden of this work is high and that costs are heavy and, therefore, some assistance is required from the education authorities (Miles, 1986). Loan services are suffering badly with the changes in Local Authority budgeting.

Several types of loan service can be identified: a loan service attached to the museum, and often receiving duplicate material from the main collections, as at Leicester (founded 1933); a loan service standing independently and purchasing its material, at least in the early days, with specific regard to the needs of schools, as in Derbyshire (founded 1936); a loan service attached to a museum, but with collections that have a broader scope, as at Oxfordshire; a loan service which includes original artefacts, but also performs the function of a large-scale resource centre, as at Wakefield; and a small-scale loan service, generally attached to a museum, but where the objects are only available by special arrangement, as at King's Lynn or Acton Scott. The larger scale loan services demand complex organization, and a great deal of time. In some museums where the loan service is extensive, and the staff numbers very limited, educational work may be limited to the administration of the loans for a considerable period each term. In general, the early and larger loan services tend to employ specific loan service officers and drivers to collect and deliver the material.

The early loan services held historical, archaeological or natural history material. Models and replicas have often been added since. Where original art work was included, this has sometimes, as in Derbyshire, had to be withdrawn owing to the increase in value of the material. Recently, loan services have begun to include material linked to specific ethnic groups to enable teachers to work with cross-cultural material. Some loan services include books, slides, or teachers' notes, although in some cases these are of some antiquity themselves.

Loan boxes vary in their construction and design but all must be light, strong, as easily carried as possible, and coded for their contents. Many boxes contain within them a method of display, so that the box becomes the pedestal for the artefact, for example, and the lid reverses to become a label. Most loan services provide a catalogue (Dundee, Leicester and Wakefield). Loan periods vary from 2 weeks to one term. Distribution is complex and ingenious schemes have been devised to keep track of up to 6000 objects in the post. Now, many services are moving towards computerization.

The value of loan material in the classroom depends on the degree of skill of the teachers concerned. Good practice exists, but tends to be uncoordinated. A recent survey on the use of museum loan services carried out by the Department of Education and Science (Department of Education and Science (1987c) describes some projects and shows intelligent use of loan material in relation to reading, writing, mathematical, historical and art work. The loan material added to the quality of the school environment and provided effective stimuli for learning. However, much of the potential of the loan material was left unexplored. There were no curriculum guidelines in schools to guide teachers in their use of artefacts, to encourage teachers, or to share useful learning strategies and experiences.

Better links between schools and loan services are proposed in the Department of Education and Science report, including in-service or pre-entry courses on the use of loan material, and the effective identification and use of feedback from schools. Links between loan-service officers in museums to learn from each other are also suggested.

Adult education

There are very few museums that fully exploit their educational potential. While this is true in general, it is more marked in the case of provision for adults. In the USA, adult education in museums is exciting, and possibilities are often exploited to the full (Gurian, 1981). One example must suffice to illustrate the scope of possibilities. At Mystic Seaport, a museum complex of buildings on a river-side site (Carr, 1986), 'adult education' includes the teaching of maritime skills (sailing, racing and boatbuilding) 'celestial naviation' (taught in the museum's planetarium), traditional wood-carving, weaving, and fireplace cookery. Both modern and traditional skills an techniques relating to the museum and its collections are taught on a regular and continuing basis to adult audiences. If a similar idea were adopted at the British Museum or the Victoria & Albert Museum, an enormous art school would be attached to the museum, with classes in stone-carving, wood-carving, ceramic work, tapes-

try, weaving, print-making of all kinds, painting, silverwork, glass-blowing, etc. This might be seen as extreme, but many museums across North America are taking exactly this approach, and with great success. Not only are visitors offered a new relationship with the collections, one aspect of the participatory experience we hear so much about, but these educational activities are also substantial income generators.

Webb (1986) points out that British and American museums use the governmental monies that they receive in very different ways. American museums use their intial income to generate more. The Metropolitan Museum of Art in New York received $20 million in grants in 1983, which generated $28 million in additional income. The British Museum and the National Gallery receiving a very similar base income generated £1.3 million, one-sixteenth as much. Now, Britain is not America, and the income received is no doubt committed in different ways. At present the national museums in Britain, for example, spend nearly 90 per cent of their income on salaries, which does not leave a lot to play with. In addition, not all of this generated income arises from educational programmes. Nonetheless, there are ideas here that we could think about. Webb goes on to say that, in general, American museums spend about 15 per cent of their income on education (not including display work). Given the vast unexplored educational potential of our museums that has been remarked on for the last 150 years, thought should be given to the possibility of practical classes in all kinds of activities for adults, on a paid basis.

Mystic Seaport runs annual research symposia in maritime history (autumn), Victorian life (spring), sea music (early summer), and conservation of artefacts (Carr, 1986). The documentation of collections is made available for scholars and other visitors through oral and video tapes, written accounts, and drawings. The video tapes include the reissue of historic film for home consumption. The area of video production in relation to the work of museums and to the exploration of the collections is another enormous currently unexploited potential. Mystic Seaport expected to sell more than $200 000 worth of home video cassettes during 1987, and are looking into extending into new video technology, seeing this as a better way to publish, instead of in book form. The museum is collaborating with the National Geographic Society in the production of video programmes for transmission through cable television, and views this as a form of educational outreach. As the museum is a not-for-profit organization, the monies gained from these enterprises will be used to finance more educational ventures. These classes, symposia, and research publications are only one small part of the museum's educational enterprises. Extensive programmes for children are also provided, as is informal education for adults.

Adult education work in British museums includes both formal and informal provisions, such as lectures, concerts, readings and films. University museums often run programmes which are linked into university coursework. At the National Gallery in London, lectures are linked into Open University courses. Curators and educators are often involved talking both in the museum and elsewhere to specialist groups of all kinds. Lunchtime handling sessions for adults proved popular at the Museum of London, as have natural history handling and discovery sessions at Liverpool Museum. The National Museum of Wales has organized family walks (Sharpe and Howe, 1982). A family room is offered during the holiday periods at the British Museum (Natural History), with objects to look at and things to do. Recently, experiments have been made with an 'art cart' in the galleries which provided both encouragement, expertise and materials for visitors to do a drawing of what they saw. The Royal Museum of Scotland provided a Discovery Room on an experimental basis for 3 weeks during the summer of 1987 which proved enormously popular. Interactive exhibits, generally concerned with principles of technology, have been installed in some museums, designed for both adults and children; Launch Pad at the Science Museum (Stevenson, 1987), Green's Mill in Nottingham, and Liverpool Museum on Merseyside are examples. Their learning potential is always quoted as their main *raison d'être*, but this has been criticized as a naive approach, given the complexities of our current everyday involvement with science and technology (Shortland, 1987).

In some cases adult education classes have been used to involve members in museum processes. A history class at Southampton resulted in new collections and new museum–visitor relationships (Jones and Major, 1986). Some museums have been working with Help the Aged doing reminiscence work, using museums objects to stimulate discussion and recall for elderly people.

Some museums have concentrated on the involvement of ethnic groups that are currently under-represented in museums (Nicholson, 1985), although the problems of this work being perceived as tokenism and the resulting negative images of museums should not be ignored (Belgrave, 1986).

Museums have long been interested in providing exhibitions that have catered for blind and partially sighted visitors. References to this kind of work can be traced back to the beginning of the century (Deas, 1913) and recently interest has revived with several major national and provincial museums putting on handling exhibitions. This kind of provision, although to be encouraged, tends to be sporadic in

any one institution, which makes the use of these exhibitions unpredictable (Coles, 1983). More qualitative and regular work would be better, and pioneering work of the Adult Education Department of the University of Leicester is relevant here (Hartley, n.d.). Adult education classes where teacher and blind students work together to develop methods of working and learning through sculpture have shown what large educational and psychological gains can be made using artefacts and practical art work. These groups have always used museum handling exhibitions as source, and have strongly developed ideas on the advantages and disadvantages of these kinds of exhibitions. Their experience in putting on their own exhibition in a museum exposed a vast communication gap between their own needs and priorities and those of the museum. If it were possible for museums to work much more closely with adult education classes such as those which had an exhibition component built into their aims, a much more profitable use of resources and expertise might be enabled, and misunderstandings might be avoided. The provision of tactile experiences on a regular basis in a part of the museum that is easy to negotiate would also be valuable. This would provide an opportunity to make contacts and establish networks which might lead to greater involvement.

The Carnegie United Kingdom Trust was instrumental in encouraging and financing a 2-year study into the arts and disabled people, which resulted in two publications which every museum should have in their library (Attenborough, 1985; Pearson, 1985). These cover a wider span of provision, both in terms of institution and type of activity, thereby placing museums within the context of specialist provision as a whole.

Some ideas for small museums

In many small museums staff act both as curators and education officers, often without educational training or experience, but often, too, with much goodwill. Possible links and ways of getting assistance and extra staff are comprehensively covered in Carter (1984). Certainly contact with the Local Education Authority, teachers' centres, advisory teachers and the local inspectorate are essential. Sponsorship may be a further way forward, although if this was to be tried, a longer rather than a shorter term sponsored appointment is likely to be more productive.

Some measures can be helpful to avoid the panic of failure of provision and the resulting knee-jerk responses: these include policies, strategies, and publicity.

A review of the existing needs and possibilities should be carried out, educational policies identified, ratified and implemented. Areas of future growth should be outlined so that the educational work which is possible is carried out within a clear analysis of where development could take place. This clear-sighted planning will pay off when unexpected opportunities present themselves.

Possible strategies of work include dividing the time available and alloting specified time (of the day, the week, the year) to educational work. Continuous haphazard demand from teachers can be limited by asking for letters rather than phone calls (with a pleasant answer-phone message to suggest a letter, while curatorial work is done).

Decisions must be made on the type of provision that is feasible; whether to teach, or to provide materials for teachers to teach the classes themselves, to do regular training sessions for teachers, to demonstrate and develop the educational possibilities, or more than one of these.

Various forms of provision should be thought about. Consider reviewing the possibilities of the museum together with advisory teachers for different subject or age-groups. Maybe some collaborative scheme could be devised. Perhaps an exploratory curriculum development project over a limited period of months might demonstrate the value and vast potential of the museum as an educational resource, and might lead on to further help or development. Most non-museum people seem very unaware of this enormous learning potential, and need to see it demonstrated in action before they can begin to understand it. The curriculum project for primary schools at the Horniman Museum provides a model which could be adopted (Mellors, 1982; Hooper-Greenhill, 1988d).

Teachers seem to ask most often for handling material. If it is possible to sort out some small collections of related objects or specimens that could be made available for handling, or demonstration by teacher or curator, or even close and sustained observation, these would probably be very popular. It would be possible to limit the availability of the collections to those teachers who had attended a short course of handling procedures. These could be held in the museum or teachers' centre after school for small numbers on a regular basis. Again, involvement with advisory teachers would be helpful. It would be possible to devise a work pattern for the curator that set aside, say 4 days of the week over a 2–3 week period during a 4–6 month period when handling groups were supervised. Most of the teaching work would be carried out by the teachers who had previously attended a training course where curatorial concerns and limits had been specified, and ideas for use had been exchanged between the teachers. These teachers' courses would need to be held some weeks before the handling sessions to enable the preparation work necessary in the schools

to be both set up and carried out. A 2-week period of 4 days in each week would enable 16 groups (two each day) to visit the museum, and would produce a group of 16 teachers trained to use at least those collections of objects. Although this seems small scale, it should result in a high standard of work, and in teachers who understood some aspects of the museum. A teacher–Friends group might evolve from such contacts which would provide a very solid base for changes in policy or for development in educational provision.

A further approach to the provision of handling material might be the development of loan kits. If it is kept to a small scale and teachers fetch and carry themselves, this might not be too overwhelming. At the Children's Museum of Boston, Mass., loan kits are only produced when sponsorship is available, and specific people can be appointed to carry out the research, identify and select the objects, design the packaging, and write the accompanying notes. This might be an idea to explore.

Written material can be useful, and not too time-consuming once it is produced. Consider writing notes on the use of the galleries, identifying possible themes that run through several galleries, or writing notes on specific objects on display so that teachers can choose their own way of using them. The writing style must be simple but succint, and the presentation of the material must enable easy and fast assimilation. The use of diagrams, flowcharts, maps, illustrations, cartoons, notes, photographs, excerpts from related documents, and so on is more interesting and more useful than several closely written A4 pages. Just imagine settling down to read what you have produced after a day at school.

Consider asking teachers who use the museum to write short notes on how they approached it and what they did as preparation or follow-up work either at school or in other places. A teachers' handbook with half-a-dozen such case studies for your museum would be very helpful for other teachers who are generally very inventive and experienced in adapting material to suit their particular needs. 'Museums and the New Exams' (Goodhew, n.d.) provides an example which could be adapted for use in one museum (or, if relevant, across several). 'Museums and the GCSE' (which in fact deals exclusively with Ironbridge Gorge Museum) provides a very elaborate model for just one museum. Simpler documents would also be useful. Visual records of the museum visit and its activities is also useful for in-service courses.

It may be possible to get sponsorship specifically for the production of written materials, either from local industry or charities, or from some of the larger firms that have sponsored museum publications over the last few years. The Local Education Authority, teachers' centre or local college may be able to help with production. Sometimes students can be available to produce some of the work, either from the Department of Museum Studies, University of Leicester, or from other institutions.

Once the educational strategy of the museum has been devised, a short document should be produced specifying what is possible and how to access it. This should be sent to all interested parties, including the Local Education Authority, and all its ramifications, schools, and libraries. It should also be available in the museum. If demand exceeds supply for the services that can be offered, this can be used as an argument for further help.

In most cases the Area Museum Service may be able to help. The Scottish Museums Council provides a model here, with their recently developed 'leisure learning' programme. The Scottish Museums Council have evolved a document that accompanies each of their travelling exhibitions which identifies a great variety of educational possibilities. These include detailed ideas for practical workshops, formal lectures, and films (useful and relevant ones listed), the names of experts and contact persons, and suggestions for community involvement. In the case of each suggestion, the estimated cost to the museum, the resources required, and other requirements are identified. The document provides a well-researched, comprehensive list of educational possibilities from which any curator hosting the exhibition can select. The Scottish Museums Council has appointed one member of staff with exclusive responsibility for this work and is now working with a number of museums on developing leisure learning programmes based on their permanent collections (Stewart, 1988).

All in all, there are many ways that curators in small museums can provide a high-quality, if small-scale, service. In general it is probably better in the long run to aim for quality rather than quantity. Supplying a minimum for many teachers results in limited achievement, and does not provide a suitable base for solid growth. Working towards a qualitative educational experience, even for limited numbers, demonstrates what can be achieved with few resources and, therefore, also indicates what could be achieved with more, and enables in-depth contact and involvement which can be built upon.

The general educational responsibility of the museum

All too often education staff are doing qualitative work with different groups while the public front of the museum is boring, difficult, and neglected. Museums are becoming much more accountable very quickly indeed. Emphasis for the way forward is undoubtedly on the overall quality of experience for the museum visitor. The educational work of the museum should be part of a general communications policy. This should be planned, organized and evaluated.

Comfort services are essential, and museums are increasingly realizing that people need to eat, drink, rest and so on if they are to remain in the building for more than a short time. But after the provision of these basic facilities how should a communications policy be evolved? One of the most vital aspects is that of the museum displays (Gurian, 1981; Patten, 1982–1983). Educational staff are used to designing effective learning experiences of all kinds for all sorts of groups, and are used to working with and adapting often inadequate displays. Together, curators, designers and educators should develop a knowledge of the visitor and the potential visitor, and should develop a unified display policy that enables first time visitors to scan and browse and repeat visitors to look, to work, to participate in an in-depth way with the collections. Galleries should be varied to provide an initial introduction to the nonspecialist lay person, and then a more detailed, more in-depth approach for someone wanting something more specific (Cameron, 1982).

The introductory galleries, or sections of the display, should assume a minimum level of knowledge, expertise and experience in the topic being introduced. The basic concepts behind the topic should be explained and demonstrated. The Bird Gallery at the Manchester Museum includes a case where it is shown by using specimens that birds have very light skeletons, that they do not all fly, and that they vary in size. A few very basic concepts are spelt out. This is not patronizing to the public. This acts as a warm-up to the topic, a way of shifting the mind from Egyptology or classical archaeology or whatever was previously being looked at. It works as a recall to people who have not thought about birds for some time, and it introduces basic concepts to those who have not been introduced to them before. A 'basic concept case' such as this could also be used to orient the viewer/reader to the approach to be adopted in the following cases and to introduce the styles of thinking which will be necessary. Are we to think like historians, or geologists? What sort of questions should we ask of the display as we view it? The current educational philosophy that lies behind the new educational approaches exemplified in the GCSE emphasizes the aquisition and use of skills, including the skills of thinking, i.e. organizing concepts, making comparisons, and detecting bias. Children are being encouraged to think like geographers, or mathematicians, and to recognize that these forms of knowing and thinking are not the same. Which do we use when in the museum? How do we know? The introductory case to the 'Lost Worlds' display in the New Walk Museum in

Leicester introduces the geologist as a detective, gives examples of the kinds of 'clues' looked for, demonstrates the comparisons made between now and then, and points out the deductive method used by geologists to draw some comparisons. This case acts as the 'thought-model' for the rest of the exhibition.

In-depth displays can concentrate less on breadth of approach and more on depth of investigation. Examples might include interdisciplinary displays on specific themes, such as the exhibit on hairdressing that forms part of the Roman Life Gallery in the Yorkshire Museum, where different types of object are assembled to show different facets of the same topic; or the 'About Face' exhibition at the Royal Museum of Scotland (summer 1988) where the topic of face decoration was explored across time, space and cultures, and related activities were organized by the education department for schools and in conjunction with local art schools and fashion courses.

Other approaches might include a multifaceted approach to one object, not presenting it in relation to its classified position within the museum collections, but looking much more broadly at who made it, when, why, who for, how it was used, how that use has changed, how the meaning of the object has changed as its context has changed. Contemporary cultural studies are beginning to explore the ideas of meaning within different discourses (Laclau and Mouffe, 1987). Museums could take the intellectual lead here with their fantastic resources which demonstrate all too well how knowledge is constructed through different combinations of material things in different social, cultural and historic contexts (Hooper-Greenhill, 1992a).

A museum communications policy should be based on the understanding that communication is only possible where shared codes are in operation. The museum code must not be isolated from the other codes that visitors are familiar with. Links must be made with what people know, understand and are comfortable with. Where, for example, archaeological fragments are on display, it cannot be assumed that the visitor can mentally complete the fragment and perceive the original artefact. Some help must be given, either by accompanying drawings (as on the labels in the Yorkshire Museum where the complete object in use is depicted) or by other means.

A communications policy should address the concept of 'the museum visitor' held by the staff of the museum. How are people conceptualized? As *tabula rasa* or as hypothesizing and meaning-making individuals? (Alt and Griggs, 1984). How is the museum experience understood? Recent research shows that attention to the exhibit diminishes after about 35 minutes, regardless of type or attractiveness of exhibit, (Falk, 1985). A museum communications

policy should pay attention to this 'concentration gap' and develop strategies that enable the lapse of concentration to occur naturally without feelings of guilt, inadequacy or boredom on the part of the visitor, and also strategies to enable a re-engagement with the displays. This means varying the museum spaces to create areas of mental relaxation, areas of high concentration, areas of sitting and listening or watching, areas of questioning or even self-testing in relation to content of near-by displays (Screven, 1986), and so on. La Villette, the new science centre in Paris, provides an example of this kind of museum planning.

Research shows that museum visitors need to feel valued, appreciated, comfortable and at home (Hood, 1983). A communications policy would start by evaluating the museum experience from the point of view of the visitor and would proceed to develop a complex, multi-faceted, co-ordinated, planned set of objectives that would provide a qualitative overall experience for many different types of visitor with many different needs. Part of these objectives would be specific in-house provision for organized groups of all ages, part would concern outreach work in different parts of the community, part would be related to displays organized to present different forms of learning experiences, with the nature of each clearly spelt out, and part would be specifically concerned with publicity and marketing. The development of management skills to enable this form of qualitative provision for 'the museum visitor' should be regarded as a priority.

The days when 'museum education' meant parties of schoolchildren being dragged round the display cases are long gone 'Museum education' is an infinitely more complex aspect of museum work, which is fast becoming one of the most necessary.

Notes

1. Foucault (1970) outlines in detail the broad epistemological frameworks within which words and things have been related and meanings have been constituted. This is presented as subject to highly significant cultural shifts over time since the Renaissance. Laclau and Mouffe (1987) discuss the ways in which objects become meaningful through the discourses in which they are positioned. The writers together offer a theory of meaningful objects which celebrates proliferations of variously constituted meanings as opposed to an essentialist understanding of the 'truth' of objects.
2. The membership secretary is currently Jeni Harrison, The Old Manse of Lynturk, Muir of Fowlis, Alford, Aberdeenshire, AB33 8HS, Scotland.
3. These include *Osborne House – A Practical Handbook for Teachers; Life on a Royal Estate – A Document Pack for Osborne House;* and *The Tudors at Hampton Court Palace – A Pack for Teachers.*

References

ALT, M. B. and GRIGGS, S. A. (1984), 'Psychology and the museum visitor', *Manual of Curatorship*, Thompson, J. (Ed.), pp. 386–393, Museum Association, Butterworths, London

AMBROSE, T. (ED.) (1987), *Education in Museums: Museums in Education* Scottish Museums Council, HMSO, Edinburgh

ATTENBOROUGH, R. (1985), *Arts and Disabled People*, Carnegie United Kingdom Trust, London

ANON. (1987), 'Meeting the GCSE challenge', *North East Museum Service News*, **16**, Newcastle-upon-Tyne

BASSETT, D. A. (1984), 'Museums and education: a brief bibliographic essay', in *Manual of Curatorship*, Thompson, J. M. A. (Ed.), pp. 448–459 Museums Association, Butterworths, London

BATEMAN, J. (1984), 'The control and financing of museum education services in Britain', *Museums Journal*, **84**(2), 51–61

BELGRAVE, R. (1986), 'Southampton's Caribbean Heritage: an analysis of the oral history project carried out by Southampton Museums 1983–1984', *Archaeological 'Objectivity' in Interpretation*, Vol. 3, World Archaeological Congress, 1–7 September, Southampton

BENNETT, T. (1988), 'Museums and the people', in *The Museum Time Machine*, Lumley, R. (Ed.), pp. 63–86, Comedia/Routledge, London

BERRY, S. and MAYER, S. (Eds.), (1989), *Museum Education: Theory and Practice*, The National Art Association, USA

BLYTH, J. (1988), *Primary Bookshelf: History 5–9*, Hodder and Stoughton, London

BOARD OF EDUCATION (1931), *Museums and the Schools: Memorandum on the Possibility of Increased Co-operation between Public Museums and Public Educational Institutions Educational Pamphlets No. 87*, HMSO, London

BRITISH ASSOCIATION FOR THE ADVANCEMENT OF SCIENCE (1920), 'Final report of the Committee on museums in relation to education', *Report of the British Association for the Advancement of Science, 1920*, pp. 267–280, London

BUSSE, F. (1880), 'Object-teaching – principles and methods', *American Journal of Education*, **30**, 471–450

CALKINS, N. A. (1880), 'Object-teaching: its purpose and province', *Education* (Boston, USA), **1**, 165–172

CAMERON, D. F. (1982), 'Museums and public access – the Glenbow approach', *International Journal of Museum Management and Curatorship*, **1**(3), 177–196

CARR, J. R. (1986), 'Education everywhere for everyone at Mystic Seaport', *The American Museum Experience: In Search of Excellence*, pp. 41–58, Scottish Museums Council, Edinburgh

CARTER, P. G. (1984), 'Educational services', in *Manual of Curatorship*, Thompson, J. (Ed.), pp. 435–447, Butterworths, London

CHADWICK, A. (1983), 'Practical aids to nineteenth century self-help – the museums: private collections into public institutions', in *Samuel Smiles and Nineteenth Century Self-help in Education*, Stephens, M. D. and Roderick, G. W. (Eds.), pp. 47–69, Department of Adult Education, University of Nottingham

COLES, P. (1983), *Please Touch: An Evaluation of the Please Touch Exhibition at the British Museum, 31 March – 18 May*, Committee of Inquiry into the Arts and Disabled People/Carnegie United Kingdom Trust

COX, A. and LOFTUS, J. (1979), 'Teaching through museums', *ILEA Contact, 11*, 9–10, Inner London Education Authority, London

DEAS, C. (1913), 'The showing of museums and art galleries to the blind', *Museums Journal*, **13**(3), 85–109

DELAHAYE, M. (1987), 'Can children be taught how to think?, *The Listener*, **22** Oct., 14

DEPARTMENT OF EDUCATION AND SCIENCE (1987a), 'Report by HM Inspectors on a survey of the use of museum made by some schools in the North West, carried out 17–21 June 1985', *HMI Report 20/87*, HMSO, London

DEPARTMENT OF EDUCATION AND SCIENCE (1987b), 'Report by HM Inspectors on a survey of the use some schools in six local education authorities make of museum services, carried out June, 1986', *HMI Report, 53/87*, HMSO, London

DEPARTMENT OF EDUCATION AND SCIENCE (1987c), 'Report by HM Inspectors on a survey of how schools in five LEAs made use of museum loan services, carried out Spring 1987', *HMI Report 290/87*, HMSO, London

DEPARTMENT OF EDUCATION AND SCIENCE (1987d), 'Report by HM Inspectors on a survey of the use some Oxfordshire schools and colleges make of museum services, carried out Sept–Nov 1986', *HMI Report 312/87*, HMSO, London

DEWEY, J. (1979), *Experience and Education*, Collier Macmillan, London

DURBIN, G. (1987), 'Practical courses for teachers', *Journal of Education in Museums*, **8**, 4–5

DURBIN, G., MORRIS, S. and WILKINSON, S. (1990), *A teachers guide to learning from objects*, English Heritage

DURRANS, B. (1988), 'The future of the other: changing cultures on display in ethnographic museums', in *The Museum Time-Machine*, Lumley, R. (Ed.), pp. 144–169, Comedia/Routledge, London

EISNER, E. W. and DOBBS, S. M. (1986), 'Museum education in twenty American art museums', *Museum News*, **65**(2), 42–49

FALK, J. F. (1985), 'Predicting visitor behaviour', *Curator*, **28**(4), 249–257

FOUCAULT, M. (1970), *The Order of Things*, Tavistock Publications, London

FRY, H. (1987), 'Worksheets as museum learning devices', *Museums Journal*, **86**(4), 219–225

GOODHEW, E. (Ed.), (n. d.), *Museums and the New Exams*, Area Museums Service for South Eastern England, London

GOODHEW, E. (Ed.), (1989), *Museums and primary science*, Area Museums Service for South Eastern England, London

GOODING, J. (1985), 'How do you begin? Museum work with undergraduates and initial teachers training students in British and American institutions', *Journal of Education in Museums*, **6**, 8–10

GURIAN, E. (1981), 'Adult learning at Children's Museum of Boston', in *Museums, Adults and the Humanities*, Collins, Z. (Ed.), pp. 271–296, American Association of Museums, Washington, DC

HALE, J. (1987), *Museum Professional Training and Career Structure*, Museums and Galleries Commission, HMSO, London

HARRISON, M. (1950), *Museum Adventure: the Story of the Geffrye Museum*, University of London, London

HARRISON, M. (1954), *Learning out of School: a Teachers'*

Guide to the Educational Use of Museums, Ward Locke Educational

HARRISON, M. (1967), *Changing Museums – Their Use and Misuse*, Longmans, London

HARTLEY, E. (n. d.) *Touch and See: Sculpture by and for the Visually Handicapped in Practice and Theory*, University of Leicester, Department of Adult Education, Leicester

HARVEY, B. (1987), *Visiting the National Portrait Gallery*, HMSO, London

HEATH, A. (1985), 'Training Teachers to use Historic Buildings for Education Purposes', *Journal of Education*, No. 6, pp. 28–31

HEIDEGGER, M. (1951), 'The age of the world view', *Measure*, **2**, 269–284

HEIN, G. E. (1982), 'Evaluation of museum programs and exhibits', in *Museums and Education*, Hansen, T. H., Anderson, K.-E. , Vestergaard, P. (Eds.), Danish ICOM/CECA, Denmark, pp. 21–26

HEWISON, R. (1987), *The Heritage Industry*, Methuen, London

HOOD, M. (1983), 'Staying away – why people choose not to visit museums', *Museum News*, **61**(4), 50–57

HOOPER-GREENHILL, E. (1980), 'The National Portrait Gallery: a case-study in cultural reproduction', M. A. thesis, Department of Sociology of Education, Institute of Education, University of London, London

HOOPER-GREENHILL, E. (1983), 'Some basic principles and issues relating to museum education', *Museums Journal*, **83**(2/3), 127–130

HOOPER-GREENHILL, E. (1985), 'Museum training at the University of Leicester', *Journal of Education in Museums*, **6**, 1–6

HOOPER-GREENHILL, E. (1987a), 'Museums in education: towards the twenty-first century', in *Museums in Education: Education in Museums*, Ambrose, T. (Ed), pp. 39–52, Scottish Museums Council, HMSO, Edinburgh

HOOPER-GREENHILL, E. (1987b), 'Knowledge in an open prison', *New Statesman*, **13 Feb.** , 21–22

HOOPER-GREENHILL, E. (1988a), 'The museum: the socio-historical articulations of knowledge and things', Ph. D. thesis, Department of the Sociology of Education, Institute of Education, University of London

HOOPER-GREENHILL, E. (1988b), 'Counting visitors or visitors who count', in *The Museum Time-Machine*, Lumley, R. (Ed.), pp. 213–232, Methuen/Routledge, London and New York

HOOPER-GREENHILL, E. (1988c), 'The art of memory and learning in the museum: museum education and GCSE', *The Internationl Journal of Museum Management and Curatorship*, **June**

HOOPER-GREENHILL, E. (1988d), 'Museums in education: working with other organizations', *Working with Museums*, Scottish Museums Council, Edinburgh

HOOPER-GREENHILL, E. (Ed.), (1989), *Initiatives in museum education*, Department of Museum Studies, University of Leicester

HOOPER-GREENHILL, E. (1991a), *Museum and gallery education*, Leicester University Press, Leicester

HOOPER-GREENHILL, E. (Ed.), (1991b), *Writing a museum education policy*, Department of Museum Studies, Department of Museum Studies, University of Leicester, Leicester

HOOPER-GREENHILL, E. (1992a), *Museums and the shaping of knowledge*, Routledge, London

HOOPER-GREENHILL, E. (1992b), *Working in museum and gallery education: 10 career experiences*, Department of Museum Studies, University of Leicester, Leicester

HORNE, D. (1984), *The Great Museum*, Pluto Press, London

HUDSON, K. (1987), *Museums of Influence*, Cambridge University Press, Cambridge

HUNTER, M. (1981), *Science and Society in Restoration England*, Cambridge University Press, Cambridge

IRONBRIDGE GORGE MUSEUM (1987), *The GCSE and Museums: a Handbook for Teachers*, Ironbridge, Telford

JONES, S. and MAJOR, C. (1986), 'Reaching the public: oral history as a survival strategy for museums', *Oral History Journal*, **14**(2), 31–38

JONES, L. S. and OTT, R. (1983), 'Self-study guides for school-age students', *Museum Studies Journal*, **1**(1), 37–45

KAUFMANN, T.D. (1978), 'Remarks on the collections of Rudolf II: the *Kunstkammer* and a form of *Representatia*', *Art Journal*, **38**, 22–28

KEATCH, S. (1987), 'Cloots, creels and claikin – drama on display', in *Education in Museums, Museums in Education*, Ambrose, T. (Ed.), pp. 77–84, Scottish Museums Council, Edinburgh

LACLAU, E. and MOUFFE, C. (1987), 'Post-Marxism without apologies', *New left Review*, **166**, 79–106

LAURENCICH-MINELLI, L. (1985), 'Museography and ethno-graphical collections in Bologna during the sixteenth and seventeenth centuries', In *The Origins of Museums*, Impey, O. and MacGregor, A. (Eds.), Clarendon Press, Oxford

LAWSON, I. (1987), 'Standard grade and Scottish museums', *Museums Journal*, **87**(3), 110–112

LAWSON, J. and SILVER, H. (1973), *A Social History of Education in England*, Methuen, London

LOCKE, S. (1984), 'Relations between educational, curatorial, and administrative staff', in *Manual of Curatorship*, Thompson, J. (Ed.), pp. 482–488, Butterworths, London

LORD, B. and LORD, G. D. (1988), 'The museum planning process', *Museums Journal*, **87**(4), 175–180

LUCE, R. (1988), Parliamentary reply to a question from Mr Tony Baldry on the future of museum training following the Hale Report, 17 March, *Office of Arts and Libraries Press Release 4047/107*, London

MACGREGOR, A. (1983), *Tradescant's Rarities* Clarendon Press, Oxford

MARKHAM, S. F. (1938), *A Report on the Museums and Art Galleries of the British Isles*, Carnegie United Kingdom Trust, Dunfermline

MELLORS, M. (1982), 'Horniman Museum and primary schools', *Journal of Education in Museums*, **3**, 19

MIERS, H. A. (1928), *A Report on the Public Museums of the British Isles*, Carnegie United Kingdom Trust, Edinburgh

MILES, H. (1986), *Museums in Scotland*, Museums and Galleries Commission, HMSO, London

MILLAR, S. (1987), 'An opportunity to be grasped', *Museums Journal*, **87**(2), 104–107

MILLER, E. (1973), *That Noble Cabinet*, Andre Deutsch, London

MOFFAT, H. (1985), 'A joint enterprise', *Journal of Education in Museums*, **6**, 20–23

MOFFAT, H. (1988), 'Museums and schools', *Museums Bulletin*, **28**(3) pp. 97–98

MORRIS, S. (1985), ' "Museum Studies" – a mode three CSE course at the National Portrait Gallery', *Journal of Education in Museums*, **6**, 37–40

MUSEUMS & GALLERIES COMMISSION (1985), *Report 1984–85*, Museums & Galleries Commission, London

MUSEUMS & GALLERIES COMMISSION (1987), *Report 1986–87*, Museums & Galleries Commission, London

MUSEUMS & GALLERIES COMMISSION (1991), *Local Authorities and Museums – report by a working party, 1991*, HMSO, London

MUSEUMS ASSOCIATION (1987), 'GCSE and museums', *Museum Journals*, **87**(1)

MUSEUMS ASSOCIATION (1991), *A national strategy for museums – Museums Association Annual Report*, 1990–1991

NATIONAL AUDIT COMMISSION (1991), *The road to Wigan Pier? Managing local authority museums and art galleries*, HMSO, London

NEWBERY, E. (1987), 'Something for all the family', *Journal of Education in Museums*, **8**, 9–10

NICHOLSON, J. (1985), 'The museum and the Indian community: findings and orientation of the Leicestershire Museums Service', *Museum Ethnographers Newsletter*, **19**, pp. 3–14

O'CONNELL, P. and ALEXANDER, M. (1979), 'Reaching the high school auidence', *Museum News*, **58**(2), 50–56

O'NEILL, M. (1987), 'Quantity vs quality or what is a community museum anyway', *Scottish Museum News*, **Spring**, 5–7

ORNSTEIN, M. (1938), *The Role of Scientific Societies in the Seventeenth Century*, The University of Chicago Press, Chicago, IL

OTTO, J. (1979), 'Learning about "neat stuff": one approach to evaluation', *Museum News*, **58**(2), 38–45

PAINE, S. (1985), 'The art classroom in the training of art and design teachers', *Journal of Education in Museums*, **6**, 15–19

PATTEN, L. H. (1982–1983), 'Education by design', *ICOM Education*, **10**, 6–7

PEARSON, A. (1985), *Arts for Everyone*, Carnegie United Kingdom Trust and Centre on Environment for the Handicapped, Edinburgh

PHELAN, B. (1987), 'The Sussex time-machine', *Journal of Education in Museums*, **8**, 11–12

POND, M. (1983), 'School history visits and Piagetian theory', *Teaching History*, **37**, 3–6

POND, M. (1984), 'Recreating a trip to York in Victorian times', *Teaching History*, **39**, 12–16

POND, M. (1985), 'The usefulness of school visits – a study', *Journal of Education in Museums*, **6**, 32–36

PORTER, J. (1982), 'Mobile exhibition services in Great Britain: a survey of their practice and potential', *Museums Journal* , **82**(3), 135–138

PRINCE, D. R. and HIGGINS-MCLOUGHLIN, B. (1987), *Museums UK: The Findings of the Museums Data-base Project*, Museums Association, London

PURVER, M. and BOWEN, E.J. (1960), *The Beginning of the Royal Society*, Clarendon Press, Oxford

REES, P. (1981), 'A mobile for the teacher', *Journal of Education in Museums*, **2**, 26–29

REEVE, J. (1983), 'Museum materials for teachers', in *Writing and Designing Interpretive Materials for Teachers*, Hall, N. (Ed.), Conference papers, Manchester Polytechnic, Manchester

RODGER, L. (1987), 'Museums in education: seizing the market opportunities', in *Education in Museums, Museums in Education*, Ambrose, T. (Ed.), pp. 27–38, Scottish Museums Council, Edinburgh

ROSSE, EARL OF (1963), *Survey of Provincial Museums and Galleries*, Standing Commission on Museums and Galleries, HMSO, London

SCREVEN, C. G. (1986), 'Exhibitions and information centres: some principles and approaches', *Curator*, **29**(2), 109–137

SHARPE, T. and HOWE, S.R. (1982), 'Family expeditions – the museum outdoors', *Museums Journal*, **82**(3), 143–147

SHORTLAND, M. (1987), 'No business like show business', *Nature*, **328**, pp. 213–214

SILIPRANDI, K. (1987), 'Playgroups and museums', *Journal of Education in Museums*, **8**, 13–14

SORSBY, B. (1985), 'Teaching Science Teachers to use Museums', *Journal of Education*, No. 6, pp. 24–27

STEVENS, T. (1981), 'Dramatic approaches to museum education', *Journal of Education in Museums*, **2**, 30–33

STEVENS, T. (1987), 'Change: a constant theme', *Journal of Education in Museums*, **8**, 15–17

STEVENSON, J. (1987), 'The philosophy behind Launchpad', *Journal of Education in Museums*, **8**, 18–20

STEWART, D. (1988), 'Leisure learning programme – update', *Scottish Museum News*, **Summer**, 2–3

WEBB, C. D. (1986), 'Museum in search of income', in *The American Museums Experience: in Search of Excellence*, Ambrose, T. (Ed.), pp. 75–83, Scottish Museums Council, HMSO, Edinburgh

WEST, B. (1988), 'The making of the English working past: a critical view of the Ironbridge Gorge Museum', in *The Museum Time-Machine*, Lumley, R. (Ed.), pp. 36–62, Comedia/Routledge, London

WHINCOP, A. (1983), 'Loan services in Great Britain – historical and philosophical account', unpublished paper, available from the Department of Museum Studies, University of Leicester, Leicester

WILLIAMS, A. (1981), *A Heritage for Scotland – Scotland's National Museums and Galleries: The Next 25 Years*, HMSO, Glasgow

WINSTANLEY, B. (1966), *Children and Museums*, Blackwell, London

WRIGHT, C. W. (1973), *Provincial Museums and Galleries*, Department of Education and Science, HMSO, London

WRIGHT, P. (1985), *On Living in an Old Country*, Verso, London

YATES, F. (1966), *The Art of Memory*, Routledge and Kegan Paul, London

Bibliography

BOOTH, J. H. and KROCKOVER, G. H. (1982), *Creative Museum Methods and Educational Techniques*, Charles C. Thomas, Springfield, IL

CHADWICK, A. and HOOPER-GREENHILL, E. (1985), 'Volunteers in museums and galleries: a discussion of some of the issues', *Museums Journal*, **84**(4), 177–178

CHEETHAM, F. W. (Ed.), (1967), *Museum School Services*, Museums Association, London

COLLINS, Z. (1981), *Museums, Adults and the Humanities*, American Association of Museums, Washington, DC

COULTER, S. (1987), 'Cables of communication', *Journal of Education in Museum*, **8**, 2–3

COUNCIL FOR MUSEUMS AND GALLERIES IN SCOTLAND (1981), *Museum Education Scotland: A Directory*, Scottish Education Department, HMSO, Edinburgh

DEPARTMENT OF EDUCATION AND SCIENCE (1971), *Museums in Eduction*, (*Education Survey 12*), HMSO, London

DEPARTMENT OF EDUCATION AND SCIENCE (1986), 'Report by HM Inspectors on a survey of the use some Hertfordshire schools make of museum services, carried out 1–4 July 1985', *HMI Report 40/86*, HMSO, London

FAIRCLOUGH, J. (1980), 'Heveningham Hall midsummer 1790: a Suffolk schools project', *Museums Journal* **80**(1), 8–9

FAIRCLOUGH, J. (1982), 'Heveningham and after', *Journal of Education in Museums*, **3**, 3–4

GRINDER, A. L. and MCCOY, E. S. (1985), *The Good Guide, a Sourcebook for Interpreters: Docents and Tour-guides*, Ironwood Press, Scotsdale, AZ

HARRISON, M. (1942), 'Thoughts on the function of museums in education', *Museums Journal*, **42**(3), 53

HOOPER-GREENHILL, E. (1982), 'Some aspects of a sociology of museums', *Museums Journal*, **82**(2), 69–70

HOOPER-GREENHILL, E. (1985), 'Art gallery audiences and class constraints', *Bullet*, 5–8

HOOPER-GREENHILL, E. (1987), 'Museum education comes of age', *Journal of Education in Museums*, **8**, 6–8

HOOPER-GREENHILL, E. (1991), *Museums and Gallery Education*, Leicester University Press, Leicester

KAVANAGH, G. (1988), 'The first world war and its implications for education in British museums', *History of Education*, **17**(2), pp. 163–176

MARR, A. (1988), 'Museums and galleries face hiving off plan', *The Independent*, **15 Mar.**

NICHOLS, S.K. (ED.), (1984), *Museum Education Anthology: 1973–1983; Perspectives on Informal Learning, a Decade of Roundtable Reports*, American Association of Museums, Washington, DC

SCHOOLS COUNCIL (1972), *Pterodactyls and Old Lace: Museums in Education*, Evans/Methuen Educational, London

SCOTTISH MUSEUMS COUNCIL (1985), *Museums are for People*, Scottish Museums Council, HMSO, Edinburgh

SIMPSON, M. (1987), 'Multi-cultural education and the role of the museum', *Journal of Education in Museums* **7**, 1–6

SORSBY, B. D. and HORNE, S. D. (1980), 'The readability of museum labels', *Museums Journal*, **80**(3), 157–159

STANDING COMMITTEE FOR MUSEUM SERVICES IN HERTFORDSHIRE (1987), *Museum Education in Hertfordshire: A Development Plan*, Hertfordshire Museums

VYGOTSKY, L.S. (1933), 'Play and its role in the mental development of the child', in *Play: Its Role in Development and Evolution*, Bruner, J. S., Jolly, A. and Sylva, K. (Eds.), pp. 537–554, Penguin, Harmondsworth

69

Approaches to summative evaluation

David R. Prince

This paper develops a number of the ideas presented in the Evaluating Exhibitions chapter in the first edition of this manual. The paper focuses on the methodologies and techniques currently available for the application of summative evaluation: essentially, evaluation undertaken on completed exhibitions. A consideration of the more important objectives of this type of evaluation helps to define it by drawing attention to its intended role in museums:

(1) To provide definitive data about the functioning of completed exhibitions in relation to their stated aims (educational or otherwise) and their intended audience.
(2) To isolate and identify problem areas that may hamper the effective communication of information carried by an exhibition.
(3) To provide a core of reliable data around which remedial action may be justifiably taken.
(4) To provide data directly applicable to the future design of related exhibitions (feedforward information).
(5) To provide data of a general nature related to the functioning of the museum itself, as part of the strategy developed for exhibition evaluation.
(6) To provide data to substantiate (or otherwise) the recommendations made by front-end and formative evaluation; that is, to aid in the evaluation of the evaluation process itself.

Although such information – perhaps idealized in the above form – is highly important to the organization and maintenance of an exhibition scheme within the overall policies of the museum towards its visitors, it is surprising that little formal evaluation has been undertaken at, or by, museums notwithstanding the work at the British Museum (Natural History), London. The emphasis continues to be placed on design and implementation, often by non-specialist staff.[1] Clearly, the role of evaluation *as part of* an exhibition programme has not been sufficiently appreciated (perhaps through a lack of knowledge, finance or incentive) with the result that the

evaluations that do occur tend to be on a qualitative level and undertaken in an *ad hoc* way, while others, through the lack of a clearly defined research perspective, operate within a theoretical vacuum.

This paper establishes a number of guidelines for undertaking summative evaluation and, by examining the current situation in museums and the techniques developed by other, but related, institutions, places such evaluation firmly at the centre of exhibition planning.

Objectives

Of primary importance to any evaluation are the exhibition criteria that the evaluation sets out to analyse. These predetermine to a considerable degree the eventual evaluative strategy developed and help shape the nature and effectiveness of the information obtained. In essence, this demands that the evaluation is geared to assess the success of the exhibition in meeting its objectives. These objectives are (or should be) established during the initial planning stage of the exhibition, but may be refined occasionally during formative evaluation when the displays themselves are being modified. At the summative stage the objectives are used as the central criteria against which the evaluation is made and are thus not available for modification or change. Thus, a lack of clearly defined objectives effectively places an exhibition outside the possibility of summative evaluation unless post-dated (and hence spurious) objectives are assigned to it. Moreover, it emphasizes the importance of keeping the evaluation process firmly in mind when formulating the overall exhibition scheme.

Therefore, objectives used as the basis for summative evaluation are gleaned from the reasons inherent in establishing the exhibition in the first instance and are thus rooted in the general perspective on exhibitions devised by the museum and develop from the overall policy objectives for the museum itself, institutionalized in, for example, policies related to the type of material collected and exhibited. In this way, the collections themselves, and the way they are used, help to define the nature of the exhibition and indirectly lay the foundations for evaluation.[2]

Hence, for most evaluative purposes, objectives are best viewed as being organized hierarchically from the most general and all-embracing to the most specific and analysable. Concentrating for the moment on exhibitions designed primarily to communicate knowledge (didactic exhibitions), it is possible to isolate five levels (or stages) in the life of an exhibition scheme where evaluation objectives may fruitfully be applied in order to generate data of summative quality (*Figure 69.1*).

In the system outlined, summative evaluation may be applied to a number of levels, depending on the type of question posed for the evaluation. Detailed questions related to the transference of knowledge, for example, would occur in level 5, while general background data on the types of visitors to the exhibition would be gleaned from level 3. Similarly, questions related to the communicational character- istics of the displays themselves (for example, attracting and holding power, visitor preference) would appear at level 4.

Equally important is the concept that each level's objectives are defined in relation to those immedi- ately preceding it, and that they in turn influence the framing of those of the subsequent level. In this way, the results of the evaluation can have an influence not only on the specific level assigned to them, but also on the preceding levels in the system. Clearly, the

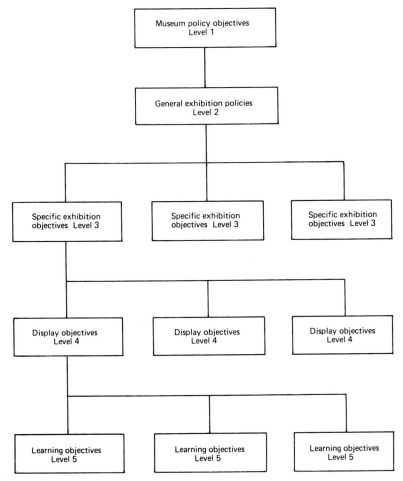

Figure 69.1 A hierarchy of evaluation objectives

emphasis here is on pairing exhibition and evaluation objectives at each level and these, by definition, vary from one institution to another and within the same institution over time. Indeed, by the very nature of exhibitions such objectives must be unique to each organization. However, a number of core features can be isolated for each level that are generally applicable to most types of exhibition, and hence to most of the demands currently made on summative evaluation. These are visitor evaluations (loosely, surveys) (level 3); display and display-based evaluations (level 4); and learning/educational assessments (level 5). Clearly, these categories are not mutually exclusive (for example, a learning evaluation must be active in all three levels), but they do provide a useful framework for discussion.

This form of objective hierarchy has long been known to be of value to exhibition evaluation. In a paper devoted entirely to this issue. Putney and Wagar (1973) isolated three levels of objectives, ranging from policy objectives (general aims), through selection objectives (for media and location), to evaluation objectives. They note (p. 44) that:

> For evaluation to be most useful, it is important to have a hierarchy of objectives in which objectives at each level are consistent with broad policy objectives but are increasingly more numerous and specific. Thus, if evaluation permits us to achieve increased effectiveness at the most specific level, we can infer that effectiveness has been increased at the more general levels; including the level of policy objectives.

Note, however, that effectiveness is inferred for previous levels, not proven.

The framing of objectives

Although the construction of a suitable framework around which to construct objectives presents few problems, the formulation of the objectives themselves is far from easy and must be devised to meet the specific requirements of the individual museum and exhibition project. A number of factors have to be taken into account, among the most important being:

(1) the nature and characteristics of the exhibition scheme;
(2) the intended function and scope of the exhibition;
(3) the relationship between the exhibition and the others of the museum;
(4) the nature and characteristics of the intended (target) audience;
(5) the type and quality of information required from the evaluation;
(6) the methods of data collection, preparation, analysis and presentation to be employed;

(7) the depth and scope of action to be taken on the conclusions and recommendations of the evaluation; and
(8) the peculiar characteristics of the test site that may influence the data through, for example, rapid changes over time.

Clearly, some of these are more directly applicable to the creation of a valid evaluative strategy, but they should be borne in mind at this stage in order to avoid the construction of erroneous objectives.

Strategies

By far the most common form of formal evaluation undertaken on exhibitions has been aimed at assessing the teaching effectiveness of displays and display units, often through the use of recall questions involving verbal answers and/or photograph or object recognition. Cameron (1967, 1968a, b). Shettel *et al* (1968), Shettel (1973). Shettel and Reilly (1965) and Screven (1969, 1974a, b, 1976) have been particularly active in developing such evaluative techniques, and are at pains to stress that objectives should be stated as clearly as possible. Defining objectives in purely *educational* terms allows an educational definition of 'objective'. Mager (1962), in an influential statement on the role of instructional objectives, defines a learning objective as:

> an *intent* communicated by a statement describing the proposed change in the learner – a statement of what the learner is to be like when he has successfully completed the learning experience. It is a description of a pattern of behaviour (performance) we want the learner to be able to demonstrate (p. 3). . . that will be accepted as evidence that the learner has achieved the objective (p. 13).

The emphasis is clearly placed on the construction of objectives in *behavioural* terms; objectives that are available for evaluation either by external observation or, more usually, by direct questioning through interviews accompanied by a battery of test items carried by a questionnaire.[3]

Against such a background, objectives are assigned *performance criteria*, for example 'name', 'list' and 'identity', and may be contrasted with the more general aims of, for example, 'knowing', 'discovering' and 'understanding'. For example, a Curator wishes to convey knowledge about the tracks produced by a number of woodland animals. The overriding aim of the exhibition is (say) 'to increase the visitors' awareness of the tracks produced, in the understanding that this will lead to a greater appreciation of woodland life'. A specific learning objective for evaluation purposes from this perspective might be:

> given eight colour photographs in two blocks of four, each containing the tracks of one of the animals on

display, the visitor will identify correctly three out of four tracks

Such an objective not only specifies the kind of behaviour involved (identifying), but also the conditions under which the behaviour is to occur ('given eight colour photographs in two blocks of four'), together with the acceptable level of performance ('three out of four tracks in each block') against which the evaluation can be made. As importantly, the objective generates a series of constraints on the evaluative strategy developed, and reflects directly on the achievement of the original aim.

Such objectives can then be assigned to individual displays, groups of displays, or to the exhibition as a whole, and thus form the basis for defining summative evaluation as (Moses, Epstein, Weisman Inc., 1977, p. 12).

the systematic examination of. . . activities where objectives are rigorously specified and performance in meeting these objectives is rigorously measured.

That is, an activity aiming to produce (Warwick and Lininger, 1975, p. 52):

an overall appraisal of a programme indicating the relationship between the major outcomes and the intended goals.

This type of definition underpins many of the evaluative techniques used to study didactic exhibitions, for example those by Shettel (1973) on the communication of scientific and technological information. The most common evaluative strategy generated by this approach is that of straightforward visitor interviewing (to gain profile information and to establish an acceptable visitor sample) accompanied by direct questioning and the recall of factual knowledge. In most cases, the results of a test sample exposed to the media are compared with those of a control group of non-users (*see*, for example, Parsons, 1965; Cameron, 1968b; Eason and Linn, 1976; Dartington Amenity Research Trust, 1978), although occasionally only one group is used (Wager, 1972; Boggs, 1977; Prince, 1982). Learning is said to have occurred from the exhibition if the members of the test group score significantly higher than those of the control group (as identified by tests of association and significance on the groups), and the displays are defined as successful (or not) following this criterion. As a direct extension, the museum itself may be defined – and evaluated – in terms of its ability to function as a 'communications system'.

Critique

Used in isolation, this approach – by concentrating on the supposedly measureable outcomes of the relationship between the visitor and the exhibition –

carries with it a number of problems. First, it underestimates the complex and subtle nature of human learning and behaviour based on that learning, particularly the role that past experience plays in shaping present perception, and learning resulting from that perception (see Neisser, 1967; Ausubel, 1968; Blumenthal, 1977; Wickelgren, 1979). Second by concentrating attention on a selected, 'observable' aspect of cognitive functioning (simply, knowledge recall) it seeks to assess learning by focusing on the characteristics of the exhibition without making sufficient reference to the characteristics of the visitor. Where such reference is made it is usually through the use of easily identifiable sociological components (age, sex and occupation); acceptable enough if that is the aim of the study, but not so for a learning assessment which must, by definition, seek to examine psychological components. Third by using direct questioning, it brings into play problems involving the successful transference of meaning through language – although Borun (1977) has been active in developing non-verbal test measures designed to lessen this problem.

As a direct consequence, few data have been gathered on the associated psychological factors that influence learning; the most immediate being *motivation*, reflected in *pre-visit intention* (Alt, 1977), and on-site factors, for example, *expressed interest* and *preference* for media, media combinations, overall strategy of communication and subject theme, and general *attitudinal orientation* towards the museum as a whole and to the exhibition in particular. Moreover, the equally important roles that aesthetic response, mood and feeling play in influencing behaviour generally (Tuan, 1974; Appleton, 1975) and hence, by implication, that within a museum, are largely undervalued.

Thus, this approach places too great an emphasis on the overtly teaching role of exhibitions and defines 'education' in too narrow a way, through making insufficient reference to other, non-measureable effects of exhibitions. This problem is acute when the approach is applied to art galleries.

However, this perspective has had a considerable influence on the way exhibitions are approached in summative evaluation, almost to the point where learning assessments based on visitor interviews accompanied by test questions are viewed by some as the only way of effectively evaluating exhibitions. As Screven (1974b, p. 68) suggests:

so far as its teaching function is concerned, the exhibit's descriptive physical components have no instructional worth in themselves. This instructional worth can be evaluated only by the effect of the exhibit on its viewers.[4]

Be that as it may, the criticisms noted earlier suggest that the results of such studies should be treated with some caution, particularly as learning implies a permanent change in the cognition of the learner, and many of the studies simply examine immediate post-visit response on a group basis.[5] As Griggs noted in the previous edition, a move away from viewing such studies as measures of learning and towards indexes of *comprehension* – where the emphasis is placed on evaluating the exhibition in terms of whether it is understandable – may render them less susceptible to this type of criticism. However, didactic exhibitions are teaching devices, and hence an evaluation in learning terms remains a goal to be striven for.

Visitor surveys

Leaving aside this issue for the moment, one of the benefits of such group-based evaluations is that they demand that visitor samples are selected carefully from the general visitor pool so that the results can be freed from sampling (evaluation-imposed) bias. Thus, the core of the methods applied here can be taken directly as background data for an analysis of the visiting public; an analysis at level 3 of the hierarchy.

Three types of information will be useful at this stage. First, visitor counts – to the museum in general and the exhibition in particular. Second, profile data of visitor-type, based on sociological criteria and employing standardized techniques of categorization that allow the data to be freed from the confines of the site, and hence comparable with those from other institutions as well as national figures. Third, specific profile data enabling the identification of the target audience as distinct from that visiting the museum generally.

It is not proposed to discuss the method of gathering data for the first two to any extent since they are well documented elsewhere,[6] save to note that the detail of the answer required of the visitor, and the way in which the responses are pre- and post-coded, depends to a large extent on the aim of the survey and the method of data preparation employed.[7] The selection of a suitable sample from the total visitor flow is a crucial aspect, and one that has a direct bearing on the validity of the results obtained.[8] The main considerations are that the value of this type of survey depends as much on the framing of questions and the categorization of answers as it does on the selection of a valid sample population, and that the background to the survey must be borne in mind when drawing conclusions and making recommendations. All too often observations are made on specific points that go far beyond the support provided by the results of a particular research programme.

The identification of the *target audience* should follow the acquisition of the profile data since it extends the knowledge gained about the visitor. The characteristics of this audience should have been defined at the exhibition's initial planning stage and translated into accessible indexes as part of formative evaluation. At the summative stage, questions are so framed as to elicit responses to reinforce this *operational definition*, and a visitor defined as being part of this audience (or not) depending on the way in which his responses fit the accepted criteria established during formative evaluation. Moreover, some indication as to this audience's representation should have been established at that stage. For example, if an exhibition is aimed primarily at 'amateur natural historians', what proportion of the total visitor pool is an acceptable measure that it has achieved this general aim – 40 per cent? 60 per cent? The figures need not be too precise at the outset, but without them the conclusions that can be drawn are limited, and since summative evaluation is concerned with the effect of the exhibition on its intended audience, then clearly this finding is of some importance. Having thus isolated this group, it is possible to proceed with a number of detailed questions aimed at drawing a closer understanding of how the visitor has interacted with the exhibition he has just seen or, indeed, may still be viewing.

Preference and interest

Visitor preference, and its associated expressed interest, are important variables available for analysis, partly because the indications brought out at the formative stage can be assessed, and partly because a body of educational psychology suggests strongly that learning is facilitated by interest through its association with intrinsic motivation,[9] an hypothesis that should have been borne in mind when undertaking front-end analysis on the proposed exhibition scheme. Two different, though not mutually exclusive, aspects can be assigned to the study of visitor preference; *what* is preferred and *why* it is preferred, and *what* is most interesting and *why*. Although both are equally important, most of the exhibition-based studies have concentrated on the 'what' aspect (see Mahaffey, 1970; Washburn and Wagar, 1972; Dick *et al.*, 1975; Dartington Amenity Research Trust, 1978; Hammitt, 1978; Griggs and Alt, 1982; Prince, 1982) and have tended to rely on supporting literature – occasionally drawing on material from perception and mass communication studies – to infer why. Considerable scope exists, therefore, to investigate this latter aspect on site, an investigation perhaps best approached through un-structured, open-ended, conversation-based inter-views associated with *naturalistic evaluation* (see Wolf and Tymitz, 1977, 1978a, b, 1979a, b) – a method rooted in the participant-observation technique of social enquiry (see Campbell, 1970; Friedrichs and

Ludtke, 1975). The formative stage may provide a useful starting point, its recommendations helping to guide the evaluator towards imposing a loose structure during summative evaluation. A further point is that visitors have occasionally been asked to identify the exhibit they found the most interesting as a basis for detailed questions about that exhibit (Alt, 1980; Prince, 1982).

Methods

Given this background, two major techniques have been employed consistently to assess visitor preference: *observation* and *interviewing*, either separately or, more commonly, in conjunction. In terms of the former, two approaches present themselves. First, a count of the total number of visitors stopping at each display within a given time span – the higher the count, the greater the preference. Second, the tracking of a selected sample of visitors through the exhibition noting the time spent at each display – the greater the time, the greater the preference. Time-lapse photography and the use of remote-controlled cameras present the possibility of unobtrusive observation in both methods (see Coker and Coker, 1973).

Although these strategies undoubtedly provide useful data – most commonly interpreted through behavioural maps[10] and important in studies of visitor orientation (Winkel *et al*, 1975) and the assessment of the *attracting* and *holding power* of the displays themselves (Lakota, 1976) – their value to summative evaluation is limited on two counts. First, no assessment of *why* the visitor has stopped can be made and, second, no analysis of what aspects of the display has proved intitially attractive can be undertaken. For summative evaluation to provide feedforward information, both aspects are important.

The only realistic method of gaining such data is to engage the visitor in conversation or interview. If this is to be done as part of a larger survey – and it is necessary if the results are to be validated – then the latter may be a more appropriate method. Although questions probing the visitors' motives and preference for theme, media and strategy of communication can be asked, there are clear dangers in making sweeping judgements based on the results due to the respondent reacting in a way he feels appropriate to the occasion, and the consideration that the questions themselves may instigate patterns of analysis and evaluation not previously contemplated by the visitor – a problem also encountered when assessing attitudes (see Shaw and Wright, 1967; Diab, 1968; Warren and Jahoda, 1973).

However, since this is the most appropriate method, the evaluation must ensure that the questions themselves are as free from internal bias as possible – a pilot survey is necessary to test both questions and interviewers – and that bias in recording the visitors' comments is reduced to a minimum.[11] Since it is probable that visitors unskilled in criticizing exhibitions (the majority) are only likely to comment briefly on the major components, this last problem may not be too severe. However, the over-zealous interviewer, prompting answers from visitors, must be warned of the potential danger.[12]

A further consideration is that such information, by its very nature, is not available for statistical analysis, except at the most fundamental levels. Although no bad thing in itself, it must be realized when drawing conclusions from the observations. In general, the techniques of eliciting value judgements from visitors are in their infancy and must be handled sympathetically in the knowledge that they are a potentially fruitful source of information.[13]

Attitudes

Data about the exhibition on this level may be termed loosely 'public reaction', and a realistic extension of such work is to assess the general attitudinal orientation of visitors towards the museum as a whole. A number of techniques are available, including those designed to elicit agreement (or disagreement) to a series of opinion or value statements – a rating-scale technique developed by Likert (1932), and refined subsequently by, amongst others, Cook and Sellitz, (1964) and Upshaw, (1968)), the evocation of social judgements (Sherif *et al.*, 1965), and the use of semantic differential scales to assess meaning (Osgood, 1964). (For reviews *see* Dawes (1972) and Lemon, (1973)). In the last case, attitudes are assessed by plotting the position of responses on a number of paired word-scales, for example 'entertaining–boring', 'interesting–dull', 'enjoyable–unenjoyable'. The true value of this type of survey comes in assessing general attitudes rather than in eliciting opinions on specific issues, and it may provide valuable information as background for a more detailed study of display preference. Comparing the views of various subgroups within the visitors (as identified by the profile and target audience data) may indicate differences of value in more effectively tailoring an exhibition to meet their needs.

Non-user surveys

To gain a wider understanding of the way in which the museum, as a social institution, is perceived by the public, a potentially fruitful area of research lies in non-user surveys. Although this is removed somewhat from exhibition evaluation, it can provide important data for the future planning of exhibition schemes by concentrating on the expectations of non-visitors in relation to the image of the museum and the type of material exhibited.[14] With the recent moves towards linking museums with other tourist attractions within a given area,[15] and the political initiatives involved in gaining commercial sponsorship, this type of research is all the more needed. However, few guidelines exist at present, since this is an area of enquiry not commonly undertaken either by museums or social research generally (for an early review see Pearson, 1978), although the results obtained can be revealing (Prince, 1983). Particular problems exist in establishing a reliable sampling frame and in the basic practicalities of handling such non-specific information. Moreover, it can be argued that the first task of museum evaluation is to look to its users in relation to their experience, rather than to non-users in relation to theirs.

Communicational effectiveness

Returning, then, to the main concern of the paper: the estimation of the quality of experience gained from an exhibition and, in particular, the assessment of the exhibition as a communications medium. Of the techniques noted earlier most, by trying to evaluate teaching effectiveness through the recall of isolated facts, are open to criticism because they take too narrow a view of learning (and indeed, the role of the museum) and assume (wrongly) that the storage and recall of such information is a valid estimation of real learning change. Grappling with this problem is difficult, not least for a museum which has little or no experience of handling such evaluations. However, the work of Lee and Uzzell (1980a) on the assessment of the educational effectiveness of farm open days for the Countryside Commission for Scotland, may provide a useful starting point for such an evaluation.

Taking a cognitive psychological perspective towards the work, a perspective which, simply, suggests that learning occurs when new material is assimilated into an organizing *schema* – this schema being the total collection of past learnings and experiences associated with, in their case, farming, for a museum, the topic of the exhibition – they suggest that learning is best assessed in terms of whether or not the visitors' schemas have been modified (or extended) in some way.[16] To facilitate this, two discrete samples of visitors are questioned, one before exposure to the exhibition and one after, with a view to probing the central *constructs* organized by the visitors in both samples. If substantial changes have taken place – as identified by significance tests on the two groups (and if the groups themselves do not differ statistically in basic, profile information) – then it can be assumed that a

learning change has taken place as a result of exposure to the exhibition.

In the survey by Lee and Uzzell, these constructs were assessed through a technique similar in style to that of the semantic-differential noted earlier, although in this case the issue was to assess how *accurate* a desciption of a type of farm or farming method was, the visitors being asked to record their answers on a scale from 1 (not at all accurate) to 7 (very accurate). If two visiting samples recorded different patterns – and the group exposed to the exhibition was similar in orientation to the information contained in the exhibition – then a favourable learning change was said to have occurred. As an extension to this work, a battery of recall, test questions was used on a self-selected sample in a similar way to that previously described.

This approach, although only sketched briefly here, offers a number of advantages over the use of isolated, recall questions.

(1) It is based on a coherent body of psychological theory that can suggest not only *how* to evaluate, but also *why* the recorded changes have occurred.
(2) It is a more realistic method of assessing learning which, as a process, is not concerned simply with the retention of isolated facts.
(3) It concentrates on the whole experience gained from an exhibition in terms of its ability to alter and reinforce preconceived ideas, and is thus more attuned to behaviour generally exhibited in museums.
(4) By not isolating specific items of information for analysis (objects, media, strategy) it is a more flexible, and powerful, analytical tool and can indicate the effectiveness of the exhibition as a whole, and not just part of it.
(5) By its very nature, it concentrates attention towards an analysis of the visitor rather than systems within the exhibition, and is thus a direct extention of the theory on which it is based.

A potential disadvantage lies in the sophisticated way in which the responses have to be treated in order to make the data amenable to the detailed assessment of the results. However, this should not be viewed as a problem and, if necessary, the museum can seek the advice of outside specialists.

Placing this discussion on a more pragmatic level may help to isolate the main points. Say, for example, that a small, thematic exhibition, containing 15 discrete display units of various sizes and complexity, has been organized to explore the theme of life in an Iron Age community. The focal point, the most significant finds from a recently excavated Celtic burial, occupies the six central units, and is supported by ancillary material from the museum's collections and others on loan from a neighbouring museum (four units). In addition, a number of interpretive aids, including photographs of the excavation process and accompanying text (two units), slides (one unit), a three dimensional model of the site (one unit) and a scale reconstruction of the burial chamber (one unit) are used to elaborate aspects of the central theme and to highlight features of the newly discovered material. The target audience has been defined as the interested layman (this definition having been translated into an operational one) with the result that some previous knowledge has been assumed in the level of presentation, particularly with regard to the selection of supporting material. A sequential information flow has been chosen as the most appropriate for interpretive purposes, and the displays have been designed and arranged accordingly.

The recall approach would tend to isolate facts from the text to act as the basic test material, and would include photograph recognition based on the artefacts in the exhibition. As a result, the presentation would be evaluated in terms of how well it had communicated this information, and the visitor said to have learned from it if he can recall it in line with pre-set criteria. It would be assumed subsequently that his understanding of the central theme had been enhanced accordingly.

Similarly, questions posed about visitor preference would seek to establish which display units had proved attractive and why. A behavioural mapping technique could be established to isolate the most popular units and to observe the pattern of movement around the gallery.

However, the approach suggested by Lee and Uzzell (1980a) would involve taking a broader view of the exhibition by focusing on Iron Age *life* and *community* as constructs, and would seek to establish whether the visitors' understanding of them had been modified as a result of exposure to the exhibition. The scales placed before both pre- and post-visit samples would be the same and might include the following:

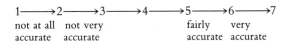

1 → 2 → 3 → 4 → 5 → 6 → 7

not at all not very   fairly very
accurate accurate   accurate accurate

How accurate are the following statements:

(1) Iron Age people lived in isolated communities.
(2) Most Iron Age people were buried in burial mounds.
(3) Most Iron Age people lived in hill forts.
(4) Iron Age people got most of their food from farming.

Clearly, the content of the statements would depend upon whether reference was made to the information in the exhibition, and the above serve only to show the style of presentation. However, they differ considerably from the type of question posed in recall based evaluation, where the emphasis might be placed on the age of a specific find, the name of a warrior king, the size and style of burial chamber. Such statements also reveal a great deal of information about the knowledge brought to the museum, not about specifics, but about a more general impression of the Iron Age: an important point when considering the amount of educationally redundant (previously known) information carried by the exhibition, and useful as feedforward data for the planning of related exhibitions. Moreover, by comparing the results recorded by various subsamples within the visitors, important considerations may emerge that help the identification of future target audiences.

A fundamental difference between this and the recall-approach is that the central variable in the evaluation is the *visitor* and not the particular characteristics of the exhibition material or style of presentation, although these may be inferred from the results. This fits in well with the overall strategy behind this evaluative technique, and may eventually prove valuable in constructing a more appropriate model of visitors and visitor behaviour – an essential factor in the development of a valid evaluative methodology.

Moreover, it is possible that this technique can be broadened to include the evaluation of exhibitions not amenable to the recall approach; that is, beyond those dealing with specific types of information on a didactic basis. It may be possible, for example, to develop a series of constructs for examining art exhibitions – perhaps by concentrating on schools and styles – and exhibitions where the communication of factual knowledge is not the primary consideration. However, there are major problems here, not least those concerned with translating a theoretical understanding of mood, feeling and aesthetic response into workable research criteria.

Conclusion

This paper, by drawing attention to the published material and techniques available for summative evaluation, has stressed that the results obtained by any survey or user analysis are governed ultimately by the objectives of the study and the type of material support available for research and analysis. It has suggested that survey objectives are best viewed as being organized hierarchically from the most general and all-embracing to the most specific, and has suggested that the observations must be placed in the context of the level from which they originate. The framing of objectives in a workable form was seen as an important part of the evaluation process – the objectives then becoming the criteria against which visitor behaviour is evaluated. Of this behaviour, learning was singled out for detailed discussion; the methods based on recall test questions and the assessment of schema changes were compared, and the suggestion was made that the latter was more acceptable. The assessment of visitor interest, preference and motivation was viewed as an essential prerequisite of summative evaluation, and care was taken to describe the isolation of a suitable target audience as part of a wider visitor survey. The role of summative evaluation was seen as extending beyond the confines of the museum into non-user surveys and attitude measurement. Various techniques were described in relation to their potential to evaluate exhibitions at a summative level.

Notes

1. Much of the 'evaluation' currently in print (especially from British sources) is highly informal and based either on descriptions (often by interested parties) or on reviews sketching their more basic components and occasionally drawing attention to their supposed educational/communicational outcomes. The *Museums Journal* (The Museums Association, London) carries a number of such reviews per issue.
2. Although this is generally the case, not all exhibitions are organized around collections. The Hall of Human Biology at the British Museum (Natural History) – described by Miles and Tout (1978) and reviewed by Duggan (1978) – is a good example. Here only one object is used – a human skull and spinal column – and even this did not come from the Museum's collections, but from a teaching hospital (Griggs, personal communication). This does not, however, devalue the central premise since in this case the approach to learning and design used lay the foundation for the evaluation, rather than the specific characteristics of the collection. The essential point is that the evaluation has a core of theory and practice upon which to work.
3. For a general criticism of this approach, see Macdonald-Ross (1973).
4. Most of the standard educational assessment techniques that are quick and easy to administer have been used in this context. Straightforward yes/no, agree/disagree formats are common, as are multiple choice questions. It should be noted that the questions need not require verbal answers; some studies have asked for a choice of objects (or representations of those objects) from a field of similar objects or representations. For a general review, *see* Stansfield (1981).
5. For a detailed criticism of this approach, *see* Alt (1977).
6. The only viable tool for collecting on-site, profile data is the questionnaire. A number of guidelines exist for their construction (see Payne, 1951; Oppenheim, 1966; Blalock, 1970; Davidson, 1970a, b; Saarinen, 1971; Countryside Recreation Research Advisory Group (CRRAG), 1973). A reading of those contained in other papers may also prove useful, bearing in mind that the final document must be tailored to the particular characteristics of the test site (see Abbey and Cameron, 1959; Cruickshank. 1972; Doughty, 1968; Mason, 1974; Digby, 1974; McWilliams and Hopwood, 1973; Mass Observation (UK) Ltd, 1978; Alt, 1980). For a brief discussion on the automated ways of achieving total visitor counts *see* Bayfield and Pickrell (1971), Bayfield and Moyes (1972), and Coker and Coker, (1972).
7. The most important questions here are:

   (1) The scope of the profile survey – is it part of a larger, more wide-ranging one, or is this the sole aim?
   (2) What method of data preparation (simply, manual or computer-assisted) is to be employed?

   Since the actual interview time will be limited (most visitors will be unwilling to give more than 15 minutes of their time) the number of questions devoted to the collection of profile data will be influenced by the overall objectives of the study. Hence, deciding on the value of this data to the final evaluation will influence the number of questions – of increasing specificity – devoted to it. The method of data handling is also crucial to the type, and depth, of questions asked, and revolves round whether or not a non-manual means of analysis is available. There can be no doubt that the true potential of such a survey can only be realized through an in-depth statistical analysis employing methods of statistical association and significance on selected, grouped variables, but that this requires a sophisticated level of data handling beyond the scope of the museum without the advantage of a computer-based statistical package capable of handling non-parametric (counted) data – especially if the number of responses is large. Indeed the depth of information this produces is beyond the normal requirements of a museum which has not yet undertaken a visitor survey beyond the level of simple visitor counts. In such a case, the placing of simple percentage points alongside the variables may be all that is required. If this is being attempted, it is important that the categories assigned to the variables are directly comparable not only with national figures, but also with similar studies elsewhere. Not to do so severely limits the scope of the final analysis.
8. Two aspects are central here:

   (1) The definition of the visiting *population*.
   (2) The method employed to extract a representative *sample*.

   The definition of (1) depends on the aims of the study and may involve just adults (what age?), children, school parties, types of visiting group and so on. A straightforward definition may be 'all adult visitors (16 and over) who have entered the museum on the day of interview', but the actual one used depends on what the evaluation is trying to demonstate. Sampling methods to select from this population for the type of survey being considered fall into one of three major classes:

   (1) Quota sampling.
   (2) Self selection.
   (3) Random sampling.

   (1) Individuals are selected on the basis of some predetermined variable or set of variables (cf. opinion polls). This is difficult to achieve if the distribution of these variables is not previously known (as in the case with most museums), and it carries the disadvantage

that statistical tests of association and significance (of which probably the most useful for general purposes is chi-square–χ^2 – see Everitt, 1977) are not amenable to this type of sampling frame.

(2) Questionnaires are left for the visitor to collect and (usually) return later. It has the major disadvantage of an unrepresented response (which effectively rules it out for use with profile data), but it may be useful in isolating 'interested' visitors for subsequent, in-depth study.

(3) Strictly determined by the use of random numbers or other non-biased sampling procedure (*see* Warwick and Lininger, 1975). Difficult to achieve if entrances and exits are many and/or difficult to observe. A useful compromise is to select 'every alternate person', but it should be noted that this tends to over-sample at slack times and under-sample at peak times. The more common method of interviewing every *n*th person may present problems due to the irregularity of arrivals and departures at the museum.

The actual method adopted is influenced by the particular characteristics of the site, and the reader is referred to Philips (1971), Atkinson, (1973), Pillay, (1973), Weisberg and Bowen, (1977) and Youngman, (1979) for an extended discussion of sampling theory, practice and methods of correlation.

9. For a general discussion on the role played by temporary motivational states in the learning process, see Logan (1969), Bruner (1973), Bourne *et al*, (1979 and Estes (1976).

10. A simple behavioural map consists of a plan of the exhibition area with all the major features (entrances, exits, display units, sales points) clearly located. The results of the survey (be they total counts or visitor tracking) are marked on at the survey points (perhaps at each display unit) together with some indication of visitor flow, usually achieved by arrows. The results indicate the most popular displays and the route taken to them. Subsequent analysis should seek to establish *why* these findings were recorded. For an example of this technique, as used in visitor centres, see Dartington Amenity Research Trust (1978), and for a brief guide to its implementations, see Lee and Uzzell (1980b).

11. For a brief, readable review of the techniques available for checking test validity and reliability, see Pidgeon and Yates (1968).

12. The type of question asked is obviously geared towards the peculiar characteristics of the test exhibition but, as a general rule, the aim is to progress from the general to the specific and, for ease of recording, to have as many pre-coded categories as possible in the test sheets. To try to take down a visitor's comment verbatim is both difficult and time consuming and may lead to substantial errors.

13. An important development in assessing visitor response within an interpretive, rather than a judgemental, framework is provided by the work of Wolf and Tymitz at the Smithsonian Institution (1977, 1978a, b). By advocating a technique involving extended, face-to-face conversation, the aim is to achieve a holistic interpretation of the visitor's total experience, rather than to the parts of it that may be exposed during a structured questionnaire interview. The technique is therefore more flexible and can accommodate spontaneous changes in mood and feeling – important when probing attitudes and values, and where the object of the exhibition is not didactic.

14. For example, Sobol (1980), in a study of 'blockbuster' exhibitions in attracting audiences to museums, found that one that captured the imagination of the public was more effective in drawing visitors than one of a more specialized nature, and that the resulting visitor profiles were more socially representative. Although this may be understood intuitively by a number of museum workers, the type of material exhibited, and the publicity involved in bringing it to the attention of a wider audience, remain problems for investigation.

15. For a description of how such a project can be undertaken, see the Dartington Amenity Research Trust (1979) project on the 'Defence of the Realm', where an attempt was made to integrate the on-site attractions of the Portsmouth area with the local museums around the theme of maritime defence.

References

ABBEY, D. S. and CAMERON, D. F. (1959), *The Museum Visitor 1 – Survey Design*, Royal Ontario Museum, Toronto

ALT, M. B. (1977), 'Evalutating didactic exhibits: a critical look at Shettel's work'. *Curator*, **20**(3), 241–258

ALT, M. B. (1980), 'Four years of visitor surveys at the British Museum (Natural History) 1976–1979', *Museums Journal*, **80**(1), 10–19

APPLETON, J. H. (1975), *The Experience of Landscape*, Wiley, London

ATKINSON, J. (1973), 'Questionnaire surveys: practical guidance in fieldwork techniques', in *The Use of Site Surveys in Countryside Recreation Planning and Management* pp. 5–7 Countryside Recreation Research Advisory Group (CRRAG)/Countryside Commission, London

AUSUBEL, D. P. (1968), *Educational Psychology: a Cognitive View*, Holt, Rinehart and Winston, New York

BAYFIELD, N. G. and MOYES, S. M. (1972), 'Simple automatic people counters', *Recreation News Supplement*, **6**, 18–20

BAYFIELD, N. G. and PICKRELL, B. G. (1971), 'The construction of a photoflux counter', *Recreation News Supplement*, **5**, 9–12

BLALOCK, H. M. JR. (1970), *An Introduction of Social Research*, Prentice-Hall, Englewood Cliffs, NJ

BLUMENTHAL, A. L. (1977), *The Process of Cognition*, Prentice-Hall, Englewood Cliffs, NJ

BOGGS, D. L. (1977), 'Visitor learning at the Ohio Historical Centre', *Curator*, **20**(3), 205–217

BORUN, M. (1977), 'Exhibit evaluation: an introduction', in *The Visitor and the Museum*, 1977 Program Planning Committee of the American Association of Museums, Seattle, Washington

BOURNE, L. E., DOMINOWSKI, R. I. and LOFTUS, E. F. (1979), *Cognitive Processes*, Prentice-Hall, Englewood Cliffs, NJ

BRUNER, J. S. (1973), *Beyond the Information Given: Studies in the Psychology of Knowing*, W.W. Norton, New York

CAMERON, D. F. (1967), 'How do we know what our visitors think?', *Museums News*, **45**(7), 31–33

CAMERON, D. F. (1968a), 'A viewpoint: the museum as a communicational system and implication for museum education', *Curator*, **11**(1), 33–40

CAMERON, D. F. (1968b), 'Measuring effectiveness: the evaluation viewpoint', *Museum News*, **46**(5), 43–45

CAMPBELL, F. L. (1970), 'Participant observation in outdoor recreation', *Journal of Leisure Research*, **2**(4), 220–236

COKER, A. M. and COKER, P. D. (1972), 'Some practical details of the use of pressure sensitive counters', *Recreation News Supplement*, **7**, 14–17

COKER, A. M. and COKER, P. D. (1973), 'A simple method of time lapse photography for use in recreation studies', *Recreation News Supplement*, **8**, 31–38

COOK, A. W. and SELLITZ, C. (1964), 'A multiple indicator approach to attitude measurement', in *Attitudes*, Warren, N. and Jahoda, M. (Eds), pp. 364–394, Penguin, Harmondsworth

COUNTRYSIDE RECREATION RESEARCH ADVISORY GROUP (CRRAG), (1973), *The Use of Site Surveys in Countryside Recreation Planning and Management*, Countryside Commission, London

CRUIKSHANK, G. (1972), 'Jewry Wall Museum, Leicester: trial by questionnaire', *Museums Journal*, **72**(2), 65–67

DART (1978), Dartington Amenity Research Trust and the Department of Psychology, the University of Surrey, *Interpretation in Visitor Centres: a Survey of the Effectiveness of Interpretive Services Provided in Visitor Centres*, Countryside Commission, Cheltenham

DARTINGTON AMENITY RESEARCH TRUST (1979), *Defence of the Realm*, Southern Tourist Board/Portsmouth City Council, Portsmouth

DAVIDSON, J. (1970a), *Outdoor Recreation Surveys: the Design of Questionnaires for Site Surveys*, Countryside Commission, London

DAVIDSON, J. (1970b), *Outdoor Recreation Information: Suggested Standard Classifications for use in Questionnaire Surveys*, Countryside Commission, London

DAWES, R. M. (1972), *Fundamentals of Attitude Measurement*, Wiley, New York

DIAB, L. N. (1968), 'Measurement of social attitudes: problems and prospects', in *Attitude, Ego-involvement and Change*, Sherif, C. W. and Sherif, M. (eds), pp. 140–158, Wiley, New York

DICK, R. E. , MYKLESTAD, E. and WAGAR, J. A. (1975), *Audience Attention as a Basis for Evaluationg Interpretive Presentation (USDA Forest Service Research Paper PNW-198)*, US Dept. of Agriculture (Forest Service), Washington, DC

DIGBY, P. W. (1974), *Visitors to Three London Museums*, London Office of Population, Censuses and Surveys, Social Survey Division, HMSO, London

DOUGHTY, P. S. (1968), 'The public of the Ulster Museum: a statistical survey', *Museums Journal*, **68**(1), 19–25 and **68**(2), 47–53

DUGGAN, A. J. (1978), 'The shape of things to come? Reflections on a visit to the Hall of Human Biology, South Kensington', *Museums Journal*, **78**(1), 5–6

EASON, L. P. and LINN, M. C. (1976), 'Evaluating the effectiveness of participatory exhibits', *Curator*, **19**(1), 45–62

ESTES, W. K. (Ed.), (1976), *Handbook of Learning and Cognitive Processes – Volume 3: Approaches to Human Learning and Motivation*, Lawrence Erlbaum, New York

EVERITT, B. S. (1977), *The Analysis of Contingency Tables*, Chapman and Hall, London

FRIEDRICHS, J. and LUDTKE, H. (1975), *Participant Observation: Theory and Practice*, Saxon House/Lexington, Farnborough, Hants

GRIGGS, S. and ALT, M. (1982), 'Visitors to the British Museum (Natural History) in 1980 and 1981', *Museums Journal*, **82**(3), 149–158

HAMMITT, W. E. (1978), 'A visual performance approach to measuring interpretive effectiveness', *Journal of Interpretation*, **3**(2), 33–37

LAKOTA, R. A. (1976), 'Techniques to improve exhibit effectiveness', in *Communicating with the Museum Visitor*, pp. 245–279, Royal Ontario Museum, Toronto

LEE, T. R. and UZZELL, D. L. (1980a), *The Educational Effectiveness of the Farm Open Day*, Countryside Commission for Scotland, Perth

LEE, T. R. and UZZELL, D. L. (1980b), *Forestry Commission Visitor Centres: an Evaluation Package*. Department of Psychology, University of Surrey

LEMON, N. (1973), *Attitudes and their Measurement*, Halsted Press/Wiley, New York

LIKERT, R. (1932), 'A technique for the measurement of attitude', *Archives of Psychology, No. 140*, New York

LOGAN, F. A. (1969), *Fundamentals of Learning and Motivation*, William C. Brown, Dubuque, IO

MACDONALD-ROSS, M. (1973), 'Behavioural objectives: a critical review', *Instructional Science*, **2**, 1–52

MAGER, R. F. (1962), *Preparing Instructional Objectives*, Lear Sieglet/Fearon, San Francisco, CA

MAHAFFEY, B. D. (1970), 'Effectiveness and preference for selected interpretive media', *Environmental Education*, **1**(4), 125–128

MASON, T. (1974), 'The visitors to Manchester Museum: a questionnaire survey', *Museums Journal*, **73**(4), 153–157

MASS OBSERVATION (UK) LTD (1978), *National Trust Visitors Survey: Part I – Report of Principle Findings: Part II – Appendix of Tables and Comments on Properties*, Mass Observation (UK) Ltd, London

McWILLIAMS, B. and HOPWOOD, J. (1973), 'The public of Norwich Castle Museum: 1971–72', *Museums Journal*, **72**(4), 153–156

MILES, R. F. and TOUT, A. F. (1978), 'Human biology and the New Exhibition Scheme in the British Museum (Natural History)', *Curator*, **21**(1), 36–50

MOSES, EPSTEIN, WISEMAN INC (1977), *Assessing the Impact of Interpretive Programmes*, prepared for the Division of Interpretation and Visitor Services, National Park Services, Washington, DC Contract PX-001-07-0702, (unpublished)

NEISSER, U. (1967), *Cognitive Psychology*, Appleton–Century–Crofts, New York

OPPENHEIM, A. N. (1966), *Questionnaire Design and Attitude Measurement*, Basic Books, New York

OSGOOD, C. E. (1964), 'Semantic differential technique in the comparative study of cultures', *American Anthropology*, **66**(3), 171–200

PARSONS, L. A. (1965), 'Systematic testing of display techniques for an anthropological exhibit', *Curator*, **8**(2), 167–189

PAYNE, S. L. (1951), *The Art of Asking Questions*, Princeton University Press, Princeton, NJ

PEARSON, L. F. (1978), *Non-work Time: A Review of the Literature (Research Memorandum No. 65)*, Centre for Urban and Regional Studies, the University of Birmingham, Birmingham

PHILIPS, D. L. (1971), *Knowledge from What?: Theories and Methods in Social Research*, Rand/McNally, Chicago, IL

PIDGEON, D. and YATES, A. (1968), *An Introduction to Educational Measurement*, Routledge and Kegan Paul, London

PILLAY, C. (1973), 'Questionnaire surveys: some sampling problems discussed and illustrated', in *The Use of Site Surveys in Countryside Recreation Planning and Management*, pp. 1–4, Countryside Commission, London

PRINCE, D. R. (1982), 'Countryside interpretation: a cognitive evaluation', *Museums Journal*, 82(3), 165–170

PRINCE, D. R. (1983), 'Behavioural consistency and visitor attraction', *International Journal of Museum Management and Curatorship*, 2, 235–247

PUTNEY, A. D. and WAGAR, J. A. (1973), 'Objectives and evaluation and interpretive planning', *Journal of Environmental Education*, 5(1), 43–44

SAARINEN, T. F. (1971), 'Research approaches and questionnaire design', in *Perceptions and Attitudes in Resource Management*, pp. 13–19, Sewell, W. R. D. and Barton, I. (Eds), Policy Research and Coordination Branch, Department of Energy, Mines and Resources, Ottawa

SCREVEN, C. G. (1969), 'The museum as a responsive learning environment', *Museum News*, 47(10), 7–10

SCREVEN, C. G. (1974a), 'Learning and exhibits: instructional design', *Museum News*, 52(5), 67–76

SCREVEN, C. G. (1974b), *The Measurement and Facilitation of Learning in the Museum Environment: An Experimental Analysis*, Smithsonian Institution Press, Washington, DC

SCREVEN, C. G. (1976), 'Exhibit evaluation: a goal-referenced approach', *Curator*, 19(5), 271–290

SHAW, M. E. and WRIGHT, J. M. (1967), *Scales for the Measurement of Attitudes*, McGraw-Hill, New York

SHERIF, C. W., SHERIF, M. and NEBERGAL, R. E. (1965), *Attitude and Attitude Change: The Social Judgement–involvement Approach*, W. B. Saunders, Philadelphia

SHETTEL, H. H. (1973), 'Exhibits: art form or educational medium?', *Museum News*, 52(1), 32–41

SHETTEL, H. H. et al., (1968), *Strategies for Determining Exhibit Effectiveness (AIR-e95-4/68-FR)* American Institute for Research, Pittsburgh, PA

SHETTEL, H. H. and REILLEY, P. C. (1965), *An Evaluation of the Existing Criteria for Judging the Quality of Science Exhibits*, American Institute for Research, Pittsburgh, PA

SOBOL, M. G. (1980), 'Do blockbusters' change the audience?', *Museums Journal*, 80(1), 25–27

STANSFIELD, G. (1981), *Effective Interpretative Exhibits*, Countryside Commission, Cheltenham

TUAN, TI-FU (1974), *Topophilia: A Study of Environmental Perception, Attitudes and Values*, Prentice-Hall, Englewood Cliffs, NJ

UPSHAW, H. S. (1968), 'Attitude measurement', in *Methodology in Social Research*, Blalock, H. M. Jr and Blalock, A. B. (Eds), pp. 60–111, McGraw-Hill, New York

WAGAR, J. J. (1972), *The Recording Quizboard: A Device for Evaluating Interpretive Services*, (Paper PNW-139) USDA Forest Research, Washington, DC

WARREN, N. and JAHODA, M. (Eds), (1973), *Attitudes*, Penguin, Harmondsworth

WARWICK, D. P. and LININGER, C. A. (1975), *The Sample Survey: Theory and Practice*, McGraw-Hill, New York

WASHBURN, R. F. and WAGAR, J. A. (1972), 'Evaluating visitor response to exhibit content', *Curator* 15(3), 248–254

WEISBERG, H. F. and BOWEN, B. D. (1977), *An Introduction to Survey Research and Data Analysis*, W. H. Freeman, San Francisco, CA

WICKELGREN, W. A. (1979), *Cognitive Psychology*, Prentice-Hall, Englewood Cliffs, NJ

WINKEL, G. H., OLSEN, R., WHEELER, F. and COHEN, H. (1975.), *The Museum Visitor and Orientational Media: An Experimental Comparison of Different Approaches at the Smithsonian Institution National Museum of History and Technology*, Smithsonian Institution, Washington, DC

WOLF, R. L. and TYMITZ, B. L. (1977), *Things to Consider when Evaluating*, Indiana Center for Evaluation, Indiana University, Bloomington, IN

WOLF, R. L. and TYMITZ, B. L. (1978a), *A Preliminary Guide for Conducting Naturalistic Evaluation in Studying Museum Environments*, Smithsonian Institution, Washington, DC

WOLF, R. L. and TYMITZ, B. L. (1978b), *Whatever Happened to the Giant Wombat?: An Investigation of the Impact of the Ice Age Mammals and the Emergence of Man Exhibit*, National Museum of Natural History, Smithsonian Institution, Smithsonian Institution, Washington, DC

WOLFE, R. L. and TYMITZ, B. L. (1979a), *The Pause that Refreshes: A Study of Visitor Reactions to the Discovery Corners in the National Museum of History and Technology*, Smithsonian Institution, Washington, DC

WOLFE, R. L. and TYMITZ, B. L. (1979b), *Do Giraffes ever Sit?: A Study of Visitor Perceptions at the National Zoological Park*, Smithsonian Institution, Smithsonian Institution, Washington, DC

YOUNGMAN, M. B. (1979), *Analysing Social and Educational Research Data*, McGraw-Hill (UK), London

70

Retailing

Mel Twelves

The museum shop

In recent years it has become more generally accepted throughout the profession that a shop can provide a valuable extension to the museum's services. On a national basis, some museums have invested substantially in shop development and sales stock. A number of the larger museums, or those more favourably placed in areas of high tourism, operate well-established shops on true commercial lines producing annual turnovers that would be the envy of many a high-street retailer. By comparison, others perform at much lower levels which make financial and staffing subsidies towards operational costs essential. This latter group at best create a trading surplus, with staff, administration and other overheads being ignored or written off. This is not an uncommon practice in public-sector-managed museums, but many are now progressing towards running retailing operations on a self-financing basis.

Historically, moves towards any commercial activity in museums have created feelings of unease. This is still the case for there is a view that such activity heralds the dissolution, or at least the lowering, of established academic standards and levels of service of which Curators are the traditional guardians. It is therefore understandable that when a museum shop is on the agenda the response is often one of unconcealed distrust. Unfortunately this can be the reason why so many shops are severely controlled in what can and cannot be sold and fall victim to management discrimination by not being allowed to play their full part in improving service to the public. This is unfortunate, because under normal circumstances a shop will only develop in relation to its position in a given market. It will only succeed by satisfying customers' needs and if it achieves this, why should there by so much concern amongst management?

A managed approach

In many ways setting up and operating a shop can be more demanding of time and other resources than temporary or permanent displays. Shops do not go away after a summer season, they have a continuing appetite for management input and trading direction needs to be regularly reviewed. An initial major difficulty particularly for those faced with the task for the first time, is deciding just where to start.

Knowing what products are to be sold is a tremendous help in considering the type of shop-fittings needed but, unless the potential customers' buying habits are identified, how can a product range be chosen? The best advice is to follow the recommendations of the popular song, 'let's start at the very beginning', which is to define clearly just what the shop is to achieve; this can be classified as its 'mission'. All subsequent activities should be subordinate to the mission and can be divided into two sections: planning and operational. This division is not absolute since there will be many grey areas in which activities are interlinked and interdependent. As a guide, however, they can be listed as follows:

Planning
Research
Sales forecasting
Choosing a site for the shop
Fitting out the shop
Stock storage and handling

Operational
Stock selection
Product or package innovation
Range development
Product life cycle
Sales monitoring
Legal obligations

The mission

This must be carefully addressed before any decisions relating to the planning, management and operation of a shop can have any positive meaning. In some eyes its purpose may be to sell a small range of items, all strictly related to the resident collection. Others may see it as offering a much broader range including souvenirs of a very general nature. There may be those who think in profit-making terms, while some may support the 'service to the visitor' principle. Equally, the motive could be to promote contact with the public or serve in a public-relations capacity. It will be possible to conceive other reasons or formulate permutations.

The adoption of a mission is, however, unlikely to be a straightforward process. Full account must be taken of the resources that are available. It may be necessary to redefine the mission several times until a workable blend of resources and objective(s) is attained. As an example, the mission might be stated initially, 'to provide a museum shop which enhances the visiting experience.' On paper this would seem to be a reasonable and simple objective. Closer examination will probably raise questions concerning operating costs, range of stock, staffing, suitable site, etc., and reality starts to take over. The outcome might be an adjustment of the mission by adding qualifications such as, 'It is recognized that a subsidy of £. . . will need to be made towards staffing and operational costs'. Another qualification could specify some self-financing or profit-making basis. Whatever mission is ultimately adopted, it must be valid and become the factor which determines the subsequent input of resources and the yardstick against which success is measured. It will be totally unreasonable to expect a mission to attain its objectives if it is to rely on resource levels dictated by other interests.

Circumstances can, of course, change and affect resource availability. In such situations the validity of a mission must be investigated. In fact a mission should be subjected to a programme of regular monitoring and review so that the best interests of both museum and public can be served. Under these conditions changes to a mission are planned and controlled. What must be avoided are internal influences that, unwittingly or otherwise, exert pressures which make the achievement of mission objectives impossible. It is worthwhile bearing in mind that the most frequently told 'sad stories' relate to profit-making and break-even missions being later subjected to strict controls governing the sales range and selling prices. These objectives and controls are not usually compatible. Running close behind are instances where shop management is given freedom to choose sales stock and set prices only to find warehouse, administration and staff support suffer as a result of a change in internal priorities. Under these and similar conditions the mission must be reconsidered.

Planning

Research

It was stated earlier that the activities comprising the two principal sections, planning and operational, are frequently interlinked. Research is an activity that links with both. Whilst it will not guarantee retailing success, it can help to remove the guesswork from much of the decision-making process. Its results can validate or invalidate the mission; if the latter, then there is no alternative but to go back to square one.

Although not exhaustive, the following list identifies points that are worthy of research.

Other museums
(1) How do their collections compare to yours?
(2) What percentage of their sales stock relates to their collections?
(3) How many visitors do they attract each year and how much do they spend? (Calculate their average spend per visitor head.)
(4) Do they have seasonal trading patterns?
(5) What percentage of annual turnover is achieved through exhibitions, special events, etc.?
(6) How long has each been operating a museum shop?
(7) What are their sales growth records?
(8) What do they sell and what are their best selling lines?
(9) Who are their suppliers and what are the trade prices and profit margins?
(10) What are the fast and slow turnover products?
(11) What percentage of the customers are adults, children?
(12) Are they satisfied with their present shop site?
(13) Are they satisfied with their shop-fittings and are those fittings standard designs or tailor made?

Your museum
(1) How many people visit your museum each year?
(2) What is the adult/child/school visiting mix?
(3) What items in the collection attract visitors most?
(4) Which exhibitions are most successful?

Competition
(1) Is there any local competition such as other museums, gift shops, etc.?
(2) What do they sell?
(3) How long have they been established?

Sales forecasting

It might be argued that the preparation of a meaningful forecast is not possible at this early stage but, as a number of other decisions are linked to income predictions, the exercise cannot be delayed. A preliminary forecast can be used to judge the mission's validity and if proven a more substantial forecast should follow. Research should have produced enough information to allow an acceptable attempt to be made and the forecast can always be modified later as the project develops.

Preliminary forecast – procedure
(1) Estimate the overhead costs including, where appropriate, rent, rates, staff, depreciation on fittings, lighting, warehousing and other support services.
(2) Calculate visitor spend per head basing your figures on the performances of the researched museums.
(3) Calculate turnover: Turnover (£) = Anticipated No. Annual Visitors × Spend Per Head.
(4) Identify a representative gross margin and apply it to turnover as follows: Turnover × % gross margin = gross profit
(5) Repeat exercise by varying spend per head to give best and worst situations. If gross profit is less than overheads check the spend per head and visitor assumptions and adjust if necessary. If the overheads still exceed gross profit, reconfirm the mission.

Detailed forecasting – procedure
(1) Estimate realistic annual sales value of each product, e.g. postcards, posters, catalogues, etc.
(2) Check accuracy of total sales estimate by calculating spend per head and compare with that used in preliminary forecast.
(3) If spend per head is excessively high/low then:
    (a) the spend used for comparison is not representative; and/or
    (b) the product mix has a significant imbalance of high/low gross margin products; and /or
    (c) estimated annual sales by product is inaccurate;
    (d) investigate (a) (b) (c) and correct.
(4) Calculate the gross profits earned by each product and add these together to give total gross profit.
(5) Estimate overheads as in preliminary forecast.
(6) Is gross profit/loss acceptable to the mission?

Choosing a site for the shop

It is obvious that a shop set to achieve a turnover measured in tens of thousands of pounds is unlikely to succeed if it is tucked away in some remote corner. However, if we ignore the extreme cases where museum management has the opportunity to include a shop in a major rebuilding project, it is rare for a museum to be so blessed that it is able to provide the perfect site. More often than not the location available is something of a compromise offering 'this but not that'. Frequently there is competition for space from other museum services; who can blame a curator for not wanting to give up valuable display space, thereby possibly condemning even more of the collection to storage? However, if the commitment to the mission is sincere, then the priorities will have been established.

Some site preferences
(1) Is in an area of high density visitor traffic, preferably situated near an entrance/exit.
(2) Has reserve wall and floor space so that future shop extension can be accommodated.
(3) Is near to adequate stock/storage facilities.
(4) Provides good and easy access for delivery of sales stock.
(5) Does not impose architectural restrictions prohibiting future repositioning of shop display fittings.
(6) Does not prohibit use of strong lighting necessary to emphasize sales displays (collection considerations).
(7) Neighbouring gallery environment is not sensitive to noise such as that created by school parties, or to high visual profile of shop and its displays.
(8) Allows quick, safe evacuation in the event of an emergency.
(9) Is capable of being independently secured if the museum is occupied after normal public hours – cleaning staff, building shared with library, used by outside groups/societies, etc. Conversely, some of these uses could be exploited by a shop that can be operated after museum closing.
(10) Does not restrict visitor flow to or from other parts of the building.

NOTE: This list does not provide for a shop selling or preparing food. If food is to be served, hygiene, ventilation and other factors must be taken into account and specialist advice sought.

Before changing the location of an existing shop or upgrading an existing 'sales counter' it is advisable to carry out some on-site research to determine visitor requirements. A simple visitor survey carried out by shop staff or Friends of the museum should suffice.

A case history
A number of years ago, there was strong feeling amongst collection management staff that shops were best sited in an inner gallery, away from the museum entrance/exit. The idea was that visitors would be obliged to pass by and be exposed to the collection displays. At least one museum put this philosophy into practice. The shop had originally been sited near a joint entrance/exit and good sales were achieved. When moved to its new 'inner' location, sales fell dramatically and, before many months had passed, plans were in hand to return it to a 'front of house' position.

The 'inner' theory had appeared fine on paper but was a theory formulated to serve collection display needs and not those of the shop or its customers. In its original position, it had attracted a 'shopper' clientele who had made substantial casual purchases. These shoppers were not prepared to spend time seeking out the new site. Sales were also lost because people visiting for more traditional reasons failed, or could not be bothered, to discover the shop – the museum was housed in a very large building.

Fitting out

If the intention is to offer only a few postcards, some leaflets plus occasional catalogues, then little in the way of display fittings will be needed. A counter or desk supplemented by a small postcard stand would probably suffice. Such a facility would be described as a sales point and should be expected to perform accordingly. It might produce good sales at times of popular exhibitions but its ability to function as a shop and create or stimulate sales would be limited.

For more ambitious projects consideration must be given to the range of stock that is to be sold and the system of retailing to be employed. These two questions cannot be divorced and only when they have been resolved should there be any attempt to brief a designer or shop-fitter.

The sales forecast should be used to assess the frequency at which the various products must sell and from this a decision can be made on whether or not a self-service or partial self-service system is necessary. For example, if the annual sales of postcards is forecast at 20 000 units and books at 2000, then it might be unrealistic to expect these figures to be achieved by operating an 'assistant served' only system. Such a system might of course be entirely suitable for products having an anticipated low turnover or high security requirement.

Although self-service can add to stock security problems, there is much to recommend it. The public are now used to it and browsing around the shelves can make shopping an enjoyable experience. It removes the physical barrier between customers and goods and the psychological barrier that can exist between customer and sales assistant. It also gives mass exposure to the stock range and encourages spontaneous purchases.

Design brief

It is possible to design and fit out a shop satisfactorily without using the services of a professional designer or shop-fitter. There are many companies who supply their own standard range of fittings and their representatives are often prepared to offer advice. As with any fittings it is a wise precaution to ensure that the range will remain available for a number of years to allow for any future expansion.

For larger projects or shops which are expected to complement a corporate image the use of professional services is recommended. However it is important to have a budget that both you and your financial controllers have agreed and of which the Designer is fully aware.

Local authority managed museums may be under an obligation to use an architect on the authority's staff. In such cases it is important to make sure that the nominated architect understands retailing needs. Joint visits to other museums shops and some leading high street shops could be helpful in creating an understanding and a good working relationship.

Whatever the source of professional input, the end product will only be as good as the initial brief. It is, therefore, important to provide as comprehensive a brief as possible and the following is provided as a sample.

Brief for the Design and Construction of a Shop Situated in the . . . . . . Art Gallery.
It has been decided that the retail facilities at the Art Gallery should be developed to fully capitalize on the retailing opportunities which it presents. The objective is to have a shop that is specially designed and constructed to meet the Gallery's needs and that the project will be completed and in operation by the . . . . . . 19. . .

Background

The Art Gallery is the principal gallery in an area embracing the Counties of A, B, C and D. It attracts approximately 100 000 visitors each year but its immediate catchment area is A and B, although the main visitor support can be considered to be generated in the City of Z and the surrounding towns of W, X and Y. Z is a University City but it also has a Polytechnic and College of Art and Technology. There are further education establishments in the neighbouring towns including a Technical College. The population of the catchment area is approximately . . . . million.

The collection at the Art Gallery comprises Fine Art of approximately . . . oils and applied art and costume. Local artists such as . . . are well represented and there are also significant works by . . . . The applied art features predominantly local material.

The retail service at the gallery is currently provided from a small sales point situated on the ground floor near the street entrance. Annual retail sales are currently in the region of £. . ., but experience has shown that a major exhibition can increase this by X per cent or more. It is felt that this level of turnover is not a true reflection of the potential. The main restrictions to increased sales are the small and limited display and selling facilities, which in turn place severe constraints on the range and type of retail stock carried. Analysis shows that the exhibition catalogues and self-published material generate about 70 per cent of the Gallery's sales. The remaining 30 per cent comes from bought-in goods comprising mainly art publications, book marks and greetings cards. Recently there has been an encouraging customer response to additional items such as craftware, designer jewellery, traditional toys and foodstuffs.

Project specifications and requirements

A ground-floor site near to the entrance hallway has been nominated for the development of a shop. It has an area of approximately. . . square metres and there is access to an adjacent room that can be used for product storage. Visitors to all galleries are likely to pass the shop but, unfortunately, this 'right of way' could cause some practical problems with shop layout and security and might reduce the usable space by about 50 per cent.

The design objective is to produce a shop that offers a self-service/merchandizing facility but at the same time allows some display accommodation for a small range of expensive goods such as jewellery and engraved glass. Some mobile display equipment should be allowed for and the shop-floor layout should be sufficiently flexible to cater for changes in display arrangements and seasonal and exhibiton themes. The design of stands, counters, etc., should provide for some on-site stock storage through the provision of lockable drawers and cupboards.

A prime objective is to keep staffing costs to a minimum and the shop design and layout should take this fully into account. It is likely that, under normal levels of operation, only one sales assistant will be available.

The range of goods to be accommodated will be publications (both self-published and brought-in), posters/prints, postcards, greetings cards, confectionery, gallery souvenirs, facsimiles/reproductions, jewellery, glassware/china ware and other three-dimensional items. The retail price range is likely to be from 15 pence up to tens of pounds. Fittings must be sympathetic to the protection, storage, lighting and general presentation of this range.

As the gallery attracts school groups as well as adults, this factor should be taken fully into account in determining equipment, design and construction and colour schemes. The overall effect should be to produce a layout and shopping environment which is cheerful, relaxed and promotes positive buying decisions. Design should also allow for future expansion of the shop floor area and retailing facilities.

Arrangement for inspecting the site can be made by appointment.

Cash registers

Although the cash register is a piece of computer hardware, it is legitimate to consider it as a shop-fitting. Modern registers incorporate electronic components and are sophisticated pieces of equipment. They have memory facilities and are pre-programmed to provide print-outs giving valuable cash sales information. Some machines are capable of transmitting this information to a centrally based computer which then adjusts stock records according to the day's sales. These are known as electronic point-of-sales systems (EPOS), but their high cost can probably only be justified by the larger retailing operations. There is a wide range of machines on the market from which to make a choice, but one of the difficulties that the first-time buyer will be faced with is understanding the terminology used in promotional catalogues and by representatives to describe the facilities. The following guide to some of the more commonly used terms may, therefore, be of some help.

Departments

Departments are memories to which product groups can be allocated and their sales recorded. For example, product groups could be grouped as:

Department 1: books/catalogues published in house.
Department 2: books/catalogues brought in.
Department 3: postcards/greetings cards.

Each department has its own numbered key which is operated as each sale is entered in the register.

Price lookups (PLUs)

This facility enables individual items of merchandise to be given numbered codes and each code subsequently assigned the appropriate retail unit price. The PLU number is also allocated to a department. When a product that has a PLU number is sold, it is only necessary to enter that number in the register and the display and recording of the price and department is automatic.

Compulsory cash/cheque declaration (CCD)

This is a security facility which requires a cashier to count the cash and cheques present in the cash drawer and enter the amount before reading or resetting the day's sales records. This highlights cash imbalances and reduces the opportunities for subsequent adjustments.

X and Z reports

These reports are produced in print-out form on the till roll.

An X reading produces a 'situation to date' report and can be used to check the takings at any time or the performance of an individual cashier.

A Z reading is usually taken at the end of a nominated period such as a day or week and resets the memories for the next period (day/week) to zero.

The information shown on the print-outs varies according to the specification of the machine but can include such details as:

(1) custom account in a time period;
(2) sales amount in a time period;
(3) average sales amount per customer;
(4) sales by department;
(5) sales by individual cashiers;
(6) value added tax totals;
(7) cash sales;
(8) credit sales;
(9) cheque-tendered sales;
(10) refunds;
(11) no-sale operations.

Stock storage and handling

Very few museum retailing operations will be able to justify the luxury of having a warehouse. In most instances the 'warehouse' will be a room in which stock can be stored and it is likely that this will, in truth, be inadequate for the task. Therefore it is more appropriate here to give some practical advice and recommend the application of common sense rather than attempt to give specifications that can only have any meaning in a modern and spacious warehouse.

(1) Products must be stored in a manner that prevents deterioration and ensures their potential sales value is maintained. Some of the storage practices recommended in the chapters on conservation and storage (Chapter 28–41) are worth adopting.

(2) If the room is to be used as an office, even on a temporary basis whilst incoming and outgoing stock is recorded, then there will be some obligation to ensure that the environment is fit as a workplace. For example, thorough consideration should be given to lighting levels, ventilation and staff safety.

(3) Safety apart, layout should be designed to provide walkways of a minimum 1 m width to allow hand trollies to be manoeuvred easily.

(4) Soap and perfumed products should not be allowed to taint other items.

(5) Shelving should be easily accessible to staff standing at floor level. Shelves that can only be reached by using a step-ladder should be restricted to storing lightweight stock. A 5 kg package that staff can easily handle when both feet are firmly placed on the ground becomes an entirely different proposition when operating from step-ladders.

(6) In bulk, paper is a very heavy material. Any shelving used for storage must be up to the job. The following examples emphasize how heavy bulk paper is:

(a) 5000 postcards, each card measuring approximately 147 mm × 105 mm, weigh 23.75 kg and occupy 0.023 m^3;

(b) 2000 copies of a 36-page booklet, *British Enamels*, (published by Tyne and Wear Museums) measuring 210 mm × 208 mm × 3 mm and weighing 130 g, weigh in total 260 kg and occupy 0.262 m^3; and

(c) 2000 copies of the 88-page book, *Maling: The Trademark of Excellence*, (published by Tyne and Wear Museums), each copy measuring 280 mm × 214 mm × 7 mm, and weighing 425 g, weigh in total 850 kg and occupy 0.838 m^3.

(7) the use of drawers, whether metal or wood, for the storage of bulk paper should be avoided, the weight can cause the sliding mechanism or runners to fail and make opening extremely difficult.

(8) Finally, there is a need for good security. This may seem an obvious point, but storage space in a museum can be at a premium and shared storage space should be avoided.

Operational

Stock selection

Shops should be developed so that they are exciting and interesting places to visit and tempt customers to spend time discovering the goods on offer. This can only be achieved by offering goods that are of interest to the visitor, yet, historically, museum shops have demonstrated a strong tendency to ignore visitor needs and offer goods which meet the 'good

taste' of staff. If this taste differs from that of the visitor then the shop will achieve little other than criticism.

No matter what the stated mission, a shop will only be successful if it sells what the customers believe they want. If it does not do this then it will fail in its role, even if that role has been identified as non-profit making, such as improving public relations or contributing to the visitor experience.

The research conducted during the planning stage will have indicated the types of products, and possibly the supply sources, that other museums sell and these will provide a good basis on which to build sales stock. What the research will most probably not have done is give much information on product innovation in each product type or on range development.

Product innovation

If a museum attracts a high percentage of first-time visitors each year then its shop can possibly survive by offering a substantial staple core stock. The more the visiting pattern progresses towards repeat visits then the more necessary it becomes to introduce products offering design variations, new colours and fresh images. Even where the first-time visitor level is high, it is essential that the product range does not stagnate; buying habits do change.

It is possible to give several illustrations of the way in which product innovation within an established product type can be introduced but the following should suffice:

(1) *Design variation.* A very simple example is the replacement of existing craft ware with work from new studios. Although pottery might be replaced by pottery and jewellery with jewellery, etc., the new designs, styles and techniques should revitalize displays.

(2) For some reason pencil erasers are currently very popular with children. This popularity might never have been achieved if manufacturers had stuck with the old dull greys, greens and reds. Now erasers come in a large assortment of bright colours and shapes (design). Similar thinking is being applied to pencils, pens and notebooks. *New colours* can give a product type new sales life.

(3) *Fresh images.* Greetings cards provide high gross margins and a good sales range. Regularly offering fresh images can stimulate demand and contribute significantly to the overall sales turnover.

Range development

Introducing new types of product is a risky business. It is a process of exploration and will by nature result in failures as well as successes. It would be an unwise manager who, on the strength of a sales representative's recommendation, ordered a large quantity of an unknown and untried product. Equally, the same lack of wisdom would be shown by accepting at face value a sales assistant's word that a certain product is always being requested. The representative or assistant may, of course be right, but the sensible approach is to first make some investigations and then carry out test marketing. Any supplier having confidence in the product will usually encourage the placing of small trial orders.

Test marketing should be carried out as scientifically as possible but, in practice, this will probably be restricted to noting whether buyers are adults or children and the rate of sales over a measured period of time. A few twists can be added by applying minor price adjustments, both up and down, or varying the shelf or display position. Remember, however, that a successful trial may not be a true reflection of what will be achieved in the longer term. Order cautiously and let the product prove itself. If the worst happens and the product turns out to be a white elephant get rid of it as quickly as possible through special offers such as two for the price of one, as free gifts or any other legitimate means. A product that does not sell well takes up valuable space and can reflect badly on the shop's image.

It can also pay to experiment by introducing the unexpected. A fine-art print offered by a shop in a museum having a science and engineering collection may seem out of place and the same may be said about sets of historic transport postcards in a prestigious art gallery. Both implants have been successfully achieved as temporary innovation exercises. They may have shocked staff but apparently not the visitors who, after all, are the people who determine whether products are right or wrong. This does not of course mean undermining a shop's corporate identify which may be dependent on a reputation for selling items which relate to the exhibits.

Product life cycle

When a particular product has sold well there is a great temptation to re-order and in larger quantities. Initially, this might be the right decision but there is a danger of falling into the trap of automatically re-ordering a product every time it sells out. All products have an economic life cycle and eventually that cycle will have run its course. The trick is knowing when the product has peaked in popularity and in determining the subsequent rate of decline. This information can be obtained by monitoring sales and re-ordering periods. Even where a decline has been identified it may still make good sense to re-order if the decline is gradual or has reached a plateau. A graphical representation of a product life-cycle curve is given in *Figure 70.1*. Plans should be in hand for new product innovation even at the

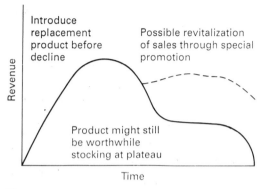

Figure 70.1   A possible product life-cycle curve

stage of sales growth. The time to introduce the replacement product is a question of management judgement, but it should be before sales of the initial product have dropped to the point where its retention on the display shelves is no longer economic.

Sales monitoring

A shop can reach a stage very quickly where the frequency of sales activity makes the manual recording of each product sold impractical. Unless an EPOS (see 'Cash registers') system is employed management must devise some means of measuring sales performance. Regular stock-taking, perhaps on a weekly or monthly basis, is one solution, but it might not be a viable proposition. An alternative is to use the stock levels in the 'warehouse' as a gauge but this makes the assumption that all stock issued to the shop is sold. A similar assumption is made if 'warehouse' re-order levels become the yardsticks. However, they are all valid systems to adopt, but the inexactness of the methods must be recognized.

It is quite common for a modern cash register to have the ability to provide printed records of sales by product groups. This facility can be a valuable source of information to which management can quickly respond. A practical example of how this information can be extracted and presented for interpretation is given in *Table 70.1*. The basic statistics in the table give an indication of product-group performance and a comparison between specified periods can show what effects special promotions, new lines, product innovation or new display positions can have.

Legal considerations

It is strongly recommended that shop management becomes fully acquainted with at least the principal requirements of the general consumer protection

Table 70.1 Sales information★

| | Product group | | | | | | |
	1	2	3	4	5	6	Total
Week 1							
Sales (£)	27	108	190	45	53	129	552
% of total	4.8	19.6	34.4	8.2	9.6	23.4	100
Gross % profit	50	35	50	30	50	40	
Gross profit (£)	13.5	37.8	95	13.5	26.5	51.6	237.9
Week 2							
Sales (£)	66	124	103	898	18	212	1421
% of total	5	9	7	63	1	15	100
Gross % profit	50	35	50	30	50	40	
Gross profit (£)	33	43.4	51.5	269.4	9	84.8	491.1

★ Product-groups: 1, postcards and greetings cards; 2, books and catalogues (zero VAT rating); 3, colouring books, notebooks and diaries; 4, foodstuffs (preserves, honey, etc.); 5, giftware (pottery, glass, etc.); 6, miscellaneous (pencils, pens, badges, etc.).

legislation. In the UK, the *Sale of Goods Act, 1979*, supported by the *Supply of Goods and Services Act, 1982*, place the retailer under three main obligations:

(1) that the goods are of 'merchantable quality' – this means that goods must be reasonably fit for their normal purpose, bearing in mind the price paid, the nature of the goods and how they are described;
(2) that the goods are 'fit for any particular purpose' made known to the retailer; and
(3) That the goods are 'as described' – as printed on packaging, displayed on signs or verbally by the retailer.

It should be noted that there are some differences between the laws of England and Wales and those of Scotland and Northern Ireland.

Other Acts relevant to retailing businesses in this country are:

The Food and Drugs Act, 1955
Prices Act, 1974
Trade Descriptions Acts, 1968 and 1972
Weights and Measures Acts, 1963 and 1979
Unfair Contract Terms Act, 1977

There are some excellent leaflets and brochures giving straightforward guidance on this legislation published by the Office of Fair Trading and the Central Office of Information, and they are available from local consumer advice points and many public libraries.

Most consumer legislation is enforced by the Local Authority (except in Northern Ireland) through their Trading Standards (sometimes called Consumer Protection or Weights and Measures) and Environmental Health Departments. Their officers are often able to give advice and guidance. Clarification of local attitudes towards Sunday trading is recommended.

Concluding comments

This chapter has been written as a practical guide for museum personnel having little or no retailing or commercial experience. Hopefully it will provide a foundation on which to build as experience is gained.

Compared with the potential new high street retailer, museums are in a favoured position having many 'friendly' sources of help within the museum network. Most will be prepared to offer helpful direction.

Membership of the Group for Museum Publishing and Shop Management (GMPSM) is recommended. It is affiliated to the Museums Association and organizes seminars covering an assortment of commercial and publishing subjects and arranges and participates in trade fairs.

Finally, it should be recognized that the recent growth of commercial activities within museums is not simply a result of economic pressures. It is more a response to visitor expectations and, as such, should be seen as a further opportunity to satisfy market needs.

Bibliography

BLUME, H. (1981), *The Charity Trading Handbook*, Charities Advisory Trust, London

BLUME, H. (1987), *The Museum Trading Handbook*, Charities Advisory Trust, London

BRAVE, J. (1983), *Law for Retailers*, Sweet & Maxwell

BYRNE, D. E. and JONES, P. H. (1977), *Retail Security, A Management Function*, 20th Century Security Education Ltd, Leatherhead, Surrey

HARRIES, J. (1983), *Consumers: Know Your rights*, Longman, London

JOY, T. (1974), *The Book Selling Business*, Pitman Publishing, London

KNEE, D. K. and WALTERS, D. W. (1985), *Strategy in Retailing, Theory in Application*, Philip Allan Deddington, Oxford

MCFADYEN, E. (Ed) (1987), *The Changing Face of British Retailing*, Newman Books, London

MOORE, J. (Ed) (1982), *A Handbook of Consumer Law*, Consumers' Association/Hodder & Stoughton, London

SMITH, K. (1983), *Marketing for Small Publishers*, Inter-Action Inprint, London

71

Enquiries

David T.-D. Clarke

Most museums visitors are in essence enquirers, for curiosity is the the human impulse from which springs the whole concept of museums. Conversely, curiosity should be the hallmark of every museum worker; a curiosity not confined to the collections themselves, but broadening into every aspect of the job.

These two elements, internal and external, are closely interrelated. Before considering them, however, it is necessary to promulgate one golden rule.

The golden rule

To the enquirer, his query is of paramount importance, and not to be satisfied is a rebuff. There is, thus, for all enquiries, one golden rule – be as helpful as possible. At the end of a long day, and with other pressing needs, every museum worker knows how difficult this can be. Even so, it is worth remembering how often such enquiries may prove to be the most rewarding. A model summary has been given by Rachel Young (1972):

> In assisting enquirers. . . museum officers perform a valuable educational function, stimulating interest as well as providing information: in return the museum may expect to acquire knowledge, material, useful friends and much public goodwill.

Good museum presentation will both satisfy and stimulate enquiries. In the front line are displays, intelligently and imaginatively conceived, and with legible and informative labels. To continue the metaphor, the entire support service in terms of general information, handbooks, catalogues, talks, guided visits, in fact the whole area of *communication* is an essential prerequisite. Monthly information leaflets, even annual reports have their part to play.

As a result of these, many visitors' queries may

find a ready answer, but equally many may not. The range of such questions will be very wide, and the enquiries will be made in person, by telephone or by letter. The first step is to sort them out properly and refer them to the appropriate officer as promptly as possible. For this purpose, all staff need to be properly informed of their respective duties, especially those at the 'receiving end,' for example, the attendant and clerical staff. The degree of information will vary with the size of the institution, but written instructions will reduce mistakes and create confidence. The potential value of a list of 'who does what' should not be overlooked. This done, consideration may be given to the form such enquiries are likely to take.

General enquiries

These may seem so self-evident as not to warrant a mention, but they will be the most frequent and it is surprising how much the image of a museum may depend upon the giving of a satisfactory answer. It may not be directly the museum's job, but a handy train timetable, a knowledge of where the buses go from, and where overnight accommodation can be obtained or information retrieved may put the finishing touch to an agreeable visit.

Under this heading the telephone warrants special mention, since its anonymity and ability to intrude on personal privacy render it particularly liable to provoke aggressive instincts. All staff at all levels should be trained to answer the telephone in an informative and friendly manner. 'Barchester museum, good morning' or 'Good morning this is John Smith speaking' are useful examples: they save repetition, and if, as sometimes happens, there is indignation at the other end of the line, it helps to defuse it. People *do* talk about these things, and the bread returns on the waters, even after many years.

Administrative enquiries

A substantial proportion of the enquiries in most museums is concerned with requests for administrative information – times of opening, dates of exhibitions, numbers of visitors, service costs and the like. For the intending visitor, a printed sheet giving opening times, brief descriptions of what services are offered, the location of car parks, access for the disabled and toilet facilities, is a useful beginning and can also serve as general publicity.

Many organizations tend to present their queries in the form of questionnaires, which can be relied on to be set out in such a way that there is insufficient space for the answers, or to be so ordered that direct copying from the previous one is impossible. It is, therefore, imperative to have statistics readily available and up to date so that prompt and accurate answers can be given.

Staff should also be aware of the needs of auditors, simply satisfied if records are properly kept, and indexes adequately maintained.

The complexities of modern life are such that enquiries will also come from staff as to their entitlements and responsibilities: the good Curator should not only anticipate them in terms of clear directives and guidelines, but also ensure that the appropriate literature is available to answer individual problems. It is a truism that little worries irritate more than big ones – an unpaid allowance rankles, and the employees may be too shy to ask about it. This area is an excellent one in which to build up a constructive relationship with trade union representatives: many crises can be avoided if they are dealt with promptly.

Specimens

The most obvious queries will be those which arise in connection with the museum's collections. They may vary from a desire to know more about a particular object on display, or a request to view a previous donation, to information on the whereabouts of similar material.

For all of these the maintenance of good internal records and organized and accessible storage are the essential prerequisites of a prompt and satisfactory answer. If this be a counsel of perfection, nevertheless the overall situation is improving, and it is our proper duty to ensure it. Attention should, however, be paid to the possible confidentiality of location records.

Acquisitions

Under this heading come offers of gifts or possible purchases, and requests for loans. For each of these it is imperative to have clear policy statements with proper delegation of decision making, and a routine to ensure the recording of appropriate data.

In the case of potential acquisitions, an interview, if not already provided, is imperative. With rising commercial values, the owner of such a piece is, alas, far less inclined to be influenced by the desire to present it rather than sell it to a public collection, and may well take fright lest he be deprived of a substantial income. It is, therefore, best to suggest that, if a sale is contemplated, one or more independent valuations are sought, and that these are suitably communicated to the owner, bearing in mind that *buying* and *selling* prices are different, and hence to suggest a point between as being of mutual advantage.

If, however, the owner wishes to make a gift, no time should be lost in providing a written acknowledgement, with such publicity as may be appropriate or acceptable.

Research enquiries

These are relatively easy, since the researcher will usually know what information is required and, again, good indexes, storage and filing systems should make individual requests relatively easy to solve. However, a few caveats are necessary. It is desirable to have a place where researchers can study, preferably under supervision, and where the objects or data can be brought to them. Regrettably, not all researchers are equally dedicated – the utmost care is necessary at all times to ensure that a record is kept of their address, and objects produced are properly noted (with a list, if necessary) and checked off in the presence of the enquirer before he leaves. Special care should be taken with small objects, such as might be eligible for substitution. This may sound hard, but it can be confirmed by experience.

Conversely, no object in a display should be so fixed that it cannot be moved to satisfy a genuine researcher if necessary. It is also worth remembering that no one has a monopoly of knowledge, and in appropriate cases a researcher should be encouraged to look at material which may have been wrongly classified in the past. Many useful discoveries have been made in drawers marked 'miscellaneous'.

Enquiries for factual information

The first essential for dealing with factual enquiries is access to a good reference library, and since no library can be fully comprehensive, 'we may not know, but we do know who does,' is an excellent precept. Nor is it difficult to achieve, since an active interest in the work of colleagues in other museums and related fields of study can usually produce an answer. Care should be taken, however, to ensure that names and addresses are not given enquirers until it has previously been ascertained that the individuals are prepared to help.

Conservation

The growing interest in private collections of all kinds also generates enquiries relating to the repair or conservation of objects collected. In museums where conservation staff are available such enquiries can readily be referred to them, or to the Conservators employed by an Area Museum Service. It should, however, hardly need emphasizing that, as with medical treatment, each problem needs to be assessed on its merits, and only the simplest tasks should be attempted by non-specialists; anything difficult should be entrusted to properly qualified personnel. Since this may require reference to commercial sources, attention is drawn to the ethical problems.

Some collectors may even seek advice as to what to collect, thus posing further ethical difficulties, which are discussed elsewhere in this manual.

Requests from students

Modern educational practices encourage personal fact-finding and staff will be familiar with letters beginning, 'Please can you tell me about. . .' usually a comprehensive subject like Roman Britain or John Constable. With these, the key is to try to relate them to the museum's collections or publications, and perhaps to provide a brief bibliography with the suggestion that the enquirer makes use of local library or school library services to obtain the relevant reading matter. As many of these enquiries come from educational establishments, this work should have been done by the appropriate teaching staff, but frequently it is not, and as the guardians of the nation's heritage, whether or not supported by public funds, museum staff have a clear duty to obey the golden rule. Children grow up to become taxpayers and ratepayers, and a polite letter, pinned on the classroom wall, may ensure that they are lifelong Friends of museums.

Requests from teachers

General educational enquiries will normally be the province of the museum's education staff who will have their own resources in terms of loan material, literature and visual aids. Whether or not such services are available, it is useful to provide a room where teachers can study and, if the museum's collections justify it, a small reference collection can prove useful. This provision also applies to older students, who may have a clear idea of what they require, but do not need to obtain other than general information on their chosen subject.

Lectures

Most Curators will receive requests for talks and lectures to local groups: Rotary Clubs, Women's Institutes and specialist societies are typical examples. Most of them will meet in the evenings, but the advantage to the museum in terms of explaining its purpose to a sympathetic audience, and even the possibility of locating a potential acquisition, is so great that every effort should be made to fulfil the request. It is useful to develop a small range of subjects, since such organizations are not always certain what they want, and they can then be given a choice. As regards fees, it is well to establish a standard practice in consultation with the museum's governing body, and even if no fees are offered, a donation to the museum's purchase fund can usually be arranged.

Requests for talks on television and radio are increasing, particularly with the growth of local radio and other television channels, and they undoubtedly represent a future growth area. The potential advantages to the museum movement are immense, and every opportunity should be taken not only to accept such requests, but actively to seek them. Possible resistance from governing bodies may arise over the allocation of fees or outdated ideas of professional anonymity, but a previously agreed policy should remove most of the implied difficulties: ethical problems are discussed elsewhere.

Objects for identification

Very many enquiries will be concerned with objects. The motivation of the enquirer will range from a simple desire to know what it is, through to the hope that the object has some financial value. The distinctions are rarely, if ever, clear cut, and the Curator may be confronted with items culled from every aspect of natural and human history, and in every sort of condition. The range and demand is so great that some system is necessary, and this is normally treated as an enquiry service.

Method

There can be no doubt that the best approach is to see the enquirer personally. This is what is expected, and offers the best method of assessing the enquirer's goodwill. Individual interviews are, however, time consuming, even if some arbitrary time limit is imposed. Sometimes too, there may be a need to consult works of reference or other persons with specialized knowledge. There is also the risk that information given verbally is misunderstood, even subsequently distorted, and, hence, a written answer may be preferable.

In some museums it may be possible to provide a duty officer, or to stipulate certain times when enquiries can be brought in. In others, enquirers may be asked to leave the object, to which a written answer will be supplied by a defined date. If the latter course is adopted, documentation is essential, and the main headings of an enquiry form are set out in *Table 71.1*. For many museums a duplicate copy will suffice, but in large institutions it may be necessary to have more than one copy for departmental or adminstrative purposes.

Table 71.1 Basic details for an enquiry form (optional items in brackets)

Name and address of enquirer (Mr Mrs, Miss, Ms, etc., post code, telephone number)	Date received By
(Name and address of owner if different from above)	
Brief description of objects, number of items, condition if damaged	Recorded by
Where found and how obtained	
Type of information required	
(Record of transit to department(s) if appropriate)	
Report (By...................................)	
Receipt to be given to enquirer and presented on retrieval	Serial number
Conditions of acceptance (Opinion only, no valuations, responsibility, possible disposal)	
Signed by enquirer	Date

Proper provision should also be made for the *immediate* photography of interesting objects which the owner may wish to retain, and other relevant details recorded in such a way that they could later, if necessary, be related to the object in question or included in general records of such data held by the museum or other bodies. Accurate map references of the find, details of previous ownership, artists' signatures, hallmarks, and similar related facts should not be overlooked.

Problems

It is obvious that no museum, however competent its staff, can be expected to identify every enquiry with accuracy. Various courses are, therefore, open. In practice, it is usually fairly easy to be able to decide whether an object may warrant further investigation or whether it does not; though the middle ground is occasionally difficult to determine. It would be wrong to trouble specialist colleagues with trivia, just as the failure to identify a masterpiece could have obvious repercussions on the reputation of the museum. As stated above, the Curator should try to build up a list of colleagues or local people who might be able to help.

There can be no definite rules, but a catholicity of interest when visiting other museums can prove of inestimable help.

Operating an enquiry service

The following rules should apply.

(1) The system must be efficient and reliable, ensuring that objects are not confused, are kept safely and are available for collection on time.
(2) If the object is damaged a note of this should be made in the presence of the enquirer.
(3) The provision of replies should always be properly delegated to the responsible officer.
(4) Written reports should be brief, but courteous and informative.
(5) It must be made clear in writing that the report is an opinion only, not a guarantee of authenticity or otherwise. Some museums also emphasize the right of an officer to refuse to give information, though this is an ethical matter which is discussed in Chapter 12.
(6) Some detachable form of receipt, recording the enquirer's aceptance of relevant conditions, is essential, and no enquiry should be returned without the presentation of this receipt.
(7) If enquiries tend to be relatively repetitive, a duplicated sheet may be useful, and can provide more detail than might otherwise be practicable.

Conditions of acceptance

The following are important.

Valuations
It must be stipulated that valuations will not be given. Apart from being the proper province of professional valuers, museum staff have not the necessary experience, nor is the practice conducive to the museum's image as a trustee. Some museums will provide a list of local licensed valuers and/or dealers, but the ethical problems are obvious, and the practice is perhaps best avoided.

Authentication
The enquiry form should state clearly that the report is an opinion only, and *not* an authentication of the object. Nevertheless, there is no satisfactory means of ensuring that the form is not subsequently used to enhance the sale value of the object. Worse, it might even be associated with a similar object which did

not fully correspond with the written report. In such circumstances, the legal position is by no means clear, and for the present the situation can only be regarded on trust. It seems unwise, therefore for opinions to be signed, and some code reference is to be preferred, if one is needed.

Responsibility for loss or damage
While it has been the practice to print a disclaimer on an enquiry receipt, it is no longer likely that this could be sustained in law, and it is, therefore, desirable to arange insurance coverage.

Disposal of uncollected items
In larger museums this is normally covered by specific legislation and by the *Local Government Act 1982* in respect of Local Authority museums. In other cases the Curator should consult the legal advisers to the governing body.

Enquiries involving external work

Some enquiries will evoke a need for a visit outside the museum by a member of staff. Advice on an object which cannot be moved or the discovery of a potentially interesting site are typical examples. Decisions in this respect are difficult and can easily become the prey of under-employed auditors. Each case will need to be judged on its merits, and the main guidelines will need to be whether the information so gained is likely to be of advantage to the museum. In practice, this apparently simple yardstick is not as simple as it appears, for though the object of the enquiry may be relatively trivial, the opportunity to talk to individuals may elicit information which can prove very helpful.

The author, leaving a house after inspecting some relative trivia, found a superb Bronze Age axe acting as a door-stop, while an anglo-Saxon vase a collegue observed maintaining a complement of geraniums in a cottage window. No line save common sense can be drawn, but certainly any total prohibition should be resisted.

General administrative problems

Priorities

It must be recognized that in some museums there is a strong feeling that internal work, by a relatively limited staff, on and with the collections, is of paramount importance and enquiries, other than those of a specialized nature, are a distraction from the primary objective. It is not the purpose of this chapter to argue this issue, and it can be appreciated that a museum of national repute will tend to attract enquiries far beyond its resources to give them individual attention. While it must be for each

museum to establish its own policy, nevertheless there would appear to be a duty – at least in museums supported by public funds – for some degree of response. As education and leisure continue to develop, it is evident that this pressure will increase, and further thought will need to be given to the best ways of dealing with it.

Charging for enquiries

Proposals for charging for enquiries are a hardy annual. In essence, if the philosophy of answering enquiries in order to obtain information for the museum and to render a service is accepted, charging can be clearly shown to be potentially counter-productive. To charge someone for bringing in a specimen which he might subsequently desire to donate would be embarrassing, to say the least. A gentle reminder and a handy donation box would seem to be the best source of revenue in this area. If a charge were made for an identification which subsequently proved to be incorrect and caused financial loss to the enquirer, it might be agreed that the payment to the museum would lend support to any claim for compensation.

Our own enquiries of others

It is relevant to give some consideration to the other side of the coin: enquiries made of others by museum staff. As a profession we should all be prepared to help our colleagues, whether it be by the provision of statistics or with detailed knowledge of our own subject. It is, therefore, incumbent upon us to ensure that the information required is clearly set out, and especially if the ubiquitous questionnaire is employed there is sufficient space for the answers and the inclusion of any limiting factors. As a simple example, bald statements of annual expenditure can be of little relevance unless distinctions are made between capital and revenue expenditure. The former will be largely determined by the size and age of the appropriate premises. Subject-based enquiries should be as specific as possible, since it is much easier to provide answers if it is known exactly what is required.

Passing on information

Thus far, enquiries have been considered in the passive sense, i.e. those directed to the museum. There is, however, an active element which is frequently overlooked. It is best defined as the stimulation of research by the communication of information gained from enquiries to potentially interested sources. For example, there is a clear responsibility to communicate new information to such organizations as biological data banks, sites and monuments records and the annual surveys of bodies concerned with particular fields of study. Similarly, a museum known to have a major, specialized holding in a particular subject area should be informed if relevant information is acquired elsewhere.

It is the proper responsibility of museum staff to be aware of the activities of kindred organizations in their chosen discipline, and to make suitable provision for them to be informed. This can only be achieved by consultation and personal co-operation, but it should not be difficult to determine, and once determined to adhere to it.

Conclusion

Few, if any of us, could honestly admit that there has never been an occasion when, just as we were starting for lunch or finishing a show-case, we have not harboured un-Christian thoughts towards the person at the other end of a ringing telephone.

As the most memorable form of instruction, therefore, two parables may form a fitting conclusion. Both are true. A certain Curator, hastening to retrieve a founder's Bronze Age hoard, just discovered on a housing estate, was approached in the entrance hall by a person holding a grubby paper bag. Resisting the temptation to refer the enquirer to the desk, he opened the bag. It was the Snettisham torc.

Three minutes before the author's museum was due to close, a man entered the office with four Charles I half-crowns.

'They look like a hoard', I said. 'Was this all you found?'

'How did you know?' he said. 'I didn't bring the other hundred'.

The hoard is now in the museum.

Acknowledgements

This paper is principally indebted to the *Museums Association's Information Sheet No. 11*, 'Museum enquiries' by Rachel M.R. Young (1972), which it condenses, but could not presume to supersede.

The author is grateful to Dr. D.A. Bassett, former Director of the National Museum of Wales, for his constructive comments. Thanks also to the many museums who have, over the years, provided information as to their enquiry services, and to all our enquirers, knowledgeable, knowledge-seeking or nutty, who, through their faith in museums, broaden our experience.

References

YOUNG, R. M. R. (1972), *Museum Enquiries (Museums Association Information Sheet 11)*, Museum Association, London

Bibliography

CAMERON, D. F. (1982), 'Museums and public access: the Glenbow approach', *The International Journal of Museum Management and Curatorship*, **1**(3), 177–196

GIBBS-SMITH, C. H. (1975), *The Arranging of Lectures (Museums Association Information Sheet 8)*, Museums Association, London

GRIGGS, S. A. and ALT, M. B. (1982), 'Visitors to the British Museum (Natural History) in 1980 and 1981', *Museums Journal*, **82**(3), 149–159

MUSEUMS ASSOCIATION (1975), *Reproduction Fees, Photography etc: Guidelines for Museums (Museums Association Information Sheet 20)*, Museums Association, London

MUSEUMS ASSOCIATION (1979), *Careers in Museums*, *(Museum Association Information Sheet)*, Museums Association, London

PARK, E. (1977), 'Why do we want your grandfather's teeth?, in *The Smithsonian Experience*, Smithsonian Institution Washington, DC

ROYAL ONTARIO MUSEUM (1976), 'Arrival and orientation', in *Communicating with the Museum Visit. Guidelines for Planning*, Royal Ontario Museum, Toronto

SHARPE, T. and ROLFE, W. D. (1979), 'Geological Enquiries', *Museums Journal*, **79**(1), 61–62

Appendix

Code of conduct for museum professionals

The Museums Association

1. Introduction

1.1 This Code is concerned with the ethical conduct of Museum Professionals, who are defined as persons working in museums and art galleries, or in organisations directly related to them on a regular basis, whether paid or unpaid, and whether full- or part-time, but whose status is recognised by the institution's governing body.

1.2 All persons employed in a museum in a professional capacity have a duty of care to the collections and to the provision of services to the public. This Code, therefore, includes not only curators, collection managers and conservators who have the primary responsibility for collections, but also all others who are involved in the work of the museum, and who may have their own professional bodies and codes of practice.

1.3 It is essential that all those working in museums should have a proper understanding of the principles involved, and the code is therefore to be interpreted in the light of individual duties, but having regard always to the best interests of the museum and the museum service as a whole.

1.4 The duty of trusteeship is vested in the governing body of the museum. Museum professionals are in a contractual relationship to the governing body whatever the capacity in which they are working for it.

1.5 The Association urges specialist groups to produce and regularly update guidelines for their members on the best current practice in their specialist areas, and which may be endorsed by the Association.

1.6 This Code assumes that museum professionals will ensure that their activities accord with at least the minimum standards set out in *Guidelines for a Registration Scheme for Museums in the United Kingdom*, (Museums and Galleries Commission), their Guidelines for Specialist Collections and that they comply with the best national and international practice.

1.7 This Code further assumes that museum professionals will undertake their duties and conduct their professional relationships in accordance with the principles of equal opportunities and other policies adopted by the Museums Association.

2. General management principles

2.1 *Rule*. Museum professionals must manage resources responsibly to achieve the highest quality of care and service. This will include advising on the formulation of objectives, and then striving to achieve targets. These policies and targets should be regularly reviewed and revised by the governing body, and should always be consistent with the *Code of Practice for Museum Authorities*.

2.2 *Rule*. Museum professionals must recognise that the success of the museum depends upon a variety of skills, and must be prepared to work together with colleagues, volunteers and outside specialists to achieve this end.

Guideline. For example, the planning of displays will be most effective if the various aspects, such as conservation, accessibility and education are taken into account in the planning stage. There is also a valuable sense of corporate achievement.

2.3 *Rule*. Museum professionals should be prepared to participate in the evaluation of their work and to take the results into account in future plans.

Guideline. Effective communication is a two-way process. Only by encouraging and analysing feedback from the public which the museum exists to serve, can the success of services be evaluated. Consideration should also be given to quality as well as to popular response.

2.4 *Rule*. Museum professionals who are responsible for other staff must ensure that opportunities for training are provided for staff development, and should advise the governing body of the need for such training.

2.5 *Rule*. Museum professionals must be aware of, and comply with, relevant law which affects their work and conditions of service. They must ensure that it is obeyed and that, where appropriate, their governing bodies are apprised of their obligations under the law.

3.   Management and care of collections

3.1 *Rule*. Museum professionals must care for the museum's existing collections and, where relevant, acquire material for their development in accordance with a properly researched, approved, and regularly updated collection management policy.

Guideline. The collections are the very core of a museum's role and existence. The integrity and development of the collections are therefore prime responsibilities of the museum professional.

In reviewing the collection management policy museum professionals should ensure that the following factors are taken into account: the role of the museum in relation to the public it serves; the nature, condition and quality of the existing collections: the nature, purpose and use of the material it seeks to preserve and interpret; the resources available for the proper long-term management of that material, including conservation, documentation and access; and the inter-relationship of the museum with other museums by virtue of geographical location or subject specialism.

An acquisition policy should, where appropriate, take into account the need for handling and loan service material. Such material may form part of the core collections of the museum or may be managed as a separate educational resource. Careful judgement must be exercised

in this respect, since material managed in a separate handling or loan collection may be put to different uses and may not necessarily be preserved indefinitely.

Where the museum is involved in fieldwork, it may not be unethical for surplus material to be collected in excess of the museum's requirements, but, such material should only be collected with due regard to the conservation requirements in that subject area, and with the intention of transferring the excess material to appropriate institutions.

When a major legacy or a mixed lot at auction might contain material inconsistent with the collection management policy, loans or transfers to other museums should be given priority.

3.2 *Rule*. Museum professionals must take every practicable step fully to protect all the items in their care so as to minimise physical deterioration, whether on display, in store, in transit, used in handling or loan collections subject to research or conservation, or on loan to or from the museum.

Guideline. Museum professionals must be aware of the actions needed for the proper care, and conservation of objects. Curatorial and conservation staff have a corporate responsibility for treatment methods, records, and the nature and extent of restorations.

3.3 *Rule*. Museum professionals must establish, maintain and regularly revise, in consultation with the appropriate specialists, safeguards against fire, theft, flood and other hazards, and procedures to secure the collections in emergency. They must apprise the governing body of the recommendations made and ensure that all safeguards and procedures subsequently adopted are enforced.

Guideline. The dangers of fire and theft are easily recognised but precautions against flood are frequently overlooked. Consideration should also be given to making provision for a major crisis such as a crashed airliner or civil disorder, so that staff are properly conversant with what is expected of them. Every effort should be made to protect the collections but in no circumstances should the lives of individuals be put at risk.

Careless or deliberate disclosure of information regarding safeguards against theft, or details of transportation can also put not only objects but persons at risk.

3.4 *Rule*. Museum professionals must ensure that all objects within their care are recorded to conform with the *Guidelines for a Registration Scheme*.

Guideline. Museum professionals are accountable for all the objects in their charge and proper documentation is essential for audit as well as management purposes. The scientific or cultural value of any object is in direct proportion to the data associated with it, and hence a secure link between the two is of fundamental importance.

3.5 *Rule.* Museum professionals must uphold the principles that there is always a strong presumption against the disposal of objects to which a museum has assumed formal title.

Guideline. Any form of disposal, whether by donation, exchange, sale or destruction should only be recommended to a governing body after appropriate curatorial specialist, and, if necessary, legal advice has been taken.

Guidance on the disposal of collections is contained in *Guidelines for a Registration Scheme*. Subject to legal considerations, the long-term loan of objects to other museums may be a satisfactory way of dealing with items which are under consideration for disposal. The recipient museum professional must take care that the provisions of such loan or transfer of material between museums are in accordance with the *Guidelines* and any existing conditions.

The best means of disposal is by transfer to another registered museum, since there is the presumption that museum collections are held for the public benefit. This may be achieved by formal transfer of ownership, or, if that is not legally possible or undesirable for other reasons, then by loan for a finite but renewable term. Formal transfer of ownership to another museum should be achieved preferably by exchange or gift, or failing that, by private treaty sale. Disposal to non-museum bodies, commercial concerns or individuals by sale or other means should be considered only as a line of last resort. Where a museum proposes to dispose of objects in contravention of the *Guidelines* it would be unethical for other museums to encourage such disposal.

3.6 *Rule.* Museum professionals must not delegate specialist functions relating to care of collections without adequate professional supervision.

Guideline. In particular, acquisition, documentation, conservation and disposal procedures must be under the direct supervision of a museum professional suitably qualified to undertake such work.

3.7 *Rule.* Museum professionals must not treat the collections as personal property or assume exclusive rights of research or publication.

Guideline. For security or other reasons, access to certain items may occasionally need to be restricted, but such circumstances should be regarded as exceptional and museum professionals should make every effort to overcome them.

3.8 *Rule.* Research undertaken by museum professionals as part of their prescribed duties must relate to the collections, functions or agreed research programme of their institution.

Guideline. Museum professionals, having direct access to the collections for which they are responsible, are best placed to study them in depth, and thus should be prepared to take advantage of the privilege and opportunity to make a positive contribution to knowledge in their chosen discipline.

The balance struck between research and other responsibilities should accord with the policy and objectives of the museum. Unpublished results of a museum professional's research or research notes should be protected from plagiarism during the reasonable term of completion, but in principle the results should be publically available wherever possible.

3.9 *Rule.* Museum professionals have a duty to seek appropriate expert advice when personal expertise or that of immediate colleagues is insufficient.

Guideline. Few museums are likely to contain all the expertise necessary for complete identification or conservation of every object in their collections or for decisions regarding such matters as security. Relevant advice should be sought from the Museums & Galleries Commission, other national or regional institutions, Area Museum Councils, universities, specialist groups or individual specialists.

3.10 *Rule.* Where a museum maintains live animals the museum professional responsible must ensure their health and well-being in accordance with the appropriate legislation and best practice. The breeding of certain animals should be in accordance with the regulations laid down by relevant breed societies.

It is essential that a veterinary surgeon be available for advice and for regular inspection of the animals and their living conditions.

The museum must prepare and follow in detail a safety code which has been approved by an expert in the veterinary field for the protection of staff and visitors.

Guideline. The introduction of living animals into the museum environment extends the range of curatorial responsibility considerably, and museum professionals must ensure that all the necessary provisions for animal welfare are made. High standards of hygiene must be maintained as a precaution against infestation and disease for both humans and livestock. Stress can be caused to animals through the behaviour of visitors, and the barriers between one and the other must be effective and secure.

Museum professionals must also be prepared to care for stock continuously, even when the museum is closed.

1 *Rule.* Where a museum or building housing a museum is isolated as a result of industrial action, the care and maintenance of the collections and/or livestock remains the primary ethical responsibility of museum professionals.

Guideline. When an industrial dispute affects the conduct of a museum professional's duties, provision must be made for the safeguarding of the collections. Should the labour of an individual be withdrawn, provision should be made as if the museum were being closed in the normal way. Any maintenance work needed to prevent damage or harm to the collections should not be interrupted.

Museum professionals should inform the relevant trade unions of the nature of their responsibilities and seek agreement with them in advance of any proposed industrial action.

2 *Rule.* Museum professionals must not evaluate, accept on loan or acquire by any means an object which there is good reason to believe was acquired by its owner in contravention of the *UNESCO Convention on the Means of Prohibiting and Preventing the Illicit Import, Export and Transfer of Ownership of Cultural Property 1970*, or by any other illegal means. This Convention has not yet been ratified by the British government but is supported by the Museums Association.

Guideline. When considering acquiring imported objects, museum professionals should take reasonable steps to ascertain the relevant laws, regulations and procedures of the country or countries of origin.

Management and care of environmental records and accessibility of data

Rule. Museum professionals must ensure as far as possible the accuracy of museum records relating to the collections and the local historic, cultural or natural environment and provide reasonable access to such records.

Guideline. In principle museum records are maintained for public use but museum professionals should exercise caution where there is good reason to believe that unrestricted access to information might lead to the abuse of significant sites or sensitive material.

Confidentiality in relation to the identity of lenders, donors, etc. must also be maintained where it is demanded.

4.2 *Rule.* Museum professionals must be aware of the implications of becoming involved, in their professional capacity, with any public pressure group or lobbying faction, since this might call into question their professional objectivity.

If an issue arises which in their professional judgement would have a detrimental effect on a sensitive site, they should make their reservations known in writing to the appropriate persons or organisations.

5. Responsibilities and services to the public

5.1 *Rule.* Museum professionals must uphold the fundamental principle of museums that the collections are maintained for the public benefit, and the implication of non-discriminatory public access which this carries.

Guideline. Museum professionals should ensure that equal opportunity of access is afforded to all and be mindful of the principles of equal opportunities in all their undertakings. They should ensure that, wherever possible, the collections are made available to those with disabilities, and that exhibitions and activities are designed with a variety of disabilities in mind.

The issues of equal opportunity relate to the particular access needs of a wide range of potential user groups. Through consultation with, and participation by user and community groups, museum professionals should assess their requirements and formulate a policy for the governing body to develop services to meet these needs.

5.2 *Rule.* Museum professionals must ensure that objects on public display, with all forms of accompanying information should present a clear, accurate and objective exposition, and should never deliberately mislead.

Guideline. Interpretation in its broadest sense is one of the core activities of a museum. This principle applies also to books and information published or otherwise disseminated by the museum, and to any educational activities, where the quality, objectivity and accuracy of information should be ensured.

Great sensitivity should be exercised when presenting contemporary cultural issues or social history. Museum professionals must clearly understand the point where professional judgement ends and personal bias begins.

From time to time, however, exhibitions will be set up by the museum or received on loan which develop a particular point of view. In such cases it is a museum professional's duty to ensure that this is made clear. The same conditions apply to educational programmes, publications and interviews.

5.3   *Rule.* Museum professionals should be aware of the positive contribution that a museum shop, cafe, restaurant or other trading activities can make to the revenue generation and the interpretive role of the museum.

Guideline. A careful balance must be maintained between the needs of revenue generation and the provision of services to visitors; the museum professional must be continually concerned that only goods of quality and reliable publications are offered for sale.

Whether or not trading activities are contracted to a commercial concern, museum professionals should ensure that the museum has the right to recommend stock or to veto merchandise on ethical grounds and that this right forms part of any formal contract.

There should be a strong presumption against the sale of historic artefacts or natural objects, as this may be confused in the public mind with material in the collections, and with the purpose of the museum itself.

All replicas of museum objects should be clearly marked in a permanent manner.

In the case of a cafe or restuarant museum professionals must ensure that their design and location preclude the generation of atmospheric conditions which might affect the conservation of the collections and avoid any conflict of alternative use.

5.4   *Rule.* Museum professionals must ensure that when museum premises are let to non-museum concerns the collections are not put at risk. The same applies to loans of objects to non-museum premises.

5.5   *Rule.* Museum professionals must ensure that, where special sales are held to raise funds for the museum it is made clear to the public that the sale does not include items from the museum's collections.

Guideline. In general it is not advisable to hold such sales on museum premises in order to avoid public misinterpretation. Museum professionals should try to avoid being personally involved in the sale of objects.

5.6   *Rule.* The museum professional must conduct the acquisition of museum items from the public with scrupulous fairness to the seller or donor.

Guideline. In the case of a dealer or auction house, the normal conditions apply. However, in the case of members of the general public it would be improper to take advantage of their unawareness of the nature or value of the objects offered. Where an object is of considerable financial value the museum professional should advise the owner that the opinion of an independent qualified valuer should be sought before a price is agreed. Where a proposed gift is of considerable value the museum professional should also inform the owner should they not previously be aware of the fact.

Where it is the intention that an object offered as a gift is to be used primarily for educational acitivities such as handling or loan collections or for purposes of demonstration, this should be made clear to the donor at the time of acquisition.

Care should be exercised before donations are accepted from minors. In all cases the parents or legal guardians of the donor should be asked for their consent to the gift after the museum professional has explained to them the significance of the proposed donation. Tactful handling of these situations is essential, the young person should not be discouraged, but equally the legal title must be clear.

5.7   *Rule.* Where an identification service is provided by the museum the relevant museum professional has a duty to identify an object submitted by a member of the public. Significant facts must not be witheld or deliberately misleading information given. In the event of the professional having insufficient specialised knowledge, this should also be stated.

Guideline. The provision of an identification service can be a fruitful source of acquisitions and afford useful contributions to knowledge, as well as developing the museum's image in the local community.

Museum professionals should be objective about their own capabilities, and seek advice when needed.

5.8 *Rule.* A museum professional must not reveal information imparted in confidence during the course of professional duty.

5.9 *Rule.* Museum professionals must be aware that the curation of human remains and material of religious significance can be a sensitive issue. A number of interested parties may claim rights over such material. These include actual and cultural descendants, legal owners and the worldwide scientific community. Museum professionals should inform themselves of the concerns of these interest groups when considering the management and display of such sensitive material.

Guideline. Despite the general obligations of access to collections (5.1), it may be appropriate to restrict access to certain specified sacred items where unrestricted access may cause offence to actual or cultural descendants. This may include the provision of separate storage facilities.

There have been a number of guidelines produced for the curation of human remains and sacred material, including *Museum Ethnographers Group Professional Guidelines Concerning the Storage, Display, Interpretation and Return of Human Remains in Ethnographical Collections in the United Kingdom Museums* (1991) and *The Vermillion Accord: Human Remains*; World Archaeological Congress (World Archaeological Bulletin, Nov. 1989) and the ICOM Code of Profesisonal Ethics section 6.7.

Governing bodies and museum professionals should therefore consider all ethical and legal implications before continuing the active or passive acquisition of human remains. Requests concerning the appropriate return of particular human remains must be resolved by individual museums on a case by case basis. This will involve the consideration of ownership, cultural significance, the scientific, educational and historical importance of the material, the cultural and religious values of the interested individuals or groups, the strength of their relationship to the remains in question, and the long term fate of the items under consideration.

All requests should be accorded respect and treated sensitively.

5.10 *Rule.* Museum professionals must ensure that in giving professional advice on any matter, such advice is consistent with good practice and given impartially.

5.11 *Rule.* Museum professionals may not delegate responsibility for services to the public to persons who lack appropriate knowledge or skill.

Guideline. A museum professional must maintain control of essential public service functions. In particular the design of educational programmes and planning of educational materials and the training of museum teachers, guides, interpreters or volunteers must be undertaken by a museum professional or under their supervision.

6. Personal activities

6.1 *Rule.* Museum professionals must at all times carry out their duties to the best of their abilities and with due regard to codes of practice in their discipline.

6.2 *Rule.* Museum professionals must not collect for themselves in competition with their employing institution. On appointment, museum professionals with private collections must inform the governing body of their scope and collecting policy. Any agreement between them must be scrupulously kept thereafter.

Guideline. It is not unethical for museum professionals to own or collect objects and it is recognised that this can enhance professional knowledge. However, extreme care must be taken to ensure that no conflict arises with the collecting policy of the employing institution. Indeed, museum professionals are advised to eschew personal collections, mindful that the best opportunity for an object to be preserved for the public is in a museum.

Staff members who collect for museums on expeditions should only engage in private collecting if:

a) the collecting is incidental and the time involved is reasonable.

b) pertinent conditions and laws are observed.

Museum professionals occupy a position of trust; this implies that they will discharge their responsibilities always giving precedence to the interests of the institution over individual interests.

Museum professionals should also be aware that they are part of a wider community concerned with the preservation of the national and international heritage, and that their actions affect the reputation of their profession worldwide.

6.3 *Rule.* Museum professionals may on no account solicit a personal gift, loan or bequest from a member of the public.

6.4 *Rule.* Museum professionals must neither solicit nor accept a gift of significant value either directly or indirectly from an artist, craftsperson or other originator of artefacts or their agent with whom the professional has come in contact through any kind of collaboration, either actual or planned involving the institution.

Guideline. The same principle identified under 6.2 applies. It is not uncommon for the organiser of an exhibition to be offered a work as a personal token of gratitude by the originator. Careful judgement must be exercised in dealing with such a situation so as to ensure that the act is not mis-interpreted. The safest course, therefore, is to accept the gift on behalf of the institution, thereby putting the integrity of the individual beyond question.

6.5   *Rule.* Museum professionals must not deal (buy or sell for profit) in material covered by the institution's collecting policy.

Guideline. The professional should also be aware that such dealing might affect other institutions, and it is thus best avoided altogether.

6.6   *Rule.* Museum professionals must not undertake authentication and identification for personal gain outside the course of normal duties, with the intention of establishing the market value of an object, without the consent of the governing body. It should then be undertaken with the highest standards of academic objectivity.

Guideline. In some countries professional rules totally prohibit museum professionals from such activities. In order to maintain an unimpeachable image the practice is best avoided. Specifically, a museum professional should never become involved in an identification or authentication when there is a possiblity that the object might be sold to any museum or fund with which that professional is associated.

A museum professional could face legal proceedings for negligence if advice is given which proved to be erroneous.

6.7   *Rule.* Museum professionals should refrain from putting a market value on objects for commercial purposes.

Guideline. Museum professionals are not normally qualified to undertake valuations and must therefore be aware of any implications of using employment for personal gain. This does not include the valuation of the museum's collection for insurance purposes.

6.8   *Rule.* Museum professionals must obtain the consent of the governing body before under-

taking private work from which regular additional remuneration may accrue, such as publication, lecturing, authorship, consultancy and contributions to the media.

Guideline. This matter is usually covered by contracts of employment and such activities should not be allowed to take precedence over, or conflict with, official duties and responsibilities.

7.   Relationship with commercial organisations

7.1   *Rule.* Museum professionals should ensure that, as far as practicable, when working with other professionals, the relevant codes of practice are mutually respected.

Guideline. Many commercial organisations operate to professional or trade codes of practice. Where appropriate the museum professional should obtain copies of such codes to ensure that proper practices are observed on both sides to their mutual benefit.

7.2   *Rule.* A museum professional must never accept from a commercial organisation any personal gift or favour which might subsequently be interpreted as an inducement to trade with that organisation.

Guideline. Paragraph 9882 of the *Civil Service Pay and Conditions of Service Code* offers a useful guide on this matter. 'The behaviour of officers as regards the acceptance of gifts, hospitality etc., should be governed by the following general guidance. The conduct of a civil servant should not foster the suspicion of a conflict of interest. Officers should therefore always have in mind the need not to give the impression to any member of the public, or organisation with whom they deal, or to their colleagues, that they may be influenced by any gift or consideration to show favour or disfavour to any person or organisation whilst acting in an official capacity. An officer must not, either directly or indirectly, accept any gift, reward or benefit from any member of the public or organisation with whom he/she has been brought in contact by reason or his/her official duties. The only exceptions to this rule are as follows:

a) isolated gifts of a trivial character or inexpensive seasonal gifts (such as calendars);

b) conventional hospitality, provided it is normal and reasonable in the circumstances. In considering what is normal and reasonable, regard should be had:

i. to the degree of narrow personal involvement. There is, of course, no objection to the acceptance of, for example, an invitation to an annual dinner of a large trade association or similar body with which a department is in much day-to-day contact; or of working lunches (provided the frequency is reasonable) in the course of official visits;

ii. to the usual conventions of returning hospitality, at least to some degree. The isolated acceptance of, for example, a meal would not offend the rule, whereas acceptance of frequent or regular invitations to lunch or dinner on a wholly one-sided basis even on a small scale might give rise to a breach of the standard required.'

When in doubt, the museum professional should consult a senior officer or the chair of the governing body, and the decision should be recorded.

7.3   *Rule*. A museum professional must ensure that the standards and objectives of the museum are not compromised in any matter of commercial sponsorship.

Guideline. Museum professionals should ensure that the precise terms of the sponsorship are agreed in writing before the project begins, in order to avoid any subsequent friction. Sponsors normally and rightly expect evidence of recognition for their assistance.

Museum professionals are also advised that in certain instances the products or activities of an intending sponsor may be open to popular criticism, and care should therefore be taken to ensure that the governing body is fully informed of the circumstances and its approval obtained.

7.4   *Rule*. A museum professional must ensure that information for the media, or publicity in any form is factually accurate and well-presented, and presents the museum in the best possible light.

Guideline. Museum professionals and governing bodies should recognise that the media are trained to approach news from a personal standpoint. There is nothing wrong in communicating information in this way provided the rule is followed.

Ethical problems might arise if, for example, a museum professional was asked to take part in a discussion on a topical issue, and in such cases the approval of a senior officer or the governing body should be obtained in advance.

The presence of museum staff can be of great advantage to the museum provided the opinions expressed are objectively presented.

8.   Relationship with professional colleagues

8.1   *Rule*. A museum professional's relationship with professional colleagues should always be courteous, both in public and private. Differences of professional opinion can be robustly expressed but never in a gratuitously personalised fashion.

Guideline. Care must be taken to avoid discourtesy by word or gesture and the museum professional should also be aware that more subtle kinds of behaviour can cause as much, or more offence. All museum professionals in positions of authority carry a concomitant responsibility to pay due respect to the feelings of others, especially to junior staff, who should be included in discussions relating to their roles in the museum wherever practicable, and whose problems should be addressed with patience and impartiality.

Museum professionals should take particular care to avoid any dispute coming to public notice so as to bring discredit on the persons concerned and the profession at large. Where a point of professional principle cannot be resolved internally, the arbitration of the President of the Museums Association or a nominee should be sought.

8.2   *Rule*. Museum professionals, especially when working outside their own area of expertise, must consult other professionals either within the museum or outside.

Guideline. Personal considerations should never be allowed to inhibit proper collaboration. Museum professionals should always be open to consultation.

8.3   *Rule*. Where acquisition policies, collecting areas or other activities overlap, the museum professionals concerned should draft mutually satisfactory agreements, which should then be submitted to respective governing bodies for approval. Where it is likely that there may be a difference of opinion over the acquisition of an object, museum professionals should make every effort to see that the matter is amicably resolved.

8.4   *Rule*. Museum professionals must conduct working relationships with people within and outside the museum with courtesy and fair-mindedness, and render professional services to others of a high standard.

Subject Index

★ = definition of term
Italic type = illustration